Healthy Hotlines:
Tips on How You Can Save a Bundle by Phone!

MATTHEW LESKO'S

HEALTHCARE HOTLINE REPORT

Healthy Hotlines:
Save a Bundle by Phone

Start living in the 90's and develop a healthy appreciation for using the phone to get the latest help, information and freebies to solve your health care problems.

Don't think of them as phone numbers, see them for what they are: a way to make money, keep your money and get better care.

All you need is an idea. Think referral. Think lower health care costs for you, your family, or your company. Just pick up the phone.

Do you want to know if your grandfather is showing signs of Alzheimer's? Call the Alzheimer's Disease Education Center at 1-800-438-4380.

They'll tell you how to spot the early warning signals.

Are you worried that you're beginning to strain to hear conversations at the dinner table? Call about a free hearing test at the Occupational Hearing Service at 1-800-222-EARS.

You can also find out about free guide dogs for your sightless friends at 1-800-548-4337, programs that can help the homeless at 1-800-444-7415, and even how to find a good plastic surgeon for your tummy tuck at 1-800-332-FACE.

Its time to help yourself. With the nation's health care system in full cardiac arrest, taxpayers need to shop

smart. It's time for a little homework.

How can you know whether you're being charged too much if you don't know the going rate? How can you know whether your doctor is reading the medical journals? Is that pill the right one? Just pick up the phone.

Jack Anderson says "Matthew Lesko teaches people how to use the government they pay for." These hotlines are a starting point for the information sources that will help you with your health care problems.

Many of these sources teach you:

- the **best treatment** for any health problem whether you're rich or poor, and

- the **latest information**, for free on any health related topic.

Eclipsing the Pill:
Birth Control in the Nineties

The new three-month contraceptive implant — Norplant — has been available for years in other Western countries. In the United States, however, the Food and Drug Administration (FDA) takes its sweet time when evaluating a drug with any controversial overtones, especially with Family Values casting a long shadow on the political landscape. Now the implant is available here, and women want to know more.

FDA makes available a number of reports on Norplant, including results of clinical trials, patient labeling information and usage warnings. Also, the Contraceptive Development Branch of the Center for Publication Research has begun collecting data on who uses Norplant and who chooses to stop using the contraceptive and why. They can be reached at 9000 Rockville Pike, Bethesda, MD 20892, (301) 496-1661.

For more information on Norplant or for a wealth of information regarding all the different forms of the Pill, contact: Center for Drug Evaluation & Research, HFD-8, FDA, 5600 Fishers Lane, Rockville, MD 20857, (301) 295-8012.

Healthcare Hotlines

Aerobics and Fitness Association of America
(800) BE FIT 86
Information on diet and exercise

Abuse
See also Violence

AIDS Clinical Trials Information Service
(800) TRIALS-A
Information on federally and privately sponsored clinical trials

AIDS Cases / HHS / Centers for Disease Control
(404) 332-4555
Recorded message on number of cases, deaths, and distribution among age groups

AIDS, Experimental Drugs (Project Inform)
(800) 822-7422
Information packet and newsletter on experimental drugs for AIDS, ARC and HIV infection

AIDS Hotline, National
(800) 342-AIDS; (800) 344-SIDA (Spanish); (800) AIDS-TTY (Hearing Impaired)
AIDS information funded by Centers for Disease Control

AIDS Information Clearinghouse, National
(800) 458-5231AIDS
Publications, posters, databases, videos

AIDS Prevention Center / Indian AIDS Hotline, National Native American
(800) 283-AIDS
Information on AIDS and AIDS prevention

AIDS Quilt / Names Project
(800) USA-NAME
Orders for "Common Thread," a documentary on the AIDS quilt

Alcohol and Drug Information, National Clearinghouse
(800) 729-6686
Publications, posters and referrals

Alcoholics, Information and counseling for family and children of
(800) 356-9996
Al-Anon Family Group Headquarters

Alcoholism and Drug Addiction Treatment Center (McDonald Center, La Jolla, California)
(800) 382-4357

Alcoholism
See also Drug Abuse

Allergy and Asthma Information Line
(800) 822-ASMA
Publications and referrals

Alzheimer's Disease Education Center
(800) 438-4380
Information packets and referrals

Alzheimer's Eldercare Institute / Brookdale Center on Aging
(800) 647-8233
Technical assistance program for instituting a respite program for individuals with Alzheimer's

Amyotrophic Lateral Sclerosis Association
(800) 782-4747
Information, publications and referrals

Anemia Foundation, Cooley's
(800) 221-3571; (212) 598-0911 in New York
Publications and referrals

Arthritis Foundation
(800) 283-7800
Information and referrals

Asbestos / Environmental Protection Agency (EPA) / Small Business Ombudsman Hotline
(800) 368-5888; (703) 305-5938 in Washington, D.C
Asbestos handling and abatement in schools, homes and workplaces information and assistance on complying with regulations

Asthma Center, Lung Line National
(800) 222-5864; (303) 355-LUNG in Denver
Information on immune system and respiratory disorders

Birth Control Care Center
(800) 255-7889
Information, referrals and treatment

Birth Defects Foundation, March of Dimes
(914) 428-7100
Health services grants to individuals or institutions

Bladder Control / Simon Foundation
(800) 23-SIMON
Information regarding loss of bladder control

Blind, American Council of the
(800) 424-8666; (202) 467-5081 in Washington, D.C.
Legislation affecting and resource materials for the blind

Blind, American Foundation for
(800) 232-5463
Referral service for information and services for the visually impaired

Blind Children's Center
(800) 222-3566; (800) 222-3567 in California
Nursery School, infant to age 5, in Los Angeles, California

Blind, Foundation for the
(800) 232-5463; (212) 620-2000 in New York
Referral services

Blind / Gallaudet Library
(202) 651-5216 TTY only; (202) 651-5217 voice and TTY
Information about library holdings for the blind

Blind, Guide Dog Foundation for
(800) 548-4337
Free guide dogs for the blind

Blind / Library of Congress / National Library for the Blind
(800) 424-8567; (202) 707-5100
Provides books and tapes to individuals with sight disabilities

Blind / Massachusetts Commission for the Blind
(800) 392-6450 (voice); (800) 392-6556 (TDD), Boston office
(800) 332-2772 (voice & TDD), Springfield office
Job counseling and job referral services

Blind / U.S. Department of Education / American Printing House for the Blind
(800) 223-1839
Information on publications regarding the blind

Cancer / American Cancer Society
(800) ACS-2345 (Maryland only)
Information, publications and referrals

Cancer, Breast / Y-Me Breast Cancer Support and Information
(800) 221-2141; (708) 799-8228 in Illinois
Counseling services and publications

Cancer Hotline / HHS / National Institutes of Health / National Cancer Institute
(800) 4-CANCER
Cancer information and publications

Cancer Information and Counseling Line of the National Cancer Institute
(800) 525-3777
Information, publications, nursing and counseling services

Chemical Manufacturers Assoc.
(800) 424-9300
Chemical spills, explosions, etc., emergency response assistance

Chemical Manufacturers Trade Association
(800) CMA-8200; (202) 887-1315 in Washington, DC
Referrals for health and safety information on industrial chemicals

Chemical Spills / Environmental Protection Agency
(800) 535-0202
Community planning and procedural information for chemical spills

Child Abuse and Neglect Information, Clearinghouse on
(800) FYI-3366
Publications and information on child abuse

Child Abuse / Parents Anonymous Hotline
(800) 421-0353
Referral service for treatment of child abuse

Child Safety Council, National
(800) 222-1464
Safety materials for children

Child Sexual Abuse, National Resource Center on
(800) KIDS-006
Child sexual abuse information, publications and training

Childbirth / ASPO / Lamaze (American Society for Psychoprophylaxis in Obstetrics)
(800) 368-4404
Information regarding certification of educators and class referrals

Children / American Academy of Pediatrics
(800) 433-9016
Although primarily an association for pediatricians, it also is an advocacy center for children

Children
(800) 237-5055
Shriner's Hospital Referral Line

Children / Adoption / Edna Gladney Center
(800) GLADNEY
Maternity home and adoption center

Children / Crisis Counseling / Covenant House
(800) 999-9999
Crisis counseling for adolescents, especially runaways and referrals

Children's Hospice International
(800) 242-4453
Referral network

Children, Missing / Kevin Collins Foundation for Missing Children
(800) 272-0012
Advice and immediate response to families of stranger-abducted children

Children, National Hotline for Missing
(800) 843-5678
Reports from parents and law enforcement officers and sightings of missing children

Children / Runaway Hotline
(800) 621-4000
Information, resources and message delivery for runaways and their parents

Children / Tough Love
(800) 333-1069
Referral service for parents with problem children

Cleft Palate Association, American
(800) 24-CLEFT
Publications and referrals

Cornelia de Lange Syndrome Foundation
(800) 223-8355; (203) 693-0159 in Connecticut; (800) 753-2357 in Canada
Supportive education and referrals for families with children with Cornelia de Lange syndrome

Cystic Fibrosis Foundation
(800) 344-4823; (301) 951-4422 in Maryland
Publications and referrals

Deafness Research Foundation
(800) 535-3323
Information and referrals

Deafness / Tripod / Grapevine
(800) 352-8888 voice and TDD; (800) 2-TRIPOD voice and TDD in California
Information and referral service regarding deafness in children

Deafness and Other Communication Disorders, National Institute on Deafness
(800) 241-1044
Publications and referrals

Diabetes Association, American
(800) ADA-DISC; (703) 549-1500 in Virginia and Washington,D.C.
Information and publications

Depressive Illness, National Foundation for
(800) 248-4344
Information on recorded message

Juvenile Diabetes Foundation
(800) JDF-CURE; (212) 889-7575 in New Jersey
Information, publications and volunteer programs

Dioxin / Environmental Protection Agency
(800) 535-0202
Dioxin information for contaminated areas in Missouri

Disabilities, Clearinghouse on Disability Information
(202) 205-8245
Publications and referrals for information of concern to those with disabilities

Disabilities, Coordinating Council for the Handicapped
(312) 939-3513;
(800) 952-4199
Information and referrals services for the those with disabilities

Disabilities / Federation of the Handicapped
(212) 727-4200
Referrals and training program for those with disabilities

Disabilities / Health Resource Center
(800) 544-3284; (202) 939-9320 in Washington, D.C.
Post-secondary education for people with disabilities

Disabilities / Information, Protection and Advocacy Center for Handicapped Individuals
(202) 966-8081
Assistance, special education and training programs for handicapped and mentally ill

Disabilities / Information Center for Individuals with Disabilities
(617) 727-5540
Information and referrals

Disabilities / Institute of Logopedics
(800) 835-1043
Residential school in Wichita, KS, for multiple-handicapped children

Disabilities / Job Accommodation
(800) ADA-WORK; (800) 526-7234; (800) 526-4698 in West Virginia; (800) 526-2262 in Canada
Information/consulting referral service for accommodating people with disabilities in the workplace

Disabilities / National Center for Youth with
(800) 333-NCYD
Information including database searches for adolescents

Disabilities / National Information Clearinghouse for Infants with Disabilities and Life-Threatening Conditions
(800) 922-9234
Referral service for ill or seriously disabled infants

Disabilities / National Information System for Health Related Svcs.
(800) 922-9234
Information regarding children born with disabilities

Disabilities / National Information Center for Children and Youth with Handicaps
(800) 999-5599
Locating services for the handicapped and information on learning disabilities

Disabilities / National Institute on Disability and Rehabilitation Research
(202) 205-8134
Research grants to individuals or institutions, providing equipment to individuals with disabilities

Disabilities / National Organization on Disability
(800) 248-ABLE
Information and publications

Disabilities / National Rehabilitation Information Center (NARIC)
(800) 346-2742
Information and referral on disability and rehabilitation

Down Syndrome Congress, National
(800) 232-6372
Information and publications

Down Syndrome Society Hotline
(800) 221-4602; (212) 460-9330 in New York
Publications, information about educational, respite and research grants programs

Drinking Water / Environmental Protection Agency
(800) 426-4791; (202) 260-7908 in Washington, D.C.
Safe drinking water information

Drug Abuse, National Institute on
(800) 662-HELP
Information on Drug Abuse

Drug and Food Complaints / HHS / Food and Drug Administration
(301) 443-1240; (202) 857-8400 weekends and holidays
Food and drugs; complaints and advice on emergencies

Drug Free Workplace Helpline
(800) 843-4971
Publications and referrals to businesses and organizations

Drug Reactions / HHS / Food and Drug Administration
(800) 638-6725; (301) 881-0256 in Maryland (call collect)
Reporting of problems with drugs and medical devices by health professionals

Dyslexia Society, Orton
(800) ABCD-123; (410) 296-0232 in Maryland
Information and referrals

Eating Disorders, Mercer Center
(410) 332-9800 in Maryland
Information and counseling

Elderly / Eldercare Hotline
(800) 677-1116
Referrals to local resources nationwide

Elderly / Legal Counseling / American Association of Retired Persons and state and Washington, D.C., governments
(800) 622-2520; (800) 652-5997; (800) 252-5997; (202) 234-0970
Free legal counsel for the elderly

Emotionally Disturbed
See also Retarded

Endometriosis Foundation
(800) 992-ENDO; (414) 355-2200 in Wisconsin
Leave name/address on recorded message to get information

Environment:
See also Asbestos, Hazardous Waste, Chemical, Superfund, Toxic

Environmental Protection Agency
program information by region:
Region I (CT, MA, VT, NH, RI)
Hazardous Waste Ombudsman
(617) 573-5707
Small Business Ombudsman
(617) 565-3420
Unleaded Fuel Hotline
(800) 631-2700 in MA; (800) 821-1237 in other Region I states

Region II (NY, NJ, Puerto Rico & Virgin Islands)
Hazardous Waste Ombudsman
(212) 264-3384
Small Business Ombudsman
(212) 264-4711
RCRA / Superfund Hotline
(800) 346-5009

Region III (Washington, DC; DE, MD, PA, VA, WV)
Hazardous Waste Ombudsman
(215) 597-0982;
Small Business Ombudsman
(800) 368-5888

Region IV (AL, FL, GA, KN, MS, NC, SC, TN)
General Number
(800) 241-1754
Hazardous Waste Ombudsman
(404) 347-7109
Small Business Ombudsman
(404) 347-7109

Region V (IN, MI, IL, MN, OH, WI)
General Number
(800) 621-8431

Region VI (AK, LA, NM, OK, TX)
Environmental Emergency Hotline—
24 hours (214) 655-2222
Hazardous Waste Ombudsman
(214) 655-6700
Small Business Ombudsman
(214) 655-2200

Region VII (NE, IA, KS, MO)
Action Line for residents:
(800) 223-0425

Region VIII (CO, MT, ND, SD, UT, WY)
General Number (800) 283-9697
Hazardous Waste Ombudsman
(303) 294-1111

Small Business Ombudsman
(303) 294-1111

Region IX (AZ, CA, HI, NV, Guam, Samoa, Northern Mariana Islands, Palau, Micronesia, and Marshall Islands)
Hazardous Waste Ombudsman
(415) 744-1730
RCRA Hotline (415) 744-2074
Small Business Ombudsman
(415) 744-1635
Superfund Hotline (415) 744-2356

Region X (WA, OR, ID, AS)
(800) 424-4-EPA

Environmental Protection Agency Research
(513) 569-7562
To order Environmental Protection Agency research reports

Environmental Protection Agency Training Institute
(202) 260-6678
Clearinghouse for all EPA training activities

Epilepsy Foundation of America
(800) EFA-1000; (301) 459-3700 in Maryland
Information

Ethics / Joseph and Rose Kennedy Institute of Ethics National Reference Center for Bioethics Literature
(800) MED-ETHX
Free online searches of database on bioethic research

Explosives, Missing / U.S. Department of Treasury
(800) 800-3855; (202) 927-7777 in Washington, DC
To report stolen or missing explosives

Explosives & Firearms / U.S. Department of the Treasury
(800) 800-3855; (202) 927-7777 in Washington, DC
Firearms, explosives, and licensing information

Eye Care Project Helpline, National
(800) 222-EYES
Assistance/care for the elderly

Fitness
See Aerobics

Foundation Center
(800) 424-9836
Information on foundations and types of grants they provide

Gas Exploration / U.S. Department of the Interior
(202) 208-3100
For information about Outer Continental Shelf oil and gas exploration off California

Handicap
See also Disabilities
See also Blind

Hazardous Waste / Environmental Protection Agency
(202) 424-9346
EPA/Hazardous Waste Ombudsman assistance on hazardous waste issues

Headache Foundation, National
(800) 843-2256; (800) 523-8858 in Illinois
Information and publications

Health Information Clearinghouse,
(800) 336-4797
To obtain publications on health, such as those contained in "Healthfinder series" and referrals to laser surgery experts

Hearing
See also Deafness

Hearing Aid Society Hearing Aid Hotline, National
(800) 521-5247
(313) 478-2610 in Michigan
Assistance in locating qualified hearing instrument specialists, consumer information kit, referrals for financial assistance

Hearing / Better Hearing Institute
(800) EAR-WELL
(703) 642-0580 in Virginia
Information and educational publications

Hearing and Speech, Action Line for National Association for
(800) 638-8255
Consumer hearing and speech hotline

Hearing Service, Occupational
(800) 222-EARS;
Hearing/screening test by telephone

Hepatitis Hotline of the American Liver Foundation, National
(800) 223-0179
Information regarding tests, availability of vaccines, etc.; physicians referral service

Hill-Burton Hospital Free Care
(800) 638-0742
(800) 492-0359 (in Maryland)
Information on hospitals and other health facilities which provide free care

Homeless and Mental Illness, National Resource Center on
(800) 444-7415
Information about services for homeless and mentally ill population

Hospice Organization, National
(800) 658-8898
Referral and information helpline on hospices

Hospice Education Institute Hospicelink
(800) 331-1620; (203) 767-1620 in Connecticut
Referral network

Human Growth Foundation
(800) 451-6434
Information regarding physical growth disorders in children

Huntington's Disease Society of America
(800) 345-4372; (212) 242-1968 in New York
Information Line

Ileitis and Colitis, National Foundation for
(800) 343-3637
Free brochures, counseling, doctor referrals and support groups

Impotency / Recovery of Male Potency
(313) 357-1314
Information and publications

Kidney Foundation, National
(800) 622-9010
Information regarding organ and tissue donation

Kidney Fund, American
(800) 638-8299
Publications, information and financial assistance

Learning Disabilities
See also Disabilities

Learning Disabilities / National Information Center for Children and Youth with Disabilities
(800) 999-5599
Locating services for the handicapped and information on learning disabilities

Library of Medicine, National
(800) 272-4787
Information and reference database searches on publications from 1913; audiovisuals from 1970

Liver Foundation, American
(800) 223-0179
Information and referrals

Lupus Foundation of America
(800) 558-0121
For free information packet

Lupus Research Institute, Terri Gotthelf
(800) 82-LUPUS
Information, publications, referrals, research grants

Lymphedema Network, National
(800) 541-3259
Information and referrals

Meat and Poultry Hotline / U.S. Department of Agriculture
(800) 535-4555
Food safety information and to report illness from meat, poultry or eggs

Mental Health, National Association
(800) 969-NMHA
Call to receive brochure

Mines, Abandoned / U.S. Department of the Interior
(412) 937-2146
Emergency response number regarding abandoned land mines

Mine Safety / U.S. Department of Labor / Mine Safety and Health Administration
(703) 557-2020
For reporting health and safety hazards

Minority Health Resource Center, Office of
(800) 444-6472
For publications, referrals and assistance

Multiple Scleroses Society, National
(800) 532-7667
For free information and information packet

Myasthenia Gravis Foundation
(800) 541-5454
Patient and professional literature and grants for research

Neurofibromatosis Foundation, National
(800) 323-7938
(212) 460-8980 in NY
To receive information packet

Nuclear Waste / Nuclear Regulatory Agency
(301) 504-3432
Recorded message announcing DOE/NRC meetings on waste management

Occupational Safety and Health Information, National Institute for
(800) 35-NIOSH
Publications/database searches on occupational safety and health, including hazards associated with fetal development and pregnancy and list of cancer-causing products

Oil Spills / U.S. Department of Transportation, Coast Guard
(800) 424-8802; (202) 426-2675 in Washington D.C.
To report adverse environmental acts (oil spills, etc.) by boats

Organ Donor Hotline
(800) 24-DONOR
Information

Organ Donor / The Living Bank
(800) 528-2971
Organ donor registry and referral service

Paralysis Foundation, American / Spinal Cord Injury Hotline
(800) 526-3456
Information, counseling and referral service

Parkinson's Education Program
(800) 344-7872
for free information packet
(714) 250-2975
for information and referrals

Parkinson Foundation, National
(800) 327-4545; (800) 433-7022 in Florida; (305) 547-6666 in Maine
Information; neurologists referrals

Parkinson Disease Association, American
(800) 223-2732
Information and referrals to doctors and hospitals

Pesticide Telecommunications Network, National
(800) 858-7378
Pesticide information on safe use and effects from Environmental Protection Agency and Texas Tech.

Plastic and Reconstructive Surgeons, American Society of
(800) 635-0635
Referral service

Plastic Surgery Information Service, Facial
(800) 332-FACE (USA)
To receive information packet

PMS Access
(800) 222-4767
Information packet, referrals, and pharmacy

Poison / American Association of Poison Control Centers
for information on accidental ingestion of chemicals, poisons or drugs (unless otherwise noted, toll-free numbers are valid only within each state):

Alabama:
(800) 292-6678
Children's Hospital of Alabama - Regional Poison Control Center, Birmingham

Arizona:
(800) 362-0101
Arizona Poison & Drug Information Center, Tucson
(602) 253-3334
Samaritan Regional Poison Center, Phoenix

California:
(209) 445-1222
Fresno Regional Poison Control Center
(800) 777-6476
Los Angeles County Medical Association Regional Poison Control Center
(800) 876-4766
San Diego Regional Poison Center
(800) 523-2222
San Francisco Bay Area Regional Poison Control Center
(800) 342-9293
UCDMC Regional Poison Control Center, Sacramento

Colorado:
(800) 332-3073
Rocky Mountain Poison and Drug Center, Denver

District of Columbia:
(202) 625-3333;
(202) 784-4660 (TTY)
National Poison Control Center Hotline (Georgetown University Hospital, Washington, D.C.)

Florida:
(800) 282-3171
Florida Poison Information Center, Tampa

Georgia:
(800) 282-5846;
(404) 525-3323 (TTY)
Georgia Poison Control Center, Atlanta

Indiana:
(800) 382-9097
Indiana Poison Center, Indianapolis

Kentucky:
(800) 722-5725
Kentucky Regional Poison Center of Kosair, Louisville

Maryland:
(800) 492-2414
Maryland Poison Center, Baltimore

Massachusetts:
(617) 232-2120
Massachusetts Poison Control System, Boston

Michigan:
(313) 745-5711; (800) 482-8254 (TTY)
Poison Control Center, Children's Hospital of Michigan, Detroit

Minnesota:
(612) 347-3141; (612) 337-7474 (TTY)
Hennepin Regional Poison Center
(800) 222-1222
Minnesota Regional Poison Center

Missouri:
(800) 392-9111; (800) 366-8888; (314) 577-5336 (TTY)
Cardinal Glennon Children's Hospital Regional Poison Center, St. Louis

Montana:
(800) 525-5042
Rocky Mountain Poison and Drug Center, Denver, Colorado

Nebraska:
(800) 955-9119
Poison Control Center, Omaha

New Jersey:
(800) 962-1253
New Jersey Poison Information and Education System, Newark

New Mexico:
(800) 432-6866
New Mexico Poison and Drug Information Center, Albuquerque

New York:
(516) 542-2323
Long Island Regional Poison Control Center, East Meadow
(212) 340-4494; (212) POISONS
New York City Poison Control Center, New York, NY

Nevada:
(702) 732-4989; (800) 446-6179 for Los Vegas
Rocky Mountain Poison and Drug Center, Denver, Colorado

Ohio:
(800) 682-7625; (614) 228-2272 (TTY)
Central Ohio Poison Center, Columbus
(800) 558-7251
Regional Poison Control System, Cincinnati Drug and Poison Information Center

Oregon:
(800) 452-7165
Oregon Poison Center, Portland

Pennsylvania:
(215) 386-2100
Delaware Valley Regional Poison Control Center, Philadelphia
(412) 681-6669
Pittsburgh Poison Center

Rhode Island:
(401) 444-5727
Rhode Island Poison Center - Rhode Island Hospital, Providence

Texas:
(800) 441-0040 in Dallas
North Texas Poison Center, Dallas
(409) 765-1420; [(800) 392-8548—medical professionals only]
Texas State Poison Center, Galveston

Utah:
(800) 456-7707
Intermountain Regional Poison Control Center, Salt Lake City:

West Virginia:
(800) 642-3625;
(304) 348-4211
West Virginia Poison Center, Charleston

Wyoming:
(800) 525-6115
Rocky Mountain Poison and Drug Center, Denver, Colorado

Radon / Environmental Protection Agency
(202) 233-9370
Information on radon issues

Retarded / Devereux Foundation
(800) 345-1292
Residential treatment in 11 states for emotionally disturbed, retarded or autistic individuals

Rural / U.S. Department of Agriculture
(800) 633-7701
Rural Information Center Hotline

Reyes' Syndrome Foundation, National
(800) 233-7393
Information and referrals

Safety Council, National
(800) 621-7619
Recorded information ; leave name/address for publications

Sarcoidosis Family Aid and Research Foundation
(800) 223-6429
Information, publications, research

Schizophrenia Association, American
(800) 847-3802
To receive information packet

Scleroderma Foundation, United
(800) 722-HOPE
(408) 728-2202 in California
Information and publications

Sexually Transmitted Diseases Resource Center, National
(800) 227-8922
Information, publications and referrals

Sickle Cell Disease, National Association for
(800) 421-8453
(213) 736-5455 in California
Publications and referrals

Soil Conservation / U.S. Department of Agriculture
(800) THE SOIL
Information on conserving soil and water resources and on volunteering

Speech
See also Hearing

Social Security Benefits / HHS / Social Security Administration
(800) 234-5772;
(800) 772-1213
Information on retirement, survivor, disability, medicare and SSI benefits

Spina Bifida Information and Referral
(800) 621-3141;
(202) 944-3285 in Washington, DC
Publications, information, referrals

Spinal Cord Injury Association, Nat'l
(800) 962-9629
Information and referrals

Stroke, National Institute of Neurological Disorders and
(800) 352-9424
Information and referrals

Sturge-Weber Foundation
(800) 627-5482
Literature, Support Services ; education on Sturge-Weber syndrome

Sudden Infant Death (SIDS) Institute, American
(800) 232-SIDS
(800) 847-7437 in Georgia
Clinical research, educational seminars and treatment facilities

Suicide and Rape 24-Hour Emergency Services of the Humanistic Mental Health Foundation
(310) 983-8383
Crisis hotline, residential treatment programs, financial assistance

Superfund / E.P.A.
(800) 424-9346
Resource Conservation and Recovery Act and the Comprehensive Environmental Response, Compensation and Liability Act information and requests for documents (Superfund)

Surgery / Second Opinion Hotline/ HHS / Health Care Financing Administration
(800) 638-6833
Referral service for second surgical opinions

Toxic / Environmental Protection Agency
(202) 554-1404
Toxic Substances Control Act regulations and program information

Tourette Syndrome Association
(800) 237-0717
To receive information packet

Trauma Society, American
(800) 556-7890
(301) 420-4189 in Maryland
Provides you with publications and information

Tuberous Sclerosis Association, National
(800) 225-6872
(301) 459-9888 in Maryland
Research, information and referrals

Violence Hotline, Domestic
(800) 288-3854
Referral service for counseling, shelter, legal information, and other types of assistance

Violence / National Child Abuse Hotline
(800) 422-4453
Information, counseling; referral service

Violence, National Council on Child Abuse and Family Violence
(800) 222-2000
Referral assistance, information and publications

Wastewater Treatment / National Small Flows Clearinghouse
(800) 624-8301
Information on wastewater treatment technologies for small communities

Water / Environmental Protection Agency
(800) 426-4791
(202) 260-7908 in Washington, DC
Safe drinking water information

Wetlands Protection Hotline
(800) 832-7828
Provides information on wetlands and their protection

Women's Bureau / U. S. Department of Labor
(800) 827-5335
Publications on child care and work and family life

Women's Sports Foundation
(800) 227-3988;
(516) 542-4700 in New York
Information packet, educational travel and training grants for individual athletes

What To Do
When You Can't Afford Health Care

An "A-to-Z" Sourcebook for the Entire Family

- **FREE Treatment**
- **FREE Hospitalization**
- **FREE Information & Advice**

by

Matthew Lesko

with

Mary Ann Martello

and

Andrew Naprawa

Research: Caroline Pharmer

Production: Beth Meserve

FIRST EDITION

Cover Design: Lester Zaiontz

Library of Congress Cataloging-in-Publication Date

Lesko, Matthew

What To Do When You Can't Afford Health Care sourcebook

ISBN # 1-878346-16-4

T O

all the federal and state bureaucrats who

eagerly share information that empowers us

to pursue our goals and dreams

Other books written by Matthew Lesko:

Getting Yours: The Complete Guide to Government Money

How to Get Free Tax Help

Information USA

The Computer Data and Database Source Book

The Maternity Sourcebook

Lesko's New Tech Sourcebook

The Investor's Information Sourcebook

The Federal Data Base Finder

The State Database Finder

The Great American Gripe Book

Lesko's Info-Power

Government Giveaways for Entrepreneurs

If you begged for, borrowed, stole or even purchased this book, I want to thank you. But I must warn you that this book comes with certain limitations.

Although by publishing my own books, I am able to go from manuscript to printed book in as little as 6 weeks instead of 12 to 18 months it took when I used New York publishers, there is still a problem with timeliness. Life around us changes so quickly that it is almost impossible to have a book 100% perfect by time the reader uses it. Phone numbers change, organizations move, and publications go out of print. If you telephone a source in this book and instead get some pizza parlor, don't distress. At least you know such an organization exists, somewhere. You can get help in locating the source's new telephone number by calling any or all of the following:

- The Information Operator in the city where the organization is located (dial the area code followed by 555-1212)
- The U.S. Government Federal Information Center (listed in the blue pages of your telephone book under U.S. Government or call your local information operator)
- Our office at Information USA in Kensington, Maryland (call 301-942-6303.)

This book will not work for you unless you know how to be nice to a bureaucrat. The sources in this book are staffed by public servants whose motives differ from professionals in the private sector. The paycheck of professionals in the private sector is dependent upon how much work they do for you. However, public servants get the same paycheck whether they work for you for two weeks for free or if they hang up on you right after you say hello. So the amount of help and information you derive from a public servant is directly related to how much they WANT to work for you. And this is a function of how well you treat them. If you are not already aware of this, you should first read the chapter entitled "The Art of Getting a Bureaucrat to Help You."

We designed this book so that most users can look up their health problem, make a single phone call, and get the information they need to solve their problem. But some problems may take three calls, seven calls, a dozen, or more. Much of our salesmanship culture wants us to believe that our problems can be solved with just one phone call, but deep down we know that most of life doesn't work that way. Finding the help and information you need can take a bit of effort, but the help is very likely to be there, and there's no magic to getting to it. You'll just have to make a few more phone calls.

Matthew Lesko
Information USA, Inc.

Table of Contents

Introduction 1

The Art Of Getting A Bureaucrat To Help You 3

Sample Success Stories 7

Free Treatment For Rich And Poor 15

    Free Medical Care for Rich and Poor By the Best Doctors in the World 16

    Doctors Who Get Grants To Study Your Illness 18

    Free Health Care At Your Hospital 20

    Local Free Health Clinics 21

    Federal Medical Programs For Elderly, Disabled And Low Income 24

    A New Law Provides Free Health Care To Children 24

    How To Get Drug Companies To Fill Your Prescription For Free 30

    It's The Law: Care At Hospital Emergency Rooms 31

    Physicians Who Volunteer In Your Area 32

    Handicapped and Disabled: The Best Places To Start For Help 35

    Free Research On Health Matters 48

Free Information And Expertise From A To Z 49

A —		Acupuncture	53
Abetalipoproteinemia	50	Acute Hemorrhagic Conjunctivitis	54
Abortion	50	Acute Leukemia	54
Abstinence	51	Acute Myocardial Infarction	54
Accident Prevention	51	Addison's Disease	55
Acetaminophen	51	Adenoma of the Thyroid	55
Achondroplasia	51	Adolescent Drug Abuse	55
Acidosis	52	Adolescent Health	56
Acne	52	Adoption	58
Acoustic Neuroma	52	Adrenal Gland Disorders	58
Acquired Immune Deficiency		Adrenoleukodystrophy	59
Disorder	53	Adynamia	59
Acromegaly	53	Agammaglobulinemia	59
Acth	53	Age-related Macular Degeneration	59

Agenesis 60
Agent Orange 60
Aging 60
Agranulocytosis 63
AIDS 63
Air Pollution 67
Albinism 68
Albright's Syndrome 68
Alcoholism 68
Aldosteronism 71
Alexander's Syndrome 71
Alkaptonuria 71
Alkylating Agents 71
Allergenics 71
Allergic Rhinitis 72
Allergies 72
Alopecia 73
Alpers Syndrome 73
Alpha-1-Antitrypsin Deficiency 74
Alternative Medicine Practices 74
Alveolar Bone 75
Alveolar Microlithiasis 75
Alveolar Proteinosis 75
Alzheimer's Disease 75
Amaurotic Idiocy 77
Ambiguous Genitalia 77
Amblyopia 78
Amebiasis 78
Amino Acid Disorders 78
Amniocentesis 78
Amosmia 79
Amyloid Polyneuropathy 79
Amyloidosis 79
Amyotonia Congenita 80
Amyotrophic Lateral Sclerosis 80
Analgesic-Associated Nephropathy 81
Anaphoresis 81
Anaplasis 81
Anemia 82
Anencephaly 82
Aneurysms 83
Angelman's Disease 83
Angina Pectoris 83
Angioedema 84
Angiography 84
Angioplasty 84
Aniline Dyes 84
Animal Research 85
Aniridia 85
Ankloglassia 85
Ankylosis Spondylitis 85
Anorexia 85
Anosmia 86
Anoxia 87
Antenatal Diagnosis 87
Anthrax 87
Antialphatrypsin 87
Antibiotics 88
Anti-Cancer Drugs 88
Anticoagulants 88
Antidiuretic Hormone 89

Antihistamines 89
Antimetabolites 89
Anti-Inflammatory Drugs 90
Antineoplastic 90
Antisocial Behavior 90
Antiviral Substances 90
Anxiety Attacks 91
Aortic Insufficiency/Stenosis 91
Aortitis 91
Aphakia 91
Aphasia 92
Aphthous Stomatitis 92
Aplastic Anemia 92
Apnea 93
Apraxia 93
Arachnoiditis 93
Aran Duchenne Spinal Muscular
 Dystrophy 93
Arnold-Chiari Malformations 94
Arrhythmias 94
Arteriosclerosis 94
Arteriovenous Malformations 95
Arteritis 95
Arthritis 95
Arthrogryposis Multiplex Congenita 96
Arthroplasty 97
Arthroscopy 97
Artificial Blood Vessels 97
Artificial Hearts 97
Artificial Insemination 98
Artificial Joints 98
Artificial Lung 98
Asbestos 99
Asbestosis 99
Asiatic Flu 100
Asparaginase 100
Aspartame 100
Asperger's Syndrome 100
Aspergillosis 101
Asphyxia 101
Aspirin Allergy 101
Asthma 101
Astigmatism 102
Asymmetric Septal Hypertrophy 103
Ataxia 103
Ataxia Telangiectasia 103
Atelectasis 104
Atherectomy 104
Atherosclerosis 104
Athetosis 105
Athlete's Foot 105
Atopic Dermatitis 105
Atrial Fibrillation 106
Attention Deficit Disorder 106
Autism 106
Autoimmune Disease 107
Autosomal Dominant Disease 107

B —
B-19 Infection 107
Baby Bottle Tooth Decay 108

Bacillus Calmette-Guerin (BCG) 108
Back Problems 108
Bacterial Meningitis 109
Bacteriology 110
Bad Breath 110
Bagassosis 110
Barlow's Syndrome 110
Bartter's Syndrome 110
Basal Cell Carcinoma 111
Batten's Disease 111
Battered Child 111
Battered Elderly 111
Battered Spouses 111
Bed Wetting 112
Bedsonia 112
Behavior and Health 112
Behavior Development 113
Behavior Modification 113
Behcet's Disease 113
Bejel 114
Bell's Palsy 114
Benign Congenital Hypotonia 114
Benign Mucosal Pemphigoid 115
Benign Prostatic Hyperplasia 115
Benzo(a)pyrene 115
Berger's Disease 116
Beriberi 116
Bernard-Soulier Syndrome 116
Beta Blocker Drugs 117
Beta-Thalassemia 117
Biliary Cirrhosis 117
Bilirubinemia 117
Binocular Vision 117
Binswanger's Disease 118
Biofeedback 118
Biomedical Engineering 119
Biomedical Research 119
Biophysics 119
Biopsies 119
Biotechnology 119
Birth 120
Birth Control 120
Birth Defects 120
Birth Weight 121
Black Lung Disease 122
Black Tongue 122
Bladder Cancer 122
Blastomycosis 123
Bleomycin 123
Blepharitis 123
Blepharospasm 123
Blindness 124
Blistering Disorders 124
Bloch-Sulzberger Syndrome 124
Blood 124
Blood Brain Barrier 125
Blood Coagulation 125
Blood Diseases 126
Blood Products 126
Blood Substitutes 126
Blood Testing 126

Blue Baby 126
Body Weight 127
Bolivian Hemorrhagic Fever 127
Bone Cancer 127
Bone Disorders 127
Bone Marrow Failure 128
Bone Marrow Transplants 128
Botulism 128
Bovine Growth Hormone 129
Bowel Disease 129
Bowen's Disease 129
Brachial Plexus Injuries 130
Bradycardia 130
Brain 130
Brain Cancer 131
Brain Death 131
Brain Injuries 132
Brain Tumors 132
Breast Cancer 133
Breastfeeding 134
Breast Implants 135
Bronchiectasis 135
Bronchitis 136
Brucellosis 136
Bruxism 136
Bubonic Plague 136
Buerger's Disease 136
Bulbar Palsy 137
Bulimia 137
Bullous Pemphigoid 138
Burkitt's Lymphoma 138
Burn Research 138
Burning Mouth Syndrome 138
Bursitis 139
Busulfan 139
Byssinosis 139

C —
Caffeine 139
Calcium 140
Canavan's Disease 140
Cancer 140
Candida 143
Canker Sores 143
Carbohydrates 143
Carcalon 143
Carcinogens 144
Carcinoma 144
Cardiomegaly 144
Cardiomyopathy 145
Cardiopulmonary Resuscitation 145
Cardiovascular Disease 145
Carditis 146
Caries 146
Carmustine 146
Carotid Endarterectomy 146
Carpal Tunnel Syndrome 146
Carpet Fumes 147
Cataphasia 147
Cataplexy 147
Cataracts 148

Cat Cry Syndrome 148
Cat Scratch Fever 148
Catheterization 148
CEA 149
Celiac Disease 149
Cellulite 149
Centenarians 150
Central Core Disease 150
Cerebellar Arteriosclerosis 150
Cerebellar Ataxia 150
Cerebellar Lesions 151
Cerebral Arteriovenous Malformations 151
Cerebral Atrophy 151
Cerebral Palsy 152
Cerebrotendious Xanthomatosis 152
Cerebrovascular Disease 152
Ceroid Lipofuscinosis 153
Cervical Cancer 153
Cervical Cap 153
Cervical Disorders 153
Cesareans 154
Cestode 154
Chagas' Disease 154
Chalazion 154
Chancroid 155
Change of Life 155
Chaparral Tea 155
Charcoal Broiling of Meat 155
Charcot-Marie-Tooth Disease 155
Charge Syndrome 156
Chediak-Higashi Syndrome 156
Cheiloaschisis 156
Chelation Therapy 156
Chemical Spills 156
Chemotherapy 157
Chewing Tobacco and Snuff 157
Chicken Pox 157
Chilblain 158
Child Abuse and Family Violence 158
Child Development 159
Child Health 160
Child Pornography 162
Child Rearing 162
Child Support 162
Childbirth 162
Childhood Arthritis 163
Childhood Asthma 163
Childhood Mental Disorders 163
Childhood Nutrition 164
Children of Alcoholics 165
Chinese Restaurant Syndrome 165
Chlamydia 165
Chloasma 165
Chlorambucil 166
Cholecystectomy 166
Cholelithotomy 166
Cholera 166
Cholesterol 166
Chondrocalcinosis 167
Chondromalacia 167
Chondrosarcoma 168

Chordoma 168
Choriocarcinoma 168
Chorionic Villus Sampling 168
Choroiditis 169
Chronic Bronchitis 169
Chronic Cough 169
Chronic Disease 169
Chronic EBV 170
Chronic Fatigue Syndrome 170
Chronic Granulomatous Disease 171
Chronic Infections 171
Chronic Myelogenous Leukemia 171
Chronic Obstructive Lung Disease 171
Chronic Pain 172
Chrysotherapy 172
Churg-Strauss Syndrome 172
Cicatricial Pemphigoid 173
Cigarettes 173
Circulation Disorders 173
Circumcision 173
Cirrhosis 173
Cisplatin 174
Claudication 174
Claustrophobia 174
Cleft Palate 174
Climacteric 175
Clinical Research 175
Cloning 175
Clotting Disorders 175
Cluster Headache 176
CMV 176
Coal Worker's Pneumoconiosis 176
Coat's Disease 176
Cobalt 176
Cocaine 176
Cockayne's Syndrome 177
Codeine 177
Coffee 177
Cogan's Syndrome 177
Cognition 178
Cold Sores 178
Coley's Mixed Toxins 178
Colic 178
Colitis 179
Collagen Disease 179
Collapsed Lungs 179
Colon Problems 180
Color Blindness 180
Colorectal Neoplasms 180
Colostomy 180
Colpocystitis 181
Comas 181
Comedo (Blackheads) 181
Common Cold 181
Communicable & Infectious
  Diseases 182
Communication Disorders 182
Compulsion 183
Computer Access 183
Condoms 184
Congenital Abnormalities 184

Congenital Adrenal Hyperplasia 184
Congenital Heart Disease 185
Congenital Infections 185
Congestive Heart Failure 185
Conjunctivitis 186
Connective Tissue Diseases 186
Constipation 186
Consumer Product Injuries 187
Contact Dermatitis 189
Contact Lenses 189
Contraception 190
Cookware 191
Cooley's Anemia 191
Cor Pulmonale 192
Corneal Disorders and Transplants 192
Cornelia deLange Syndrome 192
Coronary Angioplasty 192
Coronary Disease 193
Cosmetic Allergy 193
Cosmetic Surgery 193
Costochondritis 193
Cot Death 193
Coughing 193
Cowpox 194
Coxsackie Virus 194
CPR 194
Crack Cocaine 194
Cranial Abnormalities 195
Craniofacial Malformations 195
Cretinism 195
Creutzfeldt-Jakob Disease 195
Crib Death 196
Crigler-Najar Syndrome 196
Critical Care 196
Crohn's Disease 196
Cross-Eye 197
Cryosurgery 197
Cryptococcosis 198
Cryptosporidiosis 198
Cushing's Disease 198
Cushing's Syndrome 198
Cutis Laxa 199
Cyclic Idiopathic Edema 199
Cyclitis 199
Cyclophosphamide 200
Cyclosporine-Associated
  Hypertension 200
Cystic Acne 200
Cystic Fibrosis 200
Cystic Mastitis 201
Cystinosis 201
Cystinuria 201
Cystitis 201
Cytarabine 202
Cytomegalic Inclusion Body Disease 202
Cytomegalovirus (CMV) 202

D —
Dactinomycin 203
Daltonism 203
Dandruff 203

Dandy-Walker Syndrome 204
Darier's Disease 204
Daunorubicin 204
Day Care 204
Deafness 205
Death 205
Decarbazine 205
Decubitus Ulcers 206
Degenerative Basal Ganglia Disease 206
Degenerative Joint Disease 206
Deglutition 206
Dejerine-Sottas Disease 207
Dementia 207
Demyelinating Diseases 208
Dengue 208
Dental Care Programs 208
Dental Disease 208
Dental Procedures and Aids 209
Dental Restorative Materials 209
Dental Sealants 209
Dental X-Rays 210
Dentobacterial Plaque Infection 210
Dentures 210
Depression 210
Depth Perception 211
Dermagraphisms 211
Dermatitis Herpetiformis 212
Dermatographism 212
Dermatology 212
Dermatomyositis 212
DES 213
Developmental Disabilities 214
Devic's Syndrome 214
Dextranase 215
Dhobie Itch 215
Diabetes 215
Diabetic Neuropathy 217
Diabetic Retinopathy 217
Diagnostic Imaging 218
Dialysis 218
Diaper Rash 218
Diarrhea 218
Diet 219
Dietary Supplements 219
Diethylstilbestrol (DES) 219
Dieting 219
Diffuse Sclerosis 220
Digestive Diseases 220
Dioxin 221
Diphtheria 222
Disabilities 222
Disabled Infants 223
Disasters 223
Discoid Lupus Erythematosus 224
Disease Hotline 224
Diuretics 224
Diurnaldystonia 224
Diverticulitis 225
Divorce 225
Dizygotic Twins (Fraternal Twins) 225
Dizziness 225

DNA 226
Down's Syndrome 226
Doxorrubicin 226
DPT Vaccine (Diptheria-Pertussis
  -Tetanus) 227
Drinking and Cancer 227
Drinking Water 227
Dropsy 227
Drug Abuse 228
Drug Allergy 230
Drug Approval Process 230
Drug Development 231
Drug Evaluation 231
Drug Hemolytic Anemia 231
Drug Interactions 231
Drug Labeling 231
Drug Purpura 232
Drug Resistance 232
Drug Testing 232
Drug Treatment 233
Drunk Driving 233
Dry Eyes 234
Dry Mouth 234
Duchenne Muscular Dystrophy 235
Dupuytren's Contracture 235
Dust Inhalation Diseases 235
Dwarfism 236
Dysautonomia 236
Dysentery 236
Dyskinesia 237
Dyslexia 237
Dysmenorrhea 238
Dyspepsia 238
Dystonia 238

E —
Ear Infections 239
Eating Disorders 239
Eaton-Lambert Myasthenic Syndrome . . . 240
Echocardiography 240
Eclampsia 240
Ectodermal Dysplasias 240
Ectopic Hormones 241
Ectopic Pregnancy 241
Eczema 241
Edema 242
Eggs 242
Ehlers-Danlos Syndrome 242
Eisenmenger's Syndrome 242
EKGs 243
Elder Abuse 243
Elderly 243
Electrical Stimulation 243
Electric Blankets 244
Electrocardiogram 244
Electromagnetic Fields 244
Electro-Shock Treatment 244
Elephantiasis 245
Embolisms 245
Emphysema 245
Enamel 246

Encephalitis 246
Encephalitis Lethargica 247
Encephalomyelitis 247
Encopresis 247
Endocarditis 247
Endocrine Glands 247
Endocrinologic Muscle Disease 248
Endodontics 248
Endogenous Depression 248
Endometriosis 248
Enigmatic Blistering Disorders 249
Enteric Diseases 249
Environmental Health 250
Environmental Issues 250
Eosinophilic Granuloma 250
Epicondylitis 251
Epidemiology 251
Epidermodysplasia Verruciformis 251
Epidermolysis Bullosa 251
Epiglottitis 252
Epikeratophakia 252
Epilepsy 252
Epistaxis 253
Epstein-Barr Syndrome 253
Equine Encephalitis 253
Erythema Elevatum Diutinum 254
Erythema Multiforme 254
Erythema Nodosum 254
Erythroblastosis Fetalis 254
Erythrocytes 255
Esophageal Disorders 255
Esotropia 255
Estramustine 255
Estreptozocina 255
Estrogen 256
Ethics 257
Euthanasia 257
Ewing's Sarcoma 257
Exercise 257
Exotropia 259
Experimental Allergic Encephalomyelitis . . 259
Extended Care Facility 260
Extracorporeal Shock-Wave Lithotripsy . . . 260
Extrapyramidal Disorders 260
Eye Banks 260
Eye Care 260
Eye Exercises 261
Eye Tumors 261

F —
Fabry's Disease 261
Face Lifts 262
Facial Tics 262
Fainting 263
Falls and Frailty 263
Familial Ataxia Telangiectasia 263
Familial Multiple Endocrine Neoplasia . . . 264
Familial Spastic Paraparesis 264
Family Health 264
Family & Medical Leave 264
Family Planning 265

Family Violence 266
Fanconi's Anemia 266
Farmers Lung 266
Farsightedness 266
Fascioliasis 267
Fast Food 267
Fasting 267
Fatherhood 267
Fat Substitutes 268
Febrile Convulsions 268
Febrile Seizures 268
Feeding Impairments 268
Feet 269
Fertility 269
Fetal Alcohol Syndrome 269
Fetal Monitoring 269
Fetal Research 270
Fevers 270
Fever Blisters 270
Fiber 270
Fibrillation 271
Fibrinolysis 271
Fibrocystic Disease of the Breast 271
Fibroid Tumors 271
Fibromuscular Hyperplasia 272
Fibromyalgia 272
Fibrositis 272
Fibrotic Lung Diseases 272
Fibrous Dysplasia 273
Fifth Disease 273
Filariasis 273
First Aid 274
Floaters 274
Floppy Baby 274
Floxiridine 274
Flu 274
Fluorescein Angiography 275
Fluorescent Lamps 275
Fluoridation 275
Fluoroscopy 276
Fluorosis 276
Fluorouracil 276
Food 276
Food Additives 278
Food Allergies 279
Food and Drug Interactions 279
Food Irradiation 279
Food Labeling 280
Food Poisoning 280
Food Preservatives 281
Food Safety 281
Formaldehyde Exposure 282
Foster Care 282
Fracture Healing 282
Fragile X Syndrome 283
Friedreich's Ataxia 283
Froehlich's Syndrome 283
Fruits & Vegetables 284
Fuch's Dystrophy 284
Fungal Diseases of the Eye 284
Fungal Infections 284

Funnel Chest 285
Furry Tongue 285

G —
G6PD Deficiency 285
Galactorrhea 285
Galactosemia 285
Gallbladder 286
Gallstones 286
Gas 287
Gastric Bubble 287
Gastric Hypersecretion 287
Gastrinoma 287
Gastritis 288
Gaucher's Disease 288
Generic Drugs 288
Gene Therapy 289
Genetic Pancrea 289
Genetics 289
Genetic Testing and Counseling 291
Genital Herpes 292
Genital Warts 292
Geriatrics 293
German Measles 293
Gerontology 293
Gerson Method 293
Gerstmann's Syndrome 293
Gestation 294
Gestational Diabetes 294
Giardiasis 294
Gigantism 294
Gilbert's Syndrome 295
Gilles de la Tourette's Disease 295
Gingivitis 295
Glaucoma 295
Gliomas 296
Globoid Cell Leukodystrophy 296
Glomerulonephritis 296
Glucose Intolerance 297
Gluten Intolerance 297
Glycogen Storage Disease 297
Goiter 297
Gonads 298
Gonorrhea 298
Goodpasture's Syndrome 298
Gout 299
Grains 299
Grief 299
Granulocytopenia 300
Granulomatous Disease 300
Grape Cure 300
Grave's Disease 300
Grippe 301
Growth Hormone Deficiency 301
Guillain-Barre Syndrome 301
Gum Disease 302
Gynecomastia 302
Gyrate Atrophy 302

H —
Hailey's Disease 303

Hair Loss 303
Hair Removal 303
Hair Spray 304
Hairy Tongue 304
Halitosis 304
Hallervorden-Spatz Disease 304
Hand, Foot and Mouth Disease 304
Handicapped 305
Handicapped Children 306
Hansen's Disease 306
Happy Puppet Syndrome 307
Harada's Disease 307
Hardening of the Arteries 307
Harelip 307
Hashimoto's Disease 308
Haverhill Fever 308
Hay Fever 308
Hazardous Substances 308
Headaches 309
Head Injuries 309
Head Lice 310
Health Care Costs 310
Health Care Policy 311
Health Facilities 312
Health Foods 312
Health Fraud 312
Health Insurance 313
Health Maintenance Organizations 314
Health Professionals 314
Health Spas 315
Health Statistics 315
Hearing Aids 315
Hearing Loss 316
Heart Attacks 317
Heartburn 317
Heart Disease 318
Heart-Lung Machines 318
Heart Murmurs 319
Heart Transplants 319
Heat Stroke 319
Hebephrenia 319
Hemiplegia 320
Hemodialysis 320
Hemoglobin Genetics 320
Hemoglobinopathies 320
Hemolytic Anemia 321
Hemolytic Disease 321
Hemophilia 321
Hemophilus Influenza 322
Hemorrhagic Diathesis 322
Hemorrhoids 322
Hemosiderosis 323
Henoch-Schonlein Purpura 323
Hepatitis 323
Hernias 324
Herniated Discs 325
Heroin 325
Herpes 325
Herpes Zoster 326
Hiatal Hernias 327
Hiccups 327

High Blood Pressure 327
High-Density Lipoproteins 328
Hirschsprung's Disease 329
Hirsutism 329
Histiocytosis 329
Histoplasmosis 330
Hives 330
HIV Infection 330
Hodeolum 332
Hodgkin's Disease 332
Holistic Medicine 332
Homelessness 332
Homeopathy 333
Homocystinuria 333
Homosexuality 333
Home Test Kits 334
Hookworm Disease 334
Hormones 334
Hormone Therapy 335
Hospice Care 335
Hospital Complaints 335
Hospital Infections 335
Household Hazards 336
Human Growth Hormone 336
Human Papilloma Virus 336
Hunger 337
Hunt's Disease 337
Hunter's Syndrome 337
Huntington's Chorea 337
Hurler's Syndrome 338
Hyaline Membrane Disease 338
Hydrocephalus 339
Hydroxyurea 339
Hyperactivity 339
Hyperbaric Oxygenation 340
Hyperbilirubinemia 340
Hypercalcemia 341
Hypercalciuria 341
Hypercholesterolemia 341
Hyperglycemia 341
Hyperkinesis 341
Hyperlipidemia 342
Hyperlipoproteinemia 342
Hyperparathyroidism 342
Hyperpyrexia 342
Hypersensitivity Pneumonitis 343
Hypertension 343
Hyperthermia 343
Hyperthyroidism 343
Hypertriglyceridemia 344
Hyperuricemia 344
Hyperventilation 344
Hypobetalipoproteinemia 344
Hypocomplementemic
  Glomerulonephritis 345
Hypoglycemia 345
Hypogonadism 345
Hypokalemia 346
Hypokalemic Periodic Paralysis 346
Hypolipoproteinemia 346
Hypoparathyroidism 347

Information USA, Inc.

Hypopituitarism 347
Hypospadias 347
Hypotension 347
Hypothalamus 347
Hypothermia 348
Hypothyroidism 348
Hypotonia 348
Hypoventilation 349
Hypoxia 349
Hypsarrhythmia 349

I —
IBD and IBS 349
Iceland Disease 349
Ichthyosis 350
Identical Twins 350
Idiopathic Hypertrophic Subaortic
  Stenosis 350
Idiopathic Inflammatory Myopathy 350
Idiopathic Thrombocytopenic Purpura 351
Ileitis 351
Immune Deficiency Disease 351
Immune Thrombocytopenic Purpura 352
Immunizations 352
Impotence 353
Inappropriate Antidiuretic Hormone
  Syndrome 353
Inborn Heart Defects 353
Incontinence 354
Incontinentia Pigmenti 354
Indoor Air Pollution 355
Induced Movement Disorders 355
Infant Formula 356
Infant Health 356
Infant Nutrition 357
Infants with Disabilities 358
Infectious Arthritis 359
Infectious Diseases 359
Infectious Eye Diseases 359
Infectious Waste 359
Infertility 360
Inflammatory Bowel Disease 361
Influenza 361
Insect Stings 361
Insomnia 361
Insulin-Dependent Diabetes 362
Insulinomas 362
Interferon 362
Interleukin-2 Therapy 363
Interstitial Cystitis 363
Intestinal Malabsorption Syndrome 363
Intracranial Aneurysm 363
Intraocular Lenses 364
Intrauterine Growth Retardation 364
Intravenous Drug Therapy 364
Invasive Dental Procedures 364
In Vitro Fertilization 365
Iridocyclitis 365
Iritis 365
Iron Deficiency 365
Irradiation 366

Irritable Bowel Syndrome 366
Iscador 366
Ischemia 366
Islet Cell Hyperplasia 367
Isolated IGA Deficiency 367

J —
Jakob-Creutzfeldt Disease 367
Joint Replacement 367
Joseph's Disease 368
Juicing 368
Juvenile Delinquency 368
Juvenile Diabetes 369
Juvenile Rheumatoid Arthritis 369
Juxtaglomerular Hyperplasia 369

K —
Kanner's Syndrome 369
Kaposi's Sarcoma 370
Kawasaki Disease 370
Kearns-Sayre Syndrome 370
Keratitis 370
Keratoconus 371
Keratomileusis 371
Keratoplasty 371
Keratosis Palmaris et Plantaris 371
Kidney Cancer 372
Kidney Disease 372
Kidney Stones 373
Kidney Transplants 373
Kleine-Levin Syndrome 373
Kleptomania 374
Klinefelter's Syndrome 374
Koch Antitoxins 374
Krabbe's Disease 374
Krebiozen 374
Kugelberg-Welander Disease 375
Kuru 375

L —
Laboratory Testing 375
Labyrinthitis 375
Lacrimal Glands 376
Lactation 376
Lactose Deficiency 377
Lactose Intolerance 377
Laetrile 377
Lamaze Method of Childbirth 377
Language Disorders 377
Larynx Cancer 378
Laser Surgery 378
Lassa Fever 379
Laurence-Moon-Bardet-Biedl Syndrome . . . 380
Lead Poisoning 380
Learning Disabilities 381
Leber's Disease 382
Legg-Perthes Disease 382
Legionella Pneumophila 382
Legionnaire's Disease 382
Leigh's Disease 383
Leishmaniasis 383

Lennox-Gastaut 383
Lens Implants 383
Leprosy 384
Lesch-Nyhan Disease 384
Leukemia 384
Leukoaraiosis 385
Leukodystrophy 385
Leukoencephalopathy 385
Leukoplakia 386
Lice 386
Lichen Planus 386
Life Cycle 387
Life Expectancy 387
Lifestyle 387
Life-Sustaining Technologies 388
Lipid Research 388
Lipid Storage Diseases 388
Lipid Transport Disorders 388
Lipidemia 389
Lipidosis 389
Listeriosis 389
Lithotripsy 389
Liver Disorders 390
Living Wills 390
Locked-In Syndrome 390
Lockjaw (Tetanus) 391
Loeffler's Syndrome 391
Lomustine 391
Longevity 391
Long-Term Care 391
Lou Gehrig's Disease 392
Lower Back Pain 392
Low Birthweight 393
Low Blood Pressure 393
Low-Calorie Sweeteners 394
Low Density Lipoproteins 394
Low-Fat Diet 394
Low-Income Mothers 394
Lowe's Syndrome 395
L-Tryptophan 395
Lung Cancer 395
Lung Disease 396
Lupus 397
Lyme Disease 397
Lymphadenopathy Syndrome 398
Lymphedema 399
Lymphoblastic Lymphosarcoma 399
Lymphoma 399
Lymphosarcoma 399

M —

Macroglobulinemia and Myeloma 400
Macular Degeneration 400
Makari Test 400
Malabsorptive Disease 400
Malaria 401
Malignancies 401
Malnutrition 401
Malocclusion 402
Mammograms 402
Mandible Disorders 402

Mania 403
Manic-Depressive Psychosis 403
Maple Syrup Urine Disease 403
Marble Bone Disease 403
Marburg Virus Disease 403
Marfan Syndrome 404
Marijuana 404
Mastectomies 405
Mastocytosis 405
Maternal and Child Health 406
Mcardle's Disease 407
Measles 407
Meat and Poultry 408
Mechlorethamine 408
Meconium Aspiration Syndrome 408
Medical Devices 409
Medical Imaging 409
Medical Testing 409
Medicare and Medicaid 409
Medications 411
Medicinal Plants 413
Mediterranean Fever 413
Megaloblastic Anemia 413
Megavitamin Therapy 413
Meige's Syndrome (Facial Dystonia) 414
Melanoma 414
Melkerson's Syndrome 415
Melphalan 415
Memory Loss 415
Menier's Disease 416
Meningitis 416
Meningocele 416
Menke's Disease 417
Menopause 417
Menstruation 418
Mental Health in Children 418
Mental Illness 418
Mental Retardation 420
Mercaptopurine 421
Mercury Vapor Lamps 421
Mercy Killing 421
Metabolic Disorders 421
Metastatic Tumors 422
Methadone 423
Methotrexate 423
Microcephaly 423
Microtropia 423
Microvascular Surgery 424
Microwaves 424
Middle Ear Infections 424
Migraines 424
Military Medical Care 425
Milk 425
Minority Health Care 426
Minority Health Professionals 427
Mitochondrial Myopathies 427
Mitomycin 428
Mitotane 428
Mitral Valve Prolapse 428
Mixed Connective Tissue Disease 428
Molds 428

Mongolism 429
Mononucleosis 429
Monozygotic Twins 429
Mortality Rate 429
Motor Neuron Disease 429
Movement Disorders 430
Moya-Moya Disease 430
MRI 430
MSG 431
Mucopolysaccharidosis 431
Multi-Infarct Dementia 431
Multiple Sclerosis 431
Mumps 432
Muscular Dystrophy 432
Muscular Fatigue 433
Myasthenia Gravis 433
Mycobacterial Infections 433
Mycoses 434
Mycosis Fungoides 434
Mycotoxins 434
Myelodysplastic Syndromes 434
Myelofibrosis 435
Myeloma 435
Myocardial Infarction 436
Myoclonus 436
Myofascial Pain Syndrome 436
Myopia 436
Myositis 437
Myotonia 437

N —
Narcolepsy 438
National Health Insurance 438
Native Americans 438
Natural Childbirth 439
Nearsightedness 439
Nemaline Myopathy 439
Neoplasia 439
Neonatal Asphyxia 440
Neonatal Respiratory Distress Syndrome . . 440
Nephritis 440
Nephrocalcinosis 440
Nephrolithiasis 441
Nephrotic Syndrome 441
Nerve Damage 441
Neural Tube Defects 441
Neuralgia 442
Neurodermatitis 442
Neuro-Ophthalmology 442
Neuroaxonal Dystrophy 443
Neuroblastoma 443
Neurofibromatosis 443
Neurogenic Arthropathy 444
Neurological Disorders 444
Neuropathies 444
Neuroscience 445
Neurosclerosis 445
Neurotoxicity 445
Newborn Screening 445
Niemann-Pick Disease 445
Night Blindness 446

Noise, Effects of 446
Nongonococcal Urethritis 447
Nonprescription Drugs 447
Norplant 447
Nosebleeds 448
Nuclear Medicine 448
Nursing Homes 448
Nutrition 449
Nutritional Labeling 453
Nystagmus 453

O —
Obesity 454
Obsessive-Compulsive 455
Occupational Safety and Health 455
Ocular Hypertension 456
Odor Disorders 456
Olivopontocerebellar Atrophy 456
Onchocerciasis 456
Oncology 457
Ophthalmia Neonatorum 457
Oppenheim's Disease 457
Optic Atrophy 457
Optic Neuritis 458
Oral Cancer 458
Oral Contraceptives 458
Oral Health 459
Organ Transplants 459
Orotic Aciduria 460
Orphan Diseases 460
Orphan Drugs 460
Orthodontics 461
Orthognathic Surgery 461
Orthokeratology 461
Orthopedics 462
Orthopedic Implants 462
Orthostatic Hypotension 462
Orthotics 463
Osteitis Deformans 463
Osteoarthritis 463
Osteogenesis 464
Osteogenic Sarcoma 464
Osteomalacia 464
Osteomyelitis 464
Osteopetrosis 465
Osteoporosis 465
Osteosarcoma 466
Osteosclerosis 466
Otitis Media 467
Otosclerosis 467
Ovarian Cancer 467
Over-The-Counter Drugs 467
Ovulation 468

P —
Pacemakers 468
Paget's Disease 468
Pain 469
Palpitations 470
Palsy 470
Pancreatic Cancer 470

Pancreatitis 471
Panic Attacks 471
Panencephalitis 471
Panniculitis 472
Pap Tests 472
Papilloma Virus 472
Paralysis Agitans 473
Paramyotonia Congenita 473
Paranoia 473
Paraplegia 473
Parasitic Disease 474
Parathyroid Disorders 474
Parkinson's Disease 474
Paroxysmal Atrial Tachycardia 475
Paroxysmal Nocturnal
  Hemoglobinuria 475
Pars Planitis 476
Parvovirus Infections 476
Passive Smoking 476
PCP 476
Pectus Excavatum 477
Pediatric AIDS 477
Pediculosis 477
Pedodontics 477
Pelizaeous-Merzbacher Disease 478
Pelvic Inflammatory Disease 478
Pemphigoid 478
Penicillin 479
Peptic Ulcers 479
Periarteritis Nodosa 479
Pericarditis 479
Pericardial Tamponade 480
Perinatal Services 480
Periodontal Disease 480
Peripheral Neuropathy 481
Peripheral Vascular Disease 481
Pernicious Anemia 481
Personality Disorders 481
Pertussis 482
Pervasive Developmental
  Disorders 482
Pesticides 482
Peyronie's Disease 483
Pharmaceuticals 483
Pharmacology 484
Pharyngeal Disabilities 484
Phenylketonuria 484
Pheochromocytoma 484
Phlebitis 484
Phlebothrombosis 485
Phobias 485
Physical Fitness 485
Pick's Disease 485
The Pill 486
Pi-Mesons 486
Pimples 486
Pink Eye 486
Pinta 486
Pinworms 486
Pituitary Tumors 487
Pityriasis 487

PKD 488
PKU 488
Placenta Disorders 488
Plaque 489
Plasma Cell Cancer 489
Plastic Surgery 489
Playground Safety 489
Pleurisy 489
Plicamycin 489
PMS 490
Pneumococcal Infections 490
Pneumothorax 490
Poisoning 491
Poison Ivy 493
Polioencephalitis 493
Poliomyelitis 493
Pollen Allergy 493
Polyarteritis 494
Polycystic Kidney Disease (PKD) 494
Polycystic Ovary Syndrome 494
Polycythemia 494
Polymyalgia Rheumatica 495
Polymyositis 495
Polyneuritis 495
Polyostotic Fibrous Dysplasia 496
Polyps 496
Polyserositis 496
Pompe's Disease 497
Population Control 497
Porphyria 497
Positron Emission Tomography 498
Postnatal Care 498
Post-Polio Syndrome 499
Postural Hypotension 499
Potassium 499
Pott's Disease 500
Poultry Inspection 500
Power Lines 500
Prader-Willi Syndrome 501
Prednisone 501
Pregnancy 501
Pregnancy and Alcohol 503
Premature Babies 504
Premenstrual Syndrome 504
Prenatal Care 505
Presbycusis 505
Presbyopia 506
Prescription Drugs 506
Presenile Dementia 506
Preservatives 507
Prevention 507
Primary Care 507
Primary Lateral Sclerosis 508
Primary Ovarian Failure 508
Procarbazine 509
Progeria 509
Progestins 509
Progressive Multifocal
  Leukoencephalopathy 509
Progressive Supranuclear Palsy 509
Prostate Cancer 510

Prostate Problems 510
Prostheses 511
Prosthodontics 511
Prurigo Nodularis 511
Pruritus 512
Pseudogout 512
Pseudohypertrophic Dystrophy 512
Pseudohypoparathyroidism 512
Pseudomonas Infections 512
Pseudosenility 513
Pseudotumor Cerebri 513
Pseudoxanthoma Elasticum 513
Psittacosis 514
Psoriasis 514
Psoriatic Arthritis 514
Psychotic Episodes 514
Pterygium 515
Ptosis 515
Puberty 515
Pulmonary Alveolar Proteinosis 516
Pulmonary Disease 516
Pulmonary Toxicants 516
Pure Red Cell Aplasia 517
Purpura 517
Pyelonephritis 517
Pyogenic Infections 517
Pyorrhea 518

Q —
Quadriplegia 518

R —
Rabies 518
Radial Keratotomy 519
Radiation 519
Radon 520
Ramsey Hunt Syndrome 521
Rape 522
Rare Diseases 522
Rashes 522
Raynaud's Disease 522
Reading Disorders 523
Read Method of Childbirth 523
Recurrent Fever 523
Reflex Sympathetic Dystrophy Syndrome . . 524
Reflux Nephropathy 524
Refractory Anemia 524
Refsum's Disease 525
Regional Enteritis 525
Rehabilitation 525
Reiter's Syndrome 525
Relaxation 526
Renal Disorders 526
Renovascular Hypertension 526
Repetitive Stress Syndrome 527
Reproductive Disorders 527
Respiratory Diseases 527
Respiratory Distress Syndrome 528
Respiratory Syncytial Virus 528
Restless Leg Syndrome 529
Retardation 529

Retinal Disease 529
Rett's Syndrome 529
Reye's Syndrome 530
RH Factor 530
Rhabdomyosarcoma 530
Rheumatic Fever 531
Rheumatic Heart 531
Rheumatism 531
Rheumatoid Arthritis 532
Rhinitis 532
Rhus Dermatitis 532
Rhytidoplasty 533
Rickets 533
Riley-Day Syndrome 533
Ringworm 533
River Blindness 534
Rocky Mountain Spotted Fever 534
Root Caries 534
Rosaceae 534
Rotavirus 535
Rothmund-Thompson Syndrome 535
Rubella 535
Runaway Hotline 535

S —
Safe Sex 536
Salivary System Diseases 536
Salmonella Infections 536
Salt 536
Santavuori Disease 537
Sarcoidosis 537
Sarcoma 538
Saturated Fat 538
Scabies 538
Scarlet Fever 538
Schilder's Disease 539
Schistosomiasis 539
Schizophrenia 539
School Health 539
Schwannoma 540
Sciatica 541
Scleroderma 541
Sclerosis 541
Scoliosis 542
Seafood Inspection 542
Self-Help 542
Segawa's Dystonia 543
Seizures 543
Seminoma 543
Senility 543
Senile Macular Degeneration 544
Septal Defects 544
Sex Changes 545
Sex Determination 545
Sex Hormones 545
Sexual Abuse 545
Sexuality 545
Sexually Transmitted Diseases 546
Sezary Syndrome 547
Shaken Baby Syndrome 547
Shingles 547

Shock 548
Short Stature 548
Shy-Drager Syndrome 548
Siamese Twins 549
Sick Buildings 549
Sickle Cell 549
Sideroblastic Anemia 550
Silicone Implants 550
Sinusitis 550
Sjogren's Syndrome 550
Skin and Aging 552
Skin Cancer 552
Skin Conditions 553
Sleep Apnea 553
Sleep Disorders 553
Slow Viruses 554
Smallpox 554
Smell Disorders 554
Smokeless Tobacco 555
Smoking 556
Snacking 557
Social Security 557
Sodium 559
Solar Burns 559
Spasmodic Dysphonia 560
Spastic Conditions 560
Speech and Language Disorders 560
Sphingolipidosis 561
Spielmeyer-Sjogren's Disease 562
Spina Bifida 562
Spinal Arachnoiditis 563
Spinal Cord Injuries 563
Spinal Cord Tumors 563
Spine Curvature 564
Spinal Muscular Atrophy 564
Spine Joints 564
Spinocerebellar Degeneration 564
Sports Medicine 565
Sports Nutrition 565
Spousal Abuse 565
Squamous Cell 565
Stained Teeth 566
Staphylococcal (Staph) Infections 566
Steele-Richardson Disease 566
Steinerts Disease 566
Sterilization 567
Steroid Contraceptives 567
Steroid Hypertension 567
Steroids 568
Stevens-Johnson Syndrome 568
Stiff Man Syndrome 568
Still's Disease 569
Stomach Cancer 569
Stomatitis 569
Strabismus 569
Streptococcal (Strep) Infections 570
Streptokinase 570
Stress 570
Striatonigral Degeneration 571
Stroke 571
Strongyloidiasis (Roundworm) 572

Sturge-Weber Syndrome 573
Stuttering 573
Stye 573
Sudden Cardiac Death 573
Sudden Infant Death Syndrome 574
Suicide 575
Sulfites 575
Sunlamps 576
Sunscreens 576
Surgery 576
Surrogate Motherhood 576
Sweat Gland Disorders 576
Swine Flu 577
Sydenham's Chorea 577
Syncope 577
Synovitis 577
Syphilis 578
Syringomyelia 578
Systemic Lupus Erythematosus 578
Systemic Sclerosis 579
Systolic Hypertension 579

T —
Tachycardia 579
Takayasu's Arteritis 580
Tamoxifen 580
Tangier Disease 580
Tanning 580
Tapeworm Infection 581
Tardive Dyskinesia 581
Taste Disorders 581
Tattoo Removal 582
Tay-Sach's Disease 582
Teenagers 583
Teen Pregnancy 583
Teeth Problems 584
Temporal Arteritis 584
Tendonitis 585
Tennis Elbow 585
Test Tube Babies 585
Testicular Cancer 585
Tetanus 586
Tetralogy of Fallot 586
Thalassemia 586
Therapeutic Endoscopy 587
Thoracic-Outlet Syndrome 587
Thrombasthenia 587
Thrombocytopenia 587
Thrombolysis 588
Thrombophlebitis 588
Thrombosis 588
Thyroid Disorders 588
Thymoma 589
Thyrotoxic Myopathy 589
Thyrotoxic Periodic Paralysis 589
Tic Douloureux 589
Ticks 590
Tinnitus 590
Tobacco 590
Tongue Tied 590
Torsion Dystonia 591

Torticollis 591
Tourette Syndrome 591
Toxics 592
Toxic Shock 593
Toxocariasis 594
Toxoplasmosis 594
Trace Elements 595
Trachoma 595
Tranquilizers 595
Transdermal Delivery of Drugs 596
Transfusions 596
Transfusional Hemosiderosis 596
Transient Ischemic Attacks 596
Transplants 597
Transverse Myelitis 597
Traumatic Brain Injuries 598
Travelers' Health 598
Tremors 599
Trench Mouth 599
Trichinosis 599
Trichomoniasis 600
Trichuriasis 600
Trigeminal Neuralgia 600
Trophoblastic Cancer 600
Tropical Diseases 600
Tropical Oils 601
Truncus Arteriosus 601
Trypanosomiasis 602
Trypsinogen Deficiency 602
Tubal Ligation 602
Tuberculosis 602
Tuberous Sclerosis 602
Tularemia 603
Tumors 603
Turner Syndrome 604
Twins 604
Typhoid Fever 604

U —
Ulcers 604
Ulcerative Colitis 605
Ultrasound 605
Unconventional Medicine Practices 606
Uremia 606
Urinary Incontinence 606
Urinary Tract Disease 606
Urolithiasis 607
Urticaria 607
Uterine Cancer 607
Uveitis 608

V —
Vaccines 608
Vaginitis 609
Valvular Heart Disease 609
Varicella 610
Varicose Veins 610
Vasculitis 610
Vasectomies 611
VD 611
Vegetarianism 611

Venereal Disease 611
Venezuelan Equine Encephalitis 612
Vertigo 612
Veteran's Drug & Alcohol
  Treatment 613
Veterinary Food and Medicine 613
Video Display Terminals 613
Videos and Films 614
Vinblastine 616
Vincent's Infection 616
Vincristine 616
Viruses 617
Vision 617
Vital Statistics 618
Vitamins 618
Vitiligo 618
Vitrectomy 618
Vocal Chord Paralysis 619
Vogt-Koyanagi Disease 619
Von Recklinghausen's Disease 619
Von Willebrand's Disease 620

W —
Waardenburg Syndrome 620
Waldenstroms Macroglobulinemia 620
Walleye 620
Warts 621
Water 621
Weber-Christian Disease 621
Wegener's Granulomatosis 622
Weight Loss 622
Werdnig-Hoffmann Disease 622
Werner's Syndrome 622
Wernicke's Encephalopathy 623
Whiplash 623
Whooping Cough 623
Wife Abuse 624
Wilms' Tumor 624
Wilson Disease 624
Wiskott-Aldrich Syndrome 624
Wolff-Parkinson-White Syndrome 625
Women 625
Workplace Drug Abuse 626
Workplace Health and Safety 627
Wryneck 630

X —
Xanthinuria 630
Xanthomatosis 630
Xeroderma Pigmentosum 631
Xerophtalmia 631
Xerostomia 631
X-Rays 631

Y
Yeast Infections 632
Yellow Fever 632

Z —
Zollinger-Ellison Syndrome 633
Zoonoses 633

Free Legal Help With Your Health Care Rights **635**

    Aging-Related 636

    Cosmetics 639

    Doctors 640

    Fish and Seafood 643

    Free Medical Care 644

    Health and Safety Hazards at Work 645

    Health Fraud 647

    Health Clubs 650

    Health Maintenance Organizations 651

    Hospital Care and Service 651

    Hospital Discrimination 652

    Health Insurance 652

    Licensed Professionals 655

    Medical Bills 662

    Medical Devices 663

    Medicare Fraud and Abuse 664

    Nursing Homes 664

    Pharmacists and Pharmacies 667

    Prescription Fraud 670

    Product Safety Defects 670

    Radon 671

    Tanning Devices and Salons 675

    Getting Involved in Changing the Current Health Care System 675

Appendix A: 1992 Clinical Studies **677**

Appendix B: How To Get Drug Companies To Fill Your Prescription For Free **705**

Appendix C: State Health Statistics **713**

Index **723**

INTRODUCTION

The importance of health care in our society doesn't have to be explained here. Better people than me are doing a pretty good job of letting the public know how important health care is, how costly it has become, and how much it has to be changed.

What I want to share in this book is how to use the tools of our information society to get:

- the **best treatment** for any health problem whether your rich or poor,
- the **latest information**, for free, on any health related topic, and
- **justice** in the health care system, without hiring a lawyer.

Money Isn't Everything

Money doesn't always buy you the best treatment, the latest information, or even get you justice in our health care system. We live in a large, complex, information-oriented society, where the answers to our questions are changing daily. In this environment, some of the obvious sources of help and information are often times the worst.

Health care practitioners who barely have enough to time to care for patients, certainly don't have time to keep up on the mountains of information, data and studies that are generated daily by health care researchers. As a result, they aren't always the ones who can tell you what the latest causes, treatments and cures are to a particular illness. Hospitals that are struggling to survive financially are not likely to advertise the fact that there are federal laws that require most of them to provide a certain amount of their services for free, or that some doctors get government money to perform procedures and operations for free. And lawyers who face ever growing competition are not about to inform you that a complaint against a health care provider can be handled better by a regulatory agency that won't charge you a dime.

Learn To Use The World's Largest Source Of
Free Health Care

The government now represents approximately 37% of everything in our country. More people now work in government in our country than they do in manufacturing. Uncle Sam is a force to be reckoned with, no matter what subject you are talking about. But government has a bigger impact on health care than on any other sector of our society. In 1993, the budget for the U.S. Department of Health and Human Services is expected to be twice that of the Department of Defense. Even if you take the cost of Social Security out of the U.S. Department of Health and Human Services budget, it is still bigger than Defense. And that gap is due to get much wider in the coming years.

So why shouldn't you as a taxpayer learn to use this invaluable resource to solve some of your own health care problems. For example:

Why pay for treatment at a local hospital.......
     when some of the best doctors in the world get government money to perform procedures and operations for free?

Why pay $200 to a doctor to answer a health question........

> when you can get better answers from a FREE medical researcher who spends a lifetime and millions of dollars studying just your disease? They can tell you what will be in the medical journals next year because they are financing the research today.

Why spend money on health books at the book store......

> when you can get FREE books, pamphlets and even videos that are more complete and more up-to-date?

Why hire a lawyer when you're mistreated by a doctor, hospital or nursing home......

> when you can contact a government office who will sue them for you for free?

Why pay for a medical visit when you're unemployed or without insurance....

> when you can get free treatment at a local clinic?

Why be harassed by a hospital for not paying a bill.....

> when you can show that the hospital has to treat you for free if you can't afford to pay?

Why trust a one-minute sound bite on the nightly news by a reporter who spends maybe one hour studying a recent health discovery.....

> when you can call a government expert who spends a career studying the subject and will send you a free report showing you all the ifs, ands or buts of the discovery, and if this discovery really affects your life.

How The Book Is Organized

Once you get by the chapters on "The Art of Getting a Bureaucrat to Help You" and "Sample Success Stories," the book is basically divided into the following three sections:

Free Treatment For Rich & Poor

> This chapter describes over 400 sources of free care and treatment, including how to take advantage of free clinical studies at the National Institutes of Health and at other health facilities all over the country; how to locate low-cost and free clinics in your neighborhood; and how to find local doctors and hospitals that are willing to treat you for free.

Free Information and Expertise From A to Z

> This chapter lists over 1,500 diseases and health issues--everything from acne to accident prevention to DES, migraines, and yellow fever. It describes over 4,500 sources of clearinghouses, referral networks, publications and videos.

Free Legal Help With Your Health Care Rights

> Close to 300 consumer resources are listed that will fight to make sure you don't get taken by your insurance company, your physician, or even your Medicare office. Also included are resources on how you can fight health fraud, how to get the best nursing home care, and even how to complain about your pharmacist.

Remember, if you contact a source and they are unable to provide the exact help you need, be sure to ask them for a suggestion for another source. If they can't give you a suggestion, ask if someone else in their office would know. Never go away from your source empty handed.

The Art Of Getting A Bureaucrat To Help You

Our greatest asset to seeking help and information is that we live in a society inhabited by people who are dying to talk about what they do for a living. However, in this world of big bureaucracies and impersonal organizations, it is rare that any of us get a chance to share what we know with someone who is truly interested. Perhaps this is why psychiatrists are in such great demand.

This phenomenon can work to your advantage; most anyone can find an expert on any topic providing you expect it will take an average of seven telephone calls.

The Value Of Experts In Today's Information Age

Using experts can be your answer to coping with the information explosion. Computers handle some problems of the information explosion because they are able to categorize and index vast amounts of data. However, many computerized databases fail to contain information that is generated by non-traditional sources, such as documents that are buried in state and federal agencies.

Another problem is that many databases suffer from lack of timeliness because they offer indexes to articles and most publishers have long lead times for getting the material into print. And in our fast changing society, having the most current information is crucial.

Computers also contribute to a more serious problem. Because of their ability to store such large quantities of data, computers aggravate the information explosion by fueling the information overload. If you access one of the major databases on a subject such as Maine potatoes, most likely you will be confronted with a printout of 500 or more citations. Do you have the time to find and read all of them? Can you tell a good article from a bad one?

The first step to cut through this volume of information is to find an expert specializing in Maine potatoes. Yes, such an individual exists. This person already will have read those 500 articles and will be able to identify the relevant ones that meet your information needs. This expert will also be able to tell you what will be in the literature next year, because probably he is in the midst of writing or reviewing forthcoming articles. And if you are in search of a fact or figure, this government bureaucrat might know the answer right off the top of his head. And the best part of this research strategy is that all the information can be accumulated just for the price of a telephone call.

Case Study: How To Find Mr. Potato

The techniques for locating an expert can best be illustrated by a classic story from the days when I was struggling to start my first information brokerage company in 1975.

At the time the business amounted only to a desk and telephone crowded in the bedroom of my apartment. As so often happens in a fledgling enterprise, my first client was a friend. His problem was this: "I must have the latest information on the basic supply and demand of Maine potatoes within 24 hours."

My client represented a syndicate of commodity investors that invests millions of dollars in Maine potatoes. When he called, these potatoes were selling at double their normal price and he wanted to know why. I knew absolutely nothing about potatoes, but thought I knew where to find out. The agreement with my client was that I would be paid only if I succeeded in getting the information (no doubt you've guessed I no longer work that way).

Luck With The First Telephone Call

The first call I made was to the general information office of the U.S. Department of Agriculture. I asked to speak to an expert on potatoes. The operator referred me to Mr.

Charlie Porter. At that point, I wondered if this Mr. Porter was a department functionary with responsibility for handling crank calls, but the operator assured me that he was an agriculture economist specializing in potatoes. I called Mr. Porter and explained how I was a struggling entrepreneur who knew nothing about potatoes and needed his help to answer a client's request. Charlie graciously gave me much of the information I needed, adding that he would be happy to talk at greater length either over the phone or in person at his office. I decided to go see him.

Only Problem Was Getting Out Of Charlie Porter's Office

For two-and-one-half hours the next morning, the federal government's potato expert explained in intimate detail the supply and demand of Maine potatoes. Charlie Porter showed me computer printouts that reflected how the price had doubled in recent weeks. For any subject that arose during our conversation, Charlie had immediate access to a reference source. Rows of books in his office covered every conceivable aspect of the potato market. A strip of ticker tape that tracked the daily price of potatoes from all over the country lay across his desk.

Here in Charlie's office was everything anyone might ever want to know about potatoes. The problem, it turned out, was not in getting enough information, but how gracefully to leave his office. Once Charlie started talking, it was hard to stop him. It seemed that Charlie Porter had spent his lifetime studying the supply and demand of potatoes and finally someone with a genuine need sought his expertise.

One Potato....Two Potato....

When I was finally able to let Charlie know I had to leave, he pointed across the hall in the direction of a potato statistician whose primary responsibility was to produce a monthly report showing potato production and consumption in the United States. From the statistician I was to learn about all the categories of potatoes that are tallied. It turns out the U.S. Department of Agriculture

counts all the potato chips sold every month, even how many Pringle potato chips are consumed. The statistician offered to place me on the mailing list to receive all this free monthly data.

From Potatoes to Backaches

Government experts on potatoes and other esoteric topics have made me a lot of money from rich clients. But government experts on topics like back pain, sore feet and bone marrow transplants have also helped me with many of my personal health problems.

In the early days of my business I suffered from discomforting back pain. When I would go to my physician and discuss the problem with him, he would tell me things like "Oh, Lesko, your back pain isn't very bad. Everybody has some back pain. Come back to me when it gets worse so then we can operate." This was not very helpful advice.

One day when I was sitting in my home office waiting for the telephone to ring with a paying client, I decided to take some of my own advice. I called the National Institutes of Health to see if I could speak to a back expert. Within about three telephone calls, I was speaking to a bureaucrat who was spending millions of dollars studying the latest causes and cures to back pain. He was wonderful. He told me about research results that weren't even published yet. He told me about the results of studies that showed that 90% of all back pain was caused by the way we lead our life — tension and lack of exercise. He also told me that the YMCA had a back pain course that had a 75% cure rate. With this knowledge I signed up at a local YMCA, and within 2 lessons my back pain was cured. It was like going to some weird faith healer on television who can heal you with his hands, but this was the government.

A Cure For My Dad's Golf Swing

A few years later my father, who is retired and lives in a golfing community in Florida, called and happened to mentioned a health problem he was having with his foot. As a golfer, the use of his feet was important to him. He was losing circulation in his foot, and his doctors were trying a number of therapies without any success. Then he said that his doctor heard of a new procedure where they place a small roto-rooter in your vein to clean out any blockage. The problem was that no one in Florida was able to perform the operation.

After he told me this, I called the National Institutes of Health to see if anyone knew about this procedure. Within two calls I was talking with a physician who was studying this procedure. She was a delight. She sent me studies describing the risks of this operation, and told me who the doctors in the country were who performed this operation. She also told me who in Washington performed this procedure and what their success rate was. And the kicker was when she told me that my father could have this operation done for free at the National Institutes of Health, because they were studying the procedure.

I quickly called my Dad to brag about what I found, but he said he wasn't interested. I think that the thought of going under the knife to help his golf game was losing its appeal.

A Transplant For A Teacher In Orlando

Another personal story began when I was working one summer at the public library in Orlando, Florida. I was actually there because I was doing research on my hypothesis that "If we live in an information age, why aren't there big lines in front of the public library every day?" But that's a subject for another book. While I was in Orlando, I heard about a local school teacher who had a form of cancer that required a bone marrow transplant. However, her insurance carrier refused to pay for the operation because they believed that it was experimental surgery. The entire city was outraged and was trying to raise $50,000 in donations to pay for the operation.

I immediately changed into my "INFO-MAN" suit and called the bone marrow transplant expert at the National Institutes of Health. Over the telephone, I was given the names and telephone numbers of three doctors around the country who get government money to perform this operation on patients for free. One was at the National

Institutes of Health, another was at Duke University and the third was in Texas. No one in Orlando even knew that this resource existed.

The Art Of Getting An Expert To Talk

The information explosion requires greater reliance on experts in order to sift through the proliferation of data. Cultivating an expert, however, demands an entirely different set of skills from using a library or a publication. You must know how to treat people so that they are ready, willing and able to give the information you need. It is human nature for most anyone to want to share their knowledge, but your approach will determine whether you ultimately get the expert to open up. So it is your job to create an environment that makes an individual want to share his expertise. Remember when dealing with both public and private sector experts, they will get the same paycheck whether they give you two weeks worth of free help or if they cut the conversation short.

Expectations: The 7-Phone Call Rule

There is no magic to finding an expert. It is simply a numbers game which takes an average of seven telephone calls. Telephone enough people and keep asking each for a lead. The magic lies in how much information the expert will share once you find that individual. This is why it is essential to remember "the 7-phone call rule."

If you make several calls and begin to get upset because you are being transferred from one person to another, you will be setting yourself up to fail once you locate the right expert. What is likely to happen is that when your "Charlie Porter" picks up his telephone, he is going to hear you complaining about how sick and tired you are of getting the runaround from his organization. Well, to Charlie, you don't sound like you are going to be the highlight of his day. He will instantly figure out how to get rid of you.

This explains why some people are able to get information and others fail. Seasoned researchers know it is going to take a number of telephone calls and they will not allow themselves to get impatient. After all, the runaround is an unavoidable part of the information gathering process. Consequently, the first words that come out of your mouth are extremely important because they set the stage for letting the expert want to help you.

Ten Basic Telephone Tips

Here are a few pointers to keep in mind when you are casting about for an expert. These guidelines amount to basic common sense but are very easy to forget by the time you get to that sixth or seventh phone call.

1) Introduce Yourself Cheerfully
The way you open the conversation will set the tone for the entire interview. Your greeting and initial comment should be cordial and cheerful. They should give the feeling that this is not going to be just another telephone call, but a pleasant interlude in his or her day.

2) Be Open And Candid
You should be as candid as possible with your source since you are asking the same of him. If you are evasive or deceitful in explaining your needs or motives, your source will be reluctant to provide you with information.

3) Be Optimistic
Throughout the entire conversation you should exude a sense of confidence. If you call and say "You probably aren't the right person" or "You don't have any information, do you?" it makes it easy for the person to say "You're right, I cannot help you." A positive attitude will encourage your source to stretch his mind to see how he might be able to help you.

4) Be Humble And Courteous
You can be optimistic and still be humble. Remember the old adage that you can catch more flies with honey than you can with vinegar. People in general, and experts in particular, love to tell others what they know, as long as their position of authority are not questioned or threatened.

5) Be Concise
State your problem simply. A long-winded explanation may bore your contact and reduce your chances for getting a thorough response.

6) Don't Be A "Gimme"
A "gimme" is someone who says "give me this" or "give me that", and has little consideration for the other person's time or feelings.

7) Be Complimentary
This goes hand in hand with being humble. A well-placed compliment about your source's expertise or insight about a particular topic will serve you well. In searching for information in large organizations, you are apt to talk to many colleagues of your source, so it wouldn't hurt to convey the respect that your "Charlie Porter" commands, for example, "Everyone I spoke to said you are the person I must talk with." It is reassuring to know you have the respect of your peers.

8) Be Conversational
Avoid spending the entire time talking about the information you need. Briefly mention a few irrelevant topics such as the weather, the Washington Redskins, or the latest political campaign. The more social you are without being too chatty, the more likely that your source will open up.

9) Return The Favor
You might share with your source information or even gossip you have picked up elsewhere. However, be certain not to betray the trust of either your client or another source. If you do not have any relevant information to share at the moment, it would still be a good idea to call back when you are further along in your research.

10) Send Thank You Notes
A short note, typed or handwritten, will help ensure that your source will be just as cooperative in the future.

Sample Success Stories

Ok, all you skeptics. So, you really don't believe that if you call a government office they will actually do something good for you. I hope these case stories have the power to turn you around and make a believer out of you. Whether you are sick or well, rich or poor, or in or out of the medical profession, government resources can put you on to the fastest road to recovery, if you learn how to use them. Most of these stories were provided by the experts who work at the sources listed in this book. Others were taken from submissions to Information USA's recent "My Favorite Bureaucrat Contest."

Elderly Women With Burning Mouth Condition Finds Relief

Two sisters were concerned about the health of their elderly mother who complained of a persistent burning sensation in her mouth. They took their mother to many doctors, dentists, clinics, and even to specialists, yet none of them could find anything wrong with her. They eventually contacted the National Institute of Dental Research who told her about a rare condition called, in fact, Burning Mouth, which most often affects post-menopausal, elderly women. The Institute was then able to send the sisters information that helped them take the necessary steps toward helping their mother.

Woman With Eye Disease Gets Line On Free Treatment

A young woman diagnosed with Pseudotumor Cerebri needed help finding a local support group. The National Eye Institute referred her to the National Self Help Center and to the Self Help Clearinghouse of Greater Washington. In addition, the Institute told her about a clinical study on Idiopathic Intracranial Hypertension (another term for pseudotumor) that she might qualify for being conducted by a university medical center.

Florida Hospital Buys Patient Her Own Wheelchair

The Easter Seals Hospital in Tallahassee, Florida, gives all kinds of free health services to those who can't afford it. They offer free adult day health care for the elderly, and even bought an electric wheelchair for a woman who was a paraplegic.

They've also bought insulin level monitors for diabetics, respiratory equipment for asthmatics, as well as crutches, leg braces, and walkers. They even pay for speech and physical therapy.

Alzheimer's Patient Gets Free Care At Clinical Trial

A woman whose father is an Alzheimer's patient called the Alzheimer's Disease Education and Referral Center for information on drugs being tested for the disease. An information specialist discussed with her the types of drug trials that are going on across the country, then referred her to the nearest federally-sponsored Alzheimer's disease research center where her father could possibly receive free treatment.

State Insurance Commissioner Shows How A Cancerous Mole Is More Serious Than Breast Enlargements

A woman in North Carolina got a notice from her insurance company stating that they were not going to pay for her claim to have a cancerous mole removed from her back. She knew of a fellow worker who had just been paid by the same insurance company to have her breasts enlarged and thought she was being treated unfairly. She contacted her state insurance commissioner and within the month received payment for her medical care.

Medical Society Arranges Free Care For Ohio Woman

A 19-year-old called the Columbus, Ohio, Medical Society for help: she did not qualify for Medicaid, but she needed to see a doctor. The Medical Society called a local hospital for her and got them to agree to see her for free and to provide her with all her medications.

Woman Gets Information On Newest Breast Cancer Treatment

A newly diagnosed breast cancer patient called the National Cancer Institute for information on treatment options. The Institute provided her with the most recent and up-to-date information on the available treatment options and identified clinical trials that investigate new treatments for early stage breast cancer.

Center Locates Poem For Grieving SIDS Parent

A SIDS parent who had heard of a poem written by another SIDS parent in memory of her baby called the National Sudden Infant Death Syndrome Resource Center to get help locating it. The mother wanted to use the poem at her baby's memorial service. The staff was able to identify the poem, fax her a copy and give her contact information so she could get in touch with the author of the poem, and obtain permission to use it at her baby's funeral.

Brother of Cancer Victim Learns How to Cope

The brother of a terminally ill patient called the National Cancer Institute for information on how to care for him. They referred the man to the nearest hospice program and provided him with information and materials to assist the family in coping with the illness.

Parents Use Government To Track Down Daughter's Rare Disease Themselves And Out-Do The Doctors

A Florida couple became frustrated with the seeming lack of effort put forth by the medical community when it came to diagnosing just what was wrong with their 2-year-old daughter. Much of the advice was along the lines of, "Don't

compare her to her older sister. All children mature and progress differently," or "Bring her back in 3 months and we'll take another look at her." The couple was not satisfied with the "wait and see" approach and began doing their own research. Along the way, they came upon a brochure from the National Organization of Rare Diseases (NORD). This and subsequent information helped them rule out erroneous diagnoses made by previous specialists and helped them identify some of the other complications that accompany their child's rare ailment. The parents credit NORD's networking program with connecting them with parents of other children with the same disease.

Man Thinking About Eye Surgery Finds Out About Risks Involved

A man who was thinking about having corneal refractive surgery contacted the National Eye Institute. To help him make a more informed decision, they sent him results from the Prospective Evaluation of Radial Keratotomy (PERK), an National Eye Institute-sponsored clinical study of the procedure.

Clearinghouse Helps Woman With Bladder Problem

A woman called the National Kidney and Urologic Diseases Information Clearinghouse. She was having recurrent bladder problems and wanted to know more about her doctor's tentative diagnosis of Interstitial Cystitis (IC), which he said was a difficult disorder to diagnose and treat. She asked the clearinghouse if this was true and if they had any information regarding treatment. The clearinghouse agreed with her doctor and told her that, at present, no treatment relieves the symptoms for IC patients. The clearinghouse enclosed a list of centers they support engaged in research related to Interstitial Cystitis. They also enclosed a literature search that listed materials about IC, and a list of organizations dealing with IC.

Free Nursing Home Money After Medicaid Says No

A Worthington, Ohio, woman couldn't make it living independently any longer, but was disqualified for Medicaid coverage for a nursing home because of her savings. Through the federal Hill-Burton program she was able to receive money to cover her nursing home costs.

Woman Tracks Down Information on Cushing's Syndrome

A woman called the National Kidney and Urologic Diseases Information Clearinghouse because she needed information on a rare disorder called Cushing's Syndrome. Although they do not have publications about this syndrome, they were able to refer her to the National Organization for Rare Disorders, as well as two other organizations that deal with rare kidney conditions.

Man Gets Information on Lactose Intolerance

A man called the National Digestive Diseases Information Clearinghouse for information about his diet and lactose intolerance. They were able to provide him with publications that included general dietary guidelines. When the man asked for specific dietary advice, they referred him to a dietitian from the American Dietetic Association.

Woman With Irritable Bowel Syndrome Finds Support Network

A woman called the National Digestive Diseases Information Clearinghouse for information on Irritable Bowel Syndrome (IBS). They were able to provide her with publications and information regarding a national intestinal disease foundation. The woman also expressed some concerns about dealing with the disease and her own feelings of isolation. To help out, the clearinghouse gave her the name of a person who coordinates a telephone network support system for people with IBS.

Diabetic Gets New Information On Foot Problems

A man called the National Diabetes Information Clearinghouse for information on foot problems he was having related to diabetes. His doctor had told him that he may eventually lose his feet. The clearinghouse was able to send him information, fact sheets, and medical articles about foot problems, wound healing and infections, as well as peripheral vascular disease.

Lead Poisoning Expert Provides Worried Mother With Expert Advice

A woman in Maryland was frightened and confused when she learned that her daughter tested positive for lead poisoning. She called a number of different agencies in an attempt to discover the causes, treatments, and effects of lead poisoning. Although she found a number of offices that she thought might be able of help, no one could give her any clear answers until she spoke with Dr. Susan Binder at the Centers For Disease Control in Atlanta. Dr. Binder listened to her story in detail and outlined the possible causes of the poisoning. Together they arrived at the conclusion that recent house renovations were the likely culprit. Dr. Binder then discussed the potential long-term effects, some of the basic steps she could take to help her daughter, current research and controversies on the subject, and sent current literature. But most importantly, Dr. Binder referred her to local experts and resources in her area where she could turn for further assistance.

Car Accident Victim Gets Free Overnight Hospital Stay

The Monroe Regional Medical Center in Ocala, Florida, provided free overnight care to an emergency car accident victim with a viral illness.

Diabetic Woman Learns About Health And Pregnancy

A woman who had gestational diabetes with her first pregnancy called the National Diabetes Information Clearinghouse for information. She was trying to get pregnant again and wanted to avoid the same problems she'd had the first time. The clearinghouse provided her with a booklet, *Understanding Gestational Diabetes,* as well as several articles from a literature search. They also referred her to the American Diabetes Association, which has a booklet explaining meal planning and exchange lists of food.

Alzheimer's Center Gets Free Training Materials

The Administrator of an adult day care center for Alzheimer's patients contacted the Alzheimer's Disease Education and Referral Center for help in training staff and developing activities for patients. The Center sent her a catalog of training materials it has available and a listing of other resources for training and activities planning from its computerized database.

Stroke Victim Gets Help Finding Rehab Services

The family of a man who had recently suffered a stroke and was due to be released from the hospital needed help finding a rehabilitation facility that would accept him for speech and physical therapy. The National Rehabilitation Information Center referred them to a center in their area and also gave them information on support groups and equipment for stroke victims.

Paraplegic Gets Help Making His Home More Accessible

A recently disabled paraplegic needed to know how to make his home more accessible for his wheelchair. The National Rehabilitation Information Center sent him information and catalogs about products designed for disabled people, such as kitchen and bathroom equipment.

State Health Care Official Gets Money And Private Bill To Help Terminally Ill Boy

A Wisconsin couple's insurance company would not cover the medical expenses for their terminally ill son. They turned to a state counselor for help. An attorney who works for the service was able to get an insurance company to pay the $17,000 disputed bill. He also got the Governor to pass a new law. As a result, their son is now included in a program that provides special funds that allow him to come home from the hospital for visits three times a week when he is stable.

Business Gets Help Making Changes For Handicapped Access

A company interested in complying with the new Americans with Disabilities Act needed advice on building modifications they might have to make. The National Rehabilitation Information Center sent them precise information related to accessibility and equipment requirements under this new law.

Student Gets Free Help Writing Master's Thesis

A Master's student in Public Health contacted the National Maternal and Child Health Clearinghouse for materials on prenatal care among poor women. The clearinghouse provided a wide range of information, including current publications, resource guides listing other important titles/information sources in her area of interest, and referrals to several other government agencies and private organizations active in the area of prenatal care promotion and services.

Single Mother Finishes College With Financial Assistance from State Pregnant Women's Program

A woman in Michigan found herself in her senior year of college, unmarried and pregnant. Her due date was shortly after the end of the semester in which she would receive her degree. As the due date approached, she felt great pressures: emotional, physical, academic, and most definitely financial. At that point, she heard about the Pregnant Women's Program at the State Department of Social Services, which provides financial assistance to pregnant women in need. Her case worker guided her step-by-step through the application process and made sure she got the financial help she needed to finish college and have her baby with as little stress as possible.

Child With Learning Disability Gets Much-Needed Support

A woman whose ten-year-old son was just diagnosed with a learning disability needed help locating support groups for her son and herself. The National Institute on Deafness and Other Communication Disorders directed them to national and local organizations for more information, as well as providing them with publications and a literature search on the topic.

Health Fair Gets Free Help Organizing Event

A hospital health educator planning an annual health promotion fair for patients, staff, and the local community contacted the National Maternal and Child Health Clearinghouse for any relevant materials to help make the event a success. The clearinghouse supplied the hospital with bulk quantities of consumer-oriented publications appropriate for the general public, as well as posters and videotapes suitable for display during the event. The clearinghouse also referred them to other organizations that could provide free help in planning the event.

Pregnant Woman Gets Bilingual Information On Prenatal Care

A pregnant woman called the National Maternal and Child Health Clearinghouse for information materials that might help her properly care for her baby, both before and after birth, as well as similar materials in Spanish for her husband. The clearinghouse responded with literature on maternal nutrition, prenatal and newborn care, as well as addresses and phone numbers of sources for appropriate titles in Spanish. Since there was a history of genetic disorders in her family and she wanted to prepare for the eventual testing of her child, the clearinghouse also referred her to another office that gave her a reading list of the latest publications in print on the subject of genetic testing.

Woman With Endometriosis Gets Line On Free Treatment

A woman in her 30's had a terrible case of endometriosis and underwent a hysterectomy. But her problems continued to worsen and the endometriosis may have invaded her lungs and colon. On top of this, she was experiencing surgical menopause and needed estrogen. The National Institute of Child Health and Human Development was able to send her information on endometriosis and referred her to a national endometriosis organization that could, in turn, refer her to possible clinical studies for free treatment.

Singer Finds Out How Not To Lose Her Voice

A woman feared that the amount of singing she does would put a strain on her vocal cords. The National Institute on Deafness and Other Communication Disorders sent her information on programs to prevent voice disorders. They also directed her to researchers on this topic, and sent her relevant publications.

Down and Out, Mother of Five Gets Last Chance From Congressman

A divorced mother of five, working full-time and living on $8,000 a year with no child support, could not even afford medical service for her children. One night in desperation and on the verge of a nervous breakdown, she wrote to her Congressman, Frank Thompson of New Jersey, about her story. Within one week she received a Medicaid identification card for each of her five children which would ensure them proper medical treatment.

National Institutes of Health Helps Woman With Brain Surgery and Diabetes

A 37-year-old woman began to quickly lose her eyesight, and within two months time was told she had a pituitary tumor and would need brain surgery. An information specialist at the National Institutes of Health (NIH) directed her to a brain surgeon who was located only 45 minutes away from her home in Arkansas. Unfortunately, as a result of the surgery she now suffers from Diabetes Insipidus, which is manifested by an uncontrollable urge to drink water. At times she drinks as much as five gallons in an hour. Again, NIH directed her to the National Organization of Rare Diseases. From there, she learned all about her condition, including facts that the doctors treating her didn't know. The organization also linked her up with other people who suffer from the same condition, one whom has even started a newsletter on the disease. NORD's newsletter keeps her updated on other people, as well as current legislation dealing with Orphan drugs.

Parents of Deaf Child Get State Help

A couple in Pennsylvania decided they were ready for children after five years of marriage. When their first child was born, they were crushed to learn that the child was deaf. The woman quit her job to take care of the child's special needs. Shortly after this, the husband lost his job because of a plant closing. The woman turned to the state government for assistance and was happy to find Mr. Tornbloom who gave them a considerable amount of time, a wealth of information about programs and possibilities, and approved payment by the state for the child's hearing aid.

Mother With Premature Baby Gets Help From State Nurse

A woman in Delaware learned that her baby would be born fourteen weeks early, and she began working with a nurse from her state's Early Intervention Program. After the birth of her son, the nurse visited him frequently throughout his four-month hospital stay, and after the baby had returned to his home, she visited him many times to thoroughly evaluate his developmental progress. She was the first to spot his hearing loss and helped the couple obtain a state-funded hearing aid for him. She diagnosed his need for speech, physical, and occupational therapy, and helped enroll him in an excellent school. At this time the nurse was experiencing severe difficulties of her own at home. Her husband was dying of cancer. Despite this, she continued to be an extremely dedicated and compassionate person.

State Consumer Office Saves Employee Thousands by Getting Insurance Company To Reverse Its Policy for Covering A Pre-Existing Case of Endometriosis

Mr. Gene Hackworth of the Insurance Department of the Consumer Protection Agency in West Virginia worked for close to a year to get an insurance company to reverse an unfair decision for a woman who was being stuck for thousands of dollars as a result of exploratory surgery for endometritis. Due to his efforts, the company paid the claim.

Worried Mom Gets Bottom Line On Daughter's Acne Treatment

A mother called the National Institute of Arthritis and Musculoskeletal and Skin Diseases because her daughter had severe acne. Their dermatologist had tried many different treatments with little success. The mother wanted help understanding additional treatments the dermatologist was considering, such as putting the teenager on Acutane or birth control pills. The Institute sent the mother several articles on acne treatments, and referred her to the Acutane Hotline established by Roche Laboratories to answer consumers' questions. They also referred the mother to the American Academy of Dermatology for more information.

Center Helps Set Up New SIDS Program

A nurse with a State Maternal and Child Health Program was setting up a support group for SIDS parents, which had never been done before in her state. She called the National Sudden Infant Death Syndrome Resource Center for information, materials, publications, and examples of similar programs in other states. The staff was able to do a database search, as well as give her referrals and samples of program guidelines and publications from other states.

Man Gets Line on Hip Replacement

A man called the National Institute of Arthritis and Musculoskeletal and Skin Diseases to find out where he could get a free hip replacement. Although the institute itself does not do this operation, they were able to refer him to a hotline established in his state that could explain some options or direct him to the appropriate place in his state for more information.

State Worker Helps Couple Identify Little-Known Program To Pay For Baby's Skull Surgery

A couple in Illinois felt the financial pinch when they learned that their insurance did not cover the C-section birth of their new daughter. They were then devastated to learn that the skull surgery that was needed immediately for their new baby was also not covered. A case worker for the state Office of Crippled Children solved their problem. With his help, they sorted through the maze of forms and questions, and qualified for a program that paid for their baby's operation. (Entry #525)

Doctor Gets The Latest SIDS Information Faxed To Him

Recently, a physician from an intensive care unit in California called the National Sudden Infant Death Syndrome Resource Center for information on SIDS and other types of infant deaths. The doctor said that twins had just died in his section and he wanted information on other simultaneous deaths of twins from SIDS. The center performed a database search, and then faxed citations of articles dealing with the subject to the doctor.

Illinois Woman Sees Again

As a result of a spinal tap, a woman in Illinois contracted Multiple Sclerosis. The effects of her disease caused her to lose her eyesight, lose her job, and have a car accident. In addition to the financial strains she already faced, the roof on her house also had to be replaced. She went to the state's Office of Rehabilitation to see if they could help her find employment. The counselor questioned the diagnosis of her eye condition and paid for another eye test. As a result of the test, she had eye surgery and regained her eyesight.

Center Helps Out At A SIDS Funeral

A grandmother of a SIDS infant contacted the National Sudden Infant Death Syndrome Resource Center immediately after her grandchild's death. She wanted information sheets or other publications explaining what SIDS is so that they

could be given to those attending the funeral. This way the family would be spared the painful process of explaining the condition. The staff prepared the publications and delivered them in person to the grandmother's home the night before the funeral.

Vet Gets Help From State Counselor When Congressman Fails

When a man from upstate New York received his military discharge, he had a service-connected disability. Yet he was turned away by the Veterans Administration which refused him financial compensation. He contacted his Congressman, but even he couldn't help. Years later when a co-worker asked about his limping, he told him his military disability story. The co-worker suggested that he see his brother-in-law who was a veteran's counselor for New York state. After a thorough medical exam, a review of the paperwork, and a hearing in front of the appeal board, the Veterans Administration approved him for compensation. (Entry #202)

Woman With Rare Disease Gets Help In Treatment And Support

A woman in her late 40's who was diagnosed with a very rare and incurable disease contacted the National Organization of Rare Diseases to find out all she could and where the latest testing was being done. NORD sent her brochures and also the names of others across North America that had the same disease. The woman has managed to travel to visit some of these people and attend several organized support groups. She found these meetings, both group and individual, to be central to her ability to cope with her diagnosis and lead as full and productive a life as she can.

Disabled Woman Gets The Gift Of Life From Vocational Rehabilitation Counselor

In 1986, a woman was diagnosed with Multiple Sclerosis. She met up with Dorothy Winegrad of the Maryland State Department of Education's Division of Vocational Rehabilitation. Mrs. Winegrad assessed her situation, and recommended that she obtain a scooter and an elevator to lower her stair glide and her wheelchair to street level from her front porch. Unfortunately, the woman was unemployed and didn't have the thousands of dollars needed to purchase the items. Through the state program, Mrs. Winegrad arranged for her to obtain all the items at no cost.

Head Injury Victim Gets Help With Loss of Taste

A woman's husband had a serious fall that created trauma to his head, and as a result was unable to taste his food. The National Institute on Deafness and Other Communication Disorders sent her all kinds of publications related to such head injuries and also referred her to other organizations that could help them understand taste disorders.

Perfume Man Who Loses Sense of Smell Gets Help

For no apparent reason, a man who worked in the perfume industry lost his sense of smell. The National Institute on Deafness and Other Communication Disorders directed him to organizations that study this disorder and could inform him about current research being done on this topic.

T.V. Station Gets Help With Breast Cancer Awareness Program

The Public Service Director of a local television station called the National Cancer Institute for information on breast cancer screening. The Institute's Outreach Coordinator provided Public Service Announcements and a 30-minute video program on mammography and provided suggestions for developing a local program on breast cancer screening.

Student Gets Free Help Writing Paper On Leukemia

A high school student preparing a paper for a science class called the National Cancer Institute for background information on leukemia and the use of bone marrow transplants. They provided her with booklets and research reports to help develop the paper.

High-Risk Woman Gets Line On Free Breast Cancer Prevention

A 50-year-old woman with a family history of breast cancer called the National Cancer Institute for information on a prevention trial for women at high risk for breast cancer. They referred her to the researchers in her area conducting the study for information on free enrollment.

FREE TREATMENT FOR RICH AND POOR

For many years I was aware that hundreds of thousands of patients, both rich and poor, can receive free medical treatment from various government programs. And for many years I also believed that most people, especially those within the health care community, knew of these programs and opportunities. But my perceptions changed when I recently helped a women in my neighborhood who needed a simple examination by a cardiologist.

The woman was unemployed, had no money, and of course, no health insurance coverage. A doctor at a local clinic prescribed an anti-depressant drug but said that before he could give it to her, she needed to be examined by a cardiologist. He said she had to get the cardiologist examination on her own. I had to make over *thirty* telephone calls to get her a free examination.

What I learned by making all those telephone calls was that most people in the health care community did not even know what free services were available to the public. I even called a number of local cardiologists, and they seemed to be the least helpful of all. Not only were they not set up to handle patients for free, they had no suggestions as to how this woman could get the care she needed. They didn't even know that their own medical association provided a referral service to provide aid to those who can't afford to pay.

Our Survey Of 100 Doctors

After this experience, my staff performed an undercover investigation in which we approached one hundred cardiologists around the country with the same problem. Here is what we found:

* *4% said they would examine her even if she did not have money or insurance.*
* *5% said they would not examine her but had other suggestions that proved to be helpful.*
* *25% said they would not examine her, and suggested other solutions that proved of no value.*
* *66% said that they would not see her and had no idea where to turn.*

It's interesting that 91% of some of our country's top health professionals have no idea where to turn to if you don't have health insurance. If you would like more background on our study of cardiologists, just call our office: (301) 942-6303.

What follows in this section is a listing of those places, both nationally and locally, you can turn to for free health care and treatment. Some programs will take you only if you can't afford treatment or have no health insurance coverage, while other programs will take you no matter who you are, rich or poor.

Free Medical Care for Rich and Poor By the Best Doctors in the World

Each year hundreds of thousands of patients receive free medical care by some of the best doctors in the world. Medical research professionals receive millions of dollars each year to study the latest causes, cures and treatments to various diseases or illnesses. If your health condition is being studied somewhere, you may qualify for what is called a "clinical trial" and get treatment for free. These clinical trials can also be used when your doctor recommends an experimental new treatment.

There are several ways to find out about ongoing clinical trials across the nation. Your first call should be to the National Institutes of Health (NIH) Clinical Center. NIH is the federal government's focal point for health research and is one of the world's foremost biomedical research centers. The Clinical Center is a 540-bed hospital that has facilities and services to support research at NIH. They also have an adjacent Ambulatory Care Research Facility that provides additional space and facilities for out-patient research. Your doctor should contact

The Patient Referral Line
(301) 496-4891

to find out if your diagnosis is being studied, and to be put in contact with the primary investigator who can then tell if you meet the requirements for the study. An information brochure is available describing the Clinical Center programs.

☎ Contact:
Clinical Center
National Institutes of Health
Bethesda, MD 20892
(301) 496-2563

If your doctor diagnoses you for a disease but you can't afford treatment, you should check to see whether the National Institutes of Health is studying the disease and looking for patients to be treated at no cost.

In 1991, the Clinical Center at NIH in Bethesda, Maryland, treated 163,687 patients--so it's not as if only the lucky or the rich get to take part in the clinical studies. Keep in mind, though, that most doctors aren't even aware of what is being studied at NIH and probably won't think of a clinical study as an option for you--so *you* may very well have to tell your doctor that NIH is looking for patients with your diagnosis. The list of diseases studied at NIH includes almost everything from writers' cramp and lupus, to AIDS and PMS.

Referring doctors and dentists are welcome to visit their patients at the Clinical Center. When a patient is discharged, the referring doctor or dentist receives a full report on the results of studies and the treatment given. Cooperation of doctors, dentists and patients is appreciated for follow-up observation of patients after they have been discharged.

Patient Referrals

Again, patients are admitted to the Clinical Center *only* on referral by a doctor or dentist. Your complete diagnosis and medical history is necessary for admission.

Your doctor should make preliminary inquiries by telephone to determine if your diagnosis may be of interest to investigators. If your disease is under active investigation, your doctor may be asked to submit the diagnosis and medical history in writing to the principal investigator.

Your doctor may call the institute contact listed in *Appendix A* or the patient referral number at (301) 496-4891. To obtain telephone numbers of principal investigators or other staff not listed in *Appendix A*, call (301) 496-2351.

Financial Assistance

If necessary, the Clinical Center Social Work Department will help prospective patients with personal problems concerning their admission. This department *cannot* provide financial assistance to individuals and their families except in certain emergency situations. For more information, contact the Social Work Department at (301) 496-2381.

Patients are not financially responsible for medical, surgical or other hospital services performed at the Clinical Center; however, the patient's transportation costs *usually* cannot be paid.

Eligibility Requirements

1. You must be referred by a physician or dentist in private practice, hospital, clinic or other medical organization.

2. Your specific disease or condition must be under active investigation by NIH physicians at the time of admission.

3. Each Institute considers your age, weight, sex, general health and length of waiting list to qualify you as a patient for admission. Possibilities for long-term in-patient status and extended follow-up observations may also be

considered. Apart from the medical considerations listed above, there are no other restrictions based on race, creed, age, sex or color.

4. You must have a reasonable understanding of your role in a research study.

Length of Stay

You will be returned to the care of your referring doctors or institutions, or to your family, when your participation in a study has been completed and your medical condition permits. The clinical director of the Institute in which you are under study is responsible for making these determinations.

Accuracy of Information

The information in this section is the most up-to-date possible at the time of publication of this book. However, each year the Clinical Center publishes a new directory of clinical studies that includes the most recently-funded studies, along with those that continue to be funded. So to ensure that the following studies are still underway and looking for patients, you'll have to contact the Center. Also, an up-to-date index of the current clinical studies is carried on the AMA/GTE Telenet Medical Information Network. Quarterly index updates are available on the information network to Telenet subscribers.

Please turn to *Appendix A* for a complete list of 1992 Clinical Studies.

Doctors Who Get Grants To Study Your Illness

In addition to the free clinical studies at NIH described in the preceding section, there are thousands of other doctors who get research money and may be able to treat your condition for free. You can locate these doctors through the Division of Research Grants at NIH. This office can conduct a CRISP (Computer Retrieval for Information on Scientific Projects) search for you at no charge. The search can provide you with information on grants awarded to the National Institutes of Health, Food and Drug Administration, and other government research institutions, universities, or hospitals that deal with the topic in which you are interested. They have a free brochure available that describes their services.

☎ Contact:
Division of Research Grants
5333 Westbard Ave., Room 148
Bethesda, MD 20895
(301) 496-7543

What follows is an example of a CRISP search done on Headaches/Migraines. The information you receive includes the title of the study, the investigator, research facility, amount of grant, as well as a detailed description of the purpose of the study.

CRISP Search Request
Topic: Headache Research, 1992

Title: *Psychophysiological Assessment of Stress in Chronic Pain*
Investigator: Ohrbach, Richard, SUNY At Buffalo, 355 Squire Hall Med., Buffalo, NY 14214
Performing Organization: State University of New York at Buffalo
Award Amount: $67,303

Title: *Neural and Endothelial Regulators of Cerebrovascular Tone*
Investigator: Brayden, Joseph E., University of Vermont, Dept. of Pharmacology, Burlington, VT 05405

Performing Organization: University of Vermont & State Agricultural College
Award Amount: $52,432

Title: *Medical Care and Risks of Dysfunctional Chronic Pain*
Investigator: Von Korff, Michael R., Center for Health Studies, 1730 Minor Ave., Suite 1600, Seattle, WA 98101-1448
Performing Organization: Group Health Cooperative of Puget Sound
Award Amount: $73,600

Title: *Explanation in the Clinical Setting*
Investigator: Buchanan, Bruce G., Intelligent Systems Laboratory, Pittsburgh, PA 15260
Performing Organization: University of Pittsburgh at Pittsburgh
Award Amount: $499,187

Title: *Genetic Epidemiology of Psychiatric Disorders*
Investigator: Merikangas, Kathleen R., 40 Temple St., Lower Level, New Haven, CT 06510-3223
Performing Organization: Yale University
Award Amount: $65,433

Title: *Psychological Treatment of Headache*
Investigator: Blanchard, Edward B., 1535 Western Ave., Albany, NY 12203
Performing Organization: State University of New York at Albany
Award Amount: $116,890

Title: *Trigeminal Nerve--Control of the Brain Vasculature*
Investigator: Moskowitz, Michael A., Massachusetts General Hospital, Fruit St., Boston, MA 02114
Performing Organization: Massachusetts General Hospital
Award Amount: $282,399

Title: *Drug and Non-drug Treatment for Adult and Pediatric Migraine*
Investigator: Andrasik, Frank, University of West

Florida, 11000 University Parkway, Pensacola, FL 32514-5751
Performing Organization: University of West Florida
Award Amount: $251,602

Title: *Pentosan Polysulfate as Prophylaxis for Migraine*
Investigator: Bigelow, L.B., National Institute of Mental Health, Bethesda, MD
Performing Organization: National Institute of Mental Health
Award Amount: $0

Title: *Collaborative Studies of Less Common or Less Debilitating Neurologic Disorders*
Investigator: Roman, G.C., National Institute of Neurological Disorders and Stroke, National Institutes of Health
Performing Organization: NINDS
Award Amount: $0

Title: *Erythema Multiforme--A Clinical Pathogenetic Study*
Investigator: Weston, William L., University of Colorado School of Medicine, 4200 West Ninth Ave., Box B153, Denver, CO 80262
Performing Organization: University of Colorado Health Sciences Center
Award Amount: $167,349

Title: *Drug Dependence Clinical Research Program: Neurologic Sequelae of Cocaine Use*
Investigator: Rowbotham, Michael C., University of California, 401 Parnassus Ave., San Francisco, CA 94143
Performing Organization: University of California, San Francisco
Award Amount: $74,240

Title: *TMD Longitudinal Studies--Clinical/Chronic Pain Syndrome: Longitudinal Studies of Tempormandibular Disorders*
Investigator: Dworkin, S.F., University of Washington School of Dentistry, Seattle, WA 98195
Performing Organization: Univeristy of Washington
Award Amount: $196,489

Title: *TMD Longitudinal Studies--Clinical/Chronic*

Pain Syndrome: Longitudinal Studies of Chronic Pain Syndrome in TMD
Investigator: Von Korff, M., University of Washington School of Dentistry, Seattle, WA 98195
Performing Organization: University of Washington
Award Amount: $196,489

Title: *Compliance in the Physicians' Health Study*
Investigator: Glynn, Robert J., Brigham and Women's Hospital, 55 Pond Ave.
Performing Organization: Brigham and Women's Hospital
Award Amount: $38,563

Title: *Cost-Effective Management of HIV-related Illnesses*
Investigator: Tosteson, Anna, Dartmouth Medical School, 1 Medical Center Dr., Lebanon, NH 03756
Performing Organization: Dartmouth College
Award Amount: $196,911

Title: *The Classification of Anxiety Disorders*
Investigator: Barlow, David H., State University of New York at Albany, 1400 Washington, Ave., Albany, NY 12222
Performing Organization: State University of New York at Albany
Award Amount: $233,953

Title: *Clinical Stroke Research Center: Stroke Prevention in Young Women*
Investigator: Kettner, Steven J., University of Maryland Hospital, 22 S. Greene St., Baltimore, MD 21201
Performing Organization: University of Maryland, Baltimore Professional School
Award Amount: $312,859

Title: *General Clinical Research Center: Marijuana--Repeated Smoking in Humans (Marijuana-Alcohol Hangover)*
Investigator: Chait, Larry D., University of Chicago, 5841 S. Maryland Ave., Chicago, IL 60637
Performing Organization: University of Chicago
Award Amount: $34,508

Title: *General Clinical Research Center: Humoral*

and Cellular Mediated Immunity
Investigator: Fireman, Philip A., Children's
Hospital of Pittsburgh, 3705 Fifth Ave. at Desoto
St., Pittsburgh, PA 15213
Performing Organization: Children's Hospital of
Pittsburgh
Award Amount: $16,051

Title: *Antibody-toxin Conjugates for the Treatment
of Human Brain Tumors*
Investigator: Youle, R.J., National Institute
of Neurological Disorders and Stroke, NIH,
Bethesda, MD
Performing Organization: NINDS
Award Amount: $0

A second place to look is at the National Library
of Medicine where you can conduct a search on
their MEDLINE database (part of their
MEDLARS databases). This search can provide
you with citations and abstracts on your diagnosis
and clinical trials from 6.6 million articles from
approximately 3,600 biomedical journals published
in the United States and abroad. You can access
this system through a computer and modem. They
also sell a GRATEFUL Med software program for
$29.95 which is Macintosh and IBM-compatible,
and makes it easier to access the library's
collection. Libraries in your area, as well as
medical schools may have access to the
MEDLARS databases, and you may be able to
have someone conduct a search for you for a small
fee. Your regional medical library can also direct
you to libraries near you that have access, or they
may be able to provide the search for you. They
can be reached at (800) 338-7657. For more
information about accessing MEDLARS or buying
the GRATEFUL Med software:

☎ Contact:
MEDLARS Management Section
National Library of Medicine
Bldg. 38A, Room 4N421
8600 Rockville Pike
Bethesda, MD 20894
(800) 638-8480

Free Health Care At Your Hospital

Do you need an operation? Has an unexpected
health crisis occurred? Are you worried about
paying your hospital bills? Many hospitals, nursing
homes, and clinics offer free or low-cost health
care under the Hill-Burton free care program.
You are eligible if your income falls within the
Poverty Income Guidelines. You must request
and apply for Hill-Burton assistance (you can even
apply after you have been discharged). Each
Hill-Burton facility can choose which types of
services to provide at no charge or reduced
charge, and must give you a written individual
notice that will tell you what types of services are
covered. They also must provide a specific
amount of free care each year, but can stop once
they have given that amount. A special hotline
has been established that distributes information
on applying for Hill-Burton assistance, and can
answer questions regarding eligibility guidelines,
facilities obligated to provide services, and help
with filing a complaint. If you do not qualify for
Hill-Burton assistance, don't worry: many hospitals
have special funds to provide care for the poor.
The hospital business offices can help you apply
for various forms of government assistance, as well
as set up payment plans you can afford. They can't
help you if they don't know you have a problem.
For more information on Hill-Burton:

☎ Contact:
Office of Health Facilities
Health Resources and Services Administration
Department of Health and Human Services
5600 Fishers Lane, Room 11-03
Rockville, MD 20857
(800) 638-0742
(800) 492-0359 (in MD).

Local Free Health Clinics

Your local health department (found in the blue pages of your phone book) often operates free or sliding-fee-scale clinics and screening centers to handle non-emergency health problems. Many operate prenatal and well-baby clinics as well. The services and fees vary from place to place, so contact the health department to find out about eligibility, hours of service, and services provided. According to the National Association of Community Health Centers, federally sponsored community health centers serve six million people, and four to six million people are served at other-sponsored health centers. However, some problems exist. Because of the increase demand for low-cost health care, many centers are closing off registration and are carrying waiting lists of fifteen to twenty percent of their current case load. The demand and availability of local health centers does vary, so don't overlook this resource. To find out about local clinics:

☎ Contact:
Your State Department of Public Health
(See listing below)

Public Health Hotlines

Alabama
Department of Public Health
434 Monroe St.
Montgomery, AL 36130   (205) 242-5052

Alaska
Department of Health and Social Services
P.O. Box H
Juneau, AK 99811   (907) 465-3347

Arizona
Department of Health Services
1740 W. Adams St.
Phoenix, AZ 85007   (602) 542-1000

Arkansas
Department of Health
4815 W. Markham St.
Little Rock, AR 72205   (501) 661-2111

California
Department of Health Services
714 P St.
Sacramento, CA 95814   (916) 445-4171

Colorado
Department of Health
4210 E. 11th Ave.
Denver, CO 80220   (303) 331-4600

Connecticut
Department of Health Services
150 Washington St.
Hartford, CT 06106   (203) 566-2038

Delaware
Division of Public Health
P.O. Box 637
Dover, DE 19901   (302) 739-4701

District of Columbia
Commission of Public Health
1660 L St NW
Washington, DC 20036   (202) 673-7700

Florida
Health and Rehabilitative
 Services Department
1317 Winewood Blvd.
Tallahassee, FL 32399   (904) 487-2705

Georgia
Public Health Division
Department of Human Resources
878 Peachtree St., NE
Atlanta, GA 30309   (404) 894-7505

Hawaii
Department of Health

P.O. Box 3378
Honolulu, HI 96801   (808) 548-6505

Idaho
Department of Health and Welfare
Statehouse
Boise, ID 83720   (208) 334-5500

Illinois
Maternal and Child Health
Department of Public Health
535 W. Jefferson St.
Springfield, IL 62761   (217) 524-5989
Beautiful Babies   (800) 545-2200

Indiana
State Board of Health
1330 W. Michigan St.
Indianapolis, IN 46206   (317) 633-8400

Iowa
Department of Public Health
Lucas State Office Building
Des Moines, IA 50319   (515) 281-5605

Kansas
Department of Health and Environment
Landon Office Building
Topeka, KS 66620   (913) 296-1343

Kentucky
Department for Health Services
275 E. Main St.
Frankfort, KY 40601   (502) 564-3970

Louisiana
Department of Health and Hospitals
325 Loyola Ave.
New Orleans, LA 70112   (504) 568-5050

Maine
Department of Human Services
State House Station #11
Augusta, ME 04333   (207) 289-2736

Maryland
Department of Health and Mental Hygiene
201 W. Preston St.
Baltimore, MD 21201   (410) 225-6500

Massachusetts
Department of Public Health

150 Tremont St.
Boston, MA 02111   (617) 727-0201

Michigan
Department of Public Health
3500 N. Logan
Lansing, MI 48909   (517) 335-8024

Minnesota
Department of Health
717 Delaware St., SE
Minneapolis, MN 55440   (612) 623-5460

Mississippi
Department of Health
2423 N. State St.
Jackson, MS 39216   (601) 960-7635

Missouri
Department of Health
P.O. Box 570
Jefferson City, MO 65102   (314) 751-6001

Montana
Health Services Division
Health and Environment Sciences
Cogswell Building
Helena, MT 59620   (406) 444-4473

Nebraska
Department of Health
301 Centennial Mall S.
P.O. Box 95007
Lincoln, NE 68509   (402) 471-2133

Nevada
Department of Human Resources
505 E. King St.
Carson City, NV 89710   (703) 687-4740

New Hampshire
Department of Health and Welfare
Hazen Dr.
Concord, NH 03301   (603) 271-4501

New Jersey
Department of Health
CN 360
Trenton, NJ 08625   (609) 292-7837

New Mexico
Department of Health

1190 St. Francis Dr.
Santa Fe, NM 87502   (505) 827-2613

New York
Department of Health
Empire State Plaza
Albany, NY 12237   (518) 474-2011

North Carolina
Environment, Health and Natural Resources
225 N. McDowell St.
Raleigh, NC 27603   (919) 733-7081

North Dakota
Department of Health
State Capitol, 600 E. Boulevard
Bismarck, ND 58505   (701) 224-2372

Ohio
Department of Health
246 N. High St.
P.O. Box 118
Columbus, OH 43266   (614) 466-2253

Oklahoma
Department of Health
1000 NE 10th
P.O. Box 53551
Oklahoma City, OK 73152   (405) 271-4200

Oregon
Department of Human Resources
1400 SW 5th Ave.
Portland, OR 97201   (503) 731-4000

Pennsylvania
Department of Health
802 Health and Welfare Building
Harrisburg, PA 17120   (717) 787-6436

Rhode Island
Department of Health
75 Davis St.
Providence, RI 02908   (401) 277-2000

South Carolina
Health and Environmental Control
2600 Bull St.
Columbia, SC 29201   (803) 734-4880

South Dakota
Department of Health
Foss Building
Pierre, SD 57501   (605) 773-3361

Tennessee
Department of Health
344 Cordell Hull Building
Nashville, TN 37247   (615) 741-3111

Texas
Department of Health
1100 W. 49th St.
Austin, TX 78756   (512) 458-7111

Utah
Department of Health
288 N. 1460 W
Salt Lake City, UT 84116   (801) 538-6111

Vermont
Department of Health
60 Main St.
Burlington, VT 05401   (802) 863-7280

Virginia
Department of Health
109 Governor St.
Richmond, VA 23219   (804) 786-3561

Washington
Department of Health
1112 SE Quince
M/S: ET-12
Olympia, WA 98504   (206) 753-5871

West Virginia
Health and Human Resources Department
Building 6
Charleston, WV 25305   (304) 348-2400

Wisconsin
Health and Social Services Department
1 W. Wilson St.
Madison, WI 53703   (608) 266-1511

Wyoming
Department of Health
Hathaway Building
Cheyenne, WY 82002   (307) 777-7656

Federal Medical Programs For Elderly, Disabled And Low Income

How do you know if you qualify for Medicare or Medicaid? The Medicare Program is a federal health insurance program for persons over 65 years of age and certain disabled persons. It is funded through Social Security contributions, premiums, and general revenue. The Medicaid Program is a joint federal/state program which provides medical services to the needy and the medically needy. Eligibility and services for this program vary from state to state. To locate an office near you, look in the blue pages of your phone book under Human Services or:

☎ Contact:
Medicare Hotline
Health Care Financing Administration

330 Independence Ave., SW
Washington, DC 20201
(800) 638-6833
(800) 492-6603

This hotline can provide you with information regarding Medicare, Medicaid, and Medigap questions. They can refer you to the proper people to answer your questions, as well as provide you with publications on your topic of interest. This is also the number to call if you suspect abuse or fraud of Medicare or Medicaid, as well as if you suspect improper sales practices of Medigap policies.

A New Law Provides Free Health Care To Children

Are you pregnant or the parent of young children? Do you have a child with special needs? The federal government provides block grants, called Title V, to each state to provide maternal and child (including teens) health care services. Each state has some latitude as to how they spend the money, but 30% must go to providing services for children with special health care needs, and 30% for children and adolescents. The Maternal and Child Health Division of your state Department of Health is responsible for administering the funds. The states are required by Title V to start establishing 800 numbers to provide information regarding services available in the state (see state by state listing later in this chapter).

Federal law requires that all states provide Medicaid to pregnant women and children through the age of six whose income does not exceed 133% of the poverty line. Federal poverty thresholds in 1990 were $6,810 for one person, $9,190 for two,

$11,570 for three, and $13,950 for four people. The government is going to raise the age level for Medicaid benefits one year at a time until all children are covered to age eighteen. Many states have additional benefits for children and programs for children with special needs. The following states have extended Medicaid coverage:

- *Minnesota*: covers everyone with income below 225% of the federal poverty line, or about $31,000.
- *Vermont*: all children under eighteen with family incomes below 225% of the federal poverty line, or about $31,000.
- *Washington*: all children to age eighteen with family incomes 100% of federal poverty line, or about $13,950.
- *Wisconsin*: children one to six with family incomes below 155% of federal poverty line, or about $21,600.

- *Maine*: all children to age 18 with family incomes below 125% of poverty line, or about $17,500.
- 23 states have extended coverage for all pregnant women whose incomes are 100% of poverty line, or about $13,950.
- Several states, such as Ohio and West Virginia, have established special programs for children with special health care needs.

There are several ways to find out more about the programs available in your state. You can call the local department of health (found in the blue pages in your phone book), or the state Department of Health and the Maternal and Child Health Hotlines (listed below). Each year states enact new legislation to help provide health care for those in need. Your state representative can keep you updated regarding new legislation.

Maternal and Infant Care Hotlines

Alabama
Maternal and Infant Care
434 Monroe St.
Montgomery, AL 36103   (205) 242-5766
    (800) 654-1385 Stork Line
Referral Information   (205) 242-5661
This hotline can refer people to local maternal and infant health centers.

Alaska
Division of Public Assistance
Department of Health and Social Services
P.O. Box H
Juneau, AK 99811   (907) 465-3347

Arizona
Information Referral Service
1515 East Osbourne at the Annex
Phoenix, AZ 85014   (602) 263-8856
Health Care Referral   (800) 352-3792

Arkansas
Section of Maternal and Child Health
Arkansas State Department of Health
4815 W. Markham
Little Rock, AR 72205   (501) 661-2251
Health Care Clearinghouse   (800) 336-4797
This hotline can refer you to local resources.

California
Maternal and Child Health
State Department of Health
714 P. St., Room 740
Sacramento, CA 95814   (916) 657-1347
    (800) BABY-999 (222-9999)
This hotline can refer you to local maternal and child health resources.

Colorado
Family Health Services
Colorado Department of Health
4210 East 11th Ave.   (303) 331-8360
Denver, CO 80220   (800) 688-7777
This hotline can refer you to local maternal and child health resources.

Connecticut
Connecticut Association for Human Services
880 Asylum Ave.
Hartford, CT 06105   (203) 522-7762

INFOLINE- The following numbers can refer you to the appropriate resources in your area:
North West Region . . . . (203) 743-3819
South Central Region . . . . (203) 624-4143
North East Region . . . . (203) 774-7257
South East Region . . . . (203) 886-0516
North Central Region . . . . (203) 522-4636
South West Region . . . . (203) 333-7555
Baby-Your-Baby . . . . (800) 286-2229

Delaware
Division of Public Health
Health and Social Services Department
P.O. Box 637
Dover, DE 19901   (302) 739-4701
Help Line   (800) 451-HELP
The Helpline can refer you to local health services, as well as provide you with other state services and information.

District of Columbia
Office of Maternal And Child Health
Commission of Public Health
1660 L St NW, Suite 907
Washington, DC 20036   800-MOM-BABY

Florida
Maternal and Child Health
Health and Rehabilitative Services Department
1317 Winewood Blvd.   (904) 487-2705
Tallahassee, FL 32399   (800) 451-BABY
This hotline can refer you to local maternal and
child health resources.

Georgia
Family Health Services Section
Division of Public Health
Department of Human Resources
878 Peachtree St., NE
Suite 217   (404) 894-6622
Atlanta, GA 30309   (800) 228-9173
This hotline can refer you to local maternal and
child health resources.

Hawaii
Family Health Services Division
State of Hawaii
Department of Health
741-A Sunset Ave.   (808) 586-4410
Honolulu, HI 96816   (808) 275-2000
This number can refer you to local maternal and
child health resources.

Idaho
Bureau of Maternal and Child Health
Idaho Department of Health and Welfare
450 W. State St.   (208) 334-5949
Boise, ID 83720   (800) 926-2588
This number can refer you to local maternal and
child health resources.

Illinois
Department of Public Health
535 W. Jefferson St.
Springfield, IL 62761   (217) 782-4977
Contact your local health department.

Indiana
Division of Maternal and Child Health
Indiana State Board of Health
1330 W. Michigan St., #23D
Indianapolis, IN 46206   (317) 633-8478
Family Wellness Health Line   (800) 433-0746
This hotline can refer you to local resources for
help.

Iowa
Family and Community Health

Department of Public Health
Lucas State Office Bldg.
Des Moines, IA 50319   (515) 281-3046
Healthy Families   (800) 369-2229
This hotline can refer you to local resources.

Kansas
Electronic Data Systems- Recipients Assistance
P.O. Box 4649   (913) 273-8557
Topeka, KS 66604   (800) 658-4690

SRS- Division of Medical Services
915 SW Harrison, Room 628S
Docking State Office Building
Topeka, KS 66612   (913) 296-3981

Kentucky
Division of Maternal and Child Health
Department of Health Services
State Department of Human Resources
275 East Main St.   (502) 564-4830
Frankfort, KY 40621   (800) 372-2973
This hotline can refer you to local maternal and
child health resources.

Louisiana
Department of Health and Hospitals
325 Loyola Ave.   (504) 568-5051
New Orleans, LA 70112   (800) 922-DIAL
This hotline can refer you to local resources.

Maine
Division of Maternal and Child Health
Department of Human Services
151 Capitol St.
State House- Station 11
Augusta, ME 04333   (207) 289-3311
                  (800) 437-9300 or (207) 775-7231
This hotline can answer you maternal and child
health questions.

Maryland
Department of Health and Mental Hygiene
201 W. Preston St., 5th Fl.
Baltimore, MD 21201   (301) 225-6538
(MAC- Maryland Access to Care Program)
                                 (800) 492-5231
This 800 number can refer you to local services.

Massachusetts
Maternal and Child Health Section
Massachusetts Department of Public Health

150 Tremont St.
Boston, MA 02111   (617) 727-0940
The following numbers can refer you to the proper
maternal and child health resources:

Boston Region . . . . (800) 531-2229
Central Region . . . . (800) 227-7748
North East Region . . . . (800) 992-1895
South East Region . . . . (800) 642-4250
West Region . . . . (800) 992-6111

Michigan
Bureau of Community Health Services
Michigan Department of Public Health
3500 North Logan St.
P.O. Box 30035
Lansing, MI 38909   (517) 335-8945
                                     (800) 26-BIRTH
This hotline can refer you to local resources for all
your health and human services needs.

Minnesota
Department of Human Services
444 Lafayette Rd.
St. Paul, MN 55155   (612) 296-6117
Maternal and Child Health Referrals
                                     (800) 657-3672
Health and Human Services   (800) 652-9747

Mississippi
Department of Health
2423 N. State St.   (601) 960-7484
Jackson, MS 39216   (800) 222-7622
This hotline can refer you to local health
resources.

Missouri
Division of Child and Family Health Care
Department of Health
P.O. Box 570
Jefferson City, MO 65102
                     (800) 835-5465 TELL-LINK

Montana
Health Services and Medical Facilities Division
Department of Health and
   Environmental Sciences
Cogswell Building   (406) 444-4740
Helena, MT 59601   (800) 762-9891
This hotline can refer you to local maternal and
child health resources.

Nebraska
Maternal and Child Health
State Department of Health
301 Centennial Mall South
P.O. Box 95007
Lincoln, NE 68509   (402) 471-2907
Healthy Mother/Healthy Baby Coalition
                                     (800) 862-1889

Nevada
Family Health Services
Nevada Health Division
Kinkhead Building, #200
State Department of Human Resources
505 East King St., Room 205
Carson City, NV 89710   (702) 687-4885
                            (800) 992-0900 ext. 4885
This hotline can refer you to local maternal and
child health resources.

New Hampshire
Helpline
2 Industrial Park Dr.   (800) 852-3388
Concord, NH 03301   (603) 225-9000
This 24-hour helpline for social services answers
questions regarding emergency health, spouse or
child abuse, suicide, food, housing, clothing,
alcohol and drug problems, and more.

New Jersey
Maternal and Infant Health
New Jersey Department of Health
363 W. State St.   (609) 292-5616
Trenton, NJ 08625   (800) 328-3838
This office can answer questions regarding
maternal and infant health, and can refer to clinics
for prenatal, and child health programs. People
looking for other health services should contact
your local health department.

New Mexico
Department Of Health
1190 St. Francis Dr.
Santa Fe, NM 87502   (505) 827-2613
The Department of Health can refer you to your
local district for further information and help.

Information Center
DD Planning Council
435 St. Michael's Dr.
Bldg. D   (800) 552-8195
Santa Fe, NM 97501   (505) 827-6260

This is an information center for New Mexicans with disabilities and BABYNET. They can refer people to clinics, and handle referrals for prenatal, postnatal and well-baby care. They have an information database to direct you to services in your area.

New York
Growing Up Healthy
New York State Department of Health
8th Floor
Room 821
Empire State Plaza   (800) 522-5006
Albany, NY 12237   (518) 474-1964
This hotline can provide you with information on receiving low-cost pregnancy testing, prenatal and post natal care, as well as information on where to obtain well-baby care.

North Carolina
Care Line
Department of Human Resources
325 N. Salisbury St.   (800) 662-7030
Raleigh, NC 27603   (919) 733-4261
This hotline can answer your questions regarding where to obtain health care and other human services, such as welfare, food stamps, and other entitlement programs.

North Dakota
Division of Maternal and Child Health
State Department of Health
    and Consolidated Labs
600 E Boulevard Ave.
State Capitol Building   (701) 224-2493
Bismarck, ND 58505   (800) 472-2286
This hotline can provide you with information on family planning, health promotion and education, WIC, and other maternal and child health information.

Children With Special Health Care Needs
Department of Human Services
State Capitol Building   (701) 224-4814
Bismarck, ND 58505   (800) 472-2622 x2436
This hotline can provide answers to all your question regarding children with special health care needs. They have information on case management, special education, medical specialties, dental care, hospitalization, and much more.

Ohio
Healthy Babies Health Line
Bureau of Maternal and Child Health
Ohio Department of Health
P.O. Box 118   (614) 466-5332
Columbus, OH 43266   (800) 624-BABY
This hotline can direct you to prenatal, postnatal and well baby clinics, as well as your local WIC, Medicaid, and other human services offices.

Oklahoma
Health Line
P.O. Box 53551
Department of Health
Oklahoma City, OK 73152   (405) 271-4200
This health line can refer you to helpful clinics in the Oklahoma City area.

Community Council of Central Oklahoma
Information and Referral
P.O. Box 675
Oklahoma City, OK 73101   (405) 236-4357
This health line deals with all health concerns, referring people to health clinics in Oklahoma, Canadian and Cleveland counties.

Oregon
Safe Net
Multnamah County
426 SW Stark
Portland, OR 97204   (800) SAFE-NET
This hotline handles maternal and child health care needs (including teens). They deal with such issues as primary care, family planning, and have a roster of private physicians and clinics.

Pennsylvania
Health Hotline
Pennsylvania Department of Health
Division of Health Promotion
P.O. Box 90, Room 1003
Health and Welfare Building   (800) 692-7254
Harrisburg, PA 17108   (717) 787-5900
This hotline can provide you with community clinic information, immunizations, AIDS/STD testing, some prenatal and well-baby care, but no referrals to doctors, hospitals, or primary care.

Rhode Island
Right Start
Rhode Island Department of Health
3 Capitol Hill, Room 302

Providence, RI 02908   (800) 346-1004
This hotline is designed to hook up uninsured Pregnant women with health clinics in their area. They can also direct you to early childhood well-baby centers.

South Carolina
South Carolina Department of Health
1st Nine Care Line- MH
Robert Mills Complex
Box 101106   (803) 734-3350
Columbia, SC 29211   (800) 868-0404
This hotline serves pregnant women and women with children under the age of one. For other health care questions contact your local health department.

South Dakota
Health Services
Department of Health
Foss Bldg.   (605) 773-3737
Pierre, SD 57501   (800) 658-3080
This office can refer you to community health services, WIC, emergency services, maternal and child health care, and health promotion.

Tennessee
Maternal and Child Health Section
Tennessee Department of Health
    and Environment
Bureau of Health Services
525 Cordell Coll
Nashville, TN 37210   (800) 428-BABY (2229)
Although this hotline is set up to handle calls from pregnant women and mothers, they can direct all callers to local health services.

Texas
BABY LOVE
Maternal and Child Health
Texas Department of Health
1100 West 49th St.
Austin, TX 78756   (512) 458-7700
          (800) 4-Baby Love (422-2956)
This office can refer you to local health centers, child health clinics, WIC and Medicaid offices, and other well baby resources.

Utah
Maternal & Infant Health
44 Medical Drive
Salt Lake City, UT 84116   (801) 538-6111

Pregnancy Risk Line   (800) 826-9662
Medicine, Drugs and Chemicals   (800) 822-2229

Vermont
Medical Services
Vermont Department of Health
1193 North Ave., P. O. Box 70
Burlington, VT 05402   (800) 649-HELP
This hotline deals only with pregnancies, and can refer you to different agencies. For all other health concerns contact your local health department.

Virginia
Department of Health
400 James Madison Building
109 Governor St.
Richmond, VA 23219   (804) 786-3561
Contact your local health department.

Washington
Department of Health
1112 SE Quince, M/S: ET-21
Olympia, WA 98504   (206) 753-5871
Contact your local health department.

West Virginia
Division of Maternal and Child Health
State Department of Health
1411 Virginia St., E   (800) 642-8522
Charleston, WV 25301   (304) 558-5388
This office handles women and children's services, referrals to local health centers, early intervention programs, WIC, family planning, high risk pregnancy programs, pediatricians, birthing centers, dental heal, cancer prevention, and adolescent pregnancy programs.

Client Services
Health and Human Resources Department
State Capitol Complex   (304) 348-2400
Charleston, WV 25305   (800) 642-8589
This hotline can answer questions regarding case eligibility for benefits, and can refer callers to local health centers.

Wisconsin
Division of Health
Health and Social Services Department
1 W. Wilson St.
Madison, WI 53703   (608) 266-1511
Contact your local health department.

Wyoming
Division of Public Health
Department of Health
Hathaway Bldg.

Cheyenne, WY 82002   (307) 777-6186
This office can refer you to local health care services.

How To Get Drug Companies To Fill Your Prescription For Free

Leave it to the government to know where you can get free AZT, Halcion, Valium or Motrin but not make any effort to tell you about it. The U.S. Senate's Special Committee on Aging recently published a report on how certain eligible groups, including the elderly and the poor, can actually get their much needed prescription drugs free of charge directly from the companies that manufacture them. Here's what the committee discovered:

Taking prescription medications is often a matter of life and death for millions of Americans, yet many just can't afford the drugs they need simply because they're too expensive. Many are forced to choose between paying for food or their medications, especially the elderly. The relative lack of prescription drug insurance has been compounded by prescription cost increases that can actually surpass the rate of inflation by four times.

Though not widely known, many drug companies have programs that offer many prescription drugs free of charge to poor and other vulnerable groups that cannot afford them. However, these free drug programs are being used by only a small number of people that could truly benefit from them. And to add to this, the programs often require long waiting times for qualified patients to receive their free medications from drug manufacturers.

The Pharmaceutical Manufacturer's Association (PMA) has established a *Directory of Prescription Drug Indigent Programs*, which lists up-to-date information on individual manufacturers' patient programs. Although the directory does not always identify the drugs manufactured, it still should be your first call.

☎ Contact:
Pharmaceutical Manufacturer's Association
(800) PMA-INFO

Appendix B contains an alphabetical list of all drugs currently covered under Prescription Drug Indigent Programs, as well as the manufacturer that supplies them. We have also included some helpful tips and questions you should ask when contacting the programs:

1) If a drug is not listed in the directory, it still may be provided by the company. You should call the manufacturer directly to check.

2) Ask about the eligibility requirements. Some companies require that you have a limited income or no insurance coverage, while others require only that you get a doctor's referral.

3) Ask about the enrollment process. Many drug companies require a phone call or letter from your doctor.

4) Find out how you will receive the prescription drugs, and how you can get refills. Most companies send the medications directly to your doctor. There have been some problems with delays in receiving the drugs, so check to see what the company's shipping schedule is, and what you or your doctor should do if there is a problem.

See *Appendix B* for a list of drugs and Manufacturer Indigent Programs.

It's The Law: Care At Hospital Emergency Rooms

If you walk into an emergency room, do they have to treat you? Emergency rooms are now required by federal law to provide an initial screening to assess a patient's condition, which is designed to stop the automatic transfer of people unable to pay. Emergency rooms must also treat emergency situations until they are stabilized, then they can refer you to other hospitals or clinics for further treatment. Emergency medicine encompasses the immediate decision making and action necessary to prevent death or any further disability for patients in health crises. It also includes interventions necessary to stabilize the patient, as well as short-term assessment of the patient's condition beyond the immediate life, limb, and disability threats. If you feel you have been denied service, or received insufficient care, you should complain to your regional Health Care Financing Administration, who then will investigate your complaint. Because of the increase in the number of people who cannot afford or do not qualify for health insurance, many people wait to seek treatment until the situation becomes so terrible they end up in the emergency room. People are also using the emergency room as their primary care physician. By using some of your other options to receive health care, you can receive needed treatments sooner and from more appropriate sources.

Regional Health Care Financing Administration Offices

* Region 1
JF Kennedy Federal Building
Government Center
Boston, MA 02203 (617) 565-1188

* Region 2
26 Federal Plaza
JK Javits Federal Building
New York, NY 10278 (212) 264-4488

* Region 3
3535 Market St., Gateway Building
P.O. Box 7760
Philadelphia, PA 19101 (215) 596-1351

* Region 4
101 Marietta Tower
Atlanta, GA 30323 (404) 331-2329

* Region 5
105 W. Adams St.
Chicago, IL 60603 (312) 886-6432

* Region 6
1200 Main Tower Building
Dallas, TX 75202 (214) 767-6427

* Region 7
601 E 12th St.
Federal Building
Kansas City, MO 64106 (816) 426-5233

* Region 8
1961 Stout St.
Federal Office Building
Denver, CO 80294 (303) 844-2111

* Region 9
75 Hawthorne St.
San Francisco, CA 94105 (415) 744-3502

* Region 10
2201 Sixth Ave.
Blanchard Plaza
Mail Stop RX-40
Seattle, WA 98121 (206) 553-0425

Physicians Who Volunteer In Your Area

Where are the free clinics in your area? Do you have volunteer physician groups near you? Your local medical society can be a great resource to answer these questions. Although service varies from place to place, most medical societies know about the different county programs, groups of physicians who volunteer their services, free clinics, and other helpful information, and can refer you to the appropriate place for help. Several of the societies actually assist people in making appointments, while others direct you to an initial screening with the health department. According to a recent American Medical Association survey, physicians average 6.6 hours per week of free or reduced fee care. This amounts to $ 6.8 billion annually. To find out if there are local opportunities available for you:

☎ Contact:
Your State Medical Association
(See listing below)

Medical Association Hotlines

Alabama
Medical Association of the State of Alabama
19 S. Jackson St.
Montgomery, AL 36102 (205) 263-6441

Alaska
Alaska Medical Society
4107 Laurel St.
Anchorage, AK 99508 (907) 562-2662

Arizona
Arizona Medical Association
810 W. Bethany Home Rd.
Phoenix, AZ 85103 (602) 246-8901

Arkansas
Arkansas Medical Association
10310 W. Markum, #222
Little Rock, AR 72205 (501) 227-5210

California
California Medical Association
P.O. Box 7690
San Francisco, CA 94120 (415) 541-0900

Colorado
Colorado Medical Society
P.O. Box 17550
Denver, CO 80217 (303) 779-5455

Connecticut
Connecticut Medical Association
160 St. Ronan St.
New Haven, CT 06511 (203) 865-0587

Delaware
Delaware Medical Association
1925 Lovering Ave.
Wilmington, DE 19806 (302) 652-6512

District of Columbia
D.C. Medical Society
1707 L St., NW
Washington, DC 20036 (202) 466-1800

Florida
Florida Medical Association
760 Riverside Ave., P.O. Box 2411
Jacksonville, FL 32204 (904) 356-1571

Georgia
Georgia Medical Association
938 Peachtree St., NE
Atlanta, GA 30309 (404) 876-7535

Hawaii
Hawaii Medical Association
1360 S. Bevetania
Honolulu, HI 96814 (808) 536-7702

Idaho
Idaho Medical Association
P.O. Box 2668
Boise, ID 83701   (208) 344-7888

Illinois
Illinois Medical Society
20 N. Michigan Ave.
Suite 700
Chicago, IL 60602   (312) 782-1654

Indiana
Indiana State Medical Society
322 Canal Walk
Indianapolis, IN 46202   (317) 261-2060

Iowa
Iowa Medical Society
1001 Grand Ave.
W. Des Moines, IA 50265   (515) 223-1401

Kansas
Kansas Medical Society
623 SW 10th Ave.
Topeka, KS 66612   (913) 235-2383

Kentucky
Kentucky Medical Association
301 N. Jurstbourne Parkway
Suite 200
Louisville, KY 40222   (502) 426-6200

Louisiana
Louisiana Medical Society
3501 N. Causeway
Metairie, LA 70002   (504) 832-9815

Maine
Maine Medical Association
P.O. Box 190
Manchester, ME 04351   (207) 622-3374

Maryland
Maryland Medical Society
1211 Cathedral St.
Baltimore, MD 21201   (410) 539-0872

Massachusetts
Massachusetts Medical Society
1440 Main St.
Waltham, MA 02154   (617) 893-4610

Michigan
Michigan Medical Society
120 W. Saginaw St.
E. Lansing, MI 48823   (517) 337-1351

Minnesota
Minnesota Medical Association
2221 University Ave., SE, #400
Minneapolis, MN 55414   (612) 378-1875

Mississippi
Mississippi Medical Association
735 Riverside Dr.
Jackson, MS 39202   (601) 354-5433

Missouri
Missouri Medical Association
113 Madison St.
P.O. Box 1028
Jefferson, MO 65102   (314) 636-5151

Montana
Montana Medical Association
2021 11th Ave., Suite #1
Helena, MT 59601   (406) 443-4000

Nebraska
Nebraska Medical Association
233 S. 13th St., Suite #1512
Lincoln, NE 68508   (402) 474-4472

Nevada
Nevada Medical Association
3660 Baker West #101
Reno, NV 89509   (702) 825-6788

New Hampshire
New Hampshire Medical Society
7 North State St.
Concord, NH 03301   (603) 224-1909

New Jersey
New Jersey Medical Society
2 Princess Rd.
Lawrenceville, NJ 08648   (609) 896-1766

New Mexico
New Mexico Medical Society
7770 Jefferson N.E.
Suite #400
Albuquerque, NM 87109   (505) 828-0237

New York
New York Medical Society
420 Lakeville Rd.
Lakesuccess, NY 11042   (516) 488-6100

North Carolina
North Carolina Medical Society
P.O. Box 27167
Raleigh, NC 27611   (919) 833-3836

North Dakota
North Dakota Medical Association
204 West Thayer Ave.
Bismark, ND 58501   (701) 223-9475

Ohio
Ohio State Medical Association
1500 Lake Shore Dr.
Columbus, OH 43017   (614) 486-2401

Oklahoma
Oklahoma State Medical Association
601 N.W. Expressway
Oklahoma City, OK 73118   (405) 843-9571

Oregon
Oregon State Medical Association
5210 South Corbett
Portland, OR 97201   (503) 226-1555

Pennsylvania
Pennsylvania State Medical Society
777 E. Parl Dr.
P.O. Box 8820
Harrisburg, PA 17105   (717) 558-7750

Rhode Island
Rhode Island State Medical Society
106 Francis St.
Providence, RI 02903   (401) 331-3207

South Carolina
South Carolina State Medical Association
P.O. Box 11188
Columbia, SC 29211   (803) 798-6207

South Dakota
South Dakota State Medical Association
1323 S. Minnesota Ave.
Sioux Falls, SD 57105   (605) 336-1965
Share Care is a special program in South Dakota
for low income Medicare recipients in which
doctors accept Medicare payment in full (no
deductibles or co-payments). 50-60% of the
doctors in the state participate. You can apply for
a card with the Association.

Tennessee
Tennessee State Medical Association
P.O. Box 120909
Nashville, TN 37212   (615) 385-2100
They have the Tennessee Medical Access Program
for people over 65 and a referral program through
half of the county health agencies.

Texas
Texas State Medical Association
401 W. 15th St.
Austin, TX 78701   (512) 370-1300
The local societies can refer you to places in your
area for free or low-cost care.

Utah
Utah State Medical Association
540 E. 500 S.
Salt Lake City, UT 84102   (801) 355-7477

Vermont
Vermont State Medical Association
Box H
Montpelier, VT 05601   (802) 223-7898

Virginia
Virginia State Medical Association
4205 Dover Rd.
Richmond, VA 23221   (804) 353-2721
Some local societies have information regarding
pilot programs in their areas, as well as the
Medallion Program for Medicaid-managed care.

Washington
Washington State Medical Association
2033 6th Ave., Suite 900
Seattle, WA 98121   (206) 441-9762

West Virginia
West Virginia State Medical Association
4307 MacCorkle Ave., SE
Charleston, WV 25304   (304) 925-0342

Wisconsin
Wisconsin State Medical Association
P.O. Box 1109
Madison, WI 53701   (608) 257-6781

Wyoming
Wyoming State Medical Association

P.O. Drawer 4009
Cheyenne, WY 82003

(307) 635-2424

Handicapped and Disabled:
The Best Places To Start For Help

If you are disabled or handicapped and need help becoming more independent, there are hundreds of sources of free help and money from federal, state, local, private, and non-profit organizations.

The help available ranges from free information services, self-help groups (for specific disabilities and disabilities in general), free legal aid, and independent living programs, to free money for education, job training, living expenses, transportation, equipment and mobility aids. You can even get money to have your home retrofitted to make it more accessible to your specific handicap. And if you're denied any of these programs or services, there are several free sources of legal help to make sure that you get what you're entitled to.

The three best places where you should begin your search for information about services and money programs for the disabled and handicapped are:

The Social Security Administration
Your State Office of Vocational Rehabilitation
Client Assistance Programs

In this Section, you'll find descriptions and listings of contacts for these three programs, along with several additional best places for self-help and aid for handicapped or disabled individuals.

Free Money For The Disabled
Who Have Worked In The Past

If you're disabled and expect to be disabled for at least one year, and/or if you need extensive training to become employable again once you're ready to go back to work, you may qualify for Disability Cash Income (SSD) from the Social Security Administration. If eligible, you'll get a monthly check based on the amount of all the money you've earned in the past. If you start back to work after receiving your SSD monthly checks, you will still continue to receive SSD for one year. After one year, unless your monthly net earned income exceeds $500, you can still collect the full amount of your monthly SSD check. After three years on SSD, any net monthly income over $500 can disqualify you for SSD and make it necessary to reapply in order to restore your benefits.

If you think you might be eligible for Disability Cash Income, it is very important to apply immediately by contacting the Social Security Administration's toll-free hotline at: (800) 772-1213. If they determine that you are in fact eligible, they must grant you payments retroactive to the date on which you first applied. Keep in mind that you cannot be denied an application even if the intake worker doesn't think you would be eligible to receive money.

Free and Low-Cost Medical Insurance
For the Disabled
Who Have Worked In the Past

If you qualify for the Social Security Disability Income described above, and have been receiving it for at least two years, you will also qualify to receive Medicare. Under Medicare, you'll receive hospital visits free of charge, and you'll get your doctor visits, testing, and the prescription plan for $36.00 per month. You can apply by calling the Social Security toll-free hotline at: (800) 772-1213.

Cash For Dependents Of the Disabled

If you are eligible for Social Security Disability Income described above, your dependents (wife, children, or other in your care) may also be eligible for payments from SSD. To find out what the current total income guidelines are to qualify for the dependent benefits, you should contact the Social Security toll-free hotline at: (800) 772-1213.

Money For The Disabled Who Have Not Worked In The Past

If you are disabled but have not worked in the past, you may still be eligible to receive cash Supplemental Social Security Income benefits if your total monthly income is under a certain amount determined by federal guidelines. Contact the Social Security toll-free hotline for more information on applying: (800) 772-1213.

What To Do When Benefits Are Denied

If you are denied any of the above-mentioned Social Security cash benefits--which often happens regardless of the disability or its severity--you can get free legal help to appeal the Social Security Administration's decision on your application. Contact your state or local Department of Welfare and request the name and address of the nearest Legal Services Corporation (LSC) program, and also contact your nearest State Client Assistance Program (CAP) office. Both programs offer low-income individuals free legal help and representation in appealing application decisions. The CAP program will either provide you with free legal help and representation for your appeal or they will help you find such aid. Unlike legal help offered under the Legal Services Corporation, CAP services are not determined by your income. On the chance that neither of these agencies seem to be able to help you, contact the Disability Rights Education and Defense Fund (DREDF) at (415) 644-2555 or (415) 841-8645.

Free Money for Education and Job Training

If your disability stops you from being able to keep a full-time job or from being able to competitively look for a job, your state's Office of Vocational Rehabilitation (OVR) can help. OVR can give you up to $6,000 each year for job training or education. You can use this grant money, which you do not have to pay back, to cover any expenses related to your training or education, including tuition and fees, travel expenses, books, supplies, equipment (computers, motorized wheelchairs, etc.), a food allowance, tutoring fees, photocopies, and so on. For more information, contact your state's Office of Vocational Rehabilitation listed below.

Help For the Handicapped to Find Or Create a Job

Your state Office of Vocational Rehabilitation (OVR) also acts as an employment agency for the disabled and handicapped and can contact employers for you who have looked favorably on hiring the handicapped. OVR will act as a liaison between you and a prospective employer and help them to create a job for you by providing needed disability-related job equipment, providing needed transportation or other mobility equipment, or by providing any other help you might need to be able to work at a job for which you're qualified. For example, OVR has provided books in braille and braille-to-speech conversion equipment, and computer-robotics equipment that have allowed disabled individuals to work. For more information, contact your state's Office of Vocational Rehabilitation listed at the end of this section.

Help For the Handicapped Already On the Job

If you are working and become disabled or handicapped, your state Office of Vocational Rehabilitation (OVR) can provide you with the equipment, transportation, education, training and other help you might need to keep your job. For example, many times a disability can put someone in a wheelchair. OVR can provide you with a motorized wheelchair so you can continue in your job. Contact your state Office of Vocational Rehabilitation listed at the end of this section for more information.

Medical Help For the Disabled/Handicapped

Your state Office of Vocational Rehabilitation can pay for (or help you pay for) any medical testing or treatment that can be expected to help you, as a handicapped or disabled individual, have a more healthy, prosperous, independent, and fulfilling life. Contact your state Office of Vocational Rehabilitation listed at the end of this section for more information.

What To Do When OVR Benefits Are Denied

The first place to start when your state Office of Vocational Rehabilitation denies you handicap or disability benefits is your nearest state Client Assistance Program (CAP) office. CAP is a free information, referral, and legal service that helps disabled or handicapped individuals appeal a denial by OVR (or other agency). For a variety of reasons, it is not uncommon for a disabled individual to be turned down for services by OVR even when he/she is in fact eligible to receive them. It is sometimes helpful to get a photocopy of section 103 of Chapter 34 of the *Code of Federal Regulations of the U.S. Department of Education* from your local or county library. These are the federal guidelines that each state OVR must follow when determining eligibility. This part of the code is only a few pages and can help you explain to the Client Assistance Program officer why you believe you are eligible even though you've been denied. CAP can take your appeal process from the first stages and all the way to the U.S. Supreme Court if necessary--and it won't cost you a penny.

It is also sometimes helpful to contact the state Office of Vocational Rehabilitation (OVR) itself and make the executive director aware of your circumstances. When it appears that progress via CAP is stalled or has been dragging on for months, it can also be very helpful to contact the regional commissioner of the Rehabilitation Services Administration (RSA), a branch of the Office of Special Education Programs of the U.S. Department of Education. RSA is responsible for overseeing and funding the state OVR agencies and is generally receptive to a short explanatory phone call and letter from those who believe they

can concisely and clearly show that they have been wrongly denied OVR services. If they think you've got a case, they'll contact the OVR in question and make sure that they review your application more favorably.

To get in touch with an RSA official, contact the U.S. Department of Education, Office of Special Education and Rehabilitative Services, RSA, Washington, DC 20202: (202) 205-8870 or (202) 205-5482, and ask for the address and phone number of the regional commissioner for the ED-OSERS-RSA office serving your area.

Three Important Tips When Appealing an OVR Denial Of Services

1. If your state Office of Vocational Rehabilitation (OVR) denies you services based on other similar cases in which they have denied other prospective clients, it is important and effective to argue that such reasons for denial are not allowable under federal regulations. The 34 Code of Federal Regulations Chapter III section 361.31(b)(1) states clearly that the barriers faced by a disabled individual are unique to each individual and to each individual set of circumstances.

2. If you have previously been accepted by your state Office of Vocational Rehabilitation (OVR) as a client and you have gained employment but your handicap has not improved and you lose employment due to no fault of your own, then OVR can again provide you with their services to help you regain employment. For more specifics consult again the 34 Code of Federal Regulations, Chapter III and check under the *Post-Employment Services* sections and *Supported Employment* sections.

3. If you're currently receiving Social Security Disability (SSD), make sure that your state Office of Vocational Rehabilitation (OVR) and Client Assistance Program (CAP) are aware of this fact. Because of the more restrictive SSD definition of what it means to be disabled (compared to OVR), being on SSD almost always automatically qualifies an

SSD recipient for OVR services. It is very hard for OVR to argue otherwise.

Free Legal Help and Information Services For the Handicapped

If you think you've been wrongly denied benefits or discriminated against because of a disability or handicap, the Client Assistance Program (CAP) will help you fight for your rights when you're denied various types of disability benefits from any disability program. They will help you directly and or put you in contact with the agencies that can help you. Your state CAP office is listed at the end of this section.

More Free Legal Help for the Disabled

A national non-profit law and policy center, the Disability Rights Education and Defense Fund (DREDF) can provide you with direct legal representation and act as co-counsel in cases of disability-based discrimination. They also educate legislators and policy makers on issues affecting the rights of people with disabilities. Contact: Disability Rights Education and Defense Fund (DREDF), 2212 Sixth St., Berkeley, CA 94710; (415) 841-8645, or (415) 644-2555 (Voice/TDD).

Information Clearinghouse For All Types Of Disabilities

The Clearinghouse On Disability Information will answer your questions on a wide range of disability topics and send you all kinds of information about services for disabled and handicapped individuals at the national, state, and local levels. They have several free publications, including *Office Of Special Education and Rehabilitative Services (OSERS) News In Print* newsletter, which describes OSERS programs, research, and topical information on a broad range of disability issues. The *Summary of Existing Legislation Affecting Persons With Disabilities* is available for all federal laws through 1991. The *Pocket Guide to Federal Help For Individuals with Disabilities* is a general handy beginning reference. Contact: Clearinghouse On Disability Information,

Office Of Special Education and Rehabilitative Services, U.S. Department Of Education, Room 3132 Switzer Bldg., Washington, DC 20202-2524; (202) 205-8723, (202) 205-8241, or (202) 732-1241.

Additional Resources

1) Guide To Federally-Funded Disability Programs
Superintendent of Documents
Government Printing Office
Washington, DC 20402 (202) 783-3238
The *1992 Guide to Department of Education Programs* gives you in-depth information about the various federally-funded disability programs. This guide book can be purchased for $4.00 by writing or calling the GPO. (Stock #065-000-00449-6).

2) On-Line Information On Education For the Handicapped Or Disabled
Handicapped Educational Exchange (HEX)
11523 Charlton Dr.
Silver Spring, MD 20902
(301) 593-7033 (TDD & 300)
(301) 593-7357 (300 & 1200)
(301) 681-7372 (Voice)
The Handicapped Educational Exchange (HEX) computer bulletin board serves as a clearinghouse for information and resources available to help people who are disabled. Accessible via modem on your personal computer, it lists sources of hardware and computer software, conferences and seminars dealing with handicaps and special education, newsletters, user groups, and much more. Callers can leave public or private messages to make announcements, ask questions, or exchange information. There is no charge for the service.

3) Higher Education and Adult Training For People With Handicaps
National Clearinghouse on Postsecondary Education for Individuals with Handicaps
One Dupont Circle, NW, Suite 800
Washington, DC 20036
(202) 939-9320 (Voice/TDD)
(800) 544-3284 (outside D.C.)
The Higher Education and Adult Training for

People with Handicaps (HEATH) Resource Center is a clearinghouse and information exchange center for resources on postsecondary education programs and the handicapped. Topics include educational support services, policies, procedures, adaptations, and opportunities on American campuses, vocational-technical schools, adult education programs, independent living centers, and other training organizations after high school. Another clearinghouse, National Information Center for Children and Youth with Handicaps, handles the concerns of younger disabled persons through secondary school.

4) Rehabilitation Information Hotline

National Rehabilitation Information Center
8455 Colesville Road
Suite 935   (301) 588-9281
Silver Spring, MD 20910   (800) 346-2742
The National Rehabilitation Information Center can answer all kinds of questions on rehabilitation-related information. An information consultant will answer any questions you might have, send you literature, and/or contact you later if they need time to search further for the information you need.

5) Free Help Finding Employers Who Hire the Handicapped

Job Accommodation Network (JAN)
809 Allen Hall
West Virginia University
Morgantown, WV 26506   (800) 526-7234
                                    (800) 526-4698 (WV)
                                    (800) 526-2262 (Canada)
The Job Accommodation Network (JAN) brings together free information about practical ways employers can make accommodations for employees and job applicants with disabilities. The Network offers comprehensive information on methods and available equipment that have proven effective for a wide range of accommodations, including names, addresses, and phone numbers of appropriate resources.

State Vocational Rehabilitation (OVR) Agencies

Your state Office of Vocational Rehabilitation can provide you with the equipment, transportation, education, training and other help you might need to keep your job. They can also give you information about getting money for vocational rehabilitation education. Contact your state Office of Vocational Rehabilitation listed below for more information.

Alabama
Lamona H. Lucas, Director
Division of Rehabilitation Services
P.O. Box 11586, 2129 E. South Blvd.
Montgomery, AL 36111-0586   (205) 281-8780

Alaska
Keith Anderson, Director
Division of Vocational Rehabilitation
801 West 10th St., Suite 200
Juneau, AK 99801-1894   (907) 465-2814

American Samoa
Peter P. Galea'i, Director
Division of Vocational Rehabilitation
Dept. of Human Resources
American Samoa Government
Pago Pago, AS 96799   10288011684 - 633-2336

Arizona
James Griffin, Administrator
Rehabilitation Services Admin.
Dept. of Economic Security
1789 W. Jefferson, 2nd Floor, NW
Phoenix, AZ 85007   (602) 542-3332

Arkansas
Bobby C. Simpson, Director
Division of Rehabilitation
Services, P.O. Box 3781
Arkansas Dept. of Human Services
Little Rock, AR 72203   (501) 682-6708

James C. Hudson, Director
Division of Services for the Blind
Dept. of Human Services
P.O. Box 3237, 411 Victory Street
Little Rock, AK 72203   (501) 324-9270

California
William Tainter, Director
Dept. of Rehabilitation
830 K Street Mall, P. O. Box 94422
Sacramento, CA 95814   (916) 445-3971

Colorado
Anthony Francavilla, Manager
Rehabilitation Services
Dept. of Social Services
1575 Sherman St., 4th Floor
Denver, CO 80203-1714   (303) 866-2866

Connecticut
John F. Halliday, Director
Bureau of Rehab. Services
Dept. of Human Resources
10 Griffin Rd., North
Windsor, CT 06095   (203) 298-2003

George A. Precourt, Director
Board of Education & Services for the Blind
Dept. of Human Resources
170 Ridge Rd.
Wethersfield, CT 06109   (203) 566-5800

Delaware
Barbara P. Bennett, Acting Director
Division of Vocational Rehabilitation
Dept. of Labor, Elwyn Building
321 East 11th St.
Wilmington, DE 19801   (302) 577-2850

Dianne L. Post, Director
Div. for the Visually Impaired
Biggs Building
Health & Social Services Campus
1901 N. Dupont Highway
New Castle, DE 19720   (302) 577-4731

District of Columbia
Ruth Royall Hill, Administrator
D.C. Rehabilitation Services Administration
Commission on Social Services
Dept. of Human Services
605 G Street, N.W., Room 1111
Washington, DC 20001   (202) 727-3227

Florida
Jay Yourist, Director
Division of Vocational Rehabilitation
Dept. of Labor and Employment Security

1709-A Mahan Dr.
Tallahassee, FL 32399-0696   (904) 488-6210

Carl McCoy, Director
Division of Blind Services
Dept. of Education
2540 Executive Center Circle, W
Douglas Building
Tallahassee, FL 32301   (904) 488-1330

Georgia
Yvonne Johnson, Director
Division of Rehabilitation Services,
Dept. of Human Resources
878 Peachtree Street, N.E.
Room 706
Atlanta, GA 30309   (404) 894-6670

Guam
Norbert Ungacto, Acting Director
Dept. of Vocational Rehabilitation
Government of Guam
122 Harmon Plaza
Room B201
Harmon Industrial Park, Guam 96911
                    10288-011-671-646-9468

Hawaii
Neil Shim, Administrator
Division of Vocational Rehabilitation
Dept. of Human Services
Bishop Trust Bldg.
1000 Bishop St., Rm. 605
Honolulu, HI 96813   (808) 586-5355

Idaho
George J. Pelletier,Jr., Administrator
Division of Vocational Rehab.
Len B. Jordon Building, Rm. 150
650 West State
Boise, ID 83720   (208) 334-3390

Edward J. McHugh, Director
Idaho Commission for the Blind
341 W. Washington St.
Boise, ID 83702   (208) 334-3220

Illinois
Andrey McCrimon, Director
Illinois Dept. of Rehab. Services
623 E, Adams St., P.O. Box 19429
Springfield, IL 62794-9429   (217) 782-2093

Indiana
Richelyn Douglas, Acting Director
Division of Aging and Rehabilitation Services
Indiana Family and Social Services Admin.
P.O. Box 7083
402 W. Washington St., Room W341
Indianapolis, IN 46207-7083   (317) 232-1147

Iowa
Jerry L. Starkweather, Administrator
Division of Vocational Rehabilitation Services
Dept. of Education
510 E. 12th St.
Des Moines, IA 50319   (515) 281-6731

R. Creig Slayton, Director
Department for the Blind
524 4th St.
Des Moines, IA 50309-2364   (515) 281-1334

Kansas
Glen Yancey, Commissioner
Dept. of Social & Rehabilitation Services
300 Southwest Oakley Street
Biddle Bldg., 1st Floor
Topeka, KS 66606   (913) 296-3911

Kentucky
Caroll Burchett, Commissioner
Dept. of Vocational Rehabilitation
500 Mero St.
Frankfort, KY 40601   (502) 564-4566

Priscilla Rogers, Director
Kentucky Dept. for the Blind
427 Versailles Rd.
Frankfort, KY 40601   (502) 564-4754

Louisiana
May Nelson, Director
Rehabilitation Services
Dept. of Social Services
P.O. Box 94371
Baton Rouge, LA 70804   (504) 342-2285

Maine
Pamela A. Tetley, Director
Bureau of Rehabilitation
Dept. of Human Services
35 Anthony Ave.
Augusta, ME 04333-0011   (207) 624-5300

Maryland
James S. Jeffers
Division of Vocational Rehabilitation
Administrative Offices
2301 Argonne Dr.
Baltimore, MD 21218   (410) 554-3000

Massachusetts
Elmer C. Bartels, Commissioner
Massachusetts Rehabilitation Commission
Fort Point Place
27-43 Wormwood St.
Boston, MA 02210-1606   (617) 727-2172

Charles Crawford, Commissioner
Massachusetts Commission for the Blind
88 Kingston St.
Boston, MA 02111-2227
     (617) 727-5550, ext. 4503

Michigan
Peter Griswold, Director
Michigan Rehabilitation Services
Dept. of Education
P.O. Box 30010
Lansing, MI 48909   (517) 373-3391

Philip E. Peterson, Director
Commission for the Blind
Dept. of Labor
201 N. Washington Square
Lansing, MI 48909   (517) 373-2062

Minnesota
Mary Shortall, Assistant Commissioner
Div. of Rehabilitation Services
Dept. of Jobs and Training
390 N. Robert Street, 5th Floor
St. Paul, MN 55101   (612) 296-1822

Charles E. Hamilton
Acting Assistant Commissioner
State Services for the Blind
1745 University Avenue
St. Paul, MN 55104   (612) 642-0508

Mississippi
John Cook, Executive Director
Dept. of Rehabilitation Services
P.O. Box 22806
Jackson, MS 39225-2806   (601) 936-0285

Missouri
Don L. Gann, Assistant Commissioner
Dept. of Elementary & Secondary Education
Division of Vocational Rehab.
2401 E. McCarty St.
Jefferson City, MO 65101   (314) 751-3251

David S. Vogel, Deputy Director
Rehabilitation Services for the Blind
Division of Family Services
619 E. Capitol
Jefferson City, MO 65101   (314) 751-4249

Montana
Joe A. Mathews, Administrator
Dept. of Social & Rehabilitation Services
Rehabilitation/Visual Services Division
P.O. Box 4210, 111 Sanders
Helena, MT 59604   (406) 444-2590

Nebraska
Jason D. Andrew, Associate Commissioner &
Director
Division of Rehabilitation Services
State Dept. of Education
301 Centennial Mall South, 6th Fl.
Lincoln, NE 68509   (402) 471-3654

James S. Nyman, Director
Services for Visually Impaired
Dept. of Public Institutions
4600 Valley Rd.
Lincoln, NE 68510-4844   (402) 471-2891

Nevada
Stephen A. Shaw, Administrator
Rehabilitation Division
Dept. of Human Resources, 5th Floor
505 E. King St.
Carson City, NV 90710   (702) 687-4440

New Hampshire
Bruce Archambault, Director
Division of Vocational Rehabilitation
State Dept. of Education
78 Regional Dr.
Concord, NH 03301-9686   (603) 271-3471

New Jersey
Stephen G. Janick, III, Director
Division of Vocational Rehabilitation Services
Dept. of Labor & Industry

John Fitch Plaza
Trenton, NJ 08625   (609) 292-5987

Jamie Casabianca-Hillton
Executive Director
Commission for the Blind and Visually Impaired
Dept. of Human Services
153 Halsey Street, 6th Floor
P.O. Box 47017
Newark, NJ 07101   (201) 648-2324

New Mexico
Terry Brigance, Director
Division of Vocational Rehabilitation
State Dept. of Education
435 St. Michael Dr., Bldg. D
Santa Fe, NM 87503   (505) 827-3511

Frederick K. Schroeder, Director
Commission for the Blind
PERA Building
Room 205
Santa Fe, NM 87503   (505) 827-4479

New York
Lawrence Gloeckler, Deputy Commissioner
Vocational Educational Services
 for Individuals with Disabilities
New York State Education Dept.
One Commerce Plaza, 16th Floor
Albany, NY 12234   (518) 474-2714

John L. Ryan, Jr., Assistant Commissioner
Dept. of Social Services
Commission for the Blind & Visually Handicapped
10 Eyck Office Bldg.
40 North Pearl St.
Albany, NY 12243   (518) 473-1801

North Carolina
Claude A. Myer, Director
Division of Vocational Rehabilitation Services
Dept. of Human Resources
State Office
P.O. Box 26053
Raleigh, NC 27611   (919) 733-3364

Herman O. Gruber, Director
Division of Services for the Blind
Dept. of Human Resources
309 Ashe Ave.
Raleigh, NC 27606   (919) 733-9822

North Dakota
Gene Hysjulien, Associate Director
Office of Vocational Rehabilitation
Dept. of Human Services
Administrative Office
400 E. Broadway Ave., Suite 303
Bismarck, ND 58501-4038   (701) 224-3999

Ohio
Robert L. Rabe, Administrator
Ohio Rehabilitation Services Commission
400 E. Campus View Blvd.
Columbus, OH 43235-4604
                    (614) 438-1210 (Voice/TDD)

Oklahoma
Jerry Dunlap, Administrator
Rehabilitation Services Division
Dept. of Human Services
P.O. Box 25352
Oklahoma City, OK 73125
                    (405) 424-6006, ext. 2840

Oregon
Joil Southwell, Administrator
Vocational Rehabilitation Division
Dept. Of Human Resources
2045 Silverton Rd., N.E.
Salem, OR 97310   (503) 378-3830

Charles Young, Administrator
Commission for the Blind
535 S.E. 12th Ave.
Portland, OR 97214   (503) 731-3221

Pennsylvania
Gil Selders, Executive Director
Office of Vocational Rehabilitation
Dept. of Labor & Industry Bldg.
7th & Forster Sts.
Harrisburg, PA 17120   (717) 787-5244

Norman E. Witman, Director
Bureau of Blindness & Visual Services
Dept. of Public Welfare
1301 North 7th St.
P.O. Box 2675
Harrisburg, PA 17105   (717) 787-6176

Puerto Rico
Francisco Vallejo, Assistant Secretary
Vocational Rehabilitation

Dept. of Social Services
P.O. Box 1118
Hato Rey, PR 00919   (809) 725-1792

Rhode Island
William A. Messore, Administrator
Office of Vocational Rehabilitation Services
Dept. of Human Services
40 Fountain St.
Providence, RI 02903   (401) 421-7005

South Carolina
Joseph S. Dusenbury, Commissioner
Vocational Rehabilitation Dept.
P.O. Box 15
1410 Boston Ave.
West Columbia, SC 29171-0015   (803) 822-4300

Donald Gist, Commissioner
Commission for the Blind
1430 Confederate Ave.
Columbia, SC 29201   (803) 734-7520

South Dakota
David Miller, Director
Division of Rehabilitation Services
East Highway 34
c/o 500 East Capitol
Pierre, SD 57501-5070   (605) 773-3195

Grady Kickul, Director
Division of Service to the Blind
 and Visually Impaired
East Highway 34
c/o 500 East Capitol
Pierre, SD 57501-5070   (605) 773-4644

Tennessee
Patsy J. Mathews, Assistant Commissioner
Division of Rehabilitation Services
Dept. of Human Services
Citizen Plaza Building
15th Floor
400 Deadrick St.
Nashville, TN 37248   (615) 741-2521

Texas
Vernon M. Arrell, Commissioner
Texas Rehabilitation Commission
4900 N. Lamar, Room 7102
Austin, TX 78751-2316   (512) 483-4001

Pat D. Westbrook, Executive Director
Texas Commission for the Blind
Administration Bldg., 4800 North Lamar
Austin, TX 78711   (512) 459-2600

Utah
R. Blaine Peterson,Executive Director
Utah State Office of Rehabilitation
250 E. 500 South
Salt Lake City, UT 84111   (801) 538-7530

Vermont
Diane Dalmasse, Director
Vocational Rehabilitation Division
Agency of Human Services
Osgood Bldg., Waterbury Complex
103 S. Main St.
Waterbury, VT 05676   (802) 241-2189

David M. Mentasti, Director
Division for the Blind & Visually Impaired
Agency of Human Services
Osgood Bldg., Waterbury Complex
103 S. Main St.
Waterbury, VT 05676   (802) 241-2211

Virgin Islands
Sedonie Halbert, Administrator
Division of Disabilities
 & Rehabilitation Services
Dept. of Human Services
Barbel Plaza South
St. Thomas, VI 00802

Virginia
Susan L. Urfsky, Commissioner
Dept. of Rehabilitative Services
Commonwealth of Virginia
4901 Fitzhugh Ave., P.O. Box 11045
Richmond, VA 23230-1045   (804) 367-0316

Donald L. Cox, Commissioner
Dept. for the Visually Handicapped,
Commonwealth of Virginia
397 Azalea Ave.
Richmond, VA 23227-3697   (804) 371-3145

Washington
Jeanne Munro, Director
Division of Vocational Rehabilitation
Dept. of Social & Health Services
P.O. Box 45340
Olympia, WA 98504-5340   (206) 438-8000

Shirley Smith, Director
Dept. of Services for the Blind
521 East Legion Way, MS: FD-11
Olympia, WA 98504-1422   (206) 586-1224

West Virginia
John M. Panza, Director
Division of Vocational Rehabilitation
State Board of Rehabilitation
State Capitol Complex
Charleston, WV 25305   (304) 766-4601

Wisconsin
Judy Norman-Nunnery, Administrator
Div. of Vocational Rehabilitation
Dept. of Health and Social Services
1 West Wilson, 8th Floor
P.O. Box 7852
Madison, WI 53702   (608) 266-2168

Wyoming
Gary W. Child, Administrator
Division of Vocational Rehabilitation
Dept. of Employment
1100 Herschler Bldg.
Cheyenne, WY 82002   (307) 777-7385

State Client Assistance Program (CAP)

The first place to start when your state Office of Vocational Rehabilitation denies you handicap or disability benefits is your nearest state Client Assistance Program (CAP) office. CAP is a free information, referral, and legal service that helps disabled or handicapped individuals appeal a denial by OVR (or other agency). CAP can take your appeal process from the first stages and all

the way to the U.S. Supreme Court if necessary-- and it won't cost you a penny.

Alabama
Jerry Norsworthy
Division of Rehabilitation
 and Crippled Children Services
2129 E. South Blvd

P.O. Box 11586
Montgomery, AL 36111   (205) 281-8780

Alaska
Pam Stratton, CAP Director
ASSIST
2900 Boniface Pkwy., #100   (800) 478-0048
Anchorage, AK 99504-3195   (907) 333-2211

American Samoa
Minareta Thompson, Director
Client Assistance and P&A Program
P.O. Box 3937
Pago Pago, AS 96799   (684) 633-2441

Arizona
Ann Meyer, CAP Director
Arizona Center for Law
in the Public Interest
3724 N. Third St., Suite 300
Phoenix, AZ 85012   (602) 274-6287

Arkansas
Dale Turrentine, CAP Director
Advocacy Services,Inc.
Evergreen Place, Suite 201
1100 North University
Little Rock, AR 72207   (501) 324-9215

California
Anna Claybourne, Director
Client Assistance Program
830 K Street Mall, Room 220
Sacramento, CA 95814   (916) 322-5066

Colorado
Kimberly Hoyt, CAP Coordinator
The Legal Center
455 Sherman St., Suite 130
Denver, CO 80203   (303) 722-0300

Connecticut
Susan Werboff, CAP Director
Office of P&A for Handicapped & DD Persons
60 Weston Street
Hartford, CT 06120-1551   (203) 297-4300

Delaware
Cheryl Bates-Harris, CAP Director
United Cerebral Palsy, Inc.
700A River Rd.
Wilmington, DE 19809   (302) 764-2400

District of Columbia
Toni Fisher, CAP Coordinator
I.P.A.C.H.I.
4455 Connecticut Ave., NW
Suite B100
Washington, DC 20008   (202) 966-8081

Florida
Steve Howells, CAP Program Director
Advocacy Center for Persons with Disabilities
Webster Bldg.
2671 Executive Center Circle West, #100
Tallahassee, FL 32301-5024   (904) 488-9070

Georgia
Phil D. Payne, CAP Director
Division of Rehabilitation Services
878 Peachtree St., NE, RM. 708
Atlanta, GA 30309   (404) 894-6725

Guam
Fidela Limtiacho, President of the Board
Parent Agencies Network
130 Rehabilitation Center St.
Koro, Guam 96911

Hawaii
Executive Director
Protection and Advocacy Agency
1580 Makaloa Street, Suite 1060
Honolulu, HI 96814   (808) 949-2922

Idaho
Brent Marchbanks, Director
Co-Ad, Inc.
1409 W. Washington
Boise, ID 83702   (208) 336-5353

Illinois
Cynthia Grothaus, Manager
Illinois Client Assistance Project
100 N. First Street, 1st Floor
Springfield, IL 62702   (217) 782-5374

Indiana
Mary Lou Haines, Executive Director
Indiana Advocacy Services
850 North Meridian, Suite 2-C
Indianapolis, IN 46204   (317) 232-1150

Iowa
Harliette Heland, CAP Director

Division of Persons with Disabilities
Lucas State Office Bldg.
Des Moines, IA 50319   (515) 281-3957

Kansas
Mary Reyer, Director
Client Assistance Program
Biddle Bldg., 2nd Floor
2700 West 6th St.
Topeka, KS 66606   (913) 296-1491

Kentucky
Sharon S. Fields, Director
Client Assistance Program
Capitol Plaza Tower   (502) 564-8035
Frankfort, KY 40601   (800) 633-6283

Louisiana
Susan Howard, CAP Director
Advocacy Center for the Elderly
 and Disabled
210 O'Keefe
Suite 700
New Orleans, LA 70112   (504) 522-2337

Maine
Laura Petovello, Director
Maine Advocacy Services
1 Grandview Pl, Suite 1
P.O. Box 445   (207) 377-6202
Winthrop, ME 04364   (800) 452-1948

Maryland
Sharon Julius, CAP Program Director
State Dept of Education
Division of Vocational Rehabilitation
300 W. Preston Street
Suite 205
Baltimore, MD 21201   (301) 333-7251

Massachusetts
Barbara Lybarger, Director
Client Assistance Program
Office of Handicapped Affairs
One Ashburton Place, Room 303
Boston, MA 02108   (617) 727-7440

Michigan
Ducan O. Wyeth, CAP Director
Department of Rehabilitation Services
P.O. Box 30008
Lansing, MI 48909   (517) 373-8193

Vicky Chapman, CAP Advocate
Commission for the Blind
201 N. Washington Sq.
2nd Floor, Victor Bldg.
P.O. Box 30015
Lansing, MI 48909   (517) 373-6425

Minnesota
Valerie Brown, CAP Project Coordinator
Minnesota Disability Law Center
430 First Ave., North, Suite 300
Minneapolis, MN 55401   (612) 332-1441

Mississippi
Presley Posey, Director
Easter Seals Society
3226 N. State St.
Jackson, MS 39216   (601) 982-7051

Missouri
Cynthia N. Schloss, Executive Director
Missouri P&A Services
925 S. Country Club Dr., Unit B-1
Jefferson City, MO 65109   (314) 893-3333

Montana
Lynn Wislow, CAP Director
Montana Advocacy Program
1410 8th Ave.   (406) 444-3889
Helena, MT 59601   (800) 245-4743

Nebraska
Victoria L. Rasmussen, CAP Director
Division of Rehabilitation Services
Department of Education
301 Centennial Mall South
Lincoln, NE 68509   (402) 471-3656

Nevada
William E. Bauer, Director
Client Assistance Program
750 Silver Way
Fernly, NV 89408   (702) 688-1440

New Hampshire
Christy Goodrich, CAP Ombudsman
Governor's Commission for the Handicapped
57 Regional Dr.
Concord, NH 03301-9686   (603) 271-2773

New Jersey
Cheryl Cochran, CAP Coordinator

Department of Public Advocate
Office for Advocacy of DD
Hughes Justice Complex, CN850   (609) 292-9742
Trenton, NJ 08625   (800) 792-8600

New Mexico
Joyce Pomo, CAP Coordinator
Protection & Advocacy System, Inc.
1720 Louisiana Blvd., NE, Suite 204
Albuquerque, NM 87110   (505) 256-3100

New York
Michael Peluso, CAP Director
State Commission on Quality of Care
 for the Mentally Disabled
99 Washington Ave, Suite 1002
Albany, NY 12210   (518) 473-7378

North Carolina
Debbie Jackson, CAP Director
Division of Vocational Rehabilitation Services
P.O. Box 26053
Raleigh, NC 27611   (919) 733-3364

North Dakota
Dennis Lyon, CAP Director
Office of Vocational Rehabilitation
Dept. of Human Services
400 East Broadway
Suite 303
Bismarck, ND 58501   (701) 224-3970

Ohio
David Robinson, CAP Administrator
Governor's Office of Advocacy for
 People with Disabilities
30 East Broad Street
Room 1201
Columbus, OH 43266-0400   (614) 466-9956

Oklahoma
Helen Kutz, Director
Oklahoma Office of Handicapped Concerns
4300 N. Lincoln Blvd.
Suite 200
Oklahoma City, OK 73105   (405) 521-3756

Oregon
Mike Bullis, CAP Director
Oregon Disabilities Commission
1257 Perry St., SE
Salem, OR 97310   (503) 378-3142

Pennsylvania
Alice Paylor, Regional Manager
Client Assistance Program
Medical Center East
211 N. Whitfield, Suite 215   (412) 363-7223
Pittsburgh, PA 15206   (800) 525-7223

Stephen Pennington, Statewide Director
Client Assistance Prog. (SEPLS)
1650 Arch St., Suite 2310   (215) 557-7112
Philadelphia, PA 19103   (800)742-8877

Puerto Rico
Paul Jimenez, Cap Program Coordinator
Ombudsman for the Disabled
P.O. Box 5163   (809) 766-2388
Hato Rey, PR 00919-5163   (809) 766-2333

Rhode Island
Ted Mello, CAP Director
Rhode Island P&A System, Inc.
55 Bradford St., 2nd Floor
Providence, RI 02903   (401) 831-3150

South Carolina
J.P. Pratt, II, CAP Director
P&A for the Handicapped
3710 Landmark Dr., #208   (803) 782-0639
Columbia, SC 29204   (800) 922-5225

South Dakota
Nancy Schade, CAP Director
South Dakota Advocacy Services
221 S. Central Ave.   (605) 224-8294
Pierre, SD 57501   (800) 658-4782

Tennessee
Executive Director
Tennessee P&A, Inc.
P.O. Box 121257
Nashville, TN 37212   (615) 298-1080

Texas
Judy Sokolow, CAP Coordinator
Advocacy, Inc.
7800 Shoal Creek Blvd.
Suite 171-E
Austin, TX 78757   (512) 454-4816

Utah
Nancy Friel, CAP Director
Legal Center for People With Disabilities

455 East 400 South, Suite 201 (801) 363-1347
Salt Lake City, UT 84101 (800) 662-9080

Vermont
Diane Coates, Director
Client Assistance Program
Ladd Hall, 103 South Main St.
Waterbury, VT 05676 (802) 241-2641

Virginia
Becky Currin, CAP Manager
Department for the Rights of the Disabled
101 N 14th Street, 17th Floor (804) 225-2042
Richmond, VA 23219 (800) 552-3962

Virgin Islands
Camille Ayala, Executive Director
Commission on Advocacy for the
 Developmentally Disabled, Inc.
7A Whim St., Suite 2 (809) 776-4303
St. Croix, VI 00840 (809) 772-1200

Washington
Jerry Johnsen, Director

Client Assistance Program
P.O. Box 22510 (206) 721-4049
Seattle, WA 98122 (206) 721-4575

West Virginia
Susan Edwards, CAP Director
West Virginia Advocates
1524 Kanawha Blvd., East (303) 346-0847
Charleston, WV 25311 (800) 950-5250

Wisconsin
Bob Olson, Acting CAP Director
Governor's Commission for People
 With Disabilities
131 W Wilson St., Suite 1003
P.O. Box 7852
Madison, WI 53707 (608) 266-5378

Wyoming
Kriss Smith, CAP Director
Wyoming P&A System, Inc. (307) 638-7668
2424 Pioneer Ave., Suite 101 (307) 632-3496
Cheyenne, WY 82001 (800) 821-3091

Free Research On Health Matters

The National Health Information Center can direct you to specialized clearinghouses as well as health organizations and foundations on virtually any disease or health issue. Through its resource files and database (DIRLINE), they can respond to questions regarding health concerns and can send publications, bibliographies, and other materials. A library focusing on health topics is open to the public, and the Center also produces many different directories and resource guides, which are available for a minimal cost. A publica-

tions catalog is available free of charge. Two of the publications include a list of *Selected Federal Health Information Clearinghouses* and *Information Centers and Toll-Free Numbers for Health Information.*

☎ Contact:
National Health Information Center
P.O. Box 1133
Washington, DC 20013
(800) 336-4797
(301) 565-4167 (in MD)

FREE INFORMATION AND EXPERTISE
FROM A TO Z

This chapter brings together the hundreds of different resources on health care throughout the government into one, easy-to-use format. Subjects are listed A to Z alphabetically under topic headings, followed by the best places to contact, and any relevant publications. If the topic you're interested in doesn't have a subject heading listed in this chapter, flip to the INDEX at the back of the book, and chances are you'll find what you're looking for. If you're still stuck, you can always turn to the Health Information Clearinghouse on page 48 for help.

Here's a more detailed explanation of how we've organized the information under each subject heading:

Clearinghouses/Hotlines

Under this heading you'll find the best initial points of contact in the government for a disease or health issue. Often a toll-free telephone number is also included. Clearinghouses can provide you with all kinds of information on a topic and will often do custom searches of their computer data bases to find the most up-to-date information for you. If they can't provide you with the information you're looking for, many will also refer you to other organizations that study the topic. Many of these clearinghouses and hotlines can also help you find out about any free clinical studies undertaken on a disease where you can receive treatment free of charge.

Free Publications/Videos

Under this heading you'll find free and low-cost publications and videos available throughout the government on a given topic. Publications listed in this book are free unless otherwise noted. For more videos on any topic, see the listing under Videos. This listing describes a data base of 18,000 health-related videos available on a free loan basis through your local library.

Keep in mind, though, that just because a topic may not have any publications listed doesn't necessarily mean that there aren't any out there. The clearinghouse listed for that topic will often do a custom search for you and send you reprints of relevant journal articles, or send you a detailed bibliography of resources that you can look up on your own in your local library.

ABETALIPOPROTEINEMIA

Clearinghouses/Hotlines

The National Heart, Lung, and Blood Institute (NHLBI) can search the Combined Health Information Database (CHID) and generate a bibliography of resources on Abetalipoproteinemia for you. They also will send you any publications and journal articles they may have on hand, and will refer you to other organizations that are studying this condition. If you can't afford treatment, have your doctor call NHLBI to find out if they are conducting any clinical studies that you might qualify for.

☎ Contact:
National Heart, Lung and Blood Institute
Bldg. 31, Room 4A21
Bethesda, MD 20892
(301) 496-4236

ABORTION

Clearinghouses/Hotlines

The National Institute of Child Health and Human Development (NICHD) will send you whatever publications and reprints of journal articles they have on Abortion. If necessary, they will refer you to other experts or researchers in the field.

☎ Contact:
National Institute of Child Health
and Human Development
Bldg. 31, Room 2A32
Bethesda, MD 20892
(301) 496-5133

The Maternal Mortality Surveillance Branch Office of the National Center for Chronic Disease Prevention can provide you with research reports dealing with maternal mortality as a result of Abortions.

☎ Contact:
Maternal Mortality Surveillance Branch
National Center for Chronic Disease Prevention
and Health Promotion

1600 Clifton Road, NE
Atlanta, GA 30333
(404) 488-5144

The National Center for Health Statistics can provide you with data on the number of Abortions, age of the woman, metropolitan versus rural areas, and much more. They publish a free yearly report titled *Induced Termination of Pregnancy* and have them dating back to 1977.

☎ Contact:
National Center for Health Statistics
6525 Belcrest Road
Hyattsville, MD 20782
(301) 436-8500

Free Publications/Videos

The following Congressional Research Service (CRS) reports on Abortion are available from either of your U.S. Senators' offices at the U.S. Capitol, Washington, DC 20510, or from your Congressional Representative at the U.S. Capitol, Washington, DC 20515. You can also call in your request through the U.S. Capitol switchboard at (202) 224-3121. Be sure to include the full title and report number in your request.

- *Abortion: An Historical Perspective; Selected References, 1973-1988.* (#88-706)
- *Abortion in World Religions.* (#88-357 GOV)
- *Abortion: Info Pack.* (#IP001A)
- *Abortion: Judicial and Legislative Control: Archived Issue Brief.* (#IB74019)
- *Abortion: Judicial Control: Issue Brief.* (#IB88006)
- *Abortion Law in the Aftermath of Webster.* (#91-573 A)
- *Abortion Laws in China, Germany and Great Britain.* (#LL90-79)
- *Abortion: Legislative Control: Issue Brief.* (#IB88007)
- *Abortion: National and State Public Opinion Polls.* (#89-591 GOV)
- *A Comparative Survey of the Laws on Abortion of Selected Countries.* (#LL90-32)
- *Fetal Research: A Survey of State Law.* (#88-198 A)
- *Freedom of Speech and Government Funding: Implications of Rust v. Sullivan.* (#91-488 A)

- *The Moral Arguments in the Controversy Over Abortion, With Reference to "Human Life Amendment" Resolutions.* (#86-802 GOV)
- *Legal Analysis of Constitutional Issues Raised by the So-Called "Kemp-Hatch" Amendment Restricting Federal Funding of Abortion Counseling and Referral.* (#85-1142 A)
- *Legal Analysis of H.R. 1729, the "President's Pro-life Bill of 1987".* (#87-682 A)
- *The Proposed Freedom of Choice Act: Background Discussion.* (92-602 A)
- *Webster v Reproductive Health Services: Another Look at the Abortion Issue.* (#89-245 A)

ABSTINENCE

Free Publications/Videos

The following publications are available from the Family Life Information Exchange, P.O. Box 30146, Bethesda, MD 20814; (301) 585-6636.

- *Many Teens are Saying "NO".*
- *Adolescent Abstinence: A Guide for Family Planning Professionals.*

ACCIDENT PREVENTION

Clearinghouses/Hotlines

The National Institute on Aging (NIA) will send you whatever publications and reprints of journal articles they have on Accident Prevention and the Aging. They cannot refer you to other experts if the information they have isn't sufficient for your purposes.

☎ Contact:
National Institute on Aging
Bldg. 31, Room 5C27
Bethesda, MD 20892
(301) 496-1752

The National Center for Injury Prevention and Control has research and information relating to suicide and homicide, family violence, vehicle crashes, alcohol-related injuries, farm-related injuries, falls among the elderly, head and spinal cord injuries, and house fires. Some of the information they can send you includes research reports, statistics, and injury mortality atlases, which break things down into states, males versus females, and types of accidents.

☎ Contact:
National Center for Injury
Prevention and Control
Centers for Disease Control
1600 Clifton Road, NE
Atlanta, GA 30333
(404) 488-4936

Free Publications/Videos

The following publications are available from the National Institute on Aging, Bldg. 31, Room 5C27, Bethesda, MD 20892; (301) 496-1752.

- *Accident Prevention and the Elderly.*
- *Accidents and the Elderly.*
- *Preventing Falls and Fractures.*

ACETAMINOPHEN

Free Publications/Videos

The following publication is available from the Food & Drug Administration, (HFE-88), 5600 Fishers Ln., Rockville, MD 20857; (301) 443-3170.

- *How To Take Your Medicines: Acetaminophen-Codeine.* (#FDA91-3188)

ACHONDROPLASIA

Clearinghouses/Hotlines

The National Institute of Child Health and Human Development (NICHD) will send you whatever publications and reprints of journal articles they have on Achondroplasia. If necessary, they will refer you to other experts or researchers in the field. If you can't afford treatment, have your doctor call NICHD to find out if they are conducting any clinical studies that you might qualify for.

☎ Contact:
National Institute of Child Health
and Human Development
Bldg. 31, Room 2A32
Bethesda, MD 20892
(301) 496-5133

The National Institute of Arthritis and Musculoskeletal and Skin Diseases (NIAMS) will send you whatever publications and reprints of articles from texts and journals they have on Achondroplasia. They will also refer you to other organizations that are studying this disease. NIAMS will also let you know of any clinical studies that may be studying this disease and looking for patients.

☎ Contact:
National Institute of Arthritis
and Musculoskeletal and Skin Diseases
Box AMS
Bethesda, MD 20892
(301) 495-4484

ACIDOSIS

Clearinghouses/Hotlines

The National Institute of Child Health and Human Development (NICHD) will send you whatever publications and reprints of journal articles they have on Acidosis. If necessary, they will refer you to other experts or researchers in the field. If you can't afford treatment, have your doctor call NICHD to find out if they are conducting any clinical studies that you might qualify for.

☎ Contact:
National Institute of Child Health
and Human Development
Bldg. 31, Room 2A32
Bethesda, MD 20892
(301) 496-5133

ACNE

See also Adolescent Health
See also Cystic Acne
See also Teenagers

Clearinghouses/Hotlines

The National Institute of Arthritis and Musculoskeletal and Skin Diseases (NIAMS) conducts and supports basic and clinical research on the causes, prevention, diagnosis, and treatment of Acne and other skin problems. They have all kinds of publications to send you, and their information specialist can give you further, in-depth information on Acne and many other of related topics.

☎ Contact:
National Institute of Arthritis
and Musculoskeletal and Skin Diseases
Box AMS
Bethesda, MD 20892
(301) 495-4484

Free Publications/Videos

The following publication is available from the Consumer Information Center, P.O. Box 100, Pueblo, CO 81002.

- *Acne: Taming that Age-Old Adolescent Affliction.* (551Y)

ACOUSTIC NEUROMA

Clearinghouses/Hotlines

The National Institute on Deafness and Other Communicative Disorders (NIDCD) will send you whatever publications and reprints of journal articles they have on Acoustic Neuroma. If you need further information, they will refer you to other organizations that study this and other related disorders. NIDCD does not conduct any clinical studies for this or any other disorder.

☎ Contact:
National Institute on Deafness
and Other Communication Disorders
Bldg. 31, Room 3C35
Bethesda, MD 20892
(301) 496-7243
(800) 241-1044
(301) 402-0252 (TDD)

The National Institute of Neurological Disorders and Stroke (NINDS) can send you only information they have in their publications list on Acoustic Neuroma. They cannot refer you to any experts. This Clearinghouse cannot directly give you information about any current clinical studies NINDS might be conducting on this illness, but you can find this information for yourself by looking under the National Institute of Neurological Disorders and Stroke in *Appendix A* at the end of this book.

☎ Contact:
National Institute of Neurological
Disorders and Stroke
Bldg. 31, Room 8A06
Bethesda, MD 20892
(301) 496-5751
(800) 352-9424

ACQUIRED IMMUNE DEFICIENCY DISORDER

See AIDS

ACROMEGALY

Clearinghouses/Hotlines

The National Institute of Diabetes and Digestive and Kidney Diseases's (NIDDK) individual clearinghouses can search the Combined Health Information Database (CHID) and generate a bibliography of resources on Acromegaly for you. They also will send you any publications and journal articles they may have on hand, and will

refer you to other organizations that are studying this condition. If you can't afford treatment, have your doctor call NIDDK to find out if they are conducting any clinical studies that you might qualify for.

☎ Contact:
National Institute of Diabetes and
Digestive and Kidney Diseases
Bldg. 31, Room 9A04
Bethesda, MD 20892
(301) 496-3583

ACTH

Clearinghouses/Hotlines

The National Heart, Lung, and Blood Institute (NHLBI) can search the Combined Health Information Database (CHID) and generate a bibliography of resources on ACTH, Excessive Secretion for you. They also will send you any publications and journal articles they may have on hand, and will refer you to other organizations that are studying this condition. If you can't afford treatment, have your doctor call NHLBI to find out if they are conducting any clinical studies that you might qualify for.

☎ Contact:
National Heart, Lung and Blood Institute
Bldg. 31, Room 4A21
Bethesda, MD 20892
(301) 496-4236

ACUPUNCTURE

Clearinghouses/Hotlines

The National Institute of Neurological Disorders and Stroke conducts research on persistent pain and various therapies including drugs, Acupuncture, surgery, electrical stimulation, and also psychological techniques.

☎ Contact:
National Institute of Neurological
Disorders and Stroke

Bldg. 31, Room 8A06
Bethesda, MD 20892
(301) 496-5751
(800) 352-9424

Free Publications/Videos

The following publication on Acupuncture is available from the Science & Technology Division, Reference Section, Library of Congress, Washington, DC 20540; (202) 707-5580.

- *Acupuncture.* Reference guide designed to help locate further published material. (#85-6)

ACUTE HEMORRHAGIC CONJUNCTIVITIS

Clearinghouses/Hotlines

The National Eye Institute (NEI) can give you up-to-date information on Acute Hemorrhagic Conjunctivitis by searching the Combined Health Information Database (CHID) and MEDLINE and sending you bibliographies of resources, along with any journal articles they may have. They can also refer you to any other organizations that study this and other related diseases. NEI will also let you know of any clinical studies that may be studying this disease and looking for patients. Because of their small staff, NEI prefers that you submit your requests for information in writing.

☎ Contact:
National Eye Institute
Bldg. 31, Room 6A32
Bethesda, MD 20892
(301) 496-5248

ACUTE LEUKEMIA

Clearinghouses/Hotlines

The National Cancer Institute (NCI) will send you whatever publications and reprints of journal articles they have on Acute Leukemia. They can also give you information on the state-of-the-art treatment for this disease, including specific treatment information for your stage of cancer. They can also search their Physicians Data Query (PDQ) database to let you know if NCI is conducting any clinical studies on your disease.

☎ Contact:
National Cancer Institute
Bldg. 31, Room 10A24
Bethesda, MD 20892
(800) 4-CANCER
(301) 496-5583

ACUTE MYOCARDIAL INFARCTION

Clearinghouses/Hotlines

The National Heart, Lung, and Blood Institute (NHLBI) can search the Combined Health Information Database (CHID) and generate a bibliography of resources on Acute Myocardial Infarction for you. They also will send you any publications and journal articles they may have on hand, and will refer you to other organizations that are studying this disease. If you can't afford treatment, have your doctor call NHLBI to find out if they are conducting any clinical studies that you might qualify for.

☎ Contact:
National Heart, Lung and Blood Institute
Bldg. 31, Room 4A21
Bethesda, MD 20892
(301) 496-4236

Free Publications/Videos

The following publication is available from the National Heart, Lung and Blood Institute, Bldg. 31, Room 4A21, Bethesda, MD 20892; (301) 496-4236.

- *NHLBI Symposium on Rapid Identification and Treatment of Acute Myocardial Infarction.* (#91-3035)

ADDISON'S DISEASE

Clearinghouses/Hotlines

The National Institute of Diabetes and Digestive and Kidney Diseases's (NIDDK) individual clearinghouses can search the Combined Health Information Database (CHID) and generate a bibliography of resources on Addison's Disease for you. They also will send you any publications and journal articles they may have on hand, and will refer you to other organizations that are studying this disease. If you can't afford treatment, have your doctor call NIDDK to find out if they are conducting any clinical studies that you might qualify for.

☎ Contact:
The National Institute of Diabetes
and Digestive and Kidney Diseases
Bldg. 31, Room 9A04
Bethesda, MD 20892
(301) 496-3583

Free Publications/Videos

The following publication is available from the National Institute of Diabetes and Digestive and Kidney Diseases, Bldg. 31, Room 9A04, Bethesda, MD 20892; (301) 496-3583.

- *Addison's Disease*. (#90-2054)

ADENOMA OF THE THYROID

Clearinghouses/Hotlines

The National Institute of Diabetes and Digestive and Kidney Diseases's (NIDDK) individual clearinghouses can search the Combined Health Information Database (CHID) and generate a bibliography of resources on Adenoma of the Thyroid for you. They also will send you any publications and journal articles they may have on hand, and will refer you to other organizations that are studying this condition. If you can't

afford treatment, have your doctor call NIDDK to find out if they are conducting any clinical studies that you might qualify for.

☎ Contact:
The National Institute of Diabetes
and Digestive and Kidney Diseases
Bldg. 31, Room 9A04
Bethesda, MD 20892
(301) 496-3583

ADOLESCENT DRUG ABUSE

See also Drug Abuse

Clearinghouses/Hotlines

Are you concerned that your child may have a problem with alcohol or drugs? Do you want to know what signs to look for? The National Clearinghouse for Alcohol and Drug Information can help and has free publications available, dealing with Drug and Alcohol use.

☎ Contact:
National Clearinghouse for Alcohol
and Drug Information
P.O. Box 2345
Rockville, MD 20852
(800) 729-6686

The Office of Juvenile Justice and Delinquency Prevention (OJJDP) can send you publications, research findings, and program evaluations. They will also conduct database searches for special information, and if necessary, refer you to other organizations for further information.

☎ Contact:
Office of Juvenile Justice
and Delinquency Prevention
P.O. Box 6000
Rockville, MD 20850
(800) 638-8736

Free Publications/Videos

The following publications are available from the Office of Juvenile Justice and Delinquency

Prevention, P. O. Box 6000, Rockville, MD 20850; (800) 638-8736.

- *Juvenile Alcohol and Other Drug Abuse: A Guide to Federal Initiatives for Prevention, Treatment, and Control.* Serves as a resource for State, local, and private agencies and individuals working to combat juvenile drug and alcohol abuse.
- OJJDP Update on Statistics: *Juvenile Court Drug and Alcohol Cases: 1985-1988.*
- OJJDP Update on Programs: *Drug Recognition Techniques for Juvenile Justice Professionals.*
- OJJDP Update on Statistics: *Growth In Minority Detentions Attributed to Drug Law Violators.*
- *1990 Action Plan to Prevent Illegal Drug Use Among High-Risk Youth.*
- *Identification and Transfer of Effective Juvenile Justice Projects and Services: Effective Parenting Strategies for Families of High Risk Youth.* Assesses existing family-oriented programs that have demonstrated success in decreasing delinquency, drug use, or associated risk factors.

The following publication on Adolescent Drug Use is available from the General Accounting Office, P.O. Box 6015, Gaithersburg, MD 20877; (202) 275-6241.

- *Adolescent Drug Use Prevention: Common Features of Promising Community Programs.* Examines the design, implementation, and results of promising comprehensive, community-based drug use prevention programs for young adolescents, regardless of their funding sources.

The following publications on Adolescent Drug Use are available from the National Clearinghouse for Alcohol and Drug Information, P.O. Box 2345, Rockville, MD 20852, (800) 729-6686.

- *Growing Up Drug Free: A Parent's Guide to Prevention.*
- *Guia Practica: 10 pasos que ayudan a sus hijos a decir "No" (Quick List: 10 Steps to Help Your Child Say "No").*
- *Parent Training Is Prevention.*

- *Pointers for Parents Card.*
- *Quick List: 10 Steps to Help Your Child Say "No".*
- *10 Steps to Help Your Child Say "No". A Parent's Guide.*
- *The Adolescent Assessment/Referral System Manual.*
- *Preventing Adolescent Drug Use: From Theory to Practice.*
- *Prevention Resource Guide: Secondary School Students.*
- *Facts About Teenagers and Drug Abuse.*
- *High School Senior Drug Use: 1975-1990.*
- *News Release: High School Senior Drug Use, 1990.*
- *Steroids Mean Trouble* (poster).
- *Alcohol and Youth: Fact Sheet.*
- *Treatment for Adolescent Substance Abusers.*
- *Adolescent Drug Abuse: Analyses of Treatment Research.* NIDA Research Monograph.

ADOLESCENT HEALTH

See also Acne
See also Puberty
See also Teenagers

Clearinghouses/Hotlines

The National Maternal and Child Health Clearinghouse has an extensive list of free publications concerned with Adolescent Health. They can answer your questions, as well as refer you to national and local organizations dealing with issues with which you are concerned.

☎ Contact:
National Maternal and Child
Health Clearinghouse
38th & R Sts., NW
Washington, DC 20057
(703) 821-8955, ext. 254

The National Institute of Mental Health (NIMH) will send you whatever publications and reprints of articles from texts and journals they have on Adolescence. They will also refer you to other organizations that are studying this issue. NIMH will also let you know of any clinical studies that may be studying Adolescent Health issues and looking for patients.

☎ Contact:
National Institute of Mental Health
5600 Fishers Ln., Room 15C05
Rockville, MD 20857
(301) 443-4515

The National Institute of Child Health and Human Development (NICHD) will send you whatever publications and reprints of journal articles they have on Adolescence and Adolescent Pregnancy. If necessary, they will refer you to other experts or researchers in the field.

☎ Contact:
National Institute of Child Health
and Human Development
Bldg. 31, Room 2A32
Bethesda, MD 20892
(301) 496-5133

Free Publications/Videos

The following publications on Adolescent Health are available from the National Clearinghouse for Maternal and Child Health, 38th & R Sts., NW, Washington, DC 20057; (703) 821-8955, ext. 254.

- *Adolescent Fathers: Directory of Services*.
  Covers programs available state by state.
- *Adolescent Health: Catalog of Products*.
  Lists journal articles, videotapes, curricula materials and patient education materials focusing on adolescent health.
- *Adolescent Substance Abuse, and Promoting the Health of Adolescents: Proceedings from the 1990 Adolescent Health Coordinators Conference*.
- *Adolescent Pregnancy: Resource Guide*.
- *Health Foods, Healthy Baby*.
- *Nutrition Management of the Pregnant Adolescent*.
- *Pregnancy and Childbearing Among Homeless Adolescents: Report of a Workshop*.
- *Adolescent Fathers: Directory of Services*.
- *Patient Education Materials: A Resource Guide*. Helps identify and locate materials on maternal and child health topics that are clear, concise, easy to read and appropriate for the general public. The

guide is separated into three sections. The first is patient education materials, which is an annotated listing of source books, directories, audiovisuals, and resource guides that describe patient education materials. The second section lists publishers of patient education materials, and the third lists federal health information clearinghouses.

The following publication on Adolescent Health is available from the Office of Technology Assessment, 600 Pennsylvania Ave., SE, Washington, DC 20510; (202) 224-8996.

- *Adolescent Health: Time For a Change*.
  Assesses the health status of adolescents 10 to 18 years old and identify factors that put adolescents at risk for health problems, including racial and ethnic backgrounds, socioeconomic status, gender, and developmental stage.

The following publication on Adolescent Health is available from the National Institute of Mental Health, 5600 Fishers Ln., Room 15C05, Rockville, MD 20857; (301) 443-4515.

- *Plain Talk About Adolescence*. Covers such issues as anger and aggression in adolescents.

The following publications on Adolescent Pregnancy are available from the Family Life Information Exchange, P.O. Box 30146, Bethesda, MD 20814; (301) 585-6636.

- *Family and Adolescent Pregnancy*.
- *Trends in Adolescent Pregnancy and Childbearing*.

The following Congressional Research Service (CRS) report on Teenage Suicide is available from either of your U.S. Senators' offices at the U.S. Capitol, Washington, DC 20510, or from your Congressional Representative at the U.S. Capitol, Washington, DC 20515. You can also call in your request through the U.S. Capitol switchboard at (202) 224-3121. Be sure to include the full title and report number in your request.

- *Teenage Suicide: Bibliography-in-Brief, 1981, 1988.* (#88-652 L)

ADOPTION

Clearinghouses/Hotlines

The Family Life Information Exchange (FLIE) provides information on family planning, adolescent pregnancy, and Adoption. FLIE's primary audience consists of federally supported service agencies, but it also provides information to family planning service providers, educators, trainers, and consumers throughout the U.S.

☎ Contact:
Family Life Information Exchange
P.O. Box 37299
Washington, DC 20013
(301) 585-6636

The Administration for Children and Families of the U.S. Department of Health and Human Services has a special grants program titled, *Adoption Opportunities Program*, which provides grants and contracts to private and public non-profit organizations to improve services for the placement of children for Adoption, especially those children with special needs.

☎ Contact:
Adoption Opportunities Program
Administration for Children and Families
330 C Street, SW
Washington, DC 20201
(202) 205-8671

Free Publications/Videos

The following publications are available from the Family Life Information Exchange, P.O. Box 30146, Bethesda, MD 20814; (301) 585-6636.

- *The Adoption Option: A Guidebook for Pregnancy Counselors.* Offers numerous resources on the issue of putting up a child for adoption (#FP-10000)

The following Congressional Research Service (CRS) report is available from either of your U.S.

Senators' offices at the U.S. Capitol, Washington, DC 20510, or from your Congressional Representative at the U.S. Capitol, Washington, DC 20515. You can also call in your request through the U.S. Capitol switchboard at (202) 224-3121. Be sure to include the full title and report number in your request.

- *Adoption: Federal Programs and Issues.* (#91-131 EPW)

ADRENAL GLAND DISORDERS

Clearinghouses/Hotlines

The National Institute of Diabetes and Digestive and Kidney Diseases's (NIDDK) individual clearinghouses can search the Combined Health Information Database (CHID) and generate a bibliography of resources on the Adrenal Gland Disorders for you. They also will send you any publications and journal articles they may have on hand, and will refer you to other organizations that are studying these disorders. If you can't afford treatment, have your doctor call NIDDK to find out if they are conducting any clinical studies that you might qualify for.

☎ Contact:
National Institute of Diabetes
and Digestive and Kidney Diseases
Bldg. 31, Room 9A04
Bethesda, MD 20892
(301) 496-3583

The National Institute of Child Health and Human Development (NICHD) will send you whatever publications and reprints of journal articles they have on Adrenal Insufficiency. If necessary, they will refer you to other experts or researchers in the field. If you can't afford treatment, have your doctor call NICHD to find out if they are conducting any clinical studies that you might qualify for.

☎ Contact:
National Institute of Child Health
and Human Development

Bldg. 31, Room 2A32
Bethesda, MD 20892
(301) 496-5133

Bldg. 31, Room 8A06
Bethesda, MD 20892
(301) 496-5751
(800) 352-9424

ADRENOLEUKODYSTROPHY

Clearinghouses/Hotlines

The National Institute of Neurological Disorders and Stroke (NINDS) can send you only information they have in their publications list on Adrenoleukodystrophy. They cannot refer you to any experts. This Clearinghouse cannot directly give you information about any current clinical studies NINDS might be conducting on this illness, but you can find this information for yourself by looking under the National Institute of Neurological Disorders and Stroke in *Appendix A* at the end of this book.

☎ Contact:
National Institute of Neurological
Disorders and Stroke
Bldg. 31, Room 8A06
Bethesda, MD 20892
(301) 496-5751
(800) 352-9424

AGAMMAGLOBULINEMIA

Clearinghouses/Hotlines

The National Institute on Allergy and Infectious Diseases (NIAID) can search the Combined Health Information Database (CHID) and generate a bibliography of resources on Agammaglobulinemia for you. They will also send you any publications and journal articles they may have on hand, and will refer you to researchers who are currently studying this disease. If you can't afford treatment, have your doctor call NIAID to find out if they are conducting any clinical studies that you might qualify for.

☎ Contact:
National Institute of Allergy
and Infectious Diseases
Bldg. 31, Room 7A32
Bethesda, MD 20892
(301) 496-5717

ADYNAMIA

Clearinghouses/Hotlines

The National Institute of Neurological Disorders and Stroke (NINDS) can send you only information they have in their publications list on Adynamia. They cannot refer you to any experts. This Clearinghouse cannot directly give you information about any current clinical studies NINDS might be conducting on this illness, but you can find this information for yourself by looking under the National Institute of Neurological Disorders and Stroke in *Appendix A* at the end of this book.

☎ Contact:
National Institute of Neurological
Disorders and Stroke

AGE-RELATED MACULAR DEGENERATION

Clearinghouses/Hotlines

The National Eye Institute (NEI) can give you up-to-date information on Age-Related Macular Degeneration by searching the Combined Health Information Database (CHID) and MEDLINE and sending you bibliographies of resources, along with any journal articles they may have. They can also refer you to any other organizations that study this and other related disorders. NEI will also let you know of any clinical studies that may be studying this disease and looking for patients. Because of their small staff, NEI prefers that you submit your requests for information in writing.

☎ Contact:
The National Eye Institute
Bldg. 31, Room 6A32
Bethesda, MD 20892
(301) 496-5248

AGENESIS

Clearinghouses/Hotlines

The National Institute of Neurological Disorders and Stroke (NINDS) can send you only information they have in their publications list on Agenesis of the Corpus Callosum. They cannot refer you to any experts. This Clearinghouse cannot directly give you information about any current clinical studies NINDS might be conducting on this illness, but you can find this information for yourself by looking under the National Institute of Neurological Disorders and Stroke in *Appendix A* at the end of this book.

☎ Contact:
National Institute of Neurological
Disorders and Stroke
Bldg. 31, Room 8A06
Bethesda, MD 20892
(301) 496-5751
(800) 352-9424

AGENT ORANGE

Free Publications/Videos

The following Congressional Research Service (CRS) reports are available from either of your U.S. Senators' offices at the U.S. Capitol, Washington, DC 20510, or from your Congressional Representative at the U.S. Capitol, Washington, DC 20515. You can also call in your request through the U.S. Capitol switchboard at (202) 224-3121. Be sure to include the full title and report number in your request.

- Agent Orange: Veterans' Complaints and
Studies of Health Effect; Archived Issue

Brief. (#IB83043)
- Dioxin and Agent Orange Health Effects: An
Update. (91-195 SPR)

AGING

See also Gerontology
See also Living Wills
See also Long Term Care
See also Nursing Homes

Clearinghouses/Hotlines

The National Institute on Aging (NIA) conducts and supports biomedical, social, and behavioral research on Aging-Related issues. They can answer your questions, provide you with pamphlets, brochures, research reports, and more regarding your topic of interest, as well as refer you to current researchers in the field. NIA continues to work on the *Baltimore Longitudinal Study of Aging*, which has followed the same 650 men since 1958 to measure the changes with age.

☎ Contact:
National Institute on Aging
Federal Building
Room 6C12
Bethesda, MD 20892
(301) 496-1752

The Eldercare Locator is a new nationwide service designed to help people find needed services for the elderly. You can call (800) 677-1116 from 9 a.m.-7 p.m. weekdays and be put in touch with thousands of state and local resources throughout the country. Many of the numbers you can get are to referral agencies, who will in turn refer you to appropriate local resources. Information covers such topics as legal services, health care, social services, guardianship, and more.

☎ Contact:
Administration on Aging
Department of Health and Human Services
330 Independence Ave., SW
Washington, DC 20201
(202) 401-3498
(800) 677-1116

The Clearinghouse on Family Violence Information has information on spouse and Elder Abuse. They have brochures and audiovisual materials available, and an inhouse data base from which they can retrieve reference materials and organizations involved with family violence.

☎ Contact:
Clearinghouse on Family Violence Information
P.O. Box 1182
Washington, DC 20013
(703) 385-7565

The National Institute of Mental Health (NIMH) will send you whatever publications and reprints of articles from texts and journals they have on Aging and Mental Health. They will also refer you to other organizations that are studying this issue. NIMH will also let you know of any clinical studies that may be studying Aging and Mental Health and looking for patients.

☎ Contact:
National Institute of Mental Health
5600 Fishers Ln., Room 15C05
Rockville, MD 20857
(301) 443-4515

Free Publications/Videos

The following publication on Aging is available from the General Accounting Office (GAO), P.O. Box 6015, Gaithersburg, MD 20877; (202) 275-6241.

- *Aging Issues*. A compilation of yearly General Accounting Office reports and ongoing work conducted by GAO regarding older Americans. It covers a broad range of issues, including federal government activities in health care, housing, income security, and social and community services.

The following publications on Aging are available from the National Institute on Aging, Bldg. 31, Room 5C27, Bethesda, MD 20892; (301) 496-1752.

- *Physical Frailty: A Reducible Barrier to Independence for Older Americans*. (#92-397)
- *The National Institute on Aging*. (#83-1129)

- *Q&A: Alzheimer's Disease*. (#91-1646)
- *Normal Human Aging: The Baltimore Longitudinal Study on Aging*. (#84-2450)
- *Older and Wiser: The Baltimore Longitudinal Study on Aging*. (#89-2797)
- *Accidents and the Elderly*
- *Aging and Alcohol Abuse*
- *Aging and Your Eyes*
- *AIDS and Older Adults*
- *Arthritis Advice*
- *Be Sensible About Salt..*
- *Can Life Be Extended?*
- *Cancer Facts for People Over 50*
- *Considering Surgery?*
- *Crime and the Elderly*
- *Finding Good Medical Care*
- *Foot Care for Older People*
- *Getting Your Affairs in Order*
- *Health Quackery*
- *Health Resources for Older Women*. Provides information, organizations, and suggested readings dealing with issues of interest to older women.
- *Hints for Shopping, Cooking and Enjoying Meals*.
- *Preventing Falls and Fractures*
- *Safe Use of Medicines by Older People*
- *Safe Use of Tranquilizers*
- *Shots for Safety*
- *Sexuality in Later Life*
- *Should You Take Estrogen*
- *Urinary Incontinence*
- *What to Do About Flu*
- *When You Need A Nursing Home*
- *Who's Who in Health Care*

The following publications and videos on Aging are available from the Office of Clinical Center Communications, Bldg. 10, Room 1C255, Bethesda, MD 20892; (301) 496-2563.

- *Brain in Aging and Dementia*. (#83-2625) Booklet written to help the general public make intelligent decisions.
- *Coping with Aging Parents*. Video to help the general public make intelligent decisions.
- *Coping with Aging Parents*. A booklet to educate consumers and allow them to make informed medical decisions.
- *Coping with the Changing Seasons*. Video

to help the general public make intelligent decisions.

The following publication on Aging is available from the National Heart, Lung and Blood Institute, Bldg. 31, Room 4A21, Bethesda, MD 20892; (301) 496-4236.

- *Check Your Smoking I.Q.: An Important Quiz for the Older Smoker.* (#91-3031)

The following publication on Aging is available from the National Clearinghouse for Primary Care Information, 8201 Greensboro Drive, Suite 600, McLean, VA 22102; (703) 821-8955.

- *Easy Eating for Well-Seasoned Adults.* Collection of recipes submitted by older adults, provides an excellent resource for older adult health center clients.

The following publication on Aging is available from the Office on Smoking and Health, Centers for Disease Control, 1600 Clifton Rd., NE, MS K-50, Atlanta, GA 30333; (404) 488-5705.

- *Good News for Smokers 50 and Older.* Outlines the health benefits of quitting smoking at any age.

The following publications on Aging are available from the National Institute of Mental Health, 5600 Fishers Ln., Room 15C05, Rockville, MD 20857; (301) 443-4515.

- *If You're Over 65 and Feeling Depressed... Treatment Brings New Hope.* Explains depression, provides a depression checklist, and describes causes and treatment for depression.
- *Plain Talk About Aging.* Describes the experience of growing old and suggests ways to plan carefully in order to have aging be a positive experience.

The following publication on Aging is available from the National Health Information Center, P.O. Box 1133, Washington, DC 20013; (800) 336-4797, or (301) 565-4167 in DC metro area.

- *Long-Term Care.* Covers issues and concerns regarding long-term care, as well as a list of publications and audiovisuals available from government agencies, community organizations, foundations and many other health groups.

The following publication on Aging is available from the Food & Nutrition Information Center, National Agricultural Library, Room 304, Beltsville, MD 20705-2351; (301) 504-5719.

- *Nutrition and the Elderly.* Designed to help you locate resources on this topic.

The following publications on Aging are available from the Superintendent of Documents, Government Printing Office, Washington, DC 20402; (202) 783-3238.

- *Resident Abuse in Nursing Homes: Understanding and Preventing Abuse.* Examines the nature of abuse and ways to prevent it, and existing processes for resolving physical abuse complaints involving nursing home residents (S/N 017-022-01-12-3, $3.25).
- *The Resource Directory for Older People.* Contains information on 215 organizations that deal specifically with the elderly, including Federal Government agencies, professional societies, private groups, and voluntary programs. Each listing provides the organization's address, telephone number, its mission, services, and free publications available. It answers many questions on the treatment for the elderly, and is useful to their families, students and health professionals, librarians, legal professionals, providers of social services, and others who have a special interest in the fields of aging (S/N 017-062-00143-0, $10.00).

The following publication on Aging is available from the Office of Technology Assessment, 600 Pennsylvania Ave., SE, Washington, DC 20510; (202) 224-8996.

- *Technology and Aging in America.* A report to Congress. Ask for the summary report.

The following publication on Aging is available from the Clearinghouse on Family Violence, P.O. Box 1182, Washington, DC 20013; (703) 385-7565.

- *Abuse of the Elderly.* Provides you with reference articles and more. ($7)

The following publication on Aging is available from the Subcommittee on Health on Long-Term Care, Room 377, Ford HOB, 2nd & D Sts., SW, Washington, DC 20515; (202) 226-3381.

- *Abuses in the Sale of Long-Term Care Insurance to the Elderly.*

The following publications on Aging are available from the Subcommittee on Housing and Consumer Interests, Room 717, O'Neill HOB, 300 New Jersey Ave., SE, Washington, DC 20515; (202) 226-3344.

- *Staying Healthy, Being Aware: Health Care After Forty.*
- *Health Care for All Generations.*

The following publications on Aging are available from the Select Committee on Aging, Room 712, O'Neill HOB, 300 New Jersey Ave., SE, Washington, DC 20515; (202) 226-3375.

- *Aging Research: Benefits Outweigh the Costs.*
- *Adequate Nutrition for the Elderly.*

The following Congressional Research Service (CRS) reports on health issues for the Aging are available from either of your U.S. Senators' offices at the U.S. Capitol, Washington, DC 20510, or from your Congressional Representative at the U.S. Capitol, Washington, DC 20515. You can also call in your request through the U.S. Capitol switchboard at (202) 224-3121. Be sure to include the full title and report number in your request.

- *Older Americans Act Nutrition Program.* (#90-115 EPW)
- *Health Benefits for Retirees: An Uncertain Future.* (#IB88004)
- *Health Care Costs at the End of Life.* (#90-368 EPW)
- *Aged: Info Pack.* (#IP003A)
- *Old Age: Health Issues Aging: Health Effects and Behavior.* (#87-404 SPR)
- *The Elderly and the Health Care Dilemma: Is an Ounce of Prevention Worth a Pound of Cure?* (#85-968 SPR)
- *Health Promotion and Disease Prevention for the Elderly.* (#86-40 EPW)

The following video on Aging is available from Modern Talking Picture Service, 5000 Park St. North, St. Petersburg, FL 33709; (800) 243-MTPS.

- *You and Your Aging Parents.* Video punctures some of the myths and describes stresses of growing older.

AGRANULOCYTOSIS

Clearinghouses/Hotlines

The National Heart, Lung, and Blood Institute (NHLBI) can search the Combined Health Information Database (CHID) and generate a bibliography of resources on Agranulocytosis for you. They also will send you any publications and journal articles they may have on hand, and will refer you to other organizations that are studying Agranulocytosis. If you can't afford treatment, have your doctor call NHLBI to find out if they are conducting any clinical studies that you might qualify for.

☎ Contact:
National Heart, Lung and Blood Institute
Bldg. 31, Room 4A21
Bethesda, MD 20892
(301) 496-4236

AIDS

Clearinghouses/Hotlines

The Office of AIDS Coordination in the Food & Drug Administration (FDA) is responsible for coordinating all the efforts of the Centers within the FDA conducting AIDS research. They can tell you if certain drugs or medical devices are approved for AIDS treatment, as well as where unapproved drugs and devices are in the approval process. They handle comments on the Federal Register. They can tell you what lab tests are approved, answer your questions regarding blood transfusions and transmission of AIDS through blood, and also refer you to the right person to answer your AIDS question. They are trying to cut down the runaround through all the government agencies concerning AIDS. This office's goal is to get the answer to your question.

☎ Contact:
Office of AIDS Coordination
Office of the Commissioner
HF-12
5600 Fishers Lane
Rockville, MD 20857
(301) 443-0104

The National AIDS Information Clearinghouse can answer your questions and provide you with a wealth of information on AIDS. They have publications, brochures, posters and more, as well as having access to information on over 300 AIDS films and videotapes. They can provide you with a printout of films and videos designed to target a specific audience, ranging from teenagers to physicians. Each listing includes information on the producer, year, source, audience, and availability, as well as an abstract.

☎ Contact:
National AIDS Information Clearinghouse
P.O. Box 6003
Rockville, MD 20850
(800) 458-5231
(800) 342-AIDS
(800) 344-7432 (Servicio en Espanol)
(800) 243-7889 (TTY-Deaf Access)

The Pediatric, Adolescent, and Maternal AIDS Branch at National Institutes of Health conducts research on AIDS and AIDS-related viruses in pregnant women, mothers, infants, children, adolescents, and hemophiliac children. This office can provide you with current research results and refer you to experts or provide you with information regarding clinical studies.

☎ Contact:
Center for Research for Mothers and Children
National Institute of Child Health
and Human Development

National Institutes of Health
9000 Rockville Pike
Bethesda, MD 20892
(301) 496-7339

The National Institute of Justice AIDS Clearinghouse is the only centralized source of information on how AIDS affects criminal justice professionals and their work. Staff specialists with a broad knowledge of AIDS issues are available to answer questions, make referrals, and suggest publications pertaining to AIDS as it relates to the criminal justice system.

☎ Contact:
National Institute of Justice AIDS Clearinghouse
(301) 251-5500

The Business Response to AIDS Resource Services can give you information on workplace policy toward AIDS, as well as materials kits for employers, CEOs, managers and shop stewards. These kits contain brochures, fact sheets, labor issues, and other helpful information (the CEOs kits will contain a video). This service can also refer you to resources in your State and locality, as well as nationally.

☎ Contact:
National AIDS Information Clearinghouse
(800) 458-5231

The AIDS Clinical Trials Information Services puts callers in touch with experienced health specialists who provide information about AIDS clinical studies. These specialists access a database featuring up-to-date, accurate information on AIDS studies currently underway. The Service's health specialists are available to answer questions from individuals infected with HIV and their families, as well as from health professionals. They provide information on the purpose of the study, studies that are open, study locations, eligibility requirements and exclusion criteria, and names and telephone numbers of contact persons.

☎ Contact:
AIDS Clinical Trials Information Services
(800) 874-2572

The National Institute on Deafness and Other Communicative Disorders (NIDCD) will send you whatever publications and reprints of journal articles they have on Neurological Symptoms or Effects of AIDS. If you need further information, they will refer you to other organizations that study this and other related diseases. NIDCD does not conduct any clinical studies for this or any other disorder.

☎ Contact:
National Institute on Deafness
and Other Communication Disorders
Bldg. 31, Room 3C35
Bethesda, MD 20892
(301) 496-7243
(800) 241-1044
(301) 402-0252 (TDD)

The National Institute of Drug Abuse Helpline provides general phone information on drug abuse and on AIDS as it relates to intravenous drug users. This hotline offers referrals to drug rehab centers. Hours: 9 a.m. - 3 a.m. Monday through Friday; 12 p.m. - 3 a.m. on weekends.

☎ Contact:
National Institute of Drug Abuse Helpline
(800) 662-HELP

Free Publications/Videos

The following publications on AIDS are available from the National AIDS Information Clearinghouse, P.O. Box 6003, Rockville, MD 20850; (301) 762-5111.

- *AIDS Prevention Guide*. Written for parents and other adults concerned about young people and offers ideas to help them start a conversation about AIDS with their kids, it presents the facts about AIDS - geared to elementary and junior and senior high school students - and offers common questions and accurate answers.
- *HIV Infection and AIDS: Are You At Risk?*.
- *Voluntary HIV Counseling and Testing: Facts, Issues, and Answers.*
- *Women, Sex, and AIDS.*
- *The Connection Between TB and HIV.*
- *Surgeon General's Report on Acquired Immune Deficiency Syndrome.*
- *AIDS Health Fraud*. Video explains a variety of fraudulent cures aimed at persons infected with the HIV virus. (AD0007405).

- *AIDS: The Current Status of HIV Infection*. Video reviews basic information on the HIV virus and AIDS that physicians and other clinicians should have to provide meaningful and educational patient interactions. (AD0002529).
- *AIDS: The Litmus Test for Humanity in the 80's*. Video presents the Rev. Canon William Barcus of San Francisco, who has AIDS, speaking at the Partners in Leadership Conference on June 22, 1988. (AD0009060).
- *Beyond the Labels... The Human Side of AIDS*. Video examines the personal, social, and spiritual issues and conflicts experienced by persons with AIDS and those who care for them. (AD0001589).
- *Blood Transfusions Today*. Video of a lecture by, and an interview with, a doctor who is doing research in blood transfusions and blood substitutes. (AD0003754).
- *Drug Abuse: Meeting the Challenge*. Video presented in a documentary format. Targets substance abuse and addiction as a major public health issue. (AD0004815).
- *Drugs and AIDS: Getting the Message Out*. Video focuses on the progression of AIDS through IV needle sharing by drug abusers. (AD0002564).
- *Eating Defensively: Food Safety Advice for Persons With AIDS*. Video outlines steps to be taken by persons infected with the HIV virus to avoid exposure to food-borne pathogens such as salmonella and listeria. (AD0005743).
- *Finding Strength: A Look at the Pediatric Branch*. Video shows the health-care facilities for children at the National Institutes of Health (NIH), most of whom suffer from cancer of from HIV virus infection. (AD0008385).
- *HBO - Questions and Answers*. In this video, Surgeon General C. Everett Koop answers a group of questions about the HIV virus and AIDS collected from street interviews and telephone surveys by the Home Box Office (HBO) television organization. (AD0002464).
- *Highlights from the Launch of the National AIDS Information Campaign*. Video contains national and local television

coverage of the launch of the October 1987 campaign by the Centers for Disease Control, America Responds to AIDS. (AD0002421).

- *Nobody's Immune.* Through interviews with persons with AIDS, this video cautions against the risky lifestyles that lead to HIV transmission and AIDS. (AD0002573).
- *Nutrition Strategies in HIV Management Tele-conference.* Video documents a teleconference on the subject of nutrition and HIV virus infection. (AD0009817).
- *Screening for Tuberculosis: Administering and Reading the Mantoux Test.* Video emphasizes the importance of the Mantoux test to individuals who test positive for HIV virus antibodies, to those at risk for HIV, and to those with AIDS. (AD0003723).
- *Talking to Your Children About AIDS.* In this video, a number of physicians and other authority figures, including Surgeon General C. Everett Koop, describe ways to talk to children about HIV and AIDS. (AD0007985).
- *The Current Crisis in AIDS.* In this video, Surgeon General C. Everett Koop discusses the public health epidemic of AIDS. (AD0002463).
- *How You Won't Get AIDS.*
- *Condoms and Sexually Transmitted Diseases... Especially AIDS.* Answers 17 frequently asked questions about purchasing and using condoms. Facts about sexually transmitted diseases are also listed.

The following publications on AIDS are available from the Office of Technology Assessment, 600 Pennsylvania Ave., SE, Washington, DC 20510; (202) 224-8996.

- *AIDS and Health Insurance: An OTA Survey.* Ask for the summary report.
- *Difficult-To-Reuse Needles for the Prevention of HIV Infection Among Injection Drug Abusers.* (#OTA-BP-H-103)

The following publications on AIDS are available from the National Institute of Allergy and Infectious Diseases, Bldg. 31, Room 7A32, Bethesda, MD 20892; (301) 496-5717.

- *Where do AIDS Drugs Come From?*
- *AIDS Clinical Trials: Talking It Over.* (#89-3025)
- *NIAID AIDS Research.*
- *Where do AIDS Drugs Come From?*

The following publication is available from AIDS, P.O. Box 14252, Washington, DC 20044.

- *Surgeon General's Report on Acquired Immune Deficiency Syndrome.* Discusses the facts about this disease, how it is transmitted, the relative risks of infection, and how to protect yourself against the disease.

The following publications on AIDS are available from the Family Life Information Exchange, P.O. Box 30146, Bethesda, MD 20814; (301) 585-6636.

- *Human Immunodeficiency Virus Infection in the United States.*
- *Recommendations for Prevention of HIV in Health Care Settings.*
- *Public Health Service Guidelines for Counseling and Testing to Prevent HIV & AIDS.*

The following publication on AIDS is available from the Food & Drug Administration, (HFE-88), 5600 Fishers Ln., Rockville, MD 20857; (301) 443-3170.

- *Eating Defensively: Food Safety Advice For Persons With AIDS.* (#FDA90-2232)

The following publications on AIDS are available from the National Maternal and Child Health Clearinghouse, 38th & R Sts., NW, Washington, DC 20057; (703) 821-8955, ext. 254.

- *Building Systems of Care for Children with HIV Infection and Their Families.* (#C064)
- *Building Systems of Care for Children with HIV Infection and Their Families.*
- *Children with HIV/AIDS: A Sourcebook for Caring.*
- *Pediatric AIDS: Abstracts of Active Projects FY 1990 and FY 1991.*
- *Surgeon General's Workshop on Children with HIV Infection and Their Families, Report.*

The following publication on AIDS is available from the National Institute of Child Health and Human Development, Bldg. 31, Room 2A32, Bethesda, MD 20892; (301) 496-5133.

- *New Faces of AIDS: A Maternal and Pediatric Epidemic.* (#92-3177) .

The following publication on AIDS is available from Food & Nutrition Information Center, National Agricultural Library, Room 304, Beltsville, MD 20705-2351; (301) 504-5719.

- *Nutrition and AIDS.* A list of current references.

The following publications on AIDS are available from the Centers for Disease Control National AIDS Clearinghouse, P.O. Box 6003, Rockville, MD 20849-6003; (800) 458-5231.

- *Tuberculosis: The Connection Between TB and HIV.* (#D484)
- *HIV Infection in Two Brothers Receiving Intravenous Therapy for Hemophilia.* (#D137)
- *Update: Transmission of HIV Infection During Invasive Dental Procedures: Florida.* (#D683)
- *Condoms for Prevention of Sexually Transmitted Diseases.* (#D127)
- *Publicly Funded HIV Counseling and Testing -- United States, 1985-1989.* (#D541)
- *Open Meeting on the Risks of Transmission of Bloodborne Pathogens to Patients During Invasive Procedures.* (#D664)
- *AIDS Litigation Project: A National Survey of Federal, State, and Local Cases Before Courts and Human Rights Commissions.* (#D136)
- *American Foundation for AIDS Research AIDS/HIV Treatment Directory.* (Current Issue)
- *Information about the AIDS Clinical Trials Information Service.* (#B172)

The following publication on AIDS is available from the Technical Information Services (E06), Center for Prevention Services, Centers for Disease Control, Atlanta, GA 30333; letter requests only.

- *Resource List for Informational Materials on Sexually Transmitted Diseases.* Contains titles of STD materials of private companies and non-profit organizations.

The following videos on AIDS are available from the Modern Talking Picture Service, 5000 Park St. North, St. Petersburg, FL 33709; (800) 243-MTPS.

- *Answers About AIDS.* Video of discussion between students and Surgeon General Koop.
- *Beyond Fear: NV60.* Video on the spread of AIDS.

The following Congressional Research Service (CRS) reports on AIDS are available from either of your U.S. Senators' offices at the U.S. Capitol, Washington, DC 20510, or from your Congressional Representative at the U.S. Capitol, Washington, DC 20515. You can also call in your request through the U.S. Capitol switchboard at (202) 224-3121. Be sure to include the full title and report number in your request.

- *Acquired Immune Deficiency Syndrome (AIDS): A Brief Overview of the Major Legal Issues.* (#87-236 A)
- *AIDS: Acquired Immune Deficiency Syndrome; Selected References, 1988-1991.* (#91-419 L)
- *AIDS and Discrimination: Legal Limits on Insurance Underwriting Practices.* (#88-381 A)
- *AIDS Discrimination Issues; Legislative and Executive Actions; Archived Issue Brief.* (#IB89125)
- *AIDS in the Workplace: Employee V. Employer Interest.* (#87-510 E)
- *Blood Testing for Antibodies to the AIDS Virus: The Legal Issues.* (#87-738 A)

AIR POLLUTION

Clearinghouses/Hotlines

The Environmental Protection Agency (EPA) develops national programs, technical policies and regulations for Air Pollution control. If you have questions regarding Indoor or Outdoor Air Pollution, contact the EPA for the latest information.

☎ Contact:
Public Information Center
Environmental Protection Agency
401 M Street, SW
Washington, DC 20460
(202) 260-7751

Free Publications/Videos

The following Congressional Research Service (CRS) reports on Air Pollution are available from either of your U.S. Senators' offices at the U.S. Capitol, Washington, DC 20510, or from your Congressional Representative at the U.S. Capitol, Washington, DC 20515. You can also call in your request through the U.S. Capitol switchboard at (202) 224-3121. Be sure to include the full title and report number in your request.

- *Potential Benefits of Enacting Clean Air Act Amendments.* (#90-73 ENR)
- *Health Benefits of Air Pollution Control: A Discussion.* (#89-161 ENR)

ALBINISM

Clearinghouses/Hotlines

The National Eye Institute (NEI) can give you up-to-date information on Albinism (Eyes) by searching the Combined Health Information Database (CHID) and MEDLINE and sending you bibliographies of resources, along with any journal articles they may have. They can also refer you to any other organizations that study albinism and other related conditions. NEI will also let you know of any clinical studies that may be studying this condition and looking for patients. Because of their small staff, NEI prefers that you submit your requests for information in writing.

☎ Contact:
National Eye Institute
Bldg. 31, Room 6A32

Bethesda, MD 20892
(301) 496-5248

ALBRIGHT'S SYNDROME

Clearinghouses/Hotlines

The National Institute of Arthritis and Musculoskeletal and Skin Diseases (NIAMS) will send you whatever publications and reprints of articles from texts and journals they have on Albright's Syndrome. They will also refer you to other organizations that are studying this syndrome. NIAMS will also let you know of any clinical studies that may be studying Albright's Syndrome and looking for patients.

☎ Contact:
National Institute of Arthritis
and Musculoskeletal and Skin Diseases
Box AMS
Bethesda, MD 20892
(301) 495-4484

The National Institute of Child Health and Human Development (NICHD) will send you whatever publications and reprints of journal articles they have on Albright's Syndrome. If necessary, they will refer you to other experts or researchers in the field. If you can't afford treatment, have your doctor call NICHD to find out if they are conducting any clinical studies that you might qualify for.

☎ Contact:
National Institute of Child Health
and Human Development
Bldg. 31, Room 2A32
Bethesda, MD 20892
(301) 496-5133

ALCOHOLISM

See also Drug Abuse
See also Pregnancy and Alcohol
See also Workplace Drug Abuse

Clearinghouses/Hotlines

The National Clearinghouse for Alcohol and Drug Information can refer you to local Alcoholics Anonymous chapters and other self-help organizations as well as national associations. They can also provide you with all kinds of materials about preventing or curing substance abuse.

☎ Contact:
National Clearinghouse for Alcohol
and Drug Information
P.O. Box 2345
Rockville, MD 20852
(301) 468-2600
(800) 729-6686

The National Cancer Institute (NCI) will send you whatever publications and reprints of journal articles they have on Alcohol and Cancer. They can also give you information on the state-of-the-art treatment for this disease, including specific treatment information for your stage of cancer. They can also search their Physicians Data Query (PDQ) database to let you know if NCI is conducting any clinical studies on your disease.

☎ Contact:
National Cancer Institute
Bldg. 31, Room 10A24
Bethesda, MD 20892
(800) 4-CANCER
(301) 496-5583

The National Institute on Aging (NIA) will send you whatever publications and reprints of journal articles they have on Alcohol and Aging. They cannot refer you to other experts if the information they have isn't sufficient for your purposes.

☎ Contact:
National Institute on Aging
Bldg. 31, Room 5C27
Bethesda, MD 20892
(301) 496-1752

The National Institute on Alcohol Abuse and Alcoholism (NIAAA) looks at trends relating to treatment of alcoholism and insurance financing issues. It advocates adequate health insurance coverage for alcoholism treatment, and conducts studies on this topic, which are available to the public.

☎ Contact:
National Institute on Alcohol Abuse
and Alcoholism
National Institutes of Health
5600 Fishers Lane, Room 16-95
Rockville, MD 20857
(301) 443-2595

Free Publications/Videos

The National Clearinghouse for Alcohol Information will send you the following *Prevention Resource Guides* on alcohol abuse among students. They contain facts, figures, resources, and other relevant information. Other publications are also available. National Clearinghouse for Alcohol Information, P.O. Box 2345, Rockville, MD 20852, (800) 729-6686, (301) 468-2600.

- *Prevention Resource Guide: College Youth.*
- *Prevention Resource Guide: Secondary School Students.*
- *Prevention Resource Guide: Elementary Youth.*
- *Prevention Resource Guide: Preschool Children.*
- *Self-Help Groups for Professionals and Special Populations* (#MS330). A resource bulletin on alcoholism.
- *Prevention Resource Guide: Children of Alcoholics.* Contains facts, figures, resources, and other relevant information on alcohol abuse.
- *Prevention Resource Guide: Pregnant/Post-partum Women and Their Infants.* Contains facts, figures, resources, and other relevant information on alcohol abuse.
- *The Fact Is...There Are Specialized Mutual-Help Groups For Those With Alcohol and Drug Problems* (#MS330). Discusses self-help groups that have emerged in response to special concerns expressed by those seeking recovery for alcohol and other drug problem. The publication lists the self-help groups, providing general information about the group and a central phone number.
- *A Growing Concern: How to Provide Services for Children of Alcoholic Families.* Discusses issues and strategies for

providing help to youngsters from homes with alcoholism. Geared more to professionals and caregivers. (#PH196)

- *Alcoholic Hepatitis: A Practical Guide for Physicians and Other Health Care Professionals.* Covers diagnosis and treatment of liver disease.
- *Alcohol Alert #1: Methadone Maintenance and Patients in Alcoholism Treatment.* (#PH244).
- *Alcohol Alert #2: Alcohol and Aging.* (#PH251).
- *Alcohol Alert #3: Alcohol and Trauma.* (#PH253).
- *Alcohol Alert #4: Alcohol and Cognition.* (#PH258).
- *Alcohol Alert #5: Alcohol Withdrawal Syndrome.* (#PH270).
- *Alcohol Alert #6: Relapse and Craving.* (#PH277).
- *Alcohol Alert #7: Alcohol Use and Abuse.* (#PH278).
- *Alcohol Alert #8: Screening for Alcoholism.* (#PH285).
- *Alcohol Alert #9: Children of Alcoholics: Are They Different?* (#PH288).

The following publication on Alcoholism is available from the Superintendent of Documents, Government Printing Office, Washington, DC 20402; (202) 783-3238.

- *Alcohol Health and Research World.* A magazine published quarterly and available for $8 per year provides professionals with information regarding current research, prevention, and treatment of alcoholism, and includes comment and opinion section, along with information about upcoming events.

The following publication on Alcoholism is available from the Science & Technology Division, Reference Section, Library of Congress, Washington, DC 20540; (202) 707-5580.

- *Alcoholism.* Reference guide designed to help locate published further material. (#81-3)

The following publication on Alcoholism is available from the National Maternal and Child Health Clearinghouse, 38th & R Sts., NW, Washington, DC 20057; (703) 821-8955, ext. 254.

- *Surgeon General's Workshop on Drunk Driving.* (#C044)

The following Congressional Research Service (CRS) reports on Alcohol are available from either of your U.S. Senators' offices at the U.S. Capitol, Washington, DC 20510, or from your Congressional Representative at the U.S. Capitol, Washington, DC 20515. You can also call in your request through the U.S. Capitol switchboard at (202) 224-3121. Be sure to include the full title and report number in your request.

- *Advertising of Alcoholic Beverages in the Broadcast Media: Archived Issue Brief.* (#IB85097)
- *Alcohol Use and Abuse by Women.* (#91-680 SPR)
- *Drug and Alcohol Abuse: Prevention, Treatment, and Education.* (#86-1052 EPW)
- *Legal Analysis of Questions Regarding the National Minimum Drinking Age.* (#85-772 A)
- *Prohibiting Television Advertising of Alcoholic Beverages: A Constitutional Analysis.* (#88-22 A)
- *Drunk Driving and Raising the Drinking Age: Info Pack.* (#IP186D)
- *Drunk Driving: Bibliography-in-Brief, 1983-1988.* (#88-655 L)
- *Drunk Driving; Issue Brief.* (#IB83157)
- *Drunk Driving Laws in Foreign Countries.* (#LL89-88)
- *Nondischargeability of DWI Judgements in Bankruptcy: Survey of Case Law.* (#90-21 A)

The following video on Alcoholism is available from Modern Talking Picture Service, 5000 Park St. North, St. Petersburg, FL 33709; (800) 243-MTPS.

- *Aspects of Alcoholism.* Video outlines symptoms and diagnosis of alcoholism, including genetic factors and physical complications.

ALDOSTERONISM

Clearinghouses/Hotlines

The National Heart, Lung, and Blood Institute (NHLBI) can search the Combined Health Information Database (CHID) and generate a bibliography of resources on Aldosteronism for you. They also will send you any publications and journal articles they may have on hand, and will refer you to other organizations that are studying Aldosteronism. If you can't afford treatment, have your doctor call NHLBI to find out if they are conducting any clinical studies that you might qualify for.

☎ Contact:
National Heart, Lung and Blood Institute
Bldg. 31, Room 4A21
Bethesda, MD 20892
(301) 496-4236

ALEXANDER'S SYNDROME

Clearinghouses/Hotlines

The National Institute of Neurological Disorders and Stroke (NINDS) can send you only information they have in their publications list on Alexander's Syndrome. They cannot refer you to any experts. This Clearinghouse cannot directly give you information about any current clinical studies NINDS might be conducting on this illness, but you can find this information for yourself by looking under the National Institute of Neurological Disorders and Stroke in *Appendix A* at the end of this book.

☎ Contact:
National Institute of Neurological
Disorders and Stroke
Bldg. 31, Room 8A06
Bethesda, MD 20892
(301) 496-5751
(800) 352-9424

ALKAPTONURIA

Clearinghouses/Hotlines

The National Heart, Lung, and Blood Institute (NHLBI) can search the Combined Health Information Database (CHID) and generate a bibliography of resources on Alkaptonuria for you. They also will send you any publications and journal articles they may have on hand, and will refer you to other organizations that are studying Alkaptonuria. If you can't afford treatment, have your doctor call NHLBI to find out if they are conducting any clinical studies that you might qualify for.

☎ Contact:
National Heart, Lung and Blood Institute
Bldg. 31, Room 4A21
Bethesda, MD 20892
(301) 496-4236

ALKYLATING AGENTS

Clearinghouses/Hotlines

The National Cancer Institute (NCI) will send you whatever publications and reprints of journal articles they have on Alkylating Agents. They can also search their Physicians Data Query (PDQ) database to let you know if NCI is conducting any clinical studies on your disease.

☎ Contact:
National Cancer Institute
Bldg. 31, Room 10A24
Bethesda, MD 20892
(800) 4-CANCER
(301) 496-5583

ALLERGENICS

Clearinghouses/Hotlines

The Center for Biologics Evaluation and Research answers your questions and send you information on biologic products such as vaccines, Allergenics, blood, and blood products.

☎ Contact:
Center for Biologics Evaluation and Research
Food and Drug Administration
5600 Fishers Lane
HFB-140
Rockville, MD 20857
(301) 443-7532

ALLERGIC RHINITIS

Clearinghouses/Hotlines

The National Institute on Allergy and Infectious Diseases (NIAID) can search the Combined Health Information Database (CHID) and generate a bibliography of resources on Allergic Rhinitis for you. They will also send you any publications and journal articles they may have on hand, and will refer you to researchers who are currently studying this disease. If you can't afford treatment, have your doctor call NIAID to find out if they are conducting any clinical studies that you might qualify for.

☎ Contact:
National Institute of Allergy
and Infectious Diseases
Building 31
Room 7A32
Bethesda, MD 20892
(301) 496-5717

ALLERGIES

Clearinghouses/Hotlines

The National Institute of Allergy and Infectious Diseases (NIAID) conducts and supports research on the causes of Allergic, immunologic, and infectious diseases, and to develop better means of preventing, diagnosing, and treating illness. Some of the studies underway look at the role of the immune system in chronic diseases, such as arthritis, and at disorders of the immune system,

as in asthma. Brochures and reports are available on a wide variety of topics.

☎ Contact:
National Institute of Allergy
and Infectious Diseases
Building 31
Room 7A32
Bethesda, MD 20892
(301) 496-5717

The National Eye Institute (NEI) can give you up-to-date information on Allergies and the Eyes by searching the Combined Health Information Database (CHID) and MEDLINE and sending you bibliographies of resources, along with any journal articles they may have. They can also refer you to any other organizations that study Allergies and other related conditions. NEI will also let you know of any clinical studies that may be studying this disease and looking for patients. Because of their small staff, NEI prefers that you submit your requests for information in writing.

☎ Contact:
National Eye Institute
Building 31
Room 6A32
Bethesda, MD 20892
(301) 496-5248

Free Publications/Videos

The following publications on Allergies are available from the National Institute of Allergy and Infectious Diseases, Bldg. 31, Room 7A32, Bethesda, MD 20892; (301) 496-5717.

- *Allergic Diseases*. (#91-3221)
- *Allergies: Questions and Answers*. Answers many general questions about allergies and offers information on their symptoms, prevention, diagnosis, and treatment. (#81-189)
- *Drug Allergy*. Offers information on their symptoms, prevention, diagnosis, and treatment. (#82-703)
- *Dust Allergy*. Offers information on their symptoms, prevention, diagnosis, and treatment. (#83-490)
- *Mold Allergy*. Offers information on their symptoms, prevention, diagnosis, and

treatment. (#84-797)
- *NIAID Task Force Report on Immunology and Allergy.* (#90-2414)
- *Pollen Allergy.* Offers information on their symptoms, prevention, diagnosis, and treatment. (#76-493)

The following publications on Food Allergies are available from the Food & Drug Administration, (HFE-88), 5600 Fishers Ln., Rockville, MD 20857; (301) 443-3170.

- *Food Allergies: Separating Facts From "Hype".* (#FDA86-2213)
- *It's Spring Again and Allergies Are in Bloom.* (#FDA90-1161)

The following publication on Allergies is available from the Superintendent of Documents, Government Printing Office, Washington, DC 20402; (202) 783-3238.

- *Cooking for People with Food Allergies.*
  Provides information for those who need help managing food allergies or intolerances by helping you select and prepare foods containing no wheat, milk, eggs, corn, or gluten. Recipes are included. ($1.50, #001-000-04512-1)

The following publication on Food Allergies is available from the Food & Nutrition Information Center, National Agricultural Library, Room 304, Beltsville, MD 20705-2351; (301) 504-5719.

- *Food Allergy, Sensitivity and Tolerance.*
  Designed to help you locate resources on this topic.

The following publication and video on Allergies are available from the Office of Clinical Center Communications, Bldg. 10, Room 1C255, Bethesda, MD 20892; (301) 496-2563.

- *Allergic Diseases.* Booklet written to help the general public make intelligent decisions.
- *Allergic Diseases.* Video to help the general public make intelligent decisions.

ALOPECIA

Clearinghouses/Hotlines

The National Institute of Arthritis and Musculoskeletal and Skin Diseases (NIAMS) will send you whatever publications and reprints of articles from texts and journals they have on Alopecia. They will also refer you to other organizations that are studying this disease. NIAMS will also let you know of any clinical studies that may be studying Alopecia and looking for patients.

☎ Contact:
National Institute of Arthritis
and Musculoskeletal and Skin Diseases
Box AMS
Bethesda, MD 20892
(301) 495-4484

Free Publications/Videos

The following publication is available from the National Arthritis and Musculoskeletal and Skin Diseases Information Clearinghouse, Box AMS, Bethesda, MD 20892; (301) 495-4484.

- *Alopecia, 1989.* An annotated bibliography of resources. (#AR66, $4).

ALPERS SYNDROME

Clearinghouses/Hotlines

The National Institute of Neurological Disorders and Stroke (NINDS) can send you only information they have in their publications list on Alpers Syndrome. They cannot refer you to any experts. This Clearinghouse cannot directly give you information about any current clinical studies NINDS might be conducting on this illness, but you can find this information for yourself by looking under the National Institute of Neurological Disorders and Stroke in *Appendix A* at the end of this book.

☎ Contact:
National Institute of Neurological
Disorders and Stroke
Bldg. 31, Room 8A06
Bethesda, MD 20892
(301) 496-5751; (800) 352-9424

ALPHA-1-ANTITRYPSIN DEFICIENCY

Clearinghouses/Hotlines

The National Institute of Diabetes and Digestive and Kidney Diseases's (NIDDK) individual clearinghouses can search the Combined Health Information Database (CHID) and generate a bibliography of resources on Alpha-1-Antitrypsin Deficiency of the Liver for you. They also will send you any publications and journal articles they may have on hand, and will refer you to other organizations that are studying this disease. If you can't afford treatment, have your doctor call NIDDK to find out if they are conducting any clinical studies that you might qualify for.

☎ Contact:
National Institute of Diabetes
and Digestive and Kidney Diseases
Bldg. 31, Room 9A04
Bethesda, MD 20892
(301) 496-3583

The National Heart, Lung, and Blood Institute (NHLBI) can search the Combined Health Information Database (CHID) and generate a bibliography of resources on Alpha-1-Antitrypsin Deficiency of the Lungs for you. They also will send you any publications and journal articles they may have on hand, and will refer you to other organizations that are studying this disease. If you can't afford treatment, have your doctor call NHLBI to find out if they are conducting any clinical studies that you might qualify for.

☎ Contact:
National Heart, Lung and Blood Institute
Bldg. 31, Room 4A21
Bethesda, MD 20892
(301) 496-4236

ALTERNATIVE MEDICINE PRACTICES

Clearinghouses/Hotlines

Have you been reading about the benefits of color therapy? What about acupuncture or accupressure? Do they really help? What about the homeopathy? Will diet, herbs, and mineral and vitamin supplementation work on your illness? There has been increasing recognition and use of unconventional medical practices for the diagnosis or treatment of various diseases or conditions including cancer, arthritis, anxiety, and depression.

The U.S. Congress has provided two million dollars within the National Institutes of Health's (NIH) fiscal year 1992 appropriation to support activities to evaluate Unconventional Medical Practices and has created the Office for the Study of Unconventional Medical Practices to do just that. They will evaluate creativity and innovative thinking of individuals both inside and outside the realm of conventional medicine, while adhering to the principles of sound scientific evaluation.

Unconventional medical practices are being defined as diagnostic or therapeutic techniques that are presently considered outside the mainstream of scientific research. NIH will offer technical assistance and financial resources for the scientific evaluation of claims made about alternative medical practices. Not all alternative medical practices are amenable to traditional scientific evaluation, and some may require development of new methods to evaluate their efficacy and safety.

☎ Contact:
Office for the Study of
Unconventional Medical Practices
National Institutes of Health
Building 31
Room 2B25
Bethesda, MD 20892
(301) 496-2535

ALVEOLAR BONE

Clearinghouses/Hotlines

The National Institute of Dental Research (NIDR) will send you whatever publications and reprints of journal articles they have on the regeneration and resorption of Alveolar Bone. As a policy, NIDR will not refer you to other organizations or experts who study this condition. If you can't afford treatment, have your doctor call Dr. Albert Guckers at (301) 496-6241 to find out if NIDR is conducting any clinical studies that you might qualify for.

☎ Contact:
National Institute of Dental Research
Building 31
Room 2C35
Bethesda, MD 20892
(301) 496-4261

ALVEOLAR MICROLITHIASIS

Clearinghouses/Hotlines

The National Heart, Lung, and Blood Institute (NHLBI) can search the Combined Health Information Database (CHID) and generate a bibliography of resources on Alveolar Microlithiasis for you. They also will send you any publications and journal articles they may have on hand, and will refer you to other organizations that are studying this disease. If you can't afford treatment, have your doctor call NHLBI to find out if they are conducting any clinical studies that you might qualify for.

☎ Contact:
National Heart, Lung and Blood Institute
Building 31
Room 4A21
Bethesda, MD 20892
(301) 496-4236

ALVEOLAR PROTEINOSIS

Clearinghouses/Hotlines

The National Heart, Lung, and Blood Institute (NHLBI) can search the Combined Health Information Database (CHID) and generate a bibliography of resources on Alveolar Proteinosis for you. They also will send you any publications and journal articles they may have on hand, and will refer you to other organizations that are studying this disease. If you can't afford treatment, have your doctor call NHLBI to find out if they are conducting any clinical studies that you might qualify for.

☎ Contact:
National Heart, Lung and Blood Institute
Bldg. 31, Room 4A21
Bethesda, MD 20892
(301) 496-4236

ALZHEIMER'S DISEASE

See also Aging
See also Dementia
See also Presenile Dementia

Clearinghouses/Hotlines

The Alzheimer's Disease Education and Referral Center (ADERC) will send you all kinds of information about Alzheimer's Disease, including new research efforts, diagnosis and treatment issues. They also provide services to patients and family members, such as referring them to resources at the national and state levels.

☎ Contact:
Alzheimer's Disease Education
and Referral Center
P.O. Box 8250
Silver Spring, MD 20907
(301) 495-3311

The National Institute of Mental Health (NIMH) will send you whatever publications and reprints of articles from texts and journals they have on

Alzheimer's Disease. They will also refer you to other organizations that are studying this disease. NIMH will also let you know of any clinical studies that may be studying Alzheimer's and looking for patients.

☎ Contact:
National Institute of Mental Health
5600 Fishers Lane, Room 15C05
Rockville, MD 20857
(301) 443-4515

The National Institute of Neurological Disorders and Stroke (NINDS) can send you only information they have in their publications list on Alzheimer's. They cannot refer you to any experts. This Clearinghouse cannot directly give you information about any current clinical studies NINDS might be conducting on this illness, but you can find this information for yourself by looking under the National Institute of Neurological Disorders and Stroke in *Appendix A* at the end of this book.

☎ Contact:
The National Institute of Neurological
Disorders and Stroke
Bldg. 31, Room 8A06
Bethesda, MD 20892
(301) 496-5751
(800) 352-9424

The National Institute on Deafness and Other Communicative Disorders (NIDCD) will send you whatever publications and reprints of journal articles they have on Alzheimer's Disease. If you need further information, they will refer you to other organizations that study this and other related diseases. NIDCD does not conduct any clinical studies for this or any other disorder.

☎ Contact:
National Institute on Deafness
and Other Communication Disorders
Bldg. 31, Room 3C35
Bethesda, MD 20892
(301) 496-7243; (800) 241-1044
(301) 402-0252 (TDD)

Free Publications/Videos

The following publications on Alzheimer's are available from Alzheimer's Disease Education &

Referral Center, P.O. Box 8250, Silver Spring, MD 20907; (301) 495-3311.

- *ADEAR Center Brochure.*
- *Age Page: Confusion and Memory Loss in Old Age.*
- *Alzheimer's Disease Centers Program.*
- *Alzheimer's Disease: Q & A.*
- *Differential Diagnosis of Dementing Diseases.*
- *Fact Sheet: Alzheimer's Disease Database.*
- *Family Reading List: Caring for Memory-Impaired Elders.*
- *General Information Packet on Alzheimer's Disease.*
- *Report of the DHHS Advisory Panel on Alzheimer's Disease.*
- *Special Reports on Alzheimer's Disease.*

The following publication on Alzheimer's is available from the Office of Clinical Center Communications, Bldg. 10, Room 1C255, Bethesda, MD 20892; (301) 496-2563.

- *Alzheimer's.* A booklet to educate consumers and allow them to make informed medical decisions.

The following publications are available from the National Institute of Neurological Disorders and Stroke, P.O. Box 5801, Bethesda, MD 20824; (800) 352-9424, (301) 496-5751.

- *Alzheimer's Disease.* Contains a collection of scientific articles, patient education pamphlets, and addresses of voluntary health associations.
- *Alzheimer's Disease: A Scientific Guide for Health Practitioners.* (#84-2251)

The following publication on Alzheimer's is available from the Superintendent of Documents, Government Printing Office, Washington, DC 20402; (202) 783-3238.

- *Alzheimer's Disease Treatment and Family Stress: Directions for Research.* Presents a collection of papers giving current information on research investigations that increase understanding of the nature and consequences of family caregiving. (#017-024-01365-0, $14)

The following publications on Alzheimer's are available from the Office of Technology Assessment, 600 Pennsylvania Ave., SE, Washington, DC 20510; (202) 224-8996.

- *Confused Minds, Burdened Families: Finding Help for People With Alzheimer's and Other Dementias.* Ask for the summary report.
- *Losing a Million Minds: Confronting the Tragedy of Alzheimer's Disease and Other Dementias.* Covers existing methods of locating and arranging health and long-term care services for Alzheimer's and dementia patients. The study identifies methods that are successful in some communities and may serve as models for others.

The following publications on Alzheimer's are available from the National Institute of Mental Health, 5600 Fishers Ln., Room 15C05, Rockville, MD 20857; (301) 443-4515.

- *Differential Diagnosis of Dementing Diseases.*
- *There Were Times, Dear. . . Living With Alzheimer's Disease.*
- *Useful Information on Alzheimer's Disease.*

The following Congressional Research Service (CRS) reports on Alzheimer's Disease are available from either of your U.S. Senators' offices at the U.S. Capitol, Washington, DC 20510, or from your Congressional Representative at the U.S. Capitol, Washington, DC 20515. You can also call in your request through the U.S. Capitol switchboard at (202) 224-3121. Be sure to include the full title and report number in your request.

- *Alzheimer's Disease: Bibliography-in-Brief, 1982-1987.* (#88-312 L)
- *Alzheimer's Disease: Archived Issue Brief.* (#IB83128)
- *Consortium to Establish a Registry for Alzheimer's Disease (CERAD): A Federally Funded Research Program.* (#91-352 SPR)

AMAUROTIC IDIOCY

Clearinghouses/Hotlines

The National Institute of Neurological Disorders and Stroke (NINDS) can send you only information they have in their publications list on Amaurotic Idiocy. They cannot refer you to any experts. This Clearinghouse cannot directly give you information about any current clinical studies NINDS might be conducting on this illness, but you can find this information for yourself by looking under the National Institute of Neurological Disorders and Stroke in *Appendix A* at the end of this book.

☎ Contact:
National Institute of Neurological
Disorders and Stroke
Bldg. 31, Room 8A06
Bethesda, MD 20892
(301) 496-5751
(800) 352-9424

AMBIGUOUS GENITALIA

Clearinghouses/Hotlines

The National Institute of Child Health and Human Development (NICHD) will send you whatever publications and reprints of journal articles they have on Ambiguous Genitalia. If necessary, they will refer you to other experts or researchers in the field. If you can't afford treatment, have your doctor call NICHD to find out if they are conducting any clinical studies that you might qualify for.

☎ Contact:
National Institute of Child Health
and Human Development
Bldg. 31, Room 2A32
Bethesda, MD 20892
(301) 496-5133

AMBLYOPIA

Clearinghouses/Hotlines

The National Eye Institute (NEI) can give you up-to-date information on Amblyopia by searching the Combined Health Information Database (CHID) and MEDLINE and sending you bibliographies of resources, along with any journal articles they may have. They can also refer you to any other organizations that study this and other related disorder. NEI will also let you know of any clinical studies that may be studying this disease and looking for patients. Because of their small staff, NEI prefers that you submit your requests for information in writing.

☎ Contact:
National Eye Institute
Bldg. 31, Room 6A32
Bethesda, MD 20892
(301) 496-5248

AMEBIASIS

Clearinghouses/Hotlines

The National Institute on Allergy and Infectious Diseases (NIAID) can search the Combined Health Information Database (CHID) and generate a bibliography of resources on Amebiasis for you. They will also send you any publications and journal articles they may have on hand, and will refer you to researchers who are currently studying this disease. If you can't afford treatment, have your doctor call NIAID to find out if they are conducting any clinical studies that you might qualify for.

☎ Contact:
National Institute of Allergy
and Infectious Diseases
Bldg. 31, Room 7A32
Bethesda, MD 20892
(301) 496-5717

AMINO ACID DISORDERS

Clearinghouses/Hotlines

The National Institute of Child Health and Human Development (NICHD) will send you whatever publications and reprints of journal articles they have on Amino Acid Disorders. If necessary, they will refer you to other experts or researchers in the field. If you can't afford treatment, have your doctor call NICHD to find out if they are conducting any clinical studies that you might qualify for.

☎ Contact:
National Institute of Child Health
and Human Development
Bldg. 31, Room 2A32
Bethesda, MD 20892
(301) 496-5133

AMNIOCENTESIS

See also Pregnancy

Clearinghouses/Hotlines

The National Institute of Child Health and Human Development (NICHD) will send you whatever publications and reprints of journal articles they have on Amniocentesis. If necessary, they will refer you to other experts or researchers in the field. If you can't afford treatment, have your doctor call NICHD to find out if they are conducting any clinical studies that you might qualify for.

☎ Contact:
National Institute of Child Health
and Human Development
Bldg. 31, Room 2A32
Bethesda, MD 20892
(301) 496-5133

AMOSMIA

Clearinghouses/Hotlines

The National Institute on Deafness and Other Communicative Disorders (NIDCD) will send you whatever publications and reprints of journal articles they have on Amosmia. If you need further information, they will refer you to other organizations that study Amosmia and other related diseases. NIDCD does not conduct any clinical studies for this or any other disorder.

☎ Contact:
National Institute on Deafness
and Other Communication Disorders
Bldg. 31, Room 3C35
Bethesda, MD 20892
(301) 496-7243
(800) 241-1044
(301) 402-0252 (TDD)

AMYLOID POLYNEUROPATHY

Clearinghouses/Hotlines

The National Institute of Neurological Disorders and Stroke (NINDS) can send you only information they have in their publications list on Amyloid Polyneuropathy. They cannot refer you to any experts. This Clearinghouse cannot directly give you information about any current clinical studies NINDS might be conducting on this illness, but you can find this information for yourself by looking under the National Institute of Neurological Disorders and Stroke in *Appendix A* at the end of this book.

☎ Contact:
National Institute of Neurological
Disorders and Stroke
Bldg. 31, Room 8A06
Bethesda, MD 20892
(301) 496-5751
(800) 352-9424

AMYLOIDOSIS

Clearinghouses/Hotlines

The National Institute of Arthritis and Musculoskeletal and Skin Diseases (NIAMS) will send you whatever publications and reprints of articles from texts and journals they have on Amyloidosis. They will also refer you to other organizations that are studying this disease. NIAMS will also let you know of any clinical studies that may be studying this disease and looking for patients.

☎ Contact:
National Institute of Arthritis
and Musculoskeletal and Skin Diseases
Box AMS
Bethesda, MD 20892
(301) 495-4484

The National Institute of Diabetes and Digestive and Kidney Diseases's (NIDDK) individual clearinghouses can search the Combined Health Information Database (CHID) and generate a bibliography of resources on Amyloidosis for you. They also will send you any publications and journal articles they may have on hand, and will refer you to other organizations that are studying this disease. If you can't afford treatment, have your doctor call NIDDK to find out if they are conducting any clinical studies that you might qualify for.

☎ Contact:
National Institute of Diabetes
and Digestive and Kidney Diseases
Bldg. 31, Room 9A04
Bethesda, MD 20892
(301) 496-3583

The National Eye Institute (NEI) can give you up-to-date information on Amyloidosis by searching the Combined Health Information Database (CHID) and MEDLINE and sending you bibliographies of resources, along with any journal articles they may have. They can also refer you to any other organizations that study this and other related diseases. NEI will also let you know of any clinical studies that may be studying this disease and looking for patients. Because of their small staff, NEI prefers that you submit your requests for information in writing.

☎ Contact:
National Eye Institute
Bldg. 31, Room 6A32
Bethesda, MD 20892
(301) 496-5248

AMYOTONIA CONGENITA

Clearinghouses/Hotlines

The National Institute of Neurological Disorders and Stroke (NINDS) can send you only information they have in their publications list on Amyotonia Congenita. They cannot refer you to any experts. This Clearinghouse cannot directly give you information about any current clinical studies NINDS might be conducting on this illness, but you can find this information for yourself by looking under the National Institute of Neurological Disorders and Stroke in *Appendix A* at the end of this book.

☎ Contact:
National Institute of Neurological
Disorders and Stroke
Bldg. 31, Room 8A06
Bethesda, MD 20892
(301) 496-5751
(800) 352-9424

AMYOTROPHIC LATERAL SCLEROSIS

Clearinghouses/Hotlines

The National Institute of Diabetes and Digestive and Kidney Diseases's (NIDDK) individual clearinghouses can search the Combined Health Information Database (CHID) and generate a bibliography of resources on Amyotrophic Lateral Sclerosis (ALS) for you. They also will send you any publications and journal articles they may have on hand, and will refer you to other organizations

that are studying this disease. If you can't afford treatment, have your doctor call NIDDK to find out if they are conducting any clinical studies that you might qualify for.

☎ Contact:
National Institute of Diabetes
and Digestive and Kidney Diseases
Bldg. 31, Room 9A04
Bethesda, MD 20892
(301) 496-3583

The National Institute of Neurological Disorders and Stroke (NINDS) can send you only information they have in their publications list on Amyotrophic Lateral Sclerosis. They cannot refer you to any experts. This Clearinghouse cannot directly give you information about any current clinical studies NINDS might be conducting on this illness, but you can find this information for yourself by looking under the National Institute of Neurological Disorders and Stroke in *Appendix A* at the end of this book.

☎ Contact:
National Institute of Neurological
Disorders and Stroke
Bldg. 31, Room 8A06
Bethesda, MD 20892
(301) 496-5751
(800) 352-9424

The National Institute on Deafness and Other Communicative Disorders (NIDCD) will send you whatever publications and reprints of journal articles they have on Amyotrophic Lateral Sclerosis. If you need further information, they will refer you to other organizations that study this and other related diseases. NIDCD does not conduct any clinical studies for this or any other disorder.

☎ Contact:
National Institute on Deafness
and Other Communication Disorders
Bldg. 31, Room 3C35
Bethesda, MD 20892
(301) 496-7243
(800) 241-1044
(301) 402-0252 (TDD)

Free Publications/Videos

The following publications on Amyotrophic Lateral Sclerosis are available from the National Institute of Neurological Disorders and Stroke, Bldg. 31, Room 8A06, Bethesda, MD 20892; (301) 496-5751 or (800) 352-9424.

- *Amyotrophic Lateral Sclerosis.* Discusses the physiology and symptoms of this progressively crippling and fatal disease. (#84-916)
- *Amyotrophic Lateral Sclerosis (ALS).* Contains a collection of scientific articles, patient education pamphlets, and addresses of voluntary health associations.

The following video on ALS is available from Modern Talking Picture Service, 5000 Park St. North, St. Petersburg, FL 33709; (800) 243-MTPS.

- *One Man's Dream: To Someday Find A Cure for ALS.* Video covers current medical research on amyotrophic lateral sclerosis: Lou Gehrig's disease.

ANALGESIC-ASSOCIATED NEPHROPATHY

Clearinghouses/Hotlines

The National Institute of Diabetes and Digestive and Kidney Diseases's (NIDDK) individual clearinghouses can search the Combined Health Information Database (CHID) and generate a bibliography of resources on Analgesic- Associated Nephropathy for you. They also will send you any publications and journal articles they may have on hand, and will refer you to other organizations that are studying this disease. If you can't afford treatment, have your doctor call NIDDK to find out if they are conducting any clinical studies that you might qualify for.

☎ Contact:
National Institute of Diabetes
and Digestive and Kidney Diseases
Building 31
Room 9A04
Bethesda, MD 20892
(301) 496-3583

ANAPHORESIS

Clearinghouses/Hotlines

The National Arthritis and Musculoskeletal and Skin Diseases Information Clearinghouse can provide you with information regarding Anaphoresis, which is a lack of function of the sweat glands. The clearinghouse will send you whatever publications and reprints of articles from texts and journals they have on anaphoresis. They will also refer you to other organizations that are studying this disease.

☎ Contact:
National Arthritis and Musculoskeletal
and Skin Diseases Information Clearinghouse
9000 Rockville Pike
Box AMS
Bethesda, MD 20892
(301) 495-4484

ANAPLASIS

Clearinghouses/Hotlines

The National Cancer Institute (NCI) will send you whatever publications and reprints of journal articles they have on Anaplasis. They can also give you information on the state-of-the-art treatment for this disease, including specific treatment information for your stage of cancer. They can also search their Physicians Data Query (PDQ) database to let you know if NCI is conducting any clinical studies on your disease.

☎ Contact:
National Cancer Institute
Building 31
Room 10A24
Bethesda, MD 20892
(800) 4-CANCER
(301) 496-5583

ANEMIA

Clearinghouses/Hotlines

The National Institute of Diabetes and Digestive and Kidney Diseases's (NIDDK) individual clearinghouses can search the Combined Health Information Database (CHID) and generate a bibliography of resources on Anemia for you. They also will send you any publications and journal articles they may have on hand, and will refer you to other organizations that are studying this disease. If you can't afford treatment, have your doctor call NIDDK to find out if they are conducting any clinical studies that you might qualify for.

☎ Contact:
National Institute of Diabetes
and Digestive and Kidney Diseases
Bldg. 31, Room 9A04
Bethesda, MD 20892
(301) 496-3583

The National Cancer Institute (NCI) will send you whatever publications and reprints of journal articles they have on Hemolytic and Aplastic Anemia. They can also give you information on the state-of-the-art treatment for this disease, including specific treatment information for your stage of disease. They can also search their Physicians Data Query (PDQ) database to let you know if NCI is conducting any relevant clinical studies.

☎ Contact:
National Cancer Institute
Bldg. 31, Room 10A24
Bethesda, MD 20892
(800) 4-CANCER
(301) 496-5583

The National Heart, Lung, and Blood Institute (NHLBI) can search the Combined Health Information Database (CHID) and generate a bibliography of resources on Hemolytic and Aplastic Anemia for you. They also will send you any publications and journal articles they may have on hand, and will refer you to other organizations that are studying this condition. If you can't afford treatment, have your doctor call NHLBI to

find out if they are conducting any clinical studies that you might qualify for.

☎ Contact:
National Heart, Lung and Blood Institute
Bldg. 31, Room 4A21
Bethesda, MD 20892
(301) 496-4236

The National Institute on Allergy and Infectious Diseases (NIAID) can search the Combined Health Information Database (CHID) and generate a bibliography of resources on Hemolytic and Aplastic Anemia for you. They will also send you any publications and journal articles they may have on hand, and will refer you to researchers who are currently studying this Anemia. If you can't afford treatment, have your doctor call NIAID to find out if they are conducting any clinical studies that you might qualify for.

☎ Contact:
National Institute of Allergy
and Infectious Diseases
Bldg. 31, Room 7A32
Bethesda, MD 20892
(301) 496-5717

ANENCEPHALY

Clearinghouses/Hotlines

The National Institute of Neurological Disorders and Stroke (NINDS) can send you only information they have in their publications list on Anencephaly. They cannot refer you to any experts. This Clearinghouse cannot directly give you information about any current clinical studies NINDS might be conducting on this illness, but you can find this information for yourself by looking under the National Institute of Neurological Disorders and Stroke in *Appendix A* at the end of this book.

☎ Contact:
National Institute of Neurological
Disorders and Stroke
Bldg. 31, Room 8A06
Bethesda, MD 20892
(301) 496-5751
(800) 352-9424

ANEURYSMS

Clearinghouses/Hotlines

The National Heart, Lung, and Blood Institute (NHLBI) can search the Combined Health Information Database (CHID) and generate a bibliography of resources on Aneurysms for you. They also will send you any publications and journal articles they may have on hand, and will refer you to other organizations that are studying Aneurysms. If you can't afford treatment, have your doctor call NHLBI to find out if they are conducting any clinical studies that you might qualify for.

☎ Contact:
National Heart, Lung and Blood Institute
Bldg. 31, Room 4A21
Bethesda, MD 20892
(301) 496-4236

The National Institute of Neurological Disorders and Stroke (NINDS) can send you only information they have in their publications list on Brain or Spinal Aneurysms. They cannot refer you to any experts. This Clearinghouse cannot directly give you information about any current clinical studies NINDS might be conducting on this illness, but you can find this information for yourself by looking under the National Institute of Neurological Disorders and Stroke in *Appendix A* at the end of this book.

☎ Contact:
National Institute of Neurological
Disorders and Stroke
Bldg. 31, Room 8A06
Bethesda, MD 20892
(301) 496-5751
(800) 352-9424

ANGELMAN'S DISEASE

Clearinghouses/Hotlines

The National Institute of Neurological Disorders and Stroke (NINDS) can send you only

information they have in their publications list on Angelman's Disease. They cannot refer you to any experts. This Clearinghouse cannot directly give you information about any current clinical studies NINDS might be conducting on this illness, but you can find this information for yourself by looking under the National Institute of Neurological Disorders and Stroke in *Appendix A* at the end of this book.

☎ Contact:
National Institute of Neurological
Disorders and Stroke
Bldg. 31, Room 8A06
Bethesda, MD 20892
(301) 496-5751
(800) 352-9424

ANGINA PECTORIS

Clearinghouses/Hotlines

The National Heart, Lung, and Blood Institute (NHLBI) can search the Combined Health Information Database (CHID) and generate a bibliography of resources on Angina Pectoris for you. They also will send you any publications and journal articles they may have on hand, and will refer you to other organizations that are studying this condition. If you can't afford treatment, have your doctor call NHLBI to find out if they are conducting any clinical studies that you might qualify for.

☎ Contact:
National Heart, Lung and Blood Institute
Bldg. 31, Room 4A21
Bethesda, MD 20892
(301) 496-4236

Free Publications/Videos

The following publication on Angina is available from the National Heart, Lung and Blood Institute, Bldg. 31, Room 4A21, Bethesda, MD 20892; (301) 496-4236.

- *Facts About Angina.* (#91-2890)

ANGIOEDEMA

Clearinghouses/Hotlines

The National Institute on Allergy and Infectious Diseases (NIAID) can search the Combined Health Information Database (CHID) and generate a bibliography of resources on Angioedema and Hereditary Angioedema for you. They will also send you any publications and journal articles they may have on hand, and will refer you to researchers who are currently studying this issue. If you can't afford treatment, have your doctor call NIAID to find out if they are conducting any clinical studies that you might qualify for.

☎ Contact:
National Institute of Allergy
and Infectious Diseases
Building 31
Room 7A32
Bethesda, MD 20892
(301) 496-5717

ANGIOGRAPHY

Clearinghouses/Hotlines

The National Heart, Lung, and Blood Institute (NHLBI) can search the Combined Health Information Database (CHID) and generate a bibliography of resources on Angiography for you. They also will send you any publications and journal articles they may have on hand, and will refer you to other organizations that are studying this issue. If you can't afford treatment, have your doctor call NHLBI to find out if they are conducting any clinical studies that you might qualify for.

☎ Contact:
National Heart, Lung and Blood Institute
Building 31
Room 4A21
Bethesda, MD 20892
(301) 496-4236

ANGIOPLASTY

Clearinghouses/Hotlines

The National Heart, Lung, and Blood Institute (NHLBI) can search the Combined Health Information Database (CHID) and generate a bibliography of resources on Angioplasty for you. They also will send you any publications and journal articles they may have on hand, and will refer you to other organizations that are studying this issue. If you can't afford treatment, have your doctor call NHLBI to find out if they are conducting any clinical studies that you might qualify for.

☎ Contact:
National Heart, Lung and Blood Institute
Building 31
Room 4A21
Bethesda, MD 20892
(301) 496-4236

ANILINE DYES

Clearinghouses/Hotlines

The National Cancer Institute (NCI) will send you whatever publications and reprints of journal articles they have on Aniline Dyes. They can also give you information on the state-of-the-art treatment using these compounds, including specific treatment information for your stage of cancer. They can also search their Physicians Data Query (PDQ) database to let you know if NCI is conducting any clinical studies on your disease.

☎ Contact:
National Cancer Institute
Building 31
Room 10A24
Bethesda, MD 20892
(800) 4-CANCER
(301) 496-5583

ANIMAL RESEARCH

Free Publications/Videos

The following publication is available from the Office of Science and Health Reports, National Center for Research Resources, National Institutes of Health, Bethesda, MD 20892; (301) 496-5545.

- *NCRR Resources for Comparative Biomedical Research Directory*. Contains information about specialized animal research and supply facilities, staffs, types of resources, and major areas of research.

The following publications are available from the Office of Technology Assessment, 600 Pennsylvania Ave., SE, Washington, DC 20510; (202) 224-8996.

- *Federal Regulation and Animal Patents*. A report to Congress. Ask for the summary report.
- *Alternatives to Animal Use In Research, Testing, and Education*. A report to Congress. Ask for the summary report. (#BA-273)
- *Transgenic Animals*. A report to Congress. Ask for the summary report.

ANIRIDIA

Clearinghouses/Hotlines

The National Eye Institute (NEI) can give you up-to-date information on Aniridia by searching the Combined Health Information Database (CHID) and MEDLINE and sending you bibliographies of resources, along with any journal articles they may have. They can also refer you to any other organizations that study this and other related diseases. NEI will also let you know of any clinical studies that may be studying this disease and looking for patients. Because of their small staff, NEI prefers that you submit your requests for information in writing.

☎ Contact:
National Eye Institute
Bldg. 31, Room 6A32
Bethesda, MD 20892
(301) 496-5248

ANKLOGLASSIA

See Tongue-Tied

ANKYLOSIS SPONDYLITIS

Clearinghouses/Hotlines

The National Institute of Arthritis and Musculoskeletal and Skin Diseases (NIAMS) will send you whatever publications and reprints of articles from texts and journals they have on Ankylosis Spondylitis. They will also refer you to other organizations that are studying this disease. NIAMS will also let you know of any clinical studies that may be studying this disease and looking for patients.

☎ Contact:
National Institute of Arthritis
and Musculoskeletal and Skin Diseases
Box AMS
Bethesda, MD 20892
(301) 495-4484

ANOREXIA

See also Eating Disorders

Clearinghouses/Hotlines

The Obesity, Eating Disorders, and Energy Regulation Program at National Institutes of Health researches Obesity, Anorexia Nervosa, Bulimia and other eating disorders. They can give you information on the causes, prevention, and treatments of these conditions.

☎ Contact:
National Institute of Diabetes
and Digestive and Kidney Diseases
National Institutes of Health
Bldg. 31, Room 3A18B
Bethesda, MD 20892
(301) 496-7823

The National Institute of Child Health and Human Development (NICHD) will send you whatever publications and reprints of journal articles they have on Anorexia Nervosa. If necessary, they will refer you to other experts or researchers in the field. If you can't afford treatment, have your doctor call NICHD to find out if they are conducting any clinical studies that you might qualify for.

☎ Contact:
National Institute of Child Health
and Human Development
Bldg. 31, Room 2A32
Bethesda, MD 20892
(301) 496-5133

The National Institute of Mental Health (NIMH) will send you whatever publications and reprints of articles from texts and journals they have on Anorexia Nervosa. They will also refer you to other organizations that are studying this disorder. NIMH will also let you know of any clinical studies that may be studying this disease and looking for patients.

☎ Contact:
National Institute of Mental Health
5600 Fishers Ln., Room 15C05
Rockville, MD 20857
(301) 443-4515

Free Publications/Videos

The following publication on Anorexia is available from the Food & Nutrition Information Center, National Agricultural Library, Room 304, Beltsville, MD 20705-2351; (301) 504-5719.

- *Anorexia Nervosa and Bulimia*. Designed to help you locate resources on this topic.

The following publication on Anorexia is available from the Science & Technology Division,

Reference Section, Library of Congress, Washington, DC 20540; (202) 707-5580.

- *Anorexia Nervosa/Bulimia*. Reference guide designed to help locate further published material. (#85-8)

The following publication on Anorexia is available from the National Institute of Child Health and Human Development, Bldg. 31, Room 2A32, Bethesda, MD 20892; (301) 496-5133.

- *Facts About Anorexia Nervosa*. Explains the causes, symptoms and treatments for anorexia and bulimia as well as ongoing research efforts at the National Institutes of Health.

The following publication on Anorexia is available from the National Institute of Mental Health, 5600 Fishers Ln., Room 15C05, Rockville, MD 20857; (301) 443-4515.

- *Useful Information on Anorexia Nervosa and Bulimia*.

ANOSMIA

Clearinghouses/Hotlines

The National Institute of Neurological Disorders and Stroke (NINDS) can send you only information they have in their publications list on Anosmia. They cannot refer you to any experts. This Clearinghouse cannot directly give you information about any current clinical studies NINDS might be conducting on this illness, but you can find this information for yourself by looking under the National Institute of Neurological Disorders and Stroke in *Appendix A* at the end of this book.

☎ Contact:
National Institute of Neurological
Disorders and Stroke
Bldg. 31, Room 8A06
Bethesda, MD 20892
(301) 496-5751
(800) 352-9424

ANOXIA

Clearinghouses/Hotlines

The National Heart, Lung, and Blood Institute (NHLBI) can search the Combined Health Information Database (CHID) and generate a bibliography of resources on Anoxia for you. They also will send you any publications and journal articles they may have on hand, and will refer you to other organizations that are studying this disease. If you can't afford treatment, have your doctor call NHLBI to find out if they are conducting any clinical studies that you might qualify for.

☎ Contact:
National Heart, Lung and Blood Institute
Building 31
Room 4A21
Bethesda, MD 20892
(301) 496-4236

ANTENATAL DIAGNOSIS

Clearinghouses/Hotlines

The National Institute of Child Health and Human Development (NICHD) will send you whatever publications and reprints of journal articles they have on Antenatal Diagnosis. If necessary, they will refer you to other experts or researchers in the field. If you can't afford treatment, have your doctor call NICHD to find out if they are conducting any clinical studies that you might qualify for.

☎ Contact:
National Institute of Child Health
and Human Development
Building 31
Room 2A32
Bethesda, MD 20892
(301) 496-5133

ANTHRAX

Clearinghouses/Hotlines

The National Institute on Allergy and Infectious Diseases (NIAID) can search the Combined Health Information Database (CHID) and generate a bibliography of resources on Anthrax for you. They will also send you any publications and journal articles they may have on hand, and will refer you to researchers who are currently studying this disease. If you can't afford treatment, have your doctor call NIAID to find out if they are conducting any clinical studies that you might qualify for.

☎ Contact:
National Institute of Allergy
and Infectious Diseases
Bldg. 31, Room 7A32
Bethesda, MD 20892
(301) 496-5717

ANTIALPHATRYPSIN

Clearinghouses/Hotlines

The National Institute of Diabetes and Digestive and Kidney Diseases's (NIDDK) individual clearinghouses can search the Combined Health Information Database (CHID) and generate a bibliography of resources on Antialphatrypsin for you. They also will send you any publications and journal articles they may have on hand, and will refer you to other organizations that are studying this disease. If you can't afford treatment, have your doctor call NIDDK to find out if they are conducting any clinical studies that you might qualify for.

☎ Contact:
National Institute of Diabetes
and Digestive and Kidney Diseases
Bldg. 31, Room 9A04
Bethesda, MD 20892
(301) 496-3583

ANTIBIOTICS

Clearinghouses/Hotlines

The National Institute on Allergy and Infectious Diseases (NIAID) can search the Combined Health Information Database (CHID) and generate a bibliography of resources on Antibiotics for you. They will also send you any publications and journal articles they may have on hand, and will refer you to researchers who are currently studying this issue. If you can't afford treatment, have your doctor call NIAID to find out if they are conducting any clinical studies that you might qualify for.

☎ Contact:
National Institute of Allergy
and Infectious Diseases
Bldg. 31, Room 7A32
Bethesda, MD 20892
(301) 496-5717

Free Publications/Videos

The following Congressional Research Service (CRS) report is available from either of your U.S. Senators' offices at the U.S. Capitol, Washington, DC 20510, or from your Congressional Representative at the U.S. Capitol, Washington, DC 20515. You can also call in your request through the U.S. Capitol switchboard at (202) 224-3121. Be sure to include the full title and report number in your request.

- *Antibiotics: Health Implications of Use in Animal Feed; Archived Issue Brief.* (#IB85076)

ANTI-CANCER DRUGS

See also Cancer

Free Publications/Videos

The following fact sheets from the National

Cancer Institute provide information about side effects, proper usage, and precautions of these anti-cancer drugs. Contact the National Cancer Institute, Bldg. 31, Room 10A24, Bethesda, MD 20892, (800) 4-CANCER, (301) 496-5583.

- *Asparginasa/Asparaginase.*
- *Bleomicina/Bleomycin.*
- *Busulfano/Busulfan.*
- *Carmustina/Carmustine.*
- *Clorambucilo/Chlorambucil.*
- *Cisplatin/Cisplatin.*
- *Ciclofosfamida/Cyclophosphamide.*
- *Citarabina/Cytarabine.*
- *Decarbazino/Dacarbazine.*
- *Dactinomicina/Dactinomycin.*
- *Daunorrubicina/Daunorubicin.*
- *Doxorrubicina/Doxorubicin.*
- *Estramustina/Estramustine.*
- *Estreptozocina/Streptozocin.*
- *Floxiridina/Floxuridine.*
- *Fluorouracilo/Fluorouracil.*
- *Hidroxiurea/Hydroxyurea.*
- *Lomustina/Lomustine.*
- *Mecloretamina/Mechlorethamine.*
- *Melfalano/Melphalan.*
- *Mercaptopurina/Mercaptopurine.*
- *Metrotrexato/Methotrexate.*
- *Mitomicina/Mitomycin.*
- *Mitotano/Mitotane.*
- *Plicamicina/Plicamycin.*
- *Prednisona/Prednisone.*
- *Procarbazina/Procarbazine.*
- *Tamoxifeno/Tamoxifen.*
- *Vinblastina/Vinblastine.*
- *Vincristina/Vincristine.*

ANTICOAGULANTS

Clearinghouses/Hotlines

The National Heart, Lung, and Blood Institute (NHLBI) can search the Combined Health Information Database (CHID) and generate a bibliography of resources on Anticoagulants for you. They also will send you any publications and journal articles they may have on hand, and will refer you to other organizations that are studying this issue. If you can't afford treatment, have your doctor call NHLBI to find out if they are conducting any clinical studies that you might qualify for.

☎ Contact:
National Heart, Lung and Blood Institute
Bldg. 31, Room 4A21
Bethesda, MD 20892
(301) 496-4236

The National Institute of Diabetes and Digestive and Kidney Diseases's (NIDDK) individual clearinghouses can search the Combined Health Information Database (CHID) and generate a bibliography of resources on Native Anticoagulants for you. They also will send you any publications and journal articles they may have on hand, and will refer you to other organizations that are studying this issue. If you can't afford treatment, have your doctor call NIDDK to find out if they are conducting any clinical studies that you might qualify for.

☎ Contact:
National Institute of Diabetes
and Digestive and Kidney Diseases
Bldg. 31, Room 9A04
Bethesda, MD 20892
(301) 496-3583

ANTIDIURETIC HORMONE

Clearinghouses/Hotlines

The National Institute of Diabetes and Digestive and Kidney Diseases's (NIDDK) individual clearinghouses can search the Combined Health Information Database (CHID) and generate a bibliography of resources on Antidiuretic Hormone for you. They also will send you any publications and journal articles they may have on hand, and will refer you to other organizations that are studying this Hormone. If you can't afford treatment, have your doctor call NIDDK to find out if they are conducting any clinical studies that you might qualify for.

☎ Contact:
National Institute of Diabetes
and Digestive and Kidney Diseases

Bldg. 31, Room 9A04
Bethesda, MD 20892
(301) 496-3583

The National Heart, Lung, and Blood Institute (NHLBI) can search the Combined Health Information Database (CHID) and generate a bibliography of resources on Antidiuretic Hormone for you. They also will send you any publications and journal articles they may have on hand, and will refer you to other organizations that are studying this Hormone. If you can't afford treatment, have your doctor call NHLBI to find out if they are conducting any clinical studies that you might qualify for.

☎ Contact:
National Heart, Lung and Blood Institute
Bldg. 31, Room 4A21
Bethesda, MD 20892
(301) 496-4236

ANTIHISTAMINES

Free Publications/Videos

The following publication is available from the Food & Drug Administration, (HFE-88), 5600 Fishers Ln., Rockville, MD 20857; (301) 443-3170.

- *How To Take Your Medicines: Antihistamines.* (#FDA91-3180)

ANTIMETABOLITES

Clearinghouses/Hotlines

The National Cancer Institute (NCI) will send you whatever publications and reprints of journal articles they have on Antimetabolites. They can also give you information on this state-of-the-art treatment, including specific treatment information for your stage of cancer. They can also search their Physicians Data Query (PDQ) database to let you know if NCI is conducting any clinical studies on your disease.

☎ Contact:
National Cancer Institute
Bldg. 31, Room 10A24
Bethesda, MD 20892
(800) 4-CANCER
(301) 496-5583

ANTI-INFLAMMATORY DRUGS

Free Publications/Videos

The following publication on Anti-Inflammatory Drugs is available from the Food & Drug Administration, (HFE-88), 5600 Fishers Lane, Rockville, MD 20857; (301) 443-3170.

- *How To Take Your Medicines: Nonsteroidal Anti-inflammatory Drugs.* (#FDA90-3176)

ANTINEOPLASTIC

Free Publications/Videos

The following publication on Antineoplastic is available from the National Cancer Institute, Bldg. 31, Room 10A24, Bethesda, MD 20892; (800) 4-CANCER, or (301) 496-5583.

- *Antineoplastic.* Provides information about side effects, proper usage, and precautions of this anti-cancer drug.

ANTISOCIAL BEHAVIOR

Clearinghouses/Hotlines

The National Institute of Mental Health (NIMH) will send you whatever publications and reprints of articles from texts and journals they have on Antisocial Behavior. They will also refer you to other organizations that are studying this issue. NIMH will also let you know of any clinical studies that may be studying Antisocial Behavior and looking for patients.

☎ Contact:
National Institute of Mental Health
5600 Fishers Ln.
Room 15C05
Rockville, MD 20857
(301) 443-4515

Free Publications/Videos

The following publication on Anti-Social Behavior is available from the Clearinghouse on Child Abuse and Neglect Information, P.O. Box 1182, Washington, DC 20013; (800) FYI-3366, or (800) 394-3366.

- *Anti-Social Behavior Resulting From Abuse.* Annotated bibliography. (#07-91123, $3.50)

ANTIVIRAL SUBSTANCES

Clearinghouses/Hotlines

The National Institute on Allergy and Infectious Diseases (NIAID) can search the Combined Health Information Database (CHID) and generate a bibliography of resources on Antiviral Substances for you. They will also send you any publications and journal articles they may have on hand, and will refer you to researchers who are currently studying this issue. If you can't afford treatment, have your doctor call NIAID to find out if they are conducting any clinical studies that you might qualify for.

☎ Contact:
National Institute of Allergy
and Infectious Diseases
Building 31
Room 7A32
Bethesda, MD 20892
(301) 496-5717

ANXIETY ATTACKS

Clearinghouses/Hotlines

The National Institute of Mental Health (NIMH) maintains databases that index and abstract documents from the worldwide literature pertaining to Anxiety Attacks. In addition to scientific journals, there are references to audiovisuals, dissertations, government documents and reports. Contact NIMH for searches on specific subjects.

☎ Contact:
National Institute of Mental Health
5600 Fishers Lane
Room 15C05
Rockville, MD 20857
(301) 443-4515

AORTIC INSUFFICIENCY/ STENOSIS

Clearinghouses/Hotlines

The National Heart, Lung, and Blood Institute (NHLBI) can search the Combined Health Information Database (CHID) and generate a bibliography of resources on Aortic Insufficiency and Stenosis for you. They also will send you any publications and journal articles they may have on hand, and will refer you to other organizations that are studying this condition. If you can't afford treatment, have your doctor call NHLBI to find out if they are conducting any clinical studies that you might qualify for.

☎ Contact:
National Heart, Lung and Blood Institute
Building 31
Room 4A21
Bethesda, MD 20892
(301) 496-4236

AORTITIS

Clearinghouses/Hotlines

The National Heart, Lung, and Blood Institute (NHLBI) can search the Combined Health Information Database (CHID) and generate a bibliography of resources on Aortitis for you. They also will send you any publications and journal articles they may have on hand, and will refer you to other organizations that are studying this disease. If you can't afford treatment, have your doctor call NHLBI to find out if they are conducting any clinical studies that you might qualify for.

☎ Contact:
National Heart, Lung and Blood Institute
Bldg. 31, Room 4A21
Bethesda, MD 20892
(301) 496-4236

APHAKIA

Clearinghouses/Hotlines

The National Eye Institute (NEI) can give you up-to-date information on Aphakia by searching the Combined Health Information Database (CHID) and MEDLINE and sending you bibliographies of resources, along with any journal articles they may have. They can also refer you to any other organizations that study this and other related diseases. NEI will also let you know of any clinical studies that may be studying this disease and looking for patients. Because of their small staff, NEI prefers that you submit your requests for information in writing.

☎ Contact:
National Eye Institute
Bldg. 31, Room 6A32
Bethesda, MD 20892
(301) 496-5248

APHASIA

Clearinghouses/Hotlines

The National Institute on Deafness and Other Communicative Disorders (NIDCD) will send you whatever publications and reprints of journal articles they have on Aphasia. If you need further information, they will refer you to other organizations that study this and other related diseases. NIDCD does not conduct any clinical studies for this or any other disorder.

☎ Contact:
National Institute on Deafness
and Other Communication Disorders
Bldg. 31, Room 3C35
Bethesda, MD 20892
(301) 496-7243
(800) 241-1044
(301) 402-0252 (TDD)

The National Institute of Diabetes and Digestive and Kidney Diseases's (NIDDK) individual clearinghouses can search the Combined Health Information Database (CHID) and generate a bibliography of resources on Aphasia due to stroke for you. They also will send you any publications and journal articles they may have on hand, and will refer you to other organizations that are studying this disease. If you can't afford treatment, have your doctor call NIDDK to find out if they are conducting any clinical studies that you might qualify for.

☎ Contact:
National Institute of Diabetes
and Digestive and Kidney Diseases
Bldg. 31, Room 9A04
Bethesda, MD 20892
(301) 496-3583

The National Institute of Neurological Disorders and Stroke (NINDS) can send you only information they have in their publications list on Aphasia. They cannot refer you to any experts. This Clearinghouse cannot directly give you information about any current clinical studies NINDS might be conducting on this illness, but you can find this information for yourself by looking under the National Institute of Neurological Disorders and Stroke in *Appendix A* at the end of this book.

☎ Contact:
National Institute of Neurological
Disorders and Stroke
Bldg. 31, Room 8A06
Bethesda, MD 20892
(301) 496-5751
(800) 352-9424

Free Publications/Videos

The following publication on Aphasia is available from the National Institute of Neurological Disorders and Stroke, Bldg. 31, Room 8A06, Bethesda, MD 20892; (301) 496-5751 or (800) 352-9424.

- *Aphasia*. (#89-391)

APHTHOUS STOMATITIS

Clearinghouses/Hotlines

The National Institute of Dental Research (NIDR) will send you whatever publications and reprints of journal articles they have on Recurrent Aphthous Stomatitis. As a policy, NIDR will not refer you to other organizations or experts who study this disease. If you can't afford treatment, have your doctor call Dr. Albert Guckers at (301) 496-6241 to find out if NIDR is conducting any clinical studies that you might qualify for.

☎ Contact:
National Institute of Dental Research
Bldg. 31, Room 2C35
Bethesda, MD 20892
(301) 496-4261

APLASTIC ANEMIA

Clearinghouses/Hotlines

The National Heart, Lung, and Blood Institute

(NHLBI) can search the Combined Health Information Database (CHID) and generate a bibliography of resources on Aplastic Anemia for you. They also will send you any publications and journal articles they may have on hand, and will refer you to other organizations that are studying this disease. If you can't afford treatment, have your doctor call NHLBI to find out if they are conducting any clinical studies that you might qualify for.

☎ Contact:
National Heart, Lung and Blood Institute
Building 31
Room 4A21
Bethesda, MD 20892
(301) 496-4236

APNEA

See Sudden Infant Death Syndrome

APRAXIA

Clearinghouses/Hotlines

The National Institute of Neurological Disorders and Stroke (NINDS) can send you only information they have in their publications list on Apraxia. They cannot refer you to any experts. This Clearinghouse cannot directly give you information about any current clinical studies NINDS might be conducting on this illness, but you can find this information for yourself by looking under the National Institute of Neurological Disorders and Stroke in *Appendix A* at the end of this book.

☎ Contact:
National Institute of Neurological
Disorders and Stroke
Bldg. 31, Room 8A06
Bethesda, MD 20892
(301) 496-5751
(800) 352-9424

ARACHNOIDITIS

Clearinghouses/Hotlines

The National Institute of Neurological Disorders and Stroke (NINDS) can send you only information they have in their publications list on Arachnoiditis. They cannot refer you to any experts. This Clearinghouse cannot directly give you information about any current clinical studies NINDS might be conducting on this illness, but you can find this information for yourself by looking under the National Institute of Neurological Disorders and Stroke in *Appendix A* at the end of this book.

☎ Contact:
National Institute of Neurological
Disorders and Stroke
Bldg. 31, Room 8A06
Bethesda, MD 20892
(301) 496-5751
(800) 352-9424

Free Publications/Videos

The following publication is available from the National Institute of Neurological Disorders and Stroke, P.O. Box 5801, Bethesda, MD 20824; (800) 352-9424, or (301) 496-5751.

- *Arachnoiditis*. Contains a collection of scientific articles, patient education pamphlets, and addresses of voluntary health associations.

ARAN DUCHENNE SPINAL MUSCULAR DYSTROPHY

Clearinghouses/Hotlines

The National Institute of Neurological Disorders and Stroke (NINDS) can send you only information they have in their publications list on Aran Duchenne Spinal Muscular Dystrophy. They cannot refer you to any experts. This

Clearinghouse cannot directly give you information about any current clinical studies NINDS might be conducting on this illness, but you can find this information for yourself by looking under the National Institute of Neurological Disorders and Stroke in *Appendix A* at the end of this book.

☎ Contact:
National Institute of Neurological
Disorders and Stroke
Bldg. 31, Room 8A06
Bethesda, MD 20892
(301) 496-5751
(800) 352-9424

ARNOLD-CHIARI MALFORMATIONS

Clearinghouses/Hotlines

The National Institute of Neurological Disorders and Stroke (NINDS) can send you only information they have in their publications list on Arnold-Chiari Malformations. They cannot refer you to any experts. This Clearinghouse cannot directly give you information about any current clinical studies NINDS might be conducting on this illness, but you can find this information for yourself by looking under the National Institute of Neurological Disorders and Stroke in *Appendix A* at the end of this book.

☎ Contact:
National Institute of Neurological
Disorders and Stroke
Bldg. 31, Room 8A06
Bethesda, MD 20892
(301) 496-5751
(800) 352-9424

Free Publications/Videos

The following publication is available from the National Institute of Neurological Disorders and Stroke, P.O. Box 5801, Bethesda, MD 20824; (800) 352-9424, or (301) 496-5751.

- *Arnold-Chiari Malformation*. Contains a

collection of scientific articles, patient education pamphlets, and addresses of voluntary health associations.

ARRHYTHMIAS

Clearinghouses/Hotlines

The National Heart, Lung, and Blood Institute (NHLBI) can search the Combined Health Information Database (CHID) and generate a bibliography of resources on Arrhythmias for you. They also will send you any publications and journal articles they may have on hand, and will refer you to other organizations that are studying this condition. If you can't afford treatment, have your doctor call NHLBI to find out if they are conducting any clinical studies that you might qualify for.

☎ Contact:
National Heart, Lung and Blood Institute
Bldg. 31, Room 4A21
Bethesda, MD 20892
(301) 496-4236

Free Publications/Videos

The following publication is available from the National Heart, Lung and Blood Institute, Bldg. 31, Room 4A21, Bethesda, MD 20892; (301) 496-4236.

- *Facts About Arrhythmias/Rhythm Disorders*. (#91-2264)

ARTERIOSCLEROSIS

Clearinghouses/Hotlines

The National Heart, Lung, and Blood Institute (NHLBI) can search the Combined Health Information Database (CHID) and generate a bibliography of resources on Arteriosclerosis for you. They also will send you any publications and journal articles they may have on hand, and will refer you to other organizations that are studying this disease. If you can't afford treatment, have your doctor call NHLBI to find out if they are conducting any clinical studies that you might qualify for.

☎ Contact:
National Heart, Lung and Blood Institute
Bldg. 31, Room 4A21
Bethesda, MD 20892
(301) 496-4236

ARTERIOVENOUS MALFORMATIONS

Clearinghouses/Hotlines

The National Institute of Neurological Disorders and Stroke (NINDS) can send you only information they have in their publications list on Cerebral and Spinal Arteriovenous Malformations. They cannot refer you to any experts. This Clearinghouse cannot directly give you information about any current clinical studies NINDS might be conducting on this condition, but you can find this information for yourself by looking under the National Institute of Neurological Disorders and Stroke in *Appendix A* at the end of this book.

☎ Contact:
National Institute of Neurological
Disorders and Stroke
Bldg. 31, Room 8A06
Bethesda, MD 20892
(301) 496-5751
(800) 352-9424

Free Publications/Videos

The following publication on Arteriovenous Malformations is available from the National Institute of Neurological Disorders and Stroke, P.O. Box 5801, Bethesda, MD 20824; (800) 352-9424, or (301) 496-5751.

- *Arteriovenous Malformations (AVM)*.
Contains a collection of scientific articles,

patient education pamphlets, and addresses of voluntary health associations.

ARTERITIS

Clearinghouses/Hotlines

The National Eye Institute (NEI) can give you up-to-date information on Arteritis of the eyes by searching the Combined Health Information Database (CHID) and MEDLINE and sending you bibliographies of resources, along with any journal articles they may have. They can also refer you to any other organizations that study this and other related diseases. NEI will also let you know of any clinical studies that may be studying this disease and looking for patients. Because of their small staff, NEI prefers that you submit your requests for information in writing.

☎ Contact:
National Eye Institute
Bldg. 31, Room 6A32
Bethesda, MD 20892
(301) 496-5248

ARTHRITIS

Clearinghouses/Hotlines

The National Institute of Arthritis and Musculoskeletal and Skin Diseases (NIAMS) will send you whatever publications and reprints of articles from texts and journals they have on Arthritis. They will also refer you to other organizations that are studying this disease. NIAMS will also let you know of any clinical studies that may be studying this disease and looking for patients.

☎ Contact:
National Institute of Arthritis
and Musculoskeletal and Skin Diseases
Box AMS
Bethesda, MD 20892
(301) 495-4484

The National Institute on Aging (NIA) will send you whatever publications and reprints of journal articles they have on Arthritis. They cannot refer you to other experts if the information they have isn't sufficient for your purposes.

☎ Contact:
National Institute on Aging
Bldg. 31, Room 5C27
Bethesda, MD 20892
(301) 496-1752

Free Publications/Videos

The following publications and video on Arthritis are available from the Office of Clinical Center Communications, Bldg. 10, Room 1C255, Bethesda, MD 20892; (301) 496-2563.

- *Arthritis.* Booklet written to help the general public make intelligent decisions.
- *Arthritis Today.* Video to help the general public make intelligent decisions.
- *Arthritis Today.* Explains gout, rheumatoid arthritis, and osteoarthritis, and discusses treatment. (#83-1945)

The following publications on Arthritis are available from the National Arthritis and Musculoskeletal and Skin Diseases Information Clearinghouse, Box AMS, 9000 Rockville Pike, Bethesda, MD 20892; (301) 495-4484.

- *Arthritis in Children: Resources for Children, Parents, and Teachers, 1986.* An annotated bibliography of resources. (#AR43, $3)
- *Arthritis, Rheumatic Diseases, and Related Disorders- NIAMS 1991.*
- *Diet and Arthritis: An Annotated Bibliography, 1986* ($2)
- *Exercise and Arthritis: Patient Education Materials, 1986.* An annotated bibliography of resources. (#AR47, $4)
- *Medicine for the Layman: Arthritis.*
- *NIAMS Establishes Specialized Research Centers in Rheumatoid Arthritis, Osteoarthritis, and Osteoporosis.*
- *Sexuality and the Rheumatic Diseases: An Annotated Bibliography* ($3)
- *Therapies for People with Arthritis.*
- *Workshop on Etiopathogenesis of*

Osteoarthritis.

The following publication on Arthritis is available from the Consumer Information Center, P.O. Box 100, Pueblo, CO 81002.

- *Hocus-Pocus as Applied to Arthritis.* Discusses fraudulent cures as well as medically sound treatments for arthritis, rheumatism, and gout. (535Z).

ARTHROGRYPOSIS MULTIPLEX CONGENITA

Clearinghouses/Hotlines

The National Institute of Arthritis and Musculoskeletal and Skin Diseases (NIAMS) will send you whatever publications and reprints of articles from texts and journals they have on Arthrogryposis Multiplex Congenita. They will also refer you to other organizations that are studying this disease. NIAMS will also let you know of any clinical studies that may be studying this disease and looking for patients.

☎ Contact:
National Institute of Arthritis
and Musculoskeletal and Skin Diseases
Box AMS
Bethesda, MD 20892
(301) 495-4484

The National Institute of Child Health and Human Development (NICHD) will send you whatever publications and reprints of journal articles they have on Arthrogryposis Multiplex Congenita. If necessary, they will refer you to other experts or researchers in the field. If you can't afford treatment, have your doctor call NICHD to find out if they are conducting any clinical studies that you might qualify for.

☎ Contact:
National Institute of Child Health
and Human Development
Bldg. 31, Room 2A32
Bethesda, MD 20892
(301) 496-5133

ARTHROPLASTY

Clearinghouses/Hotlines

The National Arthritis and Musculoskeletal and Skin Diseases Information Clearinghouse can provide you with articles and reference materials on Arthroplasty, which is a reconstruction of a joint.

☎ Contact:
National Arthritis and Musculoskeletal and Skin Diseases Information Clearinghouse
Box AMS, 9000 Rockville Pike
Bethesda, MD 20892
(301) 495-4484

ARTHROSCOPY

Clearinghouses/Hotlines

The National Arthritis and Musculoskeletal and Skin Diseases Information Clearinghouse will send you whatever publications and reprints of articles from texts and journals they have on Arthroscopy. They will also refer you to other organizations that are studying this disease, and will let you know of any clinical studies that may be studying this disease and looking for patients.

☎ Contact:
National Arthritis and Musculoskeletal and Skin Diseases Information Clearinghouse
9000 Rockville Pike, Box AMS
Bethesda, MD 20892
(301) 495-4484

Free Publications/Videos

The following publication on Arthroscopy is available from the National Arthritis and Musculoskeletal and Skin Diseases Information Clearinghouse, Box AMS, 9000 Rockville Pike, Bethesda, MD 20892; (301) 495-4484.

- *Arthroscopy: A Brief Bibliography, 1989.* Annotated bibliography of resources. (#AR81)

ARTIFICIAL BLOOD VESSELS

Clearinghouses/Hotlines

The National Heart, Lung, and Blood Institute (NHLBI) can search the Combined Health Information Database (CHID) and generate a bibliography of resources on Artificial Blood Vessels for you. They also will send you any publications and journal articles they may have on hand, and will refer you to other organizations that are studying this issue. If you can't afford treatment, have your doctor call NHLBI to find out if they are conducting any clinical studies that you might qualify for.

☎ Contact:
National Heart, Lung and Blood Institute
Building 31
Room 4A21
Bethesda, MD 20892
(301) 496-4236

ARTIFICIAL HEARTS

Clearinghouses/Hotlines

The National Heart, Lung, and Blood Institute (NHLBI) can search the Combined Health Information Database (CHID) and generate a bibliography of resources on Artificial Hearts and Valves for you. They also will send you any publications and journal articles they may have on hand, and will refer you to other organizations that are studying this technology. If you can't afford treatment, have your doctor call NHLBI to find out if they are conducting any clinical studies that you might qualify for.

☎ Contact:
National Heart, Lung and Blood Institute
Building 31
Room 4A21
Bethesda, MD 20892
(301) 496-4236

Free Publications/Videos

The following publication on Artificial Hearts is available from the National Heart, Lung and Blood Institute, Building 31, Room 4A21, Bethesda, MD 20892; (301) 496-4236.

- *Artificial Heart and Assist Devices*. (#85-2723)

ARTIFICIAL INSEMINATION

See also In Vitro Fertilization

Clearinghouses/Hotlines

The National Institute of Child Health and Human Development (NICHD) will send you whatever publications and reprints of journal articles they have on Artificial Insemination. If necessary, they will refer you to other experts or researchers in the field. If you can't afford treatment, have your doctor call NICHD to find out if they are conducting any clinical studies that you might qualify for.

☎ Contact:
National Institute of Child Health
and Human Development
Building 31
Room 2A32
Bethesda, MD 20892
(301) 496-5133

Free Publications/Videos

The following publication on Artificial Insemination is available from the Office of Technology Assessment, 600 Pennsylvania Ave., SE, Washington, DC 20510; (202) 224-8996.

- *Artificial Insemination: Practice in the United States*. A report to Congress. Ask for the summary report. (#BP-BA-48)

ARTIFICIAL JOINTS

Clearinghouses/Hotlines

The National Institute of Arthritis and Musculoskeletal and Skin Diseases (NIAMS) will send you whatever publications and reprints of articles from texts and journals they have on Artificial Joints. They will also refer you to other organizations that are studying this technology. NIAMS will also let you know of any clinical studies that may be studying this issue and looking for patients.

☎ Contact:
National Institute of Arthritis
and Musculoskeletal and Skin Diseases
Box AMS
9000 Rockville Pike
Bethesda, MD 20892
(301) 495-4484

ARTIFICIAL LUNG

Clearinghouses/Hotlines

The National Heart, Lung, and Blood Institute (NHLBI) can search the Combined Health Information Database (CHID) and generate a bibliography of resources on the Artificial Lung for you. They also will send you any publications and journal articles they may have on hand, and will refer you to other organizations that are studying this technology.

☎ Contact:
National Heart, Lung and Blood Institute
Building 31
Room 4A21
Bethesda, MD 20892
(301) 496-4236

ASBESTOS

See also Asbestosis

Clearinghouses/Hotlines

Do you think there might be asbestos in your office? Was asbestos found in your child's school? The Environmental Protection Agency's (EPA) Asbestos Ombudsman Clearinghouse can provide you with all kinds of information on handling and abatement of asbestos in schools, the workplace, and the home. They can also help you interpret the asbestos-in-school requirements, and they have publications that explain recent legislation concerning asbestos.

☎ Contact:
Environmental Protection Agency
401 M St., SW
Washington, DC 20460
(800) 368-5888
(703) 557-1938

The National Cancer Institute (NCI) will send you whatever publications and reprints of journal articles they have on Asbestos and Cancer. They can also give you information on the state-of-the-art treatment for this condition, including specific treatment information for your stage of cancer. They can also search their Physicians Data Query (PDQ) database to let you know if NCI is conducting any clinical studies on your disease.

☎ Contact:
National Cancer Institute
Bldg. 31, Room 10A24
Bethesda, MD 20892
(800) 4-CANCER
(301) 496-5583

Free Publications/Videos

Are you concerned that you may have asbestos in your home or place of work? Are you not sure what to do about it? The Environmental Protection Agency's Public Information Center has several free pamphlets on asbestos. Contact: Public Information Center, Environmental Protection Agency, 401 M St., SW, Washington, DC 20460, (202) 260-7751.

- *Environmental Backgrounder: Asbestos.*
- *Asbestos in Your Home.*
- *Asbestos, Sound Science, and Public Perceptions.*

The following publication Asbestos is available from the Science & Technology Division, Reference Section, Library of Congress, Washington, DC 20540; (202) 707-5580.

- *Asbestos.* Reference guide designed to help locate further published material. (#87-1)

ASBESTOSIS

See also Asbestos

Clearinghouses/Hotlines

The National Heart, Lung, and Blood Institute (NHLBI) can search the Combined Health Information Database (CHID) and generate a bibliography of resources on Asbestosis for you. They also will send you any publications and journal articles they may have on hand, and will refer you to other organizations that are studying this disease. If you can't afford treatment, have your doctor call NHLBI to find out if they are conducting any clinical studies that you might qualify for.

☎ Contact:
National Heart, Lung and Blood Institute
Bldg. 31, Room 4A21
Bethesda, MD 20892
(301) 496-4236

The National Institute of Occupational Safety and Health (NIOSH) can provide you with information regarding Asbestosis. They can search their database for information regarding a particular work environment or health hazard. They can also send you research reports, journal articles, bibliographies and more on the topic of interest. They even have put together a publication of all their information on asbestos.

☎ Contact:
National Institute of Occupational
Safety and Health

4676 Columbia Parkway
MS C-19
Cincinnati, OH 45226
(800) 35-NIOSH

ASIATIC FLU

See Flu

ASPARAGINASE

Free Publications/Videos

The following publication is available from the National Cancer Institute, Bldg. 31, Room 10A24, Bethesda, MD 20892; (800) 4-CANCER, or (301) 496-5583.

- *Asparginasa/Asparaginase.* Provides information about side effects, proper usage, and precautions of this anti-cancer drug.

ASPARTAME

Clearinghouses/Hotlines

The National Institute of Neurological Disorders and Stroke (NINDS) can send you only information they have in their publications list on the Neurological Effects of Aspartame. They cannot refer you to any experts. This Clearinghouse cannot directly give you information about any current clinical studies NINDS might be conducting on this illness, but you can find this information for yourself by looking under the National Institute of Neurological Disorders and Stroke in *Appendix A* at the end of this book.

☎ Contact:
National Institute of Neurological
Disorders and Stroke
Building 31
Room 8A06

Bethesda, MD 20892
(301) 496-5751
(800) 352-9424

Free Publications/Videos

The following Congressional Research Service (CRS) reports on Aspartame are available from either of your U.S. Senators' offices at the U.S. Capitol, Washington, DC 20510, or from your Congressional Representative at the U.S. Capitol, Washington, DC 20515. You can also call in your request through the U.S. Capitol switchboard at (202) 224-3121. Be sure to include the full title and report number in your request.

- *Aspartame: An Artificial Sweetener.* (84-649 SPR)
- *Low-Calorie Sweeteners: Aspartame, Cyclamate, and Saccharin: Archived Issue Brief.* (IB85119)

ASPERGER'S SYNDROME

Clearinghouses/Hotlines

The National Institute of Neurological Disorders and Stroke (NINDS) can send you only information they have in their publications list on Asperger's Syndrome. They cannot refer you to any experts. This Clearinghouse cannot directly give you information about any current clinical studies NINDS might be conducting on this illness, but you can find this information for yourself by looking under the National Institute of Neurological Disorders and Stroke in *Appendix A* at the end of this book.

☎ Contact:
National Institute of Neurological
Disorders and Stroke
Building 31
Room 8A06
Bethesda, MD 20892
(301) 496-5751
(800) 352-9424

ASPERGILLOSIS

Clearinghouses/Hotlines

The National Institute on Allergy and Infectious Diseases (NIAID) can search the Combined Health Information Database (CHID) and generate a bibliography of resources on Aspergillosis for you. They will also send you any publications and journal articles they may have on hand, and will refer you to researchers who are currently studying this disease. If you can't afford treatment, have your doctor call NIAID to find out if they are conducting any clinical studies that you might qualify for.

☎ Contact:
National Institute of Allergy
and Infectious Diseases
Bldg. 31, Room 7A32
Bethesda, MD 20892
(301) 496-5717

ASPIRIN ALLERGY

Clearinghouses/Hotlines

The National Institute on Allergy and Infectious Diseases (NIAID) can search the Combined Health Information Database (CHID) and generate a bibliography of resources on Aspirin Allergy for you. They will also send you any publications and journal articles they may have on hand, and will refer you to researchers who are currently studying this condition. If you can't afford treatment, have your doctor call NIAID to find out if they are conducting any clinical studies that you might qualify for.

☎ Contact:
National Institute of Allergy
and Infectious Diseases
Bldg. 31, Room 7A32
Bethesda, MD 20892
(301) 496-5717

ASPHYXIA

Clearinghouses/Hotlines

The National Institute of Neurological Disorders and Stroke (NINDS) can send you only information they have in their publications list on Asphyxia. They cannot refer you to any experts. This Clearinghouse cannot directly give you information about any current clinical studies NINDS might be conducting on this condition, but you can find this information for yourself by looking under the National Institute of Neurological Disorders and Stroke in *Appendix A* at the end of this book.

☎ Contact:
National Institute of Neurological
Disorders and Stroke
Bldg. 31, Room 8A06
Bethesda, MD 20892
(301) 496-5751
(800) 352-9424

ASTHMA

Clearinghouses/Hotlines

The Asthma Clearinghouse will send you all kinds of publications, reports, resources, and refer you to experts on the diagnosis and therapy of asthma.

☎ Contact:
National Asthma Education Program
4733 Bethesda Ave., Suite 530
Bethesda, MD 20814
(301) 951-3260

The National Institute on Allergy and Infectious Diseases (NIAID) can search the Combined Health Information Database (CHID) and generate a bibliography of resources on Asthma for you. They will also send you any publications and journal articles they may have on hand, and will refer you to researchers who are currently studying this disease. If you can't afford treatment, have your doctor call NIAID to find out if they are conducting any clinical studies that you might qualify for.

☎ Contact:
National Institute of Allergy
and Infectious Diseases
Bldg. 31, Room 7A32
Bethesda, MD 20892
(301) 496-5717

The National Heart, Lung, and Blood Institute (NHLBI) can search the Combined Health Information Database (CHID) and generate a bibliography of resources on Asthma for you. They also will send you any publications and journal articles they may have on hand, and will refer you to other organizations that are studying this disease. If you can't afford treatment, have your doctor call NHLBI to find out if they are conducting any clinical studies that you might qualify for.

☎ Contact:
National Heart, Lung and Blood Institute
Bldg. 31, Room 4A21
Bethesda, MD 20892
(301) 496-4236

Free Publications/Videos

The following publications on Asthma are available from the National Heart, Lung and Blood Institute, Bldg. 31, Room 4A21, Bethesda, MD 20892; (301) 496-4236.

- *Air Power: Self-Management of Asthma Through Group Education.* (#85-2362)
- *Air Wise: Self-Management of Asthma Through Individual Education.* (#84-2363)
- *Check Your Asthma I.Q..* (#90-1128)
- *Facts About Asthma.* (#90-2339) Presents the basic facts about asthma and includes suggestions for avoiding and lessening asthma episodes.
- *Guidelines for Diagnosis and Management of Asthma.* (#91-3042)
- *Living With Asthma: Manual for Teaching Parents the Self-Management of Childhood Asthma.* (#87-2364)
- *Open Airways.* Designed for low-income, low-education families, offers seven sessions for inner-city children ages 4-12 and their parents. ($25)
- *Your Asthma Can Be Controlled: Expect Nothing Less.* (#91-2664)

The following publication on Asthma is available from the Science & Technology Division, Reference Section, Library of Congress, Washington, DC 20540; (202) 707-5580.

- *Allergy and Asthma.* Reference guide designed to help locate further published material. (#89-7)

The following publication on Asthma is available from the National Institute of Allergy and Infectious Diseases, Bldg. 31, Room 7A32, Bethesda, MD 20892; (301) 496-5717.

- *Asthma.* (#83-525)

The following video on Asthma is available from the Office of Clinical Center Communications, Bldg. 10, Room 1C255, Bethesda, MD 20892; (301) 496-2563.

- *Bronchial Asthma.* Video to help the general public make intelligent decisions.

The following publication on Asthma is available from the Food & Drug Administration, (HFE-88), 5600 Fishers Ln., Rockville, MD 20857; (301) 443-3170.

- *More Than Snuffles: Childhood Asthma.* (#FDA91-3181)

The following videos on Asthma are available from Modern Talking Picture Service, 5000 Park St. North, St. Petersburg, FL 33709; (800) 243-MTPS.

- *Asthma and Allergies in the School: The Importance of Cooperative Care.* Video of parents and teachers talking about managing asthmatic children in school.
- *A Regular Kid.* Video on how to manage childhood asthma.

ASTIGMATISM

Clearinghouses/Hotlines

The National Eye Institute (NEI) can give you up-to-date information on Astigmatisms by searching the Combined Health Information Database (CHID) and MEDLINE and sending you bibliographies of resources, along with any journal articles they may have. They can also refer you to any other organizations that study this and other related eye disorders. NEI will also let you know of any clinical studies that may be studying Astigmatism and looking for patients. Because of their small staff, NEI prefers that you submit your requests for information in writing.

☎ Contact:
National Eye Institute
Bldg. 31, Room 6A32
Bethesda, MD 20892
(301) 496-5248

ASYMMETRIC SEPTAL HYPERTROPHY

Clearinghouses/Hotlines

The National Heart, Lung, and Blood Institute (NHLBI) can search the Combined Health Information Database (CHID) and generate a bibliography of resources on Asymmetric Septal Hypertrophy (ASH) for you. They also will send you any publications and journal articles they may have on hand, and will refer you to other organizations that are studying this condition. If you can't afford treatment, have your doctor call NHLBI to find out if they are conducting any clinical studies that you might qualify for.

☎ Contact:
National Heart, Lung and Blood Institute
Bldg. 31, Room 4A21
Bethesda, MD 20892
(301) 496-4236

ATAXIA

Clearinghouses/Hotlines

The National Institute of Neurological Disorders and Stroke (NINDS) can send you only

information they have in their publications list on Ataxia. They cannot refer you to any experts. This Clearinghouse cannot directly give you information about any current clinical studies NINDS might be conducting on this illness, but you can find this information for yourself by looking under the National Institute of Neurological Disorders and Stroke in *Appendix A* at the end of this book.

☎ Contact:
National Institute of Neurological
Disorders and Stroke
Bldg. 31, Room 8A06
Bethesda, MD 20892
(301) 496-5751
(800) 352-9424

Free Publications/Videos

The following publication is available from the National Institute of Neurological Disorders and Stroke, Bldg. 31, Room 8A06, Bethesda, MD 20892; (301) 496-5751 or (800) 352-9424.

- *Friedreich's Ataxia*. (#82-87)

ATAXIA TELANGIECTASIA

Clearinghouses/Hotlines

The National Cancer Institute (NCI) will send you whatever publications and reprints of journal articles they have on Ataxia Telangiectasia. They can also give you information on the state-of-the-art treatment for this disease, including specific treatment information for your stage of cancer. They can also search their Physicians Data Query (PDQ) database to let you know if NCI is conducting any clinical studies on your disease.

☎ Contact:
National Cancer Institute
Bldg. 31, Room 10A24
Bethesda, MD 20892
(800) 4-CANCER
(301) 496-5583

ATELECTASIS

Clearinghouses/Hotlines

The National Heart, Lung, and Blood Institute (NHLBI) can search the Combined Health Information Database (CHID) and generate a bibliography of resources on Atelectasis for you. They also will send you any publications and journal articles they may have on hand, and will refer you to other organizations that are studying this disease. If you can't afford treatment, have your doctor call NHLBI to find out if they are conducting any clinical studies that you might qualify for.

☎ Contact:
National Heart, Lung and Blood Institute
Building 31
Room 4A21
Bethesda, MD 20892
(301) 496-4236

ATHERECTOMY

Clearinghouses/Hotlines

The National Heart, Lung, and Blood Institute (NHLBI) can search the Combined Health Information Database (CHID) and generate a bibliography of resources on Atherectomy for you. They also will send you any publications and journal articles they may have on hand, and will refer you to other organizations that are studying this disease. If you can't afford treatment, have your doctor call NHLBI to find out if they are conducting any clinical studies that you might qualify for.

☎ Contact:
National Heart, Lung and Blood Institute
Building 31
Room 4A21
Bethesda, MD 20892
(301) 496-4236

ATHEROSCLEROSIS

Clearinghouses/Hotlines

The National Institute of Child Health and Human Development (NICHD) will send you whatever publications and reprints of journal articles they have on Atherosclerosis. If necessary, they will refer you to other experts or researchers in the field. If you can't afford treatment, have your doctor call NICHD to find out if they are conducting any clinical studies that you might qualify for.

☎ Contact:
National Institute of Child Health
and Human Development
Bldg. 31, Room 2A32
Bethesda, MD 20892
(301) 496-5133

The National Heart, Lung, and Blood Institute (NHLBI) can search the Combined Health Information Database (CHID) and generate a bibliography of resources on Atherosclerosis for you. They also will send you any publications and journal articles they may have on hand, and will refer you to other organizations that are studying this disease. If you can't afford treatment, have your doctor call NHLBI to find out if they are conducting any clinical studies that you might qualify for.

☎ Contact:
National Heart, Lung and Blood Institute
Bldg. 31, Room 4A21
Bethesda, MD 20892
(301) 496-4236

The National Institute of Neurological Disorders and Stroke (NINDS) can send you only information they have in their publications list on Cerebral Atherosclerosis. They cannot refer you to any experts. This Clearinghouse cannot directly give you information about any current clinical studies NINDS might be conducting on this illness, but you can find this information for yourself by looking under the National Institute of Neurological Disorders and Stroke in *Appendix A* at the end of this book.

☎ Contact:
National Institute of Neurological
Disorders and Stroke
Bldg. 31, Room 8A06
Bethesda, MD 20892
(301) 496-5751
(800) 352-9424

The National Eye Institute (NEI) can give you up-to-date information on the Effect on Vision of Atherosclerosis by searching the Combined Health Information Database (CHID) and MEDLINE and sending you bibliographies of resources, along with any journal articles they may have. They can also refer you to any other organizations that study this and other related diseases. NEI will also let you know of any clinical studies that may be studying this disease and looking for patients. Because of their small staff, NEI prefers that you submit your requests for information in writing.

☎ Contact:
National Eye Institute
Bldg. 31, Room 6A32
Bethesda, MD 20892
(301) 496-5248

ATHETOSIS

Clearinghouses/Hotlines

The National Institute of Neurological Disorders and Stroke (NINDS) can send you only information they have in their publications list on Athetosis. They cannot refer you to any experts. This Clearinghouse cannot directly give you information about any current clinical studies NINDS might be conducting on this illness, but you can find this information for yourself by looking under the National Institute of Neurological Disorders and Stroke in *Appendix A* at the end of this book.

☎ Contact:
National Institute of Neurological
Disorders and Stroke
Bldg. 31, Room 8A06
Bethesda, MD 20892
(301) 496-5751
(800) 352-9424

ATHLETE'S FOOT

See Fungal Infections

ATOPIC DERMATITIS

Clearinghouses/Hotlines

The National Institute of Arthritis and Musculoskeletal and Skin Diseases (NIAMS) will send you whatever publications and reprints of articles from texts and journals they have on Atopic Dermatitis. They will also refer you to other organizations that are studying this disease. NIAMS will also let you know of any clinical studies that may be studying this disease and looking for patients.

☎ Contact:
National Institute of Arthritis
and Musculoskeletal and Skin Diseases
Box AMS
9000 Rockville Pike
Bethesda, MD 20892
(301) 495-4484

The National Institute on Allergy and Infectious Diseases (NIAID) can search the Combined Health Information Database (CHID) and generate a bibliography of resources on Atopic Dermatitis for you. They will also send you any publications and journal articles they may have on hand, and will refer you to researchers who are currently studying this disease. If you can't afford treatment, have your doctor call NIAID to find out if they are conducting any clinical studies that you might qualify for.

☎ Contact:
National Institute of Allergy
and Infectious Diseases
Building 31
Room 7A32
Bethesda, MD 20892
(301) 496-5717

ATRIAL FIBRILLATION

Clearinghouses/Hotlines

The National Heart, Lung, and Blood Institute (NHLBI) can search the Combined Health Information Database (CHID) and generate a bibliography of resources on Atrial Fibrillation for you. They also will send you any publications and journal articles they may have on hand, and will refer you to other organizations that are studying this disease. If you can't afford treatment, have your doctor call NHLBI to find out if they are conducting any clinical studies that you might qualify for.

☎ Contact:
National Heart, Lung and Blood Institute
Bldg. 31, Room 4A21
Bethesda, MD 20892
(301) 496-4236

ATTENTION DEFICIT DISORDER

Clearinghouses/Hotlines

The National Institute of Neurological Disorders and Stroke (NINDS) can send you only information they have in their publications list on Attention Deficit Disorder. They cannot refer you to any experts. This Clearinghouse cannot directly give you information about any current clinical studies NINDS might be conducting on this illness, but you can find this information for yourself by looking under the National Institute of Neurological Disorders and Stroke in *Appendix A* at the end of this book.

☎ Contact:
National Institute of Neurological
Disorders and Stroke
Bldg. 31, Room 8A06
Bethesda, MD 20892
(301) 496-5751
(800) 352-9424

The National Institute of Child Health and Human Development (NICHD) will send you whatever publications and reprints of journal articles they have on Attention Deficit Disorder. If necessary, they will refer you to other experts or researchers in the field. If you can't afford treatment, have your doctor call NICHD to find out if they are conducting any clinical studies that you might qualify for.

☎ Contact:
National Institute of Child Health
and Human Development
Bldg. 31, Room 2A32
Bethesda, MD 20892
(301) 496-5133

The National Institute of Mental Health (NIMH) will send you whatever publications and reprints of articles from texts and journals they have on Attention Deficit Disorder. They will also refer you to other organizations that are studying this condition. NIMH will also let you know of any clinical studies that may be studying ADD and looking for patients.

☎ Contact:
National Institute of Mental Health
5600 Fishers Ln., Room 15C05
Rockville, MD 20857
(301) 443-4515

Free Publications/Videos

The following publication is available from the National Institute of Neurological Disorders and Stroke, P.O. Box 5801, Bethesda, MD 20824; (800) 352-9424, or (301) 496-5751.

- *Attention Deficit Disorder*. Contains a collection of scientific articles, patient education pamphlets, and addresses of voluntary health associations.

AUTISM

Clearinghouses/Hotlines

The National Institute of Child Health and Human

Development (NICHD) will send you whatever publications and reprints of journal articles they have on Autism. If necessary, they will refer you to other experts or researchers in the field. If you can't afford treatment, have your doctor call NICHD to find out if they are conducting any clinical studies that you might qualify for.

☎ Contact:
National Institute of Child Health
and Human Development
Bldg. 31, Room 2A32
Bethesda, MD 20892
(301) 496-5133

The National Institute of Mental Health will send you whatever publications and reprints of articles from texts and journals they have on Autism. They will also refer you to other organizations that are studying this disease. NIMH will also let you know of any clinical studies that may be studying this disease and looking for patients.

☎ Contact:
National Institute of Mental Health
5600 Fishers Ln., Room 15C05
Rockville, MD 20857
(301) 443-4515

Free Publications/Videos

The following publications on Autism are available from the National Institute of Neurological Disorders and Stroke, P.O. Box 5801, Bethesda, MD 20824; (800) 352-9424, or (301) 496-5751.

- *Autism.* Contains a collection of scientific articles, patient education pamphlets, and addresses of voluntary health associations.
- *Autismo/Autism.* (#81-2282)

AUTOIMMUNE DISEASE

Clearinghouses/Hotlines

The National Institute of Arthritis and Musculo-skeletal and Skin Diseases (NIAMS) will send you whatever publications and reprints of articles from texts and journals they have on Autoimmune

Disease. They will also refer you to other organizations that are studying this disease. NIAMS will also let you know of any clinical studies that may be studying this disease and looking for patients.

☎ Contact:
National Institute of Arthritis
and Musculoskeletal and Skin Diseases
Box AMS
Bethesda, MD 20892
(301) 495-4484

AUTOSOMAL DOMINANT DISEASE

See Huntington's Chorea

- B -

B-19 INFECTION

Clearinghouses/Hotlines

The National Institute of Child Health and Human Development (NICHD) will send you whatever publications and reprints of journal articles they have on B-19 Infection (Human Parvovirus). If necessary, they will refer you to other experts or researchers in the field. If you can't afford treatment, have your doctor call NICHD to find out if they are conducting any clinical studies that you might qualify for.

☎ Contact:
National Institute of Child Health
and Human Development
Bldg. 31, Room 2A32
Bethesda, MD 20892
(301) 496-5133

BABY BOTTLE TOOTH DECAY

Clearinghouses/Hotlines

The National Institute of Dental Research (NIDR) will send you whatever publications and reprints of journal articles they have on Baby Bottle Tooth Decay. As a policy, NIDR will not refer you to other organizations or experts who study this issue. If you can't afford treatment, have your doctor call Dr. Albert Guckers at (301) 496-6241 to find out if NIDR is conducting any clinical studies that you might qualify for.

☎ Contact:
National Institute of Dental Research
Bldg. 31, Room 2C35
Bethesda, MD 20892
(301) 496-4261

BACILLUS CALMETTE-GUERIN (BCG)

Clearinghouses/Hotlines

The National Cancer Institute (NCI) will send you whatever publications and reprints of journal articles they have on BCG (Bacillus Calmette-Guerin). They can also give you information on the state-of-the-art treatment for this disease, including specific treatment information for your stage of cancer. They can also search their Physician's Data Query (PDQ) database to let you know if NCI is conducting any clinical studies on your disease.

☎ Contact:
National Cancer Institute
Bldg. 31, Room 10A24
Bethesda, MD 20892
(800) 4-CANCER
(301) 496-5583

The National Institute on Allergy and Infectious Diseases (NIAID) can search the Combined Health Information Database (CHID) and generate a bibliography of resources on BCG (Bacillus Calmette-Guerin) for you. They will also send you any publications and journal articles they may have on hand, and will refer you to researchers who are currently studying this disease. If you can't afford treatment, have your doctor call NIAID to find out if they are conducting any clinical studies that you might qualify for.

☎ Contact:
National Institute of Allergy
and Infectious Diseases
Bldg. 31, Room 7A32
Bethesda, MD 20892
(301) 496-5717

BACK PROBLEMS

Clearinghouses/Hotlines

The National Institute of Arthritis and Musculoskeletal and Skin Diseases (NIAMS) will send you whatever publications and reprints of articles from texts and journals they have on Back Problems. They will also refer you to other organizations that are studying this condition. NIAMS will also let you know of any clinical studies that may be studying Back Problems and looking for patients.

☎ Contact:
National Institute of Arthritis
and Musculoskeletal and Skin Diseases
Box AMS
9000 Rockville Pike
Bethesda, MD 20892
(301) 495-4484

The National Institute of Neurological Disorders and Stroke (NINDS) can send you only information they have in their publications list on Back Problems. They cannot refer you to any experts. This Clearinghouse cannot directly give you information about any current clinical studies NINDS might be conducting on this illness, but you can find this information for yourself by looking under the National Institute of Neurological Disorders and Stroke in *Appendix A* at the end of this book.

☎ Contact:
National Institute of Neurological
Disorders and Stroke
Bldg. 31, Room 8A06
Bethesda, MD 20892
(301) 496-5751
(800) 352-9424

Free Publications/Videos

The following publication on Back Pain is available from the National Institute of Neurological Disorders and Stroke, P.O. Box 5801, Bethesda, MD 20824; (800) 352-9424, or (301) 496-5751.

- *Back Pain.* Contains a collection of scientific articles, patient education pamphlets, and addresses of voluntary health associations.

The following publication on Back Pain is available from the National Arthritis and Musculoskeletal and Skin Diseases Information Clearinghouse, Box AMS, 9000 Rockville Pike, Bethesda, MD 20892; (301) 495-4484.

- *Synopsis: Workshop on Idiopathic Low-Back Pain.* (#AR16)

The following publications on Back Pain are available from the Food & Drug Administration, (HFE-88), 5600 Fishers Ln., Rockville, MD 20857; (301) 443-3170.

- *When The Spine Curves* (#FDA85-4198)
- *Back Talk: Advice for Suffering Spines.* (#FDA90-1155)

BACTERIAL MENINGITIS

Clearinghouses/Hotlines

The National Institute on Allergy and Infectious Diseases (NIAID) can search the Combined Health Information Database (CHID) and generate a bibliography of resources on Bacterial Meningitis for you. They will also send you any publications and journal articles they may have on

hand, and will refer you to researchers who are currently studying this disease. If you can't afford treatment, have your doctor call NIAID to find out if they are conducting any clinical studies that you might qualify for.

☎ Contact:
National Institute of Allergy
and Infectious Diseases
Building 31
Room 7A32
Bethesda, MD 20892
(301) 496-5717

The National Institute of Neurological Disorders and Stroke (NINDS) can send you only information they have in their publications list on Bacterial Meningitis. They cannot refer you to any experts. This Clearinghouse cannot directly give you information about any current clinical studies NINDS might be conducting on this illness, but you can find this information for yourself by looking under the National Institute of Neurological Disorders and Stroke in *Appendix A* at the end of this book.

☎ Contact:
National Institute of Neurological
Disorders and Stroke
Building 31
Room 8A06
Bethesda, MD 20892
(301) 496-5751
(800) 352-9424

The National Institute on Deafness and Other Communicative Disorders (NIDCD) will send you whatever publications and reprints of journal articles they have on Bacterial Meningitis. If you need further information, they will refer you to other organizations that study this and other related diseases. NIDCD does not conduct any clinical studies for this or any other disorder.

☎ Contact:
National Institute on Deafness
and Other Communication Disorders
Bldg. 31, Room 3C35
Bethesda, MD 20892
(301) 496-7243
(800) 241-1044
(301) 402-0252 (TDD)

BACTERIOLOGY

Clearinghouses/Hotlines

The National Institute on Allergy and Infectious Diseases (NIAID) can search the Combined Health Information Database (CHID) and generate a bibliography of resources on Bacteriology for you. They will also send you any publications and journal articles they may have on hand, and will refer you to researchers who are currently studying this issue.

☎ Contact:
National Institute of Allergy
and Infectious Diseases
Bldg. 31, Room 7A32
Bethesda, MD 20892
(301) 496-5717

BAD BREATH

See Halitosis

BAGASSOSIS

Clearinghouses/Hotlines

The National Institute of Occupational Safety and Health (NIOSH) can provide you with information regarding Bagassosis, which is a lung disease caused by inhaling sugarcane dust. NIOSH can search their data base and provide you with reprints of articles, reference materials, and more.

☎ Contact:
National Institute of Occupational
Safety and Health
4676 Columbia Parkway
MS C-19
Cincinnati, OH 45226
(800) 35-NIOSH

BARLOW'S SYNDROME

Clearinghouses/Hotlines

The National Heart, Lung, and Blood Institute (NHLBI) can search the Combined Health Information Database (CHID) and generate a bibliography of resources on Barlow's Syndrome (Mitral Valve Prolapse) for you. They also will send you any publications and journal articles they may have on hand, and will refer you to other organizations that are studying this disease. If you can't afford treatment, have your doctor call NHLBI to find out if they are conducting any clinical studies that you might qualify for.

☎ Contact:
National Heart, Lung, and Blood Institute
Building 31
Room 4A21
Bethesda, MD 20892
(301) 496-4236

BARTTER'S SYNDROME

Clearinghouses/Hotlines

The National Heart, Lung, and Blood Institute (NHLBI) can search the Combined Health Information Database (CHID) and generate a bibliography of resources on Bartter's Syndrome (Juxtaglomerular Hyperplasia) for you. They also will send you any publications and journal articles they may have on hand, and will refer you to other organizations that are studying this disease. If you can't afford treatment, have your doctor call NHLBI to find out if they are conducting any clinical studies that you might qualify for.

☎ Contact:
National Heart, Lung, and Blood Institute
Building 31
Room 4A21
Bethesda, MD 20892
(301) 496-4236

BASAL CELL CARCINOMA

Clearinghouses/Hotlines

The National Cancer Institute (NCI) will send you whatever publications and reprints of journal articles they have on Basal Cell Carcinoma. They can also give you information on the state-of-the-art treatment for this disease, including specific treatment information for your stage of cancer. They can also search their Physician's Data Query (PDQ) database to let you know if NCI is conducting any clinical studies on your disease.

☎ Contact:
National Cancer Institute
Bldg. 31, Room 10A24
Bethesda, MD 20892
(800) 4-CANCER
(301) 496-5583

BATTEN'S DISEASE

Clearinghouses/Hotlines

The National Institute of Neurological Disorders and Stroke (NINDS) can send you only information they have in their publications list on Batten's Disease. They cannot refer you to any experts. This Clearinghouse cannot directly give you information about any current clinical studies NINDS might be conducting on this illness, but you can find this information for yourself by looking under the National Institute of Neurological Disorders and Stroke in *Appendix A* at the end of this book.

☎ Contact:
National Institute of Neurological
Disorders and Stroke
Bldg. 31, Room 8A06
Bethesda, MD 20892
(301) 496-5751
(800) 352-9424

Free Publications/Videos

The following publications are available from the

National Institute of Neurological Disorders and Stroke, P.O. Box 5801, Bethesda, MD 20824; (800) 352-9424, or (301) 496-5751.

- *Batten Disease*. Fact sheet on symptoms and treatment.
- *Batten Disease*. Contains a collection of scientific articles, patient education pamphlets, and addresses of voluntary health associations.

BATTERED CHILD

See Child Abuse

BATTERED ELDERLY

See Aging
See Elder Abuse

BATTERED SPOUSES

Clearinghouses/Hotlines

The National Institute of Mental Health (NIMH) will send you whatever publications and reprints of articles from texts and journals they have on Battered Spouses. They will also refer you to other organizations that are studying this issue. NIMH will also let you know of any clinical studies that may be studying this issue and looking for patients.

☎ Contact:
National Institute of Mental Health
5600 Fishers Ln., Room 15C05
Rockville, MD 20857
(301) 443-4515

The Clearinghouse on Family Violence Information can provide you with information on Spouse and Elder Abuse. They have brochures, bibliographies, reports, and audiovisual materials available, and an in-house data base from which they can retrieve reference materials and organizations involved with family violence.

☎ Contact:
Clearinghouse on Family Violence Information
P.O. Box 1182
Washington, DC 20013
(703) 385-7565

Free Publications/Videos

This Congressional Research Service (CRS) report on Battered Spouses is available from either of your U.S. Senators' offices at the U.S. Capitol, Washington, DC 20510, or from your Congressional Representative at the U.S. Capitol, Washington, DC 20515. You can also call in your request through the U.S. Capitol switchboard at (202) 224-3121. Be sure to include the full title and report number in your request.

- *Spouse Abuse: Background and Federal
    Programs to Address the Problem.*
    (#86-1035 EPW)

BED WETTING

Clearinghouses/Hotlines

The National Institute of Child Health and Human Development (NICHD) will send you whatever publications and reprints of journal articles they have on Bed Wetting. If necessary, they will refer you to other experts or researchers in the field. If you can't afford treatment, have your doctor call NICHD to find out if they are conducting any clinical studies that you might qualify for.

☎ Contact:
National Institute of Child Health
and Human Development
Bldg. 31, Room 2A32
Bethesda, MD 20892
(301) 496-5133

The National Institute of Mental Health (NIMH) will send you whatever publications and reprints of articles from texts and journals they have on Bed Wetting. They will also refer you to other

organizations that are studying this issue. NIMH will also let you know of any clinical studies that may be studying this issue and looking for patients.

☎ Contact:
National Institute of Mental Health
5600 Fishers Ln., Room 15C05
Rockville, MD 20857
(301) 443-4515

BEDSONIA

Clearinghouses/Hotlines

The National Institute of Diabetes and Digestive and Kidney Diseases's (NIDDK) individual clearinghouses can search the Combined Health Information Database (CHID) and generate a bibliography of resources on Bedsonia for you. They also will send you any publications and journal articles they may have on hand, and will refer you to other organizations that are studying this disorder. If you can't afford treatment, have your doctor call NIDDK to find out if they are conducting any clinical studies that you might qualify for.

☎ Contact:
National Institute of Diabetes
and Digestive and Kidney Diseases
Bldg. 31, Room 9A04
Bethesda, MD 20892
(301) 496-3583

BEHAVIOR AND HEALTH

Clearinghouses/Hotlines

The National Institute of Child Health and Human Development (NICHD) will send you whatever publications and reprints of journal articles they have on Behavioral and Social Sciences. If necessary, they will refer you to other experts or researchers in the field. If you can't afford treatment, have your doctor call NICHD to find out if they are conducting any clinical studies that you might qualify for.

☎ Contact:
National Institute of Child Health
and Human Development
Bldg. 31, Room 2A32
Bethesda, MD 20892
(301) 496-5133

Free Publications/Videos

The following publication on Behavior and Health is available from the National Institutes of Health Clinical Center, Bldg. 10, Room 1C255, Bethesda, MD 20892; (301) 496-2563.

- *Behavior Patterns and Health.* (#85-2682)

BEHAVIOR DEVELOPMENT

Clearinghouses/Hotlines

The Human Learning and Behavior Branch at the National Institutes of Health studies the development of human behavior, from infancy, through childhood and adolescence, into early maturity. Studies are supported in developmental psychobiology, behavioral pediatrics, cognitive and communicative processes, social and affective development, and health related behaviors, as well as learning disabilities, dyslexia and language disorders. They can give you information about current research and reprints of journal articles.
☎ Contact:
National Institute of Child Health
and Human Development
Human Learning and Behavior Branch
National Institutes of Health
Bethesda, MD 20892
(301) 496-6591

BEHAVIOR MODIFICATION

Free Publications/Videos

The following Congressional Research Service (CRS) report is available from either of your U.S.

Senators' offices at the U.S. Capitol, Washington, DC 20510, or from your Congressional Representative at the U.S. Capitol, Washington, DC 20515. You can also call in your request through the U.S. Capitol switchboard at (202) 224-3121. Be sure to include the full title and report number in your request.

- *Constitutional and Statutory Issues Relating to the Use of Behavior Modification on Children in Institutions.* (#86-100 A)

BEHCET'S DISEASE

Clearinghouses/Hotlines

The National Eye Institute (NEI) can give you up-to-date information on Behcet's Disease of the Eyes by searching the Combined Health Information Database (CHID) and MEDLINE and sending you bibliographies of resources, along with any journal articles they may have. They can also refer you to any other organizations that study this and other related diseases. NEI will also let you know of any clinical studies that may be studying Behcet's and looking for patients. Because of their small staff, NEI prefers that you submit your requests for information in writing.
☎ Contact:
National Eye Institute
Bldg. 31, Room 6A32
Bethesda, MD 20892
(301) 496-5248

The National Institute of Dental Research (NIDR) will send you whatever publications and reprints of journal articles they have on Systemic Behcet's Disease. As a policy, NIDR will not refer you to other organizations or experts who study this disease. If you can't afford treatment, have your doctor call Dr. Albert Guckers at (301) 496-6241 to find out if NIDR is conducting any clinical studies that you might qualify for.
☎ Contact:
National Institute of Dental Research
Bldg. 31, Room 2C35
Bethesda, MD 20892
(301) 496-4261

The National Institute of Arthritis and Musculo-skeletal and Skin Diseases (NIAMS) will send you whatever publications and reprints of articles from texts and journals they have on Systemic Behcet's Disease. They will also refer you to other organizations that are studying this disease. NIAMS will also let you know of any clinical studies that may be studying this disease and looking for patients.

☎ Contact:
National Institute of Arthritis
and Musculoskeletal and Skin Diseases
Box AMS
Bethesda, MD 20892
(301) 495-4484

The National Institute of Neurological Disorders and Stroke (NINDS) can send you only information they have in their publications list on Neurological Effects of Behcet's Syndrome. They cannot refer you to any experts. This Clearinghouse cannot directly give you information about any current clinical studies NINDS might be conducting on this illness, but you can find this information for yourself by looking under the National Institute of Neurological Disorders and Stroke in *Appendix A* at the end of this book.

☎ Contact:
National Institute of Neurological
Disorders and Stroke
Bldg. 31, Room 8A06
Bethesda, MD 20892
(301) 496-5751
(800) 352-9424

BEJEL

Clearinghouses/Hotlines

The Sexually Transmitted Diseases Hotline offers valuable information to the public about a wide range of sexually transmitted diseases, including Bejel and how to protect yourself from contracting them.

☎ Contact:
National Sexually Transmitted Diseases Hotline
P.O. Box 13827
Research Triangle Park, NC 27709
(800) 227-8922

BELL'S PALSY

Clearinghouses/Hotlines

The National Institute of Neurological Disorders and Stroke (NINDS) can send you only information they have in their publications list on Bell's Palsy. They cannot refer you to any experts. This Clearinghouse cannot directly give you information about any current clinical studies NINDS might be conducting on this illness, but you can find this information for yourself by looking under the National Institute of Neurological Disorders and Stroke in *Appendix A* at the end of this book.

☎ Contact:
National Institute of Neurological
Disorders and Stroke
Bldg. 31, Room 8A06
Bethesda, MD 20892
(301) 496-5751
(800) 352-9424

Free Publications/Videos

The following publication is available from the National Institute of Neurological Disorders and Stroke, P.O. Box 5801, Bethesda, MD 20824; (800) 352-9424, or (301) 496-5751.

- *Bell's Palsy*. Contains a collection of scientific articles, patient education pamphlets, and addresses of voluntary health associations.

BENIGN CONGENITAL HYPOTONIA

Clearinghouses/Hotlines

The National Institute of Neurological Disorders and Stroke (NINDS) can send you only information they have in their publications list on Benign Congenital Hypotonia. They cannot refer you to any experts. This Clearinghouse cannot directly give you information about any current clinical studies NINDS might be conducting on this illness, but you can find this information for yourself by looking under the National Institute of Neurological Disorders and Stroke in *Appendix A* at the end of this book.

☎ Contact:
National Institute of Neurological
Disorders and Stroke
Bldg. 31, Room 8A06
Bethesda, MD 20892
(301) 496-5751
(800) 352-9424

BENIGN MUCOSAL PEMPHIGOID

Clearinghouses/Hotlines

The National Cancer Institute (NCI) will send you whatever publications and reprints of journal articles they have on Benign Mucosal Pemphigoid. They can also give you information on the state-of-the-art treatment for this disease, including specific treatment information for your stage of cancer. They can also search their Physician's Data Query (PDQ) database to let you know if NCI is conducting any clinical studies on your disease.

☎ Contact:
National Cancer Institute
Bldg. 31, Room 10A24
Bethesda, MD 20892
(800) 4-CANCER
(301) 496-5583

The National Institute of Arthritis and Musculoskeletal and Skin Diseases (NIAMS) will send you whatever publications and reprints of articles from texts and journals they have on Benign Mucosal Pemphigoid. They will also refer you to other organizations that are studying this disease. NIAMS will also let you know of any clinical studies that may be studying this disease and looking for patients.

☎ Contact:
National Institute of Arthritis
and Musculoskeletal and Skin Diseases
Box AMS

Bethesda, MD 20892
(301) 495-4484

BENIGN PROSTATIC HYPERPLASIA

Clearinghouses/Hotlines

The National Institute of Diabetes and Digestive and Kidney Diseases's (NIDDK) individual clearinghouses can search the Combined Health Information Database (CHID) and generate a bibliography of resources on Benign Prostatic Hyperplasia for you. They also will send you any publications and journal articles they may have on hand, and will refer you to other organizations that are studying this disease. If you can't afford treatment, have your doctor call NIDDK to find out if they are conducting any clinical studies that you might qualify for.

☎ Contact:
National Institute of Diabetes
and Digestive and Kidney Diseases
Bldg. 31, Room 9A04
Bethesda, MD 20892
(301) 496-3583

BENZO(A)PYRENE

Clearinghouses/Hotlines

The National Cancer Institute (NCI) will send you whatever publications and reprints of journal articles they have on Benzo(a)pyrene. They can also search their Physician's Data Query (PDQ) database to let you know if NCI is conducting any clinical studies on your disease.

☎ Contact:
National Cancer Institute
Bldg. 31, Room 10A24
Bethesda, MD 20892
(800) 4-CANCER
(301) 496-5583

BERGER'S DISEASE

Clearinghouses/Hotlines

The National Institute of Diabetes and Digestive and Kidney Diseases's (NIDDK) individual clearinghouses can search the Combined Health Information Database (CHID) and generate a bibliography of resources on Berger's Disease for you. They also will send you any publications and journal articles they may have on hand, and will refer you to other organizations that are studying this disease. If you can't afford treatment, have your doctor call NIDDK to find out if they are conducting any clinical studies that you might qualify for.

☎ Contact:
National Institute of Diabetes
and Digestive and Kidney Diseases
Bldg. 31, Room 9A04
Bethesda, MD 20892
(301) 496-3583

BERIBERI

Clearinghouses/Hotlines

The National Institute of Diabetes and Digestive and Kidney Diseases's (NIDDK) individual clearinghouses can search the Combined Health Information Database (CHID) and generate a bibliography of resources on Nutritional Beriberi for you. They also will send you any publications and journal articles they may have on hand, and will refer you to other organizations that are studying this disease. If you can't afford treatment, have your doctor call NIDDK to find out if they are conducting any clinical studies that you might qualify for.

☎ Contact:
National Institute of Diabetes
and Digestive and Kidney Diseases
Bldg. 31, Room 9A04
Bethesda, MD 20892
(301) 496-3583

The National Institute of Neurological Disorders and Stroke (NINDS) can send you only information they have in their publications list on Neurological Beriberi. They cannot refer you to any experts. This Clearinghouse cannot directly give you information about any current clinical studies NINDS might be conducting on this illness, but you can find this information for yourself by looking under the National Institute of Neurological Disorders and Stroke in *Appendix A* at the end of this book.

☎ Contact:
National Institute of Neurological
Disorders and Stroke
Building 31
Room 8A06
Bethesda, MD 20892
(301) 496-5751
(800) 352-9424

BERNARD-SOULIER SYNDROME

Clearinghouses/Hotlines

The National Institute of Diabetes and Digestive and Kidney Diseases's (NIDDK) individual clearinghouses can search the Combined Health Information Database (CHID) and generate a bibliography of resources on Bernard-Soulier Syndrome for you. They also will send you any publications and journal articles they may have on hand, and will refer you to other organizations that are studying this disease. If you can't afford treatment, have your doctor call NIDDK to find out if they are conducting any clinical studies that you might qualify for.

☎ Contact:
National Institute of Diabetes
and Digestive and Kidney Diseases
Building 31
Room 9A04
Bethesda, MD 20892
(301) 496-3583

BETA BLOCKER DRUGS

Free Publications/Videos

The following publication is available from the Food & Drug Administration, (HFE-88), 5600 Fishers Ln., Rockville, MD 20857; (301) 443-3170.

- *How To Take Your Medicines: Beta Blocker Drugs*. (FDA91-3183)

BETA-THALASSEMIA

Clearinghouses/Hotlines

The National Heart, Lung, and Blood Institute (NHLBI) can search the Combined Health Information Database (CHID) and generate a bibliography of resources on Beta-thalassemia (Cooley's Anemia) for you. They also will send you any publications and journal articles they may have on hand, and will refer you to other organizations that are studying this disorder. If you can't afford treatment, have your doctor call NHLBI to find out if they are conducting any clinical studies that you might qualify for.
☎ Contact:
National Heart, Lung, and Blood Institute
Bldg. 31, Room 4A21
Bethesda, MD 20892
(301) 496-4236

BILIARY CIRRHOSIS

Clearinghouses/Hotlines

The National Institute of Diabetes and Digestive and Kidney Diseases's (NIDDK) individual clearinghouses can search the Combined Health Information Database (CHID) and generate a bibliography of resource on Biliary Cirrhosis for you. They also will send you any publications and journal articles they may have on hand, and will

refer you to other organizations that are studying this disease. If you can't afford treatment, have your doctor call NIDDK to find out if they are conducting any clinical studies that you might qualify for.
☎ Contact:
National Institute of Diabetes
and Digestive and Kidney Diseases
Bldg. 31, Room 9A04
Bethesda, MD 20892
(301) 496-3583

BILIRUBINEMIA

Clearinghouses/Hotlines

The National Institute of Child Health and Human Development (NICHD) will send you whatever publications and reprints of journal articles they have on Bilirubinemia. If necessary, they will refer you to other experts or researchers in the field. If you can't afford treatment, have your doctor call NICHD to find out if they are conducting any clinical studies that you might qualify for.
☎ Contact:
National Institute of Child Health
and Human Development
Bldg. 31, Room 2A32
Bethesda, MD 20892
(301) 496-5133

BINOCULAR VISION

Clearinghouses/Hotlines

The National Eye Institute (NEI) can give you up-to-date information on Binocular Vision by searching the Combined Health Information Database (CHID) and MEDLINE and sending you bibliographies of resources, along with any journal articles they may have. They can also refer you to any other organizations that study this and other related issues. NEI will also let you know of any clinical studies that may be studying Binocular Vision and looking for patients.

Because of their small staff, NEI prefers that you submit your requests for information in writing.

☎ Contact:
National Eye Institute
Building 31
Room 6A32
Bethesda, MD 20892
(301) 496-5248

BINSWANGER'S DISEASE

Clearinghouses/Hotlines

The National Institute of Neurological Disorders and Stroke (NINDS) can send you only information they have in their publications list on Binswanger's Disease. They cannot refer you to any experts. This Clearinghouse cannot directly give you information about any current clinical studies NINDS might be conducting on this illness, but you can find this information for yourself by looking under the National Institute of Neurological Disorders and Stroke in *Appendix A* at the end of this book.

☎ Contact:
National Institute of Neurological
Disorders and Stroke
Building 31
Room 8A06
Bethesda, MD 20892
(301) 496-5751
(800) 352-9424

Free Publications/Videos

The following publication on Binswanger's Disease is available from the National Institute of Neurological Disorders and Stroke, P.O. Box 5801, Bethesda, MD 20824; (800) 352-9424, or (301) 496-5751.

- *Binswanger's Disease*. Contains a collection of scientific articles, patient education pamphlets, and addresses of voluntary health associations.

BIOFEEDBACK

Clearinghouses/Hotlines

The National Institute of Mental Health (NIMH) will send you whatever publications and reprints of articles from texts and journals they have on Biofeedback. They will also refer you to other organizations that are studying this issue. NIMH will also let you know of any clinical studies that may be studying biofeedback and looking for patients.

☎ Contact:
National Institute of Mental Health
5600 Fishers Lane
Room 15C05
Rockville, MD 20857
(301) 443-4515

The National Heart, Lung, and Blood Institute (NHLBI) can search the Combined Health Information Database (CHID) and generate a bibliography of resources on Biofeedback for you. They also will send you any publications and journal articles they may have on hand, and will refer you to other organizations that are studying this issue. If you can't afford treatment, have your doctor call NHLBI to find out if they are conducting any clinical studies that you might qualify for.

☎ Contact:
National Heart, Lung, and Blood Institute
Building 31
Room 4A21
Bethesda, MD 20892
(301) 496-4236

Free Publications/Videos

The following publication is available from the Science & Technology Division, Reference Section, Library of Congress, Washington, DC 20540; (202) 707-5580.

- *Biofeedback*. Reference guide designed to help locate further published material. (#83-1)

BIOMEDICAL ENGINEERING

Clearinghouses/Hotlines

The National Institute of General Medical Sciences will send you whatever information they have on Biomedical Engineering. If necessary they can also refer you to a specific researcher in this area for more information.

☎ Contact:
National Institute of General Medical Sciences
Bldg. 31, Room 4A52
Bethesda, MD 20892
(301) 496-7301

BIOMEDICAL RESEARCH

Free Publications/Videos

The following publication is available from the Office of Science and Health Reports, National Center for Research Resources, National Institutes of Health, Bethesda, MD 20892; (301) 496-5545.

- *NCRR Biomedical Research Technology Resources Directory*. Lists resource center, staffs, resources, and major areas of investigation.

The following publication is available from the Research Resources Information Center, 1601 Research Blvd., Rockville, MD 20850; (301) 984-2870.

- *Biomedical Research Technology Resources*. Lists all the current biomedical research projects funded through National Institutes of Health and the services available to other researchers.

The following publications are available from the National Center for Research Resources, Westwood Bldg., Room 10A15, Bethesda, MD 20892; (301) 496-5545.

- *Biomedical Research Technology*. (#90-1430)

- *Resources for Comparative Biomedical Research*. (#89-1431)

BIOPHYSICS

Clearinghouses/Hotlines

The National Institute of General Medical Sciences can tell you about on-going Biophysics research projects they're funding and will refer you to the researcher in charge of a particular project.

☎ Contact:
National Institutes of Health
Building 31, Room 4A52
Bethesda, MD 20892
(301) 496-7301

BIOPSIES

Clearinghouses/Hotlines

The National Cancer Institute (NCI) will send you whatever publications and reprints of journal articles they have on Biopsies. They can also search their Physician's Data Query (PDQ) database to let you know if NCI is conducting any clinical studies on your disease.

☎ Contact:
National Cancer Institute
Bldg. 31, Room 10A24
Bethesda, MD 20892
(800) 4-CANCER
(301) 496-5583

BIOTECHNOLOGY

Clearinghouses/Hotlines

The Biotechnology Information Center can give you information on genetic engineering and recombinant DNA techniques, tissue culture of plant and animal systems, single cell protein, immobilized enzymes, embryo transplants, and much more. They have access to a database, bibliographies, and other publications.

☎ Contact:
National Agricultural Library Building
Beltsville, MD 20705
(301) 504-6875

Free Publications/Videos

The following publications on Biotechnology are available from the Food & Nutrition Information Center, National Agricultural Library, Room 304, Beltsville, MD 20705-2351; (301) 504-5719.

- *Biotechnology in Food Science and Technology, January 1987 - March 1991.* A list of current resources. (#QB91-98)
- *Biotechnology in Human Health and Nutrition, January 1979 - March 1991.* A list of current resources. (#QB91-97)

The following Congressional Research Service (CRS) report on Biotechnology is available from either of your U.S. Senators' offices at the U.S. Capitol, Washington, DC 20510, or from your Congressional Representative at the U.S. Capitol, Washington, DC 20515. You can also call in your request through the U.S. Capitol switchboard at (202) 224-3121. Be sure to include the full title and report number in your request.

- *Biotechnology: Bibliography-in-Brief, 1985-1988.* (#88-566 L)

BIRTH

Clearinghouses/Hotlines

The National Institute of Child Health and Human Development (NICHD) will send you whatever publications and reprints of journal articles they have on Birth. If necessary, they will refer you to other experts or researchers in the field.

☎ Contact:
National Institute of Child Health
and Human Development

Bldg. 31, Room 2A32
Bethesda, MD 20892
(301) 496-5133

The National Center for Health Statistics (NCHS) collects and distributes data on abortions, births, deaths, marriages, and divorces, and produces annual data for the U.S., states, countries, and local areas.

☎ Contact:
Division of Vital Statistics
National Center for Health Statistics
3700 East-West Highway
Room 1-44
Hyattsville, MD 20782
(301) 436-8952

The National Maternal and Child Health Clearinghouse has all kinds of information on maternal and child health issues, such as pregnancy, child and adolescent health, and human genetics. If the answer to your question can't be answered by any of their countless free publications, they can refer you to other National or local resources. If you still need further information, they search their own reference collection and send you what they find.

☎ Contact:
National Maternal and Child
Health Clearinghouse
38th & R Sts., NW
Washington, DC 20057
(703) 821-8955, ext. 254

BIRTH CONTROL

See Contraception
See Family Planning
See Oral Contraceptives

BIRTH DEFECTS

See also Congenital Abnormalities
See also Neural Tube Defects

Clearinghouses/Hotlines

The National Institute of Child Health and Human Development (NICHD) will send you whatever publications and reprints of journal articles they have on Developmental Birth Defects. If necessary, they will refer you to other experts or researchers in the field. If you can't afford treatment, have your doctor call NICHD to find out if they are conducting any clinical studies that you might qualify for.

☎ Contact:
National Institute of Child Health
and Human Development
Bldg. 31, Room 2A32
Bethesda, MD 20892
(301) 496-5133

The National Institute of Environmental Health Sciences (NIEHS) will provide you with all the latest scientific findings on cancer-causing agents and their relationship to Birth Defects and cancer.

☎ Contact:
National Institute of Environmental
Health Sciences
Public Affairs Office
Research Triangle Park, NC 27709
(919) 541-3345

Birth defects are the leading cause of infant mortality in the U.S., accounting for more than 20% of the infant deaths each year. The Centers for Disease Control (CDC) conducts surveys of Birth Defects and developmental disabilities, especially possible preventable ones such as spina bifida, fetal alcohol syndrome, and mild mental retardation. They can send you all kinds of reports on their research results.

☎ Contact:
National Center For Environmental Health
and Injury Control
Centers for Disease Control
1600 Clifton Rd., NE
Atlanta, GA 30333
(404) 488-4706

The National Institute of Neurological Disorders and Stroke (NINDS) can send you only information they have in their publications list on Neurological Birth Defects. They cannot refer you to any experts. This Clearinghouse cannot directly give you information about any current clinical studies NINDS might be conducting on this illness, but you can find this information for yourself by looking under the National Institute of Neurological Disorders and Stroke in *Appendix A* at the end of this book.

☎ Contact:
National Institute of Neurological
Disorders and Stroke
Bldg. 31, Room 8A06
Bethesda, MD 20892
(301) 496-5751
(800) 352-9424

BIRTH WEIGHT

See also Child Health

Clearinghouses/Hotlines

The National Institute of Child Health and Human Development (NICHD) will send you whatever publications and reprints of journal articles they have on Birth Weight. If necessary, they will refer you to other experts or researchers in the field.

☎ Contact:
National Institute of Child Health
and Human Development
Bldg. 31, Room 2A32
Bethesda, MD 20892
(301) 496-5133

The National Maternal and Child Health Clearinghouse has all kinds of information on maternal and child health issues, such as pregnancy, child and adolescent health, and human genetics. If the answer to your question can't be answered by any of their countless free publications, they can refer you to other National or local resources. If you still need further information, they search their own reference collection and send you what they find.

☎ Contact:
National Maternal and Child
Health Clearinghouse
38th & R Sts., NW
Washington, DC 20057
(703) 821-8955, ext. 254

BLACK LUNG DISEASE

Clearinghouses/Hotlines

The National Heart, Lung, and Blood Institute (NHLBI) can search the Combined Health Information Database (CHID) and generate a bibliography of resources on Coal Workers' Pneumoconiosis (Black Lung Disease) for you. They also will send you any publications and journal articles they may have on hand, and will refer you to other organizations that are studying this disease. If you can't afford treatment, have your doctor call NHLBI to find out if they are conducting any clinical studies that you might qualify for.

☎ Contact:
National Heart, Lung, and Blood Institute
Bldg. 31, Room 4A21
Bethesda, MD 20892
(301) 496-4236

The National Institute for Occupational Safety and Health (NIOSH) can provide you with articles, reference materials, and more regarding Black Lung Disease, including a NIOSH report titled *Occupational Respiratory Diseases.* This report delineates the methods used to define and study occupational respiratory diseases and addresses a host of broad topics such as assessment of chest X-rays, pulmonary function data, and lung impairment, as well as looking at specific classes of these diseases.

☎ Contact:
National Institute for Occupational Safety and Health
4676 Columbia Parkway, MS C-19
Cincinnati, OH 45226
(800) 35-NIOSH

Free Publications/Videos

The following Congressional Research Service (CRS) reports are available from either of your U.S. Senators' offices at the U.S. Capitol, Washington, DC 20510, or from your Congressional Representative at the U.S. Capitol, Washington, DC 20515. You can also call in your request through the U.S. Capitol switchboard at (202) 224-3121. Be sure to include the full title and report number in your request.

- *Black Lung Programs: 1987 Issues and Action.* (#88-68 EPW)
- *Federal Black Lung Disability Benefits Program.* (81-239 EPW)

BLACK TONGUE

Clearinghouses/Hotlines

The National Institute of Dental Research (NIDR) can provide you with some reference materials on a condition called Black Tongue, which is usually caused by antibiotics.

☎ Contact:
National Institute of Dental Research
Bldg. 31, Room 2C35
Bethesda, MD 20892
(301) 496-4261

BLADDER CANCER

Clearinghouses/Hotlines

The National Cancer Institute (NCI) will send you whatever publications and reprints of journal articles they have on Bladder Cancer. They can also give you information on the state-of-the-art treatment for this disease, including specific treatment information for your stage of cancer. They can also search their Physician's Data Query (PDQ) database to let you know if NCI is conducting any clinical studies on your disease.

☎ Contact:
National Cancer Institute
Building 31, Room 10A24
Bethesda, MD 20892
(800) 4-CANCER
(301) 496-5583

Free Publications/Videos

The following publications on Bladder Cancer are

available from the National Cancer Institute, Bldg. 31, Room 10A24, Bethesda, MD 20892; (800) 4-CANCER, or (301) 496-5583.

- *What You Need to Know About Cancer of the Bladder.* (#91-1559)
- *Research Report: Cancer of the Bladder.* (#90-722)

BLASTOMYCOSIS

Clearinghouses/Hotlines

The National Institute on Allergy and Infectious Diseases (NIAID) can search the Combined Health Information Database (CHID) and generate a bibliography of resources on Blastomycosis for you. They will also send you any publications and journal articles they may have on hand, and will refer you to researchers who are currently studying this disease. If you can't afford treatment, have your doctor call NIAID to find out if they are conducting any clinical studies that you might qualify for.

☎ Contact:
National Institute of Allergy
and Infectious Diseases
Bldg. 31, Room 7A32
Bethesda, MD 20892
(301) 496-5717

BLEOMYCIN

Free Publications/Videos

The following publication is available from the National Cancer Institute, Bldg. 31, Room 10A24, Bethesda, MD 20892; (800) 4-CANCER, or (301) 496-5583.

- *Bleomicina/Bleomycin.* Provides information about side effects, proper usage, and precautions of this anti-cancer drug.

BLEPHARITIS

Clearinghouses/Hotlines

The National Eye Institute (NEI) can give you up-to-date information on Blepharitis by searching the Combined Health Information Database (CHID) and MEDLINE and sending you bibliographies of resources, along with any journal articles they may have. They can also refer you to any other organizations that study this and other related diseases. NEI will also let you know of any clinical studies that may be studying Blepharitis and looking for patients. Because of their small staff, NEI prefers that you submit your requests for information in writing.

☎ Contact:
National Eye Institute
Bldg. 31, Room 6A32
Bethesda, MD 20892
(301) 496-5248

BLEPHAROSPASM

Clearinghouses/Hotlines

The National Institute of Neurological Disorders and Stroke (NINDS) can send you only information they have in their publications list on Blepharospasm. They cannot refer you to any experts. This Clearinghouse cannot directly give you information about any current clinical studies NINDS might be conducting on this topic, but you can find this information for yourself by looking under the National Institute of Neurological Disorders and Stroke in *Appendix A* at the end of this book.

☎ Contact:
National Institute of Neurological
Disorders and Stroke
Bldg. 31, Room 8A06
Bethesda, MD 20892
(301) 496-5751
(800) 352-9424

BLINDNESS

Clearinghouses/Hotlines

The National Eye Institute (NEI) can give you up-to-date information on Blindness (Rehabilitation and Research) by searching the Combined Health Information Database (CHID) and MEDLINE and sending you bibliographies of resources, along with any journal articles they may have. They can also refer you to any other organizations that study this and other related conditions. NEI will also let you know of any clinical studies that may be studying Blindness and looking for patients. Because of their small staff, NEI prefers that you submit your requests for information in writing.

☎ Contact:
National Eye Institute
Bldg. 31, Room 6A32
Bethesda, MD 20892
(301) 496-5248

Free Publications/Videos

The following publication is available from the National Eye Institute, Bldg. 31, Room 6A32, Bethesda, MD 20892; (301) 496-5248.

- *Statistics on Blindness in the Model Reporting Area 1969-1970.* (#73-427)

BLISTERING DISORDERS

Free Publications/Videos

The following publication is available from the National Arthritis and Musculoskeletal and Skin Diseases Information Clearinghouse, Box AMS, 9000 Rockville Pike, Bethesda, MD 20892; (301) 495-4484.

- *Researchers Seek Causes of Enigmatic Blistering Disorders.* (#AR08)

BLOCH-SULZBERGER SYNDROME

Clearinghouses/Hotlines

The National Institute of Neurological Disorders and Stroke (NINDS) can send you only information they have in their publications list on the Neurological Effects of Bloch-Sulzberger Syndrome. They cannot refer you to any experts. This Clearinghouse cannot directly give you information about any current clinical studies NINDS might be conducting on this illness, but you can find this information for yourself by looking under the National Institute of Neurological Disorders and Stroke in *Appendix A* at the end of this book.

☎ Contact:
National Institute of Neurological
Disorders and Stroke
Bldg. 31, Room 8A06
Bethesda, MD 20892
(301) 496-5751
(800) 352-9424

BLOOD

Clearinghouses/Hotlines

The National Heart, Lung, and Blood Institute (NHLBI) can search the Combined Health Information Database (CHID) and generate a bibliography of resources on Inherited Blood Abnormalities for you. They also will send you any publications and journal articles they may have on hand, and will refer you to other organizations that are studying this disease. If you can't afford treatment, have your doctor call NHLBI to find out if they are conducting any clinical studies that you might qualify for.

☎ Contact:
National Heart, Lung, and Blood Institute
Bldg. 31, Room 4A21
Bethesda, MD 20892
(301) 496-4236

The National Institute of Diabetes and Digestive and Kidney Diseases's (NIDDK) individual clearinghouses can search the Combined Health Information Database (CHID) and generate a bibliography of resources on Inherited Blood Abnormalities and Platelet Abnormalities for you. They also will send you any publications and journal articles they may have on hand, and will refer you to other organizations that are studying this issue. If you can't afford treatment, have your doctor call NIDDK to find out if they are conducting any clinical studies that you might qualify for.

☎ Contact:
National Institute of Diabetes
and Digestive and Kidney Diseases
Bldg. 31, Room 9A04
Bethesda, MD 20892
(301) 496-3583

Free Publications/Videos

The following publications on Blood are available from the National Heart, Lung and Blood Institute, Bldg. 31, Room 4A21, Bethesda, MD 20892; (301) 496-4236.

- *Your Operation, Your Blood.* (#88-2967)
- *Transfusion Alert: Indications for the Use of Red Blood Cells, Platelets, and Fresh Frozen Plasma.* (#89-2974)
- *Check Your Blood I.Q.* (#88-2991)

The following publications on Blood are available from the Food & Drug Admin., (HFE-88), 5600 Fishers Ln., Rockville, MD 20857; (301) 443-3170.

- *Transfusion Alert: Use of Autologous Blood.* Discusses preoperative autologous blood donation, perioperative blood salvage, and acute normovolemic hemodilution.
- *Who Donates Better Blood For You Than You?* Discusses the advantages of donating blood for yourself before undergoing surgery.

The following video on Blood is available from Modern Talking Picture Service, 5000 Park St. North, St. Petersburg, FL 33709; (800) 243-MTPS.

- *Blood Transfusions Today.* Video addresses transfusions, donor screening, methods of

collection and preparation and storage of blood.

The following Congressional Research Service (CRS) reports on Blood are available from either of your U.S. Senators' offices at the U.S. Capitol, Washington, DC 20510, or from your Congressional Representative at the U.S. Capitol, Washington, DC 20515. You can also call in your request through the U.S. Capitol switchboard at (202) 224-3121. Be sure to include the full title and report number in your request.

- *Blood: Collection, Testing, and Processing.* (#87-641 SPR)
- *Blood Testing for Antibodies to the AIDS Virus: The Legal Issues.* (#87-738 A)

BLOOD BRAIN BARRIER

Clearinghouses/Hotlines

The National Institute of Neurological Disorders and Stroke (NINDS) can send you only information they have in their publications list on Blood Brain Barrier. They cannot refer you to any experts. This Clearinghouse cannot directly give you information about any current clinical studies NINDS might be conducting on this illness, but you can find this information for yourself by looking under the National Institute of Neurological Disorders and Stroke in *Appendix A* at the end of this book.

☎ Contact:
National Institute of Neurological
Disorders and Stroke
Bldg. 31, Room 8A06
Bethesda, MD 20892
(301) 496-5751 or (800) 352-9424

BLOOD COAGULATION

Clearinghouses/Hotlines

The National Heart, Lung, and Blood Institute

(NHLBI) can search the Combined Health Information Database (CHID) and generate a bibliography of resources on Blood Coagulation for you. They also will send you any publications and journal articles they may have on hand, and will refer you to other organizations that are studying this issue. If you can't afford treatment, have your doctor call NHLBI to find out if they are conducting any clinical studies that you might qualify for.

☎ Contact:
National Heart, Lung, and Blood Institute
Bldg. 31, Room 4A21
Bethesda, MD 20892
(301) 496-4236

BLOOD DISEASES

Clearinghouses/Hotlines

The National Heart, Lung, and Blood Institute (NHLBI) can search the Combined Health Information Database (CHID) and generate a bibliography of resources on Blood Diseases for you. They also will send you any publications and journal articles they may have on hand, and will refer you to other organizations that are studying these diseases. If you can't afford treatment, have your doctor call NHLBI to find out if they are conducting any clinical studies that you might qualify for.

☎ Contact:
National Heart, Lung, and Blood Institute
Bldg. 31, Room 4A21
Bethesda, MD 20892
(301) 496-4236

BLOOD PRODUCTS

Clearinghouses/Hotlines

The Center for Biologics Evaluation and Research answers your questions and send you information on biologic products such as vaccines, allergenics, blood, and Blood Products.

☎ Contact:
Center for Biologics Evaluation and Research
Food and Drug Administration
5600 Fishers Lane, HFB-140
Rockville, MD 20857
(301) 443-7532

BLOOD SUBSTITUTES

Clearinghouses/Hotlines

The National Heart, Lung, and Blood Institute (NHLBI) can search the Combined Health Information Database (CHID) and generate a bibliography of resources on Blood Substitutes for you. They also will send you any publications and journal articles they may have on hand, and will refer you to other organizations that are studying this issue.

☎ Contact:
National Heart, Lung, and Blood Institute
Bldg. 31, Room 4A21
Bethesda, MD 20892
(301) 496-4236

BLOOD TESTING

See Blood Products

BLUE BABY

Clearinghouses/Hotlines

The National Institute of Child Health and Human Development (NICHD) can send you information on fetal, maternal and child development, as well as materials on reproductive biology, contraception, mental retardation, and a host of other related fields.

☎ Contact:
National Institute of Child Health
and Human Development

Bldg. 31, Room 2A32
Bethesda, MD 20892
(301) 496-5133

and Infectious Diseases
Bldg. 31, Room 7A32
Bethesda, MD 20892
(301) 496-5717

BODY WEIGHT

Clearinghouses/Hotlines

The National Institute of Diabetes and Digestive and Kidney Diseases's (NIDDK) individual clearinghouses can search the Combined Health Information Database (CHID) and generate a bibliography of resources on Body Weight for you. They also will send you any publications and journal articles they may have on hand, and will refer you to other organizations that are studying this issue. If you can't afford treatment, have your doctor call NIDDK to find out if they are conducting any clinical studies that you might qualify for.

☎ Contact:
National Institute of Diabetes
and Digestive and Kidney Diseases
Bldg. 31, Room 9A04
Bethesda, MD 20892
(301) 496-3583

BOLIVIAN HEMORRHAGIC FEVER

Clearinghouses/Hotlines

The National Institute on Allergy and Infectious Diseases (NIAID) can search the Combined Health Information Database (CHID) and generate a bibliography of resources on Bolivian Hemorrhagic Fever for you. They will also send you any publications and journal articles they may have on hand, and will refer you to researchers who are currently studying this disease. If you can't afford treatment, have your doctor call NIAID to find out if they are conducting any clinical studies that you might qualify for.

☎ Contact:
National Institute of Allergy

BONE CANCER

See also Cancer

Clearinghouses/Hotlines

The National Cancer Institute (NCI) will send you whatever publications and reprints of journal articles they have on Bone Cancer. They can also give you information on the state-of-the-art treatment for this disease, including specific treatment information for your stage of cancer. They can also search their Physician's Data Query (PDQ) database to let you know if NCI is conducting any clinical studies on your disease.

☎ Contact:
National Cancer Institute
Bldg. 31, Room 10A24
Bethesda, MD 20892
(800) 4-CANCER
(301) 496-5583

Free Publications/Videos

The following publications are available from the National Cancer Institute, Bldg. 31, Room 10A24, Bethesda, MD 20892; (800) 4-CANCER, or (301) 496-5583.

- *What You Need to Know About Cancer of the Bone.* (#90-1571)
- *Research Report: Bone Cancers.* (#91-721)

BONE DISORDERS

Clearinghouses/Hotlines

The Musculoskeletal Diseases Program at National Institutes of Health focuses on orthopedic research that includes sports medicine, growth and development of bone and bone cells, as well as head injury. Their staff can answer your questions about current research and treatment issues and send you brochures and pamphlets.

☎ Contact:
National Institute of Arthritis
and Musculoskeletal and Skin Diseases
Box AMS
Bethesda, MD 20892
(301) 495-4484

BONE MARROW FAILURE

Clearinghouses/Hotlines

The National Heart, Lung, and Blood Institute (NHLBI) can search the Combined Health Information Database (CHID) and generate a bibliography of resources on Bone Marrow Failure for you. They also will send you any publications and journal articles they may have on hand, and will refer you to other organizations that are studying this disease. If you can't afford treatment, have your doctor call NHLBI to find out if they are conducting any clinical studies that you might qualify for.

☎ Contact:
National Heart, Lung, and Blood Institute
Bldg. 31, Room 4A21
Bethesda, MD 20892
(301) 496-4236

BONE MARROW TRANSPLANTS

Clearinghouses/Hotlines

The National Cancer Institute (NCI) will send you whatever publications and reprints of journal articles they have on Bone Marrow Transplants. They can also give you information on the state-of-the-art treatment for this procedure, including specific treatment information for your stage of cancer. They can also search their Physician's Data Query (PDQ) database to let you know if NCI is conducting any clinical studies on your disease.

☎ Contact:
National Cancer Institute
Bldg. 31, Room 10A24
Bethesda, MD 20892
(800) 4-CANCER
(301) 496-5583

The National Institute on Allergy and Infectious Diseases (NIAID) can search the Combined Health Information Database (CHID) and generate a bibliography of resources on Bone Marrow Transplantation for you. They will also send you any publications and journal articles they may have on hand, and will refer you to researchers who are currently studying this procedure. If you can't afford treatment, have your doctor call NIAID to find out if they are conducting any clinical studies that you might qualify for.

☎ Contact:
National Institute of Allergy
and Infectious Diseases
Bldg. 31, Room 7A32
Bethesda, MD 20892
(301) 496-5717

Free Publications/Videos

The following Congressional Research Service (CRS) report is available from either of your U.S. Senators' offices at the U.S. Capitol, Washington, DC 20510, or from your Congressional Representative at the U.S. Capitol, Washington, DC 20515. You can also call in your request through the U.S. Capitol switchboard at (202) 224-3121. Be sure to include the full title and report number in your request.

- *The Federal Role in Bone Marrow Transplantation.* (#90-303 SPR)

BOTULISM

Clearinghouses/Hotlines

The National Institute on Allergy and Infectious

Diseases (NIAID) can search the Combined Health Information Database (CHID) and generate a bibliography of resources on Botulism for you. They will also send you any publications and journal articles they may have on hand, and will refer you to researchers who are currently studying this disease. If you can't afford treatment, have your doctor call NIAID to find out if they are conducting any clinical studies that you might qualify for.

☎ Contact:
National Institute of Allergy
and Infectious Diseases
Bldg. 31, Room 7A32
Bethesda, MD 20892
(301) 496-5717

BOVINE GROWTH HORMONE

Free Publications/Videos

The following Congressional Research Service (CRS) reports on Bovine Growth Hormone are available from either of your U.S. Senators' offices at the U.S. Capitol, Washington, DC 20510, or from your Congressional Representative at the U.S. Capitol, Washington, DC 20515. You can also call in your request through the U.S. Capitol switchboard at (202) 224-3121. Be sure to include the full title and report number in your request.

- *Bovine Growth Hormone (Somatotropin): Agricultural and Regulatory Issues.* (#86-1020 ENR)
- *Bovine Somatotropin (BST or BGH): A Status Report.* (#90-576 ENR)

BOWEL DISEASE

See also Irritable Bowel Syndrome

Clearinghouses/Hotlines

The National Institute of Diabetes and Digestive

and Kidney Diseases's (NIDDK) individual clearinghouses can search the Combined Health Information Database (CHID) and generate a bibliography of resources on Bowel Disease for you. They also will send you any publications and journal articles they may have on hand, and will refer you to other organizations that are studying this disorder. If you can't afford treatment, have your doctor call NIDDK to find out if they are conducting any clinical studies that you might qualify for.

☎ Contact:
National Institute of Diabetes
and Digestive and Kidney Diseases
Bldg. 31, Room 9A04
Bethesda, MD 20892
(301) 496-3583

Free Publications/Videos

The following publications are available from the National Digestive Diseases Information Clearinghouse, Box NDDIC, Bethesda, MD 20892; (301) 468-6344.

- *Irritable Bowl Syndrome.* Information packet.
- *Inflammatory Bowel Disease.*
- *What is Irritable Bowel Syndrome?*

The following publications are available from the National Institute of Diabetes and Digestive and Kidney Diseases, Bldg. 31, Room 9A04, Bethesda, MD 20892; (301) 496-3583.

- *Irritable Bowel Syndrome.* (#90-693)
- *Bowel Diseases, Inflammatory Contact.*

BOWEN'S DISEASE

Clearinghouses/Hotlines

The National Cancer Institute (NCI) will send you whatever publications and reprints of journal articles they have on Bowen's Disease. They can also give you information on the state-of-the-art treatment for this disease, including specific treatment information for your stage of cancer.

They can also search their Physician's Data Query (PDQ) database to let you know if NCI is conducting any clinical studies on your disease.

☎ Contact:
National Cancer Institute
Bldg. 31, Room 10A24
Bethesda, MD 20892
(800) 4-CANCER
(301) 496-5583

BRACHIAL PLEXUS INJURIES

Clearinghouses/Hotlines

The National Institute of Neurological Disorders and Stroke (NINDS) can send you only information they have in their publications list on Brachial Plexus Injuries. They cannot refer you to any experts. This Clearinghouse cannot directly give you information about any current clinical studies NINDS might be conducting on this topic, but you can find this information for yourself by looking under the National Institute of Neurological Disorders and Stroke in *Appendix A* at the end of this book.

☎ Contact:
National Institute of Neurological
Disorders and Stroke
Bldg. 31, Room 8A06
Bethesda, MD 20892
(301) 496-5751
(800) 352-9424

BRADYCARDIA

Clearinghouses/Hotlines

The National Heart, Lung, and Blood Institute (NHLBI) can search the Combined Health Information Database (CHID) and generate a bibliography of resources on Bradycardia for you. They also will send you any publications and journal articles they may have on hand, and will refer you to other organizations that are studying

this disease. If you can't afford treatment, have your doctor call NHLBI to find out if they are conducting any clinical studies that you might qualify for.

☎ Contact:
National Heart, Lung, and Blood Institute
Bldg. 31, Room 4A21
Bethesda, MD 20892
(301) 496-4236

BRAIN

Clearinghouses/Hotlines

The National Institute of Neurological Disorders and Stroke (NINDS) can send you only information they have in their publications list on the Brain. They cannot refer you to any experts. This Clearinghouse cannot directly give you information about any current clinical studies NINDS might be conducting on this topic, but you can find this information for yourself by looking under the National Institute of Neurological Disorders and Stroke in *Appendix A* at the end of this book.

☎ Contact:
National Institute of Neurological
Disorders and Stroke
Bldg. 31, Room 8A06
Bethesda, MD 20892
(301) 496-5751
(800) 352-9424

Free Publications/Videos

The following publications on the Brain are available from the Office of Clinical Center Communications, National Institutes of Health, Bldg. 10, Room 5C-305, 9000 Rockville Pike, Bethesda, MD 20892; (301) 496-2563.

- *The Brain in "Aging" and Dementia*. Discusses brain anatomy and physiology, the normal process of brain aging, and senility. Vascular dementia and Alzheimer's disease are described as well as research on the causes and treatment. (#83-2625, OCCC)

- *Brain in Aging and Dementia.* (#83-2625)
- *Drugs and the Brain.* (#91-3172)

The following publication on the Brain is available from the Science & Technology Division, Reference Section, Library of Congress, Washington, DC 20540; (202) 707-5580.

- *The Brain: An Overview.* Reference guide designed to help locate further published material. (#90-10)

The following publications are available from the National Institute of Neurological Disorders and Stroke, PO Box 5801, Bethesda, MD 20824; (800) 352-9424, or (301) 496-5751.

- *Implementation of Plan: Decade of the Brain.*
- *Maximizing Human Potential: Decade of the Brain.*

The following video on the Brain is available from the National Institute of Mental Health, 5600 Fishers Ln., Room 15C05, Rockville, MD 20857; (301) 443-4515.

- *Windows Into the Brain.* Video that tells the story of three decades of scientific advances in brain imaging techniques. Include in your order a blank videocassette with enough minutes on it to tape the materials you request. (19 min.)

BRAIN CANCER

See also Cancer

Clearinghouses/Hotlines

The National Cancer Institute (NCI) will send you whatever publications and reprints of journal articles they have on Brain Cancer. They can also give you information on the state-of-the-art treatment for this disease, including specific treatment information for your stage of cancer. They can also search their Physician's Data Query (PDQ) database to let you know if NCI is conducting any clinical studies on your disease.

☎ Contact:
National Cancer Institute
Bldg. 31, Room 10A24
Bethesda, MD 20892
(800) 4-CANCER
(301) 496-5583

Free Publications/Videos

The following publication on Brain Cancer is available from the National Cancer Institute, Bldg. 31, Room 10A24, Bethesda, MD 20892; (800) 4-CANCER, or (301) 496-5583.

- *What You Need to Know About Cancer of the Brain and Spinal Cord.* (#90-1558)

The following publication on Brain Cancer is available from the National Institute of Neurological Disorders and Stroke, Bldg. 31, Room 8A06, Bethesda, MD 20892; (301) 496-5751 or (800) 352-9424.

- *Brain Tumors.* (#82-504)

BRAIN DEATH

Clearinghouses/Hotlines

The National Institute of Neurological Disorders and Stroke (NINDS) can send you only information they have in their publications list on Brain Death. They cannot refer you to any experts. This Clearinghouse cannot directly give you information about any current clinical studies NINDS might be conducting on this topic, but you can find this information for yourself by looking under the National Institute of Neurological Disorders and Stroke in *Appendix A* at the end of this book.

☎ Contact:
National Institute of Neurological
Disorders and Stroke
Bldg. 31, Room 8A06
Bethesda, MD 20892
(301) 496-5751
(800) 352-9424

BRAIN INJURIES

Clearinghouses/Hotlines

The National Rehabilitation Information Center (NRIC) has put together a free resource guide for people with traumatic Brain Injury and their families. This guide has information regarding national organizations, associations, and programs; support groups and state associations of the National Head Injury Foundation, periodicals, catalogs, directories and other sourcebooks, information resources, regional medical libraries, and rehabilitation research and training centers, and lists of books and articles in the NRIC collection that may be of interest to the newly injured person of family member.

☎ Contact:
National Rehabilitation Information Center
8455 Colesville Rd, Suite 935
Silver Spring, MD 20910
(301) 588-9284
(800) 346-2742 (Voice and TDD)

The National Institute of Neurological Disorders and Stroke (NINDS) can send you only information they have in their publications list on Brain Injuries. They cannot refer you to any experts. This Clearinghouse cannot directly give you information about any current clinical studies NINDS might be conducting on this topic, but you can find this information for yourself by looking under the National Institute of Neurological Disorders and Stroke in *Appendix A* at the end of this book.

☎ Contact:
National Institute of Neurological
Disorders and Stroke
Bldg. 31, Room 8A06
Bethesda, MD 20892
(301) 496-5751
(800) 352-9424

BRAIN TUMORS

Clearinghouses/Hotlines

The National Cancer Institute (NCI) will send you whatever publications and reprints of journal articles they have on Brain Tumors. They can also give you information on the state-of-the-art treatment for this disease, including specific treatment information for your stage of cancer. They can also search their Physician's Data Query (PDQ) database to let you know if NCI is conducting any clinical studies on your disease.

☎ Contact:
National Cancer Institute
Bldg. 31, Room 10A24
Bethesda, MD 20892
(800) 4-CANCER
(301) 496-5583

The National Institute of Neurological Disorders and Stroke (NINDS) can send you only information they have in their publications list on Brain Tumors. They cannot refer you to any experts. This Clearinghouse cannot directly give you information about any current clinical studies NINDS might be conducting on this illness, but you can find this information for yourself by looking under the National Institute of Neurological Disorders and Stroke in *Appendix A* at the end of this book.

☎ Contact:
National Institute of Neurological
Disorders and Stroke
Bldg. 31, Room 8A06
Bethesda, MD 20892
(301) 496-5751
(800) 352-9424

The National Institute on Deafness and Other Communicative Disorders (NIDCD) will send you whatever publications and reprints of journal articles they have on Brain Tumors. If you need further information, they will refer you to other organizations that study this and other related diseases. NIDCD does not conduct any clinical studies for this or any other disorder.

☎ Contact:
National Institute on Deafness
and Other Communication Disorders
Bldg. 31, Room 3C35
Bethesda, MD 20892
(301) 496-7243
(800) 241-1044
(301) 402-0252 (TDD)

Free Publications/Videos

The following publications on Brain Tumors are available from the National Institute of Neurological Disorders and Stroke, Bldg. 31, Room 8A06, Bethesda, MD 20892; (301) 496-5751 or (800) 352-9424.

- *Brain Tumors: Hope Through Research.* Explains types of tumors, warning symptoms, and treatment including chemotherapy. (#82-504)
- *Brain Tumor.* Contains a collection of scientific articles, patient education pamphlets, and addresses of voluntary health associations.
- *Brain Tumors.* Discusses hope through research.

BREAST CANCER

See also Cancer

Clearinghouses/Hotlines

The National Cancer Institute (NCI) will send you whatever publications and reprints of journal articles they have on Breast Cancer. They can also give you information on the state-of-the-art treatment for this disease, including specific treatment information for your stage of cancer. They can also search their Physician's Data Query (PDQ) database to let you know if NCI is conducting any clinical studies on your disease.

☎ Contact:
National Cancer Institute
Bldg. 31, Room 10A24
Bethesda, MD 20892
(800) 4-CANCER
(301) 496-5583

Free Publications/Videos

The following publications on Breast Cancer are available from the National Cancer Institute, Bldg. 31, Room 10A24, Bethesda, MD 20892; (800) 4-CANCER, (301) 496-5583.

- *After Breast Cancer: A Guide to Follow-up Care.* (#90-2400) Explains the importance of continuing breast self-examination, regular physical exams, possible signs of recurrence.
- *Breast Biopsy: What You Should Know.* (#90-657) Discusses biopsy procedures, what to expect in the hospital, awaiting the diagnosis, and coping with the possibility of breast cancer.
- *Breast Cancer: What You Should Know.* Discusses X-ray mammography and other breast cancer screening methods. (#85-2000)
- *Breast Cancer: Understanding Treatment Options.* (#91-2675) Summarizes the biopsy procedure, types of breast surgery, radiation therapy, adjuvant therapy and making treatment decisions.
- *Breast Cancer Digest.* (#84-1691)
- *Breast Cancer: We're Making Progress Every Day.* Summarizes the latest information about breast cancer including surgery, breast reconstruction, and rehabilitation. (#96-2409)
- *Breast Cancer: We're Making Progress.* An illustrated guide for breast self-examination. (#96-8409)
- *Breast Exams: What You Should Know.* (#91-2000)
- *Breast Lumps: Questions and Answers.*
- *Breast Reconstruction: A Matter of Choice.* (#91-2151) Discusses the techniques used in reconstructive breast surgery, possible complications, answers to common questions, criteria for choosing a plastic surgeon, and issues of emotional adjustment.
- *A Guide for Developing Public Education Programs on Breast Cancer.* (#87-2740)
- *Mastectomy: A Treatment for Breast Cancer.* (#91-658)
- *Questions and Answers About Breast Lumps.* Describes some of the most common noncancerous breast lumps and what can be done about them. (#86-2401)
- *Questions and Answers About Choosing a Mammography Facility.* (#91-3228).
- *Radiation Therapy: A Treatment for Early Stage Breast Cancer.* (#91-2227) Discusses the treatment steps, possible side

effects, precautions to take after treatment, and emotional adjustment to having breast cancer.

- *What You Need to Know About Breast Cancer.* (#91-1556)

The following publication on Breast Cancer is available from the Science & Technology Division, Reference Section, Library of Congress, Washington, DC 20540; (202) 707-5580.

- *Breast Cancer.* Reference guide designed to help locate further published material. (#91-7)

The following publication on Breast Cancer is available from the Food & Drug Administration, (HFE-88), 5600 Fishers Ln., Rockville, MD 20857; (301) 443-3170.

- *Progress Against Breast Cancer.* (#FDA91-1176)

BREASTFEEDING

Clearinghouses/Hotlines

The National Institute of Child Health and Human Development (NICHD) will send you whatever publications and reprints of journal articles they have on Breastfeeding and Breast Milk. If necessary, they will refer you to other experts or researchers in the field.

☎ Contact:
National Institute of Child Health
and Human Development
Bldg. 31, Room 2A32
Bethesda, MD 20892
(301) 496-5133

The National Maternal and Child Health Clearinghouse has all kinds of information on maternal and child health issues, such as pregnancy, child and adolescent health, and human genetics. If the answer to your question can't be answered by any of their countless free publications, they can refer you to other National or local resources. If you still need further information, they search their own reference collection and send you what they find.

☎ Contact:
National Maternal and Child
Health Clearinghouse
38th & R Sts. NW
Washington, DC 20057
(703) 821-8955, ext. 254

The Children's Nutrition Research Center at Baylor College of Medicine works to determine the unique nutrient needs of pregnant and lactating women, and of children from conception through early years of development.

☎ Contact:
Children's Nutrition Research Center
1100 Bates St.
Houston, TX 77030
(713) 798-7000

Free Publications/Videos

The following publications on Breastfeeding are available from the National Maternal and Child Health Clearinghouse, 38th & R Sts., NW, Washington, DC 20057; (703) 821-8955, ext. 254.

- *Surgeon General's Workshop on Breastfeeding and Human Lactation.* (#B163)
- *Guide to Breastfeeding the Infant with PKU.* (#B327)
- *Art and Science of Breastfeeding Manual.*
- *Breastfeeding Catalog of Products.* Includes a listing of videotapes, posters, brochures, journal articles, data bases, curricula and training aids.
- *Nutrition During Lactation.*
- *Patient Education Materials: A Resource Guide* is a free publication developed to help health professionals identify and locate materials on maternal and child health topics that are clear, concise, easy to read and appropriate for the general public. The guide is separated into three sections. The first is patient education materials, which is an annotated listing of source books, directories, audiovisuals, and resource guides that describe patient education materials. The second section lists publishers of patient education

materials, and the third lists federal health information clearinghouses.
- *Surgeon General's Workshop on Breastfeeding and Human Lactation.* Covers the physiology of breastfeeding, the unique values of human milk, current trends, and cultural factors relating to breastfeeding.

The following publication on Breastfeeding is available from the Consumer Information Center, P.O. Box 100, Pueblo, CO 81002.

- *Feeding Baby: Nature and Nurture.* Explains why breast milk is best for babies. Compares milk based and soy based formulas and explores the dangers of confusing soy beverages with soy based formulas. (506Z).

BREAST IMPLANTS

Clearinghouses/Hotlines

The Food and Drug Administration has put together an information packet to answer questions regarding breast implants. It answers questions regarding the Food and Drug Administration's moratorium on silicone gel-filled breast implants, as well as providing general information on breast implants and who to contact for more information.
☎ Contact:
Division of Consumer Affairs (HFZ-210)
Center for Devices and Radiological Health
Food and Drug Administration
Rockville, MD 20857
(301) 443-4190

Free Publications/Videos

The following publications are available from the Center for Devices and Radiological Health, (HFZ-210), Food and Drug Administration, 5600 Fishers Ln., Rockville, MD 20857; (301) 443-4690.

- *FDA Seeks Panels Advice on Silicone Breast Implants.*

- *FDA Advisory Panel Discusses Breast Implant Safety.*
- *The Body Doesn't Always Take Kindly to Breast Implants.*

The following publication is available from the Subcommittee on Housing and Consumer Interests, Room 717, O'Neill HOB, 300 New Jersey Ave., SE, Washington, DC 20515; (202) 226-3344.

- *Breast Implants: Ramifications of the FDA Ruling on Consumers.*

The following Congressional Research Service (CRS) report is available from either of your U.S. Senators' offices at the U.S. Capitol, Washington, DC 20510, or from your Congressional Representative at the U.S. Capitol, Washington, DC 20515. You can also call in your request through the U.S. Capitol switchboard at (202) 224-3121. Be sure to include the full title and report number in your request.

- *Breast Implants: Safety and FDA Regulation.* (#91-842 SPR)

BRONCHIECTASIS

Clearinghouses/Hotlines

The National Heart, Lung, and Blood Institute (NHLBI) can search the Combined Health Information Database (CHID) and generate a bibliography of resources on Bronchiectasis for you. They also will send you any publications and journal articles they may have on hand, and will refer you to other organizations that are studying this disease. If you can't afford treatment, have your doctor call NHLBI to find out if they are conducting any clinical studies that you might qualify for.
☎ Contact:
National Heart, Lung, and Blood Institute
Bldg. 31, Room 4A21
Bethesda, MD 20892
(301) 496-4236

BRONCHITIS

Clearinghouses/Hotlines

The National Heart, Lung, and Blood Institute (NHLBI) can search the Combined Health Information Database (CHID) and generate a bibliography of resources on Chronic Bronchitis for you. They also will send you any publications and journal articles they may have on hand, and will refer you to other organizations that are studying this disease. If you can't afford treatment, have your doctor call NHLBI to find out if they are conducting any clinical studies that you might qualify for.

☎ Contact:
National Heart, Lung, and Blood Institute
Building 31
Room 4A21
Bethesda, MD 20892
(301) 496-4236

BRUCELLOSIS

Clearinghouses/Hotlines

The National Institute on Allergy and Infectious Diseases (NIAID) can search the Combined Health Information Database (CHID) and generate a bibliography of resources on Brucellosis for you. They will also send you any publications and journal articles they may have on hand, and will refer you to researchers who are currently studying this disease. If you can't afford treatment, have your doctor call NIAID to find out if they are conducting any clinical studies that you might qualify for.

☎ Contact:
National Institute of Allergy
and Infectious Diseases
Building 31
Room 7A32
Bethesda, MD 20892
(301) 496-5717

BRUXISM

Clearinghouses/Hotlines

The National Institute of Dental Research (NIDR) will send you whatever publications and reprints of journal articles they have on Bruxism. As a policy, NIDR will not refer you to other organizations or experts who study this disorder. If you can't afford treatment, have your doctor call Dr. Albert Guckers at (301) 496-6241 to find out if NIDR is conducting any clinical studies that you might qualify for.

☎ Contact:
National Institute of Dental Research
Bldg. 31, Room 2C35
Bethesda, MD 20892
(301) 496-4261

BUBONIC PLAGUE

Clearinghouses/Hotlines

The National Institute on Allergy and Infectious Diseases (NIAID) can search the Combined Health Information Database (CHID) and generate a bibliography of resources on Bubonic Plague for you. They will also send you any publications and journal articles they may have on hand, and will refer you to researchers who are currently studying this disease.

☎ Contact:
National Institute of Allergy
and Infectious Diseases
Bldg. 31, Room 7A32
Bethesda, MD 20892
(301) 496-5717

BUERGER'S DISEASE

Clearinghouses/Hotlines

The National Heart, Lung, and Blood Institute

(NHLBI) can search the Combined Health Information Database (CHID) and generate a bibliography of resources on Buerger's Disease (Thromboangiitis Obliterans) for you. They also will send you any publications and journal articles they may have on hand, and will refer you to other organizations that are studying this disease. If you can't afford treatment, have your doctor call NHLBI to find out if they are conducting any clinical studies that you might qualify for.

☎ Contact:
National Heart, Lung, and Blood Institute
Bldg. 31, Room 4A21
Bethesda, MD 20892
(301) 496-4236

BULBAR PALSY

Clearinghouses/Hotlines

The National Institute of Neurological Disorders and Stroke (NINDS) can send you only information they have in their publications list on Bulbar Palsy. They cannot refer you to any experts. This Clearinghouse cannot directly give you information about any current clinical studies NINDS might be conducting on this illness, but you can find this information for yourself by looking under the National Institute of Neurological Disorders and Stroke in *Appendix A* at the end of this book.

☎ Contact:
National Institute of Neurological
Disorders and Stroke
Bldg. 31, Room 8A06
Bethesda, MD 20892
(301) 496-5751
(800) 352-9424

BULIMIA

See also Anorexia
See also Eating Disorders

Clearinghouses/Hotlines

The Obesity, Eating Disorders, and Energy Regulation Program at National Institutes of Health researches obesity, anorexia nervosa, bulimia and other eating disorders. They can give you information on the causes, prevention, and treatments of these conditions.

☎ Contact:
National Institute of Diabetes
and Digestive and Kidney Diseases
National Institutes of Health
Bldg. 31, Room 3A18B
Bethesda, MD 20892
(301) 496-7823

The National Institute of Mental Health (NIMH) will send you whatever publications and reprints of articles from texts and journals they have on Bulimia. They will also refer you to other organizations that are studying this disease. NIMH will also let you know of any clinical studies that may be studying this disease and looking for patients.

☎ Contact:
National Institute of Mental Health
5600 Fishers Ln., Room 15C05
Rockville, MD 20857
(301) 443-4515

The National Institute of Child Health and Human Development (NICHD) will send you whatever publications and reprints of journal articles they have on Bulimia. If necessary, they will refer you to other experts or researchers in the field. If you can't afford treatment, have your doctor call NICHD to find out if they are conducting any clinical studies that you might qualify for.

☎ Contact:
National Institute of Child Health
and Human Development
Bldg. 31, Room 2A32
Bethesda, MD 20892
(301) 496-5133

Free Publications/Videos

The following publication on Bulimia is available from the National Institute of Mental Health, 5600 Fishers Ln., Room 15C05, Rockville, MD 20857; (301) 443-4515.

- Useful Information on Anorexia Nervosa and Bulimia.

The following publication on Bulimia is available from the Food & Nutrition Information Center, National Agricultural Library, Room 304, Beltsville, MD 20705-2351; (301) 504-5719.

- Anorexia Nervosa and Bulimia. Designed to help you locate resources on this topic.

BULLOUS PEMPHIGOID

Clearinghouses/Hotlines

The National Institute of Arthritis and Musculoskeletal and Skin Diseases (NIAMS) will send you whatever publications and reprints of articles from texts and journals they have on Bullous Pemphigoid. They will also refer you to other organizations that are studying this disease. NIAMS will also let you know of any clinical studies that may be studying this disease and looking for patients.
☎ Contact:
National Institute of Arthritis
and Musculoskeletal and Skin Diseases
Box AMS
9000 Rockville Pike
Bethesda, MD 20892
(301) 495-4484

The National Cancer Institute (NCI) will send you whatever publications and reprints of journal articles they have on Bullous Pemphigoid. They can also give you information on the state-of-the-art treatment for this disease, including specific treatment information for your stage of cancer. They can also search their Physician's Data Query (PDQ) database to let you know if NCI is conducting any clinical studies on your disease.
☎ Contact:
National Cancer Institute
Bldg. 31, Room 10A24
Bethesda, MD 20892
(800) 4-CANCER
(301) 496-5583

BURKITT'S LYMPHOMA

Clearinghouses/Hotlines

The National Cancer Institute (NCI) will send you whatever publications and reprints of journal articles they have on Burkitt's Lymphoma. They can also give you information on the state-of-the-art treatment for this disease, including specific treatment information for your stage of cancer. They can also search their Physician's Data Query (PDQ) database to let you know if NCI is conducting any clinical studies on your disease.
☎ Contact:
National Cancer Institute
Bldg. 31, Room 10A24
Bethesda, MD 20892
(800) 4-CANCER
(301) 496-5583

BURN RESEARCH

Clearinghouses/Hotlines

The National Institute of General Medical Sciences will send you whatever information they have on Burn Research. If necessary they can also refer you to a specific researcher in this area for further information.
☎ Contact:
National Institute of General Medical Sciences
Bldg. 31, Room 4A52
Bethesda, MD 20892
(301) 496-7301

BURNING MOUTH SYNDROME

Clearinghouses/Hotlines

The National Institute of Dental Research (NIDR) will send you whatever publications and reprints of journal articles they have on Burning Mouth

Syndrome. As a policy, NIDR will not refer you to other organizations or experts who study this disease. If you can't afford treatment, have your doctor call Dr. Albert Guckers at (301) 496-6241 to find out if NIDR is conducting any clinical studies that you might qualify for.

☎ Contact:
National Institute of Dental Research
Building 31
Room 2C35
Bethesda, MD 20892
(301) 496-4261

BURSITIS

Clearinghouses/Hotlines

The National Institute of Arthritis and Musculoskeletal and Skin Diseases (NIAMS) will send you whatever publications and reprints of articles from texts and journals they have on Bursitis. They will also refer you to other organizations that are studying this disease. NIAMS will also let you know of any clinical studies that may be studying Bursitis and looking for patients.

☎ Contact:
National Institute of Arthritis
and Musculoskeletal and Skin Diseases
Box AMS
9000 Rockville Pike
Bethesda, MD 20892
(301) 495-4484

BUSULFAN

Free Publications/Videos

The following publication on Busulfan is available from the National Cancer Institute, Bldg. 31, Room 10A24, Bethesda, MD 20892; (800) 4-CANCER, or (301) 496-5583.

- *Busulfano/Busulfan.* Provides information about side effects, proper usage, and precautions of this anti-cancer drug.

BYSSINOSIS

Clearinghouses/Hotlines

The National Heart, Lung, and Blood Institute (NHLBI) can search the Combined Health Information Database (CHID) and generate a bibliography of resources on Byssinosis (Brown Lung Disease) for you. They also will send you any publications and journal articles they may have on hand, and will refer you to other organizations that are studying this disease. If you can't afford treatment, have your doctor call NHLBI to find out if they are conducting any clinical studies that you might qualify for.

☎ Contact:
National Heart, Lung, and Blood Institute
Building 31
Room 4A21
Bethesda, MD 20892
(301) 496-4236

- C -

CAFFEINE

Free Publications/Videos

The following publication on Caffeine is available from the Food & Drug Administration, (HFE-88), 5600 Fishers Ln., Rockville, MD 20857; (301) 443-3170.

- *Caffeine Jitters: Some Safety Questions Remain.* (#FDA88-2221)

CALCIUM

Free Publications/Videos

The following publication is available from the Food & Drug Administration, (HFE-88), 5600 Fishers Ln., Rockville, MD 20857; (301) 443-3170.

- *Please Pass That Woman Some More Calcium and Iron.* (#85-2198)

CANAVAN'S DISEASE

Clearinghouses/Hotlines

The National Institute of Neurological Disorders and Stroke (NINDS) can send you only information they have in their publications list on Canavan's Disease. This Clearinghouse cannot directly give you information about any current clinical studies NINDS might be conducting on this illness, but you can find this information for yourself by looking under the National Institute of Neurological Disorders and Stroke in *Appendix A* at the end of this book.

☎ Contact:
National Institute of Neurological
Disorders and Stroke
Bldg. 31, Room 8A06
Bethesda, MD 20892
(301) 496-5751
(800) 352-9424

CANCER

See also Anti-Cancer Drugs
See also Radiation
See also specific type of Cancer

Clearinghouses/Hotlines

The National Cancer Institute (NCI) can give you information on speakers who are available to talk on a variety of topics to the general public, as well as to health professionals. Topics can range from current research to environmental risks. Contact this office for more information on scheduling.

☎ Contact:
National Cancer Institute
Bldg. 31, Room 10A18
9000 Rockville Pike
Bethesda, MD 20892
(800) 4-CANCER
(301) 496-5583

The Cancer Information Service assists cancer patients, families, and medical personnel on all aspects of cancer. They have information on treatment, rehab, and detection, as well as on financial assistance and help locating resources close to home. They also have access to current research and physician referrals.

☎ Contact:
National Cancer Institute
Building 31, Room 10A18
9000 Rockville Pike
Bethesda, MD 20892
(800) 4-CANCER
(301) 427-8656 Maryland
(800) 638-6070 Alaska
(800) 524-1234 Hawaii

The National Institute of Environmental Health Sciences (NIEHS) will provide you with all the latest scientific findings on cancer-causing agents and their relationship to birth defects and cancer.

☎ Contact:
National Institute of Environmental
Health Sciences
Public Affairs Office
Research Triangle Park, NC 27709
(919) 541-3345

The National Institute on Aging (NIA) will send you whatever publications and reprints of journal articles they have on Cancer and Aging. They cannot refer you to other experts if the information they have isn't sufficient for your purposes.

☎ Contact:
National Institute on Aging
Bldg. 31, Room 5C27
Bethesda, MD 20892
(301) 496-1752

Free Publications/Videos

The following publications on Cancer are available from the National Cancer Institute, Bldg. 31, Room 10A24, Bethesda, MD 20892; (800) 4-CANCER, or (301) 496-5583.

- *Advanced Cancer: Living Each Day.* (#87-856) Addresses living with a terminal illness, how to cope, and practical considerations for the patient, the family and friends.
- *Cancer Rates and Risks.* (#85-691)
- *Cancer Treatments: Consider the Possibilities.* (#89-3060)
- *Chemotherapy and You: A Guide to Self-Help During Treatment.* (#91-2079).
- *Diet, Nutrition and Cancer Prevention: A Guide to Food Choices.* (#87-2711)
- *Everything Doesn't Cause Cancer.* Answers some common questions about the causes and prevention of cancer as well as methods for testing chemicals and test results. (#84-2039)
- *Eating Hints: Tips and Recipes for Better Nutrition During Cancer Treatment.* (#92-2079)
- *Facing Forward: A Guide for Cancer Survivors.* (#90-2424) Presents a concise overview of important survivor issues, including ongoing health needs, psychosocial concerns, insurance, and employment.
- *Good News, Better News, Best News: Cancer Prevention.* Discusses avoidable cancer risks and gives steps that one can take every day to prevent it. (#84-2671)
- *Help Yourself: Tips for Teenagers With Cancer.* (#91-2211).
- *Hospital Days, Treatment Ways.* (#91-2085) This hematology-oncology coloring book helps orient the child with cancer to hospital and treatment procedures.
- *Managing Interleukin-2 Therapy.* (#89-3071).
- *Managing Your Child's Eating Problems During Cancer Treatment.* (#92-2038) Contains information about the importance of nutrition.
- *NCI Investigational Drugs.* Covers most of the drugs in clinical cancer trials at the National Cancer Institute. It provides necessary product information for those who use these investigational drug products. (#89-2141)
- *NCI Investigational Drugs-Chemical Information.* Designed to provide selected relevant chemical and physical data to cancer investigators involved in various multidisciplinary studies of drugs which were developed or are being developed by the Developmental Therapeutics Program. (#86-2654)
- *The Pap Test: It Can Save Your Life!* (#91-3213).
- *Patient to Patient: Cancer Clinical Trials and You.* This 15-minute videocassette provides simple information for patients and families about the clinical studies process.
- *Radiation Therapy And You: A Guide To Self-Help During Treatment.* (#91-2227).
- *Skin Cancers: Basal Cell and Squamous Cell Carcinomas.* (#91-2977).
- *Students With Cancer; A Resource for the Educator.* (#87-2086)
- *Talking to Your Child About Cancer.* (#91-2761)
- *Taking Time: Support for People with Cancer and the People Who Care About Them.* (#91-2059) Addresses the feelings and concerns of others in similar situations and how they have coped.
- *A Time of Change/De Nina a Mujer.* (#88-2466)
- *What Are Clinical Trials All About?* (#90-2706).
- *What You Need to Know About Cancer of the Colon and Rectum.* (#90-1552)
- *What You Need to Know About Cancer.* (#90-1566)
- *When Someone in Your Family Has Cancer.* (#90-2685)
- *When Cancer Recurs: Meeting the Challenge Again.* (#90-2709) Details the different types of recurrence, types of treatment, and coping with cancer's return.
- *Young People With Cancer: A Handbook for Parents.* (#92-2378) Discusses the most common types of childhood cancer, treatments and side effects, and issues that may arise when a child is diagnosed with cancer.

Research Reports (Series). In-depth reports covering current knowledge of the causes and prevention, symptoms, detection and diagnosis and treatment of various types of cancer. The series includes the following:

- *Adult Kidney Cancer and Wilms' Tumor.* (#90-2342).
- *Bone Cancers.* (#91-721).
- *Bone Marrow Transplantation.* (#92-1178).
- *Cancer of the Bladder.* (#90-722).
- *Cancer of the Colon and Rectum.* (#92-95).
- *Cancer of the Lung.* (#90-526).
- *Cancer of the Ovary.* (#89-3014).
- *Cancer of the Pancreas.* (#88-2941).
- *Cancer of the Prostate.* (#91-528).
- *Cancer of the Stomach.* (#88-2978).
- *Cancer of the Uterus: Endometrial Cancer.* (#91-171).
- *Leukemia.* (#88-329).
- *Melanoma.* (#89-3020).
- *Oral Cancers.* (#92-2876).

The following Cancer publications are available from the Office of Technology Assessment, 600 Pennsylvania Ave., SE, Washington, DC 20510; (202) 224-8996.

- *Assessment of Technologies for Determining Cancer Risk From the Environment.* A report to Congress. Ask for the summary report. (#H-138)
- *Unconventional Cancer Treatments.* A report to Congress. Ask for the summary report.

The following publications and videos on Cancer are available from the Office of Clinical Center Communications, Bldg. 10, Room 1C255, Bethesda, MD 20892; (301) 496-2563.

- *Cancer and the Environment.* Video to help the general public make intelligent decisions.
- *Cancer Prevention Resource Directory.* Gives names, addresses, and telephone numbers of over 100 national associations and health departments that encourage cancer prevention activities.
- *Cancer Treatment.* Covers unproven therapies on cancer patients. (#82-1807)
- *Cancer: What Is It?* Video to help the general public make intelligent decisions.

- *Diet and Cancer Prevention.* Video to help the general public make intelligent decisions.
- *Genetics of Cancer.* Booklet written to help the general public make intelligent decisions.

The following publication on Cancer is available from the Food and Nutrition Information Center, National Agricultural Library, Room 304, Beltsville, MD 20705-2351; (301) 504-5719.

- *Diet and Cancer.* Designed to help you locate resources on this topic.

The following publications on Cancer are available from the Consumer Information Center, P.O. Box 100, Pueblo, CO 81002.

- *Diet, Nutrition and Cancer Prevention: The Good News.* (#526Y)
- *Good News For Blacks About Cancer.* (#542Y)

The following publication on Cancer is available from the Center for Devices and Radiological Health, (HFZ-210), Food and Drug Administration, 5600 Fishers Ln., Rockville, MD 20857; (301) 443-4690.

- *Heat Used To Fight Some Cancers.*

The following videos on Cancer are available from Modern Talking Picture Service, 5000 Park St. North, St. Petersburg, FL 33709; (800) 243-MTPS.

- *Cancer Treatment.* Video reviews different approaches to cancer treatment: surgery, radiation, and chemotherapy.
- *Control and Prevention of Malignant Melanoma: A Program for Melanoma-Prone Families.* A free-loan video on skin cancer.
- *Dysplastic Nevi and Melanoma: A Program for Pathologists.*
- *A Special Love.* Video chronicles family's experience with pediatric cancer.
- *Mayo Clinic: The Spirit of Hope.* Video of patients, physicians, and researchers at the Mayo.

CANDIDA

Clearinghouses/Hotlines

The National Institute on Allergy and Infectious Diseases (NIAID) can search the Combined Health Information Database (CHID) and generate a bibliography of resources on Candida for you. They will also send you any publications and journal articles they may have on hand, and will refer you to researchers who are currently studying this disease. If you can't afford treatment, have your doctor call NIAID to find out if they are conducting any clinical studies that you might qualify for.

☎ Contact:
National Institute of Allergy
and Infectious Diseases
Bldg. 31, Room 7A32
Bethesda, MD 20892
(301) 496-5717

The National Institute of Dental Research (NIDR) will send you whatever publications and reprints of journal articles they have on Candida. As a policy, NIDR will not refer you to other organizations or experts who study this disease. If you can't afford treatment, have your doctor call Dr. Albert Guckers at (301) 496-6241 to find out if NIDR is conducting any clinical studies that you might qualify for.

☎ Contact:
National Institute of Dental Research
Bldg. 31, Room 2C35
Bethesda, MD 20892
(301) 496-4261

CANKER SORES

Clearinghouses/Hotlines

The National Institute of Dental Research (NIDR) will send you whatever publications and reprints of journal articles they have on Canker Sores. As a policy, NIDR will not refer you to other organizations or experts who study this condition.

If you can't afford treatment, have your doctor call Dr. Albert Guckers at (301) 496-6241 to find out if NIDR is conducting any clinical studies that you might qualify for.

☎ Contact:
National Institute of Dental Research
Bldg. 31, Room 2C35
Bethesda, MD 20892
(301) 496-4261

Free Publications/Videos

The following publication is available from the National Institute of Dental Research, Bldg. 31, Room 2C35, Bethesda, MD 20892; (301) 496-4261.

- *Fever Blisters and Canker Sores.* (#87-247)

CARBOHYDRATES

Free Publications/Videos

The following publication on Carbohydrates is available from the Food & Drug Administration, (HFE-88), 5600 Fishers Ln., Rockville, MD 20857; (301) 443-3170.

- *A Simple Guide to Complex Carbohydrates.* (#FDA91-2230)

CARCALON

Clearinghouses/Hotlines

The National Cancer Institute (NCI) will send you whatever publications and reprints of journal articles they have on Carcalon (Krebiozen). They can also give you information on the state-of-the-art treatment for this disease, including specific treatment information for your stage of cancer. They can also search their Physician's Data Query (PDQ) database to let you know if NCI is conducting any clinical studies on your disease.

☎ Contact:
National Cancer Institute
Bldg. 31, Room 10A24
Bethesda, MD 20892
(800) 4-CANCER
(301) 496-5583

CARCINOGENS

Clearinghouses/Hotlines

The National Institute of Occupational Safety and Health (NIOSH) will send you a publication that lists the trade name products containing one or more of 16 carcinogens (substances for which evidence indicates a causal relationship between exposure to that substance and cancer). They can also provide you with other reports and information on carcinogens.

☎ Contact:
National Institute of Occupational
Safety and Health
4676 Columbia Pkwy.
Cincinnati, OH 45226
(800) 35-NIOSH
(513) 533-8326

The National Cancer Institute (NCI) will send you whatever publications and reprints of journal articles they have on Carcinogens. They can also search their Physician's Data Query (PDQ) database to let you know if NCI is conducting any clinical studies on your disease.

☎ Contact:
National Cancer Institute
Bldg. 31, Room 10A24
Bethesda, MD 20892
(800) 4-CANCER
(301) 496-5583

Free Publications/Videos

The following publication is available from the National Toxicology Program, MD B2-04, P.O. Box 12233, Research Triangle Park, NC 27709; (919) 541-3991.

- *Annual Report on Carcinogens*. Identifies some 50 substances and processes and gives summaries of the evidence for their link with cancer in humans and laboratory animals. It also provides information on production, use, population exposed, cities, and federal regulations to safeguard the public.

CARCINOMA

Clearinghouses/Hotlines

The National Cancer Institute (NCI) will send you whatever publications and reprints of journal articles they have on Carcinoma. They can also give you information on the state-of-the-art treatment for this disease, including specific treatment information for your stage of cancer. They can also search their Physician's Data Query (PDQ) database to let you know if NCI is conducting any clinical studies on your disease.

☎ Contact:
National Cancer Institute
Bldg. 31, Room 10A24
Bethesda, MD 20892
(800) 4-CANCER
(301) 496-5583

CARDIOMEGALY

Clearinghouses/Hotlines

The National Heart, Lung, and Blood Institute (NHLBI) can search the Combined Health Information Database (CHID) and generate a bibliography of resources on Cardiomegaly for you. They also will send you any publications and journal articles they may have on hand, and will refer you to other organizations studying this condition. If you can't afford treatment, have your doctor call NHLBI to find out if they are conducting any clinical studies that you might qualify for.

☎ Contact:
National Heart, Lung, and Blood Institute

Bldg. 31, Room 4A21
Bethesda, MD 20892
(301) 496-4236

CARDIOMYOPATHY

Clearinghouses/Hotlines

The National Heart, Lung, and Blood Institute (NHLBI) can search the Combined Health Information Database (CHID) and generate a bibliography of resources on Hypertrophic Cardiomyopathy for you. They also will send you any publications and journal articles they may have on hand, and will refer you to other organizations that are studying this issue. If you can't afford treatment, have your doctor call NHLBI to find out if they are conducting any clinical studies that you might qualify for.

☎ Contact:
National Heart, Lung, and Blood Institute
Bldg. 31, Room 4A21
Bethesda, MD 20892
(301) 496-4236

CARDIOPULMONARY RESUSCITATION

Clearinghouses/Hotlines

The National Heart, Lung, and Blood Institute (NHLBI) can search the Combined Health Information Database (CHID) and generate a bibliography of resources on Cardiopulmonary Resuscitation (CPR) for you. They also will send you any publications and journal articles they may have on hand, and will refer you to other organizations that are studying this procedure.

☎ Contact:
National Heart, Lung, and Blood Institute
Bldg. 31, Room 4A21
Bethesda, MD 20892
(301) 496-4236

CARDIOVASCULAR DISEASE

See also Heart Disease

Clearinghouses/Hotlines

The National Heart, Lung, and Blood Institute (NHLBI) can search the Combined Health Information Database (CHID) and generate a bibliography of resources on Cardiovascular Disease for you. They also will send you any publications and journal articles they may have on hand, and will refer you to other organizations that are studying this disease. If you can't afford treatment, have your doctor call NHLBI to find out if they are conducting any clinical studies that you might qualify for.

☎ Contact:
National Heart, Lung, and Blood Institute
Bldg. 31, Room 4A21
Bethesda, MD 20892
(301) 496-4236

Free Publications/Videos

The following publications are available from the Food and Nutrition Information Center, National Agricultural Library, Room 304, Beltsville, MD 20705; (301) 504-5719.

- *Nutrition and Cardiovascular Disease.* A list to help you locate further information or resources.
- *Childhood Obesity and Cardiovascular Disease.* A list of current references.

The following publication is available from the National Heart, Lung, and Blood Institute Information Center, 4733 Bethesda Ave., Suite 530, Bethesda, MD 20814; (301) 951-3260.

- *Directory of Cardiovascular Resources for Minority Populations.* Contains over 100 agencies, programs, publications, and other materials targeted to major minority groups.

CARDITIS

Clearinghouses/Hotlines

The National Heart, Lung, and Blood Institute (NHLBI) can search the Combined Health Information Database (CHID) and generate a bibliography of resources on Carditis for you. They also will send you any publications and journal articles they may have on hand, and will refer you to other organizations that are studying this disease. If you can't afford treatment, have your doctor call NHLBI to find out if they are conducting any clinical studies that you might qualify for.

☎ Contact:
National Heart, Lung, and Blood Institute
Building 31
Room 4A21
Bethesda, MD 20892
(301) 496-4236

CARIES

Clearinghouses/Hotlines

The National Institute of Dental Research (NIDR) will send you whatever publications and reprints of journal articles they have on Caries. As a policy, NIDR will not refer you to other organizations or experts who study Caries. If you can't afford treatment, have your doctor call Dr. Albert Guckers at (301) 496-6241 to find out if NIDR is conducting any clinical studies that you might qualify for.

☎ Contact:
National Institute of Dental Research
Building 31
Room 2C35
Bethesda, MD 20892
(301) 496-4261

CARMUSTINE

Free Publications/Videos

The following publication on Carmustine is available from the National Cancer Institute, Bldg. 31, Room 10A24, Bethesda, MD 20892; (800) 4-CANCER, or (301) 496-5583.

- *Carmustina/Carmustine.* Provides information about side effects, proper usage, and precautions of this anti-cancer drug.

CAROTID ENDARTERECTOMY

Free Publications/Videos

The following publication is available from the National Institute of Neurological Disorders and Stroke, P.O. Box 5801, Bethesda, MD 20824; (800) 352-9424, or (301) 496-5751.

- *Clinical Alert (North American Symptomatic Carotid Endarterectomy Trial).*

CARPAL TUNNEL SYNDROME

Clearinghouses/Hotlines

Carpal Tunnel Syndrome, a tingling sensation in the hands and fingers, can be caused or aggravated by repeated twisting or awkward postures, particularly when combined with high force. The population at risk includes people employed in such industries or occupations as construction, food preparation, clerical work, product fabrication and mining. The National Institute for Occupational Safety and Health has a booklet of information on the syndrome, including current research, preventive recommendations, a bibliography, and articles.

☎ Contact:
National Institute For Occupational
Safety and Health
4676 Columbia Parkway
Cincinnati, Ohio 45226
(800) 356-4674

The National Institute of Arthritis and Musculoskeletal and Skin Diseases (NIAMS) will send you
whatever publications and reprints of articles from
texts and journals they have on Carpal Tunnel
Syndrome. They will also refer you to other
organizations that are studying this condition.
NIAMS will let you know of any clinical studies
that may be studying CTS and looking for patients.

☎ Contact:
National Institute of Arthritis
and Musculoskeletal and Skin Diseases
Box AMS
Bethesda, MD 20892
(301) 495-4484

The National Institute of Neurological Disorders
and Stroke (NINDS) can send you only
information they have in their publications list on
Carpal Tunnel Syndrome. This Clearinghouse
cannot directly give you information about any
current clinical studies NINDS might be
conducting on this illness, but you can find this
information for yourself by looking under the
National Institute of Neurological Disorders and
Stroke in *Appendix A* at the end of this book.

☎ Contact:
National Institute of Neurological
Disorders and Stroke
Bldg. 31, Room 8A06
Bethesda, MD 20892
(301) 496-5751
(800) 352-9424

Free Publications/Videos

The following publication on Carpal Tunnel
Syndrome is available from the National Institute
of Neurological Disorders and Stroke, P.O. Box
5801, Bethesda, MD 20824; (800) 352-9424, or
(301) 496-5751.

- *Carpal Tunnel Syndrome*. Contains a collection of scientific articles, patient education

pamphlets, and addresses of voluntary
health associations.

CARPET FUMES

Free Publications/Videos

The following publication is available from the
Consumer Information Center, Pueblo, CO 81009.

- *Indoor Air Quality and New Carpet*. (#620Y)

CATAPHASIA

Clearinghouses/Hotlines

The National Institute of Neurological Disorders
and Stroke (NINDS) can provide you with
information regarding Aphasia, and can search for
information regarding cataphasia, as well as being
able to refer you to organizations dealing with this
condition. This Clearinghouse cannot directly give
you information about any current clinical studies
NINDS might be conducting on this illness, but
you can find this information for yourself by
looking under the National Institute of
Neurological Disorders and Stroke in *Appendix A*
at the end of this book.

☎ Contact:
National Institute of Neurological
Disorders and Stroke
Bldg. 31, Room 8A06
Bethesda, MD 20892
(301) 496-5751
(800) 352-9424

CATAPLEXY

Clearinghouses/Hotlines

The National Institute of Neurological Disorders
and Stroke (NINDS) can send you only

information they have in their publications list on Cataplexy. This Clearinghouse cannot directly give you information about any current clinical studies NINDS might be conducting on this condition, but you can find this information for yourself by looking under the National Institute of Neurological Disorders and Stroke in *Appendix A* at the end of this book.

☎ Contact:
National Institute of Neurological
Disorders and Stroke
Bldg. 31, Room 8A06
Bethesda, MD 20892
(301) 496-5751
(800) 352-9424

CATARACTS

Clearinghouses/Hotlines

The National Eye Institute (NEI) can give you up-to-date information on Cataracts and Glaucoma Prevention by searching the Combined Health Information Database (CHID) and MEDLINE and sending you bibliographies of resources, along with any journal articles they may have. They can also refer you to any other organizations that study this and other related diseases. NEI will also let you know of any clinical studies that may be studying this disease and looking for patients. Because of their small staff, NEI prefers that you submit your requests for information in writing.

☎ Contact:
National Eye Institute
Bldg. 31, Room 6A32
Bethesda, MD 20892
(301) 496-5248

CAT CRY SYNDROME

Clearinghouses/Hotlines

The National Institute of Child Health and Human Development (NICHD) will send you whatever publications and reprints of journal articles they

have on Cat Cry Syndrome (Cri Du Chat). If necessary, they will refer you to other experts or researchers in the field. If you can't afford treatment, have your doctor call NICHD to find out if they are conducting any clinical studies that you might qualify for.

☎ Contact:
National Institute of Child Health
and Human Development
Bldg. 31, Room 2A32
Bethesda, MD 20892
(301) 496-5133

CAT SCRATCH FEVER

Clearinghouses/Hotlines

The National Institute on Allergy and Infectious Diseases (NIAID) can search the Combined Health Information Database (CHID) and generate a bibliography of resources on Cat Scratch Fever for you. They will also send you any publications and journal articles they may have on hand, and will refer you to researchers who are currently studying this disease. If you can't afford treatment, have your doctor call NIAID to find out if they are conducting any clinical studies that you might qualify for.

☎ Contact:
National Institute of Allergy
and Infectious Diseases
Bldg. 31, Room 7A32
Bethesda, MD 20892
(301) 496-5717

CATHETERIZATION

Clearinghouses/Hotlines

The National Heart, Lung, and Blood Institute (NHLBI) can search the Combined Health Information Database (CHID) and generate a bibliography of resources on Cardiac or Heart Catheterization for you. They also will send you any publications and journal articles they may have on hand, and will refer you to other organizations that are studying this issue. If you can't afford treatment, have your doctor call NHLBI to find out if they are conducting any clinical studies that you might qualify for.

☎ Contact:
National Heart, Lung, and Blood Institute
Bldg. 31, Room 4A21
Bethesda, MD 20892
(301) 496-4236

CEA

Clearinghouses/Hotlines

The National Cancer Institute (NCI) will send you whatever publications and reprints of journal articles they have on CEA (Carcinoembryonic Antigen). They can give you information on state-of-the-art treatment for this disease, including specific treatment information for your stage of cancer. They can search their Physician's Data Query (PDQ) database to let you know if NCI is conducting any clinical studies on your disease.

☎ Contact:
National Cancer Institute
Bldg. 31, Room 10A24
Bethesda, MD 20892
(800) 4-CANCER
(301) 496-5583

CELIAC DISEASE

Clearinghouses/Hotlines

The National Institute of Diabetes and Digestive and Kidney Diseases's (NIDDK) individual clearinghouses can search the Combined Health Information Database (CHID) and generate a bibliography of resources on Celiac Disease for you. They also will send you any publications and journal articles they may have on hand, and will refer you to other organizations that are studying this disease. If you can't afford treatment, have your doctor call NIDDK to find out if they are

conducting any clinical studies that you might qualify for.

☎ Contact:
National Institute of Diabetes
and Digestive and Kidney Diseases
Bldg. 31, Room 9A04
Bethesda, MD 20892
(301) 496-3583

The National Cancer Institute (NCI) will send you whatever publications and reprints of journal articles they have on Celiac Disease. They can also give you information on the state-of-the-art treatment for this disease, including specific treatment information for your stage of cancer. They can also search their Physician's Data Query (PDQ) database to let you know if NCI is conducting any clinical studies on your disease.

☎ Contact:
National Cancer Institute
Bldg. 31, Room 10A24
Bethesda, MD 20892
(800) 4-CANCER
(301) 496-5583

The National Institute on Allergy and Infectious Diseases (NIAID) can search the Combined Health Information Database (CHID) and generate a bibliography of resources on Celiac Disease for you. They will also send you any publications and journal articles they may have on hand, and will refer you to researchers who are currently studying this disease. If you can't afford treatment, have your doctor call NIAID to find out if they are conducting any clinical studies that you might qualify for.

☎ Contact:
National Institute of Allergy
and Infectious Diseases
Bldg. 31, Room 7A32
Bethesda, MD 20892
(301) 496-5717

CELLULITE

Clearinghouses/Hotlines

The Food and Drug Administration monitors

many weight loss related-products and warns consumers about gimmicks sold that promise to get rid of fat on the hips and thighs. They can send you an informational package that includes consumer publications and reprints from research journals.

☎ Contact:
Food & Drug Administration
(HFE-88), 5600 Fishers Ln.
Rockville, MD 20857
(301) 443-3170

CENTENARIANS

Clearinghouses/Hotlines

The National Institute on Aging (NIA) will send you whatever publications and reprints of journal articles they have on Centenarians. They cannot refer you to other experts if the information they have isn't sufficient for your purposes.

☎ Contact:
National Institute on Aging
Bldg. 31, Room 5C27
Bethesda, MD 20892
(301) 496-1752

CENTRAL CORE DISEASE

Clearinghouses/Hotlines

The National Institute of Neurological Disorders and Stroke (NINDS) can send you only information they have in their publications list on Central Core Disease. This Clearinghouse cannot directly give you information about any current clinical studies NINDS might be conducting on this disease, but you can find this information for yourself by looking under the National Institute of Neurological Disorders and Stroke in *Appendix A* at the end of this book.

☎ Contact:
National Institute of Neurological
Disorders and Stroke
Bldg. 31, Room 8A06

Bethesda, MD 20892
(301) 496-5751
(800) 352-9424

Free Publications/Videos

The following publication is available from the National Institute of Neurological Disorders and Stroke, Bldg. 31, Room 8A06, Bethesda, MD 20892; (301) 496-5751 or (800) 352-9424.

- *Central Processing Dysfunctions in Children: A Review of Research, Monograph #9.* (#76-52)

CEREBELLAR ARTERIOSCLEROSIS

Clearinghouses/Hotlines

The National Institute of Neurological Disorders and Stroke (NINDS) can send you only information they have in their publications list on Cerebellar Arteriosclerosis. This Clearinghouse cannot directly give you information about any current clinical studies NINDS might be conducting on this illness, but you can find this information for yourself by looking under the National Institute of Neurological Disorders and Stroke in *Appendix A* at the end of this book.

☎ Contact:
National Institute of Neurological
Disorders and Stroke
Bldg. 31, Room 8A06
Bethesda, MD 20892
(301) 496-5751
(800) 352-9424

CEREBELLAR ATAXIA

Clearinghouses/Hotlines

The National Institute of Neurological Disorders and Stroke (NINDS) can send you only information they have in their publications list on

Cerebellar Ataxia. This Clearinghouse cannot directly give you information about any current clinical studies NINDS might be conducting on this illness, but you can find this information for yourself by looking under the National Institute of Neurological Disorders and Stroke in *Appendix A* at the end of this book.

☎ Contact:
National Institute of Neurological
Disorders and Stroke
Bldg. 31, Room 8A06
Bethesda, MD 20892
(301) 496-5751
(800) 352-9424

CEREBELLAR LESIONS

Clearinghouses/Hotlines

The National Institute of Neurological Disorders and Stroke (NINDS) can send you only information they have in their publications list on Hereditary Cerebellar Lesions. This Clearinghouse cannot directly give you information about any current clinical studies NINDS might be conducting on this topic, but you can find this information for yourself by looking under the National Institute of Neurological Disorders and Stroke in *Appendix A* at the end of this book.

☎ Contact:
National Institute of Neurological
Disorders and Stroke
Bldg. 31, Room 8A06
Bethesda, MD 20892
(301) 496-5751
(800) 352-9424

CEREBRAL ARTERIOVENOUS MALFORMATIONS

Clearinghouses/Hotlines

The National Institute of Neurological Disorders

and Stroke (NINDS) can send you only information they have in their publications list on Cerebral Arteriovenous Malformations. This Clearinghouse cannot directly give you information about any current clinical studies NINDS might be conducting on this topic, but you can find this information for yourself by looking under the National Institute of Neurological Disorders and Stroke in *Appendix A* at the end of this book.

☎ Contact:
National Institute of Neurological
Disorders and Stroke
Bldg. 31, Room 8A06
Bethesda, MD 20892
(301) 496-5751
(800) 352-9424

CEREBRAL ATROPHY

Clearinghouses/Hotlines

The National Institute of Neurological Disorders and Stroke (NINDS) can send you only information they have in their publications list on Cerebral Atrophy. This Clearinghouse cannot directly give you information about any current clinical studies NINDS might be conducting on this condition, but you can find this information for yourself by looking under the National Institute of Neurological Disorders and Stroke in *Appendix A* at the end of this book.

☎ Contact:
National Institute of Neurological
Disorders and Stroke
Bldg. 31, Room 8A06
Bethesda, MD 20892
(301) 496-5751
(800) 352-9424

Free Publications/Videos

The following publication is available from the National Institute of Neurological Disorders and Stroke, P.O. Box 5801, Bethesda, MD 20824; (800) 352-9424, (301) 496-5751.

- *Cerebral Atrophy*. Contains a collection of scientific articles, patient education

pamphlets, and addresses of voluntary health associations.

CEREBRAL PALSY

Clearinghouses/Hotlines

The National Institute on Deafness and Other Communicative Disorders (NIDCD) will send you whatever publications and reprints of journal articles they have on Cerebral Palsy. If you need further information, they will refer you to other organizations that study this and other related diseases. NIDCD does not conduct any clinical studies for this or any other disorder.

☎ Contact:
National Institute on Deafness
and Other Communication Disorders
Bldg. 31, Room 3C35
Bethesda, MD 20892
(301) 496-7243
(800) 241-1044
(301) 402-0252 (TDD)

The National Institute of Neurological Disorders and Stroke (NINDS) can send you only information they have in their publications list on Cerebral Palsy. This Clearinghouse cannot directly give you information about any current clinical studies NINDS might be conducting on this illness, but you can find this information for yourself by looking under the National Institute of Neurological Disorders and Stroke in *Appendix A* at the end of this book.

☎ Contact:
National Institute of Neurological
Disorders and Stroke
Bldg. 31, Room 8A06
Bethesda, MD 20892
(301) 496-5751
(800) 352-9424

Free Publications/Videos

The following publications are available from the National Institute of Neurological Disorders and Stroke, Bldg. 31, Room 8A06, Bethesda, MD

20892; (301) 496-5751 or (800) 352-9424.

- *Cerebral Palsy: Hope Through Research.* Covers the latest developments on this disease. (#84-158)
- *Cerebral Palsy.* Contains a collection of scientific articles, patient education pamphlets, and addresses of voluntary health associations.
- *Cerebral Palsy.* (#81-159)

CEREBROTENDIOUS XANTHOMATOSIS

Clearinghouses/Hotlines

The National Institute of Neurological Disorders and Stroke (NINDS) can send you only information they have in their publications list on Cerebrotendious Xanthomatosis. This Clearinghouse cannot directly give you information about any current clinical studies NINDS might be conducting on this illness, but you can find this information for yourself by looking under the National Institute of Neurological Disorders and Stroke in *Appendix A* at the end of this book.

☎ Contact:
National Institute of Neurological
Disorders and Stroke
Bldg. 31, Room 8A06
Bethesda, MD 20892
(301) 496-5751
(800) 352-9424

CEREBROVASCULAR DISEASE

Clearinghouses/Hotlines

The National Institute of Neurological Disorders and Stroke (NINDS) can send you only information they have in their publications list on Cerebrovascular Disease. This Clearinghouse cannot directly give you information about any current clinical studies NINDS might be conducting on this illness, but you can find this information for yourself by looking under the National Institute of Neurological Disorders and Stroke in *Appendix A* at the end of this book.

☎ Contact:
National Institute of Neurological
Disorders and Stroke
Bldg. 31, Room 8A06
Bethesda, MD 20892
(301) 496-5751
(800) 352-9424

CEROID LIPOFUSCINOSIS

Clearinghouses/Hotlines

The National Institute of Neurological Disorders and Stroke (NINDS) can send you only information they have in their publications list on Ceroid Lipofuscinosis. This Clearinghouse cannot directly give you information about any current clinical studies NINDS might be conducting on this illness, but you can find this information for yourself by looking under the National Institute of Neurological Disorders and Stroke in *Appendix A* at the end of this book.

☎ Contact:
National Institute of Neurological
Disorders and Stroke
Bldg. 31, Room 8A06
Bethesda, MD 20892
(301) 496-5751
(800) 352-9424

CERVICAL CANCER

See also Cancer

Clearinghouses/Hotlines

The National Cancer Institute (NCI) will send you whatever publications and reprints of journal articles they have on Cervical Cancer. They can also give you information on the state-of-the-art

treatment for this disease, including specific treatment information for your stage of cancer. They can also search their Physician's Data Query (PDQ) database to let you know if NCI is conducting any clinical studies on your disease.

☎ Contact:
National Cancer Institute
Bldg. 31, Room 10A24
Bethesda, MD 20892
(800) 4-CANCER
(301) 496-5583

Free Publications/Videos

The following publication is available from the National Cancer Institute, Bldg. 31, Room 10A24, Bethesda, MD 20892; (800) 4-CANCER, or (301) 496-5583.

- *What You Need to Know About Cancer of the Cervix.* (#90-2047)

CERVICAL CAP

See also Contraception

Free Publications/Videos

The following publication is available from the Food & Drug Administration, (HFE-88), 5600 Fishers Ln., Rockville, MD 20857; (301) 443-3170.

- *Cervical Cap? Newest Control Device.* (#FDA89-1150)

CERVICAL DISORDERS

See also Cervical Cancer

Clearinghouses/Hotlines

The National Institute of Child Health and Human Development (NICHD) will send you whatever publications and reprints of journal articles they have on Non-Malignant Cervical Disorders. If necessary, they will refer you to other experts or researchers in the field. If you can't afford treatment, have your doctor call NICHD to find out if they are conducting any clinical studies that you might qualify for.

☎ Contact:
National Institute of Child Health
and Human Development
Building 31
Room 2A32
Bethesda, MD 20892
(301) 496-5133

CESAREANS

Clearinghouses/Hotlines

The National Institute of Child Health and Human Development (NICHD) will send you whatever publications and reprints of journal articles they have on Cesarean Births. If necessary, they will refer you to other experts or researchers in the field.

☎ Contact:
National Institute of Child Health
and Human Development
Building 31
Room 2A32
Bethesda, MD 20892
(301) 496-5133

Free Publications/Videos

The following publications on Cesarean Childbirth are available from the National Institute of Child Health and Human Development, Bldg. 31, Room 2A32, Bethesda, MD 20892; (301) 496-5133.

- *Cesarean Childbirth.*
- *Facts About Cesarean Childbirth.* Discusses cesarean delivery, types of incisions, current thinking about repeat cesarean, and the pros and cons of this method of birth. (#431P)

CESTODE

See Tapeworm

CHAGAS' DISEASE

Clearinghouses/Hotlines

The National Institute on Allergy and Infectious Diseases (NIAID) can search the Combined Health Information Database (CHID) and generate a bibliography of resources on Chagas' Disease for you. They will also send you any publications and journal articles they may have on hand, and will refer you to researchers who are currently studying this disease. If you can't afford treatment, have your doctor call NIAID to find out if they are conducting any clinical studies that you might qualify for.

☎ Contact:
National Institute of Allergy
and Infectious Diseases
Bldg. 31, Room 7A32
Bethesda, MD 20892
(301) 496-5717

CHALAZION

Clearinghouses/Hotlines

The National Eye Institute (NEI) can give you up-to-date information on Chalazion by searching the Combined Health Information Database (CHID) and MEDLINE and sending you bibliographies of resources, along with any journal articles they may have. They can also refer you to any other organizations that study this and other related issues. NEI will also let you know of any clinical studies that may be studying Chalazion and looking for patients. Because of their small staff, NEI prefers that you submit your requests for information in writing.

☎ Contact:
National Eye Institute
Bldg. 31, Room 6A32
Bethesda, MD 20892
(301) 496-5248

CHANCROID

Clearinghouses/Hotlines

The Sexually Transmitted Diseases Hotline offers valuable information to the public about a wide range of sexually transmitted diseases, including Chancroid and how to protect yourself from contracting them.

☎ Contact:
National Sexually Transmitted Diseases Hotline
P.O. Box 13827
Research Triangle Park, NC 27709
(800) 227-8922

CHANGE OF LIFE

See Menopause

CHAPARRAL TEA

Clearinghouses/Hotlines

The National Cancer Institute (NCI) will send you whatever publications and reprints of journal articles they have on Chaparral Tea. They can also search their Physician's Data Query (PDQ) database to let you know if NCI is conducting any clinical studies on your disease.

☎ Contact:
National Cancer Institute
Bldg. 31, Room 10A24
Bethesda, MD 20892
(800) 4-CANCER
(301) 496-5583

CHARCOAL BROILING OF MEAT

Clearinghouses/Hotlines

The National Cancer Institute (NCI) will send you whatever publications and reprints of journal articles they have on Charcoal Broiling of Meat as it relates to cancer. They can also search their Physician's Data Query (PDQ) database to let you know if NCI is conducting any clinical studies on your disease.

☎ Contact:
National Cancer Institute
Building 31
Room 10A24
Bethesda, MD 20892
(800) 4-CANCER
(301) 496-5583

CHARCOT-MARIE-TOOTH DISEASE

Clearinghouses/Hotlines

The National Institute of Neurological Disorders and Stroke (NINDS) can send you only information they have in their publications list on Charcot-Marie-Tooth Disease. This Clearinghouse cannot directly give you information about any current clinical studies NINDS might be conducting on this illness, but you can find this information for yourself by looking under the National Institute of Neurological Disorders and Stroke in *Appendix A* at the end of this book.

☎ Contact:
National Institute of Neurological
Disorders and Stroke
Building 31
Room 8A06
Bethesda, MD 20892
(301) 496-5751
(800) 352-9424

Free Publications/Videos

The following publication on Charcot-Marie-Tooth Syndrome is available from the National Institute of Neurological Disorders and Stroke, P.O. Box 5801, Bethesda, MD 20824; (800) 352-9424, or (301) 496-5751.

- *Charcot-Marie-Tooth Syndrome.* A collection of scientific articles, patient education pamphlets, and addresses of voluntary health associations.

CHARGE SYNDROME

Clearinghouses/Hotlines

The National Institute of Child Health and Human Development (NICHD) will send you whatever publications and reprints of journal articles they have on Charge Syndrome. If necessary, they will refer you to other experts or researchers in the field. If you can't afford treatment, have your doctor call NICHD to find out if they are conducting any clinical studies that you might qualify for.

☎ Contact:
National Institute of Child Health
and Human Development
Bldg. 31, Room 2A32
Bethesda, MD 20892
(301) 496-5133

CHEDIAK-HIGASHI SYNDROME

Clearinghouses/Hotlines

The National Institute on Allergy and Infectious Diseases (NIAID) can search the Combined Health Information Database (CHID) and generate a bibliography of resources on Chediak-Higashi Syndrome for you. They will also send you any publications and journal articles they may have on hand, and will refer you to researchers who are currently studying this

disease. If you can't afford treatment, have your doctor call NIAID to find out if they are conducting any clinical studies that you might qualify for.

☎ Contact:
National Institute of Allergy
and Infectious Diseases
Bldg. 31, Room 7A32
Bethesda, MD 20892
(301) 496-5717

CHEILOASCHISIS

See Harelip

CHELATION THERAPY

Clearinghouses/Hotlines

The National Heart, Lung, and Blood Institute (NHLBI) can search the Combined Health Information Database (CHID) and generate a bibliography of resources on Chelation Therapy for Arteriosis and Hemosiderosis for you. They also will send you any publications and journal articles they may have on hand, and will refer you to other organizations that are studying this procedure. If you can't afford treatment, have your doctor call NHLBI to find out if they are conducting any clinical studies that you might qualify for.

☎ Contact:
National Heart, Lung, and Blood Institute
Bldg. 31, Room 4A21
Bethesda, MD 20892
(301) 496-4236

CHEMICAL SPILLS

Clearinghouses/Hotlines

The Environmental Protection Agency's Emergency Planning and Community Right to

Know Hotline helps communities prepare for accidental releases of toxic chemicals by providing documents and other publications necessary. Communities can call to obtain interim guidelines, *Community: Developing a Chemical Contingency Plan*, and gathering site-specific information. The hotline can also provide you with a list of more than 400 acutely toxic chemicals and direct you to sources for obtaining information about chemicals stored in your community.

☎ Contact:
Environmental Protection Agency
(800) 535-0202
(703) 920-9877

CHEMOTHERAPY

Clearinghouses/Hotlines

The National Cancer Institute (NCI) will send you whatever publications and reprints of journal articles they have on Chemotherapy for Cancer. They can also give you information on the state-of-the-art techniques, including specific treatment information for your stage of cancer. They can also search their Physician's Data Query (PDQ) database to let you know if NCI is conducting any clinical studies on your disease.

☎ Contact:
National Cancer Institute
Bldg. 31, Room 10A24
Bethesda, MD 20892
(800) 4-CANCER
(301) 496-5583

The National Institute of Dental Research (NIDR) will send you whatever publications and reprints of journal articles they have on the effects of Chemotherapy on Teeth. As a policy, NIDR will not refer you to other organizations or experts who study this disease. If you can't afford treatment, have your doctor call Dr. Albert Guckers at (301) 496-6241 to find out if NIDR is conducting any clinical studies that you might qualify for.

☎ Contact:
National Institute of Dental Research
Building 31

Room 2C35
Bethesda, MD 20892
(301) 496-4261

Free Publications/Videos

The following publication on Chemotherapy is available from the National Cancer Institute, Bldg. 31, Room 10A24, Bethesda, MD 20892; (800) 4-CANCER, or (301) 496-5583.

- *Chemotherapy and You: A Guide to Self-Help During Treatment*. (#91-1136) Addresses problems and concerns of patients receiving chemotherapy.

CHEWING TOBACCO AND SNUFF

See Smoking
See Smokeless Tobacco

CHICKEN POX

Clearinghouses/Hotlines

The National Institute on Allergy and Infectious Diseases (NIAID) can search the Combined Health Information Database (CHID) and generate a bibliography of resources on Chicken Pox for you. They will also send you any publications and journal articles they may have on hand, and will refer you to researchers who are currently studying this disease. If you can't afford treatment, have your doctor call NIAID to find out if they are conducting any clinical studies that you might qualify for.

☎ Contact:
National Institute of Allergy
and Infectious Diseases
Bldg. 31, Room 7A32
Bethesda, MD 20892
(301) 496-5717

CHILBLAIN

Clearinghouses/Hotlines

The National Arthritis and Musculoskeletal and Skin Diseases Clearinghouse can provide you with information regarding Chilblain, which is a skin condition caused by exposure to the cold. They can search their data base for articles, reference materials, and more.

☎ Contact:
National Arthritis and Musculoskeletal
and Skin Diseases Information Clearinghouse
9000 Rockville Pike
Box AMS
Bethesda, MD 20892
(301) 495-4484

CHILD ABUSE AND FAMILY VIOLENCE

Clearinghouses/Hotlines

The Clearinghouse on Child Abuse and Neglect can give you information on a variety of programs dealing with Child Abuse and neglect, including the causes, prevention, and treatment.

☎ Contact:
Administration for Children,
Youth, and Families
P.O. Box 1182
Washington, DC 20013
(800) FYI-3366

Free Publications/Videos

The following publications on Child Abuse are available from the Clearinghouse on Child Abuse & Neglect Information, P.O. Box 1182, Washington, DC 20013; (800) FYI-3366.

- *Child Abuse and Neglect: An Informed Approach To A Shared Concern.* Provides information about detecting child abuse and how to obtain help.
- *A Report to Congress: Joining Together to Fight Child Abuse.* (#20-01070)
- *Child Protection: The Role of the Courts.* (#80- 30256)
- *The Role of Law Enforcement in the Prevention and Treatment of Child Abuse and Neglect.* (#84-30193)
- *Anti-social Behavior Resulting From Abuse.* Annotated bibliography. (#07-91123, $3.50)
- *Characteristics of Abused Children.* Annotated bibliography. (#07-91135, $4.50)
- *Child Fatalities.* Annotated bibliography. (#07-91180, $3.50)
- *Day Care.* Annotated bibliography. (#07-91175, $3)
- *Shaken Baby Syndrome.* (1971-91 Publications). Annotated bibliography. (#07-91184, $1)
- *False Allegations.* Annotated bibliography covering child abuse issues. (#07-91163, $3.50)

The following publications on Child Abuse are available from the Clearinghouse on Family Violence Information, P.O. Box 1182, Washington, DC 20013; (703) 385-7565.

- *Calendar of Conferences on Child Protection and Family Violence Issues.* ($1.00)
- *Child Abuse Prevention, Adoption, and Family Services Act of 1988.*
- *Child Abuse and Neglect and Family Violence Audiovisual Catalog.* ($20.00)
- *Child Abuse and Neglect and Family Violence Thesaurus.* ($25.00)
- *Family Violence Public Awareness Materials for Adults and Children.* ($3.00)
- *Classic Literature in Family Violence: Annotated Bibliography.* ($1.00)
- *Databases Containing Family Violence Information: Annotated Bibliography.* ($1.00)
- *State Legislative Solutions to the Problem of Family Violence: Annotated Bibliography.* ($1.80)
- *Family Violence: An Overview.*
- *Organizations Concerned with Child Abuse and Neglect and Family Violence Issues.* ($5.50)

- Family Violence Research Instruments With Bibliography. ($1.50)

The following publications on Child Abuse are available from the National Resource Center on Child Sexual Abuse, Information Service, 106 Lincoln St., Huntsville, AL 35801; (800) KIDS-0006, or (205) 533-KIDS.

- *Allegations of Sexual Abuse in Child Custody and Visitation Situations.* ($12)
- *Child Protective Services: A System in Crisis.* ($12)
- *A Judicial Response to Child Sexual Abuse.* ($12)
- *Enhancing Child Sexual Abuse Services to Minority Cultures.* ($12)
- *Investigation of Ritualistic Abuse Allegations.* ($12)
- *Sibling Incest.* ($12)
- *Professionals and Volunteers with a History of Abuse.* ($12)
- *Traditional Native American Healing and Child Sexual Abuse.* ($12)
- *A Coordinated Community Approach To Child Sexual Abuse: Assessing A Model.* ($12)

The following Congressional Research Service (CRS) reports on Child Abuse are available from either of your U.S. Senators' offices at the U.S. Capitol, Washington, DC 20510, or from your Congressional Representative at the U.S. Capitol, Washington, DC 20515. You can also call in your request through the U.S. Capitol switchboard at (202) 224-3121. Be sure to include the full title and report number in your request.

- *Child Abuse Act and Related Programs: Reauthorization Issues; Issue Brief.* (IB91027)
- *Child Abuse and Neglect: Data and Federal Programs.* (89-127 EPW)
- *Child Abuse and Neglect in the United States: Legislative Issues: Selected References, 1985-1988.* (89-13 L)
- *Child Abuse: Info Pack* (IP019C)
- *The State's Duty to Child Abuse Victims: DeShaney vs. Winnebago County Department of Social Services.* (89-201 A)

CHILD DEVELOPMENT

Clearinghouses/Hotlines

The National Institute of Child Health and Human Development (NICHD) can send you information on fetal, maternal and Child Development, as well as materials on reproductive biology, contraception, mental retardation, and a host of other related fields.

☎ Contact:
National Institute of Child Health
and Human Development
Bldg. 31, Room 2A32
Bethesda, MD 20892
(301) 496-5133

Free Publications/Videos

The following publications are available from the National Institute of Mental Health, 5600 Fishers Ln., Room 15C05, Rockville, MD 20857; (301) 443-4515.

- *Importance of Play.*
- *Learning While Growing: Cognitive Development.*
- *Research on Children and Adolescents with Mental, Behavioral and Development Disorders.*
- *Stimulating Baby Senses.*

The following publication is available from the Consumer Information Center, P.O. Box 100, Pueblo, CO 81002.

- *Dealing With the Angry Child.* Practical advice to help children learn to channel and direct their anger to constructive ends. (#505Z)

The following publication is available from the National Maternal and Child Health Clearinghouse, 38th and R Sts., NW, Washington, DC 20057; (703) 821-8955, ext. 254.

- *Patient Education Materials: A Resource Guide.* Developed to help health professionals identify and locate materials on maternal and child health topics that are clear, concise, easy to read and appropriate for the general public. The guide is separated into three sections. The first is patient education materials, which is an annotated listing of source books, directories, audiovisuals, and resource guides that describe patient education materials. The second section lists publishers of patient education materials, and the third lists federal health information clearinghouses.

CHILD HEALTH

See also Lead Poisoning

Clearinghouses/Hotlines

The National Institute of Child Health and Human Development (NICHD) can send you information on fetal, maternal and child development, as well as materials on reproductive biology, contraception, mental retardation, and a host of other related fields.

☎ Contact:
National Institute of Child Health
and Human Development
Bldg. 31, Room 2A32
Bethesda, MD 20892
(301) 496-5133

The National Maternal and Child Health Clearinghouse has all kinds of information on maternal and Child Health issues, such as pregnancy, child and adolescent health, and human genetics. If the answer to your question can't be answered by any of their countless free publications, they can refer you to other national or local resources. If you still need further information, they search their own reference collection and send you what they find.

☎ Contact:
National Maternal and Child
Health Clearinghouse
38th & R Sts., NW
Washington, DC 20057
(703) 821-8955, ext. 254

Free Publications/Videos

The following publications on Child Health are available from the National Maternal and Child Health Clearinghouse, 38th & R Sts., NW, Washington, DC 20057; (703) 821-8955, ext. 254.

- *Advances in the Prevention of Low Birthweight: An International Symposium.* (#EEO2)
- *Environmental Exposures and Pregnancy: Resource Guide.* (#DOO8)
- *Prenatal Care: Resource Guide.* (#D013)
- *Newborn Screening for Genetic-Metabolic Diseases: Progress, Principles and Recommendations.* (#B048)
- *State Laws and Regulations Governing Newborn Screening.* (#B205)
- *Pre-term and Low Birthweight Infants: Resource Guide.* (#D015)
- *Nutrition During Lactation.* (#D081)
- *Nutrition During Lactation/Summary.* (#D080)
- *Recommendations for Feeding Normal Infants.* (#B060)
- *Skim Milk in Infant Feeding.* (#B042)
- *Surgeon General's Workshop on Breastfeeding and Human Lactation.* (#B163)
- *Playground Perspectives: A Curriculum Guide for Promoting Playground Safety.* (#C036)
- *Surgeon General's Workshop on Drunk Driving.* (#C044)
- *Children With Special Health Care Needs: Resource Guide.* (#D009)
- *Clinical Programs for Mentally Retarded Children.* (#B169)
- *Dental Implications of Epilepsy.* (#B053)
- *Guidelines for Purchase of Services and Assistive Devices for Individuals With Communication Disorders.* (#B180)
- *Nutrition Services For Children With Special Needs.* (#E027)
- *Pediatric Pulmonology Guidelines for the Care of Children With Chronic Lung Disease.* (#C035)
- *Surgeon General's Workshop on Children With Handicaps and Their Families.* (#B118)
- *Technology-Dependent Children: Hospital v. Home Care.* (#B316)
- *Warning Signals: Basic Criteria for Tracking At Risk Infants and Toddlers.* (#B259)

- *Four Critical Junctures: Support for Parents of Children With Special Needs.* (#C016)
- *Learning Together: Guide for Families with Genetic Disorders.* (#B076)
- *The Open Door: Parent Participation in State Policymaking About Children with Special Health Needs.* (#B339)
- *Reader's Guide for Parents of Children With Mental, Physical, or Emotional Disabilities.* (#B059)
- *Women Helping Women: Networks for Support and Caring.* (#D052)
- *Cooley's Anemia: A Psychosocial Directory.* (#B221)
- *Management and Therapy of Sickle Cell Disease.* (#E069, in press)
- *Problem Oriented Management of Sickle Cell Syndromes* (#E042)
- *Sickle Cell Anemia and Comprehensive Care: A New Horizon.* (#D065)
- *Sickle Cell: A Resource Guide for Families and Professionals.* (#D058)
- *Building Systems of Care for Children with HIV Infection and Their Families.* (#C064)
- *Children with HIV/AIDS: A Sourcebook for Caring.* (#C066)
- *A Babysitter's Guide to PKU.* (#B265)
- *Chef Lo-Phe's Phe-Nominal Cookbook.* (#B322)
- *Dental Health in Children With PKU.* (#B146)
- *Finger Foods Are Fun.* (#B279)
- *Games That Teach: Learning by Doing for Preschoolers with PKU.* (#B280)
- *Guide to Breastfeeding the Infant with PKU.* (#B327)
- *Contact: National Survey of Treatment Programs for PKU and Selected Other Inherited Metabolic Diseases.* (#C049)
- *New Parents' Guide to PKU.* (#B335)
- *Organizing Self-Help Groups: Resource Guide.* (#D012)
- *Patient Education Materials: Resource Guide.* (#E008)
- *Starting Early: A Guide to Federal Resources in Maternal and Child Health.* (#B349)
- *Surgeon General's Workshop on Self-Help and Public Health.* (#B351)
- *One-Stop Shopping for Perinatal Services.* (#D071)
- *Annotated Bibliography: Educational Materials on DNA Techniques in Genetic Testing and*

Counseling. (#E047)
- *Genetic Services: Abstracts of Active Projects FY 1991.* (#E007)
- *Genetic Services for Underserved Populations.* (#D047)
- *A Guide to Selected National Genetic Voluntary Organizations.* (#B359)
- *Human Genetics: Resource Guide.* (#D011)
- *New Human Genetics: How Gene Splicing Helps Researchers Fight Inherited Diseases.* (#B194)
- *Understanding DNA Testing: A Basic Guide for Families.* (#D088)
- *1990 Resource Guide to Organizations Concerned with Developmental Handicaps.* Focuses on children with special health care needs.
- *Pediatric AIDS: Abstracts of Active Projects FY 1990 and FY 1991.*
- *Surgeon General's Workshop on Children with HIV Infection and Their Families, Report.*

The following publication on Child Health is available from Food & Nutrition Information Center, National Agricultural Library, Room 304, Beltsville, MD 20705-2351; (301) 504-5719.

- *Children's Literature on Food and Nutrition.* Designed to help you locate resources on this topic.

The following publications on Child Health are available from the Food & Drug Administration, (HFE-88), 5600 Fishers Ln., Rockville, MD 20857; (301) 443-3170.

- *Doing More Good Than Harm With Children's Medications.* (#FDA91-3182)
- *Childhood Vaccines: A Responsibility to Remember.* (#FDA91-907)

The following publications on Child Health are available from the National Institute of Child Health and Human Development, Bldg. 31, Room 2A32, Bethesda, MD 20892; (301) 496-5133.

- *Standard Definitions for Childhood Injury Research.* (#92-1586)
- *From Cells to Selves: The National Institute of Child Health and Human Development.* (#89-83)

The following Congressional Research Service (CRS) reports on Child Health are available from either of your U.S. Senators' offices at the U.S. Capitol, Washington, DC 20510, or from your Congressional Representative at the U.S. Capitol, Washington, DC 20515. You can also call in your request through the U.S. Capitol switchboard at (202) 224-3121. Be sure to include the full title and report number in your request.

- *Federal Programs Affecting Children.* (#87-306 EPW)
- *Federal Programs for Children and Their Families.* (#90-131 EPW)
- *Health Care for Children: Federal Programs and Policies.* (#88-217 EPW)
- *Hispanic Children in Poverty.* (#85-170 EPW)
- *Right of Minors to Consent to Medical Care.* (#86-939 A)

CHILD PORNOGRAPHY

Free Publications/Videos

These Congressional Research Service (CRS) reports are available from either of your U.S. Senators' offices at the U.S. Capitol, Washington, DC 20510, or from your Congressional Representative at the U.S. Capitol, Washington, DC 20515. You can also call in your request through the U.S. Capitol switchboard at (202) 224-3121. Be sure to include the full title and report number in your request.

- *Child Pornography: Legal Considerations; Archived Issue Brief.* (#IB83148)
- *Federal Obscenity and Child Pornography Law.* (#91-118 A)

CHILD REARING

Clearinghouses/Hotlines

The National Institute of Mental Health (NIMH) will send you whatever publications and reprints of

articles from texts and journals they have on Child Rearing. They will also refer you to other organizations that are studying this issue. NIMH will also let you know of any clinical studies that may be studying this disease and looking for patients.

☎ Contact:
National Institute of Mental Health
5600 Fishers Ln., Room 15C05
Rockville, MD 20857
(301) 443-4515

CHILD SUPPORT

Free Publications/Videos

The following Congressional Research Service (CRS) report on Child Support is available from either of your U.S. Senators' offices at the U.S. Capitol, Washington, DC 20510, or from your Congressional Representative at the U.S. Capitol, Washington, DC 20515. You can also call in your request through the U.S. Capitol switchboard at (202) 224-3121. Be sure to include the full title and report number in your request.

- *The Child Support Enforcement Program: Policy and Practice.* (#89-659 EPW)

CHILDBIRTH

See also Postnatal Care

Clearinghouses/Hotlines

The National Institute of Child Health and Human Development (NICHD) will send you whatever publications and reprints of journal articles they have on Childbirth and Child Rearing. If necessary, they will refer you to other experts or researchers in the field.

☎ Contact:
National Institute of Child Health
and Human Development
Bldg. 31, Room 2A32

Bethesda, MD 20892
(301) 496-5133

The National Maternal and Child Health Clearinghouse has all kinds of information on maternal and child health issues, such as pregnancy, child and adolescent health, and human genetics. If the answer to your question can't be answered by any of their countless free publications, they can refer you to other National or local resources. If you still need further information, they search their own reference collection and send you what they find.

☎ Contact:
National Maternal and Child
Health Clearinghouse
38th & R Sts., NW
Washington, DC 20057
(703) 821-8955, ext. 254

CHILDHOOD ARTHRITIS

Clearinghouses/Hotlines

The National Institute of Arthritis and Musculoskeletal and Skin Diseases (NIAMS) will send you whatever publications and reprints of articles from texts and journals they have on Childhood Arthritis. They will also refer you to other organizations that are studying this disease. NIAMS will also let you know of any clinical studies that may be studying this disease and looking for patients.

☎ Contact:
National Arthritis and Musculoskeletal
and Skin Diseases Information Clearinghouse
Box AMS, 9000 Rockville Pike
Bethesda, MD 20892
(301) 495-4484

Free Publications/Videos

The following publication is available from the National Arthritis and Musculoskeletal and Skin Diseases Information Clearinghouse, Box AMS, 9000 Rockville Pike, Bethesda, MD 20892; (301) 495-4484.

- *Arthritis in Children: Resources for Children, Parents, and Teachers, 1986.* An annotated bibliography of resources. (#AR43, $3)

CHILDHOOD ASTHMA

See Asthma

CHILDHOOD MENTAL DISORDERS

Clearinghouses/Hotlines

The National Institute of Mental Health (NIMH) conducts research and distributes their findings on mental health issues in children.

☎ Contact:
National Institute of Mental Health
5600 Fishers Lane, Room 15C05
Rockville, MD 20857
(301) 443-4515

Free Publications/Videos

The following publications are available from the National Institute of Mental Health, 5600 Fishers Lane, Room 15C05, Rockville, MD 20857, (301) 443-4515.

- *Helping the Hyperactive Child*
- *Importance of Play*
- *Learning While Growing: Cognitive Development*
- *National Plan for Research on Child and Adolescent Mental Disorders*
- *Plain Talk about Adolescence*
- *Plain Talk About Raising Children*
- *Pre-Term Babies*
- *Research on Children and Adolescents with Mental, Behavioral and Development Disorders*
- *Stimulating Baby Senses*
- *When Parents Divorce*

- *Information Packet on Use of Mental Health
  Services by Children and Adolescents*
- *National Plan for Research on Child and
  Adolescent Mental Disorders*
- *Working Bibliography on Behavioral and
  Emotional Disorders and Assessment
  Instruments in Mental Retardation*

The following Congressional Research Service
(CRS) report on Childhood Mental Disorders is
available from either of your U.S. Senators' offices
at the U.S. Capitol, Washington, DC 20510, or
from your Congressional Representative at the
U.S. Capitol, Washington, DC 20515. You can
also call in your request through the U.S. Capitol
switchboard at (202) 224-3121. Be sure to include
the full title and report number in your request.

- *Childhood Mental Disorders: Attention-Deficit
  Hyperactivity Disorder, Autism, and Dyslexia.*
  (#91-405 SPR)

CHILDHOOD NUTRITION

Clearinghouses/Hotlines

The National Institute of Child Health and Human
Development (NICHD) will send you whatever
publications and reprints of journal articles they
have on Childhood Nutrition. If necessary, they
will refer you to other experts or researchers in
the field.

☎ Contact:
National Institute of Child Health
and Human Development
Bldg. 31, Room 2A32
Bethesda, MD 20892
(301) 496-5133

The National Maternal and Child Health
Clearinghouse has all kinds of information on
maternal and child health issues, such as
pregnancy, child and adolescent health, and human
genetics. If the answer to your question can't be
answered by any of their countless free
publications, they can refer you to other National
or local resources. If you still need further
information, they search their own reference

collection and send you what they find.

☎ Contact:
National Maternal and Child
Health Clearinghouse
38th & R Sts., NW
Washington, DC 20057
(703) 821-8955, ext. 254

Free Publications/Videos

The following publications on Childhood Nutrition
are available from the National Maternal and
Child Health Clearinghouse, 38th & R Sts., NW,
Washington, DC 20057; (703) 821-8955, ext. 254.

- *Nutritional Disorders of Children: Prevention,
  Screening, and Follow-up.*
- *Nutrition Resources for Early Childhood:
  Resource Guide.* An annotated list of
  current nutrition education publication for
  children ages 1-5 years, their parents,
  caregivers, and teachers.

The following Congressional Research Service
(CRS) reports on Child Nutrition are available
from either of your U.S. Senators' offices at the
U.S. Capitol, Washington, DC 20510, or from
your Congressional Representative at the U.S.
Capitol, Washington, DC 20515. You can also
call in your request through the U.S. Capitol
switchboard at (202) 224-3121. Be sure to include
the full title and report number in your request.

- *Child Nutrition Program Information and
  Data.* (#88-248 EPW)
- *Child Health in the Third World: U.S. and
  International Initiatives: Archived Issue
  Brief.* (#IB85189)
- *Child Nutrition: Expiring Provisions and
  Prospective Issues in the 102nd Congress.*
  (#91-110 EPW)
- *Child Nutrition: Issues in the 101st Congress.*
  (#IB89048)
- *Child Nutrition: Program Information,
  Funding, and Participation, FY1980-FY1990.*
  (#91-681 EPW)
- *Child Nutrition: 1990 Issues and Legislation;
  Archived Issue Brief.* (#IB90115)
- *Special Supplemental Food Program for
  Women, Infants, and Children (WIC):*

Description, History and Data. (86-794 EPW)

- *The WIC Program: Issues in the 102nd Congress; Issue Brief.* (IB90097)

CHILDREN OF ALCOHOLICS

Free Publications/Videos

The following publications are available from the National Clearinghouse for Alcohol Information, P.O. Box 2345, Rockville,MD 20852; (800) 729-6686, or (301) 468-2600.

- *Prevention Resource Guide: Children of Alcoholics.* Contains facts, figures, resources, and other relevant information on alcohol abuse.
- *Children of Alcoholics Kits.* Four separate kits containing background and referral information for these audiences: Helpers, Kids, Parents, and Therapists.
- *Prevention Resource Guide: Children of Alcoholics.* Provides facts and figures that put in perspective the magnitude of the problem of alcoholism and its direct effect on the family.

CHINESE RESTAURANT SYNDROME

Clearinghouses/Hotlines

The Food and Nutrition Information Center can search their database for information regarding Chinese Restaurant Syndrome which is caused by eating MSG, a seasoning often used in Chinese food.

☎ Contact:
Food and Nutrition Information Center
National Agricultural Library, Room 304
Beltsville, MD 20705
(301) 504-5719

CHLAMYDIA

Clearinghouses/Hotlines

The Sexually Transmitted Diseases Hotline offers valuable information to the public about a wide range of sexually transmitted diseases, including Chlamydia and how to protect yourself from contracting them.

☎ Contact:
National Sexually Transmitted Diseases Hotline
P.O. Box 13827
Research Triangle Park, NC 27709
(800) 227-8922

The National Institute on Allergy and Infectious Diseases (NIAID) can search the Combined Health Information Database (CHID) and generate a bibliography of resources on Chlamydial Infections for you. They will also send you any publications and journal articles they may have on hand, and will refer you to researchers who are currently studying this disease. If you can't afford treatment, have your doctor call NIAID to find out if they are conducting any clinical studies that you might qualify for.

☎ Contact:
National Institute of Allergy
and Infectious Diseases
Bldg. 31, Room 7A32
Bethesda, MD 20892
(301) 496-5717

CHLOASMA

Clearinghouses/Hotlines

The National Institute of Child Health and Human Development (NICHD) can provide you with information regarding a condition called Chloasma, which is a tan caused by pregnancy or oral contraceptives.

☎ Contact:
National Institute of Child Health
and Human Development
Bldg. 31, Room 2A32

Bethesda, MD 20892
(301) 496-5133

CHLORAMBUCIL

Free Publications/Videos

The following publication is available from the National Cancer Institute, Bldg. 31, Room 10A24, Bethesda, MD 20892; (800) 4-CANCER, or (301) 496-5583.

- *Clorambucilo/Chlorambucil.* Provides information about side effects, proper usage, and precautions of this anti-cancer drug.

CHOLECYSTECTOMY

See Gallbladder

CHOLELITHOTOMY

See Gallstones

CHOLERA

Clearinghouses/Hotlines

The National Institute on Allergy and Infectious Diseases (NIAID) can search the Combined Health Information Database (CHID) and generate a bibliography of resources on Cholera for you. They will also send you any publications and journal articles they may have on hand, and will refer you to researchers who are currently studying this disease. If you can't afford treatment, have your doctor call NIAID to find out if they are conducting any clinical studies that you might qualify for.

☎ Contact:
National Institute of Allergy
and Infectious Diseases
Bldg. 31, Room 7A32
Bethesda, MD 20892
(301) 496-5717

CHOLESTEROL

Clearinghouses/Hotlines

The National Heart, Lung, and Blood Institute (NHLBI) can search the Combined Health Information Database (CHID) and generate a bibliography of resources on Cholesterol for you. They also will send you any publications and journal articles they may have on hand, and will refer you to other organizations that are studying this issue. If you can't afford treatment, have your doctor call NHLBI to find out if they are conducting any clinical studies that you might qualify for.

☎ Contact:
National Heart, Lung, and Blood Institute
Bldg. 31, Room 4A21
Bethesda, MD 20892
(301) 496-4236

The National Cholesterol Education Program Information Center (NCEP) has specialists on staff and provides printed information on cholesterol, diet, and high blood pressure to the public and health professionals.

☎ Contact:
National Cholesterol Education Program
Information Center
4733 Bethesda Ave., Room 530
Bethesda, MD 20814
(301) 951-3260

Free Publications/Videos

The following publications on Cholesterol are available from the National Cholesterol Education Program Information Center, 4733 Bethesda Ave., Room 530, Bethesda, MD 20814; (301) 951-3260.

- *Dietary Guideline for Americans: Avoid Too Much Fat, Saturated Fat, and Cholesterol.* Tips for choosing and preparing foods.
- *Report of the Expert Panel on Detection, Evaluation, and Treatment of High Blood Cholesterol in Adults.* Practical guidelines for high blood cholesterol patients from detection to treatment.
- *Facts About...Blood Cholesterol.* Q&A on lowering high blood cholesterol.
- *Eating to Lower Your High Blood Cholesterol.* How-to booklet gives all the information needed to change eating habits and lower high blood cholesterol.
- *So You Have High Blood Cholesterol.* Easy to read pamphlet designed for patients diagnosed as having high blood cholesterol.
- *Community Guide to Cholesterol Resources.* Vital education materials on the medical and scientific aspects of cholesterol and heart disease.

The following publications on Cholesterol are available from the National Heart, Lung and Blood Institute, Bldg. 31, Room 4A21, Bethesda, MD 20892; (301) 496-4236.

- *Eating to Lower Your Blood Cholesterol.* (#89-2920)
- *Eat Right to Lower Your High Blood Cholesterol.*
- *NCEP Report of the Expert Panel on Blood Cholesterol Levels in Children: Executive Summary.* (#91-2731)
- *NCEP Report of the Expert Panel on Population Strategies for Blood Cholesterol Reduction, Executive Summary.* (#90-3046)
- *NHLBI Facts About Blood Cholesterol.* (#90-2696)
- *Nutrition and Your Health: Dietary Guidelines for Americans.*
- *Parents Guide. Cholesterol in Children. Healthy Eating is a Family Affair.* (#3099). This booklet is designed for parents who want to encourage heart-healthy eating patterns in their families.
- *So You Have High Blood Cholesterol.* (#89-2922)
- *Working Group Report on Management of Patients With Hypertension and High Blood Cholesterol.* (#90-2361)

- *1987 Report of the Expert Panel on Detection, Evaluation and Treatment of High Blood Cholesterol in Adults.* (#89-2925)

CHONDROCALCINOSIS

Clearinghouses/Hotlines

The National Institute of Arthritis and Musculoskeletal and Skin Diseases (NIAMS) will send you whatever publications and reprints of articles from texts and journals they have on Chondrocalcinosis. They will also refer you to other organizations that are studying this disease. NIAMS will also let you know of any clinical studies that may be studying this disease and looking for patients.

☎ Contact:
National Institute of Arthritis
and Musculoskeletal and Skin Diseases
Box AMS
9000 Rockville Pike
Bethesda, MD 20892
(301) 495-4484

CHONDROMALACIA

Clearinghouses/Hotlines

The National Institute of Arthritis and Musculoskeletal and Skin Diseases Clearinghouse can provide you with information regarding Chondromalacia, which is a condition where your cartilage softens. They can search their files to see if they have journal articles and other reference materials, and can also refer you to organizations dealing with this problem.

☎ Contact:
National Arthritis and Musculoskeletal
and Skin Diseases Clearinghouse
Box AMS
9000 Rockville Pike
Bethesda, MD 20892
(301) 495-4484

CHONDROSARCOMA

Clearinghouses/Hotlines

The National Cancer Institute (NCI) will send you whatever publications and reprints of journal articles they have on Chondrosarcoma. They can also give you information on the state-of-the-art treatment for this disease, including specific treatment information for your stage of cancer. They can also search their Physician's Data Query (PDQ) database to let you know if NCI is conducting any clinical studies on your disease.

☎ Contact:
National Cancer Institute
Building 31
Room 10A24
Bethesda, MD 20892
(800) 4-CANCER
(301) 496-5583

CHORIOCARCINOMA

Clearinghouses/Hotlines

The National Cancer Institute (NCI) will send you whatever publications and reprints of journal articles they have on Choriocarcinoma. They can also give you information on the state-of-the-art treatment for this disease, including specific treatment information for your stage of cancer. They can also search their Physician's Data Query (PDQ) database to let you know if NCI is conducting any clinical studies on your disease.

☎ Contact:
National Cancer Institute
Building 31
Room 10A24
Bethesda, MD 20892
(800) 4-CANCER
(301) 496-5583

CHORDOMA

Clearinghouses/Hotlines

The National Cancer Institute (NCI) will send you whatever publications and reprints of journal articles they have on Chordoma. They can also give you information on the state-of-the-art treatment for this disease, including specific treatment information for your stage of cancer. They can also search their Physician's Data Query (PDQ) database to let you know if NCI is conducting any clinical studies on your disease.

☎ Contact:
National Cancer Institute
Building 31
Room 10A24
Bethesda, MD 20892
(800) 4-CANCER
(301) 496-5583

CHORIONIC VILLUS SAMPLING

Clearinghouses/Hotlines

The National Institute of Child Health and Human Development (NICHD) will send you whatever publications and reprints of journal articles they have on Chorionic Villus Sampling (CVS). If necessary, they will refer you to other experts or researchers in the field. If you can't afford treatment, have your doctor call NICHD to find out if they are conducting any clinical studies that you might qualify for.

☎ Contact:
National Institute of Child Health and Human Development
Building 31
Room 2A32
Bethesda, MD 20892
(301) 496-5133

CHOROIDITIS

Clearinghouses/Hotlines

The National Eye Institute (NEI) can give you up-to-date information on Choroiditis by searching the Combined Health Information Database (CHID) and MEDLINE and sending you bibliographies of resources, along with any journal articles they may have. They can also refer you to any other organizations that study this and other related diseases. NEI will also let you know of any clinical studies that may be studying this disease and looking for patients. Because of their small staff, NEI prefers that you submit your requests for information in writing.

☎ Contact:
National Eye Institute
Building 31
Room 6A32
Bethesda, MD 20892
(301) 496-5248

CHRONIC BRONCHITIS

Clearinghouses/Hotlines

The National Heart, Lung, and Blood Institute (NHLBI) can search the Combined Health Information Database (CHID) and generate a bibliography of resources on Chronic Bronchitis for you. They also will send you any publications and journal articles they may have on hand, and will refer you to other organizations that are studying this disease. If you can't afford treatment, have your doctor call NHLBI to find out if they are conducting any clinical studies that you might qualify for.

☎ Contact:
National Heart, Lung, and Blood Institute
Building 31
Room 4A21
Bethesda, MD 20892
(301) 496-4236

CHRONIC COUGH

Clearinghouses/Hotlines

The National Heart, Lung, and Blood Institute (NHLBI) can search the Combined Health Information Database (CHID) and generate a bibliography of resources on Chronic Cough for you. They also will send you any publications and journal articles they may have on hand, and will refer you to other organizations that are studying this disease. If you can't afford treatment, have your doctor call NHLBI to find out if they are conducting any clinical studies that you might qualify for.

☎ Contact:
National Heart, Lung, and Blood Institute
Bldg. 31, Room 4A21
Bethesda, MD 20892
(301) 496-4236

Free Publications/Videos

The following publication on Chronic Cough is available from the National Heart, Lung and Blood Institute, Bldg. 31, Room 4A21, Bethesda, MD 20892; (301) 496-4236.

- *Do I Have a Chronic Cough?* (#559) Defines chronic cough and identifies it as a symptom of a possible chronic lung disease.

CHRONIC DISEASE

Clearinghouses/Hotlines

The Human Nutrition Research Center conducts research on dietary strategies that can delay the onset of nutritionally-related Chronic Diseases. They also study nutrient composition and nutritional qualities of food and perform studies on energy metabolism and nutritional requirements.

☎ Contact:
Human Nutrition Research Center
BARC-East
Building 308
Beltsville, MD 20705
(301) 344-2157

CHRONIC EBV

Clearinghouses/Hotlines

The National Institute on Allergy and Infectious Diseases (NIAID) can search the Combined Health Information Database (CHID) and generate a bibliography of resources on Chronic EBV (Epstein-Barr Virus) for you. They will also send you any publications and journal articles they may have on hand, and will refer you to researchers who are currently studying this disease. If you can't afford treatment, have your doctor call NIAID to find out if they are conducting any clinical studies that you might qualify for.

☎ Contact:
National Institute of Allergy
and Infectious Diseases
Bldg. 31, Room 7A32
Bethesda, MD 20892
(301) 496-5717

CHRONIC FATIGUE SYNDROME

Clearinghouses/Hotlines

The National Institute on Allergy and Infectious Diseases (NIAID) can search the Combined Health Information Database (CHID) and generate a bibliography of resources on Chronic Fatigue Syndrome for you. They will also send you any publications and journal articles they may have on hand, and will refer you to researchers who are currently studying this disease. If you can't afford treatment, have your doctor call

NIAID to find out if they are conducting any clinical studies that you might qualify for.

☎ Contact:
National Institute of Allergy
and Infectious Diseases
Bldg. 31, Room 7A32
Bethesda, MD 20892
(301) 496-5717

The Centers for Disease Control's Voice Information System allows anyone using a touchtone phone to obtain pre-recorded information on Chronic Fatigue Syndrome and many other diseases. This service offers information about this condition, symptoms and prevention methods, immunization requirements, current statistics, recent disease outbreak, and available printed materials. The system is available 24 hours a day, although the health professionals are available Monday through Friday, 8 a.m. - 4:30 p.m.

☎ Contact:
Centers for Disease Control
Information Resources Management Office
Mail Stop C-15
1600 Clifton Rd., NE
Atlanta, GA 30333
(404) 332-4555

Free Publications/Videos

The following publication is available from the Consumer Information Center, P.O. Box 100, Pueblo, CO 81002.

- *Chronic Fatigue Syndrome.* (#422Y)

The following publication is available from the Clinical Center Communications, National Institutes of Health, Building 10, Room 1C255, Bethesda, MD 20892; (301) 496-2563.

- *Chronic Fatigue Syndrome.* Describes possible causes and treatment for CFS. (#90-3059)

The following publication is available from the National Institute of Allergy and Infectious Diseases, Bldg. 31, Room 7A32, Bethesda, MD 20892; (301) 496-5717.

- Chronic Fatigue Syndrome: A Pamphlet for Physicians. (#90-484)

CHRONIC GRANULOMATOUS DISEASE

Clearinghouses/Hotlines

The National Institute on Allergy and Infectious Diseases (NIAID) can search the Combined Health Information Database (CHID) and generate a bibliography of resources on Chronic Granulomatous Disease for you. They will also send you any publications and journal articles they may have on hand, and will refer you to researchers who are currently studying this disease. If you can't afford treatment, have your doctor call NIAID to find out if they are conducting any clinical studies that you might qualify for.

☎ Contact:
National Institute of Allergy
and Infectious Diseases
Bldg. 31, Room 7A32
Bethesda, MD 20892
(301) 496-5717

CHRONIC INFECTIONS

Clearinghouses/Hotlines

The National Institute on Allergy and Infectious Diseases (NIAID) can search the Combined Health Information Database (CHID) and generate a bibliography of resources on Chronic Infections for you. They will also send you any publications and journal articles they may have on hand, and will refer you to researchers who are currently studying this disease. If you can't afford treatment, have your doctor call NIAID to find out if they are conducting any clinical studies that you might qualify for.

☎ Contact:
National Institute of Allergy
and Infectious Diseases
Bldg. 31, Room 7A32
Bethesda, MD 20892
(301) 496-5717

CHRONIC MYELOGENOUS LEUKEMIA

Clearinghouses/Hotlines

The National Cancer Institute (NCI) will send you whatever publications and reprints of journal articles they have on Chronic Myelogenous Leukemia. They can also give you information on the state-of-the-art treatment for this disease, including specific treatment information for your stage of cancer. They can also search their Physician's Data Query (PDQ) database to let you know if NCI is conducting any clinical studies on your disease.

☎ Contact:
National Cancer Institute
Bldg. 31, Room 10A24
Bethesda, MD 20892
(800) 4-CANCER
(301) 496-5583

CHRONIC OBSTRUCTIVE LUNG DISEASE

Clearinghouses/Hotlines

The National Heart, Lung, and Blood Institute (NHLBI) can search the Combined Health Information Database (CHID) and generate a bibliography of resources on Chronic Obstructive Lung Disease (COPD) for you. They also will send you any publications and journal articles they may have on hand, and will refer you to other organizations that are studying this disease. If you can't afford treatment, have your doctor call NHLBI to find out if they are conducting any clinical studies that you might qualify for.

☎ Contact:
National Heart, Lung, and Blood Institute
Bldg. 31, Room 4A21
Bethesda, MD 20892
(301) 496-4236

Free Publications/Videos

The following publication on Chronic Lung Disease is available from the National Maternal & Child Health Clearinghouse, 38th & R Sts., NW, Washington, DC 20057; (703) 821-8955, ext. 254.

- *Pediatric Pulmonology Guidelines for the Care of Children With Chronic Lung Disease.* (#C035)

CHRONIC PAIN

Clearinghouses/Hotlines

The National Institute of Neurological Disorders and Stroke (NINDS) conducts research on Chronic Pain and various therapies including drugs, acupuncture, surgery, electrical stimulation, and also psychological techniques.

☎ Contact:
National Institute of Neurological
Disorders and Stroke
Bldg. 31, Room 8A06
Bethesda, MD 20892
(301) 496-5751
(800) 352-9424

Free Publications/Videos

The following publications are available from the National Institute of Neurological Disorders and Stroke, Bldg. 31, Room 8A06, Bethesda, MD 20892; (301) 496-5751 or (800) 352-9424.

- *Chronic Pain.* (#89-2406)
- *Chronic Pain.* Discusses hope through research.

The following video is available from the Office of Clinical Center Communications, Building 10, Room 1C255, Bethesda, MD 20892; (301) 496-2563.

- *Relief of Chronic Pain.* Video to help the general public make intelligent decisions.

CHRYSOTHERAPY

Clearinghouses/Hotlines

The Arthritis and Musculoskeletal and Skin Diseases Clearinghouse can answer your questions regarding chrysotherapy, which is treatment of some diseases using chemicals which contain gold. They can look through their data base for reference materials, articles, and other information.

☎ Contact:
National Arthritis and Musculoskeletal
and Skin Diseases Clearinghouse
Box AMS
9000 Rockville Pike
Bethesda, MD 20892
(301) 495-4484

CHURG-STRAUSS SYNDROME

Clearinghouses/Hotlines

The National Institute on Allergy and Infectious Diseases (NIAID) can search the Combined Health Information Database (CHID) and generate a bibliography of resources on Churg-Strauss Syndrome for you. They will also send you any publications and journal articles they may have on hand, and will refer you to researchers who are currently studying this disease. If you can't afford treatment, have your doctor call NIAID to find out if they are conducting any clinical studies that you might qualify for.

☎ Contact:
National Institute of Allergy
and Infectious Diseases
Bldg. 31, Room 7A32
Bethesda, MD 20892
(301) 496-5717

CICATRICIAL PEMPHIGOID

Clearinghouses/Hotlines

The National Eye Institute (NEI) can give you up-to-date information on Cicatricial Pemphigoid by searching the Combined Health Information Database (CHID) and MEDLINE and sending you bibliographies of resources, along with any journal articles they may have. They can also refer you to any other organizations that study this and other related diseases. NEI will also let you know of any clinical studies that may be studying this disease and looking for patients. Because of their small staff, NEI prefers that you submit your requests for information in writing.

☎ Contact:
National Eye Institute
Bldg. 31, Room 6A32
Bethesda, MD 20892
(301) 496-5248

CIGARETTES

See Smoking

CIRCULATION DISORDERS

Clearinghouses/Hotlines

The National Heart, Lung, and Blood Institute (NHLBI) can search the Combined Health Information Database (CHID) and generate a bibliography of resources on Circulation Disorders for you. They also will send you any publications and journal articles they may have on hand, and will refer you to other organizations that are studying these disorders. If you can't afford treatment, have your doctor call NHLBI to find out if they are conducting any clinical studies that you might qualify for.

☎ Contact:
National Heart, Lung, and Blood Institute
Bldg. 31, Room 4A21
Bethesda, MD 20892
(301) 496-4236

CIRCUMCISION

Clearinghouses/Hotlines

The National Institute of Child Health and Human Development (NICHD) will send you whatever publications and reprints of journal articles they have on Circumcision. If necessary, they will refer you to other experts or researchers in the field.

☎ Contact:
National Institute of Child Health
and Human Development
Bldg. 31, Room 2A32
Bethesda, MD 20892
(301) 496-5133

CIRRHOSIS

Clearinghouses/Hotlines

The National Institute of Diabetes and Digestive and Kidney Diseases's (NIDDK) individual clearinghouses can search the Combined Health Information Database (CHID) and generate a bibliography of resources on Cirrhosis for you. They also will send you any publications and journal articles they may have on hand, and will refer you to other organizations that are studying this disease. If you can't afford treatment, have your doctor call NIDDK to find out if they are conducting any clinical studies that you might qualify for.

☎ Contact:
National Institute of Diabetes
and Digestive and Kidney Diseases
Bldg. 31, Room 9A04
Bethesda, MD 20892
(301) 496-3583

Free Publications/Videos

The following publication is available from the National Institute of Diabetes and Digestive and Kidney Diseases, Bldg. 31, Room 9A04, Bethesda, MD 20892; (301) 496-3583.

- *Cirrhosis of the Liver*. (#92-1134)

CISPLATIN

Free Publications/Videos

The following publication is available from the National Cancer Institute, Bldg. 31, Room 10A24, Bethesda, MD 20892; (800) 4-CANCER, or (301) 496-5583.

- *Cisplatin/Cisplatin*. Provides information about side effects, proper usage, and precautions of this anti-cancer drug.

CLAUDICATION

Clearinghouses/Hotlines

The National Heart, Lung, and Blood Institute (NHLBI) can search the Combined Health Information Database (CHID) and generate a bibliography of resources on Claudication for you. They also will send you any publications and journal articles they may have on hand, and will refer you to other organizations studying Claudication. If you can't afford treatment, have your doctor call NHLBI to find out if they are conducting any clinical studies that you might qualify for.

☎ Contact:
National Heart, Lung, and Blood Institute
Building 31
Room 4A21
Bethesda, MD 20892
(301) 496-4236

CLAUSTROPHOBIA

Clearinghouses/Hotlines

The National Institute of Mental Health (NIMH) maintains data bases that index and abstract documents from the worldwide literature pertaining to Mental Illness. In addition to scientific journals, there are references to audiovisuals, dissertations, government documents and reports. Contact NIMH for searches on specific subjects.

☎ Contact:
National Institute of Mental Health
5600 Fishers Lane
Room 15C05
Rockville, MD 20857
(301) 443-4515

CLEFT PALATE

Clearinghouses/Hotlines

The National Institute of Dental Research (NIDR) will send you whatever publications and reprints of journal articles they have on Cleft Palate. As a policy, NIDR will not refer you to other organizations or experts who study this condition. If you can't afford treatment, have your doctor call Dr. Albert Guckers at (301) 496-6241 to find out if NIDR is conducting any clinical studies that you might qualify for.

☎ Contact:
National Institute of Dental Research
Building 31
Room 2C35
Bethesda, MD 20892
(301) 496-4261

CLIMACTERIC

See Menopause

CLINICAL RESEARCH

Free Publications/Videos

The following publications on Clinical Research are available from the National Center for Research Resources, Office of Science and Health Reports, Bethesda, MD 20892; (301) 496-5545.

- *NCRR General Clinical Research Centers Directory*. Contains information about the centers, staffs, resources and major areas of investigation.
- *General Clinical Research Centers: A Research Resources Directory*. (#91-1433, RR)

The following publication on Clinical Research is available from the Center for Devices and Radiological Health, (HFZ-210), FDA, 5600 Fishers Ln., Rockville, MD 20857; (301) 443-4690.

- *Protecting 'Human Guinea Pigs'*.

The following publications on Clinical Research are available from the National Cancer Institute, Bldg. 31, Room 10A24, Bethesda, MD 20892; (800) 4-CANCER, or (301) 496-5583.

- *What Are Clinical Trials All About?* (#90-2706) Designed for patients who are considering taking part in research for cancer treatment.

The following publication on Clinical Research is available from the National Eye Institute, Bldg. 31, Rm 6A32, Bethesda, MD 20892; (301) 496-5248.

- *Clinical Trials Supported by the National Eye Institute*. (#90-2910)

The following publication on Clinical Research is available from the National Institutes of Health Clinical Center, Bldg. 10, Room 1C255, Bethesda, MD 20892; (301) 496-2563.

- *Current Clinical Studies and Patient Referral Procedures*. (#91-217)

The following publication on Clinical Research is available from the National Institute of Allergy and Infectious Diseases, Bldg. 31, Room 7A32, Bethesda, MD 20892; (301) 496-5717.

- *AIDS Clinical Trials: Talking It Over*. (#89-3025)

The following publication on Clinical Research is available from the National AIDS Clearinghouse, P.O. Box 6003, Rockville, MD 20849-6003; (800) 458-5231.

- *Information about the AIDS Clinical Trials Information Service*. (#B172)

CLONING

Clearinghouses/Hotlines

The National Institute of Child Health and Human Development (NICHD) will send you whatever publications and reprints of journal articles they have on Cloning & DNA Activities. If necessary, they will refer you to other experts or researchers in the field.

☎ Contact:
National Institute of Child Health
and Human Development
Bldg. 31, Room 2A32
Bethesda, MD 20892
(301) 496-5133

CLOTTING DISORDERS

Clearinghouses/Hotlines

The National Heart, Lung, and Blood Institute (NHLBI) can search the Combined Health

Information Database (CHID) and generate a bibliography of resources on Blood Clotting Disorders for you. They also will send you any publications and journal articles they may have on hand, and will refer you to other organizations that are studying this disorders. If you can't afford treatment, have your doctor call NHLBI to find out if they are conducting any clinical studies that you might qualify for.

☎ Contact:
National Heart, Lung, and Blood Institute
Bldg. 31, Room 4A21
Bethesda, MD 20892
(301) 496-4236

CLUSTER HEADACHE

See Histamine Headache

CMV

See Cytomegalovirus

COAL WORKER'S PNEUMOCONIOSIS

See Black Lung

COAT'S DISEASE

Clearinghouses/Hotlines

The National Eye Institute (NEI) can give you up-to-date information on Coat's Disease by searching the Combined Health Information Database (CHID) and MEDLINE and sending you bibliographies of resources, along with any journal articles they may have. They can also

refer you to any other organizations that study this and other related diseases. NEI will also let you know of any clinical studies that may be studying this disease and looking for patients. Because of their small staff, NEI prefers that you submit your requests for information in writing.

☎ Contact:
National Eye Institute
Bldg. 31, Room 6A32
Bethesda, MD 20892
(301) 496-5248

COBALT

Clearinghouses/Hotlines

The National Cancer Institute (NCI) will send you whatever publications and reprints of journal articles they have on Cobalt. They can also search their Physician's Data Query (PDQ) database to let you know if NCI is conducting any clinical studies on your disease.

☎ Contact:
National Cancer Institute
Bldg. 31, Room 10A24
Bethesda, MD 20892
(800) 4-CANCER
(301) 496-5583

COCAINE

See also Drug Abuse

Clearinghouses/Hotlines

The National Clearinghouse for Alcohol & Drug Information has all kinds of information to send you on Cocaine use and the latest research on its effects and treatment.

☎ Contact:
National Clearinghouse for Alcohol
and Drug Information
P.O. Box 2345
Rockville, MD 20852
(800) 729-6686 or (301) 468-2600

Free Publications/Videos

The following publications on Cocaine are available from the National Clearinghouse for Alcohol & Drug Information, P.O. Box 2345, Rockville, MD 20852; (800) 729-6686, (301) 468-2600.

- *Cocaine: Pharmacology, Effects, and Treatment of Abuse, Research Monograph.* (Series 50, 1984)
- *Cocaine Use in America: Epidemiologic and Clinical Perspectives, Research.* (Monograph Series 61, 1985)
- *Cocaine Freebase.* Describes both cocaine freebase and crack.
- *Coca Cultivation and Cocaine Processing: An Overview.*
- *Cocaine Abuse.* Fact sheet gives basic information about the psychological and physiological effects.

The following Congressional Research Service (CRS) report on Cocaine is available from either of your U.S. Senators' offices at the U.S. Capitol, Washington, DC 20510, or from your Congressional Representative at the U.S. Capitol, Washington, DC 20515. You can also call in your request through the U.S. Capitol switchboard at (202) 224-3121. Be sure to include the full title and report number in your request.

- *Cocaine and American Society: Selected References, 1985-1990.* (#90-497 L)

COCKAYNE'S SYNDROME

Clearinghouses/Hotlines

The National Institute on Aging (NIA) will send you whatever publications and reprints of journal articles they have on Cockayne's Syndrome. They cannot refer you to other experts if the information they have isn't sufficient for your purposes.

☎ Contact:
National Institute on Aging
Building 31

Room 5C27
Bethesda, MD 20892
(301) 496-1752

CODEINE

Free Publications/Videos

The following publication on Codeine is available from the Food & Drug Administration, (HFE-88), 5600 Fishers Ln., Rockville, MD 20857; (301) 443-3170.

- *How To Take Your Medicines: Acetaminophen Codeine.* (#FDA91-3188)

COFFEE

See Caffeine

COGAN'S SYNDROME

Clearinghouses/Hotlines

The National Eye Institute (NEI) can give you up-to-date information on Cogan's Syndrome by searching the Combined Health Information Database (CHID) and MEDLINE and sending you bibliographies of resources, along with any journal articles they may have. They can also refer you to any other organizations that study this and other related diseases. NEI will also let you know of any clinical studies that may be studying this disease and looking for patients. Because of their small staff, NEI prefers that you submit your requests for information in writing.

☎ Contact:
National Eye Institute
Building 31
Room 6A32
Bethesda, MD 20892
(301) 496-5248

COGNITION

Clearinghouses/Hotlines

The National Institute of Child Health and Human Development (NICHD) will send you whatever publications and reprints of journal articles they have on Cognition. If necessary, they will refer you to other experts or researchers in the field.

☎ Contact:
National Institute of Child Health
and Human Development
Building 31
Room 2A32
Bethesda, MD 20892
(301) 496-5133

The National Institute of Mental Health (NIMH) will send you whatever publications and reprints of articles from texts and journals they have on Cognition. They will also refer you to other organizations that are studying Cognition. NIMH will also let you know of any clinical studies that may be studying this issue and looking for patients.

☎ Contact:
National Institute of Mental Health
5600 Fishers Lane
Room 15C05
Rockville, MD 20857
(301) 443-4515

COLD SORES

See Fever Blisters

COLEY'S MIXED TOXINS

Clearinghouses/Hotlines

The National Cancer Institute (NCI) will send you whatever publications and reprints of journal articles they have on Coley's Mixed Toxins. They can also search their Physician's Data Query

(PDQ) database to let you know if NCI is conducting any clinical studies on your disease.

☎ Contact:
National Cancer Institute
Building 31
Room 10A24
Bethesda, MD 20892
(800) 4-CANCER
(301) 496-5583

COLIC

Clearinghouses/Hotlines

The National Institute of Child Health and Human Development (NICHD) can send you information on fetal, maternal and child development, as well as materials on reproductive biology, contraception, mental retardation, and a host of other related fields.

☎ Contact:
National Institute of Child Health
and Human Development
Building 31
Room 2A32
Bethesda, MD 20892
(301) 496-5133

The National Maternal and Child Health Clearinghouse has all kinds of information on maternal and child health issues, such as pregnancy, child and adolescent health, and human genetics. If the answer to your question can't be answered by any of their countless free publications, they can refer you to other national or local resources. If you still need further information, they search their own reference collection and send you what they find.

☎ Contact:
National Maternal and Child
Health Clearinghouse
38th & R Sts., NW
Washington, DC 20057
(703) 821-8955, ext. 254

COLITIS

Clearinghouses/Hotlines

The National Institute of Diabetes and Digestive and Kidney Diseases's (NIDDK) individual clearinghouses can search the Combined Health Information Database (CHID) and generate a bibliography of resources on Colitis for you. They also will send you any publications and journal articles they may have on hand, and will refer you to other organizations that are studying this disease. If you can't afford treatment, have your doctor call NIDDK to find out if they are conducting any clinical studies that you might qualify for.

☎ Contact:
National Institute of Diabetes
and Digestive and Kidney Diseases
Bldg. 31, Room 9A04
Bethesda, MD 20892
(301) 496-3583

Free Publications/Videos

The following publication is available from the National Institute of Diabetes and Digestive and Kidney Diseases, Bldg. 31, Room 9A04, Bethesda, MD 20892; (301) 496-3583.

- *Ulcerative Colitis.* (#90-1597)

The following video is available from the Office of Clinical Center Communications, Bldg. 10, Room 1C255, Bethesda, MD 20892; (301) 496-2563.

- *Ulcerative Colitis and Crohn's Disease.* Video to help the general public make intelligent decisions.

The following publication is available from the National Digestive Diseases Information Clearinghouse, Box NDDIC, Bethesda, MD 20892; (301) 468-6344.

- *Crohn's Disease and Ulcerative Colitis.* Information packet.

COLLAGEN DISEASE

Clearinghouses/Hotlines

The National Institute of Arthritis and Musculoskeletal and Skin Diseases (NIAMS) will send you whatever publications and reprints of articles from texts and journals they have on Collagen Disease. They will also refer you to other organizations that are studying this disease. NIAMS will also let you know of any clinical studies that may be studying this disease and looking for patients.

☎ Contact:
National Institute of Arthritis
and Musculoskeletal and Skin Diseases
Box AMS
9000 Rockville Pike
Bethesda, MD 20892
(301) 495-4484

COLLAPSED LUNGS

Clearinghouses/Hotlines

The National Heart, Lung, and Blood Institute (NHLBI) can search the Combined Health Information Database (CHID) and generate a bibliography of resources on Collapsed Lungs for you. They also will send you any publications and journal articles they may have on hand, and will refer you to other organizations that are studying this condition. If you can't afford treatment, have your doctor call NHLBI to find out if they are conducting any clinical studies that you might qualify for.

☎ Contact:
National Heart, Lung, and Blood Institute
Building 31
Room 4A21
Bethesda, MD 20892
(301) 496-4236

COLON PROBLEMS

Clearinghouses/Hotlines

The National Digestive Diseases Information Clearinghouse will respond to your requests for information about digestive diseases and distributes information to health professionals, people with digestive diseases, and the general public. They have many publications, as well as a news bulletin.

☎ Contact:
National Digestive Diseases
Information Clearinghouse
Box NDDIC
Bethesda, MD 20892
(301) 468-6344

Free Publications/Videos

The following publication is available from the National Cancer Institute, Bldg. 31, Room 10A24, Bethesda, MD 20892; (800) 4-CANCER, or (301) 496-5583.

- *Research Report: Cancer of the Colon and Rectum.* (#92-95)

The following publication is available from the Food & Drug Administration, (HFE-88), 5600 Fishers Ln., Rockville, MD 20857; (301) 443-3170.

- *The Colon Goes Up, Over, Down and Out.*
  Discusses how the colon works and is the site of many problems such as colon colitis, diverticulitis, and cancer. (#FDA89-1111)

COLOR BLINDNESS

Clearinghouses/Hotlines

The National Eye Institute (NEI) can give you up-to-date information on Color Blindness by searching the Combined Health Information Database (CHID) and MEDLINE and sending

you bibliographies of resources, along with any journal articles they may have. They can also refer you to any other organizations that study this and other related conditions. NEI will also let you know of any clinical studies that may be studying Color Blindness and looking for patients. Because of their small staff, NEI prefers that you submit your requests for information in writing.

☎ Contact:
National Eye Institute
Bldg. 31, Room 6A32
Bethesda, MD 20892
(301) 496-5248

COLORECTAL NEOPLASMS

Clearinghouses/Hotlines

The National Cancer Institute (NCI) will send you whatever publications and reprints of journal articles they have on Colorectal Neoplasms. They can also give you information on the state-of-the-art treatment for this disease, including specific treatment information for your stage of cancer. They can also search their Physician's Data Query (PDQ) database to let you know if NCI is conducting any clinical studies on your disease.

☎ Contact:
National Cancer Institute
Bldg. 31, Room 10A24
Bethesda, MD 20892
(800) 4-CANCER
(301) 496-5583

COLOSTOMY

Clearinghouses/Hotlines

The National Institute of Diabetes and Digestive and Kidney Diseases's (NIDDK) individual clearinghouses can search the Combined Health Information Database (CHID) and generate a bibliography of resources on Colostomies for you. They also will send you any publications and journal articles they may have on hand, and will refer you to other organizations that are studying this technique. If you can't afford treatment, have your doctor call NIDDK to find out if they are conducting any clinical studies that you might qualify for.

☎ Contact:
National Institute of Diabetes
and Digestive and Kidney Diseases
Bldg. 31, Room 9A04
Bethesda, MD 20892
(301) 496-3583

The National Cancer Institute (NCI) will send you whatever publications and reprints of journal articles they have on Colostomies. They can also give you information on the state-of-the-art treatment for this condition, including specific treatment information for your stage of cancer. They can also search their Physician's Data Query (PDQ) database to let you know if NCI is conducting any clinical studies on your disease.

☎ Contact:
National Cancer Institute
Bldg. 31, Room 10A24
Bethesda, MD 20892
(800) 4-CANCER
(301) 496-5583

COLPOCYSTITIS

Clearinghouses/Hotlines

The National Kidney and Urologic Diseases Information Clearinghouse can answer your questions regarding colpocystitis and other bladder conditions. They can search the Combined Health Information Database (CHID) and generate a bibliography of resources on colpocystitis. They also will send you any publications and journal articles they may have on hand, and will refer you to other organizations.

☎ Contact:
National Kidney and Urologic Diseases
Information Clearinghouse
Box NKUDIC
Bethesda, MD 20892
(301) 468-6345

COMAS

Clearinghouses/Hotlines

The National Institute of Neurological Disorders and Stroke (NINDS) can send you only information they have in their publications list on Comas. This Clearinghouse cannot directly give you information about any current clinical studies they might be conducting on this topic, but you can find this information for yourself by looking under the National Institute of Neurological Disorders and Stroke in *Appendix A* at the end of this book.

☎ Contact:
National Institute of Neurological
Disorders and Stroke
Bldg. 31, Room 8A06
Bethesda, MD 20892
(301) 496-5751
(800) 352-9424

Free Publications/Videos

The following publication is available from the National Institute of Neurological Disorders and Stroke, P.O. Box 5801, Bethesda, MD 20824; (800) 352-9424, or (301) 496-5751.

- *Coma*. Contains a collection of scientific articles, patient education pamphlets, and addresses of voluntary health associations.

COMEDO (Blackheads)

See Acne

COMMON COLD

Clearinghouses/Hotlines

The National Institute on Allergy and Infectious

Diseases (NIAID) can search the Combined Health Information Database (CHID) and generate a bibliography of resources on the Common Cold for you. They will also send you any publications and journal articles they may have on hand, and will refer you to researchers who are currently studying the Common Cold. If you can't afford treatment, have your doctor call NIAID to find out if they are conducting any clinical studies that you might qualify for.

☎ Contact:
National Institute of Allergy
and Infectious Diseases
Bldg. 31, Room 7A32
Bethesda, MD 20892
(301) 496-5717

available printed materials. Currently, you can get information on AIDS, Chronic fatigue syndrome, cytomegalovirus, encephalitis, enteric diseases, Epstein-Barr, hepatitis, Lyme disease, malaria, rabies, Vaccine-preventable disease, and yellow fever. If you need more information than the message provides, you have the option of being put in contact with a public health professional who will point you in the right direction. The system is available 24 hours a day, although the health professionals are available Monday-Friday 8 a.m.-4:30 p.m.

☎ Contact:
Disease Hotline
(404) 332-4555

COMMUNICABLE & INFECTIOUS DISEASES

Clearinghouses/Hotlines

The National Institute on Allergy and Infectious Diseases (NIAID) can search the Combined Health Information Database (CHID) and generate a bibliography of resources on Communicable and Infectious Diseases for you. They will also send you any publications and journal articles they may have on hand, and will refer you to researchers who are currently studying this disease. If you can't afford treatment, have your doctor call NIAID to find out if they are conducting any clinical studies that you might qualify for.

☎ Contact:
National Institute of Allergy
and Infectious Diseases
Bldg. 31, Room 7A32
Bethesda, MD 20892
(301) 496-5717

By calling the Centers for Disease Control's automated telephone health service, you can get all kinds of information sent to you on several diseases and health areas, including symptoms and prevention methods, immunization requirements, current statistics, recent disease outbreak, and

COMMUNICATION DISORDERS

See also Deafness

Clearinghouses/Hotlines

The National Institute on Deafness and Other Communication Disorders Clearinghouse has all kinds of resources on the normal and disordered mechanisms of hearing, balance, smell, taste, voice, speech, and language, including fact sheets, bibliographies, information packets, catalogs, and directories of information sources. They also have a directory of associations and organizations with an interest in deafness and other communication disorders.

☎ Contact:
National Institute on Deafness
and Other Communication Disorders
Bldg. 31, Room 3C35
Bethesda, MD 20892
(301) 496-7243
(800) 241-1044
(301) 402-0252 (TDD)

The National Institute of Neurological Disorders and Stroke (NINDS) can send you only information they have in their publications list on Communication Disorders. This Clearinghouse cannot directly give you information about any current clinical studies they might be conducting on this topic, but you can find this information for yourself by looking under the National Institute of Neurological Disorders and Stroke in *Appendix A* at the end of this book.

☎ Contact:
National Institute of Neurological
Disorders and Stroke
Bldg. 31, Room 8A06
Bethesda, MD 20892
(301) 496-5751
(800) 352-9424

The National Institute of Mental Health (NIMH) will send you whatever publications and reprints of articles from texts and journals they have on Communication Disorders. They will also refer you to other organizations that are studying this issue. NIMH will also let you know of any clinical studies that may be studying this disease and looking for patients.

☎ Contact:
National Institute of Mental Health
5600 Fishers Ln., Room 15C05
Rockville, MD 20857
(301) 443-4515

The National Institute of Child Health and Human Development (NICHD) will send you whatever publications and reprints of journal articles they have on Normal Human Communication. If necessary, they will refer you to other experts or researchers in the field. If you can't afford treatment, have your doctor call NICHD to find out if they are conducting any clinical studies that you might qualify for.

☎ Contact:
National Institute of Child Health
and Human Development
Bldg. 31, Room 2A32
Bethesda, MD 20892
(301) 496-5133

Free Publications/Videos

The following publication on Communication Disorders is available from the National Institute on Deafness and Other Communication Disorders, Bldg. 31, Room 3C35, Bethesda, MD 20892; (301) 496-7243, (800) 241-1044, (301) 402-0252 (TDD).

- *NIDCD Strategic Research Plan: Update on Language and Balance/Vestibular Systems.* (#91-3217, DC)

The following publication on Communication Disorders is available from the National Maternal and Child Health Clearinghouse, 38th & R Sts., NW, Washington, DC 20057; (703) 821-8955, ext. 254.

- *Guidelines for Purchase of Services and Assistive Devices for Individuals With Communication Disorders.* (#B180)

COMPULSION

Clearinghouses/Hotlines

The National Institute of Mental Health (NIMH) maintains data bases that index and abstract documents from the worldwide literature pertaining to Compulsion. In addition to scientific journals, there are references to audiovisuals, dissertations, government documents and reports. Contact NIMH for searches on specific subjects.

☎ Contact:
National Institute of Mental Health
5600 Fishers Lane, Room 15C05
Rockville, MD 20857
(301) 443-4515

COMPUTER ACCESS

Clearinghouses/Hotlines

The National Library of Medicine (NLM) has developed GRATEFUL MED, a software program that allows you to track down information in the NLM databases via your personal computer. GRATEFUL MED is available for both IBM-compatible and Macintosh computers for only $29.95. For more information about GRATEFUL MED:

☎ Contact:
National Library of Medicine
(800) 638-8480.

CONDOMS

Clearinghouses/Hotlines

The Center for Devices and Radiological Health routinely test condoms for defects, as well as conduct research on the permeability of latex condoms to the passage of viruses such as HIV. For more information about Condoms, contact the Center.

☎ Contact:
Center for Devices and Radiological Health
Food and Drug Administration
Rockville, MD 20857
(301) 443-4690

Free Publications/Videos

The following publications on Condoms are available from the Center for Devices and Radiological Health, (HFZ-210), Food and Drug Administration, 5600 Fishers Ln., Rockville, MD 20857; (301) 443-4690.

- *Condoms and Sexually Transmitted Diseases... Especially AIDS.* (#FDA 90-4239)
- *Condoms for Prevention of Sexually Transmitted Diseases.*
- *Letter to All U.S. Condom Manufacturers, Importers and Repackagers of Condoms.*

This Congressional Research Service (CRS) report on Condoms is available from either of your U.S. Senators' offices at the U.S. Capitol, Washington, DC 20510, or from your Congressional Representative at the U.S. Capitol, Washington, DC 20515. You can also call in your request through the U.S. Capitol switchboard at (202) 224-3121. Be sure to include the full title and report number in your request.

- *Advertising Condoms: Legal and Constitutional Consideration.* (#87-325 A)

CONGENITAL ABNORMALITIES

See also Birth Defects

Clearinghouses/Hotlines

The National Eye Institute (NEI) can give you up-to-date information on Congenital Abnormalities by searching the Combined Health Information Database (CHID) and MEDLINE and sending you bibliographies of resources, along with any journal articles they may have. They can also refer you to any other organizations that study this and other related conditions. NEI will also let you know of any clinical studies that may be studying Congenital Abnormalities and looking for patients. Because of their small staff, NEI prefers that you submit your requests for information in writing.

☎ Contact:
National Eye Institute
Bldg. 31, Room 6A32
Bethesda, MD 20892
(301) 496-5248

CONGENITAL ADRENAL HYPERPLASIA

Clearinghouses/Hotlines

The National Institute of Diabetes and Digestive and Kidney Diseases's (NIDDK) individual clearinghouses can search the Combined Health Information Database (CHID) and generate a bibliography of resources on Congenital Adrenal Hyperplasia for you. They also will send you any publications and journal articles they may have on hand, and will refer you to other organizations that are studying this disease. If you can't afford treatment, have your doctor call NIDDK to find out if they are conducting any clinical studies that you might qualify for.

☎ Contact:
National Institute of Diabetes
and Digestive and Kidney Diseases
Bldg. 31, Room 9A04
Bethesda, MD 20892
(301) 496-3583

The National Institute of Child Health and Human Development (NICHD) will send you whatever publications and reprints of journal articles they have on Congenital Adrenal Hyperplasia. If necessary, they will refer you to other experts or researchers in the field. If you can't afford treatment, have your doctor call NICHD to find out if they are conducting any clinical studies that you might qualify for.

☎ Contact:
National Institute of Child Health
and Human Development
Bldg. 31, Room 2A32
Bethesda, MD 20892
(301) 496-5133

CONGENITAL HEART DISEASE

Clearinghouses/Hotlines

The National Heart, Lung, and Blood Institute (NHLBI) can search the Combined Health Information Database (CHID) and generate a bibliography of resources on Congenital Heart Disease for you. They also will send you any publications and journal articles they may have on hand, and will refer you to other organizations that are studying this disease. If you can't afford treatment, have your doctor call NHLBI to find out if they are conducting any clinical studies that you might qualify for.

☎ Contact:
National Heart, Lung, and Blood Institute
Bldg. 31, Room 4A21
Bethesda, MD 20892
(301) 496-4236

CONGENITAL INFECTIONS

Clearinghouses/Hotlines

The National Institute on Allergy and Infectious Diseases (NIAID) can search the Combined Health Information Database (CHID) and generate a bibliography of resources on Congenital Infections for you. They will also send you any publications and journal articles they may have on hand, and will refer you to researchers who are currently studying this disease. If you can't afford treatment, have your doctor call NIAID to find out if they are conducting any clinical studies that you might qualify for.

☎ Contact:
National Institute of Allergy
and Infectious Diseases
Bldg. 31, Room 7A32
Bethesda, MD 20892
(301) 496-5717

CONGESTIVE HEART FAILURE

Clearinghouses/Hotlines

The National Heart, Lung, and Blood Institute (NHLBI) can search the Combined Health Information Database (CHID) and generate a bibliography of resources on Congestive Heart Failure for you. They also will send you any publications and journal articles they may have on hand, and will refer you to other organizations that are studying this disease. If you can't afford treatment, have your doctor call NHLBI to find out if they are conducting any clinical studies that you might qualify for.

☎ Contact:
National Heart, Lung, and Blood Institute
Bldg. 31, Room 4A21
Bethesda, MD 20892
(301) 496-4236

CONJUNCTIVITIS

Clearinghouses/Hotlines

The National Eye Institute (NEI) can give you up-to-date information on Conjunctivitis by searching the Combined Health Information Database (CHID) and MEDLINE and sending you bibliographies of resources, along with any journal articles they may have. They can also refer you to any other organizations that study this and other related diseases. NEI will also let you know of any clinical studies that may be studying this disease and looking for patients. Because of their small staff, NEI prefers that you submit your requests for information in writing.

☎ Contact:
National Eye Institute
Bldg. 31, Room 6A32
Bethesda, MD 20892
(301) 496-5248

CONNECTIVE TISSUE DISEASES

Clearinghouses/Hotlines

The National Institute of Arthritis and Musculoskeletal and Skin Diseases (NIAMS) will send you whatever publications and reprints of articles from texts and journals they have on Connective Tissue Diseases. They will also refer you to other organizations that are studying this disease. NIAMS will also let you know of any clinical studies that may be studying this disease and looking for patients.

☎ Contact:
National Institute of Arthritis
and Musculoskeletal and Skin Diseases
Box AMS
Bethesda, MD 20892
(301) 495-4484

The National Heart, Lung, and Blood Institute (NHLBI) can search the Combined Health Information Database (CHID) and generate a bibliography of resources on Heritable Disorders of Connective Tissue for you. They also will send you any publications and journal articles they may have on hand, and will refer you to other organizations that are studying this disease. If you can't afford treatment, have your doctor call NHLBI to find out if they are conducting any clinical studies that you might qualify for.

☎ Contact:
National Heart, Lung, and Blood Institute
Bldg. 31, Room 4A21
Bethesda, MD 20892
(301) 496-4236

CONSTIPATION

Clearinghouses/Hotlines

The National Institute of Diabetes and Digestive and Kidney Diseases's (NIDDK) individual clearinghouses can search the Combined Health Information Database (CHID) and generate a bibliography of resources on Constipation for you. They also will send you any publications and journal articles they may have on hand, and will refer you to other organizations that are studying this disease. If you can't afford treatment, have your doctor call NIDDK to find out if they are conducting any clinical studies that you might qualify for.

☎ Contact:
National Institute of Diabetes
and Digestive and Kidney Diseases
Bldg. 31, Room 9A04
Bethesda, MD 20892
(301) 496-3583

The National Institute on Aging (NIA) will send you whatever publications and reprints of journal articles they have on Constipation and Aging. They cannot refer you to other experts if the information they have isn't sufficient for your purposes.

☎ Contact:
National Institute on Aging
Bldg. 31, Room 5C27
Bethesda, MD 20892
(301) 496-1752

Free Publications/Videos

The following publication on Constipation is available from the National Digestive Diseases Information Clearinghouse, Box NDDIC, Bethesda, MD 20892; (301) 468-6344.

- *Age Page: Constipation.* (#DD-36)

The following publication on Constipation is available from the National Institute of Diabetes and Digestive and Kidney Diseases, Bldg. 31, Room 9A04, Bethesda, MD 20892; (301) 496-3583.

- *What Is Constipation?* (#86-2754)

CONSUMER PRODUCT INJURIES

Clearinghouses/Hotlines

The National Injury Information Clearinghouse gathers, investigates, analyzes, and distributes injury data relating to the causes and prevention of death, injury, and illness associated with consumer products. You can use this information center to tap into the National Electronic Injury Surveillance System (NEISS) that includes case reports on product-related injuries from hospital emergency rooms.

☎ Contact:
Consumer Product Safety Commission
5401 Westbard Avenue
Room 625
Washington, DC 20207
(301) 504-0424

Free Publications/Videos

The following publications are available from the Consumer Product Safety Commission, 5401 Westbard Avenue, Room 625, Washington, DC 20207; (301) 504-0424.

General Information
- *Who We Are and What We Do*

- *Compilation of Laws*
- *Consumer Resource Handbook (1988)*
- *CPSC Hotline Brochure*
- *Some Federal Consumer Oriented Agencies (F.S. 52)*

Bicycle Safety
- *Sprocketman (a comic book for high school age students)*
- *Mini Bikes (F.S. 38)*

Children's Furniture
- *Cribs (F.S. 43)*
- *High Chairs (F.S. 70)*
- *Bunk Beds (F.S. 71)*
- *Tips for Your Baby's Safety - Nursery Equipment Checklist (English and Spanish)*
- *The Safe Nursery - A Buyer's Guide to Nursery Equipment (English and Spanish)*
- *Be Sure It's Safe For Your Baby*

Children's Safety
- *Skateboards (F.S. 93)*
- *Protect Your Child*
- *Bumps Teachers Guide*
- *Super Sitter*

Compliance Publications
- *Retailers Guide (1/86)*
- *Guide for Manufacturers, Distributors, and Retailers*
- *Guide for Retailers (9/84)*

Curriculum Guides for Educators
- *It's No Accident - Consumer Product Safety*
- *Guide for Teachers of Grades 3-6*
- *Flammable Products: A Guide for Teachers of Secondary Grades*
- *Flammable Products: A Guide for Teachers of Elementary Grades (Spanish)*
- *Flammable Fabrics: Teacher's Guide (4T)*
- *Flammable Fabrics: Student Readings (4-S)*
- *Halloween Safety Teacher's Guide (9T)*
- *Holiday Safety Teacher's Guide (7T)*
- *Poison Prevention Teacher's Guide (6T)*

Electric Safety
- *Ranges and Ovens (F.S. 9)*
- *TV Fire and Shock (F.S. 11)*
- *Electric Blenders (F.S. 50)*
- *Clothes Dryers (F.S. 73)*

- *Ground Fault Circuit Interrupters* (F.S. 99)
- *CPSC Guide to Electrical Safety*
- *Consumer Product Safety Alert on Antennas*
- *Electrical Safety Room by Room Audit Checklist* (English and Spanish) (This is also available on "slow play disc" for the blind.)

Final Reports
- *Final Report of the National Conference on Product Safety (1982)*
- *Final Report of the National Conference on Product Safety (1984)*
- *Final Report of the National Consumer Product Safety Conference for Retailers*
- *Final Report of the National Conference on Fire Toxicity*

Fire Safety
- *Fireworks* (F.S. 12)
- *Upholstered Furniture* (F.S. 53)
- *Halloween Safety* (F.S. 100)
- *What You Should Know About Smoke Detectors*
- *Give a Gift--Give a Smoke Detector* (poster)
- *Home Fire Safety Checklist*

Hazardous Substances
- *School Science Laboratories: A Guide to Some Hazardous Products*
- *Asbestos in the Home*
- *List of Asbestos in Hair Dryers*
- *Methylene Chloride Safety Alert*

Holiday Safety
- *Merry Christmas With Safety*

Home Heating Equipment
- *Space Heaters* (F.S. 34)
- *Fireplaces* (F.S. 44)
- *Furnaces* (F.S. 79)
- *Wood Burning Stoves* (F.S. 92)
- *Kerosene Heaters* (F.S. 97)
- *Electric Space Heaters* (F.S. 98)
- *464 Chimneys Safety Alert (1984)*
- *Caution: Choosing and Using Gas Space Heaters*
- *What You Should Know About Kerosene Heaters*
- *What You Should Know About Space Heaters*

Home Insulation
- *Installing Insulation Safety*
- *Insulation Installers Guide*
- *Q&A Urea Formaldehyde Foam Insulation*

Indoor Air Quality
- *The Inside Story: A Guide to Indoor Air Quality*

Outdoor Power Equipment
- *Power Mowers* (F.S. 1)
- *Chain Saws* (F.S. 51)
- *Chain Saw Safety Guide*
- *Consumer Product Safety Alert on Chain Saws*
- *Mower Hazards and Safe Practices* (poster)
- *Power Mower and Maintenance Storage Tips*
- *Safety, Sales, and Services*
- *Power Lawn Mower Safety Kit--Teachers Manual*
- *Power Mower Hazards and Safety Features* (poster)

Older Consumers Safety
- *Home Safety Checklist for Older Consumers* (English and Spanish)

Playground Equipment
- *Play Happy, Play Safely: Little Big Kids (4-6 years)*
- *Handbook for Playground Safety, Volume I, General Guidelines*
- *Handbook for Playground Safety, Volume II, Technical Guidelines*

Poison Prevention
- *First Aid Brochure*
- *Locked-up Poisons* (English and Spanish)
- *Poison Lookout Checklist*
- *Poison Prevention Packaging: A Text for Pharmacies and Physicians*

Pool Safety
- *Children and Pool Safety Checklist*
- *Backyard Pool--CPSC Safety Alert* (5/87)

Spanish Fact Sheets
- *Power Mowers* (F.S. 1)
- *Kitchen Ranges* (F.S. 61)
- *Carbon Monoxide* (F.S. 13)
- *Infant Falls* (F.S. 20)
- *Mobile Homes* (F.S. 39)

- *Older Consumers and Stairway Accidents* (F.S. 48)
- *Kitchen Knives* (F.S. 83)
- *Trampolines* (F.S. 85)

Toys Safety
- *Toys* (F.S. 47)
- *Electric Toys* (F.S. 61)
- *Toy Chests* (F.S. 74)
- *Baby Rattles* (F.S. 86)
- *For Kids Sake, Think Toy Safety Pamphlet* (English and Spanish)
- *Toy Safety Coloring Book* (English and Spanish)
- *Which Toy For Which Child 0-5 Years*
- *Which Toy For Which Child 6-12*

Miscellaneous
- *All Terrain Vehicle (ATV) Safety Alert*
- *How to Plan and Conduct Consumer Product*
- *Safety Information Programs*
- *Ladders* (F.S. 56)
- *Clothes Dryers* (F.S. 73)
- *Publications Catalog*
- *Refuse Bins* (F.S. 81)

The following Consumer Safety video is available from Modern Talking Picture Service, 5000 Park St. North, St. Petersburg, FL 33709; (800) 243-MTPS.

- *Home Safety for the Older Consumer.* Video identifies home hazards and offers tips on reducing risk of injury.

CONTACT DERMATITIS

Free Publications/Videos

The following publication on Contact Dermatitis is available from the Food and Drug Administration, (HFE-88), 5600 Fishers Ln., Rockville, MD 20857; (301) 443-3170.

- *Contact Dermatitis: Solutions to Rash Mysteries.* (#FDA91-1166)

CONTACT LENSES

Clearinghouses/Hotlines

The National Eye Institute (NEI) can give you up-to-date information on Contact Lenses by searching the Combined Health Information Database (CHID) and MEDLINE and sending you bibliographies of resources, along with any journal articles they may have. They can also refer you to any other organizations that study this and other related issues. NEI will also let you know of any clinical studies that may be studying Contact Lenses and looking for patients. Because of their small staff, NEI prefers that you submit your requests for information in writing.

☎ Contact:
National Eye Institute
Building 31
Room 6A32
Bethesda, MD 20892
(301) 496-5248

Free Publications/Videos

The following publication on Contact Lenses is available from the Consumer Information Center, P.O. Box 100, Pueblo, CO 81002.

- *Contact Lenses: The Better the Care the Safer the Wear.* (#539Y)

The following publications on Contact Lenses are available from the Office of Technology Assessment, 600 Pennsylvania Ave., SE, Washington, DC 20510; (202) 224-8996.

- *Contact Lenses.* A report to Congress. Ask for the summary report.
- *Contact Lenses.*

The following publications on Contact Lenses are available from the Center for Devices and Radiological Health, (HFZ-210), Food and Drug Administration, 5600 Fishers Ln., Rockville, MD 20857; (301) 443-4690.

- *Homemade Saline Solutions for Contact Lenses.*
- *Acanthamoeba Eye Infections Among Contact Lens Users.*
- *An FDA Survey of U.S. Contact Lens Wearers.*
- *Are Your Contact Lenses As Safe As You Think? (#FDA 87-4220)*
- *Contact Lens Tablets to Require Sterile Fluids.*
- *FDA Advises Proper Care of Contact Lenses.*
- *Impact Resistant Lenses.*
- *ABCs of Contact Lenses. (#FDA 85-4021)*
- *Corneal Ulcers and Extended Wear Contact Lenses.*
- *Soft Contacts Need Some TLC.*

CONTRACEPTION

See also Family Planning
See also Oral Contraceptives

Clearinghouses/Hotlines

The National Institute of Child Health and Human Development (NICHD) will send you whatever publications and reprints of journal articles they have on Contraceptives. If necessary, they will refer you to other experts or researchers in the field. If you can't afford treatment, have your doctor call NICHD to find out if they are conducting any clinical studies that you might qualify for.

☎ Contact:
National Institute of Child Health
and Human Development
Bldg. 31, Room 2A32
Bethesda, MD 20892
(301) 496-5133

The Contraception Evaluation Branch at National Institutes of Health studies the safety and effectiveness of fertility control. They also provide on-going surveillance of the effectiveness of fertility regulating products and surgical procedures. A major emphasis now is to demonstrate the degree to which barrier contraceptives reduce the risk of sexually transmitted diseases, including AIDS. Staff can refer you to researchers examining a particular

birth control method, with most of their research being published in journals.

☎ Contact:
Contraception Evaluation Branch
EPN 607
9000 Rockville Pike
Bethesda, MD 20892
(301) 496-4924

The Contraceptive Development Branch at National Institutes of Health compares the effectiveness of various contraceptive methods and techniques and documents the medical side effects of oral contraceptive agents, intrauterine devices, contraceptive jellies, foams and creams. One of the areas they have focused on is the long-term effects of the use of oral contraceptives. Using health survey and epidemiologic studies of large patient populations, they also evaluate the safety and effectiveness of surgical sterilization procedures. The Center for Population Research publishes an annual progress report that outlines the accomplishments and goals in contraception development for the year.

☎ Contact:
Center for Population Research
National Institute of Child Health
and Human Development
Executive Plaza North, 6th Floor
Bethesda, MD 20892
(301) 496-1661

The Food and Drug Administration (FDA) can provide you with free reports and information regarding the new contraception called Norplant. Reports include information on patient labeling, prescribing, usage, warnings, and FDA statements regarding Norplant.

☎ Contact:
Drug Evaluation and Research
Food and Drug Administration
HFD 199
Rockville, MD 20857
(301) 295-8012

The Family Life Information Exchange (FLIE) provides information on family planning, adolescent pregnancy, and adoption. FLIE's primary audience consists of federally supported service agencies, but it also provides information to family planning service providers, educators, trainers, and consumers throughout the U.S.

☎ Contact:
Family Life Information Exchange
P.O. Box 37299
Washington, DC 20013
(301) 585-6636

Free Publications/Videos

The following publication on Contraceptives is available from the Family Life Information Exchange, P.O. Box 37299, Washington, DC 20013; (301) 585-6636.

- *Your Contraceptive Choices: For Now, For Later.*

The following publications on Contraceptives are available from the Center for Devices and Radiological Health, (HFZ-210), Food and Drug Administration, 5600 Fishers Ln., Rockville, MD 20857; (301) 443-4690.

- *Cervical Cap: Newest Birth Control Choice.*
- *New Treatments for Impotence.*

The following publications on Contraceptives are available from the Food & Drug Administration, (HFE-88), 5600 Fishers Ln., Rockville, MD 20857; (301) 443-3170.

- *Cervical Cap? Newest Control Device.* (#FDA89-1150)
- *Comparing Contraceptives.* Discusses the possible side effects and effectiveness of nine different types of birth control and also contains a chart. (#85-1123)

The following publication on Contraceptives is available from the National Institute of Child Health and Human Development, Bldg. 31, Room 2A32, Bethesda, MD 20892; (301) 496-5133.

- *Facts About Oral Contraceptives.*

The following publication on Contraceptives is available from the Consumer Information Center, P.O. Box 100, Pueblo, CO 81002.

- *The Pill: 30 Years of Safety Concerns.*

Research has improved oral contraceptives. Discusses benefits as well as side effects to watch for. (#544Z)

COOKWARE

Free Publications/Videos

The following publication is available from the Food & Drug Administration, (HFE-88), 5600 Fishers Ln., Rockville, MD 20857; (301) 443-3170.

- *Is That Newfangled Cookware Safe?* (#FDA91-2242)

COOLEY'S ANEMIA

Clearinghouses/Hotlines

The National Heart, Lung, and Blood Institute (NHLBI) can search the Combined Health Information Database (CHID) and generate a bibliography of resources on Cooley's Anemia for you. They also will send you any publications and journal articles they may have on hand, and will refer you to other organizations studying this disease. If you can't afford treatment, have your doctor call NHLBI to find out if they are conducting any clinical studies you might qualify for.

☎ Contact:
National Heart, Lung, and Blood Institute
Bldg. 31, Room 4A21
Bethesda, MD 20892
(301) 496-4236

Free Publications/Videos

The following publication is available from the National Heart, Lung and Blood Institute, Bldg. 31, Room 4A21, Bethesda, MD 20892; (301) 496-4236.

- *Cooley's Anemia: Prevention Through Understanding.* (#80-1269)

The following publication on Cooley's Anemia is available from the National Maternal and Child Health Clearinghouse, 38th & R Sts., NW, Washington, DC 20057; (703) 821-8955, ext. 254.

- *Cooley's Anemia: A Psychosocial Directory.* (#B221)

COR PULMONALE

Clearinghouses/Hotlines

The National Heart, Lung, and Blood Institute (NHLBI) can search the Combined Health Information Database (CHID) and generate a bibliography of resources on Cor Pulmonale for you. They also will send you any publications and journal articles they may have on hand, and will refer you to other organizations studying this disease. If you can't afford treatment, have your doctor call NHLBI to find out if they are conducting any clinical studies that you might qualify for.

☎ Contact:
National Heart, Lung, and Blood Institute
Bldg. 31, Room 4A21
Bethesda, MD 20892
(301) 496-4236

CORNEAL DISORDERS AND TRANSPLANTS

Clearinghouses/Hotlines

The National Eye Institute (NEI) can give you up-to-date information on Corneal Disorders and Transplants by searching the Combined Health Information Database (CHID) and MEDLINE and sending you bibliographies of resources, along with any journal articles they may have. They can also refer you to any other organizations that study this and other related diseases. NEI will also let you know of any clinical studies that may be studying this disease and looking for patients. Because of their small staff, NEI prefers that you submit your requests for information in writing.

☎ Contact:
National Eye Institute
Bldg. 31, Room 6A32
Bethesda, MD 20892
(301) 496-5248

Free Publications/Videos

The following publication is available from the National Eye Institute, Bldg. 31, Room 6A32, Bethesda, MD 20892; (301) 496-5248.

- *Vision Research: Report of the Corneal Diseases Panel, Part Two.* (#83-2472)

CORNELIA deLANGE SYNDROME

Clearinghouses/Hotlines

The National Institute of Child Health and Human Development (NICHD) will send you whatever publications and reprints of journal articles they have on Cornelia deLange Syndrome. If necessary, they will refer you to other experts or researchers in the field. If you can't afford treatment, have your doctor call NICHD to find out if they are conducting any clinical studies that you might qualify for.

☎ Contact:
National Institute of Child Health
and Human Development
Bldg. 31, Room 2A32
Bethesda, MD 20892
(301) 496-5133

CORONARY ANGIOPLASTY

Clearinghouses/Hotlines

The National Heart, Lung, and Blood Institute (NHLBI) can search the Combined Health Information Database (CHID) and generate a bibliography of resources on Coronary Angioplasty for you. They also will send you any publications and journal articles they may have on hand, and will refer you to other organizations that are studying this issue. If you can't afford treatment, have your doctor call NHLBI to find out if they are conducting any clinical studies that you might qualify for.

☎ Contact:
National Heart, Lung, and Blood Institute
Bldg. 31, Room 4A21
Bethesda, MD 20892
(301) 496-4236

CORONARY DISEASE

See Cardiovascular Disease
See Heart Disease

COSMETIC ALLERGY

Clearinghouses/Hotlines

The Office of Cosmetics and Colors of the Food and Drug Administration has a voluntary registration program for cosmetics, where cosmetic companies can register their company, manufacturers, cosmetics and cosmetic ingredients. They also operate an adverse reaction monitoring data base for complaints or allergic reactions to cosmetics. If you have a reaction to a cosmetic, you can call this office and they will register your complaint. They will also be able to tell you whether there have been other similar complaints concerning the product. This Office then informs the cosmetic company. If you have an allergic reaction to a cosmetic, this Office can tell you the steps you will need to take to determine which ingredient in the cosmetic is causing you problems.

☎ Contact:
Office of Cosmetics and Colors
Food and Drug Administration
200 C Street, SW
Washington, DC 20204
(202) 205-4094

COSMETIC SURGERY

See Face Lifts

COSTOCHONDRITIS

Clearinghouses/Hotlines

The National Institute of Arthritis and Musculoskeletal and Skin Diseases (NIAMS) will send you whatever publications and reprints of articles from texts and journals they have on Costochondritis. They will also refer you to other organizations that are studying this disease. NIAMS will also let you know of any clinical studies that may be studying this disease and looking for patients.

☎ Contact:
National Institute of Arthritis
and Musculoskeletal and Skin Diseases
Box AMS
Bethesda, MD 20892
(301) 495-4484

COT DEATH

See Sudden Infant Death Syndrome

COUGHING

Free Publications/Videos

The following publication is available from the National Heart, Lung and Blood Institute, Bldg. 31, Room 4A21, Bethesda, MD 20892; (301) 496-4236.

- *Do I Have a Chronic Cough?* (#559) Defines chronic cough and identifies it as a symptom of a possible chronic lung disease.

COWPOX

Clearinghouses/Hotlines

The National Institute of Arthritis and Musculoskeletal and Skin Diseases Clearinghouse can provide you with information regarding cowpox. They can search their files to see if they have journal articles and other reference materials on cowpox, and can also refer you to organizations dealing with skin diseases.

☎ Contact:
National Arthritis and Musculoskeletal
and Skin Diseases Clearinghouse
Box AMS
Bethesda, MD 20892
(301) 495-4484

COXSACKIE VIRUS

Clearinghouses/Hotlines

The National Institute on Allergy and Infectious Diseases (NIAID) can search the Combined Health Information Database (CHID) and generate a bibliography of resources on Coxsackie Virus (Hand-Foot & Mouth Disease) for you. They will also send you any publications and journal articles they may have on hand, and will refer you to researchers who are currently studying this disease. If you can't afford treatment, have your doctor call NIAID to find out if they are conducting any clinical studies that you might qualify for.

☎ Contact:
National Institute of Allergy
and Infectious Diseases
Bldg. 31, Room 7A32
Bethesda, MD 20892
(301) 496-5717

The National Institute of Child Health and Human Development (NICHD) will send you whatever publications and reprints of journal articles they have on Coxsackie Virus (Hand-Foot & Mouth Disease). If necessary, they will refer you to other experts or researchers in the field. If you can't afford treatment, have your doctor call NICHD to find out if they are conducting any clinical studies that you might qualify for.

☎ Contact:
National Institute of Child Health
and Human Development
Bldg. 31, Room 2A32
Bethesda, MD 20892
(301) 496-5133

CPR

See Cardiopulmonary Resuscitation

CRACK COCAINE

See also Drug Abuse

Clearinghouses/Hotlines

The National Clearinghouse for Alcohol and Drug Information is the central point within the Federal Government for current print and audiovisual materials about alcohol and other drugs. They have information tailored to parents, teachers, youth, and others, as well as information about organizations and groups concerned with alcohol and other drug problems. They have publications, reports, newsletters, videos, posters, and more, as well as being able to provide comprehensive alcohol and other drug resource referrals. Call for your free catalogue.

☎ Contact:
National Clearinghouse for Alcohol
and Drug Information
P.O. Box 2345
Rockville, MD 20852
(800) 729-6686
(301) 468-2600

Free Publications/Videos

The following Congressional Research Service

(CRS) report is available from either of your U.S. Senators' offices at the U.S. Capitol, Washington, DC 20510, or from your Congressional Representative at the U.S. Capitol, Washington, DC 20515. You can also call in your request through the U.S. Capitol switchboard at (202) 224-3121. Be sure to include the full title and report number in your request.

- *"Crack" Cocaine.* (#89-428 EPW)

CRANIAL ABNORMALITIES

Clearinghouses/Hotlines

The National Institute of Dental Research (NIDR) will send you whatever publications and reprints of journal articles they have on Cranial Abnormalities. As a policy, NIDR will not refer you to other organizations or experts who study this disease. If you can't afford treatment, have your doctor call Dr. Albert Guckers at (301) 496-6241 to find out if NIDR is conducting any clinical studies that you might qualify for.

☎ Contact:
National Institute of Dental Research
Bldg. 31, Room 2C35
Bethesda, MD 20892
(301) 496-4261

CRANIOFACIAL MALFORMATIONS

Clearinghouses/Hotlines

The National Institute of Dental Research (NIDR) will send you whatever publications and reprints of journal articles they have on Craniofacial Malformations. As a policy, NIDR will not refer you to other organizations or experts who study this disease. If you can't afford treatment, have your doctor call Dr. Albert Guckers at (301) 496-6241 to find out if NIDR is conducting any clinical studies that you might qualify for.

☎ Contact:
National Institute of Dental Research
Bldg. 31, Room 2C35
Bethesda, MD 20892
(301) 496-4261

CRETINISM

Clearinghouses/Hotlines

The National Institute of Diabetes and Digestive and Kidney Diseases's (NIDDK) individual clearinghouses can search the Combined Health Information Database (CHID) and generate a bibliography of resources on Cretinism for you. They also will send you any publications and journal articles they may have on hand, and will refer you to other organizations that are studying this disease. If you can't afford treatment, have your doctor call NIDDK to find out if they are conducting any clinical studies that you might qualify for.

☎ Contact:
National Institute of Diabetes
and Digestive and Kidney Diseases
Bldg. 31, Room 9A04
Bethesda, MD 20892
(301) 496-3583

CREUTZFELDT-JAKOB DISEASE

Clearinghouses/Hotlines

The National Institute of Neurological Disorders and Stroke (NINDS) can send you only information they have in their publications list on Creutzfeldt-Jakob Disease. This Clearinghouse cannot directly give you information about any current clinical studies they might be conducting on this illness, but you can find this information for yourself by looking under the National Institute of Neurological Disorders and Stroke in *Appendix A* at the end of this book.

☎ Contact:
National Institute of Neurological
Disorders and Stroke
Bldg. 31, Room 8A06
Bethesda, MD 20892
(301) 496-5751
(800) 352-9424

Free Publications/Videos

The following publications on Creutzfeldt-Jakob Diseaseare available from the National Institute of Neurological Disorders and Stroke, Bldg. 31, Room 8A06, Bethesda, MD 20892; (301) 496-5751 or (800) 352-9424.

- *Creutzfeldt-Jakob Disease.* (#86-2760)
- *Creutzfeldt-Jakob Disease.* Contains a collection of scientific articles, patient education pamphlets, and addresses of voluntary health associations.
- *Creutzfeldt-Jakob Disease.* Fact sheet on symptoms and treatment.

The following publication is available from the National Institute of Diabetes and Digestive and Kidney Diseases, Bldg. 31, Room 9A04, Bethesda, MD 20892; (301) 496-3583.

- *Human Growth Hormone and Creutzfeldt-Jakob Disease.* (#88-2793)

CRIB DEATH

See Sudden Infant Death Syndrome

CRIGLER-NAJAR SYNDROME

Clearinghouses/Hotlines

The National Institute of Diabetes and Digestive and Kidney Diseases's (NIDDK) individual clearinghouses can search the Combined Health Information Database (CHID) and generate a bibliography of resources on Crigler-Najar Syndrome for you. They will send you any publications and journal articles they may have on hand, and will refer you to other organizations that are studying this disease. If you can't afford treatment, have your doctor call NIDDK to find out if they are conducting any clinical studies that you might qualify for.

☎ Contact:
National Institute of Diabetes
and Digestive and Kidney Diseases
Bldg. 31, Room 9A04
Bethesda, MD 20892
(301) 496-3583

CRITICAL CARE

Free Publications/Videos

The following publication is available from the Office of Clinical Center Communications, Bldg. 10, Room 1C255, Bethesda, MD 20892; (301) 496-2563.

- *Critical Care Medicine Department.*

CROHN'S DISEASE

Clearinghouses/Hotlines

The National Institute of Diabetes and Digestive and Kidney Diseases's (NIDDK) individual clearinghouses can search the Combined Health Information Database (CHID) and generate a bibliography of resources on Crohn's Disease for you. They also will send you any publications and journal articles they may have on hand, and will refer you to other organizations studying this disease. If you can't afford treatment, have your doctor call NIDDK to find out if they are conducting any clinical studies that you might qualify for.

☎ Contact:
National Institute of Diabetes
and Digestive and Kidney Diseases

Bldg. 31, Room 9A04
Bethesda, MD 20892
(301) 496-3583

The National Digestive Diseases Information Clearinghouse can give you all kinds of information about ulcerative colitis and Crohn's Disease, clinical symptoms, epidemiological patterns, treatment strategies and experimental therapies.

☎ Contact:
National Digestive Diseases
Information Clearinghouse
Box NDDIC
Bethesda, MD 20892
(301) 468-6344

The National Institute on Allergy and Infectious Diseases (NIAID) can search the Combined Health Information Database (CHID) and generate a bibliography of resources on Crohn's Disease for you. They will also send you any publications and journal articles they may have on hand, and will refer you to researchers who are currently studying this disease. If you can't afford treatment, have your doctor call NIAID to find out if they are conducting any clinical studies that you might qualify for.

☎ Contact:
National Institute of Allergy
and Infectious Diseases
Bldg. 31, Room 7A32
Bethesda, MD 20892
(301) 496-5717

Free Publications/Videos

The following publication on Crohn's Disease is available from the National Digestive Diseases Information Clearinghouse, Box NDDIC, Bethesda, MD 20892; (301) 468-6344.

- *Crohn's Disease and Ulcerative Colitis.*
Information packet.

The following video on Crohn's Disease is available from the Office of Clinical Center Communications, Bldg. 10, Room 1C255, Bethesda, MD 20892; (301) 496-2563.

- *Ulcerative Colitis and Crohn's Disease.* Video to help the general public make intelligent decisions.

CROSS-EYE

Clearinghouses/Hotlines

The National Eye Institute (NEI) can give you up-to-date information on Cross-Eye by searching the Combined Health Information Database (CHID) and MEDLINE and sending you bibliographies of resources, along with any journal articles they may have. They can also refer you to any other organizations that study this and other related disorders. NEI will also let you know of any clinical studies that may be studying Cross-Eye and looking for patients. Because of their small staff, NEI prefers that you submit your requests for information in writing.

☎ Contact:
National Eye Institute
Bldg. 31, Room 6A32
Bethesda, MD 20892
(301) 496-5248

CRYOSURGERY

Clearinghouses/Hotlines

The National Eye Institute (NEI) can give you up-to-date information on Cryosurgery on the Eyes by searching the Combined Health Information Database (CHID) and MEDLINE and sending you bibliographies of resources, along with any journal articles they may have. They can also refer you to any other organizations that study this and other related techniques. NEI will also let you know of any clinical studies that may be studying this technique and looking for patients. Because of their small staff, NEI prefers that you submit your requests for information in writing.

☎ Contact:
National Eye Institute
Bldg. 31, Room 6A32

Bethesda, MD 20892
(301) 496-5248

The National Cancer Institute (NCI) will send you whatever publications and reprints of journal articles they have on Cryosurgery on the Eyes. They can also search their Physician's Data Query (PDQ) database to let you know if NCI is conducting any clinical studies on your disease.

☎ Contact:
National Cancer Institute
Bldg. 31, Room 10A24
Bethesda, MD 20892
(800) 4-CANCER
(301) 496-5583

CRYPTOCOCCOSIS

Clearinghouses/Hotlines

The National Institute on Allergy and Infectious Diseases (NIAID) can search the Combined Health Information Database (CHID) and generate a bibliography of resources on Cryptococcosis for you. They will also send you any publications and journal articles they may have on hand, and will refer you to researchers who are currently studying this disease. If you can't afford treatment, have your doctor call NIAID to find out if they are conducting any clinical studies that you might qualify for.

☎ Contact:
National Institute of Allergy
and Infectious Diseases
Bldg. 31, Room 7A32
Bethesda, MD 20892
(301) 496-5717

CRYPTOSPORIDIOSIS

Clearinghouses/Hotlines

The National Institute on Allergy and Infectious Diseases (NIAID) can search the Combined Health Information Database (CHID) and generate a bibliography of resources on Cryptosporidiosis for you. They will also send you any publications and journal articles they may have on hand, and will refer you to researchers who are currently studying this disease. If you can't afford treatment, have your doctor call NIAID to find out if they are conducting any clinical studies that you might qualify for.

☎ Contact:
National Institute of Allergy
and Infectious Diseases
Bldg. 31, Room 7A32
Bethesda, MD 20892
(301) 496-5717

CUSHING'S DISEASE

See Cushing's Syndrome

CUSHING'S SYNDROME

Clearinghouses/Hotlines

The National Institute of Diabetes and Digestive and Kidney Diseases's (NIDDK) individual clearinghouses can search the Combined Health Information Database (CHID) and generate a bibliography of resources on Cushing's Syndrome for you. They also will send you any publications and journal articles they may have on hand, and will refer you to other organizations that are studying this disease. If you can't afford treatment, have your doctor call NIDDK to find out if they are conducting any clinical studies that you might qualify for.

☎ Contact:
National Institute of Diabetes
and Digestive and Kidney Diseases
Bldg. 31, Room 9A04
Bethesda, MD 20892
(301) 496-3583

The National Institute of Neurological Disorders and Stroke (NINDS) can send you only information they have in their publications list on

Cushing's Syndrome. This Clearinghouse cannot directly give you information about any current clinical studies they might be conducting on this illness, but you can find this information for yourself by looking under the National Institute of Neurological Disorders and Stroke in *Appendix A* at the end of this book.

☎ Contact:
National Institute of Neurological
Disorders and Stroke
Bldg. 31, Room 8A06
Bethesda, MD 20892
(301) 496-5751
(800) 352-9424

The National Institute of Child Health and Human Development (NICHD) will send you whatever publications and reprints of journal articles they have on Cushing's Syndrome. If necessary, they will refer you to other experts or researchers in the field. If you can't afford treatment, have your doctor call NICHD to find out if they are conducting any clinical studies that you might qualify for.

☎ Contact:
National Institute of Child Health
and Human Development
Bldg. 31, Room 2A32
Bethesda, MD 20892
(301) 496-5133

Free Publications/Videos

The following publication is available from the National Institute of Diabetes and Digestive and Kidney Diseases, Bldg. 31, Room 9A04, Bethesda, MD 20892; (301) 496-3583.

- *Cushing's Syndrome.* (#89-3007)

CUTIS LAXA

Clearinghouses/Hotlines

The National Heart, Lung, and Blood Institute (NHLBI) can search the Combined Health Information Database (CHID) and generate a bibliography of resources on Cutis Laxa for you. They also will send you any publications and journal articles they may have on hand, and will refer you to other organizations that are studying this disorder. If you can't afford treatment, have your doctor call NHLBI to find out if they are conducting any clinical studies that you might qualify for.

☎ Contact:
National Heart, Lung, and Blood Institute
Bldg. 31, Room 4A21
Bethesda, MD 20892
(301) 496-4236

CYCLIC IDIOPATHIC EDEMA

Clearinghouses/Hotlines

The National Heart, Lung, and Blood Institute (NHLBI) can search the Combined Health Information Database (CHID) and generate a bibliography of resources on Cyclic Idiopathic Edema for you. They also will send you any publications and journal articles they may have on hand, and will refer you to other organizations that are studying this disease. If you can't afford treatment, have your doctor call NHLBI to find out if they are conducting any clinical studies that you might qualify for.

☎ Contact:
National Heart, Lung, and Blood Institute
Bldg. 31, Room 4A21
Bethesda, MD 20892
(301) 496-4236

CYCLITIS

Clearinghouses/Hotlines

The National Eye Institute (NEI) can give you up-to-date information on Cyclitis by searching the Combined Health Information Database (CHID) and MEDLINE and sending you bibliographies of resources, along with any journal articles they may have. They can also refer you to any other organizations that study this and other related diseases. NEI will also let you know of any clinical studies that may be studying this disease and looking for patients. Because of their small staff, NEI prefers that you submit your requests for information in writing.

☎ Contact:
National Eye Institute
Bldg. 31, Room 6A32
Bethesda, MD 20892
(301) 496-5248

CYCLOPHOSPHAMIDE

Free Publications/Videos

The following publication is available from the National Cancer Institute, Bldg. 31, Room 10A24, Bethesda, MD 20892; (800) 4-CANCER, or (301) 496-5583.

- *Ciclofosfamida/Cyclophosphamide.* Provides information about side effects, proper usage, and precautions of this anti-cancer drug.

CYCLOSPORINE-ASSOCIATED HYPERTENSION

Free Publications/Videos

The following publication is available from the National Heart, Lung and Blood Institute, Bldg. 31, Room 4A21, Bethesda, MD 20892; (301) 496-4236.

- *Cyclosporine-Associated Hypertension.* (#NN333) Information on incidence, characteristics, mechanisms, and drug management of cyclosporine-associated hypertension (CAH) are presented.

CYSTIC ACNE

Clearinghouses/Hotlines

The National Institute of Arthritis and Musculoskeletal and Skin Diseases (NIAMS) will send you whatever publications and reprints of articles from texts and journals they have on Cystic Acne. They will also refer you to other organizations that are studying this disease. NIAMS will also let you know of any clinical studies that may be studying this disease and looking for patients.

☎ Contact:
National Institute of Arthritis
and Musculoskeletal and Skin Diseases
Box AMS
Bethesda, MD 20892
(301) 495-4484

The National Cancer Institute (NCI) will send you whatever publications and reprints of journal articles they have on Cystic Acne. They can also give you information on the state-of-the-art treatment for this disease, including specific treatment information for your stage of cancer. They can also search their Physician's Data Query (PDQ) database to let you know if NCI is conducting any clinical studies on your disease.

☎ Contact:
National Cancer Institute
Bldg. 31, Room 10A24
Bethesda, MD 20892
(800) 4-CANCER
(301) 496-5583

CYSTIC FIBROSIS

Clearinghouses/Hotlines

The National Institute of Diabetes and Digestive and Kidney Diseases's (NIDDK) individual clearinghouses can search the Combined Health Information Database (CHID) and generate a bibliography of resources on Cystic Fibrosis of the Pancreas for you. They also will send you any publications and journal articles they may have on hand, and will refer you to other organizations that are studying this disease. If you can't afford treatment, have your doctor call NIDDK to find out if they are conducting any clinical studies that you might qualify for.

☎ Contact:
National Institute of Diabetes
and Digestive and Kidney Diseases
Bldg. 31, Room 9A04
Bethesda, MD 20892
(301) 496-3583

Free Publications/Videos

The following publications are available from the Office of Technology Assessment, Washington, DC 20510-8025; (202) 224-8996.

- *Genetic Counseling and Cystic Fibrosis Carrier Screening: Results of a Survey.* (#OTA-BP-BA-97)
- *Cystic Fibrosis and DNA Tests: Implications of Carrier Screening.* (#OTA-BA-532)

CYSTIC MASTITIS

See Fibrocystic Breast Disease

CYSTINOSIS

Clearinghouses/Hotlines

The National Institute of Child Health and Human Development (NICHD) will send you whatever publications and reprints of journal articles they have on Cystinosis. If necessary, they will refer you to other experts or researchers in the field. If you can't afford treatment, have your doctor call NICHD to find out if they are conducting any clinical studies that you might qualify for.

☎ Contact:
National Institute of Child Health

and Human Development
Building 31
Room 2A32
Bethesda, MD 20892
(301) 496-5133

CYSTINURIA

Clearinghouses/Hotlines

The National Institute of Diabetes and Digestive and Kidney Diseases's (NIDDK) individual clearinghouses can search the Combined Health Information Database (CHID) and generate a bibliography of resources on Cystinuria for you. They also will send you any publications and journal articles they may have on hand, and will refer you to other organizations that are studying this disease. If you can't afford treatment, have your doctor call NIDDK to find out if they are conducting any clinical studies that you might qualify for.

☎ Contact:
National Institute of Diabetes
and Digestive and Kidney Diseases
Bldg. 31, Room 9A04
Bethesda, MD 20892
(301) 496-3583

CYSTITIS

Clearinghouses/Hotlines

The National Institute of Diabetes and Digestive and Kidney Diseases's (NIDDK) individual clearinghouses can search the Combined Health Information Database (CHID) and generate a bibliography of resources on Cystitis for you. They also will send you any publications and journal articles they may have on hand, and will refer you to other organizations that are studying this disease. If you can't afford treatment, have your doctor call NIDDK to find out if they are conducting any clinical studies that you might qualify for.

☎ Contact:
National Institute of Diabetes
and Digestive and Kidney Diseases
Bldg. 31, Room 9A04
Bethesda, MD 20892
(301) 496-3583

CYTARABINE

Free Publications/Videos

The following publication is available from the National Cancer Institute, Bldg. 31, Room 10A24, Bethesda, MD 20892; (800) 4-CANCER, or (301) 496-5583.

- *Citarabina/Cytarabine.* Provides information about side effects, proper usage, and precautions of this anti-cancer drug.

CYTOMEGALIC INCLUSION BODY DISEASE

Clearinghouses/Hotlines

The National Institute of Neurological Disorders and Stroke (NINDS) can send you only information they have in their publications list on Cytomegalic Inclusion Body Disease. This Clearinghouse cannot directly give you information about any current clinical studies they might be conducting on this illness, but you can find this information for yourself by looking under the National Institute of Neurological Disorders and Stroke in *Appendix A* at the end of this book.

☎ Contact:
National Institute of Neurological
Disorders and Stroke
Bldg. 31, Room 8A06
Bethesda, MD 20892
(301) 496-5751
(800) 352-9424

CYTOMEGALOVIRUS (CMV)

Clearinghouses/Hotlines

The Centers for Disease Control's Voice Information System allows anyone using a touchtone phone to obtain pre-recorded information on Cytomegalovirus, and many other diseases. This service offers information about this condition, symptoms and prevention methods, immunization requirements, current statistics, recent disease outbreak, and available printed materials. The system is available 24 hours a day, although the health professionals are available Monday through Friday, 8 a.m.-4:30 p.m.

☎ Contact:
Centers for Disease Control
Information Resources Management Office
Mail Stop C-15
1600 Clifton Rd., NE
Atlanta, GA 30333
(404) 332-4555

The National Heart, Lung, and Blood Institute (NHLBI) can search the Combined Health Information Database (CHID) and generate a bibliography of resources on Congenital Cytomegalovirus for you. They also will send you any publications and journal articles they may have on hand, and will refer you to other organizations that are studying this disease. If you can't afford treatment, have your doctor call NHLBI to find out if they are conducting any clinical studies that you might qualify for.

☎ Contact:
National Heart, Lung, and Blood Institute
Building 31
Room 4A21
Bethesda, MD 20892
(301) 496-4236

The National Institute of Child Health and Human Development (NICHD) will send you whatever publications and reprints of journal articles they have on Congenital Cytomegalovirus. If necessary, they will refer you to other experts or researchers in the field. If you can't afford treatment, have your doctor call NICHD to find out if they are conducting any clinical studies that you might qualify for.

☎ Contact:
National Institute of Child Health
and Human Development
Building 31
Room 2A32
Bethesda, MD 20892
(301) 496-5133

The National Institute on Allergy and Infectious Diseases (NIAID) can search the Combined Health Information Database (CHID) and generate a bibliography of resources on Congenital Cytomegalovirus for you. They will also send you any publications and journal articles they may have on hand, and will refer you to researchers who are currently studying this disease. If you can't afford treatment, have your doctor call NIAID to find out if they are conducting any clinical studies that you might qualify for.

☎ Contact:
National Institute of Allergy
and Infectious Diseases
Building 31
Room 7A32
Bethesda, MD 20892
(301) 496-5717

The National Eye Institute (NEI) can give you up-to-date information on CMV by searching the Combined Health Information Database (CHID) and MEDLINE and sending you bibliographies of resources, along with any journal articles they may have. They can also refer you to any other organizations that study this and other related diseases. NEI will also let you know of any clinical studies that may be studying this disease and looking for patients. Because of their small staff, NEI prefers that you submit your requests for information in writing.

☎ Contact:
National Eye Institute
Bldg. 31, Room 6A32
Bethesda, MD 20892
(301) 496-5248

- D -

DACTINOMYCIN

Free Publications/Videos

The following publication is available from the National Cancer Institute, Bldg. 31, Room 10A24, Bethesda, MD 20892; (800) 4-CANCER, or (301) 496-5583.

- *Dactinomicina/Dactinomycin.* Provides information about side effects, proper usage, and precautions of this anti-cancer drug.

DALTONISM

See Color Blindness

DANDRUFF

Clearinghouses/Hotlines

The Over-The-Counter Drug Evaluation Division of the Food and Drug Administration has written a monograph on products claiming to reduce or alleviate Dandruff. The monograph outlines the components which have been found to be most effective and those which do nothing to remedy this problem.

☎ Contact:
Over-the-Counter Drug
Evaluation Division
Food and Drug Administration
5600 Fishers Lane
Rockville, MD 20857
(301) 295-8000

DANDY-WALKER SYNDROME

Clearinghouses/Hotlines

The National Institute of Neurological Disorders and Stroke (NINDS) can send you only information they have in their publications list on Dandy-Walker Syndrome. They cannot refer you to any experts. This Clearinghouse cannot directly give you information about any current clinical studies NINDS might be conducting on this illness, but you can find this information for yourself by looking under the National Institute of Neurological Disorders and Stroke in *Appendix A* at the end of this book.

☎ Contact:
National Institute of Neurological
Disorders and Stroke
Bldg. 31, Room 8A06
Bethesda, MD 20892
(301) 496-5751
(800) 352-9424

Free Publications/Videos

The following publication is available from the National Institute of Neurological Disorders and Stroke, P.O. Box 5801, Bethesda, MD 20824; (800) 352-9424, or (301) 496-5751.

- *Dandy Walker Syndrome*. Contains a collection of scientific articles, patient education pamphlets, and addresses of voluntary health associations.

DARIER'S DISEASE

Clearinghouses/Hotlines

The National Institute of Arthritis and Musculoskeletal and Skin Diseases (NIAMS) will send you whatever publications and reprints of articles from texts and journals they have on Darier's Disease. They will also refer you to other organizations that are studying this disease. NIAMS will also let you know of any clinical studies that may be studying this disease and looking for patients.

☎ Contact:
National Institute of Arthritis
and Musculoskeletal and Skin Diseases
Box AMS
Bethesda, MD 20892
(301) 495-4484

DAUNORUBICIN

Free Publications/Videos

The following publication is available from the National Cancer Institute, Bldg. 31, Room 10A24, Bethesda, MD 20892; (800) 4-CANCER, or (301) 496-5583.

- *Daunorrubicina/Daunorubicin*. Provides information about side effects, proper usage, and precautions of this anti-cancer drug.

DAY CARE

Free Publications/Videos

The following Congressional Research Service (CRS) report is available from either of your U.S. Senators' offices at the U.S. Capitol, Washington, DC 20510, or from your Congressional Representative at the U.S. Capitol, Washington, DC 20515. You can also call in your request through the U.S. Capitol switchboard at (202) 224-3121. Be sure to include the full title and report number in your request.

- *Child Day Care*. (#IB89011)

The following publication is available from the Clearinghouse on Child Abuse and Neglect Information, P.O. Box 1182, Washington, DC 20013; (800) FYI-3366, or (800) 394-3366.

- *Day Care*. Annotated bibliography covering child abuse issues. (#07-91175, $3)

DEAFNESS

See also Communication Disorders

Clearinghouses/Hotlines

The National Institute on Deafness and Other Communication Disorders Clearinghouse (NIDCDC) can tell you everything you always wanted to know about disorders involving hearing, balance, smell, taste, voice, speech, and language. They have countless fact sheets, bibliographies, catalogs, and directories of information sources, including a directory of associations and organizations interested in Deafness and other communication disorders.

☎ Contact:
National Institute on Deafness and Other
Communication Disorders Clearinghouse
P.O. Box 37777
Washington, DC 20013
(301) 496-7243
(301) 402-0252 (TDD)
(800) 241-1044

DEATH

See also Living Wills

Clearinghouses/Hotlines

The National Institute on Aging (NIA) will send you whatever publications and reprints of journal articles they have on Death and Dying. They cannot refer you to other experts if the information they have isn't sufficient for your purposes.

☎ Contact:
National Institute on Aging
Bldg. 31, Room 5C27
Bethesda, MD 20892
(301) 496-1752

The National Institute of Mental Health (NIMH) will send you whatever publications and reprints of articles from texts and journals they have on Death and Dying. They will also refer you to other organizations that are studying this disease.

☎ Contact:
National Institute of Mental Health
5600 Fishers Ln., Room 15C05
Rockville, MD 20857
(301) 443-4515

The National Center for Health Statistics collects and distributes data on abortions, births, deaths, marriages, and divorces, and produces annual data for the U.S., states, countries, and local areas.

☎ Contact:
Division of Vital Statistics
National Center for Health Statistics
3700 East-West Highway, Room 1-44
Hyattsville, MD 20782
(301) 436-8952

Free Publications/Videos

The following publication is available from the National Sudden Infant Death Syndrome Clearinghouse, 8201 Greensboro Drive, Suite 600, McLean, VA 22102; (703) 821-8955.

- *Talking to Children About Death*. Discusses some of the ways that parents might help children deal with a death.

DECARBAZINE

Free Publications/Videos

The following publication is available from the National Cancer Institute, Bldg. 31, Room 10A24, Bethesda, MD 20892; (800) 4-CANCER, or (301) 496-5583.

- *Decarbazino/Decarbazine*. Provides information about side effects, proper usage, and precautions of this anti-cancer drug.

DECUBITUS ULCERS

Clearinghouses/Hotlines

The National Institute of Arthritis and Musculoskeletal and Skin Diseases (NIAMS) will send you whatever publications and reprints of articles from texts and journals they have on Decubitus Ulcers. They will also refer you to other organizations that are studying this disease. NIAMS will also let you know of any clinical studies that may be studying this disease and looking for patients.

☎ Contact:
National Institute of Arthritis
and Musculoskeletal and Skin Diseases
Box AMS
Bethesda, MD 20892
(301) 495-4484

The National Institute on Aging (NIA) will send you whatever publications and reprints of journal articles they have on Decubitus Ulcers. They cannot refer you to other experts if the information they have isn't sufficient for your purposes.

☎ Contact:
National Institute on Aging
Bldg. 31, Room 5C27
Bethesda, MD 20892
(301) 496-1752

DEGENERATIVE BASAL GANGLIA DISEASE

Clearinghouses/Hotlines

The National Institute of Neurological Disorders and Stroke (NINDS) can send you only information they have in their publications list on Degenerative Basal Ganglia Disease. They cannot refer you to any experts. This Clearinghouse cannot directly give you information about any current clinical studies NINDS might be conducting on this illness, but you can find this

information for yourself by looking under the National Institute of Neurological Disorders and Stroke in *Appendix A* at the end of this book.

☎ Contact:
National Institute of Neurological
Disorders and Stroke
Bldg. 31, Room 8A06
Bethesda, MD 20892
(301) 496-5751
(800) 352-9424

DEGENERATIVE JOINT DISEASE

Clearinghouses/Hotlines

The National Institute of Arthritis and Musculoskeletal and Skin Diseases (NIAMS) will send you whatever publications and reprints of articles from texts and journals they have on Degenerative Joint Disease (DJD). They will also refer you to other organizations that are studying DJD. NIAMS will also let you know of any clinical studies that may be studying this disease and looking for patients.

☎ Contact:
National Institute of Arthritis
and Musculoskeletal and Skin Diseases
Box AMS
9000 Rockville Pike
Bethesda, MD 20892
(301) 495-4484

DEGLUTITION

Clearinghouses/Hotlines

The National Institute of Dental Research (NIDR) will send you whatever publications and reprints of journal articles they have on Deglutition. As a policy, NIDR will not refer you to other organizations or experts who study this issue. If you can't afford treatment, have your doctor call Dr. Albert Guckers at (301) 496-6241 to find out if NIDR is conducting any clinical studies that you might qualify for.

☎ Contact:
National Institute of Dental Research
Bldg. 31, Room 2C35
Bethesda, MD 20892
(301) 496-4261

DEJERINE-SOTTAS DISEASE

Clearinghouses/Hotlines

The National Institute of Neurological Disorders and Stroke (NINDS) can send you only information they have in their publications list on Dejerine-Sottas Disease. They cannot refer you to any experts. This Clearinghouse cannot directly give you information about any current clinical studies NINDS might be conducting on this illness, but you can find this information for yourself by looking under the National Institute of Neurological Disorders and Stroke in *Appendix A* at the end of this book.

☎ Contact:
National Institute of Neurological
Disorders and Stroke
Bldg. 31, Room 8A06
Bethesda, MD 20892
(301) 496-5751
(800) 352-9424

DEMENTIA

See also Mental Illness
See also Alzheimer's Disease
See also Presenile Dementia

Clearinghouses/Hotlines

The National Institute on Aging (NIA) will send you whatever publications and reprints of journal articles they have on Dementia. They cannot refer you to other experts if the information they have

isn't sufficient for your purposes.

☎ Contact:
National Institute on Aging
Bldg. 31, Room 5C27
Bethesda, MD 20892
(301) 496-1752

The National Institute of Neurological Disorders and Stroke (NINDS) can send you only information they have in their publications list on Dementia. They cannot refer you to any experts. This Clearinghouse cannot directly give you information about any current clinical studies NINDS might be conducting on this illness, but you can find this information for yourself by looking under the National Institute of Neurological Disorders and Stroke in *Appendix A* at the end of this book.

☎ Contact:
National Institute of Neurological
Disorders and Stroke
Bldg. 31, Room 8A06
Bethesda, MD 20892
(301) 496-5751
(800) 352-9424

Free Publications/Videos

The following publication on Dementia is available from the Office of Clinical Center Communications, National Institutes of Health, Bldg. 10, Room 5C-305, 9000 Rockville Pike, Bethesda, MD 20892; (301) 496-2563.

- *The Brain in "Aging" and Dementia*. Discusses brain anatomy and physiology, the normal process of brain aging, and senility. Vascular dementia and Alzheimer's disease are described as well as research on the causes and treatment. (#83-2625)

The following publication on Dementia is available from the Office of Technology Assessment, Washington, DC 20510-8025; (202) 224-8996.

- *Special Care Units for People with Alzheimer's and Other Dementias: Consumer Education, Research, Regulatory, and Reimbursement Issues*. (Free Summary Available)

DEMYELINATING DISEASES

Clearinghouses/Hotlines

The National Institute of Neurological Disorders and Stroke (NINDS) can send you only information they have in their publications list on Demyelinating Diseases. They cannot refer you to any experts. This Clearinghouse cannot directly give you information about any current clinical studies NINDS might be conducting on this illness, but you can find this information for yourself by looking under the National Institute of Neurological Disorders and Stroke in *Appendix A* at the end of this book.

☎ Contact:
National Institute of Neurological
Disorders and Stroke
Building 31
Room 8A06
Bethesda, MD 20892
(301) 496-5751
(800) 352-9424

DENGUE

Clearinghouses/Hotlines

The National Institute on Allergy and Infectious Diseases (NIAID) can search the Combined Health Information Database (CHID) and generate a bibliography of resources on Dengue for you. They will also send you any publications and journal articles they may have on hand, and will refer you to researchers who are currently studying this issue. If you can't afford treatment, have your doctor call NIAID to find out if they are conducting any clinical studies that you might qualify for.

☎ Contact:
National Institute of Allergy
and Infectious Diseases
Building 31
Room 7A32
Bethesda, MD 20892
(301) 496-5717

DENTAL CARE PROGRAMS

Free Publications/Videos

The following videos are available from Modern Talking Picture Service, 5000 Park St. North, St. Petersburg, FL 33709; (800) 243-MTPS.

- *Flossing With Charlie Brown.* Video teaches kids how to floss properly.
- *The Haunted Mouth.* Video covers preventative dentistry and tooth decay.
- *Options: Dental Health in Later Years.* Video discusses outcomes of dental neglect and focuses on prevention regimens.

DENTAL DISEASE

Clearinghouses/Hotlines

The National Institute of Dental Research (NIDR), which looks into the causes, prevention, diagnosis, and treatment of Oral and Dental Diseases, can answer your questions about the newest developments in treatment and send you publications, posters, and reports on a variety of dental topics. Publications cover canker sores, fluoride treatment, periodontal disease, and tooth decay.

☎ Contact:
National Institute of Dental Research
Bldg. 31, Room 2C35
Bethesda, MD 20892
(301) 496-4261

The Dental Disease Prevention Activity is a resource for information on prevention activities in the field of dental health. It can provide you with information on fluoridation, periodontal disease, and baby-bottle tooth decay. A list of educational materials is also available.

☎ Contact:
Centers for Disease Control
1600 Clifton Rd., NE
Atlanta, GA 30333
(404) 639-1830

Free Publications/Videos

The following publication on Dental Disease is available from the Center for Prevention Services, Centers for Disease Control, 1600 Clifton Rd., NE, Atlanta, GA 30333; (404) 693-3534.

- *Preventing the Transmission of Hepatitis B, AIDS, and Herpes in Dentistry.* Offers 13 pages of advice on preventive measures for dental health care workers to minimize their risk of the transmission of these diseases to themselves, their families, and patients.

The following publications on Dental Disease are available from Center for Devices and Radiological Health, (HFZ-210), FDA, 5600 Fishers Ln., Rockville, MD 20857; (301) 443-4690.

- *Sealing Out Decay.*
- *Today's Dentistry: A Mouthful of Marvels.*
- *Fact Sheet: Uranium in Dental Porcelain.*
- *U.S. Public Health Service Statement on the Safety of Dental Amalgam.*
- *The Selection of Patients for X-ray Examinations: Basic Concepts.* (#FDA 85-8249)

The following publication on Dental Disease is available from the National Maternal and Child Health Clearinghouse, 38th & R Sts., NW, Washington, DC 20057; (703) 821-8955, ext. 254.

- *Dental Implications of Epilepsy.* (#B053)

The following video is available from Modern Talking Picture Service, 5000 Park St. North, St. Petersburg, FL 33709; (800) 243-MTPS.

- *Periodontal Disease.* Video to help the general public make intelligent decisions.

DENTAL PROCEDURES AND AIDS

Free Publications/Videos

The following publication is available from the

Centers for Disease Control National AIDS Clearinghouse, P.O. Box 6003, Rockville, MD 20849-6003; (800) 458-5231.

- *Update: Transmission of HIV Infection During Invasive Dental Procedures: Florida.* (#D683)

DENTAL RESTORATIVE MATERIALS

Clearinghouses/Hotlines

The National Institute of Dental Research (NIDR) will send you whatever publications and reprints of journal articles they have on Dental Restorative Materials, Amalgams, and Implants. As a policy, NIDR will not refer you to other organizations or experts who study these materials. If you can't afford treatment, have your doctor call Dr. Albert Guckers at (301) 496-6241 to find out if NIDR is conducting any clinical studies that you might qualify for.

☎ Contact:
National Institute of Dental Research
Bldg. 31, Room 2C35
Bethesda, MD 20892
(301) 496-4261

DENTAL SEALANTS

Clearinghouses/Hotlines

The National Institute of Dental Research (NIDR) will send you whatever publications and reprints of journal articles they have on Dental Restorative Sealants. As a policy, NIDR will not refer you to other organizations or experts who study these compounds. If you can't afford treatment, have your doctor call Dr. Albert Guckers at (301) 496-6241 to find out if NIDR is conducting any clinical studies that you might qualify for.

☎ Contact:
National Institute of Dental Research

Bldg. 31, Room 2C35
Bethesda, MD 20892
(301) 496-4261

Free Publications/Videos

The following publication is available from the National Institute of Dental Research, Bldg. 31, Room 2C35, Bethesda, MD 20892; (301) 496-4261.

- *Seal Out Dental Decay*. (#91-489) Discusses plastic sealants.

The following publication is available from the Center for Devices and Radiological Health, (HFZ-210), Food and Drug Administration, 5600 Fishers Ln., Rockville, MD 20857; (301) 443-4690.

- *Sealing Out Decay*.

DENTAL X-RAYS

Clearinghouses/Hotlines

The National Institute of Dental Research (NIDR) will send you whatever publications and reprints of journal articles they have on Dental X-Rays. As a policy, NIDR will not refer you to other organizations or experts who study this issue.

☎ Contact:
National Institute of Dental Research
Bldg. 31, Room 2C35
Bethesda, MD 20892
(301) 496-4261

DENTOBACTERIAL PLAQUE INFECTION

Clearinghouses/Hotlines

The National Institute of Dental Research (NIDR) will send you whatever publications and reprints of journal articles they have on Dentobacterial Plaque Infection. As a policy, NIDR will not refer you to other organizations or experts who study this disease. If you can't afford treatment, have your doctor call Dr. Albert Guckers at (301) 496-6241 to find out if NIDR is conducting any clinical studies that you might qualify for.

☎ Contact:
National Institute of Dental Research
Bldg. 31, Room 2C35
Bethesda, MD 20892
(301) 496-4261

DENTURES

Clearinghouses/Hotlines

The National Institute of Dental Research (NIDR) will send you whatever publications and reprints of journal articles they have on Dentures. As a policy, NIDR will not refer you to other organizations or experts who study this issue. If you can't afford treatment, have your doctor call Dr. Albert Guckers at (301) 496-6241 to find out if NIDR is conducting any clinical studies that you might qualify for.

☎ Contact:
National Institute of Dental Research
Bldg. 31, Room 2C35
Bethesda, MD 20892
(301) 496-4261

DEPRESSION

Clearinghouses/Hotlines

The National Institute of Mental Health (NIMH) conducts research on Depression and other mental disorders, distributes information, conducts demonstration programs for the prevention, treatment, and rehabilitation of the mentally ill. A major media campaign on depression, called Project D/ART (Depression/Awareness, Recognition, Treatment), is being developed by NIMH in collaboration with other organizations to provide information on symptoms, causes, and treatments of various depressive disorders. Many publications and reports are available on various topics for professionals and the general public.

☎ Contact:
National Institute of Mental Health
5600 Fishers Ln., Room 15C05
Rockville, MD 20857
(301) 443-4515

The National Institute on Aging (NIA) will send you whatever publications and reprints of journal articles they have on Depression and Aging. They cannot refer you to other experts if the information they have isn't sufficient for your purposes.

☎ Contact:
National Institute on Aging
Bldg. 31, Room 5C27
Bethesda, MD 20892
(301) 496-1752

Free Publications/Videos

The following publications are available from the National Institute of Mental Health, 5600 Fishers Ln., Room 15C05, Rockville, MD 20857; (301) 443-4515.

- *Affective Disorders: Recent Research and Related Developments.*
- *Beating Depression: New Treatments Bring Success.*
- *Bipolar Disorder: Manic-Depressive Illness.*
- *D/ART Fact Sheet.*
- *Depression: It's a Disease and It Can Be Treated.*
- *Depressive Illnesses: Treatments Bring New Hope.*
- *Helpful Facts About Depressive Disorders.*
- *Helping the Depressed Person Get Treatment.*
- *If You're Over 65 and Feeling Depressed...Treatment Brings New Hope.* Explains depression and provides a depression checklist, and describes causes and treatment.
- *Let's Talk About Depression.*
- *Plain Talk About Depression.*
- *What to do When A Friend is Depressed: A Guide for Teenagers.*

DEPTH PERCEPTION

Clearinghouses/Hotlines

The National Eye Institute (NEI) can give you up-to-date information on Depth Perception by searching the Combined Health Information Database (CHID) and MEDLINE and sending you bibliographies of resources, along with any journal articles they may have. They can also refer you to any other organizations that study this and other related issues. NEI will also let you know of any clinical studies that may be studying this issue and looking for patients. Because of their small staff, NEI prefers that you submit your requests for information in writing.

☎ Contact:
National Eye Institute
Bldg. 31, Room 6A32
Bethesda, MD 20892
(301) 496-5248

DERMAGRAPHISMS

Clearinghouses/Hotlines

The National Institute on Allergy and Infectious Diseases (NIAID) can search the Combined Health Information Database (CHID) and generate a bibliography of resources on Dermagraphism for you. They will also send you any publications and journal articles they may have on hand, and will refer you to researchers who are currently studying this issue. If you can't afford treatment, have your doctor call NIAID to find out if they are conducting any clinical studies that you might qualify for.

☎ Contact:
National Institute of Allergy
and Infectious Diseases
Bldg. 31, Room 7A32
Bethesda, MD 20892
(301) 496-5717

DERMATITIS HERPETIFORMIS

Clearinghouses/Hotlines

The National Institute of Arthritis and Musculoskeletal and Skin Diseases (NIAMS) will send you whatever publications and reprints of articles from texts and journals they have on Dermatitis Herpetiformis. They will also refer you to other organizations that are studying this disease. NIAMS will also let you know of any clinical studies that may be studying this disease and looking for patients.

☎ Contact:
National Institute of Arthritis
and Musculoskeletal and Skin Diseases
Box AMS
9000 Rockville Pike
Bethesda, MD 20892
(301) 495-4484

DERMATOGRAPHISM

Clearinghouses/Hotlines

The National Institute on Allergy and Infectious Diseases (NIAID) can search the Combined Health Information Database (CHID) and generate a bibliography of resources on Dermatographism for you. They will also send you any publications and journal articles they may have on hand, and will refer you to researchers who are currently studying this subject. If you can't afford treatment, have your doctor call NIAID to find out if they are conducting any clinical studies that you might qualify for.

☎ Contact:
National Institute of Allergy
and Infectious Diseases
Building 31
Room 7A32
Bethesda, MD 20892
(301) 496-5717

DERMATOLOGY

Clearinghouses/Hotlines

The National Institute of Arthritis and Musculoskeletal and Skin Diseases (NIAMS) will send you whatever publications and reprints of articles from texts and journals they have on Dermatology. They will also refer you to other organizations that are studying this subject. NIAMS will also let you know of any clinical studies that may be studying related diseases and looking for patients.

☎ Contact:
National Institute of Arthritis
and Musculoskeletal and Skin Diseases
Box AMS
9000 Rockville Pike
Bethesda, MD 20892
(301) 495-4484

The National Cancer Institute (NCI) will send you whatever publications and reprints of journal articles they have on Dermatology. They can also give you information on the state-of-the-art treatment for this subject, including specific treatment information for your stage of skin cancer. They can also search their Physician's Data Query (PDQ) database to let you know if NCI is conducting any clinical studies on your disease.

☎ Contact:
National Cancer Institute
Building 31
Room 10A24
Bethesda, MD 20892
(800) 4-CANCER
(301) 496-5583

DERMATOMYOSITIS

Clearinghouses/Hotlines

The National Institute of Arthritis and Musculoskeletal and Skin Diseases (NIAMS) will send you whatever publications and reprints of articles from texts and journals they have on Dermatomyositis. They will also refer you to other organizations that are studying this disease. NIAMS will also let you know of any clinical studies that may be studying this disease and looking for patients.

☎ Contact:
National Institute of Arthritis
and Musculoskeletal and Skin Diseases
Box AMS
9000 Rockville Pike
Bethesda, MD 20892
(301) 495-4484

The National Institute of Neurological Disorders and Stroke (NINDS) can send you only information they have in their publications list on Dermatomyositis. They cannot refer you to any experts. This Clearinghouse cannot directly give you information about any current clinical studies NINDS might be conducting on this illness, but you can find this information for yourself by looking under the National Institute of Neurological Disorders and Stroke in *Appendix A* at the end of this book.

☎ Contact:
National Institute of Neurological
Disorders and Stroke
Building 31
Room 8A06
Bethesda, MD 20892
(301) 496-5751
(800) 352-9424

DES

Clearinghouses/Hotlines

The National Cancer Institute (NCI) will send you whatever publications and reprints of journal articles they have on DES (Diethylstilbestrol). They can also give you information on the state-of-the-art treatment for this disease, including specific treatment information for your stage of cancer. They can also search their Physician's Data Query (PDQ) database to let you know if NCI is conducting any clinical studies on your disease.

☎ Contact:
National Cancer Institute
Building 31
Room 10A24
Bethesda, MD 20892
(800) 4-CANCER
(301) 496-5583

The National Institute of Child Health and Human Development (NICHD) will send you whatever publications and reprints of journal articles they have on DES (Diethylstilbestrol). If necessary, they will refer you to other experts or researchers in the field. If you can't afford treatment, have your doctor call NICHD to find out if they are conducting any clinical studies that you might qualify for.

☎ Contact:
National Institute of Child Health
and Human Development
Building 31
Room 2A32
Bethesda, MD 20892
(301) 496-5133

The Center for Drug Evaluation and Research can provide you with information regarding DES and can refer you to other sources for more information.

☎ Contact:
Center for Drug Evaluation and Research
Food and Drug Administration
5600 Fishers Lane
Rockville, MD 20857
(301) 295-8012

Free Publications/Videos

The following publication is available from the National Cancer Institute, Bldg. 31, Room 10A24, Bethesda, MD 20892; (800) 4-CANCER, or (301) 496-5583.

- *Information for Physicians: Prenatal Diethylstilbestrol (DES) Exposure: Recommendations of the Diethylstilbestrol Adenosis (DESAD) Project for the Identification and Management of Exposed Individuals.* (#81-2049)

DEVELOPMENTAL DISABILITIES

Clearinghouses/Hotlines

The Center for Developmental Disabilities (CDD) can give you information about and refer you to organizations concerned with children ages 0-21 with development disabilities or special health care needs. It also can identify federal, state and non-profit agencies in every state in the country.

☎ Contact:
Center for Developmental Disabilities
Benson Building
First Floor
Columbia, SC 29208
(800) 922-9234
(800) 922-1107 in SC

The National Institute of Neurological Disorders and Stroke (NINDS) can send you only information they have in their publications list on Developmental Disorders. They cannot refer you to any experts. This Clearinghouse cannot directly give you information about any current clinical studies NINDS might be conducting on this topic, but you can find this information for yourself by looking under the National Institute of Neurological Disorders and Stroke in *Appendix A* at the end of this book.

☎ Contact:
National Institute of Neurological
Disorders and Stroke
Bldg. 31, Room 8A06
Bethesda, MD 20892
(301) 496-5751
(800) 352-9424

The National Institute on Deafness and Other Communicative Disorders (NIDCD) will send you whatever publications and reprints of journal articles they have on Developmental Disorders. If you need further information, they will refer you to other organizations that study this and other related disorders. NIDCD does not conduct any clinical studies for this or any other disorder.

☎ Contact:
National Institute on Deafness

and Other Communication Disorders
Bldg. 31, Room 3C35
Bethesda, MD 20892
(301) 496-7243
(800) 241-1044
(301) 402-0252 (TDD)

The National Institute of Child Health and Human Development (NICHD) will send you whatever publications and reprints of journal articles they have on Developmental Disorders. If necessary, they will refer you to other experts or researchers in the field. If you can't afford treatment, have your doctor call NICHD to find out if they are conducting any clinical studies that you might qualify for.

☎ Contact:
National Institute of Child Health
and Human Development
Bldg. 31, Room 2A32
Bethesda, MD 20892
(301) 496-5133

Free Publications/Videos

The following publication is available from the National Institute of Child Health and Human Development, Bldg. 31, Room 2A32, Bethesda, MD 20892; (301) 496-5133.

- *Treatment of Destructive Behaviors in Persons With Developmental Disabilities.* (#91-2410)

DEVIC'S SYNDROME

Clearinghouses/Hotlines

The National Institute of Neurological Disorders and Stroke (NINDS) can send you only information they have in their publications list on Devic's Syndrome. They cannot refer you to any experts. This Clearinghouse cannot directly give you information about any current clinical studies NINDS might be conducting on this illness, but you can find this information for yourself by looking under the National Institute of

Neurological Disorders and Stroke in *Appendix A* at the end of this book.

☎ Contact:
National Institute of Neurological
Disorders and Stroke
Bldg. 31, Room 8A06
Bethesda, MD 20892
(301) 496-5751
(800) 352-9424

DEXTRANASE

Clearinghouses/Hotlines

The National Institute of Dental Research (NIDR) will send you whatever publications and reprints of journal articles they have on Dextrans/Dextranase. As a policy, NIDR will not refer you to other organizations or experts who study this issue. If you can't afford treatment, have your doctor call Dr. Albert Guckers at (301) 496-6241 to find out if NIDR is conducting any clinical studies that you might qualify for.

☎ Contact:
National Institute of Dental Research
Bldg. 31, Room 2C35
Bethesda, MD 20892
(301) 496-4261

DHOBIE ITCH

Clearinghouses/Hotlines

The National Arthritis and Musculoskeletal and Skin Diseases Clearinghouse can provide you with information regarding Dhobie Itch, which is an infection of the skin caused by a fungus. They can search their data base for articles, reference materials, and more.

☎ Contact:
National Arthritis and Musculoskeletal
and Skin Diseases Clearinghouse
Box AMS
Bethesda, MD 20892
(301) 495-4484

DIABETES

Clearinghouses/Hotlines

The National Diabetes Information Clearinghouse will respond to your requests for information about Diabetes and its complications and distributes information appropriate to health professionals, people with diabetes and their families, and the general public. They have many publications and bibliographies, as well as *Diabetes Dateline*, a free quarterly current awareness newsletter that features news about diabetes research, upcoming meetings and events, and new publications. If you can't afford treatment, have your doctor call the National Institute of Diabetes and Digestive and Kidney Diseases to find out if they are conducting any clinical studies that you might qualify for.

☎ Contact:
National Diabetes Information Clearinghouse
Box NDIC
Bethesda, MD 20892
(301) 468-2162

The National Heart, Lung, and Blood Institute (NHLBI) can search the Combined Health Information Database (CHID) and generate a bibliography of resources on Diabetes and Arteriosclerosis for you. They also will send you any publications and journal articles they may have on hand, and will refer you to other organizations that are studying this disease. If you can't afford treatment, have your doctor call NHLBI to find out if they are conducting any clinical studies that you might qualify for.

☎ Contact:
National Heart, Lung, and Blood Institute
Building 31
Room 4A21
Bethesda, MD 20892
(301) 496-4236

The National Institute of Child Health and Human Development (NICHD) will send you whatever publications and reprints of journal articles they have on Diabetes and Pregnancy. If necessary, they will refer you to other experts or researchers in the field. If you can't afford treatment, have your doctor call NICHD to find out if they are conducting any clinical studies that you might qualify for.

☎ Contact:
National Institute of Child Health
and Human Development
Building 31
Room 2A32
Bethesda, MD 20892
(301) 496-5133

The National Institute on Allergy and Infectious Diseases (NIAID) can search the Combined Health Information Database (CHID) and generate a bibliography of resources on Diabetes with Insulin Allergy or Resistance for you. They will also send you any publications and journal articles they may have on hand, and will refer you to researchers who are currently studying this disease. If you can't afford treatment, have your doctor call NIAID to find out if they are conducting any clinical studies that you might qualify for.

☎ Contact:
National Institute of Allergy
and Infectious Diseases
Building 31
Room 7A32
Bethesda, MD 20892
(301) 496-5717

Free Publications/Videos

The following publications on Diabetes are available from the National Diabetes Information Clearinghouse, Box NDIC, Bethesda, MD 20892; (301) 468-2162.

- *Age Page: Dealing with Diabetes.*
- *Dental Tips for Diabetics.*
- *The Diabetes Dictionary.*
- *Diabetic Retinopathy.*
- *Insulin-Dependent Diabetes.*
- *Monitoring Your Blood Sugar.*
- *Noninsulin-Dependent Diabetes.*
- *Periodontal Disease and Diabetes, A Guide for Patients.*
- *The Prevention and Treatment of Five Complications of Diabetes, A Guide for Patients with an Introduction to Day-to-Day*

Management of Diabetes.
- *Understanding Gestational Diabetes.*
- *Cookbooks for People with Diabetes.* A bibliography.
- *Diabetes and Kidney Disease.* A bibliography.
- *Foot Care and Diabetes.* A bibliography.
- *Pregnancy and Diabetes.* A bibliography.
- *Sports and Exercise for People with Diabetes.* A bibliography.
- *Diabetes in Blacks.*
- *Diabetic Neuropathy.*
- *Diabetes and Kidney Disease: A Selected Annotated Bibliography.*
- *Noninsulin-Dependent Diabetes.* (#87-241)
- *Diabetes in Adults.* (#90-2904)
- *Diabetes Dictionary.* (#89-3016)
- *Diabetes in Hispanics.* (#92-3265)
- *Diabetes in Black Americans.* (#92-3266)
- *Diabetes in Education.* (#92-3267)
- *National Diabetes Advisory Board 1991 Annual Report.* (#91-1587)
- *Pregnancy and Diabetes Annotated Bibliography.*
- *Insulin-Dependent Diabetes.* (#90-2098)

The following publication on Diabetes is available from the Office of Clinical Center Communications, Bldg. 10, Room 1C255, Bethesda, MD 20892; (301) 496-2563.

- *Diabetes in Adults.* Booklet written to help the general public make intelligent decisions.

The following publication on Diabetes is available from the Science & Technology Division, Reference Section, Library of Congress, Washington, DC 20540; (202) 707-5580.

- *Diabetes Mellitus.* Reference guide designed to help locate further published material. (#86-6)

The following publication on Diabetes is available from the Food & Nutrition Information Center, National Agricultural Library, Room 304, Beltsville, MD 20705-2351; (301) 504-5719.

- *Nutrition and Diabetes.* Designed to help you locate resources on this topic.

The following publication on Diabetes is available from the National Institute of Child Health and Human Development, Bldg. 31, Room 2A32, Bethesda, MD 20892; (301) 496-5133.

- *Understanding Gestational Diabetes: A Practical Guide to a Healthy Pregnancy.* Addresses questions about diet, exercise, measurement of blood sugar levels, and general medical and obstetric care of women with gestational diabetes. It answers such questions as: Will my baby have diabetes?, What can I do to control gestational diabetes?, and Will I have diabetes in the future?

The following video on Diabetes is available from Modern Talking Picture Service, 5000 Park St. North, St. Petersburg, FL 33709; (800) 243-MTPS.

- *Don't Be Blind To Diabetes.* Video on detecting, treating, and preventing diabetes.

DIABETIC NEUROPATHY

Clearinghouses/Hotlines

The National Institute of Neurological Disorders and Stroke (NINDS) can send you only information they have in their publications list on Diabetic Neuropathy. They cannot refer you to any experts. This Clearinghouse cannot directly give you information about any current clinical studies NINDS might be conducting on this topic, but you can find this information for yourself by looking under the National Institute of Neurological Disorders and Stroke in *Appendix A* at the end of this book.

☎ Contact:
National Institute of Neurological
Disorders and Stroke
Bldg. 31, Room 8A06
Bethesda, MD 20892
(301) 496-5751
(800) 352-9424

Free Publications/Videos

The following publication is available from the National Institute of Diabetes and Digestive and Kidney Diseases, Bldg. 31, Room 9A04, Bethesda, MD 20892; (301) 496-3583.

- *Diabetic Neuropathy.* (#91-3185)

The following publication is available from the National Institute of Neurological Disorders and Stroke, P.O. Box 5801, Bethesda, MD 20824; (800) 352-9424, or (301) 496-5751.

- *Diabetic Neuropathy.* Contains a collection of scientific articles, patient education pamphlets, and addresses of voluntary health associations.

DIABETIC RETINOPATHY

Clearinghouses/Hotlines

The National Eye Institute (NEI) can give you up-to-date information Diabetic Retinopathy by searching the Combined Health Information (CHID) and MEDLINE and sending you bibliographies of along with any journal articles they may have. They can refer you to any other organizations that study this and related diseases. NEI will also let you know of any trials that may be studying this disease and looking patients. Because of their small staff, NEI prefers that submit your requests for information in writing.

☎ Contact:
National Eye Institute
Bldg. 31, Room 6A32
Bethesda, MD 20892
(301) 496-5248

Free Publications/Videos

The following publication on Diabetic Retinopathy is available from the National Eye Institute, Bldg. 31, Room 6A32, Bethesda, MD 20892; (301) 496-5248.

- *Diabetic Retinopathy.* (#90-2171)

DIAGNOSTIC IMAGING

Clearinghouses/Hotlines

The staff of the Diagnostic Imaging Research Program can also answer your questions about how this medical technology can be used to detect cancer.

☎ Contact:
National Cancer Institute
Executive Plaza North
Room 800
Rockville, MD 20892
(800) 4-CANCER
(301) 496-9531

DIALYSIS

Clearinghouses/Hotlines

The National Kidney and Urologic Diseases Information Clearinghouse (NKUDIC) can search the Combined Health Information Database (CHID) and generate a bibliography of resources on Dialysis and Continuous Ambulatory Peritoneal Dialysis (CAPD) for you. They also will send you any publications and journal articles they may have on hand, and will refer you to other organizations that are studying this issue. If you can't afford treatment, have your doctor call NIDDK to find out if they are conducting any clinical studies that you might qualify for.

☎ Contact:
National Kidney and Urologic Diseases
Information Clearinghouse
Box NKUDIC
Bethesda, MD 20892
(301) 468-6345

Free Publications/Videos

The following publications are available from the National Kidney and Urologic Diseases Information Clearinghouse, Box NKUDIC, Bethesda, MD 20892; (301) 468-6345.

- *Dialysis: Professional Materials.* Bibliography of resources.
- *Dialysis: Patient Materials.* Bibliography of resources.

The following publications are available from the Center for Devices and Radiological Health, (HFZ-210), Food and Drug Administration, 5600 Fishers Ln., Rockville, MD 20857; (301) 443-4690.

- *Kidney Disease: When Those Fabulous Filters Are Foiled.*
- *AIDS Information for the Dialysis Patient.* (#FDA 90-4240)

DIAPER RASH

Clearinghouses/Hotlines

The Over-the-Counter Drug Evaluation Division of the Food and Drug Administration has written a monograph on products claiming to reduce or alleviate Diaper Rash. The monograph outlines the components which have been found to be most effective and those which do nothing to remedy this problem.

☎ Contact:
Over-the-Counter Drug
Evaluation Division
Food and Drug Administration
5600 Fishers Lane
Rockville, MD 20857
(301) 295-8000

DIARRHEA

Clearinghouses/Hotlines

The National Institute of Diabetes and Digestive and Kidney Diseases's (NIDDK) individual clearinghouses can search the Combined Health Information Database (CHID) and generate a bibliography of resources on Diarrheal Illnesses for you. They also will send you any publications and journal articles they may have on hand, and will refer you to other organizations that are studying this disorder. If you can't afford treatment, have your doctor call NIDDK to find out if they are conducting any clinical studies that you might qualify for.

☎ Contact:
National Institute of Diabetes
and Digestive and Kidney Diseases
Bldg. 31, Room 9A04
Bethesda, MD 20892
(301) 496-3583

The National Institute on Allergy and Infectious Diseases (NIAID) can search the Combined Health Information Database (CHID) and generate a bibliography of resources on Diarrheal Illnesses for you. They will also send you any publications and journal articles they may have on hand, and will refer you to researchers who are currently studying this disorder. If you can't afford treatment, have your doctor call NIAID to find out if they are conducting any clinical studies that you might qualify for.

☎ Contact:
National Institute of Allergy
and Infectious Diseases
Building 31
Room 7A32
Bethesda, MD 20892
(301) 496-5717

Free Publications/Videos

The following publication on Diarrhea is available from the National Digestive Diseases Information Clearinghouse, Box NDDIC, Bethesda, MD 20892; (301) 468-6344.

- *Traveler's Diarrhea.* Information on prevention and control of this digestive tract disorder.

The following publication on Diarrhea is available from the National Institute of Diabetes and Digestive and Kidney Diseases, Bldg. 31, Room 9A04, Bethesda, MD 20892; (301) 496-3583.

- *Diarrhea: Infectious and Other Causes.* (#86-2749)

DIET

See Nutrition
See Food

DIETARY SUPPLEMENTS

Free Publications/Videos

The following publication on Dietary Supplements is available from the National Institute on Aging Information Center, 2209 Distribution Circle, Silver Spring, MD 20910; (301) 495-3455.

- *Dietary Supplements: More Is Not Always Better.*

DIETHYLSTILBESTROL (DES)

See DES

DIETING

Free Publications/Videos

The following publications on Dieting are available from the Food & Drug Administration, (HFE-88), 5600 Fishers Ln., Rockville, MD 20857; (301) 443-3170.

- *How to Take Weight Off Without Getting Ripped Off.* Discusses weight reduction products, fad diets, and other diet aids. (#85-1116)
- *How To Take Weight Off And Keep It Off.* (#FDA89-1116)
- *A Word About Low Sodium Diets.* (#FDA90-2179)

- *Diet Books Sell Well But...* Reviews and evaluates some of the popular diet plans. (#84-1093)

The following publication on Dieting is available from the Food & Nutrition Information Center, National Agricultural Library, Room 304, Beltsville, MD 20705-2351; (301) 504-5719.

- *Weight Control.* A list to help you locate further information or resources.

The following publications on Dieting are available from the Center for Devices and Radiological Health, (HFZ-210), Food and Drug Administration, 5600 Fishers Ln., Rockville, MD 20857; (301) 443-4690.

- *Stomach 'Bubble': Diet Device Not Without Risks.*
- *Garren Gastric Bubble.*
- *FDA Warns Weight Loss Wraps and Suits Are Frauds.*
- *About Body Wraps, Pills and Other Magic Wands for Losing Weight.*

The following publications on Dieting are available from the Consumer Information Center, P.O. Box 100, Pueblo, CO 81002.

- *An FDA Guide to Dieting.* New research on how genetics, the kinds of calories you eat, your metabolism, and the exercise you get, all affect weight. (#512Z).
- *Calories and Weight.* (#108Y)
- *Calories and Weight.* Calorie tables for hundreds of popular foods and beverages. (#107Z).
- *Modified Fast: A Sometime Solution to a Weighty Problem.* (#517Y)

The following publication on Dieting is available from the Federal Trade Commission, Office of Consumer Education, Bureau of Consumer Protection, Washington, DC 20580; (202) 326-3650.

- *Diet Programs.* Covers gimmicks and sales schemes that commercial diet programs use to lure you into spending a lot of money to lose weight.

DIFFUSE SCLEROSIS

Clearinghouses/Hotlines

The National Institute of Neurological Disorders and Stroke (NINDS) can send you only information they have in their publications list on Diffuse Sclerosis. They cannot refer you to any experts. This Clearinghouse cannot directly give you information about any current clinical studies NINDS might be conducting on this illness, but you can find this information for yourself by looking under the National Institute of Neurological Disorders and Stroke in *Appendix A* at the end of this book.

☎ Contact:
National Institute of Neurological
Disorders and Stroke
Bldg. 31, Room 8A06
Bethesda, MD 20892
(301) 496-5751
(800) 352-9424

DIGESTIVE DISEASES

Clearinghouses/Hotlines

The National Digestive Diseases Information Clearinghouse will respond to your requests for information about digestive diseases and distributes information to health professionals, people with digestive diseases, and the general public. They have many publications, as well as a news bulletin.

☎ Contact:
National Digestive Diseases
Information Clearinghouse
Box NDDIC
Bethesda, MD 20892
(301) 468-6344

Free Publications/Videos

The following publications on Digestive Diseases are available from the National Digestive Diseases

Information Clearinghouse, Box NDDIC, Bethesda, MD 20892; (301) 468-6344.

- *Diverticular Disease.* Information packet.
- *Bleeding In the Digestive Tract.*
- *Digestive Health and Disease: A Glossary.* (#DD-01)
- *Facts and Fallacies About Digestive Diseases.* (#DD-02)
- *Your Digestive System and How It Works.* (#DD-03)
- *Diagnostic Tests for Digestive Diseases: X-rays and Ultrasound.* (#DD-07)
- *Diverticulosis and Diverticulitis.*
- *Digestive Diseases and Organizations: Lay and Voluntary.* Describes and lists names, addresses, telephone numbers, and publications of 19 nonprofit, support, education, and advocacy groups related to digestive diseases. (#DD-05)
- *Smoking and Your Digestive System.* Discusses the harmful effects. of cigarette smoking on the digestive system. (#DD-52)
- *Digestive Diseases Organizations: Professional.* Describes and lists names, addresses, telephone numbers, and publications of 16 private non-profit organizations that represent digestive disease health professionals. (#DD-06)
- *NDDIC Brochure.* Describes the purpose, activities, and informational services of NDDIC. (#DD-22)
- *DD Notes.* Newsletter of NDDIC features articles about digestive diseases, voluntary and professional organizations, research, and new publications. (#DD-32)
- *Research Opportunities and Programs in the Division of Digestive Diseases and Nutrition (1990).* Provides information about the research programs of the Digestive Diseases, Nutritional Sciences, and Special Programs branches of NIDDK, mechanisms of research support, and research training and career development opportunities. (#DD-95)

The following publications on Digestive Diseases are available from the National Institute of Diabetes and Digestive and Kidney Diseases, Bldg. 31, Room 9A04, Bethesda, MD 20892; (301) 496-3583.

- *Digestive Health and Disease: A Glossary.* (#86-2750)
- *National Digestive Diseases Advisory Board: 1991 Annual Report.* (#91-2482)
- *Facts and Fallacies About Digestive Diseases.* (#92-2673)

DIOXIN

Clearinghouses/Hotlines

The Toxic Substances Control Act Hotline can provide you with free information about the dangers of dioxin.

☎ Contact:
Toxic Substances Control Act Hotline
401 M St., SW
Washington, DC 20024
(202) 554-1404

Free Publications/Videos

The following Congressional Research Service (CRS) report on Dioxin and Agent Orange is available from either of your U.S. Senators' offices at the U.S. Capitol, Washington, DC 20510, or from your Congressional Representative at the U.S. Capitol, Washington, DC 20515. You can also call in your request through the U.S. Capitol switchboard at (202) 224-3121. Be sure to include the full title and report number in your request.

- *Dioxin and Agent Orange Health Effects: An Update.* (#91-195 SPR)

The following publication on Dioxin Treatment Technologies is available from the Office of Technology Assessment, Washington, DC 20510-8025; (202) 224-8996.

- *Dioxin Treatment Technologies: Background Paper.* (#OTA-BP-O-93)

DIPHTHERIA

Clearinghouses/Hotlines

The National Institute on Allergy and Infectious Diseases (NIAID) can search the Combined Health Information Database (CHID) and generate a bibliography of resources on Diphtheria for you. They will also send you any publications and journal articles they may have on hand, and will refer you to researchers who are currently studying this disease. If you can't afford treatment, have your doctor call NIAID to find out if they are conducting any clinical studies that you might qualify for.

☎ Contact:
National Institute of Allergy
and Infectious Diseases
Building 31
Room 7A32
Bethesda, MD 20892
(301) 496-5717

DISABILITIES

See also Rehabilitation

Clearinghouses/Hotlines

The Clearinghouse on Disability Information Program is a great source of information for Federal funding of programs and services for the Disabled, Federal legislation affecting the disability community, and Federal programs benefiting people with disabilities.

☎ Contact:
U.S Department of Education
Room 3132
Mary Switzer Bldg.
Washington, DC 20202-2524
(202) 732-1723
(202) 732-1241

The National Rehabilitation Information Center (NRIC) can provide you with information on Disability-related research, resources, and products

for independent living, as well as facts sheets, resource guides, and research and technical publications, and a newsletter.

☎ Contact:
National Rehabilitation Information Center
8455 Colesville Road
Suite 935
Silver Spring, MD 20910
(800) 346-2742

Free Publications/Videos

The following publication on Disabilities is available from the U.S Department of Education, Room 3132, Mary Switzer Bldg., Washington, DC 20202-2524; (202) 732-1723, or (202) 732-1241.

- *A Pocket Guide to Federal Help for Individuals with Disabilities.*

The following publications on Disabilities are available from the Consumer Information Center, P.O. Box 100, Pueblo, CO 81002.

- *The Americans with Disabilities Act: Questions and Answers.* Explains how this law protects the civil rights of persons with disabilities at work and in public places. (#583Z).
- *Pocket Guide to Federal Help for Individuals with Disabilities.* Federally funded programs provide for vocational rehabilitation, employment, housing and more. Here's how to make use of what's available. (#112Z, $1.00).

The following reports on the *Americans With Disabilities Act* are available from either of your U.S. Senators' offices at the U.S. Capitol, Washington, DC 20510, or from your Congressional Representative at the U.S. Capitol, Washington, DC 20515. You can also call in your request through the U.S. Capitol switchboard at (202) 224-3121. Be sure to include the full title and report number in your request.

- *The Americans With Disabilities Act: An Overview of Major Provisions.* (#90-366 A)
- *The Americans With Disabilities Act: Equal Employment Opportunity Commission*

Proposed Regulations on Equal Employment Opportunity for Individuals With Disabilities. (#91-291 A)
- *The Americans With Disabilities Act: Info Pack.* (#IP443A)
- *The Possible Applicability of the Americans With Disabilities Act to Indian Tribes.* (#91-497 A)

DISABLED INFANTS

Clearinghouses/Hotlines

The National Information Clearinghouse for Infants with Disabilities and Life-Threatening Conditions offers help on legal and advocacy issues, financial assistance, community services, parent support and parent education, child protective services, home health services and other assistance to parents and professionals concerned about infants with disabilities.

☎ Contact:
National Information Clearinghouse
for Infants with Disabilities
and Life-Threatening Conditions
(NICIDLC)
Benson Building
First Floor
Columbia, SC 29208
(800) 922-9234
(800) 922-1107 (in SC)

DISASTERS

Clearinghouses/Hotlines

The National Institute of Mental Health (NIMH) (NIMH) can send you all kinds of information on the relationship between Disasters and mental illness.

☎ Contact:
National Institute of Mental Health
5600 Fishers Lane
Room 15C05

Rockville, MD 20857
(301) 443-4515

The Federal Emergency Management Agency is the Federal Government's focal point for emergency planning, preparedness, mitigation, response and recovery. They have information on how to prepare for and deal with earthquakes, floods, fires, and nuclear disasters. They have many free publications and videos listed in a free publications catalog.

☎ Contact:
Federal Emergency Management Agency
500 C St., SW
Washington, DC 20472
(202) 646-4600

Free Publications/Videos

The following publications on Disasters are available from the National Institute of Mental Health, 5600 Fishers Ln., Room 15C05, Rockville, MD 20857; (301) 443-4515.

- *Crisis Intervention Programs for Disaster Victims in Smaller Communities.*
- *Disaster Work and Mental Health: Prevention and Control of Stress Among Workers.*
- *Field Manual for Human Service Workers in Major Disasters.*
- *Human Problems in Major Disasters: A Training Curriculum for Emergency Medical Personnel.*
- *Innovations in Mental Health Services to Disaster Victims.*
- *Manual for Child Health Workers in Major Disasters.*
- *Prevention and Control of Stress Among Emergency Workers: A Pamphlet for Team Managers.*
- *Prevention and Control of Stress Among Emergency Workers: A Pamphlet for Workers.*
- *Role Stressors and Supports for Emergency Workers.*
- *Training Manual for Human Service Workers in Major Disasters.*

DISCOID LUPUS ERYTHEMATOSUS

Clearinghouses/Hotlines

The National Institute of Arthritis and Musculoskeletal and Skin Diseases (NIAMS) will send you whatever publications and reprints of articles from texts and journals they have on Discoid Lupus Erythematosus. They will also refer you to other organizations studying this disease. NIAMS will also let you know of any clinical studies that may be studying this disease and looking for patients.

☎ Contact:
National Institute of Arthritis
and Musculoskeletal and Skin Diseases
Box AMS
Bethesda, MD 20892
(301) 495-4484

DISEASE HOTLINE

Clearinghouses/Hotlines

By calling the Centers for Disease Control's automated telephone health service, you can get all kinds of information sent to you on several diseases and health areas, including symptoms and prevention methods, immunization requirements, current statistics, recent disease outbreak, and available printed materials. Currently, you can get information on AIDS, Chronic fatigue syndrome, cytomegalovirus, encephalitis, enteric diseases, Epstein-Barr, hepatitis, Lyme disease, malaria, rabies, Vaccine-preventable disease, and yellow fever. If you need more information than the message provides, you have the option of being put in contact with a public health professional who will point you in the right direction. The system is available 24 hours a day, although the health professionals are available Monday-Friday 8a.m. - 4:30p.m.

☎ Contact:
Disease Hotline
(404) 332-4555

DIURETICS

Clearinghouses/Hotlines

The National Heart, Lung, and Blood Institute (NHLBI) can search the Combined Health Information Database (CHID) and generate a bibliography of resources on Diuretics for you. They also will send you any publications and journal articles they may have on hand, and will refer you to other organizations that are studying this issue. If you can't afford treatment, have your doctor call NHLBI to find out if they are conducting any clinical studies that you might qualify for.

☎ Contact:
National Heart, Lung, and Blood Institute
Building 31
Room 4A21
Bethesda, MD 20892
(301) 496-4236

DIURNALDYSTONIA

Clearinghouses/Hotlines

The National Institute of Neurological Disorders and Stroke (NINDS) can send you only information they have in their publications list on Diurnaldystonia. They cannot refer you to any experts. This Clearinghouse cannot directly give you information about any current clinical studies NINDS might be conducting on this illness, but you can find this information for yourself by looking under the National Institute of Neurological Disorders and Stroke in *Appendix A* at the end of this book.

☎ Contact:
National Institute of Neurological
Disorders and Stroke
Building 31
Room 8A06
Bethesda, MD 20892
(301) 496-5751
(800) 352-9424

DIVERTICULITIS

Clearinghouses/Hotlines

The National Institute of Diabetes and Digestive and Kidney Diseases's (NIDDK) individual clearinghouses can search the Combined Health Information Database (CHID) and generate a bibliography of resources on Diverticulitis for you. They also will send you any publications and journal articles they may have on hand, and will refer you to other organizations that are studying this disease. If you can't afford treatment, have your doctor call NIDDK to find out if they are conducting any clinical studies that you might qualify for.

☎ Contact:
National Institute of Diabetes
and Digestive and Kidney Diseases
Bldg. 31, Room 9A04
Bethesda, MD 20892
(301) 496-3583

Free Publications/Videos

The following publication is available from the National Institute of Diabetes and Digestive and Kidney Diseases, Bldg. 31, Room 9A04, Bethesda, MD 20892; (301) 496-3583.

- *Diverticulosis and Diverticulitis*. (#92-1163)

DIVORCE

Clearinghouses/Hotlines

The National Institute of Mental Health (NIMH) (NIMH) can send you all kinds of information on the relationship between Divorce and mental illness.

☎ Contact:
National Institute of Mental Health
5600 Fishers Ln., Room 15C05
Rockville, MD 20857
(301) 443-4515

Free Publications/Videos

The following publication is available from the National Institute of Mental Health, 5600 Fishers Ln., Room 15C05, Rockville, MD 20857; (301) 443-4515.

- *When Parents Divorce*.

The following Congressional Research Service (CRS) report is available from either of your U.S. Senators' offices at the U.S. Capitol, Washington, DC 20510, or from your Congressional Representative at the U.S. Capitol, Washington, DC 20515. You can also call in your request through the U.S. Capitol switchboard at (202) 224-3121. Be sure to include the full title and report number in your request.

- *Divorce, Maintenance and Child Support Laws in Australia, Canada, England, and New Zealand*. (#LL90-65)

DIZYGOTIC TWINS (Fraternal Twins)

See Twins

DIZZINESS

Clearinghouses/Hotlines

The National Institute of Neurological Disorders and Stroke (NINDS) can send you only information they have in their publications list on Dizziness. They cannot refer you to any experts. This Clearinghouse cannot directly give you information about any current clinical studies NINDS might be conducting on this condition, but you can find this information for yourself by looking under the National Institute of Neurological Disorders and Stroke in *Appendix A* at the end of this book.

☎ Contact:
National Institute of Neurological

Disorders and Stroke
Bldg. 31, Room 8A06
Bethesda, MD 20892
(301) 496-5751
(800) 352-9424

The National Institute on Deafness and Other Communicative Disorders will send you whatever publications and reprints of journal articles they have on Dizziness. If you need further information, they will refer you to other organizations that study this and other related disorders. NIDCD does not conduct any clinical studies for this or any other disorder.

☎ Contact:
National Institute on Deafness
and Other Communication Disorders
Bldg. 31, Room 3C35
Bethesda, MD 20892
(301) 496-7243
(800) 241-1044
(301) 402-0252 (TDD)

Free Publications/Videos

The following publications on dizziness are available from the National Institute of Neurological Disorders and Stroke, Bldg. 31, Room 8A06, Bethesda, MD 20892; (301) 496-5751 or (800) 352-9424.

- *Dizziness*. (#86-76)
- *Dizziness*. Discusses hope through research.

DNA

See also Genetics
See also Genetic Testing

Clearinghouses/Hotlines

The National Cancer Institute (NCI) will send you whatever publications and reprints of journal articles they have on DNA as it relates to Cancer. They can also search their Physician's Data Query (PDQ) database to let you know if NCI is conducting any clinical studies on your disease.

☎ Contact:
National Cancer Institute
Bldg. 31, Room 10A24
Bethesda, MD 20892
(800) 4-CANCER
(301) 496-5583

Free Publications/Videos

The following publication on DNA Testing is available from the National Maternal and Child Health Clearinghouse, 38th & R Sts., NW, Washington, DC 20057; (703) 821-8955, ext. 254.

- *Understanding DNA Testing: A Basic Guide for Families*. Explains how DNA analysis can be performed for families.

DOWN'S SYNDROME

Clearinghouses/Hotlines

The National Institute of Child Health and Human Development (NICHD) can fill you in on both medical and statistical information about this birth defect. They will also send you *Facts About Down's Syndrome* and *Facts About Down's Syndrome for Women Over 35* (No. 82-536), which discuss genetic counseling and the outlook for a child born with Down's syndrome.

☎ Contact:
National Institute of Child Health
and Human Development
Bldg. 31, Room 2A32
Bethesda, MD 20892
(301) 496-5133

DOXORRUBICIN

Free Publications/Videos

The following publication is available from the National Cancer Institute, Bldg. 31, Room 10A24, Bethesda, MD 20892; (800) 4-CANCER, or (301) 496-5583.

- *Doxorrubicina/Doxorubicin.* Provides information about side effects, proper usage, and precautions of this anti-cancer drug.

DPT VACCINE
(Diptheria-Pertussis-Tetanus)

See Immunizations

DRINKING AND CANCER

Clearinghouses/Hotlines

The National Cancer Institute (NCI) will send you whatever publications and reprints of journal articles they have on Drinking and Cancer. They can also give you information on the state-of-the-art treatment for this disease, including specific treatment information for your stage of cancer. They can also search their Physician's Data Query (PDQ) database to let you know if NCI is conducting any clinical studies on your disease.

☎ Contact:
National Cancer Institute
Bldg. 31, Room 10A24
Bethesda, MD 20892
(800) 4-CANCER
(301) 496-5583

DRINKING WATER

Clearinghouses/Hotlines

Are you concerned about your drinking water? Do you want to know where in your area you can have your water tested? The Safe Drinking Water Hotline responds to questions concerning the *Safe Drinking Water Act, Water Standards & Regulations*, and the *Underground Injection Program*. They will also send you selected publications related to these issues.

☎ Contact:
Environmental Protection Agency
401 M St., SW
Washington, DC 20460
(800) 426-4791

Free Publications/Videos

The following Congressional Research Service (CRS) report on Drinking Water is available from either of your U.S. Senators' offices at the U.S. Capitol, Washington, DC 20510, or from your Congressional Representative at the U.S. Capitol, Washington, DC 20515. You can also call in your request through the U.S. Capitol switchboard at (202) 224-3121. Be sure to include the full title and report number in your request.

- *Fluoride in Drinking Water: Should the National Standard Be Made Less Stringent? Archived Issue Brief.* (#IB86014)

The following publications on Drinking Water are available from the Consumer Information Center, Pueblo, CO 81009.

- *Pesticides in Drinking-Water Wells.* Learn how to test water and what to do if it's unsafe. (434Y, $.50)

The following publication on Water Treatment is available from the Federal Trade Commission, Office of Consumer Education, Bureau of Consumer Protection, Washington, DC 20580; (202) 326-3650.

- *Buying A Home Water Treatment Unit.* Shows how to determine your need for a treatment unit, how to select options, and how to protect yourself from deceptive sales practices.

DROPSY

See Edema

DRUG ABUSE

See also Alcoholism
See also specific drug
See also Workplace Drug Abuse

Clearinghouses/Hotlines

The National Drug Abuse Information and Treatment Hotline provides drug related information to the general public, and helps drug users find and use local treatment programs and support groups and/or services. Referrals are also made to local crisis or information hotlines and support groups, such as Cocaine Anonymous and Narcotics Anonymous. They provide many pamphlets and brochures on a variety of drug topics. The hotline is in service 9a.m. to 3a.m. EST (Monday-Friday) and 12p.m. to 3a.m. EST (Saturday-Sunday).

☎ Contact:
National Drug Abuse Information
and Treatment Hotline
(800) 662-HELP
(800) 66-AYUNDA (spanish speakers)

The National Clearinghouse for Alcohol and Drug Information is the central point within the Federal Government for current print and audiovisual materials about alcohol and other drugs. They have information tailored to parents, teachers, youth, and others, as well as information about organizations and groups concerned with alcohol and other drug problems. They have publications, reports, newsletters, videos, posters, and more, as well as being able to provide comprehensive alcohol and other drug resource referrals. Call for your free catalogue.

☎ Contact:
National Clearinghouse for Alcohol
and Drug Information
P.O. Box 2345
Rockville, MD 20852
(800) 729-6686
(301) 468-2600

The House Select Committee on Narcotics Abuse and Control investigates drug abuse, conducts hearings in Washington, DC, and throughout the country, and publishes numerous studies that are available to the public.

☎ Contact:
U.S. Congress
House Select Committee on Narcotics
Abuse and Control
H2-234 House Annex 2
Washington, DC 20515
(202) 226-3040

Free Publications/Videos

The following publications on Drug Abuse are available from the National Clearinghouse for Alcohol and Drug Information, P.O. Box 2345, Rockville, MD 20852; (800) 729-6686, or (301) 468-2600.

- *Drug Abuse and AIDS: Getting the Message Out.* Video informs about prevention, transmission, consequences and treatment of AIDS.
- *Drug Abuse and Drug Abuse Research: Third Triennial Report to Congress.* Summarizes drug abuse in the U.S., its health implications, advances in treatment and prevention.
- *Drugs At Work.* Video presents information about the nature and scope of the alcohol and drug problem in the workplace.
- *Drug Testing: Handle With Care.* Video describes options available for designing a drug testing program in workplace.
- *Citizen's Alcohol and Other Drug Prevention Directory.*
- *Resources for Getting Involved.*
- *Connections.*
- *The Door to Recovery: Community Drug Abuse Treatment.*
- *The Fact Is...Communications Programs Can Help to Prevent Alcohol and Other Drug Problems.*
- *Communities Creating Change: 1990 Exemplary Alcohol and Other Drug Prevention Programs.*
- *Evaluating Faculty Development and Clinical Training Programs in Substance Abuse: A Guidebook.*
- *Finding Solutions.* Video displays drug abuse in workplace and offers solutions in

education and prevention.
- *Handbook for Evaluating Drug and Alcohol Prevention Programs.*
- *How to Start and Run an Alcohol and Other Drug Information Center: A Guide.*
- *Little League Drug Education Program* Anti-drug abuse video for kids.
- *Making Health Communication Programs Work: A Planner's Guide.*
- *Message and Material Review Process.*
- *NIDA Capsules: Drug Abuse Information and Treatment Referral Line: (800) 662-HELP.* Describes referral service that provides drug-related information to the public and helps identify services for drug users.
- *Parent Training Is Prevention.*
- *Prevention Plus II: Tools for Creating and Sustaining a Drug-Free Community.*
- *Turning Awareness Into Action.*
- *What You Can Do About Drug Use in America.*
- *Prevention: From Knowledge to Action.*
- *The Primary Prevention of Alcohol Problems: A Critical Review of the Research Literature.*
- *The Fact Is...Resources Are Available for Disabled Persons With Alcohol and Other Drug Problems.*
- *The Fact Is...Reaching Hispanic/Latino Audiences Requires Cultural Sensitivity.*
- *Safer Streets Ahead.*
- *Substance Abuse Prevention Within Inner-City Communities.*
- *Surgeon General's Workshop on Drunk Driving Proceedings.*
- *Surgeon General's Workshop on Drunk Driving: Background Papers.*
- *The Fact Is...Training Is Available for Professionals in the Field of Alcohol and Other Drug Abuse.*
- *Twenty Exemplary Prevention Programs: Helping Communities to Help Themselves.*
- *The Fact Is...You Can Effectively Launch Media Campaigns.*
- *The Fact Is...You Can Start a Student Assistance Program.*
- *Youth at High Risk for Substance Abuse.*
- *A Community Solution, Drug Abuse Treatment.*
- *Overcoming Barriers to Drug Abuse Treatment in the Community.*
- *The Fact Is...Employee Assistance Contacts Are Available In Every State.* Covers professional assessment/referral and/or short-term counseling services for motivating and helping employees with alcohol, drug, or mental health problems to seek and accept appropriate help.
- *The Fact Is...There Are Specialized Mutual-Help Groups For Those With Alcohol and Drug Problems.* (MS330) Discusses self-help groups that have emerged in response to special concerns expressed by those seeking recovery for alcohol and other drug problem. This brochure also lists the self-help groups, providing general information about the group and a central phone number.
- *Quick List: 10 Steps to Help Your Child Say "No".*
- *10 Steps to Help Your Child Say "No".* A Parent's Guide.
- *Growing Up Drug Free: A Parent's Guide to Prevention.*
- *Parent Training Is Prevention.*
- *High School Senior Drug Use: 1975-1990.*
- *The National Directory of Drug Abuse and Alcoholism Treatment and Prevention Programs.* Contains referral information about treatment and prevention programs.
- *Prevention Resource Guide: College Youth.*
- *Prevention Resource Guide: Secondary School Students.*
- *Prevention Resource Guide: Elementary Youth.*
- *Prevention Resource Guide: Preschool Children.*
- *Prevention Resource Guide: Pregnant/Post-partum Women and Their Infants.*
- *Prevention Resource Guide: Rural Communities.*

The following publication on Adolescent Drug Use is available from the General Accounting Office, P.O. Box 6015, Gaithersburg, MD 20877; (202) 275-6241.

- *Adolescent Drug Use Prevention: Common Features of Promising Community Programs.* Examines the design, implementation, and results of promising comprehensive, community-based drug use prevention programs for young adolescents, regardless of their funding sources.

The following Congressional Research Service (CRS) reports on Drug Abuse are available from either of your U.S. Senators' offices at the U.S. Capitol, Washington, DC 20510, or from your Congressional Representative at the U.S. Capitol, Washington, DC 20515. You can also call in your request through the U.S. Capitol switchboard at (202) 224-3121. Be sure to include the full title and report number in your request.

- *Drug Abuse: Treatment, Prevention and Education: Info Pack.* (#IP400D)
- *Alcohol, Drug Abuse, and Mental Health Block Grant, and Related Programs: Issue Brief.* (#IB88009)
- *Drug Abuse in America: Selected References, 1990-1992.* (#92-321 L)
- *The Drug Crisis: Federal Aid for Crime Control, Prevention, and Treatment; Selected References, 1986-1989.* (#90-9 L)
- *Drug Abuse and Control: An Alphabetical Microthesaurus of Terms Selected from the Legislative Indexing Vocabulary.* (90-143 L)
- *Drug Abuse in America: Info Pack.* (IB303D)
- *Drug Abuse: Selected References, 1986-1988.* (#88-625 L)
- *Forum: The Drug Problem, Congressional Research Service.* (#REV 11-89)
- *Substance Abuse Treatment, Prevention, and Education.* (#90-412 EPW)

DRUG ALLERGY

Clearinghouses/Hotlines

The National Institute on Allergy and Infectious Diseases (NIAID) can search the Combined Health Information Database (CHID) and generate a bibliography of resources on Drug Allergies for you. They will also send you any publications and journal articles they may have on hand, and will refer you to researchers who are currently studying this disease. If you can't afford treatment, have your doctor call NIAID to find out if they are conducting any clinical studies that you might qualify for.

☎ Contact:
National Institute of Allergy

and Infectious Diseases
Bldg. 31, Room 7A32
Bethesda, MD 20892
(301) 496-5717

Free Publications/Videos

The following publication is available from the National Institute of Allergy and Infectious Diseases, Bldg. 31, Room 7A32, Bethesda, MD 20892; (301) 496-5717.

- *Drug Allergy.* (#82-703)

DRUG APPROVAL PROCESS

Free Publications/Videos

The following Congressional Research Service (CRS) report on Drug Approval is available from either of your U.S. Senators' offices at the U.S. Capitol, Washington, DC 20510, or from your Congressional Representative at the U.S. Capitol, Washington, DC 20515. You can also call in your request through the U.S. Capitol switchboard at (202) 224-3121. Be sure to include the full title and report number in your request.

- *Drug Approval: Access to Experimental Drugs for Severely Ill Patients.* (#IB89016)

The following publication on the Drug Approval Process is available from the General Accounting Office, P.O. Box 6015, Gaithersburg, MD 20877; (202) 275-6241.

- *Nonprescription Drugs: Over the Counter and Underemphasized.* Examines the Food and Drug Administration's procedures for approving and monitoring over-the-counter drugs in order to identify potential vulnerabilities in the procedures that could result in the approval and marketing of unsafe and ineffective drugs.

DRUG DEVELOPMENT

Free Publications/Videos

The following publication is available from the Food & Drug Administration, (HFE-88), 5600 Fishers Ln., Rockville, MD 20857; (301) 443-3170.

- *From Test Tube to Patient: New Drug Development.* (#FDA90-3168)

DRUG EVALUATION

Clearinghouses/Hotlines

The Food and Drug Administration's Center for Drug Evaluation and Research responds to inquiries covering the entire spectrum of drug issues. It develops policy with regard to the safety, and labeling of all drug products and evaluate new drug applications. It also conducts research and develops scientific standards on the composition, quality, safety, and effectiveness of drugs. A list of guidelines is available to help manufacturers comply with the requirements of the regulations. The staff will respond to requests for information regarding the laws, regulations, policies, and functions of the Food and Drug Administration as it pertains to drugs. Materials are available on pharmaceuticals, drug labeling, and consumer education.

☎ Contact:
Center for Drug Evaluation and Research
Food and Drug Administration
5600 Fishers Lane
Rockville, MD 20857
(301) 295-8012

Free Publications/Videos

The following publication is available from the Consumer Information Center, P.O. Box 100, Pueblo, CO 81002.

- *Getting Information from FDA...* About drugs, foods, pesticides, medical devices, radiation safety, pet foods, and more. (593Z).

DRUG HEMOLYTIC ANEMIA

Clearinghouses/Hotlines

The National Institute of Diabetes and Digestive and Kidney Diseases's (NIDDK) individual clearinghouses can search the Combined Health Information Database (CHID) and generate a bibliography of resources on Drug Hemolytic Anemia for you. They also will send you any publications and journal articles they may have on hand, and will refer you to other organizations that are studying this disease. If you can't afford treatment, have your doctor call NIDDK to find out if they are conducting any clinical studies that you might qualify for.

☎ Contact:
National Institute of Diabetes
and Digestive and Kidney Diseases
Bldg. 31, Room 9A04
Bethesda, MD 20892
(301) 496-3583

DRUG INTERACTIONS

Free Publications/Videos

The following publication is available from the Food & Drug Administration, (HFE-88), 5600 Fishers Ln., Rockville, MD 20857; (301) 443-3170.

- *When Medications Don't Mix. Preventing Drug Interactions.* (#OM90-3009)

DRUG LABELING

Free Publications/Videos

The following publication on Drug Labeling is

available from the Food & Drug Administration, (HFE-88), 5600 Fishers Ln., Rockville, MD 20857; (301) 443-3170.

- *OTC Drug Labels: "Must Read".* (#FDA88-3157)

DRUG PURPURA

Clearinghouses/Hotlines

The National Institute of Diabetes and Digestive and Kidney Diseases's (NIDDK) individual clearinghouses can search the Combined Health Information Database (CHID) and generate a bibliography of resources on Drug Purpura for you. They also will send you any publications and journal articles they may have on hand, and will refer you to other organizations that are studying this issue. If you can't afford treatment, have your doctor call NIDDK to find out if they are conducting any clinical studies that you might qualify for.

☎ Contact:
National Institute of Diabetes
and Digestive and Kidney Diseases
Bldg. 31, Room 9A04
Bethesda, MD 20892
(301) 496-3583

DRUG RESISTANCE

Clearinghouses/Hotlines

The National Institute on Allergy and Infectious Diseases (NIAID) can search the Combined Health Information Database (CHID) and generate a bibliography of resources on Drug Resistance for you. They will also send you any publications and journal articles they may have on hand, and will refer you to researchers who are currently studying this issue. If you can't afford treatment, have your doctor call NIAID to find out if they are conducting any clinical studies that you might qualify for.

☎ Contact:
National Institute of Allergy
and Infectious Diseases
Bldg. 31, Room 7A32
Bethesda, MD 20892
(301) 496-5717

DRUG TESTING

Clearinghouses/Hotlines

The National Institute of Justice can send you all kinds of information on drug testing as it relates to the criminal justice system.

☎ Contact:
National Institute of Justice
U.S. Department of Justice
P.O. Box 6000
Rockville, MD 20850
(800) 851-3420
(301) 251-5500

The Veteran's Administration operates diverse programs to benefit veterans and their family members. These benefits include education and rehabilitation, including drug or alcohol treatment. Call or write for booklet describing benefits available for veterans and their dependents.

☎ Contact:
Department of Veterans Affairs
810 Vermont Ave., NW
Washington, DC 20420
(202) 535-7316

Free Publications/Videos

The following publications on Drug Testing are available from the National Institute of Justice, U.S. Department of Justice, P.O. Box 6000, Rockville, MD 20850; (800) 851-3420 or (301) 251-5500.

- *A Comparison of Urinalysis Technologies for Drug Testing in Criminal Justice.*
- *Mandatory and Random Drug Testing in the Honolulu Police Department.*
- *Urine Testing of Detained Juveniles To Identify*

High-Risk Youth In-Prison Programs for Drug-Involved Offenders.

The following Congressional Research Service (CRS) reports on Drug Testing are available from either of your U.S. Senators' offices at the U.S. Capitol, Washington, DC 20510, or from your Congressional Representative at the U.S. Capitol, Washington, DC 20515. You can also call in your request through the U.S. Capitol switchboard at (202) 224-3121. Be sure to include the full title and report number in your request.

- *Constitutional Analysis of Proposals to Establish a Mandatory Public Employee Drug Testing Program.* (#88-293 A)
- *Drug Free Workplace Initiatives: Federal Legislation Affecting the Private Sector.* (#88-508 E)
- *Drug Testing and the Drug-Free Workplace: A Bibliographic Guide and Reader.* (#90-6 L)
- *Drug Testing and Urinalysis in the Workplace: Legal Aspects.* (#86-996 A)
- *Drug Testing for Illegal Substances.* (#87-36 SPR)
- *Drug Testing in the Workplace: An Overview of Employee and Employer Interests: Archived Issue Brief.* (#IB87139)
- *Drug Testing in the Workplace: Federal Programs; Archived Issue Brief.* (#IB87174)
- *Drug Testing: Selected References, 1986-1987* (#88-33 L)
- *Drug Testing: The Response to Drugs in the Workplace.* (#IB350D)
- *Governmentally Mandated Drug Testing of Public Employees: A Survey of Recent Constitutional Developments.* (#90-103 A)
- *Legal Analysis of Recent Appropriation Riders to Insure a "Drug-Free Workplace".* (#88-450 A)

DRUG TREATMENT

See also Drug Abuse

Free Publications/Videos

The following publication on Drug Treatment is

available from Susan Lachter David or Audrey Yowell, National Institute on Drug Abuse, 5600 Fishers Lane, Room 10a-39, Rockville, MD 20857; (301) 443-1124.

- *Overcoming Barriers to Drug Abuse Treatment in the Community* is a flexible education model for use by communities that have funding and want to establish drug treatment facilities. This model is used in communities to educate people about drug treatment with the goal of countering resistance to the establishment of new treatment facilities. Materials are available to help local providers site facilities (How-to Resource Manual and Media package), as well as materials to assist communities groups in educating the public (Resource manual and media materials). These materials are free.

The following publications on Drug Treatment are available from the National Clearinghouse for Alcohol and Drug Information, Box 2345, Rockville, MD 20852; (800) 729-6686.

- *The National Directory of Drug Abuse and Alcoholism Treatment and Prevention Programs.* The directory contains referral information about treatment and prevention programs.
- *Adolescent Drug Abuse: Analyses of Treatment Research.* Assesses the adolescent drug user and offers theories, techniques, and findings about treatment and prevention. It also discusses family-based approaches.

DRUNK DRIVING

Clearinghouses/Hotlines

The National Center for Statistics and Analysis tabulates data on highway traffic accidents and maintains statistics on accidents and fatalities due to alcohol or drug use. They have extensive data on drunk driving, seat belts and alcohol, as well as much more send you.

☎ Contact:
National Center for Statistics and Analysis
National Highway Traffic
Safety Administration
400 7th Street SW
Washington, DC 20590
(202) 366-1470

Free Publications/Videos

The following publication on Drunk Driving is available from the National Maternal and Child Health Clearinghouse, 38th & R Sts., NW, Washington, DC 20057; (703) 821-8955, ext. 254.

- *Surgeon General's Workshop on Drunk Driving.* (#C044)

The following Congressional Research Service (CRS) reports on Drunk Driving are available from either of your U.S. Senators' offices at the U.S. Capitol, Washington, DC 20510, or from your Congressional Representative at the U.S. Capitol, Washington, DC 20515. You can also call in your request through the U.S. Capitol switchboard at (202) 224-3121. Be sure to include the full title and report number in your request.

- *Drunk Driving and Raising the Drinking Age: Info Pack.* (#IP186D)
- *Drunk Driving: Bibliography-in-Brief, 1983- 1988.* (#88-655 L)
- *Drunk Driving; Issue Brief.* (#IB83157)
- *Drunk Driving Laws in Foreign Countries.* (#LL89-88)
- *Nondischargeability of DWI Judgements in Bankruptcy: Survey of Case Law.* (#90-21 A)

DRY EYES

Clearinghouses/Hotlines

The National Eye Institute (NEI) can give you up-to-date information on Dry Eyes by searching the Combined Health Information Database (CHID) and MEDLINE and sending you bibliographies of

resources, along with any journal articles they may have. They can also refer you to any other organizations that study this and other related conditions. NEI will also let you know of any clinical studies that may be studying Dry Eyes and looking for patients. Because of their small staff, NEI prefers that you submit your requests for information in writing.

☎ Contact:
National Eye Institute
Building 31
Room 6A32
Bethesda, MD 20892
(301) 496-5248

DRY MOUTH

Clearinghouses/Hotlines

The National Institute of Dental Research (NIDR), which looks into the causes, prevention, diagnosis, and treatment of oral and dental diseases, can answer your questions about the newest developments in treatment and send you publications, posters, and reports on a variety of dental topics. Publications cover canker sores, fluoride treatment, periodontal disease, and tooth decay.

☎ Contact:
National Institute of Dental Research
Building 31
Room 2C35
Bethesda, MD 20892
(301) 496-4261

Free Publications/Videos

The following publication on Dry Mouth is available from the National Institute of Dental Research, Bldg. 31, Room 2C35, Bethesda, MD 20892; (301) 496-4261.

- *Dry Mouth (Xerostomia).* (#91-3174)

DUCHENNE MUSCULAR DYSTROPHY

Clearinghouses/Hotlines

The National Institute of Arthritis and Musculoskeletal and Skin Diseases (NIAMS) will send you whatever publications and reprints of articles from texts and journals they have on Duchenne Muscular Dystrophy. They will also refer you to other organizations that are studying this disease. NIAMS will also let you know of any clinical studies that may be studying this disease and looking for patients.

☎ Contact:
National Institute of Arthritis
and Musculoskeletal and Skin Diseases
Box AMS
Bethesda, MD 20892
(301) 495-4484

The National Institute of Neurological Disorders and Stroke (NINDS) can send you only information they have in their publications list on Duchenne Muscular Dystrophy. They cannot refer you to any experts. This Clearinghouse cannot directly give you information about any current clinical studies NINDS might be conducting on this illness, but you can find this information for yourself by looking under the National Institute of Neurological Disorders and Stroke in *Appendix A* at the end of this book.

☎ Contact:
National Institute of Neurological
Disorders and Stroke
Bldg. 31, Room 8A06
Bethesda, MD 20892
(301) 496-5751
(800) 352-9424

DUPUYTREN'S CONTRACTURE

Clearinghouses/Hotlines

The National Institute of Arthritis and Musculoskeletal and Skin Diseases (NIAMS) will send you whatever publications and reprints of articles from texts and journals they have on Dupuytren's Contracture. They will also refer you to other organizations that are studying this disorder. NIAMS will also let you know of any clinical studies that may be studying Dupuytren's and looking for patients.

☎ Contact:
National Institute of Arthritis
and Musculoskeletal and Skin Diseases
Box AMS
Bethesda, MD 20892
(301) 495-4484

The National Institute of Neurological Disorders and Stroke (NINDS) can send you only information they have in their publications list on Dupuytren's Contracture. They cannot refer you to any experts. This Clearinghouse cannot directly give you information about any current clinical studies NINDS might be conducting on this topic, but you can find this information for yourself by looking under the National Institute of Neurological Disorders and Stroke in *Appendix A* at the end of this book.

☎ Contact:
National Institute of Neurological
Disorders and Stroke
Bldg. 31, Room 8A06
Bethesda, MD 20892
(301) 496-5751
(800) 352-9424

DUST INHALATION DISEASES

Clearinghouses/Hotlines

The National Heart, Lung, and Blood Institute (NHLBI) can search the Combined Health Information Database (CHID) and generate a bibliography of resources on Dust Inhalation Diseases (Pneumoconioses) for you. They also will send you any publications and journal articles they may have on hand, and will refer you to other organizations that are studying this disease. If you can't afford treatment, have your doctor call NHLBI to find out if they are conducting any clinical studies that you might qualify for.

☎ Contact:
National Heart, Lung, and Blood Institute
Bldg. 31, Room 4A21
Bethesda, MD 20892
(301) 496-4236

The National Institute of Occupational Safety and Health (NIOSH) can provide you with information regarding Dust Inhalation Diseases. They can search their data base for information regarding a particular work environment or health hazard. They can also send you research reports, journal articles, bibliographies and more on the topic of interest.

☎ Contact:
National Institute of Occupational
Safety and Health
4676 Columbia Parkway, MS C-19
Cincinnati, OH 45226
(800) 35-NIOSH

Free Publications/Videos

The following publication is available from the National Institute of Allergy and Infectious Diseases, Bldg. 31, Room 7A32, Bethesda, MD 20892; (301) 496-5717.

- *Dust Allergy*. (#83-490)

DWARFISM

Clearinghouses/Hotlines

The National Institute of Child Health and Human Development (NICHD) will send you whatever publications and reprints of journal articles they have on Dwarfism. If necessary, they will refer you to other experts or researchers in the field. If you can't afford treatment, have your doctor call NICHD to find out if they are conducting any clinical studies that you might qualify for.

☎ Contact:
National Institute of Child Health

and Human Development
Bldg. 31, Room 2A32
Bethesda, MD 20892
(301) 496-5133.

DYSAUTONOMIA

Clearinghouses/Hotlines

The National Institute of Neurological Disorders and Stroke (NINDS) can send you only information they have in their publications list on Dysautonomia. They cannot refer you to any experts. This Clearinghouse cannot directly give you information about any current clinical studies NINDS might be conducting on this illness, but you can find this information for yourself by looking under the National Institute of Neurological Disorders and Stroke in *Appendix A* at the end of this book.

☎ Contact:
National Institute of Neurological
Disorders and Stroke
Bldg. 31, Room 8A06
Bethesda, MD 20892
(301) 496-5751
(800) 352-9424

DYSENTERY

Clearinghouses/Hotlines

The National Institute on Allergy and Infectious Diseases (NIAID) can search the Combined Health Information Database (CHID) and generate a bibliography of resources on Dysentery for you. They will also send you any publications and journal articles they may have on hand, and will refer you to researchers who are currently studying this disease. If you can't afford treatment, have your doctor call NIAID to find out if they are conducting any clinical studies that you might qualify for.

☎ Contact:
National Institute of Allergy

and Infectious Diseases
Bldg. 31, Room 7A32
Bethesda, MD 20892
(301) 496-5717

DYSKINESIA

Clearinghouses/Hotlines

The National Institute of Neurological Disorders and Stroke (NINDS) can send you only information they have in their publications list on Dyskinesia. They cannot refer you to any experts. This Clearinghouse cannot directly give you information about any current clinical studies NINDS might be conducting on this illness, but you can find this information for yourself by looking under the National Institute of Neurological Disorders and Stroke in *Appendix A* at the end of this book.

☎ Contact:
National Institute of Neurological
Disorders and Stroke
Bldg. 31, Room 8A06
Bethesda, MD 20892
(301) 496-5751
(800) 352-9424

DYSLEXIA

Clearinghouses/Hotlines

The National Institute of Child Health and Human Development (NICHD) will send you whatever publications and reprints of journal articles they have on Dyslexia. If necessary, they will refer you to other experts or researchers in the field. If you can't afford treatment, have your doctor call NICHD to find out if they are conducting any clinical studies that you might qualify for.

☎ Contact:
National Institute of Child Health
and Human Development
Bldg. 31, Room 2A32
Bethesda, MD 20892
(301) 496-5133

The National Institute on Deafness and Other Communicative Disorders (NIDCD) will send you whatever publications and reprints of journal articles they have on Dyslexia. If you need further information, they will refer you to other organizations that this and other related disorders. NIDCD does not conduct any clinical studies for Dyslexia or any other disorder.

☎ Contact:
National Institute on Deafness
and Other Communication Disorders
Building 31
Room 3C35
Bethesda, MD 20892
(301) 496-7243
(800) 241-1044
(301) 402-0252 (TDD)

The National Institute of Neurological Disorders and Stroke (NINDS) can send you only information they have in their publications list on Dyslexia. They cannot refer you to any experts. This Clearinghouse cannot directly give you information about any current clinical studies NINDS might be conducting on this condition, but you can find this information for yourself by looking under the National Institute of Neurological Disorders and Stroke in *Appendix A* at the end of this book.

☎ Contact:
National Institute of Neurological
Disorders and Stroke
Bldg. 31, Room 8A06
Bethesda, MD 20892
(301) 496-5751
(800) 352-9424

The National Institute of Mental Health (NIMH) will send you whatever publications and reprints of articles from texts and journals they have on Dyslexia. They will also refer you to other organizations that are studying this disease. NIMH will also let you know of any clinical studies that may be studying this disease and looking for patients.

☎ Contact:
National Institute of Mental Health
5600 Fishers Lane
Room 15C05
Rockville, MD 20857
(301) 443-4515

Free Publications/Videos

The following publications on Dyslexia are available from the National Institutes of Child Health and Human Development, National Institutes of Health, Building 31, Room 2A32, Bethesda, MD 20892; (301) 496-5133.

- *Developmental Dyslexia and Related Reading Disorders*. Provides an overview of what is known and what remains to be learned about dyslexia.
- *Facts About Dyslexia*.
- *Developmental Dyslexia and Related Disorders*. (#80-92)

The following publication on Dyslexia is available from the Science & Technology Division, Reference Section, Library of Congress, Washington, DC 20540; (202) 707-5580.

- *Dyslexia*. Reference guide designed to help locate further published material. (#91-3)

The following publication on Dyslexia is available from the National Institute of Neurological Disorders and Stroke, P.O. Box 5801, Bethesda, MD 20824; (800) 352-9424, or (301) 496-5751.

- *Dyslexia*. Contains a collection of scientific articles, patient education pamphlets, and addresses of voluntary health associations.

DYSMENORRHEA

Clearinghouses/Hotlines

The National Institute of Child Health and Human Development (NICHD) will send you whatever publications and reprints of journal articles they have on Dysmenorrhea. If necessary, they will refer you to other experts or researchers in the field. If you can't afford treatment, have your doctor call NICHD to find out if they are conducting any clinical studies that you might qualify for.

☎ Contact:
National Institute of Child Health

and Human Development
Bldg. 31, Room 2A32
Bethesda, MD 20892
(301) 496-5133

DYSPEPSIA

Clearinghouses/Hotlines

The National Digestive Diseases Information Clearinghouse will respond to your requests for information about digestive diseases and distributes information to health professionals, people with digestive diseases, and the general public. They have many publications, as well as a news bulletin.

☎ Contact:
National Digestive Diseases
Information Clearinghouse
Box NDDIC
Bethesda, MD 20892
(301) 468-6344

Free Publications/Videos

The following publication is available from the National Digestive Diseases Information Clearinghouse, Box NDDIC, Bethesda, MD 20892; (301) 468-6344.

- *What Is Dyspepsia?*

DYSTONIA

Clearinghouses/Hotlines

The National Institute of Neurological Disorders and Stroke (NINDS) can send you only information they have in their publications list on Dystonia Musculorum Deformans (Torsion Dystonia). They cannot refer you to any experts. This Clearinghouse cannot directly give you information about any current clinical studies NINDS might be conducting on this condition, but you can find this information for yourself by looking under the National Institute of Neurological Disorders and Stroke in *Appendix A* at the end of this book.

☎ Contact:
National Institute of Neurological
Disorders and Stroke
Bldg. 31, Room 8A06
Bethesda, MD 20892
(301) 496-5751
(800) 352-9424

Free Publications/Videos

The following publications are available from the National Institute of Neurological Disorders and Stroke, Bldg. 31, Room 8A06, Bethesda, MD 20892; (301) 496-5751, or (800) 352-9424.

- *Dystonias*. (#92-717)
- *Dystonias*. Fact sheet on symptoms and treatment.

- E -

EAR INFECTIONS

Clearinghouses/Hotlines

The National Institute on Deafness and Other Communicative Disorders (NIDCD) will send you whatever publications and reprints of journal articles they have on Ear Infections. If you need further information, they will refer you to other organizations that study this and other related conditions. NIDCD does not conduct any clinical studies for this or any other disorder.

☎ Contact:
National Institute on Deafness
and Other Communication Disorders
Bldg. 31, Room 3C35

Bethesda, MD 20892
(301) 496-7243
(800) 241-1044
(301) 402-0252 (TDD)

EATING DISORDERS

See also Anorexia

Clearinghouses/Hotlines

The Obesity, Eating Disorders, and Energy Regulation Program at the National Institutes of Health researches obesity, anorexia nervosa, bulimia and other Eating Disorders. They can give you information on the causes, prevention, and treatments of these conditions.

☎ Contact:
National Institute of Diabetes
and Digestive and Kidney Diseases
Bldg. 31, Room 3A18B
Bethesda, MD 20892
(301) 496-7823

Free Publications/Videos

The following publication on Eating Disorders is available from the Food & Drug Administration, (HFE-88), 5600 Fishers Ln., Rockville, MD 20857; (301) 443-3170.

- *Eating Disorders: When Thinness Becomes an Obsession*. Discusses bulimia and anorexia nervosa. (#86-2211)

The following Congressional Research Service (CRS) report is available from either of your U.S. Senators' offices at the U.S. Capitol, Washington, DC 20510, or from your Congressional Representative at the U.S. Capitol, Washington, DC 20515. You can also call in your request through the U.S. Capitol switchboard at (202) 224-3121. Be sure to include the full title and report number in your request.

- *Eating Disorders: Anorexia Nervosa and Bulimia*. (#87-630 SPR)

The following Congressional Research Service (CRS) report on Eating Disorders is available from either of your U.S. Senators' offices at the U.S. Capitol, Washington, DC 20510, or from your Congressional Representative at the U.S. Capitol, Washington, DC 20515. You can also call in your request through the U.S. Capitol switchboard at (202) 224-3121. Be sure to include the full title and report number in your request.

- *Eating Disorders: Anorexia Nervosa and Bulimia.* (#87-630 SPR)

EATON-LAMBERT MYASTHENIC SYNDROME

Clearinghouses/Hotlines

The National Institute of Neurological Disorders and Stroke (NINDS) can send you only information they have in their publications list on Eaton-Lambert Myasthenic Syndrome. They cannot refer you to any experts. This Clearinghouse cannot directly give you information about any current clinical studies NINDS might be conducting on this illness, but you can find this information for yourself by looking under the National Institute of Neurological Disorders and Stroke in *Appendix A* at the end of this book.

☎ Contact:
National Institute of Neurological
Disorders and Stroke
Bldg. 31, Room 8A06
Bethesda, MD 20892
(301) 496-5751
(800) 352-9424

ECHOCARDIOGRAPHY

Clearinghouses/Hotlines

The National Heart, Lung, and Blood Institute (NHLBI) can search the Combined Health Information Database (CHID) and generate a bibliography of resources on Echocardiography

(ECG) for you. They also will send you any publications and journal articles they may have on hand, and will refer you to other organizations that are studying this subject.

☎ Contact:
National Heart, Lung, and Blood Institute
Bldg. 31, Room 4A21
Bethesda, MD 20892
(301) 496-4236

ECLAMPSIA

See also Pregnancy

Clearinghouses/Hotlines

The National Institute of Child Health and Human Development (NICHD) will send you whatever publications and reprints of journal articles they have on Eclampsia/Preeclampsia. If necessary, they will refer you to other experts or researchers in the field. If you can't afford treatment, have your doctor call NICHD to find out if they are conducting any clinical studies that you might qualify for.

☎ Contact:
National Institute of Child Health
and Human Development
Bldg. 31, Room 2A32
Bethesda, MD 20892
(301) 496-5133

ECTODERMAL DYSPLASIAS

Clearinghouses/Hotlines

The National Institute of Arthritis and Musculoskeletal and Skin Diseases (NIAMS) will send you whatever publications and reprints of articles from texts and journals they have on Ectodermal Dysplasias. They will also refer you to other organizations that are studying this disease. NIAMS will also let you know of any clinical studies that may be studying this disease and looking for patients.

☎ Contact:
National Institute of Arthritis
and Musculoskeletal and Skin Diseases
Box AMS
9000 Rockville Pike
Bethesda, MD 20892
(301) 495-4484

The National Institute of Dental Research (NIDR) will send you whatever publications and reprints of journal articles they have on Ectodermal Dysplasias. As a policy, NIDR will not refer you to other organizations or experts who study this disease. If you can't afford treatment, have your doctor call Dr. Albert Guckers at (301) 496-6241 to find out if NIDR is conducting any clinical studies that you might qualify for.

☎ Contact:
National Institute of Dental Research
Building 31
Room 2C35
Bethesda, MD 20892
(301) 496-4261

ECTOPIC HORMONES

Clearinghouses/Hotlines

The National Institute of Diabetes and Digestive and Kidney Diseases's (NIDDK) individual clearinghouses can search the Combined Health Information Database (CHID) and generate a bibliography of resources on Ectopic Hormones for you. They also will send you any publications and journal articles they may have on hand, and will refer you to other organizations that are studying this subject. If you can't afford treatment, have your doctor call NIDDK to find out if they are conducting any clinical studies that you might qualify for.

☎ Contact:
National Institute of Diabetes
and Digestive and Kidney Diseases
Building 31
Room 9A04
Bethesda, MD 20892
(301) 496-3583

ECTOPIC PREGNANCY

Clearinghouses/Hotlines

The National Institute of Child Health and Human Development (NICHD) will send you whatever publications and reprints of journal articles they have on Ectopic Pregnancy. If necessary, they will refer you to other experts or researchers in the field. If you can't afford treatment, have your doctor call NICHD to find out if they are conducting any clinical studies that you might qualify for.

☎ Contact:
National Institute of Child Health
and Human Development
Building 31
Room 2A32
Bethesda, MD 20892
(301) 496-5133

ECZEMA

Clearinghouses/Hotlines

The National Institute on Allergy and Infectious Diseases (NIAID) can search the Combined Health Information Database (CHID) and generate a bibliography of resources on Eczema for you. They will also send you any publications and journal articles they may have on hand, and will refer you to researchers who are currently studying this condition. If you can't afford treatment, have your doctor call NIAID to find out if they are conducting any clinical studies that you might qualify for.

☎ Contact:
National Institute of Allergy
and Infectious Diseases
Building 31
Room 7A32
Bethesda, MD 20892
(301) 496-5717

The National Institute of Arthritis and Musculoskeletal and Skin Diseases (NIAMS) will send you whatever publications and reprints of articles from texts and journals they have on Eczema. They will also refer you to other organizations that are studying this condition. NIAMS will also let you know of any clinical studies that may be studying this disease and looking for patients.

☎ Contact:
National Institute of Arthritis
and Musculoskeletal and Skin Diseases
Box AMS
9000 Rockville Pike
Bethesda, MD 20892
(301) 495-4484

EDEMA

Clearinghouses/Hotlines

The National Heart, Lung, and Blood Institute (NHLBI) can search the Combined Health Information Database (CHID) and generate a bibliography of resources on Edema for you. They also will send you any publications and journal articles they may have on hand, and will refer you to other organizations that are studying this condition. If you can't afford treatment, have your doctor call NHLBI to find out if they are conducting any clinical studies that you might qualify for.

☎ Contact:
National Heart, Lung, and Blood Institute
Building 31
Room 4A21
Bethesda, MD 20892
(301) 496-4236

The National Institute on Aging (NIA) can provide you with information regarding Edema in the elderly.

☎ Contact:
National Institute on Aging
Federal Building
Room 6C12
Bethesda, MD 20892
(301) 496-1752

EGGS

See also Food

Free Publications/Videos

The following publication is available from the Food & Drug Administration, (HFE-88), 5600 Fishers Ln., Rockville, MD 20857; (301) 443-3170.

- *So Long, Sunny Side Up.* (#FDA92-2252)

EHLERS-DANLOS SYNDROME

Clearinghouses/Hotlines

The National Institute of Arthritis and Musculoskeletal and Skin Diseases (NIAMS) will send you whatever publications and reprints of articles from texts and journals they have on Ehlers-Danlos Syndrome. They will also refer you to other organizations that are studying this disease. NIAMS will also let you know of any clinical studies that may be studying this disease and looking for patients.

☎ Contact:
National Institute of Arthritis
and Musculoskeletal and Skin Diseases
Box AMS
Bethesda, MD 20892
(301) 495-4484

EISENMENGER'S SYNDROME

Clearinghouses/Hotlines

The National Heart, Lung, and Blood Institute (NHLBI) can search the Combined Health Information Database (CHID) and generate a bibliography of resources on Eisenmenger's

Syndrome for you. They also will send you any publications and journal articles they may have on hand, and will refer you to other organizations that are studying this disease. If you can't afford treatment, have your doctor call NHLBI to find out if they are conducting any clinical studies that you might qualify for.

☎ Contact:
National Heart, Lung, and Blood Institute
Bldg. 31, Room 4A21
Bethesda, MD 20892
(301) 496-4236

EKGs

Clearinghouses/Hotlines

The National Heart, Lung, and Blood Institute (NHLBI) can search the Combined Health Information Database (CHID) and generate a bibliography of resources on EKGs for you. They also will send you any publications and journal articles they may have on hand, and will refer you to other organizations that are studying this subject. If you can't afford treatment, have your doctor call NHLBI to find out if they are conducting any clinical studies that you might qualify for.

☎ Contact:
National Heart, Lung, and Blood Institute
Bldg. 31, Room 4A21
Bethesda, MD 20892
(301) 496-4236

ELDER ABUSE

See also Aging

Clearinghouses/Hotlines

The Clearinghouse on Family Violence Information has brochures and audiovisual materials, along with an in-house database from which they can retrieve reference materials and organizations involved with family violence for you.

☎ Contact:
Clearinghouse on Family
Violence Information
P.O. Box 1182
Washington, DC 20013
(703) 385-7565

Free Publications/Videos

The following Congressional Research Service (CRS) report on Elder Abuse is available from either of your U.S. Senators' offices at the U.S. Capitol, Washington, DC 20510, or from your Congressional Representative at the U.S. Capitol, Washington, DC 20515. You can also call in your request through the U.S. Capitol switchboard at (202) 224-3121. Be sure to include the full title and report number in your request.

- *Elder Abuse: Bibliography-in-Brief, 1980-1988.* (#88-221 L)

ELDERLY

See Aging

ELECTRICAL STIMULATION

Clearinghouses/Hotlines

The Electrophysics Branch at Food and Drug Administration conducts research on medical devices involving Electrical Stimulation to evaluate and examine their safety at the cellular level. They also examine the calibration of microwave ovens. The staff can respond to your written requests for information.

☎ Contact:
Center for Devices and Radiological Health
12721 Twinbrook Parkway
Rockville, MD 20857
(301) 443-3840

ELECTRIC BLANKETS

Clearinghouses/Hotlines

The Center for Devices and Radiological Health can answer your questions regarding the dangers or safety of Electric Blankets. They can provide you with reports and research articles on the topic.

☎ Contact:
Center for Devices and Radiological Health
(HFZ-210), Food and Drug Administration
5600 Fishers Lane
Rockville, MD 20857
(301) 443-4690

Free Publications/Videos

The following publication is available from the Center for Devices and Radiological Health, (HFZ-210), Food and Drug Administration, 5600 Fishers Ln., Rockville, MD 20857; (301) 443-4690.

- *No Known Health Hazard from Electric Blankets.*

ELECTROCARDIOGRAM

Clearinghouses/Hotlines

The National Heart, Lung, and Blood Institute (NHLBI) can search the Combined Health Information Database (CHID) and generate a bibliography of resources on Electrocardiograms for you. They also will send you any publications and journal articles they may have on hand, and will refer you to other organizations that are studying this subject. If you can't afford treatment, have your doctor call NHLBI to find out if they are conducting any clinical studies that you might qualify for.

☎ Contact:
National Heart, Lung, and Blood Institute
Bldg. 31, Room 4A21
Bethesda, MD 20892
(301) 496-4236

ELECTROMAGNETIC FIELDS

Clearinghouses/Hotlines

The Center for Devices and Radiological Health can provide you with information regarding Electromagnetic Fields and the concerns some scientists have regarding their dangers. This includes things such as televisions, electric blankets, electric razors, microwaves, and power lines. Some research has shown an increase in cancer as a result of exposure to electromagnetic fields, but the research is inconclusive at this time. The Center can send you research reports, articles, and more on the topic.

☎ Contact:
Center for Devices and Radiological Health
(HFZ-210), Food and Drug Administration
5600 Fishers Lane
Rockville, MD 20857
(301) 443-4190

Free Publications/Videos

The following Congressional Research Service (CRS) report on Electromagnetic Fields is available from either of your U.S. Senators' offices at the U.S. Capitol, Washington, DC 20510, or from your Congressional Representative at the U.S. Capitol, Washington, DC 20515. You can also call in your request through the U.S. Capitol switchboard at (202) 224-3121. Be sure to include the full title and report number in your request.

- *Power Lines and Electromagnetic Fields: Issues for Congress; Issue Brief.* (IB91051)

ELECTRO-SHOCK TREATMENT

Clearinghouses/Hotlines

The National Institute of Mental Health (NIMH)

maintains data bases that index and abstract documents from the worldwide literature pertaining to Mental Illness and Electro-Shock Treatment. In addition to scientific journals, there are references to audiovisuals, dissertations, government documents and reports. Contact NIMH for searches on specific subjects.

☎ Contact:
National Institute of Mental Health
5600 Fishers Lane, Room 15C05
Rockville, MD 20857
(301) 443-4515

Free Publications/Videos

The following publication on Electro-Shock Treatment is available from the Center for Devices and Radiological Health, (HFZ-210), Food and Drug Administration, 5600 Fishers Ln., Rockville, MD 20857; (301) 443-4690.

- *Electro-Shock Therapy: Controversy Without End.*

ELEPHANTIASIS

Clearinghouses/Hotlines

The National Institute on Allergy and Infectious Diseases (NIAID) can search the Combined Health Information Database (CHID) and generate a bibliography of resources on Elephantiasis for you. They will also send you any publications and journal articles they may have on hand, and will refer you to researchers who are currently studying this disease. If you can't afford treatment, have your doctor call NIAID to find out if they are conducting any clinical studies that you might qualify for.

☎ Contact:
National Institute of Allergy
and Infectious Diseases
Bldg. 31, Room 7A32
Bethesda, MD 20892
(301) 496-5717

EMBOLISMS

Clearinghouses/Hotlines

The National Heart, Lung, and Blood Institute (NHLBI) can search the Combined Health Information Database (CHID) and generate a bibliography of resources on Embolisms for you. They also will send you any publications and journal articles they may have on hand, and will refer you to other organizations that are studying this disease. If you can't afford treatment, have your doctor call NHLBI to find out if they are conducting any clinical studies that you might qualify for.

☎ Contact:
National Heart, Lung, and Blood Institute
Building 31
Room 4A21
Bethesda, MD 20892
(301) 496-4236

EMPHYSEMA

Clearinghouses/Hotlines

The National Heart, Lung, and Blood Institute (NHLBI) can search the Combined Health Information Database (CHID) and generate a bibliography of resources on Emphysema for you. They also will send you any publications and journal articles they may have on hand, and will refer you to other organizations that are studying this disease. If you can't afford treatment, have your doctor call NHLBI to find out if they are conducting any clinical studies that you might qualify for.

☎ Contact:
National Heart, Lung, and Blood Institute
Building 31
Room 4A21
Bethesda, MD 20892
(301) 496-4236

ENAMEL

Clearinghouses/Hotlines

The National Institute of Dental Research (NIDR) will send you whatever publications and reprints of journal articles they have on Tooth Enamel. As a policy, NIDR will not refer you to other organizations or experts who study this subject. If you can't afford treatment, have your doctor call Dr. Albert Guckers at (301) 496-6241 to find out if NIDR is conducting any clinical studies that you might qualify for.

☎ Contact:
National Institute of Dental Research
Building 31
Room 2C35
Bethesda, MD 20892
(301) 496-4261

ENCEPHALITIS

Clearinghouses/Hotlines

The National Institute on Allergy and Infectious Diseases (NIAID) can search the Combined Health Information Database (CHID) and generate a bibliography of resources on Encephalitis for you. They will also send you any publications and journal articles they may have on hand, and will refer you to researchers who are currently studying this disease. If you can't afford treatment, have your doctor call NIAID to find out if they are conducting any clinical studies that you might qualify for.

☎ Contact:
National Institute of Allergy
and Infectious Diseases
Building 31
Room 7A32
Bethesda, MD 20892
(301) 496-5717

The National Institute of Neurological Disorders and Stroke (NINDS) can send you only information they have in their publications list on Encephalitis. They cannot refer you to any experts. This Clearinghouse cannot directly give you information about any current clinical studies NINDS might be conducting on this illness, but you can find this information for yourself by looking under the National Institute of Neurological Disorders and Stroke in *Appendix A* at the end of this book.

☎ Contact:
National Institute of Neurological
Disorders and Stroke
Building 31
Room 8A06
Bethesda, MD 20892
(301) 496-5751
(800) 352-9424

The Centers for Disease Control's Voice Information System allows anyone using a touchtone phone to obtain pre-recorded information on Encephalitis, and many other diseases. This service offers information about Encephalitis, symptoms and prevention methods, immunization requirements, current statistics, recent disease outbreak, and available printed materials. The system is available 24 hours a day, although the health professionals are available Monday through Friday, 8 a.m.-4:30 p.m.

☎ Contact:
Centers for Disease Control
Information Resources Management Office
Mail Stop C-15
1600 Clifton Rd., NE
Atlanta, GA 30333
(404) 332-4555

Free Publications/Videos

The following publication is available from the National Institute of Neurological Disorders and Stroke, P.O. Box 5801, Bethesda, MD 20824; (800) 352-9424, or (301) 496-5751.

- *Encephalitis and Meningitis, Neurological Sequelae of Epilepsy.* Contains a collection of scientific articles, patient education pamphlets, and addresses of voluntary health associations.

ENCEPHALITIS LETHARGICA

Clearinghouses/Hotlines

The National Institute of Neurological Disorders and Stroke (NINDS) can send you only information they have in their publications list on Encephalitis Lethargica. They cannot refer you to any experts. This Clearinghouse cannot directly give you information about any current clinical studies NINDS might be conducting on this illness, but you can find this information for yourself by looking under the National Institute of Neurological Disorders and Stroke in *Appendix A* at the end of this book.

☎ Contact:
National Institute of Neurological
Disorders and Stroke
Bldg. 31, Room 8A06
Bethesda, MD 20892
(301) 496-5751
(800) 352-9424

ENCEPHALOMYELITIS

Clearinghouses/Hotlines

The National Institute of Neurological Disorders and Stroke (NINDS) can send you only information they have in their publications list on Encephalomyelitis. They cannot refer you to any experts. This Clearinghouse cannot directly give you information about any current clinical studies NINDS might be conducting on this illness, but you can find this information for yourself by looking under the National Institute of Neurological Disorders and Stroke in *Appendix A* at the end of this book.

☎ Contact:
National Institute of Neurological
Disorders and Stroke
Bldg. 31, Room 8A06
Bethesda, MD 20892
(301) 496-5751 or (800) 352-9424

ENCOPRESIS

Clearinghouses/Hotlines

The National Institute of Child Health and Human Development (NICHD) will send you whatever publications and reprints of journal articles they have on Encopresis. If necessary, they will refer you to other experts or researchers in the field. If you can't afford treatment, have your doctor call NICHD to find out if they are conducting any clinical studies that you might qualify for.

☎ Contact:
National Institute of Child Health
and Human Development
Bldg. 31, Room 2A32
Bethesda, MD 20892
(301) 496-5133

ENDOCARDITIS

Clearinghouses/Hotlines

The National Heart, Lung, and Blood Institute (NHLBI) can search the Combined Health Information Database (CHID) and generate a bibliography of resources on Endocarditis for you. They also will send you any publications and journal articles they may have on hand, and will refer you to other organizations that are studying this disease. If you can't afford treatment, have your doctor call NHLBI to find out if they are conducting any clinical studies that you might qualify for.

☎ Contact:
National Heart, Lung, and Blood Institute
Bldg. 31, Room 4A21
Bethesda, MD 20892
(301) 496-4236

ENDOCRINE GLANDS

Clearinghouses/Hotlines

The National Institute of Child Health and Human Development (NICHD) will send you whatever publications and reprints of journal articles they have on Endocrine Glands. If necessary, they will refer you to other experts or researchers in the field. If you can't afford treatment, have your doctor call NICHD to find out if they are conducting any clinical studies that you might qualify for.

☎ Contact:
National Institute of Child Health
and Human Development
Bldg. 31, Room 2A32
Bethesda, MD 20892
(301) 496-5133

The National Institute on Aging (NIA) will send you whatever publications and reprints of journal articles they have on the Endocrinology of Aging. They cannot refer you to other experts if the information they have isn't sufficient for your purposes.

☎ Contact:
National Institute on Aging
Bldg. 31, Room 5C27
Bethesda, MD 20892
(301) 496-1752

ENDOCRINOLOGIC MUSCLE DISEASE

Clearinghouses/Hotlines

The National Institute of Neurological Disorders and Stroke (NINDS) can send you only information they have in their publications list on Endocrinologic Muscle Disease. They cannot refer you to any experts. This Clearinghouse cannot directly give you information about any current clinical studies NINDS might be conducting on this illness, but you can find this information for yourself by looking under the National Institute of Neurological Disorders and Stroke in *Appendix A* at the end of this book.

☎ Contact:
National Institute of Neurological
Disorders and Stroke

Bldg. 31, Room 8A06
Bethesda, MD 20892
(301) 496-5751
(800) 352-9424

ENDODONTICS

Clearinghouses/Hotlines

The National Institute of Dental Research (NIDR) will send you whatever publications and reprints of journal articles they have on Endodontics. As a policy, NIDR will not refer you to other organizations or experts who study this subject. If you can't afford treatment, have your doctor call Dr. Albert Guckers at (301) 496-6241 to find out if NIDR is conducting any clinical studies that you might qualify for.

☎ Contact:
National Institute of Dental Research
Bldg. 31, Room 2C35
Bethesda, MD 20892
(301) 496-4261

ENDOGENOUS DEPRESSION

See Depression

ENDOMETRIOSIS

Clearinghouses/Hotlines

The National Institute of Child Health and Human Development (NICHD) will send you whatever publications and reprints of journal articles they have on Endometriosis. If necessary, they will refer you to other experts or researchers in the field. If you can't afford treatment, have your doctor call NICHD to find out if they are conducting any clinical studies that you might qualify for.

☎ Contact:
National Institute of Child Health
and Human Development
Bldg. 31, Room 2A32
Bethesda, MD 20892
(301) 496-5133

Free Publications/Videos

The following publication on Endometriosis is available from the National Institute of Child Health and Human Development, Bldg. 31, Room 2A32, Bethesda, MD 20892; (301) 496-5133.

- *Facts About Endometriosis.* (#91-2413)

The following publication on Endometriosis is available from the Center for Devices and Radiological Health, (HFZ-210), Food and Drug Administration, 5600 Fishers Ln., Rockville, MD 20857; (301) 443-4690.

- *Endometriosis: A Growing Cause of Infertility in Women.*

ENIGMATIC BLISTERING DISORDERS

Clearinghouses/Hotlines

The National Institute of Arthritis and Musculoskeletal and Skin Diseases (NIAMS) will send you whatever publications and reprints of articles from texts and journals they have on Enigmatic Blistering Disorders. They will also refer you to other organizations that are studying this disease. NIAMS will also let you know of any clinical studies that may be studying this disease and looking for patients.

☎ Contact:
National Institute of Arthritis
and Musculoskeletal and Skin Diseases
Box AMS
9000 Rockville Pike
Bethesda, MD 20892
(301) 495-4484

Free Publications/Videos

The following publications on Enigmatic Blistering Disorders are available from the National Institute of Arthritis and Musculoskeletal and Skin Diseases, Box AMS, Bethesda, MD 20892; (301) 495-4484.

- *Researchers Seek Causes of Enigmatic Blistering Disorders.*
- *Researchers Seek Causes of Enigmatic Blistering Disorders.* (#AR08)

ENTERIC DISEASES

Clearinghouses/Hotlines

The Centers for Disease Control's Voice Information System allows anyone using a touchtone phone to obtain pre-recorded information on Enteric Diseases, and many other conditions. This service offers information about symptoms and prevention methods, immunization requirements, current statistics, recent disease outbreak, and available printed materials. The system is available 24 hours a day, although the health professionals are available Monday through Friday, 8-4:30.

☎ Contact:
Centers for Disease Control
Information Resources Management Office
Mail Stop C-15
1600 Clifton Rd., NE
Atlanta, GA 30333
(404) 332-4555

The National Institute of Diabetes and Digestive and Kidney Diseases's (NIDDK) individual clearinghouses can search the Combined Health Information Database (CHID) and generate a bibliography of resources on Enteritis for you. They also will send you any publications and journal articles they may have on hand, and will refer you to other organizations that are studying this disease. If you can't afford treatment, have your doctor call NIDDK to find out if they are conducting any clinical studies that you might qualify for.

☎ Contact:
National Institute of Diabetes
and Digestive and Kidney Diseases
Bldg. 31, Room 9A04
Bethesda, MD 20892
(301) 496-3583

ENVIRONMENTAL HEALTH

Clearinghouses/Hotlines

The National Cancer Institute (NCI) will send you whatever publications and reprints of journal articles they have on Environmental Carcinogens. They can also give you information on the state-of-the-art treatment for this disease, including specific treatment information for your stage of cancer. They can also search their Physician's Data Query (PDQ) database to let you know if NCI is conducting any clinical studies on your disease.

☎ Contact:
National Cancer Institute
Bldg. 31, Room 10A24
Bethesda, MD 20892
(800) 4-CANCER
(301) 496-5583

The National Institute of Environmental Health Sciences (NIEHS) will send you whatever publications and journal articles they can locate on specific questions about Environmental Health and Mutagenesis. If necessary, they can put you in contact with researchers who are studying this issue. NIEHS does not conduct any clinical studies.

☎ Contact:
National Institute of Environmental
Health Sciences
P.O. Box 12233
Research Triangle Park, NC 27709
(919) 541-3345

Free Publications/Videos

The following publication on Environmental Health is available from the Agency for Toxic Substances and Disease Registry, Division of Health Education, E-33, 1600 Clifton Rd., Atlanta, GA 30333; (404) 639-0734.

- *Case Studies in Environmental Medicine.*
Discusses diagnosis and treatment of cases involving arsenic, asbestos, benzene, cadmium, chromium, cyanide, dioxins, lead, radon, methylene, chloride, vinyl chloride, trichloroethylene, tetra-chloroethylene, polyaromatic hydrocarbons, and polychlorinated biphenyls.

ENVIRONMENTAL ISSUES

Clearinghouses/Hotlines

The Environmental Protection Agency's (EPA) Public Information Center offers information about the EPA, its programs, and activities. They can refer callers to the appropriate technical program or regional office, and free materials are available on such topics as hazardous wastes, asbestos, air and water pollution, pesticides, and drinking water.

☎ Contact:
Environmental Protection Agency
Public Information Center
401 M St., SW, PM211B
Washington, DC 20460
(202) 260-7751

EOSINOPHILIC GRANULOMA

Clearinghouses/Hotlines

The National Heart, Lung, and Blood Institute (NHLBI) can search the Combined Health Information Database (CHID) and generate a bibliography of resources on Eosinophilic Granuloma of the Lung for you. They also will send you any publications and journal articles they may have on hand, and will refer you to other organizations that are studying this disease. If you can't afford treatment, have your doctor call NHLBI to find out if they are conducting any clinical studies that you might qualify for.

☎ Contact:
National Heart, Lung, and Blood Institute
Bldg. 31, Room 4A21
Bethesda, MD 20892
(301) 496-4236

The National Institute on Allergy and Infectious Diseases (NIAID) can search the Combined Health Information Database (CHID) and generate a bibliography of resources on Eosinophilic Syndrome for you. They will also send you any publications and journal articles they may have on hand, and will refer you to researchers who are currently studying this disease. If you can't afford treatment, have your doctor call NIAID to find out if they are conducting any clinical studies that you might qualify for.

☎ Contact:
National Institute of Allergy
and Infectious Diseases
Bldg. 31, Room 7A32
Bethesda, MD 20892
(301) 496-5717

EPICONDYLITIS

See Tennis Elbow

EPIDEMIOLOGY

Free Publications/Videos

The following publication is available from the National Heart, Lung and Blood Institute, Bldg. 31, Room 4A21, Bethesda, MD 20892; (301) 496-4236.

- *Poland USA Collaborative Study on Epidemiology: Polish Data Book*. (#92-2886)

EPIDERMODYSPLASIA VERRUCIFORMIS

Clearinghouses/Hotlines

The National Institute of Arthritis and Musculoskeletal and Skin Diseases (NIAMS) will send you whatever publications and reprints of articles from texts and journals they have on Epidermodysplasia Verruciformis. They will also refer you to other organizations that are studying this disease. NIAMS will also let you know of any clinical studies that may be studying this disease and looking for patients.

☎ Contact:
National Institute of Arthritis
and Musculoskeletal and Skin Diseases
Box AMS, 9000 Rockville Pike
Bethesda, MD 20892
(301) 495-4484

EPIDERMOLYSIS BULLOSA

Clearinghouses/Hotlines

The National Institute of Arthritis and Musculoskeletal and Skin Diseases (NIAMS) will send you whatever publications and reprints of articles from texts and journals they have on Epidermolysis Bullosa. They will also refer you to other organizations that are studying this disease. NIAMS will also let you know of any clinical studies that may be studying this disease and looking for patients.

☎ Contact:
National Institute of Arthritis
and Musculoskeletal and Skin Diseases
Box AMS, 9000 Rockville Pike
Bethesda, MD 20892
(301) 495-4484

Free Publications/Videos

The following publication is available from the

National Institute of Arthritis and Musculoskeletal and Skin Diseases, Box AMS, Bethesda, MD 20892; (301) 495-4484.

- *Living With Epidermolysis Bullosa.* (#AR19, NIH 84-663)

EPIGLOTTITIS

Clearinghouses/Hotlines

The National Institute on Allergy and Infectious Diseases (NIAID) can search the Combined Health Information Database (CHID) and generate a bibliography of resources on Epiglottitis for you. They will also send you any publications and journal articles they may have on hand, and will refer you to researchers who are currently studying this disease. If you can't afford treatment, have your doctor call NIAID to find out if they are conducting any clinical studies that you might qualify for.

☎ Contact:
National Institute of Allergy
and Infectious Diseases
Bldg. 31, Room 7A32
Bethesda, MD 20892
(301) 496-5717

EPIKERATOPHAKIA

Clearinghouses/Hotlines

The National Eye Institute (NEI) can give you up-to-date information on Epikeratophakia by searching the Combined Health Information Database (CHID) and MEDLINE and sending you bibliographies of resources, along with any journal articles they may have. They can also refer you to any other organizations that study this technique. NEI will also let you know of any clinical studies that may be studying this topic and looking for patients. Because of their small staff, NEI prefers that you submit your requests for information in writing.

☎ Contact:
National Eye Institute
Bldg. 31, Room 6A32
Bethesda, MD 20892
(301) 496-5248

EPILEPSY

Clearinghouses/Hotlines

The National Institute of Neurological Disorders and Stroke (NINDS) can send you only information they have in their publications list on Epilepsy. They cannot refer you to any experts. This Clearinghouse cannot directly give you information about any current clinical studies NINDS might be conducting on this illness, but you can find this information for yourself by looking under the National Institute of Neurological Disorders and Stroke in *Appendix A* at the end of this book.

☎ Contact:
National Institute of Neurological
Disorders and Stroke
Bldg. 31, Room 8A06
Bethesda, MD 20892
(301) 496-5751
(800) 352-9424

Free Publications/Videos

The following publication on Epilepsy is available from the Science & Technology Division, Reference Section, Library of Congress, Washington, DC 20540; (202) 707-5580.

- *Epilepsy.* Reference guide designed to help locate further published material. (#81-17)

The following publication on Epilepsy is available from the Office of Clinical Center Communications, Bldg. 10, Room 1C255, Bethesda, MD 20892; (301) 496-2563.

- *Epilepsy.* Discusses types of seizures and medical and surgical therapies. (#82-2369)

The following publication on Epilepsy is available from the National Institute of Neurological Disorders and Stroke, P.O. Box 5801, Bethesda, MD 20824; (800) 352-9424, or (301) 496-5751.

- *Epilepsy*. Discusses hope through research. (#81-156)
- *Epilepsy Bibliography 1900-1950*.
- *Epilepsy Bibliography 1950-1975*.

The following publication on Epilepsy is available from the National Maternal and Child Health Clearinghouse, 38th & R Sts., NW, Washington, DC 20057; (703) 821-8955, ext. 254.

- *Dental Implications of Epilepsy*. (#B053)

EPISTAXIS

See Nosebleeds

EPSTEIN-BARR SYNDROME

Clearinghouses/Hotlines

The National Institute on Allergy and Infectious Diseases (NIAID) can search the Combined Health Information Database (CHID) and generate a bibliography of resources on Epstein-Barr Syndrome for you. They will also send you any publications and journal articles they may have on hand, and will refer you to researchers who are currently studying this disease. If you can't afford treatment, have your doctor call NIAID to find out if they are conducting any clinical studies that you might qualify for.

☎ Contact:
National Institute of Allergy
and Infectious Diseases
Bldg. 31, Room 7A32
Bethesda, MD 20892
(301) 496-5717

The Centers for Disease Control's Voice Information System allows anyone using a touchtone phone to obtain pre-recorded information on Epstein-Barr, and many other conditions. This service offers information about symptoms and prevention methods, immunization requirements, current statistics, recent disease outbreak, and available printed materials. The system is available 24 hours a day, although the health professionals are available Monday through Friday, 8 a.m.-4:30 p.m.

☎ Contact:
Centers for Disease Control
Information Resources Management Office
Mail Stop C-15, 1600 Clifton Rd., NE
Atlanta, GA 30333
(404) 332-4555

The National Institute on Allergy and Infectious Diseases (NIAID) can search the Combined Health Information Database (CHID) and generate a bibliography of resources on Epstein-Barr Virus for you. They will also send you any publications and journal articles they may have on hand, and will refer you to researchers who are currently studying this disease. If you can't afford treatment, have your doctor call NIAID to find out if they are conducting any clinical studies that you might qualify for.

☎ Contact:
National Institute of Allergy
and Infectious Diseases
Bldg. 31, Room 7A32
Bethesda, MD 20892
(301) 496-5717

EQUINE ENCEPHALITIS

Clearinghouses/Hotlines

The National Institute of Allergy and Infectious Diseases Clearinghouse can provide you with information regarding Equine Encephalitis.

☎ Contact:
National Institute of Allergy
and Infectious Diseases
Bldg. 31, Room 7A32
Bethesda, MD 20892
(301) 496-5717

ERYTHEMA ELEVATUM DIUTINUM

Clearinghouses/Hotlines

The National Institute of Arthritis and Musculoskeletal and Skin Diseases (NIAMS) will send you whatever publications and reprints of articles from texts and journals they have on Erythema Elevatum Diutinum. They will also refer you to other organizations that are studying this disease. NIAMS will also let you know of any clinical studies that may be studying this disease and looking for patients.

☎ Contact:
National Institute of Arthritis
and Musculoskeletal and Skin Diseases
Box AMS
9000 Rockville Pike
Bethesda, MD 20892
(301) 495-4484

ERYTHEMA MULTIFORME

Clearinghouses/Hotlines

The National Institute on Allergy and Infectious Diseases (NIAID) can search the Combined Health Information Database (CHID) and generate a bibliography of resources on Erythema Multiforme for you. They will also send you any publications and journal articles they may have on hand, and will refer you to researchers who are currently studying this condition. If you can't afford treatment, have your doctor call NIAID to find out if they are conducting any clinical studies that you might qualify for.

☎ Contact:
National Institute of Allergy
and Infectious Diseases
Building 31
Room 7A32
Bethesda, MD 20892
(301) 496-5717

ERYTHEMA NODOSUM

Clearinghouses/Hotlines

The National Institute on Allergy and Infectious Diseases (NIAID) can search the Combined Health Information Database (CHID) and generate a bibliography of resources on Erythema Nodosum for you. They will also send you any publications and journal articles they may have on hand, and will refer you to researchers who are currently studying this condition. If you can't afford treatment, have your doctor call NIAID to find out if they are conducting any clinical studies that you might qualify for.

☎ Contact:
National Institute of Allergy
and Infectious Diseases
Building 31
Room 7A32
Bethesda, MD 20892
(301) 496-5717

ERYTHROBLASTOSIS FETALIS

Clearinghouses/Hotlines

The National Institute of Child Health and Human Development (NICHD) will send you whatever publications and reprints of journal articles they have on Erythroblastosis Fetalis. If necessary, they will refer you to other experts or researchers in the field. If you can't afford treatment, have your doctor call NICHD to find out if they are conducting any clinical studies that you might qualify for.

☎ Contact:
National Institute of Child Health
and Human Development
Building 31
Room 2A32
Bethesda, MD 20892
(301) 496-5133

ERYTHROCYTES

See Blood

ESOPHAGEAL DISORDERS

Clearinghouses/Hotlines

The National Institute of Diabetes and Digestive and Kidney Diseases's (NIDDK) individual clearinghouses can search the Combined Health Information Database (CHID) and generate a bibliography of resources on Esophageal Disorders for you. They also will send you any publications and journal articles they may have on hand, and will refer you to other organizations that are studying this subject. If you can't afford treatment, have your doctor call NIDDK to find out if they are conducting any clinical studies that you might qualify for.

☎ Contact:
National Institute of Diabetes
and Digestive and Kidney Diseases
Building 31
Room 9A04
Bethesda, MD 20892
(301) 496-3583

The National Cancer Institute (NCI) will send you whatever publications and reprints of journal articles they have on Carcinoma of the Esophagus. They can also give you information on the state-of-the-art treatment for this disease, including specific treatment information for your stage of cancer. They can also search their Physician's Data Query (PDQ) database to let you know if NCI is conducting any clinical studies on your disease.

☎ Contact:
National Cancer Institute
Building 31
Room 10A24
Bethesda, MD 20892
(800) 4-CANCER
(301) 496-5583

Free Publications/Videos

The following publication on Esophageal Disorders is available from the National Cancer Institute, Bldg. 31, Room 10A24, Bethesda, MD 20892; (800) 4-CANCER, or (301) 496-5583.

- *What You Need to Know About Cancer of the Esophagus.* (#91-1557)

ESOTROPIA

See Cross-Eye

ESTRAMUSTINE

Free Publications/Videos

The following publication on Estramustine is available from the National Cancer Institute, Bldg. 31, Room 10A24, Bethesda, MD 20892; (800) 4-CANCER, or (301) 496-5583.

- *Estramustina/Estramustine.* Provides information about side effects, proper usage, and precautions of this anti-cancer drug.

ESTREPTOZOCINA

Free Publications/Videos

The following publication on Estreptozocina is available from the National Cancer Institute, Bldg. 31, Room 10A24, Bethesda, MD 20892; (800) 4-CANCER, or (301) 496-5583.

- *Estreptozocina/Streptozocin.* Provides information about side effects, proper usage, and precautions of this anti-cancer drug.

ESTROGEN

Clearinghouses/Hotlines

The National Institute of Child Health and Human Development (NICHD) will send you whatever publications and reprints of journal articles they have on Estrogen Replacement Therapy. If necessary, they will refer you to other experts or researchers in the field. If you can't afford treatment, have your doctor call NICHD to find out if they are conducting any clinical studies that you might qualify for.

☎ Contact:
National Institute of Child Health
and Human Development
Bldg. 31, Room 2A32
Bethesda, MD 20892
(301) 496-5133

The National Cancer Institute (NCI) will send you whatever publications and reprints of journal articles they have on Estrogen Replacement Therapy. They can also search their Physician's Data Query (PDQ) database to let you know if NCI is conducting any clinical studies on your disease.

☎ Contact:
National Cancer Institute
Bldg. 31, Room 10A24
Bethesda, MD 20892
(800) 4-CANCER
(301) 496-5583

The National Institute of Arthritis and Musculoskeletal and Skin Diseases (NIAMS) will send you whatever publications and reprints of articles from texts and journals they have on Estrogen Replacement Therapy. They will also refer you to other organizations that are studying this issue. NIAMS will also let you know of any clinical studies that may be studying this disease and looking for patients.

☎ Contact:
National Institute of Arthritis
and Musculoskeletal and Skin Diseases
Box AMS
Bethesda, MD 20892
(301) 495-4484

The National Institute on Aging (NIA) will send you whatever publications and reprints of journal articles they have on Estrogen Replacement Therapy. They cannot refer you to other experts if the information they have isn't sufficient for your purposes.

☎ Contact:
National Institute on Aging
Building 31
Room 5C27
Bethesda, MD 20892
(301) 496-1752

Estrogen is taken by millions of women and does help relieve the symptoms of menopause such as hot flashes, as well as relieve vaginal changes that can cause dryness, burning, itching, and pain during intercourse in middle and later life. There is some concern now that women who take estrogen for long periods of time will develop cancer of the uterus. The Food and Drug Administration is encouraging doctors to examine the needs of their patients on estrogen, as evidence is lacking that post menopausal estrogens are necessary. The Center for Drug Evaluation and Research has up-to-the-minute information on estrogen use and has put together a packet of information on estrogen so women can know the benefits and risks when deciding the best course of therapy.

☎ Contact:
Center for Drug Evaluation and Research
Food and Drug Administration
HFD 100
Room 14B45
5600 Fishers Lane
Rockville, MD 20857
(301) 295-8012

Free Publications/Videos

The following publication on Estrogen is available from the Food & Drug Administration, (HFE-88), 5600 Fishers Ln., Rockville, MD 20857; (301) 443-3170.

- *How To Take Your Medicines: Estrogens.* (FDA91-3186)

ETHICS

Free Publications/Videos

The following Congressional Research Service (CRS) reports on Medical Ethics are available from either of your U.S. Senators' offices at the U.S. Capitol, Washington, DC 20510, or from your Congressional Representative at the U.S. Capitol, Washington, DC 20515. You can also call in your request through the U.S. Capitol switchboard at (202) 224-3121. Be sure to include the full title and report number in your request.

- *Biomedical Ethics and Congress: History and Current Legislative Activity; Issue Brief.* (#IB86078)
- *Biomedical Ethics: Audio Brief.* (#AB50004)

EUTHANASIA

See Living Wills

EWING'S SARCOMA

Clearinghouses/Hotlines

The National Cancer Institute (NCI) will send you whatever publications and reprints of journal articles they have on Ewing's Sarcoma. They can also give you information on the state-of-the-art treatment for this disease, including specific treatment information for your stage of cancer. They can also search their Physician's Data Query (PDQ) database to let you know if NCI is conducting any clinical studies on your disease.

☎ Contact:
National Cancer Institute
Bldg. 31, Room 10A24
Bethesda, MD 20892
(800) 4-CANCER
(301) 496-5583

EXERCISE

See also Worksite Health and Safety

Clearinghouses/Hotlines

The National Institute of Arthritis and Musculoskeletal and Skin Diseases (NIAMS) will send you whatever publications and reprints of articles from texts and journals they have on Exercise Physiology. They will also refer you to other organizations that are studying this issue. NIAMS will also let you know of any clinical studies that may be studying this disease and looking for patients.

☎ Contact:
National Institute of Arthritis
and Musculoskeletal and Skin Diseases
Box AMS
Bethesda, MD 20892
(301) 495-4484

The National Institute on Aging (NIA) will send you whatever publications and reprints of journal articles they have on Exercise and Aging. They cannot refer you to other experts if the information they have isn't sufficient for your purposes.

☎ Contact:
National Institute on Aging
Bldg. 31, Room 5C27
Bethesda, MD 20892
(301) 496-1752

The National Heart, Lung, and Blood Institute (NHLBI) can search the Combined Health Information Database (CHID) and generate a bibliography of resources on Exercise and the Heart for you. They also will send you any publications and journal articles they may have on hand, and will refer you to other organizations that are studying this issue. If you can't afford treatment, have your doctor call NHLBI to find out if they are conducting any clinical studies that you might qualify for.

☎ Contact:
National Heart, Lung, and Blood Institute
Bldg. 31, Room 4A21
Bethesda, MD 20892
(301) 496-4236

Are you concerned about continuing your current exercise program now that you are pregnant? What about if you want to start exercising, but aren't sure which exercises are good for you. The National Institute of Child Health and Human Development can provide you with relevant articles and information regarding exercises and pregnancy.

☎ Contact:
National Institute of Child Health
and Human Development
Building 31, Room 2A32
Bethesda, MD 20892
(301) 496-5133

The President's Council on Physical Fitness and Sports will send you a free quarterly newsletter on physical fitness and related books, conferences, and articles, including *Everybody's Walking For Fitness* and *Walking for Exercise and Pleasure*.

☎ Contact:
President's Council on Physical Fitness
and Sports
450 5th St., NW, Suite 7103
Washington, DC 20001
(202) 272-3421

Free Publications/Videos

The following publications on Exercise and Nutrition are available from the Food and Nutrition Information Center, National Agricultural Library, 10301 Baltimore Blvd., Beltsville, MD 20705; (301) 504-5719.

- *Sports Nutrition Nutri-Topic*. Lists books, journal articles, pamphlets, booklets, and other resources to contact regarding sports fitness and nutrition. Included is a list of videos produced outside the government, but available for free loan from the Food and Nutrition Information Center, dealing with exercise and fitness.
- *Sports Nutrition*. A list to help you locate further information or resources.

The following publication on Exercise and Nutrition is available from the Office of Clinical Center Communications, National Institutes of Health, Building 10, Room 5C305, Bethesda, MD

20892; (301) 496-2563.

- *Obesity and Energy Metabolism*. Explains the relationship between too much food and too little exercise.

The following publication on Exercise and Nutrition is available from the National Arthritis and Musculoskeletal and Skin Diseases Information Clearinghouse, Box AMS, 9000 Rockville Pike, Bethesda, MD 20892; (301) 495-4484.

- *Exercise and Arthritis, 1986*. A bibliography of sources. ($4)
- *Exercise and Arthritis: An Annotated Bibliography, 1986*. Contains 37 references with abstracts, books, reports, and audiovisuals along with resources for developing an aquatic exercise regime, a home maintenance program, and exercises specifically for children.

The following publication on Exercise is available from the National Institute on Aging Information Center, Federal Bldg., Room 6C12, Bethesda, MD 20892; (301) 496-1752.

- *Don't Take It Easy - Exercise!* Suggests ways for older Americans to remain active and healthy.

The following publications on Exercise are available from the National Heart, Lung, and Blood Institute, Bldg. 31, Room 4A21, Bethesda, MD 20892; (301) 496-4236.

- *Exercise and Your Heart* (#81-1677)
- *NHLBI Facts About Exercise: How To Get Started*.
- *NHLBI Facts About Exercise: Sample Exercise Programs*.
- *NHLBI Facts About Exercise: What Is Fact and What Is Fiction?*

The following publication on Exercise is available from the National Institute of Mental Health, 5600 Fishers Ln., Room 15C05, Rockville, MD 20857; (301) 443-4515.

- *Plain Talk About Physical Fitness and Mental*

Health. Presents ideas about exercise and its connection to mental stability, particularly for special groups of people. (#84-1364)

The following publications on Exercise are available from the President's Council on Physical Fitness and Sports, 450 5th St., NW, Suite 7103, Washington, DC 20001; (202) 272-3421.

- *Fitness Fundamentals.*
- *Fitness in the Workplace.*
- *One Step At A Time (An Introduction to Running).*
- *Physical Education: A Performance Checklist.*

The following publications on Exercise are available from the Superintendent of Documents, Government Printing Office, Washington, DC 20402; (202) 783-3238.

- *Adult Physical Fitness.* Explains benefits of regular, vigorous exercise. ($4.50)
- *Aqua Dynamics.* Comprehensive program of strength, flexibility and endurance exercises for the water. ($3.75)
- *Fitness Fundamentals.* Outlines basic guidelines to follow to begin and maintain a personal exercise program. ($25/100)
- *Introduction to Running: One Step At A Time.* Handbook for beginning runners. ($1)
- *Promoting Health, Preventing Disease: Objectives for the Nation.* National objectives in health and fitness for 1990. ($5)
- *Physical Fitness/Sports Medicine.* Quarterly bibliographic listing of references in more than 300 subject areas. ($9/yr)
- *1985 GPO Youth Fitness Survey.* Report on the 1985 School Population Fitness Survey, conducted by the University of Michigan. ($5)

The following publication on Exercise is available from the National Diabetes Information Clearinghouse, Box NDIC, Bethesda, MD 20892; (301) 468-2162.

- *Sports and Exercise for People with Diabetes.* A bibliography.

EXOTROPIA

Clearinghouses/Hotlines

The National Eye Institute (NEI) can give you up-to-date information on Exotropia by searching the Combined Health Information Database (CHID) and MEDLINE and sending you bibliographies of resources, along with any journal articles they may have. They can also refer you to any other organizations that study this and other related conditions. NEI will also let you know of any clinical studies that may be studying this disease and looking for patients. Because of their small staff, NEI prefers that you submit your requests for information in writing.

☎ Contact:
National Eye Institute
Bldg. 31, Room 6A32
Bethesda, MD 20892
(301) 496-5248

EXPERIMENTAL ALLERGIC ENCEPHALOMYELITIS

Clearinghouses/Hotlines

The National Institute of Neurological Disorders and Stroke (NINDS) can send you only information they have in their publications list on Experimental Allergic Encephalomyelitis (EAE). They cannot refer you to any experts. This Clearinghouse cannot directly give you information about any current clinical studies NINDS might be conducting on this illness, but you can find this information for yourself by looking under the National Institute of Neurological Disorders and Stroke in *Appendix A* at the end of this book.

☎ Contact:
National Institute of Neurological Disorders and Stroke
Bldg. 31, Room 8A06
Bethesda, MD 20892
(301) 496-5751
(800) 352-9424

EXTENDED CARE FACILITY

See Long Term Care
See Nursing Homes

EXTRACORPOREAL SHOCK-WAVE LITHOTRIPSY

Free Publications/Videos

The following publication on Extracorporeal Shock-Wave Lithotripsy is available from the National Institute of Diabetes and Digestive and Kidney Diseases, Bldg. 31, Room 9A04, Bethesda, MD 20892; (301) 496-3583.

- *Extracorporeal Shock-Wave Lithotripsy.* (#88-859)

EXTRAPYRAMIDAL DISORDERS

Clearinghouses/Hotlines

The National Institute of Neurological Disorders and Stroke (NINDS) can send you only information they have in their publications list on Extrapyramidal Disorders. They cannot refer you to any experts. This Clearinghouse cannot directly give you information about any current clinical studies NINDS might be conducting on this topic, but you can find this information for yourself by looking under the National Institute of Neurological Disorders and Stroke in *Appendix A* at the end of this book.

☎ Contact:
National Institute of Neurological
Disorders and Stroke
Bldg. 31, Room 8A06
Bethesda, MD 20892

(301) 496-5751
(800) 352-9424

EYE BANKS

Clearinghouses/Hotlines

The National Eye Institute (NEI) can give you up-to-date information on Eye Banks by searching the Combined Health Information Database (CHID) and MEDLINE and sending you bibliographies of resources, along with any journal articles they may have. They can also refer you to any other organizations that study this and other related subjects. NEI will also let you know of any clinical studies that may be studying this disease and looking for patients. Because of their small staff, NEI prefers that you submit your requests for information in writing.

☎ Contact:
National Eye Institute
Bldg. 31, Room 6A32
Bethesda, MD 20892
(301) 496-5248

EYE CARE

See also Vision
See also Contact Lenses

Clearinghouses/Hotlines

The National Eye Institute (NEI) conducts and supports research, including clinical studies, related to the cause, natural history, prevention, diagnosis, and treatment of disorders of the eye and visual system. Several brochures and reports are available on a wide variety of related topics.

☎ Contact:
National Eye Institute
Building 31
Room 6A32
Bethesda, MD 20892
(301) 496-5248

The Center for Devices and Radiological Health can provide you with information regarding the dangers of x-rays on the eyes.

☎ Contact:
Center for Devices and Radiological Health
Food and Drug Administration
HFZ-210
Rockville, MD 20857
(301) 443-4190

Free Publications/Videos

The following publications on Eye Care are available from the Center for Devices and Radiological Health, (HFZ-210), Food and Drug Administration, 5600 Fishers Ln., Rockville, MD 20857; (301) 443-4690.

- *Protecting Your Eyes From Everyday Hazards.*
- *Pursuing 20/20 at 40+.*
- *Ulcerative Keratitis.*
- *Eyeing Glasses: The Focus Is On Function.*
- *A Beholder Tells of a Lens Implant.*
- *IOL's New Lenses for Old Eyes.*

The following publication on Eye Care is available from the National Eye Institute, Bldg. 31, Room 6A32, Bethesda, MD 20892; (301) 496-5248.

- *Age-Related Macular Degeneration.* Explains how the eye works and how the degeneration occurs with the aging process. It tells how patients can check their own eyes and describes laser photocoagulation for treating this disease. (#85-2294)
- *Diabetes and Your Eyes.*

EYE EXERCISES

Clearinghouses/Hotlines

The National Eye Institute (NEI) can give you up-to-date information on Eye Exercises by searching the Combined Health Information Database (CHID) and MEDLINE and sending you bibliographies of resources, along with any journal articles they may have. They can also refer you to

any other organizations that study this and other related issues. Because of their small staff, NEI prefers that you submit your requests for information in writing.

☎ Contact:
National Eye Institute
Building 31, Room 6A32
Bethesda, MD 20892
(301) 496-5248

EYE TUMORS

Clearinghouses/Hotlines

The National Eye Institute (NEI) can give you up-to-date information on Eye Tumors by searching the Combined Health Information Database (CHID) and MEDLINE and sending you bibliographies of resources, along with any journal articles they may have. They can also refer you to any other organizations that study this and other related diseases. NEI will also let you know of any clinical studies that may be studying this disease and looking for patients. Because of their small staff, NEI prefers that you submit your requests for information in writing.

☎ Contact:
National Eye Institute
Building 31
Room 6A32
Bethesda, MD 20892
(301) 496-5248

- F -

FABRY'S DISEASE

Clearinghouses/Hotlines

The National Institute of Neurological Disorders and Stroke (NINDS) can send you only information they have in their publications list on Fabry's Disease. They cannot refer you to any experts. This Clearinghouse cannot directly give you information about any current clinical studies NINDS might be conducting on this illness, but you can find this information for yourself by looking under the National Institute of Neurological Disorders and Stroke in *Appendix A* at the end of this book.

☎ Contact:
National Institute of Neurological
Disorders and Stroke
Building 31
Room 8A06
Bethesda, MD 20892
(301) 496-5751
(800) 352-9424

The National Institute of Child Health and Human Development (NICHD) will send you whatever publications and reprints of journal articles they have on Fabry's Disease. If necessary, they will refer you to other experts or researchers in the field. If you can't afford treatment, have your doctor call NICHD to find out if they are conducting any clinical studies that you might qualify for.

☎ Contact:
National Institute of Child Health
and Human Development
Building 31
Room 2A32
Bethesda, MD 20892
(301) 496-5133

Free Publications/Videos

The following publication on Fabry's Disease is available from the National Institute of Neurological Disorders and Stroke, P.O. Box 5801, Bethesda, MD 20824; (800) 352-9424, or (301) 496-5751.

- *Fabry's Disease*. A collection of scientific articles, patient education pamphlets, and addresses of voluntary health associations.

FACE LIFTS

Clearinghouses/Hotlines

The Center for Devices and Radiological Health does not regulate Face Lifts, although they do have some information regarding the injection of liquid silicone for use in facial injections.

☎ Contact:
Center for Devices and Radiological Health
Food and Drug Administration, HFZ-210
Rockville, MD 20857
(301) 443-4190

Free Publications/Videos

The following publication is available from the Center for Devices and Radiological Health, (HFZ-210), Food and Drug Administration, 5600 Fishers Ln., Rockville, MD 20857; (301) 443-4690.

- *New Face Lift Not All Smiles.*

FACIAL TICS

Clearinghouses/Hotlines

The National Institute of Neurological Disorders and Stroke (NINDS) can send you only information they have in their publications list on Facial Tics (Tic Douloureux). They cannot refer you to any experts. This Clearinghouse cannot directly give you information about any current clinical studies NINDS might be conducting on this condition, but you can find this information for yourself by looking under the National Institute of Neurological Disorders and Stroke in *Appendix A* at the end of this book.

☎ Contact:
National Institute of Neurological
Disorders and Stroke
Bldg. 31, Room 8A06
Bethesda, MD 20892
(301) 496-5751
(800) 352-9424

FAINTING

Clearinghouses/Hotlines

The National Heart, Lung, and Blood Institute (NHLBI) can search the Combined Health Information Database (CHID) and generate a bibliography of resources on Fainting (Syncope) for you. They also will send you any publications and journal articles they may have on hand, and will refer you to other organizations that are studying this condition. If you can't afford treatment, have your doctor call NHLBI to find out if they are conducting any clinical studies that you might qualify for.

☎ Contact:
National Heart, Lung, and Blood Institute
Building 31
Room 4A21
Bethesda, MD 20892
(301) 496-4236

FALLS AND FRAILTY

See also Aging

Clearinghouses/Hotlines

The National Institute on Aging (NIA) will send you whatever publications and reprints of journal articles they have on Falls and Frailty. They cannot refer you to other experts if the information they have isn't sufficient for your purposes.

☎ Contact:
National Institute on Aging
Building 31
Room 5C27
Bethesda, MD 20892
(301) 496-1752

FAMILIAL ATAXIA TELANGIECTASIA

Clearinghouses/Hotlines

The National Cancer Institute (NCI) will send you whatever publications and reprints of journal articles they have on Familial Ataxia Telangiectasia. They can also give you information on the state-of-the-art treatment for this disease, including specific treatment information for your stage of cancer. They can also search their Physician's Data Query (PDQ) database to let you know if NCI is conducting any clinical studies on your disease.

☎ Contact:
National Cancer Institute
Building 31
Room 10A24
Bethesda, MD 20892
(800) 4-CANCER
(301) 496-5583

The National Institute of Neurological Disorders and Stroke (NINDS) can send you only information they have in their publications list on Familial Ataxia Telangiectasia. They cannot refer you to any experts. This Clearinghouse cannot directly give you information about any current clinical studies NINDS might be conducting on this illness, but you can find this information for yourself by looking under the National Institute of Neurological Disorders and Stroke in *Appendix A* at the end of this book.

☎ Contact:
National Institute of Neurological Disorders and Stroke
Building 31
Room 8A06
Bethesda, MD 20892
(301) 496-5751
(800) 352-9424

FAMILIAL MULTIPLE ENDOCRINE NEOPLASIA

Free Publications/Videos

The following publication is available from the National Institute of Diabetes and Digestive and Kidney Diseases, Bldg. 31, Room 9A04, Bethesda, MD 20892; (301) 496-3583.

- *Familial Multiple Endocrine Neoplasia Type 1.* (#92-3048)

FAMILIAL SPASTIC PARAPARESIS

Clearinghouses/Hotlines

The National Institute of Neurological Disorders and Stroke (NINDS) can send you only information they have in their publications list on Familial Spastic Paraparesis. They cannot refer you to any experts. This Clearinghouse cannot directly give you information about any current clinical studies NINDS might be conducting on this illness, but you can find this information for yourself by looking under the National Institute of Neurological Disorders and Stroke in *Appendix A* at the end of this book.

☎ Contact:
National Institute of Neurological
Disorders and Stroke
Bldg. 31, Room 8A06
Bethesda, MD 20892
(301) 496-5751
(800) 352-9424

FAMILY HEALTH

Clearinghouses/Hotlines

The U.S. Department of Agriculture's Family Information Center will answer your questions about families throughout the lifecycle, from marital relationships and childbearing families to empty nest families and retirement. They also deal with matters concerning social environment and family economics education.

☎ Contact:
U.S. Department of Agriculture
Family Information Center
National Agricultural Library, Room 304
Beltsville, MD 20705
(301) 504-5204

The National Institute on Aging (NIA) will send you whatever publications and reprints of journal articles they have on Family and Aging. They cannot refer you to other experts if the information they have isn't sufficient for your purposes.

☎ Contact:
National Institute on Aging
Bldg. 31, Room 5C27
Bethesda, MD 20892
(301) 496-1752

Free Publications/Videos

The following publication is available from the National Health Information Center, P.O. Box 1133, Washington, DC 20013; (800) 336-4797, or (301) 565-4167 in DC metro area.

- *Family Care.* Lists organizations, self-help and support groups, as well as books about home care for the chronically or terminally ill or the disabled child or aging parent. Suggested resources for preparing for death such as living wills and organ or tissue donation are also included.

FAMILY & MEDICAL LEAVE

Free Publications/Videos

The following Congressional Research Service (CRS) reports on Family and Medical Leave are available from either of your U.S. Senators' offices at the U.S. Capitol, Washington, DC 20510, or from your Congressional Representative at the U.S. Capitol, Washington, DC 20515. You can also call in your request through the U.S. Capitol switchboard at (202) 224-3121. Be sure to include the full title and report number in your request.

- *Parental leave: Info Pack.* (#IP367P)
- *Family and Medical Leave Legislation: Summary Comparison of H.R. 2, S. 5, H.R. 319, S 418, and S. 688.* (#91-434 GOV)
- *Maternity and Parental Leave Policies: A Comparative Analysis.* (#85-148 GOV)
- *Parental Leave: Legislation in the 100th Congress; Issue Brief.* (#IB86132)

FAMILY PLANNING

See also Contraception

Clearinghouses/Hotlines

The National Institute of Child Health and Human Development (NICHD) will send you whatever publications and reprints of journal articles they have on Family Planning Research. If necessary, they will refer you to other experts or researchers in the field.

☎ Contact:
National Institute of Child Health
and Human Development
Bldg. 31, Room 2A32
Bethesda, MD 20892
(301) 496-5133

The Family Life Information Exchange (FLIE) provides information on Family Planning, adolescent pregnancy, and adoption. FLIE's primary audience consists of federally supported service agencies, but it also provides information to family planning service providers, educators, trainers, and consumers throughout the U.S.

☎ Contact:
Family Life Information Exchange
P.O. Box 37299
Washington, DC 20013
(301) 585-6636

Free Publications/Videos

The following publications on Family Planning are available from the Family Life Information Exchange, P.O. Box 37299, Washington, DC 20013; (301) 585-6636.

- *Information for Men: Your Sterilization Operation.*
- *Information for Women: Your Sterilization Operation.*
- *Many Teens are Saying "NO".*
- *Trends in Adolescent Pregnancy and Child-bearing.*
- *Teenage Pregnancy and Fertility in the U.S.*
- *Your Contraceptive Choices: For Now, For Later.*
- *OPA Program Instructions: Norplant Education in Title X.*
- *Program Guidelines for Project Grants for Family Planning Services.*
- *The Adoption Option, Guidebook for Pregnancy Counselors.*
- *OAPP Funded Curricula.*
- *AFL Research Projects Summary.*
- *Family Planning Grantees, Delegates, and Clinics 1991/1992 Directory.*
- *Title X National Family Planning Program Fact Sheet.*
- *Recommendations for Prevention of HIV in Health Care Settings*
- *PHS Guidelines for Counseling and Testing to Prevent HIV & AIDS.*
- *OPA Program Instructions: AIDS Education in Title X.*
- *Family and Adolescent Pregnancy.*
- *Adolescent Abstinence: A Guide for Family Planning Professionals.*
- *Improving the Quality of Clinician Pap Smear.*
- *AFL Demonstration Projects: Program and Evaluation Summaries.*
- *Sexually Transmitted Diseases Treatment Guidelines.*

The following Congressional Research Service (CRS) reports on Family Planning are available from either of your U.S. Senators' offices at the U.S. Capitol, Washington, DC 20510, or from your Congressional Representative at the U.S. Capitol, Washington, DC 20515. You can also call in your request through the U.S. Capitol switchboard at (202) 224-3121. Be sure to include the full title and report number in your request.

- *Family Planning: Title X of the Public Health Service Act: Issue Brief.* (IB88005)
- *Family Planning: Title X of the Public Health Service Act: Issue Brief.* (IB91096)

FAMILY VIOLENCE

Clearinghouses/Hotlines

The Clearinghouse on Family Violence Information can send you all kinds of information on spouse and elder abuse including brochures, audiovisual materials, and an in-house database from which they can retrieve reference materials and organizations involved with family violence.

☎ Contact:
Clearinghouse on Family Violence Information
P.O. Box 1182
Washington, DC 20013
(703) 385-7565

Free Publications/Videos

The following publication is available from the Consumer Information Center, P.O. Box 100, Pueblo, CO 81002.

- *Plain Talk About Wife Abuse.* (#567Y)

FANCONI'S ANEMIA

Clearinghouses/Hotlines

The National Heart, Lung, and Blood Institute (NHLBI) can search the Combined Health Information Database (CHID) and generate a bibliography of resources on Fanconi's Anemia for you. They also will send you any publications and journal articles they may have on hand, and will refer you to other organizations that are studying this disease. If you can't afford treatment, have

your doctor call NHLBI to find out if they are conducting any clinical studies that you might qualify for.

☎ Contact:
National Heart, Lung, and Blood Institute
Bldg. 31, Room 4A21
Bethesda, MD 20892
(301) 496-4236

FARMERS LUNG

Clearinghouses/Hotlines

The National Institute of Occupational Safety and Health (NIOSH) can provide you with information regarding Farmers Lung, which is a lung disease caused by moldy hay. NIOSH can search their data base and provide you with reprints of articles, reference materials, and more.

☎ Contact:
National Institute of Occupational
Safety and Health
4676 Columbia Parkway
MS C-19
Cincinnati, OH 45226
(800) 35-NIOSH

FARSIGHTEDNESS

Clearinghouses/Hotlines

The National Eye Institute (NEI) can give you up-to-date information on Farsightedness by searching the Combined Health Information Database (CHID) and MEDLINE and sending you bibliographies of resources, along with any journal articles they may have. They can also refer you to any other organizations that study this and other related conditions. NEI will also let you know of any clinical studies that may be studying this disease and looking for patients. Because of their small staff, NEI prefers that you submit your requests for information in writing.

☎ Contact:
National Eye Institute

Bldg. 31, Room 6A32
Bethesda, MD 20892
(301) 496-5248

through the U.S. Capitol switchboard at (202) 224-3121. Be sure to include the full title and report number in your request.

- *Fast Food Restaurant Labeling.* (#87-736 SPR)

FASCIOLIASIS

Clearinghouses/Hotlines

The National Institute of Allergy and Infectious Diseases Clearinghouse can provide you with information regarding Fascioliasis, which is a disease of the liver which is caused by eating uncooked aquatic plants.

☎ Contact:
National Institute of Allergy
and Infectious Diseases
Bldg. 31, Room 7A32
Bethesda, MD 20892
(301) 496-5717

FAST FOOD

See also Food

Clearinghouses/Hotlines

The Food and Drug Administration has information on the nutritional value and other concerns dealing with Fast Food.

☎ Contact:
Food and Drug Administration
HFE-88
5600 Fishers Lane
Rockville, MD 20857
(301) 443-3170

Free Publications/Videos

The following Congressional Research Service (CRS) report is available from either of your U.S. Senators' offices at the U.S. Capitol, Washington, DC 20510, or from your Congressional Representative at the U.S. Capitol, Washington, DC 20515. You can also call in your request

FASTING

Clearinghouses/Hotlines

The Food and Nutrition Information Center can provide you with a wealth of information on food and nutrition topics. They have bibliographies ready and a data base through which they can search any food or nutrition subject.

☎ Contact:
Food and Nutrition Information Center
National Agricultural Library
Room 304
Beltsville, MD 20705
(301) 504-5719

FATHERHOOD

Clearinghouses/Hotlines

The National Institute of Child Health and Human Development (NICHD) can send you information on fetal, maternal and child development, as well as materials on reproductive biology, contraception, mental retardation, and a host of other related fields.

☎ Contact:
National Institute of Child Health
and Human Development
Bldg. 31, Room 2A32
Bethesda, MD 20892
(301) 496-5133

Free Publications/Videos

The following publication on Adolescent Fatherhood is available from the National

Maternal and Child Health Clearinghouse, 38th and R Sts., NW, Washington, DC 20057; (703) 821-8955, ext. 254.

- *Adolescent Fathers*. A resource directory geared to help unwed adolescent fathers accept their responsibilities. It lists, state-by-state, services and outreach programs currently available to help adolescent fathers.

FAT SUBSTITUTES

See also Food
See also Nutrition

Free Publications/Videos

The following publication on Fat Substitutes is available from the Food & Drug Administration, (HFE-88), 5600 Fishers Ln., Rockville, MD 20857; (301) 443-3170.

- *Fat Substitutes. A Taste of the Future?* (#FDA91-2247)

FEBRILE CONVULSIONS

Clearinghouses/Hotlines

The National Institute of Neurological Disorders and Stroke (NINDS) can send you only information they have in their publications list on Febrile Convulsions. They cannot refer you to any experts. This Clearinghouse cannot directly give you information about any current clinical studies NINDS might be conducting on this condition, but you can find this information for yourself by looking under the National Institute of Neurological Disorders and Stroke in *Appendix A* at the end of this book.

☎ Contact:
National Institute of Neurological
Disorders and Stroke
Bldg. 31, Room 8A06

Bethesda, MD 20892
(301) 496-5751
(800) 352-9424

FEBRILE SEIZURES

Clearinghouses/Hotlines

The National Institute of Child Health and Human Development (NICHD) will send you whatever publications and reprints of journal articles they have on Febrile Seizures. If necessary, they will refer you to other experts or researchers in the field. If you can't afford treatment, have your doctor call NICHD to find out if they are conducting any clinical studies that you might qualify for.

☎ Contact:
National Institute of Child Health
and Human Development
Building 31
Room 2A32
Bethesda, MD 20892
(301) 496-5133

FEEDING IMPAIRMENTS

Clearinghouses/Hotlines

The National Institute of Dental Research (NIDR) will send you whatever publications and reprints of journal articles they have on Feeding Impairments. As a policy, NIDR will not refer you to other organizations or experts who study this issue. If you can't afford treatment, have your doctor call Dr. Albert Guckers at (301) 496-6241 to find out if NIDR is conducting any clinical studies that you might qualify for.

☎ Contact:
National Institute of Dental Research
Building 31
Room 2C35
Bethesda, MD 20892
(301) 496-4261

FEET

Free Publications/Videos

The following publication on Feet is available from the Office of Clinical Center Communications, Bldg. 10, Room 1C255, Bethesda, MD 20892; (301) 496-2563.

- *Your Problem Feet: Care and Management.* Video to help the general public make intelligent decisions.

The following videos on Feet are available from the Modern Talking Picture Service, 5000 Park St. North, St. Petersburg, FL 33709; (800) 243-MTPS.

- *As Young As Your Feet.* Video stresses importance of good foot health for older Americans.
- *Feet: A Key To Keeping Fit.* Video discusses the use of orthoses for athletes to prevent sports injuries.

FERTILITY

Clearinghouses/Hotlines

The National Institute of Child Health and Human Development (NICHD) will send you whatever publications and reprints of journal articles they have on Fertility and Fertility Drugs. If necessary, they will refer you to other experts or researchers in the field. If you can't afford treatment, have your doctor call NICHD to find out if they are conducting any clinical studies that you might qualify for.

☎ Contact:
National Institute of Child Health
and Human Development
Building 31
Room 2A32
Bethesda, MD 20892
(301) 496-5133

FETAL ALCOHOL SYNDROME

Clearinghouses/Hotlines

The National Institute of Child Health and Human Development (NICHD) will send you whatever publications and reprints of journal articles they have on Fetal Alcohol Syndrome. If necessary, they will refer you to other experts or researchers in the field. If you can't afford treatment, have your doctor call NICHD to find out if they are conducting any clinical studies that you might qualify for.

☎ Contact:
National Institute of Child Health
and Human Development
Bldg. 31, Room 2A32
Bethesda, MD 20892
(301) 496-5133

The National Clearinghouse for Alcohol and Drug Information is the central point within the Federal Government for current print and audiovisual materials about alcohol and other drugs. They have information tailored to parents, teachers, youth, and others, as well as information about organizations and groups concerned with alcohol and other drug problems. They have publications, reports, newsletters, videos, posters, and more, as well as being able to provide comprehensive alcohol and other drug resource referrals. Call for your free catalog.

☎ Contact:
National Clearinghouse for Alcohol
and Drug Information
P.O. Box 2345
Rockville, MD 20852
(800) 729-6686
(301) 468-2600

FETAL MONITORING

See also Sudden Infant Death Syndrome

Clearinghouses/Hotlines

The National Institute of Child Health and Human Development (NICHD) will send you whatever publications and reprints of journal articles they have on Fetal Monitoring. If necessary, they will refer you to other experts or researchers in the field.

☎ Contact:
National Institute of Child Health
and Human Development
Bldg. 31, Room 2A32
Bethesda, MD 20892
(301) 496-5133

FETAL RESEARCH

Free Publications/Videos

The following Congressional Research Service (CRS) reports on human Fetal Research are available from either of your U.S. Senators' offices at the U.S. Capitol, Washington, DC 20510, or from your Congressional Representative at the U.S. Capitol, Washington, DC 20515. You can also call in your request through the U.S. Capitol switchboard at (202) 224-3121. Be sure to include the full title and report number in your request.

- *Fetal Research: A Survey of State Law.*
  (#88-198 A)
- *Human Fetal Research and Tissue Transplantation: Issue Brief.* (#IB88100)

FEVERS

Clearinghouses/Hotlines

The National Institute on Allergy and Infectious Diseases (NIAID) can search the Combined Health Information Database (CHID) and generate a bibliography of resources on Recurrent Fevers for you. They will also send you any publications and journal articles they may have on hand, and will refer you to researchers who are

currently studying this subject. If you can't afford treatment, have your doctor call NIAID to find out if they are conducting any clinical studies that you might qualify for.

☎ Contact:
National Institute of Allergy
and Infectious Diseases
Bldg. 31, Room 7A32
Bethesda, MD 20892
(301) 496-5717

FEVER BLISTERS

Clearinghouses/Hotlines

The National Institute of Dental Research (NIDR) will send you whatever publications and reprints of journal articles they have on Fever Blisters. As a policy, NIDR will not refer you to other organizations or experts who study this condition. If you can't afford treatment, have your doctor call Dr. Albert Guckers at (301) 496-6241 to find out if NIDR is conducting any clinical studies that you might qualify for.

☎ Contact:
National Institute of Dental Research
Bldg. 31, Room 2C35
Bethesda, MD 20892
(301) 496-4261

Free Publications/Videos

The following publication on Fever Blisters is available from the National Institute of Dental Research, Bldg. 31, Room 2C35, Bethesda, MD 20892; (301) 496-4261.

- *Fever Blisters and Canker Sores.* (#87-247)

FIBER

Free Publications/Videos

The following publication on Fiber is available from the Food & Drug Administration, (HFE-88),

5600 Fishers Ln., Rockville, MD 20857; (301) 443-3170.

- *Fiber: Something Healthy to Chew On.*
    Discusses the role of fiber in nutrition. (#85-2206)

FIBRILLATION

Clearinghouses/Hotlines

The National Heart, Lung, and Blood Institute (NHLBI) can search the Combined Health Information Database (CHID) and generate a bibliography of resources on Fibrillation for you. They also will send you any publications and journal articles they may have on hand, and will refer you to other organizations that are studying this subject. If you can't afford treatment, have your doctor call NHLBI to find out if they are conducting any clinical studies that you might qualify for.

☎ Contact:
National Heart, Lung, and Blood Institute
Bldg. 31, Room 4A21
Bethesda, MD 20892
(301) 496-4236

FIBRINOLYSIS

Clearinghouses/Hotlines

The National Heart, Lung, and Blood Institute (NHLBI) can search the Combined Health Information Database (CHID) and generate a bibliography of resources on Fibrinolysis for you. They also will send you any publications and journal articles they may have on hand, and will refer you to other organizations that are studying this subject. If you can't afford treatment, have your doctor call NHLBI to find out if they are conducting any clinical studies that you might qualify for.

☎ Contact:
National Heart, Lung, and Blood Institute

Bldg. 31, Room 4A21
Bethesda, MD 20892
(301) 496-4236

FIBROCYSTIC DISEASE OF THE BREAST

Clearinghouses/Hotlines

The National Cancer Institute (NCI) can provide you with information regarding Fibrocystic Disease of the Breast. They have a publication, listed below, and can search their medical texts for more information.

☎ Contact:
National Cancer Institute
Bldg. 31, Room 10A24
Bethesda, MD 20892
(800) 4-CANCER
(301) 496-5583

Free Publications/Videos

The following publication is available from the National Cancer Institute, Bldg. 31, Room 10A24, Bethesda, MD 20892; (800) 4-CANCER or (301) 496-5583.

- *Questions and Answers Regarding Breast Lumps.* Explains breast lumps, their causes, as well as breast exams.

FIBROID TUMORS

Clearinghouses/Hotlines

The National Institute of Child Health and Human Development (NICHD) will send you whatever publications and reprints of journal articles they have on Fibroid Tumors. If necessary, they will refer you to other experts or researchers in the field. If you can't afford treatment, have your doctor call NICHD to find out if they are conducting any clinical studies that you might qualify for.

☎ Contact:
National Institute of Child Health
and Human Development
Bldg. 31, Room 2A32
Bethesda, MD 20892
(301) 496-5133

FIBROMUSCULAR HYPERPLASIA

Clearinghouses/Hotlines

The National Institute of Arthritis and Musculoskeletal and Skin Diseases (NIAMS) will send you whatever publications and reprints of articles from texts and journals they have on Fibromuscular Hyperplasia. They will also refer you to other organizations that are studying this disease. NIAMS will also let you know of any clinical studies that may be studying this disease and looking for patients.

☎ Contact:
National Institute of Arthritis
and Musculoskeletal and Skin Diseases
Box AMS
Bethesda, MD 20892
(301) 495-4484

The National Heart, Lung and Blood Institute (NHLBI) has information on Fibromuscular Hyperplasia, including research reports and descriptive information, which they will send to you for free.

☎ Contact:
National Heart, Lung and Blood Institute
Bldg. 31, Room 4A21
Bethesda, MD 20892
(301) 496-4236

FIBROMYALGIA

Clearinghouses/Hotlines

The National Institute of Arthritis and Musculoskeletal and Skin Diseases (NIAMS) will send you whatever publications and reprints of articles from texts and journals they have on Fibromyalgia. They will also refer you to other organizations that are studying this disease. NIAMS will also let you know of any clinical studies that may be studying this disease and looking for patients.

☎ Contact:
National Institute of Arthritis
and Musculoskeletal and Skin Diseases
Box AMS
Bethesda, MD 20892
(301) 495-4484

FIBROSITIS

Clearinghouses/Hotlines

The National Institute of Arthritis and Musculoskeletal and Skin Diseases (NIAMS) will send you whatever publications and reprints of articles from texts and journals they have on Fibrositis. They will also refer you to other organizations that are studying this disease. NIAMS will also let you know of any clinical studies that may be studying this disease and looking for patients.

☎ Contact:
National Institute of Arthritis
and Musculoskeletal and Skin Diseases
Box AMS
Bethesda, MD 20892
(301) 495-4484

FIBROTIC LUNG DISEASES

Clearinghouses/Hotlines

The National Heart, Lung, and Blood Institute (NHLBI) can search the Combined Health Information Database (CHID) and generate a bibliography of resources on Fibrotic Lung Diseases for you. They also will send you any publications and journal articles they may have on hand, and will refer you to other organizations that are studying this technique. If you can't afford treatment, have your doctor call NHLBI to find out if they are conducting any clinical studies that you might qualify for.

☎ Contact:
National Heart, Lung, and Blood Institute
Bldg. 31, Room 4A21
Bethesda, MD 20892
(301) 496-4236

FIBROUS DYSPLASIA

Clearinghouses/Hotlines

The National Institute of Neurological Disorders and Stroke (NINDS) can send you only information they have in their publications list on Fibrous Dysplasia. They cannot refer you to any experts. This Clearinghouse cannot directly give you information about any current clinical studies NINDS might be conducting on this illness, but you can find this information for yourself by looking under the National Institute of Neurological Disorders and Stroke in *Appendix A* at the end of this book.

☎ Contact:
National Institute of Neurological
Disorders and Stroke
Bldg. 31, Room 8A06
Bethesda, MD 20892
(301) 496-5751
(800) 352-9424

The National Institute of Arthritis and Musculoskeletal and Skin Diseases (NIAMS) will send you whatever publications and reprints of articles from texts and journals they have on Fibrous Dysplasia. They will also refer you to other organizations that are studying this disease. NIAMS will also let you know of any clinical studies that may be studying this disease and looking for patients.

☎ Contact:
National Institute of Arthritis
and Musculoskeletal and Skin Diseases
Box AMS
Bethesda, MD 20892

(301) 495-4484

FIFTH DISEASE

Clearinghouses/Hotlines

The National Institute on Allergy and Infectious Diseases (NIAID) can search the Combined Health Information Database (CHID) and generate a bibliography of resources on Fifth Disease for you. They will also send you any publications and journal articles they may have on hand, and will refer you to researchers who are currently studying this disease. If you can't afford treatment, have your doctor call NIAID to find out if they are conducting any clinical studies that you might qualify for.

☎ Contact:
National Institute of Allergy
and Infectious Diseases
Bldg. 31, Room 7A32
Bethesda, MD 20892
(301) 496-5717

FILARIASIS

Clearinghouses/Hotlines

The National Institute on Allergy and Infectious Diseases (NIAID) can search the Combined Health Information Database (CHID) and generate a bibliography of resources on Filariasis for you. They will also send you any publications and journal articles they may have on hand, and will refer you to researchers who are currently studying this subject. If you can't afford treatment, have your doctor call NIAID to find out if they are conducting any clinical studies that you might qualify for.

☎ Contact:
National Institute of Allergy
and Infectious Diseases
Bldg. 31, Room 7A32
Bethesda, MD 20892
(301) 496-5717

FIRST AID

Free Publications/Videos

The following publication is available from the Superintendent of Documents, Government Printing Office, Washington, DC 20402; (202) 783-3238.

- *First Aid Book*. Recommends procedures for dealing with emergencies which require first aid. It includes sections on human anatomy and patient assessment, artificial ventilation, CPR, control of bleeding, shock, wounds and dressings, and more. ($6.50)

FLOATERS

Clearinghouses/Hotlines

The National Eye Institute (NEI) can give you up-to-date information on Floaters by searching the Combined Health Information Database (CHID) and MEDLINE and sending you bibliographies of resources, along with any journal articles they may have. They can also refer you to any other organizations that study this and other related condition. NEI will also let you know of any clinical studies that may be studying Floaters and looking for patients. Because of their small staff, NEI prefers that you submit your requests for information in writing.

☎ Contact:
National Eye Institute
Bldg. 31, Room 6A32
Bethesda, MD 20892
(301) 496-5248

FLOPPY BABY

Clearinghouses/Hotlines

The National Institute of Neurological Disorders and Stroke (NINDS) can send you only information they have in their publications list on Floppy Baby (Nemaline Myopathy). They cannot refer you to any experts. This Clearinghouse cannot directly give you information about any current clinical studies NINDS might be conducting on this topic, but you can find this information for yourself by looking under the National Institute of Neurological Disorders and Stroke in *Appendix A* at the end of this book.

☎ Contact:
National Institute of Neurological
Disorders and Stroke
Bldg. 31, Room 8A06
Bethesda, MD 20892
(301) 496-5751
(800) 352-9424

FLOXIRIDINE

Free Publications/Videos

The following publication on Floxiridine is available from the National Cancer Institute, Bldg. 31, Room 10A24, Bethesda, MD 20892; (800) 4-CANCER, or (301) 496-5583.

- *Floxiridina/Floxuridine*. Provides information about side effects, proper usage, and precautions of this anti-cancer drug.

FLU

Clearinghouses/Hotlines

The National Institute on Allergy and Infectious Diseases (NIAID) can search the Combined Health Information Database (CHID) and generate a bibliography of resources on the Flu for you. They will also send you any publications and journal articles they may have on hand, and will refer you to researchers who are currently studying this condition. If you can't afford treatment, have your doctor call NIAID to find out if they are conducting any clinical studies that you might qualify for.

☎ Contact:
National Institute of Allergy
and Infectious Diseases
Building 31
Room 7A32
Bethesda, MD 20892
(301) 496-5717

The Centers for Disease Control has set up a special hotline number from which you can get all kinds of information sent to you on several diseases and health areas, including symptoms and prevention methods, immunization requirements, current statistics, recent disease outbreaks, and available printed materials. One of the illnesses you can learn more about is the Flu. The hotline will tell you about the different strains of flu currently going around the country, as well as the immunization available. If you need more information than the message provides, you have the option of being put in contact with a public health professional who will point you in the right direction. The system is available 24 hours a day, although the health professionals are available Monday-Friday, 8 a.m.-4:30 p.m.

☎ Contact:
Disease Hotline
(404) 332-4555

Free Publications/Videos

The following publication on Flu is available from the National Institute of Allergy and Infectious Diseases, Bldg. 31, Room 7A32, Bethesda, MD 20892; (301) 496-5717.

- *Flu.* (#87-187)

The following publication on Flu Shots is available from the Food & Drug Administration, (HFE-88), 5600 Fishers Ln., Rockville, MD 20857; (301) 443-3170.

- *Flu Shots. Do You Need One?* (#FDA90-3175)

FLUORESCEIN ANGIOGRAPHY

Clearinghouses/Hotlines

The National Eye Institute (NEI) can give you up-to-date information on Fluorescein Angiography by searching the Combined Health Information Database (CHID) and MEDLINE and sending you bibliographies of resources, along with any journal articles they may have. They can also refer you to any other organizations that study this procedure. NEI will also let you know of any clinical studies that may be studying this subject and looking for patients. Because of their small staff, NEI prefers that you submit your requests for information in writing.

☎ Contact:
National Eye Institute
Bldg. 31, Room 6A32
Bethesda, MD 20892
(301) 496-5248

FLUORESCENT LAMPS

Free Publications/Videos

The following publication is available from the Center for Devices and Radiological Health, (HFZ-210), Food and Drug Administration, 5600 Fishers Ln., Rockville, MD 20857; (301) 443-4690.

- *Fact Sheet: Fluorescent Lamps.*

FLUORIDATION

Clearinghouses/Hotlines

The National Institute of Dental Research (NIDR) will send you whatever publications and reprints of journal articles they have on Fluoridation. As a policy, NIDR will not refer you to other organizations or experts who study this disease. If you can't afford treatment, have your doctor call Dr. Albert Guckers at (301) 496-6241 to find out if NIDR is conducting any clinical studies that you might qualify for.

☎ Contact:
National Institute of Dental Research
Bldg. 31, Room 2C35
Bethesda, MD 20892
(301) 496-4261

Free Publications/Videos

The following publications on Fluoridation are available from the National Institute of Dental Research, Bldg. 31, Room 2C35, Bethesda, MD 20892; (301) 496-4261.

- *Fluoride Mouthrinsing in Schools...Protection for Children's Teeth.* (#82-1131)
- *A Healthy Start...Fluoride Tablets for Children in Preschool Programs.* (#82-1838)
- *Fluoride to Protect the Teeth of Adults.* (#87-2329)

FLUOROSCOPY

Free Publications/Videos

The following publication is available from the Center for Devices and Radiological Health, (HFZ-210), Food and Drug Administration, 5600 Fishers Ln., Rockville, MD 20857; (301) 443-4690.

- *Fact Sheet: Fluoroscopy.*

FLUOROSIS

Clearinghouses/Hotlines

The National Institute of Dental Research (NIDR) will send you whatever publications and reprints of journal articles they have on Fluorosis. As a policy, NIDR will not refer you to other

organizations or experts who study this disease. If you can't afford treatment, have your doctor call Dr. Albert Guckers at (301) 496-6241 to find out if NIDR is conducting any clinical studies that you might qualify for.

☎ Contact:
National Institute of Dental Research
Bldg. 31, Room 2C35
Bethesda, MD 20892
(301) 496-4261

FLUOROURACIL

Free Publications/Videos

The following publication is available from the National Cancer Institute, Bldg. 31, Room 10A24, Bethesda, MD 20892; (800) 4-CANCER, or (301) 496-5583.

- *Fluorouracilo/Fluorouracil.* Provides information about side effects, proper usage, and precautions of this anti-cancer drug.

FOOD

See also Nutrition

Clearinghouses/Hotlines

The Food Marketing and Economics Branch of the Economics Research Service produces studies and will share their expertise on such topics as the convenience food markets, food purchases away from home, the fast food industry, the relationship between consumer attitudes about nutrition and actual food expenditures, and the economic effects of food safety regulations.

☎ Contact:
Food Marketing and Economics Branch
Economics Research Service
1301 New York Ave., NW
Washington, DC 20005-4788
(202) 786-1862

The U.S. Department of Agriculture's Meat & Poultry Hotline inspects and analyzes domestic and imported meat and poultry and establishes standards for processed meat and poultry products. They will answer your questions about the proper handling, preparation, and refrigeration, food poisoning, food additives, food labeling, sodium, and herbs.

☎ Contact:
U.S. Department of Agriculture
Room 1165-S
Washington, DC 20205
(800) 535-4555
(202) 447-9351

Food and Nutrition Information Center can provide you with a wealth of information on food and nutrition topics. They have bibliographies ready and a data base through which they can search any food or nutrition subject.

☎ Contact:
Food and Nutrition Information Center
National Agricultural Library
Room 304
Beltsville, MD 20705
(301) 504-5719

The Center for Food Safety and Applied Nutrition regulates what has to be on food labels, as well as food additives, and food safety. If you have a question regarding a food label, food label requirements, or if you find some foreign material in your non-meat food product, this office can be of assistance.

☎ Contact:
Center for Food Safety
and Applied Nutrition
Food and Drug Administration
Office of Constituents
200 C Street, SW, HFF-11
Washington, DC 20204
(202) 205-4317

The Human Nutrition Information Service (HNIS) shares its research in nutritive value of foods and of the nutritional adequacy of diets and food supplies. It also maintains the Nutrient Data Bank which contains surveys and data on the nutrient values in foods and descriptions of foods. Various consumer materials are available as well as a publications list including over 20 publications on the nutrient composition of foods. HNIS has several publications dealing with dietary guidelines for Americans, which are seven basic principles for developing and maintaining a healthier diet and are the basis for all Federal nutrition information and education programs for healthy Americans.

☎ Contact:
Human Nutrition Information Service
U.S. Department of Agriculture
6505 Belcrest Rd., Room 363
Hyattsville, MD 20782
(301) 436-8617

The Food and Nutrition Service (FNS) publishes a variety of brochures explaining the various food assistance programs it operates both for those eligible for the programs and for those who administer them. Programs include the Child Nutrition Program, Food Distribution Program, Women, Infants, and Children (WIC) Program, Food Stamp Program, and various nutrition education materials. You can contact FNS for a publications list, and most publications are free.

☎ Contact:
Food and Nutrition Service
3101 Park Center Dr.
Park Office Bldg.
Alexandria, VA 22302
(703) 305-2554

Free Publications/Videos

The following publication on Food Consumption is available from the U.S. Department of Agriculture, 6505 Belcrest Rd., Room 368, Hyattsville, MD 20782; (301) 436-8498.

- *Nationwide Food Consumption Survey.* (NFCS 1987-88) Conducted every 10 years, this survey provides comprehensive information on the consumption of foods and nutrients and on the dietary status of U.S. households and individuals.

The following publication on Food is available from the National Institute of Allergy and Infectious Diseases, Bldg. 31, Room 7A32, Bethesda, MD 20892; (301) 496-5717.

- *Adverse Reactions to Foods.* (#84-2442)

The following publications on Food are available from the Food & Drug Admin., (HFE-88), 5600 Fishers Ln., Rockville, MD 20857; (301) 443-3170.

- *The Consumer's Guide to Food Labels.* Translates the nutrition information that appears on food labels. (#85-2083)
- *Food and Drug Interactions.* Explains why some foods and medicines may interfere with each other, and suggests whys to avoid the problem. (#94-3070)
- *More Than You Ever Thought You Would Know About Food Additives.* (#82-2160)
- *Sweetness Minus Calories = Controversy.* (#85-2205)
- *Getting Information from FDA...* about drugs, foods, pesticides, medical devices, radiation safety, pet foods, and more. (593Z).

The following Food publications are available from the Food and Nutrition Information Center, National Agricultural Library, Room 304, Beltsville, MD 20705; (301) 504-5719.

- *Cultural Perspectives on Food and Nutrition.* A list of current references.
- *Food Safety: Ready-Prepared Foods.* A list to help you locate further information or resources.
- *Food Service: Printed Materials and Audio-visuals.* A list of current references.
- *Nutrient Composition of Selected Grains as Food, January 1986 -- September 1990.* A list of current resources. (#QB91-34)
- *Pesticide Residues in Food.* A list of current references.

The following Food publication is available from the National Heart, Lung and Blood Institute, Bldg. 31, Room 4A21, Bethesda, MD 20892; (301) 496-4236.

- *Eating With Your Heart in Mind.* (#3100). This booklet is for children ages 7 to 10, particularly those with high blood cholesterol.

The following Food publication is available from the National Institute on Aging Information Clearinghouse, 2209 Distribution Circle, Silver Spring, MD 20910; (301) 495-3455.

- *Food: Staying Healthy After 65*.

The following publications on Food Safety are available from the Consumer Information Center, P.O. Box 100, Pueblo, CO 81002.

- *Preventing Food-Borne Illness.* (#534Y)
- *Quick Consumer Guide to Safe Food Handling.* (#535Y)
- *Weighing Food Safety Risks.* (#537Y)

The following publications on Food are available from Human Nutrition Information Service, U.S. Department of Agriculture, 6505 Belcrest Rd., Room 363, Hyattsville, MD 20782; (301) 436-8617.

- *Nutrition and Your Health: Dietary Guidelines for Americans.* (free, also in Spanish)
- *Dietary Guidelines and Your Diet.* ($4.50)
- *Preparing Foods and Planning Menus Using the Dietary Guidelines.* ($2.50)
- *Making Bag Lunches, Snacks, and Desserts Using the Dietary Guidelines.* ($2.50)
- *Shopping for Food and Making Meals in Minutes Using the Dietary Guidelines.* ($3.00)
- *Eating Better When Eating Out Using the Dietary Guidelines.* ($1.50)
- *Calories and Weight: The USDA Pocket Guide.* ($1.75)
- *Nutritive Value of Foods.* ($3.75)
- *Your Money's Worth in Foods.* ($2.25)
- *The Sodium Content of Your Food.* ($2.25)
- *Thrifty Meals for Two: Making Your Food Dollars Count.* ($2.50)
- *Cooking for People with Food Allergies.* ($1.50)
- *Good Sources of Nutrients.* ($5.00)

FOOD ADDITIVES

Clearinghouses/Hotlines

The Center for Food Safety and Applied Nutrition regulates what has to be on food labels, as well as Food Additives, and food safety. If you have a question regarding a food additive, such as what is an additive or the amount allowed, this Office can be of assistance. They also respond to inquiries regarding reactions to food additives.

☎ Contact:
Center for Food Safety
and Applied Nutrition
Food and Drug Administration
Office of Constituents
200 C Street, SW, HFF-11
Washington, DC 20204
(202) 205-4317

Free Publications/Videos

The following publication on Food Additives is available from the Science & Technology Division, Reference Section, Library of Congress, Washington, DC 20540; (202) 707-5580.

- *Food Additives*. Reference guide designed to help locate further published material. (#82-1)

The following publication is available from the Food & Drug Administration, (HFE-88), 5600 Fishers Ln., Rockville, MD 20857; (301) 443-3170.

- *Food Additives*. (#FDA92-2251)

The following Congressional Research Service (CRS) reports on Food Additives are available from either of your U.S. Senators' offices at the U.S. Capitol, Washington, DC 20510, or from your Congressional Representative at the U.S. Capitol, Washington, DC 20515. You can also call in your request through the U.S. Capitol switchboard at (202) 224-3121. Be sure to include the full title and report number in your request.

- *Food and Color Additives: "De Minimis"* (#IB85119)
- *Low-Calorie Sweeteners: Aspartame, Cyclamate, and Saccharin: Archived Issue Brief.* (#IB85119)
- *Nonfat Solids Standards for Milk: Proposed Legislative Changes.* (#91-772 ENR)
- *Sulfites: Food Preservatives.* (#86-887 SPR)
- *Fast Food Restaurant Labeling.* (#87-736 SPR)
- *Antibiotics: Health Implications of Use in*

Animal Feed; Archived Issue Brief. (#IB85076)

FOOD ALLERGIES

See Allergies

FOOD AND DRUG INTERACTIONS

Free Publications/Videos

The following publication is available from the Food & Drug Administration, (HFE-88), 5600 Fishers Ln., Rockville, MD 20857; (301) 443-3170.

- *Food and Drug Interactions.* (#OM89-3023)

FOOD IRRADIATION

Clearinghouses/Hotlines

The Center for Food Safety and Applied Nutrition regulates what has to be on food labels, as well as food additives, and food safety. If you have a question regarding a food label, food label requirements, food additives, or if you find some foreign material in your non-meat food product, this office can be of assistance. For questions regarding meat products, which includes soups containing meat or frozen pizza with meat toppings, call the U.S. Department of Agriculture's Food Safety and Inspection Service at (800) 535-4555.

☎ Contact:
Center for Food Safety and Applied Nutrition
Food and Drug Administration
Office of Constituents
200 C Street, SW, HFF-11
Washington, DC 20204
(202) 205-4317

Free Publications/Videos

The following publications on Food Irradiation are available from the Food & Drug Administration, (HFE-88), 5600 Fishers Ln., Rockville, MD 20857; (301) 443-3170.

- *The Growing Use of Irradiation To Preserve Food.* (#FDA88-2212)
- *Food Irradiation: Toxic To Bacteria, Safe For Humans.* (#FDA91-2241)

The following Congressional Research Service (CRS) report on Food Irradiation is available from either of your U.S. Senators' offices at the U.S. Capitol, Washington, DC 20510, or from your Congressional Representative at the U.S. Capitol, Washington, DC 20515. You can also call in your request through the U.S. Capitol switchboard at (202) 224-3121. Be sure to include the full title and report number in your request.

- *Preservation of Food by Irradiation.* (86-1046 SPR)

FOOD LABELING

Clearinghouses/Hotlines

In November of 1991, the Bush Administration announced proposals for sweeping changes in food labels that will affect virtually all foods. The new law calls for consistent serving sizes in easily understandable measurements, definitions of nine core descriptive terms, and much more. The new food labels will be on a large percentage of foods by 1993 and on all food by 1994, but do you read labels? Part of the Nutrition Labeling Education Act calls for activities that educate consumers about the availability of nutrition information on the food label and the importance of using that information to maintain healthful dietary practices. A key feature of the Food Labeling Education Information Center is designed to encourage public and private sector organizations to exchange information about their food labeling education activities. The center is to develop a data base of activities and materials relevant to food labeling

education. Among materials to be included are: books, fact sheets, bibliographies, articles, reports, posters, brochures, newsletters, slides, videos, media kits, and programs and program materials. Call for more information or if you have materials you would like to share.

☎ Contact:
Food Labeling Education Information Center
National Exchange for Food Labeling Education
Food and Nutrition Information Center
National Agricultural Library
10301 Baltimore Blvd., Room 304
Beltsville, MD 20704
(301) 504-5472

Free Publications/Videos

The following Congressional Research Service (CRS) reports on Food Labeling are available from either of your U.S. Senators' offices at the U.S. Capitol, Washington, DC 20510, or from your Congressional Representative at the U.S. Capitol, Washington, DC 20515. You can also call in your request through the U.S. Capitol switchboard at (202) 224-3121. Be sure to include the full title and report number in your request.

- *Food Labeling: Issue Brief.* (#IB80055)
- *National Standards for Organic Food Production and Labeling.* (#90-244 ENR)
- *Fast Food Restaurant Labeling.* (#87-736 SPR)
- *Nutrition Labeling: Status of Reform Efforts; Proceedings of a Seminar.* (#91-579 SPR)
- *Labeling of Tropical Oils: Legislation, Health, and Trade Issues.* (#87-910 SPR)
- *Nutrition Labeling and Education Act of 1990: P.L. 101-535.* (#91-146 SPR)

FOOD POISONING

Clearinghouses/Hotlines

The National Institute on Allergy and Infectious Diseases (NIAID) can search the Combined Health Information Database (CHID) and generate a bibliography of resources on Food

Poisoning for you. They will also send you any publications and journal articles they may have on hand, and will refer you to researchers who are currently studying this subject. If you can't afford treatment, have your doctor call NIAID to find out if they are conducting any clinical studies that you might qualify for.

☎ Contact:
National Institute of Allergy
and Infectious Diseases
Bldg. 31, Room 7A32
Bethesda, MD 20892
(301) 496-5717

Free Publications/Videos

The following publication on Food Poisoning is available from the Food & Drug Administration, (HFE-88), 5600 Fishers Ln., Rockville, MD 20857; (301) 443-3170.

- *The Unwelcome Dinner Guest: Preventing Foodborne Illness.* (#FDA91-2244)

FOOD PRESERVATIVES

Free Publications/Videos

The following publication is available from the Food & Drug Administration, (HFE-88), 5600 Fishers Ln., Rockville, MD 20857; (301) 443-3170.

- *Food Preservatives: A Fresh Report.* (#FDA84-2194)

The following Congressional Research Service (CRS) reports on Food Preservation are available from either of your U.S. Senators' offices at the U.S. Capitol, Washington, DC 20510, or from your Congressional Representative at the U.S. Capitol, Washington, DC 20515. You can also call in your request through the U.S. Capitol switchboard at (202) 224-3121. Be sure to include the full title and report number in your request.

- *Preservation of Food by Irradiation.* (#86-1046 SPR)

- *Sulfites: Food Preservatives.* (86-887 SPR)

FOOD SAFETY

Clearinghouses/Hotlines

The Center for Food Safety and Applied Nutrition regulates what has to be on food labels, as well as food additives, and Food Safety. If you have a question regarding a food label, food label requirements, or if you find some foreign material in your non-meat food product, this office can be of assistance. For questions regarding meat products, which includes soups containing meat or frozen pizza with meat toppings, call the USDA's Food Safety and Inspection Service at (800) 535-4555.

☎ Contact:
Center for Food Safety
and Applied Nutrition
Food and Drug Administration
Office of Constituents
200 C Street, SW
HFF-11
Washington, DC 20204
(202) 205-4317

Free Publications/Videos

The following publications on Food Safety are available from the Food & Drug Administration, (HFE-88), 5600 Fishers Ln., Rockville, MD 20857; (301) 443-3170.

- *Mother Nature's Regulations On Food Safety.* (#FDA88-2223)
- *Food Safety And The Microwave.* (#OM91-3007)
- *What Happens If The Packaging Gets Into The Food.* (#FDA92-2250)

The following publications on Food Safety are available from the Food & Nutrition Information Center, National Agricultural Library, Room 304, Beltsville, MD 20705-2351; (301) 504-5719.

- *Food Safety: Ready-Prepared Foods.* Designed to help you locate resources on this topic.
- *Food Safety: Teacher's Guide.* Designed to

help you locate resources on this topic.

- *Making Your Food Dollars Count: A Project Guide*. Suggests ways to spend money and food stamps on nutritious foods and explains how to setup such a education campaign within a community. This reference is available on loan or can be borrowed through an interlibrary loan.

The following Congressional Research Service (CRS) reports on Food Safety are available from either of your U.S. Senators' offices at the U.S. Capitol, Washington, DC 20510, or from your Congressional Representative at the U.S. Capitol, Washington, DC 20515. You can also call in your request through the U.S. Capitol switchboard at (202) 224-3121. Be sure to include the full title and report number in your request.

- *Food Safety: Issues in the 101st Congress.* (#IB90096)
- *Food Safety Policy: Selected Scientific and Regulatory Issues.* (#IB83158)
- *The Safety of Imported Foods.* (#91-644 SPR)
- *Fruit and Vegetable Issues in the 102nd Congress.* (#91-409 ENR)

FORMALDEHYDE EXPOSURE

Clearinghouses/Hotlines

The Environmental Protection Agency will send you their booklet that tells you about Formaldehyde found in indoor air. It tells you where you may come in contact with formaldehyde, how it may affect your health, and how you might reduce your exposure to it.

☎ Contact:
Public Information Center
Environmental Protection Agency
401 M St., SW
Washington, DC 20460
(202) 260-7751

FOSTER CARE

Free Publications/Videos

The following Congressional Research Service (CRS) reports on Foster Care are available from either of your U.S. Senators' offices at the U.S. Capitol, Washington, DC 20510, or from your Congressional Representative at the U.S. Capitol, Washington, DC 20515. You can also call in your request through the U.S. Capitol switchboard at (202) 224-3121. Be sure to include the full title and report number in your request.

- *Foster Care and Federal Law: Significant Developments and Continuing Issues.* (#91-539 A)
- *Foster Care Protections under Titles IV-B and IV-E of the Social Security Act.* (#88-165 EPW)

FRACTURE HEALING

Clearinghouses/Hotlines

The National Institute of Arthritis and Musculoskeletal and Skin Diseases (NIAMS) will send you whatever publications and reprints of articles from texts and journals they have on Fracture Healing. They will also refer you to other organizations that are studying this subject. NIAMS will also let you know of any clinical studies that may be studying this disease and looking for patients.

☎ Contact:
National Institute of Arthritis
and Musculoskeletal and Skin Diseases
Box AMS
9000 Rockville Pike
Bethesda, MD 20892
(301) 495-4484

FRAGILE X SYNDROME

Clearinghouses/Hotlines

The National Institute of Child Health and Human Development (NICHD) will send you whatever publications and reprints of journal articles they have on Fragile X Syndrome. If necessary, they will refer you to other experts or researchers in the field. If you can't afford treatment, have your doctor call NICHD to find out if they are conducting any clinical studies that you might qualify for.

☎ Contact:
National Institute of Child Health
and Human Development
Bldg. 31, Room 2A32
Bethesda, MD 20892
(301) 496-5133

FRIEDREICH'S ATAXIA

Clearinghouses/Hotlines

The National Institute of Neurological Disorders and Stroke (NINDS) can send you only information they have in their publications list on Friedreich's Ataxia. They cannot refer you to any experts. This Clearinghouse cannot directly give you information about any current clinical studies NINDS might be conducting on this illness, but you can find this information for yourself by looking under the National Institute of Neurological Disorders and Stroke in *Appendix A* at the end of this book.

☎ Contact:
National Institute of Neurological
Disorders and Stroke
Bldg. 31, Room 8A06
Bethesda, MD 20892
(301) 496-5751
(800) 352-9424

Free Publications/Videos

The following publications are available from the National Institute of Neurological Disorders and Stroke, Bldg. 31, Room 8A06, Bethesda, MD 20892; (301) 496-5751 or (800) 352-9424.

- *Friedreich's Ataxia*. (#82-87)
- *Friedreich's Ataxia*. Fact sheet on symptoms and treatment.

FROEHLICH'S SYNDROME

Clearinghouses/Hotlines

The National Institute of Diabetes and Digestive and Kidney Diseases's (NIDDK) individual clearinghouses can search the Combined Health Information Database (CHID) and generate a bibliography of resources on Froehlich's Syndrome (Adiposogenital Dystrophy) for you. They also will send you any publications and journal articles they may have on hand, and will refer you to other organizations that are studying this disease. If you can't afford treatment, have your doctor call NIDDK to find out if they are conducting any clinical studies that you might qualify for.

☎ Contact:
National Institute of Diabetes
and Digestive and Kidney Diseases
Bldg. 31, Room 9A04
Bethesda, MD 20892
(301) 496-3583

The National Institute of Child Health and Human Development (NICHD) will send you whatever publications and reprints of journal articles they have on Froehlich's Syndrome (Adiposogenital Dystrophy). If necessary, they will refer you to other experts or researchers in the field. If you can't afford treatment, have your doctor call NICHD to find out if they are conducting any clinical studies that you might qualify for.

☎ Contact:
National Institute of Child Health
and Human Development
Bldg. 31, Room 2A32
Bethesda, MD 20892
(301) 496-5133

The National Institute of Neurological Disorders and Stroke (NINDS) can provide you with information regarding Froehlich's Syndrome, including research reports and descriptive information. This information is free.

☎ Contact:
National Institute of Neurological
Disorders and Stroke
Bldg. 31, Room 8A06
Bethesda, MD 20892
(301) 496-5751
(800) 352-9424

FRUITS & VEGETABLES

See also Food

Free Publications/Videos

The following publication is available from the Food & Drug Administration, (HFE-88), 5600 Fishers Ln., Rockville, MD 20857; (301) 443-3170.

- *Produce and Pesticides.* (#OM89-3020)
- *Fruit, Something Good That's Not Illegal, Immoral or Fattening.* (#FDA88-2226)

FUCH'S DYSTROPHY

Clearinghouses/Hotlines

The National Eye Institute (NEI) can give you up-to-date information on Fuch's Dystrophy by searching the Combined Health Information Database (CHID) and MEDLINE and sending you bibliographies of resources, along with any journal articles they may have. They can also refer you to any other organizations that study this and other related diseases. NEI will also let you know of any clinical studies that may be studying this disease and looking for patients. Because of their small staff, NEI prefers that you submit your requests for information in writing.

☎ Contact:
National Eye Institute
Bldg. 31, Room 6A32

Bethesda, MD 20892
(301) 496-5248

FUNGAL DISEASES OF THE EYE

Clearinghouses/Hotlines

The National Eye Institute (NEI) can give you up-to-date information on Fungal Diseases (Eyes) by searching the Combined Health Information Database (CHID) and MEDLINE and sending you bibliographies of resources, along with any journal articles they may have. They can also refer you to any other organizations that study this and other related diseases. NEI will also let you know of any clinical studies that may be studying this disease and looking for patients. Because of their small staff, NEI prefers that you submit your requests for information in writing.

☎ Contact:
National Eye Institute
Building 31, Room 6A32
Bethesda, MD 20892
(301) 496-5248

FUNGAL INFECTIONS

Clearinghouses/Hotlines

The National Institute on Allergy and Infectious Diseases (NIAID) can search the Combined Health Information Database (CHID) and generate a bibliography of resources on Fungal Infections for you. They will also send you any publications and journal articles they may have on hand, and will refer you to researchers who are currently studying this subject. If you can't afford treatment, have your doctor call NIAID to find out if they are conducting any clinical studies that you might qualify for.

☎ Contact:
National Institute of Allergy
and Infectious Diseases

Bldg. 31, Room 7A32
Bethesda, MD 20892
(301) 496-5717

FUNNEL CHEST

Clearinghouses/Hotlines

The National Heart, Lung, and Blood Institute (NHLBI) can search the Combined Health Information Database (CHID) and generate a bibliography of resources on Funnel Chest (Pectus Excavatum) for you. They also will send you any publications and journal articles they may have on hand, and will refer you to other organizations that are studying this condition. If you can't afford treatment, have your doctor call NHLBI to find out if they are conducting any clinical studies that you might qualify for.

☎ Contact:
National Heart, Lung, and Blood Institute
Bldg. 31, Room 4A21
Bethesda, MD 20892
(301) 496-4236

FURRY TONGUE

See Black Tongue

- G -

G6PD DEFICIENCY

Clearinghouses/Hotlines

The National Heart, Lung, and Blood Institute

(NHLBI) can search the Combined Health Information Database (CHID) and generate a bibliography of resources on G6PD Deficiency for you. They also will send you any publications and journal articles they may have on hand, and will refer you to other organizations that are studying this disease. If you can't afford treatment, have your doctor call NHLBI to find out if they are conducting any clinical studies that you might qualify for.

☎ Contact:
National Heart, Lung, and Blood Institute
Building 31, Room 4A21
Bethesda, MD 20892
(301) 496-4236

GALACTORRHEA

Clearinghouses/Hotlines

The National Institute of Diabetes and Digestive and Kidney Diseases's (NIDDK) individual clearinghouses can search the Combined Health Information Database (CHID) and generate a bibliography of resources on Galactorrhea for you. They also will send you any publications and journal articles they may have on hand, and will refer you to other organizations that are studying this disease. If you can't afford treatment, have your doctor call NIDDK to find out if they are conducting any clinical studies that you might qualify for.

☎ Contact:
National Institute of Diabetes
and Digestive and Kidney Diseases
Building 31, Room 9A04
Bethesda, MD 20892
(301) 496-3583

GALACTOSEMIA

Clearinghouses/Hotlines

The National Institute of Diabetes and Digestive and Kidney Diseases's (NIDDK) individual clearinghouses can search the Combined Health Information Database (CHID) and generate a bibliography of resources on Galactosemia for you. They also will send you any publications and journal articles they may have on hand, and will refer you to other organizations that are studying this disease. If you can't afford treatment, have your doctor call NIDDK to find out if they are conducting any clinical studies that you might qualify for.

☎ Contact:
National Institute of Diabetes
and Digestive and Kidney Diseases
Bldg. 31, Room 9A04
Bethesda, MD 20892
(301) 496-3583

The National Institute of Child Health and Human Development (NICHD) will send you whatever publications and reprints of journal articles they have on Galactosemia. If necessary, they will refer you to other experts or researchers in the field. If you can't afford treatment, have your doctor call NICHD to find out if they are conducting any clinical studies that you might qualify for.

☎ Contact:
National Institute of Child Health
and Human Development
Bldg. 31, Room 2A32
Bethesda, MD 20892
(301) 496-5133

The National Institute of Neurological Disorders and Stroke (NINDS) can send you only information they have in their publications list on Galactosemia. They cannot refer you to any experts. This Clearinghouse cannot directly give you information about any current clinical studies NINDS might be conducting on this illness, but you can find this information for yourself by looking under the National Institute of Neurological Disorders and Stroke in *Appendix A* at the end of this book.

☎ Contact:
National Institute of Neurological
Disorders and Stroke
Bldg. 31, Room 8A06
Bethesda, MD 20892
(301) 496-5751
(800) 352-9424

GALLBLADDER

Clearinghouses/Hotlines

The National Institute of Diabetes and Digestive and Kidney Diseases's (NIDDK) individual clearinghouses can search the Combined Health Information Database (CHID) and generate a bibliography of resources on Gallbladder Disease for you. They also will send you any publications and journal articles they may have on hand, and will refer you to other organizations that are studying this disease. If you can't afford treatment, have your doctor call NIDDK to find out if they are conducting any clinical studies that you might qualify for.

☎ Contact:
National Institute of Diabetes
and Digestive and Kidney Diseases
Bldg. 31, Room 9A04
Bethesda, MD 20892
(301) 496-3583

GALLSTONES

Clearinghouses/Hotlines

The National Institute of Diabetes and Digestive and Kidney Diseases's (NIDDK) individual clearinghouses can search the Combined Health Information Database (CHID) and generate a bibliography of resources on Gallstones for you. They also will send you any publications and journal articles they may have on hand, and will refer you to other organizations that are studying this disease. If you can't afford treatment, have your doctor call NIDDK to find out if they are conducting any clinical studies that you might qualify for.

☎ Contact:
National Institute of Diabetes
and Digestive and Kidney Diseases
Bldg. 31, Room 9A04
Bethesda, MD 20892
(301) 496-3583

Free Publications/Videos

The following publications on Gallstone Disease are available from the National Digestive Diseases Information Clearinghouse, Box NDDIC, Bethesda, MD 20892; (301) 468-6344.

- *Gallstone Disease.* Addresses questions about surgery and complications as well as the reasons for the formation of gallstones. (#85-2752)
- *Gallstones.* Information packet.

GAS

Clearinghouses/Hotlines

The National Digestive Diseases Information Clearinghouse will respond to your requests for information about Gas and digestive diseases and distributes information to health professionals, people with digestive diseases, and the general public. They have many publications, as well as a news bulletin.

☎ Contact:
National Digestive Diseases
Information Clearinghouse
Box NDDIC
Bethesda, MD 20892
(301) 468-6344

Free Publications/Videos

The following publication on Gas is available from the National Digestive Diseases Information Clearinghouse, Box NDDIC, Bethesda, MD 20892; (301) 468-6344.

- *Gas in the Digestive Tract.* (#90-883)

GASTRIC BUBBLE

Free Publications/Videos

The following publications are available from the Center for Devices and Radiological Health, (HFZ-210), Food and Drug Administration, 5600 Fishers Ln., Rockville, MD 20857; (301) 443-4690.

- *Stomach 'Bubble': Diet Device Not Without Risks.*
- *Garren Gastric Bubble.*
- *FDA Drug Bulletin, Nov. 1986.*

GASTRIC HYPERSECRETION

Clearinghouses/Hotlines

The National Institute of Diabetes and Digestive and Kidney Diseases's (NIDDK) individual clearinghouses can search the Combined Health Information Database (CHID) and generate a bibliography of resources on Gastric Hypersecretion for you. They also will send you any publications and journal articles they may have on hand, and will refer you to other organizations that are studying this disease. If you can't afford treatment, have your doctor call NIDDK to find out if they are conducting any clinical studies that you might qualify for.

☎ Contact:
National Institute of Diabetes
and Digestive and Kidney Diseases
Bldg. 31, Room 9A04
Bethesda, MD 20892
(301) 496-3583

GASTRINOMA

Clearinghouses/Hotlines

The National Institute of Diabetes and Digestive and Kidney Diseases's (NIDDK) individual clearinghouses can search the Combined Health Information Database (CHID) and generate a bibliography of resources on Gastrinoma for you. They also will send you any publications and journal articles they may have on hand, and will refer you to other organizations that are studying this disease. If you can't afford treatment, have your doctor call NIDDK to find out if they are conducting any clinical studies that you might qualify for.

☎ Contact:
National Institute of Diabetes
and Digestive and Kidney Diseases
Building 31
Room 9A04
Bethesda, MD 20892
(301) 496-3583

GASTRITIS

Clearinghouses/Hotlines

The National Institute of Diabetes and Digestive and Kidney Diseases's (NIDDK) individual clearinghouses can search the Combined Health Information Database (CHID) and generate a bibliography of resources on Gastritis for you. They also will send you any publications and journal articles they may have on hand, and will refer you to other organizations that are studying this disease. If you can't afford treatment, have your doctor call NIDDK to find out if they are conducting any clinical studies that you might qualify for.

☎ Contact:
National Institute of Diabetes
and Digestive and Kidney Diseases
Building 31
Room 9A04
Bethesda, MD 20892
(301) 496-3583

GAUCHER'S DISEASE

Clearinghouses/Hotlines

The National Institute of Neurological Disorders and Stroke (NINDS) can send you only information they have in their publications list on Gaucher's Disease. They cannot refer you to any

experts. This Clearinghouse cannot directly give you information about any current clinical studies NINDS might be conducting on this illness, but you can find this information for yourself by looking under the National Institute of Neurological Disorders and Stroke in *Appendix A* at the end of this book.

☎ Contact:
National Institute of Neurological
Disorders and Stroke
Bldg. 31, Room 8A06
Bethesda, MD 20892
(301) 496-5751
(800) 352-9424

Free Publications/Videos

The following publication on Gaucher's Disease is available from the Office of Technology Assessment, Washington, DC 20510-8025; (202) 224-8996.

- *Federal and Private Roles in the Development and Provision of Alglucerase Therapy for Gaucher Disease.* (#OTA-BP-H-104)

The following publication Gaucher's Disease is available from the National Institute of Neurological Disorders and Stroke, P.O. Box 5801, Bethesda, MD 20824; (800) 352-9424, or (301) 496-5751.

- *Gaucher's Disease.* Contains a collection of scientific articles, patient education pamphlets, and addresses of voluntary health associations.

GENERIC DRUGS

Clearinghouses/Hotlines

Do you want to know if the medicine you are taking has a generic equivalent? Call the Center for Drug Evaluation and they can provide you with information regarding Generic Drugs, as well as information as to whether or not a generic exists for your particular medicine.

☎ Contact:
Center for Drug Evaluation and Research
Food and Drug Administration
HFD 100
Room 14B45
5600 Fishers Lane
Rockville, MD 20857
(301) 295-8012

Free Publications/Videos

The following Congressional Research Service (CRS) report on Generic Drugs is available from either of your U.S. Senators' offices at the U.S. Capitol, Washington, DC 20510, or from your Congressional Representative at the U.S. Capitol, Washington, DC 20515. You can also call in your request through the U.S. Capitol switchboard at (202) 224-3121. Be sure to include the full title and report number in your request.

- *Generic Drugs and the Elderly: Issues and Policy Considerations.* (#91-792 SPR)

GENE THERAPY

Free Publications/Videos

The following Congressional Research Service (CRS) reports on Gene Therapy are available from either of your U.S. Senators' offices at the U.S. Capitol, Washington, DC 20510, or from your Congressional Representative at the U.S. Capitol, Washington, DC 20515. You can also call in your request through the U.S. Capitol switchboard at (202) 224-3121. Be sure to include the full title and report number in your request.

- *Human Gene Therapy: Archived Issue Brief.* (#IB84119)
- *Human Gene Therapy: Issue Brief.* (#IB87040)
- *Patenting Life: Issue Brief.* (#IB87222)
- *Proposal to Map and Sequence the Human Genome: Issue Brief.* (#IB88012)

GENETIC PANCREA

Clearinghouses/Hotlines

The National Institute of Diabetes and Digestive and Kidney Diseases's (NIDDK) individual clearinghouses can search the Combined Health Information Database (CHID) and generate a bibliography of resources on Genetic Pancrea. (Involvement not due to Cystic Fibrosis) for you. They also will send you any publications and journal articles they may have on hand, and will refer you to other organizations that are studying this disease. If you can't afford treatment, have your doctor call NIDDK to find out if they are conducting any clinical studies that you might qualify for.

☎ Contact:
National Institute of Diabetes
and Digestive and Kidney Diseases
Bldg. 31, Room 9A04
Bethesda, MD 20892
(301) 496-3583

GENETICS

See also DNA

Clearinghouses/Hotlines

The National Maternal and Child Health Clearinghouse has all kinds of information on maternal and child health issues, such as pregnancy, child and adolescent health, and human Genetics. If the answer to your question can't be answered by any of their countless free publications, they can refer you to other National or local resources. If you still need further information, they search their own reference collection and send you what they find.

☎ Contact:
National Maternal and Child
Health Clearinghouse
38th & R Sts., NW
Washington, DC 20057
(703) 821-8955, ext. 254

The National Institute of General Medical Sciences can tell you about on-going Genetics research projects they're funding and will refer you to the researcher in charge of a particular project.

☎ Contact:
National Institutes of Health
Building 31, Room 4A52
Bethesda, MD 20892
(301) 496-7301

The National Institute of Neurological Disorders and Stroke (NINDS) can send you only information they have in their publications list on Genetics. They cannot refer you to any experts. This Clearinghouse cannot directly give you information about any current clinical studies NINDS might be conducting on this topic, but you can find this information for yourself by looking under the National Institute of Neurological Disorders and Stroke in *Appendix A* at the end of this book.

☎ Contact:
National Institute of Neurological
Disorders and Stroke
Bldg. 31, Room 8A06
Bethesda, MD 20892
(301) 496-5751
(800) 352-9424

The National Institute of Dental Research (NIDR) will send you whatever publications and reprints of journal articles they have on Genetics. As a policy, NIDR will not refer you to other organizations or experts who study this subject. If you can't afford treatment, have your doctor call Dr. Albert Guckers at (301) 496-6241 to find out if NIDR is conducting any clinical studies that you might qualify for.

☎ Contact:
National Institute of Dental Research
Bldg. 31, Room 2C35
Bethesda, MD 20892
(301) 496-4261

The National Institute of Child Health and Human Development (NICHD) will send you whatever publications and reprints of journal articles they have on Genetics. If necessary, they will refer you to other experts or researchers in the field. If you can't afford treatment, have your doctor call NICHD to find out if they are conducting any clinical studies that you might qualify for.

☎ Contact:
National Institute of Child Health
and Human Development
Bldg. 31, Room 2A32
Bethesda, MD 20892
(301) 496-5133

The National Institute on Deafness and Other Communicative Disorders (NIDCD) will send you whatever publications and reprints of journal articles they have on Genetics. If you need further information, they will refer you to other organizations that study this issue. NIDCD does not conduct any clinical studies for this or any other disorder.

☎ Contact:
National Institute on Deafness
and Other Communication Disorders
Bldg. 31, Room 3C35
Bethesda, MD 20892
(301) 496-7243
(800) 241-1044
(301) 402-0252 (TDD)

The National Institute on Aging (NIA) will send you whatever publications and reprints of journal articles they have on the Genetics of Aging. They cannot refer you to other experts if the information they have isn't sufficient for your purposes.

☎ Contact:
National Institute on Aging
Bldg. 31, Room 5C27
Bethesda, MD 20892
(301) 496-1752

Free Publications/Videos

The following publications on Genetics are available from the Office of Technology Assessment, 600 Pennsylvania Ave., SE, Washington, DC 20510; (202) 224-8996.

- *Genetic Monitoring and Screening in the Workplace.* Examines the impact of genetic testing; relevant ethical issues; and legal issues, including employment discrimination.
- *Mapping Our Genes: Genome Projects: How*

Big, How Fast? A report to Congress. Ask for the summary report. (#BA-373)

- *The Role of Genetic Testing in the Prevention of Occupational Disease.* A report to Congress. Ask for the summary report. (#BA-194)
- *Technologies for Detecting Heritable Mutations in Human Beings.* A report to Congress. Ask for the summary report. (#H-298)
- *Commercial Development of Tests for Human Genetic Disorders.* A report to Congress. Ask for the summary report.
- *Humane Gene Therapy.* A report to Congress. Ask for the summary report. (#BP-BA-32)
- *Genetic Tests and Health Insurance: Results of a Survey.* (#OTA-BP-BA-98)
- *Genetic Counseling and Cystic Fibrosis Carrier Screening: Results of a Survey.* (#OTA-BP-BA-97)

The following publication and video on Genetics is available from the Office of Clinical Center Communications, Bldg. 10, Room 1C255, Bethesda, MD 20892; (301) 496-2563.

- *Control and Therapy of Genetic Diseases.* Video to help the general public make intelligent decisions.
- *Genetics of Cancer.* Booklet written to help the general public make intelligent decisions.

The following publications on Genetics are available from the National Maternal and Child Health Clearinghouse, 38th & R Sts., NW, Washington, DC 20057; (703) 821-8955, ext. 254.

- *Genetics: Abstract of Active Projects FY 1991.*
- *Genetics Support Groups, Human Genetics: Resource Guide.*
- *Resources for Clergy in Human Genetic Problems.*
- *State Laws and Regulations Governing Newborn Screening.* (#B205)
- *Learning Together: Guide for Families with Genetic Disorders.* (#B076)

The following video on Genetics is available from Modern Talking Picture Service, 5000 Park St. North, St. Petersburg, FL 33709; (800) 243-MTPS.

- *Genetic Engineering: The Nature of Change.* Video explores potentials and limitations of genetic engineering.

GENETIC TESTING AND COUNSELING

Clearinghouses/Hotlines

The National Maternal and Child Health Clearinghosue has all kinds of information on maternal and child health issues, such as pregnancy, child and adolescent health, and human genetics. If the answer to your question can't be answered by any of their countless free publications, they can refer you to other National or local resources. If you still need further information, they search their own reference collection and send you what they find.

☎ Contact:
National Maternal and Child Health Clearinghosue
38th & R Sts. NW
Washington, DC 20057
(703) 821-8955, ext. 254

Free Publications/Videos

The following publications on Genetic Testing are available from the National Maternal and Child Health Clearinghouse, 38th & R Sts., NW, Washington, DC 20057; (703) 821-8955, ext. 254.

- *Annotated Bibliography: Educational Materials on DNA Techniques in Genetic Testing and Counseling.* (#E047)
- *Human Genetics: Resource Guide.* (#D011)
- *New Human Genetics: How Gene Splicing Helps Researchers Fight Inherited Diseases.* (#B194)
- *Understanding DNA Testing: A Basic Guide for Families.* (#D088)
- *Annotated Bibliography: Educational Materials on DNA Techniques in Genetic Testing and Counseling.* (#E047)
- *Genetic Services: Abstracts of Active Projects FY 1991.* (#E007)

- *Genetic Services for Underserved Populations.* (#D047)
- *A Guide to Selected National Genetic Voluntary Organizations.* (#B359)

The following Congressional Research Service (CRS) report on Genetic Screening is available from either of your U.S. Senators' offices at the U.S. Capitol, Washington, DC 20510, or from your Congressional Representative at the U.S. Capitol, Washington, DC 20515. You can also call in your request through the U.S. Capitol switchboard at (202) 224-3121. Be sure to include the full title and report number in your request.

- *Genetic Screening; Archived Issue Brief.* (#IB90121)

GENITAL HERPES

Clearinghouses/Hotlines

The National Institute on Allergy and Infectious Diseases (NIAID) can search the Combined Health Information Database (CHID) and generate a bibliography of resources on Genital Herpes for you. They will also send you any publications and journal articles they may have on hand, and will refer you to researchers who are currently studying this disease. If you can't afford treatment, have your doctor call NIAID to find out if they are conducting any clinical studies that you might qualify for.

☎ Contact:
National Institute of Allergy
and Infectious Diseases
Bldg. 31, Room 7A32
Bethesda, MD 20892
(301) 496-5717

The Sexually Transmitted Diseases Hotline offers valuable information to the public about a wide range of sexually transmitted diseases, including Genital Herpes and how to protect yourself from contracting them.

☎ Contact:
National Sexually Transmitted Diseases Hotline
P.O. Box 13827

Research Triangle Park, NC 27709
(800) 227-8922

Free Publications/Videos

The following publication on Genital Herpes is available from the National Institute of Allergy and Infectious Diseases, Bldg. 31, Room 7A32, Bethesda, MD 20892; (301) 496-5717.

- *Genital Herpes.* (#84-2005)

GENITAL WARTS

Clearinghouses/Hotlines

The National Institute on Allergy and Infectious Diseases (NIAID) can search the Combined Health Information Database (CHID) and generate a bibliography of resources on Genital Warts for you. They will also send you any publications and journal articles they may have on hand, and will refer you to researchers who are currently studying this disease. If you can't afford treatment, have your doctor call NIAID to find out if they are conducting any clinical studies that you might qualify for.

☎ Contact:
National Institute of Allergy
and Infectious Diseases
Building 31
Room 7A32
Bethesda, MD 20892
(301) 496-5717

The Sexually Transmitted Diseases Hotline offers valuable information to the public about a wide range of sexually transmitted diseases, including Genital Warts and how to protect yourself from contracting them.

☎ Contact:
National Sexually Transmitted Diseases Hotline
P.O. Box 13827
Research Triangle Park, NC 27709
(800) 227-8922

GERIATRICS

See Aging
See Gerontology

GERMAN MEASLES

Clearinghouses/Hotlines

The National Institute on Allergy and Infectious Diseases (NIAID) can search the Combined Health Information Database (CHID) and generate a bibliography of resources on German Measles (Rubella) for you. They will also send you any publications and journal articles they may have on hand, and will refer you to researchers who are currently studying this disease. If you can't afford treatment, have your doctor call NIAID to find out if they are conducting any clinical studies that you might qualify for.

☎ Contact:
National Institute of Allergy
and Infectious Diseases
Bldg. 31, Room 7A32
Bethesda, MD 20892
(301) 496-5717

GERONTOLOGY

See also Aging
See also Long-Term Care

Clearinghouses/Hotlines

The Gerontology Research Center offer a wide range of pamphlets and reports on aging research for professionals and the general public, including information on the *Baltimore Longitudinal Study on Aging*.

☎ Contact:
Francis Scott Key Medical Center
4940 Eastern Ave.
Baltimore, MD 21224

(301) 558-8114

The National Institute on Aging (NIA) will send you whatever publications and reprints of journal articles they have on Gerontology. They cannot refer you to other experts if the information they have isn't sufficient for your purposes.

☎ Contact:
National Institute on Aging
Bldg. 31, Room 5C27
Bethesda, MD 20892
(301) 496-1752

GERSON METHOD

Clearinghouses/Hotlines

The National Cancer Institute (NCI) will send you whatever publications and reprints of journal articles they have on the Gerson Method. They can also search their Physician's Data Query (PDQ) database to let you know if NCI is conducting any clinical studies on your disease.

☎ Contact:
National Cancer Institute
Bldg. 31, Room 10A24
Bethesda, MD 20892
(800) 4-CANCER
(301) 496-5583

GERSTMANN'S SYNDROME

Clearinghouses/Hotlines

The National Institute of Neurological Disorders and Stroke (NINDS) can send you only information they have in their publications list on Gerstmann's Syndrome. They cannot refer you to any experts. This Clearinghouse cannot directly give you information about any current clinical studies NINDS might be conducting on this illness, but you can find this information for yourself by looking under the National Institute of Neurological Disorders and Stroke in *Appendix A* at the end of this book.

☎ Contact:
National Institute of Neurological
Disorders and Stroke
Building 31
Room 8A06
Bethesda, MD 20892
(301) 496-5751
(800) 352-9424

GESTATION

Clearinghouses/Hotlines

The National Institute of Child Health and Human Development (NICHD) will send you whatever publications and reprints of journal articles they have on Gestation. If necessary, they will refer you to other experts or researchers in the field.

☎ Contact:
National Institute of Child Health
and Human Development
Building 31
Room 2A32
Bethesda, MD 20892
(301) 496-5133

GESTATIONAL DIABETES

Clearinghouses/Hotlines

The National Institute of Child Health and Human Development (NICHD) will send you whatever publications and reprints of journal articles they have on Gestational Diabetes. If necessary, they will refer you to other experts or researchers in the field.

☎ Contact:
National Institute of Child Health
and Human Development
Building 31
Room 2A32
Bethesda, MD 20892
(301) 496-5133

Free Publications/Videos

The following publication on Gestational Diabetes is available from the National Institute of Child Health and Human Development, Bldg. 31, Room 2A32, Bethesda, MD 20892; (301) 496-5133.

- *Understanding Gestational Diabetes: A Practical Guide to a Healthy Pregnancy.* (#89-2788)

GIARDIASIS

Clearinghouses/Hotlines

The National Institute on Allergy and Infectious Diseases (NIAID) can search the Combined Health Information Database (CHID) and generate a bibliography of resources on Giardiasis for you. They will also send you any publications and journal articles they may have on hand, and will refer you to researchers who are currently studying this disease. If you can't afford treatment, have your doctor call NIAID to find out if they are conducting any clinical studies that you might qualify for.

☎ Contact:
National Institute of Allergy
and Infectious Diseases
Bldg. 31, Room 7A32
Bethesda, MD 20892
(301) 496-5717

GIGANTISM

Clearinghouses/Hotlines

The National Institute of Diabetes and Digestive and Kidney Diseases's (NIDDK) individual clearinghouses can search the Combined Health Information Database (CHID) and generate a bibliography of resources on Gigantism for you. They also will send you any publications and journal articles they may have on hand, and will refer you to other organizations that are studying this disease. If you can't afford treatment, have your doctor call NIDDK to find out if they are conducting any clinical studies that you might qualify for.

☎ Contact:
National Institute of Diabetes
and Digestive and Kidney Diseases
Bldg. 31, Room 9A04
Bethesda, MD 20892
(301) 496-3583

GILBERT'S SYNDROME

Clearinghouses/Hotlines

The National Institute of Diabetes and Digestive and Kidney Diseases's (NIDDK) individual clearinghouses can search the Combined Health Information Database (CHID) and generate a bibliography of resources on Gilbert's Syndrome for you. They also will send you any publications and journal articles they may have on hand, and will refer you to other organizations that are studying this disease. If you can't afford treatment, have your doctor call NIDDK to find out if they are conducting any clinical studies that you might qualify for.

☎ Contact:
National Institute of Diabetes
and Digestive and Kidney Diseases
Bldg. 31, Room 9A04
Bethesda, MD 20892
(301) 496-3583

GILLES DE LA TOURETTE'S DISEASE

Clearinghouses/Hotlines

The National Institute of Neurological Disorders and Stroke (NINDS) can send you only information they have in their publications list on Gilles de la Tourette's Disease. They cannot refer you to any experts. This Clearinghouse cannot

directly give you information about any current clinical studies NINDS might be conducting on this disorder, but you can find this information for yourself by looking under the National Institute of Neurological Disorders and Stroke in *Appendix A* at the end of this book.

☎ Contact:
National Institute of Neurological
Disorders and Stroke
Bldg. 31, Room 8A06
Bethesda, MD 20892
(301) 496-5751
(800) 352-9424

GINGIVITIS

Clearinghouses/Hotlines

The National Institute of Dental Research (NIDR) will send you whatever publications and reprints of journal articles they have on Gingivitis. As a policy, NIDR will not refer you to other organizations or experts who study this disease. If you can't afford treatment, have your doctor call Dr. Albert Guckers at (301) 496-6241 to find out if NIDR is conducting any clinical studies that you might qualify for.

☎ Contact:
National Institute of Dental Research
Bldg. 31, Room 2C35
Bethesda, MD 20892
(301) 496-4261

GLAUCOMA

Clearinghouses/Hotlines

The National Eye Institute (NEI) conducts research aimed at the prevention and nonsurgical treatment of cataracts and prevention of Glaucoma. They have publications on these topics and can answer your questions regarding current research.

☎ Contact:
National Eye Institute

Bldg. 31, Room 6A32
Bethesda, MD 20892
(301) 496-5248

Free Publications/Videos

The following publication on Glaucoma is available from the Food & Drug Administration, HFE-88, 5600 Fishers Lane, Rockville, MD 20857; (301) 443-3170.

- *Keeping An Eye on Glaucoma*. Discusses the control of glaucoma with drugs and surgery. (#80-3105)

The following publications on Glaucoma are available from the National Eye Institute, Bldg. 31, Room 6A32, Bethesda, MD 20892; (301) 496-5248.

- *Glaucoma*. (#89-651)
- *Vision Research: Report of the Glaucoma Panel, Part Four*. (#83-2474)

GLIOMAS

Clearinghouses/Hotlines

The National Institute of Neurological Disorders and Stroke (NINDS) can send you only information they have in their publications list on Gliomas. They cannot refer you to any experts. This Clearinghouse cannot directly give you information about any current clinical studies NINDS might be conducting on this topic, but you can find this information for yourself by looking under the National Institute of Neurological Disorders and Stroke in *Appendix A* at the end of this book.

☎ Contact:
National Institute of Neurological
Disorders and Stroke
Bldg. 31, Room 8A06
Bethesda, MD 20892
(301) 496-5751
(800) 352-9424

GLOBOID CELL LEUKODYSTROPHY

Clearinghouses/Hotlines

The National Institute of Neurological Disorders and Stroke (NINDS) can send you only information they have in their publications list on Globoid Cell Leukodystrophy. They cannot refer you to any experts. This Clearinghouse cannot directly give you information about any current clinical studies NINDS might be conducting on this illness, but you can find this information for yourself by looking under the National Institute of Neurological Disorders and Stroke in *Appendix A* at the end of this book.

☎ Contact:
National Institute of Neurological
Disorders and Stroke
Bldg. 31, Room 8A06
Bethesda, MD 20892
(301) 496-5751 or (800) 352-9424

GLOMERULONEPHRITIS

Clearinghouses/Hotlines

The National Institute of Diabetes and Digestive and Kidney Diseases's (NIDDK) individual clearinghouses can search the Combined Health Information Database (CHID) and generate a bibliography of resources on Glomerulonephritis for you. They also will send you any publications and journal articles they may have on hand, and will refer you to other organizations that are studying this disease. If you can't afford treatment, have your doctor call NIDDK to find out if they are conducting any clinical studies that you might qualify for.

☎ Contact:
National Institute of Diabetes
and Digestive and Kidney Diseases
Bldg. 31, Room 9A04
Bethesda, MD 20892
(301) 496-3583

GLUCOSE INTOLERANCE

Clearinghouses/Hotlines

The National Institute of Diabetes and Digestive and Kidney Diseases's (NIDDK) individual clearinghouses can search the Combined Health Information Database (CHID) and generate a bibliography of resources on Glucose Intolerance for you. They also will send you any publications and journal articles they may have on hand, and will refer you to other organizations that are studying this disease. If you can't afford treatment, have your doctor call NIDDK to find out if they are conducting any clinical studies that you might qualify for.

☎ Contact:
National Institute of Diabetes
and Digestive and Kidney Diseases
Bldg. 31, Room 9A04
Bethesda, MD 20892
(301) 496-3583

GLUTEN INTOLERANCE

Clearinghouses/Hotlines

The National Institute of Diabetes and Digestive and Kidney Diseases's (NIDDK) individual clearinghouses can search the Combined Health Information Database (CHID) and generate a bibliography of resources on Gluten Intolerance for you. They also will send you any publications and journal articles they may have on hand, and will refer you to other organizations that are studying this disease. If you can't afford treatment, have your doctor call NIDDK to find out if they are conducting any clinical studies that you might qualify for.

☎ Contact:
National Institute of Diabetes
and Digestive and Kidney Diseases
Bldg. 31, Room 9A04
Bethesda, MD 20892
(301) 496-3583

GLYCOGEN STORAGE DISEASE

Clearinghouses/Hotlines

The National Institute of Diabetes and Digestive and Kidney Diseases's (NIDDK) individual clearinghouses can search the Combined Health Information Database (CHID) and generate a bibliography of resources on Glycogen Storage Disease for you. They also will send you any publications and journal articles they may have on hand, and will refer you to other organizations that are studying this disease. If you can't afford treatment, have your doctor call NIDDK to find out if they are conducting any clinical studies that you might qualify for.

☎ Contact:
National Institute of Diabetes
and Digestive and Kidney Diseases
Bldg. 31, Room 9A04
Bethesda, MD 20892
(301) 496-3583

The National Institute of Child Health and Human Development (NICHD) will send you whatever publications and reprints of journal articles they have on Glycogen Storage Disease. If necessary, they will refer you to other experts or researchers in the field. If you can't afford treatment, have your doctor call NICHD to find out if they are conducting any clinical studies that you might qualify for.

☎ Contact:
National Institute of Child Health
and Human Development
Bldg. 31, Room 2A32
Bethesda, MD 20892
(301) 496-5133

GOITER

Clearinghouses/Hotlines

The National Institute of Diabetes and Digestive

and Kidney Diseases's (NIDDK) individual clearinghouses can search the Combined Health Information Database (CHID) and generate a bibliography of resources on Goiter for you. They also will send you any publications and journal articles they may have on hand, and will refer you to other organizations that are studying this disease. If you can't afford treatment, have your doctor call NIDDK to find out if they are conducting any clinical studies that you might qualify for.

☎ Contact:
National Institute of Diabetes
and Digestive and Kidney Diseases
Bldg. 31, Room 9A04
Bethesda, MD 20892
(301) 496-3583

GONADS

Clearinghouses/Hotlines

The National Institute of Child Health and Human Development (NICHD) will send you whatever publications and reprints of journal articles they have on Gonads. If necessary, they will refer you to other experts or researchers in the field. If you can't afford treatment, have your doctor call NICHD to find out if they are conducting any clinical studies that you might qualify for.

☎ Contact:
National Institute of Child Health
and Human Development
Bldg. 31, Room 2A32
Bethesda, MD 20892
(301) 496-5133

GONORRHEA

Clearinghouses/Hotlines

The National Institute on Allergy and Infectious Diseases (NIAID) can search the Combined Health Information Database (CHID) and generate a bibliography of resources on Gonorrhea

for you. They will also send you any publications and journal articles they may have on hand, and will refer you to researchers who are currently studying this disease. If you can't afford treatment, have your doctor call NIAID to find out if they are conducting any clinical studies that you might qualify for.

☎ Contact:
National Institute of Allergy
and Infectious Diseases
Bldg. 31, Room 7A32
Bethesda, MD 20892
(301) 496-5717

The Sexually Transmitted Diseases Hotline offers valuable information to the public about a wide range of sexually transmitted diseases, including Gonorrhea and how to protect yourself from contracting them.

☎ Contact:
National Sexually Transmitted Diseases Hotline
P.O. Box 13827
Research Triangle Park, NC 27709
(800) 227-8922

GOODPASTURE'S SYNDROME

Clearinghouses/Hotlines

The National Heart, Lung, and Blood Institute (NHLBI) can search the Combined Health Information Database (CHID) and generate a bibliography of resources on Goodpasture's Syndrome for you. They also will send you any publications and journal articles they may have on hand, and will refer you to other organizations that are studying this disease. If you can't afford treatment, have your doctor call NHLBI to find out if they are conducting any clinical studies that you might qualify for.

☎ Contact:
National Heart, Lung, and Blood Institute
Bldg. 31, Room 4A21
Bethesda, MD 20892
(301) 496-4236

The National Institute of Diabetes and Digestive and Kidney Diseases's (NIDDK) individual clearinghouses can search the Combined Health Information Database (CHID) and generate a bibliography of resources on Goodpasture's Syndrome for you. They also will send you any publications and journal articles they may have on hand, and will refer you to other organizations that are studying this disease. If you can't afford treatment, have your doctor call NIDDK to find out if they are conducting any clinical studies that you might qualify for.

☎ Contact:
National Institute of Diabetes
and Digestive and Kidney Diseases
Bldg. 31, Room 9A04
Bethesda, MD 20892
(301) 496-3583

GOUT

Clearinghouses/Hotlines

The National Institute of Arthritis and Musculoskeletal and Skin Diseases (NIAMS) will send you whatever publications and reprints of articles from texts and journals they have on Gout. They will also refer you to other organizations that are studying this disease. NIAMS will also let you know of any clinical studies that may be studying this disease and looking for patients.

☎ Contact:
National Institute of Arthritis
and Musculoskeletal and Skin Diseases
Box AMS
9000 Rockville Pike
Bethesda, MD 20892
(301) 495-4484

Free Publications/Videos

The following publication is available from the Office of Clinical Center Communications, Bldg. 10, Room 1C255, Bethesda, MD 20892; (301) 496-2563.

- *Arthritis Today*. Explains gout, rheumatoid

arthritis, and osteoarthritis, and discusses treatment. (#83-1945)

GRAINS

Free Publications/Videos

The following publication on Grains is available from the Food & Nutrition Information Center, National Agricultural Library, Room 304, Beltsville, MD 20705-2351; (301) 504-5719.

- *Nutrient Composition of Selected Grains as Food, January 1986 - September 1990*. A list of current resources. (#QB91-34)

GRIEF

Clearinghouses/Hotlines

The National Institute of Mental Health (NIMH) maintains data bases that index and abstract documents from the worldwide literature pertaining to Grief. In addition to scientific journals, there are references to audiovisuals, dissertations, government documents and reports. Contact NIMH for searches on specific subjects.

☎ Contact:
National Institute of Mental Health
5600 Fishers Lane
Room 15C05
Rockville, MD 20857
(301) 443-4515

Free Publications/Videos

The following publication on Grief is available from the National Sudden Infant Death Syndrome Clearinghouse, 8201 Greensboro Dr., Suite 600, McLean, VA 22102; (703) 821-8955.

- *The Grief of Children*. Discusses some of the ways that children express grief and that adults can help.

GRANULOCYTOPENIA

Clearinghouses/Hotlines

The National Institute of Arthritis and Musculoskeletal and Skin Diseases (NIAMS) will send you whatever publications and reprints of articles from texts and journals they have on Granulocytopenia. They will also refer you to other organizations that are studying this condition. NIAMS will also let you know of any clinical studies that may be studying this condition and looking for patients.

☎ Contact:
National Institute of Arthritis
and Musculoskeletal and Skin Diseases
Box AMS
Bethesda, MD 20892
(301) 495-4484

The National Institute of Diabetes and Digestive and Kidney Diseases's (NIDDK) individual clearinghouses can search the Combined Health Information Database (CHID) and generate a bibliography of resources on Granulocytopenia for you. They also will send you any publications and journal articles they may have on hand, and will refer you to other organizations that are studying this condition. If you can't afford treatment, have your doctor call NIDDK to find out if they are conducting any clinical studies that you might qualify for.

☎ Contact:
National Institute of Diabetes
and Digestive and Kidney Diseases
Bldg. 31, Room 9A04
Bethesda, MD 20892
(301) 496-3583

GRANULOMATOUS DISEASE

Clearinghouses/Hotlines

The National Institute on Allergy and Infectious Diseases (NIAID) can search the Combined Health Information Database (CHID) and generate a bibliography of resources on Granulomatous Diseases for you. They will also send you any publications and journal articles they may have on hand, and will refer you to researchers who are currently studying this disease. If you can't afford treatment, have your doctor call NIAID to find out if they are conducting any clinical studies that you might qualify for.

☎ Contact:
National Institute of Allergy
and Infectious Diseases
Bldg. 31, Room 7A32
Bethesda, MD 20892
(301) 496-5717

GRAPE CURE

Clearinghouses/Hotlines

The National Cancer Institute (NCI) will send you whatever publications and reprints of journal articles they have on the Grape Cure. They can also search their Physician's Data Query (PDQ) database to let you know if NCI is conducting any clinical studies on your disease.

☎ Contact:
National Cancer Institute
Bldg. 31, Room 10A24
Bethesda, MD 20892
(800) 4-CANCER
(301) 496-5583

GRAVE'S DISEASE

Clearinghouses/Hotlines

The National Eye Institute (NEI) can give you up-to-date information on Grave's Disease (Eye Complications). by searching the Combined Health Information Database (CHID) and MEDLINE and sending you bibliographies of resources, along with any journal articles they may have. They can also refer you to any other organizations that study this and other related diseases. NEI will also let you know of any clinical studies that may be studying this disease and looking for patients. Because of their small staff, NEI prefers that you submit your requests for information in writing.

☎ Contact:
National Eye Institute
Bldg. 31, Room 6A32
Bethesda, MD 20892
(301) 496-5248

The National Institute of Diabetes and Digestive and Kidney Diseases's (NIDDK) individual clearinghouses can search the Combined Health Information Database (CHID) and generate a bibliography of resources on Grave's Disease (General Information) for you. They also will send you any publications and journal articles they may have on hand, and will refer you to other organizations that are studying this disease. If you can't afford treatment, have your doctor call NIDDK to find out if they are conducting any clinical studies that you might qualify for.

☎ Contact:
National Institute of Diabetes
and Digestive and Kidney Diseases
Bldg. 31, Room 9A04
Bethesda, MD 20892
(301) 496-3583

bibliography of resources on Growth Hormone Deficiency for you. They also will send you any publications and journal articles they may have on hand, and will refer you to other organizations that are studying this disease. If you can't afford treatment, have your doctor call NIDDK to find out if they are conducting any clinical studies that you might qualify for.

☎ Contact:
National Institute of Diabetes
and Digestive and Kidney Diseases
Bldg. 31, Room 9A04
Bethesda, MD 20892
(301) 496-3583

The National Institute of Child Health and Human Development (NICHD) will send you whatever publications and reprints of journal articles they have on Growth Hormone Deficiency. If necessary, they will refer you to other experts or researchers in the field. If you can't afford treatment, have your doctor call NICHD to find out if they are conducting any clinical studies that you might qualify for.

☎ Contact:
National Institute of Child Health
and Human Development
Bldg. 31, Room 2A32
Bethesda, MD 20892
(301) 496-5133

GRIPPE

See Flu

GROWTH HORMONE DEFICIENCY

Clearinghouses/Hotlines

The National Institute of Diabetes and Digestive and Kidney Diseases's (NIDDK) individual clearinghouses can search the Combined Health Information Database (CHID) and generate a

GUILLAIN-BARRE SYNDROME

Clearinghouses/Hotlines

The National Institute of Neurological Disorders and Stroke (NINDS) can send you only information they have in their publications list on Guillain-Barre Syndrome (Polyneuritis). They cannot refer you to any experts. This Clearinghouse cannot directly give you information about any current clinical studies NINDS might be conducting on this illness, but you can find this information for yourself by looking under the National Institute of Neurological Disorders and Stroke in *Appendix A* at the end of this book.

☎ Contact:
National Institute of Neurological
Disorders and Stroke
Bldg. 31, Room 8A06
Bethesda, MD 20892
(301) 496-5751 or (800) 352-9424

Free Publications/Videos

The following publication on Guillain-Barre Syndrome is available from the National Institute of Neurological Disorders and Stroke, P.O. Box 5801, Bethesda, MD 20824; (800) 352-9424, or (301) 496-5751.

- *Guillain-Barre Syndrome.* Collection of scientific articles, patient education pamphlets, and addresses of voluntary health associations.

GUM DISEASE

Clearinghouses/Hotlines

The National Institute of Dental Research (NIDR) will send you whatever publications and reprints of journal articles they have on Gum Disease. As a policy, NIDR will not refer you to other organizations or experts who study this disease. If you can't afford treatment, have your doctor call Dr. Albert Guckers at (301) 496-6241 to find out if NIDR is conducting any clinical studies that you might qualify for.

☎ Contact:
National Institute of Dental Research
Bldg. 31, Room 2C35
Bethesda, MD 20892
(301) 496-4261

GYNECOMASTIA

Clearinghouses/Hotlines

The National Institute of Child Health and Human

Development (NICHD) will send you whatever publications and reprints of journal articles they have on Gynecomastia. If necessary, they will refer you to other experts or researchers in the field. If you can't afford treatment, have your doctor call NICHD to find out if they are conducting any clinical studies that you might qualify for.

☎ Contact:
National Institute of Child Health
and Human Development
Bldg. 31, Room 2A32
Bethesda, MD 20892
(301) 496-5133

The National Institute of Diabetes and Digestive and Kidney Diseases's (NIDDK) individual clearinghouses can search the Combined Health Information Database (CHID) and generate a bibliography of resources on Gynecomastia for you. They also will send you any publications and journal articles they may have on hand, and will refer you to other organizations that are studying this disease. If you can't afford treatment, have your doctor call NIDDK to find out if they are conducting any clinical studies that you might qualify for.

☎ Contact:
National Institute of Diabetes
and Digestive and Kidney Diseases
Bldg. 31, Room 9A04
Bethesda, MD 20892
(301) 496-3583

GYRATE ATROPHY

Clearinghouses/Hotlines

The National Eye Institute (NEI) can give you up-to-date information on Gyrate Atrophy by searching the Combined Health Information Database (CHID) and MEDLINE and sending you bibliographies of resources, along with any journal articles they may have. They can also refer you to any other organizations that study this and other related diseases. NEI will also let you know of any clinical studies that may be studying this disease and looking for patients. Because of

their small staff, NEI prefers that you submit your requests for information in writing.

☎ Contact:
National Eye Institute
Bldg. 31, Room 6A32
Bethesda, MD 20892
(301) 496-5248

- H -

HAILEY'S DISEASE

Clearinghouses/Hotlines

The National Institute of Diabetes and Digestive and Kidney Diseases's (NIDDK) individual clearinghouses can search the Combined Health Information Database (CHID) and generate a bibliography of resources on Hailey's Disease for you. They also will send you any publications and journal articles they may have on hand, and will refer you to other organizations that are studying this disease. If you can't afford treatment, have your doctor call NIDDK to find out if they are conducting any clinical studies that you might qualify for.

☎ Contact:
National Institute of Diabetes
and Digestive and Kidney Diseases
Bldg. 31, Room 9A04
Bethesda, MD 20892
(301) 496-3583

HAIR LOSS

Clearinghouses/Hotlines

The National Institute of Arthritis and Musculoskeletal and Skin Diseases (NIAMS) will send you whatever publications and reprints of articles from texts and journals they have on Hair Loss. They will also refer you to other organizations that are studying this disease. NIAMS will also let you know of any clinical studies that may be studying this disease and looking for patients.

☎ Contact:
National Institute of Arthritis
and Musculoskeletal and Skin Diseases
Box AMS, 9000 Rockville Pike
Bethesda, MD 20892
(301) 495-4484

Is your hair line receding or are you thinning on top? Our government's hair and drug experts have determined that over the counter hair grower or hair loss prevention drug products don't do their job.

☎ Contact:
Center for Drug Evaluation and Research
Food and Drug Administration
HFD-100, Room 14B45
5600 Fishers Lane
Rockville, MD 20857
(301) 295-8012

Free Publications/Videos

The following publication is available from the Center for Devices and Radiological Health, (HFZ-210), Food and Drug Administration, 5600 Fishers Ln., Rockville, MD 20857; (301) 443-4690.

- *Hair Too Little: Synthetic Hair Implants.*

HAIR REMOVAL

Free Publications/Videos

The following publication is available from the Center for Devices and Radiological Health, (HFZ-210), Food and Drug Administration, 5600 Fishers Ln., Rockville, MD 20857; (301) 443-4690.

- *Hair Too Little: Some Basics on Hair Removal Products.*

The following publication on Hair Removal is available from the Consumer Information Center, P.O. Box 100, Pueblo, CO 81002.

- *Hair: A Personal Statement.* Get the latest research on hair loss; what's been tested and what does and does not work, transplants, how everyday hair grooming influences hair growth, and more. (#534Z).

HAIR SPRAY

Clearinghouses/Hotlines

The Office of Cosmetics at the Food and Drug Administration handles questions and concerns about hair sprays. There is no mandatory registration of hair spray, but they can provide you with some information regarding the product, and will take complaints.

☎ Contact:
Office of Cosmetics and Colors
Food and Drug Administration
200 C St., SW
Washington, DC 20204
(202) 245-1061

HAIRY TONGUE

See Black Tongue

HALITOSIS

Clearinghouses/Hotlines

The National Institute of Dental Research (NIDR) can provide you with some information regarding Halitosis (bad breath).

☎ Contact:
National Institute of Dental Research
Bldg. 31, Room 2C35

Bethesda, MD 20892
(301) 496-4261

HALLERVORDEN-SPATZ DISEASE

Clearinghouses/Hotlines

The National Institute of Neurological Disorders and Stroke (NINDS) can send you only information they have in their publications list on Hallervorden-Spatz Disease. They cannot refer you to any experts. This Clearinghouse cannot directly give you information about any current clinical studies NINDS might be conducting on this illness, but you can find this information for yourself by looking under the National Institute of Neurological Disorders and Stroke in *Appendix A* at the end of this book.

☎ Contact:
National Institute of Neurological
Disorders and Stroke
Bldg. 31, Room 8A06
Bethesda, MD 20892
(301) 496-5751
(800) 352-9424

HAND, FOOT AND MOUTH DISEASE

Clearinghouses/Hotlines

The National Institute on Allergy and Infectious Diseases (NIAID) can search the Combined Health Information Database (CHID) and generate a bibliography of resources on Coxsackie Virus (Hand-Foot & Mouth Disease) for you. They will also send you any publications and journal articles they may have on hand, and will refer you to researchers who are currently studying this disease. If you can't afford treatment, have your doctor call NIAID to find out if they are conducting any clinical studies that you might qualify for.

☎ Contact:
National Institute of Allergy
and Infectious Diseases
Bldg. 31, Room 7A32
Bethesda, MD 20892
(301) 496-5717

The National Institute of Child Health and Human Development (NICHD) will send you whatever publications and reprints of journal articles they have on Coxsackie Virus (Hand-Foot & Mouth Disease). If necessary, they will refer you to other experts or researchers in the field. If you can't afford treatment, have your doctor call NICHD to find out if they are conducting any clinical studies that you might qualify for.

☎ Contact:
National Institute of Child Health
and Human Development
Bldg. 31, Room 2A32
Bethesda, MD 20892
(301) 496-5133

HANDICAPPED

See also Disabilities

Clearinghouses/Hotlines

The Clearinghouse on the Handicapped will respond to your questions by referring you to organizations that supply information to and about handicapped individuals. They also can send you material on federal benefits, funding, and legislation for the handicapped.

☎ Contact:
Switzer Building
Room 3132, 330 C Street SW
Washington, DC 20202
(202) 732-1250

The ERIC Clearinghouse on Handicapped and Gifted Children gathers and distributes educational information on all disabilities across all age levels. They have publications, digests (2-4 page summaries of current topics), *Research Briefs*, *Issue Briefs*, Directories of currently funded research, topical **INFO** packets and *Flyer Files*.

☎ Contact:
Council for Exceptional Children
1920 Association Dr.
Reston, VA 22091
(703) 264-9474

The National Information Center for Children and Youth with Handicaps helps parents of Handicapped children locate services and parent support groups. It also focuses on the needs of rural areas, culturally diverse populations, and severely handicapped people. This center also provides information on vocational/transitional issues, special education, and legal rights and advocacy. It provides fact sheets on specific disabilities, including autism, cerebral palsy, hearing impairments, Down's syndrome, epilepsy, learning disabilities, mental retardation, physical disabilities, speech and language impairments, spina bifida, visual impairments.

☎ Contact:
The National Information Center
for Children and Youth with Handicaps
P.O. Box 1492
Washington, DC 20013
(800) 999-5599

The National Institute on Disability and Rehabilitation Research can fill you in on the newest developments in rehabilitation methods and devices for people of all ages with physical and mental handicaps, especially those who are severely disabled. They also have all kinds of statistical data on disabilities and research funding information are also available. Ask for a copy of their program directory which includes information on the projects they are funding for the year.

☎ Contact:
Department of Education
Mary E. Switzer Building
MS-2305
330 C St., SW
Washington, DC 20202
(202) 732-6151

Free Publications/Videos

The following publications on the Handicapped are available from the National Information Center for Handicapped Children and Youth, P.O.

Box 1492, Washington, DC 20013; (800) 999-5599, (703) 893-6061.

- *Parents' Guide to Accessing Programs for Infants, Toddlers, Preschoolers with Handicaps.*
- *Parents' Guide to Accessing Parent Programs, Community Services, and Record Keeping.*
- *Life After School for Children with Disabilities: Answers to Questions.*
- *Parents Ask about Employment and Financial Assistance.*
- *A Parent's Guide: Accessing the ERIC Resource Collection.*
- *A Parent's Guide to Doctors, Disabilities, and the Family.*
- *A Parent's Guide: Planning a Move; Mapping Your Strategy.*
- *A Parent's Guide: Special Education and Related Services: Communicating Through Letter Writing.*

The following publication on Devices for the Handicapped is available from the Center for Devices and Radiological Health, (HFZ-210), Food and Drug Administration, 5600 Fishers Ln., Rockville, MD 20857; (301) 443-4690.

- *Regulatory Requirements for Devices for the Handicapped.* (#FDA 87-4221)

The following publication on the Handicapped is available from the National Health Information Center, P.O. Box 1133, Washington, DC 20013; (800) 336-4797, or (301) 565-4167 in DC metro area.

- *Healthfinder: Family Care.* Provides information on support services offered by national organizations and foundations as well as government services available to individuals with handicaps or disabilities.

The following publication on the Handicapped is available from the Food & Nutrition Information Center, National Agricultural Library, Room 304, Beltsville, MD 20705-2351; (301) 504-5719.

- *Nutrition and the Handicapped.* Designed to help you locate resources on this topic.

HANDICAPPED CHILDREN

Clearinghouses/Hotlines

The National Information Center for Handicapped Children and Youth (NICHCY) helps parents of Handicapped Children and disabled adults locate services for the handicapped, along with providing information on learning disabilities through newsletters, parent guides, and other helpful publications.

☎ Contact:
The National Information Center
for Handicapped Children and Youth
P.O. Box 1492
Washington, DC 20013
(800) 999-5599
(703) 893-6061

Free Publications/Videos

The following publications are available from the National Maternal and Child Health Clearinghouse, 38th & R Sts., NW, Washington, DC 20057; (703) 821-8955, ext. 254.

- *Surgeon General's Workshop on Children With Handicaps and Their Families.* (#B118)
- *Technology-Dependent Children: Hospital v. Home Care.* (#B316)
- *Four Critical Junctures: Support for Parents of Children With Special Needs.* (#C016)

HANSEN'S DISEASE

Clearinghouses/Hotlines

The National Institute on Allergy and Infectious Diseases (NIAID) can search the Combined Health Information Database (CHID) and generate a bibliography of resources on Hansen's Disease for you. They will also send you any publications and journal articles they may have on hand, and will refer you to researchers who are currently studying this disease. If you can't afford treatment, have your doctor call NIAID to find out if they are conducting any clinical studies that you might qualify for.

☎ Contact:
National Institute of Allergy
and Infectious Diseases
Bldg. 31, Room 7A32
Bethesda, MD 20892
(301) 496-5717

HAPPY PUPPET SYNDROME

Clearinghouses/Hotlines

The National Institute of Neurological Disorders and Stroke (NINDS) can send you only information they have in their publications list on Happy Puppet Syndrome. They cannot refer you to any experts. This Clearinghouse cannot directly give you information about any current clinical studies NINDS might be conducting on this illness, but you can find this information for yourself by looking under the National Institute of Neurological Disorders and Stroke in *Appendix A* at the end of this book.

☎ Contact:
National Institute of Neurological
Disorders and Stroke
Bldg. 31, Room 8A06
Bethesda, MD 20892
(301) 496-5751
(800) 352-9424

HARADA'S DISEASE

Clearinghouses/Hotlines

The National Eye Institute (NEI) can give you up-to-date information on Harada's Disease by searching the Combined Health Information Database (CHID) and MEDLINE and sending you bibliographies of resources, along with any journal articles they may have. They can also

refer you to any other organizations that study this and other related diseases. NEI will also let you know of any clinical studies that may be studying this disease and looking for patients. Because of their small staff, NEI prefers that you submit your requests for information in writing.

☎ Contact:
National Eye Institute
Building 31
Room 6A32
Bethesda, MD 20892
(301) 496-5248

HARDENING OF THE ARTERIES

Clearinghouses/Hotlines

The National Heart, Lung, and Blood Institute (NHLBI) can search the Combined Health Information Database (CHID) and generate a bibliography of resources on Hardening of the Arteries for you. They also will send you any publications and journal articles they may have on hand, and will refer you to other organizations that are studying this disease. If you can't afford treatment, have your doctor call NHLBI to find out if they are conducting any clinical studies that you might qualify for.

☎ Contact:
National Heart, Lung, and Blood Institute
Bldg. 31, Room 4A21
Bethesda, MD 20892
(301) 496-4236

HARELIP

Clearinghouses/Hotlines

The National Institute on Deafness and Other Communication Disorders Clearinghouse can provide you with information regarding Harelip, as well as directing you to other organizations dealing with this condition.

☏ Contact:
National Institute on Deafness and Other
Communication Disorders Clearinghouse
1010 Wayne Ave., Suite 300
Silver Spring, MD 20910
(800) 241-1044
(301) 402-0252 (TDD)

HASHIMOTO'S DISEASE

Clearinghouses/Hotlines

The National Institute of Diabetes and Digestive and Kidney Diseases's (NIDDK) individual clearinghouses can search the Combined Health Information Database (CHID) and generate a bibliography of resources on Hashimoto's Disease for you. They also will send you any publications and journal articles they may have on hand, and will refer you to other organizations that are studying this disease. If you can't afford treatment, have your doctor call NIDDK to find out if they are conducting any clinical studies that you might qualify for.

☏ Contact:
National Institute of Diabetes
and Digestive and Kidney Diseases
Bldg. 31, Room 9A04
Bethesda, MD 20892
(301) 496-3583

HAVERHILL FEVER
(Rat Bite Fever)

Clearinghouses/Hotlines

The National Institute of Allergy and Infectious Diseases can provide you with reference materials on Haverhill Fever, which is an infectious disease transmitted by a rat bite.

☏ Contact:
National Institute of Allergy
and Infectious Diseases
Bldg. 31, Room 7A32

Bethesda, MD 20892
(301) 496-5717

HAY FEVER

Clearinghouses/Hotlines

The National Institute on Allergy and Infectious Diseases (NIAID) can search the Combined Health Information Database (CHID) and generate a bibliography of resources on Hay Fever for you. They will also send you any publications and journal articles they may have on hand, and will refer you to researchers who are currently studying this disease. If you can't afford treatment, have your doctor call NIAID to find out if they are conducting any clinical studies that you might qualify for.

☏ Contact:
National Institute of Allergy
and Infectious Diseases
Bldg. 31, Room 7A32
Bethesda, MD 20892
(301) 496-5717

HAZARDOUS SUBSTANCES

Clearinghouses/Hotlines

When Hazardous Substances are released into a specific area, such as when a train car carrying chlorine derails or a truck with pesticides overturns, the Agency for Toxic Substances and Disease Registry evaluates the potential impact the accident may have on the health of the surrounding community. If such an accident has occurred in your neighborhood, you can request that a health assessment be conducted. This office also sponsors Citizens' Roundtables, which give communities the opportunity to express their needs and concerns. They also offer educational materials on the health effects and medical surveillance of people exposed to hazardous substances, including a series of self-instructional documents called *Case Studies in Environmental Medicine*.

☎ Contact:
Agency for Toxic Substances
and Disease Registry
1600 Clifton Rd., NE
Atlanta, GA 30333
(404) 639-0600

Are you concerned that your home or environment may be polluted by a Hazardous Substance? The Public Information Center can provide you with information regarding hazardous substances, as well as direct you to other hotlines and sources of information more specific to your request.

☎ Contact:
Public Information Center
Environmental Protection Agency
401 M St., SW
Washington, DC 20460
(202) 260-7751

Free Publications/Videos

The following publication on Hazardous Substances is available from the Public Information Center PM211 B, Environmental Protection Agency, 401 M St., SW, Washington, DC 20460; (202) 260-2080.

- *Hazardous Substances In Our Environment: A Citizen's Guide to Understanding Health Risks and Reducing Exposure.* Helps answer your questions about health risks from hazardous substances after reading statements in newspapers, book and government reports. Part 1 describes different hazardous substances and how they get into your environment, and Part 2 describes government actions, community activities and personal actions you can take. Also included is a list of publications and resources for further information.

HEADACHES

Clearinghouses/Hotlines

The National Institute of Neurological Disorders and Stroke (NINDS) can send you only information they have in their publications list on Headaches. They cannot refer you to any experts. This Clearinghouse cannot directly give you information about any current clinical studies NINDS might be conducting on this topic, but you can find this information for yourself by looking under the National Institute of Neurological Disorders and Stroke in *Appendix A* at the end of this book.

☎ Contact:
National Institute of Neurological
Disorders and Stroke
Building 31
Room 8A06
Bethesda, MD 20892
(301) 496-5751
(800) 352-9424

Free Publications/Videos

The following publications are available from the National Institute of Neurological Disorders and Stroke, Bldg. 31, Room 8A06, Bethesda, MD 20892; (301) 496-5751 or (800) 352-9424.

- *Headache*. (#84-158)
- *Headache*. Discusses hope through research.
- *Headache*. Contains a collection of scientific articles, patient education pamphlets, and addresses of voluntary health associations.

HEAD INJURIES

Clearinghouses/Hotlines

The National Institute of Neurological Disorders and Stroke (NINDS) can send you only information they have in their publications list on Head Injuries. They cannot refer you to any experts. This Clearinghouse cannot directly give you information about any current clinical studies NINDS might be conducting on this topic, but you can find this information for yourself by looking under the National Institute of Neurological Disorders and Stroke in *Appendix A* at the end of this book.

☎ Contact:
National Institute of Neurological
Disorders and Stroke
Bldg. 31, Room 8A06
Bethesda, MD 20892
(301) 496-5751
(800) 352-9424

The National Institute on Deafness and Other Communicative Disorders (NIDCD) will send you whatever publications and reprints of journal articles they have on Head Injuries. If you need further information, they will refer you to other organizations that this and other related diseases. NIDCD does not conduct any clinical studies for this or any other disorder.

☎ Contact:
National Institute on Deafness
and Other Communication Disorders
Bldg. 31, Room 3C35
Bethesda, MD 20892
(301) 496-7243
(800) 241-1044
(301) 402-0252 (TDD)

Free Publications/Videos

The following publications are available from the National Institute of Neurological Disorders and Stroke, Bldg. 31, Room 8A06, Bethesda, MD 20892; (301) 496-5751 or (800) 352-9424.

- *Head Injury: Hope through Research*. Discusses ways to prevent head injuries and the resulting damage from different types of injuries, as well as rehabilitation techniques. (#84-2478)
- *Head Injury*. Discusses hope through research.

HEAD LICE

Clearinghouses/Hotlines

The National Institute on Allergy and Infectious Diseases (NIAID) can search the Combined Health Information Database (CHID) and generate a bibliography of resources on Head Lice (Pediculosis) for you. They will also send you any publications and journal articles they may have on hand, and will refer you to researchers who are currently studying this disease. If you can't afford treatment, have your doctor call NIAID to find out if they are conducting any clinical studies that you might qualify for.

☎ Contact:
National Institute of Allergy
and Infectious Diseases
Bldg. 31, Room 7A32
Bethesda, MD 20892
(301) 496-5717

HEALTH CARE COSTS

Clearinghouses/Hotlines

The Health Care Financing Administration and Social Security Administration collect statistics on health, health care, and health care financing. They distribute data on a wide variety of topics, such as spending on health care services, the age of recipients of services, and health problems.

☎ Contact:
Health Care Financing Administration
200 Independence Ave., SW, Room 423-H
Washington, DC 20201
(202) 245-8056
and
Office of Research and Statistics
Social Security Administration
1875 Connecticut Ave., NW
Washington, DC 20009
(202) 965-1234

Free Publications/Videos

The following Congressional Research Service (CRS) reports on Health Care Costs are available from either of your U.S. Senators' offices at the U.S. Capitol, Washington, DC 20510, or from your Congressional Representative at the U.S. Capitol, Washington, DC 20515. You can also call in your request through the U.S. Capitol switchboard at (202) 224-3121. Be sure to include the full title and report number in your request.

- *AIDS: Acquired Immune Deficiency Syndrome; Selected References.* (#89-333 L)
- *Appropriations for Selected Health Programs, FY 1980-FY 1991* (#91-769 EPW)
- *Controlling Health Care Costs.* (#90-64 EPW)
- *Elderly Home Care: Tax Incentives and Proposals for Change.* (#89-662 E)
- *Generic Drugs and the Elderly; Issues and Policy Considerations.* (#91-792 SPR)
- *Health Care: Archived Issue Brief.* (#IB87009)
- *Health Care Costs and Cost Containment, Audio Brief.* (#AB50216)
- *Health Care Costs and Cost Containment.* (#LTR91-878)
- *Health Care Costs at the End of Life.* (#90-368 EPW)
- *Health Care Cost Containment: Bibliography-in-Brief, 1986-1988.* (#88-376 L)
- *Health Care Costs: Info Pack.* (#IP223H)
- *Health Care Expenditures and Prices: Issue Brief.* (#IB77066)
- *Health Care Financing and Health Insurance: A Glossary of Terms.* (#88-539 EPW)
- *Health Care: Issue Brief.* (#IB87009)
- *Health Care Issues for the 102nd Congress.* (#91-128 EPW)
- *Health Insurance and the Uninsured: Background Data and Analysis.* (#88-537 EPW)
- *Health Insurance Coverage: Characteristics of the Insured and Uninsured Populations.* (#91-618 EPW)
- *National Health Expenditures: Trends from 1960-1989.* (#91-588 EPW)

HEALTH CARE POLICY

Clearinghouses/Hotlines

The Agency for Health Care Policy and Research (AHCPR) is the primary source of Federal support for research on problems related to the quality and delivery of health services. AHCPR programs evaluate health services, assess technologies, improve access to new scientific and technical information for research users. Research

findings are disseminated through publications, conferences, and workshops. Materials are available on medical treatment effectiveness, health care costs and utilizations, health care expenditures, health information systems, health technology assessment, and funding opportunities for grants and contracts.

☎ Contact:
Agency for Health Care Policy
and Research
5600 Fishers Lane
Rockville, MD 20857
(301) 443-4100

Free Publications/Videos

The following publication is available from the Subcommittee on Housing and Consumer Interests, Room 717, O'Neill HOB, 300 New Jersey Ave., SE, Washington, DC 20515; (202) 226-3344.

- *Women Health Care Consumers: Shortchanges in Medical Research and Treatment.*

The following publication is available from the Subcommittee on Health on Long-Term Care, Room 377, Ford HOB, 2nd & D Sts., SW, Washington, DC 20515; (202) 226-3381.

- *The Nation's Long-Term Health Care Crisis.*

The following video is available from Modern Talking Picture Service, 5000 Park St. North, St. Petersburg, FL 33709; (800) 243-MTPS.

- *First Comes Caring.* Video on physicians and medical advances.

The following Congressional Research Service (CRS) reports on Health Care Policy are available from either of your U.S. Senators' offices at the U.S. Capitol, Washington, DC 20510, or from your Congressional Representative at the U.S. Capitol, Washington, DC 20515. You can also call in your request through the U.S. Capitol switchboard at (202) 224-3121. Be sure to include the full title and report number in your request.

- *The Canadian Health Care System.* (#90-95 EPQ)

- *Catastrophic Health Insurance: Medicare.*
  (#IB87106)
- *Catastrophic Health Insurance: Bibliography-in-Brief, 1986-1988.* (#88-401 L)
- *Catastrophic Health Insurance: Info Pack.*
  (#IP370C)
- *Catastrophic Health Insurance: Medicare; Issue Brief.* (#IB87106)
- *Financing Catastrophic Health Care: Possible Effects on Marginal and Average Income Tax Rates.* (#89-132 E)
- *Health Care Access: Federal Policy Issues; Info Pack.* (#IP421H)
- *Health Care: Archived Issue Brief.* (#IB87009)
- *Health Care Financing and Health Insurance: A Glossary of Terms.* (#88-539 EPW)
- *Health Care for Children: Federal Programs and Policies.* (#88-217 EPW)
- *Health Care: Issue Brief.* (#IB87009)
- *Health Care.* (#IB87009)
- *Health Care Expenditures and Prices.*
  (#IB77066)
- *The Japanese Health Care System.* (#89-572 EPW)
- *Medicare Catastrophic Coverage Act of 1988 (P.L. 100-360).* (#89-155 EPW)

HEALTH FACILITIES

Free Publications/Videos

The following Congressional Research Service (CRS) reports on Health Facilities are available from either of your U.S. Senators' offices at the U.S. Capitol, Washington, DC 20510, or from your Congressional Representative at the U.S. Capitol, Washington, DC 20515. You can also call in your request through the U.S. Capitol switchboard at (202) 224-3121. Be sure to include the full title and report number in your request.

- *Community Health Centers and the Primary Care Block Grant.* (#86-899 EPW)
- *Community Services under Medicaid for Persons With Mental Retardation: Archived Issue Brief.* (#IB89135)
- *Description of Residential Facilities for the Elderly.* (#84-19 EPW)

- *Rural Hospitals.* (#89-296 EPW)
- *Rural Hospitals under Medicare's Prospective Payment System and the Omnibus Budget Reconciliation Act of 1986 (P.L. 99-509).*
  (#87-816 EPW)
- *Advance Directives and Health Care Facilities.*
  (#91-117 EPW)

HEALTH FOODS

See also Food
See also Nutrition

Clearinghouses/Hotlines

Food and Nutrition Information Center can provide you with a wealth of information on food and nutrition topics. They have bibliographies ready and a data base through which they can search any food or nutrition subject.

☎ Contact:
Food and Nutrition Information Center
National Agricultural Library
Room 304
Beltsville, MD 20705
(301) 504-5719

Free Publications/Videos

The following publication is available from the Food & Drug Administration, (HFE-88), 5600 Fishers Ln., Rockville, MD 20857; (301) 443-3170.

- *The Confusing World of Health Foods.*
  Provides general information about foods sold as health foods and about such terms as "organic". (#84-2108)

HEALTH FRAUD

Free Publications/Videos

The following publications are available from the Center for Devices and Radiological Health,

(HFZ-210), Food and Drug Administration, 5600 Fishers Ln., Rockville, MD 20857; (301) 443-4690.

- *Top 10 Health Frauds.*
- *Quackery Targets Teens.*
- *EMS: Electrical Muscle Stimulaters.*
- *Critiquing Quack Ads.*
- *Quackery: The Billion Dollar Miracle Business.* (#FDA 85-4200)
- *EMS Fraudulent Flab Remover.*
- *Open Season on Quacks.*
- *The Big Quack Attack.* (#FDA 80-4022)
- *The Gadget Quacks.*

The following publication is available from the Subcommittee on Health on Long-Term Care, Room 377, Ford HOB, 2nd & D Sts., SW, Washington, DC 20515; (202) 226-3381.

- *Innovation in Telemarketing Frauds and Scams.*

HEALTH INSURANCE

Clearinghouses/Hotlines

The National Institute on Alcohol Abuse and Alcoholism (NIAAA) looks at trends relating to treatment of alcoholism and insurance financing issues. It advocates adequate health insurance coverage for alcoholism treatment, and conducts studies on this topic, which are available to the public.

☎ Contact:
National Institute on Alcohol
Abuse and Alcoholism
5600 Fishers Lane, Room 16-95
Rockville, MD 20857
(301) 443-2595

Free Publications/Videos

The following publication on Health Insurance is available from the Agency for Health Care Policy and Research Publications Clearinghouse, P.O. Box 8547, Silver Spring, MD 20907; (800) 358-9295.

- *Checkup on Health Insurance Choices.* Describes different types of health insurance, worksheets, checklists, and a glossary of health insurance terms to help people understand their insurance options.

The following publications on Health Insurance are available from the Office of Technology Assessment, Washington, DC 20510-8025; (202) 224-8996.

- *Genetic Tests and Health Insurance: Results of a Survey.* (#OTA-BP-BA-98)
- *Does Health Insurance Make A Difference?.* (#OTA-BP-H-99)

The following publication on Health Insurance is available from the Subcommittee on Health on Long-Term Care, Room 377, Ford HOB, 2nd & D Sts., SW, Washington, DC 20515; (202) 226-3381.

- *Abuses in the Sale of Long-Term Care Insurance to the Elderly.*

The following publication on Health Insurance is available from the Subcommittee on Retirement Income and Employment, Room 714, O'Neill HOB, 300 New Jersey Ave., SE, Washington, DC 20515; (202) 226-3335.

- *Nationalized Health Insurance: The Lessons of Catastrophic Care.*

The following Congressional Research Service (CRS) reports on Health Insurance are available from either of your U.S. Senators' offices at the U.S. Capitol, Washington, DC 20510, or from your Congressional Representative at the U.S. Capitol, Washington, DC 20515. You can also call in your request through the U.S. Capitol switchboard at (202) 224-3121. Be sure to include the full title and report number in your request.

- *Health Insurance: Issue Brief.* (#IB91093)
- *Health Insurance: Info Pack.* (#IP072H)
- *Health Insurance: Approaches for Universal Coverage.* (#90-568 EPW)
- *Health Insurance and the Uninsured: Background Data and Analysis, Education and Public Welfare Division.* (#88-537 EPW)
- *Increasing Access to Health Insurance: Audio*

Brief. (#AB50166)
- *Catastrophic Health Insurance: Medicare.* (#IB87106)
- *Catastrophic Health Insurance: Info Pack.* (#IP370C)
- *Catastrophic Health Insurance: Bibliography-in-Brief, 1986-1988.* (#88-401 L)
- *Long-Term Care for the Elderly.* (#IB88098)
- *Mandated Employer Provided Health Insurance.* (#IB87168)
- *Private Health Insurance: Continuation Coverage.* (#IB87182)
- *Access to Health Care and Health Insurance: Bibliography-in-Brief, 1986-1987.* (#88-27 L)
- *The Canadian Health Care System.* (#90-95 EPQ)
- *Employees Group Health Insurance Benefits Continuation under COBRA.* (#91-97 A)
- *Employer Provided Health Insurance: Comparison of the Major Provisions of the "Minimum Health Benefits for All Workers Act" (S. 1265/H.R. 2508).* (#88-588 EPW)
- *Health Insurance Continuation Coverage under COBRA: Issue Brief.* (#IB87182)
- *Health Insurance Coverage: Characteristics of the Insured and Uninsured Populations.* (#91-618 EPW)
- *Health Insurance: Employer Benefits Required under COBRA and Pending Proposals.* (#IP389H)
- *Health Insurance Legislation in the 102nd Congress.* (#91-564 EPW)
- *Health Insurance that Supplements Medicare: Background Material and Data.* (#89-421 EPW)
- *Private Health Insurance Continuation Coverage; Issue Brief.* (#IB87182)
- *Private Health Insurance Continuation Coverage: Legislative History of Title X of COBRA.* (#87-613 EPW)

HEALTH MAINTENANCE ORGANIZATIONS

Free Publications/Videos

The following Congressional Research Service (CRS) reports on Health Maintenance

Organizations are available from either of your U.S. Senators' offices at the U.S. Capitol, Washington, DC 20510, or from your Congressional Representative at the U.S. Capitol, Washington, DC 20515. You can also call in your request through the U.S. Capitol switchboard at (202) 224-3121. Be sure to include the full title and report number in your request.

- *Health Maintenance Organizations (HMO) and Employer Group Health Plans.* (#91-261 EPW)
- *Health Maintenance Organizations: Bibliography-in-Brief, 1983-1987.* (#88-87 L)

HEALTH PROFESSIONALS

Free Publications/Videos

The following Congressional Research Service (CRS) reports on Health Professionals are available from either of your U.S. Senators' offices at the U.S. Capitol, Washington, DC 20510, or from your Congressional Representative at the U.S. Capitol, Washington, DC 20515. You can also call in your request through the U.S. Capitol switchboard at (202) 224-3121. Be sure to include the full title and report number in your request.

- *Clinical Laboratory Improvement Amendments of 1988 (CLIA).* (#90-421 EPW)
- *Health Professions Education and Nurse Training Programs: Titles VI and VIII; Issue Brief.* (#IB88055)
- *Health Professions Education and Nurse Training Programs: Titles VII and VIII of the Public Health Service Act.* (#IB88055)
- *HIV Infected Health Care Workers: The Legal Issues.* (#91-598 A)
- *HIV Infected Health Care Workers: The Medical and Scientific Issues.* (#91-622 SPR)
- *Life-Sustaining Technologies: Medical and Moral Issues.* (#91-45 SPR)
- *Medicare Payments to Hospitals and Physicians: Info Pack.* (#IP317M)
- *Medicare Physician Payment Reform.* (#91-643 EPW)

- *Medicare: Physicians Payments.* (88-658 EPW)
- *Medicare: Physician Referrals to Clinical Laboratories.* (#90-439 EPW)
- *Medicare's Peer Review Organizations.* (#90-273 EPW)
- *National Health Service Corps.* (91-729 EPW)
- *Nurses: Supply and Demand; Bibliography-in-Brief 1981-1988.* (#88-729 L)

HEALTH SPAS

Free Publications/Videos

The following publication is available from the Federal Trade Commission, Washington, DC 20580; (202) 326-2222.

- *Health Spas: Exercise Your Rights.* Explains what to consider when you join a health spa, as well as what to do when you have a complaint. The Consumer Protection Division of your State Attorney General's Office can handle complaints against health spas.

HEALTH STATISTICS

See also Appendix C

Clearinghouses/Hotlines

The National Center for Health Statistics collects, analyzes, and distributes data on health in the United States. Materials available include statistical data on health, nutrition, vital statistics such as births and divorces, health care delivery, dental health, health resources utilization, health care personnel, families, contraception, and health care economics.

☎ Contact:
Centers for Disease Control
6525 Belcrest Rd., Room 1064
Hyattsville, MD 20782
(301) 436-8500

The *Morbidity and Mortality Weekly Report* is published by the Centers for Disease Control (CDC), and in each issue the CDC examines the data on a specific health topic, including such things as abortion, AIDS, measles, pediatric nutrition, smoking and more. At the end of each report, references are listed. You can call the Morbidity and Mortality Weekly Report office to see if they have a report on your topic of interest, but you must order the publication from the Superintendent of Documents, Government Printing Office, Washington, DC 20402; (202) 783-3238.

☎ Contact:
Morbidity and Mortality Weekly Report
Centers for Disease Control
1600 Clifton Rd., NE
Atlanta, GA 30333
(404) 639-2104

A state's health care registration system is often the best place to start researching specific health data for an entire state's population. In addition, each state makes available its annual health report in a number of formats. See *Appendix C* for information about your state's health statistics, as well as the services and products they offer.

Free Publications/Videos

The following publication is available from the Health Resources and Services Administration, Office of Data Analysis and Management, Parklawn Bldg. Room 8-43, 5600 Fishers Ln., Rockville, MD 20857; (301) 443-6936.

- *Inventory of U.S. Health Care Databases, 1976-1987.* Presents abstracts of more than 300 health care databases created or maintained by both public and private sector agencies and organizations.

HEARING AIDS

Clearinghouses/Hotlines

The National Institute on Deafness and Other

Communication Disorders (NICHD) can send you a packet of information regarding Hearing Aids, including such pamphlets to explain the different types of hearing loss, hearing aids, hearing aid use and maintenance and more. Call for your free packet.

☎ Contact:
National Institute on Deafness and
Other Communication Disorders Clearinghouse
1010 Wayne Ave., Suite 300
Silver Spring, MD 20910
(800) 241-1044
(301) 402-0252 (TDD)

Free Publications/Videos

The following publication on Hearing Aids is available from the Food & Drug Administration, (HFE-88), 5600 Fishers Ln., Rockville, MD 20857; (301) 443-3170.

- *Facts about Hearing and Hearing Aids.*
Discusses the causes of and treatment for hearing loss and the selection, use, and care of hearing aids. (#79-4016)

The following publications are available from the Center for Devices and Radiological Health, (HFZ-210), Food and Drug Administration, 5600 Fishers Ln., Rockville, MD 20857; (301) 443-4690.

- *Hearing Aids: A Link to the World.*
- *When Bells Are Ringing (But There Aren't Any Bells).*
- *Cochlear Implant.*
- *It's Not Only A Good Idea, It's Also The Law.*
- *Tuning In On Hearing Aids.*
- *Facts About Hearing and Hearing Aids.*
(#FDA 79-4016)

The following publication on Hearing Aids is available from the Federal Trade Commission, Office of Consumer Education, Bureau of Consumer Protection, Washington, DC 20580; (202) 326-3650.

- *Hearing Aids.* Describes the types of hearing loss, purchase suggestions for hearing aids, purchase agreements and Federal standards for sales.

HEARING LOSS

Clearinghouses/Hotlines

The National Institute of Neurological Disorders and Stroke (NINDS) can send you only information they have in their publications list on Hearing Disorders. They cannot refer you to any experts. This Clearinghouse cannot directly give you information about any current clinical studies NINDS might be conducting on this condition, but you can find this information for yourself by looking under the National Institute of Neurological Disorders and Stroke in *Appendix A* at the end of this book.

☎ Contact:
National Institute of Neurological
Disorders and Stroke
Bldg. 31, Room 8A06
Bethesda, MD 20892
(301) 496-5751
(800) 352-9424

The National Institute on Aging (NIA) will send you whatever publications and reprints of journal articles they have on Hearing Loss and Aging. They cannot refer you to other experts if the information they have isn't sufficient for your purposes.

☎ Contact:
National Institute on Aging
Bldg. 31, Room 5C27
Bethesda, MD 20892
(301) 496-1752

The National Institute on Deafness and Other Communicative Disorders (NIDCD) will send you whatever publications and reprints of journal articles they have on Hearing Loss. If you need further information, they will refer you to other organizations that this and other related diseases. NIDCD does not conduct any clinical studies for this or any other disorder.

☎ Contact:
National Institute on Deafness
and Other Communication Disorders
Bldg. 31, Room 3C35
Bethesda, MD 20892
(301) 496-7243

(800) 241-1044
(301) 402-0252 (TDD)

Free Publications/Videos

The following publication is available from the Office of Technology Assessment, 600 Pennsylvania Ave., SE, Washington, DC 20510; (202) 224-8996.

- *Hearing Impairment and Elderly People.* A report to Congress. Ask for the summary report. (#BP-BA-30)

The following publication and video on Hearing Loss are available from the Office of Clinical Center Communications, Bldg. 10, Room 1C255, Bethesda, MD 20892; (301) 496-2563.

- *Hearing Impairment.* A booklet to educate consumers and allow them to make informed medical decisions.
- *Hearing Impairment: The Invisible Handicap.* Video to help the general public make intelligent decisions.

The following publication is available from the National Institute on Deafness and Other Communication Disorders, Bldg. 31, Room 3C35, Bethesda, MD 20892; (301) 496-7243.

- *Hearing Loss.* (#82-157)

The following video is available from Modern Talking Picture Service, 5000 Park St. North, St. Petersburg, FL 33709; (800) 243-MTPS.

- *The Pleasure of Hearing.* Video helps recognize hearing impairment, overcome inhibitions about seeking help.

HEART ATTACKS

Clearinghouses/Hotlines

The National Heart, Lung, and Blood Institute (NHLBI) can search the Combined Health Information Database (CHID) and generate a bibliography of resources on Heart Attacks for you. They also will send you any publications and journal articles they may have on hand, and will refer you to other organizations that are studying this disease. If you can't afford treatment, have your doctor call NHLBI to find out if they are conducting any clinical studies that you might qualify for.

☎ Contact:
National Heart, Lung, and Blood Institute
Bldg. 31, Room 4A21
Bethesda, MD 20892
(301) 496-4236

Free Publications/Videos

The following publication is available from the High Blood Pressure Information Center, 4733 Bethesda Ave., Suite 530, Bethesda, MD 20814; (301) 951-3260.

- *Heart Attacks.* Facts about the leading cause of death in the U.S.

The following video is available from Modern Talking Picture Service, 5000 Park St. North, St. Petersburg, FL 33709; (800) 243-MTPS.

- *Heart Attacks.* Video talks about heart attacks: symptoms, causes, risk factors, treatment and research.

HEARTBURN

Clearinghouses/Hotlines

The National Digestive Diseases Information Clearinghouse will respond to your requests for information about Heartburn and distributes information to health professionals, people with digestive diseases, and the general public. They have many publications, as well as a news bulletin.

☎ Contact:
National Digestive Diseases
Information Clearinghouse
Box NDDIC

Bethesda, MD 20892
(301) 468-6344

Free Publications/Videos

The following publications are available from the National Digestive Diseases Information Clearinghouse, Box NDDIC, Bethesda, MD 20892; (301) 468-6344.

- *Heartburn.*
- *Esophageal Reflux.* Information packet.

HEART DISEASE

See also Cardiovascular Disease

Clearinghouses/Hotlines

The National Cholesterol Education Program acts as a clearinghouse to inform the public about Cardiovascular Disease. The Program works to increase the general public's awareness about the importance of having their blood cholesterol levels checked, knowing what their cholesterol levels are, and taking steps to lower elevated levels. They also develop materials for the worksite and the schools.

☎ Contact:
National Institutes of Health
Building 31, Room 4A-21
9000 Rockville Pike
Bethesda, MD 20892
(301) 951-3260

Free Publications/Videos

The following publications are available from the National Heart, Lung, and Blood Institute, Bldg. 31, Room 4A21, Bethesda, MD 20892; (301) 496-4236.

- *Foods For Health: Report of the Pilot Program.* Shares the results of a one-year experiment to increase consumer awareness and knowledge about nutrition as it relates to cardiovascular risk factors. (#83-2036)
- *Artificial Heart and Assist Devices.* (#85-2723)
- *The Healthy Heart Handbook for Women.* Self-help guide answers many questions about women and cardiovascular disease.
- *With Every Beat of Your Heart: An Ideabook for Community Heart Health Programs.* Basic information for use in starting or expanding a heart health program.
- *Test Your Healthy Heart "I.Q.".* True-false test of heart disease. (#88-2724)
- *Directory of Cardiovascular Resources for Minority Population.* Describes available materials on cardiovascular disease.
- *Small Business Basics: Guidelines for Heart and Lung Health at the Workplace.* Guidelines for establishing heart and lung health programs and practices in the workplace.
- *Play Your Cards Right...Stay Young at Heart: A Heart Health Nutrition Education Program.* Kit designed to help program planners implement a heart healthy eating program at their worksite cafeteria, restaurant, school, or other eating establishment.

The following publication is available from the Office of Clinical Center Communications, Bldg. 10, Room 1C255, Bethesda, MD 20892; (301) 496-2563.

- *Risk of Heart Disease.* (#89-2985) Discusses new findings in clinical cardiology, new techniques to diagnose abnormalities in the pumping function of the heart, and new concepts in treating people who come to the hospital with an acute heart attack.

HEART-LUNG MACHINES

Clearinghouses/Hotlines

The National Heart, Lung, and Blood Institute (NHLBI) can search the Combined Health Information Database (CHID) and generate a bibliography of resources on Heart-Lung Machines for you. They also will send you any publications and journal articles they may have on hand, and will refer you to other organizations that are studying these devices. If you can't afford treatment, have your doctor call NHLBI to find out if they are conducting any clinical studies that you might qualify for.

☎ Contact:
National Heart, Lung, and Blood Institute
Bldg. 31, Room 4A21
Bethesda, MD 20892
(301) 496-4236

HEART MURMURS

Clearinghouses/Hotlines

The National Heart, Lung, and Blood Institute (NHLBI) can search the Combined Health Information Database (CHID) and generate a bibliography of resources on Heart Murmurs for you. They also will send you any publications and journal articles they may have on hand, and will refer you to other organizations that are studying this disease. If you can't afford treatment, have your doctor call NHLBI to find out if they are conducting any clinical studies that you might qualify for.

☎ Contact:
National Heart, Lung, and Blood Institute
Bldg. 31, Room 4A21
Bethesda, MD 20892
(301) 496-4236

HEART TRANSPLANTS

Clearinghouses/Hotlines

The National Heart, Lung, and Blood Institute (NHLBI) can search the Combined Health Information Database (CHID) and generate a bibliography of resources on Heart Transplantation for you. They also will send you any publications and journal articles they may have on hand, and will refer you to other organizations

that are studying this disease. If you can't afford treatment, have your doctor call NHLBI to find out if they are conducting any clinical studies that you might qualify for.

☎ Contact:
National Heart, Lung, and Blood Institute
Building 31
Room 4A21
Bethesda, MD 20892
(301) 496-4236

HEAT STROKE

Clearinghouses/Hotlines

The National Institute on Aging (NIA) will send you whatever publications and reprints of journal articles they have on Heat Stroke and Aging. They cannot refer you to other experts if the information they have isn't sufficient for your purposes.

☎ Contact:
National Institute on Aging
Bldg. 31, Room 5C27
Bethesda, MD 20892
(301) 496-1752

HEBEPHRENIA

Clearinghouses/Hotlines

The National Institute of Mental Health (NIMH) maintains data bases that index and abstract documents from the worldwide literature pertaining to Hebephrenia and Mental Illness. In addition to scientific journals, there are references to audiovisuals, dissertations, government documents and reports. Contact NIMH for searches on specific subjects.

☎ Contact:
National Institute of Mental Health
5600 Fishers Lane
Room 15C05
Rockville, MD 20857
(301) 443-4515

HEMIPLEGIA

Clearinghouses/Hotlines

The National Institute of Neurological Disorders and Stroke (NINDS) can send you only information they have in their publications list on Hemiplegia. They cannot refer you to any experts. This Clearinghouse cannot directly give you information about any current clinical studies NINDS might be conducting on this illness, but you can find this information for yourself by looking under the National Institute of Neurological Disorders and Stroke in *Appendix A* at the end of this book.

☎ Contact:
National Institute of Neurological
Disorders and Stroke
Building 31
Room 8A06
Bethesda, MD 20892
(301) 496-5751
(800) 352-9424

HEMODIALYSIS

Clearinghouses/Hotlines

The National Institute on Deafness and Other Communicative Disorders (NIDCD) will send you whatever publications and reprints of journal articles they have on Hemodialysis. If you need further information, they will refer you to other organizations that this and other related diseases. NIDCD does not conduct any clinical studies for this or any other disorder.

☎ Contact:
National Institute of Diabetes
and Digestive and Kidney Diseases
Building 31
Room 9A04
Bethesda, MD 20892
(301) 496-3583
(800) 241-1044
(301) 402-0252 (TDD)

HEMOGLOBIN GENETICS

Clearinghouses/Hotlines

The National Institute of Diabetes and Digestive and Kidney Diseases's (NIDDK) individual clearinghouses can search the Combined Health Information Database (CHID) and generate a bibliography of resources on Hemoglobin Genetics for you. They also will send you any publications and journal articles they may have on hand, and will refer you to other organizations that are studying this topic.

☎ Contact:
National Institute of Diabetes
and Digestive and Kidney Diseases
Building 31
Room 9A04
Bethesda, MD 20892
(301) 496-3583

HEMOGLOBINOPATHIES

Clearinghouses/Hotlines

The National Institute of Diabetes and Digestive and Kidney Diseases's (NIDDK) individual clearinghouses can search the Combined Health Information Database (CHID) and generate a bibliography of resources on Hemoglobinopathies for you. They also will send you any publications and journal articles they may have on hand, and will refer you to other organizations that are studying this disease. If you can't afford treatment, have your doctor call NIDDK to find out if they are conducting any clinical studies that you might qualify.

☎ Contact:
National Institute of Diabetes
and Digestive and Kidney Diseases
Building 31
Room 9A04
Bethesda, MD 20892
(301) 496-3583

HEMOLYTIC ANEMIA

Clearinghouses/Hotlines

The National Institute of Diabetes and Digestive and Kidney Diseases's (NIDDK) individual clearinghouses can search the Combined Health Information Database (CHID) and generate a bibliography of resources on Hemolytic Anemia for you. They also will send you any publications and journal articles they may have on hand, and will refer you to other organizations that are studying this disease. If you can't afford treatment, have your doctor call NIDDK to find out if they are conducting any clinical studies that you might qualify.

☎ Contact:
National Institute of Diabetes
and Digestive and Kidney Diseases
Bldg. 31, Room 9A04
Bethesda, MD 20892
(301) 496-3583

The National Institute on Allergy and Infectious Diseases (NIAID) can search the Combined Health Information Database (CHID) and generate a bibliography of resources on Hemolytic Anemia for you. They will also send you any publications and journal articles they may have on hand, and will refer you to researchers who are currently studying this disease. If you can't afford treatment, have your doctor call NIAID to find out if they are conducting any clinical studies that you might qualify for.

☎ Contact:
National Institute of Allergy
and Infectious Diseases
Bldg. 31, Room 7A32
Bethesda, MD 20892
(301) 496-5717

HEMOLYTIC DISEASE

Clearinghouses/Hotlines

The National Institute of Child Health and Human Development (NICHD) will send you whatever publications and reprints of journal articles they have on Hemolytic Disease in Newborns. If necessary, they will refer you to other experts or researchers in the field. If you can't afford treatment, have your doctor call NICHD to find out if they are conducting any clinical studies that you might qualify for.

☎ Contact:
National Institute of Child Health
and Human Development
Bldg. 31, Room 2A32
Bethesda, MD 20892
(301) 496-5133

The National Heart, Lung, and Blood Institute (NHLBI) can search the Combined Health Information Database (CHID) and generate a bibliography of resources on Hemolytic Disease (Newborn) for you. They also will send you any publications and journal articles they may have on hand, and will refer you to other organizations that are studying this disease. If you can't afford treatment, have your doctor call NHLBI to find out if they are conducting any clinical studies that you might qualify for.

☎ Contact:
National Heart, Lung, and Blood Institute
Bldg. 31, Room 4A21
Bethesda, MD 20892
(301) 496-4236

HEMOPHILIA

Clearinghouses/Hotlines

The National Heart, Lung, and Blood Institute (NHLBI) can search the Combined Health Information Database (CHID) and generate a bibliography of resources on Hemophilia for you. They also will send you any publications and journal articles they may have on hand, and will refer you to other organizations that are studying this disease. If you can't afford treatment, have your doctor call NHLBI to find out if they are conducting any clinical studies that you might qualify for.

☎ Contact:
National Heart, Lung, and Blood Institute
Bldg. 31, Room 4A21
Bethesda, MD 20892
(301) 496-4236

HEMOPHILUS INFLUENZA

Clearinghouses/Hotlines

The National Institute on Allergy and Infectious Diseases (NIAID) can search the Combined Health Information Database (CHID) and generate a bibliography of resources on Hemophilus Influenza for you. They will also send you any publications and journal articles they may have on hand, and will refer you to researchers who are currently studying this disease. If you can't afford treatment, have your doctor call NIAID to find out if they are conducting any clinical studies that you might qualify for.

☎ Contact:
National Institute of Allergy
and Infectious Diseases
Bldg. 31, Room 7A32
Bethesda, MD 20892
(301) 496-5717

HEMORRHAGIC DIATHESIS

Clearinghouses/Hotlines

The National Institute of Diabetes and Digestive and Kidney Diseases's (NIDDK) individual clearinghouses can search the Combined Health Information Database (CHID) and generate a bibliography of resources on Hemorrhagic Diathesis for you. They also will send you any publications and journal articles they may have on hand, and will refer you to other organizations that are studying this disease. If you can't afford treatment, have your doctor call NIDDK to find out if they are conducting any clinical studies that you might qualify for.

☎ Contact:
National Institute of Diabetes
and Digestive and Kidney Diseases
Bldg. 31, Room 9A04
Bethesda, MD 20892
(301) 496-3583

The National Heart, Lung, and Blood Institute (NHLBI) can search the Combined Health Information Database (CHID) and generate a bibliography of resources on Hemorrhagic Diathesis for you. They also will send you any publications and journal articles they may have on hand, and will refer you to other organizations that are studying this disease. If you can't afford treatment, have your doctor call NHLBI to find out if they are conducting any clinical studies that you might qualify for.

☎ Contact:
National Heart, Lung, and Blood Institute
Bldg. 31, Room 4A21
Bethesda, MD 20892
(301) 496-4236

HEMORRHOIDS

Clearinghouses/Hotlines

The National Institute of Diabetes and Digestive and Kidney Diseases's (NIDDK) individual clearinghouses can search the Combined Health Information Database (CHID) and generate a bibliography of resources on Hemorrhoids for you. They also will send you any publications and journal articles they may have on hand, and will refer you to other organizations that are studying this disease. If you can't afford treatment, have your doctor call NIDDK to find out if they are conducting any clinical studies that you might qualify for.

☎ Contact:
National Institute of Diabetes
and Digestive and Kidney Diseases
Bldg. 31, Room 9A04
Bethesda, MD 20892
(301) 496-3583

The National Heart, Lung, and Blood Institute (NHLBI) can search the Combined Health Information Database (CHID) and generate a bibliography of resources on Hemorrhoids for you. They also will send you any publications and journal articles they may have on hand, and will refer you to other organizations that are studying this disease. If you can't afford treatment, have your doctor call NHLBI to find out if they are conducting any clinical studies that you might qualify for.

☎ Contact:
National Heart, Lung, and Blood Institute
Bldg. 31, Room 4A21
Bethesda, MD 20892
(301) 496-4236

Free Publications/Videos

The following publication is available from the National Digestive Diseases Information Clearinghouse, Box NDDIC, Bethesda, MD 20892; (301) 468-6344.

- *Hemorrhoids*.

HEMOSIDEROSIS

Clearinghouses/Hotlines

The National Heart, Lung, and Blood Institute (NHLBI) can search the Combined Health Information Database (CHID) and generate a bibliography of resources on Hemosiderosis for you. They also will send you any publications and journal articles they may have on hand, and will refer you to other organizations that are studying this disease. If you can't afford treatment, have your doctor call NHLBI to find out if they are conducting any clinical studies that you might qualify for.

☎ Contact:
National Heart, Lung, and Blood Institute
Bldg. 31, Room 4A21
Bethesda, MD 20892
(301) 496-4236

HENOCH-SCHONLEIN PURPURA

Clearinghouses/Hotlines

The National Institute on Allergy and Infectious Diseases (NIAID) can search the Combined Health Information Database (CHID) and generate a bibliography of resources on Henoch-Schonlein Purpura for you. They will also send you any publications and journal articles they may have on hand, and will refer you to researchers who are currently studying this disease. If you can't afford treatment, have your doctor call NIAID to find out if they are conducting any clinical studies that you might qualify for.

☎ Contact:
National Institute of Allergy
and Infectious Diseases
Bldg. 31, Room 7A32
Bethesda, MD 20892
(301) 496-5717

The National Institute of Child Health and Human Development (NICHD) will send you whatever publications and reprints of journal articles they have on Henoch-Schonlein Purpura. If necessary, they will refer you to other experts or researchers in the field. If you can't afford treatment, have your doctor call NICHD to find out if they are conducting any clinical studies that you might qualify for.

☎ Contact:
National Institute of Child Health
and Human Development
Bldg. 31, Room 2A32
Bethesda, MD 20892
(301) 496-5133

HEPATITIS

Clearinghouses/Hotlines

The National Institute on Allergy and Infectious Diseases (NIAID) can search the Combined

Health Information Database (CHID) and generate a bibliography of resources on Hepatitis for you. They will also send you any publications and journal articles they may have on hand, and will refer you to researchers who are currently studying this disease. If you can't afford treatment, have your doctor call NIAID to find out if they are conducting any clinical studies that you might qualify for.

☎ Contact:
National Institute of Allergy
and Infectious Diseases
Bldg. 31, Room 7A32
Bethesda, MD 20892
(301) 496-5717

The National Digestive Diseases Information Clearinghouse (NDDIC) can search the Combined Health Information Database (CHID) and generate a bibliography of resources on Hepatitis for you. They also will send you any publications and journal articles they may have on hand, and will refer you to other organizations that are studying this disease. If you can't afford treatment, have your doctor call NDDIC to find out if they are conducting any clinical studies that you might qualify.

☎ Contact:
National Digestive Diseases
Information Clearinghouse
Box NDDIC
Bethesda, MD 20892
(301) 468-6344

The Centers for Disease Control's Voice Information System allows anyone using a touchtone phone to obtain pre-recorded information on Hepatitis, and many other conditions. This service offers information about Hepatitis, symptoms and prevention methods, immunization requirements, current statistics, recent disease outbreak, and available printed materials. The system is available 24 hours a day, although the health professionals are available Monday through Friday, 8-4:30.

☎ Contact:
Centers for Disease Control
Information Resources Management Office
Mail Stop C-15, 1600 Clifton Rd., NE
Atlanta, GA 30333
(404) 332-4555

Free Publications/Videos

The following publication on Hepatitis is available from the National Digestive Diseases Information Clearinghouse, Box NDDIC, 9000 Rockville Pike, Bethesda, MD 20892; (301) 468-6344.

- *Hepatitis B Prevention: A Resource Guide 1990*. Directory of 64 national, state, and local organizations that provide hepatitis B prevention services. Also includes a bibliography with 347 citations to professional and patient literature about hepatitis B prevention. 251 pages. (#DD-90)

The following publication on Hepatitis is available from the National Clearinghouse for Alcohol and Drug Information, P.O. Box 2345, Rockville, MD 20850; (301) 468-2600.

- *Alcoholic Hepatitis: A Practical Guide for Physicians and Other Health Care Professionals*. Covers diagnosis and treatment of liver disease.

HERNIAS

Clearinghouses/Hotlines

The National Digestive Diseases Information Clearinghouse (NDDIC) can search the Combined Health Information Database (CHID) and generate a bibliography of resources on Abdominal and Bladder Hernias for you. They also will send you any publications and journal articles they may have on hand, and will refer you to other organizations that are studying this disease. If you can't afford treatment, have your doctor call NDDIC to find out if they are conducting any clinical studies that you might qualify.

☎ Contact:
National Digestive Diseases
Information Clearinghouse
Box NDDIC
Bethesda, MD 20892
(301) 468-6344

Free Publications/Videos

The following publication is available from the National Digestive Diseases Information Clearinghouse, Box NDDIC, Bethesda, MD 20892; (301) 468-6344.

- *Hiatal Hernia.*

HERNIATED DISCS

See also Back Problems

Clearinghouses/Hotlines

The National Institute of Arthritis and Musculoskeletal and Skin Diseases (NIAMS) will send you whatever publications and reprints of articles from texts and journals they have on Herniated Discs. They will also refer you to other organizations that are studying this disease. NIAMS will also let you know of any clinical studies that may be studying this disease and looking for patients.

☎ Contact:
National Institute of Arthritis
and Musculoskeletal and Skin Diseases
Box AMS
Bethesda, MD 20892
(301) 495-4484

HEROIN

See also Drug Abuse

Clearinghouses/Hotlines

The National Clearinghouse for Alcohol and Drug Information is the central point within the Federal Government for current print and audiovisual materials about alcohol and other drugs. They have information tailored to parents, teachers, youth, and others, as well as information about organizations and groups concerned with alcohol and other drug problems. They have publications,

reports, newsletters, videos, posters, and more, as well as being able to provide comprehensive alcohol and other drug resource referrals. Call for your free catalogue.

☎ Contact:
National Clearinghouse for Alcohol
and Drug Information
P.O. Box 2345
Rockville, MD 20852
(800) 729-6686
(301) 468-2600

Free Publications/Videos

The following publication is available from the National Clearinghouse for Alcohol and Drug Information, P.O. Box 2345, Rockville, MD 20852; (301) 468-2600.

- *Heroin.* Fact sheet gives basic information about the psychological and physiological effects.

The following Congressional Research Service (CRS) report is available from either of your U.S. Senators' offices at the U.S. Capitol, Washington, DC 20510, or from your Congressional Representative at the U.S. Capitol, Washington, DC 20515. You can also call in your request through the U.S. Capitol switchboard at (202) 224-3121. Be sure to include the full title and report number in your request.

- *Heroin: Legalization for Medical Use.* (#88-86 SPR)

HERPES

Clearinghouses/Hotlines

The Sexually Transmitted Diseases Hotline offers valuable information to the public about a wide range of sexually transmitted diseases, including Herpes and how to protect yourself from contracting them.

☎ Contact:
National Sexually Transmitted Diseases Hotline

P.O. Box 13827
Research Triangle Park, NC 27709
(800) 227-8922

The National Institute on Allergy and Infectious Diseases (NIAID) can search the Combined Health Information Database (CHID) and generate a bibliography of resources on Herpes Simplex Virus (Type II) for you. They will also send you any publications and journal articles they may have on hand, and will refer you to researchers who are currently studying this disease. If you can't afford treatment, have your doctor call NIAID to find out if they are conducting any clinical studies that you might qualify for.

☎ Contact:
National Institute of Allergy
and Infectious Diseases
Bldg. 31, Room 7A32
Bethesda, MD 20892
(301) 496-5717

The National Institute of Dental Research (NIDR) will send you whatever publications and reprints of journal articles they have on Herpes Simplex Virus and Oral Lesions. As a policy, NIDR will not refer you to other organizations or experts who study this disease. If you can't afford treatment, have your doctor call Dr. Albert Guckers at (301) 496-6241 to find out if NIDR is conducting any clinical studies that you might qualify for.

☎ Contact:
National Institute of Dental Research
Bldg. 31, Room 2C35
Bethesda, MD 20892
(301) 496-4261

The National Eye Institute (NEI) can give you up-to-date information on the Effect of Herpes Simplex on the Eyes by searching the Combined Health Information Database (CHID) and MEDLINE and sending you bibliographies of resources, along with any journal articles they may have. They can also refer you to any other organizations that study this and other related diseases. NEI will also let you know of any clinical studies that may be studying this disease and looking for patients. Because of their small staff, NEI prefers that you submit your requests for information in writing.

☎ Contact:
National Eye Institute
Bldg. 31, Room 6A32
Bethesda, MD 20892
(301) 496-5248

Free Publications/Videos

The following publication on Herpes is available from the Office of Clinical Center Communications, Bldg. 10, Room 1C255, Bethesda, MD 20892; (301) 496-2563.

- *Herpes*. Booklet written to help the general public make intelligent decisions.

The following publication is available from the National Institute of Allergy and Infectious Diseases, Bldg. 31, Room 7A32, Bethesda, MD 20892; (301) 496-5717.

- *Genital Herpes*. Discusses symptoms, treatment, and prevention. (#84-2005)

The following publication on Herpes is available from the National Institutes of Health Clinical Center, Bldg. 10, Room 1C255, Bethesda, MD 20892; (301) 496-2563.

- *Herpes (Medicine for the Public)*. (#85-858)

HERPES ZOSTER (SHINGLES)

Clearinghouses/Hotlines

The National Institute on Allergy and Infectious Diseases (NIAID) can search the Combined Health Information Database (CHID) and generate a bibliography of resources on Herpes Zoster-Varicella Infections for you. They will also send you any publications and journal articles they may have on hand, and will refer you to researchers who are currently studying this disease. If you can't afford treatment, have your doctor call NIAID to find out if they are conducting any clinical studies that you might qualify for.

☎ Contact:
National Institute of Allergy
and Infectious Diseases
Bldg. 31, Room 7A32
Bethesda, MD 20892
(301) 496-5717

The National Institute of Neurological Disorders and Stroke (NINDS) can send you only information they have in their publications list on Herpes Zoster (Shingles). They cannot refer you to any experts. This Clearinghouse cannot directly give you information about any current clinical studies NINDS might be conducting on this illness, but you can find this information for yourself by looking under the National Institute of Neurological Disorders and Stroke in *Appendix A* at the end of this book.

☎ Contact:
National Institute of Neurological
Disorders and Stroke
Bldg. 31, Room 8A06
Bethesda, MD 20892
(301) 496-5751
(800) 352-9424

HIATAL HERNIAS

Clearinghouses/Hotlines

The National Institute of Diabetes and Digestive and Kidney Diseases's (NIDDK) individual clearinghouses can search the Combined Health Information Database (CHID) and generate a bibliography of resources on Hiatal Hernias for you. They also will send you any publications and journal articles they may have on hand, and will refer you to other organizations that are studying this disease. If you can't afford treatment, have your doctor call NIDDK to find out if they are conducting any clinical studies that you might qualify.

☎ Contact:
National Institute of Diabetes
and Digestive and Kidney Diseases
Bldg. 31, Room 9A04
Bethesda, MD 20892
(301) 496-3583

Free Publications/Videos

The following publication is available from the National Institute of Diabetes and Digestive and Kidney Diseases, Bldg. 31, Room 9A04, Bethesda, MD 20892; (301) 496-3583.

- *Hiatal Hernia*. (#92-498)

HICCUPS

Clearinghouses/Hotlines

The National Heart, Lung, and Blood Institute (NHLBI) can search the Combined Health Information Database (CHID) and generate a bibliography of resources on Hiccups for you. They also will send you any publications and journal articles they may have on hand, and will refer you to other organizations that are studying this disease. If you can't afford treatment, have your doctor call NHLBI to find out if they are conducting any clinical studies that you might qualify for.

☎ Contact:
National Heart, Lung, and Blood Institute
Bldg. 31, Room 4A21
Bethesda, MD 20892
(301) 496-4236

HIGH BLOOD PRESSURE

Clearinghouses/Hotlines

The High Blood Pressure Information Center is a source of information and educational materials on controlling high blood pressure. Print and audiovisual materials (for professionals and the public), as well as information on locations and services of community programs and activities are available. A free newsletter, *Info Memo*, covers topics of interest concerning blood pressure, cholesterol and smoking and is published as needed.

☎ Contact:
High Blood Pressure Information Center
4733 Bethesda Ave., Suite 530
Bethesda, MD 20814
(301) 951-3260

The National Heart, Lung, and Blood Institute (NHLBI) can search the Combined Health Information Database (CHID) and generate a bibliography of resources on High Blood Pressure for you. They also will send you any publications and journal articles they may have on hand, and will refer you to other organizations that are studying this disease. If you can't afford treatment, have your doctor call NHLBI to find out if they are conducting any clinical studies that you might qualify for.

☎ Contact:
National Heart, Lung, and Blood Institute
Bldg. 31, Room 4A21
Bethesda, MD 20892
(301) 496-4236

The National Institute on Aging (NIA) will send you whatever publications and reprints of journal articles they have on High Blood Pressure. They cannot refer you to other experts if the information they have isn't sufficient for your purposes.

☎ Contact:
National Institute on Aging
Bldg. 31, Room 5C27
Bethesda, MD 20892
(301) 496-1752

Free Publications/Videos

The following publications on High Blood Pressure are available from the High Blood Pressure Information Center, 4733 Bethesda Ave., Suite 530, Bethesda, MD 20814, (301) 951-3260.

- *Community Guide to High Blood Pressure* (#82-2333)
- *High Blood Pressure: Things You and Your Family Should Know* (#86-2025)
- *High Blood Pressure and What You Can Do About It.*
- *Blacks and High Blood Pressure.* Offers information on prevalence, and need for treatment.
- *Heart Attacks.* Facts about the leading cause of death in the U.S.
- *High Blood Pressure & What You Can Do About It.* An overview of high blood pressure.
- *High Blood Pressure: Things You and Your Family Should Know.* Basic leaflet about high blood pressure (Spanish).
- *Living With Hypertension.* Series of five pamphlets lets patients know they are in control of their hypertension.
- *The Physician's Guide: How to Help Your Hypertensive Patients Stop Smoking.* Shows what doctors can do within a busy office practice to persuade hypertensive patients to stop smoking. (#84-1271)

The following publications are available from the National Heart, Lung and Blood Institute, Bldg. 31, Room 4A21, Bethesda, MD 20892; (301) 496-4236.

- *Questions About Weight, Salt and High Blood Pressure.* (#88-1459)
- *The Public and High Blood Pressure.* (#85-2118)
- *The 1988 Report of the Joint National Committee on Detection, Evaluation, and Treatment of High Blood Pressure.* (#88-1088)
- *Cyclosporine-Associated Hypertension.* (#NN333) Information on incidence, characteristics, mechanisms, and drug management of cyclosporine-associated hypertension (CAH) are presented.
- *Diagnosis and Management of Hypertension-- 1987.* (#89-2968)
- *Physician's Guide: How to Help Your Hypertensive Patients Stop Smoking.* (#84-1271)
- *Working Group Report on the Heart in Hypertension.* (#91-3033)

HIGH-DENSITY LIPOPROTEINS

See also Cholesterol

Clearinghouses/Hotlines

The National Heart, Lung, and Blood Institute

(NHLBI) can search the Combined Health Information Database (CHID) and generate a bibliography of resources on High-Density Lipoproteins (HDL) for you. They also will send you any publications and journal articles they may have on hand, and will refer you to other organizations that are studying this disease. If you can't afford treatment, have your doctor call NHLBI to find out if they are conducting any clinical studies that you might qualify for.

☎ Contact:
National Heart,Lung and Blood Institute
Bldg. 31, Room 4A21
Bethesda, MD 20892
(301) 496-4236

HIRSCHSPRUNG'S DISEASE

Clearinghouses/Hotlines

The National Institute of Diabetes and Digestive and Kidney Diseases (NIDDK) can search the Combined Health Information Database (CHID) and generate a bibliography of resources on Hirschsprung's Diseases, which is a problem with the colon. They will send you any journal articles they may have on hand, and will refer you to other organizations.

☎ Contact:
National Institute of Diabetes
and Digestive and Kidney Diseases
Bldg. 31, Room 9A04
Bethesda, MD 20892
(301) 496-3583

HIRSUTISM

Clearinghouses/Hotlines

The National Institute of Arthritis and Musculoskeletal and Skin Diseases (NIAMS) will send you whatever publications and reprints of articles from texts and journals they have on Hirsutism. They will also refer you to other organizations that are studying this disease.

NIAMS will also let you know of any clinical studies that may be studying this disease and looking for patients.

☎ Contact:
National Institute of Arthritis
and Musculoskeletal and Skin Diseases
Box AMS
9000 Rockville Pike
Bethesda, MD 20892
(301) 495-4484

HISTIOCYTOSIS

Clearinghouses/Hotlines

The National Cancer Institute (NCI) will send you whatever publications and reprints of journal articles they have on Histiocytosis. They can also give you information on the state-of-the-art treatment for this disease, including specific treatment information for your stage of cancer. They can also search their Physician's Data Query (PDQ) database to let you know if NCI is conducting any clinical studies on your disease.

☎ Contact:
National Cancer Institute
Bldg. 31, Room 10A24
Bethesda, MD 20892
(800) 4-CANCER
(301) 496-5583

The National Heart, Lung, and Blood Institute (NHLBI) can search the Combined Health Information Database (CHID) and generate a bibliography of resources on Histiocytosis for you. They also will send you any publications and journal articles they may have on hand, and will refer you to other organizations that are studying this disease. If you can't afford treatment, have your doctor call NHLBI to find out if they are conducting any clinical studies that you might qualify for.

☎ Contact:
National Heart, Lung, and Blood Institute
Bldg. 31, Room 4A21
Bethesda, MD 20892
(301) 496-4236

HISTOPLASMOSIS

Clearinghouses/Hotlines

The National Institute on Allergy and Infectious Diseases (NIAID) can search the Combined Health Information Database (CHID) and generate a bibliography of resources on Histoplasmosis for you. They will also send you any publications and journal articles they may have on hand, and will refer you to researchers who are currently studying this disease. If you can't afford treatment, have your doctor call NIAID to find out if they are conducting any clinical studies that you might qualify for.

☎ Contact:
National Institute of Allergy
and Infectious Diseases
Bldg. 31, Room 7A32
Bethesda, MD 20892
(301) 496-5717

The National Eye Institute (NEI) can give you up-to-date information on Histoplasmosis of the Eyes by searching the Combined Health Information Database (CHID) and MEDLINE and sending you bibliographies of resources, along with any journal articles they may have. They can also refer you to any other organizations that study this and other related diseases. NEI will also let you know of any clinical studies that may be studying this disease and looking for patients. Because of their small staff, NEI prefers that you submit your requests for information in writing.

☎ Contact:
National Eye Institute
Bldg. 31, Room 6A32
Bethesda, MD 20892
(301) 496-5248

HIVES

Clearinghouses/Hotlines

The National Institute on Allergy and Infectious Diseases (NIAID) can search the Combined Health Information Database (CHID) and generate a bibliography of resources on Hives for you. They will also send you any publications and journal articles they may have on hand, and will refer you to researchers who are currently studying this disease. If you can't afford treatment, have your doctor call NIAID to find out if they are conducting any clinical studies that you might qualify for.

☎ Contact:
National Institute of Allergy
and Infectious Diseases
Bldg. 31, Room 7A32
Bethesda, MD 20892
(301) 496-5717

HIV INFECTION

See also AIDS

Clearinghouses/Hotlines

The Sexually Transmitted Diseases Hotline offers valuable information to the public about a wide range of sexually transmitted diseases, including HIV Infection and how to protect yourself from contracting it.

☎ Contact:
National Sexually Transmitted Diseases Hotline
P.O. Box 13827
Research Triangle Park, NC 27709
(800) 227-8922

The National Institute of Drug Abuse Helpline provides general phone information on drug abuse and on AIDS as it relates to intravenous drug users. This hotline offers referrals to drug rehab centers. Hours: 9 a.m. - 3 a.m. Monday through Friday; 12 p.m. - 3 a.m. on weekends.

☎ Contact:
National Institute of Drug Abuse Helpline
(800) 662-HELP.

The National AIDS Information Clearinghouse can answer all your questions regarding HIV Infection. They can make referrals, as well as send you brochures, posters, and reports. They have access to information on over 300 AIDS films and videotapes, and can provide you with a printout of films and videos designed to target a specific audience, ranging from teenagers to physicians. Each listing includes information on the producer, year, source, audience, and availability, as well as an abstract.

☎ Contact:
National AIDS Information Clearinghouse
P.O. Box 6003
Rockville, MD 20850
(800) 458-5231
(800) 342-AIDS
(800) 344-7432 (Servicio en Espanol)
(800) 243-7889 (TTY-Deaf Access)

The National Institute on Allergy and Infectious Diseases (NIAID) can search the Combined Health Information Database (CHID) and generate a bibliography of resources on HIV Infection for you. They will also send you any publications and journal articles they may have on hand, and will refer you to researchers who are currently studying this disease. If you can't afford treatment, have your doctor call NIAID to find out if they are conducting any clinical studies that you might qualify for.

☎ Contact:
National Institute of Allergy
and Infectious Diseases
Bldg. 31, Room 7A32
Bethesda, MD 20892
(301) 496-5717

The National Cancer Institute (NCI) will send you whatever publications and reprints of journal articles they have on HIV Infection. They can also give you information on the state-of-the-art treatment for this disease, including specific treatment information for your stage of cancer. They can also search their Physician's Data Query (PDQ) database to let you know if NCI is conducting any clinical studies on your disease.

☎ Contact:
National Cancer Institute
Bldg. 31, Room 10A24
Bethesda, MD 20892
(800) 4-CANCER
(301) 496-5583

The National Institute of Dental Research (NIDR) will send you whatever publications and reprints of

journal articles they have on HIV and Oral Complications. As a policy, NIDR will not refer you to other organizations or experts who study this disease. If you can't afford treatment, have your doctor call Dr. Albert Guckers at (301) 496-6241 to find out if NIDR is conducting any clinical studies that you might qualify for.

☎ Contact:
National Institute of Dental Research
Building 31
Room 2C35
Bethesda, MD 20892
(301) 496-4261

Free Publications/Videos

The following publication on HIV Infection is available from the Office of Technology Assessment, Washington, DC 20510-8025; (202) 224-8996.

- *Difficult-To-Reuse Needles for the Prevention of HIV Infection Among Injection Drug Abusers.* (#OTA-BP-H-103)

The following publications on HIV Infection are available from the Centers for Disease Control National AIDS Clearinghouse, P.O. Box 6003, Rockville, MD 20849-6003; (800) 458-5231.

- *HIV Infection in Two Brothers Receiving Intravenous Therapy for Hemophilia.* (#D137)
- *Tuberculosis: The Connection Between TB and HIV.* (#D484)
- *HIV Infection in Two Brothers Receiving Intravenous Therapy for Hemophilia.* (#D137)
- *Update: Transmission of HIV Infection During Invasive Dental Procedures - Florida.* (#D683)
- *Condoms for Prevention of Sexually Transmitted Diseases.* (#D127)
- *Publicly Funded HIV Counseling and Testing-United States, 1985-1989.* (#D541)
- *Open Meeting on the Risks of Transmission of Bloodborne Pathogens to Patients During Invasive Procedures.* (#D664)
- *AIDS Litigation Project: A National Survey of Federal, State, and Local Cases Before*

Courts and Human Rights Commissions. (#D136)
- *American Foundation for AIDS Research AIDS/HIV Treatment Directory.* (Current Issue)
- *Information about the AIDS Clinical studies Information Service.* (#B172)

The following Congressional Research Service (CRS) report on HIV Infection is available from either of your U.S. Senators' offices at the U.S. Capitol, Washington, DC 20510, or from your Congressional Representative at the U.S. Capitol, Washington, DC 20515. You can also call in your request through the U.S. Capitol switchboard at (202) 224-3121. Be sure to include the full title and report number in your request.

- *Pediatric HIV Infection: Selected Research Issues.* (#IB89099)

HODEOLUM

See Stye

HODGKIN'S DISEASE

Clearinghouses/Hotlines

The National Cancer Institute (NCI) will send you whatever publications and reprints of journal articles they have on Hodgkin's Disease. They can also give you information on the state-of-the-art treatment for this disease, including specific treatment information for your stage of cancer. They can also search their Physician's Data Query (PDQ) database to let you know if NCI is conducting any clinical studies on your disease.

☎ Contact:
National Cancer Institute
Bldg. 31, Room 10A24
Bethesda, MD 20892
(800) 4-CANCER
(301) 496-5583

Free Publications/Videos

The following publication on Hodgkin's Disease is available from the National Cancer Institute, Bldg. 31, Room 10A24, Bethesda, MD 20892; (800) 4-CANCER, or (301) 496-5583.

- *What You Need to Know About Hodgkin's Disease.* (#90-1555)

HOLISTIC MEDICINE

See Alternative Medicine

HOMELESSNESS

Clearinghouses/Hotlines

The National Resource Center On Homelessness and Mental Illness develops and distributes the newest information on the coordination of housing and services for homeless, mentally ill persons. Supported in part by the Department of Housing and Urban Development, this program features an increased emphasis on the development, financing, and operation of housing for homeless, mentally ill persons. This Center publishes *Access*, a bi-monthly newsletter, and has free information packets and database searches. They also have an organizational referral list, *Organizations Concerned with Homelessness and Mental Illness*, which includes information on more than 100 federal programs and national and state organizations working in the fields of homelessness and/or mental health.

☎ Contact:
Policy Research Associates, Inc.
262 Delaware Ave.
Delmar, NY 12054
(800) 444-7415

Free Publications/Videos

The following Congressional Research Service (CRS) reports are available from either of your

U.S. Senators' offices at the U.S. Capitol, Washington, DC 20510, or from your Congressional Representative at the U.S. Capitol, Washington, DC 20515. You can also call in your request through the U.S. Capitol switchboard at (202) 224-3121. Be sure to include the full title and report number in your request.

- *Homelessness: Medical Conditions.* (#91-201 SPR)
- *Homelessness and Commitment: The Cases of Joyce Brown (a/k/a Billie Boggs).* (#88-186 A)
- *Homeless Mentally Ill Persons: Problems and Programs.* (#91-344 EPW)

HOMEOPATHY

See Alternative Medicine

HOMOCYSTINURIA

Clearinghouses/Hotlines

The National Institute of Child Health and Human Development (NICHD) will send you whatever publications and reprints of journal articles they have on Homocystinuria. If necessary, they will refer you to other experts or researchers in the field. If you can't afford treatment, have your doctor call NICHD to find out if they are conducting any clinical studies that you might qualify for.

☎ Contact:
National Institute of Child Health
and Human Development
Bldg. 31, Room 2A32
Bethesda, MD 20892
(301) 496-5133

The National Heart, Lung, and Blood Institute (NHLBI) can search the Combined Health Information Database (CHID) and generate a bibliography of resources on Homocystinuria for you. They also will send you any publications and

journal articles they may have on hand, and will refer you to other organizations that are studying this disease. If you can't afford treatment, have your doctor call NHLBI to find out if they are conducting any clinical studies that you might qualify for.

☎ Contact:
National Heart, Lung, and Blood Institute
Bldg. 31, Room 4A21
Bethesda, MD 20892
(301) 496-4236

HOMOSEXUALITY

Clearinghouses/Hotlines

The National Institute of Child Health and Human Development (NICHD) can send you information on fetal, maternal and child development, as well as materials on reproductive biology, contraception, mental retardation, and a host of other related fields.

☎ Contact:
National Institute of Child Health
and Human Development
Building 31
Room 2A32
Bethesda, MD 20892
(301) 496-5133

Free Publications/Videos

The following Congressional Research Service (CRS) reports on Homosexuality are available from either of your U.S. Senators' offices at the U.S. Capitol, Washington, DC 20510, or from your Congressional Representative at the U.S. Capitol, Washington, DC 20515. You can also call in your request through the U.S. Capitol switchboard at (202) 224-3121. Be sure to include the full title and report number in your request.

- *Homosexuality and Immigration Law After the Immigration Act of 1990.* (#91-495 A)
- *Homosexual Rights: Legal Analysis of H.R. 709/S 464, the "Civil Rights Amendments Act of 1987".* (#87-593 A)

- *An Overview of Legal Developments in Homosexual Rights.* (#85-717 A)
- *Prohibiting Discrimination on the Basis of Affectional or Sexual Orientation: Arguments for and Against Proposed Legislation.* (#87-825 GOV)
- *Prohibiting Discrimination on the Basis of Sexual Orientation: Arguments for and Against Proposed Legislation.* (#89-222 GOV)

HOME TEST KITS

Free Publications/Videos

The following publication is available from the Office of Technology Assessment, Washington, DC 20510-8025; (202) 224-8996.

- *Home Drug Infusion Therapy Under Medicare.* (#OTA-H-509)

The following publications are available from the Center for Devices and Radiological Health, (HFZ-210), Food and Drug Administration, 5600 Fishers Ln., Rockville, MD 20857; (301) 443-4690.

- *Urinalysis: Looking Into the Void.*
- *Do It Yourself Medical Testing.* (#FDA 86-4206)
- *How Am I? Let Me Check.*
- *Fact Sheet: Drugs of Abuse Tests.*

HOOKWORM DISEASE

Clearinghouses/Hotlines

The National Institute of Allergy and Infectious Diseases can provide you with reference materials on Hookworm Disease and can refer you to other organizations.

☎ Contact:
National Institute of Allergy and Infectious Diseases
Bldg. 31, Room 7A32

Bethesda, MD 20892
(301) 496-5717

HORMONES

See also Menopause

Clearinghouses/Hotlines

The National Institute of Diabetes and Digestive and Kidney Diseases's (NIDDK) individual clearinghouses can search the Combined Health Information Database (CHID) and generate a bibliography of resources on Hormones for you. They also will send you any publications and journal articles they may have on hand, and will refer you to other organizations that are studying this issue. If you can't afford treatment, have your doctor call NIDDK to find out if they are conducting any clinical studies that you might qualify for.

☎ Contact:
National Institute of Diabetes and Digestive and Kidney Diseases
Bldg. 31, Room 9A04
Bethesda, MD 20892
(301) 496-3583

The National Institute of Child Health and Human Development (NICHD) will send you whatever publications and reprints of journal articles they have on Sex Hormones. If necessary, they will refer you to other experts or researchers in the field. If you can't afford treatment, have your doctor call NICHD to find out if they are conducting any clinical studies that you might qualify for.

☎ Contact:
National Institute of Child Health and Human Development
Bldg. 31, Room 2A32
Bethesda, MD 20892
(301) 496-5133

The National Cancer Institute (NCI) will send you whatever publications and reprints of journal articles they have on Hormones and Cancer. They can also give you information on the state-of-the-art treatment for this disease, including specific treatment information for your stage of cancer. They can also search their Physician's Data Query (PDQ) database to let you know if NCI is conducting any clinical studies on your disease.

☎ Contact:
National Cancer Institute
Bldg. 31, Room 10A24
Bethesda, MD 20892
(800) 4-CANCER
(301) 496-5583

specific treatment information for your stage of cancer. They can also search their Physician's Data Query (PDQ) database to let you know if NCI is conducting any clinical studies on your disease.

☎ Contact:
National Cancer Institute
Bldg. 31, Room 10A24
Bethesda, MD 20892
(800) 4-CANCER
(301) 496-5583

HORMONE THERAPY

Free Publications/Videos

The following publication on Hormone Therapy is available from the Office of Technology Assessment, Washington, DC 20510-8025; (202) 224-8996.

- *The Menopause, Hormone Therapy, and Women's Health-Background Paper.* (#OTA-BP-BA-88)

HOSPICE CARE

Clearinghouses/Hotlines

The National Institute on Aging (NIA) will send you whatever publications and reprints of journal articles they have on Hospice Care. They cannot refer you to other experts if the information they have isn't sufficient for your purposes.

☎ Contact:
National Institute on Aging
Bldg. 31, Room 5C27
Bethesda, MD 20892
(301) 496-1752

The National Cancer Institute (NCI) will send you whatever publications and reprints of journal articles they have on Hospice Care and Cancer. They can also give you information on the state-of-the-art treatment for this disease, including

HOSPITAL COMPLAINTS

Clearinghouses/Hotlines

On a toll-free hotline, the Office of Health Facilities will respond to your complaints about health facilities that offer free health care under the Hill-Burton law. Complaints include denial of health care, discrimination, sanitary conditions, among others.

☎ Contact:
Health Resource Service Administration
5600 Fishers Lane
Room 11-03
Rockville, MD 20857
(800) 638-0742
(800) 492-0359 in MD

HOSPITAL INFECTIONS

Clearinghouses/Hotlines

The National Institute on Allergy and Infectious Diseases (NIAID) can search the Combined Health Information Database (CHID) and generate a bibliography of resources on Hospital Infections for you. They will also send you any publications and journal articles they may have on hand, and will refer you to researchers who are currently studying this disease. If you can't afford treatment, have your doctor call NIAID to find out if they are conducting any clinical studies that you might qualify for.

☎ Contact:
National Institute of Allergy
and Infectious Diseases
Bldg. 31, Room 7A32
Bethesda, MD 20892
(301) 496-5717

☎ Contact:
National Institute of Child Health
and Human Development
Bldg. 31, Room 2A32
Bethesda, MD 20892
(301) 496-5133

HOUSEHOLD HAZARDS

Free Publications/Videos

The following publication Household Hazards is available from the RCRA Hotline, Environmental Protection Agency, 401 M St., SW, Washington, DC 20460; (800) 424-9346, or (703) 920-9810.

- *A Survey of Household Hazardous Wastes and Related Collection Programs.* Defines household hazardous wastes, their presence in our solid waste, different types of collection programs.

The following publication on Environmental Hazards is available from the Consumer Information Center, Pueblo, CO 81009.

- *Homebuyer's Guide to Environmental Hazards.* (#432&, $.50) Learn about environmental hazards, what to do, and where to get help.

HUMAN GROWTH HORMONE

Clearinghouses/Hotlines

The National Institute of Child Health and Human Development (NICHD) will send you whatever publications and reprints of journal articles they have on the Human Growth Hormone. If necessary, they will refer you to other experts or researchers in the field. If you can't afford treatment, have your doctor call NICHD to find out if they are conducting any clinical studies that you might qualify for.

HUMAN PAPILLOMA VIRUS

Clearinghouses/Hotlines

The National Cancer Institute (NCI) will send you whatever publications and reprints of journal articles they have on Human Papilloma Virus (HPV). They can also give you information on the state-of-the-art treatment for this disease, including specific treatment information for your stage of cancer. They can also search their Physician's Data Query (PDQ) database to let you know if NCI is conducting any clinical studies on your disease.

☎ Contact:
National Cancer Institute
Bldg. 31, Room 10A24
Bethesda, MD 20892
(800) 4-CANCER
(301) 496-5583

The National Institute on Allergy and Infectious Diseases (NIAID) can search the Combined Health Information Database (CHID) and generate a bibliography of resources on Human Papilloma Virus (HPV) Hospital Infections for you. They will also send you any publications and journal articles they may have on hand, and will refer you to researchers who are currently studying this disease. If you can't afford treatment, have your doctor call NIAID to find out if they are conducting any clinical studies that you might qualify for.

☎ Contact:
National Institute of Allergy
and Infectious Diseases
Bldg. 31, Room 7A32
Bethesda, MD 20892
(301) 496-5717

HUNGER

Free Publications/Videos

The following Congressional Research Service (CRS) reports on Hunger are available from either of your U.S. Senators' offices at the U.S. Capitol, Washington, DC 20510, or from your Congressional Representative at the U.S. Capitol, Washington, DC 20515. You can also call in your request through the U.S. Capitol switchboard at (202) 224-3121. Be sure to include the full title and report number in your request.

- *Hunger in Brief: Reports and Proposals for Expanded Federal Efforts.* (#86-703 SPR)
- *Summary of Reports Concerning Hunger in America, 1983-1986.* (#86-791 SPR)

HUNT'S DISEASE

Clearinghouses/Hotlines

The National Institute of Neurological Disorders and Stroke (NINDS) can send you only information they have in their publications list on Hunt's Disease. They cannot refer you to any experts. This Clearinghouse cannot directly give you information about any current clinical studies NINDS might be conducting on this illness, but you can find this information for yourself by looking under the National Institute of Neurological Disorders and Stroke in *Appendix A* at the end of this book.

☎ Contact:
National Institute of Neurological
Disorders and Stroke
Building 31
Room 8A06
Bethesda, MD 20892
(301) 496-5751
(800) 352-9424

HUNTER'S SYNDROME

Clearinghouses/Hotlines

The National Institute of Diabetes and Digestive and Kidney Diseases's (NIDDK) individual clearinghouses can search the Combined Health Information Database (CHID) and generate a bibliography of resources on Hunter's Syndrome for you. They also will send you any publications and journal articles they may have on hand, and will refer you to other organizations that are studying this issue. If you can't afford treatment, have your doctor call NIDDK to find out if they are conducting any clinical studies that you might qualify for.

☎ Contact:
National Institute of Diabetes
and Digestive and Kidney Diseases
Bldg. 31, Room 9A04
Bethesda, MD 20892
(301) 496-3583

HUNTINGTON'S CHOREA

Clearinghouses/Hotlines

The National Institute of Neurological Disorders and Stroke (NINDS) can send you only information they have in their publications list on Huntington's Disease. They cannot refer you to any experts. This Clearinghouse cannot directly give you information about any current clinical studies NINDS might be conducting on this illness, but you can find this information for yourself by looking under the National Institute of Neurological Disorders and Stroke in *Appendix A* at the end of this book.

☎ Contact:
National Institute of Neurological
Disorders and Stroke
Bldg. 31, Room 8A06
Bethesda, MD 20892
(301) 496-5751
(800) 352-9424

The National Institutes of Health (NIH) and Indiana University Medical Center, Indianapolis, (IUMC) maintain a roster of Huntington's Disease patients and families. Each of the families complete a family history questionnaire, and the statistics are used for research. IUMC also acts as a broker between families and researchers, who can request patients for a particular project from IUMC's database of patients and families.

☎ Contact:
Medical Research Bldg.
975 W. Walnut St.
Indianapolis, IN 46202-5251
(317) 274-2245

Free Publications/Videos

The following publications on Huntington's Disease are available from the National Institute of Neurological Disorders and Stroke, P.O. Box 5801, Bethesda, MD 20824; (800) 352-9424, or (301) 496-5751.

- *Huntington's Disease*. A collection of scientific articles, patient education pamphlets, and addresses of voluntary health associations.
- *Huntington's Disease 1992*. Annual or Biennial Research Updates.

HURLER'S SYNDROME

Clearinghouses/Hotlines

The National Institute of Child Health and Human Development (NICHD) will send you whatever publications and reprints of journal articles they have on Hurler's Syndrome. If necessary, they will refer you to other experts or researchers in the field. If you can't afford treatment, have your doctor call NICHD to find out if they are conducting any clinical studies that you might qualify for.

☎ Contact:
National Institute of Child Health
and Human Development
Bldg. 31, Room 2A32

Bethesda, MD 20892
(301) 496-5133

The National Institute of Diabetes and Digestive and Kidney Diseases's (NIDDK) individual clearinghouses can search the Combined Health Information Database (CHID) and generate a bibliography of resources on Hurler's Syndrome for you. They also will send you any publications and journal articles they may have on hand, and will refer you to other organizations that are studying this disease. If you can't afford treatment, have your doctor call NIDDK to find out if they are conducting any clinical studies that you might qualify for.

☎ Contact:
National Institute of Diabetes
and Digestive and Kidney Diseases
Bldg. 31, Room 9A04
Bethesda, MD 20892
(301) 496-3583

HYALINE MEMBRANE DISEASE

Clearinghouses/Hotlines

The National Institute of Child Health and Human Development (NICHD) will send you whatever publications and reprints of journal articles they have on Hyaline Membrane Disease. If necessary, they will refer you to other experts or researchers in the field. If you can't afford treatment, have your doctor call NICHD to find out if they are conducting any clinical studies that you might qualify for.

☎ Contact:
National Institute of Child Health
and Human Development
Bldg. 31, Room 2A32
Bethesda, MD 20892
(301) 496-5133

The National Heart, Lung, and Blood Institute (NHLBI) can search the Combined Health Information Database (CHID) and generate a bibliography of resources on Hyaline Membrane

Disease for you. They also will send you any publications and journal articles they may have on hand, and will refer you to other organizations that are studying this disease. If you can't afford treatment, have your doctor call NHLBI to find out if they are conducting any clinical studies that you might qualify for.

☎ Contact:
National Heart, Lung, and Blood Institute
Bldg. 31, Room 4A21
Bethesda, MD 20892
(301) 496-4236

HYDROCEPHALUS

Clearinghouses/Hotlines

The National Institute of Neurological Disorders and Stroke (NINDS) can send you only information they have in their publications list on Hydrocephalus. They cannot refer you to any experts. This Clearinghouse cannot directly give you information about any current clinical studies NINDS might be conducting on this condition, but you can find this information for yourself by looking under the National Institute of Neurological Disorders and Stroke in *Appendix A* at the end of this book.

☎ Contact:
National Institute of Neurological
Disorders and Stroke
Bldg. 31, Room 8A06
Bethesda, MD 20892
(301) 496-5751
(800) 352-9424

The National Institute of Child Health and Human Development (NICHD) will send you whatever publications and reprints of journal articles they have on Hydrocephalus. If necessary, they will refer you to other experts or researchers in the field. If you can't afford treatment, have your doctor call NICHD to find out if they are conducting any clinical studies that you might qualify for.

☎ Contact:
National Institute of Child Health
and Human Development
Bldg. 31, Room 2A32

Bethesda, MD 20892
(301) 496-5133

HYDROXYUREA

Free Publications/Videos

The following publication on Hydroxyurea is available from the National Cancer Institute, Bldg. 31, Room 10A24, Bethesda, MD 20892; (800) 4-CANCER, or (301) 496-5583.

- *Hidroxiurea/Hydroxyurea.* Provides information about side effects, proper usage, and precautions of this anti-cancer drug.

HYPERACTIVITY

Clearinghouses/Hotlines

The National Institute of Mental Health (NIMH) will send you whatever publications and reprints of articles from texts and journals they have on Hyperactivity. They will also refer you to other organizations that are studying this disease. NIMH will also let you know of any clinical studies that may be studying this disease and looking for patients.

☎ Contact:
National Institute of Mental Health
5600 Fishers Lane, Room 15C05
Rockville, MD 20857
(301) 443-4515

The National Institute of Child Health and Human Development (NICHD) will send you whatever publications and reprints of journal articles they have on Hyperactivity. If necessary, they will refer you to other experts or researchers in the field. If you can't afford treatment, have your doctor call NICHD to find out if they are conducting any clinical studies that you might qualify for.

☎ Contact:
National Institute of Child Health
and Human Development

Bldg. 31, Room 2A32
Bethesda, MD 20892
(301) 496-5133

The National Institute of Neurological Disorders and Stroke (NINDS) can send you only information they have in their publications list on Hyperactivity. They cannot refer you to any experts. This Clearinghouse cannot directly give you information about any current clinical studies NINDS might be conducting on this topic, but you can find this information for yourself by looking under the National Institute of Neurological Disorders and Stroke in *Appendix A* at the end of this book.

☎ Contact:
National Institute of Neurological
Disorders and Stroke
Bldg. 31, Room 8A06
Bethesda, MD 20892
(301) 496-5751
(800) 352-9424

Free Publications/Videos

The following publication on Hyperactivity is available from the National Institute of Child Health and Human Development, Bldg. 31, Room 2A32, Bethesda, MD 20892; (301) 496-5133.

- *Facts About Childhood Hyperactivity.*

The following publication on Hyperactivity is available from the National Institute of Mental Health, 5600 Fishers Ln., Room 15C05, Rockville, MD 20857; (301) 443-4515.

- *Helping the Hyperactive Child.*

HYPERBARIC OXYGENATION

Clearinghouses/Hotlines

The National Heart, Lung, and Blood Institute (NHLBI) can search the Combined Health Information Database (CHID) and generate a

bibliography of resources on Hyperbaric Oxygenation for you. They also will send you any publications and journal articles they may have on hand, and will refer you to other organizations that are studying this disease. If you can't afford treatment, have your doctor call NHLBI to find out if they are conducting any clinical studies that you might qualify for.

☎ Contact:
National Heart, Lung, and Blood Institute
Bldg. 31, Room 4A21
Bethesda, MD 20892
(301) 496-4236

HYPERBILIRUBINEMIA

Clearinghouses/Hotlines

The National Institute of Child Health and Human Development (NICHD) will send you whatever publications and reprints of journal articles they have on Hyperbilirubinemia. If necessary, they will refer you to other experts or researchers in the field. If you can't afford treatment, have your doctor call NICHD to find out if they are conducting any clinical studies that you might qualify for.

☎ Contact:
National Institute of Child Health
and Human Development
Bldg. 31, Room 2A32
Bethesda, MD 20892
(301) 496-5133

The National Institute of Diabetes and Digestive and Kidney Diseases's (NIDDK) individual clearinghouses can search the Combined Health Information Database (CHID) and generate a bibliography of resources on Hyperbilirubinemia for you. They also will send you any publications and journal articles they may have on hand, and will refer you to other organizations that are studying this disease. If you can't afford treatment, have your doctor call NIDDK to find out if they are conducting any clinical studies that you might qualify for.

☎ Contact:
National Institute of Diabetes
and Digestive and Kidney Diseases

Bldg. 31, Room 9A04
Bethesda, MD 20892
(301) 496-3583

HYPERCALCEMIA

See also Paget's Disease

Clearinghouses/Hotlines

The National Institute of Diabetes and Digestive and Kidney Diseases's (NIDDK) individual clearinghouses can search the Combined Health Information Database (CHID) and generate a bibliography of resources on Hypercalcemia for you. They also will send you any publications and journal articles they may have on hand, and will refer you to other organizations that are studying this disease. If you can't afford treatment, have your doctor call NIDDK to find out if they are conducting any clinical studies that you might qualify for.

☎ Contact:
National Institute of Diabetes
and Digestive and Kidney Diseases
Bldg. 31, Room 9A04
Bethesda, MD 20892
(301) 496-3583

HYPERCALCIURIA

See also Osteoporosis

Clearinghouses/Hotlines

The National Institute of Diabetes and Digestive and Kidney Diseases's (NIDDK) individual clearinghouses can search the Combined Health Information Database (CHID) and generate a bibliography of resources on Hypercalciuria for you. They also will send you any publications and journal articles they may have on hand, and will refer you to other organizations that are studying this disease. If you can't afford treatment, have your doctor call NIDDK to find out if they are

conducting any clinical studies that you might qualify for.

☎ Contact:
National Institute of Diabetes
and Digestive and Kidney Diseases
Bldg. 31, Room 9A04
Bethesda, MD 20892
(301) 496-3583

HYPERCHOLESTEROLEMIA

See Cholesterol

HYPERGLYCEMIA

Clearinghouses/Hotlines

The National Institute of Diabetes and Digestive and Kidney Diseases's (NIDDK) individual clearinghouses can search the Combined Health Information Database (CHID) and generate a bibliography of resources on Hyperglycemia for you. They also will send you any publications and journal articles they may have on hand, and will refer you to other organizations that are studying this disease. If you can't afford treatment, have your doctor call NIDDK to find out if they are conducting any clinical studies that you might qualify for.

☎ Contact:
National Institute of Diabetes
and Digestive and Kidney Diseases
Bldg. 31, Room 9A04
Bethesda, MD 20892
(301) 496-3583

HYPERKINESIS

Clearinghouses/Hotlines

The National Institute of Mental Health (NIMH) will send you whatever publications and reprints of articles from texts and journals they have on Hyperkinesis. They will also refer you to other organizations that are studying this disease. NIMH will also let you know of any clinical studies that may be studying this disease and looking for patients.

☎ Contact:
National Institute of Mental Health
5600 Fishers Ln., Room 15C05
Rockville, MD 20857
(301) 443-4515

HYPERLIPIDEMIA

Clearinghouses/Hotlines

The National Heart, Lung, and Blood Institute (NHLBI) can search the Combined Health Information Database (CHID) and generate a bibliography of resources on Hyperlipidemia for you. They also will send you any publications and journal articles they may have on hand, and will refer you to other organizations that are studying this disease. If you can't afford treatment, have your doctor call NHLBI to find out if they are conducting any clinical studies that you might qualify for.

☎ Contact:
National Heart, Lung, and Blood Institute
Bldg. 31, Room 4A21
Bethesda, MD 20892
(301) 496-4236

HYPERLIPOPROTEINEMIA

Clearinghouses/Hotlines

The National Heart, Lung, and Blood Institute (NHLBI) can search the Combined Health Information Database (CHID) and generate a bibliography of resources on Hyperlipoproteinemia for you. They also will send you any publications and journal articles they may have on hand, and will refer you to other organizations that are studying this disease. If you can't afford

treatment, have your doctor call NHLBI to find out if they are conducting any clinical studies that you might qualify for.

☎ Contact:
National Heart, Lung, and Blood Institute
Bldg. 31, Room 4A21
Bethesda, MD 20892
(301) 496-4236

HYPERPARATHYROIDISM

Clearinghouses/Hotlines

The National Institute of Diabetes and Digestive and Kidney Diseases's (NIDDK) individual clearinghouses can search the Combined Health Information Database (CHID) and generate a bibliography of resources on Hyperparathyroidism for you. They also will send you any publications and journal articles they may have on hand, and will refer you to other organizations that are studying this disease. If you can't afford treatment, have your doctor call NIDDK to find out if they are conducting any clinical studies that you might qualify for.

☎ Contact:
National Institute of Diabetes
and Digestive and Kidney Diseases
Bldg. 31, Room 9A04
Bethesda, MD 20892
(301) 496-3583

HYPERPYREXIA

Clearinghouses/Hotlines

The National Institute on Aging (NIA) will send you whatever publications and reprints of journal articles they have on Hyperpyrexia (heat stroke/heat exhaustion). They cannot refer you to other experts if the information they have isn't sufficient for your purposes.

☎ Contact:
National Institute on Aging
Bldg. 31, Room 5C27

Bethesda, MD 20892
(301) 496-1752

HYPERSENSITIVITY PNEUMONITIS

Clearinghouses/Hotlines

The National Institute on Allergy and Infectious Diseases (NIAID) can search the Combined Health Information Database (CHID) and generate a bibliography of resources on Hypersensitivity Pneumonitis for you. They will also send you any publications and journal articles they may have on hand, and will refer you to researchers who are currently studying this disease. If you can't afford treatment, have your doctor call NIAID to find out if they are conducting any clinical studies that you might qualify for.

☎ Contact:
National Institute of Allergy
and Infectious Diseases
Bldg. 31, Room 7A32
Bethesda, MD 20892
(301) 496-5717

HYPERTENSION

See High Blood Pressure

HYPERTHERMIA

Clearinghouses/Hotlines

The National Institute on Aging (NIA) will send you whatever publications and reprints of journal articles they have on Hyperthermia (Heat Stroke/Heat Exhaustion). They cannot refer you to other experts if the information they have isn't sufficient for your purposes.

☎ Contact:
National Institute on Aging
Bldg. 31, Room 5C27
Bethesda, MD 20892
(301) 496-1752

The National Cancer Institute (NCI) will send you whatever publications and reprints of journal articles they have on Hyperthermia (Heat Stroke/Exhaustion). They can also give you information on the state-of-the-art treatment for this disease, including specific treatment information for your stage of cancer. They can also search their Physician's Data Query (PDQ) database to let you know if NCI is conducting any clinical studies on your disease.

☎ Contact:
National Cancer Institute
Bldg. 31, Room 10A24
Bethesda, MD 20892
(800) 4-CANCER
(301) 496-5583

Free Publications/Videos

The following publication is available from the Center for Devices and Radiological Health, (HFZ-210), Food and Drug Administration, 5600 Fishers Ln., Rockville, MD 20857; (301) 443-4690.

- *Heat Used To Fight Some Cancers.*

The following publication is available from the National Institute on Aging, Bldg. 31, Room 5C27, Bethesda, MD 20892; (301) 496-1752.

- *A Hot Weather Hazard for Older People: Hyperthermia.* (#89-2763)

HYPERTHYROIDISM

Clearinghouses/Hotlines

The National Institute of Diabetes and Digestive and Kidney Diseases's (NIDDK) individual clearinghouses can search the Combined Health Information Database (CHID) and generate a bibliography of resources on Hyperthyroidism for you. They also will send you any publications and journal articles they may have on hand, and will refer you to other organizations that are studying this disease. If you can't afford treatment, have your doctor call NIDDK to find out if they are conducting any clinical studies that you might qualify for.

☎ Contact:
National Institute of Diabetes
and Digestive and Kidney Diseases
Bldg. 31, Room 9A04
Bethesda, MD 20892
(301) 496-3583

HYPERTRIGLYCERIDEMIA

Clearinghouses/Hotlines

The National Heart, Lung, and Blood Institute (NHLBI) can search the Combined Health Information Database (CHID) and generate a bibliography of resources on Hypertriglyceridemia for you. They also will send you any publications and journal articles they may have on hand, and will refer you to other organizations that are studying this disease. If you can't afford treatment, have your doctor call NHLBI to find out if they are conducting any clinical studies that you might qualify for.

☎ Contact:
National Heart, Lung, and Blood Institute
Bldg. 31, Room 4A21
Bethesda, MD 20892
(301) 496-4236

HYPERURICEMIA

Clearinghouses/Hotlines

The National Institute of Diabetes and Digestive and Kidney Diseases's (NIDDK) individual clearinghouses can search the Combined Health Information Database (CHID) and generate a bibliography of resources on Hyperuricemia for

you. They also will send you any publications and journal articles they may have on hand, and will refer you to other organizations that are studying this disease. If you can't afford treatment, have your doctor call NIDDK to find out if they are conducting any clinical studies that you might qualify for.

☎ Contact:
National Institute of Diabetes
and Digestive and Kidney Diseases
Bldg. 31, Room 9A04
Bethesda, MD 20892
(301) 496-3583

HYPERVENTILATION

Clearinghouses/Hotlines

The National Heart, Lung, and Blood Institute (NHLBI) can search the Combined Health Information Database (CHID) and generate a bibliography of resources on Hyperventilation for you. They also will send you any publications and journal articles they may have on hand, and will refer you to other organizations that are studying this disease. If you can't afford treatment, have your doctor call NHLBI to find out if they are conducting any clinical studies that you might qualify for.

☎ Contact:
National Heart, Lung, and Blood Institute
Bldg. 31, Room 4A21
Bethesda, MD 20892
(301) 496-4236

HYPOBETALIPO-PROTEINEMIA

Clearinghouses/Hotlines

The National Heart, Lung, and Blood Institute (NHLBI) can search the Combined Health Information Database (CHID) and generate a bibliography of resources on Hypobetalipoproteinemia for you. They also will send you any publications and journal articles they may have on hand, and will refer you to other organizations that are studying this disease. If you can't afford treatment, have your doctor call NHLBI to find out if they are conducting any clinical studies that you might qualify for.

☎ Contact:
National Heart, Lung, and Blood Institute
Bldg. 31, Room 4A21
Bethesda, MD 20892
(301) 496-4236

HYPOCOMPLEMENTEMIC GLOMERULONEPHRITIS

Clearinghouses/Hotlines

The National Institute on Allergy and Infectious Diseases (NIAID) can search the Combined Health Information Database (CHID) and generate a bibliography of resources on Hypocomplementemic Glomerulonephritis for you. They will also send you any publications and journal articles they may have on hand, and will refer you to researchers who are currently studying this disease. If you can't afford treatment, have your doctor call NIAID to find out if they are conducting any clinical studies that you might qualify for.

☎ Contact:
National Institute of Allergy
and Infectious Diseases
Bldg. 31, Room 7A32
Bethesda, MD 20892
(301) 496-5717

HYPOGLYCEMIA

Clearinghouses/Hotlines

The National Heart, Lung, and Blood Institute (NHLBI) can search the Combined Health Information Database (CHID) and generate a

bibliography of resources on Hypoglycemia for you. They also will send you any publications and journal articles they may have on hand, and will refer you to other organizations that are studying this disease. If you can't afford treatment, have your doctor call NHLBI to find out if they are conducting any clinical studies that you might qualify for.

☎ Contact:
National Heart, Lung, and Blood Institute
Building 31
Room 4A21
Bethesda, MD 20892
(301) 496-4236

The National Institute of Diabetes and Digestive and Kidney Diseases's (NIDDK) individual clearinghouses can search the Combined Health Information Database (CHID) and generate a bibliography of resources on Hypoglycemia for you. They also will send you any publications and journal articles they may have on hand, and will refer you to other organizations that are studying this disease. If you can't afford treatment, have your doctor call NIDDK to find out if they are conducting any clinical studies that you might qualify for.

☎ Contact:
National Institute of Diabetes
and Digestive and Kidney Diseases
Bldg. 31, Room 9A04
Bethesda, MD 20892
(301) 496-3583

HYPOGONADISM

Clearinghouses/Hotlines

The National Institute of Diabetes and Digestive and Kidney Diseases's (NIDDK) individual clearinghouses can search the Combined Health Information Database (CHID) and generate a bibliography of resources on Hypogonadism for you. They also will send you any publications and journal articles they may have on hand, and will refer you to other organizations that are studying this disease. If you can't afford treatment, have your doctor call NIDDK to find out if they are conducting any clinical studies that you might qualify for.

☎ Contact:
National Institute of Diabetes
and Digestive and Kidney Diseases
Building 31
Room 9A04
Bethesda, MD 20892
(301) 496-3583

The National Institute of Child Health and Human Development (NICHD) will send you whatever publications and reprints of journal articles they have on Hypogonadism. If necessary, they will refer you to other experts or researchers in the field. If you can't afford treatment, have your doctor call NICHD to find out if they are conducting any clinical studies that you might qualify for.

☎ Contact:
National Institute of Child Health
and Human Development
Building 31
Room 2A32
Bethesda, MD 20892
(301) 496-5133

HYPOKALEMIA

Clearinghouses/Hotlines

The National Heart, Lung, and Blood Institute (NHLBI) can search the Combined Health Information Database (CHID) and generate a bibliography of resources on Hypokalemia for you. They also will send you any publications and journal articles they may have on hand, and will refer you to other organizations that are studying this disease. If you can't afford treatment, have your doctor call NHLBI to find out if they are conducting any clinical studies that you might qualify for.

☎ Contact:
National Heart, Lung, and Blood Institute
Building 31, Room 4A21
Bethesda, MD 20892
(301) 496-4236

HYPOKALEMIC PERIODIC PARALYSIS

Clearinghouses/Hotlines

The National Institute of Neurological Disorders and Stroke (NINDS) can send you only information they have in their publications list on Hypokalemic Periodic Paralysis. They cannot refer you to any experts. This Clearinghouse cannot directly give you information about any current clinical studies NINDS might be conducting on this illness, but you can find this information for yourself by looking under the National Institute of Neurological Disorders and Stroke in *Appendix A* at the end of this book.

☎ Contact:
National Institute of Neurological
Disorders and Stroke
Building 31
Room 8A06
Bethesda, MD 20892
(301) 496-5751
(800) 352-9424

HYPOLIPOPROTEINEMIA

Clearinghouses/Hotlines

The National Heart, Lung, and Blood Institute (NHLBI) can search the Combined Health Information Database (CHID) and generate a bibliography of resources on Hypolipoproteinemia for you. They also will send you any publications and journal articles they may have on hand, and will refer you to other organizations that are studying this disease. If you can't afford treatment, have your doctor call NHLBI to find out if they are conducting any clinical studies that you might qualify for.

☎ Contact:
National Heart, Lung, and Blood Institute
Bldg. 31, Room 4A21
Bethesda, MD 20892
(301) 496-4236

HYPOPARATHYROIDISM

Clearinghouses/Hotlines

The National Institute of Diabetes and Digestive and Kidney Diseases's (NIDDK) individual clearinghouses can search the Combined Health Information Database (CHID) and generate a bibliography of resources on Hypoparathyroidism for you. They also will send you any publications and journal articles they may have on hand, and will refer you to other organizations that are studying this disease. If you can't afford treatment, have your doctor call NIDDK to find out if they are conducting any clinical studies that you might qualify for.

☎ Contact:
National Institute of Diabetes
and Digestive and Kidney Diseases
Building 31
Room 9A04
Bethesda, MD 20892
(301) 496-3583

HYPOPITUITARISM

Clearinghouses/Hotlines

The National Institute of Diabetes and Digestive and Kidney Diseases's (NIDDK) individual clearinghouses can search the Combined Health Information Database (CHID) and generate a bibliography of resources on Hypopituitarism for you. They also will send you any publications and journal articles they may have on hand, and will refer you to other organizations that are studying this disease. If you can't afford treatment, have your doctor call NIDDK to find out if they are conducting any clinical studies that you might qualify for.

☎ Contact:
National Institute of Diabetes
and Digestive and Kidney Diseases
Bldg. 31, Room 9A04
Bethesda, MD 20892
(301) 496-3583

HYPOSPADIAS

Clearinghouses/Hotlines

The National Institute of Child Health and Human Development (NICHD) will send you whatever publications and reprints of journal articles they have on Hypospadias. If necessary, they will refer you to other experts or researchers in the field. If you can't afford treatment, have your doctor call NICHD to find out if they are conducting any clinical studies that you might qualify for.

☎ Contact:
National Institute of Child Health
and Human Development
Bldg. 31, Room 2A32
Bethesda, MD 20892
(301) 496-5133

HYPOTENSION

See Low Blood Pressure

HYPOTHALAMUS

Clearinghouses/Hotlines

The National Institute of Diabetes and Digestive and Kidney Diseases's (NIDDK) individual clearinghouses can search the Combined Health Information Database (CHID) and generate a bibliography of resources on the Hypothalamus for you. They also will send you any publications and journal articles they may have on hand, and will refer you to other organizations that are studying related diseases. If you can't afford treatment, have your doctor call NIDDK to find out if they are conducting any clinical studies that you might qualify for.

☎ Contact:
National Institute of Diabetes
and Digestive and Kidney Diseases
Bldg. 31, Room 9A04

Bethesda, MD 20892
(301) 496-3583

The National Institute of Child Health and Human Development (NICHD) will send you whatever publications and reprints of journal articles they have on the Hypothalamus. If necessary, they will refer you to other experts or researchers in the field. If you can't afford treatment, have your doctor call NICHD to find out if they are conducting any clinical studies that you might qualify for.

☎ Contact:
National Institute of Child Health
and Human Development
Building 31
Room 2A32
Bethesda, MD 20892
(301) 496-5133

HYPOTHERMIA

Clearinghouses/Hotlines

The National Institute on Aging (NIA) will send you whatever publications and reprints of journal articles they have on Accidental Hypothermia. They cannot refer you to other experts if the information they have isn't sufficient for your purposes.

☎ Contact:
National Institute on Aging
Bldg. 31, Room 5C27
Bethesda, MD 20892
(301) 496-1752

Free Publications/Videos

The following publication on Hypothermia is available from the National Institute on Aging Information Center, 2209 Distribution Circle, Silver Spring, MD 20910; (301) 495-3455.

- *A Winter Hazard for Older People: Accidental Hypothermia* warns elderly persons to protect themselves against a progressive drop in deep body temperature that can be

fatal if not detected in time and properly treated. (#81-1464)

HYPOTHYROIDISM

Clearinghouses/Hotlines

The National Institute of Diabetes and Digestive and Kidney Diseases's (NIDDK) individual clearinghouses can search the Combined Health Information Database (CHID) and generate a bibliography of resources on Goitrous Hypothyroidism for you. They also will send you any publications and journal articles they may have on hand, and will refer you to other organizations that are studying this disease. If you can't afford treatment, have your doctor call NIDDK to find out if they are conducting any clinical studies that you might qualify for.

☎ Contact:
National Institute of Diabetes
and Digestive and Kidney Diseases
Bldg. 31, Room 9A04
Bethesda, MD 20892
(301) 496-3583

HYPOTONIA

Clearinghouses/Hotlines

The National Institute of Neurological Disorders and Stroke (NINDS) can send you only information they have in their publications list on Hypotonia. They cannot refer you to any experts. This Clearinghouse cannot directly give you information about any current clinical studies NINDS might be conducting on this illness, but you can find this information for yourself by looking under the National Institute of Neurological Disorders and Stroke in *Appendix A* at the end of this book.

☎ Contact:
National Institute of Neurological
Disorders and Stroke
Bldg. 31, Room 8A06

Bethesda, MD 20892
(301) 496-5751
(800) 352-9424

HYPOVENTILATION

Clearinghouses/Hotlines

The National Heart, Lung, and Blood Institute (NHLBI) can search the Combined Health Information Database (CHID) and generate a bibliography of resources on Hypoventilation for you. They also will send you any publications and journal articles they may have on hand, and will refer you to other organizations that are studying this disease. If you can't afford treatment, have your doctor call NHLBI to find out if they are conducting any clinical studies that you might qualify for.

☎ Contact:
National Heart, Lung, and Blood Institute
Bldg. 31, Room 4A21
Bethesda, MD 20892
(301) 496-4236

HYPOXIA

Clearinghouses/Hotlines

The National Heart, Lung, and Blood Institute (NHLBI) can search the Combined Health Information Database (CHID) and generate a bibliography of resources on Hypoxia for you. They also will send you any publications and journal articles they may have on hand, and will refer you to other organizations that are studying this disease. If you can't afford treatment, have your doctor call NHLBI to find out if they are conducting any clinical studies that you might qualify for.

☎ Contact:
National Heart, Lung, and Blood Institute
Bldg. 31, Room 4A21
Bethesda, MD 20892
(301) 496-4236

HYPSARRHYTHMIA

Clearinghouses/Hotlines

The National Institute of Neurological Disorders and Stroke (NINDS) can send you only information they have in their publications list on Hypsarrhythmia. They cannot refer you to any experts. This Clearinghouse cannot directly give you information about any current clinical studies NINDS might be conducting on this condition, but you can find this information for yourself by looking under the National Institute of Neurological Disorders and Stroke in *Appendix A* at the end of this book.

☎ Contact:
National Institute of Neurological Disorders and Stroke
Building 31, Room 8A06
Bethesda, MD 20892
(301) 496-5751
(800) 352-9424

- I -

IBD AND IBS

See Irritable Bowel Syndrome

ICELAND DISEASE

Clearinghouses/Hotlines

The National Institute of Neurological Disorders and Stroke (NINDS) can send you only information they have in their publications list on Iceland Disease. They cannot refer you to any experts. This Clearinghouse cannot directly give you information about any current clinical studies NINDS might be conducting on this illness, but you can find this information for yourself by looking under the National Institute of Neurological Disorders and Stroke in *Appendix A* at the end of this book.

☎ Contact:
National Institute of Neurological
Disorders and Stroke
Bldg. 31, Room 8A06
Bethesda, MD 20892
(301) 496-5751
(800) 352-9424

ICHTHYOSIS

Clearinghouses/Hotlines

The National Institute of Arthritis and Musculoskeletal and Skin Diseases (NIAMS) will send you whatever publications and reprints of articles from texts and journals they have on Ichthyosis. They will also refer you to other organizations that are studying this disease. NIAMS will also let you know of any clinical studies that may be studying this disease and looking for patients.

☎ Contact:
National Institute of Arthritis
and Musculoskeletal and Skin Diseases
Box AMS
Bethesda, MD 20892
(301) 495-4484

Free Publications/Videos

The following publication is available from the National Arthritis and Musculoskeletal and Skin Diseases Information Clearinghouse, Box AMS, 9000 Rockville Pike, Bethesda, MD 20892; (301) 495-4484.

- *Ichthyosis and Related Disorders: An Annotated Bibliography*, 1989. An annotated bibliography of resources. (#AR65, $4)

IDENTICAL TWINS

See Twins

IDIOPATHIC HYPERTROPHIC SUBAORTIC STENOSIS

Clearinghouses/Hotlines

The National Heart, Lung, and Blood Institute (NHLBI) can search the Combined Health Information Database (CHID) and generate a bibliography of resources on Idiopathic Hypertrophic Subaortic Stenosis (IHSS) for you. They also will send you any publications and journal articles they may have on hand, and will refer you to other organizations that are studying this disease. If you can't afford treatment, have your doctor call NHLBI to find out if they are conducting any clinical studies that you might qualify for.

☎ Contact:
National Heart, Lung, and Blood Institute
Bldg. 31, Room 4A21
Bethesda, MD 20892
(301) 496-4236

IDIOPATHIC INFLAMMATORY MYOPATHY

Clearinghouses/Hotlines

The National Institute of Neurological Disorders and Stroke (NINDS) can send you only information they have in their publications list on Idiopathic Inflammatory Myopathy. They cannot refer you to any experts. This Clearinghouse cannot directly give you information about any current clinical studies NINDS might be conducting on this illness, but you can find this information for yourself by looking under the National Institute of Neurological Disorders and Stroke in *Appendix A* at the end of this book.

☎ Contact:
National Institute of Neurological
Disorders and Stroke
Bldg. 31, Room 8A06
Bethesda, MD 20892
(301) 496-5751
(800) 352-9424

IDIOPATHIC THROMBOCYTOPENIC PURPURA

Clearinghouses/Hotlines

The National Heart, Lung, and Blood Institute (NHLBI) can search the Combined Health Information Database (CHID) and generate a bibliography of resources on Idiopathic Thrombo-cytopenic Purpura (ITP) for you. They also will send you any publications and journal articles they may have on hand, and will refer you to other organizations that are studying this disease. If you can't afford treatment, have your doctor call NHLBI to find out if they are conducting any clinical studies that you might qualify for.

☎ Contact:
National Heart, Lung, and Blood Institute
Bldg. 31, Room 4A21
Bethesda, MD 20892
(301) 496-4236

The National Institute of Diabetes and Digestive and Kidney Diseases's (NIDDK) individual clearinghouses can search the Combined Health Information Database (CHID) and generate a bibliography of resources on Idiopathic Thrombocytopenic Purpura (ITP) for you. They also will send you any publications and journal articles they may have on hand, and will refer you to other organizations that are studying this disease. If you can't afford treatment, have your doctor call NIDDK to find out if they are conducting any clinical studies that you might qualify for.

☎ Contact:
National Institute of Diabetes
and Digestive and Kidney Diseases
Bldg. 31, Room 9A04
Bethesda, MD 20892
(301) 496-3583

ILEITIS

Clearinghouses/Hotlines

The National Institute of Diabetes and Digestive and Kidney Diseases's (NIDDK) individual clearinghouses can search the Combined Health Information Database (CHID) and generate a bibliography of resources on Ileitis for you. They also will send you any publications and journal articles they may have on hand, and will refer you to other organizations that are studying this condition. If you can't afford treatment, have your doctor call NIDDK to find out if they are conducting any clinical studies that you might qualify for.

☎ Contact:
National Institute of Diabetes
and Digestive and Kidney Diseases
Bldg. 31, Room 9A04
Bethesda, MD 20892
(301) 496-3583

IMMUNE DEFICIENCY DISEASE

Clearinghouses/Hotlines

The National Institute on Allergy and Infectious Diseases (NIAID) can search the Combined Health Information Database (CHID) and generate a bibliography of resources on Immune Deficiency Diseases for you. They will also send you any publications and journal articles they may have on hand, and will refer you to researchers who are currently studying this disease. If you can't afford treatment, have your doctor call NIAID to find out if they are conducting any clinical studies that you might qualify for.

☎ Contact:
National Institute of Allergy
and Infectious Diseases
Bldg. 31, Room 7A32
Bethesda, MD 20892
(301) 496-5717

The National Cancer Institute (NCI) will send you whatever publications and reprints of journal articles they have on Immune Deficiency Diseases. They can also give you information on the state-of-the-art treatment for this disease, including specific treatment information for your stage of cancer. They can also search their Physician's Data Query (PDQ) database to let you know if NCI is conducting any clinical studies on your disease.

☎ Contact:
National Cancer Institute
Bldg. 31, Room 10A24
Bethesda, MD 20892
(800) 4-CANCER
(301) 496-5583

Free Publications/Videos

The following publications on Immune Deficiency Diseases are available from the National Institute of Allergy and Infectious Diseases, Bldg. 31, Room 7A32, Bethesda, MD 20892; (301) 496-5717.

- *Understanding the Immune System.* (#92-529)
- *Understanding the Immune System.* Discusses antigens, the immune system, disorders (including AIDS), the immunology of transplants, and new diagnostic methods. (#84-529)

IMMUNE THROMBOCYTOPENIC PURPURA

Free Publications/Videos

The following publication is available from the National Heart, Lung and Blood Institute, Bldg.

31, Room 4A21, Bethesda, MD 20892; (301) 496-4236.

- *Facts About Immune Thrombocytopenic Purpura.*

IMMUNIZATIONS

Clearinghouses/Hotlines

The Centers for Disease Control will answer all your questions and send you publications about immunization against vaccine-preventable diseases of young children. They can also send you reports of the recommendations of the Immunization Practices Advisory Committee, as well as informational pamphlets on the various vaccines all of our children should receive.

☎ Contact:
Centers for Disease Control
1600 Tullie Circle
Atlanta, GA 30333
(404) 639-1830

The Centers for Disease Control (CDC) and the Agency for Toxic Substances and Disease Registry have developed a Voice Information System that allows anyone using a touchtone phone, to obtain prerecorded information on a particular health issue. The most complex system is for international travelers' health. The system can also transfer the caller to a public health professional for additional information. The system is available 24 hours per day, although the health professionals are available Monday-Friday, 8 a.m. - 4:30 p.m.

☎ Contact:
Disease Information
Centers for Disease Control
Information Resources Management Office
Mail Stop C-15, 1600 Clifton Road, NE
Atlanta, GA 30333
(404) 332-4555

Free Publications/Hotlines

The following publication on Vaccines is available from the Centers for Disease Control, National Center for Prevention Services, (E06), 1600

Clifton Rd., NE, Atlanta, GA 30333; (404) 639-1838.

- *Vaccine Preventable Disease Highlights.*
  Provides a forum for the exchange of ideas about immunization activities, primarily at state and local levels.

IMPOTENCE

Clearinghouses/Hotlines

The National Institute of Mental Health (NIMH) will send you whatever publications and reprints of articles from texts and journals they have on Impotence. They will also refer you to other organizations studying this condition. NIMH will also let you know of any clinical studies that may be studying this disease and looking for patients.

☎ Contact:
National Institute of Mental Health
5600 Fishers Ln., Room 15C05
Rockville, MD 20857
(301) 443-4515

The National Kidney and Urological Diseases Information Clearinghouse (NKUDIC) can search the Combined Health Information Database (CHID) and generate a bibliography of resources on Impotence for you. They also will send you any publications and journal articles they may have on hand, and will refer you to other organizations that are studying Impotence. If you can't afford treatment, have your doctor call NKUDIC to find out if they are conducting any clinical studies that you might qualify for.

☎ Contact:
National Kidney and Urological Diseases
Information Clearinghouse
Box NKUDIC
Bethesda, MD 20892
(301) 468-6345

Free Publications/Videos

The following publication on Impotence is available from the National Kidney and Urological

Diseases Information Clearinghouse, Box NKUDIC, Bethesda, MD 20892; (301) 468-6345.

- *Impotence.* Bibliography of resources.

INAPPROPRIATE ANTIDIURETIC HORMONE SYNDROME

Clearinghouses/Hotlines

The National Heart, Lung, and Blood Institute (NHLBI) can search the Combined Health Information Database (CHID) and generate a bibliography of resources on Inappropriate Antidiuretic Hormone Syndrome for you. They also will send you any publications and journal articles they may have on hand, and will refer you to other organizations that are studying this disease. If you can't afford treatment, have your doctor call NHLBI to find out if they are conducting any clinical studies that you might qualify for.

☎ Contact:
National Heart, Lung, and Blood Institute
Bldg. 31, Room 4A21
Bethesda, MD 20892
(301) 496-4236

INBORN HEART DEFECTS

Clearinghouses/Hotlines

The National Heart, Lung, and Blood Institute (NHLBI) can search the Combined Health Information Database (CHID) and generate a bibliography of resources on Inborn Heart Defects for you. They also will send you any publications and journal articles they may have on hand, and will refer you to other organizations that are studying this disease. If you can't afford treatment, have your doctor call NHLBI to find out if they are conducting any clinical studies that you might qualify for.

☎ Contact:
National Heart, Lung, and Blood Institute
Bldg. 31, Room 4A21
Bethesda, MD 20892
(301) 496-4236

INCONTINENCE

Clearinghouses/Hotlines

The National Institute on Aging (NIA) will send you whatever publications and reprints of journal articles they have on Incontinence. They cannot refer you to other experts if the information they have isn't sufficient for your purposes.

☎ Contact:
National Institute on Aging
Bldg. 31, Room 5C27
Bethesda, MD 20892
(301) 496-1752

The National Kidney and Urological Diseases Information Clearinghouse (NKUDIC) can search the Combined Health Information Database (CHID) and generate a bibliography of resources on Incontinence for you. They also will send you any publications and journal articles they may have on hand, and will refer you to other organizations that are studying this disease. If you can't afford treatment, have your doctor call NKUDIC to find out if they are conducting any clinical studies that you might qualify for.

☎ Contact:
National Kidney and Urological Diseases
Information Clearinghouse
Box NKUDIC
Bethesda, MD 20892
(301) 468-6345

Free Publications/Videos

The following publications on Incontinence are available from the National Kidney and Urological Diseases Information Clearinghouse, Box NKUDIC, Bethesda, MD 20892; (301) 468-6345.

- *Prevention and Treatment of Kidney Stones.*

Describes diagnosis, treatment, and types of urinary incontinence.
- *Urinary Incontinence.* Describes diagnosis, treatment, and types of urinary incontinence.
- *Urinary Incontinence in Adults.* Summary statement of National Institutes of Health Consensus Development Conference.
- *Urinary Incontinence: Professional Materials.* Bibliography of resources.
- *Urinary Incontinence: Patient Materials.* Bibliography of resources.

The following publication is available from the National Institute on Aging Information Center, 2209 Distribution Circle, Silver Spring, MD 20910; (301) 495-3455.

- *Urinary Incontinence.* Facts for the aging.

The following publication is available from the Office of Technology Assessment, 600 Pennsylvania Ave., SE, Washington, DC 20510; (202) 224-8996.

- *Technologies for Managing Urinary Incontinence.* A report to Congress. Ask for the summary report. (#HCS-33)

INCONTINENTIA PIGMENTI

Clearinghouses/Hotlines

The National Institute of Neurological Disorders and Stroke (NINDS) can send you only information they have in their publications list on Incontinentia Pigmenti. They cannot refer you to any experts. This Clearinghouse cannot directly give you information about any current clinical studies NINDS might be conducting on this illness, but you can find this information for yourself by looking under the National Institute of Neurological Disorders and Stroke in *Appendix A* at the end of this book.

☎ Contact:
National Institute of Neurological
Disorders and Stroke
Bldg. 31, Room 8A06

Bethesda, MD 20892
(301) 496-5751
(800) 352-9424

INDOOR AIR POLLUTION

Clearinghouses/Hotlines

The Environmental Protection Agency's Indoor Air Division can provide you with fact sheets on a wide variety of Indoor Air Problems such as Sick Building Syndrome, tobacco smoke, office ventilation, and air cleaners. They'll send you a summary of *Air Cleaning Devices*, as well as a directory of State Indoor Air Contacts. *Building Air Quality: A Guide for Building Owners and Facility Managers* is another handbook for all air quality questions and remedies.

☎ Contact:
Indoor Air Division
Environmental Protection Agency
ANR-445W
Washington, DC 20460
(703) 308-8470

Free Publications/Videos

The following publication is available from the Science & Technology Division, Reference Section, Library of Congress, Washington, DC 20540; (202) 707-5580.

- *Indoor Air Pollution*. Reference guide designed to help locate further published material. (#86-8)

The following Congressional Research Service (CRS) reports on Indoor Air Pollution are available from either of your U.S. Senators' offices at the U.S. Capitol, Washington, DC 20510, or from your Congressional Representative at the U.S. Capitol, Washington, DC 20515. You can also call in your request through the U.S. Capitol switchboard at (202) 224-3121. Be sure to include the full title and report number in your request.

- *Indoor Air Pollution: Audio Brief.* (#AB50188)

- *Indoor Air Pollution: Cause for Concern?* (#88-745 ENR)
- *Indoor Air Pollution: Issue Brief.* (#IB88902)
- *Indoor Air Quality Problems: Present and Future; Videoprogram.* (#LTR91-858)
- *Radon: An Overview of Health and Environmental Issues.* (#IP363R)
- *Radon and Indoor Air Pollution: Bibliography-in-Brief, 1986-1987.* (#87-853 L)
- *Radon: Congressional and Federal Concerns: Issue Brief.* (#IB86144)

The following publications on Indoor Air Pollution are available from the Consumer Information Center, Pueblo, CO 81009.

- *Biological Pollutants in Your Home.* Describes indoor air pollutants and what to do about them. (#469Y, $.50)
- *The Inside Story: A Guide to Indoor Air Quality.* Alerts you to the ways air pollutants may affect you and what to do. (#433Y, $.50)

INDUCED MOVEMENT DISORDERS

Clearinghouses/Hotlines

The National Institute of Neurological Disorders and Stroke (NINDS) can send you only information they have in their publications list on Induced Movement Disorders. They cannot refer you to any experts. This Clearinghouse cannot directly give you information about any current clinical studies NINDS might be conducting on this topic, but you can find this information for yourself by looking under the National Institute of Neurological Disorders and Stroke in *Appendix A* at the end of this book.

☎ Contact:
National Institute of Neurological
Disorders and Stroke
Bldg. 31, Room 8A06
Bethesda, MD 20892
(301) 496-5751
(800) 352-9424

INFANT FORMULA

Free Publications/Videos

The following Congressional Research Service (CRS) report on Infant Formula is available from either of your U.S. Senators' offices at the U.S. Capitol, Washington, DC 20510, or from your Congressional Representative at the U.S. Capitol, Washington, DC 20515. You can also call in your request through the U.S. Capitol switchboard at (202) 224-3121. Be sure to include the full title and report number in your request.

- *Infant Formula: National Problems; Archived Mini Brief.* (#MB82244)

INFANT HEALTH

Clearinghouses/Hotlines

The National Maternal and Child Health Clearinghouse has all kinds of information on maternal and child health issues, such as pregnancy, child and adolescent health, and human genetics. If the answer to your question can't be answered by any of their countless free publications, they can refer you to other National or local resources. If you still need further information, they search their own reference collection and send you what they find.

☎ Contact:
National Maternal and Child
Health Clearinghouse
38th & R Sts. NW
Washington, DC 20057
(703) 821-8955, ext. 254

The National Center for Clinical Infant Programs (NCCIP) supports professional initiatives in Infant Health, mental health and development. *Project Zero to Three*, funded by the Bureau of Maternal and Child Health and Resources Development, focuses on infants who are disabled or at risk. Publications are available on clinical issues targeted at disciplines concerned with infants,

toddlers, and their families.

☎ Contact:
National Center for
Clinical Infant Programs
P.O. Box 25494
Richmond, VA 23260
(800) 544-0155
(703) 528-4300

The National Institute of Child Health and Human Development (NICHD) will send you whatever publications and reprints of journal articles they have on Infant Health and Mortality. If necessary, they will refer you to other experts or researchers in the field.

☎ Contact:
National Institute of Child Health
and Human Development
Building 31
Room 2A32
Bethesda, MD 20892
(301) 496-5133

The National Information Clearinghouse for Infants with Disabilities and Life-Threatening Conditions offers parents of infants with disabilities help with legal and advocacy issues, and finding financial assistance, community services, parent support and parent education, child protective services, home health services and other assistance.

☎ Contact:
Benson Building
First Floor
Columbia, SC 29208
(800) 922-9234
(800) 922-1107 in SC

The Healthy Start Program is a Presidential initiative to reduce infant mortality through additional support for comprehensive service delivery in 15 high-risk communities, with the goal of reducing infant mortality by 50% over five years. The Health Resources and Services Administration has put together an information packet that includes some background information and a listing of grantees (including a breakdown of features and contact people).

☎ Contact:
Health Resources and Services Administration

5600 Fishers Lane
Room 1443
Rockville, MD 20857
(301) 443-2086

The National Center for Health Statistics (NCHS) can provide you with statistics regarding infant mortality, such as age, location, information on mothers and more. Call the center for your free report.

☎ Contact:
National Center for Health Statistics
6525 Belcrest Rd.
Hyattsville, MD 20782
(301) 436-8500

Free Publications/Videos

The following publication on Infant Health is available from the Superintendent of Documents, Government Printing Office, Washington, DC 20402; (202) 783-3238.

- *Infant Care*. Presents the latest information on caring for a new baby from birth through the first year. Special attention is given to the all-important first few weeks of life, including advice on feeding and bathing a newborn and the minor illnesses and injuries that are common to infants. ($4, S/N 017-091-00241-0)

The following publications on Infant Health are available from the National Maternal and Child Health Clearinghouse, 38th & R Sts., NW, Washington, DC 20057; (703) 821-8955, ext. 254.

- *Warning Signals: Basic Criteria for Tracking At Risk Infants and Toddlers*. (#B259)
- *Four Critical Junctures: Support for Parents of Children With Special Needs*. (#C016)
- *The Open Door: Parent Participation in State Policymaking About Children with Special Health Needs*. (#B339)
- *Skim Milk in Infant Feeding*. (#B042)
- *Newborn Screening for Genetic-Metabolic Diseases: Progress, Principles and Recommendations*. (#B048)
- *Pre-term and Low Birthweight Infants: Resource Guide*. (#D015)

- *Nutrition During Lactation*. (#D081)
- *Recommendations for Feeding Normal Infants*. (#B060)
- *Patient Education Materials: A Resource Guide*. This guide was developed to help health professionals identify and locate materials on maternal and child health topics that are clear, concise, easy to read and appropriate for the general public. The guide is separated into three sections. The first is patient education materials, which is an annotated listing of source books, directories, audiovisuals, and resource guides that describe patient education materials. The second section lists publishers of patient education materials, and the third lists federal health information clearinghouses.

The following Congressional Research Service (CRS) report on Infant Health is available from either of your U.S. Senators' offices at the U.S. Capitol, Washington, DC 20510, or from your Congressional Representative at the U.S. Capitol, Washington, DC 20515. You can also call in your request through the U.S. Capitol switchboard at (202) 224-3121. Be sure to include the full title and report number in your request.

- *Demographic and Social Patterns of Infant Mortality*. (#86-133 EPW)

INFANT NUTRITION

Clearinghouses/Hotlines

The National Maternal and Child Health Clearinghouse has all kinds of information on maternal and child health issues, such as pregnancy, child and adolescent health, and human genetics. If the answer to your question can't be answered by any of their countless free publications, they can refer you to other National or local resources. If you still need further information, they search their own reference collection and send you what they find.

☎ Contact:
National Maternal and Child

Health Clearinghouse
38th & R Sts. NW
Washington, DC 20057
(703) 821-8955, ext. 254

The National Institute of Child Health and Human Development (NICHD) will send you whatever publications and reprints of journal articles they have on Infant Nutrition. If necessary, they will refer you to other experts or researchers in the field. If you can't afford treatment, have your doctor call NICHD to find out if they are conducting any clinical studies that you might qualify for.

☎ Contact:
National Institute of Child Health
and Human Development
Bldg. 31, Room 2A32
Bethesda, MD 20892
(301) 496-5133

The National Center for Clinical Infant Programs supports professional initiatives in infant health, mental health and development. *Project Zero to Three*, for example, is an effort funded by the Bureau of Maternal and Child Health and Resources Development that focuses on infants who are disabled or at risk. Publications are available on clinical issues targeted at disciplines concerned with infants, toddlers, and their families.

☎ Contact:
National Center for Clinical Infant Programs
P.O. Box 25494
Richmond, VA 23260
(800) 544-0155
(703) 528-4300

Free Publications/Videos

The following publication on Infant Nutrition is available from the Food & Nutrition Information Center, National Agricultural Library, Room 304, Beltsville, MD 20705-2351; (301) 504-5719.

- *Infant Nutrition.* A list of current references.

The following publication on Infant Nutrition is available from the Food & Drug Administration, (HFE-88), 5600 Fishers Ln., Rockville, MD 20857; (301) 443-3170.

- *Good Nutrition For the High Chair Set.* (#FDA92-2208)

The following publication on Infant Nutrition is available from the National Maternal and Child Health Clearinghouse, 38th & R Sts., NW, Washington, DC 20057; (703) 821-8955, ext. 254.

- *Patient Education Materials: A Resource Guide.* Developed to help health professionals identify and locate materials on maternal and child health topics that are clear, concise, easy to read and appropriate for the general public. The guide is separated into three sections. The first is patient education materials, which is an annotated listing of source books, directories, audiovisuals, and resource guides that describe patient education materials. The second section lists publishers of patient education materials, and the third lists federal health information clearinghouses.

INFANTS WITH DISABILITIES

Clearinghouses/Hotlines

The National Information Clearinghouse for Infants with Disabilities and Life-Threatening Conditions offers help on legal and advocacy issues, financial assistance, community services, parent support and parent education, child protective services, home health services and other assistance to parents and professionals concerned about infants with disabilities.

☎ Contact:
National Information Clearinghouse
for Infants with Disabilities
and Life-Threatening Conditions
Benson Building
First Floor
Columbia, SC 29208
(800) 922-9234
(800) 922-1107 (in SC)

INFECTIOUS ARTHRITIS

Clearinghouses/Hotlines

The National Institute of Arthritis and Musculoskeletal and Skin Diseases (NIAMS) will send you whatever publications and reprints of articles from texts and journals they have on Infectious Arthritis. They will also refer you to other organizations that are studying this disease. NIAMS will also let you know of any clinical studies that may be studying this disease and looking for patients.

☎ Contact:
National Institute of Arthritis
and Musculoskeletal and Skin Diseases
Box AMS
Bethesda, MD 20892
(301) 495-4484

Free Publications/Videos

The following publication is available from the National Arthritis and Musculoskeletal and Skin Diseases Information Clearinghouse, Box AMS, 9000 Rockville Pike, Bethesda, MD 20892; (301) 495-4484.

- *Infectious Arthritis, 1985*. An annotated bibliography of resources. (#AR48, $2)

INFECTIOUS DISEASES

Clearinghouses/Hotlines

The National Institute on Allergy and Infectious Diseases (NIAID) can search the Combined Health Information Database (CHID) and generate a bibliography of resources on Infectious Diseases for you. They will also send you any publications and journal articles they may have on hand, and will refer you to researchers who are currently studying these diseases. If you can't afford treatment, have your doctor call NIAID to find out if they are conducting any clinical studies

that you might qualify for.

☎ Contact:
National Institute of Allergy
and Infectious Diseases
Bldg. 31, Room 7A32
Bethesda, MD 20892
(301) 496-5717

Free Publications/Videos

The following publication is available from the National Institute of Allergy and Infectious Diseases, Bldg. 31, Room 7A32, Bethesda, MD 20892; (301) 496-5717.

- *NIAID: The Edge of Discovery*. (#88-2773)

INFECTIOUS EYE DISEASES

Clearinghouses/Hotlines

The National Eye Institute (NEI) can give you up-to-date information on Infectious Eye Diseases by searching the Combined Health Information Database (CHID) and MEDLINE and sending you bibliographies of resources, along with any journal articles they may have. They can also refer you to any other organizations that study this and other related diseases. NEI will also let you know of any clinical studies that may be studying this disease and looking for patients. Because of their small staff, NEI prefers that you submit your requests for information in writing.

☎ Contact:
National Eye Institute
Bldg. 31, Room 6A32
Bethesda, MD 20892
(301) 496-5248

INFECTIOUS WASTE

Free Publications/Videos

The following Congressional Research Service

(CRS) reports on Infectious Waste are available from either of your U.S. Senators' offices at the U.S. Capitol, Washington, DC 20510, or from your Congressional Representative at the U.S. Capitol, Washington, DC 20515. You can also call in your request through the U.S. Capitol switchboard at (202) 224-3121. Be sure to include the full title and report number in your request.

- *Brief Summary of Several Federal Statutes Which Arguably Provide the Federal Government the Authority to Control the Disposal of Infectious Hospital.* (#87-658 A)
- *Infectious Waste and Beach Closings.* (#88-596 ENR)

INFERTILITY

Clearinghouses/Hotlines

The National Institute of Child Health and Human Development (NICHD) can provide you with information on Infertility, including journal articles and other relevant information. The Reproductive Sciences Branch (301-496-6515) supports basic research in reproductive sciences, such as the alleviation of human infertility, curing human reproductive diseases and disorders, development of healthy embryos, and the discovery of safe methods of contraception. They conduct research on endometriosis, fibroids, tubal and ectopic pregnancies, and abnormal puberty. They are also supporting the National Reproductive Medicine Network, which is a group of cooperating sites designed to carry out large-scale clinical studies on infertility and reproductive diseases. The first trial is a comparison of intrauterine and intracervical insemination, either with or without ovulation induction. These trials are free for participants. For more information contact NICHD or one of the following sites near you listed below.

☎ Contact:
National Institute of Child Health
and Human Development
Reproductive Sciences Branch
Center for Population Research
6130 Executive Boulevard
Room 603

Bethesda, MD 20892
(301) 496-5133

Magee- Women's Hospital (Pittsburgh)
Kathleen Baffone, RN
(412) 647-4135

New England Medical Center (Boston)
Judith Carleo, RN
(617) 956-4621

University of Pennsylvania (Philadelphia)
Linda Martino, CRNP
(215) 662-2936

University of Tennessee (Memphis)
Renee Samuels, RN
(901) 528-5859

University of California (Davis)
Lois Wisner, RNC
(916) 752-3863

Free Publications/Videos

The following publication on Infertility is available from the Food & Drug Admin., (HFE-88), 5600 Fishers Ln., Rockville, MD 20857; (301) 443-3170.

- *Infertility and How It's Treated.* (#83-3136)

The following publication on Infertility is available from the Office of Technology Assessment, 600 Pennsylvania Ave., SE, Washington, DC 20510; (202) 224-8996.

- *Infertility: Medical and Social Choices.* A report to Congress. Ask for the summary report. (#BA-358)

The following publication on Infertility is available from the Federal Trade Commission, Office of Consumer Education, Bureau of Consumer Protection, Washington, DC 20580; (202) 326-3650.

- *Infertility Services.* Reviews success-rate claims of these services and provides information to help you evaluate these claims and select the best program for your needs.

INFLAMMATORY BOWEL DISEASE

Clearinghouses/Hotlines

The National Institute of Diabetes and Digestive and Kidney Diseases's (NIDDK) individual clearinghouses can search the Combined Health Information Database (CHID) and generate a bibliography of resources on Inflammatory Bowel Disease for you. They also will send you any publications and journal articles they may have on hand, and will refer you to other organizations that are studying this disease. If you can't afford treatment, have your doctor call NIDDK to find out if they are conducting any clinical studies that you might qualify for.

☎ Contact:
National Institute of Diabetes
and Digestive and Kidney Diseases
Bldg. 31, Room 9A04
Bethesda, MD 20892
(301) 496-3583

The National Institute on Allergy and Infectious Diseases (NIAID) can search the Combined Health Information Database (CHID) and generate a bibliography of resources on Inflammatory Bowel Disease for you. They will also send you any publications and journal articles they may have on hand, and will refer you to researchers who are currently studying this disease. If you can't afford treatment, have your doctor call NIAID to find out if they are conducting any clinical studies that you might qualify for.

☎ Contact:
National Institute of Allergy
and Infectious Diseases
Bldg. 31, Room 7A32
Bethesda, MD 20892
(301) 496-5717

Free Publications/Videos

The following publication is available from the National Institute of Diabetes and Digestive and Kidney Diseases, Bldg. 31, Room 9A04, Bethesda, MD 20892; (301) 496-3583.

- *Inflammatory Bowel Disease.* (#86-884)

INFLUENZA

See Flu

INSECT STINGS

Clearinghouses/Hotlines

The National Institute on Allergy and Infectious Diseases (NIAID) can search the Combined Health Information Database (CHID) and generate a bibliography of resources on Insect Sting Allergy for you. They will also send you any publications and journal articles they may have on hand, and will refer you to researchers who are currently studying this issue. If you can't afford treatment, have your doctor call NIAID to find out if they are conducting any clinical studies that you might qualify for.

☎ Contact:
National Institute of Allergy
and Infectious Diseases
Building 31
Room 7A32
Bethesda, MD 20892
(301) 496-5717

INSOMNIA

Clearinghouses/Hotlines

The National Institute of Mental Health (NIMH) will send you whatever publications and reprints of articles from texts and journals they have on Insomnia. They will also refer you to other organizations that are studying this disorder. NIMH will also let you know of any clinical studies that may be studying Insomnia and looking for patients.

☎ Contact:
National Institute of Mental Health
5600 Fishers Lane
Room 15C05
Rockville, MD 20857
(301) 443-4515

Free Publications/Videos

The following publication on Insomnia is available from the Food & Drug Administration, (HFE-88), 5600 Fishers Ln., Rockville, MD 20857; (301) 443-3170.

- *Why Aren't You Asleep Yet? A Bedtime Story.* (#FDA90-1154)

INSULIN-DEPENDENT DIABETES

See also Diabetes

Clearinghouses/Hotlines

The National Diabetes Information Clearinghouse will respond to your requests for information about diabetes and its complications and distributes information appropriate to health professionals, people with diabetes and their families, and the general public. They have many publications and bibliographies, as well as *Diabetes Dateline*, a free quarterly current awareness newsletter that features news about diabetes research, upcoming meetings and events, and new publications. If you can't afford treatment, have your doctor call the National Institute of Diabetes and Digestive and Kidney Diseases to find out if they are conducting any clinical studies that you might qualify for.

☎ Contact:
National Diabetes Information Clearinghouse
Box NDIC
Bethesda, MD 20892
(301) 468-2162

Free Publications/Videos

The following publication is available from the National Institute of Diabetes and Digestive and Kidney Diseases, Bldg. 31, Room 9A04, Bethesda, MD 20892; (301) 496-3583.

- *Insulin-Dependent Diabetes.* (#90-2098)

INSULINOMAS

Clearinghouses/Hotlines

The National Institute of Diabetes and Digestive and Kidney Diseases's (NIDDK) individual clearinghouses can search the Combined Health Information Database (CHID) and generate a bibliography of resources on Insulinomas for you. They also will send you any publications and journal articles they may have on hand, and will refer you to other organizations that are studying this topic. If you can't afford treatment, have your doctor call NIDDK to find out if they are conducting any clinical studies that you might qualify for.

☎ Contact:
National Institute of Diabetes
and Digestive and Kidney Diseases
Bldg. 31, Room 9A04
Bethesda, MD 20892
(301) 496-3583

INTERFERON

Clearinghouses/Hotlines

The National Institute on Allergy and Infectious Diseases (NIAID) can search the Combined Health Information Database (CHID) and generate a bibliography of resources on Interferon for you. They will also send you any publications and journal articles they may have on hand, and will refer you to researchers who are currently studying this treatment. If you can't afford treatment, have your doctor call NIAID to find out if they are conducting any clinical studies that you might qualify for.

☎ Contact:
National Institute of Allergy
and Infectious Diseases
Bldg. 31, Room 7A32
Bethesda, MD 20892
(301) 496-5717

INTERLEUKIN-2 THERAPY

Free Publications/Videos

The following publication is available from the National Cancer Institute, Bldg. 31, Room 10A24, Bethesda, MD 20892; (800) 4-CANCER, or (301) 496-5583.

- *Managing Interleukin-2 Therapy*. (#89-3071) Explains what patients can expect during treatment, possible side effects and management of these symptoms.

INTERSTITIAL CYSTITIS

Clearinghouses/Hotlines

The National Institute of Diabetes and Digestive and Kidney Diseases's (NIDDK) individual clearinghouses can search the Combined Health Information Database (CHID) and generate a bibliography of resources on Interstitial Cystitis for you. They also will send you any publications and journal articles they may have on hand, and will refer you to other organizations that are studying this disease. If you can't afford treatment, have your doctor call NIDDK to find out if they are conducting any clinical studies that you might qualify for.

☎ Contact:
National Institute of Diabetes
and Digestive and Kidney Diseases
Bldg. 31, Room 9A04
Bethesda, MD 20892
(301) 496-3583

INTESTINAL MALABSORPTION SYNDROME

Clearinghouses/Hotlines

The National Institute of Diabetes and Digestive and Kidney Diseases's (NIDDK) individual clearinghouses can search the Combined Health Information Database (CHID) and generate a bibliography of resources on Intestinal Malabsorption Syndrome for you. They also will send you any publications and journal articles they may have on hand, and will refer you to other organizations that are studying this disease. If you can't afford treatment, have your doctor call NIDDK to find out if they are conducting any clinical studies that you might qualify for.

☎ Contact:
National Institute of Diabetes
and Digestive and Kidney Diseases
Building 31
Room 9A04
Bethesda, MD 20892
(301) 496-3583

INTRACRANIAL ANEURYSM

Clearinghouses/Hotlines

The National Institute of Neurological Disorders and Stroke (NINDS) can send you only information they have in their publications list on Intracranial Aneurysm. They cannot refer you to any experts. This Clearinghouse cannot directly give you information about any current clinical studies NINDS might be conducting on this condition, but you can find this information for yourself by looking under the National Institute of Neurological Disorders and Stroke in *Appendix A* at the end of this book.

☎ Contact:
National Institute of Neurological
Disorders and Stroke
Building 31

Room 8A06
Bethesda, MD 20892
(301) 496-5751
(800) 352-9424

and Human Development
Building 31
Room 2A32
Bethesda, MD 20892
(301) 496-5133

INTRAOCULAR LENSES

Clearinghouses/Hotlines

The National Eye Institute (NEI) can give you up-to-date information on Intraocular Lenses by searching the Combined Health Information Database (CHID) and MEDLINE and sending you bibliographies of resources, along with any journal articles they may have. They can also refer you to any other organizations that study this and other related topics. NEI will also let you know of any clinical studies that may be studying this disease and looking for patients. Because of their small staff, NEI prefers that you submit your requests for information in writing.

☎ Contact:
National Eye Institute
Building 31
Room 6A32
Bethesda, MD 20892
(301) 496-5248

INTRAUTERINE GROWTH RETARDATION

Clearinghouses/Hotlines

The National Institute of Child Health and Human Development (NICHD) will send you whatever publications and reprints of journal articles they have on Intrauterine Growth Retardation. If necessary, they will refer you to other experts or researchers in the field. If you can't afford treatment, have your doctor call NICHD to find out if they are conducting any clinical studies that you might qualify for.

☎ Contact:
National Institute of Child Health

INTRAVENOUS DRUG THERAPY

Clearinghouses/Hotlines

At present, Medicare payment for Intravenous (IV) drug therapy is limited to hospital-based care, but new devices, new drugs, and new treatment protocols are available to patients in the home. An Office of Technology Assessment study is examining the potential impact of coverage for Medicare.

☎ Contact:
Elaine Power, project director
Office of Technology Assessment
Washington, DC 20510
(202) 228-6590

INVASIVE DENTAL PROCEDURES

Clearinghouses/Hotlines

The National Institute of Dental Research (NIDR) will send you whatever publications and reprints of journal articles they have on Invasive Dental Procedures. As a policy, NIDR will not refer you to other organizations or experts who study this disease. If you can't afford treatment, have your doctor call Dr. Albert Guckers at (301) 496-6241 to find out if NIDR is conducting any clinical studies that you might qualify for.

☎ Contact:
National Institute of Dental Research
Bldg. 31, Room 2C35
Bethesda, MD 20892
(301) 496-4261

Free Publications/Videos

The following publication on Invasive Dental Procedures is available from the Centers for Disease Control National AIDS Clearinghouse, P.O. Box 6003, Rockville, MD 20849-6003; (800) 458-5231.

- *Update: Transmission of HIV Infection During Invasive Dental Procedures - Florida.* (#D683)

IN VITRO FERTILIZATION

See also Artificial Insemination

Clearinghouses/Hotlines

The National Institute of Child Health and Human Development (NICHD) will send you whatever publications and reprints of journal articles they have on In Vitro Fertilization. If necessary, they will refer you to other experts or researchers in the field. If you can't afford treatment, have your doctor call NICHD to find out if they are conducting any clinical studies that you might qualify for.

☎ Contact:
National Institute of Child Health
and Human Development
Bldg. 31, Room 2A32
Bethesda, MD 20892
(301) 496-5133

IRIDOCYCLITIS

Clearinghouses/Hotlines

The National Eye Institute (NEI) can give you up-to-date information on Iridocyclitis by searching the Combined Health Information Database (CHID) and MEDLINE and sending you bibliographies of resources, along with any journal articles they may have. They can also refer you to any other organizations that study this and other related diseases. NEI will also let you know of any

clinical studies that may be studying this disease and looking for patients. Because of their small staff, NEI prefers that you submit your requests for information in writing.

☎ Contact:
National Eye Institute
Bldg. 31, Room 6A32
Bethesda, MD 20892
(301) 496-5248

IRITIS

Clearinghouses/Hotlines

The National Eye Institute (NEI) can give you up-to-date information on Iritis by searching the Combined Health Information Database (CHID) and MEDLINE and sending you bibliographies of resources, along with any journal articles they may have. They can also refer you to any other organizations that study this and other related diseases. NEI will also let you know of any clinical studies that may be studying this disease and looking for patients. Because of their small staff, NEI prefers that you submit your requests for information in writing.

☎ Contact:
National Eye Institute
Bldg. 31, Room 6A32
Bethesda, MD 20892
(301) 496-5248

IRON DEFICIENCY

Clearinghouses/Hotlines

The National Institute of Diabetes and Digestive and Kidney Diseases's (NIDDK) individual clearinghouses can search the Combined Health Information Database (CHID) and generate a bibliography of resources on Iron Deficiency Anemia for you. They also will send you any publications and journal articles they may have on hand, and will refer you to other organizations that are studying this disease. If you can't afford treatment, have your doctor call NIDDK to find out if they are conducting any clinical studies that you might qualify for.

☎ Contact:
National Institute of Diabetes
and Digestive and Kidney Diseases
Bldg. 31, Room 9A04
Bethesda, MD 20892
(301) 496-3583

IRRADIATION

See Food Irradiation

IRRITABLE BOWEL SYNDROME

See also Bowel Disease

Clearinghouses/Hotlines

The National Institute of Diabetes and Digestive and Kidney Diseases's (NIDDK) individual clearinghouses can search the Combined Health Information Database (CHID) and generate a bibliography of resources on Irritable Bowel Syndrome for you. They also will send you any publications and journal articles they may have on hand, and will refer you to other organizations that are studying this disease. If you can't afford treatment, have your doctor call NIDDK to find out if they are conducting any clinical studies that you might qualify for.

☎ Contact:
National Institute of Diabetes
and Digestive and Kidney Diseases
Bldg. 31, Room 9A04
Bethesda, MD 20892
(301) 496-3583

Free Publications/Videos

The following publication is available from the National Institute of Diabetes and Digestive and Kidney Diseases, Bldg. 31, Room 9A04, Bethesda, MD 20892; (301) 496-3583.

- *Irritable Bowel Syndrome.* (#90-693)

The following publication is available from the National Institute of Diabetes and Digestive and Kidney Diseases, Bldg. 31, Room 9A04, Bethesda, MD 20892; (301) 496-3583.

- *IBD and IBS: Two Very Different Problems.* (#90-3079)

ISCADOR

Clearinghouses/Hotlines

The National Cancer Institute (NCI) will send you whatever publications and reprints of journal articles they have on Iscador. They can also search their Physician's Data Query (PDQ) database to let you know if NCI is conducting any clinical studies on your disease.

☎ Contact:
National Cancer Institute
Bldg. 31, Room 10A24
Bethesda, MD 20892
(800) 4-CANCER
(301) 496-5583

ISCHEMIA

Clearinghouses/Hotlines

The National Heart, Lung, and Blood Institute (NHLBI) can search the Combined Health Information Database (CHID) and generate a bibliography of resources on Ischemia for you. They also will send you any publications and journal articles they may have on hand, and will refer you to other organizations that are studying this disease. If you can't afford treatment, have your doctor call NHLBI to find out if they are conducting any clinical studies that you might qualify for.

☎ Contact:
National Heart, Lung, and Blood Institute
Bldg. 31, Room 4A21
Bethesda, MD 20892
(301) 496-4236

ISLET CELL HYPERPLASIA

Clearinghouses/Hotlines

The National Institute of Diabetes and Digestive and Kidney Diseases's (NIDDK) individual clearinghouses can search the Combined Health Information Database (CHID) and generate a bibliography of resources on Islet Cell Hyperplasia for you. They also will send you any publications and journal articles they may have on hand, and will refer you to other organizations that are studying this disease. If you can't afford treatment, have your doctor call NIDDK to find out if they are conducting any clinical studies that you might qualify for.

☎ Contact:
National Institute of Diabetes
and Digestive and Kidney Diseases
Bldg. 31, Room 9A04
Bethesda, MD 20892
(301) 496-3583

ISOLATED IGA DEFICIENCY

Clearinghouses/Hotlines

The National Cancer Institute (NCI) will send you whatever publications and reprints of journal articles they have on Isolated IGA Deficiency. They can also give you information on the state-of-the-art treatment for this disease, including specific treatment information for your stage of cancer. They can search their Physician's Data Query (PDQ) database to let you know if NCI is conducting any clinical studies on your disease.

☎ Contact:
National Cancer Institute
Bldg. 31, Room 10A24
Bethesda, MD 20892
(800) 4-CANCER
(301) 496-5583

- J -

JAKOB-CREUTZFELDT DISEASE

Clearinghouses/Hotlines

The National Institute of Neurological Disorders and Stroke (NINDS) can send you only information they have in their publications list on Jakob-Creutzfeldt Disease. They cannot refer you to any experts. This Clearinghouse cannot directly give you information about any current clinical studies they might be conducting on this illness, but you can find this information for yourself by looking under the National Institute of Neurological Disorders and Stroke in *Appendix A* at the end of this book.

☎ Contact:
National Institute of Neurological
Disorders and Stroke
Bldg. 31, Room 8A06
Bethesda, MD 20892
(301) 496-5751
(800) 352-9424

JOINT REPLACEMENT

Clearinghouses/Hotlines

The National Institute of Arthritis and Musculoskeletal and Skin Diseases (NIAMS) conducts and supports basic and clinical research on the causes, prevention, diagnosis, and treatment of Joint Replacement. They have all kinds of publications to send you, and their information specialist can give you further, in-depth information on joint replacements and many other related topics.

☎ Contact:
National Institute of Arthritis
and Musculoskeletal and Skin Diseases
Box AMS
9000 Rockville Pike
Bethesda, MD 20892
(301) 495-4484

Free Publications/Videos

The following publication on Joint Replacement is available from the National Arthritis and Musculoskeletal and Skin Diseases Information Clearinghouse, Box AMS, 9000 Rockville Pike, Bethesda, MD 20892; (301) 495-4484.

- *Joint Replacement Patient Education Materials, 1987.* An annotated bibliography of resources. (#AR85)

JOSEPH'S DISEASE

Clearinghouses/Hotlines

The National Institute of Neurological Disorders and Stroke (NINDS) can send you only information they have in their publications list on Joseph's Disease. They cannot refer you to any experts. This Clearinghouse cannot directly give you information about any current clinical studies they might be conducting on this illness, but you can find this information for yourself by looking under the National Institute of Neurological Disorders and Stroke in *Appendix A* at the end of this book.

☎ Contact:
National Institute of Neurological
Disorders and Stroke
Building 31
Room 8A06

Bethesda, MD 20892
(301) 496-5751
(800) 352-9424

Free Publications/Videos

The following publication on Joseph's Disease is available from the National Institute of Neurological Disorders and Stroke, Bldg. 31, Room 8A06, Bethesda, MD 20892; (301) 496-5751 or (800) 352-9424.

- *Joseph's Disease.* Fact sheet on symptoms and treatment. (#85-2716)

JUICING

Clearinghouses/Hotlines

Does the recent fad about the reputed health benefits of Juicing your fruits and vegetables have any scientific validity? The Food and Nutrition Information Center can answer your questions regarding juices and the benefits of eating more fruits and vegetables.

☎ Contact:
Food and Nutrition Information Center
National Agricultural Library
10301 Baltimore Blvd.
Beltsville, MD 20705
(301) 504-5719

JUVENILE DELINQUENCY

Clearinghouses/Hotlines

The National Institute of Mental Health (NIMH) will send you whatever publications and reprints of articles from texts and journals they have on Juvenile Delinquency. They will also refer you to other organizations that are studying this issue. NIMH will also let you know of any clinical studies that may be studying this issue and looking for patients.

☎ Contact:
National Institute of Mental Health
5600 Fishers Lane
Room 15C05
Rockville, MD 20857
(301) 443-4515

☎ Contact:
National Institute of Arthritis
and Musculoskeletal and Skin Diseases
Box AMS, 9000 Rockville Pike
Bethesda, MD 20892
(301) 495-4484

JUVENILE DIABETES

Clearinghouses/Hotlines

The National Institute of Diabetes and Digestive and Kidney Diseases's (NIDDK) individual clearinghouses can search the Combined Health Information Database (CHID) and generate a bibliography of resources on Juvenile Diabetes for you. They also will send you any publications and journal articles they may have on hand, and will refer you to other organizations that are studying this disease. If you can't afford treatment, have your doctor call NIDDK to find out if they are conducting any clinical studies that you might qualify for.

☎ Contact:
National Institute of Diabetes
and Digestive and Kidney Diseases
Bldg. 31, Room 9A04
Bethesda, MD 20892
(301) 496-3583

JUVENILE RHEUMATOID ARTHRITIS

Clearinghouses/Hotlines

The National Institute of Arthritis and Musculoskeletal and Skin Diseases (NIAMS) will send you whatever publications and reprints of articles from texts and journals they have on Juvenile Rheumatoid Arthritis. They will also refer you to other organizations that are studying this disease. NIAMS will also let you know of any clinical studies that may be studying this disease and looking for patients.

JUXTAGLOMERULAR HYPERPLASIA

Clearinghouses/Hotlines

The National Heart, Lung, and Blood Institute (NHLBI) can search the Combined Health Information Database (CHID) and generate a bibliography of resources on Juxtaglomerular Hyperplasia (Bartter's Syndrome) for you. They also will send you any publications and journal articles they may have on hand, and will refer you to other organizations that are studying this disease. If you can't afford treatment, have your doctor call NHLBI to find out if they are conducting any clinical studies that you might qualify for.

☎ Contact:
National Heart, Lung, and Blood Institute
Bldg. 31, Room 4A21
Bethesda, MD 20892
(301) 496-4236

- K -

KANNER'S SYNDROME

Clearinghouses/Hotlines

The National Institute of Neurological Disorders and Stroke (NINDS) can send you only information they have in their publications list on

Kanner's Syndrome (Infantile Autism). They cannot refer you to any experts. This Clearinghouse cannot directly give you information about any current clinical studies NINDS might be conducting on this illness, but you can find this information for yourself by looking under the National Institute of Neurological Disorders and Stroke in *Appendix A* at the end of this book.

☎ Contact:
National Institute of Neurological
Disorders and Stroke
Bldg. 31, Room 8A06
Bethesda, MD 20892
(301) 496-5751
(800) 352-9424

KAPOSI'S SARCOMA

Clearinghouses/Hotlines

The National Cancer Institute (NCI) will send you whatever publications and reprints of journal articles they have on Kaposi's Sarcoma. They can also give you information on the state-of-the-art treatment for this disease, including specific treatment information for your stage of cancer. They can also search their Physician's Data Query (PDQ) database to let you know if NCI is conducting any clinical studies on your disease.

☎ Contact:
National Cancer Institute
Bldg. 31, Room 10A24
Bethesda, MD 20892
(800) 4-CANCER
(301) 496-5583

KAWASAKI DISEASE

Clearinghouses/Hotlines

The National Institute on Allergy and Infectious Diseases (NIAID) can search the Combined Health Information Database (CHID) and generate a bibliography of resources on Kawasaki Disease for you. They will also send you any

publications and journal articles they may have on hand, and will refer you to researchers who are currently studying this disease. If you can't afford treatment, have your doctor call NIAID to find out if they are conducting any clinical studies that you might qualify for.

☎ Contact:
National Institute of Allergy
and Infectious Diseases
Bldg. 31, Room 7A32
Bethesda, MD 20892
(301) 496-5717

KEARNS-SAYRE SYNDROME

Clearinghouses/Hotlines

The National Institute of Neurological Disorders and Stroke (NINDS) can send you only information they have in their publications list on Kearns-Sayre Syndrome. They cannot refer you to any experts. This Clearinghouse cannot directly give you information about any current clinical studies NINDS might be conducting on this illness, but you can find this information for yourself by looking under the National Institute of Neurological Disorders and Stroke in *Appendix A* at the end of this book.

☎ Contact:
National Institute of Neurological
Disorders and Stroke
Bldg. 31, Room 8A06
Bethesda, MD 20892
(301) 496-5751
(800) 352-9424

KERATITIS

Clearinghouses/Hotlines

The National Eye Institute (NEI) can give you up-to-date information on Keratitis by searching the Combined Health Information Database (CHID) and MEDLINE and sending you bibliographies of resources, along with any journal articles they may have. They can also refer you to any other organizations that study this and other related diseases. NEI will also let you know of any clinical studies that may be studying this disease and looking for patients. Because of their small staff, NEI prefers that you submit your requests for information in writing.

☎ Contact:
National Eye Institute
Bldg. 31, Room 6A32
Bethesda, MD 20892
(301) 496-5248

KERATOCONUS

Clearinghouses/Hotlines

The National Eye Institute (NEI) can give you up-to-date information on Keratoconus by searching the Combined Health Information Database (CHID) and MEDLINE and sending you bibliographies of resources, along with any journal articles they may have. They can also refer you to any other organizations that study this and other related diseases. NEI will also let you know of any clinical studies that may be studying this disease and looking for patients. Because of their small staff, NEI prefers that you submit your requests for information in writing.

☎ Contact:
National Eye Institute
Bldg. 31, Room 6A32
Bethesda, MD 20892
(301) 496-5248

KERATOMILEUSIS

Clearinghouses/Hotlines

The National Eye Institute (NEI) can give you up-to-date information on Keratomileusis by searching the Combined Health Information Database (CHID) and MEDLINE and sending

you bibliographies of resources, along with any journal articles they may have. They can also refer you to any other organizations that study this and other related diseases. NEI will also let you know of any clinical studies that may be studying this disease and looking for patients. Because of their small staff, NEI prefers that you submit your requests for information in writing.

☎ Contact:
National Eye Institute
Building 31, Room 6A32
Bethesda, MD 20892
(301) 496-5248

KERATOPLASTY

Clearinghouses/Hotlines

The National Eye Institute (NEI) can give you up-to-date information on Keratoplasty by searching the Combined Health Information Database (CHID) and MEDLINE and sending you bibliographies of resources, along with any journal articles they may have. They can also refer you to any other organizations that study this issue. NEI will also let you know of any clinical studies that may be studying Keratoplasty and looking for patients. Because of their small staff, NEI prefers that you submit your requests for information in writing.

☎ Contact:
National Eye Institute
Building 31, Room 6A32
Bethesda, MD 20892
(301) 496-5248

KERATOSIS PALMARIS ET PLANTARIS

Clearinghouses/Hotlines

The National Cancer Institute (NCI) will send you whatever publications and reprints of journal articles they have on Keratosis Palmaris et

Plantaris. They can also give you information on the state-of-the-art treatment for this disease, including specific treatment information for your stage of cancer. They can also search their Physician's Data Query (PDQ) database to let you know if NCI is conducting any clinical studies on your disease.

☎ Contact:
National Cancer Institute
Building 31
Room 10A24
Bethesda, MD 20892
(800) 4-CANCER
(301) 496-5583

KIDNEY CANCER

Clearinghouses/Hotlines

The National Cancer Institute (NCI) will send you whatever publications and reprints of journal articles they have on Kidney Cancer. They can also give you information on the state-of-the-art treatment for this disease, including specific treatment information for your stage of cancer. They can also search their Physician's Data Query (PDQ) database to let you know if NCI is conducting any clinical studies on your disease.

☎ Contact:
National Cancer Institute
Building 31
Room 10A24
Bethesda, MD 20892
(800) 4-CANCER
(301) 496-5583

Free Publications/Videos

The following publications on Kidney Cancer are available from the National Cancer Institute, Bldg. 31, Room 10A24, Bethesda, MD 20892; (800) 4-CANCER, or (301) 496-5583.

- *What You Need to Know About Cancer of the Kidney.* (#90-1569)
- *Adult Kidney Cancer and Wilms' Tumor.* (#90-2342)

KIDNEY DISEASE

Clearinghouses/Hotlines

National Kidney and Urological Diseases Information Clearinghouse has all kinds of information on Kidney Diseases and their causes, treatment, and prevention.

☎ Contact:
National Kidney and Urological Diseases
Information Clearinghouse
Box NKUDIC
Bethesda, MD 20892
(301) 468-6345

Free Publications/Videos

The following publications on Kidney Disease are available from the National Kidney and Urological Diseases Information Clearinghouse, Box NKUDIC, Bethesda, MD 20892; (301) 468-6345.

- *National Kidney and Urologic Diseases Information Clearinghouse.* Main government contact point for information on these diseases.
- *Directory of Kidney and Urologic Disease-Related Organizations.* Lists professional, patient, and voluntary organizations.
- *Diabetes and Kidney Disease: A Selected Annotated Bibliography.*
- *End-Stage Renal Disease: Choosing a Treatment That's Right for You.*
- *Renal Nutrition.* Bibliography of resources.
- *Transplantation: Professional Materials.* Bibliography of resources.
- *Transplantation: Patient Materials.* Bibliography of resources.
- *National Kidney and Urologic Diseases Advisory Board: 1991 Annual Report.* (#91-3004)

The following publication on Kidney Disease is available from the National Institute of Diabetes and Digestive and Kidney Diseases, Bldg. 31, Room 9A04, Bethesda, MD 20892; (301) 496-3583.

- National Kidney and Urologic Diseases Advisory Board Long-Range Plan, Executive Summary. (#90-1510)

KIDNEY STONES

Clearinghouses/Hotlines

The National Kidney and Urological Diseases Information Clearinghouse (NKUDIC) can search the Combined Health Information Database (CHID) and generate a bibliography of resources on Kidney Stones for you. They also will send you any publications and journal articles they may have on hand, and will refer you to other organizations that are studying this disease. If you can't afford treatment, have your doctor call NKUDIC to find out if they are conducting any clinical studies that you might qualify for.

☎ Contact:
National Kidney and Urological Diseases
Information Clearinghouse
Box NKUDIC
Bethesda, MD 20892
(301) 468-6345

Free Publications/Videos

The following publications on Kidney Stones are available from the National Kidney and Urological Diseases, Information Clearinghouse, Box NKUDIC, Bethesda, MD 20892; (301) 468-6345.

- *Prevention and Treatment of Kidney Stones.* Describes diagnosis, treatment, and types of urinary incontinence.
- *Extracorporeal Shock-Wave Lithotripsy.* Describes the removal of kidney and urinary tract stones.
- *Urinary Stones: Professional Materials.* Bibliography of resources.
- *Urinary Stones: Patient Materials.* Bibliography of resources.

The following publication on Kidney Stones is available from the National Institute of Diabetes and Digestive and Kidney Diseases, Bldg. 31,

Room 9A04, Bethesda, MD 20892; (301) 496-3583.

- Prevention and Treatment of Kidney Stones. (#83-2495)

KIDNEY TRANSPLANTS

Clearinghouses/Hotlines

The National Institute of Diabetes and Digestive and Kidney Diseases (NIDDK) conducts research on Kidney Transplants. The staff can refer you to current researchers working on this procedure, as well as send you relevant brochures and reports.

☎ Contact:
National Institute of Diabetes
and Digestive and Kidney Diseases
Building 31
Room 9A04
Bethesda, MD 20892
(301) 496-3583

KLEINE-LEVIN SYNDROME

Clearinghouses/Hotlines

The National Institute of Neurological Disorders and Stroke (NINDS) can send you only information they have in their publications list on Kleine-Levin Syndrome. They cannot refer you to any experts. This Clearinghouse cannot directly give you information about any current clinical studies NINDS might be conducting on this illness, but you can find this information for yourself by looking under the National Institute of Neurological Disorders and Stroke in *Appendix A* at the end of this book.

☎ Contact:
National Institute of Allergy
and Infectious Diseases
Building 31
Room 7A32
Bethesda, MD 20892
(301) 496-5717

KLEPTOMANIA

Clearinghouses/Hotlines

The National Institute of Mental Health (NIMH) maintains data bases that index and abstract documents from the worldwide literature pertaining to Kleptomania. In addition to scientific journals, there are references to audiovisuals, dissertations, government documents and reports. Contact NIMH for searches on specific subjects.

☎ Contact:
National Institute of Mental Health
5600 Fishers Lane, Room 15C05
Rockville, MD 20857
(301) 443-4515

KLINEFELTER'S SYNDROME

Clearinghouses/Hotlines

The National Institute of Child Health and Human Development (NICHD) will send you whatever publications and reprints of journal articles they have on Klinefelter's Syndrome. If necessary, they will refer you to other experts or researchers in the field. If you can't afford treatment, have your doctor call NICHD to find out if they are conducting any clinical studies that you might qualify for.

☎ Contact:
National Institute of Child Health
and Human Development
Bldg. 31, Room 2A32
Bethesda, MD 20892
(301) 496-5133

KOCH ANTITOXINS

Clearinghouses/Hotlines

The National Cancer Institute (NCI) will send you whatever publications and reprints of journal articles they have on Koch Antitoxins. They can also search their Physician's Data Query (PDQ) database to let you know if NCI is conducting any clinical studies on your disease.

☎ Contact:
National Cancer Institute
Bldg. 31, Room 10A24
Bethesda, MD 20892
(800) 4-CANCER
(301) 496-5583

KRABBE'S DISEASE

Clearinghouses/Hotlines

The National Institute of Neurological Disorders and Stroke (NINDS) can send you only information they have in their publications list on Krabbe's Disease. They cannot refer you to any experts. This Clearinghouse cannot directly give you information about any current clinical studies NINDS might be conducting on this illness, but you can find this information for yourself by looking under the National Institute of Neurological Disorders and Stroke in *Appendix A* at the end of this book.

☎ Contact:
National Institute of Allergy
and Infectious Diseases
Bldg. 31, Room 7A32
Bethesda, MD 20892
(301) 496-5717

KREBIOZEN

Clearinghouses/Hotlines

The National Cancer Institute (NCI) will send you whatever publications and reprints of journal articles they have on Krebiozen (Carcalon). They can also search their Physician's Data Query (PDQ) database to let you know if NCI is conducting any clinical studies on your disease.

☎ Contact:
National Cancer Institute

Bldg. 31, Room 10A24
Bethesda, MD 20892
(800) 4-CANCER
(301) 496-5583

KUGELBERG-WELANDER DISEASE

Clearinghouses/Hotlines

The National Institute of Neurological Disorders and Stroke (NINDS) can send you only information they have in their publications list on Kugelberg-Welander Disease (Juvenile Spinal Muscular Atrophy). They cannot refer you to any experts. This Clearinghouse cannot directly give you information about any current clinical studies NINDS might be conducting on this illness, but you can find this information for yourself by looking under the National Institute of Neurological Disorders and Stroke in *Appendix A* at the end of this book.

☎ Contact:
National Institute of Allergy
and Infectious Diseases
Building 31
Room 7A32
Bethesda, MD 20892
(301) 496-5717

KURU

Clearinghouses/Hotlines

The National Institute on Allergy and Infectious Diseases (NIAID) can search the Combined Health Information Database (CHID) and generate a bibliography of resources on Kuru for you. They will also send you any publications and journal articles they may have on hand, and will refer you to researchers who are currently studying this subject. If you can't afford treatment, have your doctor call NIAID to find out if they are conducting any clinical studies that you might qualify for.

☎ Contact:
National Institute of Allergy
and Infectious Diseases
Building 31
Room 7A32
Bethesda, MD 20892
(301) 496-5717

- L -

LABORATORY TESTING

Free Publications/Videos

The following publication is available from the Food & Drug Administration, (HFE-88), 5600 Fishers Ln., Rockville, MD 20857; (301) 443-3170.

- *A Consumer Guide to Laboratory Testing.*
  (#FDA90-3177)

LABYRINTHITIS

Clearinghouses/Hotlines

The National Institute on Deafness and Other Communicative Disorders (NIDCD) will send you whatever publications and reprints of journal articles they have on Labyrinthitis. If you need further information, they will refer you to other organizations that study this and other related disorders. NIDCD does not conduct any clinical studies for Labyrinthitis or any other disorder.

☎ Contact:
National Institute on Deafness
and Other Communication Disorders
Building 31
Room 3C35
Bethesda, MD 20892

(301) 496-7243
(800) 241-1044
(301) 402-0252 (TDD)

The National Institute of Neurological Disorders and Stroke (NINDS) can send you only information they have in their publications list on Labyrinthitis. They cannot refer you to any experts. This Clearinghouse cannot directly give you information about any current clinical studies NINDS might be conducting on this illness, but you can find this information for yourself by looking under the National Institute of Neurological Disorders and Stroke in *Appendix A* at the end of this book.

☎ Contact:
National Institute of Neurological
Disorders and Stroke
Building 31
Room 8A06
Bethesda, MD 20892
(301) 496-5751
(800) 352-9424

LACRIMAL GLANDS

Clearinghouses/Hotlines

The National Eye Institute (NEI) can give you up-to-date information on Lacrimal Glands by searching the Combined Health Information Database (CHID) and MEDLINE and sending you bibliographies of resources, along with any journal articles they may have. They can also refer you to any other organizations that study this and other related subjects. NEI will also let you know of any clinical studies that may be studying Lacrimal Glands and looking for patients. Because of their small staff, NEI prefers that you submit your requests for information in writing.

☎ Contact:
National Eye Institute
Building 31
Room 6A32
Bethesda, MD 20892
(301) 496-5248

LACTATION

Clearinghouses/Hotlines

The National Maternal and Child Health Clearinghouse has all kinds of information on maternal and child health issues, such as pregnancy, child and adolescent health, and human genetics. If the answer to your question can't be answered by any of their countless free publications, they can refer you to other National or local resources. If you still need further information, they search their own reference collection and send you what they find.

☎ Contact:
National Maternal and Child
Health Clearinghouse
38th & R Sts. NW
Washington, DC 20057
(703) 821-8955, ext. 254

The National Institute of Diabetes and Digestive and Kidney Diseases's (NIDDK) individual clearinghouses can search the Combined Health Information Database (CHID) and generate a bibliography of resources on Lactation for you. They also will send you any publications and journal articles they may have on hand, and will refer you to other organizations that are studying this subject. If you can't afford treatment, have your doctor call NIDDK to find out if they are conducting any clinical studies that you might qualify for.

☎ Contact:
National Institute of Diabetes
and Digestive and Kidney Diseases
Bldg. 31, Room 9A04
Bethesda, MD 20892
(301) 496-3583

Free Publications/Videos

The following publications are available from the National Maternal and Child Health Clearinghouse, 38th & R Sts., NW, Washington, DC 20057; (703) 821-8955, ext. 254.

- *Nutrition During Lactation.* (#D081)

- *Surgeon General's Workshop on Breastfeeding and Human Lactation.* (#B163)
- *Nutrition During Lactation/Summary.* (#D080)
- *Recommendations for Feeding Normal Infants.* (#B060)

LACTOSE DEFICIENCY

See Lactose Intolerance

LACTOSE INTOLERANCE

Clearinghouses/Hotlines

The National Digestive Diseases Information Clearinghouse can search the Combined Health Information Database (CHID) and generate a bibliography of resources on Lactose Intolerance for you. They also will send you any publications and journal articles they may have on hand, and will refer you to other organizations that are studying this condition. If you can't afford treatment, have your doctor call The National Digestive Diseases Information Clearinghouse to find out if they are conducting any clinical studies that you might qualify for.

☎ Contact:
National Digestive Diseases
Information Clearinghouse
Box NDDIC
Bethesda, MD 20892
(301) 496-3583

Free Publications/Videos

The following publication on Lactose Intolerance is available from the National Digestive Diseases Information Clearinghouse, Box NDDIC, Bethesda, MD 20892; (301) 468-6344.

- *Lactose Intolerance.* Information packet.

LAETRILE

Clearinghouses/Hotlines

The National Cancer Institute (NCI) will send you whatever publications and reprints of journal articles they have on Laetrile. They can also give you information on the state-of-the-art treatment, including specific treatment information for your stage of cancer. They can also search their Physician's Data Query (PDQ) database to let you know if NCI is conducting any clinical studies on your disease.

☎ Contact:
National Cancer Institute
Bldg. 31, Room 10A24
Bethesda, MD 20892
(800) 4-CANCER
(301) 496-5583

LAMAZE METHOD OF CHILDBIRTH

See Childbirth

LANGUAGE DISORDERS

Clearinghouses/Hotlines

The National Institute on Deafness and Other Communicative Disorders (NIDCD) will send you whatever publications and reprints of journal articles they have on Language Disorders. If you need further information, they will refer you to other organizations that study this and other related disorders. NIDCD does not conduct any clinical studies for this or any other disorder.

☎ Contact:
National Institute on Deafness
and Other Communication Disorders
Bldg. 31, Room 3C35
Bethesda, MD 20892

(301) 496-7243
(800) 241-1044
(301) 402-0252 (TDD)

The National Institute of Child Health and Human Development (NICHD) will send you whatever publications and reprints of journal articles they have on Language Development. If necessary, they will refer you to other experts or researchers in the field. If you can't afford treatment, have your doctor call NICHD to find out if they are conducting any clinical studies that you might qualify for.

☎ Contact:
National Institute of Child Health
and Human Development
Bldg. 31, Room 2A32
Bethesda, MD 20892
(301) 496-5133

The National Institute of Neurological Disorders and Stroke (NINDS) can send you only information they have in their publications list on Language Disorders. They cannot refer you to any experts. This Clearinghouse cannot directly give you information about any current clinical studies NINDS might be conducting on this topic, but you can find this information for yourself by looking under the National Institute of Neurological Disorders and Stroke in *Appendix A* at the end of this book.

☎ Contact:
National Institute of Neurological
Disorders and Stroke
Bldg. 31, Room 8A06
Bethesda, MD 20892
(301) 496-5751
(800) 352-9424

Free Publications/Videos

The following publication on Language Disorders is available from the National Institute on Deafness and Other Communication Disorders, Bldg. 31, Room 3C35, Bethesda, MD 20892; (301) 496-7243.

- *NIDCD Strategic Research Plan: Update on Language and Balance/Vestibular Systems.* (#91-3217, DC)

The following publication on Language Disorders is available from the National Institute of Neurological Disorders and Stroke, P.O. Box 5801, Bethesda, MD 20824; (800) 352-9424, or (301) 496-5751.

- *Developmental Speech and Language Disorders.* Discusses hope through research.

LARYNX CANCER

Free Publications/Videos

The following publication is available from the National Cancer Institute, Bldg. 31, Room 10A24, Bethesda, MD 20892; (800) 4-CANCER, or (301) 496-5583.

- *What You Need to Know About Cancer of the Larynx.* (#90-1568)

LASER SURGERY

Clearinghouses/Hotlines

The National Cancer Institute (NCI) will send you whatever publications and reprints of journal articles they have on Laser Surgery on Cancer. They can also give you information on the state-of-the-art treatments, including specific treatment information for your stage of cancer. They can also search their Physician's Data Query (PDQ) database to let you know if NCI is conducting any clinical studies on your disease.

☎ Contact:
National Cancer Institute
Bldg. 31, Room 10A24
Bethesda, MD 20892
(800) 4-CANCER
(301) 496-5583

The National Institute of Arthritis and Musculoskeletal and Skin Diseases (NIAMS) will send you whatever publications and reprints of articles from texts and journals they have on Laser Removal of Tattoos. They will also refer you to other organizations that are studying this technique. NIAMS will also let you know of any clinical studies that may be studying this technique and looking for patients.

☎ Contact:
National Institute of Arthritis
and Musculoskeletal and Skin Diseases
Box AMS
Bethesda, MD 20892
(301) 495-4484

The National Heart, Lung, and Blood Institute (NHLBI) can search the Combined Health Information Database (CHID) and generate a bibliography of resources on Laser Angioplasty for you. They also will send you any publications and journal articles they may have on hand, and will refer you to other organizations that are studying this procedure. If you can't afford treatment, have your doctor call NHLBI to find out if they are conducting any clinical studies that you might qualify for.

☎ Contact:
National Heart, Lung, and Blood Institute
Bldg. 31, Room 4A21
Bethesda, MD 20892
(301) 496-4236

The National Eye Institute (NEI) can give you up-to-date information on Laser Treatment for Eye disorders by searching the Combined Health Information Database (CHID) and MEDLINE and sending you bibliographies of resources, along with any journal articles they may have. They can also refer you to any other organizations that study this and other related treatments. NEI will also let you know of any clinical studies that may be studying this technique and looking for patients. Because of their small staff, NEI prefers that you submit your requests for information in writing.

☎ Contact:
National Eye Institute
Bldg. 31, Room 6A32
Bethesda, MD 20892
(301) 496-5248

The National Health Information Center can give you the names of organizations and agencies, which can then refer you to experts in the field of Laser Surgery.

☎ Contact:
National Health Information Center
P.O. Box 1133
Washington, DC 20013
(301) 565-4167 (DC area)
(800) 336-4797

Free Publications/Videos

The following publications on Laser Surgery are available from the Center for Devices and Radiological Health, (HFZ-210), Food and Drug Administration, 5600 Fishers Ln., Rockville, MD 20857; (301) 443-4690.

- *FDA Approves First Laser Device for Clearing Arteries.*
- *Laser Treatment To Go: Outpatient Uses of Healing Light Abound.*
- *Laser Light Show Safety: Who's Responsible?* (#FDA 86-8262)
- *Fact Sheet: Laser Biostimulation. The Surgeon's Newest Scalpel Is A Laser.* (#FDA 83-8200)

LASSA FEVER

Clearinghouses/Hotlines

The National Institute on Allergy and Infectious Diseases (NIAID) can search the Combined Health Information Database (CHID) and generate a bibliography of resources on Lassa Fever for you. They will also send you any publications and journal articles they may have on hand, and will refer you to researchers who are currently studying this condition. If you can't afford treatment, have your doctor call NIAID to find out if they are conducting any clinical studies that you might qualify for.

☎ Contact:
National Institute of Allergy
and Infectious Diseases
Bldg. 31, Room 7A32
Bethesda, MD 20892
(301) 496-5717

LAURENCE-MOON-BARDET-BIEDL SYNDROME

Clearinghouses/Hotlines

The National Institute of Neurological Disorders and Stroke (NINDS) can send you only information they have in their publications list on Laurence-Moon-Bardet-Biedl Syndrome. They cannot refer you to any experts. This Clearinghouse cannot directly give you information about any current clinical studies NINDS might be conducting on this illness, but you can find this information for yourself by looking under the National Institute of Neurological Disorders and Stroke in *Appendix A* at the end of this book.

☎ Contact:
National Institute of Neurological
Disorders and Stroke
Bldg. 31, Room 8A06
Bethesda, MD 20892
(301) 496-5751
(800) 352-9424

LEAD POISONING

Clearinghouses/Hotlines

The National Institute of Environmental Health Sciences (NIEHS) will send you whatever publications and journal articles they can locate on specific questions about Lead Poisoning. If necessary they can put you in contact with researchers studying this issue. NIEHS does not conduct any clinical studies.

☎ Contact:
National Institute of Environmental
Health Sciences
P.O. Box 12233
Research Triangle Park, NC 27709
(919) 541-3345

The National Heart, Lung, and Blood Institute (NHLBI) can search the Combined Health Information Database (CHID) and generate a bibliography of resources on Lead-Poisoning Anemia for you. They also will send you any publications and journal articles they may have on hand, and will refer you to other organizations that are studying this disease. If you can't afford treatment, have your doctor call NHLBI to find out if they are conducting any clinical studies that you might qualify for.

☎ Contact:
National Heart, Lung, and Blood Institute
Bldg. 31, Room 4A21
Bethesda, MD 20892
(301) 496-4236

The National Institute of Neurological Disorders and Stroke (NINDS) can send you only information they have in their publications list on Lead Encephalopathy. They cannot refer you to any experts. This Clearinghouse cannot directly give you information about any current clinical studies NINDS might be conducting on this illness, but you can find this information for yourself by looking under the National Institute of Neurological Disorders and Stroke in *Appendix A* at the end of this book.

☎ Contact:
National Institute of Neurological
Disorders and Stroke
Bldg. 31, Room 8A06
Bethesda, MD 20892
(301) 496-5751
(800) 352-9424

Free Publications/Videos

The following publications on Lead Poisoning are available from the Lead Poisoning Prevention Branch, National Center for Environmental Health and Injury Control, Centers for Disease Control, 1600 Clifton Rd., NE, Atlanta, GA 3033; (404) 488-4880.

- *Preventing Lead Poisoning in Young Children.*
- *Strategic Plan For the Elimination of Childhood Lead Poisoning.*

The following publications on Lead Poisoning are available from the National Maternal and Child Health Clearinghouse, 38th and R Sts., NW, Washington, DC 20057; (703) 821-8955, ext. 254.

- *Childhood Lead Poisoning: Current Perspectives, Childhood Lead-Poisoning Prevention: A Resource Guide, Historical Perspective on Health Effects of Lead*
- *Manual for the Identification and Abatement of Environmental Lead Hazards.*

The following publications on Lead Poisoning are available from the Food & Drug Administration, (HFE-88), 5600 Fishers Ln., Rockville, MD 20857; (301) 443-3170.

- *An Unwanted Souvenir: Lead in Ceramic Ware.* (#FDA90-1157)
- *Getting The Lead Out Of Just About Everything.* (#FDA92-2249)

The following publication on Lead Poisoning is available from the Agency for Toxic Substances and Disease Registry, 1600 Clifton Rd., NE, Atlanta, GA 30333; (404) 639-0607.

- *The Nature and Extent of Lead Poisoning in Children in the United States: A Report to Congress.*

LEARNING DISABILITIES

Clearinghouses/Hotlines

The National Institute of Child Health and Human Development (NICHD) will send you whatever publications and reprints of journal articles they have on Learning Disabilities. If necessary, they will refer you to other experts or researchers in the field. If you can't afford treatment, have your doctor call NICHD to find out if they are conducting any clinical studies that you might qualify for.

☎ Contact:
National Institute of Child Health
and Human Development
Bldg. 31, Room 2A32
Bethesda, MD 20892
(301) 496-5133

The National Institute of Mental Health (NIMH) will send you whatever publications and reprints of

articles from texts and journals they have on Learning Disabilities. They will also refer you to other organizations that are studying this disease. NIMH will also let you know of any clinical studies that may be studying this disease and looking for patients.

☎ Contact:
National Institute of Mental Health
5600 Fishers Lane
Room 15C05
Rockville, MD 20857
(301) 443-4515

The National Institute of Neurological Disorders and Stroke (NINDS) can send you only information they have in their publications list on Learning Disabilities. They cannot refer you to any experts. This Clearinghouse cannot directly give you information about any current clinical studies NINDS might be conducting on this topic, but you can find this information for yourself by looking under the National Institute of Neurological Disorders and Stroke in *Appendix A* at the end of this book.

☎ Contact:
National Institute of Neurological
Disorders and Stroke
Bldg. 31, Room 8A06
Bethesda, MD 20892
(301) 496-5751
(800) 352-9424

Free Publications/Videos

The following publication on Learning Disabilities is available from the National Institute of Child Health and Human Development, Bldg. 31, Room 2A32, Bethesda, MD 20892; (301) 496-5133.

- *Learning Disabilities: A Report to the U.S. Congress.*

The following publication on Learning Disabilities is available from the National Institute of Neurological Disorders and Stroke, P.O. Box 5801, Bethesda, MD 20824; (800) 352-9424, or (301) 496-5751.

- *Learning Disabilities.* Contains a collection of scientific articles, patient education

pamphlets, and addresses of voluntary health associations.

LEBER'S DISEASE

Clearinghouses/Hotlines

The National Eye Institute (NEI) can give you up-to-date information on Leber's Disease by searching the Combined Health Information Database (CHID) and MEDLINE and sending you bibliographies of resources, along with any journal articles they may have. They can also refer you to any other organizations that study this and other related diseases. NEI will also let you know of any clinical studies that may be studying this disease and looking for patients. Because of their small staff, NEI prefers that you submit your requests for information in writing.

☎ Contact:
National Eye Institute
Bldg. 31, Room 6A32
Bethesda, MD 20892
(301) 496-5248

LEGG-PERTHES DISEASE

Clearinghouses/Hotlines

The National Institute of Arthritis and Musculoskeletal and Skin Diseases (NIAMS) will send you whatever publications and reprints of articles from texts and journals they have on Legg-Perthes Disease. They will also refer you to other organizations that are studying this disease. NIAMS will also let you know of any clinical studies that may be studying this disease and looking for patients.

☎ Contact:
National Institute of Arthritis
and Musculoskeletal and Skin Diseases
Box AMS
9000 Rockville Pike
Bethesda, MD 20892
(301) 495-4484

LEGIONELLA PNEUMOPHILA

Clearinghouses/Hotlines

The National Institute on Allergy and Infectious Diseases (NIAID) can search the Combined Health Information Database (CHID) and generate a bibliography of resources on Legionella Pneumophila for you. They will also send you any publications and journal articles they may have on hand, and will refer you to researchers who are currently studying this disease. If you can't afford treatment, have your doctor call NIAID to find out if they are conducting any clinical studies that you might qualify for.

☎ Contact:
National Institute of Allergy
and Infectious Diseases
Building 31
Room 7A32
Bethesda, MD 20892
(301) 496-5717

LEGIONNAIRE'S DISEASE

Clearinghouses/Hotlines

The National Institute on Allergy and Infectious Diseases (NIAID) can search the Combined Health Information Database (CHID) and generate a bibliography of resources on Legionnaire's Disease for you. They will also send you any publications and journal articles they may have on hand, and will refer you to researchers who are currently studying this disease. If you can't afford treatment, have your doctor call NIAID to find out if they are conducting any clinical studies that you might qualify for.

☎ Contact:
National Institute of Allergy
and Infectious Diseases
Building 31, Room 7A32
Bethesda, MD 20892
(301) 496-5717

LEIGH'S DISEASE

Clearinghouses/Hotlines

The National Institute of Neurological Disorders and Stroke (NINDS) can send you only information they have in their publications list on Leigh's Disease (Subacute Necrotizing Encephalitis). They cannot refer you to any experts. This Clearinghouse cannot directly give you information about any current clinical studies NINDS might be conducting on this illness, but you can find this information for yourself by looking under the National Institute of Neurological Disorders and Stroke in *Appendix A* at the end of this book.

☎ Contact:
National Institute of Neurological
Disorders and Stroke
Bldg. 31, Room 8A06
Bethesda, MD 20892
(301) 496-5751
(800) 352-9424

LEISHMANIASIS

Clearinghouses/Hotlines

The National Institute on Allergy and Infectious Diseases (NIAID) can search the Combined Health Information Database (CHID) and generate a bibliography of resources on Leishmaniasis for you. They will also send you any publications and journal articles they may have on hand, and will refer you to researchers who are currently studying this disease. If you can't afford treatment, have your doctor call NIAID to find out if they are conducting any clinical studies that you might qualify for.

☎ Contact:
National Institute of Allergy
and Infectious Diseases
Bldg. 31, Room 7A32
Bethesda, MD 20892
(301) 496-5717

LENNOX-GASTAUT SYNDROME

Clearinghouses/Hotlines

The National Institute of Neurological Disorders and Stroke (NINDS) can send you only information they have in their publications list on Lennox-Gastaut Syndrome. They cannot refer you to any experts. This Clearinghouse cannot directly give you information about any current clinical studies NINDS might be conducting on this illness, but you can find this information for yourself by looking under the National Institute of Neurological Disorders and Stroke in *Appendix A* at the end of this book.

☎ Contact:
National Institute of Neurological
Disorders and Stroke
Bldg. 31, Room 8A06
Bethesda, MD 20892
(301) 496-5751
(800) 352-9424

LENS IMPLANTS

Clearinghouses/Hotlines

The National Eye Institute (NEI) can give you up-to-date information on Lens Implants by searching the Combined Health Information Database (CHID) and MEDLINE and sending you bibliographies of resources, along with any journal articles they may have. They can also refer you to any other organizations that study this and other related techniques. NEI will also let you know of any clinical studies that may be studying this technique and looking for patients. Because of their small staff, NEI prefers that you submit your requests for information in writing.

☎ Contact:
National Eye Institute
Bldg. 31, Room 6A32
Bethesda, MD 20892
(301) 496-5248

LEPROSY

Clearinghouses/Hotlines

The Gillis W. Long Hansen's Disease Center primarily provides Hansen's Disease (leprosy) patients a place to receive a complete free evaluation and treatment. Any person with a confirmed diagnosis of leprosy is eligible for admission. The Center conducts an extensive patient care and rehabilitation program, as well as research, training and education activities.

☎ Contact:
Gillis W. Long Hansen's Disease Center
Carville, LA 70721
(504) 642-4706

The National Institute on Allergy and Infectious Diseases (NIAID) can search the Combined Health Information Database (CHID) and generate a bibliography of resources on Leprosy for you. They will also send you any publications and journal articles they may have on hand, and will refer you to researchers who are currently studying this disease. If you can't afford treatment, have your doctor call NIAID to find out if they are conducting any clinical studies that you might qualify for.

☎ Contact:
National Institute of Allergy
and Infectious Diseases
Bldg. 31, Room 7A32
Bethesda, MD 20892
(301) 496-5717

LESCH-NYHAN DISEASE

Clearinghouses/Hotlines

The National Institute of Diabetes and Digestive and Kidney Diseases's (NIDDK) individual clearinghouses can search the Combined Health Information Database (CHID) and generate a bibliography of resources on Lesch-Nyhan Disease for you. They also will send you any publications and journal articles they may have on hand, and

will refer you to other organizations studying this disease. If you can't afford treatment, have your doctor call NIDDK to find out if they are conducting any clinical studies that you might qualify for.

☎ Contact:
National Institute of Diabetes
and Digestive and Kidney Diseases
Bldg. 31, Room 9A04
Bethesda, MD 20892
(301) 496-3583

The National Institute of Neurological Disorders and Stroke (NINDS) can send you only information they have in their publications list on Lesch-Nyhan Disease. They cannot refer you to any experts. This Clearinghouse cannot directly give you information about any current clinical studies NINDS might be conducting on this illness, but you can find this information for yourself by looking under the National Institute of Neurological Disorders and Stroke in *Appendix A* at the end of this book.

☎ Contact:
National Institute of Neurological
Disorders and Stroke
Bldg. 31, Room 8A06
Bethesda, MD 20892
(301) 496-5751
(800) 352-9424

The National Institute of Mental Health (NIMH) will send you whatever publications and reprints of articles from texts and journals they have on Lesch-Nyhan Disease. They will refer you to other organizations studying this disease. NIMH will also let you know of any clinical studies that may be studying this disease and looking for patients.

☎ Contact:
National Institute of Mental Health
5600 Fishers Ln., Room 15C05
Rockville, MD 20857
(301) 443-4515

LEUKEMIA

Clearinghouses/Hotlines

The National Cancer Institute (NCI) will send you

whatever publications and reprints of journal articles they have on Leukemia. They can also give you information on the state-of-the-art treatment for this disease, including specific treatment information for your stage of cancer. They can also search their Physician's Data Query (PDQ) database to let you know if NCI is conducting any clinical studies on your disease.

☏ Contact:
National Cancer Institute
Bldg. 31, Room 10A24
Bethesda, MD 20892
(800) 4-CANCER
(301) 496-5583

Free Publications/Videos

The following publications on Leukemia are available from the National Cancer Institute, Bldg. 31, Room 10A24, Bethesda, MD 20892; (800) 4-CANCER, or (301) 496-5583.

- *What You Need to Know About Adult Leukemia.* (#88-1572)
- *What You Need to Know About Childhood Leukemia.* (#89-1573)
- *Research Report: Leukemia.* (#88-329)

LEUKOARAIOSIS

Clearinghouses/Hotlines

The National Institute of Neurological Disorders and Stroke (NINDS) can send you only information they have in their publications list on Leukoaraiosis. They cannot refer you to any experts. This Clearinghouse cannot directly give you information about any current clinical studies NINDS might be conducting on this illness, but you can find this information for yourself by looking under the National Institute of Neurological Disorders and Stroke in *Appendix A* at the end of this book.

☏ Contact:
National Institute of Neurological
Disorders and Stroke
Building 31

Room 8A06
Bethesda, MD 20892
(301) 496-5751
(800) 352-9424

LEUKODYSTROPHY

Clearinghouses/Hotlines

The National Institute of Neurological Disorders and Stroke (NINDS) can send you only information they have in their publications list on Leukodystrophy. They cannot refer you to any experts. This Clearinghouse cannot directly give you information about any current clinical studies NINDS might be conducting on this illness, but you can find this information for yourself by looking under the National Institute of Neurological Disorders and Stroke in *Appendix A* at the end of this book.

☏ Contact:
National Institute of Neurological
Disorders and Stroke
Building 31
Room 8A06
Bethesda, MD 20892
(301) 496-5751
(800) 352-9424

LEUKOENCEPHALOPATHY

Clearinghouses/Hotlines

The National Institute of Neurological Disorders and Stroke (NINDS) can send you only information they have in their publications list on Leukoencephalopathy. They cannot refer you to any experts. This Clearinghouse cannot directly give you information about any current clinical studies NINDS might be conducting on this illness, but you can find this information for yourself by looking under the National Institute of Neurological Disorders and Stroke in *Appendix A* at the end of this book.

☎ Contact:
National Institute of Neurological
Disorders and Stroke
Building 31
Room 8A06
Bethesda, MD 20892
(301) 496-5751
(800) 352-9424

LEUKOPLAKIA

Clearinghouses/Hotlines

The National Institute of Dental Research (NIDR) will send you whatever publications and reprints of journal articles they have on Leukoplakia. As a policy, NIDR will not refer you to other organizations or experts who study this disease. If you can't afford treatment, have your doctor call Dr. Albert Guckers at (301) 496-6241 to find out if NIDR is conducting any clinical studies that you might qualify for.

☎ Contact:
National Institute of Dental Research
Building 31
Room 2C35
Bethesda, MD 20892
(301) 496-4261

LICE

Clearinghouses/Hotlines

The National Institute on Allergy and Infectious Diseases (NIAID) can search the Combined Health Information Database (CHID) and generate a bibliography of resources on Lice for you. They will also send you any publications and journal articles they may have on hand, and will refer you to researchers who are currently studying Lice. If you can't afford treatment, have your doctor call NIAID to find out if they are conducting any clinical studies that you might qualify for.

☎ Contact:
National Institute of Allergy
and Infectious Diseases
Building 31
Room 7A32
Bethesda, MD 20892
(301) 496-5717

Free Publications/Videos

The following publication on Lice is available from the Food & Drug Administration, (HFE-88), 5600 Fishers Ln., Rockville, MD 20857; (301) 443-3170.

- *Going To The Head Of The Class (Of Lice And Children).* (FDA90-1153)

LICHEN PLANUS

Clearinghouses/Hotlines

The National Institute of Dental Research (NIDR) will send you whatever publications and reprints of journal articles they have on Lichen Planus. As a policy, NIDR will not refer you to other organizations or experts who study this disease. If you can't afford treatment, have your doctor call Dr. Albert Guckers at (301) 496-6241 to find out if NIDR is conducting any clinical studies that you might qualify for.

☎ Contact:
National Institute of Dental Research
Building 31
Room 2C35
Bethesda, MD 20892
(301) 496-4261

The National Institute of Arthritis and Musculoskeletal and Skin Diseases (NIAMS) will send you whatever publications and reprints of articles from texts and journals they have on Lichen Planus. They will also refer you to other organizations that are studying this disease. NIAMS will also let you know of any clinical studies that may be studying this disease and looking for patients.

☎ Contact:
National Institute of Arthritis
and Musculoskeletal and Skin Diseases
Box AMS
9000 Rockville Pike
Bethesda, MD 20892
(301) 495-4484

LIFE CYCLE

Clearinghouses/Hotlines

This center answers questions about families throughout the Life Cycle, from marital relationships and childbearing families to empty nest families and retirement, and deals with matters concerning social environment and family economics education.

☎ Contact:
Family Branch
U.S. Department of Agriculture
10301 Baltimore Blvd.
Beltsville, MD 20705
(301) 504-5204

The National Institute on Aging (NIA) will send you whatever publications and reprints of journal articles they have on Life Cycle. They cannot refer you to other experts if the information they have isn't sufficient for your purposes.

☎ Contact:
National Institute on Aging
Bldg. 31, Room 5C27
Bethesda, MD 20892
(301) 496-1752

LIFE EXPECTANCY

Clearinghouses/Hotlines

The National Center for Health Statistics (NCHS) collects, analyzes, and distributes data on health-related issues, such as Life Expectancy. Materials available include statistical data on health, nutrition, vital statistics such as births and divorces, health care delivery, dental health, health resources utilization, health care personnel, families, contraception, and health care economics.

☎ ·Contact:
Centers for Disease Control
6525 Belcrest Rd., Room 1064
Hyattsville, MD 20782
(301) 436-8500

The National Institute on Aging will send you whatever publications and reprints of journal articles they have on Life Expectancy and Extension. They cannot refer you to other experts if the information they have isn't sufficient for your purposes.

☎ Contact:
National Institute on Aging
Bldg. 31, Room 5C27
Bethesda, MD 20892
(301) 496-1752

LIFESTYLE

Free Publications/Videos

The following publication is available from the Office of Clinical Center Communications, Bldg. 10, Room 1C255, Bethesda, MD 20892; (301) 496-2563.

- *Behavior Patterns and Health*. Discusses the scientific evidence linking behavior to disease and suggests ways to reduce the risks of heart attack, lung cancer, and stroke by changing our lifestyle. (#85-2682)

The following publication is available from the National Health Information Center, P.O. Box 1133, Washington, DC 20013; (800) 336-4797, or (301) 565-4167 in DC metro area.

- *Health Risk Appraisals*. Identifies several different tests that will help you analyze your health history and current lifestyle to determine your risk for preventable death or chronic illness. This publications also contains a vendor list of many corporate health promotion centers, medical research institutions, and private organizations that offer such tests and the costs of each. ($1)

LIFE-SUSTAINING TECHNOLOGIES

See Living Wills

LIPID RESEARCH

Clearinghouses/Hotlines

The National Heart, Lung, and Blood Institute (NHLBI) can search the Combined Health Information Database (CHID) and generate a bibliography of resources on Lipid Research for you. They also will send you any publications and journal articles they may have on hand, and will refer you to other organizations that are studying this disease. If you can't afford treatment, have your doctor call NHLBI to find out if they are conducting any clinical studies that you might qualify for.

☎ Contact:
National Heart, Lung, and Blood Institute
Building 31
Room 4A21
Bethesda, MD 20892
(301) 496-4236

Free Publications/Videos

The following publications on Lipid Research are available from National Heart, Lung and Blood Institute, Bldg. 31, Room 4A21, Bethesda, MD 20892; (301) 496-4236.

- *Lipid Research Clinics Population Studies Data Book.* (#87-2727)
- *The Lipid Research Clinics Population Studies Data Book: Vol. IV: The USSR Second Prevalence Study.* (#90-2992)

LIPID STORAGE DISEASES

Clearinghouses/Hotlines

The National Institute of Neurological Disorders and Stroke (NINDS) can send you only information they have in their publications list on Lipid Storage Diseases. They cannot refer you to any experts. This Clearinghouse cannot directly give you information about any current clinical studies NINDS might be conducting on this illness, but you can find this information for yourself by looking under the National Institute of Neurological Disorders and Stroke in *Appendix A* at the end of this book.

☎ Contact:
National Institute of Neurological
Disorders and Stroke
Bldg. 31, Room 8A06
Bethesda, MD 20892
(301) 496-5751
(800) 352-9424

Free Publications/Videos

The following publications are available from the National Institute of Neurological Disorders and Stroke, Bldg. 31, Room 8A06, Bethesda, MD 20892; (301) 496-5751 or (800) 352-9424.

- *Lipid Storage Disease.* (#84-2628)
- *Lipid Storage Diseases.* Fact sheet on symptoms and treatment.

LIPID TRANSPORT DISORDERS

Clearinghouses/Hotlines

The National Heart, Lung, and Blood Institute (NHLBI) can search the Combined Health Information Database (CHID) and generate a bibliography of resources on Lipid Transport Disorders for you. They also will send you any publications and journal articles they may have on hand, and will refer you to other organizations that are studying this disorder. If you can't afford treatment, have your doctor call NHLBI to find out if they are conducting any clinical studies that you might qualify for.

☎ Contact:
National Heart, Lung, and Blood Institute
Bldg. 31, Room 4A21
Bethesda, MD 20892
(301) 496-4236

LIPIDEMIA

Clearinghouses/Hotlines

The National Heart, Lung, and Blood Institute (NHLBI) can search the Combined Health Information Database (CHID) and generate a bibliography of resources on Lipidemia for you. They also will send you any publications and journal articles they may have on hand, and will refer you to other organizations that are studying this disease. If you can't afford treatment, have your doctor call NHLBI to find out if they are conducting any clinical studies that you might qualify for.

☎ Contact:
National Heart, Lung, and Blood Institute
Bldg. 31, Room 4A21
Bethesda, MD 20892
(301) 496-4236

LIPIDOSIS

Clearinghouses/Hotlines

The National Institute of Neurological Disorders and Stroke (NINDS) can send you only information they have in their publications list on Lipidosis. They cannot refer you to any experts. This Clearinghouse cannot directly give you information about any current clinical studies NINDS might be conducting on this illness, but you can find this information for yourself by looking under the National Institute of

Neurological Disorders and Stroke in *Appendix A* at the end of this book.

☎ Contact:
National Institute of Neurological
Disorders and Stroke
Building 31
Room 8A06
Bethesda, MD 20892
(301) 496-5751
(800) 352-9424

LISTERIOSIS

Clearinghouses/Hotlines

The National Institute on Allergy and Infectious Diseases (NIAID) can search the Combined Health Information Database (CHID) and generate a bibliography of resources on Listeriosis for you. They will also send you any publications and journal articles they may have on hand, and will refer you to researchers who are currently studying this disease. If you can't afford treatment, have your doctor call NIAID to find out if they are conducting any clinical studies that you might qualify for.

☎ Contact:
National Institute of Allergy
and Infectious Diseases
Building 31
Room 7A32
Bethesda, MD 20892
(301) 496-5717

LITHOTRIPSY

Free Publications/Videos

The following publication is available from the National Institute of Diabetes and Digestive and Kidney Diseases, Bldg. 31, Room 9A04, Bethesda, MD 20892; (301) 496-3583.

- *Extracorporeal Shock-Wave Lithotripsy.* (#88-859)

LIVER DISORDERS

Clearinghouses/Hotlines

The National Institute of Diabetes and Digestive and Kidney Diseases's (NIDDK) individual clearinghouses can search the Combined Health Information Database (CHID) and generate a bibliography of resources on the Liver for you. They also will send you any publications and journal articles they may have on hand, and will refer you to other organizations that are studying liver disease. If you can't afford treatment, have your doctor call NIDDK to find out if they are conducting any clinical studies that you might qualify for.

☎ Contact:
National Institute of Diabetes
and Digestive and Kidney Diseases
Building 31
Room 9A04
Bethesda, MD 20892
(301) 496-3583

Free Publications/Videos

The following publication on Liver Disorders is available from the National Institute of Diabetes and Digestive and Kidney Diseases, Bldg. 31, Room 9A04, Bethesda, MD 20892; (301) 496-3583.

- *Cirrhosis of the Liver.* (#92-1134)

LIVING WILLS

See also Aging

Free Publications/Videos

The following Congressional Research Service (CRS) reports are available from either of your U.S. Senators' offices at the U.S. Capitol, Washington, DC 20510, or from your Congressional Representative at the U.S. Capitol,

Washington, DC 20515. You can also call in your request through the U.S. Capitol switchboard at (202) 224-3121. Be sure to include the full title and report number in your request.

- *Treatment and Appointment Directives: Living Wills, Powers of Attorney, and Other Advance Medical Care Documents.* (#91-87 A)
- *Life-Sustaining Technologies: Medical and Moral Issues.* (#91-45 SPR)
- *Advance Directives and Health Care Facilities.* (#91-117 EPW)
- *Advance Medical Directives.* (#91-27 A)
- *Birth, Life and Death: Fundamental Life Decisions and the Right to Privacy.* (#90-180 A)
- *The Right to Die: Fundamental Life Decisions After Cruzan v. Director, Missouri Dept. of Health.* (#90-371 A)
- *A Survey of the Statutory Definitions of Death.* (#91-635 A)

LOCKED-IN SYNDROME

Clearinghouses/Hotlines

The National Institute of Neurological Disorders and Stroke (NINDS) can send you only information they have in their publications list on Locked-In Syndrome. They cannot refer you to any experts. This Clearinghouse cannot directly give you information about any current clinical studies NINDS might be conducting on this illness, but you can find this information for yourself by looking under the National Institute of Neurological Disorders and Stroke in *Appendix A* at the end of this book.

☎ Contact:
National Institute of Neurological
Disorders and Stroke
Building 31
Room 8A06
Bethesda, MD 20892
(301) 496-5751
(800) 352-9424

LOCKJAW (Tetanus)

Clearinghouses/Hotlines

The National Institute of Allergy and Infectious Diseases (NIAID) can provide you some basic information regarding Lockjaw.

☎ Contact:
National Institute of Allergy
and Infectious Diseases
Bldg. 31, Room 7A32
Bethesda, MD 20892
(301) 496-5717

LOEFFLER'S SYNDROME

Clearinghouses/Hotlines

The National Institute on Allergy and Infectious Diseases (NIAID) can search the Combined Health Information Database (CHID) and generate a bibliography of resources on Loeffler's Syndrome for you. They will also send you any publications and journal articles they may have on hand, and will refer you to researchers who are currently studying this disease. If you can't afford treatment, have your doctor call NIAID to find out if they are conducting any clinical studies that you might qualify for.

☎ Contact:
National Institute of Allergy
and Infectious Diseases
Bldg. 31, Room 7A32
Bethesda, MD 20892
(301) 496-5717

LOMUSTINE

Free Publications/Videos

The following publication on Lomustine is available from the National Cancer Institute, Bldg. 31, Room 10A24, Bethesda, MD 20892; (800) 4-

CANCER, or (301) 496-5583.

- *Lomustina/Lomustine.* Provides information about side effects, proper usage, and precautions of this anti-cancer drug.

LONGEVITY

Clearinghouses/Hotlines

The National Center for Health Statistics collects, analyzes, and distributes data on health-related issues, such as Longevity. Materials available include statistical data on health, nutrition, vital statistics such as births and divorces, health care delivery, dental health, health resources utilization, health care personnel, families, contraception, and health care economics.

☎ Contact:
Centers for Disease Control
6525 Belcrest Rd., Room 1064
Hyattsville, MD 20782
(301) 436-8500

The National Institute on Aging (NIA) will send you whatever publications and reprints of journal articles they have on Longevity Statistics. They cannot refer you to other experts if the information they have isn't sufficient for your purposes.

☎ Contact:
National Institute on Aging
Bldg. 31, Room 5C27
Bethesda, MD 20892
(301) 496-1752

LONG-TERM CARE

See also Aging
See also Gerontology
See also Nursing Homes

Clearinghouses/Hotlines

The National Institute on Aging (NIA) conducts and supports biomedical, social, and behavioral research on aging related issues. They can answer your questions, provide you with pamphlets, brochures, research reports, and more regarding your topic of interest, as well as refer you to current researchers in the field. NIA continues to work on the *Baltimore Longitudinal Study of Aging*, which has followed the same 650 men since 1958 to measure the changes with age.

☎ Contact:
National Institute on Aging
Federal Building, Room 6C12
Bethesda, MD 20892
(301) 496-1752

Free Publications/Videos

The following publication on Long-Term Care is available from the ODPHP Health Information Center, P.O. Box 1133, Washington, DC 20013; (800) 336-4797, or (301) 565-4167.

- *Long-Term Care*. Explains issues and concerns regarding long-term care, and includes a list of publications and audiovisuals available from government agencies, community organizations, foundations and many other health groups.

The following Congressional Research Service (CRS) reports on Long-Term Care are available from either of your U.S. Senators' offices at the U.S. Capitol, Washington, DC 20510, or from your Congressional Representative at the U.S. Capitol, Washington, DC 20515. You can also call in your request through the U.S. Capitol switchboard at (202) 224-3121. Be sure to include the full title and report number in your request.

- *Financing and Delivery of Long-Term Care Services for the Elderly*. (#88-379 EPW)
- *Financing Long-Term Care for the Elderly: Audio Brief*. (#AB50187)
- *Hospital Capital Cost Reimbursement under Medicare*. (#86-598 EPW)
- *Long Term Care Financing: Selected References*. (#89-42 L)
- *Long Term Care for the Elderly*. (#IB88098)
- *Long-Term Care Legislation: Summary of Selected Bills*. (#89-238 EPW)
- *Public Opinion on Long-Term Health Care Needs, Costs and Financing*. (#90-151 GOV)

- *Tax Options for Financing Long-Term Care for the Elderly*. (#89-329 E)

LOU GEHRIG'S DISEASE

Clearinghouses/Hotlines

The National Institute of Neurological Disorders and Stroke (NINDS) can send you only information they have in their publications list on Lou Gehrig's Disease. They cannot refer you to any experts. This Clearinghouse cannot directly give you information about any current clinical studies NINDS might be conducting on this illness, but you can find this information for yourself by looking under the National Institute of Neurological Disorders and Stroke in *Appendix A* at the end of this book.

☎ Contact:
National Institute of Neurological
Disorders and Stroke
Bldg. 31, Room 8A06
Bethesda, MD 20892
(301) 496-5751
(800) 352-9424

Free Publications/Videos

The following publications are available from the National Institute of Neurological Disorders and Stroke, Bldg. 31, Room 8A06, Bethesda, MD 20892; (301) 496-5751 or (800) 352-9424.

- *Amyotrophic Lateral Sclerosis*. (#84-916)
- *Amyotrophic Lateral Sclerosis (ALS)*. Contains a collection of scientific articles, patient education pamphlets, and addresses of voluntary health associations.

LOWER BACK PAIN

Clearinghouses/Hotlines

The National Institute of Arthritis and Musculoskeletal and Skin Diseases (NIAMS) will send you whatever publications and reprints of articles from texts and journals they have on Lower Back Pain (Disk and Musculoskeletal). They will also refer you to other organizations that are studying this condition. NIAMS will also let you know of any clinical studies that may be studying this disease and looking for patients.

☎ Contact:
National Institute of Arthritis
and Musculoskeletal and Skin Diseases
Box AMS, 9000 Rockville Pike
Bethesda, MD 20892
(301) 495-4484

The National Institute of Neurological Disorders and Stroke (NINDS) can send you only information they have in their publications list on Lower Back Pain (Sciatica). They cannot refer you to any experts. This Clearinghouse cannot directly give you information about any current clinical studies NINDS might be conducting on this topic, but you can find this information for yourself by looking under the National Institute of Neurological Disorders and Stroke in *Appendix A* at the end of this book.

☎ Contact:
National Institute of Neurological
Disorders and Stroke
Bldg. 31, Room 8A06
Bethesda, MD 20892
(301) 496-5751
(800) 352-9424

LOW BIRTHWEIGHT

Clearinghouses/Hotlines

The National Institute of Child Health and Human Development (NICHD) will send you whatever publications and reprints of journal articles they have on Low Birthweight. If necessary, they will refer you to other experts or researchers in the field. If you can't afford treatment, have your doctor call NICHD to find out if they are conducting any clinical studies that you might qualify for.

☎ Contact:
National Institute of Child Health
and Human Development

Bldg. 31, Room 2A32
Bethesda, MD 20892
(301) 496-5133

The National Maternal and Child Health Clearinghouse has all kinds of information on maternal and child health issues, such as pregnancy, child and adolescent health, and human genetics. If the answer to your question can't be answered by any of their countless free publications, they can refer you to other National or local resources. If you still need further information, they search their own reference collection and send you what they find.

☎ Contact:
National Maternal and Child
Health Clearinghouse
38th & R Sts., NW
Washington, DC 20057
(703) 821-8955, ext. 254

Free Publications/Videos

The following publication on Low Birthweight is available from the Office of Technology Assessment, 600 Pennsylvania Ave., SE, Washington, DC 20510; (202) 224-8996.

- *Neonatal Intensive Care for Low Birthweight Infants: Costs and Effectiveness.* A report to Congress. Ask for the summary report.

The following publications on Low Birthweight are available from the National Maternal and Child Health Clearinghouse, 38th & R Sts., NW, Washington, DC 20057; (703) 821-8955, ext. 254.

- *Advances in the Prevention of Low Birthweight: An International Symposium.* (#EEO2) .
- *Pre-term and Low Birthweight Infants: Resource Guide.* (#D015)

LOW BLOOD PRESSURE

Clearinghouses/Hotlines

The National Heart, Lung, and Blood Institute

(NHLBI) can search the Combined Health Information Database (CHID) and generate a bibliography of resources on Low Blood Pressure for you. They also will send you any publications and journal articles they may have on hand, and will refer you to other organizations that are studying this condition. If you can't afford treatment, have your doctor call NHLBI to find out if they are conducting any clinical studies that you might qualify for.

☎ Contact:
National Heart, Lung, and Blood Institute
Bldg. 31, Room 4A21
Bethesda, MD 20892
(301) 496-4236

LOW-CALORIE SWEETENERS

Free Publications/Videos

This Congressional Research Service (CRS) report is available from either of your U.S. Senators' offices at the U.S. Capitol, Washington, DC 20510, or from your Congressional Representative at the U.S. Capitol, Washington, DC 20515. You can also call in your request through the U.S. Capitol switchboard at (202) 224-3121. Be sure to include the full title and report number in your request.

- *Low-Calorie Sweeteners: Aspartame, Cyclamate, and Saccharin.* (#IB85119)

LOW DENSITY LIPOPROTEINS

Clearinghouses/Hotlines

The National Heart, Lung, and Blood Institute (NHLBI) can search the Combined Health Information Database (CHID) and generate a bibliography of resources on Low Density Lipoproteins (LDL) for you. They also will send

you any publications and journal articles they may have on hand, and will refer you to other organizations that are studying this issue. If you can't afford treatment, have your doctor call NHLBI to find out if they are conducting any clinical studies that you might qualify for.

☎ Contact:
National Heart, Lung, and Blood Institute
Building 31
Room 4A21
Bethesda, MD 20892
(301) 496-4236

LOW-FAT DIET

See also Food

Clearinghouses/Hotlines

The Food and Nutrition Information Center can provide you with a wealth of information on food and nutrition topics. They have bibliographies ready and a data base through which they can search any food or nutrition subject.

☎ Contact:
Food and Nutrition Information Center
National Agricultural Library
Room 304
Beltsville, MD 20705
(301) 504-5719

LOW-INCOME MOTHERS

Free Publications/Videos

The following publication on Low-Income Mothers is available from the National Clearinghouse for Primary Care Information, 8201 Greensboro Drive, Suite 600, McLean, VA 22102; (703) 821-8955.

- *Healthy Mothers, Healthy Babies: A Compendium of Program Ideas for Servicing Low-Income Women.* Provides useful suggestions to health care providers who work with low income populations, and suggests program planning and policy directions for State and national organizations concerned with maternal and infant health.

LOWE'S SYNDROME

Clearinghouses/Hotlines

The National Institute of Child Health and Human Development (NICHD) will send you whatever publications and reprints of journal articles they have on Lowe's Syndrome (Oculocerebrorenal). If necessary, they will refer you to other experts or researchers in the field. If you can't afford treatment, have your doctor call NICHD to find out if they are conducting any clinical studies that you might qualify for.

☎ Contact:
National Institute of Child Health
and Human Development
Building 31
Room 2A32
Bethesda, MD 20892
(301) 496-5133

The National Eye Institute (NEI) can give you up-to-date information on Lowe's Syndrome. by searching the Combined Health Information Database (CHID) and MEDLINE and sending you bibliographies of resources, along with any journal articles they may have. They can also refer you to any other organizations that study this and other related diseases. NEI will also let you know of any clinical studies that may be studying this disease and looking for patients. Because of their small staff, NEI prefers that you submit your requests for information in writing.

☎ Contact:
National Eye Institute
Building 31
Room 6A32
Bethesda, MD 20892
(301) 496-5248

L-TRYPTOPHAN

Free Publications/Videos

The following Congressional Research Service (CRS) report is available from either of your U.S. Senators' offices at the U.S. Capitol, Washington, DC 20510, or from your Congressional Representative at the U.S. Capitol, Washington, DC 20515. You can also call in your request through the U.S. Capitol switchboard at (202) 224-3121. Be sure to include the full title and report number in your request.

- *L-Tryptophan: Health Problems, Production and Regulatory Status: Proceedings of a CRS Seminar.* (#91-758 SPR)

LUNG CANCER

Clearinghouses/Hotlines

The National Cancer Institute (NCI) will send you whatever publications and reprints of journal articles they have on Lung Cancer. They can also give you information on the state-of-the-art treatment for this disease, including specific treatment information for your stage of cancer. They can also search their Physician's Data Query (PDQ) database to let you know if NCI is conducting any clinical studies on your disease.

☎ Contact:
National Cancer Institute
Bldg. 31, Room 10A24
Bethesda, MD 20892
(800) 4-CANCER
(301) 496-5583

Free Publications/Videos

The following publications are available from the National Cancer Institute, Bldg. 31, Room 10A24, Bethesda, MD 20892; (800) 4-CANCER, or (301) 496-5583.

- *Research Report: Cancer of the Lung. (#90-526)*
- *What You Need to Know About Cancer of the Lung. (#91-1553)*

LUNG DISEASE

Clearinghouses/Hotlines

The National Institute on Allergy and Infectious Diseases (NIAID) can search the Combined Health Information Database (CHID) and generate a bibliography of resources on Infectious and Allergenic Lung Disease for you. They will also send you any publications and journal articles they may have on hand, and will refer you to researchers who are currently studying this disease. If you can't afford treatment, have your doctor call NIAID to find out if they are conducting any clinical studies that you might qualify for.

☎ Contact:
National Institute of Allergy
and Infectious Diseases
Building 31
Room 7A32
Bethesda, MD 20892
(301) 496-5717

The National Heart, Lung, and Blood Institute (NHLBI) can search the Combined Health Information Database (CHID) and generate a bibliography of resources on Interstitial and Non-infectious, Non-allergenic, Non-tumorous Lung Disease for you. They also will send you any publications and journal articles they may have on hand, and will refer you to other organizations that are studying this disease. If you can't afford treatment, have your doctor call NHLBI to find out if they are conducting any clinical studies that you might qualify for.

☎ Contact:
National Heart, Lung, and Blood Institute
Building 31
Room 4A21
Bethesda, MD 20892
(301) 496-4236

The National Cancer Institute (NCI) will send you whatever publications and reprints of journal articles they have on Cancerous Lung Disease. They can also give you information on the state-of-the-art treatment for this disease, including specific treatment information for your stage of cancer. They can also search their Physician's Data Query (PDQ) database to let you know if NCI is conducting any clinical studies on your disease.

☎ Contact:
National Cancer Institute
Bldg. 31, Room 10A24
Bethesda, MD 20892
(800) 4-CANCER
(301) 496-5583

The National Institute of Environmental Health Sciences (NIEHS) will send you whatever publications and journal articles they can locate on specific questions about Asbestosis lung disease. If necessary they can put you in contact with researchers studying this issue. NIEHS does not conduct any clinical studies.

☎ Contact:
National Institute of Environmental
Health Sciences
P.O. Box 12233
Research Triangle Park, NC 27709
(919) 541-3345

Free Publications/Videos

The following publication is available from the Office of Technology Assessment, Washington, DC 20510-8025; (202) 224-8996.

- *Identifying and Controlling Pulmonary Toxicants: Background Paper. (#OTA-BP-BA-91)*

The following publication is available from the National Maternal and Child Health Clearinghouse, 38th & R Sts., NW, Washington, DC 20057; (703) 821-8955, ext. 254.

- *Pediatric Pulmonology Guidelines for the Care of Children With Chronic Lung Disease. (#C035)*

LUPUS

Clearinghouses/Hotlines

The National Institute of Arthritis and Musculoskeletal and Skin Diseases (NIAMS) will send you whatever publications and reprints of articles from texts and journals they have on Lupus Erythematosus. They will also refer you to other organizations that are studying this disease. NIAMS will also let you know of any clinical studies that may be studying this disease and looking for patients.

☎ Contact:
National Institute of Arthritis
and Musculoskeletal and Skin Diseases
Box AMS
Bethesda, MD 20892
(301) 495-4484

The National Institute of Neurological Disorders and Stroke (NINDS) can send you only information they have in their publications list on Lupus Erythematosus. They cannot refer you to any experts. This Clearinghouse cannot directly give you information about any current clinical studies NINDS might be conducting on this illness, but you can find this information for yourself by looking under the National Institute of Neurological Disorders and Stroke in *Appendix A* at the end of this book.

☎ Contact:
National Institute of Neurological
Disorders and Stroke
Bldg. 31, Room 8A06
Bethesda, MD 20892
(301) 496-5751
(800) 352-9424

The National Institute on Allergy and Infectious Diseases (NIAID) can search the Combined Health Information Database (CHID) and generate a bibliography of resources on Lupus Erythematosus for you. They will also send you any publications and journal articles they may have on hand, and will refer you to researchers who are currently studying this disease. If you can't afford treatment, have your doctor call NIAID to find out if they are conducting any clinical studies that you might qualify for.

☎ Contact:
National Institute of Allergy
and Infectious Diseases
Bldg. 31, Room 7A32
Bethesda, MD 20892
(301) 496-5717

Free Publications/Videos

The following publications on Lupus are available from the National Institute of Arthritis and Musculoskeletal and Skin Diseases, Box AMS, Bethesda, MD 20892; (301) 495-4484.

- *Conference Report: Education Strategies for Improving the Outcome of Lupus in High Risk Populations.*
- *Update: Lupus Erythematosus Research.*
- *What Black Women Should Know About Lupus.* 8 page booklet. (#AR130, NIH91-3219)
- *Lupus: Patient Education Materials, 1990.* An annotated bibliography of resources. (#AR51, $4)

The following publication on Lupus is available from the Food & Drug Administration, (HFE-88), 5600 Fishers Ln., Rockville, MD 20857; (301) 443-3170.

- *Living With Lupus.* (#FDA90-3178)

The following publication on Lupus is available from the National Institute of Neurological Disorders and Stroke, P.O. Box 5801, Bethesda, MD 20824; (800) 352-9424, or (301) 496-5751.

- *Lupus, Neurological Sequelae of.* Collection of scientific articles, patient education pamphlets, and addresses of voluntary health associations.

LYME DISEASE

Clearinghouses/Hotlines

The National Institute on Allergy and Infectious

Diseases (NIAID) can search the Combined Health Information Database (CHID) and generate a bibliography of resources on Lyme Arthritis and Lyme Disease for you. They will also send you any publications and journal articles they may have on hand, and will refer you to researchers who are currently studying this disease. If you can't afford treatment, have your doctor call NIAID to find out if they are conducting any clinical studies that you might qualify for.

☎ Contact:
National Institute of Allergy
and Infectious Diseases
Building 31
Room 7A32
Bethesda, MD 20892
(301) 496-5717

The National Institute of Arthritis and Musculoskeletal and Skin Diseases (NIAMS) will send you whatever publications and reprints of articles from texts and journals they have on Lyme Arthritis and Lyme Disease. They will also refer you to other organizations that are studying this disease. NIAMS will also let you know of any clinical studies that may be studying this disease and looking for patients.

☎ Contact:
National Institute of Arthritis
and Musculoskeletal and Skin Diseases
Box AMS
Bethesda, MD 20892
(301) 495-4484

The Centers for Disease Control's Voice Information System allows anyone using a touchtone phone to obtain pre-recorded information on Lyme Disease, and many other conditions. This service offers information about this condition, symptoms and prevention methods, immunization requirements, current statistics, recent disease outbreak, and available printed materials. The system is available 24 hours a day, although the health professionals are available Monday through Friday, 8 a.m.-4:30 p.m.

☎ Contact:
Centers for Disease Control
Information Resources Management Office
Mail Stop C-15
1600 Clifton Rd., NE

Atlanta, GA 30333
(404) 332-4555

Free Publications/Videos

The following publication on Lyme Disease is available from the Office of Clinical Center Communications, Bldg. 10, Room 1C255, Bethesda, MD 20892; (301) 496-2563.

- *Lyme Disease*. Video to help the general public make intelligent decisions.

The following publication on Lyme Disease is available from the National Arthritis and Musculoskeletal and Skin Diseases Information Clearinghouse, Box AMS, 9000 Rockville Pike, Bethesda, MD 20892; (301) 495-4484.

Lyme Disease: An Annotated Bibliography, 1989.
An annotated bibliography of resources. (#AR67, $5)

LYMPHADENOPATHY SYNDROME

Clearinghouses/Hotlines

The National Institute on Allergy and Infectious Diseases (NIAID) can search the Combined Health Information Database (CHID) and generate a bibliography of resources on Lymphadenopathy Syndrome (LAD) for you. They will also send you any publications and journal articles they may have on hand, and will refer you to researchers who are currently studying this disease. If you can't afford treatment, have your doctor call NIAID to find out if they are conducting any clinical studies that you might qualify for.

☎ Contact:
National Institute of Allergy
and Infectious Diseases
Bldg. 31, Room 7A32
Bethesda, MD 20892
(301) 496-5717

LYMPHEDEMA

Clearinghouses/Hotlines

The National Cancer Institute (NCI) will send you whatever publications and reprints of journal articles they have on Lymphedema. They can also give you information on the state-of-the-art treatment for this disease, including specific treatment information for your stage of cancer. They can also search their Physician's Data Query (PDQ) database to let you know if NCI is conducting any clinical studies on your disease.

☎ Contact:
National Cancer Institute
Building 31
Room 10A24
Bethesda, MD 20892
(800) 4-CANCER
(301) 496-5583

LYMPHOBLASTIC LYMPHOSARCOMA

Clearinghouses/Hotlines

The National Cancer Institute (NCI) will send you whatever publications and reprints of journal articles they have on Lymphoblastic Lymphosarcoma. They can also give you information on the state-of-the-art treatment for this disease, including specific treatment information for your stage of cancer. They can also search their Physician's Data Query (PDQ) database to let you know if NCI is conducting any clinical studies on your disease.

☎ Contact:
National Cancer Institute
Building 31
Room 10A24
Bethesda, MD 20892
(800) 4-CANCER
(301) 496-5583

LYMPHOMA

Clearinghouses/Hotlines

The National Cancer Institute (NCI) will send you whatever publications and reprints of journal articles they have on Lymphoma. They can also give you information on the state-of-the-art treatment for this disease, including specific treatment information for your stage of cancer. They can also search their Physician's Data Query (PDQ) database to let you know if NCI is conducting any clinical studies on your disease.

☎ Contact:
National Cancer Institute
Bldg. 31, Room 10A24
Bethesda, MD 20892
(800) 4-CANCER
(301) 496-5583

Free Publications/Videos

The following publication on Lymphoma is available from the National Cancer Institute, Bldg. 31, Room 10A24, Bethesda, MD 20892; (800) 4-CANCER, or (301) 496-5583.

- *What You Need to Know About Non-Hodgkins Lymphoma*. (#90-1567)

LYMPHOSARCOMA

Clearinghouses/Hotlines

The National Cancer Institute (NCI) will send you whatever publications and reprints of journal articles they have on Lymphosarcoma. They can also give you information on the state-of-the-art treatment for this disease, including specific treatment information for your stage of cancer. They can also search their Physician's Data Query (PDQ) database to let you know if NCI is conducting any clinical studies on your disease.

☎ Contact:
National Cancer Institute

Bldg. 31, Room 10A24
Bethesda, MD 20892
(800) 4-CANCER
(301) 496-5583

- M -

refer you to any other organizations that study this and other related diseases. NEI will also let you know of any clinical studies that may be studying this disease and looking for patients. Because of their small staff, NEI prefers that you submit your requests for information in writing.

☎ Contact:
National Eye Institute
Bldg. 31, Room 6A32
Bethesda, MD 20892
(301) 496-5248

MACROGLOBULINEMIA AND MYELOMA

Clearinghouses/Hotlines

The National Cancer Institute (NCI) will send you whatever publications and reprints of journal articles they have on Macroglobulinemia and Myeloma. They can also give you information on the state-of-the-art treatment for this disease, including specific treatment information for your stage of cancer. They can also search their Physician's Data Query (PDQ) database to let you know if NCI is conducting any clinical studies on your disease.

☎ Contact:
National Cancer Institute
Bldg. 31, Room 10A24
Bethesda, MD 20892
(800) 4-CANCER
(301) 496-5583

MACULAR DEGENERATION

Clearinghouses/Hotlines

The National Eye Institute (NEI) can give you up-to-date information on Macular Degeneration by searching the Combined Health Information Database (CHID) and MEDLINE and sending you bibliographies of resources, along with any journal articles they may have. They can also

MAKARI TEST

Clearinghouses/Hotlines

The National Cancer Institute (NCI) will send you whatever publications and reprints of journal articles they have on the Makari Test. They can also search their Physician's Data Query (PDQ) database to let you know if NCI is conducting any clinical studies on your disease.

☎ Contact:
National Cancer Institute
Bldg. 31, Room 10A24
Bethesda, MD 20892
(800) 4-CANCER
(301) 496-5583

MALABSORPTIVE DISEASE

Clearinghouses/Hotlines

The National Institute of Diabetes and Digestive and Kidney Diseases's (NIDDK) individual clearinghouses can search the Combined Health Information Database (CHID) and generate a bibliography of resources on Malabsorptive Disease for you. They also will send you any publications and journal articles they may have on hand, and will refer you to other organizations that are studying this disease. If you can't afford treatment, have your doctor call NIDDK to find out if they are conducting any clinical studies that you might qualify for.

☎ Contact:
National Institute of Diabetes
and Digestive and Kidney Diseases
Building 31
Room 9A04
Bethesda, MD 20892
(301) 496-3583

MALARIA

Clearinghouses/Hotlines

The National Institute on Allergy and Infectious Diseases (NIAID) can search the Combined Health Information Database (CHID) and generate a bibliography of resources on Malaria for you. They will also send you any publications and journal articles they may have on hand, and will refer you to researchers who are currently studying this disease. If you can't afford treatment, have your doctor call NIAID to find out if they are conducting any clinical studies that you might qualify for.

☎ Contact:
National Institute of Allergy
and Infectious Diseases
Bldg. 31, Room 7A32
Bethesda, MD 20892
(301) 496-5717

The Centers for Disease Control's Voice Information System allows anyone using a touchtone phone to obtain pre-recorded information on Malaria, and many other conditions. This service offers information about Malaria, its symptoms and prevention methods, immunization requirements, current statistics, recent disease outbreak, and available printed materials. The system is available 24 hours a day, although the health professionals are available Monday through Friday, 8 a.m.-4:30 p.m.

☎ Contact:
Centers for Disease Control
Information Resources Management Office
Mail Stop C-15
1600 Clifton Rd., NE
Atlanta, GA 30333
(404) 332-4555

MALIGNANCIES

Clearinghouses/Hotlines

The National Cancer Institute (NCI) will send you whatever publications and reprints of journal articles they have on Malignancies. They can also give you information on the state-of-the-art treatment for this disease, including specific treatment information for your stage of cancer. They can also search their Physician's Data Query (PDQ) database to let you know if NCI is conducting any clinical studies on your disease.

☎ Contact:
National Cancer Institute
Bldg. 31, Room 10A24
Bethesda, MD 20892
(800) 4-CANCER
(301) 496-5583

MALNUTRITION

Clearinghouses/Hotlines

The National Institute of Diabetes and Digestive and Kidney Diseases's (NIDDK) individual clearinghouses can search the Combined Health Information Database (CHID) and generate a bibliography of resources on Malnutrition for you. They also will send you any publications and journal articles they may have on hand, and will refer you to other organizations that are studying this disease. If you can't afford treatment, have your doctor call NIDDK to find out if they are conducting any clinical studies that you might qualify for.

☎ Contact:
National Institute of Diabetes
and Digestive and Kidney Diseases
Bldg. 31, Room 9A04
Bethesda, MD 20892
(301) 496-3583

The National Institute of Child Health and Human Development (NICHD) will send you whatever publications and reprints of journal articles they have on Malnutrition. If necessary, they will refer you to other experts or researchers in the field. If you can't afford treatment, have your doctor call NICHD to find out if they are conducting any clinical studies that you might qualify for.

☎ Contact:
National Institute of Child Health
and Human Development
Bldg. 31, Room 2A32
Bethesda, MD 20892
(301) 496-5133

MALOCCLUSION

Clearinghouses/Hotlines

The National Institute of Dental Research (NIDR) will send you whatever publications and reprints of journal articles they have on Malocclusion. As a policy, however, NIDR will not refer you to other organizations or experts who study this condition. If you can't afford treatment, have your doctor call Dr. Albert Guckers at (301) 496-6241 to find out if NIDR is conducting any clinical studies that you might qualify for.

☎ Contact:
National Institute of Dental Research
Bldg. 31, Room 2C35
Bethesda, MD 20892
(301) 496-4261

MAMMOGRAMS

See also Breast Cancer

Clearinghouses/Hotlines

The National Cancer Institute (NCI) will send you whatever publications and reprints of journal articles they have on Mammography. They can also search their Physician's Data Query (PDQ) database to let you know if NCI is conducting any clinical studies on your disease.

☎ Contact:
National Cancer Institute

Bldg. 31, Room 10A24
Bethesda, MD 20892
(800) 4-CANCER
(301) 496-5583

Free Publications/Videos

The following publication is available from the Food & Drug Administration, (HFE-88), 5600 Fishers Ln., Rockville, MD 20857; (301) 443-3170.

- *Why Women Don't Get Mammograms (And Why They Should).* (#FDA90-1137)

The following publication is available from the Consumer Information Center, P.O. Box 100, Pueblo, CO 81002.

- *Smart Advice for Women 40 and Over: Have a Mammogram.* (#543Y)

The following publications are available from the Center for Devices and Radiological Health, (HFZ-210), Food and Drug Administration, 5600 Fishers Ln., Rockville, MD 20857; (301) 443-4690.

- *Center Supporting Efforts to Improve Mammography Quality.*
- *Mammography Benefits.*
- *Progress Against Breast Cancer.*
- *Breast Exposure: Nationwide Trends (BENT)*

The following publication is available from the National Cancer Institute, Bldg. 31, Room 10A24, Bethesda, MD 20892; (800) 4-CANCER, or (301) 496-5583.

- *Questions and Answers About Choosing a Mammography Facility.* (#91-3228)

MANDIBLE DISORDERS

Clearinghouses/Hotlines

The National Institute of Dental Research (NIDR) will send you whatever publications and reprints of journal articles they have on Mandible Disorders.

As a policy, however, NIDR will not refer you to other organizations or experts who study this condition. If you can't afford treatment, have your doctor call Dr. Albert Guckers at (301) 496-6241 to find out if NIDR is conducting any clinical studies that you might qualify for.

☎ Contact:
National Institute of Dental Research
Bldg. 31, Room 2C35
Bethesda, MD 20892
(301) 496-4261

MANIA

Clearinghouses/Hotlines

The National Institute of Mental Health (NIMH) will send you whatever publications and reprints of articles from texts and journals they have on Mania. They will also refer you to other organizations that are studying this condition. NIMH will also let you know of any clinical studies that may be studying Mania and looking for patients.

☎ Contact:
National Institute of Mental Health
5600 Fishers Lane
Room 15C05
Rockville, MD 20857
(301) 443-4515

MANIC-DEPRESSIVE PSYCHOSIS

Clearinghouses/Hotlines

The National Institute of Mental Health (NIMH) will send you whatever publications and reprints of articles from texts and journals they have on Manic-Depressive Psychosis. They will also refer you to other organizations that are studying this condition. NIMH will also let you know of any clinical studies that may be studying Manic-Depressive Psychosis and looking for patients.

☎ Contact:
National Institute of Mental Health
5600 Fishers Ln., Room 15C05
Rockville, MD 20857
(301) 443-4515

MAPLE SYRUP URINE DISEASE

Clearinghouses/Hotlines

The National Institute of Diabetes and Digestive and Kidney Diseases's (NIDDK) individual clearinghouses can search the Combined Health Information Database (CHID) and generate a bibliography of resources on Maple Syrup Urine Disease for you. They also will send you any publications and journal articles they may have on hand, and will refer you to other organizations that are studying this disease. If you can't afford treatment, have your doctor call NIDDK to find out if they are conducting any clinical studies that you might qualify for.

☎ Contact:
National Institute of Diabetes
and Digestive and Kidney Diseases
Bldg. 31, Room 9A04
Bethesda, MD 20892
(301) 496-3583

MARBLE BONE DISEASE

See Osteopetrosis

MARBURG VIRUS DISEASE

Clearinghouses/Hotlines

The National Institute on Allergy and Infectious Diseases (NIAID) can search the Combined Health Information Database (CHID) and generate a bibliography of resources on Marburg Virus Disease for you. They will also send you any publications and journal articles they may have on hand, and will refer you to researchers who are currently studying this disease. If you can't afford treatment, have your doctor call NIAID to find out if they are conducting any clinical studies that you might qualify for.

☎ Contact:
National Institute of Allergy
and Infectious Diseases
Bldg. 31, Room 7A32
Bethesda, MD 20892
(301) 496-5717

MARFAN SYNDROME

Clearinghouses/Hotlines

The National Institute on Allergy and Infectious Diseases (NIAID) can search the Combined Health Information Database (CHID) and generate a bibliography of resources on Marfan Syndrome for you. They will also send you any publications and journal articles they may have on hand, and will refer you to researchers who are currently studying this disease. If you can't afford treatment, have your doctor call NIAID to find out if they are conducting any clinical studies you might qualify for.

☎ Contact:
National Institute of Allergy
and Infectious Diseases
Bldg. 31, Room 7A32
Bethesda, MD 20892
(301) 496-5717

The National Institute of Arthritis and Musculo-skeletal and Skin Diseases (NIAMS) will send you whatever publications and reprints of articles from texts and journals they have on Marfan Syndrome. They will also refer you to other organizations that are studying this disease. NIAMS will also let you know of any clinical studies that may be studying this disease and looking for patients.

☎ Contact:
National Institute of Arthritis
and Musculoskeletal and Skin Diseases

Box AMS
Bethesda, MD 20892
(301) 495-4484

The National Heart, Lung, and Blood Institute (NHLBI) can search the Combined Health Information Database (CHID) and generate a bibliography of resources on Marfan Syndrome for you. They also will send you any publications and journal articles they may have on hand, and will refer you to other organizations that are studying this disease. If you can't afford treatment, have your doctor call NHLBI to find out if they are conducting any clinical studies that you might qualify for.

☎ Contact:
National Heart, Lung, and Blood Institute
Bldg. 31, Room 4A21
Bethesda, MD 20892
(301) 496-4236

Free Publications/Videos

The following publication is available from the National Arthritis and Musculoskeletal and Skin Diseases Information Clearinghouse, Box AMS, 9000 Rockville Pike, Bethesda, MD 20892; (301) 495-4484.

- *Advances in Treatment of the Marfan Syndrome.* (#AR06)

MARIJUANA

See also Drug Abuse

Clearinghouses/Hotlines

The National Clearinghouse for Alcohol and Drug Information is the central point within the Federal Government for current print and audiovisual materials about alcohol and other drugs. They have information tailored to parents, teachers, youth, and others, as well as information about organizations and groups concerned with alcohol and other drug problems. They have publications, reports, newsletters, videos, posters, and more, as well as being able to provide comprehensive alcohol and other drug resource referrals. Call for your free catalog.

☎ Contact:
National Clearinghouse for Alcohol
and Drug Information
P.O. Box 2345
Rockville, MD 20852
(800) 729-6686
(301) 468-2600

The National Eye Institute (NEI) can give you up-to-date information on Marijuana's Effect on Glaucoma. by searching the Combined Health Information Database (CHID) and MEDLINE and sending you bibliographies of resources, along with any journal articles they may have. They can also refer you to any other organizations that study this and other related diseases. NEI will also let you know of any clinical studies that may be studying this disease and looking for patients. Because of their small staff, NEI prefers that you submit your requests for information in writing.

☎ Contact:
National Eye Institute
Bldg. 31, Room 6A32
Bethesda, MD 20892
(301) 496-5248

Free Publications/Videos

The following publication on Marijuana is available from the National Clearinghouse for Alcohol and Drug Information, P.O. Box 2345, Rockville, Md 20852; (301) 468-2600.

- *Marijuana Update*. Gives basic information about the psychological and physiological effects.

MASTECTOMIES

See also Breast Cancer

Clearinghouses/Hotlines

The National Cancer Institute (NCI) will send you

whatever publications and reprints of journal articles they have on Mastectomies. They can also search their Physician's Data Query (PDQ) database to let you know if NCI is conducting any clinical studies on your disease.

☎ Contact:
National Cancer Institute
Building 31
Room 10A24
Bethesda, MD 20892
(800) 4-CANCER
(301) 496-5583

Free Publications/Videos

The following publication on Mastectomies is available from the National Cancer Institute, Bldg. 31, Room 10A24, Bethesda, MD 20892; (800) 4-CANCER, or (301) 496-5583.

- *Mastectomy: A Treatment for Breast Cancer*. (#91-658) Presents information about the different types of breast surgery.

MASTOCYTOSIS

Clearinghouses/Hotlines

The National Institute on Allergy and Infectious Diseases (NIAID) can search the Combined Health Information Database (CHID) and generate a bibliography of resources on Mastocytosis for you. They will also send you any publications and journal articles they may have on hand, and will refer you to researchers who are currently studying this disease. If you can't afford treatment, have your doctor call NIAID to find out if they are conducting any clinical studies that you might qualify for.

☎ Contact:
National Institute of Allergy
and Infectious Diseases
Building 31
Room 7A32
Bethesda, MD 20892
(301) 496-5717

MATERNAL AND CHILD HEALTH

Clearinghouses/Hotlines

The National Maternal and Child Health Clearinghouse has all kinds of information on maternal and child health issues. If the answer to your question can't be answered by any of their countless free publications, they can refer you to other national or local resources. If you still need further information, they search their own reference collection and send you what they find.

☎ Contact:
National Maternal and Child
Health Clearinghouse
38th & R Sts., NW
Washington, DC 20057
(703) 821-8955, ext. 254

Free Publications/Videos

The following publications on Maternal and Child Health are available from the National Maternal and Child Health Clearinghouse, 38th & R Sts., NW, Washington, DC 20057; (703) 821-8955, ext. 254.

- *Advances in the Prevention of Low Birthweight: An International Symposium.* (#EE02)
- *Annotated Bibliography: Educational Materials on DNA Techniques in Genetic Testing and Counseling.* (#E047)
- *Building Systems of Care for Children with HIV Infection and Their Families.* (#C064)
- *A Babysitter's Guide to PKU.* (#B265)
- *Chef Lo-Phe's Phe-Nominal Cookbook.* (#B322)
- *Children with HIV/AIDS: A Sourcebook for Caring.* (#C066)
- *Children With Special Health Care Needs: Resource Guide.* (#D009)
- *Clinical Programs for Mentally Retarded Children.* (#B169)
- *Cooley's Anemia: A Psychosocial Directory.* (#B221)
- *Dental Implications of Epilepsy.* (#B053)

- *Dental Health in Children With PKU.* (#B146)
- *Environmental Exposures and Pregnancy: Resource Guide.* (#DOO8)
- *Four Critical Junctures: Support for Parents of Children With Special Needs.* (#C016)
- *Finger Foods Are Fun.* (#B279)
- *Games That Teach: Learning by Doing for Preschoolers with PKU.* (#B280)
- *Guide to Breastfeeding the Infant with PKU.* (#B327)
- *Guidelines for Purchase of Services and Assistive Devices for Individuals With Communication Disorders.* (#B180)
- *Genetic Services: Abstracts of Active Projects FY 1991.* (#E007)
- *Genetic Services for Underserved Populations.* (#D047)
- *A Guide to Selected National Genetic Voluntary Organizations.* (#B359)
- *Human Genetics: Resource Guide.* (#D011)
- *Learning Together: Guide for Families with Genetic Disorders.* (#B076)
- *Management and Therapy of Sickle Cell Disease.* (#E069)
- *Newborn Screening for Genetic-Metabolic Diseases: Progress, Principles and Recommendations.* (#B048)
- *New Human Genetics: How Gene Splicing Helps Researchers Fight Inherited Diseases.* (#B194)
- *Nutrition During Lactation.* (#D081)
- *Nutrition During Lactation/Summary.* (#D080)
- *Nutrition Services For Children With Special Needs.* (#E027)
- *National Survey of Treatment Programs for PKU and Selected Other Inherited Metabolic Diseases.* (#C049)
- *New Parents' Guide to PKU.* (#B335)
- *Organizing Self-Help Groups: Resource Guide.* (#D012)
- *One-Stop Shopping for Perinatal Services.* (#D071)
- *The Open Door: Parent Participation in State Policymaking About Children with Special Health Needs.* (#B339)
- *Patient Education Materials: Resource Guide.* (#E008)
- *Pediatric Pulmonology Guidelines for the Care of Children With Chronic Lung Disease.* (#C035)

- *Playground Perspectives: A Curriculum Guide for Promoting Playground Safety.* (#C036)
- *Prenatal Care: Resource Guide.* (#D013)
- *Pre-term and Low Birthweight Infants: Resource Guide.* (#D015)
- *Problem Oriented Management of Sickle Cell Syndromes.* (#E042)
- *Recommendations for Feeding Normal Infants.* (#B060)
- *Reader's Guide for Parents of Children With Mental, Physical, or Emotional Disabilities.* (#B059)
- *Skim Milk in Infant Feeding.* (#B042)
- *Sickle Cell Anemia and Comprehensive Care: A New Horizon.* (#D065)
- *Sickle Cell: A Resource Guide for Families and Professionals.* (#D058)
- *Starting Early: A Guide to Federal Resources in Maternal and Child Health.* (#B349)
- *Surgeon General's Workshop on Self-Help and Public Health.* (#B351)
- *State Laws and Regulations Governing Newborn Screening.* (#B205)
- *Surgeon General's Workshop on Breastfeeding and Human Lactation.* (#B163)
- *Surgeon General's Workshop on Drunk Driving.* (#C044)
- *Surgeon General's Workshop on Children With Handicaps and Their Families.* (#B118)
- *Technology-Dependent Children: Hospital v. Home Care.* (#B316)
- *Understanding Your Health Insurance Options: A Guide For Families Who Have Children With Special Health Care Needs.* (#B353)
- *Understanding DNA Testing: A Basic Guide for Families.* (#D088)
- *Warning Signals: Basic Criteria for Tracking At Risk Infants and Toddlers.* (#B259)
- *Women Helping Women: Networks for Support and Caring.* (#D052)
- *The Federal Resource Directory.* Describes over 500 publications and audiovisual materials related to maternal and child health, an annotated listing of over 80 federal agencies and information centers, and a directory of federal, regional, and state maternal and child health programs.

MCARDLE'S DISEASE

Clearinghouses/Hotlines

The National Institute of Neurological Disorders and Stroke (NINDS) can send you only information they have in their publications list on McArdle's Disease. They cannot refer you to any experts. This Clearinghouse cannot directly give you information about any current clinical studies NINDS might be conducting on this illness, but you can find this information for yourself by looking under the National Institute of Neurological Disorders and Stroke in *Appendix A* at the end of this book.

☎ Contact:
National Institute of Neurological
Disorders and Stroke
Building 31
Room 8A06
Bethesda, MD 20892
(301) 496-5751
(800) 352-9424

MEASLES

See also Immunizations

Clearinghouses/Hotlines

The National Institute on Allergy and Infectious Diseases (NIAID) can search the Combined Health Information Database (CHID) and generate a bibliography of resources on Measles and Measles Encephalitis for you. They will also send you any publications and journal articles they may have on hand, and will refer you to researchers who are currently studying this disease. If you can't afford treatment, have your doctor call NIAID to find out if they are conducting any clinical studies that you might qualify for.

☎ Contact:
National Institute of Allergy
and Infectious Diseases
Bldg. 31, Room 7A32

Bethesda, MD 20892
(301) 496-5717

The National Institute of Neurological Disorders and Stroke (NINDS) can send you only information they have in their publications list on Measles Encephalitis. They cannot refer you to any experts. This Clearinghouse cannot directly give you information about any current clinical studies NINDS might be conducting on this illness, but you can find this information for yourself by looking under the National Institute of Neurological Disorders and Stroke in *Appendix A* at the end of this book.

☎ Contact:
National Institute of Neurological
Disorders and Stroke
Bldg. 31, Room 8A06
Bethesda, MD 20892
(301) 496-5751
(800) 352-9424

MEAT AND POULTRY

Clearinghouses/Hotlines

The U.S. Department of Agriculture's Meat & Poultry Hotline inspects and analyzes domestic and imported meat and poultry and establishes standards for processed meat and poultry products. They will answer your questions about the proper handling, preparation, and refrigeration, food poisoning, food additives, food labeling, sodium, and herbs.

☎ Contact:
U.S. Department of Agriculture
Room 1165-S
Washington, DC 20205
(800) 535-4555
(202) 447-9351

Free Publications/Videos

The following Congressional Research Service (CRS) report is available from either of your U.S. Senators' offices at the U.S. Capitol, Washington, DC 20510, or from your Congressional

Representative at the U.S. Capitol, Washington, DC 20515. You can also call in your request through the U.S. Capitol switchboard at (202) 224-3121. Be sure to include the full title and report number in your request.

- *Meat and Poultry Inspection: Background and Current Issues.* (#89-448 ENR)
- *HACCP (Hazard Analysis and Critical Control Point) in Meat, Poultry, and Seafood Inspection.* (#91-832 ENR)

MECHLORETHAMINE

Free Publications/Videos

The following publication is available from the National Cancer Institute, Bldg. 31, Room 10A24, Bethesda, MD 20892; (800) 4-CANCER, or (301) 496-5583.

- *Mecloretamina/Mechlorethamine.* Provides information about side effects, proper usage, and precautions of this anti-cancer drug.

MECONIUM ASPIRATION SYNDROME

Clearinghouses/Hotlines

The National Institute of Child Health and Human Development (NICHD) will send you whatever publications and reprints of journal articles they have on Meconium Aspiration Syndrome. If necessary, they will refer you to other experts or researchers in the field. If you can't afford treatment, have your doctor call NICHD to find out if they are conducting any clinical studies that you might qualify for.

☎ Contact:
National Institute of Child Health
and Human Development
Building 31, Room 2A32

Bethesda, MD 20892
(301) 496-5133

MEDICAL DEVICES

Clearinghouses/Hotlines

The Food and Drug Administration's Center for Devices and Radiological Health has all kinds of information on laws, regulations, and safe use of medical devices.

☎ Contact:
Center for Devices and Radiological
Health (HFZ-210)
Food and Drug Administration
5600 Fishers Ln.
Rockville, MD 20857
(301) 443-4690

Free Publications/Videos

The following publications on Medical Devises are available from the Center for Devices and Radiological Health (HFZ-210), Food and Drug Administration, 5600 Fishers Ln., Rockville, MD 20857, (301) 443-4690.

- *An Introduction to Medical Device Regulations.* (#FDA 87-4222)
- *Classifying Your Medical Devices.* (#FDA 87-4223)
- *Through the Bureaucratic Jungle: A Guide for the Confused Consumer.*
- *The Medical Device Amendments: 10 Years After.* (#FDA 86-4207)
- *Everything You Always Wanted to Know About the Medical Device Amendments...And Weren't Afraid to Ask.* (#FDA 84-4173)
- *Home Is Where The Medical Device Is.*
- *When You And Your Partner The Doctor Talk About Diagnosis.*
- *Medical Devices: Strengthening Consumer Protection.*
- *Medical Device Problem Reporting.* (#FDA 85-4196)

The following publication is available from the

Consumer Information Center, P.O. Box 100, Pueblo, CO 81002.

- *Getting Information from FDA...* about drugs, foods, pesticides, medical devices, radiation safety, pet foods, and more. (#593Z).

MEDICAL IMAGING

Free Publications/Videos

The following publication is available from the Food & Drug Administration, (HFE-88), 5600 Fishers Ln., Rockville, MD 20857; (301) 443-3170.

- *A Primer On Medical Imaging.* (#FDA90-3179)

The following publication is available from the Subcommittee on Health on Long-Term Care, Room 377, Ford HOB, 2nd & D Sts., SW, Washington, DC 20515; (202) 226-3381.

- *Recent Trends in Dubious and Quack Medical Devices.*

MEDICAL TESTING

Free Publications/Videos

The following publication is available from the Food & Drug Administration, (HFE-88), 5600 Fishers Ln., Rockville, MD 20857; (301) 443-3170.

- *Do It Yourself Medical Testing.* (#FDA89-4206)

MEDICARE AND MEDICAID

Clearinghouses/Hotlines

The Medicare Hotline can answer your questions

about Medicare, Medicaid, and Medigap. They can also refer you to the proper people to answer your questions they can't answer, as well as provide you with publications on your topic of interest. This is also the number to call if you suspect abuse or fraud of Medicare or Medicaid, as well as if you suspect improper sales practices of Medigap policies.

☎ Contact:
Health Care Financing Administration
330 Independence Ave., SW
Washington, DC 20201
(800) 638-6833
(800) 492-6603

The Health Care Financing Administration (HCFA) compiles statistics on Medicaid, health coverage for low-income, and Medicare, health coverage for the elderly. The data are broken down many ways such as populations, expenditures, and utilization. Each year they publish a HCFA statistics booklet that gives you significant summary information about health expenditures and HCFA programs.

☎ Contact:
Health Care Financing Administration
6325 Security Blvd.
Baltimore, MD 21207
(301) 597-3933

Free Publications/Videos

The following Medicare publications are available from the Health Care Financing Administration, 330 Independence Ave., SW, Washington, DC 20201, (800) 638-6833, (800) 492-6603.

- *Medicare 1991 Highlights.*
- *1992 Guide To Health Insurance for People With Medicare.*
- *The Medicare 1992 Handbook.*
- *Medicare Employer Health Plans 1991.*
- *Medicare and Coordinated Care Plans.*
- *Medicare Coverage for Second Surgical Opinions.*
- *Medicare Hospice Benefits.*
- *Medicare Savings For Qualified Beneficiaries.*

The following publications on Medicare are available from Health Care Financing

Administration, Room 577, East High Rise Building, 6325 Security Blvd., Baltimore, MD 21207.

- *How To Fill Out A Medicare Claim Form.* Gives you a step-by-step explanation of how to fill out this basic form in order to get reimbursed for medical bills.
- *A Brief Explanation of Medicare* and *A Guide to Health Insurance for People with Medicare.* Discuss what Medicare does and does not cover. They also cover Medigap and other supplementary private health insurance plans.

The following publication on Medicare is available from the Office of Technology Assessment, Washington, DC 20510-8025; (202) 224-8996.

- *Evaluation of the Oregon Medicaid Proposal.* (#OTA-H-531)

The following publications on Medicare are available from the Consumer Information Center, P.O. Box 100, Pueblo, CO 81002.

- *Medicare and Advance Directives.* Explains how to set up a living will or durable power of attorney to help you receive the medical treatment you want if you become physically or mentally unable to communicate. (#516Z).
- *Medicare Q&A.* Answers 60 commonly asked questions about Medicare - eligibility, enrollment, who pays deductibles, services, benefits and much more. (#517Z).
- *Medicare and Your Physician's Bill.* Explains how Medicare determines its payments for physicians' services and what to do if you disagree with a payment or charge. (#518Z).

The following video on Medicare is available from Modern Talking Picture Service, 5000 Park St. North, St. Petersburg, FL 33709; (800) 243-MTPS.

- *Understanding Insurance To Supplement Medicare.* Video explains recent changes to Medicare benefits and offers advice on how to shop around for supplemental insurance.

The following Congressional Research Service (CRS) reports on Medicare and Medicaid are available from either of your U.S. Senators' offices at the U.S. Capitol, Washington, DC 20510, or from your Congressional Representative at the U.S. Capitol, Washington, DC 20515. You can also call in your request through the U.S. Capitol switchboard at (202) 224-3121. Be sure to include the full title and report number in your request.

- *Medicaid: FY 90 Budget and Child Health Initiatives.* (#IB89031)
- *Medicaid: Reimbursement for Outpatient Prescription Drugs.* (#91-235 EPW)
- *Medicaid Services for Persons With Mental Retardation or Related Conditions.* (88-759)
- *Medicare: Geographic Variations in Payments for Physician Services.* (#88-775 EPW)
- *Medicare, Medicaid, and Maternal and Child Health Programs: An Overview of Major Legislation Enacted from 1980 Through 1986.* (#87-296 EPW)
- *Medicare: Prospective Payments for Inpatient Hospital Services; Archived Issue Brief.* (#IB87180)
- *Medicare's Prospective Payment System: An Analysis of the Financial Risk of Outlier Cases.* (#87-877 EPW)
- *Medicare's Prospective Payment System: The 98th and 99th Congresses.* (#87-862 EPW)
- *Medicare: Recalculating Payment Rates under the Prospective Payment System.* (#87-574 EPW)
- *Medicare Reimbursement: Selected References, 1986-1988.* (#88-679 L)
- *Medicare: Risk Contracts With Health Maintenance Organizations and Competitive Medical Plans.* (#88-138 EPW)
- *Medigap and Related Private Health Insurance Legislation in the 101st Congress.* (#91-140 EPW)
- *National Health Expenditures: Trends from 1960-1989.* (#91-588 EPW)
- *National Health Spending, 1989: A Description of Spending by Services and Payers.* (#91-527 EPW)
- *National Health Spending, 1990: A Description of Spending by Services and Payers.* (#91-814 EPW)
- *Patient Outcome Research and Practice Guidelines: A Plan for Research and Policy.* (#91-50 SPR)
- *A Prospective Payment System for Hospital-Based Physician Services under Medicare; a Report Prepared for the Subcommittee on Health.* (#87-715 EPW)
- *Public Health and the Congress: Selected References.* (#89-147 L)
- *Rationing Health Care.* (#90-346 EPW)
- *Rural Hospitals under Medicare's Prospective Payment System and the Omnibus Budget Reconciliation Act of 1986 (P.L. 99-509).* (#87-816 EPW)

MEDICATIONS

See also Drug Approval Process
See also Drug Evaluation

Clearinghouses/Hotlines

Are you taking a drug and want to know more about it? Are you considering taking a drug and want to know if it will really work for you? The Center for Drug Evaluation and Research is responsible for making sure that drugs and vaccines are safe and work the way they are supposed to, as well as making sure these products are labeled truthfully with the information that people need. This Center can provide you with free package inserts for drugs, which include information on dosage, chemistry, effects, recommendations, counter indications and more.

☎ Contact:
Drug Information Clearinghouse
Center for Drug Evaluation and Research
Food and Drug Administration
HFD 100, Room 14B45
5600 Fishers Lane
Rockville, MD 20857
(301) 295-8012

If you would like more information such as the research behind the approval of a particular drug, you need to submit a Freedom of Information Act (FOIA) request for that drug to the address below. The information you will receive is called the Summary Basis of Approval, which consists of the approval letter, approved label, the chemist's review, pharmacist's review and medical officer's review. There is a search and copy charge for this information.

☎ Contact:
FOIA Staff
HFI-35
Food and Drug Administration
5600 Fishers Lane
Rockville, MD 20857

Free Publications/Videos

The following publications on Medications are available from the Food & Drug Administration, (HFE-88), 5600 Fishers Ln., Rockville, MD 20857; (301) 443-3170.

- *Buying Medicine? Stop, Look, Look Again!.* (#FDA91-1175)
- *Questions About Your Medicines: Go Ahead, Ask.* (#FDA91-3166)
- *When Medications Don't Mix. Preventing Drug Interactions.* (#OM90-3009)
- *Doing More Good Than Harm With Children's Medications.* (#FDA91-3182)
- *Food and Drug Interactions.* (#OM89-3023)
- *Know The Right Way To Take Your Medicine.* (#FDA88-3164)
- *Here Are Some Things You Should Know About Prescription Drugs.* (#FDA84-3124)
- *Pharmacists Help Solve Medication Mysteries.* (#FDA91-3187)

The following publication on Medications is available from the Food and Drug Administration, (HFI-42), 5600 Fishers Ln., Rockville, MD 20857; (301) 443-3220.

- *Drug Bulletin.* Tracks the latest developments in the drug field, such drug reactions and new medical devices. Published on an as-needed basis.

The following publication on Medications is available from the General Accounting Office, P.O. Box 6015, Gaithersburg, MD 20877; (202) 275-6241.

- *Nonprescription Drugs: Over the Counter and Underemphasized.* Examines the Food and Drug Administration's procedures for approving and monitoring over-the-counter drugs in order to identify potential vulnerabilities in the procedures that could result in the approval and marketing of unsafe and ineffective drugs.

The following publications on Medications are available from the Consumer Information Center, P.O. Box 100, Pueblo, CO 81002.

- *Buying Medicine? Help Protect Yourself Against Tampering.* (#540Z).
- *Rx to OTC.* What you need to know about prescription medications that have become available over-the-counter. (#545Z).
- *Safe and Sure Self-Care with Over-the Counter Medicines.* Protect yourself by learning about labeling requirements and warnings. (#546Z).
- *When Do You Need An Antacid?* What an antacid is, and when and how to use one most effectively. Side effects to watch for and when to consult your doctor. (#547Z).

The following publication on Medications is available from the National Institute of General Medical Sciences, Bldg. 31, Room 4A52, Bethesda, MD 20892; (301) 496-7301.

- *Medicines And You.* Describes how your age, genes, and diet can affect the way medicines work in your body. (#81-2140)

The following Congressional Research Service (CRS) report on Medications is available from either of your U.S. Senators' offices at the U.S. Capitol, Washington, DC 20510, or from your Congressional Representative at the U.S. Capitol, Washington, DC 20515. You can also call in your request through the U.S. Capitol switchboard at (202) 224-3121. Be sure to include the full title and report number in your request.

- *Pharmaceutical Pricing and Patent Law.* (#91-748 E)

The following publication on Medications is available from the Superintendent of Documents, Government Printing Office, Washington, DC 20402; (202) 738-3238.

- *Prescription Drug Programs for Older Americans.* ($3.75) Taking Prescription medications is often a matter of life and death for millions of Americans. Many older Americans are unable to buy the drugs they need because the drugs are too expensive. The purpose of this report is to update Congress about the impact of using drug costs on public and private insurance programs, and analyze the extent to which they meet the need of providing drugs. This report includes a directory of pharmaceutical manufacturer indigent patient programs, listing names, addresses, program characteristics, names of drug products, and patient eligibility criteria. This directory is not only for the elderly, but for all indigent people. For more information, see the "How to Get Drug Companies to Fill Your Prescription For Free" section at the beginning of the book.

MEDICINAL PLANTS

Free Publications/Videos

The following publication on Medicinal Plants is available from the Science & Technology Division, Reference Section, Library of Congress, Washington, DC 20540; (202) 707-5580.

- *Medicinal Plants.* Reference guide designed to help locate further published material. (#91-8)

MEDITERRANEAN FEVER

Clearinghouses/Hotlines

The National Institute on Allergy and Infectious Diseases (NIAID) can search the Combined Health Information Database (CHID) and generate a bibliography of resources on Mediterranean Fever for you. They will also send you any publications and journal articles they may

have on hand, and will refer you to researchers who are currently studying this disease. If you can't afford treatment, have your doctor call NIAID to find out if they are conducting any clinical studies that you might qualify for.

☎ Contact:
National Institute of Allergy
and Infectious Diseases
Building 31
Room 7A32
Bethesda, MD 20892
(301) 496-5717

The National Institute of Arthritis and Musculoskeletal and Skin Diseases (NIAMS) will send you whatever publications and reprints of articles from texts and journals they have on Mediterranean Fever. They will also refer you to other organizations that are studying this condition. NIAMS will also let you know of any clinical studies that may be studying this disease and looking for patients.

☎ Contact:
National Institute of Arthritis
and Musculoskeletal and Skin Diseases
Box AMS
9000 Rockville Pike
Bethesda, MD 20892
(301) 495-4484

MEGALOBLASTIC ANEMIA

See Anemia

MEGAVITAMIN THERAPY

Clearinghouses/Hotlines

The Food and Nutrition Information Center can provide you with information regarding Vitamins and Vitamin Therapy. They can provide you with bibliographies on other information on the subject.

☎ Contact:
Food and Nutrition Information Service
National Agricultural Library

Room 304
Beltsville, MD 20705
(301) 504-5719

MEIGE'S SYNDROME (FACIAL DYSTONIA)

Clearinghouses/Hotlines

The National Institute on Deafness and Other Communicative Disorders (NIDCD) will send you whatever publications and reprints of journal articles they have on Meige's Syndrome (Facial Dystonia). If you need further information, they will refer you to other organizations that study this and other related disorders. NIDCD does not conduct any clinical studies for this or any other disorder.

☎ Contact:
National Institute on Deafness
and Other Communication Disorders
Building 31
Room 3C35
Bethesda, MD 20892
(301) 496-7243
(800) 241-1044
(301) 402-0252 (TDD)

The National Institute of Neurological Disorders and Stroke (NINDS) can send you only information they have in their publications list on Meige's Syndrome (Facial Dystonia). They cannot refer you to any experts. This Clearinghouse cannot directly give you information about any current clinical studies NINDS might be conducting on this illness, but you can find this information for yourself by looking under the National Institute of Neurological Disorders and Stroke in *Appendix A* at the end of this book.

☎ Contact:
National Institute of Neurological
Disorders and Stroke
Building 31
Room 8A06
Bethesda, MD 20892
(301) 496-5751
(800) 352-9424

MELANOMA

See also Cancer

Clearinghouses/Hotlines

The National Cancer Institute (NCI) will send you whatever publications and reprints of journal articles they have on Melanoma. They can also give you information on the state-of-the-art treatment for this disease, including specific treatment information for your stage of cancer. They can also search their Physician's Data Query (PDQ) database to let you know if NCI is conducting any clinical studies on your disease.

☎ Contact:
National Cancer Institute
Building 31
Room 10A24
Bethesda, MD 20892
(800) 4-CANCER
(301) 496-5583

The National Eye Institute (NEI) can give you up-to-date information on Melanoma by searching the Combined Health Information Database (CHID) and MEDLINE and sending you bibliographies of resources, along with any journal articles they may have. They can also refer you to any other organizations that study this and other related diseases. NEI will also let you know of any clinical studies that may be studying this disease and looking for patients. Because of their small staff, NEI prefers that you submit your requests for information in writing.

☎ Contact:
National Eye Institute
Building 31
Room 6A32
Bethesda, MD 20892
(301) 496-5248

Free Publications/Videos

The following publications on Melanoma are available from the National Cancer Institute, Bldg. 31, Room 10A24, Bethesda, MD 20892; (800) 4-CANCER, or (301) 496-5583.

- *Research Report: Melanoma.* (#89-3020)
- *What You Need to Know About Melanoma.* (#90-1563)

MELKERSON'S SYNDROME

Clearinghouses/Hotlines

The National Institute of Neurological Disorders and Stroke (NINDS) can send you only information they have in their publications list on Melkerson's Syndrome. They cannot refer you to any experts. This Clearinghouse cannot directly give you information about any current clinical studies NINDS might be conducting on this illness, but you can find this information for yourself by looking under the National Institute of Neurological Disorders and Stroke in *Appendix A* at the end of this book.

☎ Contact:
National Institute of Neurological
Disorders and Stroke
Building 31
Room 8A06
Bethesda, MD 20892
(301) 496-5751
(800) 352-9424

MELPHALAN

Free Publications/Videos

The following publication on Melphalan is available from the National Cancer Institute, Bldg. 31, Room 10A24, Bethesda, MD 20892; (800) 4-CANCER, or (301) 496-5583.

- *Melfalano/Melphalan.* Provides information about side effects, proper usage, and precautions of this anti-cancer drug.

MEMORY LOSS

Clearinghouses/Hotlines

The National Institute of Mental Health (NIMH) will send you whatever publications and reprints of articles from texts and journals they have on Memory Loss. They will also refer you to other organizations that are studying this condition. NIMH will also let you know of any clinical studies that may be studying this disease and looking for patients.

☎ Contact:
National Institute of Mental Health
5600 Fishers Ln., Room 15C05
Rockville, MD 20857
(301) 443-4515

The National Institute on Aging (NIA) will send you whatever publications and reprints of journal articles they have on Memory Loss. They cannot refer you to other experts if the information they have isn't sufficient for your purposes.

☎ Contact:
National Institute on Aging
Bldg. 31, Room 5C27
Bethesda, MD 20892
(301) 496-1752

The National Institute of Neurological Disorders and Stroke (NINDS) can send you only information they have in their publications list on Memory Loss. They cannot refer you to any experts. This Clearinghouse cannot directly give you information about any current clinical studies NINDS might be conducting on this topic, but you can find this information for yourself by looking under the National Institute of Neurological Disorders and Stroke in *Appendix A* at the end of this book.

☎ Contact:
National Institute of Neurological
Disorders and Stroke
Bldg. 31, Room 8A06
Bethesda, MD 20892
(301) 496-5751
(800) 352-9424

Free Publications/Videos

The following publication on Memory Loss is available from the National Institute of Neurological Disorders and Stroke, P.O. Box 5801, Bethesda, MD 20824; (800) 352-9424, or (301) 496-5751.

- *Memory Loss.* A collection of scientific articles, patient education pamphlets, and addresses of voluntary health associations.

MENIER'S DISEASE

Clearinghouses/Hotlines

The National Institute of Neurological Disorders and Stroke (NINDS) can send you only information they have in their publications list on Menier's Disease. They cannot refer you to any experts. This Clearinghouse cannot directly give you information about any current clinical studies NINDS might be conducting on this illness, but you can find this information for yourself by looking under the National Institute of Neurological Disorders and Stroke in *Appendix A* at the end of this book.

☎ Contact:
National Institute of Neurological
Disorders and Stroke
Bldg. 31, Room 8A06
Bethesda, MD 20892
(301) 496-5751
(800) 352-9424

MENINGITIS

Clearinghouses/Hotlines

The National Institute on Allergy and Infectious Diseases (NIAID) can search the Combined Health Information Database (CHID) and generate a bibliography of resources on Meningitis for you. They will also send you any publications and journal articles they may have on hand, and

will refer you to researchers who are currently studying this disease. If you can't afford treatment, have your doctor call NIAID to find out if they are conducting any clinical studies that you might qualify for.

☎ Contact:
National Institute of Allergy
and Infectious Diseases
Bldg. 31, Room 7A32
Bethesda, MD 20892
(301) 496-5717

The National Institute of Neurological Disorders and Stroke (NINDS) can send you only information they have in their publications list on Meningitis. They cannot refer you to any experts. This Clearinghouse cannot directly give you information about any current clinical studies NINDS might be conducting on this illness, but you can find this information for yourself by looking under the National Institute of Neurological Disorders and Stroke in *Appendix A* at the end of this book.

☎ Contact:
National Institute of Neurological
Disorders and Stroke
Bldg. 31, Room 8A06
Bethesda, MD 20892
(301) 496-5751
(800) 352-9424

Free Publications/Videos

The following publication is available from the National Institute of Neurological Disorders and Stroke, P.O. Box 5801, Bethesda, MD 20824; (800) 352-9424, or (301) 496-5751.

- *Encephalitis and Meningitis, Neurological Sequelae of Epilepsy.* A collection of scientific articles, patient education pamphlets, and addresses of voluntary health associations.

MENINGOCELE

Clearinghouses/Hotlines

The National Institute of Child Health and Human

Development (NICHD) will send you whatever publications and reprints of journal articles they have on Meningocele. If necessary, they will refer you to other experts or researchers in the field. If you can't afford treatment, have your doctor call NICHD to find out if they are conducting any clinical studies that you might qualify for.

☎ Contact:
National Institute of Child Health
and Human Development
Building 31
Room 2A32
Bethesda, MD 20892
(301) 496-5133

The National Institute of Neurological Disorders and Stroke (NINDS) can send you only information they have in their publications list on Meningocele. They cannot refer you to any experts. This Clearinghouse cannot directly give you information about any current clinical studies NINDS might be conducting on this topic, but you can find this information for yourself by looking under the National Institute of Neurological Disorders and Stroke in *Appendix A* at the end of this book.

☎ Contact:
National Institute of Neurological
Disorders and Stroke
Building 31
Room 8A06
Bethesda, MD 20892
(301) 496-5751
(800) 352-9424

MENKE'S DISEASE

Clearinghouses/Hotlines

The National Institute of Neurological Disorders and Stroke (NINDS) can send you only information they have in their publications list on Menke's Disease. They cannot refer you to any experts. This Clearinghouse cannot directly give you information about any current clinical studies NINDS might be conducting on this illness, but you can find this information for yourself by looking under the National Institute of

Neurological Disorders and Stroke in *Appendix A* at the end of this book.

☎ Contact:
National Institute of Neurological
Disorders and Stroke
Building 31
Room 8A06
Bethesda, MD 20892
(301) 496-5751
(800) 352-9424

MENOPAUSE

See also Estrogen

Clearinghouses/Hotlines

The National Institute on Aging (NIA) will send you whatever publications and reprints of journal articles they have on Menopause. They cannot refer you to other experts if the information they have isn't sufficient for your purposes.

☎ Contact:
National Institute on Aging
Building 31
Room 5C27
Bethesda, MD 20892
(301) 496-1752

Free Publications/Videos

The following publication on Menopause is available from the Office of Technology Assessment, Washington, DC 20510-8025; (202) 224-8996.

- *The Menopause, Hormone Therapy, and
    Women's Health-Background Paper.*
    (#OTA-BP-BA-88)

The following publication on Menopause is available from the National Institute on Aging, Bldg. 31, Room 5C27, Bethesda, MD 20892; (301) 496-1752.

- *The Menopause Time of Life.* (#86-2461)

MENSTRUATION

Clearinghouses/Hotlines

The National Institute of Child Health and Human Development (NICHD) will send you whatever publications and reprints of journal articles they have on Menstruation. If necessary, they will refer you to other experts or researchers in the field.

☎ Contact:
National Institute of Child Health
and Human Development
Building 31
Room 2A32
Bethesda, MD 20892
(301) 496-5133

Free Publications/Videos

The following video on Menstruation is available from Modern Talking Picture Service, 5000 Park St. North, St. Petersburg, FL 33709; (800) 243-MTPS.

- *Feminine Hygiene And You.* Video explains female reproductive system, menstrual cycle, vaginal secretions and infections.

MENTAL HEALTH IN CHILDREN

Free Publications/Videos

The National Institute of Mental Health (NIMH) conducts research and distributes their findings on Mental Health issues in Children. The following publications are available from NIMH, 5600 Fishers Lane, Room 15C05, Rockville, MD 20857; (301) 443-4515.

- *Helping the Hyperactive Child.*
- *Importance of Play.*
- *Learning While Growing: Cognitive Development.*

- *National Plan for Research on Child and Adolescent Mental Disorders.*
- *Plain Talk About Adolescence.*
- *Plain Talk About Raising Children.*
- *Pre-Term Babies.*
- *Research on Children and Adolescents with Mental, Behavioral and Development Disorders.*
- *Stimulating Baby Senses.*
- *When Parents Divorce.*
- *Information Packet on Use of Mental Health Services by Children and Adolescents.*
- *National Plan for Research on Child and Adolescent Mental Disorders.*
- *Working Bibliography on Behavioral and Emotional Disorders and Assessment Instruments in Mental Retardation.*

MENTAL ILLNESS

Clearinghouses/Hotlines

The National Institute of Mental Health (NIMH) maintains databases that index and abstract documents from the worldwide literature pertaining to Mental Illness. In addition to scientific journals, there are references to audiovisuals, dissertations, government documents and reports. Contact NIMH for searches on specific subjects.

☎ Contact:
National Institute of Mental Health
5600 Fishers Lane
Room 15C05
Rockville, MD 20857
(301) 443-4515

The National Institute on Aging (NIA) will send you whatever publications and reprints of journal articles they have on Mental Health and Aging. They cannot refer you to other experts if the information they have isn't sufficient for your purposes.

☎ Contact:
National Institute on Aging
Building 31
Room 5C27
Bethesda, MD 20892
(301) 496-1752

Free Publications/Videos

The following publications and videos on Mental Illness are available from the National Institute of Mental Health, 5600 Fishers Lane, Room 15C05, Rockville, MD 20857; (301) 443-4515.

- *Plain Talk About Physical Fitness and Mental Health.*
- *Plain Talk About Mutual Help Groups.*
- *You Are Not Alone: Facts About Mental Health and Mental Illness.*
- *Information Packet on Use of Mental Health Services by Children and Adolescents.*
- *National Plan for Research on Child and Adolescent Mental Disorders.*
- *Working Bibliography on Behavioral and Emotional Disorders and Assessment.*
- *Instruments in Mental Retardation.*
- *Caring for People with Severe Mental Disorders: A National Plan of Research to Improve Services.*
- *Medications for Mental Illness: What You Should Know About the Drugs Doctors Prescribe for Anxiety, Depression, Schizophrenia and Other Mental Disorders.* Booklet designed to help people understand how and why drugs can be used as part of the treatment for mental health problems. It includes questions you should ask your doctor, provides information on different classes of drugs, and things needing special consideration.
- *Just Like You and Me.* A video that features former mental patients who have made transition from hospitalization back to the community through the Transitional Employment Program. Include in your order a blank videocassette with enough minutes on it to tape the materials you request. (32 min.)
- *Making the Numbers Work for You.* A video that points out the need for timely, accurate statistical information from each State. Such information assists the Federal Government to compile figures on the needs and opportunities in promoting better mental health. Include in your order a blank videocassette with enough minutes on it to tape the materials you

request. (35 min.)
- *More Than A Grant.* A video that describes some of NIMH's programs and encourages Historically Black Colleges and Universities faculties and students to explore ways of obtaining support for research projects in the field of mental health. Include in your order a blank videocassette with enough minutes on it to tape the materials you request. (19 min.)
- *More Than A Passing Acquaintance.* Video that tells the story of how one community support program meets the challenge in providing services and opportunities for person who have made the transition from hospitalization back into the community. Include in your order a blank videocassette with enough minutes on it to tape the materials you request. (24 min.)
- *Windows Into the Brain.* Video that tells the story of three decades of scientific advances in brain imaging techniques. Include in your order a blank videocassette with enough minutes on it to tape the materials you request. (19 min.)
- *Plain Talk About the Stigma of Mental Illness.*
- *A Consumer's Guide to Mental Health Services.* Describes the services available from community mental health centers, details different kinds of therapy and mental health professionals, and provides a list of warning signals and tells what to do in a crisis situation.

The following Congressional Research Service (CRS) report on Mental Illness is available from either of your U.S. Senators' offices at the U.S. Capitol, Washington, DC 20510, or from your Congressional Representative at the U.S. Capitol, Washington, DC 20515. You can also call in your request through the U.S. Capitol switchboard at (202) 224-3121. Be sure to include the full title and report number in your request.

- *The Constitutional Rights of Mental Patients.* (#85-585 A)

The following publication on Mental Disorders is available from the Office of Technology Assessment, Washington, DC 20510-8025; (202) 224-8996.

- *The Biology of Mental Disorders*. (#OTA-BA-538)

The following publication on Mental Health is available from the Superintendent of Documents, Government Printing Office, Washington, DC 20402; (202) 783-3238.

- *Mental Health Directory 1990*. A comprehensive state-by-state listing of outpatient mental health clinics, psychiatric hospitals, Veterans Administration medical centers, residential treatment centers for emotionally disturbed children, mental health day/night facilities, community mental health centers, and general hospitals with separate psychiatric services. (#017-024-01419-2, $23)

The following publication on Mental Illness is available from the Office of Programs for the Homeless Mentally Ill, NIMH, Room 7C-06, 5600 Fishers Ln., Rockville, MD 20857; (301) 443-3706.

- *Synopses of NIMH-Funded Mental Health Services Demonstration Projects for the Homeless Mentally Ill.*

The following video on Mental Illness is available from the Office of Clinical Center Communications, Bldg. 10, Room 1C255, Bethesda, MD 20892; (301) 496-2563.

- *Phobias and Panic Disorders*. Video to help the general public make intelligent decisions.

MENTAL RETARDATION

Clearinghouses/Hotlines

The President's Committee on Mental Retardation has information on prevention of biomedical and environmental causes of Retardation, and family and community support services. Materials are also available on the legal rights of the mentally retarded and employment programs.

☎ Contact:
President's Committee on Mental Retardation
330 Independence Ave., SW, Room 4262
North Building
Washington, DC 20201
(202) 619-0634

The National Institute of Child Health and Human Development (NICHD) will send you whatever publications and reprints of journal articles they have on Mental Retardation. If necessary, they will refer you to other experts or researchers in the field. If you can't afford treatment, have your doctor call NICHD to find out if they are conducting any clinical studies that you might qualify for.

☎ Contact:
National Institute of Child Health
and Human Development
Bldg. 31, Room 2A32
Bethesda, MD 20892
(301) 496-5133

Free Publications/Videos

The following publication is available from the Science & Technology Division, Reference Section, Library of Congress, Washington, DC 20540; (202) 707-5580.

- *Mental Retardation*. Reference guide designed to help locate further published material. (#83-6)

The following publication is available from the National Institute of Child Health and Human Development, Bldg. 31, Room 2A32, Bethesda, MD 20892; (301) 496-5133.

- *Centers of Excellence: The Mental Retardation Research Centers*. (#86-2882)

The following publication is available from the National Maternal and Child Health Clearinghouse, 38th & R Sts., NW, Washington, DC 20057; (703) 821-8955, ext. 254.

- *Clinical Programs for Mentally Retarded Children*. (#B169)

The following publication is available from the National Institute of Mental Health, 5600 Fishers Ln., Room 15C05, Rockville, MD 20857; (301) 443-4515.

- *Instruments in Mental Retardation.*

MERCAPTOPURINE

Free Publications/Videos

The following publication is available from the National Cancer Institute, Bldg. 31, Room 10A24, Bethesda, MD 20892; (800) 4-CANCER, or (301) 496-5583.

- *Mercaptopurina/Mercaptopurine.* Provides information about side effects, proper usage, and precautions of this anti-cancer drug.

MERCURY POISONING

See also Seafood Inspection

Clearinghouses/Hotlines

The National Institute of Neurological Disorders and Stroke (NINDS) can send you only information they have in their publications list on Minamata Disease (Mercury Poisoning). They cannot refer you to any experts. This Clearinghouse cannot directly give you information about any current clinical studies NINDS might be conducting on this illness, but you can find this information for yourself by looking under the National Institute of Neurological Disorders and Stroke in *Appendix A* at the end of this book.

☎ Contact:
National Institute of Neurological
Disorders and Stroke
Bldg. 31, Room 8A06
Bethesda, MD 20892
(301) 496-5751
(800) 352-9424

MERCURY VAPOR LAMPS

Clearinghouses/Hotlines

The Food and Drug Administration's Center for Devices and Radiological Health has all kinds of information on laws, regulations, and safe use of medical devices.

☎ Contact:
Center for Devices and Radiological
Health (HFZ-210)
Food and Drug Administration
5600 Fishers Ln.
Rockville, MD 20857
(301) 443-4690

Free Publications/Videos

The following publications are available from the Center for Devices and Radiological Health, (HFZ-210), Food and Drug Administration, 5600 Fishers Ln., Rockville, MD 20857; (301) 443-4690.

- *Fact Sheet: The Hazards From Broken Mercury Vapor and Metal Halide Lamps.*
- *When A Broken Lamp Burns.*

MERCY KILLING

See Living Wills

METABOLIC DISORDERS

Clearinghouses/Hotlines

The National Institute of Diabetes and Digestive and Kidney Diseases's (NIDDK) individual clearinghouses can search the Combined Health Information Database (CHID) and generate a bibliography of resources on Metabolic Disorders for you. They also will send you any publications and journal articles they may have on hand, and will refer you to other organizations that are studying these disorders. If you can't afford treatment, have your doctor call NIDDK to find out if they are conducting any clinical studies that you might qualify for.

☎ Contact:
National Institute of Diabetes
and Digestive and Kidney Diseases
Bldg. 31, Room 9A04
Bethesda, MD 20892
(301) 496-3583

The National Institute of Child Health and Human Development (NICHD) will send you whatever publications and reprints of journal articles they have on Inborn Errors of Metabolism. If necessary, they will refer you to other experts or researchers in the field. If you can't afford treatment, have your doctor call NICHD to find out if they are conducting any clinical studies that you might qualify for.

☎ Contact:
National Institute of Child Health
and Human Development
Bldg. 31, Room 2A32
Bethesda, MD 20892
(301) 496-5133

The National Institute of Neurological Disorders and Stroke (NINDS) can send you only information they have in their publications list on Inborn Errors of Metabolism. They cannot refer you to any experts. This Clearinghouse cannot directly give you information about any current clinical studies NINDS might be conducting on this illness, but you can find this information for yourself by looking under the National Institute of Neurological Disorders and Stroke in *Appendix A* at the end of this book.

☎ Contact:
National Institute of Neurological
Disorders and Stroke
Bldg. 31, Room 8A06
Bethesda, MD 20892
(301) 496-5751
(800) 352-9424

Free Publications/Videos

The following publication on Metabolic Disorders

is available from the Office of Clinical Center Communications, National Institutes of Health, Building 10, Room 5C305, Bethesda, MD 20892; (301) 496-2563.

- *Obesity and Energy Metabolism.* Explains the relationship between too much food and too little exercise.

The following publications on Metabolic Disorders are available from the National Maternal and Child Health Clearinghouse, 38th & R Streets., NW, Washington, DC 20057; (703) 821-8955, ext. 254.

- *National Survey of Treatment Programs for PKU and Selected Other Inherited Metabolic Diseases.* (#C049)
- *Newborn Screening for Genetic-Metabolic Diseases: Progress, Principles and Recommendations.* (#B048)

METASTATIC TUMORS

See also Cancer

Clearinghouses/Hotlines

The National Institute of Neurological Disorders and Stroke (NINDS) can send you only information they have in their publications list on Metastatic Tumors of the Central Nervous System. They cannot refer you to any experts. This Clearinghouse cannot directly give you information about any current clinical studies NINDS might be conducting on this topic, but you can find this information for yourself by looking under the National Institute of Neurological Disorders and Stroke in *Appendix A* at the end of this book.

☎ Contact:
National Institute of Neurological
Disorders and Stroke
Building 31
Room 8A06
Bethesda, MD 20892
(301) 496-5751
(800) 352-9424

METHADONE

Clearinghouses/Hotlines

The Food and Drug Administration (FDA) is also responsible for regulating the dispensing of drugs for treatment of opiate addiction, including methadone. Contact the FDA for more information on this and other anti-addiction drugs and their uses.

☎ Contact:
Food and Drug Administration
5600 Fishers Lane
Rockville, MD 20857
(301) 295-8029

METHOTREXATE

Free Publications/Videos

The following publication is available from the National Cancer Institute, Bldg. 31, Room 10A24, Bethesda, MD 20892; (800) 4-CANCER, or (301) 496-5583.

- *Metrotrexato/Methotrexate*. Provides information about side effects, proper usage, and precautions of this anti-cancer drug.

MICROCEPHALY

Clearinghouses/Hotlines

The National Institute of Child Health and Human Development (NICHD) will send you whatever publications and reprints of journal articles they have on Microcephaly. If necessary, they will refer you to other experts or researchers in the field. If you can't afford treatment, have your doctor call NICHD to find out if they are conducting any clinical studies that you might qualify for.

☎ Contact:
National Institute of Child Health

and Human Development
Building 31
Room 2A32
Bethesda, MD 20892
(301) 496-5133

The National Institute of Neurological Disorders and Stroke (NINDS) can send you only information they have in their publications list on Microcephaly. They cannot refer you to any experts. This Clearinghouse cannot directly give you information about any current clinical studies NINDS might be conducting on this topic, but you can find this information for yourself by looking under the National Institute of Neurological Disorders and Stroke in *Appendix A* at the end of this book.

☎ Contact:
National Institute of Neurological
Disorders and Stroke
Building 31
Room 8A06
Bethesda, MD 20892
(301) 496-5751
(800) 352-9424

MICROTROPIA

Clearinghouses/Hotlines

The National Eye Institute (NEI) can give you up-to-date information on Microtropia by searching the Combined Health Information Database (CHID) and MEDLINE and sending you bibliographies of resources, along with any journal articles they may have. They can also refer you to any other organizations that study this and other related subjects. NEI will also let you know of any clinical studies that may be studying Microtropia and looking for patients. Because of their small staff, NEI prefers that you submit your requests for information in writing.

☎ Contact:
National Eye Institute
Building 31
Room 6A32
Bethesda, MD 20892
(301) 496-5248

MICROVASCULAR SURGERY

Clearinghouses/Hotlines

The National Institute of Neurological Disorders and Stroke (NINDS) can send you only information they have in their publications list on Microvascular Surgery. They cannot refer you to any experts. This Clearinghouse cannot directly give you information about any current clinical studies NINDS might be conducting on this topic, but you can find this information for yourself by looking under the National Institute of Neurological Disorders and Stroke in *Appendix A* at the end of this book.

☎ Contact:
National Institute of Neurological
Disorders and Stroke
Building 31
Room 8A06
Bethesda, MD 20892
(301) 496-5751
(800) 352-9424

MICROWAVES

Free Publications/Videos

The following publications on Microwaves are available from the Center for Devices and Radiological Health, (HFZ-210), Food and Drug Administration, 5600 Fishers Ln., Rockville, MD 20857; (301) 443-4690.

- *Keeping Up With The Microwave Revolution.*
- *Microwave Oven Radiation.* (#FDA 86-8120)

The following publication on Microwaves is available from the Food & Drug Administration, (HFE-88), 5600 Fishers Ln., Rockville, MD 20857; (301) 443-3170.

- *Food Safety And The Microwave.* (#OM91-3007)

MIDDLE EAR INFECTIONS

Clearinghouses/Hotlines

The National Institute on Deafness and Other Communicative Disorders (NIDCD) will send you whatever publications and reprints of journal articles they have on Middle Ear Infections. If you need further information, they will refer you to other organizations that study this and other related diseases. NIDCD does not conduct any clinical studies for this or any other disorder.

☎ Contact:
National Institute on Deafness
and Other Communication Disorders
Bldg. 31, Room 3C35
Bethesda, MD 20892
(301) 496-7243
(800) 241-1044
(301) 402-0252 (TDD)

The National Institute of Neurological Disorders and Stroke (NINDS) can send you only information they have in their publications list on Middle Ear Infection. They cannot refer you to any experts. This Clearinghouse cannot directly give you information about any current clinical studies NINDS might be conducting on this condition, but you can find this information for yourself by looking under the National Institute of Neurological Disorders and Stroke in *Appendix A* at the end of this book.

☎ Contact:
National Institute of Neurological
Disorders and Stroke
Bldg. 31, Room 8A06
Bethesda, MD 20892
(301) 496-5751
(800) 352-9424

MIGRAINES

Clearinghouses/Hotlines

The National Institute of Neurological Disorders and Stroke (NINDS) can send you only

information they have in their publications list on Migraine Headaches. They cannot refer you to any experts. This Clearinghouse cannot directly give you information about any current clinical studies NINDS might be conducting on this topic, but you can find this information for yourself by looking under the National Institute of Neurological Disorders and Stroke in *Appendix A* at the end of this book.

☎ Contact:
National Institute of Neurological
Disorders and Stroke
Bldg. 31, Room 8A06
Bethesda, MD 20892
(301) 496-5751
(800) 352-9424

MILITARY MEDICAL CARE

Clearinghouses/Hotlines

The following Congressional Research Service (CRS) reports on Military Medical Care are available from either of your U.S. Senators' offices at the U.S. Capitol, Washington, DC 20510, or from your Congressional Representative at the U.S. Capitol, Washington, DC 20515. You can also call in your request through the U.S. Capitol switchboard at (202) 224-3121. Be sure to include the full title and report number in your request.

- *Acquired Immune Deficiency Syndrome and Military Manpower Policy: Issue Brief.* (#IB87202)
- *Military Health Care/CHAMPUS Management Initiatives.* (#91-420 F)
- *Military Medical Care Services: Questions and Answers; Issue Brief.* (#IB87155)
- *Military Medical Care Services: Questions and Answers; Archived Issue Brief.* (#IB87155)

MILK

See also Lactose Intolerance

Clearinghouses/Hotlines

The National Institute of Diabetes and Digestive and Kidney Diseases's (NIDDK) individual clearinghouses can search the Combined Health Information Database (CHID) and generate a bibliography of resources on Milk Intolerance for you. They also will send you any publications and journal articles they may have on hand, and will refer you to other organizations that are studying this disease. If you can't afford treatment, have your doctor call NIDDK to find out if they are conducting any clinical studies that you might qualify for.

☎ Contact:
National Institute of Diabetes
and Digestive and Kidney Diseases
Bldg. 31, Room 9A04
Bethesda, MD 20892
(301) 496-3583

Food and Nutrition Information Center can provide you with a wealth of information on food and nutrition topics. They have bibliographies ready and a data base through which they can search any food or nutrition subject.

☎ Contact:
Food and Nutrition Information Center
National Agricultural Library
Room 304
Beltsville, MD 20705
(301) 504-5719

Free Publications/Videos

The following publication on Lactose Intolerance is available from the National Institute of Diabetes and Digestive and Kidney Diseases, Bldg. 31, Room 9A04, Bethesda, MD 20892; (301) 496-3583.

- *Lactose Intolerance.* (#91-2751)

The following Congressional Research Service (CRS) reports are available from either of your U.S. Senators' offices at the U.S. Capitol, Washington, DC 20510, or from your Congressional Representative at the U.S. Capitol, Washington, DC 20515. You can also call in your request through the U.S. Capitol switchboard at

(202) 224-3121. Be sure to include the full title and report number in your request.

- *Milk Standards: Grade A vs. Grade B.* (#91-589 ENR)
- *Nonfat Solids Standards for Milk: Proposed Legislative Changes.* (91-772 ENR)

MINORITY HEALTH CARE

Clearinghouses/Hotlines

The Office of Minority Health Resource Center (OMHRC) works to improve the health status of Asians, Pacific Islanders, Blacks, Hispanics, and Native Americans. They distribute accurate and timely information on health care issues through conferences and workshops, awarding of grants for innovative community health strategies developed by minority coalitions, and research on risk factors affecting these populations. The Resource Center has information on minority health-related data and information resources available at the Federal, state, and local levels and provides assistance and information to people interested in minority health.

OMHRC developed a strategy guide on methods for achieving the minority health goals. The *Closing the Gap* series of fact sheets on the priority areas that describe the extent to which specific minority groups are affected, detail avenues for prevention, and offer resources for additional information. They have a database of minority health-related publications, organizations and programs that concentrate on minority health. The Resource Persons Network consists of more than 2200 physicians, nurses, social workers, and health educators who provide expert technical assistance to minority community-based organizations, voluntary groups, and individuals needing assistance. The Resource Center can also provide you with information regarding audiovisual materials for minority populations and health-related funding resources.

☎ Contact:
Office of Minority Health
Resource Center

P.O. Box 37337
Washington, DC 20013
(800) 444-6472

Free Publications/Videos

The following publications on Minority Health Care are available from the Office of Minority Health Resource Center, P.O. Box 37337, Washington, DC 20013; (800) 444-6472.

- *Program/Project Description.*
- *Report of the Secretary's Task Force on Black and Minority Health.*
- *Violence and Homicide in Hispanic Communities: Conference Proceedings.*
- *Grants Fact Sheets.*
- *Closing the Gap.* A series of fact sheets that describe how specific minority groups are affected, detail avenues for prevention, and offer resources for additional information.
- *Infant Mortality Among U.S. Minority Populations (Part 1: Organizations and Programs)*
- *Infant Mortality Among U.S. Minority Populations (Part II: Publications and Audiovisual Materials)*
- *Health Aims*
- *Health Education*
- *Prevention & Beyond: A Framework for Collective Action*
- *Health Materials for Black Americans.*
- *Sources of Health Materials for Native Americans.*

The following publication on Minority Health Care is available from National Health Information Center, P.O. Box 1133, Washington, DC 20013; (800) 336-4797, (301) 565-4167.

- *Minority Health Care.* A resource list used in support of health education, will provide you with information about the symptoms of diseases, the link between lifestyle and diseases, and the importance of early detection and treatment as a necessary component of any health communication program. It also includes materials aimed specifically at minority audiences, with some in other languages.

The following publication on Minority Health Care is available from the National Clearinghouse for Alcohol Information, P.O. Box 2345, Rockville, MD 20852; (800) 729-6686, or (301) 468-2600.

- *Prevention Resource Guide: Asian and Pacific Islander Americans.* Contains facts, figures, resources, and other relevant information on alcohol abuse.

The following publication on Minority Health Care is available from the National Cancer Institute, Bldg. 31, Room 10A24, Bethesda, MD 20892; (800) 4-CANCER, or (301) 496-5583.

- *What Black Americans Should Know About Cancer.* Explains the rates and risks of cancer among Blacks and answers the most often asked questions as well as prevention, detection, treatment, and rehabilitation. (#82-1635)

The following publication on Minority Health Care is available from the National Arthritis and Musculoskeletal and Skin Diseases Information Clearinghouse, Box AMS, 9000 Rockville Pike, Bethesda, MD 20892; (301) 495-4484.

- *What Black Women Should Know About Lupus.* (#AR130, NIH91-3219)

The following publication on Minority Health Care is available from the High Blood Pressure Information Center, 4733 Bethesda Ave., Suite 530, Bethesda, MD 20814; (301) 951-3260.

- *Blacks and High Blood Pressure.* Offers information on prevalence and need for treatment.

The following publications on Minority Health Care are available from the National Institute of Diabetes and Digestive and Kidney Diseases, Bldg. 31, Room 9A04, Bethesda, MD 20892; (301) 496-3583.

- *Diabetes in Hispanics.* (#92-3265)
- *Diabetes in Black Americans.* (#92-3266)

MINORITY HEALTH PROFESSIONALS

Clearinghouses/Hotlines

The Bureau of Health Professions has produced fourteen videos to help recruit minorities and disadvantaged students into the health professions. The minority focus includes Blacks, American Indians, Alaskan Natives, and Hispanics, and covers a wide variety of medical professions.

☎ Contact:
Division of Disadvantaged Assistance
Bureau of Health Professions
5600 Fishers Lane
Room 8-20
Rockville, MD 20857
(301) 443-3843

MITOCHONDRIAL MYOPATHIES

Clearinghouses/Hotlines

The National Institute of Neurological Disorders and Stroke (NINDS) can provide you with information about Mitochondrial Myopathies, such as articles, pamphlets, and reports.

☎ Contact:
National Institute of Neurological
Disorders and Stroke
P.O. Box 5801
Bethesda, MD 20824
(800) 352-9424

Free Publications/Videos

The following publication is available from the National Institute of Neurological Disorders and Stroke, P.O. Box 5801, Bethesda, MD 20824; (800) 352-9424, or (301) 496-5751.

- *Mitochondrial Myopathies.* A collection of s cientific articles, patient education

pamphlets, and addresses of voluntary health associations.

MITOMYCIN

Free Publications/Videos

The following publication is available from the National Cancer Institute, Bldg. 31, Room 10A24, Bethesda, MD 20892; (800) 4-CANCER, or (301) 496-5583.

- *Mitomicina/Mitomycin.* Provides information about side effects, proper usage, and precautions of this anti-cancer drug.

MITOTANE

Free Publications/Videos

The following publication is available from the National Cancer Institute, Bldg. 31, Room 10A24, Bethesda, MD 20892; (800) 4-CANCER, or (301) 496-5583.

- *Mitotano/Mitotane.* Provides information about side effects, proper usage, and precautions of this anti-cancer drug.

MITRAL VALVE PROLAPSE

Clearinghouses/Hotlines

The National Heart, Lung, and Blood Institute (NHLBI) can search the Combined Health Information Database (CHID) and generate a bibliography of resources on Mitral Valve Prolapse for you. They also will send you any publications and journal articles they may have on hand, and will refer you to other organizations that are studying this subject. If you can't afford treatment, have your doctor call NHLBI to find out if they are conducting any clinical studies that you might qualify for.

☎ Contact:
National Heart, Lung, and Blood Institute
Bldg. 31, Room 4A21
Bethesda, MD 20892
(301) 496-4236

Free Publications/Videos

The following publication is available from the National Heart, Lung, and Blood Institute, Bldg. 31, Room 4A21, Bethesda, MD 20892; (301) 496-4236.

- *NHLBI Facts About...Mitral Valve Prolapse.* Discusses the condition and treatment.

MIXED CONNECTIVE TISSUE DISEASE

Clearinghouses/Hotlines

The National Institute of Arthritis and Musculoskeletal and Skin Diseases (NIAMS) will send you whatever publications and reprints of articles from texts and journals they have on Mixed Connective Tissue Disease. They will also refer you to other organizations that are studying this disease. NIAMS will also let you know of any clinical studies that may be studying this disease and looking for patients.

☎ Contact:
National Institute of Arthritis
and Musculoskeletal and Skin Diseases
Box AMS
Bethesda, MD 20892
(301) 495-4484

MOLDS

Clearinghouses/Hotlines

The National Institute of Allergy and Infectious

Diseases (NIAID) conducts and supports research on the causes of allergic, immunologic, and infectious diseases, and to develop better means of preventing, diagnosing, and treating illness. Some of the studies underway look at the role of the immune system in chronic diseases, such as arthritis, and at disorders of the immune system, as in asthma. Brochures and reports are available on a wide variety of topics.

☎ Contact:
National Institute of Allergy
and Infectious Diseases
Bldg. 31, Room 7A32
Bethesda, MD 20892
(301) 496-5717

Free Publications/Videos

The following publication on Molds is available from the National Institute of Allergy and Infectious Diseases, Bldg. 31, Room 7A32, Bethesda, MD 20892; (301) 496-5717.

- *Mold Allergy.* (#84-797)

The following publication on Molds is available from the Food & Drug Administration, (HFE-88), 5600 Fishers Ln., Rockville, MD 20857; (301) 443-3170.

- *Danger Lurks Among the Molds.* (#FDA81-2143)

MONGOLISM

See Down Syndrome

MONONUCLEOSIS

Clearinghouses/Hotlines

The National Institute on Allergy and Infectious Diseases (NIAID) can search the Combined Health Information Database (CHID) and generate a bibliography of resources on Mononucleosis for you. They will also send you any publications and journal articles they may have on hand, and will refer you to researchers who are currently studying this disease. If you can't afford treatment, have your doctor call NIAID to find out if they are conducting any clinical studies that you might qualify for.

☎ Contact:
National Institute of Allergy
and Infectious Diseases
Bldg. 31, Room 7A32
Bethesda, MD 20892
(301) 496-5717

MONOZYGOTIC TWINS

See Twins

MORTALITY RATE

Clearinghouses/Hotlines

The National Center for Health Statistics (NCHS) collects, analyzes, and distributes data on health in the United States. Materials available include statistical data on health, nutrition, vital statistics such as births and divorces, health care delivery, dental health, health resources utilization, health care personnel, families, contraception, and health care economics.

☎ Contact:
National Center for Health Statistics
6525 Belcrest Rd., Room 1064
Hyattsville, MD 20782
(301) 436-8500

MOTOR NEURON DISEASE

Clearinghouses/Hotlines

The National Institute of Neurological Disorders

and Stroke (NINDS) can send you only information they have in their publications list on Motor Neuron Disease. They cannot refer you to any experts. This Clearinghouse cannot directly give you information about any current clinical studies NINDS might be conducting on this illness, but you can find this information for yourself by looking under the National Institute of Neurological Disorders and Stroke in *Appendix A* at the end of this book.

☎ Contact:
National Institute of Neurological
Disorders and Stroke
Bldg. 31, Room 8A06
Bethesda, MD 20892
(301) 496-5751
(800) 352-9424

MOVEMENT DISORDERS

Clearinghouses/Hotlines

The National Institute of Neurological Disorders and Stroke (NINDS) can send you only information they have in their publications list on Hereditary Movement Disorders. They cannot refer you to any experts. This Clearinghouse cannot directly give you information about any current clinical studies NINDS might be conducting on this topic, but you can find this information for yourself by looking under the National Institute of Neurological Disorders and Stroke in *Appendix A* at the end of this book.

☎ Contact:
National Institute of Neurological
Disorders and Stroke
Bldg. 31, Room 8A06
Bethesda, MD 20892
(301) 496-5751
(800) 352-9424

MOYA-MOYA DISEASE

Clearinghouses/Hotlines

The National Institute of Neurological Disorders and Stroke (NINDS) can send you only information they have in their publications list on Moya-Moya Disease. They cannot refer you to any experts. This Clearinghouse cannot directly give you information about any current clinical studies NINDS might be conducting on this illness, but you can find this information for yourself by looking under the National Institute of Neurological Disorders and Stroke in *Appendix A* at the end of this book.

☎ Contact:
National Institute of Neurological
Disorders and Stroke
Bldg. 31, Room 8A06
Bethesda, MD 20892
(301) 496-5751
(800) 352-9424

Free Publications/Videos

The following publication on Moya-Moya is available from the National Institute of Neurological Disorders and Stroke, P.O. Box 5801, Bethesda, MD 20824; (800) 352-9424, or (301) 496-5751.

- *Moya-moya Disease*. A collection of scientific articles, patient education pamphlets, and addresses of voluntary health associations.

MRI

Clearinghouses/Hotlines

The Food and Drug Administration's Center for Devices and Radiological Health has all kinds of information on laws, regulations, and safe use of Medical Resonance Imaging.

☎ Contact:
Center for Devices and Radiological
Health (HFZ-210)
Food and Drug Administration
5600 Fishers Ln.
Rockville, MD 20857
(301) 443-4690

Free Publications/Videos

The following publications on MRI are available from the Center for Devices and Radiological Health, (HFZ-210), Food and Drug Admin., 5600 Fishers Ln., Rockville, MD 20857; (301) 443-4690.

- *Panel Finds MRI A Generally Safe Modality for Imaging.*
- *NMR Offers a Better Focus on What's Inside Us.*
- *NMR Imaging Devices.*

MSG

See Chinese Restaurant Syndrome

MUCOPOLY-SACCHARIDOSIS

Clearinghouses/Hotlines

The National Institute of Arthritis and Musculoskeletal and Skin Diseases (NIAMS) will send you whatever publications and reprints of articles from texts and journals they have on Mucopolysaccharidosis. They will also refer you to other organizations that are studying this disease. NIAMS will also let you know of any clinical studies that may be studying this disease and looking for patients.

☎ Contact:
National Institute of Arthritis
and Musculoskeletal and Skin Diseases
Box AMS
Bethesda, MD 20892
(301) 495-4484

MULTI-INFARCT DEMENTIA

See also Aging

Clearinghouses/Hotlines

The National Institute on Aging (NIA) will send you whatever publications and reprints of journal articles they have on Multi-Infarct Dementia. They cannot refer you to other experts if the information they have isn't sufficient for your purposes.

☎ Contact:
National Institute on Aging
Bldg. 31, Room 5C27
Bethesda, MD 20892
(301) 496-1752

The National Institute of Neurological Disorders and Stroke (NINDS) can send you only information they have in their publications list on Multi-Infarct Dementia. They cannot refer you to any experts. This Clearinghouse cannot directly give you information about any current clinical studies NINDS might be conducting on this illness, but you can find this information for yourself by looking under the National Institute of Neurological Disorders and Stroke in *Appendix A* at the end of this book.

☎ Contact:
National Institute of Neurological
Disorders and Stroke
Bldg. 31, Room 8A06
Bethesda, MD 20892
(301) 496-5751
(800) 352-9424

MULTIPLE SCLEROSIS

Clearinghouses/Hotlines

The National Institute of Neurological Disorders and Stroke (NINDS) can send you only information they have in their publications list on Multiple Sclerosis. They cannot refer you to any experts. This Clearinghouse cannot directly give you information about any current clinical studies NINDS might be conducting on this illness, but you can find this information for yourself by looking under the National Institute of Neurological Disorders and Stroke in *Appendix A* at the end of this book.

☎ Contact:
National Institute of Neurological
Disorders and Stroke
Building 31
Room 8A06
Bethesda, MD 20892
(301) 496-5751
(800) 352-9424

The National Institute on Deafness and Other
Communicative Disorders (NIDCD) will send you
whatever publications and reprints of journal
articles they have on Multiple Sclerosis. If you
need further information, they will refer you to
other organizations that study this and other
related diseases. NIDCD does not conduct any
clinical studies for this or any other disorder.

☎ Contact:
National Institute on Deafness
and Other Communication Disorders
Building 31
Room 3C35
Bethesda, MD 20892
(301) 496-7243
(800) 241-1044
(301) 402-0252 (TDD)

Free Publications/Videos

The following publication on Multiple Sclerosis is
available from the National Institutes of Health
Clinical Center, Bldg. 10, Room 1C255, Bethesda,
MD 20892; (301) 496-2563.

- *Multiple Sclerosis*. Booklet written to help the
  general public make intelligent decisions.
  (#90-3015)

The following publications on Multiple Sclerosis
are available from the National Institute of
Neurological Disorders and Stroke, Bldg. 31,
Room 8A06, Bethesda, MD 20892; (301) 496-
5751, or (800) 352-9424.

- *Multiple Sclerosis*. (#81-75)
- *Multiple Sclerosis*. Discusses hope through
  research.
- *Multiple Sclerosis 1990*. Annual or Biennial
  Research Updates.

MUMPS

See also Immunizations

Clearinghouses/Hotlines

The National Institute on Allergy and Infectious
Diseases (NIAID) can search the Combined
Health Information Database (CHID) and
generate a bibliography of resources on Mumps
for you. They will also send you any publications
and journal articles they may have on hand, and
will refer you to researchers who are currently
studying this disease. If you can't afford
treatment, have your doctor call NIAID to find out
if they are conducting any clinical studies that you
might qualify for.

☎ Contact:
National Institute of Allergy
and Infectious Diseases
Bldg. 31, Room 7A32
Bethesda, MD 20892
(301) 496-5717

MUSCULAR DYSTROPHY

Clearinghouses/Hotlines

The National Institute of Neurological Disorders
and Stroke (NINDS) can send you only
information they have in their publications list on
Muscular Dystrophy. They cannot refer you to
any experts. This Clearinghouse cannot directly
give you information about any current clinical
studies NINDS might be conducting on this illness,
but you can find this information for yourself by
looking under the National Institute of
Neurological Disorders and Stroke in *Appendix A*
at the end of this book.

☎ Contact:
National Institute of Neurological
Disorders and Stroke
Bldg. 31, Room 8A06
Bethesda, MD 20892
(301) 496-5751
(800) 352-9424

The National Institute of Arthritis and Musculoskeletal and Skin Diseases (NIAMS) will send you whatever publications and reprints of articles from texts and journals they have on Infantile Muscular Atrophy. They will also refer you to other organizations that are studying this disease. NIAMS will also let you know of any clinical studies that may be studying this disease and looking for patients.

☎ Contact:
National Institute of Arthritis
and Musculoskeletal and Skin Diseases
Box AMS
Bethesda, MD 20892
(301) 495-4484

Free Publications/Videos

The following publication is available from the National Institute of Neurological Disorders and Stroke, P.O. Box 5801, Bethesda, MD 20824; (800) 352-9424, or (301) 496-5751.

- *Muscular Dystrophy*. Contains a collection of scientific articles, patient education pamphlets, and addresses of voluntary health associations.

MUSCULAR FATIGUE

Clearinghouses/Hotlines

The National Institute of Neurological Disorders and Stroke (NINDS) can send you only information they have in their publications list on Muscular Fatigue. They cannot refer you to any experts. This Clearinghouse cannot directly give you information about any current clinical studies NINDS might be conducting on this condition, but you can find this information for yourself by looking under the National Institute of Neurological Disorders and Stroke in *Appendix A* at the end of this book.

☎ Contact:
National Institute of Neurological
Disorders and Stroke
Bldg. 31, Room 8A06

Bethesda, MD 20892
(301) 496-5751
(800) 352-9424

MYASTHENIA GRAVIS

Clearinghouses/Hotlines

The National Institute of Neurological Disorders and Stroke (NINDS) can send you only information they have in their publications list on Myasthenia Gravis. They cannot refer you to any experts. This Clearinghouse cannot directly give you information about any current clinical studies NINDS might be conducting on this illness, but you can find this information for yourself by looking under the National Institute of Neurological Disorders and Stroke in *Appendix A* at the end of this book.

☎ Contact:
National Institute of Neurological
Disorders and Stroke
Bldg. 31, Room 8A06
Bethesda, MD 20892
(301) 496-5751
(800) 352-9424

Free Publications/Videos

The following publication is available from the National Institute of Neurological Disorders and Stroke, P.O. Box 5801, Bethesda, MD 20824; (800) 352-9424, or (301) 496-5751.

- *Myasthenia Gravis*. Collection of scientific articles, patient education pamphlets, and addresses of voluntary health associations.

MYCOBACTERIAL INFECTIONS

Clearinghouses/Hotlines

The National Institute on Allergy and Infectious Diseases (NIAID) can search the Combined

Health Information Database (CHID) and generate a bibliography of resources on Mycobacterial Infections for you. They will also send you any publications and journal articles they may have on hand, and will refer you to researchers who are currently studying this disease. If you can't afford treatment, have your doctor call NIAID to find out if they are conducting any clinical studies that you might qualify for.

☎ Contact:
National Institute of Allergy
and Infectious Diseases
Bldg. 31, Room 7A32
Bethesda, MD 20892
(301) 496-5717

MYCOSES

Clearinghouses/Hotlines

The National Institute on Allergy and Infectious Diseases (NIAID) can search the Combined Health Information Database (CHID) and generate a bibliography of resources on Mycoses for you. They will also send you any publications and journal articles they may have on hand, and will refer you to researchers who are currently studying this disease. If you can't afford treatment, have your doctor call NIAID to find out if they are conducting any clinical studies that you might qualify for.

☎ Contact:
National Institute of Allergy
and Infectious Diseases
Bldg. 31, Room 7A32
Bethesda, MD 20892
(301) 496-5717

MYCOSIS FUNGOIDES

Clearinghouses/Hotlines

The National Cancer Institute (NCI) will send you whatever publications and reprints of journal

articles they have on Mycosis Fungoides. They can also give you information on the state-of-the-art treatment for this disease, including specific treatment information for your stage of cancer. They can also search their Physician's Data Query (PDQ) database to let you know if NCI is conducting any clinical studies on your disease.

☎ Contact:
National Cancer Institute
Bldg. 31, Room 10A24
Bethesda, MD 20892
(800) 4-CANCER
(301) 496-5583

MYCOTOXINS

Clearinghouses/Hotlines

National Institute of Environmental Health Sciences (NIEHS) will send you whatever publications and journal articles they can locate on specific questions about Mycotoxins. If necessary they can put you in contact with researchers studying this issue. NIEHS does not conduct any clinical studies.

☎ Contact:
National Institute of Environmental
Health Sciences
P.O. Box 12233
Research Triangle Park, NC 27709
(919) 541-3345

MYELODYSPLASTIC SYNDROMES

Clearinghouses/Hotlines

The National Heart, Lung, and Blood Institute (NHLBI) can search the Combined Health Information Database (CHID) and generate a bibliography of resources on Myelodysplastic Syndromes for you. They also will send you any publications and journal articles they may have on hand, and will refer you to other organizations that are studying this disease. If you can't afford treatment, have your doctor call NHLBI to find out if they are conducting any clinical studies that you might qualify for.

☎ Contact:
National Heart, Lung, and Blood Institute
Bldg. 31, Room 4A21
Bethesda, MD 20892
(301) 496-4236

MYELOFIBROSIS

Clearinghouses/Hotlines

The National Institute of Arthritis and Musculoskeletal and Skin Diseases (NIAMS) will send you whatever publications and reprints of articles from texts and journals they have on Myelofibrosis. They will also refer you to other organizations that are studying this disease. NIAMS will also let you know of any clinical studies that may be studying this disease and looking for patients.

☎ Contact:
National Institute of Arthritis
and Musculoskeletal and Skin Diseases
Box AMS
9000 Rockville Pike
Bethesda, MD 20892
(301) 495-4484

The National Heart, Lung, and Blood Institute (NHLBI) can search the Combined Health Information Database (CHID) and generate a bibliography of resources on Myelofibrosis for you. They also will send you any publications and journal articles they may have on hand, and will refer you to other organizations that are studying this disease. If you can't afford treatment, have your doctor call NHLBI to find out if they are conducting any clinical studies that you might qualify for.

☎ Contact:
National Heart, Lung, and Blood Institute
Bldg. 31, Room 4A21
Bethesda, MD 20892
(301) 496-4236

The National Cancer Institute (NCI) will send you whatever publications and reprints of journal articles they have on Myelofibrosis. They can also give you information on the state-of-the-art treatment for this disease, including specific treatment information for your stage of cancer. They can also search their Physician's Data Query (PDQ) database to let you know if NCI is conducting any clinical studies on your disease.

☎ Contact:
National Cancer Institute
Bldg. 31, Room 10A24
Bethesda, MD 20892
(800) 4-CANCER
(301) 496-5583

MYELOMA

Clearinghouses/Hotlines

The National Cancer Institute (NCI) will send you whatever publications and reprints of journal articles they have on Myeloma. They can also give you information on the state-of-the-art treatment for this disease, including specific treatment information for your stage of cancer. They can also search their Physician's Data Query (PDQ) database to let you know if NCI is conducting any clinical studies on your disease.

☎ Contact:
National Cancer Institute
Bldg. 31, Room 10A24
Bethesda, MD 20892
(800) 4-CANCER
(301) 496-5583

Free Publications/Videos

The following publication is available from the National Cancer Institute, Bldg. 31, Room 10A24, Bethesda, MD 20892; (800) 4-CANCER, or (301) 496-5583.

- *What You Need to Know About Multiple Myeloma.* (#90-1575)

MYOCARDIAL INFARCTION

See also Heart Disease

Clearinghouses/Hotlines

The National Heart, Lung, and Blood Institute (NHLBI) can search the Combined Health Information Database (CHID) and generate a bibliography of resources on Myocardial Infarction for you. They also will send you any publications and journal articles they may have on hand, and will refer you to other organizations that are studying this subject. If you can't afford treatment, have your doctor call NHLBI to find out if they are conducting any clinical studies that you might qualify for.

☎ Contact:
National Heart, Lung, and Blood Institute
Bldg. 31, Room 4A21
Bethesda, MD 20892
(301) 496-4236

MYOCLONUS

Clearinghouses/Hotlines

The National Institute of Neurological Disorders and Stroke (NINDS) can send you only information they have in their publications list on Myoclonus. They cannot refer you to any experts. This Clearinghouse cannot directly give you information about any current clinical studies NINDS might be conducting on this condition, but you can find this information for yourself by looking under the National Institute of Neurological Disorders and Stroke in *Appendix A* at the end of this book.

☎ Contact:
National Institute of Neurological
Disorders and Stroke
Bldg. 31, Room 8A06
Bethesda, MD 20892
(301) 496-5751
(800) 352-9424

MYOFASCIAL PAIN SYNDROME

Clearinghouses/Hotlines

The National Institute of Arthritis and Musculoskeletal and Skin Diseases (NIAMS) will send you whatever publications and reprints of articles from texts and journals they have on Myofascial Pain Syndrome. They will also refer you to other organizations that are studying this disease. NIAMS will also let you know of any clinical studies that may be studying this disease and looking for patients.

☎ Contact:
National Institute of Arthritis
and Musculoskeletal and Skin Diseases
Box AMS
9000 Rockville Pike
Bethesda, MD 20892
(301) 495-4484

MYOPIA

Clearinghouses/Hotlines

The National Eye Institute (NEI) can give you up-to-date information on Myopia by searching the Combined Health Information Database (CHID) and MEDLINE and sending you bibliographies of resources, along with any journal articles they may have. They can also refer you to any other organizations that study this and other related conditions. NEI will also let you know of any clinical studies that may be studying this disease and looking for patients. Because of their small staff, NEI prefers that you submit your requests for information in writing.

☎ Contact:
National Eye Institute
Bldg. 31, Room 6A32
Bethesda, MD 20892
(301) 496-5248

MYOSITIS

Clearinghouses/Hotlines

The National Institute of Arthritis and Musculoskeletal and Skin Diseases (NIAMS) will send you whatever publications and reprints of articles from texts and journals they have on Myositis. They will also refer you to other organizations that are studying this disease. NIAMS will also let you know of any clinical studies that may be studying this disease and looking for patients.

☎ Contact:
National Institute of Arthritis
and Musculoskeletal and Skin Diseases
Box AMS
9000 Rockville Pike
Bethesda, MD 20892
(301) 495-4484

The National Institute of Neurological Disorders and Stroke (NINDS) can send you only information they have in their publications list on Myositis. They cannot refer you to any experts. This Clearinghouse cannot directly give you information about any current clinical studies NINDS might be conducting on this condition, but you can find this information for yourself by looking under the National Institute of Neurological Disorders and Stroke in *Appendix A* at the end of this book.

☎ Contact:
National Institute of Neurological
Disorders and Stroke
Bldg. 31, Room 8A06
Bethesda, MD 20892
(301) 496-5751
(800) 352-9424

MYOTONIA

Clearinghouses/Hotlines

The National Institute of Arthritis and Musculoskeletal and Skin Diseases (NIAMS) will send you whatever publications and reprints of articles from texts and journals they have on Myotonia. They will also refer you to other organizations that are studying this disease. NIAMS will also let you know of any clinical studies that may be studying this disease and looking for patients.

☎ Contact:
National Institute of Arthritis
and Musculoskeletal and Skin Diseases
Box AMS
9000 Rockville Pike
Bethesda, MD 20892
(301) 495-4484

The National Institute of Neurological Disorders and Stroke (NINDS) can send you only information they have in their publications list on Myotonia. They cannot refer you to any experts. This Clearinghouse cannot directly give you information about any current clinical studies NINDS might be conducting on this illness, but you can find this information for yourself by looking under the National Institute of Neurological Disorders and Stroke in *Appendix A* at the end of this book.

☎ Contact:
National Institute of Neurological
Disorders and Stroke
Bldg. 31, Room 8A06
Bethesda, MD 20892
(301) 496-5751
(800) 352-9424

The National Institute of Child Health and Human Development (NICHD) will send you whatever publications and reprints of journal articles they have on Myotonia Congenita. If necessary, they will refer you to other experts or researchers in the field. If you can't afford treatment, have your doctor call NICHD to find out if they are conducting any clinical studies that you might qualify for.

☎ Contact:
National Institute of Child Health
and Human Development
Building 31
Room 2A32
Bethesda, MD 20892
(301) 496-5133

- N -

NARCOLEPSY

Clearinghouses/Hotlines

The National Institute of Neurological Disorders and Stroke (NINDS) can send you only information they have in their publications list on Narcolepsy. They cannot refer you to any experts. This Clearinghouse cannot directly give you information about any current clinical studies NINDS might be conducting on this illness, but you can find this information for yourself by looking under the National Institute of Neurological Disorders and Stroke in *Appendix A* at the end of this book.

☎ Contact:
National Institute of Neurological
Disorders and Stroke
Bldg. 31, Room 8A06
Bethesda, MD 20892
(301) 496-5751
(800) 352-9424

Free Publications/Videos

The following publications are available from the National Institute of Neurological Disorders and Stroke, P.O. Box 5801, Bethesda, MD 20824; (800) 352-9424, or (301) 496-5751.

- *Narcolepsy*. Contains a collection of scientific articles, patient education pamphlets, and addresses of voluntary health associations.
- *Narcolepsy*. (#89-1637) Fact sheet on symptoms and treatment.

NATIONAL HEALTH INSURANCE

See Health Insurance

NATIVE AMERICANS

See also Minority Health Care

Clearinghouses/Hotlines

The Indian Health Services (IHS) provides comprehensive health services through IHS facilities, tribally contracted hospitals, health centers, school health centers, and health stations. Reports, directories, brochures, and pamphlets are available.

☎ Contact:
Indian Health Service
5600 Fishers Lane
Rockville, MD 20857
(301) 443-3593

Free Publications/Videos

The following publication on Native American Health Care is available from the Office of Technology Assessment, 600 Pennsylvania Ave., SE, Washington, DC 20510; (202) 224-8996.

- *Indian Health Care*. A report to Congress. Ask for the summary report.

The following publication on Native American Health Care is available from the National Clearinghouse for Alcohol Information, P.O. Box 2345, Rockville, MD 20852; (800) 729-6686, or (301) 468-2600.

- *Prevention Resource Guide: American Indians/Native Alaskans*. Contains facts, figures, resources, and other relevant information on alcohol abuse.

The following Congressional Research Service (CRS) report on Native American Health Care is available from either of your U.S. Senators' offices at the U.S. Capitol, Washington, DC 20510, or from your Congressional Representative at the U.S. Capitol, Washington, DC 20515. You can also call in your request through the U.S. Capitol switchboard at (202) 224-3121. Be sure to include the full title and report number in your request.

- *Native Americans: Nutrition and Diet-Related Diseases.* (#87-246 SPR)

NATURAL CHILDBIRTH

See Childbirth

NEARSIGHTEDNESS

Clearinghouses/Hotlines

The National Eye Institute (NEI) can give you up-to-date information on Nearsightedness by searching the Combined Health Information Database (CHID) and MEDLINE and sending you bibliographies of resources, along with any journal articles they may have. They can also refer you to any other organizations that study this and other related conditions. NEI will also let you know of any clinical studies that may be studying Nearsightedness and looking for patients. Because of their small staff, NEI prefers that you submit your requests for information in writing.

☎ Contact:
National Eye Institute
Building 31
Room 6A32
Bethesda, MD 20892
(301) 496-5248

NEMALINE MYOPATHY

Clearinghouses/Hotlines

The National Institute of Neurological Disorders and Stroke (NINDS) can send you only information they have in their publications list on Nemaline Myopathy (Floppy Baby). They cannot refer you to any experts. This Clearinghouse cannot directly give you information about any current clinical studies NINDS might be conducting on this illness, but you can find this information for yourself by looking under the National Institute of Neurological Disorders and Stroke in *Appendix A* at the end of this book.

☎ Contact:
National Institute of Neurological
Disorders and Stroke
Building 31
Room 8A06
Bethesda, MD 20892
(301) 496-5751
(800) 352-9424

NEOPLASIA

Clearinghouses/Hotlines

The National Institute of Diabetes and Digestive and Kidney Diseases's (NIDDK) individual clearinghouses can search the Combined Health Information Database (CHID) and generate a bibliography of resources on Neoplasia for you. They also will send you any publications and journal articles they may have on hand, and will refer you to other organizations that are studying this issue. If you can't afford treatment, have your doctor call NIDDK to find out if they are conducting any clinical studies that you might qualify for.

☎ Contact:
National Institute of Diabetes
and Digestive and Kidney Diseases
Building 31
Room 9A04
Bethesda, MD 20892
(301) 496-3583

Free Publications/Videos

The following publication on Neoplasia is available from the National Institute of Diabetes and Digestive and Kidney Diseases, Bldg. 31, Room 9A04, Bethesda, MD 20892; (301) 496-3583.

- *Familial Multiple Endocrine Neoplasia Type 1.* (#92-3048)

NEONATAL ASPHYXIA

Clearinghouses/Hotlines

The National Institute of Neurological Disorders and Stroke (NINDS) can send you only information they have in their publications list on Neonatal Asphyxia. They cannot refer you to any experts. This Clearinghouse cannot directly give you information about any current clinical studies NINDS might be conducting on this topic, but you can find this information for yourself by looking under the National Institute of Neurological Disorders and Stroke in *Appendix A* at the end of this book.

☎ Contact:
National Institute of Neurological
Disorders and Stroke
Bldg. 31, Room 8A06
Bethesda, MD 20892
(301) 496-5751
(800) 352-9424

NEONATAL RESPIRATORY DISTRESS SYNDROME

Free Publications/Videos

The following publication is available from the National Heart, Lung and Blood Institute, Bldg. 31, Room 4A21, Bethesda, MD 20892; (301) 496-4236.

- *Neonatal Respiratory Distress Syndrome.* (#87-2893)

NEPHRITIS

Clearinghouses/Hotlines

The National Institute of Diabetes and Digestive and Kidney Diseases's (NIDDK) individual clearinghouses can search the Combined Health Information Database (CHID) and generate a bibliography of resources on Nephritis for you. They also will send you any publications and journal articles they may have on hand, and will refer you to other organizations that are studying this disease. If you can't afford treatment, have your doctor call NIDDK to find out if they are conducting any clinical studies that you might qualify for.

☎ Contact:
National Institute of Diabetes
and Digestive and Kidney Diseases
Building 31
Room 9A04
Bethesda, MD 20892
(301) 496-3583

NEPHROCALCINOSIS

Clearinghouses/Hotlines

The National Institute of Diabetes and Digestive and Kidney Diseases's (NIDDK) individual clearinghouses can search the Combined Health Information Database (CHID) and generate a bibliography of resources on Nephrocalcinosis for you. They also will send you any publications and journal articles they may have on hand, and will refer you to other organizations that are studying this disease. If you can't afford treatment, have your doctor call NIDDK to find out if they are conducting any clinical studies that you might qualify for.

☎ Contact:
National Institute of Diabetes
and Digestive and Kidney Diseases
Bldg. 31, Room 9A04
Bethesda, MD 20892
(301) 496-3583

The National Institute of Arthritis and Musculoskeletal and Skin Diseases (NIAMS) will send you whatever publications and reprints of articles from texts and journals they have on Nephrocalcinosis. They will also refer you to other organizations that are studying this condition. NIAMS will also let you know of any clinical studies that may be studying this disease and looking for patients.

☎ Contact:
National Institute of Arthritis
and Musculoskeletal and Skin Diseases
Box AMS
9000 Rockville Pike
Bethesda, MD 20892
(301) 495-4484

NEPHROLITHIASIS

Clearinghouses/Hotlines

The National Institute of Diabetes and Digestive and Kidney Diseases's (NIDDK) individual clearinghouses can search the Combined Health Information Database (CHID) and generate a bibliography of resources on Nephrolithiasis for you. They also will send you any publications and journal articles they may have on hand, and will refer you to other organizations that are studying this disease. If you can't afford treatment, have your doctor call NIDDK to find out if they are conducting any clinical studies that you might qualify for.

☎ Contact:
National Institute of Diabetes
and Digestive and Kidney Diseases
Bldg. 31, Room 9A04
Bethesda, MD 20892
(301) 496-3583

NEPHROTIC SYNDROME

Clearinghouses/Hotlines

The National Institute of Diabetes and Digestive and Kidney Diseases's (NIDDK) individual clearinghouses can search the Combined Health Information Database (CHID) and generate a bibliography of resources on Nephrotic Syndrome for you. They also will send you any publications and journal articles they may have on hand, and will refer you to other organizations that are

studying this disease. If you can't afford treatment, have your doctor call NIDDK to find out if they are conducting any clinical studies that you might qualify for.

☎ Contact:
National Institute of Diabetes
and Digestive and Kidney Diseases
Bldg. 31, Room 9A04
Bethesda, MD 20892
(301) 496-3583

NERVE DAMAGE

Clearinghouses/Hotlines

The National Institute of Neurological Disorders and Stroke (NINDS) can send you only information they have in their publications list on Nerve Damage. They cannot refer you to any experts. This Clearinghouse cannot directly give you information about any current clinical studies NINDS might be conducting on this topic, but you can find this information for yourself by looking under the National Institute of Neurological Disorders and Stroke in *Appendix A* at the end of this book.

☎ Contact:
National Institute of Neurological
Disorders and Stroke
Bldg. 31, Room 8A06
Bethesda, MD 20892
(301) 496-5751
(800) 352-9424

NEURAL TUBE DEFECTS

See also Birth Defects

Clearinghouses/Hotlines

The National Institute of Neurological Disorders and Stroke (NINDS) can send you only information they have in their publications list on Neural Tube Defects. They cannot refer you to any experts. This Clearinghouse cannot directly give you information about any current clinical studies NINDS might be conducting on this topic, but you can find this information for yourself by looking under the National Institute of Neurological Disorders and Stroke in *Appendix A* at the end of this book.

☎ Contact:
National Institute of Neurological
Disorders and Stroke
Bldg. 31, Room 8A06
Bethesda, MD 20892
(301) 496-5751
(800) 352-9424

The National Institute of Child Health and Human Development (NICHD) will send you whatever publications and reprints of journal articles they have on Neural Tube Defects. If necessary, they will refer you to other experts or researchers in the field. If you can't afford treatment, have your doctor call NICHD to find out if they are conducting any clinical studies that you might qualify for.

☎ Contact:
National Institute of Child Health
and Human Development
Bldg. 31, Room 2A32
Bethesda, MD 20892
(301) 496-5133

NEURALGIA

Clearinghouses/Hotlines

The National Institute of Neurological Disorders and Stroke (NINDS) can send you only information they have in their publications list on Neuralgia. They cannot refer you to any experts. This Clearinghouse cannot directly give you information about any current clinical studies NINDS might be conducting on this condition, but you can find this information for yourself by looking under the National Institute of Neurological Disorders and Stroke in *Appendix A* at the end of this book.

☎ Contact:
National Institute of Neurological
Disorders and Stroke

Bldg. 31, Room 8A06
Bethesda, MD 20892
(301) 496-5751
(800) 352-9424

NEURODERMATITIS

Clearinghouses/Hotlines

The National Institute of Arthritis and Musculoskeletal and Skin Diseases Clearinghouse can provide you with information regarding Neurodermatitis. They can search the Combined Health Information Database (CHID) and send you reprints of texts and journal articles, as well as refer you to other organizations.

☎ Contact:
National Arthritis and Musculoskeletal
and Skin Diseases Information Clearinghouse
Box AMS
9000 Rockville Pike
Bethesda, MD 20892
(301) 495-4484

NEURO-OPHTHALMOLOGY

Clearinghouses/Hotlines

The National Eye Institute (NEI) can give you up-to-date information on Neuro-Ophthalmology by searching the Combined Health Information Database (CHID) and MEDLINE and sending you bibliographies of resources, along with any journal articles they may have. They can also refer you to any other organizations that study this and other related subjects. Because of their small staff, NEI prefers that you submit your requests for information in writing.

☎ Contact:
National Eye Institute
Building 31
Room 6A32
Bethesda, MD 20892
(301) 496-5248

NEUROAXONAL DYSTROPHY

Clearinghouses/Hotlines

The National Institute of Neurological Disorders and Stroke (NINDS) can send you only information they have in their publications list on Neuroaxonal Dystrophy. They cannot refer you to any experts. This Clearinghouse cannot directly give you information about any current clinical studies NINDS might be conducting on this illness, but you can find this information for yourself by looking under the National Institute of Neurological Disorders and Stroke in *Appendix A* at the end of this book.

☎ Contact:
National Institute of Neurological
Disorders and Stroke
Building 31
Room 8A06
Bethesda, MD 20892
(301) 496-5751
(800) 352-9424

NEUROBLASTOMA

Clearinghouses/Hotlines

The National Cancer Institute (NCI) will send you whatever publications and reprints of journal articles they have on Neuroblastoma. They can also give you information on the state-of-the-art treatment for this disease, including specific treatment information for your stage of cancer. They can also search their Physician's Data Query (PDQ) database to let you know if NCI is conducting any clinical studies on your disease.

☎ Contact:
National Cancer Institute
Bldg. 31, Room 10A24
Bethesda, MD 20892
(800) 4-CANCER
(301) 496-5583

NEUROFIBROMATOSIS

Clearinghouses/Hotlines

The National Institute on Deafness and Other Communicative Disorders (NIDCD) will send you whatever publications and reprints of journal articles they have on Neurofibromatosis (von Recklinghausen's). If you need further information, they will refer you to other organizations that study this and other related diseases. NIDCD does not conduct any clinical studies for this or any other disorder.

☎ Contact:
National Institute on Deafness
and Other Communication Disorders
Bldg. 31, Room 3C35
Bethesda, MD 20892
(301) 496-7243
(800) 241-1044
(301) 402-0252 (TDD)

The National Institute of Neurological Disorders and Stroke (NINDS) can send you only information they have in their publications list on Neurofibromatosis (von Recklinghausen's). They cannot refer you to any experts. This Clearinghouse cannot directly give you information about any current clinical studies NINDS might be conducting on this illness, but you can find this information for yourself by looking under the National Institute of Neurological Disorders and Stroke in *Appendix A* at the end of this book.

☎ Contact:
National Institute of Neurological
Disorders and Stroke
Bldg. 31, Room 8A06
Bethesda, MD 20892
(301) 496-5751
(800) 352-9424

Free Publications/Videos

The following publications on Neurofibromatosis are available from the National Institute of Neurological Disorders and Stroke, P.O. Box 5801, Bethesda, MD 20824; (800) 352-9424, or (301) 496-5751.

- *Neurofibromatosis*. (#83-2126) Fact sheet on symptoms and treatment.
- *Neurofibromatosis*. Contains a collection of scientific articles, patient education pamphlets, and addresses of voluntary health associations.

NEUROGENIC ARTHROPATHY

Clearinghouses/Hotlines

The National Institute of Neurological Disorders and Stroke (NINDS) can send you only information they have in their publications list on Neurogenic Arthropathy. They cannot refer you to any experts. This Clearinghouse cannot directly give you information about any current clinical studies NINDS might be conducting on this topic, but you can find this information for yourself by looking under the National Institute of Neurological Disorders and Stroke in *Appendix A* at the end of this book.

☎ Contact:
National Institute of Neurological
Disorders and Stroke
Building 31
Room 8A06
Bethesda, MD 20892
(301) 496-5751
(800) 352-9424

NEUROLOGICAL DISORDERS

Clearinghouses/Hotlines

The National Institute of Neurological Disorders and Stroke (NINDS) can send you only information they have in their publications list on Neurological Disorders. They cannot refer you to any experts. This Clearinghouse cannot directly give you information about any current clinical studies NINDS might be conducting on this topic,

but you can find this information for yourself by looking under the National Institute of Neurological Disorders and Stroke in *Appendix A* at the end of this book.

☎ Contact:
National Institute of Neurological
Disorders and Stroke
Building 31
Room 8A06
Bethesda, MD 20892
(301) 496-5751
(800) 352-9424

Free Publications/Videos

The following publication on Neurological Disorders is available from the National Institute of Neurological Disorders and Stroke, P.O. Box 5801, Bethesda, MD 20824; (800) 352-9424, or (301) 496-5751.

- *Neurological Disorders: Voluntary Health Agencies and Other Patient Resources (a directory)*.

NEUROPATHIES

Clearinghouses/Hotlines

The National Institute of Neurological Disorders and Stroke (NINDS) can send you only information they have in their publications list on Neuropathies. They cannot refer you to any experts. This Clearinghouse cannot directly give you information about any current clinical studies NINDS might be conducting on this condition, but you can find this information for yourself by looking under the National Institute of Neurological Disorders and Stroke in *Appendix A* at the end of this book.

☎ Contact:
National Institute of Neurological
Disorders and Stroke
Bldg. 31, Room 8A06
Bethesda, MD 20892
(301) 496-5751
(800) 352-9424

NEUROSCIENCE

Free Publications/Videos

The following publication on Neuroscience is available from the Office of Technology Assessment, 600 Pennsylvania Ave., SE, Washington, DC 20510; (202) 224-8996.

- *Impacts of Neuroscience*. A report to Congress. Ask for the summary report. (#BP-BA-24)

NEUROSCLEROSIS

Clearinghouses/Hotlines

The National Institute of Neurological Disorders and Stroke (NINDS) can send you only information they have in their publications list on Neurosclerosis. They cannot refer you to any experts. This Clearinghouse cannot directly give you information about any current clinical studies NINDS might be conducting on this illness, but you can find this information for yourself by looking under the National Institute of Neurological Disorders and Stroke in *Appendix A* at the end of this book.

☎ Contact:
National Institute of Neurological
Disorders and Stroke
Bldg. 31, Room 8A06
Bethesda, MD 20892
(301) 496-5751
(800) 352-9424

NEUROTOXICITY

Free Publications/Videos

The following publication is available from the National Institute of Neurological Disorders and Stroke, P.O. Box 5801, Bethesda, MD 20824;

(800) 352-9424, or (301) 496-5751.

- *Neurotoxicity*. Contains a collection of scientific articles, patient education pamphlets, and addresses of voluntary health associations.

NEWBORN SCREENING

Clearinghouses/Hotlines

The National Maternal and Child Health Clearinghouse has all kinds of information on maternal and child health issues, such as pregnancy, child and adolescent health, and human genetics. If the answer to your question can't be answered by any of their countless free publications, they can refer you to other National or local resources. If you still need further information, they search their own reference collection and send you what they find.

☎ Contact:
National Maternal and Child
Health Clearinghouse
38th & R Sts., NW
Washington, DC 20057
(703) 821-8955, ext. 254

Free Publications/Videos

The following publication is available from the National Maternal and Child Health Clearinghouse, 38th & R Sts., NW, Washington, DC 20057; (703) 821-8955, ext. 254.

- *State Laws and Regulations Governing New- -born Screening.* (#B205)

NIEMANN-PICK DISEASE

Clearinghouses/Hotlines

The National Institute of Neurological Disorders and Stroke (NINDS) can send you only

information they have in their publications list on Niemann-Pick Disease. They cannot refer you to any experts. This Clearinghouse cannot directly give you information about any current clinical studies NINDS might be conducting on this illness, but you can find this information for yourself by looking under the National Institute of Neurological Disorders and Stroke in *Appendix A* at the end of this book.

☎ Contact:
National Institute of Neurological
Disorders and Stroke
Building 31
Room 8A06
Bethesda, MD 20892
(301) 496-5751
(800) 352-9424

The National Eye Institute (NEI) can give you up-to-date information on Niemann-Pick Disease. by searching the Combined Health Information Database (CHID) and MEDLINE and sending you bibliographies of resources, along with any journal articles they may have. They can also refer you to any other organizations that study this and other related diseases. NEI will also let you know of any clinical studies that may be studying this disease and looking for patients. Because of their small staff, NEI prefers that you submit your requests for information in writing.

☎ Contact:
National Eye Institute
Building 31
Room 6A32
Bethesda, MD 20892
(301) 496-5248

Free Publications/Videos

The following publication on Niemann-Pick Disease is available from the National Institute of Neurological Disorders and Stroke, P.O. Box 5801, Bethesda, MD 20824; (800) 352-9424, or (301) 496-5751.

- *Niemann-Pick Disease.* Contains a collection of scientific articles, patient education pamphlets, and addresses of voluntary health associations.

NIGHT BLINDNESS

Clearinghouses/Hotlines

The National Eye Institute (NEI) can give you up-to-date information on Night Blindness by searching the Combined Health Information Database (CHID) and MEDLINE and sending you bibliographies of resources, along with any journal articles they may have. They can also refer you to any other organizations that study this and other related conditions. NEI will also let you know of any clinical studies that may be studying Night Blindness and looking for patients. Because of their small staff, NEI prefers that you submit your requests for information in writing.

☎ Contact:
National Eye Institute
Bldg. 31, Room 6A32
Bethesda, MD 20892
(301) 496-5248

NOISE, EFFECTS OF

Clearinghouses/Hotlines

The National Institute of Environmental Health Sciences (NIEHS) will send you whatever publications and journal articles they can locate on specific questions about the health effects of Noise. If necessary they can put you in contact with researchers studying this issue. NIEHS does not conduct any clinical studies.

☎ Contact:
National Institute of Environmental
Health Sciences
P.O. Box 12233
Research Triangle Park, NC 27709
(919) 541-3345

The National Institute on Deafness and Other Communicative Disorders (NIDCD) will send you whatever publications and reprints of journal articles they have on the health effects of Noise. If you need further information, they will refer you to other organizations that study this and other related diseases. NIDCD does not conduct any clinical studies for this or any other disorder.

☎ Contact:
National Institute on Deafness
and Other Communication Disorders
Building 31
Room 3C35
Bethesda, MD 20892
(301) 496-7243
(800) 241-1044
(301) 402-0252 (TDD)

The National Institute of Neurological Disorders and Stroke (NINDS) can send you only information they have in their publications list on the neurological effects of Noise. They cannot refer you to any experts. This Clearinghouse cannot directly give you information about any current clinical studies NINDS might be conducting on this topic, but you can find this information for yourself by looking under the National Institute of Neurological Disorders and Stroke in *Appendix A* at the end of this book.

☎ Contact:
National Institute of Neurological
Disorders and Stroke
Building 31
Room 8A06
Bethesda, MD 20892
(301) 496-5751
(800) 352-9424

NONGONOCOCCAL URETHRITIS

Clearinghouses/Hotlines

The Sexually Transmitted Diseases Hotline offers valuable information to the public about a wide range of sexually transmitted diseases, including Nongonococcal Urethritis and how to protect yourself from contracting them.

☎ Contact:
National Sexually Transmitted Diseases Hotline
P.O. Box 13827
Research Triangle Park, NC 27709
(800) 227-8922

NONPRESCRIPTION DRUGS

See also Medications

Free Publications/Videos

The following publication is available from the General Accounting Office, P.O. Box 6015, Gaithersburg, MD 20877; (202) 275-6241.

- *Nonprescription Drugs: Over the Counter and Underemphasized*. Examines the Food and Drug Administration's procedures for approving and monitoring over-the-counter drugs in order to identify potential vulnerabilities in the procedures that could result in the approval and marketing of unsafe and ineffective drugs.

NORPLANT

See also Contraception

Clearinghouses/Hotlines

The Food and Drug Administration (FDA) can provide you with free reports and information regarding the new contraception called Norplant. Reports include information on patient labeling, prescribing, usage, warnings, and FDA statements regarding Norplant.

☎ Contact:
Drug Evaluation and Research
Food and Drug Administration
HFD 199
Rockville, MD 20857
(301) 295-8012

The Contraceptive Development Branch of the Center for Population Research is beginning to conduct research regarding who chooses to use Norplant, and who chooses to discontinue it.

☎ Contact:
Contraceptive Development Branch of
the Center for Population Research
9000 Rockville Pike

Bethesda, MD 20892
(301) 496-1661

Free Publications/Videos

The following publication on Norplant is available from the Family Life Information Exchange, P.O. Box 30146, Bethesda, MD 20814; (301) 585-6636.

- *OPA Program Instructions: Norplant Education in Title X.*

NOSEBLEEDS

Clearinghouses/Hotlines

The National Heart, Lung, and Blood Institute (NHLBI) can search the Combined Health Information Database (CHID) and generate a bibliography of resources on Nosebleeds (Epistaxis) for you. They also will send you any publications and journal articles they may have on hand, and will refer you to other organizations that are studying this disease. If you can't afford treatment, have your doctor call NHLBI to find out if they are conducting any clinical studies that you might qualify for.

☎ Contact:
National Heart, Lung, and Blood Institute
Bldg. 31, Room 4A21
Bethesda, MD 20892
(301) 496-4236

NUCLEAR MEDICINE

Free Publications/Videos

The following publications are available from the Center for Devices and Radiological Health, (HFZ-210), Food and Drug Administration, 5600 Fishers Ln., Rockville, MD 20857; (301) 443-4690.

- *Fact Sheet: Nuclear Medicine.*
- *Using Medical Radiation From The Inside Out.*

NURSING HOMES

See also Long-Term Care

Clearinghouses/Hotlines

The National Institute on Aging (NIA) will send you whatever publications and reprints of journal articles they have on Nursing Homes. They cannot refer you to other experts if the information they have isn't sufficient for your purposes.

☎ Contact:
National Institute on Aging
Building 31
Room 5C27
Bethesda, MD 20892
(301) 496-1752

Free Publications/Videos

The following publication on Nursing Homes is available from the National Institute on Aging, Federal Building, Room 6C12, Bethesda, MD 20892; (301) 496-1752.

- *When You Need A Nursing Home.*

The following publication on Nursing Homes is available from the ODPHP Health Information Center, P.O. Box 1133, Washington, DC 20013; (800) 336-4797, or (301) 565-4167.

- *Long-Term Care.* Explains issues and concerns regarding long-term care, and includes a list of publications and audiovisuals available from government agencies, community organizations, foundations and many other health groups.

The following publication on Nursing Homes is available from the Superintendent of Documents, Government Printing Office, Washington, DC 20402; (202) 783-3238.

- *Resident Abuse in Nursing Homes: Understanding and Preventing Abuse.* Contains results of a study to promote a better understanding of abuse in nursing homes. It examines the nature of abuse and ways to prevent it, and existing processes for resolving physical abuse complaints involving nursing home residents. (S/N 017-022-01-12-3, $3.25)

The following publication on Nursing Homes is available from the Consumer Information Center, P.O. Box 100, Pueblo, CO 81002.

- *Guide to Choosing a Nursing Home.* Suggestions to help plan, visit and evaluate your need. Includes information on food services, payment, Medicare/Medicaid coverage, insurance, contracts, and more. (#533Z).

NUTRITION

Clearinghouses/Hotlines

The National Institute of Child Health and Human Development (NICHD) will send you whatever publications and reprints of journal articles they have on Nutrition. If necessary, they will refer you to other experts or researchers in the field. If you can't afford treatment, have your doctor call NICHD to find out if they are conducting any clinical studies that you might qualify for.

☎ Contact:
National Institute of Child Health
and Human Development
Building 31
Room 2A32
Bethesda, MD 20892
(301) 496-5133

The National Institute of Diabetes and Digestive and Kidney Diseases's (NIDDK) individual clearinghouses can search the Combined Health Information Database (CHID) and generate a bibliography of resources on Nutrition for you. They also will send you any publications and journal articles they may have on hand, and will refer you to other organizations that are studying nutrition related diseases. If you can't afford treatment, have your doctor call NIDDK to find

out if they are conducting any clinical studies that you might qualify for.

☎ Contact:
National Institute of Diabetes
and Digestive and Kidney Diseases
Building 31
Room 9A04
Bethesda, MD 20892
(301) 496-3583

The National Institute on Aging (NIA) will send you whatever publications and reprints of journal articles they have on Nutrition and Aging. They cannot refer you to other experts if the information they have isn't sufficient for your purposes.

☎ Contact:
National Institute on Aging
Building 31
Room 5C27
Bethesda, MD 20892
(301) 496-1752

The U.S. Department of Agriculture's Food and Nutrition Information Center (FNIC) has all kinds of information publications to send you on food, nutrition, and health.

☎ Contact:
Food and Nutrition Information Center
National Agricultural Library
Room 304
Beltsville, MD 20705
(301) 504-5719

The National Maternal and Child Health Clearinghouse has all kinds of information on maternal and child health issues, such as pregnancy, child and adolescent health, and human genetics. If the answer to your question can't be answered by any of their countless free publications, they can refer you to other National or local resources. If you still need further information, they search their own reference collection and send you what they find.

☎ Contact:
National Maternal and Child
Health Clearinghouse
38th & R Streets., NW
Washington, DC 20057
(703) 821-8955, ext. 254

The Human Nutrition Information Service (HNIS) shares its research in nutritive value of foods and of the nutritional adequacy of diets and food supplies. It also maintains the Nutrient Data Bank, which contains surveys and data on the nutrient values in foods and descriptions of foods. Various consumer materials are available as well as a publications list, including over 20 publications on the nutrient composition of foods. HNIS has several publications dealing with dietary guidelines for Americans, which are seven basic principles for developing and maintaining a healthier diet and are the basis for all Federal nutrition information and education programs for health conscious Americans.

☎ Contact:
Human Nutrition Information Service
U.S. Department of Agriculture
6505 Belcrest Road
Room 363
Hyattsville, MD 20782
(301) 436-8617

The Food and Nutrition Service (FNS) publishes a variety of brochures explaining the various food assistance programs it operates both for those eligible for the programs and for those who administer them. Programs include the Child Nutrition Program, Food Distribution Program, Women, Infants, and Children (WIC) Program, Food Stamp Program, and various nutrition education materials. You can contact FNS for a publications list, and most of the publications are free.

☎ Contact:
Food and Nutrition Service
3101 Park Center Drive
Park Office Bldg.
Alexandria, VA 22302
(703) 305-2554

Free Publications/Videos

The following publications on Nutrition are available from the Human Nutrition Information Service, U.S. Department of Agriculture, 6505 Belcrest Rd., Room 363, Hyattsville, MD 20782; (301) 436-8617.

- *Nutrition and Your Health: Dietary Guidelines for Americans*. (free, also in Spanish)
- *Dietary Guidelines and Your Diet*. ($4.50)
- *Calories and Weight: The USDA Pocket Guide*. ($1.75)
- *Nutritive Value of Foods*. ($3.75)
- *Your Money's Worth in Foods*. ($2.25)
- *The Sodium Content of Your Food*. ($2.25)
- *Thrifty Meals for Two: Making Your Food Dollars Count*. ($2.50)
- *Cooking for People with Food Allergies*. ($1.50)
- *Good Sources of Nutrients*. ($5.00)

The following publications on Nutrition are available from the Food and Nutrition Information Center, National Agricultural Library, Room 304, Beltsville, MD 20705; (301) 504-5719.

- *Children's Literature on Food and Nutrition*. A list to help you locate further information or resources.
- *Nutrition and Cardiovascular Disease*. A list to help you locate further information or resources.
- *Nutrition, Learning and Behavior*. A list to help you locate further information or resources.
- *Sensible Nutrition*. A list to help you locate further information or resources.
- *Vegetarian Nutrition*. A list to help you locate further information or resources.
- *Adult/Patient Nutrition Education Materials*. A list of current references.
- *Fish Oil: Role of Omega-3s in Health and Nutrition*. A list of current references.
- *Nutrition Education Materials and Audiovisuals: Grades Preschool-6*. A list of current references.
- *Nutrition Education Printed Materials and Audiovisuals: Grades 7-12*. A list of current references.
- *Adult/Patient Nutrition Education Materials*. An annotated bibliography contains 130 citations on nutrition education materials for adults on a variety of topics including weight control, anorexia/bulimia, diabetes, heart disease, oral health and food quackery.
- *Sources of Free or Low-cost Food and Nutrition Materials*. A list of organizations that provide free or low-cost food and nutrition

materials for consumers.
- *Adult/Patient Nutrition Education Materials, January 1982 -September 1990.* A list of current resources. (#QB91-29)
- *Biotechnology in Human Health and Nutrition, January 1979 - March 1991.* A list of current resources. (#QB91-97)
- *Cultural Perspectives on Food and Nutrition, April 1992.* A list of current resources. (#SRB 92-11)
- *Infant Nutrition, January 1987 - March 1991.* (#QB91-34) A list of current resources.
- *Sports Nutrition Nutri-Topic.* Lists books, journal articles, pamphlets, booklets, and other resources to contact regarding sports fitness and nutrition. Included is a list of videos produced outside the government, but available for free loan from the Food and Nutrition Information Center, dealing with exercise and fitness.
- *Eating For Better Health.* Contains nutrition and weight loss information as well as inexpensive recipes and menus.
- *Diet and Cancer.* Designed to help you locate resources on this topic.

The following publications on Nutrition are available from the National Maternal and Child Health Clearinghouse, 38th & R Streets., NW, Washington, DC 20057; (703) 821-8955, ext. 254.

- *Nutritional Disorders of Children: Prevention, Screening, and Follow-up.*
- *Nutrition Resources for Early Childhood: Resource Guide.* An annotated list of current nutrition education publication for children ages 1-5 years, their parents, caregivers, and teachers.
- *Nutrition Services For Children With Special Needs.*
- *Patient Education Materials: A Resource Guide* is a free publication developed to help health professionals identify and locate materials on maternal and child health topics that are clear, concise, easy to read and appropriate for the general public. The guide is separated into three sections. The first is patient education materials, which is an annotated listing of source books, directories, audiovisuals, and resource guides that describe patient

education materials. The second section lists publishers of patient education materials, and the third lists federal health information clearinghouses.

The following publications on Nutrition are available from the Consumer Information Center, P.O. Box 100, Pueblo, CO 81002.

- *Food Guide Pyramid.* Your daily diet should look like a pyramid - a lot of breads and cereals at the base; and only a few fats, oils, and sweets at the top. Here's how to use this concept to eat right and maintain a healthy weight. ($1.00).
- *Nutrition and the Elderly.* (#533Y)
- *Eating for Life.* (#113Y, $1.00)
- *Fat Substitutes.* (#528Y)
- *Fish and Seafood Made Easy.* (#421Y, $.50)
- *Food News for Consumers: 4 issues.* (#251Y, $5)
- *Is That Newfangled Cookware Safe?* (#531Y)
- *Keeping Up with the Microwave Revolution.* (#532Y)
- *A Word About Low Sodium Diets.* (#538Y)

The following publications on Nutrition are available from the National Cancer Institute, Bldg. 31, Room 10A24, Bethesda, MD 20892; (800) 4-CANCER, or (301) 496-5583.

- *Diet, Nutrition, and Cancer Prevention: The Good News.* (#87-2878)
- *Diet, Nutrition and Cancer Prevention: A Guide to Food Choices.* Describes what is known about the interrelationships of diet and certain cancers. (#85-2711)
- *Eating Hints: Tips and Recipes for Better Nutrition During Cancer Treatment.* (#91-2079) Includes recipes and suggestions for maintaining optimum, yet realistic, good nutrition during treatment.

The following publications on Nutrition are available from the Superintendent of Documents, Government Printing Office, Washington, DC 20402; (202) 783-3238.

- *Shopping for Food and Making Meals in Minutes Using the Dietary Guidelines.* Describes quick meal hints, tips on reading food labels, an aisle-by-aisle shopping guide, and 18 timesaving recipe ideas. ($3, #S/N 001-000-04529-6)

- *Preparing Foods and Planning Menus Using the Dietary Guidelines.* Contains tips for cooking with less sugar, fat, and sodium; a daily guide to food choices; making the menu fit the family; and 10 recipe ideas. ($2.50, S/N 001-000-04527-0)
- *Making Bag Lunches, Snacks, and Desserts Using the Dietary Guidelines.* Provides a muncher's guide; great-tasting desserts with less fat and sugar; the best in bag lunches, hot or cold; and 27 recipe ideas. ($2.50, S/N 001-000-04528-8)
- *Eating Better When Eating Out Using the Dietary Guidelines.* Discusses ordering foods "your way," how to read menus, and fact and fiction about fast foods. ($1.50, S/N 001-000-04530-0)
- *The Healthy Heart Cookbook.* An enjoyable and exciting new way of cooking to keep your heart healthy and diet wise. Suggests ways to shop wisely, discusses good and bad cooking oils, and provides numerous tasty menu suggestions. ($3, S/N 008-070-00632-4)

The following publication on Nutrition is available from the National Health Information Center, P.O. Box 1133, Washington, DC 20013; (800) 336-4797, or (301) 565-4167 in DC metro area.

- *Worksite Nutrition: A Decision Maker's Guide.* A 58 page program for implementing nutrition programs in the workplace, describes what resources employers need to conduct such a health initiative. ($2.00)

The following publications on Nutrition are available from the Food & Drug Administration, (HFE-88), 5600 Fishers Ln., Rockville, MD 20857; (301) 443-3170.

- *Good Nutrition For the Highchair Set.* (#FDA92-2208)
- *Women and Nutrition: A Menu of Special Needs.* (#FDA91-2247)
- *The Nutritional Gender Gap at the Dinner Table.* (#84-2197)
- *Nutrition Labels and U.S. RDA.* Explains the

evolution of the Recommended Daily Allowances (RDAs) and the intention of nutritional labeling information.

- *Eating Defensively: Food Safety Advice For Persons With AIDS.* (#FDA90-2232)
- *Fruit, Something Good That's Not Illegal, Immoral or Fattening.* (#FDA88-2226)
- *Fiber: Something Healthy to Chew On.* (#FDA91-2206)
- *The "Grazing" Of America: A Guide to Healthy Snacking.* (#FDA89-2229)
- *What About Nutrients In Fast Foods?* Examines the pros and cons of "fast foods" and analyses the nutritional value of various menus.
- *Planning The Diet For A Healthy Heart.* (#FDA91-2220)
- *A Simple Guide to Complex Carbohydrates.* (#FDA91-2230)

The following publication on Nutrition is available from the National Clearinghouse for Primary Care Information, 8201 Greensboro Dr., Suite 600, McLean, VA 22102; (703) 821-8955.

- *Easy Eating For Well-Seasoned Adults.* A collection of recipes submitted by older adults.

The following publication on Nutrition is available from the National Arthritis and Musculoskeletal and Skin Diseases Information Clearinghouse, Box AMS, 9000 Rockville Pike, Bethesda, MD 20892; (301) 495-4484.

- *Diet and Arthritis: An Annotated Bibliography, 1986* ($2)

The following publications on Nutrition are available from the National Heart, Lung, and Blood Institute, Bldg. 31, Room 4A21, Bethesda, MD 20892; (301) 496-4236.

- *Dietary Guidelines for Americans: Avoid Too Much Fat, Saturated Fat and Cholesterol.*
- *Check Your Weight and Heart Disease I.Q.* (#90-3034)
- *Eating to Lower Your Blood Cholesterol.* (#89-2920)
- *Eat Right to Lower Your High Blood Cholesterol.* (#90-2972)

- *Home and Garden Bulletin.*
- *Check Your Weight and Heart Disease I.Q.*
 (#3034) Addresses the independent relationship of obesity and being overweight to coronary heart disease and its relationship to high blood pressure, high blood cholesterol, and smoking habits.

The following publication on Nutrition is available from the Science & Technology Division, Reference Section, Library of Congress, Washington, DC 20540; (202) 707-5580.

- *Human Diet & Nutrition.* Reference guide designed to help locate further published material. (#89-5)

The following publication on Nutrition is available from Subcommittee on Human Services, Room 715, O'Neill HOB, 300 New Jersey Ave., SE, Washington, DC 20515; (202) 226-3348.

- *Hunger and Nutrition: Challenges to Older Americans' Health.*

The following videos on Nutrition are available from the Modern Talking Picture Service, 5000 Park St. North, St. Petersburg, FL 33709; (800) 243-MTPS.

- *The Munchers: A Fable.* Video presents information on nutrition and dental health.
- *The Fitness Formula.* Video showing proper cooking methods for turkey.

The following Congressional Research Service (CRS) reports on Nutrition are available from either of your U.S. Senators' offices at the U.S. Capitol, Washington, DC 20510, or from your Congressional Representative at the U.S. Capitol, Washington, DC 20515. You can also call in your request through the U.S. Capitol switchboard at (202) 224-3121. Be sure to include the full title and report number in your request.

- *A National Nutrition Monitoring System: Background and Legislative Mandate.* (91-785 SPR)
- *Native Americans: Nutrition and Diet-Related Diseases.* (87-246 SPR)

The following software program on **Nutrition** is available from the National Technical Information Service, 5285 Port Royal Rd., Springfield, VA 22261; (703) 487-4650.

- *The Dietary Analysis Program* is a simple software program for IBM PC-compatible computers that will give you a dietary analysis of the foods you eat in a meal or for each day. Just by entering the names of the foods you have eaten, this program, developed by the U.S. Department of Agriculture's Human Nutrition Information Service, will give you nutrient data information, calories, and recommended daily allowances on over 850 foods. The software program is available for $60.

NUTRITIONAL LABELING

See Food Labeling

NYSTAGMUS

Clearinghouses/Hotlines

The National Eye Institute (NEI) can give you up-to-date information on Nystagmus by searching the Combined Health Information Database (CHID) and MEDLINE and sending you bibliographies of resources, along with any journal articles they may have. They can also refer you to any other organizations that study this and other related subjects. NEI will also let you know of any clinical studies that may be studying Nystagmus and looking for patients. Because of their small staff, NEI prefers that you submit your requests for information in writing.

☎ Contact:
National Eye Institute
Building 31
Room 6A32
Bethesda, MD 20892
(301) 496-5248

OBESITY

See also Dieting

Clearinghouses/Hotlines

The Obesity, Eating Disorders, and Energy Regulation Program at National Institutes of Health researches obesity, anorexia nervosa, bulimia and other eating disorders. They can give you information on the causes, prevention, and treatments of these conditions.

☎ Contact:
National Institute of Diabetes
and Digestive and Kidney Diseases
National Institutes of Health
Building 31
Room 3A18B
Bethesda, MD 20892
(301) 496-7823

The National Institute of Diabetes and Digestive and Kidney Diseases's (NIDDK) individual clearinghouses can search the Combined Health Information Database (CHID) and generate a bibliography of resources for you on Obesity. They also will send you any publications and journal articles they may have on hand, and will refer you to other organizations that are studying this condition. If you can't afford treatment, have your doctor call NIDDK to find out if they are conducting any clinical studies that you might qualify for.

☎ Contact:
National Institute of Diabetes
and Digestive and Kidney Diseases
Building 31
Room 9A04
Bethesda, MD 20892
(301) 496-3583

The National Institute of Mental Health (NIMH) will send you whatever publications and reprints of articles from texts and journals they have on Obesity. They will also refer you to other organizations that are studying this disorder. NIAMS will also let you know of any clinical studies that may be studying this disorder and looking for patients.

☎ Contact:
National Institute of Mental Health
5600 Fishers Ln., Room 15C05
Rockville, MD 20857
(301) 443-4515

The National Institute of Child Health and Human Development (NICHD) will send you whatever publications and reprints of journal articles they have on Obesity in Children. If necessary, they will refer you to other experts or researchers in the field. If you can't afford treatment, have your doctor call NICHD to find out if they are conducting any clinical studies that you might qualify for.

☎ Contact:
National Institute of Child Health
and Human Development
Bldg. 31, Room 2A32
Bethesda, MD 20892
(301) 496-5133

Free Publications/Videos

The following publication is available from the Office of Clinical Center Communications, Bldg. 10, Room 1C255, Bethesda, MD 20892; (301) 496-2563.

- *Obesity and Energy Metabolism.* Explains the relationship between too much food and too little exercise. A videotape based on this publication is available and can be purchased or available on a free loan basis. (#86-1805)

The following publication is available from the Food and Nutrition Information Center, National Agricultural Library, Room 304, Beltsville, MD 20705; (301) 504-5719.

- *Childhood Obesity and Cardiovascular Disease.* A list of current references.

The following publication is available from the Obesity Initiative, National Heart, Lung, and Blood Institute, P.O. Box 30105, Bethesda, MD 20824-0105; (301) 951-3260.

- *Check Your Weight and Heart IQ.*

OBSESSIVE-COMPULSIVE

Clearinghouses/Hotlines

The National Institute of Mental Health (NIMH) maintains data bases that index and abstract documents from the worldwide literature pertaining to Obsessive-Compulsive Disorder. In addition to scientific journals, there are references to audiovisuals, dissertations, government documents and reports. Contact NIMH for searches on specific subjects.

☎ Contact:
National Institute of Mental Health
5600 Fishers Lane, Room 15C05
Rockville, MD 20857
(301) 443-4515

Free Publications/Videos

The following publication is available from the National Institute of Mental Health, 5600 Fishers Ln., Room 15C05, Rockville, MD 20857; (301) 443-4515.

- *Obsessive-Compulsive Disorder: Useful Information from the NIMH.*

OCCUPATIONAL SAFETY AND HEALTH

Clearinghouses/Hotlines

The National Institute for Occupational Safety and Health (NIOSH) conducts research and recommends Occupational Safety and Health standards. Information is available about any aspect of occupational safety and health including lung diseases, cancer, reproductive disorders, neurotoxic disorders, and musculoskeletal injuries. They also have information on chemical hazards, physical hazards, carpal tunnel syndrome, video display terminals, indoor air quality, construction hazards, agricultural hazards, and information for health care workers.

☎ Contact:
Technical Information Branch
National Institute for Occupational
Safety and Health
4676 Columbia Parkway
Cincinnati, OH 45226
(800) 35-NIOSH

Free Publications/Videos

The following Congressional Research Service (CRS) reports on Occupational Safety and Health are available from either of your U.S. Senators' offices at the U.S. Capitol, Washington, DC 20510, or from your Congressional Representative at the U.S. Capitol, Washington, DC 20515. You can also call in your request through the U.S. Capitol switchboard at (202) 224-3121. Be sure to include the full title and report number in your request.

- *AIDS in the Workplace: Employee Vs Employer Interest.* (#87-510 E)
- *Black Lung Programs: 1987 Issues and Action.* (#88-68 EPW)
- *Construction Workers: Safety and Health Legislation; Issue Brief.* (#IB90150)
- *Federal Agency Workers: How Safe Are They?* (#91-412 E)
- *High Risk Occupational Disease Notification and Prevention Act of 1987: Side-by-Side Comparison of H.R. 162 and S. 79.* (#88-43 E)
- *Occupational Disease Notification Proposals: Is Legislation Necessary? Issue Brief.* (#IB86150)
- *Occupational Safety and Health Issues: Info Pack.* (#IP456O)
- *Tort Liability of the Federal Government and Its Contractors to Veterans Exposed to Atomic Radiation.* (#86-979 A)
- *Video Display Terminals (VDT's): Health, Safety, and Labor-Management Issues.* (#87-314 SPR)
- *Video Display Terminals and Problems of Modern Office Health, Safety and Policy: An Update.* (#89-684 SPR)

OCULAR HYPERTENSION

Clearinghouses/Hotlines

The National Eye Institute (NEI) can give you up-to-date information on Ocular Hypertension by searching the Combined Health Information Database (CHID) and MEDLINE and sending you bibliographies of resources, along with any journal articles they may have. They can also refer you to any other organizations that study this and other related conditions. NEI will also let you know of any clinical studies that may be studying this disease and looking for patients. Because of their small staff, NEI prefers that you submit your requests for information in writing.

☎ Contact:
National Eye Institute
Bldg. 31, Room 6A32
Bethesda, MD 20892
(301) 496-5248

ODOR DISORDERS

Clearinghouses/Hotlines

The National Institute on Deafness and Other Communication Disorders (NIDCD) will send you whatever publications and reprints of journal articles they have on Odor Disorders. If you need further information, they will refer you to other organizations that this and other related conditions. NIDCD does not conduct any clinical studies for this or any other disorder.

☎ Contact:
National Institute on Deafness
and Other Communication Disorders
Bldg. 31, Room 3C35
Bethesda, MD 20892
(301) 496-7243
(800) 241-1044
(301) 402-0252 (TDD)

The National Institute of Neurological Disorders and Stroke (NINDS) can send you only information they have in their publications list on Odor Disorders. They cannot refer you to any experts. This Clearinghouse cannot directly give you information about any current clinical studies NINDS might be conducting on this disorder, but you can find this information for yourself by looking under the National Institute of Neurological Disorders and Stroke in *Appendix A* at the end of this book.

☎ Contact:
National Institute of Neurological
Disorders and Stroke
Bldg. 31, Room 8A06
Bethesda, MD 20892
(301) 496-5751
(800) 352-9424

OLIVOPONTOCEREBELLAR ATROPHY

Free Publications/Videos

The following publication is available from the National Institute of Neurological Disorders and Stroke, P.O. Box 5801, Bethesda, MD 20824; (800) 352-9424, or (301) 496-5751.

- *Olivopontocerebellar Atrophy*. Contains a collection of scientific articles, patient education pamphlets, and addresses of voluntary health associations.

ONCHOCERCIASIS

Clearinghouses/Hotlines

The National Eye Institute (NEI) can give you up-to-date information on Onchocerciasis by searching the Combined Health Information Database (CHID) and MEDLINE and sending you bibliographies of resources, along with any journal articles they may have. They can also refer you to any other organizations that study this and other related conditions. NEI will also let you know of any clinical studies that may be studying this disease and looking for patients. Because of

their small staff, NEI prefers that you submit your requests for information in writing.

☎ Contact:
National Eye Institute
Bldg. 31, Room 6A32
Bethesda, MD 20892
(301) 496-5248

ONCOLOGY

See also Cancer

Clearinghouses/Hotlines

The National Cancer Institute (NCI) will send you whatever publications and reprints of journal articles they have on Oncology. They can also give you information on the state-of-the-art treatment for this issue, including specific treatment information for your stage of cancer. They can also search their Physician's Data Query (PDQ) database to let you know if NCI is conducting any clinical studies on your disease.

☎ Contact:
National Cancer Institute
Bldg. 31, Room 10A24
Bethesda, MD 20892
(800) 4-CANCER
(301) 496-5583

OPHTHALMIA NEONATORUM

Clearinghouses/Hotlines

The National Eye Institute (NEI) can give you up-to-date information on Ophthalmia Neonatorum by searching the Combined Health Information Database (CHID) and MEDLINE and sending you bibliographies of resources, along with any journal articles they may have. They can also refer you to any other organizations that study this and other related conditions. NEI will also let you know of any clinical studies that may be studying

this disease and looking for patients. Because of their small staff, NEI prefers that you submit your requests for information in writing.

☎ Contact:
National Eye Institute
Bldg. 31, Room 6A32
Bethesda, MD 20892
(301) 496-5248

OPPENHEIM'S DISEASE

Clearinghouses/Hotlines

The National Institute of Neurological Disorders and Stroke (NINDS) can send you only information they have in their publications list on Oppenheim's Disease (Amyotonia Congenita). They cannot refer you to any experts. This Clearinghouse cannot directly give you information about any current clinical studies NINDS might be conducting on this illness, but you can find this information for yourself by looking under the National Institute of Neurological Disorders and Stroke in *Appendix A* at the end of this book.

☎ Contact:
National Institute of Neurological
Disorders and Stroke
Bldg. 31, Room 8A06
Bethesda, MD 20892
(301) 496-5751
(800) 352-9424

OPTIC ATROPHY

Clearinghouses/Hotlines

The National Eye Institute (NEI) can give you up-to-date information on Optic Atrophy by searching the Combined Health Information Database (CHID) and MEDLINE and sending you bibliographies of resources, along with any journal articles they may have. They can also refer you to any other organizations that study this and other related conditions. NEI will also let you know of any clinical studies that may be studying this disease and looking for patients. Because of their small staff, NEI prefers that you submit your requests for information in writing.

☎ Contact:
National Eye Institute
Bldg. 31, Room 6A32
Bethesda, MD 20892
(301) 496-5248

OPTIC NEURITIS

Clearinghouses/Hotlines

The National Eye Institute (NEI) can give you up-to-date information on Optic Neuritis by searching the Combined Health Information Database (CHID) and MEDLINE and sending you bibliographies of resources, along with any journal articles they may have. They can also refer you to any other organizations that study this and other related conditions. NEI will also let you know of any clinical studies that may be studying this disease and looking for patients. Because of their small staff, NEI prefers that you submit your requests for information in writing.

☎ Contact:
National Eye Institute
Bldg. 31, Room 6A32
Bethesda, MD 20892
(301) 496-5248

ORAL CANCER

See also Cancer

Clearinghouses/Hotlines

The National Institute of Dental Research (NIDR) will send you whatever publications and reprints of journal articles they have on Oral Cancer. As a policy, however, NIDR will not refer you to other organizations or experts who study this disease. If you can't afford treatment, have your doctor call Dr. Albert Guckers at (301) 496-6241 to find out if NIDR is conducting any clinical studies that you

might qualify for.

☎ Contact:
National Institute of Dental Research
Bldg. 31, Room 2C35
Bethesda, MD 20892
(301) 496-4261

Free Publications/Videos

The following publication on Oral Cancer is available from the National Institute of Dental Research, Bldg. 31, Room 2C35, Bethesda, MD 20892; (301) 496-4261.

- *Research Report: Oral Cancer.* (#88-2876)

The following publication is available from the National Cancer Institute, Bldg. 31, Room 10A24, Bethesda, MD 20892; (800) 4-CANCER, (301) 496-5583.
- *What You Need to Know About Oral Cancer.* (#91-1574)

ORAL CONTRACEPTIVES

See also Contraception

Clearinghouses/Hotlines

The National Institute of Child Health and Human Development (NICHD) will send you whatever publications and reprints of journal articles they have on Oral Contraceptives. If necessary, they will refer you to other experts or researchers in the field. If you can't afford treatment, have your doctor call NICHD to find out if they are conducting any clinical studies that you might qualify for.

☎ Contact:
National Institute of Child Health
and Human Development
Bldg. 31, Room 2A32
Bethesda, MD 20892
(301) 496-5133

The Center for Drug Evaluation and Research can provide you with research reports and articles dealing with Oral Contraceptives.

☎ Contact:
Center for Drug Evaluation and Research
Food and Drug Administration
HFD 100, Room 14B45
5600 Fishers Lane
Rockville, MD 20857
(301) 295-8012

Free Publications/Videos

The following publication on Oral Contraceptives is available from the National Institute of Child Health and Human Development, Bldg. 31, Room 2A32, Bethesda, MD 20892; (301) 496-5133.

- *Facts About Oral Contraceptives*.

ORAL HEALTH

Clearinghouses/Hotlines

The National Institute of Dental Research (NIDR), which looks into the causes, prevention, diagnosis, and treatment of Oral and Dental Diseases, can answer your questions about the newest developments in treatment and send you publications, posters, and reports on a variety of dental topics. Publications cover canker sores, fluoride treatment, periodontal disease, and tooth decay.

☎ Contact:
National Institute of Dental Research
Bldg. 31, Room 2C35
Bethesda, MD 20892
(301) 496-4261

Free Publications/Videos

The following publications are available from the National Institute of Dental Research, Bldg. 31, Room 2C35, Bethesda, MD 20892; (301) 496-4261.

- *Oral Health of United States Adults: National Findings*. (#87-2868)

- *Oral Health of U.S. Adults: Regional Findings*. (#88-2869)

ORGAN TRANSPLANTS

Clearinghouses/Hotlines

The Health Resources and Services Administration's Division of Organ Transplantation conducts a program to foster relationships with public and private organizations to promote organ donation and transplantation. The program provides information to professional associations, health providers, consumers and insurers, medical societies, state health departments, and the general public. The Center also supports the National Organ Procurement and Transplantation Network, which is designed to ensure equitable distribution of available organs to patients and transplant centers, and a Scientific Registry of demographic and clinical information on transplant recipients. An annual report, information on the Transplantation Network, a fact sheet on organ transplantation, and a Q&A publication are available.

☎ Contact:
Bureau of Health Resources Development
Health Resources and Services Administration
5600 Fishers Lane, Room 11A-22
Rockville, MD 20857
(301) 443-7577

Free Publications/Videos

The following publication is available from the National Clearinghouse for Primary Care Information, 8201 Greensboro Dr., Suite 600, McLean, VA 22102; (703) 821-8955.

- *Organ Transplantation: Questions and Answers*. Provides answers to some of the most frequently asked questions about transplants.

The following publication is available from the Select Committee on Aging, Room 712, O'Neill HOB, 300 New Jersey Ave., SE, Washington, DC 20515; (202) 226-3375.

- Organ Transplants: Choices and Criteria, Who Lives, Who Dies, Who Pays?

This Congressional Research Service (CRS) report on Organ Transplantation is available from either of your U.S. Senators' offices at the U.S. Capitol, Washington, DC 20510, or from your Congressional Representative at the U.S. Capitol, Washington, DC 20515. You can also call in your request through the U.S. Capitol switchboard at (202) 224-3121. Be sure to include the full title and report number in your request.

- Organ Transplantation in the United States: Analysis of Selected Ethical Issues. (#89-103 SPR)

OROTIC ACIDURIA

Clearinghouses/Hotlines

The National Institute of Arthritis and Musculoskeletal and Skin Diseases (NIAMS) will send you whatever publications and reprints of articles from texts and journals they have on Orotic Aciduria. They will also refer you to other organizations that are studying this condition. NIAMS will also let you know of any clinical studies that may be studying this condition and looking for patients.

☎ Contact:
National Institute of Arthritis
and Musculoskeletal and Skin Diseases
Box AMS
Bethesda, MD 20892
(301) 495-4484

The National Institute of Diabetes and Digestive and Kidney Diseases's (NIDDK) individual clearinghouses can search the Combined Health Information Database (CHID) and generate a bibliography of resources for you on Orotic Aciduria. They also will send you any publications and journal articles they may have on hand, and will refer you to other organizations that are studying this condition. If you can't afford treatment, have your doctor call NIDDK to find out if they are conducting any clinical studies that you might qualify for.

☎ Contact:
National Institute of Diabetes
and Digestive and Kidney Diseases
Bldg. 31, Room 9A04
Bethesda, MD 20892
(301) 496-3583

ORPHAN DISEASES

Clearinghouses/Hotlines

The National Information Center for Orphan Drugs and Rare Diseases responds to inquiries on diseases with a prevalence of 200,000 or fewer cases in the United States and provides a mutual support network for families with similar disorders. Some examples of Orphan/Rare Diseases include amenorrhea, apnea, bacteremia, cachexia, carnitine deficiency, causalgia, donor tissue damage, germ cell tumors, leishmaniasis, myoclonus, renal cancer, skin ulcers, strabismus, and Wilson's disease. This Clearinghouse, sponsored by the Food and Drug Administration, also gathers and distributes information on medicines not widely researched or available.

☎ Contact:
National Information Center
for Orphan Drugs and Rare Diseases
450 5th St., NW, Room 7103
Washington, DC 20001
(800) 456-3505

ORPHAN DRUGS

Clearinghouses/Hotlines

The National Information Center for Orphan Drugs and Rare Diseases responds to inquiries on diseases with a prevalence of 200,000 or fewer cases in the United States and provides a mutual support network for families with similar disorders. This Clearinghouse, sponsored by the Food and Drug Administration, also gathers and distributes information on medicines not widely researched or available.

☎ Contact:
National Information Center
for Orphan Drugs and Rare Diseases
450 5th St., NW
Room 7103
Washington, DC 20001
(800) 456-3505

The National Institute of Neurological Disorders and Stroke (NINDS) can send you only information they have in their publications list on Orphan Drugs. They cannot refer you to any experts. This Clearinghouse cannot directly give you information about any current clinical studies NINDS might be conducting on this topic, but you can find this information for yourself by looking under the National Institute of Neurological Disorders and Stroke in *Appendix A* at the end of this book.

☎ Contact:
National Institute of Neurological
Disorders and Stroke
Building 31
Room 8A06
Bethesda, MD 20892
(301) 496-5751
(800) 352-9424

ORTHODONTICS

Clearinghouses/Hotlines

The National Institute of Dental Research (NIDR) will send you whatever publications and reprints of journal articles they have on Orthodontics. As a policy, however, NIDR will not refer you to other organizations or experts who study this subject. If you can't afford treatment, have your doctor call Dr. Albert Guckers at (301) 496-6241 to find out if NIDR is conducting any clinical studies that you might qualify for.

☎ Contact:
National Institute of Dental Research
Building 31
Room 2C35
Bethesda, MD 20892
(301) 496-4261

Free Publications/Videos

The following videos are available from Modern Talking Picture Service, 5000 Park St. North, St. Petersburg, FL 33709; (800) 243-MTPS.

- *Adult Orthodontics: A Healthy Smile At Any Age.* Video showing how orthodontics aren't just for kids.
- *Orthodontics: Not Just Smiles.* Video shows how people of all ages can benefit from braces.

ORTHOGNATHIC SURGERY

Clearinghouses/Hotlines

The National Institute of Dental Research (NIDR) will send you whatever publications and reprints of journal articles they have on Orthognathic Surgery. As a policy, however, NIDR will not refer you to other organizations or experts who study this issue. If you can't afford treatment, have your doctor call Dr. Albert Guckers at (301) 496-6241 to find out if NIDR is conducting any clinical studies that you might qualify for.

☎ Contact:
National Institute of Dental Research
Bldg. 31, Room 2C35
Bethesda, MD 20892
(301) 496-4261

ORTHOKERATOLOGY

Clearinghouses/Hotlines

The National Eye Institute (NEI) can give you up-to-date information on Orthokeratology by searching the Combined Health Information Database (CHID) and MEDLINE and sending you bibliographies of resources, along with any journal articles they may have. They can also refer you to any other organizations that study this and other related issues. NEI will also let you know of any clinical studies that may be studying

Orthokeratology and looking for patients. Because of their small staff, NEI prefers that you submit your requests for information in writing.

☎ Contact:
National Eye Institute
Bldg. 31, Room 6A32
Bethesda, MD 20892
(301) 496-5248

ORTHOPEDICS

Clearinghouses/Hotlines

The National Institute of Arthritis and Musculoskeletal and Skin Diseases (NIAMS) will send you whatever publications and reprints of articles from texts and journals they have on Orthopedic Disorders. They will also refer you to other organizations that are studying these conditions. NIAMS will also let you know of any clinical studies that may be studying Orthopedics disorders and looking for patients.

☎ Contact:
National Institute of Arthritis
and Musculoskeletal and Skin Diseases
Box AMS
Bethesda, MD 20892
(301) 495-4484

ORTHOPEDIC IMPLANTS

Clearinghouses/Hotlines

The National Institute of Arthritis and Musculoskeletal and Skin Diseases (NIAMS) will send you whatever publications and reprints of articles from texts and journals they have on Orthopedic Implants. They will also refer you to other organizations that are studying this issue. NIAMS will also let you know of any clinical studies that may be studying implants and looking for patients.

☎ Contact:
National Institute of Arthritis
and Musculoskeletal and Skin Diseases

Box AMS
9000 Rockville Pike
Bethesda, MD 20892
(301) 495-4484

ORTHOSTATIC HYPOTENSION

Clearinghouses/Hotlines

The National Heart, Lung, and Blood Institute (NHLBI) can search the Combined Health Information Database (CHID) and generate a bibliography of resources for you on Orthostatic Hypotension. They also will send you any publications and journal articles they may have on hand, and will refer you to other organizations that are studying this condition. If you can't afford treatment, have your doctor call NHLBI to find out if they are conducting any clinical studies that you might qualify for.

☎ Contact:
National Heart, Lung, and Blood Institute
Building 31
Room 4A21
Bethesda, MD 20892
(301) 496-4236

The National Institute of Neurological Disorders and Stroke (NINDS) can send you only information they have in their publications list on Orthostatic Hypotension. They cannot refer you to any experts. This Clearinghouse cannot directly give you information about any current clinical studies NINDS might be conducting on this disorder, but you can find this information for yourself by looking under the National Institute of Neurological Disorders and Stroke in *Appendix A* at the end of this book.

☎ Contact:
National Institute of Neurological
Disorders and Stroke
Building 31
Room 8A06
Bethesda, MD 20892
(301) 496-5751
(800) 352-9424

ORTHOTICS

Clearinghouses/Hotlines

The National Institute of Arthritis and Musculoskeletal and Skin Diseases (NIAMS) will send you whatever publications and reprints of articles from texts and journals they have on Orthotics. They will also refer you to other organizations that are studying this issue. NIAMS will also let you know of any clinical studies that may be studying orthotics and looking for patients.

☎ Contact:
National Institute of Arthritis
and Musculoskeletal and Skin Diseases
Box AMS
9000 Rockville Pike
Bethesda, MD 20892
(301) 495-4484

OSTEITIS DEFORMANS

Clearinghouses/Hotlines

The National Institute of Arthritis and Musculoskeletal and Skin Diseases (NIAMS) will send you whatever publications and reprints of articles from texts and journals they have on Osteitis Deformans. They will also refer you to other organizations that are studying this condition. NIAMS will also let you know of any clinical studies that may be studying this condition and looking for patients.

☎ Contact:
National Institute of Arthritis
and Musculoskeletal and Skin Diseases
Box AMS
9000 Rockville Pike
Bethesda, MD 20892
(301) 495-4484

OSTEOARTHRITIS

Clearinghouses/Hotlines

The National Institute of Arthritis and Musculoskeletal and Skin Diseases (NIAMS) will send you whatever publications and reprints of articles from texts and journals they have on Osteoarthritis. They will also refer you to other organizations that are studying this condition. NIAMS will also let you know of any clinical studies that may be studying this condition and looking for patients.

☎ Contact:
National Institute of Arthritis
and Musculoskeletal and Skin Diseases
Box AMS
9000 Rockville Pike
Bethesda, MD 20892
(301) 495-4484

The National Institute on Aging (NIA) will send you whatever publications and reprints of journal articles they have on Osteoarthritis and Aging. They cannot refer you to other experts if the information they have isn't sufficient for your purposes.

☎ Contact:
National Institute on Aging
Bldg. 31, Room 5C27
Bethesda, MD 20892
(301) 496-1752

Free Publications/Videos

The following publication on Osteoarthritis is available from the National Arthritis and Musculoskeletal and Skin Diseases Information Clearinghouse, Box AMS, 9000 Rockville Pike, Bethesda, MD 20892; (301) 495-4484.

- *Osteoarthritis Patient Education Materials: An Annotated Bibliography.* ($3)

OSTEOGENESIS

Clearinghouses/Hotlines

The National Institute of Arthritis and Musculoskeletal and Skin Diseases (NIAMS) will send you whatever publications and reprints of articles from texts and journals they have on Osteogenesis. They will also refer you to other organizations that are studying this condition. NIAMS will also let you know of any clinical studies that may be studying this condition and looking for patients.

☎ Contact:
National Institute of Arthritis
and Musculoskeletal and Skin Diseases
Box AMS
9000 Rockville Pike
Bethesda, MD 20892
(301) 495-4484

The National Institute of Child Health and Human Development (NICHD) will send you whatever publications and reprints of journal articles they have on Osteogenesis Imperfecta. If necessary, they will refer you to other experts or researchers in the field. If you can't afford treatment, have your doctor call NICHD to find out if they are conducting any clinical studies that you might qualify for.

☎ Contact:
National Institute of Child Health
and Human Development
Bldg. 31, Room 2A32
Bethesda, MD 20892
(301) 496-5133

OSTEOGENIC SARCOMA

Clearinghouses/Hotlines

The National Cancer Institute (NCI) will send you whatever publications and reprints of journal articles they have on Osteogenic Sarcoma. They can also give you information on the state-of-the-art treatment for this condition, including specific

treatment information for your stage of cancer. They can also search their Physician's Data Query (PDQ) database to let you know if NCI is conducting any clinical studies on your disease.

☎ Contact:
National Cancer Institute
Bldg. 31, Room 10A24
Bethesda, MD 20892
(800) 4-CANCER
(301) 496-5583

OSTEOMALACIA

Clearinghouses/Hotlines

The National Institute of Arthritis and Musculoskeletal and Skin Diseases (NIAMS) will send you whatever publications and reprints of articles from texts and journals they have on Osteomalacia. They will also refer you to other organizations that are studying this condition. NIAMS will also let you know of any clinical studies that may be studying this condition and looking for patients.

☎ Contact:
National Institute of Arthritis
and Musculoskeletal and Skin Diseases
Box AMS
9000 Rockville Pike
Bethesda, MD 20892
(301) 495-4484

OSTEOMYELITIS

Clearinghouses/Hotlines

The National Institute of Allergy and Infectious Diseases (NIAID) can search the Combined Health Information Database (CHID) and generate a bibliography of resources for you on Osteomyelitis. They will also send you any publications and journal articles they may have on hand, and will refer you to researchers who are currently studying this disease. If you can't afford treatment, have your doctor call NIAID to find out if they are conducting any clinical studies that you might qualify for.

☎ Contact:
National Institute of Allergy
and Infectious Diseases
Building 31
Room 7A32
Bethesda, MD 20892
(301) 496-5717

The National Institute of Arthritis and Musculoskeletal and Skin Diseases (NIAMS) will send you whatever publications and reprints of articles from texts and journals they have on Osteomyelitis. They will also refer you to other organizations that are studying this condition. NIAMS will also let you know of any clinical studies that may be studying this condition and looking for patients.

☎ Contact:
National Institute of Arthritis
and Musculoskeletal and Skin Diseases
Box AMS
9000 Rockville Pike
Bethesda, MD 20892
(301) 495-4484

OSTEOPETROSIS

Clearinghouses/Hotlines

The National Institute of Child Health and Human Development (NICHD) will send you whatever publications and reprints of journal articles they have on Osteopetrosis. If necessary, they will refer you to other experts or researchers in the field. If you can't afford treatment, have your doctor call NICHD to find out if they are conducting any clinical studies that you might qualify for.

☎ Contact:
National Institute of Child Health
and Human Development
Building 31
Room 2A32
Bethesda, MD 20892
(301) 496-5133

OSTEOPOROSIS

Clearinghouses/Hotlines

The National Institute on Aging (NIA) will send you whatever publications and reprints of journal articles they have on Osteoporosis with Age. They cannot refer you to other experts if the information they have isn't sufficient for your purposes.

☎ Contact:
National Institute on Aging
Bldg. 31, Room 5C27
Bethesda, MD 20892
(301) 496-1752

The National Arthritis and Musculoskeletal and Skin Diseases Information Clearinghouse has all kinds of up-to-date information on the causes, prevention, and treatment of Osteoporosis.

☎ Contact:
National Arthritis and Musculoskeletal
and Skin Diseases Information Clearinghouse
Box AMS, 9000 Rockville Pike
Bethesda, MD 20892
(301) 495-4484

The Office of Technology Assessment (OTA) is studying the capacity of existing technologies to detect bone loss in the early stages of Osteoporosis and the cost of the technologies.

☎ Contact:
Katie Maslow, project director
Office of Technology Assessment
Washington, DC 20510
(202) 228-6590

Free Publications/Videos

The following publications on Osteoporosis are available from the National Arthritis and Musculoskeletal and Skin Diseases Information Clearinghouse, Box AMS, 9000 Rockville Pike, Bethesda, MD 20892, (301) 495-4484.

- *Osteoporosis.*
- *Osteoporosis: Cause, Treatment, Prevention.*
- *Osteoporosis: Patient Education Materials.*

- *Osteoporosis: Professional Education Materials.*
- *Osteoporosis: A Growing National Problem.*
- *Osteoporosis: Consensus Development Conference Statement.*
- *Scientific Workshop: Research Directions in Osteoporosis.*
- *Medicine for the Layman: Osteoporosis.*
- *Osteoporosis Research, Education and Health Promotion.*
- *Workshop on Etiopathogenesis of Osteo-arthritis.*

The following Congressional Research Service (CRS) report on Osteoporosis is available from either of your U.S. Senators' offices at the U.S. Capitol, Washington, DC 20510, or from your Congressional Representative at the U.S. Capitol, Washington, DC 20515. You can also call in your request through the U.S. Capitol switchboard at (202) 224-3121. Be sure to include the full title and report number in your request.

- *Osteoporosis: An Overview of Recent Developments.* (#87-843 SPR)

The following publication on Osteoporosis is available from the National Institute on Aging Clearinghouse, 2209 Distribution Circle, Silver Spring, MD 20910; (301) 495-3455.

- *Osteoporosis: The Bone Thinner.* Facts for the aging.

The following publication on Osteoporosis is available from the Science & Technology Division, Reference Section, Library of Congress, Washington, DC 20540; (202) 707-5580.

- *Osteoporosis.* Reference guide designed to help locate further published material. (#87-7)

The following publication on Osteoporosis is available from the Food & Drug Administration, (HFE-88), 5600 Fishers Ln., Rockville, MD 20857; (301) 443-3170.

- *Osteoporosis: Calcium and Estrogens.* Discusses the causes of this weakening of the bones, especially in older women, and how diet and estrogen treatment can help. (#85-1117, FDA)

OSTEOSARCOMA

See also Papilloma Virus

Clearinghouses/Hotlines

The National Cancer Institute (NCI) will send you whatever publications and reprints of journal articles they have on Osteosarcoma. They can also give you information on the state-of-the-art treatment for this disease, including specific treatment information for your stage of cancer. They can also search their Physician's Data Query (Physician's Data Query (PDQ)) database to let you know if NCI is conducting any clinical studies on your disease.

☎ Contact:
National Cancer Institute
Bldg. 31, Room 10A24
Bethesda, MD 20892
(800) 4-CANCER
(301) 496-5583

OSTEOSCLEROSIS

Clearinghouses/Hotlines

The National Institute of Child Health and Human Development (NICHD) will send you whatever publications and reprints of journal articles they have on Osteosclerosis. If necessary, they will refer you to other experts or researchers in the field. If you can't afford treatment, have your doctor call NICHD to find out if they are conducting any clinical studies that you might qualify for.

☎ Contact:
National Institute of Child Health
and Human Development
Bldg. 31, Room 2A32
Bethesda, MD 20892
(301) 496-5133

OTITIS MEDIA

See Ear Infections

OTOSCLEROSIS

Clearinghouses/Hotlines

The National Institute on Deafness and Other Communication Disorders (NIDCD) will send you whatever publications and reprints of journal articles they have on Otosclerosis. If you need further information, they will refer you to other organizations that study this and other related conditions. NIDCD does not conduct any clinical studies for this or any other disorder.

☎ Contact:
National Institute on Deafness
and Other Communication Disorders
Building 31
Room 3C35
Bethesda, MD 20892
(301) 496-7243
(800) 241-1044
(301) 402-0252 (TDD)

The National Institute of Neurological Disorders and Stroke (NINDS) can send you only information they have in their publications list on Otosclerosis. They cannot refer you to any experts. This Clearinghouse cannot directly give you information about any current clinical studies NINDS might be conducting on this illness, but you can find this information for yourself by looking under the National Institute of Neurological Disorders and Stroke in *Appendix A* at the end of this book.

☎ Contact:
National Institute of Neurological
Disorders and Stroke
Building 31
Room 8A06
Bethesda, MD 20892
(301) 496-5751
(800) 352-9424

OVARIAN CANCER

See also Cancer

Clearinghouses/Hotlines

The National Cancer Institute (NCI) will send you whatever publications and reprints of journal articles they have on Ovarian Cancer. They can also give you information on the state-of-the-art treatment for this disease, including specific treatment information for your stage of cancer. They can also search their Physician's Data Query (PDQ) database to let you know if NCI is conducting any clinical studies on your disease.

☎ Contact:
National Cancer Institute
Building 31
Room 10A24
Bethesda, MD 20892
(800) 4-CANCER
(301) 496-5583

Free Publications/Videos

The following publications on Ovarian Cancer are available from the National Cancer Institute, Bldg. 31, Room 10A24, Bethesda, MD 20892; (800) 4-CANCER, (301) 496-5583.

- *Research Report: Cancer of the Ovary.* (#89-3014)
- *What You Need to Know About Cancer of the Ovary.* (#91-1561)

OVER-THE-COUNTER DRUGS

See also Medications

Clearinghouses/Hotlines

The Over-the-Counter Drug Evaluation Division of the Center for Drug Evaluation and Research can provide information on the Over-The-Counter

Drug approval process or information on a specific over-the-counter drug category.

☎ Contact:
Over-the Counter Drug Evaluation Division
Center for Drug Evaluation and Research
Food and Drug Administration
5600 Fishers Lane
Rockville, MD 20857
(301) 295-8000

Free Publications/Videos

The following publication on Over-The-Counter Drugs is available from the Food & Drug Administration, (HFE-88), 5600 Fishers Lane, Rockville, MD 20857; (301) 443-3170.

- *OTC Drug Labels: "Must Read".* (#FDA88-3157)

OVULATION

Clearinghouses/Hotlines

The National Institute of Child Health and Human Development (NICHD) will send you whatever publications and reprints of journal articles they have on Ovulation. If necessary, they will refer you to other experts or researchers in the field. If you can't afford treatment, have your doctor call NICHD to find out if they are conducting any clinical studies that you might qualify for.

☎ Contact:
National Institute of Child Health
and Human Development
Building 31
Room 2A32
Bethesda, MD 20892
(301) 496-5133

- P -

PACEMAKERS

Clearinghouses/Hotlines

The National Heart, Lung, and Blood Institute (NHLBI) can search the Combined Health Information Database (CHID) and generate a bibliography of resources for you on Pacemakers. They also will send you any publications and journal articles they may have on hand, and will refer you to other organizations that are studying this issue. If you can't afford treatment, have your doctor call NHLBI to find out if they are conducting any clinical studies that you might qualify for.

☎ Contact:
National Heart, Lung, and Blood Institute
Bldg. 31, Room 4A21
Bethesda, MD 20892
(301) 496-4236

Free Publications/Videos

The following publications are available from the Center for Devices and Radiological Health, (HFZ-210), Food and Drug Administration, 5600 Fishers Ln., Rockville, MD 20857; (301) 443-4690.

- *Cardiac Pacemakers: Keeping Up The Beat.* (#FDA 81-4026)
- *Cordis Pleads Guilty, Four Executives of Pacemaker Company Indicted.*

PAGET'S DISEASE

Clearinghouses/Hotlines

The National Institute of Arthritis and Musculoskeletal and Skin Diseases (NIAMS) will send you whatever publications and reprints of articles from texts and journals they have on Paget's Disease of Bone (Osteitis Deformans) and Skin. They will also refer you to other organizations that are studying this disease. NIAMS will also let you know of any clinical studies that may be studying this disease and looking for patients.

☎ Contact:
National Institute of Arthritis
and Musculoskeletal and Skin Diseases
Box AMS
9000 Rockville Pike
Bethesda, MD 20892
(301) 495-4484

The National Cancer Institute (NCI) will send you whatever publications and reprints of journal articles they have on Paget's Disease of the Skin. They can also give you information on the state-of-the-art treatment for this disease, including specific treatment information for your stage of cancer. They can also search their Physician's Data Query (PDQ) database to let you know if NCI is conducting any clinical studies on your disease.

☎ Contact:
National Cancer Institute
Building 31
Room 10A24
Bethesda, MD 20892
(800) 4-CANCER
(301) 496-5583

Free Publications/Videos

The following publications on Paget's Disease are available from the National Institute of Arthritis and Musculoskeletal and Skin Diseases, Box AMS, 9000 Rockville Pike, Bethesda, MD 20892; (301) 495-4484.

- *Understanding Paget's Disease.* Describes this disease of the bone that occurs most frequently between the ages of 50 and 70. (#85-2241)
- *Researching the Cause and Treatment of Paget's Disease of Bone.*

PAIN

Clearinghouses/Hotlines

The National Cancer Institute (NCI) will send you whatever publications and reprints of journal articles they have on Cancer Related Pain. They can also give you information on the state-of-the-art treatment for this condition, including specific treatment information for your stage of cancer. They can also search their Physician's Data Query (PDQ) database to let you know if NCI is conducting any clinical studies on your disease.

☎ Contact:
National Cancer Institute
Bldg. 31, Room 10A24
Bethesda, MD 20892
(800) 4-CANCER
(301) 496-5583

The National Institute of Neurological Disorders and Stroke (NINDS) can send you information they have only in their publications list on Pain. They cannot refer you to any experts. This Clearinghouse cannot directly give you information about any current clinical studies NINDS might be conducting on this topic, but you can find this information for yourself by looking under the National Institute of Neurological Disorders and Stroke in *Appendix A* at the end of this book.

☎ Contact:
National Institute of Neurological
Disorders and Stroke
Bldg. 31, Room 8A06
Bethesda, MD 20892
(301) 496-5751
(800) 352-9424

The National Institute of Dental Research (NIDR) will send you whatever publications and reprints of journal articles they have on Oral-Facial Pain. As a policy, however, NIDR will not refer you to other organizations or experts who study this condition. If you can't afford treatment, have your doctor call Dr. Albert Guckers at (301) 496-6241 to find out if NIDR is conducting any clinical studies that you might qualify for.

☎ Contact:
National Institute of Dental Research

Bldg. 31, Room 2C35
Bethesda, MD 20892
(301) 496-4261

The National Institute on Aging (NIA) will send you whatever publications and reprints of journal articles they have on Pain and the Elderly. They cannot refer you to other experts if the information they have isn't sufficient for your purposes.

☎ Contact:
National Institute on Aging
Bldg. 31, Room 5C27
Bethesda, MD 20892
(301) 496-1752

Free Publications/Videos

The following publication on Pain is available from the Office of Clinical Center Communications, Bldg. 10, Room 1C255, Bethesda, MD 20892; (301) 496-2563.

- *Relief of Chronic Pain*. Video to help the general public make intelligent decisions.

The following publications on Pain are available from the Center for Devices and Radiological Health, (HFZ-210), Food and Drug Administration, 5600 Fishers Ln., Rockville, MD 20857; (301) 443-4690.

- *TENS, Current That Switches Off Pain.*
- *TENS 21DFD Part 882.*

The following publication on Pain is available from the National Institute of Neurological Disorders and Stroke, Bldg. 31, Room 8A06, Bethesda, MD 20892; (301) 496-5751 or (800) 352-9424.

- *Chronic Pain.* (#89-2406)

PALPITATIONS

Clearinghouses/Hotlines

The National Heart, Lung, and Blood Institute (NHLBI) can search the Combined Health Infor-

mation Database (CHID) and generate a bibliography of resources for you on Palpitations. They also will send you any publications and journal articles they may have on hand, and will refer you to other organizations that are studying this condition. If you can't afford treatment, have your doctor call NHLBI to find out if they are conducting any clinical studies that you might qualify for.

☎ Contact:
National Heart, Lung, and Blood Institute
Bldg. 31, Room 4A21
Bethesda, MD 20892
(301) 496-4236

PALSY

Clearinghouses/Hotlines

The National Institute of Neurological Disorders and Stroke (NINDS) can send you information they have only in their publications list on Progressive Supranuclear Palsy. They cannot refer you to any experts. This Clearinghouse cannot directly give you information about any current clinical studies NINDS might be conducting on this illness, but you can find this information for yourself by looking under the National Institute of Neurological Disorders and Stroke in *Appendix A* at the end of this book.

☎ Contact:
National Institute of Neurological
Disorders and Stroke
Bldg. 31, Room 8A06
Bethesda, MD 20892
(301) 496-5751
(800) 352-9424

PANCREATIC CANCER

See also Cancer

Clearinghouses/Hotlines

The National Cancer Institute (NCI) will send you whatever publications and reprints of journal

articles they have on Pancreatic Cancer. They can also give you information on the state-of-the-art treatment for this condition, including specific treatment information for your stage of cancer. They can also search their Physician's Data Query (PDQ) database to let you know if NCI is conducting any clinical studies on your disease.

☎ Contact:
National Cancer Institute
Bldg. 31, Room 10A24
Bethesda, MD 20892
(800) 4-CANCER
(301) 496-5583

Free Publications/Videos

The following publications on Pancreatic Cancer are available from the National Cancer Institute, Bldg. 31, Room 10A24, Bethesda, MD 20892; (800) 4-CANCER, or (301) 496-5583.

- *Research Report: Cancer of the Pancreas.* (#88-2941)
- *What You Need to Know About Cancer of the Pancreas.* (#90-1560)

PANCREATITIS

Clearinghouses/Hotlines

The National Digestive Diseases Information Clearinghouse (NDDIC) can search the Combined Health Information Database (CHID) and generate a bibliography of resources for you on Pancreatic Disease. They also will send you any publications and journal articles they may have on hand, and will refer you to other organizations that are studying this disease. If you can't afford treatment, have your doctor call NDDIC to find out if they are conducting any clinical studies that you might qualify for.

☎ Contact:
National Digestive Diseases
Information Clearinghouse
Box NDDIC
Bethesda, MD 20892
(301) 468-6344

Free Publications/Videos

The following publications are available from the National Digestive Diseases Information Clearinghouse, Box NDDIC, Bethesda, MD 20892; (301) 468-6344.

- *Pancreatitis.*
- *What Is Pancreatitis?* (#91-1596).

PANIC ATTACKS

Clearinghouses/Hotlines

The National Institute of Mental Health (NIMH) maintains data bases that index and abstract documents from the worldwide literature pertaining to Panic Attacks. In addition to scientific journals, there are references to audiovisuals, dissertations, government documents and reports. Contact NIMH for searches on specific subjects.

☎ Contact:
National Institute of Mental Health
5600 Fishers Lane, Room 15C05
Rockville, MD 20857
(301) 443-4515

Free Publications/Videos

The following video is available from the Office of Clinical Center Communications, Bldg. 10, Room 1C255, Bethesda, MD 20892; (301) 496-2563.

- *Phobias and Panic Disorder.* Video to help the general public make intelligent decisions.

PANENCEPHALITIS

Clearinghouses/Hotlines

The National Institute of Neurological Disorders and Stroke (NINDS) can send you information they have only in their publications list on Panencephalitis. They cannot refer you to any experts. This Clearinghouse cannot directly give you information about any current clinical studies NINDS might be conducting on this illness, but you can find this information for yourself by looking under the National Institute of Neurological Disorders and Stroke in *Appendix A* at the end of this book.

☎ Contact:
National Institute of Neurological
Disorders and Stroke
Bldg. 31, Room 8A06
Bethesda, MD 20892
(301) 496-5751
(800) 352-9424

PANNICULITIS

Clearinghouses/Hotlines

The National Institute of Diabetes and Digestive and Kidney Diseases's (NIDDK) individual clearinghouses can search the Combined Health Information Database (CHID) and generate a bibliography of resources for you on Panniculitis. They also will send you any publications and journal articles they may have on hand, and will refer you to other organizations studying this disease. If you can't afford treatment, have your doctor call NIDDK to find out if they are conducting any clinical studies that you might qualify for.

☎ Contact:
National Institute of Diabetes
and Digestive and Kidney Diseases
Bldg. 31, Room 9A04
Bethesda, MD 20892
(301) 496-3583

PAP TESTS

Clearinghouses/Hotlines

The National Cancer Institute (NCI) will send you whatever publications and reprints of journal articles they have on Pap Smears. They can also give you information on the state-of-the-art treatment for this issue.

☎ Contact:
National Cancer Institute
Bldg. 31, Room 10A24
Bethesda, MD 20892
(800) 4-CANCER
(301) 496-5583

Free Publications/Videos

The following publications on Pap Tests are available from the Family Life Information Exchange, P.O. Box 37299, Washington, DC 20013; (301) 585-6636.

- *Improving the Quality of Clinician Pap Smear.*

The following publication on Pap Tests is available from the Food & Drug Administration, (HFE-88), 5600 Fishers Ln., Rockville, MD 20857; (301) 443-3170.

- *Controversial PAP Test: It Could Save Your Life.* (#FDA90-1159)

The following publication on Pap Tests is available from the National Cancer Institute, Bldg. 31, Room 10A24, Bethesda, MD 20892; (800) 4-CANCER, or (301) 496-5583.

- *The Pap Test: It Can Save Your Life!* (#91-3213)

PAPILLOMA VIRUS

See also Cancer

Clearinghouses/Hotlines

The National Cancer Institute (NCI) will send you whatever publications and reprints of journal articles they have on Papilloma Virus and Cancer. They can also give you information on the state-of-the-art treatment for this condition, including specific treatment information for your stage of cancer. They can also search their Physician's Data Query (PDQ) database to let you know if NCI is conducting any clinical studies on your disease.

☎ Contact:
National Cancer Institute
Bldg. 31, Room 10A24
Bethesda, MD 20892
(800) 4-CANCER
(301) 496-5583

PARALYSIS AGITANS

Clearinghouses/Hotlines

The National Institute of Neurological Disorders and Stroke (NINDS) can send you information they have only in their publications list on Paralysis Agitans. They cannot refer you to any experts. This Clearinghouse cannot directly give you information about any current clinical studies NINDS might be conducting on this disorder, but you can find this information for yourself by looking under the National Institute of Neurological Disorders and Stroke in *Appendix A* at the end of this book.

☎ Contact:
National Institute of Neurological
Disorders and Stroke
Bldg. 31, Room 8A06
Bethesda, MD 20892
(301) 496-5751
(800) 352-9424

PARAMYOTONIA CONGENITA

Clearinghouses/Hotlines

The National Institute of Neurological Disorders and Stroke (NINDS) can send you information they have only in their publications list on Paramyotonia Congenita. They cannot refer you to any experts. This Clearinghouse cannot directly give you information about any current clinical

studies NINDS might be conducting on this illness, but you can find this information for yourself by looking under the National Institute of Neurological Disorders and Stroke in *Appendix A* at the end of this book.

☎ Contact:
National Institute of Neurological
Disorders and Stroke
Bldg. 31, Room 8A06
Bethesda, MD 20892
(301) 496-5751
(800) 352-9424

PARANOIA

Clearinghouses/Hotlines

The National Institute of Mental Health (NIMH) maintains data bases that index and abstract documents from the worldwide literature pertaining to Paranoia. In addition to scientific journals, there are references to audiovisuals, dissertations, government documents and reports. Contact NIMH for searches on specific subjects.

☎ Contact:
National Institute of Mental Health
5600 Fishers Lane, Room 15C05
Rockville, MD 20857
(301) 443-4515

Free Publications/Videos

The following publication is available from the National Institute of Mental Health, 5600 Fishers Ln., Room 15C05, Rockville, MD 20857; (301) 443-4515.

- *Useful Information on Paranoia.*

PARAPLEGIA

Clearinghouses/Hotlines

The National Institute of Neurological Disorders and Stroke (NINDS) can send you information they have only in their publications list on Paraplegia. They cannot refer you to any experts. This Clearinghouse cannot directly give you information about any current clinical studies NINDS might be conducting on this illness, but you can find this information for yourself by looking under the National Institute of Neurological Disorders and Stroke in *Appendix A* at the end of this book.

☎ Contact:
National Institute of Neurological
Disorders and Stroke
Bldg. 31, Room 8A06
Bethesda, MD 20892
(301) 496-5751
(800) 352-9424

PARASITIC DISEASE

Clearinghouses/Hotlines

The National Institute of Allergy and Infectious Diseases (NIAID) can search the Combined Health Information Database (CHID) and generate a bibliography of resources for you on Parasitic Disease. They will also send you any publications and journal articles they may have on hand, and will refer you to researchers who are currently studying this disease. If you can't afford treatment, have your doctor call NIAID to find out if they are conducting any clinical studies that you might qualify for.

☎ Contact:
National Institute of Allergy
and Infectious Diseases
Bldg. 31, Room 7A32
Bethesda, MD 20892
(301) 496-5717

PARATHYROID DISORDERS

Clearinghouses/Hotlines

The National Institute of Diabetes and Digestive and Kidney Diseases's (NIDDK) individual

clearinghouses can search the Combined Health Information Database (CHID) and generate a bibliography of resources for you on Parathyroid Disorders. They also will send you any publications and journal articles they may have on hand, and will refer you to other organizations that are studying this disease. If you can't afford treatment, have your doctor call NIDDK to find out if they are conducting any clinical studies that you might qualify for.

☎ Contact:
National Institute of Diabetes
and Digestive and Kidney Diseases
Bldg. 31, Room 9A04
Bethesda, MD 20892
(301) 496-3583

PARKINSON'S DISEASE

Clearinghouses/Hotlines

The National Institute of Neurological Disorders and Stroke (NINDS) can send you information they have only in their publications list on Parkinson's Disease. They cannot refer you to any experts. This Clearinghouse cannot directly give you information about any current clinical studies NINDS might be conducting on this illness, but you can find this information for yourself by looking under the National Institute of Neurological Disorders and Stroke in *Appendix A* at the end of this book.

☎ Contact:
National Institute of Neurological
Disorders and Stroke
Bldg. 31, Room 8A06
Bethesda, MD 20892
(301) 496-5751
(800) 352-9424

The National Institute on Deafness and Other Communication Disorders (NIDCD) will send you whatever publications and reprints of journal articles they have on Parkinson's Disease. If you need further information, they will refer you to other organizations that study this and other related diseases. NIDCD does not conduct any clinical studies for this or any other disorder.

☎ Contact:
National Institute on Deafness
and Other Communication Disorders
Bldg. 31, Room 3C35
Bethesda, MD 20892
(301) 496-7243
(800) 241-1044
(301) 402-0252 (TDD)

Free Publications/Videos

The following publication and video on Parkinson's Disease are available from the Office of Clinical Center Communications, Bldg. 10, Room 1C255, Bethesda, MD 20892; (301) 496-2563.

- *Parkinson's Disease: Natural and Drug-Induced Causes*. Video to help the general public make intelligent decisions.
- *Parkinson's Disease*. A booklet to educate consumers and allow them to make informed medical decisions.

The following publications on Parkinson's are available from the National Institute of Neurological Disorders and Stroke, Bldg. 31, Room 8A06, Bethesda, MD 20892; (301) 496-5751 or (800) 352-9424.

- *Parkinson's Disease: Hope Through Research*. Outlines the possible causes and treatments for Parkinson's disease and summarizes both research efforts and therapies. (#83-139)
- *Parkinson's Disease*. Discusses hope through research. (#83-139)
- *Parkinson's Disease*. Contains a collection of scientific articles, patient education pamphlets, and addresses of voluntary health associations.

PAROXYSMAL ATRIAL TACHYCARDIA

Clearinghouses/Hotlines

The National Heart, Lung, and Blood Institute (NHLBI) can search the Combined Health Information Database (CHID) and generate a bibliography of resources for you on Paroxysmal Atrial Tachycardia (PAT). They also will send you any publications and journal articles they may have on hand, and will refer you to other organizations that are studying this condition. If you can't afford treatment, have your doctor call NHLBI to find out if they are conducting any clinical studies that you might qualify for.

☎ Contact:
National Heart, Lung, and Blood Institute
Bldg. 31, Room 4A21
Bethesda, MD 20892
(301) 496-4236

PAROXYSMAL NOCTURNAL HEMOGLOBINURIA

Clearinghouses/Hotlines

The National Heart, Lung, and Blood Institute (NHLBI) can search the Combined Health Information Database (CHID) and generate a bibliography of resources for you on Paroxysmal Nocturnal Hemoglobinuria. They also will send you any publications and journal articles they may have on hand, and will refer you to other organizations that are studying this condition. If you can't afford treatment, have your doctor call NHLBI to find out if they are conducting any clinical studies that you might qualify for.

☎ Contact:
National Heart, Lung, and Blood Institute
Bldg. 31, Room 4A21
Bethesda, MD 20892
(301) 496-4236

The National Institute of Allergy and Infectious Diseases (NIAID) can search the Combined Health Information Database (CHID) and generate a bibliography of resources for you on Paroxysmal Nocturnal Hemoglobinuria. They will also send you any publications and journal articles they may have on hand, and will refer you to researchers who are currently studying this disease. If you can't afford treatment, have your doctor call NIAID to find out if they are conducting any clinical studies that you might qualify for.

☎ Contact:
National Institute of Allergy
and Infectious Diseases
Bldg. 31, Room 7A32
Bethesda, MD 20892
(301) 496-5717

PARS PLANITIS

Clearinghouses/Hotlines

The National Eye Institute (NEI) can give you up-to-date information on Pars Planitis by searching the Combined Health Information Database (CHID) and MEDLINE and sending you bibliographies of resources, along with any journal articles they may have. They can also refer you to any other organizations that study this and other related conditions. NEI will also let you know of any clinical studies that may be studying this disease and looking for patients. Because of their small staff, NEI prefers that you submit your requests for information in writing.

☎ Contact:
National Eye Institute
Bldg. 31, Room 6A32
Bethesda, MD 20892
(301) 496-5248

PARVOVIRUS INFECTIONS

Clearinghouses/Hotlines

The National Institute of Allergy and Infectious Diseases (NIAID) can search the Combined Health Information Database (CHID) and generate a bibliography of resources for you on Parvovirus Infections. They will also send you any publications and journal articles they may have on hand, and will refer you to researchers who are currently studying this disease. If you can't afford treatment, have your doctor call NIAID to find out if they are conducting any clinical studies that you might qualify for.

☎ Contact:
National Institute of Allergy
and Infectious Diseases
Bldg. 31, Room 7A32
Bethesda, MD 20892
(301) 496-5717

PASSIVE SMOKING

See also Smoking

Clearinghouses/Hotlines

The Office on Smoking and Health offers all kinds of information services on smoking and health issues. They can send you numerous publications in the field, and through its database can provide you with further bibliographic information. Their Smoking Studies Section designs and conducts national surveys on smoking behavior, attitude, knowledge, and beliefs regarding tobacco use.

☎ Contact:
Office on Smoking and Health
Centers for Disease Control
1600 Clifton Rd., NE
MS K-50
Atlanta, GA 30333
(404) 488-5705

Free Publications/Videos

The following publication is available from the Office of Technology Assessment, 600 Pennsylvania Ave., SE, Washington, DC 20510; (202) 224-8996.

- *Passive Smoking in the Workplace: Selected Issues*. A report to Congress. Ask for the summary report.

PCP

See also Drug Abuse

Clearinghouses/Hotlines

The National Clearinghouse for Alcohol and Drug Information is the central point within the Federal Government for current print and audiovisual materials about alcohol and other drugs. They have information tailored to parents, teachers, youth, and others, as well as information about organizations and groups concerned with alcohol and other drug problems. They have publications, reports, newsletters, videos, posters, and more, as well as being able to provide comprehensive alcohol and other drug resource referrals. Call for your free catalog.

☎ Contact:
National Clearinghouse for Alcohol
and Drug Information
P.O. Box 2345
Rockville, MD 20852
(800) 729-6686
(301) 468-2600

Free Publications/Videos

The following publications on PCP are available from the National Clearinghouse for Alcohol and Drug Information, P.O. Box 2345, Rockville, MD 20852; (301) 468-2600.

- *PCP* and *PCP: Update on Abuse*. Fact sheets give basic information about the psychological and physiological effects.

PECTUS EXCAVATUM

Clearinghouses/Hotlines

The National Heart, Lung, and Blood Institute (NHLBI) can search the Combined Health Information Database (CHID) and generate a bibliography of resources for you on Pectus Excavatum (Funnel Chest). They also will send you any publications and journal articles they may have on hand, and will refer you to other organizations that are studying this condition. If you can't afford treatment, have your doctor call NHLBI to find out if they are conducting any clinical studies that you might qualify for.

☎ Contact:
National Heart, Lung, and Blood Institute
Bldg. 31, Room 4A21
Bethesda, MD 20892
(301) 496-4236

The National Institute of Arthritis and Musculoskeletal and Skin Diseases (NIAMS) will send you whatever publications and reprints of articles from texts and journals they have on Pectus Excavatum (as related to Marfans only). They will also refer you to other organizations that are studying this disease. NIAMS will also let you know of any clinical studies that may be studying this disease and looking for patients.

☎ Contact:
National Institute of Arthritis
and Musculoskeletal and Skin Diseases
Box AMS
9000 Rockville Pike
Bethesda, MD 20892
(301) 495-4484

PEDIATRIC AIDS

See AIDS

PEDICULOSIS

See Lice

PEDODONTICS

Clearinghouses/Hotlines

The National Institute of Dental Research (NIDR) will send you whatever publications and reprints of journal articles they have on Pedodontics. As a policy, however, NIDR will not refer you to other organizations or experts who study this issue. If you can't afford treatment, have your doctor call

Dr. Albert Guckers at (301) 496-6241 to find out if NIDR is conducting any clinical studies that you might qualify for.

☎ Contact:
National Institute of Dental Research
Bldg. 31, Room 2C35
Bethesda, MD 20892
(301) 496-4261

PELIZAEOUS-MERZBACHER DISEASE

Clearinghouses/Hotlines

The National Institute of Neurological Disorders and Stroke (NINDS) can send you information they have only in their publications list on Pelizaeous-Merzbacher Disease. They cannot refer you to any experts. This Clearinghouse cannot directly give you information about any current clinical studies NINDS might be conducting on this illness, but you can find this information for yourself by looking under the National Institute of Neurological Disorders and Stroke in *Appendix A* at the end of this book.

☎ Contact:
National Institute of Neurological
Disorders and Stroke
Bldg. 31, Room 8A06
Bethesda, MD 20892
(301) 496-5751
(800) 352-9424

PELVIC INFLAMMATORY DISEASE

Clearinghouses/Hotlines

The National Institute of Allergy and Infectious Diseases (NIAID) can search the Combined Health Information Database (CHID) and generate a bibliography of resources for you on Pelvic Inflammatory Disease. They will also send you any publications and journal articles they may

have on hand, and will refer you to researchers who are currently studying this disease. If you can't afford treatment, have your doctor call NIAID to find out if they are conducting any clinical studies that you might qualify for.

☎ Contact:
National Institute of Allergy
and Infectious Diseases
Bldg. 31, Room 7A32
Bethesda, MD 20892
(301) 496-5717

PEMPHIGOID

Clearinghouses/Hotlines

The National Cancer Institute (NCI) will send you whatever publications and reprints of journal articles they have on Pemphigoid. They can also give you information on the state-of-the-art treatment for this condition, including specific treatment information for your stage of cancer. They can also search their Physician's Data Query (PDQ) database to let you know if NCI is conducting any clinical studies on your disease.

☎ Contact:
National Cancer Institute
Bldg. 31, Room 10A24
Bethesda, MD 20892
(800) 4-CANCER
(301) 496-5583

The National Institute of Arthritis and Musculoskeletal and Skin Diseases (NIAMS) will send you whatever publications and reprints of articles from texts and journals they have on Pemphigoid. They will also refer you to other organizations that are studying this disease. NIAMS will also let you know of any clinical studies that may be studying this disease and looking for patients.

☎ Contact:
National Institute of Arthritis
and Musculoskeletal and Skin Diseases
Box AMS
9000 Rockville Pike
Bethesda, MD 20892
(301) 495-4484

PENICILLIN

Free Publications/Videos

The following publication on Penicillin is available from the Food & Drug Administration, (HFE-88), 5600 Fishers Ln., Rockville, MD 20857; (301) 443-3170.

- *How To Take Your Medicines: Penicillins.* (#FDA91-3184)

PEPTIC ULCERS

Clearinghouses/Hotlines

The National Institute of Diabetes and Digestive and Kidney Diseases's (NIDDK) individual clearinghouses can search the Combined Health Information Database (CHID) and generate a bibliography of resources for you on Peptic Ulcers. They also will send you any publications and journal articles they may have on hand, and will refer you to other organizations that are studying this disease. If you can't afford treatment, have your doctor call NIDDK to find out if they are conducting any clinical studies that you might qualify for.

☎ Contact:
National Institute of Diabetes
and Digestive and Kidney Diseases
Building 31
Room 9A04
Bethesda, MD 20892
(301) 496-3583

Free Publications/Videos

The following publication on Peptic Ulcers is available from the National Institute of Diabetes and Digestive and Kidney Diseases, Bldg. 31, Room 9A04, Bethesda, MD 20892; (301) 496-3583.

- *Peptic Ulcer.* (#85-38)

PERIARTERITIS NODOSA

Clearinghouses/Hotlines

The National Heart, Lung, and Blood Institute (NHLBI) can search the Combined Health Information Database (CHID) and generate a bibliography of resources for you on Periarteritis Nodosa. They also will send you any publications and journal articles they may have on hand, and will refer you to other organizations that are studying this condition. If you can't afford treatment, have your doctor call NHLBI to find out if they are conducting any clinical studies that you might qualify for.

☎ Contact:
National Heart, Lung, and Blood Institute
Building 31
Room 4A21
Bethesda, MD 20892
(301) 496-4236

The National Institute of Allergy and Infectious Diseases (NIAID) can search the Combined Health Information Database (CHID) and generate a bibliography of resources for you on Periarteritis Nodosa. They will also send you any publications and journal articles they may have on hand, and will refer you to researchers who are currently studying this disease. If you can't afford treatment, have your doctor call NIAID to find out if they are conducting any clinical studies that you might qualify for.

☎ Contact:
National Institute of Allergy
and Infectious Diseases
Building 31
Room 7A32
Bethesda, MD 20892
(301) 496-5717

PERICARDITIS

Clearinghouses/Hotlines

The National Heart, Lung, and Blood Institute

(NHLBI) can search the Combined Health Information Database (CHID) and generate a bibliography of resources for you on Pericarditis. They also will send you any publications and journal articles they may have on hand, and will refer you to other organizations that are studying this condition. If you can't afford treatment, have your doctor call NHLBI to find out if they are conducting any clinical studies that you might qualify for.

☎ Contact:
National Heart, Lung, and Blood Institute
Building 31
Room 4A21
Bethesda, MD 20892
(301) 496-4236

PERICARDIAL TAMPONADE

Clearinghouses/Hotlines

The National Heart, Lung, and Blood Institute (NHLBI) can search the Combined Health Information Database (CHID) and generate a bibliography of resources for you on Pericardial Tamponade. They also will send you any publications and journal articles they may have on hand, and will refer you to other organizations studying this condition. If you can't afford treatment, have your doctor call NHLBI to find out if they are conducting any clinical studies you might qualify for.

☎ Contact:
National Heart, Lung, and
Blood Institute
Building 31
Room 4A21
Bethesda, MD 20892
(301) 496-4236

PERINATAL SERVICES

See Prenatal

PERIODONTAL DISEASE

Clearinghouses/Hotlines

The National Institute of Dental Research (NIDR) will send you whatever publications and reprints of journal articles they have on Periodontal Disease. As a policy, however, NIDR will not refer you to other organizations or experts who study this disease. If you can't afford treatment, have your doctor call Dr. Albert Guckers at (301) 496-6241 to find out if NIDR is conducting any clinical studies that you might qualify for.

☎ Contact:
National Institute of
Dental Research
Building 31
Room 2C35
Bethesda, MD 20892
(301) 496-4261

Free Publications/Videos

The following video on Periodontal Disease is available from the Office of Clinical Center Communications, Building 10, Room 1C255, Bethesda, MD 20892; (301) 496-2563.

- *Periodontal Disease*. Video to help the general public make intelligent decisions.

The following publications on Periodontal Disease are available from the National Institute of Dental Research, Building 31, Room 2C35, Bethesda, MD 20892; (301) 496-4261.

- *Periodontal (Gum) Disease*.
- *Detection and Prevention of Periodontal Disease in Diabetes*. (#86-1148)
- *Tooth Decay*. (#82-1146)
- *Preventing Tooth Decay: A Guide to Implementing Self-Applied Fluoride Programs in School Settings*.

PERIPHERAL NEUROPATHY

Clearinghouses/Hotlines

The National Institute of Neurological Disorders and Stroke (NINDS) can send you information they have only in their publications list on Peripheral Neuropathy. They cannot refer you to any experts. This Clearinghouse cannot directly give you information about any current clinical studies NINDS might be conducting on this disorder, but you can find this information for yourself by looking under the National Institute of Neurological Disorders and Stroke in *Appendix A* at the end of this book.

☎ Contact:
National Institute of Neurological
Disorders and Stroke
Bldg. 31, Room 8A06
Bethesda, MD 20892
(301) 496-5751
(800) 352-9424

Free Publications/Videos

The following publication on Peripheral Neuropathy is available from the National Institute of Neurological Disorders and Stroke, P.O. Box 5801, Bethesda, MD 20824; (800) 352-9424, or (301) 496-5751.

- *Peripheral Neuropathy*. Collection of scientific articles, patient education pamphlets, and addresses of voluntary health associations.

PERIPHERAL VASCULAR DISEASE

Clearinghouses/Hotlines

The National Heart, Lung, and Blood Institute (NHLBI) can search the Combined Health Information Database (CHID) and generate a bibliography of resources for you on Peripheral Vascular Disease. They also will send you any publications and journal articles they may have on

hand, and will refer you to other organizations that are studying this condition. If you can't afford treatment, have your doctor call NHLBI to find out if they are conducting any clinical studies that you might qualify for.

☎ Contact:
National Heart, Lung, and Blood Institute
Bldg. 31, Room 4A21
Bethesda, MD 20892
(301) 496-4236

PERNICIOUS ANEMIA

Clearinghouses/Hotlines

The National Institute of Diabetes and Digestive and Kidney Diseases's (NIDDK) individual clearinghouses can search the Combined Health Information Database (CHID) and generate a bibliography of resources for you on Pernicious Anemia. They also will send you any publications and journal articles they may have on hand, and will refer you to other organizations that are studying this disease. If you can't afford treatment, have your doctor call NIDDK to find out if they are conducting any clinical studies that you might qualify for.

☎ Contact:
National Institute of Diabetes
and Digestive and Kidney Diseases
Bldg. 31, Room 9A04
Bethesda, MD 20892
(301) 496-3583

PERSONALITY DISORDERS

Clearinghouses/Hotlines

The National Institute of Mental Health (NIMH) will send you whatever publications and reprints of articles from texts and journals they have on Personality Disorders. They will also refer you to other organizations that are studying this issue. NIMH will also let you know of any clinical studies that may be studying this disorder and looking for patients.

☎ Contact:
National Institute of Mental Health
5600 Fishers Lane
Room 15C05
Rockville, MD 20857
(301) 443-4515

PERTUSSIS

See also Immunizations

Clearinghouses/Hotlines

The National Institute of Allergy and Infectious Diseases (NIAID) can search the Combined Health Information Database (CHID) and generate a bibliography of resources for you on Pertussis. They will also send you any publications and journal articles they may have on hand, and will refer you to researchers who are currently studying this disease. If you can't afford treatment, have your doctor call NIAID to find out if they are conducting any clinical studies that you might qualify for.

☎ Contact:
National Institute of Allergy
and Infectious Diseases
Bldg. 31, Room 7A32
Bethesda, MD 20892
(301) 496-5717

PERVASIVE DEVELOPMENTAL DISORDERS

See also Developmental Disabilities

Free Publications/Videos

The following publication is available from the National Institute of Neurological Disorders and Stroke, P.O. Box 5801, Bethesda, MD 20824; (800) 352-9424, or (301) 496-5751.

- *Pervasive Developmental Disorders*. Contains a collection of scientific articles, patient education pamphlets, and addresses of voluntary health associations.

PESTICIDES

Clearinghouses/Hotlines

The National Pesticide Telecommunications Network, a service of the U.S. Environmental Protection Agency and Texas Tech University, will respond to your non-emergency questions about the effects of Pesticides, toxicology and symptoms, environmental effects, disposal and cleanup, and safe use of pesticides. It's open 24 hours, 7 days a week.

☎ Contact:
National Pesticide Telecommunications Network
(800) 858-7378

The Environmental Protection Agency is interested in receiving information on any adverse effects associated with Pesticide exposure. You should provide as complete information as possible, including any official investigation report of the incident and medical records concerning adverse health effects. Medical records will be held in confidence.

☎ Contact:
Frank Davido
Pesticide Incident Response Officer
Field Operations Division (H-7506C)
Office of Pesticide Programs
Environmental Protection Agency
401 M St., SW
Washington, DC 20460
(703) 305-0576

National Institute of Environmental Health Sciences (NIEHS) will send you whatever publications and journal articles they can locate on specific questions about Pesticides. If necessary they can put you in contact with researchers studying this issue. NIEHS does not conduct any clinical studies.

☎ Contact:
National Institute of Environmental

Health Sciences
P.O. Box 12233
Research Triangle Park, NC 27709
(919) 541-3345

Free Publications/Videos

The following publication on Pesticides is available from the Food and Nutrition Information Center, National Agricultural Library, Room 304, Beltsville, MD 20705; (301) 504-5719.

- *Pesticide Residues in Food.* A list of current references.

The following publication on Pesticides is available from the Food & Drug Administration, (HFE-88), 5600 Fishers Ln., Rockville, MD 20857; (301) 443-3170.

- *Produce and Pesticides.* (#OM89-3020)

The following publications on Pesticides are available from the Public Information Center, PM-211B, Environmental Protection Agency, 401 M St., SW, Washington, DC 20460; (202) 260-7751.

- *Citizen's Guide to Pesticides*. Describes how to choose and use pesticides, how to pick a pest control company, and what to do in the event of a problem.
- *Regulating Pesticides*. Explains Environmental Protection Agency's registration process and how they classify pesticides.
- *EPA's Pesticide Programs*. Pesticide registration and food safety are discussed first, followed by other pesticide programs.

The following publication on Pesticides is available from the Consumer Information Center, Pueblo, CO 81009.

- *Pesticides in Drinking-Water Wells*. Learn how to test water and what to do if it's unsafe. (#434Y, $.50)

The following Congressional Research Service (CRS) reports on Pesticide Residues are available from either of your U.S. Senators' offices at the U.S. Capitol, Washington, DC 20510, or from your Congressional Representative at the U.S. Capitol, Washington, DC 20515. You can also call in your request through the U.S. Capitol switchboard at (202) 224-3121. Be sure to include the full title and report number in your request.

- *Apple Alarm: Public Concern About Pesticide Residues in Fruits and Vegetables.* (#89-166 ENR)
- *Pesticide Monitoring Program: Developing New Methods to Detect Pesticide Residues in Food.* (#87-413 SPR)
- *Pesticides in Food: A Checklist of CRS Products.* (#91-918 L)

PEYRONIE'S DISEASE

Clearinghouses/Hotlines

The National Institute of Diabetes and Digestive 0and Kidney Diseases's (NIDDK) individual clearinghouses can search the Combined Health Information Database (CHID) and generate a bibliography of resources for you on Peyronie's Disease. They also will send you any publications and journal articles they may have on hand, and will refer you to other organizations that are studying this disease. If you can't afford treatment, have your doctor call NIDDK to find out if they are conducting any clinical studies that you might qualify for.

☎ Contact:
National Institute of Diabetes
and Digestive and Kidney Diseases
Bldg. 31, Room 9A04
Bethesda, MD 20892
(301) 496-3583

PHARMACEUTICALS

See Medications
See Drug Approval Process
See Drug Evaluation

PHARMACOLOGY

Clearinghouses/Hotlines

The National Institute of General Medical Sciences can tell you about on-going Pharmacology research projects they're funding and will refer you to the researcher in charge of a particular project.

☎ Contact:
National Institutes of Health
Building 31, Room 4A52
Bethesda, MD 20892
(301) 496-7301

National Institute of Environmental Health Sciences (NIEHS) will send you whatever publications and journal articles they can locate on specific questions about Pharmacology and Toxicology. If necessary they can put you in contact with researchers studying this issue. NIEHS does not conduct any clinical studies.

☎ Contact:
National Institute of Environmental
Health Sciences
P.O. Box 12233
Research Triangle Park, NC 27709
(919) 541-3345

PHARYNGEAL DISABILITIES

Clearinghouses/Hotlines

The National Institute of Dental Research (NIDR) will send you whatever publications and reprints of journal articles they have on Pharyngeal Disabilities. As a policy, however, NIDR will not refer you to other organizations or experts who study this condition. If you can't afford treatment, have your doctor call Dr. Albert Guckers at (301) 496-6241 to find out if NIDR is conducting any clinical studies that you might qualify for.

☎ Contact:
National Institute of Dental Research
Bldg. 31, Room 2C35
Bethesda, MD 20892
(301) 496-4261

PHENYLKETONURIA

See PKU

PHEOCHROMOCYTOMA

Clearinghouses/Hotlines

The National Heart, Lung, and Blood Institute (NHLBI) can search the Combined Health Information Database (CHID) and generate a bibliography of resources for you on Pheochromocytoma. They also will send you any publications and journal articles they may have on hand, and will refer you to other organizations that are studying this condition. If you can't afford treatment, have your doctor call NHLBI to find out if they are conducting any clinical studies that you might qualify for.

☎ Contact:
National Heart, Lung, and Blood Institute
Bldg. 31, Room 4A21
Bethesda, MD 20892
(301) 496-4236

PHLEBITIS

Clearinghouses/Hotlines

The National Heart, Lung, and Blood Institute (NHLBI) can search the Combined Health Information Database (CHID) and generate a bibliography of resources for you on Phlebitis. They also will send you any publications and journal articles they may have on hand, and will refer you to other organizations that are studying this condition. If you can't afford treatment, have your doctor call NHLBI to find out if they are conducting any clinical studies that you might qualify for.

☎ Contact:
National Heart, Lung, and Blood Institute
Building 31

Room 4A21
Bethesda, MD 20892
(301) 496-4236

PHLEBOTHROMBOSIS

Clearinghouses/Hotlines

The National Heart, Lung, and Blood Institute (NHLBI) can search the Combined Health Information Database (CHID) and generate a bibliography of resources for you on Phlebothrombosis. They also will send you any publications and journal articles they may have on hand, and will refer you to other organizations that are studying this condition. If you can't afford treatment, have your doctor call NHLBI to find out if they are conducting any clinical studies that you might qualify for.

☎ Contact:
National Heart, Lung, and Blood Institute
Building 31
Room 4A21
Bethesda, MD 20892
(301) 496-4236

PHOBIAS

Clearinghouses/Hotlines

The National Institute of Mental Health (NIMH) will send you whatever publications and reprints of articles from texts and journals they have on Phobias. They will also refer you to other organizations that are studying this issue. NIMH will also let you know of any clinical studies that may be studying these disorders and looking for patients.

☎ Contact:
National Institute of Mental Health
5600 Fishers Lane
Room 15C05
Rockville, MD 20857
(301) 443-4515

Free Publications/Videos

The following video is available from the Office of Clinical Center Communications, Bldg. 10, Room 1C255, Bethesda, MD 20892; (301) 496-2563.

- *Phobias and Panic Disorder*. Video to help the general public make intelligent decisions.

PHYSICAL FITNESS

See Exercise

PICK'S DISEASE

Clearinghouses/Hotlines

The National Institute of Neurological Disorders and Stroke (NINDS) can send you information they have only in their publications list on Pick's Disease. They cannot refer you to any experts. This Clearinghouse cannot directly give you information about any current clinical studies NINDS might be conducting on this illness, but you can find this information for yourself by looking under the National Institute of Neurological Disorders and Stroke in *Appendix A* at the end of this book.

☎ Contact:
National Institute of Neurological Disorders and Stroke
Bldg. 31, Room 8A06
Bethesda, MD 20892
(301) 496-5751
(800) 352-9424

Free Publications/Videos

The following publication is available from the National Institute of Neurological Disorders and Stroke, P.O. Box 5801, Bethesda, MD 20824; (800) 352-9424, or (301) 496-5751.

- Pick's Disease. Collection of scientific articles, patient education pamphlets, and addresses of voluntary health associations.

THE PILL

See Oral Contraceptives

PI-MESONS

Clearinghouses/Hotlines

The National Cancer Institute (NCI) will send you whatever publications and reprints of journal articles they have on Pi-Mesons Cancer Treatment. They can also give you information on the state-of-the-art treatment for this issue, including specific treatment information for your stage of cancer. They can also search their Physician's Data Query (PDQ) database to let you know if NCI is conducting any clinical studies on your disease.

☎ Contact:
National Cancer Institute
Bldg. 31, Room 10A24
Bethesda, MD 20892
(800) 4-CANCER
(301) 496-5583

PIMPLES

See Acne

PINK EYE

Clearinghouses/Hotlines

The National Eye Institute (NEI) can give you up-to-date information on Pink Eye by searching the

Combined Health Information Database (CHID) and MEDLINE and sending you bibliographies of resources, along with any journal articles they may have. They can also refer you to any other organizations that study this and other related conditions. NEI will also let you know of any clinical studies that may be studying this disorder and looking for patients. Because of their small staff, NEI prefers that you submit your requests for information in writing.

☎ Contact:
National Eye Institute
Bldg. 31, Room 6A32
Bethesda, MD 20892
(301) 496-5248

PINTA

Clearinghouses/Hotlines

The National Arthritis and Musculoskeletal and Skin Diseases Clearinghouse can provide you with information regarding Pinta. They can search the Combined Health Information Database (CHID) for information regarding this condition and can refer you to other organizations.

☎ Contact:
National Arthritis and Musculoskeletal and Skin Diseases Clearinghouse
Box AMS
Bethesda, MD 20892
(301) 495-4484

PINWORMS

Clearinghouses/Hotlines

The National Institute of Allergy and Infectious Diseases (NIAID) can search the Combined Health Information Database (CHID) and generate a bibliography of resources for you on Pinworms. They will also send you any publications and journal articles they may have on hand, and will refer you to researchers who are currently studying this condition. If you can't afford treatment, have your doctor call NIAID to find out if they are conducting any clinical studies that you might qualify for.

☎ Contact:
National Institute of Allergy
and Infectious Diseases
Bldg. 31, Room 7A32
Bethesda, MD 20892
(301) 496-5717

PITUITARY TUMORS

Clearinghouses/Hotlines

The National Institute of Neurological Disorders and Stroke (NINDS) can send you information they have only in their publications list on Pituitary Tumors. They cannot refer you to any experts. This Clearinghouse cannot directly give you information about any current clinical studies NINDS might be conducting on this topic, but you can find this information for yourself by looking under the National Institute of Neurological Disorders and Stroke in *Appendix A* at the end of this book.

☎ Contact:
National Institute of Neurological
Disorders and Stroke
Bldg. 31, Room 8A06
Bethesda, MD 20892
(301) 496-5751
(800) 352-9424

The National Institute of Diabetes and Digestive and Kidney Diseases's (NIDDK) individual clearinghouses can search the Combined Health Information Database (CHID) and generate a bibliography of resources for you on Pituitary Tumors. They also will send you any publications and journal articles they may have on hand, and will refer you to other organizations that are studying this disease. If you can't afford treatment, have your doctor call NIDDK to find out if they are conducting any clinical studies that you might qualify for.

☎ Contact:
National Institute of Diabetes
and Digestive and Kidney Diseases

Bldg. 31, Room 9A04
Bethesda, MD 20892
(301) 496-3583

The National Institute of Child Health and Human Development (NICHD) will send you whatever publications and reprints of journal articles they have on Pituitary Tumors. If necessary, they will refer you to other experts or researchers in the field. If you can't afford treatment, have your doctor call NICHD to find out if they are conducting any clinical studies that you might qualify for.

☎ Contact:
National Institute of Child Health
and Human Development
Bldg. 31, Room 2A32
Bethesda, MD 20892
(301) 496-5133

PITYRIASIS

Clearinghouses/Hotlines

The National Institute of Arthritis and Musculoskeletal and Skin Diseases (NIAMS) will send you whatever publications and reprints of articles from texts and journals they have on Pityriasis Rosea and Rubra Pilaris. They will also refer you to other organizations that are studying these diseases. NIAMS will also let you know of any clinical studies that may be studying this disease and looking for patients.

☎ Contact:
National Institute of Arthritis
and Musculoskeletal and Skin Diseases
Box AMS
Bethesda, MD 20892
(301) 495-4484

The National Cancer Institute (NCI) will send you whatever publications and reprints of journal articles they have on Pityriasis Rubra Pilaris. They can also give you information on the state-of-the-art treatment for this condition, including specific treatment information for your stage of cancer. They can also search their Physician's Data Query (PDQ) database to let you know if

NCI is conducting any clinical studies on your disease.

☎ Contact:
National Cancer Institute
Building 31
Room 10A24
Bethesda, MD 20892
(800) 4-CANCER
(301) 496-5583

PKD

See Polycystic Kidney Disease

PKU

Clearinghouses/Hotlines

The National Institute of Child Health and Human Development (NICHD) will send you whatever publications and reprints of journal articles they have on PKU (Phenylketonuria). If necessary, they will refer you to other experts or researchers in the field. If you can't afford treatment, have your doctor call NICHD to find out if they are conducting any clinical studies that you might qualify for.

☎ Contact:
National Institute of Child Health
and Human Development
Building 31
Room 2A32
Bethesda, MD 20892
(301) 496-5133

The National Maternal and Child Health Clearinghouse has all kinds of information on maternal and child health issues, such as pregnancy, child and adolescent health, and human genetics. If the answer to your question can't be answered by any of their countless free publications, they can refer you to other National or local resources. If you still need further information, they search their own reference collection and send you what they find.

☎ Contact:
National Maternal and Child
Health Clearinghouse
38th & R Sts., NW
Washington, DC 20057
(703) 821-8955, ext. 254

Free Publications/Videos

The following publications on PKU are available from the National Maternal and Child Health Clearinghouse, 38th & R Sts., NW, Washington, DC 20057; (703) 821-8955, ext. 254.

- *A Babysitter's Guide to PKU.* (#B265)
- *Chef Lo-Phe's Phe-Nominal Cookbook.* (#B322)
- *Dental Health in Children With PKU.* (#B146)
- *Finger Foods Are Fun.* (#B279)
- *Games That Teach: Learning by Doing for Preschoolers with PKU.* (#B280)
- *Guide to Breastfeeding the Infant with PKU.* (#B327)
- *National Survey of Treatment Programs for PKU and Selected Other Inherited Metabolic Diseases.* (#C049)
- *New Parents' Guide to PKU.* (#B335)

PLACENTA DISORDERS

Clearinghouses/Hotlines

The National Institute of Child Health and Human Development (NICHD) will send you whatever publications and reprints of journal articles they have on Placenta Disorders. If necessary, they will refer you to other experts or researchers in the field. If you can't afford treatment, have your doctor call NICHD to find out if they are conducting any clinical studies that you might qualify for.

☎ Contact:
National Institute of Child Health
and Human Development
Bldg. 31, Room 2A32
Bethesda, MD 20892
(301) 496-5133

PLAQUE

Clearinghouses/Hotlines

The National Institute of Dental Research (NIDR) will send you whatever publications and reprints of journal articles they have on Plaque. As a policy, however, NIDR will not refer you to other organizations or experts who study this condition. If you can't afford treatment, have your doctor call Dr. Albert Guckers at (301) 496-6241 to find out if NIDR is conducting any clinical studies that you might qualify for.

☎ Contact:
National Institute of Dental Research
Bldg. 31, Room 2C35
Bethesda, MD 20892
(301) 496-4261

PLASMA CELL CANCER

Clearinghouses/Hotlines

The National Cancer Institute (NCI) will send you whatever publications and reprints of journal articles they have on Plasma Cell Cancer. They can also give you information on the state-of-the-art treatment for this condition, including specific treatment information for your stage of cancer. They can also search their Physician's Data Query (PDQ) database to let you know if NCI is conducting any clinical studies on your disease.

☎ Contact:
National Cancer Institute
Bldg. 31, Room 10A24
Bethesda, MD 20892
(800) 4-CANCER
(301) 496-5583

PLASTIC SURGERY

See Face Lifts

PLAYGROUND SAFETY

Free Publications/Videos

The following publication is available from the National Maternal and Child Health Clearinghouse, 38th & R Sts., NW, Washington, DC 20057; (703) 821-8955, ext. 254.

- *Playground Perspectives: A Curriculum Guide for Promoting Playground Safety.* (#C036)

PLEURISY

Clearinghouses/Hotlines

The National Heart, Lung, and Blood Institute (NHLBI) can search the Combined Health Information Database (CHID) and generate a bibliography of resources for you on Pleurisy. They also will send you any publications and journal articles they may have on hand, and will refer you to other organizations that are studying this condition. If you can't afford treatment, have your doctor call NHLBI to find out if they are conducting any clinical studies that you might qualify for.

☎ Contact:
National Heart, Lung, and Blood Institute
Bldg. 31, Room 4A21
Bethesda, MD 20892
(301) 496-4236

PLICAMYCIN

Free Publications/Videos

The following publication is available from the National Cancer Institute, Bldg. 31, Room 10A24, Bethesda, MD 20892; (800) 4-CANCER, or (301) 496-5583.

- *Plicamicina/Plicamycin.* Provides information

about side effects, proper usage, and precautions of this anti-cancer drug.

PMS

Clearinghouses/Hotlines

The National Institute of Child Health and Human Development (NICHD) will send you whatever publications and reprints of journal articles they have on PMS (Premenstrual Syndrome). If necessary, they will refer you to other experts or researchers in the field. If you can't afford treatment, have your doctor call NICHD to find out if they are conducting any clinical studies that you might qualify for.

☎ Contact:
National Institute of Child Health
and Human Development
Bldg. 31, Room 2A32
Bethesda, MD 20892
(301) 496-5133

The National Institute of Mental Health (NIMH) will send you whatever publications and reprints of articles from texts and journals they have on PMS (Premenstrual Syndrome). They will also refer you to other organizations that are studying this issue. NIMH will also let you know of any clinical studies that may be studying this disorder and looking for patients.

☎ Contact:
National Institute of Mental Health
5600 Fishers Lane
Room 15C05
Rockville, MD 20857
(301) 443-4515

Free Publications/Videos

The following publication is available from the National Institute of Child Health and Human Development, Bldg. 31, Room 2A32, Bethesda, MD 20892; (301) 496-5133.

- *Facts About Dysmenorrhea and Premenstrual Syndrome.*

PNEUMOCOCCAL INFECTIONS

Clearinghouses/Hotlines

The National Institute of Allergy and Infectious Diseases (NIAID) can search the Combined Health Information Database (CHID) and generate a bibliography of resources for you on Pneumococcal Infections. They will also send you any publications and journal articles they may have on hand, and will refer you to researchers currently studying this condition. If you can't afford treatment, have your doctor call NIAID to find out if they are conducting any clinical studies that you might qualify for.

☎ Contact:
National Institute of Allergy
and Infectious Diseases
Bldg. 31, Room 7A32
Bethesda, MD 20892
(301) 496-5717

The National Heart, Lung, and Blood Institute (NHLBI) can search the Combined Health Information Database (CHID) and generate a bibliography of resources for you on Pneumoconioses (Dust Inhalation Disease). They also will send you any publications and journal articles they may have on hand, and will refer you to other organizations that are studying this condition. If you can't afford treatment, have your doctor call NHLBI to find out if they are conducting any clinical studies that you might qualify for.

☎ Contact:
National Heart, Lung, and Blood Institute
Bldg. 31, Room 4A21
Bethesda, MD 20892
(301) 496-4236

PNEUMOTHORAX

Clearinghouses/Hotlines

The National Heart, Lung, and Blood Institute

(NHLBI) can search the Combined Health Information Database (CHID) and generate a bibliography of resources for you on Pneumothorax. They also will send you any publications and journal articles they may have on hand, and will refer you to other organizations that are studying this condition. If you can't afford treatment, have your doctor call NHLBI to find out if they are conducting any clinical studies that you might qualify for.

☎ Contact:
National Heart, Lung, and Blood Institute
Bldg. 31, Room 4A21
Bethesda, MD 20892
(301) 496-4236

POISONING

Clearinghouses/Hotlines

The Poison Control Centers answer specific questions about situations involving poisons. While most calls received involve questions regarding children, a significant number of calls involve adults exposed to some form of toxic substance. These Centers provide medical treatment guidance and can answer general questions about air toxics, including paint fumes and pesticides. Regional Poison Control Centers service many areas throughout the United States.

☎ Contact:
Alabama Poison Center
205-345-0600
800-462-0800 (AL only)

Arizona Poison Control System
602-626-7899
602-626-6016 (Tucson)
602-253-3334 (Phoenix)
800-362-0101 (AZ only)

Central Ohio Poison Center
614-461-2012
614-228-1323
800-682-7625

Blodgett Regional Poison Center
616-774-7854

800-442-4571 (616 area code only)

Cardinal Glennon Children's Hospital
Regional Poison Center
314-772-8300
314-772-5200
800-392-9111 (MO only)

Maryland Poison Center
301-528-7606
301-528-7701
800-492-2414 (MD only)

Duke University Poison Control Center
919-684-4438
919-684-8111
800-672-1697 (NC only)

Georgia Poison Control Center
404-589-4400
800-282-5846 (GA only)
404-525-3323 (TTY)

Hennepin Regional Poison Center (Minnesota)
612-347-3144
612-347-3141
612-347-6219 (TTY)

Intermountain Regional Poison Control Center
801-581-7504
801-581-2151
800-662-0062 (UT only)

Kentucky Regional Poison Center
of Kosair Children's Hospital
502-562-7263
502-589-8222
800-722-5725 (KY only) (TDD)

Long Island Regional Poison Control Center
516-542-3707
516-542-2323

Los Angeles County Medical Association
Regional Poison Control Center
213-664-1212
213-484-5151

Louisiana Regional Poison Control Center
318-674-6364
318-425-1524
800-535-0525 (LA only)

Massachusetts Poison Control System
617-735-6607
617-232-2120
800-492-2414 (MD only)

Michigan Poison Control Center
313-745-5329
313-745-5711
800-462-6642 (313 area code only)
800-572-1655 (remainder of MI)

Mid-Plains Poison Center
402-390-5434
402-390-5400
800-642-999 (NE only)
800-228-9515 (surrounding states)

New Jersey Poison Information
and Education System
201-926-7443
201-923-0764
800-432-6866 (NJ only)

New Mexico Poison and Drug
Information Center
505-277-4261
505-843-2551
800-432-6866 (NM only)

New York City Poison Control Center
212-340-4497
212-340-4494

North Central Texas Poison Center
214-920-2586
214-920-2400
800-441-0040 (TX only)

Oregon Poison Control and
Drug Information Center
503-225-7799
503-225-8968 (Portland, OR)
800-452-7165

Pittsburgh Poison Center
412-647-5600
412-681-6669

Rocky Mountain Poison Center
303-893-7774
303-629-1123
800-332-3073 (CO only)

800-525-5042 (MT only)
800-442-2702 (WY only)

San Diego Regional Poison Center
619-294-3666
619-294-6000

San Francisco Bay Area
Regional Poison Control Center
415-821-8324
415-476-6600

Southwest Ohio Regional
Poison Control System
513-872-5111
800-872-5111

Tampa Bay Regional Control System
813-251-6911
813-253-444
800-282-3171

Texas State Poison Center
409-761-3332
409-765-1701 (Houston)
713-654-1701 (Austin)
800-392-8548 (TX only)

UCDMC Regional Poison Control Center
916-453-3414
916-453-3692

West Virginia Poison Center
304-347-1212
304-348-4211
800-642-3625 (WV only)

Washington DC
(202) 625-3333

Free Publications/Videos

The following publications on Poisoning are available from the Food & Drug Administration, (HFE-88), 5600 Fishers Ln., Rockville, MD 20857; (301) 443-3170.

- *The Poison Safety Game.* (#FDA90-1099)
- *At Home Antidotes For Poisoning Emergencies.* (#FDA86-1125)

- Dennis the Menace Takes A Poke At Poison.

POISON IVY

Clearinghouses/Hotlines

The National Institute of Allergy and Infectious Diseases (NIAID) can search the Combined Health Information Database (CHID) and generate a bibliography of resources for you on Poison Ivy. They will also send you any publications and journal articles they may have on hand, and will refer you to researchers who are currently studying this condition.

☎ Contact:
National Institute of Allergy
and Infectious Diseases
Bldg. 31, Room 7A32
Bethesda, MD 20892
(301) 496-5717

Free Publications/Videos

The following publication is available from the National Institute of Allergy and Infectious Diseases, Bldg. 31, Room 7A32, Bethesda, MD 20892; (301) 496-5717.

- *Poison Ivy Allergy.* (#82-897) Offers information on their symptoms, prevention, diagnosis, and treatment. (#82-897)

POLIOENCEPHALITIS

Clearinghouses/Hotlines

The National Institute of Neurological Disorders and Stroke (NINDS) can send you information they have only in their publications list on Polioencephalitis (Cerebral Poliomyelitis). They cannot refer you to any experts. This Clearinghouse cannot directly give you information about any current clinical studies NINDS might be conducting on this illness, but you can find this

information for yourself by looking under the National Institute of Neurological Disorders and Stroke in *Appendix A* at the end of this book.

☎ Contact:
National Institute of Neurological
Disorders and Stroke
Bldg. 31, Room 8A06
Bethesda, MD 20892
(301) 496-5751
(800) 352-9424

POLIOMYELITIS

Clearinghouses/Hotlines

The National Institute of Allergy and Infectious Diseases (NIAID) can search the Combined Health Information Database (CHID) and generate a bibliography of resources for you on Poliomyelitis. They will also send you any publications and journal articles they may have on hand, and will refer you to researchers who are currently studying this condition. If you can't afford treatment, have your doctor call NIAID to find out if they are conducting any clinical studies that you might qualify for.

☎ Contact:
National Institute of Allergy
and Infectious Diseases
Bldg. 31, Room 7A32
Bethesda, MD 20892
(301) 496-5717

POLLEN ALLERGY

Clearinghouses/Hotlines

The National Institute of Allergy and Infectious Diseases (NIAID) can search the Combined Health Information Database (CHID) and generate a bibliography of resources for you on Pollen Allergy. They will also send you any publications and journal articles they may have on hand, and will refer you to researchers who are currently studying this condition. If you can't afford treatment, have your doctor call NIAID to find out if they are conducting any clinical studies that you might qualify for.

☎ Contact:
National Institute of Allergy
and Infectious Diseases
Bldg. 31, Room 7A32
Bethesda, MD 20892
(301) 496-5717

POLYARTERITIS

Clearinghouses/Hotlines

The National Heart, Lung, and Blood Institute (NHLBI) can search the Combined Health Information Database (CHID) and generate a bibliography of resources for you on Polyarteritis. They also will send you any publications and journal articles they may have on hand, and will refer you to other organizations that are studying this condition. If you can't afford treatment, have your doctor call NHLBI to find out if they are conducting any clinical studies that you might qualify for.

☎ Contact:
National Heart, Lung, and Blood Institute
Bldg. 31, Room 4A21
Bethesda, MD 20892
(301) 496-4236

POLYCYSTIC KIDNEY DISEASE (PKD)

Clearinghouses/Hotlines

The National Kidney and Urologic Diseases Information Clearinghouse can provide you with information regarding Polycystic Kidney Disease (PKD). They can search the Combined Health Information Database (CHID) and generate a bibliography of resources for you. They can also send relevant articles and reference materials if they have them for you, as well as referring you to other organizations for further assistance.

☎ Contact:
National Kidney and Urologic Diseases
Information Clearinghouse
Box NKUDIC
Bethesda, MD 20892
(301) 468-6345

POLYCYSTIC OVARY SYNDROME

Clearinghouses/Hotlines

The National Institute of Child Health and Human Development (NICHD) will send you whatever publications and reprints of journal articles they have on Polycystic Ovary Syndrome. If necessary, they will refer you to other experts or researchers in the field. If you can't afford treatment, have your doctor call NICHD to find out if they are conducting any clinical studies that you might qualify for.

☎ Contact:
National Institute of Child Health
and Human Development
Bldg. 31, Room 2A32
Bethesda, MD 20892
(301) 496-5133

POLYCYTHEMIA

Clearinghouses/Hotlines

The National Heart, Lung, and Blood Institute (NHLBI) can search the Combined Health Information Database (CHID) and generate a bibliography of resources for you on Secondary Polycythemia. They also will send you any publications and journal articles they may have on hand, and will refer you to other organizations studying this condition. If you can't afford treatment, have your doctor call NHLBI to find out if they are conducting any clinical studies that you might qualify for.

☎ Contact:
National Heart, Lung, and Blood Institute

Bldg. 31, Room 4A21
Bethesda, MD 20892
(301) 496-4236

The National Cancer Institute (NCI) will send you whatever publications and reprints of journal articles they have on Polycythemia (Vera). They can also give you information on the state-of-the-art treatment for this condition, including specific treatment information for your stage of cancer. They can also search their Physician's Data Query (PDQ) database to let you know if NCI is conducting any clinical studies on your disease.

☎ Contact:
National Cancer Institute
Bldg. 31, Room 10A24
Bethesda, MD 20892
(800) 4-CANCER
(301) 496-5583

POLYMYALGIA RHEUMATICA

Clearinghouses/Hotlines

The National Institute of Arthritis and Musculoskeletal and Skin Diseases (NIAMS) will send you whatever publications and reprints of articles from texts and journals they have on Polymyalgia Rheumatica. They will also refer you to other organizations that are studying this disease. NIAMS will also let you know of any clinical studies that may be studying this disease and looking for patients.

☎ Contact:
National Institute of Arthritis
and Musculoskeletal and Skin Diseases
Box AMS
Bethesda, MD 20892
(301) 495-4484

POLYMYOSITIS

Clearinghouses/Hotlines

The National Institute of Arthritis and Musculoskeletal and Skin Diseases (NIAMS) will send you whatever publications and reprints of articles from texts and journals they have on Polymyositis. They will also refer you to other organizations that are studying this disease. NIAMS will also let you know of any clinical studies that may be studying this disease and looking for patients.

☎ Contact:
National Institute of Arthritis
and Musculoskeletal and Skin Diseases
Box AMS
Bethesda, MD 20892
(301) 495-4484

The National Institute of Neurological Disorders and Stroke (NINDS) can send you information they have only in their publications list on Polymyositis. They cannot refer you to any experts. This Clearinghouse cannot directly give you information about any current clinical studies NINDS might be conducting on this disorder, but you can find this information for yourself by looking under the National Institute of Neurological Disorders and Stroke in *Appendix A* at the end of this book.

☎ Contact:
National Institute of Neurological
Disorders and Stroke
Bldg. 31, Room 8A06
Bethesda, MD 20892
(301) 496-5751
(800) 352-9424

POLYNEURITIS

Clearinghouses/Hotlines

The National Institute of Arthritis and Musculoskeletal and Skin Diseases (NIAMS) will send you whatever publications and reprints of articles from texts and journals they have on Polyneuritis (Guillain-Barre Syndrome). They will also refer you to other organizations that are studying this disease. NIAMS will also let you know of any clinical studies that may be studying this disease and looking for patients.

☎ Contact:
National Institute of Arthritis
and Musculoskeletal and Skin Diseases
Box AMS
Bethesda, MD 20892
(301) 495-4484

The National Institute of Neurological Disorders and Stroke (NINDS) can send you information they have only in their publications list on Polyneuritis (Guillain-Barre Syndrome). They cannot refer you to any experts. This Clearinghouse cannot directly give you information about any current clinical studies NINDS might be conducting on this illness, but you can find this information for yourself by looking under the National Institute of Neurological Disorders and Stroke in *Appendix A* at the end of this book.

☎ Contact:
National Institute of Neurological
Disorders and Stroke
Bldg. 31, Room 8A06
Bethesda, MD 20892
(301) 496-5751
(800) 352-9424

POLYOSTOTIC FIBROUS DYSPLASIA

Clearinghouses/Hotlines

The National Institute of Arthritis and Musculoskeletal and Skin Diseases (NIAMS) will send you whatever publications and reprints of articles from texts and journals they have on Polyostotic Fibrous Dysplasia (Albright's Syndrome). They will also refer you to other organizations that are studying this disease. NIAMS will also let you know of any clinical studies that may be studying this disease and looking for patients.

☎ Contact:
National Institute of Arthritis
and Musculoskeletal and Skin Diseases
Box AMS
Bethesda, MD 20892
(301) 495-4484

POLYPS

Clearinghouses/Hotlines

The National Cancer Institute (NCI) will send you whatever publications and reprints of journal articles they have on Colon Polyps and Cancer. They can also give you information on the state-of-the-art treatment for this condition, including specific treatment information for your stage of cancer. They can also search their Physician's Data Query (PDQ) database to let you know if NCI is conducting any clinical studies on your disease.

☎ Contact:
National Cancer Institute
Bldg. 31, Room 10A24
Bethesda, MD 20892
(800) 4-CANCER
(301) 496-5583

The National Institute of Diabetes and Digestive and Kidney Diseases's (NIDDK) individual clearinghouses can search the Combined Health Information Database (CHID) and generate a bibliography of resources for you on Colon Polyps. They also will send you any publications and journal articles they may have on hand, and will refer you to other organizations that are studying this disease. If you can't afford treatment, have your doctor call NIDDK to find out if they are conducting any clinical studies that you might qualify for.

☎ Contact:
National Institute of Diabetes
and Digestive and Kidney Diseases
Bldg. 31, Room 9A04
Bethesda, MD 20892
(301) 496-3583

POLYSEROSITIS

Clearinghouses/Hotlines

The National Institute of Allergy and Infectious Diseases (NIAID) can search the Combined

Health Information Database (CHID) and generate a bibliography of resources for you on Polyserositis. They will also send you any publications and journal articles they may have on hand, and will refer you to researchers who are currently studying this condition. If you can't afford treatment, have your doctor call NIAID to find out if they are conducting any clinical studies that you might qualify for.

☎ Contact:
National Institute of Allergy
and Infectious Diseases
Bldg. 31, Room 7A32
Bethesda, MD 20892
(301) 496-5717

POMPE'S DISEASE

Clearinghouses/Hotlines

The National Institute of Neurological Disorders and Stroke (NINDS) can send you information they have only in their publications list on Pompe's Disease. They cannot refer you to any experts. This Clearinghouse cannot directly give you information about any current clinical studies NINDS might be conducting on this illness, but you can find this information for yourself by looking under the National Institute of Neurological Disorders and Stroke in *Appendix A* at the end of this book.

☎ Contact:
National Institute of Neurological
Disorders and Stroke
Bldg. 31, Room 8A06
Bethesda, MD 20892
(301) 496-5751
(800) 352-9424

The National Institute of Diabetes and Digestive and Kidney Diseases's (NIDDK) individual clearinghouses can search the Combined Health Information Database (CHID) and generate a bibliography of resources for you on Pompe's Disease. They also will send you any publications and journal articles they may have on hand, and will refer you to other organizations that are studying this disease. If you can't afford

treatment, have your doctor call NIDDK to find out if they are conducting any clinical studies that you might qualify for.

☎ Contact:
National Institute of Diabetes
and Digestive and Kidney Diseases
Bldg. 31, Room 9A04
Bethesda, MD 20892
(301) 496-3583

POPULATION CONTROL

Clearinghouses/Hotlines

The National Institute of Child Health and Human Development (NICHD) will send you whatever publications and reprints of journal articles they have on Population Dynamics and Problems. If necessary, they will refer you to other experts or researchers in the field.

☎ Contact:
National Institute of Child Health
and Human Development
Bldg. 31, Room 2A32
Bethesda, MD 20892
(301) 496-5133

Free Publications/Videos

The following publication is available from the Office of Technology Assessment, 600 Pennsylvania Ave., SE, Washington, DC 20510; (202) 224-8996.

- *World Population and Fertility Planning Technologies: The Next 20 Years*. A report to Congress. Ask for the summary report. (#HR-157)

PORPHYRIA

Clearinghouses/Hotlines

The National Institute of Arthritis and

Musculoskeletal and Skin Diseases (NIAMS) will send you whatever publications and reprints of articles from texts and journals they have on Porphyria. They will also refer you to other organizations that are studying this disease. NIAMS will also let you know of any clinical studies that may be studying this disease and looking for patients.

☎ Contact:
National Institute of Arthritis
and Musculoskeletal and Skin Diseases
Box AMS, 9000 Rockville Pike
Bethesda, MD 20892
(301) 495-4484

The National Institute of Diabetes and Digestive and Kidney Diseases's (NIDDK) individual clearinghouses can search the Combined Health Information Database (CHID) and generate a bibliography of resources for you on Porphyria. They also will send you any publications and journal articles they may have on hand, and will refer you to other organizations that are studying this disease. If you can't afford treatment, have your doctor call NIDDK to find out if they are conducting any clinical studies that you might qualify for.

☎ Contact:
National Institute of Diabetes
and Digestive and Kidney Diseases
Building 31
Room 9A04
Bethesda, MD 20892
(301) 496-3583

POSITRON EMISSION TOMOGRAPHY

Free Publications/Videos

The following publication on Positron Emission Tomography is available from the National Institute of Neurological Disorders and Stroke, P.O. Box 5801, Bethesda, MD 20824; (800) 352-9424, or (301) 496-5751.

- *Positron Emission Tomography.*

POSTNATAL CARE

See also Childbirth
See also Child Health

Clearinghouses/Hotlines

The National Institute of Child Health and Human Development (NICHD) will send you whatever publications and reprints of journal articles they have on Postnatal Care. If necessary, they will refer you to other experts or researchers in the field. If you can't afford treatment, have your doctor call NICHD to find out if they are conducting any clinical studies that you might qualify for.

☎ Contact:
National Institute of Child Health
and Human Development
Bldg. 31, Room 2A32
Bethesda, MD 20892
(301) 496-5133

The National Maternal and Child Health Clearinghouse has all kinds of information on maternal and child health issues, such as pregnancy, child and adolescent health, and human genetics. If the answer to your question can't be answered by any of their countless free publications, they can refer you to other National or local resources. If you still need further information, they search their own reference collection and send you what they find.

☎ Contact:
National Maternal and Child
Health Clearinghouse
38th & R Sts., NW
Washington, DC 20057
(703) 821-8955, ext. 254

Free Publications/Videos

The following publication is available from the National Maternal and Child Health Clearinghouse, 38th & R Sts., NW, Washington, DC 20057; (703) 821-8955, ext. 254.

- *Patient Education Materials: A Resource*

Guide is a free publication developed to help health professionals identify and locate materials on maternal and child health topics that are clear, concise, easy to read and appropriate for the general public. The guide is separated into three sections. The first is patient education materials, which is an annotated listing of source books, directories, audiovisuals, and resource guides that describe patient education materials. The second section lists publishers of patient education materials, and the third lists federal health information clearinghouses.

POST-POLIO SYNDROME

Clearinghouses/Hotlines

The National Institute of Neurological Disorders and Stroke (NINDS) can send you information they have only in their publications list on Post-polio Syndrome. They cannot refer you to any experts. This Clearinghouse cannot directly give you information about any current clinical studies NINDS might be conducting on this illness, but you can find this information for yourself by looking under the National Institute of Neurological Disorders and Stroke in *Appendix A* at the end of this book.

☎ Contact:
National Institute of Neurological
Disorders and Stroke
Building 31
Room 8A06
Bethesda, MD 20892
(301) 496-5751
(800) 352-9424

Free Publications/Videos

The following publication on Post-Polio Syndrome is available from the National Institute of Neurological Disorders and Stroke, P.O. Box 5801, Bethesda, MD 20824; (800) 352-9424, or (301) 496-5751.

- *Post-Polio Syndrome.* Contains a collection of scientific articles, patient education pamphlets, and addresses of voluntary health associations.

POSTURAL HYPOTENSION

Clearinghouses/Hotlines

The National Heart, Lung, and Blood Institute (NHLBI) can search the Combined Health Information Database (CHID) and generate a bibliography of resources for you on Postural Hypotension. They also will send you any publications and journal articles they may have on hand, and will refer you to other organizations that are studying this condition. If you can't afford treatment, have your doctor call NHLBI to find out if they are conducting any clinical studies that you might qualify for.

☎ Contact:
National Heart, Lung, and Blood Institute
Bldg. 31, Room 4A21
Bethesda, MD 20892
(301) 496-4236

POTASSIUM

See also Food

Clearinghouses/Hotlines

The National Heart, Lung, and Blood Institute (NHLBI) can search the Combined Health Information Database (CHID) and generate a bibliography of resources for you on the Potassium Content of Foods. They also will send you any publications and journal articles they may have on hand, and will refer you to other organizations that are studying this issue.

☎ Contact:
National Heart, Lung, and Blood Institute
Bldg. 31, Room 4A21
Bethesda, MD 20892
(301) 496-4236

POTT'S DISEASE

Clearinghouses/Hotlines

The National Institute of Neurological Disorders and Stroke (NINDS) can send you information they have only in their publications list on Pott's Disease. They cannot refer you to any experts. This Clearinghouse cannot directly give you information about any current clinical studies NINDS might be conducting on this illness, but you can find this information for yourself by looking under the National Institute of Neurological Disorders and Stroke in *Appendix A* at the end of this book.
☎ Contact:
National Institute of Neurological
Disorders and Stroke
Bldg. 31, Room 8A06
Bethesda, MD 20892
(301) 496-5751
(800) 352-9424

POULTRY INSPECTION

See also Meat & Poultry

Clearinghouses/Hotlines

The U.S. Department of Agriculture's Meat & Poultry Hotline inspects and analyzes domestic and imported Meat and Poultry and establishes standards for processed meat and poultry products. They will answer your questions about the proper handling, preparation, and refrigeration, food poisoning, food additives, food labeling, sodium, and herbs.
☎ Contact:
U.S. Department of Agriculture
Room 1165-S
Washington, DC 20205
(800) 535-4555
(202) 447-9351

Free Publications/Videos

The following Congressional Research Service

(CRS) report on Poultry Inspection is available from either of your U.S. Senators' offices at the U.S. Capitol, Washington, DC 20510, or from your Congressional Representative at the U.S. Capitol, Washington, DC 20515. You can also call in your request through the U.S. Capitol switchboard at (202) 224-3121. Be sure to include the full title and report number in your request.

- *Federal Poultry Inspection: A Brief.* (#87-432 ENR)

The following publication on Poultry Inspection is available from the Food & Drug Administration, (HFE-88), 5600 Fishers Ln., Rockville, MD 20857; (301) 443-3170.

- *Salmonella Enteritidis: From The Chicken To The Egg.* (#FDA91-2238)

POWER LINES

Clearinghouses/Hotlines

The Center for Devices and Radiological Health can send you reports and studies regarding the danger of Power Lines, and their possible linkage to cancer.
☎ Contact:
Center for Devices and Radiological Health
HFZ-210
Food and Drug Administration
5600 Fishers Lane
Rockville, MD 20857
(301) 443-4190

Free Publications/Videos

The following Congressional Research Service (CRS) report is available from either of your U.S. Senators' offices at the U.S. Capitol, Washington, DC 20510, or from your Congressional Representative at the U.S. Capitol, Washington, DC 20515. You can also call in your request through the U.S. Capitol switchboard at (202) 224-3121. Be sure to include the full title and report number in your request.

- Power Lines and Electromagnetic Fields: Issues for Congress; Issue Brief. (#IB91051)

PRADER-WILLI SYNDROME

Clearinghouses/Hotlines

The National Institute of Child Health and Human Development (NICHD) will send you whatever publications and reprints of journal articles they have on Prader-Willi Syndrome. If necessary, they will refer you to other experts or researchers in the field. If you can't afford treatment, have your doctor call NICHD to find out if they are conducting any clinical studies that you might qualify for.

☎ Contact:
National Institute of Child Health
and Human Development
Bldg. 31, Room 2A32
Bethesda, MD 20892
(301) 496-5133

PREDNISONE

Free Publications/Videos

The following publication is available from the National Cancer Institute, Bldg. 31, Room 10A24, Bethesda, MD 20892; (800) 4-CANCER, or (301) 496-5583.

- Prednisona/Prednisone. Provides information about side effects, proper usage, and precautions of this anti-cancer drug.

PREGNANCY

See also Amniocentesis

Clearinghouses/Hotlines

The National Institute of Child Health and Human Development (NICHD) will send you whatever publications and reprints of journal articles they have on Pregnancy. If necessary, they will refer you to other experts or researchers in the field. If you can't afford treatment, have your doctor call NICHD to find out if they are conducting any clinical studies that you might qualify for.

☎ Contact:
National Institute of Child Health
and Human Development
Bldg. 31, Room 2A32
Bethesda, MD 20892
(301) 496-5133

The National Maternal and Child Health Clearinghouse has all kinds of information on Pregnancy, and prenatal and infant care.

☎ Contact:
National Maternal and Child Health
Clearinghouse
38th & R Sts., NW
Washington, DC 20057
(703) 821-8955, ext. 254

The Office on Smoking Health will give you information on the effects that smoking has on Pregnancy and newborns. Some of the free pamphlets available include *Is Your Baby Smoking?* which explains the dangers of passive smoke on the baby; *Baby In The House Stickers*, which remind pregnant women that when they smoke, they smoke for two.

☎ Contact:
Office on Smoking Health
Centers for Disease Control
Mail Stop K-50
1600 Clifton Rd., NE
Atlanta, GA 30333
(404) 488-5705

Free Publications/Videos

The following publications on Pregnancy are available from the National Maternal and Child Health Clearinghouse, 38th & R Sts., NW, Washington, DC 20057; (703) 821-8955, ext. 254.

- Advances in the Prevention of Low Birth-weight: An International Symposium.
- Caring for Our Future: The Content of Prenatal Care.

- *Prenatal Care.*
- *Prenatal Care: Resource Guide.*
- *Prevention of Hemolytic Disease of the Fetus and Newborn Due to RH Isoimmunization.*
- *Adolescent Pregnancy- Resource Guide.*
- *Health Foods, Healthy Baby.*
- *Nutrition Management of the Pregnant Adolescent.*
- *Pregnancy and Childbearing Among Homeless Adolescents: Report of a Workshop.*
- *Adolescent Fathers: Directory of Services.*
- *Resource Guide: Environmental Exposures and Pregnancy.* Includes an annotated list of current publications and journal articles, a list of organizations that can provide additional information, and a list of teratogen information services. Federal and state government maternal and child health agencies may also be able to provide further assistance.
- *Environmental Exposures and Pregnancy: Resource Guide.* (#DOO8)

The following publications on Pregnancy are available from the National Institute of Child Health and Human Development, Bldg. 31, Room 2A32, Bethesda, MD 20892; (301) 496-5133.

- *Understanding Gestational Diabetes: A Practical Guide to a Healthy Pregnancy.* Addresses questions about diet, exercise, measurement of blood sugar levels, and general medical and obstetric care of women with gestational diabetes. It answers such questions as: Will my baby have diabetes?, What can I do to control gestational diabetes?, and Will I have diabetes in the future?.
- *Pregnancy Basics: What You Need to Know and Do to Have a Good Healthy Baby.* Examines weight gain, vitamins, nutrition, exercise, smoking, drinking, drugs, and X-rays.
- *Diagnostic Ultrasound Imaging in Pregnancy.* (#84-667)
- *Pregnancy Basics.*

The following publications are available from the National Clearinghouse for Alcohol and Drug Information, P.O. Box 2345, Rockville, MD 20852; (800) 729-6686, or (301) 468-2600.

- *Prevention Resource Guide: Pregnant/Postpartum Women and Their Infants.* Contains facts, figures, resources, and other relevant information on alcohol abuse.
- *An Inner Voice Tells You Not to Drink or Use Other Drugs.* Poster depicts an artistic rendition of a pregnant American Indian Woman (#AV161)
- *Alcohol, Tobacco, and Other Drugs May Harm the Unborn.* Presents the most recent finding of basic research and clinical studies (#PH291)
- *Drug Abuse and Pregnancy.* An overview of the scope of the problem and effects of maternal drug use on the mother, fetus, and infant (#CAP33)
- *How To Take Care of Your Baby Before Birth.* A low-literacy brochure that describes what pregnant women should and should not do, emphasizing a no use of alcohol and other drugs message (#PH239, also in Spanish)
- *Women and Alcohol.* Discussion of women and alcohol. (RPO716).
- *Prenatal Drug Exposure: Kinetics and Dynamics.* Research studies on the effects of maternal use of drugs on the fetus. (#M60)
- *Alcohol, Tobacco, and Other Drugs May Harm the Unborn.*
- *Drug Abuse and Pregnancy.*
- *How to Take Care of Your Baby Before Birth.*

The following publications on Pregnancy are available from the Food & Drug Administration, (HFE-88), 5600 Fishers Ln., Rockville, MD 20857; (301) 443-3170.

- *Drugs and Pregnancy.* (#80-3083, FDA) Explains how medications, drugs, alcohol and tobacco are shared with the unborn baby. Other related hazards to the fetus are also discussed.
- *All About Eating for Two.* (#84-2183) Discusses how pregnancy and breastfeeding affect a woman's nutritional needs.

The following publication on Pregnancy is available from the National Institute of Diabetes and Digestive and Kidney Diseases, Bldg. 31, Room 9A04, Bethesda, MD 20892; (301) 496-3583.

- Pregnancy and Diabetes Annotated Bibliography. (#91-2083)

The following publication on Pregnancy is available from the National Heart, Lung and Blood Institute, Bldg. 31, Room 4A21, Bethesda, MD 20892; (301) 496-4236.

- Working Group Report on High Blood Pressure in Pregnancy. (#90-3029)

The following publication on Pregnancy is available from the Food and Nutrition Information Center, National Agricultural Library, Room 304, Beltsville, MD 20705; (301) 504-5719.

- Adolescent Pregnancy and Nutrition. A list to help you locate further information or resources.

The following publication on Pregnancy is available from the Consumer Information Center, P.O. Box 100, Pueblo, CO 81002.

- Getting Fit Your Way. (#109Y)

The following publication on Pregnancy is available from the Center for Devices and Radiological Health, (HFZ-210), Food and Drug Administration, 5600 Fishers Ln., Rockville, MD 20857; (301) 443-4690.

- X-Rays, Pregnancy and You.... (#FDA 79-8087)

The following publication on Pregnancy is available from the Office of Technology Assessment, 600 Pennsylvania Ave., SE, Washington, DC 20510; (202) 224-8996.

- Reproductive Health Hazards in the Workplace. A report to Congress. Ask for the summary report.

The following Congressional Research Service (CRS) reports are available from either of your U.S. Senators' offices at the U.S. Capitol, Washington, DC 20510, or from your Congressional Representative at the U.S. Capitol, Washington, DC 20515. You can also call in your request through the U.S. Capitol switchboard at (202) 224-3121. Be sure to include the full title and report number in your request.

- The Judicial and Legislative Treatment of Pregnancy: A Review of Developments from Unprotected Status to Anti-Discrimination-Equal Treatment. (87-277 A)
- Teenage Pregnancy: Selected Reference, 1986-1988. (89-119 L)

PREGNANCY AND ALCOHOL

See also Alcoholism
See also Drug Abuse

Clearinghouses/Hotlines

The National Clearinghouse for Alcohol and Drug Information has several free publications dealing with drinking and drug use during pregnancy.
☎ Contact:
National Clearinghouse for Alcohol and Drug Information
P.O. Box 2345
Rockville, MD 20852
(800) 729-6686

Free Publications/Videos

The following publications on Pregnancy and Alcohol are available from the National Clearinghouse for Alcohol and Drug Information, P.O. Box 2345, Rockville, MD 20852; (800) 729-6686.

- Alcohol, Tobacco, and Other Drugs May Harm the Unborn. Presents the most recent finding of basic research and clinical studies. (PH291)
- Drug Abuse and Pregnancy. Provides an overview of the scope of the problem and effects of maternal drug use on the mother, fetus, and infant. (CAP33)
- How To Take Care of Your Baby Before Birth. A low-literacy brochure aimed at pregnant women that describes what they should

and should not do during their pregnancy, emphasizing a no use of alcohol and other drugs message. (#PH239, also in Spanish)

- *An Inner Voice Tells You Not to Drink or Use Other Drugs.* Poster depicts an artistic rendition of a pregnant American Indian Woman. (#AV161)
- *Prenatal Drug Exposure: Kinetics and Dynamics.* NIDA Research Monograph 60-presents research studies on the effects of maternal use of drugs on the fetus. (#M60)
- *Prevention Resource Guide: Pregnant/Postpartum Women and Their Infants.* Resource Guide targets pregnant and postpartum women, women between the ages of 15-44, counselors, health care providers, and prevention program planners. It provides a high-demand, comprehensive resource for information concerning alcohol and other drug prevention among pregnant and postpartum women and their infants. (#MS420)
- *Women and Alcohol.* Discussion of women and alcohol. (#RPO716)

PREMATURE BABIES

Clearinghouses/Hotlines

The National Institute of Child Health and Human Development (NICHD) will send you whatever publications and reprints of journal articles they have on Premature Babies. If necessary, they will refer you to other experts or researchers in the field. If you can't afford treatment, have your doctor call NICHD to find out if they are conducting any clinical studies that you might qualify for.

☎ Contact:
National Institute of Child Health
and Human Development
Bldg. 31, Room 2A32
Bethesda, MD 20892
(301) 496-5133

The National Maternal and Child Health Clearinghouse has all kinds of information on maternal and child health issues, such as pregnancy, child and adolescent health, and human genetics. If the answer to your question can't be answered by any of their countless free publications, they can refer you to other National or local resources. If you still need further information, they search their own reference collection and send you what they find.

☎ Contact:
National Maternal and Child
Health Clearinghouse
38th & R Sts., NW
Washington, DC 20057
(703) 821-8955, ext. 254

Free Publications/Videos

The following publication on Premature Babies is available from the National Maternal and Child Health Clearinghouse, 38th & R Sts., NW, Washington, DC 20057; (703) 821-8955, ext. 254.

- *Preterm and Low Birthweight Infants: Resource Guide.* Includes an annotated listing of selected educational materials and a list of genetic services providers and voluntary and professional organizations, which may be able to provide additional information. Federal and state government maternal and child health agencies may also be able to provide further information.

The following publications on Premature Birth are available from the National Institute of Child Health and Human Development, Bldg. 31, Room 2A32, Bethesda, MD 20892; (301) 496-5133.

- *Facts About Premature Birth.*
- *Little Babies Born Too Soon, Born Too Small.* Covers premature labor and birth. (#77-1079)

PREMENSTRUAL SYNDROME

See PMS

PRENATAL CARE

Clearinghouses/Hotlines

The National Institute of Child Health and Human Development (NICHD) will send you whatever publications and reprints of journal articles they have on Prenatal Care. If necessary, they will refer you to other experts or researchers in the field. If you can't afford treatment, have your doctor call NICHD to find out if they are conducting any clinical studies that you might qualify for.

☎ Contact:
National Institute of Child Health
and Human Development
Bldg. 31, Room 2A32
Bethesda, MD 20892
(301) 496-5133

The National Maternal and Child Health Clearinghouse has all kinds of information on maternal and child health issues, such as pregnancy, child and adolescent health, and human genetics. If the answer to your question can't be answered by any of their countless free publications, they can refer you to other National or local resources. If you still need further information, they search their own reference collection and send you what they find.

☎ Contact:
National Maternal and Child
Health Clearinghouse
38th & R Sts., NW
Washington, DC 20057
(703) 821-8955, ext. 254

Free Publications/Videos

The following publications on Prenatal Care are available from the National Maternal and Child Health Clearinghouse, 38th & R Sts., NW, Washington, DC 20057; (703) 821-8955, ext. 254.

- *One-Stop Shopping for Perinatal Services.* (#D071)
- *Prenatal Care*. The federal government's popular 98-page "Dr. Spock" that provides basic information to pregnant women on caring for herself and her unborn baby. (#H50)
- *Patient Education Materials: A Resource Guide* is a free publication developed to help health professionals identify and locate materials on maternal and child health topics that are clear, concise, easy to read and appropriate for the general public. The guide is separated into three sections. The first is patient education materials, which is an annotated listing of source books, directories, audiovisuals, and resource guides that describe patient education materials. The second section lists publishers of patient education materials, and the third lists federal health information clearinghouses.
- *Prenatal Care: Resource Guide.* (#D013)

The following publication on Prenatal Care is available from the National Institute of Child Health and Human Development, Bldg. 31, Room 2A32, Bethesda, MD 20892; (301) 496-5133.

- *Caring for Our Future: The Content of Prenatal Care.* (#90-3182)

The following publication on Prenatal Care is available from the National Clearinghouse for Alcohol and Drug Information, P.O. Box 2345, Rockville, MD 20852; (301) 468-2600.

- *Prenatal Drug Exposure: Kinetics and Dynamics*. NIDA Research Monograph 60.

PRESBYCUSIS

Clearinghouses/Hotlines

The National Institute on Deafness and Other Communication Disorders (NIDCD) will send you whatever publications and reprints of journal articles they have on Presbycusis. If you need further information, they will refer you to other organizations that study this and other related diseases. NIDCD does not conduct any clinical studies for this or any other disorder.

☎ Contact:
National Institute on Deafness
and Other Communication Disorders
Building 31
Room 3C35
Bethesda, MD 20892
(301) 496-7243
(800) 241-1044
(301) 402-0252 (TDD)

The National Institute of Neurological Disorders and Stroke (NINDS) can send you information they have only in their publications list on Presbycusis. They cannot refer you to any experts. This Clearinghouse cannot directly give you information about any current clinical studies NINDS might be conducting on this disorder, but you can find this information for yourself by looking under the National Institute of Neurological Disorders and Stroke in *Appendix A* at the end of this book.

☎ Contact:
National Institute of Neurological
Disorders and Stroke
Building 31
Room 8A06
Bethesda, MD 20892
(301) 496-5751
(800) 352-9424

The National Institute on Aging (NIA) will send you whatever publications and reprints of journal articles they have on Presbycusis: Hearing and Aging. They cannot refer you to other experts if the information they have isn't sufficient for your purposes.

☎ Contact:
National Institute on Aging
Building 31, Room 5C27
Bethesda, MD 20892
(301) 496-1752

PRESBYOPIA

Clearinghouses/Hotlines

The National Eye Institute (NEI) can give you up-to-date information on Presbyopia by searching the Combined Health Information Database (CHID) and MEDLINE and sending you bibliographies of resources, along with any journal articles they may have. They can also refer you to any other organizations that study this and other related conditions. NEI will also let you know of any clinical studies that may be studying this disorder and looking for patients. Because of their small staff, NEI prefers that you submit your requests for information in writing.

☎ Contact:
National Eye Institute
Building 31
Room 6A32
Bethesda, MD 20892
(301) 496-5248

PRESCRIPTION DRUGS

See Medications
See Appendix B

PRESENILE DEMENTIA

See also Dementia
See also Alzheimer's Disease

Clearinghouses/Hotlines

The National Institute on Aging (NIA) will send you whatever publications and reprints of journal articles they have on Presenile Dementia. They cannot refer you to other experts if the information they have isn't sufficient for your purposes.

☎ Contact:
National Institute on Aging
Building 31
Room 5C27
Bethesda, MD 20892
(301) 496-1752

The National Institute of Neurological Disorders and Stroke (NINDS) can send you information they have only in their publications list on

Presenile Dementia. They cannot refer you to any experts. This Clearinghouse cannot directly give you information about any current clinical studies NINDS might be conducting on this illness, but you can find this information for yourself by looking under the National Institute of Neurological Disorders and Stroke in *Appendix A* at the end of this book.

☎ Contact:
National Institute of Neurological
Disorders and Stroke
Building 31
Room 8A06
Bethesda, MD 20892
(301) 496-5751
(800) 352-9424

The National Institute of Mental Health (NIMH) will send you whatever publications and reprints of articles from texts and journals they have on Presenile Dementia. They will also refer you to other organizations studying this disorder. NIMH will also let you know of any clinical studies that may be studying this disorder and looking for patients.

☎ Contact:
National Institute of Mental Health
5600 Fishers Lane
Room 15C05
Rockville, MD 20857
(301) 443-4515

PRESERVATIVES

See Food Preservatives

PREVENTION

Free Publications/Videos

The following publication on Prevention is available from the National Health Information Center, P.O. Box 1133, Washington, DC 20013; (800) 336-4797, or (301) 565-4167 in DC metro area.

- *Health Risk Appraisals.* Identifies several different tests that will help you analyze your health history and current lifestyle to determine your risk for preventable death or chronic illness. This publication also contains a vendor list of many corporate health promotion centers, medical research institutions, and private organizations that offer such tests and the costs of each. ($1)

The following publication on Prevention is available from the National Heart, Lung and Blood Institute, Bldg. 31, Room 4A21, Bethesda, MD 20892; (301) 496-4236.

- *Good News, Better News, Best News...Cancer Prevention.* (#86-2671)

The following publication on Prevention is available from the National Cancer Institute, Bldg. 31, Room 10A24, Bethesda, MD 20892; (800) 4-CANCER, or (301) 496-5583.

- *Cancer Prevention Resource Directory.* (#86-2827)

PRIMARY CARE

Clearinghouses/Hotlines

Administrators or practitioners at Federally funded community/migrant health centers have a vital need to know recent development in Federal guidance and policies affecting primary care delivery, resources available to support service delivery programs, and basic clinical, administrative, and financial management systems that can help establish and operate an efficient center. The National Clearinghouse for Primary Care Information provides information services to support the planning, development, and delivery of ambulatory health care to urban and rural areas that have shortages of medical personnel and services. They distribute materials on ambulatory care, financial management, primary health care, medical personnel and services primarily to health professionals. They also distribute publications on community health centers, migrant health centers, childhood injury prevention efforts, clinical care and many other health concerns.

☎ Contact:
National Clearinghouse for Primary
Care Information
8201 Greensboro Drive
Suite 600
McLean, VA 22102
(703) 821-8955

Free Publications/Videos

The following publications on Primary Care are available from the National Clearinghouse for Primary Care Information, 8201 Greensboro Dr., Suite 600, McLean, VA 22102; (703) 821-8955.

- *How To Speak Primary Care.* Defines acronyms commonly used in primary care programs.
- *Prescription for Primary Care: A Community Guidebook.* A guide to developing a successful primary care program.
- *Annotated Bibliography of Primary Care Research.* Subject areas include quality assurance and practice patterns, health promotion and disease prevention, health needs and access to care, patient-provider communication, and technology assessment.
- *Health Hotlines: Toll-Free Numbers from DIRLINE.* A compilation of health information and services organizations with toll-free 800 telephone numbers.
- *330/329-Funded Community and Migrant Health Center: Directory.* Lists the community and migrant health centers funded by Public Health Service.

The following publication on Primary Care is available from Office of Programs for the Homeless Mentally Ill, National Institute of Mental Health, Room 7C-06, 5600 Fishers Ln., Rockville, MD 20857; (301) 443-3706.

- *Somatization Disorder in the Medical Setting.* Intended to help primary care givers diagnose, treat, and manage patients with this disorder.

PRIMARY LATERAL SCLEROSIS

Clearinghouses/Hotlines

The National Institute of Neurological Disorders and Stroke (NINDS) can send you information they have only in their publications list on Primary Lateral Sclerosis. They cannot refer you to any experts. This Clearinghouse cannot directly give you information about any current clinical studies NINDS might be conducting on this illness, but you can find this information for yourself by looking under the National Institute of Neurological Disorders and Stroke in *Appendix A* at the end of this book.

☎ Contact:
National Institute of Neurological
Disorders and Stroke
Bldg. 31, Room 8A06
Bethesda, MD 20892
(301) 496-5751
(800) 352-9424

PRIMARY OVARIAN FAILURE

Clearinghouses/Hotlines

The National Institute of Child Health and Human Development (NICHD) will send you whatever publications and reprints of journal articles they have on Primary Ovarian Failure. If necessary, they will refer you to other experts or researchers in the field. If you can't afford treatment, have your doctor call NICHD to find out if they are conducting any clinical studies that you might qualify for.

☎ Contact:
National Institute of Child Health
and Human Development
Bldg. 31, Room 2A32
Bethesda, MD 20892
(301) 496-5133

PROCARBAZINE

Free Publications/Videos

The following publication on Procarbazine is available from the National Cancer Institute, Bldg. 31, Room 10A24, Bethesda, MD 20892; (800) 4-CANCER, or (301) 496-5583.

- *Procarbazina/Procarbazine*. Provides information about side effects, proper usage, and precautions of this anti-cancer drug.

PROGERIA

Clearinghouses/Hotlines

The National Institute on Aging (NIA) will send you whatever publications and reprints of journal articles they have on Progeria. They cannot refer you to other experts if the information they have isn't sufficient for your purposes.

☎ Contact:
National Institute on Aging
Building 31
Room 5C27
Bethesda, MD 20892
(301) 496-1752

PROGESTINS

Clearinghouses/Hotlines

The National Institute of Child Health and Human Development (NICHD) will send you whatever publications and reprints of journal articles they have on Progestins and Progesterone. If necessary, they will refer you to other experts or researchers in the field. If you can't afford treatment, have your doctor call NICHD to find out if they are conducting any clinical studies that you might qualify for.

☎ Contact:
National Institute of Child Health
and Human Development
Building 31
Room 2A32
Bethesda, MD 20892
(301) 496-5133

PROGRESSIVE MULTIFOCAL LEUKOENCEPHALOPATHY

Free Publications/Videos

The following publication on Progressive Multifocal Leukoencephalopathy is available from the National Institute of Neurological Disorders and Stroke, P.O. Box 5801, Bethesda, MD 20824; (800) 352-9424, or (301) 496-5751.

- *Progressive Multifocal Leukoencephalopathy*. Collection of scientific articles, patient education pamphlets, and addresses of voluntary health associations.

PROGRESSIVE SUPRANUCLEAR PALSY

Free Publications/Videos

The following publication on Progressive Supranuclear Palsy is available from the National Institute of Neurological Disorders and Stroke, P.O. Box 5801, Bethesda, MD 20824; (800) 352-9424, or (301) 496-5751.

- *Progressive Supranuclear Palsy*. Contains a collection of scientific articles, patient education pamphlets, and addresses of voluntary health associations.

PROSTATE CANCER

See also Cancer

Clearinghouses/Hotlines

The National Cancer Institute (NCI) will send you whatever publications and reprints of journal articles they have on Prostate Cancer. They can also give you information on the state-of-the-art treatment for this disease, including specific treatment information for your stage of cancer. They can also search their Physician's Data Query (PDQ) database to let you know if NCI is conducting any clinical studies on your disease.

☎ Contact:
National Cancer Institute
Bldg. 31, Room 10A24
Bethesda, MD 20892
(800) 4-CANCER
(301) 496-5583

Free Publications/Videos

The following publications are available from the National Cancer Institute, Bldg. 31, Room 10A24, Bethesda, MD 20892; (800) 4-CANCER, or (301) 496-5583.

- *What You Need to Know About Prostate Cancer.* (#90-1576)
- *Research Report: Cancer of the Prostate.* (#89-528)

PROSTATE PROBLEMS

Clearinghouses/Hotlines

The National Institute of Diabetes and Digestive and Kidney Diseases's (NIDDK) individual clearinghouses can search the Combined Health Information Database (CHID) and generate a bibliography of resources for you on Prostate Enlargement. They also will send you any publications and journal articles they may have on

hand, and will refer you to other organizations that are studying this condition. If you can't afford treatment, have your doctor call NIDDK to find out if they are conducting any clinical studies that you might qualify for.

☎ Contact:
National Institute of Diabetes
and Digestive and Kidney Diseases
Bldg. 31, Room 9A04
Bethesda, MD 20892
(301) 496-3583

The National Institute on Aging (NIA) will send you whatever publications and reprints of journal articles they have on Hyperplasia of the Prostate. They cannot refer you to other experts if the information they have isn't sufficient for your purposes.

☎ Contact:
National Institute on Aging
Bldg. 31, Room 5C27
Bethesda, MD 20892
(301) 496-1752

Free Publications/Videos

The following publications on Prostate Problems are available from the National Kidney and Urological Diseases Information Clearinghouse, Box NKUDIC, Bethesda, MD 20892; (301) 468-6345.

- *Prostate Problems.* Describes common prostate problems such as prostatitis, benign prostatic hypertrophy, and prostate cancer.
- *Prostate Enlargement: Benign Prostatic Hyperplasia.* Basic information about the prostate gland and prostate enlargement.
- *Prostate Disorders: Professional Materials.* Bibliography of resources.
- *Prostate Disorders: Patient Materials.* Bibliography of resources.
- *Prostate Problems: Safety Belt Sense.* Facts for the aging.

The following publication on Prostate Problems is available from the National Institute of Diabetes and Digestive and Kidney Diseases, Bldg. 31, Room 9A04, Bethesda, MD 20892; (301) 496-3583.

- Benign Prostatic Hyperplasia: Vol. II. (#87-2881)

PROSTHESES

Clearinghouses/Hotlines

The National Center for Medical Rehabilitation Research conducts research in restoring, replacing, or improving functional capability lost as a consequence of injury, disease, or congenital disorder. Currently the Center is assessing the current status of medical rehabilitation, identifying medical rehabilitation research issues and opportunities, and recommending program priorities.

☎ Contact:
National Center for Medical
Rehabilitation Research
National Institutes of Health
Building 31, Room 2A03
Bethesda, MD 20892
(301) 496-3454

The National Institute of Arthritis and Musculoskeletal and Skin Diseases (NIAMS) will send you whatever publications and reprints of articles from texts and journals they have on Prostheses (Orthotics). They will also refer you to other organizations studying this subject. NIAMS will also let you know of any clinical studies that may be studying this issue and looking for patients.

☎ Contact:
National Institute of Arthritis
and Musculoskeletal and Skin Diseases
Box AMS, 9000 Rockville Pike
Bethesda, MD 20892
(301) 495-4484

The National Heart, Lung, and Blood Institute (NHLBI) can search the Combined Health Information Database (CHID) and generate a bibliography of resources for you on Heart and Blood Vessel Prostheses. They also will send you any publications and journal articles they may have on hand, and will refer you to other organizations that are studying this issue. If you can't afford treatment, have your doctor call NHLBI to find out if they are conducting any clinical studies that

you might qualify for.

☎ Contact:
National Heart, Lung, and Blood Institute
Bldg. 31, Room 4A21
Bethesda, MD 20892
(301) 496-4236

PROSTHODONTICS

Clearinghouses/Hotlines

The National Institute of Dental Research (NIDR) will send you whatever publications and reprints of journal articles they have on Prosthodontics. As a policy, however, NIDR will not refer you to other organizations or experts who study this subject. If you can't afford treatment, have your doctor call Dr. Albert Guckers at (301) 496-6241 to find out if NIDR is conducting any clinical studies that you might qualify for.

☎ Contact:
National Institute of Dental Research
Bldg. 31, Room 2C35
Bethesda, MD 20892
(301) 496-4261

PRURIGO NODULARIS

Clearinghouses/Hotlines

The National Institute of Arthritis and Musculoskeletal and Skin Diseases (NIAMS) will send you whatever publications and reprints of articles from texts and journals they have on Prurigo Nodularis. They will also refer you to other organizations that are studying this disorder. NIAMS will also let you know of any clinical studies that may be studying this disease and looking for patients.

☎ Contact:
National Institute of Arthritis
and Musculoskeletal and Skin Diseases
Box AMS
9000 Rockville Pike
Bethesda, MD 20892
(301) 495-4484

PRURITUS

Clearinghouses/Hotlines

The National Arthritis and Musculoskeletal and Skin Diseases Clearinghouse can provide you with information regarding Pruritus. They can search the Combined Health Information Database (CHID) for information regarding this condition and can refer you to other organizations.

☎ Contact:
National Arthritis and Musculoskeletal
and Skin Diseases Clearinghouse
Box AMS
Bethesda, MD 20892
(301) 495-4484

PSEUDOGOUT

Clearinghouses/Hotlines

The National Institute of Arthritis and Musculoskeletal and Skin Diseases (NIAMS) will send you whatever publications and reprints of articles from texts and journals they have on Pseudogout. They will also refer you to other organizations that are studying this disorder. NIAMS will also let you know of any clinical studies that may be studying this disease and looking for patients.

☎ Contact:
National Institute of Arthritis
and Musculoskeletal and Skin Diseases
Box AMS
Bethesda, MD 20892
(301) 495-4484

PSEUDOHYPERTROPHIC DYSTROPHY

See Muscular Dystrophy

PSEUDOHYPO-PARATHYROIDISM

Clearinghouses/Hotlines

The National Institute of Diabetes and Digestive and Kidney Diseases's (NIDDK) individual clearinghouses can search the Combined Health Information Database (CHID) and generate a bibliography of resources for you on Pseudohypoparathyroidism. They also will send you any publications and journal articles they may have on hand, and will refer you to other organizations that are studying this condition. If you can't afford treatment, have your doctor call NIDDK to find out if they are conducting any clinical studies that you might qualify for.

☎ Contact:
National Institute of Diabetes
and Digestive and Kidney Diseases
Building 31
Room 9A04
Bethesda, MD 20892
(301) 496-3583

PSEUDOMONAS INFECTIONS

Clearinghouses/Hotlines

The National Institute of Allergy and Infectious Diseases (NIAID) can search the Combined Health Information Database (CHID) and generate a bibliography of resources for you on Pseudomonas Infections. They will also send you any publications and journal articles they may have on hand, and will refer you to researchers who are currently studying this condition. If you can't afford treatment, have your doctor call NIAID to find out if they are conducting any clinical studies that you might qualify for.

☎ Contact:
National Institute of Allergy
and Infectious Diseases
Building 31

Room 7A32
Bethesda, MD 20892
(301) 496-5717

PSEUDOSENILITY

Clearinghouses/Hotlines

The National Institute on Aging (NIA) will send you whatever publications and reprints of journal articles they have on Pseudosenility. They cannot refer you to other experts if the information they have isn't sufficient for your purposes.

☎ Contact:
National Institute on Aging
Bldg. 31, Room 5C27
Bethesda, MD 20892
(301) 496-1752

PSEUDOTUMOR CEREBRI

Clearinghouses/Hotlines

The National Eye Institute (NEI) can give you up-to-date information on Pseudotumor Cerebri by searching the Combined Health Information Database (CHID) and MEDLINE and sending you bibliographies of resources, along with any journal articles they may have. They can also refer you to any other organizations that study this and other related conditions. NEI will also let you know of any clinical studies that may be studying this disorder and looking for patients. Because of their small staff, NEI prefers that you submit your requests for information in writing.

☎ Contact:
National Eye Institute
Bldg. 31, Room 6A32
Bethesda, MD 20892
(301) 496-5248

The National Institute of Neurological Disorders and Stroke (NINDS) can send you information they have only in their publications list on Pseudotumor Cerebri. They cannot refer you to any experts. This Clearinghouse cannot directly give you information about any current clinical studies NINDS might be conducting on this disorder, but you can find this information for yourself by looking under the National Institute of Neurological Disorders and Stroke in *Appendix A* at the end of this book.

☎ Contact:
National Institute of Neurological
Disorders and Stroke
Bldg. 31, Room 8A06
Bethesda, MD 20892
(301) 496-5751
(800) 352-9424

Free Publications/Videos

The following publication is available from the National Institute of Neurological Disorders and Stroke, P.O. Box 5801, Bethesda, MD 20824; (800) 352-9424, or (301) 496-5751.

- *Pseudotumor Cerebri*. Collection of scientific articles, patient education pamphlets, and addresses of voluntary health associations.

PSEUDOXANTHOMA ELASTICUM

Clearinghouses/Hotlines

The National Heart, Lung, and Blood Institute (NHLBI) can search the Combined Health Information Database (CHID) and generate a bibliography of resources for you on Pseudoxanthoma Elasticum. They also will send you any publications and journal articles they may have on hand, and will refer you to other organizations that are studying this condition. If you can't afford treatment, have your doctor call NHLBI to find out if they are conducting any clinical studies that you might qualify for.

☎ Contact:
National Heart, Lung, and Blood Institute
Bldg. 31, Room 4A21
Bethesda, MD 20892
(301) 496-4236

PSITTACOSIS

Clearinghouses/Hotlines

The National Institute of Allergy and Infectious Diseases (NIAID) can search the Combined Health Information Database (CHID) and generate a bibliography of resources for you on Psittacosis. They will also send you any publications and journal articles they may have on hand, and will refer you to researchers who are currently studying this condition. If you can't afford treatment, have your doctor call NIAID to find out if they are conducting any clinical studies that you might qualify for.

☎ Contact:
National Institute of Allergy
and Infectious Diseases
Building 31, Room 7A32
Bethesda, MD 20892
(301) 496-5717

PSORIASIS

Clearinghouses/Hotlines

The National Institute of Arthritis and Musculoskeletal and Skin Diseases (NIAMS) will send you whatever publications and reprints of articles from texts and journals they have on Psoriasis. They will also refer you to other organizations that are studying this condition. NIAMS will also let you know of any clinical studies that may be studying this condition and looking for patients.

☎ Contact:
National Institute of Arthritis
and Musculoskeletal and Skin Diseases
Box AMS, 9000 Rockville Pike
Bethesda, MD 20892
(301) 495-4484

Free Publications/Videos

The following publication on Psoriasis is available

from the Center for Devices and Radiological Health, (HFZ-210), Food and Drug Administration, 5600 Fishers Ln., Rockville, MD 20857; (301) 443-4690.

- *PUVA's Double Whammy on Psoriasis.*

The following publication on Psoriasis is available from the National Arthritis and Musculoskeletal and Skin Diseases Information Clearinghouse, Box AMS, 9000 Rockville Pike, Bethesda, MD 20892; (301) 495-4484.

- *Psoriasis: Patient Education Materials, 1989.*
An annotated bibliography of resources. (#AR38, $2)

PSORIATIC ARTHRITIS

Clearinghouses/Hotlines

The National Institute of Arthritis and Musculoskeletal and Skin Diseases (NIAMS) will send you whatever publications and reprints of articles from texts and journals they have on Psoriatic Arthritis. They will also refer you to other organizations that are studying this condition. NIAMS will also let you know of any clinical studies that may be studying this condition and looking for patients.

☎ Contact:
National Institute of Arthritis
and Musculoskeletal and Skin Diseases
Box AMS
9000 Rockville Pike
Bethesda, MD 20892
(301) 495-4484

PSYCHOTIC EPISODES

Clearinghouses/Hotlines

The National Institute of Mental Health (NIMH) will send you whatever publications and reprints of articles from texts and journals they have on

Office of Technology Assessment, Washington, DC
20510-8025; (202) 224-8996.

- *Identifying and Controlling Pulmonary Toxi-cants: Background Paper.* (#OTA-BP-BA-91)

PURE RED CELL APLASIA

Clearinghouses/Hotlines

The National Heart, Lung, and Blood Institute (NHLBI) can search the Combined Health Information Database (CHID) and generate a bibliography of resources for you on Pure Red Cell Aplasia. They also will send you any publications and journal articles they may have on hand, and will refer you to other organizations that are studying this condition. If you can't afford treatment, have your doctor call NHLBI to find out if they are conducting any clinical studies that you might qualify for.
☎ Contact:
National Heart, Lung, and Blood Institute
Bldg. 31, Room 4A21
Bethesda, MD 20892
(301) 496-4236

PURPURA

Clearinghouses/Hotlines

The National Institute of Arthritis and Musculoskeletal and Skin Diseases (NIAMS) will send you whatever publications and reprints of articles from texts and journals they have on Purpura. They will also refer you to other organizations that are studying this condition. NIAMS will also let you know of any clinical studies that may be studying this condition and looking for patients.
☎ Contact:
National Institute of Arthritis
and Musculoskeletal and Skin Diseases
Box AMS

Bethesda, MD 20892
(301) 495-4484

PYELONEPHRITIS

Clearinghouses/Hotlines

The National Institute of Diabetes and Digestive and Kidney Diseases's (NIDDK) individual clearinghouses can search the Combined Health Information Database (CHID) and generate a bibliography of resources for you on Pyelonephritis. They also will send you any publications and journal articles they may have on hand, and will refer you to other organizations that are studying this condition. If you can't afford treatment, have your doctor call NIDDK to find out if they are conducting any clinical studies that you might qualify for.
☎ Contact:
National Institute of Diabetes
and Digestive and Kidney Diseases
Bldg. 31, Room 9A04
Bethesda, MD 20892
(301) 496-3583

PYOGENIC INFECTIONS

Clearinghouses/Hotlines

The National Institute of Allergy and Infectious Diseases (NIAID) can search the Combined Health Information Database (CHID) and generate a bibliography of resources for you on Recurrent Pyogenic Infections. They will also send you any publications and journal articles they may have on hand, and will refer you to researchers who are currently studying this condition. If you can't afford treatment, have your doctor call NIAID to find out if they are conducting any clinical studies that you might qualify for.
☎ Contact:
National Institute of Allergy
and Infectious Diseases

Bldg. 31, Room 7A32
Bethesda, MD 20892
(301) 496-5717

PYORRHEA

Clearinghouses/Hotlines

The National Institute of Dental Research (NIDR) will send you whatever publications and reprints of journal articles they have on Pyorrhea. As a policy, however, NIDR will not refer you to other organizations or experts who study this disease. If you can't afford treatment, have your doctor call Dr. Albert Guckers at (301) 496-6241 to find out if NIDR is conducting any clinical studies that you might qualify for.

☎ Contact:
National Institute of Dental Research
Building 31
Room 2C35
Bethesda, MD 20892
(301) 496-4261

- Q -

QUADRIPLEGIA

Clearinghouses/Hotlines

The National Institute of Neurological Disorders and Stroke (NINDS) can send you information they have only in their publications list on Quadriplegia. They cannot refer you to any experts. This Clearinghouse cannot directly give you information about any current clinical studies NINDS might be conducting on this illness, but you can find this information for yourself by looking under the National Institute of

Neurological Disorders and Stroke in *Appendix A* at the end of this book.

☎ Contact:
National Institute of Neurological
Disorders and Stroke
Bldg. 31, Room 8A06
Bethesda, MD 20892
(301) 496-5751
(800) 352-9424

- R -

RABIES

Clearinghouses/Hotlines

The National Institute of Allergy and Infectious Diseases (NIAID) can search the Combined Health Information Database (CHID) and generate a bibliography of resources for you on Rabies. They will also send you any publications and journal articles they may have on hand, and will refer you to researchers who are currently studying this disease. If you can't afford treatment, have your doctor call NIAID to find out if they are conducting any clinical studies that you might qualify for.

☎ Contact:
National Institute of Allergy
and Infectious Diseases
Bldg. 31, Room 7A32
Bethesda, MD 20892
(301) 496-5717

The Centers for Disease Control's Voice Information System allows anyone using a touchtone phone to obtain pre-recorded information on Rabies, and many other conditions. This service offers information about this condition, symptoms and prevention methods, immunization requirements, current statistics, recent disease outbreak, and available printed materials. The system is available 24 hours a day, although the health professionals are available Monday through Friday, 8-4:30.

☎ Contact:
Centers for Disease Control
Information Resources Management Office
Mail Stop C-15
1600 Clifton Rd., NE
Atlanta, GA 30333
(404) 332-4555

Free Publications/Videos

The following publication is available from the National Institute of Allergy and Infectious Diseases, Bldg. 31, Room 7A32, Bethesda, MD 20892; (301) 496-5717.

- *Rabies*. (#83-221)

The following video is available from Modern Talking Picture Service, 5000 Park St. North, St. Petersburg, FL 33709; (800) 243-MTPS.

- *Rabies*. Video teaches symptoms to be aware of and their threat to the nervous system.

RADIAL KERATOTOMY

Clearinghouses/Hotlines

The National Eye Institute (NEI) can give you up-to-date information on Radial Keratotomy by searching the Combined Health Information Database (CHID) and MEDLINE and sending you bibliographies of resources, along with any journal articles they may have. They can also refer you to any other organizations that study this and other related issue. NEI will also let you know of any clinical studies that may be studying this procedure and looking for patients. Because of their small staff, NEI prefers that you submit your requests for information in writing.

☎ Contact:
National Eye Institute
Bldg. 31, Room 6A32

Bethesda, MD 20892
(301) 496-5248

RADIATION

Clearinghouses/Hotlines

The National Cancer Institute (NCI) will send you whatever publications and reprints of journal articles they have on Radiation. They can also give you information on the state-of-the-art treatment for this issue, including specific treatment information for your stage of cancer. They can also search their Physician's Data Query (PDQ) database to let you know if NCI is conducting any clinical studies on your disease.

☎ Contact:
National Cancer Institute
Bldg. 31, Room 10A24
Bethesda, MD 20892
(800) 4-CANCER
(301) 496-5583

The National Eye Institute (NEI) can give you up-to-date information on the Effect of Radiation on the Eyes by searching the Combined Health Information Database (CHID) and MEDLINE and sending you bibliographies of resources, along with any journal articles they may have. They can also refer you to any other organizations that study this and other related issue. NEI will also let you know of any clinical studies that may be studying this procedure and looking for patients. Because of their small staff, NEI prefers that you submit your requests for information in writing.

☎ Contact:
National Eye Institute
Bldg. 31, Room 6A32
Bethesda, MD 20892
(301) 496-5248

The National Institute of Dental Research (NIDR) will send you whatever publications and reprints of journal articles they have on the effects of Radiation on Teeth. As a policy, however, NIDR will not refer you to other organizations or experts who study this issue. If you can't afford treatment, have your doctor call Dr. Albert Guckers at (301) 496-6241 to find out if NIDR is conducting any clinical studies that you might qualify for.

☎ Contact:
National Institute of Dental Research
Building 31
Room 2C35
Bethesda, MD 20892
(301) 496-4261

The National Institute of Neurological Disorders and Stroke (NINDS) can send you information they have only in their publications list on Radiation of the Nervous System. They cannot refer you to any experts. This Clearinghouse cannot directly give you information about any current clinical studies NINDS might be conducting on this topic, but you can find this information for yourself by looking under the National Institute of Neurological Disorders and Stroke in *Appendix A* at the end of this book.

☎ Contact:
National Institute of Neurological
Disorders and Stroke
Bldg. 31, Room 8A06
Bethesda, MD 20892
(301) 496-5751
(800) 352-9424

National Institute of Environmental Health Sciences (NIEHS) will send you whatever publications and journal articles they can locate on specific questions about Non-ionizing Radiation. If necessary they can put you in contact with researchers studying this issue. NIEHS does not conduct any clinical studies.

☎ Contact:
National Institute of Environmental
Health Sciences
P.O. Box 12233
Research Triangle Park, NC 27709
(919) 541-3345

The Center for Devices and Radiological Health regulates radiating emitting devices and can answer your questions regarding the danger of X-rays on a fetus.

☎ Contact:
Center for Devices and Radiological Health
Food and Drug Administration

5600 Fishers Lane, HFZ-210
Rockville, MD 20857
(301) 443-4190

Free Publications/Videos

The following publication on Radiation is available from the Office of Clinical Center Communications, Bldg. 10, Room 1C255, Bethesda, MD 20892; (301) 496-2563.

- *Radiation Risks and Radiation Therapy.* Covers unproven therapies on cancer patients to help make intelligent decisions. (#83-2367)

The following publication on Radiation is available from the Consumer Information Center, P.O. Box 100, Pueblo, CO 81002.

- *Food Irradiation: Toxic to Bacteria, Safe for Humans.* (#529Y)

The following publications on Radiation are available from the National Cancer Institute, Bldg. 31, Room 10A24, Bethesda, MD 20892; (800) 4-CANCER, or (301) 496-5583.

- *Radiation Therapy and You: A Guide to Self-Help During Treatment.* (#91-2227) Addresses concerns of patients receiving external and internal forms of radiation therapy.
- *Radiation Therapy: A Treatment for Early Stage Breast Cancer.* (#91-659)

RADON

Clearinghouses/Hotlines

The Radon Hotline is a 24-hour toll-free hotline where a message records your name and address and a brochure on Radon is sent via first class mail. The brochure gives some basic information concerning radon, as well as information on a radon detection kit available from the National Safety Council.

☎ Contact:
National Radon Hotline
Box 16622
Alexandria, VA 22302
(800) 767-7236

Free Publications/Videos

The Environmental Protection Agency's Public Information Center is the government's central depository for information on Radon and its removal. The following publications are available from the Public Information Center PM211-B, Environmental Protection Agency, 401 M St., SW, Washington, DC 20460; (202) 260-7751.

- *A Citizen's Guide to Radon: What It Is And What To Do About It*. Designed to help readers understand the radon problem and decide if they need to take action to reduce radon levels in their homes.
- *Removal Of Radon From Household Water*. Studies ways to reduce radon in houses; including methods to remove the gas from water to prevent its release in houses when the water is used.
- *Radon Reduction in New Construction*. Designed to provide radon information for those involved in new construction and to introduce methods that can be used during construction to minimizer radon entry and facilitate its removal after construction is complete.
- *Radon Reduction Methods: A Homeowner's Guide*. Designed for homeowners who have already tested their houses for radon and decided that they need to take some action, as well as those who are still uncertain.
- *Reducing Radon Risks*. Describes ways to test for radon, and myths about radon.
- *Environmental Backgrounder: Radon*. Explains issues, sources, concerns, laws, and Federal approaches.

The following Congressional Research Service (CRS) reports on Radon are available from either of your U.S. Senators' offices at the U.S. Capitol, Washington, DC 20510, or from your Congressional Representative at the U.S. Capitol, Washington, DC 20515. You can also call in your request through the U.S. Capitol switchboard at (202) 224-3121. Be sure to include the full title and report number in your request.

- *Radon: Issues and Congress; Issue Brief.* (#IB92095)
- *Radon: An Overview of Health and Environmental Issues; Info Pack.* (#IP363R)

RAMSEY HUNT SYNDROME

Clearinghouses/Hotlines

The National Institute of Neurological Disorders and Stroke (NINDS) can send you information they have only in their publications list on Ramsey Hunt Syndrome. They cannot refer you to any experts. This Clearinghouse cannot directly give you information about any current clinical studies NINDS might be conducting on this illness, but you can find this information for yourself by looking under the National Institute of Neurological Disorders and Stroke in *Appendix A* at the end of this book.

☎ Contact:
National Institute of Neurological
Disorders and Stroke
Bldg. 31, Room 8A06
Bethesda, MD 20892
(301) 496-5751
(800) 352-9424

The National Institute on Deafness and Other Communication Disorders (NIDCD) will send you whatever publications and reprints of journal articles they have on Ramsey Hunt Syndrome. If you need further information, they will refer you to other organizations that study this and other related disorders. NIDCD does not conduct any clinical studies for this or any other disorder.

☎ Contact:
National Institute on Deafness
and Other Communication Disorders
Bldg. 31, Room 3C35
Bethesda, MD 20892
(301) 496-7243
(800) 241-1044
(301) 402-0252 (TDD)

RAPE

Clearinghouses/Hotlines

The National Institute of Mental Health (NIMH) will send you whatever publications and reprints of articles from texts and journals they have on Rape. They will also refer you to other organizations that are studying this issue. NIMH will also let you know of any clinical studies that may be studying this issue and looking for patients.

☎ Contact:
National Institute of Mental Health
5600 Fishers Ln., Room 15C05
Rockville, MD 20857
(301) 443-4515

RARE DISEASES

Clearinghouses/Hotlines

The National Information Center for Orphan Drugs and Rare Diseases responds to inquiries on diseases with a prevalence of 200,000 or fewer cases in the United States and provides a mutual support network for families with similar disorders. This Clearinghouse, sponsored by the Food and Drug Administration, also gathers and distributes information on medicines not widely researched or available.

☎ Contact:
National Information Center
for Orphan Drugs and Rare Diseases
450 5th St., NW, Room 7103
Washington, DC 20001
(800) 456-3505

RASHES

Clearinghouses/Hotlines

The National Institute of Allergy and Infectious Diseases (NIAID) conducts and supports research on the causes of allergic, immunologic, and infectious diseases, and to develop better means of preventing, diagnosing, and treating illness. Some of the studies underway look at the role of the immune system in chronic diseases, such as arthritis, and at disorders of the immune system, as in asthma. Brochures and reports are available on a wide variety of topics.

☎ Contact:
National Institute of Allergy
and Infectious Diseases
Building 31
Room 7A32
Bethesda, MD 20892
(301) 496-5717

Free Publications/Videos

The following publication on Rashes is available from the Food & Drug Administration, (HFE-88), 5600 Fishers Ln., Rockville, MD 20857; (301) 443-3170.

- *Contact Dermatitis: Solutions to Rash Mysteries*. (#FDA91-1166)

RAYNAUD'S DISEASE

Clearinghouses/Hotlines

The National Heart, Lung, and Blood Institute (NHLBI) can search the Combined Health Information Database (CHID) and generate a bibliography of resources for you on Raynaud's Disease. They also will send you any publications and journal articles they may have on hand, and will refer you to other organizations that are studying this condition. If you can't afford treatment, have your doctor call NHLBI to find out if they are conducting any clinical studies that you might qualify for.

☎ Contact:
National Heart, Lung, and Blood Institute
Building 31
Room 4A21
Bethesda, MD 20892
(301) 496-4236

The National Institute of Arthritis and Musculoskeletal and Skin Diseases (NIAMS) will send you whatever publications and reprints of articles from texts and journals they have on Raynaud's Disease. They will also refer you to other organizations that are studying this disease. NIAMS will also let you know of any clinical studies that may be studying this disease and looking for patients.

☎ Contact:
National Institute of Arthritis
and Musculoskeletal and Skin Diseases
Box AMS
9000 Rockville Pike
Bethesda, MD 20892
(301) 495-4484

Free Publications/Videos

The following publication on Raynaud's Disease is available from the National Heart, Lung and Blood Institute, Bldg. 31, Room 4A21, Bethesda, MD 20892; (301) 496-4236.

- *Facts About Raynaud's Phenomenon.* (#90-2263)

READING DISORDERS

Clearinghouses/Hotlines

The National Institute of Child Health and Human Development (NICHD) will send you whatever publications and reprints of journal articles they have on Reading Disorders. If necessary, they will refer you to other experts or researchers in the field. If you can't afford treatment, have your doctor call NICHD to find out if they are conducting any clinical studies that you might qualify for.

☎ Contact:
National Institute of Child Health
and Human Development
Bldg. 31, Room 2A32
Bethesda, MD 20892
(301) 496-5133

The National Institute on Deafness and Other Communication Disorders (NIDCD) will send you whatever publications and reprints of journal articles they have on Reading Disorders. If you need further information, they will refer you to other organizations that study this and other related disorders. NIDCD does not conduct any clinical studies for this or any other disorder.

☎ Contact:
National Institute on Deafness
and Other Communication Disorders
Bldg. 31, Room 3C35
Bethesda, MD 20892
(301) 496-7243
(800) 241-1044
(301) 402-0252 (TDD)

READ METHOD OF CHILDBIRTH

See Childbirth

RECURRENT FEVER

Clearinghouses/Hotlines

The National Institute of Allergy and Infectious Diseases (NIAID) can search the Combined Health Information Database (CHID) and generate a bibliography of resources for you on Recurrent Fever. They will also send you any publications and journal articles they may have on hand, and will refer you to researchers who are currently studying this condition. If you can't afford treatment, have your doctor call NIAID to find out if they are conducting any clinical studies that you might qualify for.

☎ Contact:
National Institute of Allergy
and Infectious Diseases
Bldg. 31, Room 7A32
Bethesda, MD 20892
(301) 496-5717

REFLEX SYMPATHETIC DYSTROPHY SYNDROME

Clearinghouses/Hotlines

The National Institute of Arthritis and Musculoskeletal and Skin Diseases (NIAMS) will send you whatever publications and reprints of articles from texts and journals they have on Reflex Sympathetic Dystrophy Syndrome. They will also refer you to other organizations that are studying this disease. NIAMS will also let you know of any clinical studies that may be studying this condition and looking for patients.

☎ Contact:
National Institute of Arthritis
and Musculoskeletal and Skin Diseases
Bldg. 31, Room 4C05
Bethesda, MD 20892
(301) 495-4484

The National Institute of Neurological Disorders and Stroke (NINDS) can send you information they have only in their publications list on Reflex Sympathetic Dystrophy Syndrome. They cannot refer you to any experts. This Clearinghouse cannot directly give you information about any current clinical studies NINDS might be conducting on this illness, but you can find this information for yourself by looking under the National Institute of Neurological Disorders and Stroke in *Appendix A* at the end of this book.

☎ Contact:
National Institute of Neurological
Disorders and Stroke
Bldg. 31, Room 8A06
Bethesda, MD 20892
(301) 496-5751
(800) 352-9424

Free Publications/Videos

The following publication on Reflex Sympathetic Dystrophy Syndrome is available from the National Institute of Neurological Disorders and Stroke, P.O. Box 5801, Bethesda, MD 20824; (800) 352-9424, or (301) 496-5751.

- *Reflex Sympathetic Dystrophy Syndrome (RSDS)*. Contains a collection of scientific articles, patient education pamphlets, and addresses of voluntary health associations.

REFLUX NEPHROPATHY

Clearinghouses/Hotlines

The National Institute of Diabetes and Digestive and Kidney Diseases's (NIDDK) individual clearinghouses can search the Combined Health Information Database (CHID) and generate a bibliography of resources for you on Reflux Nephropathy. They also will send you any publications and journal articles they may have on hand, and will refer you to other organizations that are studying this disease. If you can't afford treatment, have your doctor call NIDDK to find out if they are conducting any clinical studies that you might qualify for.

☎ Contact:
National Institute of Diabetes
and Digestive and Kidney Diseases
Bldg. 31, Room 9A04
Bethesda, MD 20892
(301) 496-3583

REFRACTORY ANEMIA

Clearinghouses/Hotlines

The National Heart, Lung, and Blood Institute (NHLBI) can search the Combined Health Information Database (CHID) and generate a bibliography of resources for you on Refractory Anemia. They also will send you any publications and journal articles they may have on hand, and will refer you to other organizations that are studying Refractory Anemia. If you can't afford treatment, have your doctor call NHLBI to find out if they are conducting any clinical studies that you might qualify for.

☎ Contact:
National Heart, Lung, and Blood Institute

Bldg. 31, Room 4A21
Bethesda, MD 20892
(301) 496-4236

REFSUM'S DISEASE

Clearinghouses/Hotlines

The National Institute of Neurological Disorders and Stroke (NINDS) can send you information they have only in their publications list on Refsum's Disease. They cannot refer you to any experts. This Clearinghouse cannot directly give you information about any current clinical studies NINDS might be conducting on this illness, but you can find this information for yourself by looking under the National Institute of Neurological Disorders and Stroke in *Appendix A* at the end of this book.

☎ Contact:
National Institute of Neurological
Disorders and Stroke
Bldg. 31, Room 8A06
Bethesda, MD 20892
(301) 496-5751
(800) 352-9424

REGIONAL ENTERITIS

See Crohn's Disease

REHABILITATION

See also Disabilities

Clearinghouses/Hotlines

The National Institute on Disability and Rehabilitation Research can fill you in on the newest developments in rehabilitation methods and devices for people of all ages with physical and mental handicaps, especially those who are

severely disabled. They also have all kinds of statistical data on disabilities and research funding information are also available. Ask for a copy of their program directory, which includes information on the projects they are funding for the year.

☎ Contact:
U.S. Department of Education
Mary E. Switzer Bldg.
MS-2305, 330 C St., SW
Washington, DC 20202
(202) 732-6151

The National Institute on Aging (NIA) will send you whatever publications and reprints of journal articles they have on Rehabilitation. They cannot refer you to other experts if the information they have isn't sufficient for your purposes.

☎ Contact:
National Institute on Aging
Bldg. 31, Room 5C27
Bethesda, MD 20892
(301) 496-1752

The National Rehabilitation Information Center (NRIC) can provide you with all kinds of information on disability-related research, resources and products for independent living as well as fact sheets, resource guides, research and technical publications, newsletters, and database information. The NRIC collection includes materials relevant to the rehabilitation of all disability groups.

☎ Contact:
National Rehabilitation Information Center
8455 Colesville Rd., Suite 935
Silver Spring, MD 20910
(800) 346-2742 (voice and TDD)

REITER'S SYNDROME

Clearinghouses/Hotlines

The National Institute of Arthritis and Musculoskeletal and Skin Diseases (NIAMS) will send you whatever publications and reprints of articles from texts and journals they have on Reiter's Syndrome. They will also refer you to other organizations that are studying this Syndrome. NIAMS will also let you know of any clinical studies that may be studying this disease and looking for patients.

☎ Contact:
National Institute of Arthritis
and Musculoskeletal and Skin Diseases
Bldg. 31, Room 4C05
Bethesda, MD 20892
(301) 495-4484

RELAXATION

Clearinghouses/Hotlines

The National Institute of Mental Health (NIMH) maintains data bases that index and abstract documents from the worldwide literature pertaining to Mental Illness and Relaxation. In addition to scientific journals, there are references to audiovisuals, dissertations, government documents and reports. Contact NIMH for searches on specific subjects.

☎ Contact:
National Institute of Mental Health
5600 Fishers Lane, Room 15C05
Rockville, MD 20857
(301) 443-4515

Free Publications/Videos

The following publication is available from the National Institute of Mental Health, 5600 Fishers Ln., Room 15C05, Rockville, MD 20857; (301) 443-4515.

- *Plain Talk About the Art of Relaxation.*

RENAL DISORDERS

Clearinghouses/Hotlines

The National Institute of Diabetes and Digestive and Kidney Diseases's (NIDDK) individual

clearinghouses can search the Combined Health Information Database (CHID) and generate a bibliography of resources for you on Renal Disorders such as renal glycosuria, hypertension, tubular acidosis, and vascular disease. They also will send you any publications and journal articles they may have on hand, and will refer you to other organizations that are studying this disease. If you can't afford treatment, have your doctor call NIDDK to find out if they are conducting any clinical studies that you might qualify for.

☎ Contact:
National Institute of Diabetes
and Digestive and Kidney Diseases
Bldg. 31, Room 9A04
Bethesda, MD 20892
(301) 496-3583

Free Publications/Videos

The following publication is available from the National Heart, Lung and Blood Institute, Bldg. 31, Room 4A21, Bethesda, MD 20892; (301) 496-4236.

- *Working Group Report on Hypertension and Chronic Renal Failure.* (#90-3032)

The following publications are available from the National Institute of Diabetes and Digestive and Kidney Diseases, Bldg. 31, Room 9A04, Bethesda, MD 20892; (301) 496-3583.

- *End-Stage Renal Disease: Choosing a Treatment That's Right for You.* (#92-2412)
- *United States Renal Data System 1991 Annual Data Report.* (#91-3176)

RENOVASCULAR HYPERTENSION

Clearinghouses/Hotlines

The National Institute of Diabetes and Digestive and Kidney Diseases's (NIDDK) individual clearinghouses can search the Combined Health Information Database (CHID) and generate a bibliography of resources for you on Renovascular Hypertension. They also will send you any publications and journal articles they may have on hand, and will refer you to other organizations that are studying this disease. If you can't afford treatment, have your doctor call NIDDK to find out if they are conducting any clinical studies that you might qualify for.

☎ Contact:
National Institute of Diabetes
and Digestive and Kidney Diseases
Bldg. 31, Room 9A04
Bethesda, MD 20892
(301) 496-3583

The National Heart, Lung, and Blood Institute (NHLBI) can search the Combined Health Information Database (CHID) and generate a bibliography of resources for you on Renovascular Hypertension. They also will send you any publications and journal articles they may have on hand, and will refer you to other organizations that are studying this condition. If you can't afford treatment, have your doctor call NHLBI to find out if they are conducting any clinical studies that you might qualify for.

☎ Contact:
National Heart, Lung, and Blood Institute
Bldg. 31, Room 4A21
Bethesda, MD 20892
(301) 496-4236

REPETITIVE STRESS SYNDROME

Clearinghouses/Hotlines

The National Institute of Occupational Safety and Health (NIOSH) can provide you with information regarding Repetitive Stress Syndrome. They can search their data base for relevant materials and send you articles and reference materials they may have.

☎ Contact:
National Institute of Occupational
Safety and Health
4676 Columbia Parkway, MS C-19

Cincinnati, OH 45226
(800) 35-NIOSH

REPRODUCTIVE DISORDERS

Clearinghouses/Hotlines

The National Institute of Child Health and Human Development (NICHD) will send you whatever publications and reprints of journal articles they have on Reproductive Disorders. If necessary, they will refer you to other experts or researchers in the field. If you can't afford treatment, have your doctor call NICHD to find out if they are conducting any clinical studies that you might qualify for.

☎ Contact:
National Institute of Child Health
and Human Development
Bldg. 31, Room 2A32
Bethesda, MD 20892
(301) 496-5133

RESPIRATORY DISEASES

Clearinghouses/Hotlines

The National Institute of Allergy and Infectious Diseases (NIAID) can search the Combined Health Information Database (CHID) and generate a bibliography of resources for you on Infectious and Allergenic Respiratory Diseases. They will also send you any publications and journal articles they may have on hand, and will refer you to researchers who are currently studying this disease. If you can't afford treatment, have your doctor call NIAID to find out if they are conducting any clinical studies that you might qualify for.

☎ Contact:
National Institute of Allergy
and Infectious Diseases
Bldg. 31, Room 7A32

Bethesda, MD 20892
(301) 496-5717

The National Heart, Lung, and Blood Institute (NHLBI) can search the Combined Health Information Database (CHID) and generate a bibliography of resources for you on Respiratory Disease. They also will send you any publications and journal articles they may have on hand, and will refer you to other organizations that are studying this condition. If you can't afford treatment, have your doctor call NHLBI to find out if they are conducting any clinical studies that you might qualify for.

☎ Contact:
National Heart, Lung, and Blood Institute
Bldg. 31, Room 4A21
Bethesda, MD 20892
(301) 496-4236

The National Cancer Institute (NCI) will send you whatever publications and reprints of journal articles they have on Tumorous and Cancerous Respiratory Diseases. They can also give you information on the state-of-the-art treatment for this disease, including specific treatment information for your stage of cancer. They can also search their Physician's Data Query (PDQ) database to let you know if NCI is conducting any clinical studies on your disease.

☎ Contact:
National Cancer Institute
Bldg. 31, Room 10A24
Bethesda, MD 20892
(800) 4-CANCER
(301) 496-5583

RESPIRATORY DISTRESS SYNDROME

Clearinghouses/Hotlines

The National Heart, Lung, and Blood Institute (NHLBI) can search the Combined Health Information Database (CHID) and generate a bibliography of resources for you on Respiratory Distress Syndrome. They also will send you any

publications and journal articles they may have on hand, and will refer you to other organizations that are studying this condition. If you can't afford treatment, have your doctor call NHLBI to find out if they are conducting any clinical studies that you might qualify for.

☎ Contact:
National Heart, Lung, and Blood Institute
Building 31
Room 4A21
Bethesda, MD 20892
(301) 496-4236

Free Publications/Videos

The following publication on Respiratory Distress Syndrome is available from the National Heart, Lung and Blood Institute, Bldg. 31, Room 4A21, Bethesda, MD 20892; (301) 496-4236.

- *Prevention of Respiratory Distress Syndrome.* (#85-2695)

RESPIRATORY SYNCYTIAL VIRUS

Clearinghouses/Hotlines

The National Institute of Allergy and Infectious Diseases (NIAID) can search the Combined Health Information Database (CHID) and generate a bibliography of resources for you on Respiratory Syncytial Virus. They will also send you any publications and journal articles they may have on hand, and will refer you to researchers who are currently studying this disease. If you can't afford treatment, have your doctor call NIAID to find out if they are conducting any clinical studies that you might qualify for.

☎ Contact:
National Institute of Allergy
and Infectious Diseases
Building 31
Room 7A32
Bethesda, MD 20892
(301) 496-5717

RESTLESS LEG SYNDROME

Clearinghouses/Hotlines

The National Institute of Neurological Disorders and Stroke (NINDS) can send you information they have only in their publications list on Restless Leg Syndrome. They cannot refer you to any experts. This Clearinghouse cannot directly give you information about any current clinical studies NINDS might be conducting on this disorder, but you can find this information for yourself by looking under the National Institute of Neurological Disorders and Stroke in *Appendix A* at the end of this book.

☎ Contact:
National Institute of Neurological
Disorders and Stroke
Bldg. 31, Room 8A06
Bethesda, MD 20892
(301) 496-5751
(800) 352-9424

Free Publications/Videos

The following publication is available from the National Institute of Neurological Disorders and Stroke, P.O. Box 5801, Bethesda, MD 20824; (800) 352-9424, or (301) 496-5751.

- *Restless Leg Syndrome*. Collection of scientific articles, patient education pamphlets, and addresses of voluntary health associations.

RETARDATION

See Mental Retardation

RETINAL DISEASE

Clearinghouses/Hotlines

The National Eye Institute (NEI) can give you up-to-date information on Retinal Diseases by searching the Combined Health Information Database (CHID) and MEDLINE and sending you bibliographies of resources, along with any journal articles they may have. These diseases include retinal degeneration, detachment, vascular disease, retinitis pigmentosa, retinoblastomas, and retinopathies. They can also refer you to any other organizations that study this and other related condition. NEI will also let you know of any clinical studies that may be studying this issue and looking for patients. Because of their small staff, NEI prefers that you submit your requests for information in writing.

☎ Contact:
National Eye Institute
Bldg. 31, Room 6A32
Bethesda, MD 20892
(301) 496-5248

Free Publications/Videos

The following publication is available from the National Eye Institute, Bldg. 31, Room 6A32, Bethesda, MD 20892; (301) 496-5248.

- *Vision Research: Report of the Retinal and Choroidal Diseases Panel, Part One.* (#83-2471)

RETT'S SYNDROME

Clearinghouses/Hotlines

The National Institute of Neurological Disorders and Stroke (NINDS) can send you information they have only in their publications list on Rett's Syndrome. They cannot refer you to any experts. This Clearinghouse cannot directly give you information about any current clinical studies NINDS might be conducting on this illness, but you can find this information for yourself by looking under the National Institute of Neurological Disorders and Stroke in *Appendix A* at the end of this book.

☎ Contact:
National Institute of Neurological

Disorders and Stroke
Bldg. 31, Room 8A06
Bethesda, MD 20892
(301) 496-5751
(800) 352-9424

Free Publications/Videos

The following publication on Rett's Syndrome is available from the National Institute of Neurological Disorders and Stroke, P.O. Box 5801, Bethesda, MD 20824; (800) 352-9424, or (301) 496-5751.

- *Rett Syndrome*. A collection of scientific articles, patient education pamphlets, and addresses of voluntary health associations.

REYE'S SYNDROME

Clearinghouses/Hotlines

The National Institute of Neurological Disorders and Stroke (NINDS) can send you information they have only in their publications list on Reye's Syndrome. They cannot refer you to any experts. This Clearinghouse cannot directly give you information about any current clinical studies NINDS might be conducting on this illness, but you can find this information for yourself by looking under the National Institute of Neurological Disorders and Stroke in *Appendix A* at the end of this book.

☎ Contact:
National Institute of Neurological
Disorders and Stroke
Bldg. 31, Room 8A06
Bethesda, MD 20892
(301) 496-5751
(800) 352-9424

Free Publications/Videos

The following publication on Reye's Syndrome is available from the National Institute of Neurological Disorders and Stroke, P.O. Box 5801,

Bethesda, MD 20824; (800) 352-9424, or (301) 496-5751.

- *Reye's Syndrome*. Contains a collection of scientific articles, patient education pamphlets, and addresses of voluntary health associations.

The following publication is available from the Food & Drug Administration, (HFE-88), 5600 Fishers Ln., Rockville, MD 20857; (301) 443-3170.

- *Reye Syndrome: The Decline Of A Disease*. (#FDA91-1172)

RH FACTOR

Clearinghouses/Hotlines

The National Heart, Lung, and Blood Institute (NHLBI) can search the Combined Health Information Database (CHID) and generate a bibliography of resources for you on Rh Factor. They also will send you any publications and journal articles they may have on hand, and will refer you to other organizations that are studying this issue. If you can't afford treatment, have your doctor call NHLBI to find out if they are conducting any clinical studies that you might qualify for.

☎ Contact:
National Heart, Lung, and Blood Institute
Bldg. 31, Room 4A21
Bethesda, MD 20892
(301) 496-4236

RHABDOMYOSARCOMA

Clearinghouses/Hotlines

The National Cancer Institute (NCI) will send you whatever publications and reprints of journal articles they have on Sarcoma of Bone and Soft Tissue. They can also give you information on the state-of-the-art treatment for this disease, including specific treatment information for your stage of cancer. They can also search their Physician's Data Query (PDQ) database to let you know if NCI is conducting any clinical studies on your disease.

☎ Contact:
National Cancer Institute
Bldg. 31, Room 10A24
Bethesda, MD 20892
(800) 4-CANCER
(301) 496-5583

will refer you to other organizations that are studying this disease. If you can't afford treatment, have your doctor call NHLBI to find out if they are conducting any clinical studies that you might qualify for.

☎ Contact:
National Heart, Lung, and Blood Institute
Building 31
Room 4A21
Bethesda, MD 20892
(301) 496-4236

RHEUMATIC FEVER

Clearinghouses/Hotlines

The National Institute of Allergy and Infectious Diseases (NIAID) can search the Combined Health Information Database (CHID) and generate a bibliography of resources for you on Rheumatic Fever. They will also send you any publications and journal articles they may have on hand, and will refer you to researchers who are currently studying this disease. If you can't afford treatment, have your doctor call NIAID to find out if they are conducting any clinical studies that you might qualify for.

☎ Contact:
National Institute of Allergy
and Infectious Diseases
Building 31
Room 7A32
Bethesda, MD 20892
(301) 496-5717

RHEUMATIC HEART

Clearinghouses/Hotlines

The National Heart, Lung, and Blood Institute (NHLBI) can search the Combined Health Information Database (CHID) and generate a bibliography of resources for you on Rheumatic Heart. They also will send you any publications and journal articles they may have on hand, and

RHEUMATISM

Clearinghouses/Hotlines

The National Institute of Arthritis and Musculoskeletal and Skin Diseases (NIAMS) will send you whatever publications and reprints of articles from texts and journals they have on Rheumatism. They will also refer you to other organizations that are studying this disease. NIAMS will also let you know of any clinical studies that may be studying this disease and looking for patients.

☎ Contact:
National Institute of Arthritis
and Musculoskeletal and Skin Diseases
Box AMS
Bethesda, MD 20892
(301) 495-4484

Free Publications/Videos

The following publication on Rheumatism is available from the National Arthritis and Musculoskeletal and Skin Diseases Clearinghouse, Box AMS, 9000 Rockville Pike, Bethesda, MD 20892; (301) 495-4484.

- *Rheumatic Diseases and the Older Adult: An Annotated Bibliography, 1986.* Contains 86 references with abstracts to the medical literature for physicians, allied health professionals, and others interested in geriatric medicine and rheumatology. ($4)

The following publications on Rheumatic Diseases are available from the National Arthritis and Musculoskeletal and Skin Diseases Information Clearinghouse, Box AMS, 9000 Rockville Pike, Bethesda, MD 20892; (301) 495-4484.

- *Psychosocial Aspects of Rheumatic Diseases, 1985.* An annotated bibliography of resources. (#AR56, $3)
- *Sexuality and the Rheumatic Diseases, 1986.* An annotated bibliography of resources. (#AR59, $2)

RHEUMATOID ARTHRITIS

Clearinghouses/Hotlines

The National Institute of Arthritis and Musculoskeletal and Skin Diseases (NIAMS) will send you whatever publications and reprints of articles from texts and journals they have on Rheumatoid Arthritis. They will also refer you to other organizations that are studying this disease. NIAMS will also let you know of any clinical studies that may be studying this disease and looking for patients.

☎ Contact:
National Institute of Arthritis
and Musculoskeletal and Skin Diseases
Box AMS
9000 Rockville Pike
Bethesda, MD 20892
(301) 495-4484

Free Publications/Videos

The following publication is available from the National Arthritis and Musculoskeletal and Skin Diseases Information Clearinghouse, Box AMS, 9000 Rockville Pike, Bethesda, MD 20892; (301) 495-4484.

- *Rheumatoid Arthritis: Patient Education Materials, 1984.* An annotated bibliography of resources. (#AR57, $4)

RHINITIS

Clearinghouses/Hotlines

The National Institute of Allergy and Infectious Diseases (NIAID) can search the Combined Health Information Database (CHID) and generate a bibliography of resources for you on Rhinitis. They will also send you any publications and journal articles they may have on hand, and will refer you to researchers who are currently studying this disease. If you can't afford treatment, have your doctor call NIAID to find out if they are conducting any clinical studies that you might qualify for.

☎ Contact:
National Institute of Allergy
and Infectious Diseases
Building 31
Room 7A32
Bethesda, MD 20892
(301) 496-5717

RHUS DERMATITIS

Clearinghouses/Hotlines

The National Arthritis and Musculoskeletal and Skin Diseases Clearinghouse can provide you with information regarding Rhus Dermatitis, which is a skin condition you get when you come in contact with such plants as poison ivy or poison sumac. They can search the Combined Health Information Database (CHID) for information regarding this condition and can refer you to other organizations.

☎ Contact:
National Arthritis and Musculoskeletal
and Skin Diseases Clearinghouse
Box AMS
9000 Rockville Pike
Bethesda, MD 20892
(301) 495-4484

RHYTIDOPLASTY

See Face Lift

RICKETS

Clearinghouses/Hotlines

The National Institute of Diabetes and Digestive and Kidney Diseases's (NIDDK) individual clearinghouses can search the Combined Health Information Database (CHID) and generate a bibliography of resources for you on Vitamin-D Resistant Rickets. They also will send you any publications and journal articles they may have on hand, and will refer you to other organizations that are studying this disease. If you can't afford treatment, have your doctor call NIDDK to find out if they are conducting any clinical studies that you might qualify for.

☎ Contact:
National Institute of Diabetes
and Digestive and Kidney Diseases
Bldg. 31, Room 9A04
Bethesda, MD 20892
(301) 496-3583

The National Institute of Allergy and Infectious Diseases (NIAID) can search the Combined Health Information Database (CHID) and generate a bibliography of resources for you on Rickettsial Diseases. They will also send you any publications and journal articles they may have on hand, and will refer you to researchers who are currently studying this condition. If you can't afford treatment, have your doctor call NIAID to find out if they are conducting any clinical studies that you might qualify for.

☎ Contact:
National Institute of Allergy
and Infectious Diseases
Bldg. 31, Room 7A32
Bethesda, MD 20892
(301) 496-5717

RILEY-DAY SYNDROME

Clearinghouses/Hotlines

The National Institute of Neurological Disorders and Stroke (NINDS) can send you information they have only in their publications list on Riley-Day Syndrome. They cannot refer you to any experts. This Clearinghouse cannot directly give you information about any current clinical studies NINDS might be conducting on this illness, but you can find this information for yourself by looking under the National Institute of Neurological Disorders and Stroke in *Appendix A* at the end of this book.

☎ Contact:
National Institute of Neurological
Disorders and Stroke
Bldg. 31, Room 8A06
Bethesda, MD 20892
(301) 496-5751
(800) 352-9424

RINGWORM

Clearinghouses/Hotlines

The National Institute of Allergy and Infectious Diseases (NIAID) can search the Combined Health Information Database (CHID) and generate a bibliography of resources for you on Ringworm. They will also send you any publications and journal articles they may have on hand, and will refer you to researchers who are currently studying this condition. If you can't afford treatment, have your doctor call NIAID to find out if they are conducting any clinical studies that you might qualify for.

☎ Contact:
National Institute of Allergy
and Infectious Diseases
Bldg. 31, Room 7A32
Bethesda, MD 20892
(301) 496-5717

RIVER BLINDNESS

Clearinghouses/Hotlines

The National Eye Institute (NEI) can give you up-to-date information on River Blindness by searching the Combined Health Information Database (CHID) and MEDLINE and sending you bibliographies of resources, along with any journal articles they may have. They can also refer you to any other organizations that study this and other related condition. NEI will also let you know of any clinical studies that may be studying this condition and looking for patients. Because of their small staff, NEI prefers that you submit your requests for information in writing.

☎ Contact:
National Eye Institute
Bldg. 31, Room 6A32
Bethesda, MD 20892
(301) 496-5248

The National Institute of Allergy and Infectious Diseases (NIAID) can search the Combined Health Information Database (CHID) and generate a bibliography of resources for you on River Blindness. They will also send you any publications and journal articles they may have on hand, and will refer you to researchers currently studying this condition. If you can't afford treatment, have your doctor call NIAID to find out if they are conducting any clinical studies that you might qualify for.

☎ Contact:
National Institute of Allergy
and Infectious Diseases
Bldg. 31, Room 7A32
Bethesda, MD 20892
(301) 496-5717

ROCKY MOUNTAIN SPOTTED FEVER

Clearinghouses/Hotlines

The National Institute of Allergy and Infectious Diseases (NIAID) can search the Combined Health Information Database (CHID) and generate a bibliography of resources for you on Rocky Mountain Spotted Fever. They will also send you any publications and journal articles they may have on hand, and will refer you to researchers currently studying this condition. If you can't afford treatment, have your doctor call NIAID to find out if they are conducting any clinical studies that you might qualify for.

☎ Contact:
National Institute of Allergy
and Infectious Diseases
Bldg. 31, Room 7A32
Bethesda, MD 20892
(301) 496-5717

ROOT CARIES

Clearinghouses/Hotlines

The National Institute of Dental Research (NIDR) will send you whatever publications and reprints of journal articles they have on Root Caries. As a policy, however, NIDR will not refer you to other organizations or experts who study this condition. If you can't afford treatment, have your doctor call Dr. Albert Guckers at (301) 496-6241 to find out if NIDR is conducting any clinical studies that you might qualify for.

☎ Contact:
National Institute of Dental Research
Bldg. 31, Room 2C35
Bethesda, MD 20892
(301) 496-4261

ROSACEAE

Clearinghouses/Hotlines

The National Arthritis and Musculoskeletal and Skin Diseases Clearinghouse can provide you with information regarding Rosaceae. They can search the Combined Health Information Database (CHID) for information regarding this condition and can refer you to other organizations.

☎ Contact:
National Arthritis and Musculoskeletal
and Skin Diseases Clearinghouse
Box AMS, 9000 Rockville Pike
Bethesda, MD 20892
(301) 495-4484

ROTAVIRUS

Clearinghouses/Hotlines

The National Institute of Allergy and Infectious Diseases (NIAID) can search the Combined Health Information Database (CHID) and generate a bibliography of resources for you on Rotavirus. They will also send you any publications and journal articles they may have on hand, and will refer you to researchers currently studying this condition. If you can't afford treatment, have your doctor call NIAID to find out if they are conducting any clinical studies that you might qualify for.

☎ Contact:
National Institute of Allergy
and Infectious Diseases
Bldg. 31, Room 7A32
Bethesda, MD 20892
(301) 496-5717

ROTHMUND-THOMPSON SYNDROME

Clearinghouses/Hotlines

The National Cancer Institute (NCI) will send you whatever publications and reprints of journal articles they have on Rothmund-Thompson Syndrome. They can also give you information on the state-of-the-art treatment for this disease, including specific treatment information for your stage of cancer. They can also search their Physician's Data Query (PDQ) database to let you know if NCI is conducting any clinical studies on your disease.

☎ Contact:
National Cancer Institute
Bldg. 31, Room 10A24
Bethesda, MD 20892
(800) 4-CANCER
(301) 496-5583

RUBELLA

See also Immunizations

Clearinghouses/Hotlines

The National Institute of Allergy and Infectious Diseases (NIAID) can search the Combined Health Information Database (CHID) and generate a bibliography of resources for you on Rubella and Rubeola. They will also send you any publications and journal articles they may have on hand, and will refer you to researchers who are currently studying this disease. If you can't afford treatment, have your doctor call NIAID to find out if they are conducting any clinical studies that you might qualify for.

☎ Contact:
National Institute of Allergy
and Infectious Diseases
Bldg. 31, Room 7A32
Bethesda, MD 20892
(301) 496-5717

RUNAWAY HOTLINE

Clearinghouses/Hotlines

The National Runaway Hotline provides information and resources to parents and runaways. It will deliver messages to parents from their children and offer advice to runaways regarding places to go for help. The Hotline operates 24 hours per day, and all information is confidential.

☎ Contact:
National Runaway Hotline
(800) 621-4000

SAFE SEX

See also AIDS
See also Sexually Transmitted Diseases

Clearinghouses/Hotlines

The National AIDS Information Clearinghouse can provide you with information, including pamphlets and reports on how to have safe sex.

☎ Contact:
National AIDS Information Clearinghouse
P.O. Box 6003
Rockville, MD 20850
(800) 342-AIDS

SALIVARY SYSTEM DISEASES

Clearinghouses/Hotlines

The National Institute of Dental Research (NIDR) will send you whatever publications and reprints of journal articles they have on Salivary System Diseases. As a policy, however, NIDR will not refer you to other organizations or experts who study these diseases. If you can't afford treatment, have your doctor call Dr. Albert Guckers at (301) 496-6241 to find out if NIDR is conducting any clinical studies that you might qualify for.

☎ Contact:
National Institute of Dental Research
Bldg. 31, Room 2C35
Bethesda, MD 20892
(301) 496-4261

SALMONELLA INFECTIONS

Clearinghouses/Hotlines

The National Institute of Allergy and Infectious Diseases (NIAID) can search the Combined Health Information Database (CHID) and generate a bibliography of resources for you on Salmonella Infections. They will also send you any publications and journal articles they may have on hand, and will refer you to researchers who are currently studying salmonella infections. If you can't afford treatment, have your doctor call NIAID to find out if they are conducting any clinical studies that you might qualify for.

☎ Contact:
National Institute of Allergy
and Infectious Diseases
Bldg. 31, Room 7A32
Bethesda, MD 20892
(301) 496-5717

Free Publications/Videos

The following publication on Salmonella Infections is available from the Food & Drug Administration, (HFE-88), 5600 Fishers Ln., Rockville, MD 20857; (301) 443-3170.

- *Salmonella Enteritidis From The Chicken To The Egg.* (#FDA91-2238)

SALT

Clearinghouses/Hotlines

Food and Nutrition Information Center can provide you with a wealth of information on food and nutrition topics. They have bibliographies ready and a data base through which they can search any food or nutrition subject.

☎ Contact:
Food and Nutrition Information Center
National Agricultural Library
Room 304
Beltsville, MD 20705
(301) 504-5719

Free Publications/Videos

The following publication on Salt is available from the Human Nutrition Information Service 6505 Belcrest Rd., Room 363, Hyattsville, MD 20782; (301) 436-8617.

- *The Sodium Content of Your Food.* ($2.25,

The following publication on Salt is available from the National Heart, Lung and Blood Institute, Bldg. 31, Room 4A21, Bethesda, MD 20892; (301) 496-4236.

- *Questions About Weight, Salt and High Blood Pressure.* (#88-1459)

The following publication on Salt is available from the National Institute on Aging Information Center, 2209 Distribution Circle, Silver Spring, MD 20910; (301) 495-3455.

- *Be Sensible About Salt.* Facts for the aging.

The following publication on Salt is available from the Food & Drug Administration, (HFE-88), 5600 Fishers Ln., Rockville, MD 20857; (301) 443-3170.

- *A Word About Low Sodium Diets.* Suggests ways consumers can lower sodium intake and lists foods that are naturally low in sodium. (#FDA90-2179)

SANTAVUORI DISEASE

Clearinghouses/Hotlines

The National Institute of Neurological Disorders and Stroke (NINDS) can send you only information they have in their current publications on Santavuori Disease. They cannot refer you to any experts. This Clearinghouse cannot directly give you information about any current clinical studies NINDS might be conducting on this illness, but you can find this information for yourself by looking under the National Institute of Neurological Disorders and Stroke in *Appendix A* at the end of this book.

☎ Contact:
National Institute of Neurological
Disorders and Stroke
Bldg. 31, Room 8A06
Bethesda, MD 20892
(301) 496-5751
(800) 352-9424

SARCOIDOSIS

Clearinghouses/Hotlines

The National Institute of Allergy and Infectious Diseases (NIAID) can search the Combined Health Information Database (CHID) and generate a bibliography of resources for you on Sarcoidosis. They will also send you any publications and journal articles they may have on hand, and will refer you to researchers who are currently studying sarcoidosis. If you can't afford treatment, have your doctor call NIAID to find out if they are conducting any clinical studies that you might qualify for.

☎ Contact:
National Institute of Allergy
and Infectious Diseases
Bldg. 31, Room 7A32
Bethesda, MD 20892
(301) 496-5717

The National Heart, Lung, and Blood Institute (NHLBI) can search the Combined Health Information Database (CHID) and generate a bibliography of resources for you on Sarcoidosis. They also will send you any publications and journal articles they may have on hand, and will refer you to other organizations that are studying sarcoidosis. If you can't afford treatment, have your doctor call NHLBI to find out if they are conducting any clinical studies that you might qualify for.

☎ Contact:
National Heart, Lung, and Blood Institute
Bldg. 31, Room 4A21
Bethesda, MD 20892
(301) 496-4236

The National Eye Institute (NEI) can give you up-to-date information on Sarcoidosis by searching the Combined Health Information Database (CHID) and MEDLINE and sending you bibliographies of resources, along with any journal articles they may have. They can also refer you to any other organizations that study sarcoidosis and other related conditions. NEI will also let you know of any clinical studies that may be studying this disease and looking for patients. Because of

their small staff, NEI prefers that you submit your requests for information in writing.

☎ Contact:
National Eye Institute
Bldg. 31, Room 6A32
Bethesda, MD 20892
(301) 496-5248

Free Publications/Videos

The following publication on Sarcoidosis is available from the National Heart, Lung and Blood Institute, Bldg. 31, Room 4A21, Bethesda, MD 20892; (301) 496-4236.

- *Sarcoidosis*. (#91-3093)

SARCOMA

Clearinghouses/Hotlines

The National Cancer Institute (NCI) will send you whatever publications and reprints of journal articles they have on Sarcoma of Bone and Soft Tissue. They can also give you information on the state-of-the-art treatment for this disease, including specific treatment information for your stage of cancer. They can also search their Physician's Data Query (PDQ) database to let you know if NCI is conducting any clinical studies on your disease.

☎ Contact:
National Cancer Institute
Bldg. 31, Room 10A24
Bethesda, MD 20892
(800) 4-CANCER
(301) 496-5583

SATURATED FAT

Clearinghouses/Hotlines

The Food and Nutrition Information Center (FNIC) can provide you with information regarding Saturated Fats. They can provide you with bibliographies on other information on the subject.

☎ Contact:
Food and Nutrition Information Center
National Agricultural Library
Room 304
Beltsville, MD 20705
(301) 504-5719

SCABIES

Clearinghouses/Hotlines

The National Institute of Allergy and Infectious Diseases (NIAID) can search the Combined Health Information Database (CHID) and generate a bibliography of resources for you on Scabies. They will also send you any publications and journal articles they may have on hand, and will refer you to researchers who are currently studying this condition. If you can't afford treatment, have your doctor call NIAID to find out if they are conducting any clinical studies that you might qualify for.

☎ Contact:
National Institute of Allergy
and Infectious Diseases
Bldg. 31, Room 7A32
Bethesda, MD 20892
(301) 496-5717

SCARLET FEVER

Clearinghouses/Hotlines

The National Institute of Allergy and Infectious Diseases (NIAID) can provide you with some basic information on Scarlet Fever.

☎ Contact:
National Institute of Allergy
and Infectious Diseases
Bldg. 31, Room 7A32
Bethesda, MD 20892
(301) 496-5717

SCHILDER'S DISEASE

Clearinghouses/Hotlines

The National Institute of Neurological Disorders and Stroke (NINDS) can send you only information they have in their current publications on Schilder's Disease. They cannot refer you to any experts. This Clearinghouse cannot directly give you information about any current clinical studies NINDS might be conducting on this illness, but you can find this information for yourself by looking under the National Institute of Neurological Disorders and Stroke in *Appendix A* at the end of this book.

☎ Contact:
National Institute of Neurological
Disorders and Stroke
Bldg. 31, Room 8A06
Bethesda, MD 20892
(301) 496-5751
(800) 352-9424

SCHISTOSOMIASIS

Clearinghouses/Hotlines

The National Institute of Allergy and Infectious Diseases (NIAID) can search the Combined Health Information Database (CHID) and generate a bibliography of resources for you on Schistosomiasis. They will also send you any publications and journal articles they may have on hand, and will refer you to researchers who are currently studying this condition. If you can't afford treatment, have your doctor call NIAID to find out if they are conducting any clinical studies that you might qualify for.

☎ Contact:
National Institute of Allergy
and Infectious Diseases
Bldg. 31, Room 7A32
Bethesda, MD 20892
(301) 496-5717

SCHIZOPHRENIA

Clearinghouses/Hotlines

The National Institute of Mental Health (NIMH) will send you whatever publications and reprints of articles from texts and journals they have on Schizophrenia. They will also refer you to other organizations studying this disorder. NIMH will also let you know of any clinical studies that may be studying this disease and looking for patients.

☎ Contact:
National Institute of Mental Health
5600 Fishers Ln., Room 15C05
Rockville, MD 20857
(301) 443-4515

Free Publications/Videos

The following publications on Schizophrenia are available from the National Institute of Mental Health, 5600 Fishers Ln., Room 15C05, Rockville, MD 20857; (301) 443-4515.

- *A National Plan for Schizophrenia Research: Panel Recommendations.*
- *A National Plan for Schizophrenia Research: Report of the National.*
- *Advisory Mental Health Council.*
- *Schizophrenia: Questions and Answers.*
- *Special Report: Schizophrenia 1987.*

The following publication on Schizophrenia is available from the Superintendent of Documents, Government Printing Office, Washington, DC 20402; (202) 783-3238.

- *Schizophrenia Bulletin.* Publishes articles on all facets of schizophrenia research and treatment. (4 issues/yr., $19)

SCHOOL HEALTH

Clearinghouses/Hotlines

The Department of Education's Drug Abuse

Prevention Oversight Staff provides materials to schools and communities in developing a comprehensive program to prevent the use of alcohol and other drugs, including tobacco and steroids.

☎ Contact:
Office of the Secretary
U.S. Department of Education
400 Maryland Ave., SW, Room 4145
Washington, DC 20202-0100
(202) 401-3030

Free Publications/Videos

The National Clearinghouse for Alcohol and Drug Information will send you the following *Prevention Resource Guides* on alcohol abuse among students. They contain facts, figures, resources, and other relevant information. Contact: National Clearinghouse for Alcohol Information, P.O. Box 2345, Rockville, MD 20852; (800) 729-6686, or (301) 468-2600.

- *Prevention Resource Guide: College Youth*.
- *Prevention Resource Guide: Secondary School Students*.
- *Prevention Resource Guide: Elementary Youth*.
- *Prevention Resource Guide: Preschool Children*.

National Health Information Center can send you all kinds of free and low-cost resources on health issues concerning schools and students. The following publications are available from the National Health Information Center, P.O. Box 1133, Washington, DC 20013; (800) 336-4797, or (301) 565-4167 in DC metro area.

- *Healthy Schools: A Directory of Federal Activities Related to Health Promotion through the Schools*. Presents information on activities of all Federal departments including contact information and brief program descriptions. ($4)
- *Healthy Kids For the Year 2000: An Action Plan for Schools*. Presents a 12-step action plan that school leaders can use to attack the health problems facing youth by implementing a comprehensive school health program. ($6)

- *Achieving the 1990 Health Objectives For The Nation: Agenda for the Nation's Schools*. A step-by-step description of strategies that schools and communities can implement in 14 key health areas. ($25)
- *National Adolescent Student Health Survey*. Results of the first national survey in more than 20 years on teens' behavior, knowledge, and attitudes on health and sex-related issues. ($17.95)
- *Coalition Index: A Guide to School Health Education Materials*. Lists materials from nearly 20 national health-related organizations and categorizes the materials by content area. ($10)
- *How Health Is Your School?* Guide for assessing, planning, and implementing quality school health services, environment, and health education programs. ($12)
- *Promoting Health Education in Schools: Problems and Solutions*. An informative overview of issues involved in providing health education and health promotion through the schools. ($13.95)

The following publication on School Health is available from the National Institute of Dental Research, Bldg. 31, Room 2C35, Bethesda, MD 20892; (301) 496-4261.

- *Oral Health of U.S. Children: The National Survey of Dental Care in U.S. School Children*. (#89-2247)

The following publication on School Health is available from the National Cancer Institute, Bldg. 31, Room 10A24, Bethesda, MD 20892; (800) 4-CANCER, or (301) 496-5583.

- *School Programs to Prevent Smoking*. (#90-500)

SCHWANNOMA

Clearinghouses/Hotlines

The National Cancer Institute (NCI) will send you whatever publications and reprints of journal

articles they have on Schwannoma. They can also give you information on the state-of-the-art treatment for this disease, including specific treatment information for your stage of cancer. They can also search their Physician's Data Query (PDQ) database to let you know if NCI is conducting any clinical studies on your disease.

☎ Contact:
National Cancer Institute
Bldg. 31, Room 10A24
Bethesda, MD 20892
(800) 4-CANCER
(301) 496-5583

SCIATICA

See also Back Problems

Clearinghouses/Hotlines

The National Institute of Arthritis and Musculoskeletal and Skin Diseases (NIAMS) will send you whatever publications and reprints of articles from texts and journals they have on Sciatica. They will also refer you to other organizations that are studying this condition. NIAMS will also let you know of any clinical studies that may be studying this disease and looking for patients.

☎ Contact:
National Institute of Arthritis
and Musculoskeletal and Skin Diseases
Box AMS
Bethesda, MD 20892
(301) 495-4484

The National Institute of Neurological Disorders and Stroke (NINDS) can send you only information they have in their current publications on Sciatica. They cannot refer you to any experts. This Clearinghouse cannot directly give you information about any current clinical studies NINDS might be conducting on this disorder, but you can find this information for yourself by looking under the National Institute of Neurological Disorders and Stroke in *Appendix A* at the end of this book.

☎ Contact:
National Institute of Neurological

Disorders and Stroke
Bldg. 31, Room 8A06
Bethesda, MD 20892
(301) 496-5751
(800) 352-9424

SCLERODERMA

Clearinghouses/Hotlines

The National Institute of Arthritis and Musculoskeletal and Skin Diseases (NIAMS) will send you whatever publications and reprints of articles from texts and journals they have on Scleroderma. They will also refer you to other organizations that are studying this disease. NIAMS will also let you know of any clinical studies that may be studying this disease and looking for patients.

☎ Contact:
National Institute of Arthritis
and Musculoskeletal and Skin Diseases
Box AMS
Bethesda, MD 20892
(301) 495-4484

Free Publications/Videos

The following publication is available from the National Arthritis and Musculoskeletal and Skin Diseases Information Clearinghouse, Box AMS, 9000 Rockville Pike, Bethesda, MD 20892; (301) 495-4484.

- *Scleroderma, 1992.* An annotated bibliography of resources. (#AR140, $6)

SCLEROSIS

Clearinghouses/Hotlines

The National Institute of Neurological Disorders and Stroke (NINDS) can send you only information they have in their current publications on Sclerosis. They cannot refer you to any experts. This Clearinghouse cannot directly give you information about any current clinical studies NINDS might be conducting on this illness, but you can find this information for yourself by looking under the National Institute of Neurological Disorders and Stroke in *Appendix A* at the end of this book.

☎ Contact:
National Institute of Neurological
Disorders and Stroke
Bldg. 31, Room 8A06
Bethesda, MD 20892
(301) 496-5751
(800) 352-9424

SCOLIOSIS

Clearinghouses/Hotlines

The National Institute of Arthritis and Musculoskeletal and Skin Diseases (NIAMS) will send you whatever publications and reprints of articles from texts and journals they have on Scoliosis. They will also refer you to other organizations that are studying this condition. NIAMS will also let you know of any clinical studies that may be studying this disease and looking for patients.

☎ Contact:
National Institute of Arthritis
and Musculoskeletal and Skin Diseases
9000 Rockville Pike
Box AMS
Bethesda, MD 20892
(301) 495-4484

Free Publications/Videos

The following publications are available from the Center for Devices and Radiological Health, (HFZ-210), Food and Drug Administration, 5600 Fishers Ln., Rockville, MD 20857; (301) 443-4690.

- *When The Spine Curves.* (#FDA 85-4198)
- *Reducing Patient Exposure During Scoliosis Radiography.*

SEAFOOD INSPECTION

Clearinghouses/Hotlines

The Office of Seafood at the Food and Drug Administration has an automated telephone system which can answer your questions regarding seafood storage, cooking, safety, handling, labeling, or any problems you may have concerning seafood. They can mail or fax you materials, and take reports of suspected seafood problems, as well as answer your recreational fishing questions.

☎ Contact:
Office of Seafood
(202) 205-4314

Free Publications/Videos

The following Congressional Research Service (CRS) reports on Seafood Inspection are available from either of your U.S. Senators' offices at the U.S. Capitol, Washington, DC 20510, or from your Congressional Representative at the U.S. Capitol, Washington, DC 20515. You can also call in your request through the U.S. Capitol switchboard at (202) 224-3121. Be sure to include the full title and report number in your request.

- *Mandatory Federal Seafood Inspection: An Overview.* (#83-198 ENR)
- *Seafood Inspection Issues; Archived Issue Brief.* (#IB89126)

The following publication is available from the Food & Drug Administration, (HFE-88), 5600 Fishers Ln., Rockville, MD 20857; (301) 443-3170.

- *Get Hooked On Seafood Safety.* (#FDA92-2246)

SELF-HELP

Free Publications/Videos

The following publication on Self-Help is available

from the National Maternal and Child Health Clearinghouse, 38th & R Sts., NW, Washington, DC 20057; (703) 821-8955, ext. 254.

- *Surgeon General's Workshop on Self-Help and Public Health.* (#B351)

The following publication on Self-Help is available from the National Clearinghouse for Alcohol and Drug Information, P.O. Box 2345, Rockville, MD 20852; (800) 729-6686.

- *The Fact Is...There Are Specialized Mutual-Help Groups For Those With Alcohol and Drug Problems.* (#MS330) Discusses self-help groups that have emerged in response to special concerns expressed by those seeking recovery for alcohol and other drug problem. The publication lists the self-help groups, providing general information about the group and a central phone number.

SEGAWA'S DYSTONIA

Clearinghouses/Hotlines

The National Institute of Neurological Disorders and Stroke (NINDS) can send you only information they have in their current publications on Segawa's Dystonia. They cannot refer you to any experts. This Clearinghouse cannot directly give you information about any current clinical studies NINDS might be conducting on this disorder, but you can find this information for yourself by looking under the National Institute of Neurological Disorders and Stroke in *Appendix A* at the end of this book.

☎ Contact:
National Institute of Neurological
Disorders and Stroke
Building 31
Room 8A06
Bethesda, MD 20892
(301) 496-5751
(800) 352-9424

SEIZURES

See also Epilepsy

Clearinghouses/Hotlines

The National Institute of Neurological Disorders and Stroke (NINDS) can send you pamphlets and other information about seizures.

☎ Contact:
National Institute of Neurological
Disorders and Stroke
Building 31
Bethesda, MD 20892
(301) 496-5751
(800) 352-9424

Free Publications/Videos

The following video is available from the Office of Clinical Center Communications, Bldg. 10, Room 1C255, Bethesda, MD 20892; (301) 496-2563.

- *Understanding Seizure Disorders*. Video to help the general public make intelligent decisions.

SEMINOMA

See Testicular Cancer

SENILITY

See also Aging
See also Alzheimer's Disease

Clearinghouses/Hotlines

The National Institute on Aging (NIA) will send you whatever publications and reprints of journal articles they have on Senile Dementia. They cannot refer you to other experts if the information they have isn't sufficient for your purposes.

☎ Contact:
National Institute on Aging
Bldg. 31, Room 5C27
Bethesda, MD 20892
(301) 496-1752

The National Institute of Mental Health (NIMH) will send you whatever publications and reprints of articles from texts and journals they have on Senile Dementia. They will also refer you to other organizations that are studying this disorder. NIMH will also let you know of any clinical studies that may be studying this disease and looking for patients.

☎ Contact:
National Institute of Mental Health
5600 Fishers Ln., Room 15C05
Rockville, MD 20857
(301) 443-4515

The National Institute of Neurological Disorders and Stroke (NINDS) can send you only information they have in their current publications on Senile Dementia. They cannot refer you to any experts. This Clearinghouse cannot directly give you information about any current clinical studies NINDS might be conducting on this illness, but you can find this information for yourself by looking under the National Institute of Neurological Disorders and Stroke in *Appendix A* at the end of this book.

☎ Contact:
National Institute of Neurological
Disorders and Stroke
Bldg. 31, Room 8A06
Bethesda, MD 20892
(301) 496-5751
(800) 352-9424

Free Publications/Videos

The following publication on Senility is available from the National Institute on Aging Information Center, 2209 Distribution Circle, Silver Spring, MD 20910; (301) 495-3455.

- *Senility: Myth or Madness?* Facts for the aging.

SENILE MACULAR DEGENERATION

Clearinghouses/Hotlines

The National Eye Institute (NEI) can give you up-to-date information on Senile Macular Degeneration by searching the Combined Health Information Database (CHID) and MEDLINE and sending you bibliographies of resources, along with any journal articles they may have. They can also refer you to any other organizations that study this and other related conditions. NEI will also let you know of any clinical studies that may be studying this disease and looking for patients. Because of their small staff, NEI prefers that you submit your requests for information in writing.

☎ Contact:
National Eye Institute
Building 31
Room 6A32
Bethesda, MD 20892
(301) 496-5248

SEPTAL DEFECTS

Clearinghouses/Hotlines

The National Heart, Lung, and Blood Institute (NHLBI) can search the Combined Health Information Database (CHID) and generate a bibliography of resources for you on Septal Defects. They also will send you any publications and journal articles they may have on hand, and will refer you to other organizations that are studying this condition. If you can't afford treatment, have your doctor call NHLBI to find out if they are conducting any clinical studies that you might qualify for.

☎ Contact:
National Heart, Lung, and Blood Institute
Building 31
Room 4A21
Bethesda, MD 20892
(301) 496-4236

SEX CHANGES

Clearinghouses/Hotlines

The National Institute of Child Health and Human Development (NICHD) will send you whatever publications and reprints of journal articles they have on Sex Changes. If necessary, they will refer you to other experts or researchers in the field.

☎ Contact:
National Institute of Child Health
and Human Development
Bldg. 31, Room 2A32
Bethesda, MD 20892
(301) 496-5133

SEX DETERMINATION

Clearinghouses/Hotlines

The National Institute of Child Health and Human Development (NICHD) will send you whatever publications and reprints of journal articles they have on Sex Determination. If necessary, they will refer you to other experts or researchers in the field. If you can't afford treatment, have your doctor call NICHD to find out if they are conducting any clinical studies that you might qualify for.

☎ Contact:
National Institute of Child Health
and Human Development
Bldg. 31, Room 2A32
Bethesda, MD 20892
(301) 496-5133

SEX HORMONES

Clearinghouses/Hotlines

The National Institute of Child Health and Human Development (NICHD) will send you whatever publications and reprints of journal articles they have on Sex Hormones. If necessary, they will

refer you to other experts or researchers in the field. If you can't afford treatment, have your doctor call NICHD to find out if they are conducting any clinical studies that you might qualify for.

☎ Contact:
National Institute of Child Health
and Human Development
Bldg. 31, Room 2A32
Bethesda, MD 20892
(301) 496-5133

SEXUAL ABUSE

See also Child Abuse
See also Family Violence

Clearinghouses/Hotlines

The Clearinghouse on Child Abuse and Neglect can provide you with publications, reports, videos and more regarding Sexual Abuse, and can direct you to organizations that can provide further assistance.

☎ Contact:
Clearinghouse on Child Abuse
and Neglect Information
P.O. Box 1182
Washington, DC 20013
(800) FYI-3366

Free Publications/Videos

The following publication is available from the Clearinghouse on Child Abuse and Neglect Information, P.O. Box 1182, Washington, DC 20013; (800) FYI-3366, or (800) 394-3366.

- *Child Sexual Abuse Prevention: Tips to Parents*. Brochure. (#20-01036)

SEXUALITY

Clearinghouses/Hotlines

The National Institute of Child Health and Human

Development (NICHD) will send you whatever publications and reprints of journal articles they have on Sexuality. If necessary, they will refer you to other experts or researchers in the field. If you can't afford treatment, have your doctor call NICHD to find out if they are conducting any clinical studies that you might qualify for.

☎ Contact:
National Institute of Child Health
and Human Development
Building 31
Room 2A32
Bethesda, MD 20892
(301) 496-5133

Free Publications/Videos

The following publications on Sexuality are available from the National Arthritis and Musculoskeletal and Skin Diseases Information Clearinghouse, Box AMS, 9000 Rockville Pike, Bethesda, MD 20892; (301) 495-4484.

- *Sexuality and the Rheumatic Diseases: An Annotated Bibliography* ($3)
- *Sexuality and the Rheumatic Diseases, 1986.* An annotated bibliography of resources. (#AR59, $2)

The following publication on Sexuality is available from the National Institute on Aging Information Center, 2209 Distribution Circle, Silver Spring, MD 20910; (301) 495-3455.

- *Sexuality in Later Life.* Facts for the aging.

SEXUALLY TRANSMITTED DISEASES

See also Safe Sex

Clearinghouses/Hotlines

The National AIDS Information Clearinghouse can provide you with information, including pamphlets and reports on how to have safe sex.

☎ Contact:
National AIDS Information Clearinghouse
P.O. Box 6003
Rockville, MD 20850
(800) 342-AIDS

The Sexually Transmitted Diseases Hotline can give you all kinds of information on STDs. They will also refer you to free or low-cost clinics in your area to get checked out and treated. The hotline also can refer you to support groups in your area for those with specific diseases. Their hours are 8 a.m. to 8 p.m. (Pacific Standard Time).

☎ Contact:
Sexually Transmitted Diseases Hotline
(800) 227-8922

The National Institute of Allergy and Infectious Diseases (NIAID) can search the Combined Health Information Database (CHID) and generate a bibliography of resources for you on Sexually Transmitted Diseases. They will also send you any publications and journal articles they may have on hand, and will refer you to researchers who are currently studying this issue. If you can't afford treatment, have your doctor call NIAID to find out if they are conducting any clinical studies that you might qualify for.

☎ Contact:
National Institute of Allergy
and Infectious Diseases
Bldg. 31, Room 7A32
Bethesda, MD 20892
(301) 496-5717

Free Publications/Videos

The following publication is available from the National Institute of Allergy and Infectious Diseases, Bldg. 31, Room 7A32, Bethesda, MD 20892; (301) 496-5717.

- *Sexually Transmitted Diseases.* Discusses symptoms, treatment, and prevention of a variety of STDs, such as herpes and AIDS.

The following publication is available from the Centers for Disease Control National AIDS Clearinghouse, P.O. Box 6003, Rockville, MD 20849-6003; (800) 458-5231.

- Condoms for Prevention of Sexually Transmitted Diseases. (#D127)

The following publication on Sexually Transmitted Diseases is available from the Family Life Information Exchange, P.O. Box 30146, Bethesda, MD 20814; (301) 585-6636.

- Sexually Transmitted Diseases Treatment Guidelines.

SEZARY SYNDROME

Clearinghouses/Hotlines

The National Cancer Institute (NCI) will send you whatever publications and reprints of journal articles they have on Sezary Syndrome. They can also give you information on the state-of-the-art treatment for this disease, including specific treatment information for your stage of cancer. They can also search their Physician's Data Query (PDQ) database to let you know if NCI is conducting any clinical studies on your disease.

☎ Contact:
National Cancer Institute
Building 31
Room 10A24
Bethesda, MD 20892
(800) 4-CANCER
(301) 496-5583

The National Institute of Arthritis and Musculoskeletal and Skin Diseases (NIAMS) will send you whatever publications and reprints of articles from texts and journals they have on Sezary Syndrome. They will also refer you to other organizations that are studying this condition. NIAMS will also let you know of any clinical studies that may be studying this disease and looking for patients.

☎ Contact:
National Institute of Arthritis
and Musculoskeletal and Skin Diseases
Box AMS
9000 Rockville Pike
Bethesda, MD 20892
(301) 495-4484

SHAKEN BABY SYNDROME

Free Publications/Videos

The following publication on Shaken Baby Syndrome is available from the Clearinghouse on Child Abuse and Neglect Information, P.O. Box 1182, Washington, DC 20013; (800) FYI-3366, or (800) 394-3366.

- Shaken Baby Syndrome. (1971-91 Publications) Annotated bibliography. (07-91184, $1)

SHINGLES

Clearinghouses/Hotlines

The National Institute of Neurological Disorders and Stroke (NINDS) can send you only information they have in their current publications on Shingles (Herpes Zoster). They cannot refer you to any experts. This Clearinghouse cannot directly give you information about any current clinical studies NINDS might be conducting on this illness, but you can find this information for yourself by looking under the National Institute of Neurological Disorders and Stroke in *Appendix A* at the end of this book.

☎ Contact:
National Institute of Neurological
Disorders and Stroke
Building 31
Room 8A06
Bethesda, MD 20892
(301) 496-5751
(800) 352-9424

The National Institute of Allergy and Infectious Diseases (NIAID) can search the Combined Health Information Database (CHID) and generate a bibliography of resources for you on Shingles (Herpes Zoster). They will also send you any publications and journal articles they may have on hand, and will refer you to researchers who are currently studying this issue. If you can't afford treatment, have your doctor call NIAID to find out if they are conducting any clinical studies you might qualify for.

☎ Contact:
National Institute of Allergy
and Infectious Diseases
Building 31
Room 7A32
Bethesda, MD 20892
(301) 496-5717

Free Publications/Videos

The following publications on Shingles are available from the National Institute of Neurological Disorders and Stroke, P.O. Box 5801, Bethesda, MD 20824; (800) 352-9424, or (301) 496-5751.

- *Shingles*. Contains a collection of scientific articles, patient education pamphlets, and addresses of voluntary health associations.
- *Shingles (Herpes Zoster)*. Discusses hope through research.

SHOCK

Clearinghouses/Hotlines

The National Heart, Lung, and Blood Institute (NHLBI) can search the Combined Health Information Database (CHID) and generate a bibliography of resources for you on Cardiogenic and Hemorrhagic Shock. They also will send you any publications and journal articles they may have on hand, and will refer you to other organizations that are studying this condition. If you can't afford treatment, have your doctor call NHLBI to find out if they are conducting any clinical studies that you might qualify for.

☎ Contact:
National Heart, Lung, and Blood Institute
Building 31
Room 4A21
Bethesda, MD 20892
(301) 496-4236

SHORT STATURE

Clearinghouses/Hotlines

The National Institute of Child Health and Human Development (NICHD) will send you whatever publications and reprints of journal articles they have on Short Stature. If necessary, they will refer you to other experts or researchers in the field. If you can't afford treatment, have your doctor call NICHD to find out if they are conducting any clinical studies that you might qualify for.

☎ Contact:
National Institute of Child Health
and Human Development
Bldg. 31, Room 2A32
Bethesda, MD 20892
(301) 496-5133

SHY-DRAGER SYNDROME

Clearinghouses/Hotlines

The National Institute of Neurological Disorders and Stroke (NINDS) can send you only information they have in their current publications on Shy-Drager Syndrome. They cannot refer you to any experts. This Clearinghouse cannot directly give you information about any current clinical studies NINDS might be conducting on this illness, but you can find this information for yourself by looking under the National Institute of Neurological Disorders and Stroke in *Appendix A* at the end of this book.

☎ Contact:
National Institute of Neurological
Disorders and Stroke
Bldg. 31, Room 8A06
Bethesda, MD 20892
(301) 496-5751
(800) 352-9424

The National Institute of Mental Health (NIMH) will send you whatever publications and reprints of articles from texts and journals they have on Shy-Drager Syndrome. They will also refer you to other organizations that are studying this disorder. NIMH will also let you know of any clinical studies that may be studying this disease and looking for patients.

☎ Contact:
National Institute of Mental Health
5600 Fishers Lane
Room 15C05
Rockville, MD 20857
(301) 443-4515

Free Publications/Videos

The following publication on Shy-Drager Syndrome is available from the National Institute of Neurological Disorders and Stroke, P.O. Box 5801, Bethesda, MD 20824; (800) 352-9424, or (301) 496-5751.

- *Shy-Drager Syndrome.* Collection of scientific articles, patient education pamphlets, and addresses of voluntary health associations.

SIAMESE TWINS

See Twins

SICK BUILDINGS

Clearinghouses/Hotlines

The Environmental Protection Agency's Indoor Air Division can provide you with fact sheets on a wide variety of indoor air problems such as Sick Building Syndrome, tobacco smoke, office ventilation, and air cleaners. They'll send you a summary of *Air Cleaning Devices*, as well as a directory of State Indoor Air Contacts. *Building Air Quality: A Guide for Building Owners and Facility Managers* is another handbook for all air quality questions and remedies.

☎ Contact:
Indoor Air Division
Environmental Protection Agency
ANR-445W

Washington, DC 20460
(703) 308-8470

SICKLE CELL

Clearinghouses/Hotlines

The National Heart, Lung, and Blood Institute (NHLBI) can search the Combined Health Information Database (CHID) and generate a bibliography of resources for you on Sickle Cell Anemia. They also will send you any publications and journal articles they may have on hand, and will refer you to other organizations that are studying this condition. If you can't afford treatment, have your doctor call NHLBI to find out if they are conducting any clinical studies that you might qualify for.

☎ Contact:
National Heart, Lung, and Blood Institute
Bldg. 31, Room 4A21
Bethesda, MD 20892
(301) 496-4236

Free Publications/Videos

The following publication on Sickle Cell Anemia is available from the Office of Clinical Center Communications, Bldg. 10, Room 1C255, Bethesda, MD 20892; (301) 496-2563.

- *Sickle Cell Anemia.* (#90-3058) Booklet written to help the general public make intelligent decisions.

The following publication on Sickle Cell Disease is available from the National Heart, Lung and Blood Institute, Bldg. 31, Room 4A21, Bethesda, MD 20892; (301) 496-4236.

- *Management and Therapy of Sickle Cell Disease.* (#91-2117)

The following publication on Sickle Cell Disease is available from the Superintendent of Documents, Government Printing Office, Washington, DC 20402; (202) 783-3238.

- *Management and Therapy of Sickle Cell Disease*. Presents articles on the treatment and management of sickle cell diseases for physicians. It covers laboratory diagnosis and newborn screening, sickle cell trait, nursing management, and psychosocial management. ($3.25, S/N 017-043-00120-6)

The following publication on Sickle Cell Anemia is available from the Science & Technology Division, Reference Section, Library of Congress, Washington, DC 20540; (202) 707-5580.

- *Sickle Cell Anemia.* Reference guide designed to help locate further published material. (#82-9)

The following publications on Sickle Cell Disease are available from the National Maternal and Child Health Clearinghouse, 38th & R Sts., NW, Washington, DC 20057; (703) 821-8955, ext. 254.

- *Management and Therapy of Sickle Cell Disease.* (#E069)
- *Problem-Oriented Management of Sickle Cell Syndromes.* (#E042)
- *Sickle Cell Anemia and Comprehensive Care: A New Horizon.* (#D065)
- *Sickle Cell: A Resource Guide for Families and Professionals.* (#D058)

SIDEROBLASTIC ANEMIA

Clearinghouses/Hotlines

The National Heart, Lung, and Blood Institute (NHLBI) can search the Combined Health Information Database (CHID) and generate a bibliography of resources for you on Sideroblastic Anemia. They also will send you any publications and journal articles they may have on hand, and will refer you to other organizations that are studying this condition. If you can't afford treatment, have your doctor call NHLBI to find out if they are conducting any clinical studies that you might qualify for.

☎ Contact:
National Heart, Lung, and Blood Institute

Building 31
Room 4A21
Bethesda, MD 20892
(301) 496-4236

SILICONE IMPLANTS

See Breast Implants

SINUSITIS

Clearinghouses/Hotlines

The National Institute of Allergy and Infectious Diseases (NIAID) can search the Combined Health Information Database (CHID) and generate a bibliography of resources for you on Sinusitis. They will also send you any publications and journal articles they may have on hand, and will refer you to researchers who are currently studying this issue. If you can't afford treatment, have your doctor call NIAID to find out if they are conducting any clinical studies that you might qualify for.

☎ Contact:
National Institute of Allergy
and Infectious Diseases
Bldg. 31, Room 7A32
Bethesda, MD 20892
(301) 496-5717

SJOGREN'S SYNDROME

Clearinghouses/Hotlines

The National Institute of Arthritis and Musculoskeletal and Skin Diseases (NIAMS) will send you whatever publications and reprints of articles from texts and journals they have on Sjogren's Syndrome. They will also refer you to other organizations that are studying this condition. NIAMS will also let you know of any clinical studies that may be studying this disease and looking for patients.

☎ Contact:
National Institute of Arthritis
and Musculoskeletal and Skin Diseases
Box AMS
Bethesda, MD 20892
(301) 495-4484

The National Institute of Allergy and Infectious Diseases (NIAID) can search the Combined Health Information Database (CHID) and generate a bibliography of resources for you on Sjogren's Syndrome. They will also send you any publications and journal articles they may have on hand, and will refer you to researchers who are currently studying this issue. If you can't afford treatment, have your doctor call NIAID to find out if they are conducting any clinical studies that you might qualify for.

☎ Contact:
National Institute of Allergy
and Infectious Diseases
Bldg. 31, Room 7A32
Bethesda, MD 20892
(301) 496-5717

The National Institute of Neurological Disorders and Stroke (NINDS) can send you only information they have in their current publications on Sjogren's Syndrome. They cannot refer you to any experts. This Clearinghouse cannot directly give you information about any current clinical studies NINDS might be conducting on this illness, but you can find this information for yourself by looking under the National Institute of Neurological Disorders and Stroke in *Appendix A* at the end of this book.

☎ Contact:
National Institute of Neurological
Disorders and Stroke
Bldg. 31, Room 8A06
Bethesda, MD 20892
(301) 496-5751
(800) 352-9424

The National Eye Institute (NEI) can give you up-to-date information on Sjogren's Syndrome by searching the Combined Health Information Database (CHID) and MEDLINE and sending you bibliographies of resources, along with any journal articles they may have. They can also refer you to any other organizations that study this and other related conditions. NEI will also let you know of any clinical studies that may be studying this disease and looking for patients. Because of their small staff, NEI prefers that you submit your requests for information in writing.

☎ Contact:
National Eye Institute
Bldg. 31, Room 6A32
Bethesda, MD 20892
(301) 496-5248

The National Institute of Dental Research (NIDR) will send you whatever publications and reprints of journal articles they have on Sjogren's Syndrome. As a policy, however, NIDR will not refer you to other organizations or experts who study this disease. If you can't afford treatment, have your doctor call Dr. Albert Guckers at (301) 496-6241 to find out if NIDR is conducting any clinical studies that you might qualify for.

☎ Contact:
National Institute of Dental Research
Bldg. 31, Room 2C35
Bethesda, MD 20892
(301) 496-4261

The National Institute on Deafness and Other Communication Disorders (NIDCD) will send you whatever publications and reprints of journal articles they have on Sjogren's Syndrome. If you need further information, they will refer you to other organizations that study this and other related conditions. NIDCD does not conduct any clinical studies for this or any other disorder.

☎ Contact:
National Institute on Deafness
and Other Communication Disorders
Bldg. 31, Room 3C35
Bethesda, MD 20892
(301) 496-7243
(800) 241-1044
(301) 402-0252 (TDD)

Free Publications/Videos

The following publication is available from the National Arthritis and Musculoskeletal and Skin Diseases Information Clearinghouse, Box AMS,

9000 Rockville Pike, Bethesda, MD 20892; (301) 495-4484.

- *Sjogren's Syndrome: Patient Education Materials, 1987.* An annotated bibliography of resources. (#AR62, $2)

SKIN AND AGING

Clearinghouses/Hotlines

The National Institute on Aging (NIA) will send you whatever publications and reprints of journal articles they have on Skin and Aging. They cannot refer you to other experts if the information they have isn't sufficient for your purposes.

☎ Contact:
National Institute on Aging
Building 31
Room 5C27
Bethesda, MD 20892
(301) 496-1752

The National Institute of Arthritis and Musculoskeletal and Skin Diseases (NIAMS) will send you whatever publications and reprints of articles from texts and journals they have on Skin and Aging. They will also refer you to other organizations that are studying this issue. NIAMS will also let you know of any clinical studies that may be studying this disease and looking for patients.

☎ Contact:
National Institute of Arthritis
and Musculoskeletal and Skin Diseases
Box AMS
Bethesda, MD 20892
(301) 495-4484

The National Cancer Institute (NCI) will send you whatever publications and reprints of journal articles they have on Skin and Sunlight. They can also give you information on the state-of-the-art treatment for this disease, including specific treatment information for your stage of cancer. They can also search their Physician's Data Query (PDQ) database to let you know if NCI is conducting any clinical studies on your disease.

☎ Contact:
National Cancer Institute
Bldg. 31, Room 10A24
Bethesda, MD 20892
(800) 4-CANCER
(301) 496-5583

SKIN CANCER

Clearinghouses/Hotlines

The National Cancer Institute (NCI) will send you whatever publications and reprints of journal articles they have on Skin Cancer. They can also give you information on the state-of-the-art treatment for this disease, including specific treatment information for your stage of cancer. They can also search their Physician's Data Query (PDQ) database to let you know if NCI is conducting any clinical studies on your disease.

☎ Contact:
National Cancer Institute
Bldg. 31, Room 10A24
Bethesda, MD 20892
(800) 4-CANCER
(301) 496-5583

Free Publications/Videos

The following video on Skin Cancer is available from Modern Talking Picture Service, 5000 Park St. North, St. Petersburg, FL 33709; (800) 243-MTPS.

- *Control and Prevention of Malignant Melanoma: A Program for Melanoma-Prone Families.* A free-loan video on skin cancer.

The following publications on Skin Cancer are available from the National Cancer Institute, Bldg. 31, Room 10A24, Bethesda, MD 20892; (800) 4-CANCER, or (301) 496-5583.

- *Research Report: Skin Cancers: Basal and Squamous Cell Carcinomas.* (#92-2977)
- *What You Need to Know About Melanoma.* (#90-1563)

- *What You Need to Know About Skin Cancer*.
  (#90-1564)

The following publication on Skin Cancer is available from the Federal Trade Commission, Office of Consumer Education, Bureau of Consumer Protection, Washington, DC 20580; (202) 326-3650.

- *Sunscreens*. Offers a quiz to help you decide how much sun you should be exposed to and what precautions to take to protect yourself.

SKIN CONDITIONS

Clearinghouses/Hotlines

The National Institute of Arthritis and Musculoskeletal and Skin Diseases (NIAMS) will send you whatever publications and reprints of articles from texts and journals they have on Skin Diseases. They will also refer you to other organizations that are studying this condition. NIAMS will also let you know of any clinical studies that may be studying this disease and looking for patients.

☎ Contact:
National Institute of Arthritis
and Musculoskeletal and Skin Diseases
Box AMS
9000 Rockville Pike
Bethesda, MD 20892
(301) 495-4484

SLEEP APNEA

Free Publications/Videos

The following publication is available from the National Institute of Neurological Disorders and Stroke, P.O. Box 5801, Bethesda, MD 20824; (800) 352-9424, or (301) 496-5751.

- *Sleep Apnea*. Collection of scientific

articles, patient education pamphlets, and addresses of voluntary health associations.

SLEEP DISORDERS

Clearinghouses/Hotlines

The National Institute of Neurological Disorders and Stroke (NINDS) can send you only information they have in their current publications on Sleep Disorders. They cannot refer you to any experts. This Clearinghouse cannot directly give you information about any current clinical studies NINDS might be conducting on this topic, but you can find this information for yourself by looking under the National Institute of Neurological Disorders and Stroke in *Appendix A* at the end of this book.

☎ Contact:
National Institute of Neurological
Disorders and Stroke
Bldg. 31, Room 8A06
Bethesda, MD 20892
(301) 496-5751
(800) 352-9424

The National Institute of Mental Health (NIMH) will send you whatever publications and reprints of articles from texts and journals they have on Sleep Disorders. They will also refer you to other organizations that are studying this disorder. NIMH will also let you know of any clinical studies that may be studying this disease and looking for patients.

☎ Contact:
National Institute of Mental Health
5600 Fishers Ln., Room 15C05
Rockville, MD 20857
(301) 443-4515

The National Institute on Aging (NIA) will send you whatever publications and reprints of journal articles they have on Sleep and Aging. They cannot refer you to other experts if the information they have isn't sufficient for your purposes.

☎ Contact:
National Institute on Aging
Bldg. 31, Room 5C27

Bethesda, MD 20892
(301) 496-1752

Free Publications/Videos

The following video on Sleep Disorders is available from the Office of Clinical Center Communications, Bldg. 10, Room 1C255, Bethesda, MD 20892; (301) 496-2563.

- *Sleep and Its Disorders.* Video to help the general public make intelligent decisions.

The following publication on Sleep Disorders is available from the National Institute of Mental Health, 5600 Fishers Ln., Room 15C05, Rockville, MD 20857; (301) 443-4515.

- *Useful Information on Sleep Disorders.*

The following publication on Sleep Disorders is available from the FDA, (HFE-88), 5600 Fishers Ln., Rockville, MD 20857; (301) 443-3170.

- *Why Aren't You Asleep Yet? A Bedtime Story.* (#FDA90-1154)

The following publication on Sleep Disorders is available from the Office of Medical Applications of Research, National Institutes of Health, Bldg. 1, Room 260, Bethesda, MD 20892; (301) 496-1143.

- *Treatment of Sleep Disorders of Older People.* Discusses diagnosis and treatment of sleep disorders in the elderly.

SLOW VIRUSES

Clearinghouses/Hotlines

The National Institute of Neurological Disorders and Stroke (NINDS) can send you only information they have in their current publications on Slow Viruses. They cannot refer you to any experts. This Clearinghouse cannot directly give you information about any current clinical studies NINDS might be conducting on this topic, but you can find this information for yourself by looking

under the National Institute of Neurological Disorders and Stroke in *Appendix A* at the end of this book.

☎ Contact:
National Institute of Neurological
Disorders and Stroke
Bldg. 31, Room 8A06
Bethesda, MD 20892
(301) 496-5751
(800) 352-9424

SMALLPOX

Clearinghouses/Hotlines

The National Institute of Allergy and Infectious Diseases (NIAID) can search the Combined Health Information Database (CHID) and generate a bibliography of resources for you on Smallpox. They will also send you any publications and journal articles they may have on hand, and will refer you to researchers who are currently studying this disease. If you can't afford treatment, have your doctor call NIAID to find out if they are conducting any clinical studies that you might qualify for.

☎ Contact:
National Institute of Allergy
and Infectious Diseases
Bldg. 31, Room 7A32
Bethesda, MD 20892
(301) 496-5717

SMELL DISORDERS

Clearinghouses/Hotlines

The National Institute on Deafness and Other Communication Disorders (NIDCD) will send you whatever publications and reprints of journal articles they have on Smell Disorders. If you need further information, they will refer you to other organizations that study this and other related disorders. NIDCD does not conduct any clinical studies for this or any other disorder.

☎ Contact:
National Institute on Deafness
and Other Communication Disorders
Bldg. 31, Room 3C35
Bethesda, MD 20892
(301) 496-7243
(800) 241-1044
(301) 402-0252 (TDD)

The National Institute of Neurological Disorders and Stroke (NINDS) can send you only information they have in their current publications on Smell Disorders. They cannot refer you to any experts. This Clearinghouse cannot directly give you information about any current clinical studies NINDS might be conducting on this topic, but you can find this information for yourself by looking under the National Institute of Neurological Disorders and Stroke in *Appendix A* at the end of this book.

☎ Contact:
National Institute of Neurological
Disorders and Stroke
Bldg. 31, Room 8A06
Bethesda, MD 20892
(301) 496-5751
(800) 352-9424

Free Publications/Videos

The following publication on Smell Disorders is available from the National Institute on Deafness and Other Communication Disorders, Bldg. 31, Room 3C35, Bethesda, MD 20892; (301) 496-7243.

- *Because You Asked About Smell and Taste Disorders.* (#91-3231)

SMOKELESS TOBACCO

See also Smoking

Clearinghouses/Hotlines

The Office on Smoking and Health (OSH) offers all kinds of information services on smoking and health issues. They can send you numerous publications in the field, and through its database can provide you with further bibliographic information. Their Smoking Studies Section designs and conducts national surveys on smoking behavior, attitude, knowledge, and beliefs regarding tobacco use.

☎ Contact:
Office on Smoking and Health
Centers for Disease Control
1600 Clifton Rd., NE
MS K-50
Atlanta, GA 30333
(404) 488-5705

Free Publications/Videos

The following publication on Smokeless Tobacco is available from the Dental Disease Prevention Activity, Centers for Disease Control, 1600 Clifton Road NE, Atlanta, GA 30333; (404) 693-1830.

- *Smokeless Tobacco Education Resources.* An annotated list of educational materials on snuff and chewing tobacco available from federal, state and local agencies and from private sources.

The following Congressional Research Service (CRS) reports on smokeless tobacco are available from either of your U.S. Senators' offices at the U.S. Capitol, Washington, DC 20510, or from your Congressional Representative at the U.S. Capitol, Washington, DC 20515. You can also call in your request through the U.S. Capitol switchboard at (202) 224-3121. Be sure to include the full title and report number in your request.

- *Smokeless Tobacco: Health Concerns Spark Advertising and Labeling Controversy.* (#86-519 E)
- *Smokeless Tobacco: Snuff and Chewing Tobacco; Bibliography in Brief, 1983-1987.* (#88-115 L)

The following video is available from Modern Talking Picture Service, 5000 Park St. North, St. Petersburg, FL 33709; (800) 243-MTPS.

- *Smokeless Tobacco: (Check It Out!).* Video covers the hazards of smokeless tobacco.

SMOKING

Clearinghouses/Hotlines

The Office on Smoking and Health (OSH) offers all kinds of information services on smoking and health issues. They can send you numerous publications in the field, and through its database can provide you with further bibliographic information. Their Smoking Studies Section designs and conducts national surveys on smoking behavior, attitude, knowledge, and beliefs regarding tobacco use.

☎ Contact:
Office on Smoking and Health
Centers for Disease Control
1600 Clifton Rd., NE
MS K-50
Atlanta, GA 30333
(404) 488-5705

The National Cancer Institute (NCI) will send you whatever publications and reprints of journal articles they have on Cigarette Research and Smoking-related Cancer. They can also give you information on the state-of-the-art treatment for addiction to cigarettes, including specific treatment information on the different stages of lung cancer and other cancers. They can also search their Physician's Data Query (PDQ) database to let you know if NCI is conducting any clinical studies on your disease.

☎ Contact:
National Cancer Institute
Bldg. 31, Room 10A24
Bethesda, MD 20892
(800) 4-CANCER
(301) 496-5583

The National Heart, Lung, and Blood Institute (NHLBI) can search the Combined Health Information Database (CHID) and generate a bibliography of resources for you on Smoking and Heart Disease. They also will send you any publications and journal articles they may have on hand, and will refer you to other organizations studying this issue. If you can't afford treatment, have your doctor call NHLBI to find out if they are conducting any clinical studies that you might qualify for.

☎ Contact:
National Heart, Lung, and Blood Institute
Bldg. 31, Room 4A21
Bethesda, MD 20892
(301) 496-4236

Free Publications/Videos

The following publications on Smoking are available from the Office on Smoking and Health, Centers for Disease Control, 1600 Clifton Rd., NE, MS K-50, Atlanta, GA 30333; (404) 488-5705.

- *Smoking, Tobacco and Health*. (#87-8397) Discusses the health risks and prevalence of smoking as well as tobacco growing, cigarette manufacturing, and marketing.
- *Out of the Ashes: Choosing a Method to Quit Smoking*. A guide to assist smokers in selecting a quitting program.
- *Review and Evaluation of Smoking Cessation Methods*. An in-depth analysis of the variety of methods available to help smokers quit, including the effectiveness, benefits, and drawbacks of each method.
- *State and Local Programs on Smoking and Health: A Catalog of Local Programs Throughout the Country on Smoking and Health*. (#82-50189. A catalog packed with descriptions of cessation clinics, prevention efforts, school programs, community and patient education programs, mass media campaigns, and individual self-help strategies.
- *Good News for Smokers 50 and Older*. Outlines the health benefits of quitting smoking for older smokers.
- *At A Glance: The Health Benefits Of Smoking Cessation: A Report Of the Surgeon General*. Highlights the benefits of quitting smoking.
- *Smoking And Health: A National Status Report*. Discusses the status of smoking programs in the U.S.
- *Bibliography on Smoking and Health*. A compilation of 1989 scientific information on tobacco and tobacco use.
- *Is Your Baby Smoking?* Explains the dangers of passive smoke on the baby.
- *Baby In The House Stickers*. Remind pregnant women that when they smoke, they smoke for two.

The following publications on Smoking are available from the National Cancer Institute, Bldg. 31, Room 10A24, Bethesda, MD 20892; (800) 4-CANCER, or (301) 496-5583.

- *Smoking Policy Package.* Examines different questions and issues about smoking in the workplace.
- *Why Do You Smoke?* (#88-1822)
- *Clearing the Air: A Guide to Quitting Smoking.* Suggests various approaches to quit smoking. (#86-1647)
- *How to Help Your Patients Stop Smoking: A National Cancer Institute Manual for Physicians.* (#90-3064)
- *Self-Guided Programs for Smoking Cessation: A Program Planner's Guide.* (#91-3104)
- *How To Help Your Patients Stop Using Tobacco: A National Cancer Institute Manual For The Oral Health Team.*
- *Pharmacists Helping Smokers Quit Kit.*
- *Quit for Good Kit.* Packet designed for health professionals to assist their smoking patients to quit.

The following publications on Smoking are available from the National Digestive Diseases Information Clearinghouse, Box NDDIC, Bethesda, MD 20892; (301) 468-6344.

- *Smoking and Your Digestive System.* Discusses the harmful effects of cigarette smoking on the digestive system. (#DD-52)

The following publication on Smoking is available from the Office of Technology Assessment, 600 Pennsylvania Ave., SE, Washington, DC 20510; (202) 224-8996.

- *Passive Smoking in the Workplace: Selected Issues.*

The following Congressional Research Service (CRS) reports on Cigarettes are available from either of your U.S. Senators' offices at the U.S. Capitol, Washington, DC 20510, or from your Congressional Representative at the U.S. Capitol, Washington, DC 20515. You can also call in your request through the U.S. Capitol switchboard at (202) 224-3121. Be sure to include the full title and report number in your request.

- *Cigarettes and Other Tobacco Products; Should Congress Bank All Advertising and Promotion?* (#IB86105)
- *The Constitutionality of Banning Cigarette Advertising.* (#90-82 A)

SNACKING

Clearinghouses/Hotlines

The Food and Nutrition Information Center (FNIC) can provide you with a wealth of information on food and nutrition topics. They have bibliographies ready and a database through which they can search any food or nutrition subject.

☎ Contact:
Food and Nutrition Information Center
National Agricultural Library
Room 304
Beltsville, MD 20705
(301) 504-5719

Free Publications/Videos

The following publication is available from the Food & Drug Administration, (HFE-88), 5600 Fishers Ln., Rockville, MD 20857; (301) 443-3170.

- *The "Grazing" Of America: A Guide to Healthy Snacking.* (#FDA89-2229)

SOCIAL SECURITY

Clearinghouses/Hotlines

The Social Security Administration produces a wide variety of informational material designed to help people--both taxpayers and beneficiaries--gain a better understanding of the Social Security, Supplemental Security Income (SSI), and Medicare programs. A free catalog lists leaflets, booklets, posters, and other print materials, including those available in Spanish and Pacific/Asian languages.

☎ Contact:
Social Security Administration
Office of Public Affairs
P.O. Box 17743
Baltimore, MD 21235
(410) 965-0945

Free Publications/Videos

The following video on Social Security is available from the Office of Public Affairs, Social Security Administration, P.O. Box 17743, Baltimore, MD 21235; (410) 965-4031.

- *Serving as a Representative Payee.* Describes the responsibilities of representative payees and how to keep records of expenditures.

The following publications on Social Security are available from the Social Security Administration, Office of Public Affairs, P.O. Box 17743, Baltimore, MD 21235; (410) 965-0945.

- *Understanding Social Security.* Gives a general overview of all Social Security programs, and Medicare. (#05-10024)
- *Retirement.* Provides specific information about retirement benefits. (#05-10035)
- *Survivors.* Provides specific information about survivors benefits, including who is eligible, how benefits are figured, and how to apply. (#05-10084)
- *Disability.* Provides specific information about Social Security disability insurance benefits. (#05-10029)
- *Medicare.* Provides specific information about both parts of Medicare. (#05-10043)
- *SSI.* Provides general information in simple understandable language about the Supplemental Security Income (SSI) program. (#05-11090)
- *Your Social Security Taxes-What They're Paying For And Where The Money Goes.* Written for workforce members, it explains that their Social Security taxes pay for more than just retirement benefits and reminds them that their employers pay an equal share of taxes. (#05-10010)
- *An Employer's Investment In Social Security.* Reminds employers that they are helping to pay for Social Security benefits for their employees and provides tips to make sure they provide accurate information when they report employee earnings to Social Security. (#05-10059)
- *Social Security Numbers for Newborns.* Explains how easy it is to get a Social Security number for a newborn. (#05-10023)
- *Food Stamps and Other Nutrition Programs.* Explains who can get food stamps and how to apply. (#05-10100)
- *Social Security and SSI Benefits for Children with Disabilities.* Provides an overview of Social Security disability/survivors and SSI benefit for children, with emphasis on benefits available to children with disabilities. (#05-10026)
- *If You Are a Farm Worker.* Explains why and when wages must be reported to Social Security and discusses the importance of reporting wages accurately. (#05-10074)
- *A Guide to Social Security for Farmers, Growers, and Crew Leaders.* Tells farm owners/operators and crew leaders their responsibilities to their farm workers and how to report their own farm income. (#05-10025)
- *A Guide to Social Security and SSI Disability Benefits for People with HIV Infection.* Provides information about disability and SSI benefits. (#05-10020)
- *A Guide for Representative Payees.* Explains the responsibilities of the representative payee in handling Social Security and/or SSI payments on behalf of a beneficiary. (#05-10076)
- *A Guide to SSI For Groups and Organizations.* Gives a comprehensive explanation of SSI for groups and organizations that serve as representatives or advocates for potentially eligible populations. (#05-11015)
- *A Desktop Guide to SSI Eligibility Requirements.* Includes State variable information. (#05-11001)
- *Benefits for People with Disabilities Who Work.* Gives a summary of Social Security and SSI work incentives. (#05-11002)
- *Working While Disabled-A Guide To Plans For Achieving Self-Support While Receiving SSI.* Explains how to develop a plan for

achieving self-support and how it can help people with disabilities re-enter the workforce. (#05-11017)
- *A Summary Guide to Social Security and Supplemental Security Income Work Incentives for the Disabled and Blind.* A comprehensive and detailed explanation of the disability work incentives provisions. (#64-030)
- *Understanding SSI.* SSI materials used to train staffs of organizations to help eligible SSI beneficiaries obtain or continue to receive benefits. (#17-008)
- *Social Security Programs and Benefits.* This cassette recording is a compilation of six program booklets. It is available through the Library of Congress' network of 160 branch libraries across the United States. It requires a special tape player available from branch libraries. A braille version is available from the Library of Congress' braille lending libraries.
- *Serving As a Representative Payee.* Guide containing materials for the recruitment and training of volunteers.

Fact Sheets
- *Social Security Update.* (#05-10003)
- *Financing Social Security.* (#05-10094)
- *If You Are Self-Employed.* (#05-10022)
- *Food Stamp Facts.* (#10101)
- *The Appeals Process.* (#05-10041)
- *Social Security and Your Right to Representation.* (#05-10075)
- *Government Pension Offset.* (#05-10007)
- *A Pension From Work Not Covered by Social Security.* (#05-10045)
- *Household Workers.* (#05-10021)
- *Military Service and Social Security.* (#05-10017)
- *If You Work For a Nonprofit Organization.* (#05-10027)
- *The Notch...What It Is and What It Isn't.* (#05-10042)
- *How Your Retirement Benefit is Figured.* (#05-10070)
- *How Work Affects Your Social Security Benefits.* (#05-10069)
- *Reviewing Your Disability.* (#05-10068)
- *You Should Know About QMB.* (#05-10079)

Posters
- *Elderly Woman With Cane.* English only.
- *Elderly Man With Rose.* English only.
- *Children With Disabilities-Reaching Hands.*
- *Heart in Hand.*
- *Elderly Person with Cane.* Spanish only.
- *Homeless Person.* English only.
- *You don't have to hear us to get our message.* English only.
- *Not being able to see shouldn't keep you in the dark.* English only.
- *Just because you can't always see childhood disabilities...* English only.
- *Did you have a disability as a child?* English only.
- *We're looking for some special children.*
- *If You Are Applying for Social Security Benefits.*
- *When You Apply For A Social Security Number.*
- *Applying For Disability Benefits?*
- *You Can Get Supplemental Security Income (SSI) Checks If...*

The following publication on Social Security is available from the Consumer Information Center, P.O. Box 100, Pueblo, CO 81002.

- *Request for Earnings and Benefit Estimate Statement.* A form to complete and return to Social Security to get your earnings history and an estimate of future benefits. (#519Z).

SODIUM

See Salt

SOLAR BURNS

Clearinghouses/Hotlines

The National Eye Institute (NEI) can give you up-to-date information on the effect of Solar Burns on the eye by searching the Combined Health

Information Database (CHID) and MEDLINE and sending you bibliographies of resources, along with any journal articles they may have. They can also refer you to any other organizations that study this and other related conditions. NEI will also let you know of any clinical studies that may be studying this disease and looking for patients. Because of their small staff, NEI prefers that you submit your requests for information in writing.

☎ Contact:
National Eye Institute
Building 31
Room 6A32
Bethesda, MD 20892
(301) 496-5248

SPASMODIC DYSPHONIA

Clearinghouses/Hotlines

The National Institute on Deafness and Other Communication Disorders (NIDCD) will send you whatever publications and reprints of journal articles they have on Spasmodic Dysphonia. If you need further information, they will refer you to other organizations that study this and other related diseases. NIDCD does not conduct any clinical studies for this or any other disorder.

☎ Contact:
National Institute on Deafness
and Other Communication Disorders
Bldg. 31, Room 3C35
Bethesda, MD 20892
(301) 496-7243
(800) 241-1044
(301) 402-0252 (TDD)

The National Institute of Neurological Disorders and Stroke (NINDS) can send you only information they have in their current publications on Spasmodic Dysphonia. They cannot refer you to any experts. This Clearinghouse cannot directly give you information about any current clinical studies NINDS might be conducting on this illness, but you can find this information for yourself by looking under the National Institute of Neurological Disorders and Stroke in *Appendix A* at the end of this book.

☎ Contact:
National Institute of Neurological
Disorders and Stroke
Bldg. 31, Room 8A06
Bethesda, MD 20892
(301) 496-5751
(800) 352-9424

SPASTIC CONDITIONS

Clearinghouses/Hotlines

The National Institute of Neurological Disorders and Stroke (NINDS) can send you only information they have in their current publications on Spastic Hemiplegia, Paraplegia, Quadriplegia, and Torticollis. They cannot refer you to any experts. This Clearinghouse cannot directly give you information about any current clinical studies NINDS might be conducting on this topic, but you can find this information for yourself by looking under the National Institute of Neurological Disorders and Stroke in *Appendix A* at the end of this book.

☎ Contact:
National Institute of Neurological
Disorders and Stroke
Bldg. 31, Room 8A06
Bethesda, MD 20892
(301) 496-5751
(800) 352-9424

SPEECH AND LANGUAGE DISORDERS

Clearinghouses/Hotlines

The National Institute on Deafness and Other Communication Disorders (NIDCD) will send you whatever publications and reprints of journal articles they have on Speech and Language Disorders. If you need further information, they will refer you to other organizations that study this and other related diseases. NIDCD does not conduct any clinical studies for this or any other disorder.

☎ Contact:
National Institute on Deafness
and Other Communication Disorders
Bldg. 31, Room 3C35
Bethesda, MD 20892
(301) 496-7243
(800) 241-1044
(301) 402-0252 (TDD)

The National Institute of Dental Research (NIDR) will send you whatever publications and reprints of journal articles they have on Speech Disorders. As a policy, however, NIDR will not refer you to other organizations or experts who study this disease. If you can't afford treatment, have your doctor call Dr. Albert Guckers at (301) 496-6241 to find out if NIDR is conducting any clinical studies that you might qualify for.

☎ Contact:
National Institute of Dental Research
Bldg. 31, Room 2C35
Bethesda, MD 20892
(301) 496-4261

The National Institute of Child Health and Human Development (NICHD) will send you whatever publications and reprints of journal articles they have on Speech and Language Disorders. If necessary, they will refer you to other experts or researchers in the field. If you can't afford treatment, have your doctor call NICHD to find out if they are conducting any clinical studies that you might qualify for.

☎ Contact:
National Institute of Child Health
and Human Development
Bldg. 31, Room 2A32
Bethesda, MD 20892
(301) 496-5133

The National Institute of Neurological Disorders and Stroke (NINDS) can send you only information they have in their current publications on Speech and Language Disorders. They cannot refer you to any experts. This Clearinghouse cannot directly give you information about any current clinical studies NINDS might be conducting on this topic, but you can find this information for yourself by looking under the

National Institute of Neurological Disorders and Stroke in *Appendix A* at the end of this book.

☎ Contact:
National Institute of Neurological
Disorders and Stroke
Bldg. 31, Room 8A06
Bethesda, MD 20892
(301) 496-5751
(800) 352-9424

Free Publications/Videos

The following publication on Speech is available from the National Institute on Deafness and Other Communication Disorders, Bldg. 31, Room 3C35, Bethesda, MD 20892; (301) 496-7243.

- *Assessment of Speech and Voice Production: Research and Clinical Applications*. (#91-3236)

The following publication on Speech is available from the National Institute of Neurological Disorders and Stroke, P.O. Box 5801, Bethesda, MD 20824; (800) 352-9424, or (301) 496-5751.

- *Developmental Speech and Language Disorders*. Discusses hope through research.

SPHINGOLIPIDOSIS

Clearinghouses/Hotlines

The National Institute of Neurological Disorders and Stroke (NINDS) can send you only information they have in their current publications on Sphingolipidosis. They cannot refer you to any experts. This Clearinghouse cannot directly give you information about any current clinical studies NINDS might be conducting on this illness, but you can find this information for yourself by looking under the National Institute of Neurological Disorders and Stroke in *Appendix A* at the end of this book.

☎ Contact:
National Institute of Neurological

Disorders and Stroke
Bldg. 31, Room 8A06
Bethesda, MD 20892
(301) 496-5751
(800) 352-9424

SPIELMEYER-SJOGREN'S DISEASE

Clearinghouses/Hotlines

The National Institute of Neurological Disorders and Stroke (NINDS) can send you only information they have in their current publications on Spielmeyer-Sjogren's Disease. They cannot refer you to any experts. This Clearinghouse cannot directly give you information about any current clinical studies NINDS might be conducting on this illness, but you can find this information for yourself by looking under the National Institute of Neurological Disorders and Stroke in *Appendix A* at the end of this book.

☎ Contact:
National Institute of Neurological
Disorders and Stroke
Bldg. 31, Room 8A06
Bethesda, MD 20892
(301) 496-5751
(800) 352-9424

SPINA BIFIDA

Clearinghouses/Hotlines

The National Institute of Neurological Disorders and Stroke (NINDS) can send you only information they have in their current publications on Spina Bifida. They cannot refer you to any experts. This Clearinghouse cannot directly give you information about any current clinical studies NINDS might be conducting on this disorder, but you can find this information for yourself by looking under the National Institute of Neurological Disorders and Stroke in *Appendix A* at the end of this book.

☎ Contact:
National Institute of Neurological
Disorders and Stroke
Bldg. 31, Room 8A06
Bethesda, MD 20892
(301) 496-5751
(800) 352-9424

The National Institute of Child Health and Human Development (NICHD) will send you whatever publications and reprints of journal articles they have on Spina Bifida. If necessary, they will refer you to other experts or researchers in the field. If you can't afford treatment, have your doctor call NICHD to find out if they are conducting any clinical studies that you might qualify for.

☎ Contact:
National Institute of Child Health
and Human Development
Bldg. 31, Room 2A32
Bethesda, MD 20892
(301) 496-5133

The National Institute on Deafness and Other Communication Disorders (NIDCD) will send you whatever publications and reprints of journal articles they have on Spina Bifida. If you need further information, they will refer you to other organizations that study Spina Bifida and other related diseases. NIDCD does not conduct any clinical studies for this or any other disorder.

☎ Contact:
National Institute on Deafness
and Other Communication Disorders
Bldg. 31, Room 3C35
Bethesda, MD 20892
(301) 496-7243
(800) 241-1044
(301) 402-0252 (TDD)

Free Publications/Videos

The following publications are available from the National Institute of Neurological Disorders and Stroke, Bldg. 31, Room 8A06, Bethesda, MD 20892; (301) 496-5751 or (800) 352-9424.

- *Spina Bifida: Hope through Research.*
    Discusses the prevailing views about the causes, diagnosis, and medical care of this congenital spinal cord defect. (#86-309)

- *Spina Bifida*. (#85-309)
- *Spina Bifida*. Collection of scientific articles, patient education pamphlets, and addresses of voluntary health associations.

SPINAL ARACHNOIDITIS

Clearinghouses/Hotlines

The National Institute of Neurological Disorders and Stroke (NINDS) can send you only information they have in their current publications on Spinal Arachnoiditis. They cannot refer you to any experts. This Clearinghouse cannot directly give you information about any current clinical studies NINDS might be conducting on this illness, but you can find this information for yourself by looking under the National Institute of Neurological Disorders and Stroke in *Appendix A* at the end of this book.

☎ Contact:
National Institute of Neurological
Disorders and Stroke
Bldg. 31, Room 8A06
Bethesda, MD 20892
(301) 496-5751
(800) 352-9424

Free Publications/Videos

The following publication is available from the National Institute of Neurological Disorders and Stroke, P.O. Box 5801, Bethesda, MD 20824; (800) 352-9424, or (301) 496-5751.

- *Spinal Cord Injuries 1990*. Annual or Biennial Research Updates.

SPINAL CORD INJURIES

Clearinghouses/Hotlines

The National Rehabilitation Information Center (NRIC) has put together a free resource guide for people with spinal cord injuries (SCI) and their families. Included in the guide is information about SCI-related magazines and newsletters; SCI organizations that assist people with SCI from point of injury onward, and organizations that focus on specific aspects of SCI; SCI membership organizations, and the names and addresses of their chapters; and a short listing of some of the documents available from the NRIC library that discuss topics of interest of people with SCI.

☎ Contact:
National Rehabilitation Information Center
8455 Colesville, Rd, Suite 935
Silver Spring, MD 20910
(301) 588-9284
(800) 346-2742 (Voice and TDD)

The National Institute of Neurological Disorders and Stroke (NINDS) can give you information about the causes, implications, and outlook for spinal cord injuries and drug therapy, neural prostheses, and rehabilitation.

☎ Contact:
National Institute of Neurological
Disorders and Stroke
Bldg. 31, Room 8A06
Bethesda, MD 20892
(301) 496-5751
(800) 352-9424

Free Publications/Videos

The following publications are available from the National Institute of Neurological Disorders and Stroke, Bldg. 31, Room 8A06, Bethesda, MD 20892; (301) 496-5751 or (800) 352-9424.

- *Spinal Cord Injury*. (#81-160)
- *National Head and Spinal Cord Injury Survey*. (#81-2240)
- *Spinal Cord Injury*. Discusses hope through research.

SPINAL CORD TUMORS

Clearinghouses/Hotlines

The National Institute of Neurological Disorders

and Stroke (NINDS) can send you only information they have in their current publications on Spinal Cord Tumors. They cannot refer you to any experts. This Clearinghouse cannot directly give you information about any current clinical studies NINDS might be conducting on this topic, but you can find this information for yourself by looking under the National Institute of Neurological Disorders and Stroke in *Appendix A* at the end of this book.

☎ Contact:
National Institute of Neurological
Disorders and Stroke
Bldg. 31, Room 8A06
Bethesda, MD 20892
(301) 496-5751
(800) 352-9424

SPINE CURVATURE

See Scoliosis

SPINAL MUSCULAR ATROPHY

Clearinghouses/Hotlines

The National Institute of Arthritis and Musculoskeletal and Skin Diseases (NIAMS) will send you whatever publications and reprints of articles from texts and journals they have on Juvenile Spinal Muscular Atrophy (Kug-Wel Disease). They will also refer you to other organizations that are studying this disease. NIAMS will also let you know of any clinical studies that may be studying this disease and looking for patients.

☎ Contact:
National Institute of Arthritis
and Musculoskeletal and Skin Diseases
Box AMS
9000 Rockville Pike
Bethesda, MD 20892
(301) 495-4484

The National Institute of Neurological Disorders and Stroke (NINDS) can send you only information they have in their current publications on Spinal Muscular Atrophy. They cannot refer you to any experts. This Clearinghouse cannot directly give you information about any current clinical studies NINDS might be conducting on this disorder, but you can find this information for yourself by looking under the National Institute of Neurological Disorders and Stroke in *Appendix A* at the end of this book.

☎ Contact:
National Institute of Neurological
Disorders and Stroke
Building 31
Room 8A06
Bethesda, MD 20892
(301) 496-5751
(800) 352-9424

Free Publications/Videos

The following publication on Spinal Muscular Atrophy is available from the National Institute of Neurological Disorders and Stroke, P.O. Box 5801, Bethesda, MD 20824; (800) 352-9424, or (301) 496-5751.

- *Spinal Muscular Atrophy (Pediatric)*. Contains a collection of scientific articles, patient education pamphlets, and addresses of voluntary health associations.

SPINE JOINTS

See Ankylosing Spondylitis

SPINOCEREBELLAR DEGENERATION

Clearinghouses/Hotlines

The National Institute of Neurological Disorders and Stroke (NINDS) can send you only

information they have in their current publications on Spinocerebellar Degeneration. They cannot refer you to any experts. This Clearinghouse cannot directly give you information about any current clinical studies NINDS might be conducting on this disorder, but you can find this information for yourself by looking under the National Institute of Neurological Disorders and Stroke in *Appendix A* at the end of this book.

☎ Contact:
National Institute of Neurological
Disorders and Stroke
Building 31
Room 8A06
Bethesda, MD 20892
(301) 496-5751
(800) 352-9424

SPORTS MEDICINE

Clearinghouses/Hotlines

Are you suffering from a sports-related injury? Contemplating surgery to correct the problem? Want to know the latest information regarding sports medicine? The National Institute of Arthritis and Musculoskeletal and Skin Diseases (NIAMS) is the place to go as the staff can answer questions regarding current research and treatment of sports injuries and medicine, as well as providing you with a list of sports medicine groups. The Institute is currently soliciting research grant applications to provide a new foundation of knowledge related to fitness and sports medicine. Some of the topics to be studied include muscle pathophysiology, epidemiology of injuries, functional assessments, injury mechanisms, healing and prevention and training.

☎ Contact:
National Institute of Arthritis
and Musculoskeletal and Skin Diseases
Box AMS
9000 Rockville Pike
Bethesda, MD 20892
(301) 495-4484

SPORTS NUTRITION

Clearinghouses/Hotlines

The Food and Nutrition Information Center (FNIC) can provide you with a wealth of information on food and nutrition topics. They have bibliographies ready and a database through which they can search any food or nutrition subject.

☎ Contact:
Food and Nutrition Information Center
National Agricultural Library
Room 304
Beltsville, MD 20705
(301) 504-5719

Free Publications/Videos

The following publication is available from the Food and Nutrition Information Center, National Agricultural Library, 10301 Baltimore Blvd., Beltsville, MD 20705; (301) 504-5719.

- *Sports Nutrition Nutri-Topic.* Lists books, journal articles, pamphlets, booklets, and other resources to contact regarding sports fitness and nutrition. Included is a list of videos produced outside the government, but available for free loan from the Food and Nutrition Information Center, dealing with exercise and fitness.

SPOUSAL ABUSE

See Battered Spouses
See Family Violence

SQUAMOUS CELL

Clearinghouses/Hotlines

The National Cancer Institute (NCI) will send you

whatever publications and reprints of journal articles they have on Squamous Cell. They can also give you information on the state-of-the-art treatment for this disease, including specific treatment information for your stage of cancer. They can also search their Physician's Data Query (PDQ) database to let you know if NCI is conducting any clinical studies on your disease.

☎ Contact:
National Cancer Institute
Bldg. 31, Room 10A24
Bethesda, MD 20892
(800) 4-CANCER
(301) 496-5583

STAINED TEETH

Clearinghouses/Hotlines

The National Institute of Dental Research (NIDR) will send you whatever publications and reprints of journal articles they have on Stained Teeth from tetracycline use. As a policy, however, NIDR will not refer you to other organizations or experts who study this disease. If you can't afford treatment, have your doctor call Dr. Albert Guckers at (301) 496-6241 to find out if NIDR is conducting any clinical studies that you might qualify for.

☎ Contact:
National Institute of Dental Research
Bldg. 31, Room 2C35
Bethesda, MD 20892
(301) 496-4261

STAPHYLOCOCCAL (STAPH) INFECTIONS

Clearinghouses/Hotlines

The National Institute of Allergy and Infectious Diseases (NIAID) can search the Combined Health Information Database (CHID) and generate a bibliography of resources for you on Staphylococcal (Staph) Infections. They will also send you any publications and journal articles they may have on hand, and will refer you to researchers who are currently studying this disease. If you can't afford treatment, have your doctor call NIAID to find out if they are conducting any clinical studies that you might qualify for.

☎ Contact:
National Institute of Allergy
and Infectious Diseases
Building 31
Room 7A32
Bethesda, MD 20892
(301) 496-5717

STEELE-RICHARDSON DISEASE

Clearinghouses/Hotlines

The National Institute of Neurological Disorders and Stroke (NINDS) can send you only information they have in their current publications on Steele-Richardson Disease. They cannot refer you to any experts. This Clearinghouse cannot directly give you information about any current clinical studies NINDS might be conducting on this illness, but you can find this information for yourself by looking under the National Institute of Neurological Disorders and Stroke in *Appendix A* at the end of this book.

☎ Contact:
National Institute of Neurological
Disorders and Stroke
Building 31
Room 8A06
Bethesda, MD 20892
(301) 496-5751
(800) 352-9424

STEINERTS DISEASE

See Muscular Dystrophy

STERILIZATION

See also Vasectomies

Clearinghouses/Hotlines

The National Institute of Child Health and Human Development (NICHD) will send you whatever publications and reprints of journal articles they have on Sterilization. If necessary, they will refer you to other experts or researchers in the field. If you can't afford treatment, have your doctor call NICHD to find out if they are conducting any clinical studies that you might qualify for.

☎ Contact:
National Institute of Child Health
and Human Development
Bldg. 31, Room 2A32
Bethesda, MD 20892
(301) 496-5133

Using health survey and epidemiologic studies of large patient populations, the Contraceptive Development Branch at National Institutes of Health evaluates the safety and effectiveness of different surgical Sterilization procedures. The Center for Population Research publishes an annual progress report that outlines the accomplishments and goals in contraception development for the year.

☎ Contact:
Center for Population Research
National Institute of Child Health
and Human Development
Executive Plaza North, 6th Floor
Bethesda, MD 20892
(301) 496-1661

Free Publications/Videos

The following publications on Sterilization are available from the Family Life Information Exchange, P.O. Box 30146, Bethesda, MD 20814; (301) 585-6636.

- *Information for Men: Your Sterilization Operation.*
- *Information for Women: Your Sterilization Operation.* Covers tubal ligation and other methods of birth control (#10015)

STEROID CONTRACEPTIVES

Clearinghouses/Hotlines

The National Institute of Child Health and Human Development (NICHD) will send you whatever publications and reprints of journal articles they have on Steroid Contraceptives. If necessary, they will refer you to other experts or researchers in the field. If you can't afford treatment, have your doctor call NICHD to find out if they are conducting any clinical studies that you might qualify for.

☎ Contact:
National Institute of Child Health
and Human Development
Bldg. 31, Room 2A32
Bethesda, MD 20892
(301) 496-5133

STEROID HYPERTENSION

Clearinghouses/Hotlines

The National Heart, Lung, and Blood Institute (NHLBI) can search the Combined Health Information Database (CHID) and generate a bibliography of resources for you on Steroid Hypertension. They also will send you any publications and journal articles they may have on hand, and will refer you to other organizations that are studying this condition. If you can't afford treatment, have your doctor call NHLBI to find out if they are conducting any clinical studies that you might qualify for.

☎ Contact:
National Heart, Lung, and Blood Institute
Bldg. 31, Room 4A21
Bethesda, MD 20892
(301) 496-4236

STEROIDS

Clearinghouses/Hotlines

The Food and Drug Administration's Center for Drug Evaluation and Research has put together a free information packet containing brochures, regulations, reports, and a poster on the dangers of steroids.

☎ Contact:
Center for Drug Evaluation and Research
Food and Drug Administration
5600 Fishers Lane, HFD-365
Rockville, MD 20857
(301) 295-8012

The Department of Education's Drug Abuse Prevention Oversight Staff provides materials to schools and communities in developing a comprehensive program to prevent the use of alcohol and other drugs, including tobacco and steroids.

☎ Contact:
Office of the Secretary
U.S. Department of Education
400 Maryland Ave., SW, Room 4145
Washington, DC 20202-0100
(202) 401-3030

Free Publications/Videos

The following publications on Steroids are available from the National Clearinghouse for Alcohol and Drug Information, P.O. Box 2345, Rockville, MD 20852; (301) 468-2600.

- *Anabolic Steroids and You.*
- *The Fact is...The Use of Steroids in Sports Can Be Dangerous.*
- *Pumping Trouble: The Problem of Steroid Use.*
- *Steroids Mean Trouble.* Anti-drug abuse poster.

The following publication on Steroids is available from the Consumer Information Center, P.O. Box 100, Pueblo, CO 81002.

- *Anabolic Steroids: Losing at Winning.* (#516Y)

STEVENS-JOHNSON SYNDROME

Clearinghouses/Hotlines

The National Institute of Allergy and Infectious Diseases (NIAID) can search the Combined Health Information Database (CHID) and generate a bibliography of resources for you on Stevens-Johnson Syndrome. They will also send you any publications and journal articles they may have on hand, and will refer you to researchers who are currently studying this Syndrome. If you can't afford treatment, have your doctor call NIAID to find out if they are conducting any clinical studies that you might qualify for.

☎ Contact:
National Institute of Allergy
and Infectious Diseases
Bldg. 31, Room 7A32
Bethesda, MD 20892
(301) 496-5717

STIFF MAN SYNDROME

Clearinghouses/Hotlines

The National Institute of Neurological Disorders and Stroke (NINDS) can send you only information they have in their current publications on Stiff Man Syndrome. They cannot refer you to any experts. This Clearinghouse cannot directly give you information about any current clinical studies NINDS might be conducting on this disorder, but you can find this information for yourself by looking under the National Institute of Neurological Disorders and Stroke in *Appendix A* at the end of this book.

☎ Contact:
National Institute of Neurological
Disorders and Stroke
Bldg. 31, Room 8A06
Bethesda, MD 20892
(301) 496-5751
(800) 352-9424

STILL'S DISEASE

Clearinghouses/Hotlines

The National Institute of Arthritis and Musculoskeletal and Skin Diseases (NIAMS) will send you whatever publications and reprints of articles from texts and journals they have on Still's Disease. They will also refer you to other organizations that are studying this disease. NIAMS will also let you know of any clinical studies that may be studying this disease and looking for patients.

☎ Contact:
National Institute of Arthritis
and Musculoskeletal and Skin Diseases
Box AMS
9000 Rockville Pike
Bethesda, MD 20892
(301) 495-4484

STOMACH CANCER

Clearinghouses/Hotlines

The National Cancer Institute (NCI) will send you whatever publications and reprints of journal articles they have on Stomach Cancer. They can also give you information on the state-of-the-art treatment for this disease, including specific treatment information for your stage of cancer. They can also search their Physician's Data Query (PDQ) database to let you know if NCI is conducting any clinical studies on your disease.

☎ Contact:
National Cancer Institute
Bldg. 31, Room 10A24
Bethesda, MD 20892
(800) 4-CANCER
(301) 496-5583

Free Publications/Videos

The following publications are available from the National Cancer Institute, Bldg. 31, Room 10A24,

Bethesda, MD 20892; (800) 4-CANCER, or (301) 496-5583.

- *Research Report: Cancer of the Stomach.* (#88-2978)
- *What You Need to Know About Cancer of the Stomach.* (#90-1544)

STOMATITIS

Clearinghouses/Hotlines

The National Institute of Dental Research (NIDR) will send you whatever publications and reprints of journal articles they have on Stomatitis. As a policy, however, NIDR will not refer you to other organizations or experts who study this condition. If you can't afford treatment, have your doctor call Dr. Albert Guckers at (301) 496-6241 to find out if NIDR is conducting any clinical studies that you might qualify for.

☎ Contact:
National Institute of Dental Research
Bldg. 31, Room 2C35
Bethesda, MD 20892
(301) 496-4261

STRABISMUS

Clearinghouses/Hotlines

The National Eye Institute (NEI) can give you up-to-date information on Strabismus by searching the Combined Health Information Database (CHID) and MEDLINE and sending you bibliographies of resources, along with any journal articles they may have. They can also refer you to any other organizations that study Strabismus and other related conditions. NEI will also let you know of any clinical studies that may be studying this disease and looking for patients. Because of their small staff, NEI prefers that you submit your requests for information in writing.

☎ Contact:
National Eye Institute

Bldg. 31, Room 6A32
Bethesda, MD 20892
(301) 496-5248

Free Publications/Videos

The following publication on Strabismus is available from the National Eye Institute, Bldg. 31, Room 6A32, Bethesda, MD 20892; (301) 496-5248.

- *Vision Research: Report of the Strabismus Amblyopia and Visual Processing Panel, Part Five.* (#83-2475)

STREPTOCOCCAL (STREP) INFECTIONS

Clearinghouses/Hotlines

The National Institute of Allergy and Infectious Diseases (NIAID) can search the Combined Health Information Database (CHID) and generate a bibliography of resources for you on Streptococcal (Strep) Infections. They will also send you any publications and journal articles they may have on hand, and will refer you to researchers who are currently studying this kind of infection. If you can't afford treatment, have your doctor call NIAID to find out if they are conducting any clinical studies that you might qualify for.

☎ Contact:
National Institute of Allergy
and Infectious Diseases
Bldg. 31, Room 7A32
Bethesda, MD 20892
(301) 496-5717

STREPTOKINASE

Clearinghouses/Hotlines

The National Heart, Lung, and Blood Institute (NHLBI) can search the Combined Health

Information Database (CHID) and generate a bibliography of resources for you on Streptokinase. They also will send you any publications and journal articles they may have on hand, and will refer you to other organizations that are studying Streptokinase. If you can't afford treatment, have your doctor call NHLBI to find out if they are conducting any clinical studies that you might qualify for.

☎ Contact:
National Heart, Lung, and Blood Institute
Bldg. 31, Room 4A21
Bethesda, MD 20892
(301) 496-4236

STRESS

Clearinghouses/Hotlines

The National Institute of Mental Health (NIMH) will send you whatever publications and reprints of articles from texts and journals they have on Stress. They will also refer you to other organizations that are studying this issue. NIMH will also let you know of any clinical studies that may be studying this disease and looking for patients.

☎ Contact:
National Institute of Mental Health
5600 Fishers Lane
Room 15C05
Rockville, MD 20857
(301) 443-4515

The National Heart, Lung, and Blood Institute (NHLBI) can search the Combined Health Information Database (CHID) and generate a bibliography of resources for you on Stress (EKG). They also will send you any publications and journal articles they may have on hand, and will refer you to other organizations that are studying this issue. If you can't afford treatment, have your doctor call NHLBI to find out if they are conducting any clinical studies that you might qualify for.

☎ Contact:
National Heart, Lung, and Blood Institute
Bldg. 31, Room 4A21

Bethesda, MD 20892
(301) 496-4236

The National Institute on Aging (NIA) will send you whatever publications and reprints of journal articles they have on Stress and Aging. They cannot refer you to other experts if the information they have isn't sufficient for your purposes.

☎ Contact:
National Institute on Aging
Building 31
Room 5C27
Bethesda, MD 20892
(301) 496-1752

Free Publications/Videos

The following publications on Stress are available from the National Institute of Mental Health, 5600 Fishers Ln., Room 15C05, Rockville, MD 20857; (301) 443-4515.

- *Plain Talk About Handling Stress.*
- *Plain Talk About the Art of Relaxation.*
  Discusses the stages of physical and mental stress, describes the symptoms and offers suggestions for stress reduction.

The following publication on Stress is available from the Superintendent of Documents, Government Printing Office, Washington, DC 20402; (202) 783-3238

- *Stress Management in Work Settings.*
  Summarizes and reviews scientific evidence and practical issues relating to worksite stress management, and includes a collection of resources for training materials, products, and equipment. ($9.50, S/N 017-033-00428-5)

The following publication on Stress is available from the Science & Technology Division, Reference Section, Library of Congress, Washington, DC 20540; (202) 707-5580.

- *Stress: Physiological and Psychological Aspects.*
  Reference guide designed to help locate further published material. (#87-6)

The following publication on Stress is available from the National Heart, Lung and Blood Institute, Bldg. 31, Room 4A21, Bethesda, MD 20892; (301) 496-4236.

- *Proceedings of the Working Conference on Stress, Reactivity, and Cardiovascular Disease.* (#85-2698)

STRIATONIGRAL DEGENERATION

Clearinghouses/Hotlines

The National Institute of Neurological Disorders and Stroke (NINDS) can send you only information they have in their current publications on Striatonigral Degeneration. They cannot refer you to any experts. This Clearinghouse cannot directly give you information about any current clinical studies NINDS might be conducting on this disorder, but you can find this information for yourself by looking under the National Institute of Neurological Disorders and Stroke in *Appendix A* at the end of this book.

☎ Contact:
National Institute of Neurological
Disorders and Stroke
Bldg. 31, Room 8A06
Bethesda, MD 20892
(301) 496-5751
(800) 352-9424

STROKE

Clearinghouses/Hotlines

The National Institute of Neurological Disorders and Stroke (NINDS) conducts and guides research on the causes, prevention, diagnosis, and treatment of Stroke. They can give all kinds of information about this area of study. Other areas of research include cerebral palsy, autism, dyslexia, multiple sclerosis, Parkinson's and Huntington's diseases, and epilepsy.

☎ Contact:
National Institute of Neurological
Disorders and Stroke
Building 31
Room 8A06
Bethesda, MD 20892
(301) 496-5751
(800) 352-9424

The National Heart, Lung, and Blood Institute (NHLBI) can search the Combined Health Information Database (CHID) and generate a bibliography of resources for you on Stroke (Hypertension). They also will send you any publications and journal articles they may have on hand, and will refer you to other organizations that are studying stroke. If you can't afford treatment, have your doctor call NHLBI to find out if they are conducting any clinical studies that you might qualify for.

☎ Contact:
National Heart, Lung, and
Blood Institute
Building 31
Room 4A21
Bethesda, MD 20892
(301) 496-4236

The National Institute on Deafness and Other Communication Disorders (NIDCD) will send you whatever publications and reprints of journal articles they have on Stroke. If you need further information, they will refer you to other organizations that study this and other related diseases. NIDCD does not conduct any clinical studies for this or any other disorder.

☎ Contact:
National Institute on Deafness
and Other Communication Disorders
Building 31
Room 3C35
Bethesda, MD 20892
(301) 496-7243
(800) 241-1044
(301) 402-0252 (TDD)

Free Publications/Videos

The following publication on Stroke is available from the Office of Clinical Center Communications, Bldg. 10, Room 1C255, Bethesda, MD 20892; (301) 496-2563.

- *Stroke Update*. (#88-2989) Booklet written to help the general public make intelligent decisions.

The following publications on Stroke are available from the National Institute of Neurological Disorders and Stroke, Bldg. 31, Room 8A06, Bethesda, MD 20892; (301) 496-5751 or (800) 352-9424.

- *What You Should Know About Stroke and Stroke Prevention*. (#81-1909)
- *Stroke: Hope through Research*. (#83-2222)
- *Stroke 1990*. Annual or Biennial Research Updates.
- *Stroke*. Discusses hope through research.
- *Fundamentals of Stroke Care*. (#76-14016)
- *Stroke*. Collection of scientific articles, patient education pamphlets, and addresses of voluntary health associations.

The following publication on Stroke is available from the National Institute on Aging Information Center, 2209 Distribution Circle, Silver Spring, MD 20910; (301) 495-3455.

- *Stroke*. Facts for the aging.

STRONGYLOIDIASIS (ROUNDWORM)

Clearinghouses/Hotlines

The National Institute of Allergy and Infectious Diseases (NIAID) can provide you with reference materials on Roundworm, and can refer you to other organizations.

☎ Contact:
National Institute of Allergy
and Infectious Diseases
Building 31
Room 7A32
Bethesda, MD 20892
(301) 496-5717

STURGE-WEBER SYNDROME

Clearinghouses/Hotlines

The National Institute of Neurological Disorders and Stroke (NINDS) can send you only information they have in their current publications on Sturge-Weber Syndrome. They cannot refer you to any experts. This Clearinghouse cannot directly give you information about any current clinical studies NINDS might be conducting on this illness, but you can find this information for yourself by looking under the National Institute of Neurological Disorders and Stroke in *Appendix A* at the end of this book.

☎ Contact:
National Institute of Neurological
Disorders and Stroke
Bldg. 31, Room 8A06
Bethesda, MD 20892
(301) 496-5751
(800) 352-9424

STUTTERING

Clearinghouses/Hotlines

The National Institute on Deafness and Other Communication Disorders (NIDCD) will send you whatever publications and reprints of journal articles they have on Stuttering. If you need further information, they will refer you to other organizations that study this and other related disorders. However, NIDCD does not conduct any clinical studies for stuttering.

☎ Contact:
National Institute on Deafness
and Other Communication Disorders
Building 31
Room 3C35
Bethesda, MD 20892
(301) 496-7243
(800) 241-1044
(301) 402-0252 (TDD)

The National Institute of Neurological Disorders and Stroke (NINDS) can send you only information they have in their current publications on Stuttering. They cannot refer you to any experts. This Clearinghouse cannot directly give you information about any current clinical studies NINDS might be conducting on this disorder, but you can find this information for yourself by looking under the National Institute of Neurological Disorders and Stroke in *Appendix A* at the end of this book.

☎ Contact:
National Institute of Neurological
Disorders and Stroke
Bldg. 31, Room 8A06
Bethesda, MD 20892
(301) 496-5751
(800) 352-9424

STYE

Clearinghouses/Hotlines

The National Eye Institute (NEI) can provide you with reference materials and other information regarding a Stye, which is an infection of a gland by the eyelash.

☎ Contact:
National Eye Institute
Bldg. 31, Room 6A32
Bethesda, MD 20892
(301) 496-5248

SUDDEN CARDIAC DEATH

Clearinghouses/Hotlines

The National Heart, Lung, and Blood Institute (NHLBI) can search the Combined Health Information Database (CHID) and generate a bibliography of resources for you on Sudden Cardiac Death. They also will send you any publications and journal articles they may have on hand, and will refer you to other organizations that are studying this issue. If you can't afford treatment, have your doctor call NHLBI to find out if they are conducting any clinical studies that you might qualify for.

☎ Contact:
National Heart, Lung, and Blood Institute
Bldg. 31, Room 4A21
Bethesda, MD 20892
(301) 496-4236

SUDDEN INFANT DEATH SYNDROME

Clearinghouses/Hotlines

The National Sudden Infant Death Syndrome Clearinghouse can provide you with information, research, reports, brochures, and referrals dealing with Sudden Infant Death Syndrome.

☎ Contact:
National Sudden Infant Death
Syndrome Clearinghouse
8201 Greensboro Dr., Suite 600
McLean, VA 22102
(703) 821-8955

The National Institute of Child Health and Human Development (NICHD) will send you whatever publications and reprints of journal articles they have on Sudden Infant Death Syndrome. If necessary, they will refer you to other experts or researchers in the field.

☎ Contact:
National Institute of Child Health
and Human Development
Bldg. 31, Room 2A32
Bethesda, MD 20892
(301) 496-5133

Free Publications/Videos

The following Sudden Infant Death Syndrome (SIDS) publications are available from the National Sudden Infant Death Syndrome Clearinghouse, 8201 Greensboro Dr., Suite 600, McLean, VA 22102; (703) 821-8955.

- *Crib Death*. Explains SIDS in easy to read booklet form.
- *Current Research in Sudden Infant Death*
- *Directory of State Title V Maternal and Child Health Directors and SIDS Program Coordinators*. Lists MCH directors and SIDS coordinators by state; Federal and Federally supported programs; and private SIDS and SIDS-related programs.
- *Examination of the SIDS Infant: Investigative and Autopsy Protocols*. Reports the results of a 1975 national conference.
- *Fact Sheet: Facts about Apnea and Other Apparent Life-threatening Events*.
- *Fact Sheet: Grief of Children*. Discusses some of the common expressions of children's grief and offers way in which adults can help during the grieving process.
- *Fact Sheet: Parents and The Grieving Process*. Defines grief, presents common reactions and emotions expressed by people who are bereaved, and highlights the process by which resolution and recovery may be achieved.
- *Fact Sheet: SIDS Information for the EMT*. Provides suggestions for first response of EMTs and others at the time of sudden infant death.
- *Fact Sheet: What Is SIDS?* Provides basic facts about SIDS and discusses reactions of the surviving family members and ways they can be helped.
- *FDA Safety Alert: Important Tips for Apnea Monitor Users*. Lists important tips to help parents and caregivers understand the limitations of infant apnea monitors and offers guidelines for their proper use.
- *A Guide to Resources in Perinatal Bereavement*. Offers selected resources for professionals working with parents who have lost a child.
- *Infantile Apnea and Home Monitoring: Consensus Statement*. The October 1986 National Institutes of Health Consensus Development Conference on Infantile Apnea and Home Monitoring.
- *Information Exchange*. Quarterly newsletter of SIDS Clearinghouse.
- *Joint Hearing on SIDS Before the committees on Post Office and Civil Service, Committee on Energy and Commerce, and the Select*

Committee on Children, Youth, and Families, 99th Congress. Testimony to bring the issue of SIDS into the public domain, to generate support for educating the public and professionals about SIDS, and to encourage further research.

- *Nosology Guideline.* Supplement to the medical examiner's cause-of-death coding manual describing death certificate coding information for SIDS.
- *SIDS Information for the EMT.*
- *Sudden Infant Death Syndrome and Other Infant Losses Among Adolescent Parents: An Annotate Bibliography and Resource Guide.* An overview of adolescent bereavement, abstract of articles, and resources for adolescents.
- *Sudden Unexplained Infant Death 1970-1975: An Evolution of Understanding.* Examines changes in understanding of sudden, unexpected, and unexplained infant death.
- *Talking to Children About Death.* Helps prepare parents and other adults to talk to children about death.

SUICIDE

Clearinghouses/Hotlines

The National Institute of Mental Health (NIMH) will send you whatever publications and reprints of articles from texts and journals they have on Suicide. They will also refer you to other organizations that are studying suicide. NIMH will also let you know of any clinical studies that may be studying this issue and looking for patients

☎ Contact:
National Institute of Mental Health
5600 Fishers Lane
Room 15C05
Rockville, MD 20857
(301) 443-4515

Free Publications/Videos

The following Congressional Research Service (CRS) report on Suicide is available from either of

your U.S. Senators' offices at the U.S. Capitol, Washington, DC 20510, or from your Congressional Representative at the U.S. Capitol, Washington, DC 20515. You can also call in your request through the U.S. Capitol switchboard at (202) 224-3121. Be sure to include the full title and report number in your request.

- *Teenage Suicide: Bibliography-in-Brief, 1981, 1988.* (#88-652)

SULFITES

Clearinghouses/Hotlines

The Food and Nutrition Information Center can provide you with a wealth of information on food and nutrition topics. They have bibliographies ready and a data base through which they can search any food or nutrition subject.

☎ Contact:
Food and Nutrition Information Center
National Agricultural Library
Room 304
Beltsville, MD 20705
(301) 504-5719

Free Publications/Videos

The following Congressional Research Service (CRS) report on Sulfites is available from either of your U.S. Senators' offices at the U.S. Capitol, Washington, DC 20510, or from your Congressional Representative at the U.S. Capitol, Washington, DC 20515. You can also call in your request through the U.S. Capitol switchboard at (202) 224-3121. Be sure to include the full title and report number in your request.

- *Sulfites: Food Preservatives.* (#86-887 SPR)

The following publication on Sulfites is available from the Food & Drug Administration, (HFE-88), 5600 Fishers Ln., Rockville, MD 20857; (301) 443-3170.

- *Reacting to Sulfites.* (#FDA90-2209)

SUNLAMPS

Free Publications/Videos

The following publications on Sunlamps are available from the Center for Devices and Radiological Health, (HFZ-210), Food and Drug Administration, 5600 Fishers Ln., Rockville, MD 20857; (301) 443-4690.

- *Fact Sheet: Sunlamps.*
- *Federal Register: Sunlamp Products; Performance Standard; Final Rule.*
- *Sunlamps: Putting Safety First.*

SUNSCREENS

Free Publications/Videos

The following publications are available from the Center for Devices and Radiological Health, (HFZ-210), Food and Drug Administration, 5600 Fishers Ln., Rockville, MD 20857; (301) 443-4690.

- *Sunbathing Without Burning.* (#FDA 78-7022)
- *Out of the Bronzed Age.*

SURGERY

Clearinghouses/Hotlines

The National Second Surgical Opinion Program is an information resource for people faced with the possibility of non-emergency or Elective Surgery. By calling its toll-free number, the staff will help you locate a surgeon or other specialist enrolled in the program who can offer you a second opinion. Pamphlets are available containing questions that patients looking for second opinions should ask.

☎ Contact:
Health Care Financing Administration
330 Independence Ave., SW
Washington, DC 20201

(800) 638-6833
(800) 492-6603 in MD

Free Publications/Videos

The following publication is available from the Consumer Information Center, P.O. Box 100, Pueblo, CO 81002.

- *Getting a Second Opinion.* (#557Y)

SURROGATE MOTHERHOOD

Free Publications/Videos

The following Congressional Research Service (CRS) reports on Surrogate Motherhood are available from either of your U.S. Senators' offices at the U.S. Capitol, Washington, DC 20510, or from your Congressional Representative at the U.S. Capitol, Washington, DC 20515. You can also call in your request through the U.S. Capitol switchboard at (202) 224-3121. Be sure to include the full title and report number in your request.

- *Analysis of Legal and Constitutional Issues Involved in Surrogate Motherhood.* (#88-240 A)
- *Surrogate Mothers: Bibliography-in-Brief, 1985-1988.* (#88-268 L)

SWEAT GLAND DISORDERS

See also Anaphoresis

Clearinghouses/Hotlines

The National Institute of Arthritis and Musculoskeletal and Skin Diseases (NIAMS) will send you whatever publications and reprints of articles from texts and journals they have on Sweat Gland Disorders. They will also refer you to other organizations that are studying this condition.

NIAMS will also let you know of any clinical studies that may be studying these disorders looking for patients.

☎ Contact:
National Institute of Arthritis
and Musculoskeletal and Skin Diseases
Box AMS
9000 Rockville Pike
Bethesda, MD 20892
(301) 495-4484

SWINE FLU

See also Flu

Clearinghouses/Hotlines

The National Institute of Allergy and Infectious Diseases (NIAID) can search the Combined Health Information Database (CHID) and generate a bibliography of resources for you on Swine Flu. They will also send you any publications and journal articles they may have on hand, and will refer you to researchers who are currently studying Swine Flu. If you can't afford treatment, have your doctor call NIAID to find out if they are conducting any clinical studies that you might qualify for.

☎ Contact:
National Institute of Allergy
and Infectious Diseases
Bldg. 31, Room 7A32
Bethesda, MD 20892
(301) 496-5717

SYDENHAM'S CHOREA

Clearinghouses/Hotlines

The National Institute of Neurological Disorders and Stroke (NINDS) can send you only information they have in their current publications on Sydenham's Chorea. They cannot refer you to any experts. This Clearinghouse cannot directly give you information about any current clinical

studies NINDS might be conducting on this disorder, but you can find this information for yourself by looking under the National Institute of Neurological Disorders and Stroke in *Appendix A* at the end of this book.

☎ Contact:
National Institute of Neurological
Disorders and Stroke
Bldg. 31, Room 8A06
Bethesda, MD 20892
(301) 496-5751
(800) 352-9424

SYNCOPE

See also Fainting

Clearinghouses/Hotlines

The National Heart, Lung, and Blood Institute (NHLBI) can search the Combined Health Information Database (CHID) and generate a bibliography of resources for you on Syncope (Fainting). They also will send you any publications and journal articles they may have on hand, and will refer you to other organizations that are studying fainting. If you can't afford treatment, have your doctor call NHLBI to find out if they are conducting any clinical studies that you might qualify for.

☎ Contact:
National Heart, Lung, and Blood Institute
Bldg. 31, Room 4A21
Bethesda, MD 20892
(301) 496-4236

SYNOVITIS

Clearinghouses/Hotlines

The National Institute of Arthritis and Musculoskeletal and Skin Diseases (NIAMS) will send you whatever publications and reprints of articles from texts and journals they have on Synovitis. They will also refer you to other organizations that are studying Synovitis. NIAMS will also let you know of any clinical studies that may be studying this disease and looking for patients.

☎ Contact:
National Institute of Arthritis
and Musculoskeletal and Skin Diseases
Box AMS
9000 Rockville Pike
Bethesda, MD 20892
(301) 495-4484

SYPHILIS

Clearinghouses/Hotlines

The Sexually Transmitted Diseases Hotline offers valuable information to the public about a wide range of sexually transmitted diseases, including Syphilis and how to protect yourself from contracting them.

☎ Contact:
National Sexually Transmitted Diseases Hotline
P.O. Box 13827
Research Triangle Park, NC 27709
(800) 227-8922

The National Institute of Allergy and Infectious Diseases (NIAID) can search the Combined Health Information Database (CHID) and generate a bibliography of resources for you on Syphilis. They will also send you any publications and journal articles they may have on hand, and will refer you to researchers who are currently studying Syphilis. If you can't afford treatment, have your doctor call NIAID to find out if they are conducting any clinical studies that you might qualify for.

☎ Contact:
National Institute of Allergy
and Infectious Diseases
Building 31
Room 7A32
Bethesda, MD 20892
(301) 496-5717

SYRINGOMYELIA

Clearinghouses/Hotlines

The National Institute of Neurological Disorders and Stroke (NINDS) can send you only information they have in their current publications on Syringomyelia. They cannot refer you to any experts. This Clearinghouse cannot directly give you information about any current clinical studies NINDS might be conducting on this illness, but you can find this information for yourself by looking under the National Institute of Neurological Disorders and Stroke in *Appendix A* at the end of this book.

☎ Contact:
National Institute of Neurological
Disorders and Stroke
Building 31
Room 8A06
Bethesda, MD 20892
(301) 496-5751
(800) 352-9424

Free Publications/Videos

The following publication on Syringomyelia is available from the National Institute of Neurological Disorders and Stroke, P.O. Box 5801, Bethesda, MD 20824; (800) 352-9424, or (301) 496-5751.

- *Syringomyelia*. Collection of scientific
    articles, patient education pamphlets, and
    addresses of voluntary health associations.

SYSTEMIC LUPUS ERYTHEMATOSUS

See Lupus

SYSTEMIC SCLEROSIS

Clearinghouses/Hotlines

The National Institute of Neurological Disorders and Stroke (NINDS) can send you only information they have in their current publications on Progressive Systemic Sclerosis. They cannot refer you to any experts. This Clearinghouse cannot directly give you information about any current clinical studies NINDS might be conducting on this illness, but you can find this information for yourself by looking under the National Institute of Neurological Disorders and Stroke in *Appendix A* at the end of this book.

☎ Contact:
National Institute of Neurological
Disorders and Stroke
Bldg. 31, Room 8A06
Bethesda, MD 20892
(301) 496-5751
(800) 352-9424

The National Institute of Arthritis and Musculoskeletal and Skin Diseases (NIAMS) will send you whatever publications and reprints of articles from texts and journals they have on Progressive Systemic Sclerosis. They will also refer you to other organizations that are studying systemic sclerosis. NIAMS will also let you know of any clinical studies that may be studying this disease and looking for patients.

☎ Contact:
National Institute of Arthritis
and Musculoskeletal and Skin Diseases
Box AMS
9000 Rockville Pike
Bethesda, MD 20892
(301) 495-4484

SYSTOLIC HYPERTENSION

Clearinghouses/Hotlines

The National Heart, Lung, and Blood Institute (NHLBI) can search the Combined Health Information Database (CHID) and generate a bibliography of resources for you on Systolic Hypertension in the Elderly. They also will send you any publications and journal articles they may have on hand, and will refer you to other organizations that are studying this condition. If you can't afford treatment, have your doctor call NHLBI to find out if they are conducting any clinical studies that you might qualify for.

☎ Contact:
National Heart, Lung, and
Blood Institute
Building 31
Room 4A21
Bethesda, MD 20892
(301) 496-4236

- T -

TACHYCARDIA

Clearinghouses/Hotlines

The National Heart, Lung, and Blood Institute (NHLBI) can search the Combined Health Information Database (CHID) and generate a bibliography of resources for you on Tachycardia. They also will send you any publications and journal articles they may have on hand, and will refer you to other organizations that are studying this issue. If you can't afford treatment, have your doctor call NHLBI to find out if they are conducting any clinical studies that you might qualify for.

☎ Contact:
National Heart, Lung, and
Blood Institute
Building 31
Room 4A21
Bethesda, MD 20892
(301) 496-4236

TAKAYASU'S ARTERITIS

Clearinghouses/Hotlines

The National Institute of Allergy and Infectious Diseases (NIAID) can search the Combined Health Information Database (CHID) and generate a bibliography of resources for you on Takayasu's Arteritis. They will also send you any publications and journal articles they may have on hand, and will refer you to researchers who are currently studying this disease. If you can't afford treatment, have your doctor call NIAID to find out if they are conducting any clinical studies that you might qualify for.

☎ Contact:
National Institute of Allergy
and Infectious Diseases
Bldg. 31, Room 7A32
Bethesda, MD 20892
(301) 496-5717

TAMOXIFEN

Free Publications/Videos

The following publication is available from the National Cancer Institute, Bldg. 31, Room 10A24, Bethesda, MD 20892; (800) 4-CANCER, or (301) 496-5583.

- *Tamoxifeno/Tamoxifen.* Provides information about side effects, proper usage, and precautions of this anti-cancer drug.

TANGIER DISEASE

Clearinghouses/Hotlines

The National Heart, Lung, and Blood Institute (NHLBI) can search the Combined Health Information Database (CHID) and generate a bibliography of resources for you on Tangier

Disease. They also will send you any publications and journal articles they may have on hand, and will refer you to other organizations that are studying this disease. If you can't afford treatment, have your doctor call NHLBI to find out if they are conducting any clinical studies that you might qualify for.

☎ Contact:
National Heart, Lung, and Blood Institute
Building 31
Room 4A21
Bethesda, MD 20892
(301) 496-4236

The National Institute of Neurological Disorders and Stroke (NINDS) can send you information they have only in their publications list on Tangier Disease. They cannot refer you to any experts. This Clearinghouse cannot directly give you information about any current clinical studies NINDS might be conducting on this illness, but you can find this information for yourself by looking under the National Institute of Neurological Disorders and Stroke in *Appendix A* at the end of this book.

☎ Contact:
National Institute of Neurological
Disorders and Stroke
Building 31
Room 8A06
Bethesda, MD 20892
(301) 496-5751
(800) 352-9424

TANNING

Clearinghouses/Hotlines

The Food and Drug Administration's Center for Devices and Radiological Health acts as a clearinghouse for information on the hazards of Tanning and Tanning Salons and devices. They can send you all kinds of consumer information on tanning, including reprints of journal articles, statistics, and government regulations on the tanning industry. This Center also responds to consumer complaints involving tanning devices and misrepresentative claims by tanning salons.

☎ Contact:
Center for Devices and
Radiological Health
(HFZ-210)
Food and Drug Administration
5600 Fishers Lane
Rockville, MD 20857
(301) 443-4690

Free Publications/Videos

The following publications on Tanning are available from the Center for Devices and Radiological Health, (HFZ-210), Food and Drug Administration, 5600 Fishers Ln., Rockville, MD 20857; (301) 443-4690.

- *The Darker Side of Indoor Tanning.* (#FDA 87-8272)
- *Out of the Bronzed Age.*
- *Notes on the Science Seminar: Tanning Booths.*
- *AMA News Release: Sun-Tan Parlors Called Potentially Dangerous.*
- *Tanning Beds Are Not Without Drawbacks.* (#FDA 84-8228)
- *Tan Now, Pay Later?*
- *A Careful Look Into Tanning Booths.* (#FDA 81-8149)
- *A Word of Caution on Tanning Booths.* (#FDA 80-8118)

TAPEWORM INFECTION

Clearinghouses/Hotlines

The National Institute of Allergy and Infectious Diseases (NIAID) can provide you with reference materials on Tapeworm, and can refer you to other organizations.

☎ Contact:
National Institute of Allergy
and Infectious Diseases
Bldg. 31, Room 7A32
Bethesda, MD 20892
(301) 496-5717

TARDIVE DYSKINESIA

Clearinghouses/Hotlines

The National Institute of Mental Health (NIMH) will send you whatever publications and reprints of articles from texts and journals they have on Tardive Dyskinesia. They will also refer you to other organizations that are studying this disorder. NIMH will also let you know of any clinical studies that may be studying this disorder and looking for patients.

☎ Contact:
National Institute of Mental Health
5600 Fishers Ln., Room 15C05
Rockville, MD 20857
(301) 443-4515

The National Institute of Neurological Disorders and Stroke (NINDS) can send you information they have only in their publications list on Tardive Dyskinesia. They cannot refer you to any experts. This Clearinghouse cannot directly give you information about any current clinical studies NINDS might be conducting on this illness, but you can find this information for yourself by looking under the National Institute of Neurological Disorders and Stroke in *Appendix A* at the end of this book.

☎ Contact:
National Institute of Neurological
Disorders and Stroke
Bldg. 31, Room 8A06
Bethesda, MD 20892
(301) 496-5751
(800) 352-9424

TASTE DISORDERS

Clearinghouses/Hotlines

The National Institute on Deafness and Other Communication Disorders (NIDCD) will send you whatever publications and reprints of journal articles they have on Taste and Smell Dysfunction. If you need further information, they will refer you to other organizations that study this and other related diseases. NIDCD does not conduct any clinical studies for this or any other disorder.

☎ Contact:
National Institute on Deafness
and Other Communication Disorders
Bldg. 31, Room 3C35
Bethesda, MD 20892
(301) 496-7243
(800) 241-1044
(301) 402-0252 (TDD)

The National Institute of Neurological Disorders and Stroke (NINDS) can send you information they have only in their publications list on Taste and Smell Dysfunction. They cannot refer you to any experts. This Clearinghouse cannot directly give you information about any current clinical studies NINDS might be conducting on this topic, but you can find this information for yourself by looking under the National Institute of Neurological Disorders and Stroke in *Appendix A* at the end of this book.

☎ Contact:
National Institute of Neurological
Disorders and Stroke
Bldg. 31, Room 8A06
Bethesda, MD 20892
(301) 496-5751
(800) 352-9424

The National Institute of Dental Research (NIDR) will send you whatever publications and reprints of journal articles they have on Taste Disorders. As a policy, however, NIDR will not refer you to other organizations or experts who study this disease. If you can't afford treatment, have your doctor call Dr. Albert Guckers at (301) 496-6241 to find out if NIDR is conducting any clinical studies that you might qualify for.

☎ Contact:
National Institute of Dental Research
Bldg. 31, Room 2C35
Bethesda, MD 20892
(301) 496-4261

Free Publications/Videos

The following publication on Taste Disorders is available from the National Institute on Deafness

and Other Communication Disorders, Bldg. 31, Rm. 3C35, Bethesda, MD 20892; (301) 496-7243.

- *Because You Asked About Smell and Taste Disorders.* (#91-3231)

TATTOO REMOVAL

Clearinghouses/Hotlines

The National Institute of Arthritis and Musculoskeletal and Skin Diseases (NIAMS) will send you whatever publications and reprints of articles from texts and journals they have on Laser Removal of Tattoos. They will also refer you to other organizations that are studying this procedure. NIAMS will also let you know of any clinical studies that may be studying this procedure and looking for patients.

☎ Contact:
National Institute of Arthritis
and Musculoskeletal and Skin Diseases
Box AMS
Bethesda, MD 20892
(301) 495-4484

TAY-SACH'S DISEASE

Clearinghouses/Hotlines

The National Institute of Neurological Disorders and Stroke (NINDS) can send you information they have only in their publications list on Tay-Sach's Disease. They cannot refer you to any experts. This Clearinghouse cannot directly give you information about any current clinical studies NINDS might be conducting on this illness, but you can find this information for yourself by looking under the National Institute of Neurological Disorders and Stroke in *Appendix A* at the end of this book.

☎ Contact:
National Institute of Neurological
Disorders and Stroke
Bldg. 31, Room 8A06

Bethesda, MD 20892
(301) 496-5751
(800) 352-9424

TEENAGERS

See also Adolescent Health

Clearinghouses/Hotlines

The National Institute of Child Health and Human Development (NICHD) will send you whatever publications and reprints of journal articles they have on Teenagers. If necessary, they will refer you to other experts or researchers in the field.

☎ Contact:
National Institute of Child Health
and Human Development
Bldg. 31, Room 2A32
Bethesda, MD 20892
(301) 496-5133

Free Publications/Videos

The following publication is available from the Family Life Information Exchange, P.O. Box 30146, Bethesda, MD 20814; (301) 585-6636.

- *Teenage Pregnancy and Fertility in the US.*

The following publications on Teenagers are available from the Office on Smoking and Health, Centers for Disease Control, 1600 Clifton Rd., NE, MS K-50, Atlanta, GA 30333; (404) 488-5705.

- *If Your Kids Think Everybody Smokes, They Don't Know Everybody. A Parent's Guide to Smoking and Teenagers.* Explains why some teenagers become smokers. (#83-50199)
- *Teenage Cigarette Smoking Self Test.* A quiz designed to help teens understand their feelings about smoking.

The following publication on Teenagers is available from the National Clearinghouse for Alcohol Information, P.O. Box 2345, Rockville, MD 20852; (800) 729-6686, or (301) 468-2600.

- *Facts About Teenagers and Drug Abuse.*

The following publication on Teenagers is available from the National Cancer Institute, Bldg. 31, Room 10A24, Bethesda, MD 20892; (800) 4-CANCER, or (301) 496-5583.

- *Help Yourself: Tips for Teenagers with Cancer.* (#91-2211) Designed to provide information and support to adolescents with cancer.

The following Congressional Research Service (CRS) report on Teenagers is available from either of your U.S. Senators' offices at the U.S. Capitol, Washington, DC 20510, or from your Congressional Representative at the U.S. Capitol, Washington, DC 20515. You can also call in your request through the U.S. Capitol switchboard at (202) 224-3121. Be sure to include the full title and report number in your request.

- *Teenage Sexual Activity and Childbearing: An Analysis of the Relationships of Behavior to Family and, Personal Background.* (#87-637 EPW)

TEEN PREGNANCY

Clearinghouses/Hotlines

The National Institute of Child Health and Human Development (NICHD) will send you whatever publications and reprints of journal articles they have on Teenage Pregnancy. If necessary, they will refer you to other experts or researchers in the field.

☎ Contact:
National Institute of Child Health
and Human Development
Bldg. 31, Room 2A32
Bethesda, MD 20892
(301) 496-5133

Free Publications/Videos

The following publication on Teenage Pregnancy is available from the Food & Nutrition

Information Center, National Agricultural Library, Room 304, Beltsville, MD 20705-2351; (301) 504-5719.

- *Adolescent Pregnancy and Nutrition.* Designed to help you locate resources on this topic.

The following Congressional Research Service (CRS) reports on Teen Pregnancy are available from either of your U.S. Senators' offices at the U.S. Capitol, Washington, DC 20510, or from your Congressional Representative at the U.S. Capitol, Washington, DC 20515. You can also call in your request through the U.S. Capitol switchboard at (202) 224-3121. Be sure to include the full title and report number in your request.

- *Teenage Pregnancy: Selected Reference, 1986-1988.* (#89-119 L)
- *Adolescent Pregnancy: Programs and Issues; Issue Brief.* (#IB91118)
- *The Children of Teenage Mothers.* (#87-94 EPW)
- *Teenage Pregnancy and Childbearing: Incidence Data.* (#87-11 EPW)
- *Teenage Pregnancy: Issues and Legislation: Issue Brief.* (#IB86128)
- *Teenage Sexual Activity and Childbearing: An Analysis of the Relationships of Behavior to Family and Personal Background.* (#87-637 EPW)

TEETH PROBLEMS

Clearinghouses/Hotlines

The National Institute of Dental Research (NIDR) will send you whatever publications and reprints of journal articles they have on specific Teeth Problems. As a policy, however, NIDR will not refer you to other organizations or experts who study this disease. If you can't afford treatment, have your doctor call Dr. Albert Guckers at (301) 496-6241 to find out if NIDR is conducting any clinical studies that you might qualify for.

☎ Contact:
National Institute of Dental Research
Bldg. 31, Room 2C35

Bethesda, MD 20892
(301) 496-4261

Free Publications/Videos

The following publications are available from the National Institute of Dental Research, Bldg. 31, Room 2C35, Bethesda, MD 20892; (301) 496-4261.

- *Periodontal Disease and Diabetes: A Guide for Patients.*
- *Rx for Sound Teeth.* (#91-3245)

TEMPORAL ARTERITIS

Clearinghouses/Hotlines

The National Eye Institute (NEI) can give you up-to-date information on Temporal Arteritis by searching the Combined Health Information Database (CHID) and MEDLINE and sending you bibliographies of resources, along with any journal articles they may have. They can also refer you to any other organizations that study this and other related conditions. NEI will also let you know of any clinical studies that may be studying this disease and looking for patients. Because of their small staff, NEI prefers that you submit your requests for information in writing.

☎ Contact:
National Eye Institute
Bldg. 31, Room 6A32
Bethesda, MD 20892
(301) 496-5248

The National Institute of Neurological Disorders and Stroke (NINDS) can send you information they have only in their publications list on the Neurological Aspects of Temporal Arteritis. They cannot refer you to any experts. This Clearinghouse cannot directly give you information about any current clinical studies NINDS might be conducting on this topic, but you can find this information for yourself by looking under the National Institute of Neurological Disorders and Stroke in *Appendix A* at the end of this book.

☎ Contact:
National Institute of Neurological
Disorders and Stroke
Building 31
Room 8A06
Bethesda, MD 20892
(301) 496-5751
(800) 352-9424

TENDONITIS

Clearinghouses/Hotlines

The National Institute of Arthritis and Musculoskeletal and Skin Diseases (NIAMS) will send you whatever publications and reprints of articles from texts and journals they have on Tendonitis. They will also refer you to other organizations that are studying this condition. NIAMS will also let you know of any clinical studies that may be studying tendonitis and looking for patients.

☎ Contact:
National Institute of Arthritis
and Musculoskeletal and Skin Diseases
Box AMS
9000 Rockville Pike
Bethesda, MD 20892
(301) 495-4484

TENNIS ELBOW

Clearinghouses/Hotlines

The National Arthritis and Musculoskeletal and Skin Diseases Information Clearinghouse can provide you with reference materials on Tennis Elbow.

☎ Contact:
National Arthritis and Musculoskeletal
and Skin Diseases Information Clearinghouse
Box AMS
9000 Rockville Pike
Bethesda, MD 20892
(301) 495-4484

TEST TUBE BABIES

Clearinghouses/Hotlines

The National Institute of Child Health and Human Development (NICHD) will send you whatever publications and reprints of journal articles they have on Test Tube Babies. If necessary, they will refer you to other experts or researchers in the field.

☎ Contact:
National Institute of Child Health
and Human Development
Bldg. 31, Room 2A32
Bethesda, MD 20892
(301) 496-5133

TESTICULAR CANCER

See also Cancer

Clearinghouses/Hotlines

The National Cancer Institute (NCI) will send you whatever publications and reprints of journal articles they have on Testicular Cancer. They can also give you information on the state-of-the-art treatment for this disease, including specific treatment information for your stage of cancer. They can also search their Physician's Data Query (PDQ) database to let you know if NCI is conducting any clinical studies on your disease.

☎ Contact:
National Cancer Institute
Bldg. 31, Room 10A24
Bethesda, MD 20892
(800) 4-CANCER
(301) 496-5583

Free Publications/Videos

The following publications on Testicular Cancer are available from the National Cancer Institute, Bldg. 31, Room 10A24, Bethesda, MD 20892; (800) 4-CANCER, or (301) 496-5583.

- *Testicular Self-Examination.* Provides information about risks and symptoms of testicular cancer and suggestions effective self-examinations. (#86-2636)
- *What You Need to Know About Testicular Cancer.* (#88-1565)

The following publication on Testicular Cancer is available from the National Heart, Lung and Blood Institute, Bldg. 31, Room 4A21, Bethesda, MD 20892; (301) 496-4236.

- *Testicular Self-Examination.* (#90-2636)

TETANUS

Clearinghouses/Hotlines

The National Institute of Allergy and Infectious Diseases (NIAID) can search the Combined Health Information Database (CHID) and generate a bibliography of resources for you on Tetanus. They will also send you any publications and journal articles they may have on hand, and will refer you to researchers who are currently studying this disease. If you can't afford treatment, have your doctor call NIAID to find out if they are conducting any clinical studies that you might qualify for.

☎ Contact:
National Institute of Allergy
and Infectious Diseases
Bldg. 31, Room 7A32
Bethesda, MD 20892
(301) 496-5717

TETRALOGY OF FALLOT

Clearinghouses/Hotlines

The National Heart, Lung, and Blood Institute (NHLBI) can search the Combined Health Information Database (CHID) and generate a bibliography of resources for you on Tetralogy of Fallot. They also will send you any publications

and journal articles they may have on hand, and will refer you to other organizations that are studying this disease. If you can't afford treatment, have your doctor call NHLBI to find out if they are conducting any clinical studies that you might qualify for.

☎ Contact:
National Heart, Lung, and Blood Institute
Bldg. 31, Room 4A21
Bethesda, MD 20892
(301) 496-4236

THALASSEMIA

Clearinghouses/Hotlines

The National Heart, Lung, and Blood Institute (NHLBI) can search the Combined Health Information Database (CHID) and generate a bibliography of resources for you on Thalassemia. They also will send you any publications and journal articles they may have on hand, and will refer you to other organizations that are studying this disease. If you can't afford treatment, have your doctor call NHLBI to find out if they are conducting any clinical studies that you might qualify for.

☎ Contact:
National Heart, Lung, and Blood Institute
Bldg. 31, Room 4A21
Bethesda, MD 20892
(301) 496-4236

The National Institute of Diabetes and Digestive and Kidney Diseases's (NIDDK) individual clearinghouses can search the Combined Health Information Database (CHID) and generate a bibliography of resources for you on Thalassemia. They also will send you any publications and journal articles they may have on hand, and will refer you to other organizations that are studying this disease. If you can't afford treatment, have your doctor call NIDDK to find out if they are conducting any clinical studies that you might qualify for.

☎ Contact:
National Institute of Diabetes
and Digestive and Kidney Diseases

Bldg. 31, Room 9A04
Bethesda, MD 20892
(301) 496-3583

(301) 496-5751
(800) 352-9424

THERAPEUTIC ENDOSCOPY

Free Publications/Videos

The following publication on Therapeutic Endoscopy is available from the National Digestive Diseases Information Clearinghouse, Box NDDIC, 9000 Rockville Pike, Bethesda, MD 20892; (301) 468-6344.

- *Therapeutic Endoscopy and Bleeding Ulcers.* 1989 National Institutes of Health Consensus Development Conference Statement issued by an expert panel about the effectiveness and safety of therapeutic endoscopy in the treatment of high-risk patients with bleeding ulcers. (#DD-41)

THORACIC-OUTLET SYNDROME

Clearinghouses/Hotlines

The National Institute of Neurological Disorders and Stroke (NINDS) can send you information they have only in their publications list on the Thoracic-Outlet Syndrome. They cannot refer you to any experts. This Clearinghouse cannot directly give you information about any current clinical studies NINDS might be conducting on this illness, but you can find this information for yourself by looking under the National Institute of Neurological Disorders and Stroke in *Appendix A* at the end of this book.

☎ Contact:
National Institute of Neurological
Disorders and Stroke
Bldg. 31, Room 8A06
Bethesda, MD 20892

THROMBASTHENIA

Clearinghouses/Hotlines

The National Institute of Diabetes and Digestive and Kidney Diseases's (NIDDK) individual clearinghouses can search the Combined Health Information Database (CHID) and generate a bibliography of resources for you on Thrombasthenia. They also will send you any publications and journal articles they may have on hand, and will refer you to other organizations that are studying this disease. If you can't afford treatment, have your doctor call NIDDK to find out if they are conducting any clinical studies that you might qualify for.

☎ Contact:
National Institute of Diabetes
and Digestive and Kidney Diseases
Bldg. 31, Room 9A04
Bethesda, MD 20892
(301) 496-3583

THROMBOCYTOPENIA

Clearinghouses/Hotlines

The National Institute of Diabetes and Digestive and Kidney Diseases's (NIDDK) individual clearinghouses can search the Combined Health Information Database (CHID) and generate a bibliography of resources for you on Thrombocytopenia. They also will send you any publications and journal articles they may have on hand, and will refer you to other organizations that are studying this disease. If you can't afford treatment, have your doctor call NIDDK to find out if they are conducting any clinical studies that you might qualify for.

☎ Contact:
National Institute of Diabetes
and Digestive and Kidney Diseases

Building 31
Room 9A04
Bethesda, MD 20892
(301) 496-3583

Room 4A21
Bethesda, MD 20892
(301) 496-4236

THROMBOLYSIS

Clearinghouses/Hotlines

The National Heart, Lung, and Blood Institute (NHLBI) can search the Combined Health Information Database (CHID) and generate a bibliography of resources for you on Thrombolysis. They also will send you any publications and journal articles they may have on hand, and will refer you to other organizations that are studying this disease. If you can't afford treatment, have your doctor call NHLBI to find out if they are conducting any clinical studies that you might qualify for.

☎ Contact:
National Heart, Lung, and Blood Institute
Building 31
Room 4A21
Bethesda, MD 20892
(301) 496-4236

THROMBOPHLEBITIS

Clearinghouses/Hotlines

The National Heart, Lung, and Blood Institute (NHLBI) can search the Combined Health Information Database (CHID) and generate a bibliography of resources for you on Thrombophlebitis. They also will send you any publications and journal articles they may have on hand, and will refer you to other organizations that are studying this disease. If you can't afford treatment, have your doctor call NHLBI to find out if they are conducting any clinical studies that you might qualify for.

☎ Contact:
National Heart, Lung, and Blood Institute
Building 31

THROMBOSIS

Clearinghouses/Hotlines

The National Heart, Lung, and Blood Institute (NHLBI) can search the Combined Health Information Database (CHID) and generate a bibliography of resources for you on Thrombosis. They also will send you any publications and journal articles they may have on hand, and will refer you to other organizations that are studying this disease. If you can't afford treatment, have your doctor call NHLBI to find out if they are conducting any clinical studies that you might qualify for.

☎ Contact:
National Heart, Lung, and Blood Institute
Bldg. 31, Room 4A21
Bethesda, MD 20892
(301) 496-4236

THYROID DISORDERS

Clearinghouses/Hotlines

The National Institute of Diabetes and Digestive and Kidney Diseases's (NIDDK) individual clearinghouses can search the Combined Health Information Database (CHID) and generate a bibliography of resources for you on Thyroid Disorders. They also will send you any publications and journal articles they may have on hand, and will refer you to other organizations that are studying this condition. If you can't afford treatment, have your doctor call NIDDK to find out if they are conducting any clinical studies that you might qualify for.

☎ Contact:
National Institute of Diabetes
and Digestive and Kidney Diseases
Bldg. 31, Room 9A04

Bethesda, MD 20892
(301) 496-3583

THYMOMA

Clearinghouses/Hotlines

The National Cancer Institute (NCI) will send you whatever publications and reprints of journal articles they have on Thymoma. They can also give you information on the state-of-the-art treatment for this disease, including specific treatment information for your stage of cancer. They can also search their Physician's Data Query (PDQ) database to let you know if NCI is conducting any clinical studies on your disease.

☎ Contact:
National Cancer Institute
Bldg. 31, Room 10A24
Bethesda, MD 20892
(800) 4-CANCER
(301) 496-5583

THYROTOXIC MYOPATHY

Clearinghouses/Hotlines

The National Institute of Neurological Disorders and Stroke (NINDS) can send you information they have only in their publications list on Thyrotoxic Myopathy. They cannot refer you to any experts. This Clearinghouse cannot directly give you information about any current clinical studies NINDS might be conducting on this illness, but you can find this information for yourself by looking under the National Institute of Neurological Disorders and Stroke in *Appendix A* at the end of this book.

☎ Contact:
National Institute of Neurological
Disorders and Stroke
Bldg. 31, Room 8A06
Bethesda, MD 20892
(301) 496-5751
(800) 352-9424

THYROTOXIC PERIODIC PARALYSIS

Clearinghouses/Hotlines

The National Institute of Neurological Disorders and Stroke (NINDS) can send you information they have only in their publications list on Thyrotoxic Periodic Paralysis. They cannot refer you to any experts. This Clearinghouse cannot directly give you information about any current clinical studies NINDS might be conducting on this illness, but you can find this information for yourself by looking under the National Institute of Neurological Disorders and Stroke in *Appendix A* at the end of this book.

☎ Contact:
National Institute of Neurological
Disorders and Stroke
Building 31
Room 8A06
Bethesda, MD 20892
(301) 496-5751
(800) 352-9424

TIC DOULOUREUX

Clearinghouses/Hotlines

The National Institute of Neurological Disorders and Stroke (NINDS) can send you information they have only in their publications list on Tic Douloureux (Trigeminal Neuralgia). They cannot refer you to any experts. This Clearinghouse cannot directly give you information about any current clinical studies NINDS might be conducting on this disorder, but you can find this information for yourself by looking under the National Institute of Neurological Disorders and Stroke in *Appendix A* at the end of this book.

☎ Contact:
National Institute of Neurological
Disorders and Stroke
Bldg. 31, Room 8A06
Bethesda, MD 20892

(301) 496-5751
(800) 352-9424

TICKS

Clearinghouses/Hotlines

The National Institute of Allergy and Infectious Diseases (NIAID) can search the Combined Health Information Database (CHID) and generate a bibliography of resources for you on Ticks. They will also send you any publications and journal articles they may have on hand, and will refer you to researchers who are currently studying this condition. If you can't afford treatment, have your doctor call NIAID to find out if they are conducting any clinical studies that you might qualify for.

☎ Contact:
National Institute of Allergy
and Infectious Diseases
Building 31
Room 7A32
Bethesda, MD 20892
(301) 496-5717

TINNITUS

Clearinghouses/Hotlines

The National Institute on Deafness and Other Communication Disorders (NIDCD) will send you whatever publications and reprints of journal articles they have on Tinnitus. If you need further information, they will refer you to other organizations that study this and other related disorders. NIDCD does not conduct any clinical studies for this or any other disorder.

☎ Contact:
National Institute on Deafness
and Other Communication Disorders
Building 31
Room 3C35
Bethesda, MD 20892
(301) 496-7243

(800) 241-1044
(301) 402-0252 (TDD)

The National Institute of Neurological Disorders and Stroke (NINDS) can send you information they have only in their publications list on Tinnitus. They cannot refer you to any experts. This Clearinghouse cannot directly give you information about any current clinical studies NINDS might be conducting on this disorder, but you can find this information for yourself by looking under the National Institute of Neurological Disorders and Stroke in *Appendix A* at the end of this book.

☎ Contact:
National Institute of Neurological
Disorders and Stroke
Building 31
Room 8A06
Bethesda, MD 20892
(301) 496-5751
(800) 352-9424

TOBACCO

See Passive Smoking
See Smoking
See Smokeless Tobacco

TONGUE TIED

Clearinghouses/Hotlines

The National Institute of Deafness and Other Communication Disorders Clearinghouse can provide you with information regarding organizations dealing with this condition.

☎ Contact:
National Institute of Deafness and Other
Communication Disorders Clearinghouse
1010 Wayne Ave.
Suite 300
Silver Spring, MD 20910
(800) 241-1044
(301) 402-9252 (TDD)

TORSION DYSTONIA

Clearinghouses/Hotlines

The National Institute of Neurological Disorders and Stroke (NINDS) can send you information they have only in their publications list on Torsion Dystonia (Dystonia Musculorum Deformans). They cannot refer you to any experts. This Clearinghouse cannot directly give you information about any current clinical studies NINDS might be conducting on this illness, but you can find this information for yourself by looking under the National Institute of Neurological Disorders and Stroke in *Appendix A* at the end of this book.

☎ Contact:
National Institute of Neurological
Disorders and Stroke
Bldg. 31, Room 8A06
Bethesda, MD 20892
(301) 496-5751
(800) 352-9424

TORTICOLLIS

Clearinghouses/Hotlines

The National Institute of Neurological Disorders and Stroke (NINDS) can send you information they have only in their publications list on Torticollis (Wryneck). They cannot refer you to any experts. This Clearinghouse cannot directly give you information about any current clinical studies NINDS might be conducting on this disorder, but you can find this information for yourself by looking under the National Institute of Neurological Disorders and Stroke in *Appendix A* at the end of this book.

☎ Contact:
National Institute of Neurological
Disorders and Stroke
Bldg. 31, Room 8A06
Bethesda, MD 20892
(301) 496-5751
(800) 352-9424

TOURETTE SYNDROME

Clearinghouses/Hotlines

The National Institute of Neurological Disorders and Stroke (NINDS) can send you information they have only in their publications list on Tourette Syndrome. They cannot refer you to any experts. This Clearinghouse cannot directly give you information about any current clinical studies NINDS might be conducting on this disorder, but you can find this information for yourself by looking under the National Institute of Neurological Disorders and Stroke in *Appendix A* at the end of this book.

☎ Contact:
National Institute of Neurological
Disorders and Stroke
Bldg. 31, Room 8A06
Bethesda, MD 20892
(301) 496-5751
(800) 352-9424

The National Institute of Mental Health (NIMH) will send you whatever publications and reprints of articles from texts and journals they have on Tourette Syndrome. They will also refer you to other organizations that are studying this disorder. NIMH will also let you know of any clinical studies that may be studying this disorder and looking for patients.

☎ Contact:
National Institute of Mental Health
5600 Fishers Ln., Room 15C05
Rockville, MD 20857
(301) 443-4515

The National Institute on Deafness and Other Communication Disorders (NIDCD) will send you whatever publications and reprints of journal articles they have on Tourette Syndrome. If you need further information, they will refer you to other organizations that study this and other related disorders. NIDCD does not conduct any clinical studies for this or any other disorder.

☎ Contact:
National Institute on Deafness
and Other Communication Disorders
Bldg. 31, Room 3C35

Bethesda, MD 20892
(301) 496-7243
(800) 241-1044
(301) 402-0252 (TDD)

Free Publications/Videos

The following publications on Tourette Syndrome are available from the National Institute of Neurological Disorders and Stroke, Bldg. 31, Room 8A06, Bethesda, MD 20892; (301) 496-5751 or (800) 352-9424.

- *Tourette Syndrome.* Contains a collection of scientific articles, patient education pamphlets, and addresses of voluntary health associations.
- *Tourette Syndrome.* Fact sheet on symptoms and treatment.

TOXICS

Clearinghouses/Hotlines

The National Pesticide Telecommunications Network, a service of the U.S. Environmental Protection Agency and Texas Tech University, will respond to your non-emergency questions about the effects of pesticides, toxicology and symptoms, environmental effects, disposal and cleanup, and safe use of pesticides. Answers to information requests are given on the telephone or in the next day's mail. Phones are staffed by pesticide specialists with agricultural, environmental and public health backgrounds. It's open 24 hours, 7 days a week.

☎ Contact:
Texas Tech University
Health Sciences Center
Department of Preventative Medicine
and Community Health
National Pesticide Telecommunication
Network (NPTN)
Lubbock, TX 79430
(800) 858-PEST

The Clinical Biochemistry Branch of the Centers

for Disease Control is working to develop technologies to detect, treat, and prevent human toxicant exposures and any adverse health effects resulting from that exposure.

☎ Contact:
Division of Environmental Health
Laboratory Sciences
Centers for Disease Control
1600 Clifton Rd.
Atlanta, GA 30333
(404) 488-4132

The National Institute of General Medical Sciences (NIGMS) will send you whatever information they have on Toxicology and Pharmacology. If necessary they can also refer you to a specific researcher in this area for more information. Keep in mind, though, that NIGMS does not conduct any clinical studies on this or any other issue.

☎ Contact:
National Institute of General
Medical Sciences
Building 31
Room 4A52
Bethesda, MD 20892
(301) 496-7301

National Institute of Environmental Health Sciences (NIEHS) will send you whatever publications and journal articles they can locate on questions about specific Toxics. If necessary they can put you in contact with researchers studying this issue. NIEHS does not conduct any clinical studies.

☎ Contact:
National Institute of Environmental
Health Sciences
P.O. Box 12233
Research Triangle Park, NC 27709
(919) 541-3345

Free Publications/Videos

The following publication on Toxicology is available from the Science & Technology Division, Reference Section, Library of Congress, Washington, DC 20540; (202) 707-5580.

- *Chemical Exposures: Toxicology, Safety, and Risk Assessment.* Reference guide designed to help locate further published material. (#91-11)

The following publications and video on Toxics are available from the Public Information Center, Environmental Protection Agency, 401 M St., SW, Washington, DC 20460; (202) 260-7751.

- *What It Means To You.* A 15-minute video tells businesses and community members about actions they can take to learn about chemicals in the community and steps they can take to plan for the possibility of chemical accidents. They can send you an informational brochure and order form. ($21.50)
- *The Layman's Guide to the Toxic Substances Control Act.*
- *TSCA Assistance Information Service.* Explains the law and how they help in answering your questions.

The following Congressional Research Service (CRS) report on Toxics is available from either of your U.S. Senators' offices at the U.S. Capitol, Washington, DC 20510, or from your Congressional Representative at the U.S. Capitol, Washington, DC 20515. You can also call in your request through the U.S. Capitol switchboard at (202) 224-3121. Be sure to include the full title and report number in your request.

- *Toxic Chemicals: Environmental and Health Issues; Audio Brief.* (#AB50104)

TOXIC SHOCK

Clearinghouses/Hotlines

The Center for Devices and Radiological Health can provide you with information on tampons and Toxic Shock.

☎ Contact:
Center for Devices and
Radiological Health
Food and Drug Administration
HFZ-210
5600 Fishers Lane
Rockville, MD 20857
(301) 443-4690

The National Institute of Child Health and Human Development (NICHD) will send you whatever publications and reprints of journal articles they have on Toxic Shock Syndrome. If necessary, they will refer you to other experts or researchers in the field. If you can't afford treatment, have your doctor call NICHD to find out if they are conducting any clinical studies that you might qualify for.

☎ Contact:
National Institute of Child Health
and Human Development
Bldg. 31, Room 2A32
Bethesda, MD 20892
(301) 496-5133

The National Institute of Allergy and Infectious Diseases (NIAID) can search the Combined Health Information Database (CHID) and generate a bibliography of resources for you on Toxic Shock Syndrome. They will also send you any publications and journal articles they may have on hand, and will refer you to researchers who are currently studying this condition. If you can't afford treatment, have your doctor call NIAID to find out if they are conducting any clinical studies that you might qualify for.

☎ Contact:
National Institute of Allergy
and Infectious Diseases
Building 31
Room 7A32
Bethesda, MD 20892
(301) 496-5717

The Centers for Disease Control's Voice Information System allows anyone using a touchtone phone to obtain pre-recorded information on Toxic Shock Syndrome, and many other conditions. This service offers information about this condition, symptoms and prevention methods, immunization requirements, current statistics, recent disease outbreak, and available printed materials. The system is available 24 hours a day, although the health professionals are available Monday through Friday, 8 a.m.-4:30 p.m. The system can also transfer the caller to a public health professional for additional information.

☎ Contact:
Centers for Disease Control
Information Resources Management Office
Mail Stop C-15
1600 Clifton Rd., NE
Atlanta, GA 30333
(404) 332-4555

The National Institute of Mental Health (NIMH) will send you whatever publications and reprints of articles from texts and journals they have on Toxic Shock Syndrome. They will also refer you to other organizations that are studying this disorder. NIMH will also let you know of any clinical studies that may be studying this disorder and looking for patients.

☎ Contact:
National Institute of Mental Health
5600 Fishers Lane
Room 15C05
Rockville, MD 20857
(301) 443-4515

Free Publications/Videos

The following publication on Toxic Shock Syndrome is available from the Food & Drug Administration, (HFE-88), 5600 Fishers Ln., Rockville, MD 20857; (301) 443-3170.

- *Toxic Shock Syndrome and Tampons*. Explains the symptoms and causes of this syndrome. (#85-4169, FDA)

The following publications on Toxic Shock Syndrome are available from the Center for Devices and Radiological Health, (HFZ-210), Food and Drug Administration, 5600 Fishers Ln., Rockville, MD 20857; (301) 443-4690.

- *Using New Tampon Absorbency Labeling to Help Prevent TSS.*
- *Preventing TSS.*
- *FDA Proposes New Terms For Tampon Absorbency Labeling.*
- *Tampon Absorbency Not Material Increases TSS Risk.*
- *Tampon Standardized Absorbency Information.*
- *Toxic Shock Syndrome and Tampons.* (#FDA 83-4169)

TOXOCARIASIS

Clearinghouses/Hotlines

The National Eye Institute (NEI) can give you up-to-date information on Toxocariasis by searching the Combined Health Information Database (CHID) and MEDLINE and sending you bibliographies of resources, along with any journal articles they may have. They can also refer you to any other organizations that study this and other related conditions. NEI will also let you know of any clinical studies that may be studying this disease and looking for patients. Because of their small staff, NEI prefers that you submit your requests for information in writing.

☎ Contact:
National Eye Institute
Building 31
Room 6A32
Bethesda, MD 20892
(301) 496-5248

TOXOPLASMOSIS

Clearinghouses/Hotlines

The National Institute of Allergy and Infectious Diseases (NIAID) can search the Combined Health Information Database (CHID) and generate a bibliography of resources for you on Toxoplasmosis. They will also send you any publications and journal articles they may have on hand, and will refer you to researchers who are currently studying this disease. If you can't afford treatment, have your doctor call NIAID to find out if they are conducting any clinical studies that you might qualify for.

☎ Contact:
National Institute of Allergy
and Infectious Diseases
Building 31
Room 7A32
Bethesda, MD 20892
(301) 496-5717

The National Eye Institute (NEI) can give you up-to-date information on Toxoplasmosis by searching the Combined Health Information Database (CHID) and MEDLINE and sending you bibliographies of resources, along with any journal articles they may have. They can also refer you to any other organizations that study this and other related conditions. NEI will also let you know of any clinical studies that may be studying this disease and looking for patients.

☎ Contact:
National Eye Institute
Building 31
Room 6A32
Bethesda, MD 20892
(301) 496-5248

Free Publications/Videos

The following publication on Toxoplasmosis is available from the National Institute of Allergy and Infectious Diseases, Building 31, Room 7A32, Bethesda, MD 20892; (301) 496-5717.

- *Toxoplasmosis.* Discusses the hazards to the fetus of the toxoplasma parasites and suggests precautions to prevent the disease. (#83-308)

TRACE ELEMENTS

Clearinghouses/Hotlines

The Grand Forks Human Nutrition Research Center works on defining human requirements for Trace Elements and the physiological and biochemical factors that influence those requirements.

☎ Contact:
Grand Forks Human Nutrition
Research Center
P.O. Box 7166
University Station
Grand Forks, ND 58202-7166
(701) 795-8456

TRACHOMA

Clearinghouses/Hotlines

The National Eye Institute (NEI) can give you up-to-date information on Trachoma by searching the Combined Health Information Database (CHID) and MEDLINE and sending you bibliographies of resources, along with any journal articles they may have. They can also refer you to any other organizations that study this and other related conditions. NEI will also let you know of any clinical studies that may be studying this disease and looking for patients.

☎ Contact:
National Eye Institute
Bldg. 31, Room 6A32
Bethesda, MD 20892
(301) 496-5248

TRANQUILIZERS

Clearinghouses/Hotlines

The National Institute of Mental Health (NIMH) maintains data bases that index and abstract documents from the worldwide literature pertaining to Mental Illness and Tranquilizers. In addition to scientific journals, there are references to audiovisuals, dissertations, government documents and reports. Contact NIMH for searches on specific subjects.

☎ Contact:
National Institute of Mental Health
5600 Fishers Lane, Room 15C05
Rockville, MD 20857
(301) 443-4515

Free Publications/Videos

The following publication on Tranquilizers is available from the Food & Drug Administration, (HFE-88), 5600 Fishers Ln., Rockville, MD 20857; (301) 443-3170.

- *A Guide to the Proper Use of Tranquilizers.* On the safe use of this medicines used for treating intense anxiety disorders. (#86-3158, FDA)

TRANSDERMAL DELIVERY OF DRUGS

Clearinghouses/Hotlines

The Center for Drug Evaluation and Research can provide you with information regarding the Transdermal Delivery of Drugs. They have research reports and articles on the topic.

☎ Contact:
Center for Drug Evaluation and Research
Food and Drug Administration
5600 Fishers Lane
Rockville, MD 20857
(301) 295-8012

Free Publications/Videos

The following publication is available from the National Institute of Child Health and Human Development, Bldg. 31, Room 2A32, Bethesda, MD 20892; (301) 496-5133.

- *Transdermal Delivery of Drugs.* (#91-3075)

TRANSFUSIONS

Clearinghouses/Hotlines

The Center for Biologics Evaluation and Research answers your questions and send you information on biologic products such as vaccines, allergenics, blood, and blood products.

☎ Contact:
Center for Biologics Evaluation and Research
Food and Drug Administration
5600 Fishers Lane
HFB-140

Rockville, MD 20857
(301) 443-7532

Free Publications/Videos

The following publication is available from the National Heart, Lung and Blood Institute, Bldg. 31, Room 4A21, Bethesda, MD 20892; (301) 496-4236.

- *Transfusion Alert: Indications for the Use of Red Blood Cells, Platelets, and Fresh Frozen Plasma.* (#89-2974)

TRANSFUSIONAL HEMOSIDEROSIS

Clearinghouses/Hotlines

The National Heart, Lung, and Blood Institute (NHLBI) can search the Combined Health Information Database (CHID) and generate a bibliography of resources for you on Transfusional Hemosiderosis. They also will send you any publications and journal articles they may have on hand, and will refer you to other organizations that are studying this disease. If you can't afford treatment, have your doctor call NHLBI to find out if they are conducting any clinical studies that you might qualify for.

☎ Contact:
National Heart, Lung, and Blood Institute
Bldg. 31, Room 4A21
Bethesda, MD 20892
(301) 496-4236

TRANSIENT ISCHEMIC ATTACKS

Clearinghouses/Hotlines

The National Institute of Neurological Disorders and Stroke (NINDS) can send you information they have only in their publications list on

Transient Ischemic Attacks. They cannot refer you to any experts. This Clearinghouse cannot directly give you information about any current clinical studies NINDS might be conducting on this topic, but you can find this information for yourself by looking under the National Institute of Neurological Disorders and Stroke in *Appendix A* at the end of this book.

☎ Contact:
National Institute of Neurological
Disorders and Stroke
Building 31
Room 8A06
Bethesda, MD 20892
(301) 496-5751
(800) 352-9424

TRANSPLANTS

Clearinghouses/Hotlines

The National Heart, Lung, and Blood Institute (NHLBI) does experimental research on Heart and Lung Transplants. Current research focuses on immune modulation and organ rejection, as well as on long-term preservation of the heart to allow for transplantation. The staff can refer you to current researchers, and can send you brochures and reports on this procedure.

☎ Contact:
National Heart, Lung, and
Blood Institute
Building 31
Room 5A-52
9000 Rockville Pike
Bethesda, MD 20892
(301) 496-4236

The National Eye Institute (NEI) can give you up-to-date information on Transplantation of the Cornea by searching the Combined Health Information Database (CHID) and MEDLINE and sending you bibliographies of resources, along with any journal articles they may have. They can also refer you to any other organizations that study this and other related conditions. NEI will also let you know of any clinical studies that may be studying this disease and looking for patients.

☎ Contact:
National Eye Institute
Bldg. 31, Room 6A32
Bethesda, MD 20892
(301) 496-5248

The National Institute of Diabetes and Digestive and Kidney Diseases's (NIDDK) individual clearinghouses can search the Combined Health Information Database (CHID) and generate a bibliography of resources for you on Transplants of the Liver, Pancreas, and Kidneys. They also will send you any publications and journal articles they may have on hand, and will refer you to other organizations that are studying this issue. If you can't afford treatment, have your doctor call NIDDK to find out if they are conducting any clinical studies that you might qualify for.

☎ Contact:
National Institute of Diabetes
and Digestive and Kidney Diseases
Bldg. 31, Room 9A04
Bethesda, MD 20892
(301) 496-3583

TRANSVERSE MYELITIS

Clearinghouses/Hotlines

The National Institute of Neurological Disorders and Stroke (NINDS) can send you information they have only in their publications list on Transverse Myelitis. They cannot refer you to any experts. This Clearinghouse cannot directly give you information about any current clinical studies NINDS might be conducting on this illness, but you can find this information for yourself by looking under the National Institute of Neurological Disorders and Stroke in *Appendix A* at the end of this book.

☎ Contact:
National Institute of Neurological
Disorders and Stroke
Bldg. 31, Room 8A06
Bethesda, MD 20892
(301) 496-5751
(800) 352-9424

Free Publications/Videos

The following publication on Transverse Myelitis is available from the National Institute of Neurological Disorders and Stroke, P.O. Box 5801, Bethesda, MD 20824; (800) 352-9424, or (301) 496-5751.

- *Transverse Myelitis*. Contains a collection of scientific articles, patient education pamphlets, and addresses of voluntary health associations.

TRAUMATIC BRAIN INJURIES

See also Head Injuries

Clearinghouses/Hotlines

The National Rehabilitation Information Center (NRIC) has put together a free resource guide for people with traumatic brain injury and their families. This guide has information regarding national organizations, associations, and programs; support groups and state associations of the National Head Injury Foundation, periodicals, catalogs, directories and other sourcebooks, information resources, regional medical libraries, and rehabilitation research and training centers, and lists of books and articles in the NRIC collection that may be of interest to the newly injured person of family member.

☎ Contact:
National Rehabilitation Information Center
8455 Colesville Rd, Suite 935
Silver Spring, MD 20910
(301) 588-9284
(800) 346-2742 (Voice and TDD)

The National Institute of General Medical Sciences will send you whatever information they have on Trauma Research. If necessary they can also refer you to a specific researcher in this area for more information. Keep in mind, though, that NIGMS does not conduct any clinical studies on this or any other condition.

☎ Contact:
National Institute of General
Medical Sciences
Bldg. 31, Room 4A52
Bethesda, MD 20892
(301) 496-7301

The National Institute on Deafness and Other Communication Disorders (NIDCD) will send you whatever publications and reprints of journal articles they have on Trauma Research. If you need further information, they will refer you to other organizations that study this and other related disorders. NIDCD does not conduct any clinical studies for this or any other disorder.

☎ Contact:
National Institute on Deafness
and Other Communication Disorders
Bldg. 31, Room 3C35
Bethesda, MD 20892
(301) 496-7243
(800) 241-1044
(301) 402-0252 (TDD)

TRAVELERS' HEALTH

Clearinghouses/Hotlines

If you're going to be traveling outside the U.S., you might be interested in checking up on any disease outbreaks in the countries you'll be visiting, along with any vaccine requirements you need to follow. The Centers for Disease Control's Voice Information System allows anyone using a touchtone phone to obtain pre-recorded information on international Travelers' Health issues. The system can also transfer the caller to a public health professional for additional information. The system is available 24 hours a day, although the health professionals are available Monday through Friday, 8 a.m.-4:30 p.m.

☎ Contact:
Centers for Disease Control
Information Resources Management Office
Mail Stop C-15, 1600 Clifton Rd., NE
Atlanta, GA 30333
(404) 332-4555

Free Publications/Videos

The following publication on Travelers' Health is available from the National Clearinghouse for Primary Care Information, 8201 Greensboro Dr., Suite 600, McLean, VA 22102; (703) 821-8955.

- *Caribbean Medical Problems*. Reviews tropical and other diseases contracted by visitors to and immigrants from the Caribbean.

TREMORS

Clearinghouses/Hotlines

The National Institute of Neurological Disorders and Stroke (NINDS) can send you information they have only in their publications list on Tremors. They cannot refer you to any experts. This Clearinghouse cannot directly give you information about any current clinical studies NINDS might be conducting on this disorder, but you can find this information for yourself by looking under the National Institute of Neurological Disorders and Stroke in *Appendix A* at the end of this book.

☎ Contact:
National Institute of Neurological
Disorders and Stroke
Bldg. 31, Room 8A06
Bethesda, MD 20892
(301) 496-5751
(800) 352-9424

The National Institute on Deafness and Other Communication Disorders (NIDCD) will send you whatever publications and reprints of journal articles they have on Tremors. If you need further information, they will refer you to other organizations that study this and other related disorders. NIDCD does not conduct any clinical studies for this or any other disorder.

☎ Contact:
National Institute on Deafness
and Other Communication Disorders
Bldg. 31, Room 3C35
Bethesda, MD 20892

(301) 496-7243
(800) 241-1044
(301) 402-0252 (TDD)

Free Publications/Videos

The following publication on Tremors is available from the National Institute of Neurological Disorders and Stroke, P.O. Box 5801, Bethesda, MD 20824; (800) 352-9424, or (301) 496-5751.

- *Tremor*. Contains a collection of scientific articles, patient education pamphlets, and addresses of voluntary health associations.

TRENCH MOUTH

Clearinghouses/Hotlines

The National Institute of Dental Research (NIDR) will send you whatever publications and reprints of journal articles they have on Trench Mouth. As a policy, however, NIDR will not refer you to other organizations or experts who study this condition. If you can't afford treatment, have your doctor call Dr. Albert Guckers at (301) 496-6241 to find out if NIDR is conducting any clinical studies that you might qualify for.

☎ Contact:
National Institute of Dental Research
Bldg. 31, Room 2C35
Bethesda, MD 20892
(301) 496-4261

TRICHINOSIS

Clearinghouses/Hotlines

The National Institute of Allergy and Infectious Diseases (NIAID) can search the Combined Health Information Database (CHID) and generate a bibliography of resources for you on Trichinosis. They will also send you any publications and journal articles they may have on hand, and will refer you to researchers who are currently studying this disease. If you can't afford treatment, have your doctor call NIAID to find out if they are conducting any clinical studies that you might qualify for.

☎ Contact:
National Institute of Allergy
and Infectious Diseases
Bldg. 31, Room 7A32
Bethesda, MD 20892
(301) 496-5717

TRICHOMONIASIS

Clearinghouses/Hotlines

The National Institute of Allergy and Infectious Diseases (NIAID) can search the Combined Health Information Database (CHID) and generate a bibliography of resources for you on Trichomoniasis. They will also send you any publications and journal articles they may have on hand, and will refer you to researchers who are currently studying this disease. If you can't afford treatment, have your doctor call NIAID to find out if they are conducting any clinical studies that you might qualify for.

☎ Contact:
National Institute of Allergy
and Infectious Diseases
Bldg. 31, Room 7A32
Bethesda, MD 20892
(301) 496-5717

TRICHURIASIS

See Strongyloidiasis

TRIGEMINAL NEURALGIA

Free Publications/Videos

The following publication on Trigeminal Neuralgia

is available from the National Institute of Neurological Disorders and Stroke, P.O. Box 5801, Bethesda, MD 20824; (800) 352-9424, or (301) 496-5751.

- *Trigeminal Neuralgia.* Collection of scientific articles, patient education pamphlets, and addresses of voluntary health associations.

TROPHOBLASTIC CANCER

Clearinghouses/Hotlines

The National Cancer Institute (NCI) will send you whatever publications and reprints of journal articles they have on Trophoblastic Cancer. They can also give you information on the state-of-the-art treatment for this disease, including specific treatment information for your stage of cancer. They can also search their Physician's Data Query (Physician's Data Query (PDQ)) database to let you know if NCI is conducting any clinical studies on your disease.

☎ Contact:
National Cancer Institute
Bldg. 31, Room 10A24
Bethesda, MD 20892
(800) 4-CANCER
(301) 496-5583

TROPICAL DISEASES

Clearinghouses/Hotlines

The National Institute of Allergy and Infectious Diseases (NIAID) can search the Combined Health Information Database (CHID) and generate a bibliography of resources for you on Tropical Diseases. They will also send you any publications and journal articles they may have on hand, and will refer you to researchers who are currently studying this disease. If you can't afford treatment, have your doctor call NIAID to find out if they are conducting any clinical studies that you might qualify for.

☎ Contact:
National Institute of Allergy
and Infectious Diseases
Building 31
Room 7A32
Bethesda, MD 20892
(301) 496-5717

The National Institute of Neurological Disorders
and Stroke (NINDS) can send you information
they have only in their publications list on Tropical
Spastic Paraparesis. They cannot refer you to any
experts. This Clearinghouse cannot directly give
you information about any current clinical studies
NINDS might be conducting on this illness, but
you can find this information for yourself by
looking under the National Institute of
Neurological Disorders and Stroke in *Appendix A*
at the end of this book.

☎ Contact:
National Institute of Neurological
Disorders and Stroke
Building 31
Room 8A06
Bethesda, MD 20892
(301) 496-5751
(800) 352-9424

Free Publications/Videos

The following publication on Tropical Diseases is
available from the Office of Technology
Assessment, 600 Pennsylvania Ave., SE,
Washington, DC 20510; (202) 224-8996.

- *Status of Biomedical Research and Related
  Technology for Tropical Diseases*. A report
  to Congress. Ask for the summary report.
  (#H-258)

TROPICAL OILS

Clearinghouses/Hotlines

The Food and Nutrition Information Center can
provide you with a wealth of information on food
and nutrition topics. They have bibliographies

ready and a database through which they can
search any food or nutrition subject.

☎ Contact:
Food and Nutrition Information Center
National Agricultural Library
Room 304
Beltsville, MD 20705
(301) 504-5719

Free Publications/Videos

The following Congressional Research Service
(CRS) report on Tropical Oils is available from
either of your U.S. Senators' offices at the U.S.
Capitol, Washington, DC 20510, or from your
Congressional Representative at the U.S. Capitol,
Washington, DC 20515. You can also call in your
request through the U.S. Capitol switchboard at
(202) 224-3121. Be sure to include the full title
and report number in your request.

- *Labeling of Tropical Oils: Legislation, Health,
  and Trade Issues*. (#87-910 SPR)

TRUNCUS ARTERIOSUS

Clearinghouses/Hotlines

The National Heart, Lung, and Blood Institute
(NHLBI) can search the Combined Health
Information Database (CHID) and generate a
bibliography of resources for you on Truncus
Arteriosus. They also will send you any
publications and journal articles they may have on
hand, and will refer you to other organizations
that are studying this disease. If you can't afford
treatment, have your doctor call NHLBI to find
out if they are conducting any clinical studies that
you might qualify for.

☎ Contact:
National Heart, Lung, and
Blood Institute
Building 31
Room 4A21
Bethesda, MD 20892
(301) 496-4236

TRYPANOSOMIASIS

Clearinghouses/Hotlines

The National Institute of Allergy and Infectious Diseases (NIAID) can search the Combined Health Information Database (CHID) and generate a bibliography of resources for you on Trypanosomiasis. They will also send you any publications and journal articles they may have on hand, and will refer you to researchers who are currently studying this disease. If you can't afford treatment, have your doctor call NIAID to find out if they are conducting any clinical studies that you might qualify for.

☎ Contact:
National Institute of Allergy
and Infectious Diseases
Building 31
Room 7A32
Bethesda, MD 20892
(301) 496-5717

TRYPSINOGEN DEFICIENCY

Clearinghouses/Hotlines

The National Institute of Diabetes and Digestive and Kidney Diseases's (NIDDK) individual clearinghouses can search the Combined Health Information Database (CHID) and generate a bibliography of resources for you on Trypsinogen Deficiency. They also will send you any publications and journal articles they may have on hand, and will refer you to other organizations that are studying this condition. If you can't afford treatment, have your doctor call NIDDK to find out if they are conducting any clinical studies that you might qualify for.

☎ Contact:
National Institute of Diabetes
and Digestive and Kidney Diseases
Building 31
Room 9A04
Bethesda, MD 20892
(301) 496-3583

TUBAL LIGATION

See Contraception
See Sterilization

TUBERCULOSIS

Clearinghouses/Hotlines

The National Institute of Allergy and Infectious Diseases (NIAID) can search the Combined Health Information Database (CHID) and generate a bibliography of resources for you on Tuberculosis. They will also send you any publications and journal articles they may have on hand, and will refer you to researchers who are currently studying this disease. If you can't afford treatment, have your doctor call NIAID to find out if they are conducting any clinical studies that you might qualify for.

☎ Contact:
National Institute of Allergy
and Infectious Diseases
Bldg. 31, Room 7A32
Bethesda, MD 20892
(301) 496-5717

Free Publications/Videos

The following publication is available from the Centers for Disease Control National AIDS Clearinghouse, P.O. Box 6003, Rockville, MD 20849-6003; (800) 458-5231.

- *Tuberculosis: The Connection Between TB and HIV.* (#D484)

TUBEROUS SCLEROSIS

Clearinghouses/Hotlines

The National Institute of Neurological Disorders

and Stroke (NINDS) can send you information they have only in their publications list on Tuberous Sclerosis. They cannot refer you to any experts. This Clearinghouse cannot directly give you information about any current clinical studies NINDS might be conducting on this illness, but you can find this information for yourself by looking under the National Institute of Neurological Disorders and Stroke in *Appendix A* at the end of this book.

☎ Contact:
National Institute of Neurological
Disorders and Stroke
Bldg. 31, Room 8A06
Bethesda, MD 20892
(301) 496-5751
(800) 352-9424

Free Publications/Videos

The following publication on Tuberous Sclerosis is available from the National Institute of Neurological Disorders and Stroke, Bldg. 31, Room 8A06, Bethesda, MD 20892; (301) 496-5751 or (800) 352-9424.

- *Tuberous Sclerosis*. Fact sheet on symptoms and treatment.

TULAREMIA

Clearinghouses/Hotlines

The National Institute of Allergy and Infectious Diseases (NIAID) can search the Combined Health Information Database (CHID) and generate a bibliography of resources for you on Tularemia. They will also send you any publications and journal articles they may have on hand, and will refer you to researchers who are currently studying this disease. If you can't afford treatment, have your doctor call NIAID to find out if they are conducting any clinical studies that you might qualify for.

☎ Contact:
National Institute of Allergy
and Infectious Diseases
Bldg. 31, Room 7A32

Bethesda, MD 20892
(301) 496-5717

TUMORS

See also Cancer

Clearinghouses/Hotlines

The National Cancer Institute (NCI) will send you whatever publications and reprints of journal articles they have on Tumors. They can also give you information on the state-of-the-art treatment for related diseases, including specific treatment information for your stage of cancer. They can also search their Physician's Data Query (PDQ) database to let you know if NCI is conducting any clinical studies on your disease.

☎ Contact:
National Cancer Institute
Bldg. 31, Room 10A24
Bethesda, MD 20892
(800) 4-CANCER
(301) 496-5583

The National Eye Institute (NEI) can give you up-to-date information on Tumors of the Eye by searching the Combined Health Information Database (CHID) and MEDLINE and sending you bibliographies of resources, along with any journal articles they may have. They can also refer you to any other organizations that study this and other related condition. NEI will also let you know of any clinical studies that may be studying this disease and looking for patients.

☎ Contact:
National Eye Institute
Bldg. 31, Room 6A32
Bethesda, MD 20892
(301) 496-5248

The National Institute of Diabetes and Digestive and Kidney Diseases's (NIDDK) individual clearinghouses can search the Combined Health Information Database (CHID) and generate a bibliography of resources for you on Tumors with Endocrine Function. They also will send you any publications and journal articles they may have on hand, and will refer you to other organizations that are studying this condition. If you can't afford treatment, have your doctor call NIDDK to find out if they are conducting any clinical studies that you might qualify for.

☎ Contact:
National Institute of Diabetes
and Digestive and Kidney Diseases
Bldg. 31, Room 9A04
Bethesda, MD 20892
(301) 496-3583

TURNER SYNDROME

Clearinghouses/Hotlines

The National Institute of Child Health and Human Development (NICHD) will send you whatever publications and reprints of journal articles they have on Turner Syndrome. If necessary, they will refer you to other experts or researchers in the field. If you can't afford treatment, have your doctor call NICHD to find out if they are conducting any clinical studies that you might qualify for.

☎ Contact:
National Institute of Child Health
and Human Development
Bldg. 31, Room 2A32
Bethesda, MD 20892
(301) 496-5133

TWINS

Clearinghouses/Hotlines

The National Institute of Child Health and Human Development (NICHD) can provide you with a wealth of information regarding Identical, Fraternal, and Siamese Twins, including articles, research reports, reference materials, and more.

☎ Contact:
National Institute of Child Health
and Human Development
Bldg. 31, Room 2A32

Bethesda, MD 20892
(301) 496-5133

TYPHOID FEVER

Clearinghouses/Hotlines

The National Institute of Allergy and Infectious Diseases (NIAID) can search the Combined Health Information Database (CHID) and generate a bibliography of resources for you on Typhoid Fever. They will also send you any publications and journal articles they may have on hand, and will refer you to researchers who are currently studying this disease. If you can't afford treatment, have your doctor call NIAID to find out if they are conducting any clinical studies that you might qualify for.

☎ Contact:
National Institute of Allergy
and Infectious Diseases
Bldg. 31, Room 7A32
Bethesda, MD 20892
(301) 496-5717

- U -

ULCERS

See also Peptic Ulcers

Clearinghouses/Hotlines

The National Digestive Diseases Information Clearinghouse (NDDIC) can search the Combined Health Information Database (CHID) and generate a bibliography of resources for you on Ulcers. They also will send you any publications and journal articles they may have on hand, and will refer you to other organizations that are studying this condition. If you can't afford treatment, have your doctor call NDDIC to find out if they are conducting any clinical studies that you might qualify for.

☎ Contact:
National Digestive Diseases
Information Clearinghouse
Box NDDIC
Bethesda, MD 20892
(301) 468-6344

Free Publications/Videos

The following publications on Ulcers are available from the National Digestive Diseases Information Clearinghouse, Box NDDIC, Bethesda, MD 20892; (301) 468-6344.

- *Stomach Ulcers.*
- *Ulcers.* Information packet.
- *Therapeutic Endoscopy and Bleeding Ulcers.*
- *Peptic Ulcer.* Discusses diagnosis and treatment. (#85-3800).
- *Therapeutic Endoscopy and Bleeding Ulcers.* 1989 National Institutes of Health Consensus Development Conference Statement issued by an expert panel about the effectiveness and safety of therapeutic endoscopy in the treatment of high-risk patients with bleeding ulcers. (#DD-41)

The following publications on Ulcers are available from the Food & Drug Administration, (HFE-88), 5600 Fishers Ln., Rockville, MD 20857; (301) 443-3170.

- *Ulcers: Screaming Or Silent. Watch 'Em With Care.* (#FDA90-1160)
- *When Digestive Juices Corrode, You've Got An Ulcer.* (#FDA84-1133)

ULCERATIVE COLITIS

Clearinghouses/Hotlines

The National Institute of Diabetes and Digestive and Kidney Diseases's (NIDDK) individual clearinghouses can search the Combined Health Information Database (CHID) and generate a bibliography of resources for you on Ulcerative Colitis. They also will send you any publications and journal articles they may have on hand, and will refer you to other organizations that are studying this disease. If you can't afford treatment, have your doctor call NIDDK to find out if they are conducting any clinical studies that you might qualify for.

☎ Contact:
National Institute of Diabetes
and Digestive and Kidney Diseases
Bldg. 31, Room 9A04
Bethesda, MD 20892
(301) 496-3583

Free Publications/Videos

The following publication on Ulcerative Colitis is available from the National Institute of Diabetes and Digestive and Kidney Diseases, Bldg. 31, Room 9A04, Bethesda, MD 20892; (301) 496-3583.

- *Ulcerative Colitis.* (#90-1597)

ULTRASOUND

Clearinghouses/Hotlines

The National Institute of Child Health and Human Development (NICHD) will send you whatever publications and reprints of journal articles they have on Ultrasound. If necessary, they will refer you to other experts or researchers in the field. If you can't afford treatment, have your doctor call NICHD to find out if they are conducting any clinical studies that you might qualify for.

☎ Contact:
National Institute of Child Health
and Human Development
Bldg. 31, Room 2A32
Bethesda, MD 20892
(301) 496-5133

Free Publications/Videos

The following publications on Ultrasound are available from the National Institute of Child Health and Human Development, Bldg. 31, Room 2A32, Bethesda, MD 20892; (301) 496-5133.

- *Diagnostic Ultrasound Imaging in Pregnancy.* Discusses the biophysics and bioeffects of sonograms, clinical applications, epidemiological studies, and the psychological, legal, and ethical dimensions of ultrasound imaging. (#84-667)
- *The Unknowns of Ultrasound.* Addresses the limitations of ultrasound. (#83-8201)

The following publications on Ultrasound are available from the Center for Devices and Radiological Health, (HFZ-210), FDA, 5600 Fishers Ln., Rockville, MD 20857; (301) 443-4690.

- *A Primer on Medical Imaging: Part II.*
- *The Ultrasonic Therapy Equipment Standard.* (#FDA 85-8240)
- *The Medical Use of Sound.*

UNCONVENTIONAL MEDICINE PRACTICES

See Alternative Medicine Practices

UREMIA

Clearinghouses/Hotlines

The National Institute of Diabetes and Digestive and Kidney Diseases's (NIDDK) individual clearinghouses can search the Combined Health Information Database (CHID) and generate a bibliography of resources for you on Uremia. They also will send you any publications and journal articles they may have on hand, and will refer you to other organizations that are studying this disease. If you can't afford treatment, have your doctor call NIDDK to find out if they are conducting any clinical studies that you might qualify for.

☎ Contact:
National Institute of Diabetes
and Digestive and Kidney Diseases
Bldg. 31, Room 9A04
Bethesda, MD 20892
(301) 496-3583

URINARY INCONTINENCE

See Incontinence

URINARY TRACT DISEASE

Clearinghouses/Hotlines

The National Kidney and Urological Diseases Information Clearinghouse (NKUDIC) can search the Combined Health Information Database (CHID) and generate a bibliography of resources for you on Urinary Tract Diseases and Tumors. They also will send you any publications and journal articles they may have on hand, and will refer you to other organizations that are studying this disease. If you can't afford treatment, have your doctor call NKUDIC to find out if they are conducting any clinical studies that you might qualify for.

☎ Contact:
National Kidney and Urological Diseases
Information Clearinghouse
Box NKUDIC
Bethesda, MD 20892
(301) 468-6345

The National Cancer Institute (NCI) will send you whatever publications and reprints of journal articles they have on Urinary Tract Tumors. They can also give you information on the state-of-the-art treatment for this disease, including specific treatment information for your stage of cancer. They can also search their Physician's Data Query (PDQ) database to let you know if NCI is conducting any clinical studies on your disease.

☎ Contact:
National Cancer Institute
Building 31
Room 10A24
Bethesda, MD 20892
(800) 4-CANCER
(301) 496-5583

Free Publications/Videos

The following publications on Urinary Tract Disease are available from the National Kidney and Urological Diseases Information Clearinghouse, Box NKUDIC, Bethesda, MD 20892; (301) 468-6345.

- *National Kidney and Urologic Diseases Information Clearinghouse.* Main government contact point for information on urologic diseases.
- *Understanding Urinary Tract Infections.* Patient and public education booklet.
- *Urinary Tract Infections.* Bibliography of resources.

UROLITHIASIS

Clearinghouses/Hotlines

The National Institute of Diabetes and Digestive and Kidney Diseases's (NIDDK) individual clearinghouses can search the Combined Health Information Database (CHID) and generate a bibliography of resources for you on Urolithiasis. They also will send you any publications and journal articles they may have on hand, and will refer you to other organizations that are studying this condition. If you can't afford treatment, have your doctor call NIDDK to find out if they are conducting any clinical studies that you might qualify for.

☎ Contact:
National Institute of Diabetes
and Digestive and Kidney Diseases
Bldg. 31, Room 9A04
Bethesda, MD 20892
(301) 496-3583

URTICARIA

Clearinghouses/Hotlines

The National Institute of Allergy and Infectious Diseases (NIAID) can search the Combined Health Information Database (CHID) and generate a bibliography of resources for you on Urticaria. They will also send you any publications and journal articles they may have on hand, and will refer you to researchers who are currently studying this disease. If you can't afford treatment, have your doctor call NIAID to find out if they are conducting any clinical studies that you might qualify for.

☎ Contact:
National Institute of Allergy
and Infectious Diseases
Bldg. 31, Room 7A32
Bethesda, MD 20892
(301) 496-5717

UTERINE CANCER

See also Cancer

Clearinghouses/Hotlines

The National Institute of Child Health and Human Development (NICHD) will send you whatever publications and reprints of journal articles they have on Uterine Cancer. If necessary, they will refer you to other experts or researchers in the field. If you can't afford treatment, have your doctor call NICHD to find out if they are conducting any clinical studies that you might qualify for.

☎ Contact:
National Institute of Child Health
and Human Development
Bldg. 31, Room 2A32
Bethesda, MD 20892
(301) 496-5133

The National Cancer Institute (NCI) will send you whatever publications and reprints of journal

articles they have on Uterine Cancer. They can also give you information on the state-of-the-art treatment for this disease, including specific treatment information for your stage of cancer. They can also search their Physician's Data Query (PDQ) database to let you know if NCI is conducting any clinical studies on your disease.

☎ Contact:
National Cancer Institute
Bldg. 31, Room 10A24
Bethesda, MD 20892
(800) 4-CANCER
(301) 496-5583

Free Publications/Videos

The following publications on Uterine Cancer are available from the National Cancer Institute, Bldg. 31, Room 10A24, Bethesda, MD 20892; (800) 4-CANCER, or (301) 496-5583.

- *Research Report: Cancer of the Uterus.* (#87-171)
- *What You Need to Know About Cancer of the Uterus.* (#91-1562)

UVEITIS

Clearinghouses/Hotlines

The National Eye Institute (NEI) can give you up-to-date information on Uveitis by searching the Combined Health Information Database (CHID) and MEDLINE and sending you bibliographies of resources, along with any journal articles they may have. They can also refer you to any other organizations that study this and other related conditions. NEI will also let you know of any clinical studies that may be studying this disease and looking for patients. Because of their small staff, NEI prefers that you submit your requests for information in writing.

☎ Contact:
National Eye Institute
Bldg. 31, Room 6A32
Bethesda, MD 20892
(301) 496-5248

- V -

VACCINES

Clearinghouses/Hotlines

The Immunization Division of the Centers for Disease Control will send you all kinds of free information and publications about immunization against Vaccine-preventable diseases of young children. They can provide you with reports of the recommendations of the Immunization Practices Advisory Committee, as well as informational pamphlets on the various vaccines all of our children should receive.

☎ Contact:
Immunization Division
Centers for Disease Control
1600 Tullie Circle
Atlanta, GA 30333
(404) 639-1830

The National Institute of Allergy and Infectious Diseases (NIAID) can search the Combined Health Information Database (CHID) and generate a bibliography of resources for you on Vaccines. They will also send you any publications and journal articles they may have on hand, and will refer you to researchers who are currently studying this issue. If you can't afford treatment, have your doctor call NIAID to find out if they are conducting any clinical studies that you might qualify for.

☎ Contact:
National Institute of Allergy
and Infectious Diseases
Building 31
Room 7A32
Bethesda, MD 20892
(301) 496-5717

The Center for Biologics Evaluation and Research answers your questions and sends you information on biologic products such as Vaccines, allergenics, blood, and blood products.

☎ Contact:
Center for Biologics Evaluation and Research
Food and Drug Administration
5600 Fishers Lane
HFB-140
Rockville, MD 20857
(301) 443-7532

By calling this automated telephone health service, you can get all kinds of information sent to you on several diseases and health areas, including symptoms and prevention methods, immunization requirements, current statistics, recent disease outbreak, and available printed materials. Currently, you can get information on AIDS, Chronic fatigue syndrome, cytomegalovirus, encephalitis, enteric diseases, Epstein-Barr, hepatitis, Lyme disease, malaria, rabies, Vaccine-preventable disease, and yellow fever. If you need more information than the message provides, you have the option of being put in contact with a public health professional who will point you in the right direction. The system is available 24 hours a day, although the health professionals are available Monday-Friday 8a.m.-4:30p.m.

☎ Contact:
Disease Hotline
(404) 332-4555

Free Publications/Videos

The following publications on Vaccines are available from the Food & Drug Administration, (HFE-88), 5600 Fishers Ln., Rockville, MD 20857; (301) 443-3170.

- *New Vaccine Protects Against Serious "Day Care" Disease.*
- *Vaccines: Precious Ounces of Prevention.*
- *Shots Adults Shouldn't Do Without.*
- *Childhood Vaccines: A Responsibility to Remember.* (#FDA91-907)
- *Flu Shots. Do You Need One?* (#FDA90-3175)

VAGINITIS

Clearinghouses/Hotlines

The National Institute of Allergy and Infectious Diseases (NIAID) can search the Combined Health Information Database (CHID) and generate a bibliography of resources for you on Vaginitis. They will also send you any publications and journal articles they may have on hand, and will refer you to researchers who are currently studying this condition. If you can't afford treatment, have your doctor call NIAID to find out if they are conducting any clinical studies that you might qualify for.

☎ Contact:
National Institute of Allergy
and Infectious Diseases
Bldg. 31, Room 7A32
Bethesda, MD 20892
(301) 496-5717

VALVULAR HEART DISEASE

Clearinghouses/Hotlines

The National Heart, Lung, and Blood Institute (NHLBI) can search the Combined Health Information Database (CHID) and generate a bibliography of resources for you on Valvular Heart Disease. They also will send you any publications and journal articles they may have on hand, and will refer you to other organizations that are studying this condition. If you can't afford treatment, have your doctor call NHLBI to find out if they are conducting any clinical studies that you might qualify for.

☎ Contact:
National Heart, Lung, and Blood Institute
Bldg. 31, Room 4A21
Bethesda, MD 20892
(301) 496-4236

VARICELLA

Clearinghouses/Hotlines

The National Institute of Neurological Disorders and Stroke (NINDS) can send you information they have only in their publications list on Varicella--Zoster Virus. They cannot refer you to any experts. This Clearinghouse cannot directly give you information about any current clinical studies NINDS might be conducting on this illness, but you can find this information for yourself by looking under the National Institute of Neurological Disorders and Stroke in *Appendix A* at the end of this book.

☎ Contact:
National Institute of Neurological
Disorders and Stroke
Building 31
Room 8A06
Bethesda, MD 20892
(800) 352-9424
(301) 496-5751

VARICOSE VEINS

Clearinghouses/Hotlines

The National Heart, Lung, and Blood Institute (NHLBI) can search the Combined Health Information Database (CHID) and generate a bibliography of resources for you on Varicose Veins. They also will send you any publications and journal articles they may have on hand, and will refer you to other organizations that are studying this condition. If you can't afford treatment, have your doctor call NHLBI to find out if they are conducting any clinical studies that you might qualify for.

☎ Contact:
National Heart, Lung, and Blood Institute
Building 31
Room 4A21
Bethesda, MD 20892
(301) 496-4236

VASCULITIS

Clearinghouses/Hotlines

The National Heart, Lung, and Blood Institute (NHLBI) can search the Combined Health Information Database (CHID) and generate a bibliography of resources for you on Vasculitis. They also will send you any publications and journal articles they may have on hand, and will refer you to other organizations that are studying this condition. If you can't afford treatment, have your doctor call NHLBI to find out if they are conducting any clinical studies that you might qualify for.

☎ Contact:
National Heart, Lung, and Blood Institute
Bldg. 31, Room 4A21
Bethesda, MD 20892
(301) 496-4236

The National Institute of Allergy and Infectious Diseases (NIAID) can search the Combined Health Information Database (CHID) and generate a bibliography of resources for you on Vasculitis. They will also send you any publications and journal articles they may have on hand, and will refer you to researchers who are currently studying this condition. If you can't afford treatment, have your doctor call NIAID to find out if they are conducting any clinical studies that you might qualify for.

☎ Contact:
National Institute of Allergy
and Infectious Diseases
Building 31
Room 7A32
Bethesda, MD 20892
(301) 496-5717

The National Cancer Institute (NCI) will send you whatever publications and reprints of journal articles they have on Vasculitis. They can also give you information on the state-of-the-art treatment for this disease, including specific treatment information for your stage of cancer. They can also search their Physician's Data Query (PDQ) database to let you know if NCI is conducting any clinical studies on your disease.

☎ Contact:
National Cancer Institute
Building 31
Room 10A24
Bethesda, MD 20892
(800) 4-CANCER
(301) 496-5583

VASECTOMIES

See also Contraception
See also Sterilization

Clearinghouses/Hotlines

The National Institute of Child Health and Human Development (NICHD) will send you whatever publications and reprints of journal articles they have on Vasectomies. If necessary, they will refer you to other experts or researchers in the field.

☎ Contact:
National Institute of Child Health
and Human Development
Building 31
Room 2A32
Bethesda, MD 20892
(301) 496-5133

Free Publications/Videos

The following publication on Vasectomies is available from the Family Life Information Exchange, P.O. Box 30146, Bethesda, MD 20814; (301) 585-6636.

- *Information for Men: Your Sterilization Operation*. Includes information on the operation and a 3-part consent form used for all federally funded vasectomies. (#100014)

The following publication on Vasectomies is available from the National Institute of Child Health and Human Development, Bldg. 31, Room 2A32, Bethesda, MD 20892; (301) 496-5133.

- *Facts About Vasectomy Safety.*

VD

See Venereal Disease

VEGETARIANISM

See also Food
See also Nutrition

Free Publications/Videos

The following publication is available from the Food & Nutrition Information Center, National Agricultural Library, Room 304, Beltsville, MD 20705-2351; (301) 504-5719.

- *Vegetarian Nutrition*. Designed to help you locate resources on this topic.

VENEREAL DISEASE

Clearinghouses/Hotlines

The Sexually Transmitted Diseases Hotline offers valuable information to the public about a wide range of sexually transmitted diseases, including Venereal Disease and how to protect yourself from contracting them.

☎ Contact:
National Sexually Transmitted Diseases Hotline
P.O. Box 13827
Research Triangle Park, NC 27709
(800) 227-8922

The National Institute of Allergy and Infectious Diseases (NIAID) can search the Combined Health Information Database (CHID) and generate a bibliography of resources for you on Venereal Disease. They will also send you any publications and journal articles they may have on hand, and will refer you to researchers who are currently studying this condition. If you can't afford treatment, have your doctor call NIAID to find out if they are conducting any clinical studies that you might qualify for.

☎ Contact:
National Institute of Allergy
and Infectious Diseases
Building 31
Room 7A32
Bethesda, MD 20892
(301) 496-5717

Free Publications/Videos

The following Congressional Research Service (CRS) report on Venereal Disease is available from either of your U.S. Senators' offices at the U.S. Capitol, Washington, DC 20510, or from your Congressional Representative at the U.S. Capitol, Washington, DC 20515. You can also call in your request through the U.S. Capitol switchboard at (202) 224-3121. Be sure to include the full title and report number in your request.

- *Fifty State Survey of States Statutes Concerning Venereal Disease as It May Relate to AIDS.* (#87-240 A)

VENEZUELAN EQUINE ENCEPHALITIS

Clearinghouses/Hotlines

The National Institute of Allergy and Infectious Diseases (NIAID) can search the Combined Health Information Database (CHID) and generate a bibliography of resources for you on Venezuelan Equine Encephalitis. They will also send you any publications and journal articles they may have on hand, and will refer you to researchers who are currently studying this condition. If you can't afford treatment, have your doctor call NIAID to find out if they are conducting any clinical studies that you might qualify for.

☎ Contact:
National Institute of Allergy
and Infectious Diseases

Building 31
Room 7A32
Bethesda, MD 20892
(301) 496-5717

VERTIGO

Clearinghouses/Hotlines

The National Institute of Neurological Disorders and Stroke (NINDS) can send you information they have only in their publications list on Vertigo. They cannot refer you to any experts. This Clearinghouse cannot directly give you information about any current clinical studies NINDS might be conducting on this disorder, but you can find this information for yourself by looking under the National Institute of Neurological Disorders and Stroke in *Appendix A* at the end of this book.

☎ Contact:
National Institute of Neurological
Disorders and Stroke
Building 31
Room 8A06
Bethesda, MD 20892
(800) 352-9424
(301) 496-5751

The National Institute on Deafness and Other Communication Disorders (NIDCD) will send you whatever publications and reprints of journal articles they have on Vertigo. If you need further information, they will refer you to other organizations that study this and other related conditions. NIDCD does not conduct any clinical studies for this or any other disorder.

☎ Contact:
National Institute on Deafness
and Other Communication Disorders
Building 31
Room 3C35
Bethesda, MD 20892
(301) 496-7243
(800) 241-1044
(301) 402-0252 (TDD)

VETERAN'S DRUG & ALCOHOL TREATMENT

Clearinghouses/Hotlines

The Veteran's Administration operates diverse programs to benefit veterans and their family members. These benefits include education and rehabilitation, including drug or alcohol treatment. Call or write for booklet describing benefits available for veterans and their dependents.

☎ Contact:
U.S. Department of Veterans Affairs
810 Vermont Ave., NW
Washington, DC 20420
(202) 535-7316

Free Publications/Videos

The following publication on Veterans Benefits is available from the Consumer Information Center, P.O. Box 100, Pueblo, CO 81002.

- *Federal Benefits for Veterans and Dependents.* Lists medical, educational, loan, insurance, compensation, pension, and other programs of the VA and other agencies. (#110Z).

VETERINARY FOOD AND MEDICINE

Clearinghouses/Hotlines

The Center for Veterinary Medicine regulates drugs for all animals, medical devices on the market, and makes sure that food is safe and not mislabeled. Vaccines are regulated by the U.S. Department of Agriculture. This Center makes sure that food labeled as complete and balanced nutrition really is. They also handle all consumer complaints regarding veterinary medicines and food. If your animal gets sick after getting a shot or after eating dinner, the Center can tell you if

other animals have had a similar reaction. They investigate complaints and deal with the companies regarding problem products. For animal vaccines and serums contact the Animal and Plant Health Inspection Service, U.S. Department of Agriculture, Washington, DC 20250; (301) 436-7279.

☎ Contact:
Center for Veterinary Medicine
Communication and Education Branch
Food and Drug Administration
7500 Standish Place
Rockville, MD 20855
(301) 295-8755

VIDEO DISPLAY TERMINALS

Clearinghouses/Hotlines

Over a million people each day sit down to work in front of a terminal, inputting and outputting information. There have been concerns about the risks these terminals present. The National Institute for Occupational Safety and Health (NIOSH) has put together an information booklet, describing Video Display Terminals, the current research on their use, a listing of articles for further information. For your free copy contact:

☎ Contact:
National Institute For Occupational
Safety and Health
4676 Columbia Parkway
Cincinnati, Ohio 45226
(800) 356-4674

Free Publications/Videos

The following Congressional Research Service (CRS) reports on Video Display Terminals are available from either of your U.S. Senators' offices at the U.S. Capitol, Washington, DC 20510, or from your Congressional Representative at the U.S. Capitol, Washington, DC 20515. You can also call in your request through the U.S. Capitol switchboard at (202) 224-3121. Be sure to include the full title and report number in your request.

- *Video Display Terminals (VDT's): Health, Safety, and Labor-Management Issues.* (#87-314 SPR)
- *Video Display Terminals and Problems of Modern Office Health, Safety and Policy: An Update.* (#89-684 SPR)

The following publications on Video Display Terminals are available from the Center for Devices and Radiological Health, (HFZ-210), Food and Drug Administration, 5600 Fishers Lane, Rockville, MD 20857; (301) 443-4690.

- *Use of Video Display Terminals by Pregnant Women.*
- *VDT's Pass Medical Tests.*

VIDEOS AND FILMS

Free Publications/Videos

The U.S. Government's National Library of Medicine contains approximately 22,000 audiovisuals in a variety of formats including Videocassettes, audio-cassettes, 16mm Films, filmstrips, slides, videodiscs and computer software. The best way to identify specific titles is to access a database called AVLINE which is available on the MEDLARS database system. Almost any local university library or hospital library can access this database for you. If you have trouble finding a local source for this database:

☎ Contact:
Reference Section
National Library of Medicine
8600 Rockville Pike
Bethesda, MD 20894
(800) 272-4787

Borrowing Procedures

These audiovisuals are available to the public but only through interlibrary loans. This means that a library has to act as your middleman for obtaining your Video. The library that performs your AVLINE database search or even your local public library can perform the middleman service for you.

The loan period is four weeks, including transit time, and no renewals are granted. The only fee involved is a $7 charge to the library for processing an interlibrary loan request. Your local public library may pass along this charge to you.

Next On Oprah

You can get a video on any medical condition, problem or procedure you can imagine. Below is a sampling of the kinds of titles that are available. You can easily see that you are not likely to find these at your local video store (even in the back room section). But, after this book is printed, you may start seeing some of these videos on the daytime talk shows like Donahue, Oprah and Geraldo. The database shows can even get the following videos:

- *Male Transsexual Case #4 Before Surgery.* An interview between a psychiatrist and a transsexual patient shortly before surgery to remove the testicles and penis, a vagina constructed and silastic implantation in both breasts.
- *Male Transsexual Case #4 After Surgery.* An interview between a psychiatrist and a male transsexual who recently had the surgery mentioned above.
- *Mother of Male Transsexual.* Mother discusses her reaction to the surgery scheduled for the next day in which her son will have his testicles and penis removed and a vaginoplasty performed.
- *Easy To Get* and *Penicillin and Venereal Disease.* These two WWII area, U.S. Army training films portray stories of how military men pick up girls at drug stores and night clubs and have to suffer the consequences of venereal disease.

Sampling Of Available Videos

Chemotherapy
- *Radiation Therapy: Cancer And You*
- *Recent Advances In Drug Therapy*
- *Safety Issues In Handling Cancer Chemotherapy*
- *General Principles Of Cancer Chemotherapy*
- *Chemotherapy*

- Chemotherapy Side-Effects
- Chemotherapy Administration: Current
  Methods
- Cancer Treatment Issues

Cholesterol
- Controlling Cholesterol: American Heart
  Association
- Cholesterol, Diet And Heart Disease

Circumcision
- Newborn Circumcision: Retracting Old Myths
  And Managing New Problems
- Circumcision

Death
- Dealing With Death And Dying
- When The Time Comes
- Hospice: The Special Touch
- Facing Death

Headaches
- Recurrent Headache
- Pitfalls And Pointers In The Management Of
  Chronic Headaches
- The Burdened Shoulder, Diagnosing Joint Pain
- Medical Treatment Of Headache
- Diagnosis & Treatment Of Headache
- Headache (Mechanisms, Causes, Evaluation,
  and Treatment)

Holistic Health
- Holistic Health: Treating The Whole Person
- Mind Over Medicine
- Holistic Medicine In Primary Care
- Dr. Deepak Chopra: Witnessing Spontaneous
  Cures To Seemingly Terminal Illnesses
- Recovering The Soul: A Scientific And Spiritual
  Search
- Stress And The Family: A Holistic Approach
- Health, Mind And Behavior: In Space, Toward
  Peace
- Well & Strong: A Story of Vera Henderson
  Who Cured Her Illness By Using A Holistic
  Medical Center Instead Of Surgery
  Recommended By Her Doctor
- The Primary Prevention Of Coronary Heart
  Disease (A Holistic Approach To Managing
  The Condition)
- Other Lives/Other Selves (The Therapeutic
  Power Of Past Life Regression)

- Medicine Woman, Medicine Man: Traditional
  Holistic Medicine In Middle America

Infertility
- Laparoscopic Infertility Surgery
- Six Phases Of Infertility Treatment: Medical
  And Emotional Aspects
- Hazardous Inheritance: Workplace Dangers To
  Reproductive Health
- Diagnostic Imaging In Fertility Disorders
- Hi-Tech Babies
- Infertility
- In Search Of A Child
- Investigation Of The Infertile Couple
- Male Infertility
- Medical Assistance In Procreation; Should
  Doctors Impose
- Non-Medical Restrictions

Malpractice
- Ten Procedures For Avoiding Medical
  Malpractice
- Malpractice
- Understanding Emergency Room Medical
  Malpractice
- Anatomy Of A Nursing Negligence Case
- Analysis Of Dental Malpractice
- Negligence: Legal Aspects Of Negligence
- Psychological Impact of Malpractice On
  Physicians
- The Malpractice Suit: A Survival Guide For
  Physicians And Their Families
- Medical Risk Management: How To Reduce
  Your Chances Of Being Sued
- Even The Good Guys Get Sued
- Understanding Obstetric Malpractice
- Help With Your Deposition

Masturbation
- Child And Adolescent Behavior
- Sexuality: Its Implications For Nursing Practice

Menopause
- A Clinical Approach To Estrogen Replacement
  Therapy

Penile Implants
- Impotency: Prosthetic Approach To Impotency
- Implantation Of An Inflatable Penile
  Prosthesis In The Treatment Of Erectile
  Impotence

- *Implantation Of A Penile Prosthesis*
- *Transscrotal Approach For Penile Prosthesis Insertion*
- *Evaluation And Treatment Of Impotence With The Jonas Penile Prosthesis*
- *Diagnosing Erectile Problems*

Premenstrual Syndrome
- *Menstrual Cycle Related Mood Disorders*

Prostate
- *Cancer Of The Prostate: An Overview Of Therapies*
- *Screening For Carcinoma Of The Prostate*
- *The Prostate: Ultrasound With MRI Confirmation*
- *Ultrasonically Guided Prostate Biopsy*
- *Anatomy And Pathology Of The Prostate*
- *Cancer Screening (Complete Screening Examination For Skin, Lung, Breast, Cervical, Ovarian, Prostate, And Colorectal Cancers)*
- *Hormonal Treatment For Prostate Cancer*
- *Male Reproductive System*
- *Male Genitalia, Rectum, And Hernias*

Stress Management
- *Time And Stress Management*
- *Less Stress In 5 Easy Steps* (With Ed Asner)
- *Stress Ulcer Disease*
- *Neck Pain: Etiology, Diagnosis, and Management*
- *Occupational Disorders Of Musicians*
- *Lifestyle Modification And Stress Management Objectives*
- *Smokeless Tobacco*
- *Stress-Related Disorders And Their Management Through Biofeedback And Relaxation Training*
- *Managing Stress*
- *Managing Job Related Stress*

Vasectomy
- *Vasectomy (The Five Minute Vasectomy And The Mini Vasectomy)*
- *Vasovasostomy: Vasectomy Reversal*
- *Bob's Vasectomy*
- *Pre-Vasectomy Family Consultation*
- *Vasectomy Operating Procedure*
- *Technique For Office Vasectomy*

VINBLASTINE

Free Publications/Videos

The following publication on Vinblastine is available from the National Cancer Institute, Bldg. 31, Room 10A24, Bethesda, MD 20892; (800) 4-CANCER, or (301) 496-5583.

- *Vinblastina/Vinblastine.* Provides information about side effects, proper usage, and precautions of this anti-cancer drug.

VINCENT'S INFECTION

Clearinghouses/Hotlines

The National Institute of Dental Research (NIDR) will send you whatever publications and reprints of journal articles they have on Vincent's Infection. As a policy, however, NIDR will not refer you to other organizations or experts who study this condition. If you can't afford treatment, have your doctor call Dr. Albert Guckers at (301) 496-6241 to find out if NIDR is conducting any clinical studies that you might qualify for.

☎ Contact:
National Institute of Dental Research
Building 31
Room 2C35
Bethesda, MD 20892
(301) 496-4261

VINCRISTINE

Free Publications/Videos

The following publication on Vincristine is available from the National Cancer Institute, Bldg. 31, Room 10A24, Bethesda, MD 20892; (800) 4-CANCER, or (301) 496-5583.

- *Vincristina/ Vincristine.* Provides information

about side effects, proper usage, and precautions of this anti-cancer drug.

VIRUSES

Clearinghouses/Hotlines

The National Institute of Allergy and Infectious Diseases (NIAID) conducts and supports research on the causes of allergic, immunologic, and infectious diseases, and to develop better means of preventing, diagnosing, and treating illness. Some of the studies underway look at the role of the immune system in chronic diseases, such as arthritis, and at disorders of the immune system, as in asthma. Brochures and reports are available on a wide variety of topics.

☎ Contact:
National Institute of Allergy
and Infectious Diseases
Bldg. 31, Room 7A32
Bethesda, MD 20892
(301) 496-5717

Free Publications/Videos

The following publication is available from the National Institute of Allergy and Infectious Diseases, Bldg. 31, Room 7A32, Bethesda, MD 20892; (301) 496-5717.

- *At the Edge of Life: An Introduction to Viruses.* (#80-433)

VISION

See also Eye Care

Clearinghouses/Hotlines

The National Eye Institute (NEI) can give you up-to-date information on Vision and Aging by searching the Combined Health Information Database (CHID) and MEDLINE and sending you bibliographies of resources, along with any journal articles they may have. They can also refer you to any other organizations that study this and other related issues. NEI will also let you know of any clinical studies that may be studying this issue and looking for patients. Because of their small staff, NEI prefers that you submit your requests for information in writing.

☎ Contact:
National Eye Institute
Bldg. 31, Room 6A32
Bethesda, MD 20892
(301) 496-5248

The National Institute on Aging (NIA) will send you whatever publications and reprints of journal articles they have on Vision and Aging. They cannot refer you to other experts if the information they have isn't sufficient for your purposes.

☎ Contact:
National Institute on Aging
Building 31
Room 5C27
Bethesda, MD 20892
(301) 496-1752

Free Publications/Videos

The following publications on Vision are available from the National Eye Institute, Bldg. 31, Room 6A32, Bethesda, MD 20892; (301) 496-5248.

- *Vision Research: National Plan.* (#83-2469)
- *Vision Research: Report of the Panel on Visual Impairment and Its Rehabilitation, Part Six.* (#83-2476)
- *Measuring the Quality of Life of People With Visual Impairment: Proceedings of a Workshop.* (#90-3078)

The following videos on Vision are available from the Modern Talking Picture Service, 5000 Park St. North, St. Petersburg, FL 33709; (800) 243-MTPS.

- *Rites of Sight - Your Vision: The Second 50 Years.* Video explains normal vision changes and shows how to keep your eyes healthy with proper care.
- *Your Vision, Your Life.* Video introduces different aspects of optometric care.

VITAL STATISTICS

See Health Statistics

VITAMINS

Clearinghouses/Hotlines

The National Institute on Aging (NIA) will send you whatever publications and reprints of journal articles they have on Vitamin Supplements and Aging. They cannot refer you to other experts if the information they have isn't sufficient for your purposes.

☎ Contact:
National Institute on Aging
Building 31
Room 5C27
Bethesda, MD 20892
(301) 496-1752

The National Heart, Lung, and Blood Institute (NHLBI) can search the Combined Health Information Database (CHID) and generate a bibliography of resources for you on Vitamin C, D and E, and Cardiovascular Disease. They also will send you any publications and journal articles they may have on hand, and will refer you to other organizations that are studying this issue. If you can't afford treatment, have your doctor call NHLBI to find out if they are conducting any clinical studies that you might qualify for.

☎ Contact:
National Heart, Lung, and Blood Institute
Building 31
Room 4A21
Bethesda, MD 20892
(301) 496-4236

Free Publications/Videos

The following publication on Vitamins is available from the Food & Drug Administration, (HFE-88), 5600 Fishers Ln., Rockville, MD 20857; (301) 443-3170.

- *Some Facts and Myths of Vitamins*. Covers the government's recommended dietary allowances. (#82-2164)

VITILIGO

Clearinghouses/Hotlines

The National Institute of Arthritis and Musculoskeletal and Skin Diseases (NIAMS) will send you whatever publications and reprints of articles from texts and journals they have on Vitiligo. They will also refer you to other organizations that are studying this disease. NIAMS will also let you know of any clinical studies that may be studying this disease and looking for patients.

☎ Contact:
National Institute of Arthritis
and Musculoskeletal and Skin Diseases
Box AMS
Bethesda, MD 20892
(301) 495-4484

Free Publications/Videos

The following publication is available from the National Arthritis and Musculoskeletal and Skin Diseases Information Clearinghouse, Box AMS, 9000 Rockville Pike, Bethesda, MD 20892; (301) 495-4484.

- *What You Should Know About Vitiligo*. (#AR05, NIH 80-2088)

VITRECTOMY

Clearinghouses/Hotlines

The National Eye Institute (NEI) can give you up-to-date information on Vitrectomy by searching the Combined Health Information Database (CHID) and MEDLINE and sending you bibliographies of resources, along with any journal articles they may have. They can also refer you to any other organizations that study this and other related issues. NEI will also let you know of any clinical studies that may be studying this issue and looking for patients. Because of their small staff, NEI prefers that you submit your requests for information in writing.

☎ Contact:
National Eye Institute
Bldg. 31, Room 6A32
Bethesda, MD 20892
(301) 496-5248

VOCAL CHORD PARALYSIS

Clearinghouses/Hotlines

The National Institute of Neurological Disorders and Stroke (NINDS) can send you information they have only in their publications list on Vocal Cord Paralysis. They cannot refer you to any experts. This Clearinghouse cannot directly give you information about any current clinical studies NINDS might be conducting on this disorder, but you can find this information for yourself by looking under the National Institute of Neurological Disorders and Stroke in *Appendix A* at the end of this book.

☎ Contact:
National Institute of Neurological
Disorders and Stroke
Bldg. 31, Room 8A06
Bethesda, MD 20892
(800) 352-9424
(301) 496-5751

The National Institute on Deafness and Other Communication Disorders (NIDCD) will send you whatever publications and reprints of journal articles they have on Vocal Cord Paralysis. If you need further information, they will refer you to other organizations that this and other related conditions. NIDCD does not conduct any clinical studies for this or any other disorder.

☎ Contact:
National Institute on Deafness
and Other Communication Disorders
Bldg. 31, Room 3C35

Bethesda, MD 20892
(301) 496-7243
(800) 241-1044
(301) 402-0252 (TDD)

VOGT-KOYANAGI DISEASE

Clearinghouses/Hotlines

The National Eye Institute (NEI) can give you up-to-date information on Vogt-Koyanagi Disease by searching the Combined Health Information Database (CHID) and MEDLINE and sending you bibliographies of resources, along with any journal articles they may have. They can also refer you to any other organizations that study this and other related condition. NEI will also let you know of any clinical studies that may be studying this condition and looking for patients. Because of their small staff, NEI prefers that you submit your requests for information in writing.

☎ Contact:
National Eye Institute
Building 31
Room 6A32
Bethesda, MD 20892
(301) 496-5248

VON RECKLINGHAUSEN'S DISEASE

Clearinghouses/Hotlines

The National Institute of Neurological Disorders and Stroke (NINDS) can send you information they have only in their publications list on Von Recklinghausen's Disease. They cannot refer you to any experts. This Clearinghouse cannot directly give you information about any current clinical studies NINDS might be conducting on this illness, but you can find this information for yourself by looking under the National Institute of Neurological Disorders and Stroke in *Appendix A* at the end of this book.

☎ Contact:
National Institute of Neurological
Disorders and Stroke
Bldg. 31, Room 8A06
Bethesda, MD 20892
(800) 352-9424
(301) 496-5751

VON WILLEBRAND'S DISEASE

Clearinghouses/Hotlines

The National Heart, Lung, and Blood Institute (NHLBI) can search the Combined Health Information Database (CHID) and generate a bibliography of resources for you on Von Willebrand's Disease. They also will send you any publications and journal articles they may have on hand, and will refer you to other organizations that are studying this condition. If you can't afford treatment, have your doctor call NHLBI to find out if they are conducting any clinical studies that you might qualify for.

☎ Contact:
National Heart, Lung, and Blood Institute
Bldg. 31, Room 4A21
Bethesda, MD 20892
(301) 496-4236

- W -

WAARDENBURG SYNDROME

Free Publications/Videos

The following publication is available from the

National Institute on Deafness and Other Communication Disorders, Bldg. 31, Room 3C35, Bethesda, MD 20892; (301) 496-7243.

- *Because You Asked About Waardenburg Syndrome.* (#91-3260)

WALDENSTROMS MACROGLOBULINEMIA

Clearinghouses/Hotlines

The National Cancer Institute (NCI) will send you whatever publications and reprints of journal articles they have on Waldenstroms Macroglobulinemia. They can also give you information on the state-of-the-art treatment for this disease, including specific treatment information for your stage of cancer. They can also search their Physician's Data Query (PDQ) database to let you know if NCI is conducting any clinical studies on your disease.

☎ Contact:
National Cancer Institute
Bldg. 31, Room 10A24
Bethesda, MD 20892
(800) 4-CANCER
(301) 496-5583

WALLEYE

Clearinghouses/Hotlines

The National Eye Institute (NEI) can give you up-to-date information on Walleye by searching the Combined Health Information Database (CHID) and MEDLINE and sending you bibliographies of resources, along with any journal articles they may have. They can also refer you to any other organizations that study this and other related condition. NEI will also let you know of any clinical studies that may be studying this disease and looking for patients. • Because of their small staff, NEI prefers that you submit your requests for information in writing.

☎ Contact:
National Eye Institute
Bldg. 31, Room 6A32
Bethesda, MD 20892
(301) 496-5248

WARTS

Clearinghouses/Hotlines

The National Institute of Allergy and Infectious Diseases (NIAID) can search the Combined Health Information Database (CHID) and generate a bibliography of resources for you on Warts. They will also send you any publications and journal articles they may have on hand, and will refer you to researchers who are currently studying this condition.   If you can't afford treatment, have your doctor call NIAID to find out if they are conducting any clinical studies that you might qualify for.

☎ Contact:
National Institute of Allergy
and Infectious Diseases
Bldg. 31, Room 7A32
Bethesda, MD 20892
(301) 496-5717

The National Cancer Institute (NCI) will send you whatever publications and reprints of journal articles they have on Multiple Warts. They can also give you information on the state-of-the-art treatment for this disease, including specific treatment information for your stage of cancer. They can also search their Physician's Data Query (PDQ) database to let you know if NCI is conducting any clinical studies on your disease.

☎ Contact:
National Cancer Institute
Bldg. 31, Room 10A24
Bethesda, MD 20892
(800) 4-CANCER
(301) 496-5583

The National Institute of Arthritis and Musculoskeletal and Skin Diseases (NIAMS) will send you whatever publications and reprints of articles from texts and journals they have on

Multiple Warts. They will also refer you to other organizations that are studying this disease. NIAMS will also let you know of any clinical studies that may be studying this disease and looking for patients.

☎ Contact:
National Institute of Arthritis
and Musculoskeletal and Skin Diseases
Box AMS
Bethesda, MD 20892
(301) 495-4484

WATER

See Drinking Water

WEBER-CHRISTIAN DISEASE

Clearinghouses/Hotlines

The National Institute of Arthritis and Musculoskeletal and Skin Diseases (NIAMS) will send you whatever publications and reprints of articles from texts and journals they have on Weber-Christian Disease. They will also refer you to other organizations that are studying this disease. NIAMS will also let you know of any clinical studies that may be studying this disease and looking for patients.

☎ Contact:
National Institute of Arthritis
and Musculoskeletal and Skin Diseases
Box AMS
Bethesda, MD 20892
(301) 495-4484

The National Institute of Allergy and Infectious Diseases (NIAID) can search the Combined Health Information Database (CHID) and generate a bibliography of resources for you on Weber-Christian Disease. They will also send you any publications and journal articles they may have on hand, and will refer you to researchers who are currently studying this condition. If you can't afford treatment, have your doctor call NIAID to find out if they are conducting any clinical studies that you might qualify for.

☎ Contact:
National Institute of Allergy
and Infectious Diseases
Bldg. 31, Room 7A32
Bethesda, MD 20892
(301) 496-5717

WEGENER'S GRANULOMATOSIS

Clearinghouses/Hotlines

The National Institute of Arthritis and Musculoskeletal and Skin Diseases (NIAMS) will send you whatever publications and reprints of articles from texts and journals they have on Wegener's Granulomatosis. They will also refer you to other organizations that are studying this condition. NIAMS will also let you know of any clinical studies that may be studying this disease and looking for patients.

☎ Contact:
National Institute of Arthritis
and Musculoskeletal and Skin Diseases
Box AMS
Bethesda, MD 20892
(301) 495-4484

The National Institute of Allergy and Infectious Diseases (NIAID) can search the Combined Health Information Database (CHID) and generate a bibliography of resources for you on Wegener's Granulomatosis. They will also send you any publications and journal articles they may have on hand, and will refer you to researchers who are currently studying this condition. If you can't afford treatment, have your doctor call NIAID to find out if they are conducting any clinical studies that you might qualify for.

☎ Contact:
National Institute of Allergy
and Infectious Diseases
Bldg. 31, Room 7A32

Bethesda, MD 20892
(301) 496-5717

WEIGHT LOSS

See Dieting

WERDNIG-HOFFMANN DISEASE

Clearinghouses/Hotlines

The National Institute of Neurological Disorders and Stroke (NINDS) can send you information they have only in their publications list on Werdnig-Hoffmann Disease. They cannot refer you to any experts. This Clearinghouse cannot directly give you information about any current clinical studies NINDS might be conducting on this illness, but you can find this information for yourself by looking under the National Institute of Neurological Disorders and Stroke in *Appendix A* at the end of this book.

☎ Contact:
National Institute of Neurological
Disorders and Stroke
Bldg. 31, Room 8A06
Bethesda, MD 20892
(800) 352-9424
(301) 496-5751

WERNER'S SYNDROME

Clearinghouses/Hotlines

The National Institute of Diabetes and Digestive and Kidney Diseases's (NIDDK) individual clearinghouses can search the Combined Health Information Database (CHID) and generate a bibliography of resources for you on Werner's Syndrome. They also will send you any publications and journal articles they may have on hand, and will refer you to other organizations that are studying this disorder. If you can't afford treatment, have your doctor call NIDDK to find out if they are conducting any clinical studies that you might qualify for.

☎ Contact:
National Institute of Diabetes
and Digestive and Kidney Diseases
Bldg. 31, Room 9A04
Bethesda, MD 20892
(301) 496-3583

WERNICKE'S ENCEPHALOPATHY

Clearinghouses/Hotlines

The National Institute of Neurological Disorders and Stroke (NINDS) can send you information they have only in their publications list on Wernicke's Encephalopathy (Cerebral Beriberi). They cannot refer you to any experts. This Clearinghouse cannot directly give you information about any current clinical studies NINDS might be conducting on this illness, but you can find this information for yourself by looking under the National Institute of Neurological Disorders and Stroke in *Appendix A* at the end of this book.

☎ Contact:
National Institute of Neurological
Disorders and Stroke
Bldg. 31, Room 8A06
Bethesda, MD 20892
(800) 352-9424
(301) 496-5751

WHIPLASH

Clearinghouses/Hotlines

The National Institute of Neurological Disorders and Stroke (NINDS) can send you information they have only in their publications list on Whiplash. They cannot refer you to any experts. This Clearinghouse cannot directly give you information about any current clinical studies NINDS might be conducting on this condition, but you can find this information for yourself by looking under the National Institute of Neurological Disorders and Stroke in *Appendix A* at the end of this book.

☎ Contact:
National Institute of Neurological
Disorders and Stroke
Building 31
Room 8A06
Bethesda, MD 20892
(800) 352-9424
(301) 496-5751

WHOOPING COUGH

Clearinghouses/Hotlines

The National Institute of Allergy and Infectious Diseases (NIAID) can search the Combined Health Information Database (CHID) and generate a bibliography of resources for you on Whooping Cough. They will also send you any publications and journal articles they may have on hand, and will refer you to researchers who are currently studying this condition. If you can't afford treatment, have your doctor call NIAID to find out if they are conducting any clinical studies that you might qualify for.

☎ Contact:
National Institute of Allergy
and Infectious Diseases
Building 31
Room 7A32
Bethesda, MD 20892
(301) 496-5717

Free Publications/Videos

The following publication is available from the Food & Drug Administration, (HFE-88), 5600 Fishers Ln., Rockville, MD 20857; (301) 443-3170.

- *Whooping Cough Still Threatens U.S. Children.*

WIFE ABUSE

See Battered Spouses

WILMS' TUMOR

Clearinghouses/Hotlines

The National Cancer Institute (NCI) will send you whatever publications and reprints of journal articles they have on Wilms' Tumor. They can also give you information on the state-of-the-art treatment for this disease, including specific treatment information for your stage of cancer. They can also search their Physician's Data Query (PDQ) database to let you know if NCI is conducting any clinical studies on your disease.

☎ Contact:
National Cancer Institute
Bldg. 31, Room 10A24
Bethesda, MD 20892
(800) 4-CANCER
(301) 496-5583

Free Publications/Videos

The following publication is available from the National Cancer Institute, Bldg. 31, Room 10A24, Bethesda, MD 20892; (800) 4-CANCER, or (301) 496-5583.

- *Adult Kidney Cancer and Wilms' Tumor.*
(#90-2342)

WILSON DISEASE

Clearinghouses/Hotlines

The National Institute of Diabetes and Digestive and Kidney Diseases's (NIDDK) individual clearinghouses can search the Combined Health Information Database (CHID) and generate a bibliography of resources for you on Wilson Disease. They also will send you any publications and journal articles they may have on hand, and will refer you to other organizations that are studying this disorder. If you can't afford treatment, have your doctor call NIDDK to find out if they are conducting any clinical studies that you might qualify for.

☎ Contact:
National Institute of Diabetes
and Digestive and Kidney Diseases
Building 31
Room 9A04
Bethesda, MD 20892
(301) 496-3583

The National Institute of Neurological Disorders and Stroke (NINDS) can send you information they have only in their publications list on Wilson Disease. They cannot refer you to any experts. This Clearinghouse cannot directly give you information about any current clinical studies NINDS might be conducting on this illness, but you can find this information for yourself by looking under the National Institute of Neurological Disorders and Stroke in *Appendix A* at the end of this book.

☎ Contact:
National Institute of Neurological
Disorders and Stroke
Building 31
Room 8A06
Bethesda, MD 20892
(800) 352-9424
(301) 496-5751

WISKOTT-ALDRICH SYNDROME

Clearinghouses/Hotlines

The National Cancer Institute (NCI) will send you whatever publications and reprints of journal articles they have on Wiskott-Aldrich Syndrome. They can also give you information on the state-of-the-art treatment for this disease, including specific treatment information for your stage of cancer. They can also search their Physician's Data Query (PDQ) database to let you know if NCI is conducting any clinical studies on your disease.

☎ Contact:
National Cancer Institute
Bldg. 31, Room 10A24
Bethesda, MD 20892
(800) 4-CANCER
(301) 496-5583

WOLFF-PARKINSON-WHITE SYNDROME

Clearinghouses/Hotlines

The National Heart, Lung, and Blood Institute (NHLBI) can search the Combined Health Information Database (CHID) and generate a bibliography of resources for you on Wolff-Parkinson-White Syndrome (WPW). They also will send you any publications and journal articles they may have on hand, and will refer you to other organizations that are studying this condition. If you can't afford treatment, have your doctor call NHLBI to find out if they are conducting any clinical studies that you might qualify for.

☎ Contact:
National Heart, Lung, and Blood Institute
Bldg. 31, Room 4A21
Bethesda, MD 20892
(301) 496-4236

WOMEN

See also Battered Spouses

Clearinghouses/Hotlines

The National Heart, Lung, and Blood Institute (NHLBI) can search the Combined Health Information Database (CHID) and generate a bibliography of resources for you on Women's

Health Issues. They also will send you any publications and journal articles they may have on hand, and will refer you to other organizations that are studying this issue. If you can't afford treatment, have your doctor call NHLBI to find out if they are conducting any clinical studies that you might qualify for.

☎ Contact:
National Heart, Lung, and Blood Institute
Building 31
Room 4A21
Bethesda, MD 20892
(301) 496-4236

The National Institute on Aging will send you whatever publications and reprints of journal articles they have on Older Women. They cannot refer you to other experts if the information they have isn't sufficient for your purposes.

☎ Contact:
National Institute on Aging
Building 31
Room 5C27
Bethesda, MD 20892
(301) 496-1752

Free Publications/Videos

The following publication on Women is available from the Family Life Information Exchange, P.O. Box 37299, Washington, DC 20013; (301) 585-6636.

- *Information for Women: Your Sterilization Operation.*

The following publication on Women is available from the National Clearinghouse for Alcohol and Drug Information, P.O. Box 2345, Rockville, MD 20852; (800) 729-6686.

- *Women and Alcohol.* Discussion of women and alcohol. (#RPO716).

The following publication on Women is available from the National Health Information Center, P.O. Box 1133, Washington, DC 20013; (800) 336-4797, or (301) 565-4167 in DC metro area.

- *Women's Health.* Lists many organizations

that provide information on a broad range of topics including gynecological, mitral valve prolapse, osteoporosis. This 6-page reference illustrates the array of organizations offering expertise and information.

The following publication on Women is available from the National Institute on Aging, Bldg. 31, Room 5C27, Bethesda, MD 20892; (301) 496-1752.

- *Resource Directory for Older Women.* (#89-738)

The following publication on Women is available from National Institute of Arthritis and Musculoskeletal and Skin Diseases, Box AMS, 9000 Rockville Pike, Bethesda, MD 20892; (301) 495-4484.

- *What Black Women Should Know About Lupus.* (#91-3219)

The following publication on Women is available from the National Heart, Lung and Blood Institute, Bldg. 31, Room 4A21, Bethesda, MD 20892; (301) 496-4236.

- *The Healthy Heart Handbook for Women.* Answers many questions about women and cardiovascular disease. (#92-2720)

The following publications on Women are available from the Food & Drug Administration, (HFE-88), 5600 Fishers Ln., Rockville, MD 20857; (301) 443-3170.

- *Why Women Don't Get Mammograms (And Why They Should).* (#FDA90-1137)
- *Women and Nutrition: A Menu of Special Needs.* (#FDA91-2247)
- *Women's Health (An FDA Consumer Special Report).* (#FDA91-1181)
- *How To Take Your Medicines: Estrogens.* (FDA91-3186)

The following publication on Women is available from the National Maternal and Child Health Clearinghouse, 38th & R Sts., NW, Washington, DC 20057; (703) 821-8955, ext. 254.

- *Women Helping Women: Networks for Support and Caring.* (#D052)

The following publication on Women is available from the Office of Technology Assessment, Washington, DC 20510-8025; (202) 224-8996.

- *The Menopause, Hormone Therapy, and Women's Health-Background Paper.* (#OTA-BP-BA-88)

The following Congressional Research Service (CRS) reports on Women's health issues are available from either of your U.S. Senators' offices at the U.S. Capitol, Washington, DC 20510, or from your Congressional Representative at the U.S. Capitol, Washington, DC 20515. You can also call in your request through the U.S. Capitol switchboard at (202) 224-3121. Be sure to include the full title and report number in your request.

- *Women's Health Issues; Selected References, 1986-1991.* (#91-606 L)
- *Women and AIDS: Selected References, 1986-1991.* (#91-607 L)
- *Alcohol Use and Abuse by Women.* (#91-680 SPR)
- *Breast Implants: Safety and FDA Regulation.* (#91-842 SPR)
- *Surrogate Mothers: Bibliography-in-Brief 1985-1988.* (#88-268 L)

WORKPLACE DRUG ABUSE

See also Drug Abuse
See also Alcoholism

Clearinghouses/Hotlines

The National Clearinghouse for Alcohol and Drug Information has several free publications and videos dealing with drugs and the workplace.

☎ Contact:
National Clearinghouse for Alcohol and Drug Information
P.O. Box 2345

Rockville, MD 20852
(800) 729-6686

Free Publications/Videos

The following publications on Workplace Drug Abuse are available from the National Clearinghouse for Alcohol and Drug Information, P.O. Box 2345, Rockville, MD 20852; (800) 729-6686.

- *AIDS/HIV Infection and the Workplace: NIDA Workgroup Report Assessment of Laboratory Quality in Urine Drug Testing.*
- *Comprehensive Procedures for Drug Testing in the Workplace.*
- *Drug Abuse Curriculum for Employee Assistance Program Professionals.*
- *Drug Abuse in the Workplace Videotape Series.*
- *Drug-Free Federal Workplace: Executive Order 12564 of September 15, 1988.*
- *Drug-Free Workplace Requirements; Notice and Interim Final Rules.*
- *Drugs in the Workplace, Research and Evaluation Data.*
- *The Fact is...Employee Assistance Contacts Are Available in Every State.*
- *An Employer's Guide to Dealing with Substance Abuse.*
- *Listing of Drug Testing Laboratories Certified by the Department of Health and Human Services.*
- *Mandatory Guidelines for Federal Drug Testing.*
- *Mandatory Guidelines for Federal Workplace Drug Testing Programs; Final Guidelines.*
- *Model Plan for a Comprehensive Drug-Free Workplace Program.*
- *NIDA Capsule: Resources to Address Drugs in the Workplace.*
- *NIDA's Drug-Free Workplace Helpline.*
- *Public Law 100-690. Subtitle D-Drug-Free Workplace Act of 1988.*
- *Drug-Free Workplace Act.*
- *Research on Drugs and the Workplace.*
- *Technical, Scientific, and Procedural Issues of Employee Drug Testing.*
- *What Works: Workplaces Without Drugs.*
- *Workers at Risk: Drugs and Alcohol on the Job.*

WORKPLACE HEALTH AND SAFETY

Clearinghouses/Hotlines

The National Institute for Occupational Safety and Health (NIOSH) conducts research to make workplaces healthier and safer. They respond to urgent requests for assistance from employers, employees, and their representatives where imminent hazards are suspected. Information is available about any aspect of occupational safety and health including lung diseases, cancer, reproductive disorders, neurotoxic disorders, and musculoskeletal injuries. They also have information on chemical hazards, physical hazards, carpal tunnel syndrome, video display terminals, indoor air quality, construction hazards, agricultural hazards, and information for health care workers. They conduct inspections, laboratory and epidemiologic research, publish their findings, and make recommendations for improved working conditions to regulatory agencies. For information on NIOSH or job-related hazards contact the address below.

☏ Contact:
National Institute for Occupational
Safety and Health
4676 Columbia Parkway
Cincinnati, OH 45226
(800) 356-4674

The Occupational Safety and Health Administration (OSHA) encourages employers and employees to reduce workplace hazards and to implement new or improve existing safety and health programs. They provide research on innovative ways of dealing the these problems, maintain a recordkeeping system to monitor job-related injuries and illnesses, develop standards and enforce them, as well as establish training programs. OSHA has an extensive list of publications on a variety of job hazards.

☏ Contact:
Occupational Safety and
Health Administration
U.S. Department of Labor
200 Constitution Ave., NW

Washington, DC 20210
(202) 523-8151

The National Resource Center on Worksite Health Promotion has information about currently operating worksite health promotion programs in American corporations. They also can send you bibliographies of low-cost and free worksite health promotion materials, along with lists of companies that offer health promotion services. The Center's database contains information on descriptions of health promotion programs, information on organizations that can help employers, and abstracts of program evaluations, cost-effectiveness studies, research-based guidelines, and other information.

☎ Contact:
National Resource Center on
Worksite Health Promotion
777 North Capitol St., NE
Suite 800
Washington, DC 20002
(202) 408-9320

Free Publications/Videos

The following publications on Workplace Health and Safety are available from the Occupational Safety and Health Administration, U.S. Department of Labor, 200 Constitution Ave., NW, Washington, DC 20210; (202) 523-8151.

- *Controlling Electrical Hazards*
- *Asbestos Standard for Construction Industry*
- *Hand and Power Tools*
- *Grain Handling*
- *Hearing Conservation*
- *Respiratory Protection*
- *Working Safely with Video Display Terminals*
- *Workplace Health Programs*
- *Program Highlights*. Description of hazards, standards, of OSHA programs or policies.
- *Fatal Facts*. Summarize fatal accidents occurring in the construction industry, the citations issued against the company involved, and the precautions that could be taken to avoid such accidents.
- *Safe Works*. News sheets that provide a brief summary of the results of a small business employer's request for workplace

safety and health assistance from OSHA-funded consultation services.

The following publications on Worksite Health Promotion are available from the National Resource Center on Worksite Health Promotion, 777 North Capitol St., NE, #800, Washington, DC 20002; (202) 408-9320.

- *Healthy People 2000 at Work: Strategies for Employers* ($20)
- *Working for Good Health: Small Business and Health Promotion* ($25)
- *Financial Incentives for Healthy Lifestyles* ($30)
- *Directory of Worksite Health Promotion Resources* ($5)
- *Directory of State Health Promotion Resources for Employers* ($15)
- Worksite Health Promotion Sourcebook (TBA)

The following publications on Workplace Health and Safety are available from the National Clearinghouse for Alcohol and Drug Information, P.O. Box 2345, Rockville, MD 20852; (800) 729-6686.

- *The Fact Is...Employee Assistance Contacts Are Available In Every State*. Covers professional assessment/referral and/or short-term counseling services for motivating and helping employees with alcohol, drug, or mental health problems to seek and accept appropriate help.
- *The Fact Is...Employee Assistance Contacts Are Available In Every State*. Employees with alcohol, drug, or mental health problems can get help through the Employee Assistance Program, which will either give them short term counseling or refer them to other treatment programs.

The following publications on Workplace Health and Safety are available from the National Health Information Center, P.O. Box 1133, Washington, DC 20013; (800) 336-4797, or (301) 565-4167 in the DC metro area.

- *Worksite Nutrition: A Decision Maker's Guide*. Shows employers how to implement nutrition programs in the workplace. ($2, #U-0010)

- *Worksite Nutrition Guide: Health Menu Program.* Practical information about developing worksite nutrition education programs. ($3)
- *Achieving the Year 2000 Health Objectives for the Nation: Strategies for Business and Labor.* What employers can do to promote good health among their employees and to meet the goals for a healthier Nation. ($20)
- *Financial Incentives for Health Lifestyles: Potential and Pitfalls.* A discussion of monetary incentives for promoting healthier lifestyles among employees. Covers practical, legal, ethical, and medical aspects of such plans. ($30)
- *Health Promoting Policies and Programs for Small Business.* A discussion of the challenges facing small businesses that want to improve the health of their employees. ($25)
- *Directory of Federal Worksite Health Promotion Initiatives.* Compilation of projects and research sponsored by the Federal Government to stimulate and improve worksite health promotion in public and private sectors. ($3)
- *The Future of Work and Health: Implications for Health Strategies.* Summarizes emerging trends in work and health and explores issues concerning the development of health care strategies for worksites in the future. ($7)
- *National Survey of Worksite Health Promotion Activities: A Summary.* Reviews the findings of a 1985 telephone survey of a representative sample of worksites with 50 or more employees. ($2)
- *Worksite Wellness Media Reports.* Presents in one volume comprehensive reports on health facts and examples of worksite wellness programs in areas of health especially important to employers and employees. ($3)
- *Worksite Wellness Reports.* Background papers on which some of the reports appearing in the volume cited above are based. ($15)
- *Worksite Nutrition: A Decision Maker's Guide.* Presents rationale for implementing

nutrition programs in the workplace and describes what resources employers need to conduct worksite nutrition programs. ($2)

The following publication on Workplace Health Promotion is available from the National Institute for Occupational Safety and Health, 4676 Columbia Parkway, Cincinnati, OH 45226; (800) 356-4674.

- *Healthy People 2000: National Health Promotion and Disease Prevention Objectives: Occupational Safety and Health.* Outlines the objectives for health promotion and disease prevention in the workplace.

The following publication on Workplace Health and Safety is available from the Office of Technology Assessment, 600 Pennsylvania Ave., SE, Washington, DC 20510; (202) 224-8996.

- *Preventing Illness and Injury in the Workplace.* A report to Congress. Ask for the summary report.

The following publication on Workplace Health and Safety is available from the Superintendent of Documents, Government Printing Office, Washington, DC 20402; (202) 783-3238.

- *Stress Management in Work Settings.* Summarizes and reviews scientific evidence and practical issues relating to worksite stress management, and includes a collection of resources for training materials, products, and equipment. ($9.50, S/N 017-033-00428-5)

The following publications on Workplace Health are available from the National Heart, Lung and Blood Institute, Bldg. 31, Room 4A21, Bethesda, MD 20892; (301) 496-4236.

- *Small Business Basics: Guidelines for Heart and Lung Health at the Workplace.* Guidelines for establishing heart and lung health programs and practices in the workplace. (#87-2719)
- *Play Your Cards Right...Stay Young at Heart:*

A Heart Health Nutrition Education Program. Kit designed to help program planners implement a heart healthy eating program at their worksite cafeteria, restaurant, school, or other eating establishment.

- *National Heart, Lung, and Blood Institute Demonstration Projects in the Workplace: High Blood Pressure Control.* (#84-2119)
- *Worksite Health Promotion and Human Resources: A Hard Look at the Data, Program Summary.* (#85-2644)
- *Make Workplace Wellness Programs Work for Your Company.* (#90-2648)

The following publication on Workplace Health is available from the National Cancer Institute, Bldg. 31, Room 10A24, Bethesda, MD 20892; (800) 4-CANCER or (301) 496-5583.

- *Smoking Policy Package*

WRYNECK

Clearinghouses/Hotlines

The National Institute of Neurological Disorders and Stroke (NINDS) can send you information they have only in their publications list on Wryneck (Torticollis). They cannot refer you to any experts. This Clearinghouse cannot directly give you information about any current clinical studies NINDS might be conducting on this disorder, but you can find this information for yourself by looking under the National Institute of Neurological Disorders and Stroke in *Appendix A* at the end of this book.

☎ Contact:
National Institute of Neurological
Disorders and Stroke
Building 31
Room 8A06
Bethesda, MD 20892
(800) 352-9424
(301) 496-5751

- X -

XANTHINURIA

Clearinghouses/Hotlines

The National Institute of Diabetes and Digestive and Kidney Diseases's (NIDDK) individual clearinghouses can search the Combined Health Information Database (CHID) and generate a bibliography of resources for you on Xanthinuria. They also will send you any publications and journal articles they may have on hand, and will refer you to other organizations that are studying this disease. If you can't afford treatment, have your doctor call NIDDK to find out if they are conducting any clinical studies that you might qualify for.

☎ Contact:
National Institute of Diabetes
and Digestive and Kidney Diseases
Building 31
Room 9A04
Bethesda, MD 20892
(301) 496-3583

XANTHOMATOSIS

Clearinghouses/Hotlines

The National Heart, Lung, and Blood Institute (NHLBI) can search the Combined Health Information Database (CHID) and generate a bibliography of resources for you on Xanthomatosis. They also will send you any publications and journal articles they may have on hand, and will refer you to other organizations that are studying this condition. If you can't afford treatment, have your doctor call NHLBI to find out if they are conducting any clinical studies that you might qualify for.

☎ Contact:
National Heart, Lung, and Blood Institute
Building 31
Room 4A21
Bethesda, MD 20892
(301) 496-4236

XERODERMA PIGMENTOSUM

Clearinghouses/Hotlines

The National Institute of Arthritis and Musculoskeletal and Skin Diseases (NIAMS) will send you whatever publications and reprints of articles from texts and journals they have on Xeroderma Pigmentosum. They will also refer you to other organizations that are studying this condition. NIAMS will also let you know of any clinical studies that may be studying this disease and looking for patients.

☎ Contact:
National Institute of Arthritis
and Musculoskeletal and Skin Diseases
Box AMS
9000 Rockville Pike
Bethesda, MD 20892
(301) 495-4484

The National Cancer Institute (NCI) will send you whatever publications and reprints of journal articles they have on Xeroderma Pigmentosum. They can also give you information on the state-of-the-art treatment for this disease, including specific treatment information for your stage of cancer. They can also search their Physician's Data Query (PDQ) database to let you know if NCI is conducting any clinical studies on your disease.

☎ Contact:
National Cancer Institute
Building 31
Room 10A24
Bethesda, MD 20892
(800) 4-CANCER
(301) 496-5583

XEROPHTALMIA

Clearinghouses/Hotlines

The National Eye Institute (NEI) can give you up-to-date information on Xerophtalmia by searching the Combined Health Information Database (CHID) and MEDLINE and sending you bibliographies of resources, along with any journal articles they may have. They can also refer you to any other organizations that study this and other related condition. NEI will also let you know of any clinical studies that may be studying this disease and looking for patients. Because of their small staff, NEI prefers that you submit your requests for information in writing.

☎ Contact:
National Eye Institute
Bldg. 31, Room 6A32
Bethesda, MD 20892
(301) 496-5248

XEROSTOMIA

See Dry Mouth

X-RAYS

See also Radiation

Clearinghouses/Hotlines

The Food and Drug Administration's Center for Devices and Radiological Health can give you all kinds of information on X-rays and their potential side effects.

☎ Contact:
Center for Devices and Radiological Health
(HFZ-210)
Food and Drug Administration
5600 Fishers Ln.
Rockville, MD 20857
(301) 443-4690

Free Publications/Videos

The following publications on X-Rays are available from the Center for Devices and Radiological Health, (HFZ-210), Food and Drug Administration, 5600 Fishers Ln., Rockville, MD 20857, (301) 443-4690.

- *A Primer on Medical Imaging: Parts I & II.*
- *Dyes Inject Contrast Into X-rays Shades of Gray.*
- *Are Routine Chest X-Rays Really Necessary?* (#FDA 84-8205)
- *Fact Sheet: Diagnostic X-Ray Exposure and Dose.*
- *FDA X-Ray Record Cards.* (#FDA 80-8024)
- *X-Rays: Get The Picture On Protection.* (#FDA 80-8088)
- *Primer on Radiation.* (#FDA 79-8099)
- *Reducing Genetic Risk From X-Rays.* (#FDA 77-8019)
- *We Want You To Know About Television Radiation.* (#FDA 76-8041)
- *Radiation: Benefit vs. Risk.* (#FDA 75-8014)

- Y -

YEAST INFECTIONS

Clearinghouses/Hotlines

The National Institute of Allergy and Infectious Diseases (NIAID) can search the Combined Health Information Database (CHID) and generate a bibliography of resources for you on Yeast Infections. They will also send you any publications and journal articles they may have on hand, and will refer you to researchers who are currently studying this condition. If you can't afford treatment, have your doctor call NIAID to find out if they are conducting any clinical studies that you might qualify for.

☎ Contact:
National Institute of Allergy
and Infectious Diseases
Bldg. 31, Room 7A32
Bethesda, MD 20892
(301) 496-5717

Free Publications/Videos

The following publication is available from the Food & Drug Administration, (HFE-88), 5600 Fishers Ln., Rockville, MD 20857; (301) 443-3170.

- *On Yeast Infections And Other Female Irritations.* (#FDA85-1121)

YELLOW FEVER

Clearinghouses/Hotlines

The National Institute of Allergy and Infectious Diseases (NIAID) can search the Combined Health Information Database (CHID) and generate a bibliography of resources for you on Yellow Fever. They will also send you any publications and journal articles they may have on hand, and will refer you to researchers who are currently studying this condition. If you can't afford treatment, have your doctor call NIAID to find out if they are conducting any clinical studies that you might qualify for.

☎ Contact:
National Institute of Allergy
and Infectious Diseases
Bldg. 31, Room 7A32
Bethesda, MD 20892
(301) 496-5717

The Centers for Disease Control's Voice Information System allows anyone using a touchtone phone to obtain pre-recorded information on Yellow Fever, and many other conditions. This service offers information about this condition, symptoms and prevention methods, immunization requirements, current statistics, recent disease outbreak, and available printed materials. The system is available 24 hours a day,

although the health professionals are available Monday through Friday, 8 a.m.-4:30 p.m. The system can also transfer the caller to a public health professional for additional information.

☎ Contact:
Centers for Disease Control
Information Resources Management Office
Mail Stop C-15
1600 Clifton Rd., NE
Atlanta, GA 30333
(404) 332-4555

- Z -

ZOLLINGER-ELLISON SYNDROME

Clearinghouses/Hotlines

The National Institute of Diabetes and Digestive and Kidney Diseases's (NIDDK) individual clearinghouses can search the Combined Health Information Database (CHID) and generate a bibliography of resources for you on Zollinger-Ellison Syndrome. They also will send you any publications and journal articles they may

have on hand, and will refer you to other organizations that are studying this disorder. If you can't afford treatment, have your doctor call NIDDK to find out if they are conducting any clinical studies that you might qualify for.

☎ Contact:
National Institute of Diabetes
and Digestive and Kidney Diseases
Bldg. 31, Room 9A04
Bethesda, MD 20892
(301) 496-3583

ZOONOSES

Clearinghouses/Hotlines

The National Institute of Allergy and Infectious Diseases (NIAID) can search the Combined Health Information Database (CHID) and generate a bibliography of resources for you on Zoonoses. They will also send you any publications and journal articles they may have on hand, and will refer you to researchers who are currently studying this condition. If you can't afford treatment, have your doctor call NIAID to find out if they are conducting any clinical studies that you might qualify for.

☎ Contact:
National Institute of Allergy
and Infectious Diseases
Bldg. 31, Room 7A32
Bethesda, MD 20892
(301) 496-5717

FREE LEGAL HELP
WITH YOUR HEALTH CARE RIGHTS

The Health Maintenance Organization (HMO) you belong to won't treat you for a condition that your contract says it would.

Your Medicare payments have stopped and you can't get a straight answer about why they have.

Your nursing home is expensive and cold.

You pay thousands a year in insurance premiums, but when it comes time for them to honor your claim, they fight you for every last dime.

That weight loss center told you one thing but you got another, plus a huge bill.

It's not bad enough that health care is expensive, but when you add to that all those out there trying to take advantage of you—not giving you your money's worth, not paying your insurance claim, and just giving you second-rate treatment—it's not surprising that some people just want to give up on the idea of ever getting proper care.

To help you get the care and services you've paid for and are entitled to, we've put together this Section on consumer help. You'll find out where to get action on complaints about nursing homes, doctors, dentists, hospitals, HMOs, insurance companies, and much more.

Many of these consumer resources are federal and state agencies that have been set up especially to combat abuse in the health care field--and they are experts at getting results.

After all, it's one thing for you to tell an insurance company to pay up, but then they get a call from your state's Insurance Commissioner who issued their license to do business, your case will get resolved. Your Medicare/Medicaid case worker might not see things your way, but a call from your U.S. Senator's office might help them be a little more sympathetic to your position. If a hospital turns you down for treatment, a call from the federal agency that pays their bills could help clear up the problem.

Health care is just too expensive to allow yourself to be taken advantage of--the people who work for these agencies enjoy catching people who try to this to you. Give them a call--make their day, and your own.

AGING-RELATED

Type of Complaint

■ The Social Security Administration has stopped your monthly checks because they say you've died.

■ Because of a physical disability, you can no longer walk to the bus stop to go shopping.

■ The food in your nursing home is often cold and horrible tasting.

■ You're having trouble paying your heating bills because your house isn't insulated.

■ Your social security checks aren't enough to pay your monthly bills.

☎ Contact:
State Agencies on Aging
See listing below

Help Available
Information: yes
Investigation: yes
Mediation/Arbitration: yes
Legal advice: yes
Legal representation: no

Besides the general consumer protection services available to the elderly through the state and local consumer protection offices, each state also has Agencies on Aging that help the elderly with all kinds of special problems, such as:

- sheltered housing
- insurance counseling
- adult day care
- in-home care
- employment opportunities
- home delivered meals
- transportation
- recreation
- pharmacy problems
- tax relief on investments
- income finance assistance
- medicaid/medicare counseling
- nursing home information and complaints
- weatherization and home repair
- fuel assistance
- continuing care
- home equity conversion
- social security benefits
- unemployment insurance
- veterans benefits
- legal services
- education

The state Agencies on Aging will often act on your behalf to help you resolve problems that are special to older people. This could involve calling a nursing home, a bus company, or the Social Security Administration for you. And if the aging agencies can't solve the problems directly, they'll often refer you to the state or federal agency that can. For aging-related problems, the state Agencies on Aging are simply the best starting places.

State Agencies on Aging

Alabama
Commission on Aging, 770 Washington Street, ASA Plaza, Suite 470, Montgomery, AL 36130; (205) 242-5743; toll free in-state: (800) 243-5463.

Alaska
Older Alaskans Commission, P.O. Box C, Juneau, AK 99811-0209; (907) 465-3250.

American Samoa
Territorial Administration on Aging, Government of American Samoa, Pago Pago, AS 96799; 011 (684)-1251.

Arizona
Aging and Adult Administration, 1789 West Washington, 958, Phoenix, AZ 85007; (602) 542-4446.

Arkansas
Division of Aging and Adult Services, Department of Human Services, P.O. Box 1437, Little Rock, AR 72203-1437; (501) 682-2441.

California
Department of Aging, 1600 K St., Sacramento, CA 95814; (916) 322-5290.

Colorado
Aging and Adult Services Division, Department of Social Services, 1575 Sherman St., 4th Floor, Denver, CO 80203-1714; (303) 866-3851.

Connecticut
Department on Aging, 175 Main St., Hartford, CT 06106; (203) 566-3238, or toll free in-state: (800) 443-9946.

Delaware
Department of Health and Social Services, Division of Aging, 1901 North DuPont Highway, New Castle, DE 19720; (302) 577-4660, or toll free in-state: (800) 223-9074.

District of Columbia
Office on Aging, 1424 K St., NW, 2nd Floor, Washington, D.C. 20005; (202) 724-5623.

Florida
Aging and Adult Services, 1321 Winewood Blvd., Room 323, Tallahassee, FL 32399-0700; (904) 488-2881.

Georgia
Office of Aging, 878 Peachtree St., NE, Suite 632, Atlanta, GA 30309; (404) 894-5333.

Guam
Office of Aging Government of Guam, P.O. Box 2816, Agana, GU 96910; 011 (671) 734-2942.

Hawaii
Executive Office on Aging, 335 Merchant St., Room 241, Honolulu, HI 96813; (808) 586-0100.

Idaho
Office on Aging, State House, Room 108, Boise, ID 83720; (208) 334-3833.

Illinois
Department on Aging, 421 East Capitol Ave., Springfield, IL 62701; (217) 785-3140, or toll free (800) 252-8966.

Indiana
Division of Aging and Rehabilitation Service, I.N.H.S., 402 W. Washington, Indianapolis, IN 46207-7083; (317) 232-7020, or toll free in-state: (800) 622-4972.

Iowa
Department of Elder Affairs, 914 Grand Ave., Suite 236, Des Moines, IA 50309; (515) 281-5187, or toll free in-state: (800) 532-3213.

Kansas
Department on Aging, Docking State Office Building, 122 South, 915 Southwest Harrison St., Room R122 S, Topeka, KS 66612-4986; (913) 296-4986, or toll free in-state: (800) 432-3535.

Kentucky
Division for Aging Services, Department for Social Services, 275 East Main St., 6th Floor West, Frankfort, KY 40621; (502) 564-6930, or toll free in-state: (800) 372-2991.

Louisiana
Governors Office of Elder Affairs, P.O. Box 80374, Baton Rouge, LA 70898; (504) 925-1700.

Maine
Bureau of the Elderly and Adult Service, Statehouse #11, Station 11, Augusta, ME 04333-0011; (207) 624-5335.

Maryland
Office on Aging, 301 West Preston St., 10th Floor, Baltimore, MD 21201; (301) 225-1100, or toll free in-state: (800) 338-0153.

Massachusetts
Executive Office of Elder Affairs, 1 Ashburton Place, Boston, MA 02108; (617) 727-7750, or toll free in-state: (800) 872-0166.

Michigan
Office of Services to the Aging, P.O. Box 30026, Lansing, MI 48909; (517) 373-8230.

Minnesota
Board on Aging, 444 Lafayette Rd., St. Paul, MN 55155-3843; (612) 296-2544, or toll free in-state: (800) 652- 9747.

Mississippi
Department of Human Services, Division of Aging and Adult Services, 421 West Pascagoula St., Jackson, MS 39203; (601) 949-2070, or toll free in-state: (800) 345-6347.

Missouri
Division of Aging, P.O. Box 1337, Jefferson City, MO 65102; (314) 751-3082, or toll free in-state: (800) 392-0210.

Montana
Governor's Office on Aging, Aging Services Bureau, State Capital Building, P.O. Box 8005, Helena, MT 59604; (406) 444-3111, or toll free in-state: (800) 332-2272.

Nebraska
Department on Aging, State Office Building, P.O. Box 95044, Lincoln, NE 68509; (402) 471-2306, or toll free in-state: (800) 942-7830.

Nevada
Division for Aging Services, Department of Human Resources, 1665 Hot Springs Road, Suite 158, Carson City, NV 89710; (702) 687-4210.

New Hampshire
Division of Elderly and Adult Services, 6 Hazen Dr., Concord, NH 03301; (603) 271-4680, or toll free in-state: (800) 852-3345.

New Jersey
Division on Aging, Department of Community Affairs, 101 South Broad St., CN 807, Trenton, NJ 08625; (609) 292-4833, or toll free in-state: (800) 792-8820.

New Mexico
Agency on Aging, 224 East Palace Ave., Ground Floor, Santa Fe, NM 87501; (505) 827-7640, or toll free in-state: (800) 432-2080.

New York
Office for the Aging, Agency Building 2, ESP, Albany, NY 12223; (518) 474-5731, or toll free in-state: (800) 342-9871.

North Carolina
Division of Aging, Department of Human Resources, 693 Palmer Drive, Call Box 29531, Raleigh, NC 27626-0531; (919) 733-3983.

North Dakota
Aging Services, Department of Human Services, 600 East Blvd., Bismarck, ND 58505; (701) 224-2310, or toll free in-state: (800) 472-2622.

Ohio
Department of Aging, 50 West Broad St., 9th Floor, Columbus, OH 43266-0501; (614) 466-5500, or toll free in-state: (800) 282-1206.

Oklahoma
Special Unit on Aging, P.O. Box 25352, Oklahoma City, OK 73125; (405) 521-2281.

Oregon
Senior Services Division, Department of Human Resources, State of Oregon, 313 Public Service Building, Salem, OR 97310; (503) 378-4728, or toll free in-state: (800) 232-3020.

Pennsylvania
Department of Aging, 231 State St., Barto Building, Harrisburg, PA 17101; (717) 783-1549.

Puerto Rico
Office of Elder Affairs, Call Box 50063, Old San Juan Station, San Juan, PR 00902; (809) 721-0753.

Rhode Island
Department of Elderly Affairs, 160 Pine St., Providence, RI 02903; (401) 277-2880, or toll free in-state: (800) 322-2880.

South Carolina
Commission on Aging, 400 Arbor Drive, Suite 500B, Columbia, SC 29223; (803) 735-0210, or toll free in-state: (800) 868-9095.

South Dakota
Office of Adult Services and Aging, 700 Governors Dr., Pierre, SD 57501; (605) 773- 3656.

Tennessee
Commission on Aging, 706 Church St., Suite 201, Nashville, TN 37243-0860; (615) 741-2056.

Texas
Department on Aging, P.O. Box 12786, Capitol Station, Austin, TX 78711; (512) 444-2727, or toll free in-state: (800) 252-9240.

Utah
Division of Aging and Adult Services, P.O. Box 45500, Salt Lake City, UT 84145-9500; (801) 538-3920.

Vermont
Department of Aging and Disability, 103 South Main St., Waterbury, VT 05671; (802) 241-2400, or toll free in-state: (800) 642-5119.

Virgin Islands
Department of Human Services, Barbel Plaza South, Charlotte Amalie, St. Thomas, VI 00802; (809) 774-0930.

Virginia
Department for the Aging, 700 East Franklin St., 10th Floor, Richmond, VA 23219; (804) 225-2271, or toll free in-state: (800) 552-4464.

Washington
Aging and Adult Services Administration, P.O. Box 15600, Olympia, WA 98504-5600; (206) 493-2500, or toll free in-state: (800) 422-3263.

West Virginia
Commission on Aging, 1900 Kanawha Blvd., East, Charleston, WV 25305-0160; (304) 558-3317.

Wisconsin
Bureau on Aging, P.O. Box 7851, Madison, WI 53707; (608) 266-2536.

Wyoming
Commission on Aging, Hathaway Building, Cheyenne, WY 82002; (307) 777-7986, or toll free in-state: (800) 442-2766.

COSMETICS

Type of Complaint

■ Your lipstick burns your lips.

■ A skin cream gives you a rash.

■ An eyeliner causes eye irritation.

☎ **Contact:**
Food and Drug Administration
5600 Fishers Lane
Rockville, MD 20857
(301) 443-1240

Help Available
Information: yes
Investigation: yes
Mediation/Arbitration: no
Legal advice: yes
Legal representation: no

If you have any complaints about the performance of any cosmetic product, contact the Food and Drug Administration (FDA) regional office nearest you (listed below). When reporting cosmetics complaints involving injury or illness, make sure that you have all of the relevant information available, including where and when you bought it, who manufactured it, the product code on the packaging, and so on.

Although the FDA can't take action against a company based on a product opened by an individual consumer, they may investigate other unopened products from the same manufacturing lot and use those findings to take action against the company if they find further contamination. This may include ordering the product off the store shelves, product recalls, or even fines, depending on the severity of the violation.

Depending on the situation, the FDA may ask you to send the product in question to them, or in urgent cases, they may even arrange to pick up the product from your home. After a laboratory test, the FDA will then send you the results of their chemical analysis of the product. Although the FDA will not sue or seek compensation for you from a company, you can use the FDA analysis report for any action you decide to take on your own.

Food and Drug Administration Regional Offices

California
FDA (HFR-P145), 50 United Nations Plaza, Rm. 524, San Francisco, CA 94102; (415) 556-1364.
FDA (HFR-P245), 1521 West Pico Blvd., Los Angeles, CA 90015; (213) 252-7597.

Colorado
FDA (HFR-SW245), P.O. Box 25087, 6th and Kipling, Denver, CO 80225-0087; (303) 236-3000.

Florida
FDA (HFR-SE245), 7200 Lack Ellenor Dr., Suite

120, Orlando, FL 32809; (407) 855-0900.
FDA (HFR-SE2575), 6601 NW 25th St., P.O. Box 59-2256, Miami, FL 33159-2256; (305) 526-2919.

Georgia
FDA (HFR-SE145), 60 Eighth St., NE, Atlanta, GA 30309; (404) 347-7355.

Illinois
FDA (HFR-MW145), 300 S. Riverside Plaza, Suite 550 South, Chicago, IL 60606; (312) 353-7126.

Indiana
FDA, 101 W. Ohio Street, Suite 1310, Indianapolis, IN 46204; (317) 226-6500.

Louisiana
FDA (HFR-SE445), 4298 Elysian Fields Ave., New Orleans, LA 70122; (504) 589-2420.

Maryland
FDA (HFR-MA245), 900 Madison Ave., Baltimore, MD 21201; (301) 962-3731.

Massachusetts
FDA (HFR-NE245), One Montvale Ave., Stoneham, MA 02180; (617) 279-1675.

Michigan
FDA (HFR-MW245), 1560 E. Jefferson Ave., Detroit, MI 48207; (313) 226-6260.

Minnesota
FDA (HFR-MW345), 240 Hennepin Ave., Minneapolis, MN 55401; (612) 334-4103.

Missouri
FDA (HFR-SW245), Laclede's Landing, 808 N. Collins St., St. Louis, MO 63102; (314) 425-5021.
FDA (HFR-SW345), 1009 Cherry St., Kansas City, MO 64106; (816) 374-6371.

New Jersey
FDA (HFR-MA345), 61 Main St., West Orange, NJ 07052; (201) 645-3265.

New York
FDA, 850 Third Ave., Brooklyn, NY 11232; (718) 965-5725.
FDA (HFR-NE345), 599 Delaware Ave., Buffalo, NY 14202; (716) 846-4483.

Ohio
FDA (HFR-MA445), 1141 Central Parkway, Cincinnati, OH 45202; (513) 684-3501.
FDA (HFR-MA4525), 3820 Central Rd., P.O. Box 838, Brunswick, OH 44212; (216) 273-1038.

Pennsylvania
FDA (HFR-MA145), Room 900 US Customhouse, 2nd and Chestnut Sts., Philadelphia, PA 19106; (215) 597-0837.

Puerto Rico
FDA (HFR-SE545), P.O. Box 5719, Puerto de Tierra Station, San Juan, PR 00906-5719.

Tennessee
FDA (HFR-SE345), 297 Plus Park Blvd., Nashville, TN 37217; (615) 781-5372.

Texas
FDA (HFR-SW145), 3032 Bryan St., Dallas, TX 75204; (214) 655-5315.
FDA (HFR-SW1580), 1445 North Loop West, Suite 420, Houston, TX 77008; (713) 220-2322.
FDA, 10127 Morraco, Suite 119, Room B-406, San Antonio, TX 78206; (512) 229-4528.

Virginia
FDA, 1110 N. Glebe Rd., Suite 250, Arlington, VA 22201; (703) 285-2578.

Washington
FDA (HFR-P345), 22201 23rd Dr., SE, P.O. Box 3012, Bothell, WA 98041-4421; (206) 483-4953.

DOCTORS

Type of Complaint

- Your new nose job makes you look like Porky Pig.

- Your doctor charges you for procedures that weren't performed.

- You thought you were going to have your broken arm set in a cast but ended up having it amputated.

■ Your doctor makes repeated sexual advances toward you, even with his assistants in the room.

■ The surgeon who operated on your hernia left a sponge in your stomach.

☎ **Contact:**
State Medical Examining Boards
See listing below

Help Available
Information: yes
Investigation: yes
Mediation/Arbitration: yes
Legal advice: yes
Legal representation: no

Each state licenses the doctors who practice in it, and each Medical Examining Board will take your complaint and bring it before a panel of doctors and lawyers for review. If they find evidence that a violation of the law or ethical code has taken place, the panel may decide to bring the case up in front of the state Medical Board.

Depending on the complaint, if the doctor is found guilty, he or she could face formal reprimands, suspensions, and license revocations. You can also call these offices and find out if a doctor has been brought up on any public formal hearings involving his/her conduct.

The Medical Boards will also look into billing complaints that you have with your doctor. They'll contact the doctor for his or her side of the dispute and then decide what action should be taken to resolve the problem.

State Medical Examining Boards

Alabama
State Board of Medical Examiners, 848 Washington Ave., or P.O. Box 946, Montgomery, AL 36102-0946; (205) 242-4116.

Alaska
State Medical Board, Frontier State of Alaska Bldg., 3601 C St., Suite 722, Anchorage, AK 99503; (907) 561-2878.

Arizona
State Board of Medical Examiners, 2001 W. Camelback Rd., #300, Phoenix, AZ 85015; (602) 255-3751.

Arkansas
State Medical Board, 2100 River Front Drive, Suite 200, Little Rock, AR 72202; (501) 324-9410.

California
Medical Board of California, 1426 Howe Avenue, Sacramento, CA 98525; (916) 920-6343.

Colorado
Board of Medical Examiners, 1560 Broadway, Suite 1300, Denver, CO 80202-5140; (303) 894-7690.

Connecticut
Division of Medical Quality Assurance, 150 Washington St., Hartford, CT 06106; (203) 566-7398.

Delaware
Board of Medical Practice, Margaret o'Neill Building, 2nd Floor, Federal & Court Sts., Dover, DE 19903; (302) 739-4522.

District of Columbia
Board of Medicine, 605 G St., NW, Room 202, Lower Level, or P.O. Box 37200, Washington, DC 20001-7200; (202) 727-9794.

Florida
Board of Medicine, Northwood Centre #60, 1940 N. Monroe St., Tallahassee, FL 32399-0792; (904) 488-0595.

Georgia
Composite State Board of Medical Examiners, 166 Pryor St., SW, Atlanta, GA 30303; (404) 656-3913.

Hawaii
Board of Medical Examiners, Department of Commerce and Consumer Affairs, 1010 Richard St., or P.O. Box 3469, Honolulu, HI 96801; (808) 586-2708.

Idaho
State Board of Medicine, 280 N. 8th, Suite 202, Statehouse Mail, Boise, ID 83720-2680; (208) 334-2822.

Illinois
Dept. of Professional Regulation, 320 W. Washington St., Springfield, IL 62786; (217) 785-0822.

Indiana
Health Professions Service Bureau, 402 W. Washington, Room 041, Indianapolis, IN 46204; (317) 232-2960.

Iowa
State Board of Medical Examiners, State Capitol Complex, 1209 E. Court Ave., Executive Hills West, Des Moines, IA 50319-0180; (515) 281-5171.

Kansas
State Board of Healing Arts, 235 S. Topeka Blvd., Topeka, KS 66603; (913) 296-7413.

Kentucky
Board of Medical Licensure, Hurtuburne Medical Center, 310 Whittington Pkwy, Suite 1B, Louisville, KY 40222; (502) 429-8046.

Louisiana
State Board of Medical Examiners, 830 Union St. #100, New Orleans, LA 70112; (504) 524-6763.

Maine
Board of Registration In Medicine, State House Station #137, or Two Bangor St., Augusta, ME 04333; (207) 287-3601.

Maryland
Board of Physician Quality Assurance, 4201 Patterson Ave., 3rd Floor, or P.O. Box 2571, Baltimore, MD 21215; (301) 764-4777.

Massachusetts
Board of Registration In Medicine, Ten West St., Boston, MA 02111; (617) 727-3086.

Michigan
Board of Medicine, 611 W. Ottawa Street, or P.O. Box 30018, Lansing, MI 48933; (517) 373-6650.

Minnesota
Board of Medical Examiners, 2700 University Ave. S.E., Suite 106, St. Paul, MN 55114-1080; (612) 642-0538.

Mississippi
State Board of Medical Licensure, 2688-D Insurance Center Dr., Jackson, MS 39216; (601) 354-6645.

Missouri
State Board of Registration For The Healing Arts, 3605 Missouri Blvd., or P.O. Box 4, Jefferson City, MO 65102; (314) 751-0098.

Montana
Board of Medical Examiners, P.O. Box 200513, 111 N. Jackson, Helena, MT 59620-0513; (406) 444-4284.

Nebraska
State Board of Examiners in Medicine and Surgery, 301 Centennial Mall South, or P.O. Box 95007, Lincoln, NE 68509-5007; (402) 471-2115.

Nevada
State Board of Medical Examiners, 1105 Terminal Way, Suite 301, or P.O. Box 7238, Reno, NV 89510; (702) 688-2559.

New Hampshire
Board of Registration in Medicine, Health and Welfare Building, Hazen Dr., Concord, NH 03301; (603) 271-1203.

New Jersey
State Board of Medical Examiners, 28 W. State St., Room 602, Trenton, NJ 08608; (609) 292-4843.

New Mexico
State Board of Medical Examiners, 491 Old Santa Fe Trail, Lamy Building, 2nd Floor, or P.O. Box 20001, Santa Fe, NM 87504; (505) 827-7317.

New York
State Board for Medicine, Room 3023, Cultural Education Center, Empire State Plaza, Albany, NY 12230; (518) 474-3841.

New York Board for Professional Medial Conduct, New York State Department of Health, #438, Corning Tower Building, Empire State Plaza, Albany, NY 12237-0614; (518) 474-8357.

North Carolina
Board of Medical Examiners, P.O. Box 26808, or 1203 Front Street, Raleigh, NC 27609-6608; (919) 828-1212.

North Dakota
State Board of Medical Examiners, City Center Plaza, 418 E. Broadway, Suite 12, Bismarck, ND 58501; (701) 223-9485.

Ohio
State Medical Board, 77 S. High St., 17th Floor, Columbus, OH 43266-0315; (614) 466-3934.

Oklahoma
State Board of Medical Licensure and Supervision, 5104 N. Francis, Suite C, Oklahoma City, OK 73118; (405) 848-2189.

Oregon
Board of Medical Examiners, 620 Crown Plaza, 1500 SW First Ave., Portland, OR 97201-5826; (503) 229-5770.

Pennsylvania
State Board of Medicine, Transportation and Safety Building, Room 612, Commonwealth Ave. & Forster St., Harrisburg, PA 17120; (717) 787-2381.

Puerto Rico
Board of Medical Examiners, Kennedy Ave., ILA Building, Hogar del Obrero Portuario, Piso 8, Puerto Nuevo, PR 00920; (809) 725-8161.

Rhode Island
Board of Licensure and Discipline, Department of Health, 3 Capitol Hill, Cannon Building, Room 205, Providence, RI 02908; (401) 277-3855.

South Carolina
State Board of Medical Examiners, P.O. Box 12245, 1220 Pickens St., Columbia, SC 29211; (803) 734-8901.

South Dakota
State Board of Medical and Osteopathic Examiners, 1323 S. Minnesota Ave., Sioux Falls, SD 57105; (605) 336-1965.

Tennessee
State Board of Medical Examiners, 283 Plus Park Blvd., Nashville, TN 37247-1010; (615) 367-6251.

Texas
State Board of Medical Examiners, 12 Center Creek, #300, Austin, TX 78754; (512) 834-7728.

Utah
Physicians Licensing Board, Division of Occupational and Professional Licensing, Heber M Wells Building, 4th Floor, 160 E. 300 South, Salt Lake City, UT 84145; (801) 530-6628.

Vermont
Board of Medical Practice, Licensing and Registration, Pavilion Office Building, 109 State Street, Montpelier, VT 05609; (802) 828-2674, (800) 439-8683 (VT).

Virginia
Board of Medicine, 6606 W. Broad Street, 4th Floor, Richmond, VA 23230-1770; (804) 662-9925.

Virgin Islands
Board of Medical Examiners, Department of Health, 48 Sugar Estate, St. Thomas, VI 00802; (809) 774-0117.

Washington
Board of Medical Examiners, Department of Health Licensing, 1300 Quince St., EY25, or P.O. Box 866, Olympia, WA 98504; (206) 753-2999.

West Virginia
Board of Medicine, 101 Dee Dr., Charleston, WV 25311; (304) 558-2921.

Wisconsin
Medical Examining Board, 1400 E. Washington Ave., or P.O. Box 8935, Madison, WI 53708; (608) 266-2811.

Wyoming
Board of Medical Examiners, 2301 Central Ave., 2nd floor, Barrett Building, Cheyenne, WY 82002; (307) 777-6463.

FISH AND SEAFOOD

Type of Complaint

■ A can of tuna you opened has bones in it.

■ The processed lobster substitute you bought smells like beef.

■ The clam chowder you bought has half an inch of sand on the bottom of the can.

☎ Contact:
National Marine Fisheries Service
National Oceanic and
Atmospheric Administration
U.S. Department of Commerce
1335 East-West Hwy., Room 6142
Silver Spring, MD 20910
(301) 443-8910

Help Available
Information: yes
Investigation: yes
Mediation/Arbitration: yes
Legal advice: n/a
Legal representation: no

Unlike meat and poultry, the processing of seafood is not regulated by the federal government. The National Marine Fisheries Service (NMFS), however, has a voluntary inspection program for seafood processors that want their products and facilities inspected and graded. Currently only about 12 percent of the seafood processors in the U.S. participate in this program, but the ones that do have to obey any findings of NMFS inspections.

If you've got a complaint about a seafood product, and you want to report it to the NMFS, you'll have to keep a couple of things in mind: 1) The NMFS has authority only over the processing of the seafood, which means that if your complaint has to do with, say, spoilage, the problem could have been caused by the store you bought it from or by the company that shipped the product from the processor. That is not to say that spoilage can't be caused by the processing, but the chances of pinpointing the cause will be more difficult. Whereas finding a rock in your can of tuna is more clearly a processing problem. 2) For the NMFS to act on your complaint, the product must have been processed by a company that is participating in their inspection program.

Once you submit a complaint to the NMFS (see list below for the office nearest you), they'll first look to see if the company that processed the seafood is participating in their inspection program. If the company is participating, the NMFS will contact the company about the complaint and ask them to look into it, or, depending on the seriousness of the problem, the NMFS may inspect the processing company first hand. Either way, if the investigation shows that the processor has a problem with the way they're making the seafood, the NMFS can force them to correct the problem, and if they don't, they can be dropped from participating in the inspection program.

National Marine Fisheries Service Offices

Alaska
P.O. Box 021668, Juneau, AK 99802-1668; (907) 586-7225

Northeast
8484 Georgia Ave., Silver Spring, MD 20910; (301) 427-2300.

Northwest
7600 Sandpoint Way, NE C15700, Seattle, WA 98115; (206) 526-6133

Southeast
9450 Koger Blvd., Suite 106, St. Petersburg, FL 33702; (813) 893-3145

Southwest
300 S. Ferry, Room 2022, Terminal Island, CA.

FREE MEDICAL CARE

Type of Complaint

■ When you ask for information about free medical care at your hospital, they say they don't have any, even though they do.

■ A hospital won't give you free medical care because they say your income is too high, even though it isn't.

■ You end up paying for medical care at a hospital that you wouldn't have had to if they had let you know about how you could get it for free.

☎ **Contact:**
U.S. Department of Health
and Human Resources
Health Resource and Services Administration
Rockville, MD 20857
(800) 492-0359 (in MD)
(800) 638-0742 (outside MD)

Help Available
Information: yes
Investigation: yes
Mediation/Arbitration: yes
Legal advice: yes
Legal representation: no

Under the federal Hill-Burton law, hospitals and other health facilities that receive money for construction and modernization from the federal government must provide certain services free to those who are unable to pay. If you think a facility that is participating in the Hill-Burton program has unfairly denied you free medical care, write the regional office of the U.S. Department of Health and Human Services serving your state listed below.

Be sure to include copies of all relevant documents, along with the names of people and facilities involved. Your complaint will be looked into, and if the investigator finds that a facility has unfairly denied you health care that you are entitled to under the Hill-Burton law, they can demand that the facility provide you with the health care coming to you. In the unlikely event that the hospital refuses to comply, it could have its federal funding cut off.

U.S. Department of Health and Human Services

Region I
John F. Kennedy Federal Building, Room 2100, Government Center, Boston, MA 02203; (617) 565-1500. Serving: Connecticut, Maine, Massachusetts, New Hampshire, Rhode Island, and Vermont.

Region II
Federal Building, 26 Federal Plaza, New York, NY 10278; (212) 264-4600. Serving: New York, New Jersey, Puerto, Rico, and the Virgin Islands.

Region III
P.O. Box 13716, 3535 Market St., Philadelphia, PA 19101; (215) 596-6492. Serving: Delaware, Maryland, Pennsylvania, Virginia, West Virginia, and District of Columbia.

Region IV
101 Marietta Tower, 15th Floor, Atlanta, GA 30323; (404) 331-2442. Serving: Alabama, Florida, Georgia, Kentucky, Mississippi, North Carolina, South Carolina, and Tennessee.

Region V
105 W. Adams St., Chicago, IL 60603; (312) 353-5160. Serving: Illinois, Indiana, Michigan, Minnesota, Ohio, and Wisconsin.

Region VI
1200 Main Tower Building, Room 1100, Dallas, TX 75202; (214) 767-3301. Serving: Arkansas, Louisiana, New Mexico, Oklahoma, and Texas.

Region VII
601 E. 12th St., Kansas City, MO 64106; (816) 426-2821. Serving: Iowa, Kansas, Missouri, and Nebraska.

Region VIII
1961 Stout St., Denver, CO 80294; (303) 844-3372. Serving: Colorado, Montana, North Dakota South Dakota, Utah, and Wyoming.

Region IX
Federal Office Building, 50 United Nations Plaza, San Francisco, CA 94102; (415) 556-6746. Serving: Arizona, California, Hawaii, Nevada, Guam, Trust Territory of Pacific Islands, and American Samoa.

Region X
2201 6th Ave., Seattle, WA 98121; (206) 553-0420. Serving: Alaska, Idaho, Oregon, and Washington.

HEALTH AND SAFETY HAZARDS AT WORK

Type of Complaint

■ The repetitious work on the assembly line at

work is causing chronic pain in your arms and hands.

■ You were fired because you pointed out health hazards on the job to your boss.

■ There is asbestos insulation falling from the ceiling above your desk at work.

■ Your boss continues to make you use power tools with faulty wiring even after you've pointed it out to him.

☎ **Contact:**
Office of Field Programs
Occupational Safety and Health Administration
U.S. Department of Labor
200 Constitution Ave., NW, Room N3603
Washington, DC 20210
(202) 523-8111

Help Available
Information: yes
Investigation: yes
Mediation/Arbitration: yes
Legal advice: yes
Legal representation: yes

Without knowing it, you might be exposed to situations on the job that violate federal health and safety standards. But if you suspect that conditions on your job threaten your health or safety, contact the nearest Occupational Safety and Health Administration (OSHA) regional office nearest you (listed below).

OSHA will review your complaint and decide if a federal OSHA safety standard is possibly being violated. To do this, they will send out an investigator to inspect your work place. If the inspection proves that OSHA laws have been violated, they may give your company a citation, impose financial penalties, and force the company to correct the violation. If the company refuses, OSHA may take them to court to enforce the law.

If you think you've been fired, demoted, transferred, or have experienced other forms of discipline for bringing health and safety violations to the attention to your boss, OSHA will investigate your complaint, and if they find that

you've been mistreated for reporting an OSHA violation, they can force your company to reinstate you with back pay to your former position. Keep in mind, though, that if you feel that you might lose your job by reporting a health violation, contact OSHA directly. To protect your job, OSHA will not tell your company who filed the complaint against them.

Occupational Health and Safety Administration Regional Offices

Atlanta
U.S. Department of Labor, 1371 Peachtree St., NE, Room 111, Atlanta, GA 30367; (404) 347-4495; OSHA: (404) 347-3573.

Boston
U.S. Department of Labor, JFK Building, Room 1612-C, Government Center, Boston, MA 02203; (617) 565-2072; OSHA (617) 565-7164.

Chicago
U.S. Department of Labor, New Federal Building, Room 570B, 230 S. Dearborn St., IL 60604; (312) 353-6976; OSHA: (312) 353-2220.

Dallas
U.S. Department of Labor, 525 Griffin St., Federal Building, Room 840, Dallas, TX 75202; (214) 767-4776; OSHA: (214) 767-4731.

Denver
U.S. Department of Labor, 1412 Federal Office Building, 1961 Stout St., Denver, CO 80294; (303) 844-4235; OSHA: (303) 844-4235.

Kansas City
U.S. Department of Labor, Federal Office Building, Room 2011, 911 Walnut St., Kansas City, MO 64106; (816) 426-5481; OSHA: (816) 426-5861.

New York
U.S. Department of Labor, 201 Varick St., New York, NY 10014; (212) 337-2319; OSHA: (212) 337-2325.

Philadelphia
U.S. Department of Labor, Gateway Building, Room 1310, 3535 Market St., Philadelphia, PA 19104; (215) 596-1139; OSHA: (215) 596-1201.

San Francisco
U.S. Department of Labor, 450 Golden Gate Ave., Room 9418, San Francisco, CA 94102; (415) 744-6673; OSHA: (415) 744-6670.

Seattle
U.S. Department of Labor, Federal Office Building, 909 First Ave., Room 3048, Seattle, WA 98174; (206) 442-7620; OSHA (206) 442-5930.

HEALTH FRAUD

Type of Complaint

- A medical supply company sells you a miracle cure for cancer that turns out to be aspirin.

- A man, posing as a doctor, promises to cure your arthritis by giving you injections of a new drug that turns out to be sugar water.

- The $1,000 cure for AIDS you bought is actually a bottle of multi-vitamins along with advice to drink a lot of water.

☎ Contact:
Your State Consumer Protection Office
See listing below

Help Available
Information: yes
Investigation: yes
Mediation/Arbitration: yes
Legal advice: yes
Legal representation: no

Con artists have been selling miracle cures for diabetes, cancer, arthritis, old age, and hair loss for centuries, and unsuspecting people have been making them rich for just as long. And if you find yourself the victim of one of these scams, contact your state's Consumer Protection Office (listed below).

After receiving your complaint, they will investigate it by contacting the company in question and getting their side of the story. They may then decide to mediate a settlement between you and the company, which could result in you getting your money back and getting the company stopped from continuing their illegal practices.

If a state's Consumer Protection Office gets enough complaints about a particular company, they may decide to start a formal investigation that could result in legal action against the company. If the company is found guilty of fraud, it may be forced to pay back money to the people they cheated and stop selling their product, and they may even have their business license revoked and have to pay civil fines.

State Consumer Protection Offices

Alabama
Consumer Protection Division, Office of Attorney General, 11 S. Union St., Montgomery, AL 36130; (205) 242-7334, or (800) 392-5658 (toll-free in AL).

Alaska
Attorney General, 1031 W. Fourth Ave., Suite 200, Anchorage, AK 99501; (907) 276-3550.

Arizona
Consumer Protection Division, Office of Attorney General, 1275 W. Washington St., Room 259, Phoenix, AZ 85007; (602) 542-3702, or (800) 352-8431 (toll-free in AZ).

Arkansas
Consumer Protection Division, Office of Attorney General, 200 Tower Building, 323 Center St., Suite 200, Little Rock, AR 72201; (501) 682-2341, or (800) 482-8982 (toll-free in AR).

California
Public Inquiry Unit, Office of Attorney General, 1515 K St., Suite 511, or P.O. Box 944255, Sacramento, CA 94244-2550; (916) 322-3360, or (800) 952-5225 (toll-free in CA).

California Department of Consumer Affairs, 1020 N St., Sacramento, CA 95814; (916) 445-0660, (800) 344-9940.

Bureau of Automotive Repair, California Dept. of Consumer Affairs, 10240 Systems Parkway, Sacramento, CA 95827; (916) 366-5100, or (800) 952-5210 (toll-free in CA--auto repair only).

Colorado
Consumer Protection Unit, Office of Attorney General, 1525 Sherman Street, 5th Floor, Denver, CO 80203; (303) 866-5189, (800) 332-2071.

Connecticut
Department of Consumer Protection, State Office Building, 165 Capitol Avenue, Hartford, CT 06106; (203) 566-4999, or (800) 538-CARS, (800) 842-2649 government information (toll-free in CT).

Delaware
Division of Consumer Affairs, Department of Community Affairs, 820 N. French St., 4th Floor, Wilmington, DE 19801; (302) 577-3250.

District of Columbia
Department of Consumer and Regulatory Affairs, 614 H St., N.W., Washington, DC 20001; (202) 727-7000.

Florida
Division of Consumer Services, Mayo Building, Tallahassee, FL 32399-0800; (904) 488-2226, or (800) HELP-FLA (toll-free in FL).

Georgia
Office of Consumer Affairs, 2 Martin Luther King, Jr. Drive, Plaza Level-East Tower, Atlanta, GA 30334; (404) 656-3790, or (800) 869-1123 (toll-free in GA).

Hawaii
Office of Consumer Protection, Department of Commerce and Consumer Affairs, 828 Fort Street Mall, Suite 600B, or P.O. Box 3767, Honolulu, HI 96813-3767; (808) 587-3222.

Illinois
Governor's Office of Citizens Assistance, 222 South College, Room 106, Springfield, IL 62706; (217) 782-0244, or (800) 642-3112 (toll-free in IL).

Indiana
Consumer Protection Division, Office of Attorney General, 219 State House, 200 W. Washington, Indianapolis, IN 46204; (317) 232-6330, or (800) 382-5516 (toll-free in IN).

Iowa
Iowa Citizens' Aide Ombudsman, 215 E. 7th St., Capitol Complex, Des Moines, IA 50319; (515) 281-3592, or (800) 358-5510 (toll-free in IA).

Kansas
Consumer Protection Division, Office of Attorney General, Kansas Judicial Center, 301 West 10th St., Topeka, KS 66612; (913) 296-3751, or (800) 432-2310 (toll-free in KS).

Kentucky
Consumer Protection Division, Office of Attorney General, 209 St. Clair St., Frankfort, KY 40601; (502) 564-2200, or (800) 432-9257 (toll-free in KY).

Louisiana
Consumer Protection Section, Office of Attorney General, State Capitol Building, P.O. Box 94005; Baton Rouge, LA 70804; (504) 342-7013.

Maine
Consumer Assistance Services, Office of Attorney General, State House Station No. 6, Augusta, ME 04333; (207) 289-3716.

Maryland
Consumer Protection Division, Office of Attorney General, 200 St. Paul Pl., Baltimore, MD 21202; (410) 528-8662, or (202) 727-7000 in the Washington, DC metro area.

Massachusetts
Consumer Protection Division, Department of Attorney General, 131 Tremont St., Boston, MA 02111; (617) 727-8400.

Michigan
Consumer Protection Division, Office of Attorney General, P.O. Box 30213, Lansing, MI 48909; (517) 373-1140.

Minnesota
Office of Consumer Services, Office of Attorney General, 1440 N.C.L. Tower, 455 Minnesota Street, St. Paul, MN 55101; (612) 296-3353.

Mississippi
Consumer Protection Division, Office of Attorney General, P.O. Box 22947, Jackson, MS 39225; (601) 354-6018.

Missouri
Public Protection Division, Office of Attorney

General, P.O. Box 899, Jefferson City, MO 65102; (314) 751-3321, or (800) 392-8222 (toll-free in MO).

Montana
Office of Consumer Affairs, Department of Commerce, 1424 9th Ave., Helena, MT 59620; (406) 444-4312.

Nebraska
Consumer Protection Division, Office of Attorney General, 2115 State Capitol, Room 2115, Lincoln, NE 68509; (402) 471-2682.

Nevada
Consumer Affairs Division, Department of Commerce, 4600 Kietezke Lane, Bldg B, Suite 113, Reno, NV 89502; (702) 688-1800, or (800) 992-0900 (NV only).

New Hampshire
Consumer Protection and Antitrust Bureau, Office of Attorney General, 25 Capitol St., Concord, NH 03301-0397; (603) 271-3641.

New Jersey
Department of the Public Advocate, 25 Market St., CN 850, Trenton, NJ 08625; (609) 292-7087, or (800) 792-8600 (toll-free in NJ).

New Mexico
Consumer and Economic Crime Division, Office of Attorney General, P.O. Drawer 1508, Santa Fe, NM 87504; (505) 827-6060, or (800) 678-1508 (toll-free in NM).

New York
Bureau of Consumer Frauds and Protection, NY State Department of Law, The Capitol, Albany, NY 12224; (518) 474-5481.

Bureau of Consumer Frauds and Protection, Office of Attorney General, 120 Broadway, Manhattan, NY 10271; (212) 416-8345.

North Carolina
Consumer Protection Division, Office of Attorney General, P.O. Box 629, Raleigh, NC 27602; (919) 733-7741.

North Dakota
Consumer Fraud Division, Office of Attorney

General, 600 E. Boulevard, Bismarck, ND 58505; (701) 224-3404, or (800) 472-2600 (toll-free in ND).

Ohio
Consumer Protection Division, Office of Attorney General, 30 E. Broad St., State Office Tower, 25th Floor, Columbus, OH 43266-0410; (614) 466-4986, or (800) 282-0515 (toll-free in OH).

Oklahoma
Consumer Protection Unit, Office of Attorney General, 2300 N. Lincoln, Room 112, 112 State Capitol Building, Oklahoma City, OK 73105-4894; (405) 521-3921.

Oregon
Financial Fraud Section, Consumer Complaints, Department of Justice, Justice Building, Salem, OR 97310; (503) 378-4320.

Pennsylvania
Bureau of Consumer Protection, Office of Attorney General, Strawberry Square, 14th Floor, Harrisburg, PA 17120; (717) 787-9707, or (800) 441-2555 (toll-free in PA).

Puerto Rico
Department of Consumer Affairs, Minillas Station, P.O. Box 41059, Santurce, PR 00940; (809) 722-7555.

Rhode Island
Consumer Protection Division, Department of Attorney General, 72 Pine St., Providence, RI 02903; (401) 277-2104.

South Carolina
Department of Consumer Affairs, P.O. Box 5757, Columbia, SC 29250; (803) 734-9452, or (800) 922-1594 (toll-free in SC).

South Dakota
Division of Consumer Affairs, Office of Attorney General, 500 East Capitol, Capitol Building, Pierre, SD 57501; (605) 773-4400, (800) 300-1986.

Tennessee
Division of Consumer Affairs, 500 James Robertson Parkway, 5th Floor, Nashville, TN 37243-0600; (615) 741-4737, or (800) 342-8385 (toll-free in TN).

Texas
Consumer Protection Division, Office of Attorney General, Capitol Station, P.O. Box 12548, Austin, TX 78711; (512) 463-2070, or (800) 621-0508.

Utah
Division of Consumer Protection, Department of Commerce, 160 E. 3rd South, or P.O. Box 45804, Salt Lake City, UT 84145-0804; (801) 530-6601.

Vermont
Public Protection Division, Office of Attorney General, 109 State St., Montpelier, VT 05609; (802) 828-3171.

Virgin Islands
Department of Licensing and Consumer Affairs, Property and Procurement Building, Subbase #1, Room 205, St. Thomas, VI 00802; (809) 774-3130.

Virginia
Division of Consumer Affairs, P.O. Box 1163, Richmond, VA 23209; (804) 786-2042.

Washington
Consumer and Business Fair Practice Division, Office of Attorney General, 900 4th Avenue, Suite 2000, Seattle, WA 98164; (206) 464-6684, or (800) 551-4636 (toll-free in WA).

West Virginia
Consumer Protection Division, Office of Attorney General, 812 Quarrier St., 6th Floor, Charleston, WV 25301; (304) 558-8986, or (800) 368-8808 (toll-free in WV).

Wisconsin
Office of Consumer Protection and Citizen Advocacy, Department of Justice, P.O. Box 7856, Madison, WI 53707-7856; (608) 266-1852, or (800) 362-8189 (toll-free in WI).

Wyoming
Consumer Affairs, Office of Attorney General, 123 State Capitol Building, Cheyenne, WY 82002; (307) 777-7841.

HEALTH CLUBS

Type of Complaint

■ You pay $500 for a membership to a health club but they close down the very next day.

■ You buy a membership to a health club because they claimed they'd have an olympic size swimming pool built within two months. Six months later, there's still no pool.

■ That personal fitness trainer the health club promised you turns out to be the personal trainer for the other 500 members too and has no time for you.

☎ **Contact:**
Your State Consumer Protection Office
See listing on page 647

Help Available
Information: yes
Investigation: yes
Mediation/Arbitration: yes
Legal advice: yes
Legal representation: no

Because of the increasing complaints about health clubs, many states have enacted special laws specifically to protect consumers against unfair practices. In fact, some states now require that new health clubs post a bond or put money into a special account before they open just in case any problems arise.

If you have been lied to or cheated out of money by a health club, contact your state's Consumer Protection Office. They'll investigate your complaint and find out if the club has acted dishonestly. They may decide to set up a meeting between you and the health club to mediate a settlement, or if the case is clear cut, they may simply ask the club to refund your money.

When a Consumer Protection Office gets several complaints against the same health club, they will often conduct an investigation that could result in legal action against the club. Penalties might include revoking the club's operating license, imposing civil fines, and forcing the club to refund their clients' money.

HEALTH MAINTENANCE ORGANIZATIONS

Type of Complaint

- An HMO won't provide you with care because you're too old.

- The physician at your HMO treats you for the same condition three times in the last month with no improvement, and then he says the pain is all in your head.

- Medicare paid for your gallstone treatment, but the HMO still billed you for it.

☎ Contact:
Office of Prepaid Health Care
Operation and Oversite Office of Operation
Health Care Financing Administration
Cohen Building, Room 4406
330 Independence Ave., SW
Washington, DC 20201
(202) 619-3555

Help Available
Information: yes
Investigation: yes
Mediation/Arbitration: yes
Legal advice: yes
Legal representation: no

If a Health Maintenance Organization (HMO) receives Medicare or Medicaid payments, and most do, they've got to follow certain federal guidelines regarding the quality of care they provide. If you feel that the care you received from a federally-qualified HMO was less than what you expected, contact the Health Care Financing Administration (HCFA).

The HCFA will look into your complaint by first finding out if what you're complaining about is something that they have jurisdiction over, and if

it is, they'll contact the HMO on your behalf and ask for their side of the story. If the HMO's response shows that they have violated a federal guideline, the Health Care Financing Administration will ask the HMO to promptly correct the problem. If the HMO still doesn't do anything about your complaint, the HCFA has the ability to deny the HMO's participation in the Medicare and Medicaid programs, which could severely hurt them financially.

HOSPITAL CARE AND SERVICE

Type of Complaint

- You had to wait three hours in the emergency room with a compound fracture in your leg before you were taken care of.

- The hospital insisted on discharging you after surgery even though you were still in extreme pain.

- Dirty towels and bed sheets were piled in the hallways in the hospital where you stayed.

- The linens on your hospital bed were dirty and the food was cold.

- The nurse who took care of you was rude and impatient when she was explaining how you were supposed to take your medication.

☎ Contact:
Health Care Financing Administration
U.S. Department of Health and Human Services
Meadows East Building, 2-D-2
6300 Security Blvd.
Baltimore, MD 21207
(301) 966-6823

Help Available
Information: yes
Investigation: yes
Mediation/Arbitration: yes
Legal advice: yes
Legal representation: no

Visits to the hospital are stressful enough without having to also deal with rude nurses, unsanitary conditions, long waits, and any other annoying problems that sometimes come up. If you have a complaint about your treatment while at the hospital, contact the U.S. Department of Health and Human Services regional office serving your area listed on page 645.

The Health Care Financing Administration (HCFA) is the federal agency that handles complaints involving any hospital that participates in the Medicare funding program, and that covers about 95 percent of all hospitals in the U.S. Once they receive your written complaint, HCFA will review it to determine if there's enough evidence to warrant them taking any action. If they decide that there is, they'll refer the complaint to one of their regional offices or to the Medicare state agencies who will investigate the complaint and relay the results back to the HCFA.

If the investigation of your complaint finds that a violation of federal guidelines has taken place, they will contact the hospital in question and request that it correct the problem, whether this means making sure the nurses are more courteous, the linens are cleaned properly, or the food is heated and served more efficiently. If the hospital doesn't do anything about remedying the complaints, the HCFA, depending of the seriousness of the violation, may choose to cut the hospital off from participating in the Medicare funding program.

HOSPITAL DISCRIMINATION

Type of Complaint

■ You are denied dialysis because you are HIV positive.

■ A hospital refuses to allow your Seeing Eye dog to accompany you during your stay.

■ You were denied medical services at a hospital because your physician doesn't have staff privileges.

☎ **Contact:**
Office for Civil Rights
U.S. Department of Health and Human Services
330 Independence Ave., SW, Room 5250
Washington, DC 20201
(202) 619-0403

Help Available
Information: yes
Investigation: yes
Mediation/Arbitration: yes
Legal advice: yes
Legal representation: no

These and other discriminatory acts occur more often that you might think. If you feel that a hospital, nursing home, or mental health facility that receives funding from the U.S. Department of Health and Human Services (HHS) has denied you services or discriminated against you in other ways based on your race, color, age, religion, national origin, or medical condition, contact the HHS regional office nearest you (listed on page 645).

If the HHS investigator determines that your complaint has cause for action, HHS will arrange a meeting with the health care facility representatives, hear the evidence, and make a decision. If they decide in your favor, the health care facility can be forced to treat you and others like you or risk losing their federal funding. And if your case is life-threatening and requires that the investigation process be speeded up, HHS will do that so that you can get the services you need as soon as possible.

HEALTH INSURANCE

Type of Complaint

■ Your insurance company cancels your car insurance without properly notifying you.

■ Your health insurance premium goes up after one year even though your broker said it would go down.

■ An insurance company won't honor your claim for reasons you can't understand.

☎ Contact:
State Insurance Commissioners
See listing below for the office nearest you

Help Available
Information: yes
Investigation: yes
Mediation/Arbitration: yes
Legal advice: yes
Legal representation: no

Contact your state's Insurance Commissioner if you have any complaints involving insurance policies, including premiums, deductibles, claims, or anything else related to your insurance coverage. They will review your complaint, and if they find that your insurance company has acted in an unlawful or unethical way, they have the power to force the insurance dealer to compensate you or correct whatever mistake they've made.

If you have a policy claim, but your state-licensed insurance company goes out of business before you can collect, you may not be completely out of luck. Some states, like Maryland, have organizations funded by the insurance industry that pay policy claims if your state-licensed insurance company goes out of business. These funds, though, do not pay all types of claims, and because they are not insured by the state, there is no guarantee that your claim against them will be paid. Contact your state's Insurance Commission to find out if your state has such an organization.

State Insurance Commissioners

Alabama
Insurance Commissioner, 135 S. Union St. #181, Montgomery, AL 36130-3401; (205) 269-3550.

Alaska
Division of Insurance, Director of Insurance, P.O. Box D, Juneau, AK 99811; (907) 465-2515.

Arizona
Director of Insurance, 3030 N. 3rd St., Suite 1100, Phoenix, AZ 85012; (602) 255-5400.

Arkansas
Insurance Commissioner, 400 University Tower Building, Little Rock, AR 72204; (501) 371-1325.

California
Commissioner of Insurance, 100 Van Ness Ave., San Francisco, CA 94102; (415) 557-3245 (in San Francisco), or (213) 736-2551 (in Los Angeles), or (800) 233-9045 (toll free in CA).

Colorado
Commissioner of Insurance, 303 W. Colfax Ave., Suite 500, Denver, CO 80204; (303) 866-6221/6248.

Connecticut
Insurance Commissioner, P.O. Box 816, Hartford, CT 06142-0816; (203) 297-3800, (800) 842-2220 (within CT).

Delaware
Insurance Commissioner, 841 Silver Lake Blvd., Dover, DE 19901; (302) 739-4251.

District of Columbia
Superintendent of Insurance, 613 G St., N.W., Suite 516, Washington, DC 20001; (202) 727-7424.

Florida
Insurance Commissioner, Plaza Level Eleven--The Capitol, Tallahassee, FL 32399-0300; (904) 488-3440, or (800) 342-2762 (toll free in FL).

Georgia
Insurance Commissioner, 2 Martin L. King, Jr., Dr., West Tower, Room 716, Atlanta, GA 30334; (404) 656-2056.

Guam
Insurance Commissioner, P.O. Box 2796, Agana, GU 96910.

Hawaii
Insurance Commissioner, P.O. Box 3614, Honolulu, HI 96811; (808) 586-2790.

Idaho
Director of Insurance, 500 S. 10th St., Boise, ID 83720; (208) 334-2250.

Illinois
Director of Insurance, 320 W. Washington St., 4th

Floor, Springfield, IL 62767; (217) 782-4515.

Indiana
Commissioner of Insurance, 311 W. Washington St., Suite 300, Indianapolis, IN 46204; (317) 232-2385, or (800) 622-4461 (toll-free in IN).

Iowa
Insurance Commissioner, Lucas State Office Building, 6th Floor, Des Moines, IA 50319; (515) 281-5705.

Kansas
Commissioner of Insurance, 420 S.W. 9th St., Topeka, KS 66612; (913) 296-7801, or (800) 432-2484 (toll free in KS).

Kentucky
Insurance Commissioner, 229 W. Main St., or P.O. Box 517, Frankfort, KY 40601; (502) 564-3630.

Louisiana
Commissioner of Insurance, P.O. Box 94214, Baton Rouge, LA 70804-9214; (504) 342-5900.

Maine
Superintendent of Insurance, State House Station 34, Augusta, ME 04333; (207) 582-8707.

Maryland
Insurance Commissioner Office, 501 St. Paul Place, 7th Floor South, Baltimore, MD 21202; (301) 333-2520, or (800) 492-7521 (toll free in MD).

Massachusetts
Commissioner of Insurance, 280 Friend St., Boston, MA 02114; (617) 727-7189, ext. 300.

Michigan
Michigan Insurance Bureau, P.O. Box 30220, Lansing, MI 48909; (517) 373-9273.

Minnesota
Commissioner of Commerce, 133 E. 7th St., St. Paul, MN 55101; (612) 296-2594, (800) 652-9747 (in MN).

Mississippi
Commissioner of Insurance, 1804 Walter Sillers Building, Jackson, MS 39201; (601) 359-3569.

Missouri
Director of Insurance, 301 W. High St., Room 630, P.O. Box 690, Jefferson City, MO 65102-0690; (314) 751-4126, (800) 726-7390 (MO only).

Montana
Commissioner of Insurance, 126 North Sanders, Mitchell Building, Room 270, Helena, MT 59620; (406) 444-2040, or (800) 332-6148 (toll free in MT).

Nebraska
Director of Insurance, 941 "O" St., Suite 400, Lincoln, ME 68508; (402) 471-2201.

Nevada
Commissioner of Insurance, 1165 Hotspring Road, Capitol Complex 152, Carson City, NV 89710; (702) 687-4270, or (800) 992-0900 (toll free in NV).

New Hampshire
Insurance Commissioner, 169 Manchester St., Concord, NH 03301; (603) 271-2261, or (800) 852-3416 (toll free in NH).

New Jersey
Commissioner, Department of Insurance, CN325-20 West State St., Trenton, NJ 08625; (609) 292-5363.

New Mexico
Superintendent of Insurance, PERA Building, Room 428, P.O. Drawer 1269, Santa Fe, NM 87504; (505) 827-4500.

New York
Superintendent of Insurance, 160 W. Broadway, Consumer Bureau, 19th Floor, New York, NY 10013; (212) 602-0429, or (800) 342-3736 (toll free in NY).

North Carolina
Commissioner of Insurance, Dobbs Building, P.O. Box 26387, Raleigh, NC 27611; (919) 733-7343, (800) 662-7777 (within NC).

North Dakota
Commissioner of Insurance, State Capitol Building, 5th Floor, 600 East Boulevard Ave., Bismarck, ND 58505-0520; (701) 224-2440, or (800) 247-0560 (toll free in ND).

Ohio
Director of Insurance, 2100 Stella Court, Columbus, OH 43266-0566; (614) 644-2651, or (800) 282-4658 and (800) 843-8356 (toll free in OH).

Oklahoma
Insurance Commissioner, P.O. Box 53408, Oklahoma City, OK 73152; (405) 521-2828, or (800) 522-0071 (toll free in OK).

Oregon
Insurance Commissioner, 440 Labor and Industries Building, Salem, OR 97310; (503) 378-4271.

Pennsylvania
Insurance Commissioner, Strawberry Square, 13th Floor, Harrisburg, PA 17120; (717) 787-5173.

Puerto Rico
Commissioner of Insurance, P.O. Box 8330, Fernandez Juncos Station, Santurce, PR 00910; (809) 722-8686.

Rhode Island
Insurance Commissioner, 233 Richmond St., Providence, RI 02903; (401) 277-2246.

South Carolina
Insurance Commissioner, 1612 Marion St., or P.O. Box 100105, Columbia, SC 29202-3105; (803) 737-6117.

South Dakota
Director of Insurance, 910 E. Sioux Ave., Pierre, SD 57501-3940; (605) 773-3563.

Tennessee
Commissioner of Insurance, 500 James Robertson Parkway, Volunteer Plaza, Nashville, TN 37243; (615) 741-2241, (800) 342-4029 (toll free in TN).

Texas
Claims and Compliance Division, State Board of Insurance, 1110 San Jacinto Blvd., Austin, TX 78701; (512) 463-6501, or (800) 252-3439 (toll free in TX).

Utah
Commissioner of Insurance, 3110 State Office Bldg., Salt Lake City, UT 84114; (801) 530-6400.

Vermont
Commissioner of Insurance, State Office Building, 120 State St., Montpelier, VT 05602; (802) 828-3301.

Virgin Islands
Commissioner of Insurance, 18 Kongens Garde, St. Thomas, VI 00802; (809) 774-2991.

Virginia
Commissioner of Insurance, 700 Jefferson Building, or P.O. Box 1157, Richmond, VA 23209; (804) 786-3741, (800) 552-7945 (toll free in VA).

Washington
Insurance Commissioner Office, Insurance Building, Mail Stop AQ121, Olympia, WA 98504; (206) 753-7301, (800) 562-6900 (toll free in WA).

West Virginia
Insurance Commissioner, 2019 Washington St., East, Charleston, WV 25305; (304) 348-3394, or (800) 642-9004 (toll free in WV).

Wisconsin
Commissioner of Insurance, P.O. Box 7873, Madison, WI 53707-7873; (608) 266-3585, or (800) 236-8517 (toll free in WI).

Wyoming
Commissioner of Insurance, 122 W. 25th St., Cheyenne, WY 82002; (307) 777-7401, (800) 442-4333 (within WY).

LICENSED PROFESSIONALS

Type of Complaint

- While treating you for back pain, your acupuncturist punctures your eardrum.

- Your hearing aid salesman sells you a product that picks up music from your local rock station.

- Your visiting nurse is rude.

☎ **Contact:**
State Licensing Boards
See listing below for the office nearest you

Help Available
Information: yes
Investigation: yes
Mediation/Arbitration: yes
Legal advice: yes
Legal representation: no

Depending on the state, you may be surprised to find out what professionals require business licenses, like manicurists, taxidermists, or even morticians. If you've got a complaint against someone who has to have a license to do business, you've got an advantage when you go to complain: they can't cut hair, stuff your dog, or bury your favorite aunt without that license. And if they've got a lot of unresolved complaints lodged against them at your state Licensing Board, they are going to have a tough time getting that license renewed.

Your state's Licensing Board can tell you which professions it licenses, along with whatever disciplinary actions resulting from consumer complaints that it can carry out. Although most require that you submit a written complaint, they can often listen to the facts over the phone and advise you whether or not you have a legitimate grievance. Depending upon the situation, the state Licensing Boards have the power to investigate and take disciplinary action, including probation, license suspension, or license revocation, against the professional in question.

Although each state differs in the professions it regulates, here is a sampling of those licensed across the 50 states. Remember, though, not every state licenses the professions listed here. You'll have to contact your state's licensing board to find out if the professional you are having a problem with is licensed.

Acupuncturists
Audiologists
Chiropractors
Dental Hygienists
Dentists
Dieticians
Doctors

Electrologists
Emergency Medical Technicians
Family Support Counselors
Health Insurance Agents
Hearing Aid Specialists
Marriage Counselors
Midwives
Nurses
Occupational Therapists
Optometrists
Osteopaths
Pharmacists
Physical Therapists
Podiatrists
Psychologists
Speech Pathologists

State Licensing Boards

Alabama
State Occupational Information Coordinating Community (SOICC), P.O. Box 5690, 401 Adams Ave., Montgomery, AL 36104; (205) 242-2990. Licensing boards & professions: audiologists, speech pathologists, cosmetologists, counselors, dentists, dental hygienists, chiropractors, doctors of medicine, physician's assistants, surgeon's assistants, hearing aid specialists, insurance agents, nurses, nursing home administrators, optometrists, pharmacists, physical therapists, physical therapist assistants, podiatrists, psychologists.

Alaska
Division of Occupational Licensing, Department of Commerce and Economic Development, State of Alaska, PO Box 110806, Juneau, AK 99811-0806; (907) 465-2534. Licensing boards & professions: audiologists, chiropractors, dental professionals, dispensing opticians, hearing aid dealers, physicians, naturopaths, nursing, nursing home administrators, optometrists, pharmacists, physical therapists, psychologists.

Arizona
Arizona Department of Revenue, 1600 West Monroe, Phoenix, AZ 85007; (602) 542-4576. Licensing boards & professions: pharmacists, physical therapists, podiatrists, psychologists, chiropractors, dentists, homeopathic specialists, medical examiners, radiologic technicians, naturopathic physicians, nurses, opticians, optometrists,

osteopaths, cosmetologists, insurance agents, physician assistants, nursing care administrators.

Arkansas
Governor's Office, State Capitol Building, Little Rock, AR 72201; (501) 682-2345. Licensing boards & professions: cosmetologists, dental examiners, speech pathologists, audiologists, nurses, pharmacists, chiropractors, counselors, physicians, opticians, optometrists, podiatrists, psychologists, social workers, therapy technologists.

California
State of California, Department of Consumer Affairs, Director and Executives Office, 400 R Street, Suite 3000, Sacramento, CA 95814; (916) 323-2191 (Northern CA), or (415) 553-1814 (San Francisco Bay area), or (213) 974-1452 (Southern CA), or (800) 344-9940 (toll-free in CA). Licensing boards professions: cosmetologists, physical therapists, medical quality assurance, physician's assistants, chiropractors, acupuncture specialists, psychologists, registered nurses, pharmacists, dentists, dental auxiliaries, behavioral scientists, optometrists, athletic trainers, vocational nurses, psychiatric technicians, osteopaths, dispensing opticians/contact lens examiners, respiratory care specialists, nursing home administrators, podiatrists, hearing aid dispensers, speech pathologists, audiologists.

Colorado
Department of Regulatory Agencies, State Services Building, 1560 Broadway, Suite 1550, Denver, CO 80202; (303) 894-7855. Licensing Board/Professions: cosmetologists, chiropractors, dentists, hearing aid dealers, insurance agents, nurses, nursing home administrators, optometrists, pharmacists & pharmacies, physical therapists, physicians, psychologists, social workers.

Connecticut
Department of Health Services, 150 Washington St., Hartford, CT 06106; (203) 566-7398. Licensed Health Professions: physicians, dentists, optometrists, osteopaths, Naturopaths, homeopaths, chiropractors, psychologists, registered nurses, licensed practical nurses, dental hygienists, registered physical therapists, hypertrichologists, audiologists, speech pathologists, podiatrists, registered sanitarians, nursing home administrators, hearing aid dealers, opticians, occupational therapists.

Other Licensed Professions: Contact Professional Licensing Division, 165 Capitol Avenue, Room G1, Hartford, CT 06106 (203) 566-1814: pharmacists, patent medicine distributors.

Delaware
Division of Professional Regulation, P.O. Box 1401, O'Neil Building, Dover, DE 19903; (302) 739-4522. Complaints in writing only. Licensed Professionals: cosmetologists, podiatrists, chiropractors, dentists, physicians, nurses, nursing home administrators, social workers, speech pathologists, hearing aid dealers, audiologists, psychologists, optometrists, occupational therapists, pharmacists.

District of Columbia
Department of Consumer and Regulatory Affairs, 614 H Street NW, Room 104, Washington, DC 20001; (202) 727-7000. Licensing Board/Professions: cosmetologists, dentists, dieticians, physicians, nurses, nursing home administrators, occupational therapists, optometrists, pharmacists, physical therapists, podiatrists, psychologists, social workers.

Florida
Florida Department of Professional Regulation, Consumer Services, 1940 N. Monroe St., Tallahassee, FL 32399-075; (904) 488-6602. Licensing boards & professions: chiropractors, cosmetologists, dentists, dispensing opticians, medical examiners, hearing aid dispensers, naturopathics, nursing home administrators, nurses, optometrists, osteopaths, pharmacists, podiatrists, psychologists, acupuncture technicians, radiological health technicians, laboratory services, entomology specialists, emergency medical personnel.

Georgia
Examining Board Division, Secretary of State, 166 Pryor Street, SW, Atlanta, GA 30303; (404) 656-3900. Licensing boards & professions: athletic trainers, chiropractors, cosmetologists, professional counselors, social workers, marriage and family therapists, dietitians, dentists, hearing aid dealers and dispensers, physicians, nurses, nursing home administrators, occupational therapists, dispensing opticians, optometrists, pharmacists, physical therapists, podiatrists, practical nurses, psychologists, sanitarians, speech pathologists, audiologists, laboratory analysts.

Hawaii
Office of the Director, Department of Commerce and Consumer Affairs, P.O. Box 3469, Honolulu, HI 96801; (808) 586-2846. Licensing boards & professions: acupuncture specialists, chiropractors, cosmetologists, dental examiners, hearing aid dealers and fitters, massage specialists, physicians, naturopaths, nurses, nursing home administrators, dispensing opticians, optometrists, osteopaths, pharmacists, physical therapists, psychologists, speech pathologists, audiologists.

Idaho
State of Idaho, Department of Self-Governing Agencies, Bureau of Occupational Licenses, Owyhua Plaza, 1109 Main Street #220, Boise, ID 83702; (208) 334-3233. Licensing boards & professions: athletic directors, dentists, physicians, chiropractors, cosmetologists, counselors, dentists, environmental health specialists, hearing aid dealers and fitters, nursing home administrators, optometrists, podiatrists, psychologists, social workers, pharmacists.

Illinois
State of Illinois, Department of Professional Regulations, 320 W. Washington, Third Floor, Springfield, IL 62786; (217) 785-0800. Licensed professions: athletic trainers, cosmetologists, chiropractors, dentists and dental auxiliaries, physicians, nurses, nursing home administrators, occupational therapists, optometrists, pharmacists, physical therapists, podiatrists, psychologists, social workers.

Indiana
Indiana Health Professional Bureau, 402 W. Washington, Room 041, Indianapolis, IN 46282; (317) 232-2960. Licensed health professionals: chiropractors, dentists, health facility administrators, nurses, optometrists, pharmacists, sanitarians, speech pathologists, audiologists, psychologists, hearing aid dealers, podiatrists, physical therapists.

Iowa
Bureau of Professional Licensing, Iowa Department of Health, Lucas State Office Building, Des Moines, IA 50319; (515) 281-4401. Licensed professionals: dietitians, hearing aid dealers, nursing home administrators, optometrists, ophthalmology dispensers, podiatrists, psychologists, physical and occupational therapists, occu-pational therapist assistants, social workers, speech pathologists and audiologists, respiratory care therapists, cosmetologists, chiropractors, nurses, physicians, dentists, pharmacists, veterinarians.

Kansas
Secretary of State, State Capitol, Consumer Affairs, 200 SE 7th Street, #214, Topeka, KS 66611; (913) 291-4340. Licensing boards: adult home administrators, cosmetologists, dentists and dental auxiliaries, emergency medical services, healing arts specialists, hearing aid dispensers, insurance agents, nurses, optometrists, pharmacists, physical therapists, podiatrists.

Kentucky
Division of Occupations and Professions, P.O. Box 456, Frankfort, KY 40602; (502) 564-3296. Licensing boards & professions: hearing aid dealers, nurses, psychologists, social workers, speech and audiologists. Other licensed professionals: Kentucky Occupational Information Coordinating Committee, 275 E. Main St., Two Center, Frankfort, KY 40621; (502) 564-4258: chiropractors, dentists, cosmetologists, emergency medical technicians services, radiation and product safety specialists, insurance agents, medical licensure supervisors, nursing home administrators, ophthalmic dispensers, optometric examiners, pharmacists, physical therapists, podiatrists.

Louisiana
Department of Economic Development, 101 France St., Baton Rouge, LA 70802; (504) 342--5361. Licensing boards & professions: acupuncture assistants, adult day care administrators, ambulatory surgical centers, blood alcohol analysts, chiropractors, pesticide applicators, dentists, drug manufacturers, emergency medical technicians, family support counselors, hearing aid dealers, hemodialysis clinics, home health centers, independent laboratories, insurance, maternity homes, mental and substance abuse clinics, midwives, nursing home administrators, occupational therapists, optometrists, pharmacists, physical therapists, physicians, podiatrists, psychologists, radiation therapists, radiologic technologists, sanitarians, social workers, speech pathologists and audiologists.

Maine
Department of Professional and Financial

Regulation, State House Station 35, Augusta, ME 04333; (207) 582-8700. Licensing boards & professions: insurance agents, athletic trainers, hearing aid dealers and fitters, speech pathologists and audiologists, dietitians, nursing home administrators, substance abuse counselors, physical therapists, psychologists, social workers, radiological technicians, occupational therapists, respiratory care therapists, nurses, dentists, chiropractors, osteopaths, podiatrists, physicians.

Maryland

Division of Maryland Occupational and Professional Licensing, 501 St. Paul Pl., 9th Floor, Baltimore, MD 21202; (301) 333-6209. Licensed professionals: hearing aid dealers, cosmetologists. Referral to the licensing agency for insurance agents can be provided by the office listed above. Other licensed professions: Boards and Commissions, Department of Health and Mental Hygiene, 4201 Patterson Ave., Baltimore, MD 21215; (410) 764-4747: audiologists, chiropractors, dentists, dietitians, electrologists, medical examiners, nurses, nursing home administrators, optometrists, occupational therapists, pharmacists, physical therapists, podiatrists, professional counselors, psychologists, speech pathologists, social workers.

Massachusetts

Division of Registration, 100 Cambridge St., Boston, MA 02202; (617) 727-3074. Licensing boards & professions: electrologists, health officers, licensed practical nurses, nursing home administrators, optometrists, physician's assistants, podiatrists, pharmacists, psychologists, registered nurses, sanitarians, speech pathologists, audiologists, social workers, physical therapists, occupational therapists, athletic trainers, chiropractors, dental hygienists, dentists, dispensing opticians, pharmacies.

Michigan

Michigan Department of License and Regulation, P.O. Box 30018, Lansing, MI 48909; (517) 373--1870. Licensing board & professions: cosmetologists.

Minnesota

Office of Consumer Services, Office of Attorney General, 1440 N.C.L. Tower, 455 Minnesota St., St. Paul, MN 55101; (612) 296-3353. Licensing

boards & professions: chiropractors, cosmetologists, dentists, dental assistants, dental hygienists, hearing aid dispensers, insurance agents, midwives, nursing home administrators, optometrists, osteopathic physicians, pawnbrokers, pharmacists, physical therapists, physicians, surgeons, physician's assistants, podiatrists, practical nurses, psychologists, registered nurses, rehabilitation consultants.

Mississippi

Secretary of State, P.O. Box 136, Jackson, MS 39205; (601) 359-3123. Licensing boards & professions: athletic trainers, chiropractors, dentists, physicians, nurses, nursing home administrators, optometrists, pharmacists, physical therapists, psychologists, cosmetologists.

Missouri

Division of Professional Registration, Department of Economic Development, P.O. Box 1335, 3605 Missouri Blvd., Jefferson City, MO 65102; (314) 751-0293. Licensing boards & professions: athletic trainers, chiropractors, cosmetologists, professional counselors, dentists, healing arts specialists, hearing aid dealers/fitters, nurses, optometrists, podiatrists, pharmacists, insurance agents, nursing home administrators, dental hygienists, physicians, physical therapists, speech pathologists and audiologists, psychologists.

Montana

Professional and Occupational Licensing, Business Regulation, Department of Commerce, 111 N. Jackson St., Helena, MT 59620; (406) 444-3737. Licensing boards & professions: acupuncturists, athletic trainers, chiropractors, cosmetologists, dental hygienists, dentists, denturists, electrologists, hearing aid dispensers, insurance, medical doctors, nurses, nursing home administrators, occupational therapists, optometrists, osteopathic physicians, physical therapists, radiologic technologists, sanitarians, social workers and counselors, speech pathologists and audiologists.

Nebraska

Bureau of Examining Boards, Nebraska Department of Health, P.O. Box 95007, Lincoln, NE 68509; (402) 471-2115. Licensing boards & health professions: athletic trainers, advanced emergency medical technicians, audiologist/speech pathologists, cosmetologists, chiropractors, dentists/dental hygienists, hearing aid dealers and fitters, pharmacists, podiatrists, optometrists, physical therapists, nurses, nursing home administrators, occupational therapists, professional counselors, psychologists, respiratory care specialists, social workers, sanitarians.

Nevada
Professional and Occupational Licensing, 1 East Liberty, Suite 311, Reno, NV 89501; (702) 786-0231. Licensing boards & professions: athletic trainers, audiologists and speech pathologists, chiropractors, dentists, hearing aid specialists, homeopaths, marriage and family counselors, physicians, naturopathic healing arts specialists, nurses, dispensing opticians, optometrists, oriental medicine, osteopaths, pharmacists, physical therapists, podiatrists, psychologists.

New Hampshire
SOICC of New Hampshire, 64 B Old Sun Cook Rd., Concord, NH 03301; (603) 228-9500. Licensing boards & professions: emergency medical technicians, cosmetologists, chiropractors, dentists, physicians, nurses, nursing home administrators, occupational therapists, optometrists, psychologists, pharmacists, podiatrists.

New Jersey
Director, Centralized Licensing for the Licensing Boards, Division of Consumer Affairs, 375 West State Street, Trenton, NJ 08625; (609) 292-4670. Licensing boards & professions: dentists, marriage counselors, nurses, ophthalmic dispensing technicians, optometrists, pharmacists, physical therapists, acupuncture specialists, athletic trainers, hearing aid dispensers, chiropractors, opthomologists.

New Mexico
Regulation and Licensing Department, P.O. Box 25101, Santa Fe, NM 87504-1388; (505) 827-7000. Licensing boards & professions: athletic promoters, chiropractors, cosmetologists, dentists, physicians, nurses, nursing home administrators, occupational therapists, optometrists, osteopaths, pharmacists, physical therapists, podiatrists, psychologists.

New York
New York State Education Department, Division of Professional Licensing, Cultural Education Center, Empire State Plaza, Albany, NY 12230; (518) 474-3852, or (800) 342-3729 (toll-free in NY). Licensed professionals: acupuncturists, audiologists, chiropractors, dentists, physicians, osteopaths, nurses, occupational therapists, ophthalmic dispensers, optometrists, pharmacists, physical therapists, podiatrists, psychologists, social workers, speech pathologists.

North Carolina
North Carolina Center for Public Policy Research, P.O. Box 430, Raleigh, NC 27602; (919) 832-2839. Licensing boards & professions: chiropractors, cosmetologists, registered counselors, dental, hearing aid dealers and fitters, marital and family therapists, physicians, nurses, nursing home administrators, opticians, optometrists, osteopaths, pharmacists, physical therapists, podiatrists, practicing psychologists, social workers, speech and language pathologists.

North Dakota
North Dakota Legislative Council Library, 600 East Boulevard Avenue, Bismarck, ND 58505; (701) 224-2916. Licensing boards & professions: athletic trainers, audiologists and speech pathologists, chiropractors, cosmetologists, dentists, dietitians, emergency medical services, hearing aid dealers and fitters, physicians, nurses, nursing home administrators, occupational therapists, optometrists, pharmacists, physical therapists, podiatrists, psychologists, respiratory care specialists, social workers.

Ohio
State of Ohio, Department of Administrative Services, Division of Computer Services, 30 East Broad St., 40th Floor, Columbus, OH 43215-0409; (614) 466-8029. Licensed professionals: wholesale distributors of dangerous drugs, terminal distributors of dangerous drugs, pharmacists, managing cosmetologists, cosmetologists, practical nurses, registered nurses, dentists, dental hygienists, osteopaths, physicians, podiatrists, chiropractors, midwives.

Oklahoma
Governor's Office, State Capitol, Oklahoma City, OK 73117-1299; (405) 521-2342 or State Information Operator (405) 521-1601. Licensing board & professions: physicians, medico-legals, nursing homes, nurses, optometrists, osteopaths, physi-

cians, pharmacists, psychologists, social workers, speech pathologists, chiropractors, cosmetologists, dentists. For other licensed professionals, contact Occupational Licensing, OK State Health Department, 1000 North East, 10th Street, Oklahoma City, OK 73152; (405) 271-5217: hearing aid dealers.

Oregon
Department of Economic Development, Small Business Advocates, 775 Summer Street NE, Salem, OR 97310; (800) 233-3306 (toll-free in OR). Licensing boards & professions: insurance agents.

Pennsylvania
Bureau of Professional and Occupational Affairs, Secretary of State, 618 Transportation and Safety Building, Harrisburg, PA 17120; (717) 783-1400. Licensed health professions: dentists, physicians, nurses, nursing home administrators, occupational therapists, optometrists, osteopaths, pharmacists, physical therapists, podiatrists, psychologists, speech-language and hearing specialists.

Rhode Island
State Attorney General, Consumer Protection, 72 Pine Street, Providence, RI 02903; (401) 274-4400. Licensing boards & professions: nurses aides, psychologists, respiratory therapists, sanitarians, speech pathologists, physical therapists, podiatrists, prosthetists, nurses, nursing home administrators, occupational therapists, opticians, optometrists, osteopaths, physician assistants, cosmetologists, physicians, midwives, acupuncturists, athletic trainers, audiologists, chiropractors, dentists, dental hygienists, electrologist.

South Carolina
South Carolina State Library, 1500 Senate St., Columbia, SC 29211; (803) 734-8666. Licensing boards & professions: chiropractors, cosmetologists, dentists, physicians, nurses, nursing home administrators, occupational therapists, opticians, optometrists, pharmacists, physical therapists, professional counselors, marriage and family therapists, psychologists, sanitarians, social workers, speech pathologist/audiologists.

South Dakota
Department of Commerce and Regulation, 910 E. Sioux, Pierre, SD 57105; (605) 773-3178. South Dakota Medical and Osteopath examiners, 1323 A. Minnesota Avenue, Sioux Falls, SD 57104; (605) 336-1965. Licensing boards & professions: physicians, osteopaths, physician's assistants, physical therapists, medical corporations, emergency technicians, chiropractors, cosmetologists, hearing aid dispensers, medical/osteopaths, nurses, nursing home administrators, optometrists, pharmacists, podiatrists, psychologists, social workers.

Tennessee
Division of Regulatory Boards, Department of Commerce & insurance, 500 James Robertson Parkway, Nashville, TN 37243; (615) 741-3449. Licensing boards & professions: cosmetologists, pharmacists. For other licensed health professionals, contact Division of Health Related Professions, Department of Health and Environment, 283 Plus Park Blvd Complex, Nashville, TN 37247; (615) 367-6220: dentists, dental hygienists, podiatrists, physicians, physician's assistants, osteopaths, optometrists, nursing home administrators, dispensing opticians, chiropractors, social workers, hearing aid dispensers, registered professional environmentalists, marital and family counselors, speech pathology/audiologists, occupational and physical therapists, x-ray technicians, registered nurses, licensed practical nurses.

Texas
Texas Department of Commerce, Office of Business Permit Assistance, P.O. Box 12728, Capitol Station, Austin, TX 78711; (512) 320-0110, or (800) 888-0511 (toll-free in TX). Licensing boards & professions: cosmetologists, chiropractors, psychologists, dentists, insurance agents, fitting and dispensing of hearing aids, vocational nurses, nursing home administrators, physicians, optometrists, pharmacists, physical therapists, podiatrists, professional counselors, dietitians, speech-language pathology and audiology.

Utah
Division of Occupational and Professional Licensing, Department of Business Regulation, Heber M. Wells Building, 160 East 300 South, P.O. Box 45805, Salt Lake City, UT 84145-0805; (801) 530-6628. Licensing boards & professions: cosmetologists, electrologists, chiropractors, podiatrists, dentists, dental hygienists, physicians, surgeons, naturopaths, registered nurses, licensed

practical nurses, nurse midwives, nurse anesthetists, nurse specialists, prescriptive practice specialist, IV therapists, optometrists, osteopaths, pharmacists, pharmacies, manufacturing pharmacies, health facility administrators, sanitarians, physical therapists, psychologists, clinical social workers, conduct research on controlled substance, marriage and family therapists, master therapeutic recreational specialists, speech pathologists, audiologists, occupational therapists, hearing aid specialists, massage therapists, acupuncture practitioners, physician assistants, dieticians.

Vermont
Division of Licensing and Registration, Secretary of State, Pavilion Office Building, 109 State St., Montpelier, VT 05609; (802) 828-2363. Licensing boards & professions: chiropractors, cosmetologists, dentists, medical board (physicians), podiatrists, physical therapists, social workers, physician assistants, nurses, nursing home administrators, opticians, optometrists, osteopaths, pharmacies, pharmacist, psychologists, radiological technicians.

Virginia
Virginia Department of Commerce, 3600 W. Broad St., 5th Floor, Richmond, VA 23230; (804) 367-8500. Licensed professions: audiologists, hearing aid dealers and fitters, nursing home administrators, opticians, speech pathologists. For licensed health professions, contact receptionist, Health Professionals: (804) 662-9900. The office listed above can provide you with phone numbers for the following licensing boards: dentists, physicians, medical/legal assistants, nurses, optometrists, pharmacists, psychologists, professional counselors, social workers.

Washington
Department of Health, P.O. Box 1099, Olympia, WA 98507; (206) 586-4561. Licensed professions: acupuncturists, chiropractors, cosmetology schools/ instructors, cosmetologists, dentists, dental hygienists, drugless therapeutic-naturopaths, hearing aid dispensers/trainees, midwives, nursing home administrators, occularists, occupational therapists, dispensing opticians, optometrists, osteopaths, osteopathic physician/surgeon, osteopathic physician assistants, physicians, surgeons, physician's assistants, limited physician, podiatrists, practical nurses, psychologists, physical therapists, registered nurses.

West Virginia
Administrative Law Division, Secretary of State, State Capitol, Charleston, WV 25305; (304) 345-4000. Licensing boards & professions: chiropractors, dentists, and dental hygienists, hearing-aid dealers, physicians, practical nurses, registered nurses, nursing home administrators, occupational therapists, optometrists, osteopaths, pharmacists, physical therapists, psychologists, radiologic technicians, sanitarians.

Wisconsin
Department of Regulation and Licensing, P.O. Box 8935, Madison, WI 53708; (608) 266-7482. Licensed professions: chiropractors, cosmetologists, distributors of dangerous drugs, dental hygienists, dentists, drug manufacturers, electrologists, hearing aid dealers/fitters, physicians, surgeons, nurse midwives, registered nurses, licensed practical nurses, nursing home administrators, optometrists, pharmacists, physical therapists, physician's assistants, podiatrists, psychologists.

Wyoming
Governor's Office, State Capitol, Cheyenne, WY 82002; (307) 777-7434. Licensing boards & professions: health service administrators, medical record technicians, medical laboratory workers, dental laboratory technicians, opticians, radiological technicians, respiratory technicians, insurance agents, physicians, physician's assistants, chiropractors, pharmacists, occupational therapists, activity therapists, physical therapists, speech pathologist and audiologist, optometrist, dietitians, dentists, dental hygienists, registered nurses, licensed practical nurses, emergency medical technicians, nurse's aides, medical assistants, counselors, cosmetologists.

MEDICAL BILLS

Type of Complaint

■ You pay your doctor for a lab test, and he also receives payment for the tests from Medicare, but he won't give you a refund.

■ Even after repeated calls to your insurance company, they give you the runaround about sending you a refund for doctor's fees that you paid for out-of-pocket.

■ You overpaid your doctor for a visit, but you haven't received the refund she promised you months ago.

☎ **Contact:**
State Consumer Protection Office
See page 647 for the office nearest you

State Medical Boards
See page 641 for the office nearest you

Help Available
Information: yes
Investigation: yes
Mediation/Arbitration: yes
Legal advice: yes
Legal representation: no

Errors in your medical bills and insurance claims are more common than you might think. If you find problems with your medical bill and your physician or Health Maintenance Organization (HMO) isn't responding to your complaint, contact your state's Consumer Protection Office or Medical Board. If necessary, they will contact your doctor or hospital on your behalf to help solve your problems with your medical records, billing errors, insurance claim delays, denied or delayed refunds, and much more.

Keep in mind, though, that your state's Consumer Protection Office does not handle complaints about the quality or accuracy of your doctor's treatment and diagnosis. For information on this subject contact your state Medical Board.

MEDICAL DEVICES

Type of Complaint

■ A piece of your new hearing aid falls off and gets lodged in your ear canal.

■ The baby monitor you bought shuts off whenever you use the television remote control.

■ Your in-home respirator has the annoying habit of switching off after you've fallen asleep.

☎ **Contact:**
Consumer Affairs and Information Staff
Food and Drug Administration
(HFE-88)
U.S. Department of Health
and Human Services
5600 Fishers Lane, Room 1364
Rockville, MD 20857
(301) 443-1240

Help Available
Information: yes
Investigation: yes
Mediation/Arbitration: no
Legal advice: yes
Legal representation: no

The Food and Drug Administration (FDA) is the federal agency that regulates the manufacture of medical devices, and they take all kinds of complaints about the performance of these devices. And if you think the one you have may have some kind of defect, you should contact the FDA (see page 639 for the office nearest you) along with the place where you bought it.

Although the FDA won't act on your behalf to recover damages from the manufacturer of a defective medical device, they will look into your complaint to see if they should take some kind of action against the manufacturer to make sure that the problem isn't widespread or life threatening. If the FDA determines that there is a serious threat to the public from a defective medical device, they can insist that the manufacturer stop making the product and issue a recall on those they've already sold.

As far as your own case against the manufacturer, the FDA will make the results of their investigation available to you and anyone else so that if you wish to take the company to court on your own, you can use the FDA results to help you prove your case.

MEDICARE FRAUD AND ABUSE

Type of Complaint

■ You think your doctor is billing Medicare for procedures that you may not have needed.

■ A pharmacist dispenses generic drugs to fill prescriptions and then bills Medicare for more expensive, non-generic drugs.

■ The ambulance company you work for is billing Medicare for transporting patients who never existed.

☎ Contact:
U.S. Department of Health and Human Services
OIG Hotline, P.O. Box 17303
Baltimore, MD 21203-7303
(800) 368-5779 (toll-free)

Help Available
Information: yes
Investigation: yes
Mediation/Arbitration: n/a
Legal advice: yes
Legal representation: n/a

The U.S. Department of Health and Human Services, the federal agency that administers the Medicare program, has set up a toll-free hotline so that you can report Medicare fraud or abuse. Your report will be investigated, and if it is found to be true, the case may be referred to the U.S. Department of Justice for criminal prosecution, which could lead to imprisonment and fines. If you wish, your call will be kept anonymous.

NURSING HOMES

Type of Complaint

■ The food at your nursing home is often served cold.

■ The fees seem to rise every month without notice.

■ The staff has treated you abusively.

■ You've been unfairly denied admission to a nursing home for reasons that don't make sense to you.

☎ Contact:
Nursing Home Ombudsmen
See listing below for the office nearest you

Help Available
Information: yes
Investigation: yes
Mediation/Arbitration: yes
Legal advice: yes
Legal representation: no

There are many complaints common to nursing homes and other health care facilities across the country. To help resolve these special complaints, most states have established Ombudsman offices that act to ensure that these facilities provide their services appropriately and fairly.

Ombudsman offices act as mediators or go-betweens in disputes involving consumer complaints. The Ombudsman, however, are not enforcement agencies: they don't "police" nursing homes and other health agencies in their areas to make sure these facilities are conforming to regulations. And they cannot force a nursing home to change or correct their practices--this can be done through the state office which licenses the nursing home.

What they can do is contact the nursing home on your behalf and try to work out a voluntary solution to your complaint. Often a phone call or a letter is enough to correct the situation, but in more serious cases, a formal meeting between the nursing home, you, and an Ombudsman staff member may be necessary. Since it's to the nursing home's advantage to take care of problems before they are referred to enforcement agencies, such as the state Office of the Attorney General or the state Department of Health and Social Services, you may find that the help of the Ombudsman is all you'll need to correct the problem. If it isn't, the Ombudsman may in fact send your complaint on to an enforcement agency for you.

Of course if you aren't satisfied with the Ombudsman's help, you don't have to accept their findings, and you can always contact the state's Consumer Protection Office (see page 647 for the office nearest you) or the Licensing Board (see page 656 for the office nearest you), who will also investigate your complaint.

Nursing Home Ombudsmen

Alabama
Commission on Aging, 7070 Washington Ave., R.F.A. Plaza, #470, Montgomery, AL 36130; (205) 242-5743, (800) 243-5463.

Alaska
Office of the Older Alaskans Ombudsman, 3601 C St., Suite 260, Anchorage, AK 99503-5209; (907) 279-2232, (800) 478-9996 (long term care); also accepts collect calls from older persons.

Arizona
Aging and Adult Administration, 1789 W. Jefferson, P.O. Box 950A, Phoenix, AZ 85007; (602) 542-4446.

Arkansas
Division of Aging and Adult Services, 1417 Donaghey Plaza South, P.O. Box 1437, Little Rock, AR 72203-1437; (501) 682-2441.

California
Department of Aging, 1600 K St., Sacramento, CA 95814; (916) 323-6681, or toll free in-state: (800) 231-4024.

Colorado
The Legal Center, 455 Sherman St., Suite 130, Denver, CO 80203; (303) 722-0300, or toll free in-state: (800) 288-1376.

Connecticut
Department on Aging, 175 Main St., Hartford, CT 06106; (203) 566-3238, or toll free in-state: (800) 443-9946.

Delaware
Division on Aging, 11-13 North Church Ave., Milford, DE 19963; (302) 422-1386, or toll free in-

state: (800) 292-1515.

District of Columbia
Legal Counsel for the Elderly, 601 E Street, NW, Building A, 4th Floor, Washington, DC 20049; (202) 662-4933.

Georgia
Office of Aging, Department of Human Resources, 878 Peachtree St., NE, Suite 632, Atlanta, GA 30309; (404) 894-5336.

Hawaii
Executive Office on Aging, 335 Merchant St., Room 241, Honolulu, HI 96813; (808) 586-0100.

Idaho
Office on Aging, State House, Room 108, Boise, ID 83720; (208) 334-3833.

Illinois
Department on Aging, 421 East Capitol Ave., Springfield, IL 62701; (217) 785-3140, or toll free: (800) 252-8966.

Indiana
Aging Division, Department of Human Services, P.O. Box 7083, Indianapolis, IN 46207-7083; (317) 232-7020, or toll free in-state: (800) 622-4484.

Iowa
Department of Elder Affairs, 914 Grand Ave., 200 Jewett Building, Suite 236, Des Moines, IA 50319; (515) 281-5187, or toll free in-state: (800) 532-3213.

Kansas
Department on Aging, Docking State Office Building, 122 South, 915 Southwest Harrison St., Topeka, KS 66612-4986; (913) 296-4986, or toll free in-state: (800) 432-3535.

Kentucky
Division for Aging Services, Department for Social Services, 275 East Main St., 6th Floor West, Frankfort, KY 40621; (502) 564-6930, or toll free in-state: (800) 372-2991.

Louisiana
Governors Office of Elder Affairs, P.O. Box 80374, Baton Rouge, LA 70898-3074; (504) 925-1700, (800) 259-4990.

Maryland
Office on Aging, 301 West Preston St., 10th Floor, Baltimore, MD 21201; (410) 225-1100, or toll free in-state: (800) 243-3425.

Massachusetts
Executive Office of Elder Affairs, 1 Ashburton Place, Boston, MA 02101; (617) 727-7750, or toll free in-state: (800) 872-0166.

Michigan
Citizens for Better Care, 416 N. Homer, Suite 101, Lansing, MI 48912-4700; (517) 336-6753, or toll free in-state: (800) 292-7852.

Minnesota
Board on Aging, Office of Ombudsman for Older Minnesotans, 444 Lafayette Rd., St. Paul, MN 55155-3843; (612) 296-2770, or (800) 333-2433.

Mississippi
Division of Aging and Adult Services, 421 West Pascagoula St., Jackson, MS 39201; (601) 949-2070, or toll free in-state: (800) 222-7622.

Missouri
Division of Aging, P.O. Box 1337, Jefferson City, MO 65102; (314) 751-3082, or toll free in-state: (800) 392-0210.

Montana
Governor's Office on Aging, Capitol Station, Helena, MT 59620; (406) 444-4204, or toll free in-state: (800) 332-2272.

Nebraska
Department on Aging, State Office Building, P.O. Box 95044, Lincoln, NE 68509; (402) 471-2306, or -2307, (800) 942-7830.

Nevada
Division for Aging Services, Department of Human Resources, 1665 Hot Springs Road, #158, Carson City, NV 89710; (702) 687-4210.

New Hampshire
Division of Elderly and Adult Services, 6 Hazen Dr., Concord, NH 03301; (603) 271-4375, or toll free in-state: (800) 442-5640.

New Mexico
Agency on Aging, 224 East Palace Ave., Ground Floor, Santa Fe, NM 87501; (505) 827-7640, or toll free in-state: (800) 432-2080.

New York
Office for the Aging, Nelson A. Rockefeller Building, ESP, Albany, NY 12223; (518) 474-5731, or toll free in-state: (800) 342-9871.

North Carolina
Division of Aging, Department of Human Resources, 693 Palmer Drive, Raleigh, NC 27603; (919) 733-3983, toll free in-state: (800) 662-7030.

North Dakota
Aging Services, Department of Human Services, 600 East Blvd., Bismarck, ND 58505; (701) 224-2310, or toll free in-state: (800) 472-2622.

Ohio
Department of Aging, 50 West Broad St., 9th Floor, Columbus, OH 43266-0501; (614) 466-5500, toll free in-state: (800) 282-1206.

Oklahoma
Special Unit on Aging, P.O. Box 25352, Oklahoma City, OK 73125; (405) 521-2281.

Oregon
Office of LTC Ombudsman, 2475 Lancaster Dr., Bldg. B, #9, Salem, OR 97310; (503) 378-6533, or toll free in-state: (800) 522-2602.

Pennsylvania
Department of Aging, 231 State St., Harrisburg, PA 17101; (717) 783-3126.

Puerto Rico
Office of Elder Affairs, Call Box 50063, Old San Juan Station, San Juan, PR 00902; (809) 722-2429.

Rhode Island
Department of Elderly Affairs, 160 Pine St., Providence, RI 02903; (401) 277-2880, or toll free in-state: (800) 322-2880.

South Carolina
Office of the Governor, Division of Ombudsman and Citizens' Service, 1205 Pendleton St., Columbia, SC 29201; (803) 734-0457.

South Dakota
Office of Adult Services and Aging, 700 Governors Dr., Pierre, SD 57501; (605) 773-3656.

Tennessee
Commission on Aging, 706 Church St., Suite 201, Nashville, TN 37219; (615) 741-2056.

Texas
Department on Aging, P.O. Box 12786, Capitol Station, Austin, TX 78711; (512) 444-2727, or toll free in-state: (800) 252-9240.

Utah
Division of Aging and Adult Services, P.O. Box 45500, Salt Lake City, UT 84145-9500; (801) 538-3920.

Vermont
Department of Rehabilitation and Aging, 103 South Main St., Waterbury, VT 05676; (802) 241-2400.

Virginia
Department for the Aging, 700 East Franklin St., 10th Floor, Richmond, VA 23219; (804) 225-2271, toll free in-state: (800) 552-4464, or (800) 552-3402 (long term care).

Washington
South King County Multi-Service Center, 1200 South, 336 St., P.O. Box 23699, Federal Way, WA 98903-0699; (206) 838-6810; (800) 422-1384.

West Virginia
Commission on Aging, State Capitol, 1900 Kanola East, Holly Grove, WV 25325-0160; (304) 558-3317, or toll free in-state: (800) 642-3671.

Wisconsin
Board on Aging and Long Term Care, 214 North Hamilton St., Madison, WI 53703; (608) 266-8944.

Wyoming
Long Term Care Ombudsman, 900 8th St., Wheatland, WY 82201; (307) 322-5553.

PHARMACISTS AND PHARMACIES

Type of Complaint

■ Your pharmacist neglects to warn you about taking a certain drug while operating heavy machinery.

■ You were charged for 100 pills, but the pharmacist gave you only 75.

■ Your pharmacist is rude and impatient with you when you ask questions about your prescription.

■ Your pharmacist dispenses the wrong prescription for you and you have a serious allergic reaction to the drug.

☎ **Contact:**
State Pharmacy Boards
See listing below
for the Board in your state

Help Available
Information: yes
Investigation: yes
Mediation/Arbitration: yes
Legal advice: yes
Legal representation: no

Like many licensed professionals, pharmacists are required to be licensed by the state they practice their trade in. Although that license doesn't guarantee that the pharmacist will always do his or her job correctly, it does give you some recourse if you feel that the pharmacist has acted unprofessionally or negligently. If you have a complaint about a pharmacist, contact your state's Pharmacy Board (listed below), either by calling or writing, and they will look into the matter for you.

If the Board's investigation shows that you do have a legitimate complaint, they will decide what action to take against the pharmacist. Depending on the seriousness of the complaint, the Board may just tell the pharmacist to cease his or her offensive behavior, or they may conduct a formal hearing that could result in a suspension or revoking of their license to practice.

State Pharmacy Boards

Alabama
Alabama State Board of Pharmacy, 1 Perimeter Park South, Suite 425 South, Birmingham, AL 35243; (205) 967-0130.

Alaska
Department of Commerce and Economic Development, Division of Occupational Licensing, P.O. Box 110806, Juneau, AK 99811; (907) 465-2534.

Arizona
State Board of Pharmacy, 5060 N. 19th Ave. Suite 101, Phoenix, AZ 85015; (602) 255-5125. Complaints in writing only.

Arkansas
Board of Pharmacy, 320 W. Capital, Suite 802, Little Rock, AR 72201; (501) 324-9200.

California
State Board of Pharmacy, 400 R Street, #4070, Sacramento, CA 95814; (916) 445-5014.

Colorado
Board of Pharmacy, 1560 Broadway, Suite 1310, Denver, CO 80202; (303) 894-7750.

Connecticut
Drug Control Division, 165 Capital Ave., Room G-37, Hartford, CT 06106, (203) 566-4490.

Delaware
Board of Pharmacies, Cooper Bldg., Room 205, Federal & Waters St., Dover, DE 19901; (302) 739-4708.

District of Columbia
Board of Pharmacy, Department of Consumer and Regulatory Affairs, Pharmaceutical and Medical Control Division, 614 H Street, NW, Washington, D.C. 20001; (202) 727-7218. Complaints in writing only.

Florida
State Department of Health and Rehabilitative Services, Pharmacy Program Office, 1317 Winewood Blvd. Tallahassee, FL 32399; (904) 487-1257.

Georgia
Board of Pharmacy, 166 Pryor St. S.W., Atlanta, GA 30303; (404) 656-3912. Complaints in writing only.

Hawaii
R.I.C.O., P.O. Box 2399, Honolulu, HI 96804; (808) 586-2698.

Idaho
Board of Pharmacy, 280 North 8th St., Suite 204, Boise, ID 83720; (208) 334-2356.

Illinois
State Board of Pharmacy, 100 W. Randolph, Chicago, IL 60601; (312) 814-4573.

Indiana
State Board of Pharmacy, 402 W. Washington St., #041, P.O. Box 82067, Indianapolis, IN 46024; (317) 232-2960.

Iowa
Board of Pharmacy, Attn: Chief Investigator, 1209 East Court, Des Moines, IA 50319; (515) 281-5944.

Kansas
Board of Pharmacy, Landon State Office Building, 900 Jackson St., Room 513, Topeka, KS 66612; (913) 296-4056.

Kentucky
Board of Pharmacy, 1228 U.S. 127 South, Frankfort, KY 40601; (502) 564-3833.

Louisiana
Board of Pharmacy, 5615 Corporate Blvd. Suite 8E, Baton Rouge, LA 70808-2537; (504) 925-6496.

Maine
Department of Professional Regulations, State House #35, Augusta, ME 04333; (207) 582-8723.

Maryland
Board of Pharmacy, 4201 Patterson Ave., Baltimore, MD 21215; (410) 764-4755.

Massachusetts
State Board of Pharmacy, State Office Building, Government Center, 100 Cambridge St., Boston, MA 02202; (617) 727-9954.

Michigan
Board of Pharmacy, P.O. Box 30018, Lansing, MI 48909; (517) 373-9196.

Minnesota
Board of Pharmacy, 2700 University Ave., West #107, St. Paul, MN 55114-1079; (612) 642-0541.

Mississippi
State Board of Pharmacy, Suite D, C & F Plaza, 2310 Hwy. 80 West, Jackson, MS 39204; (601) 354-6750.

Missouri
State Board of Pharmacy, 3605 Missouri Blvd., Jefferson City, MO 65109; (314) 751-0091.

Montana
State Board of Pharmacy, 111 N. Jackson Street, P.O. Box 200513, Helena, MT 59620-0513; (406) 444-3737.

Nebraska
Bureau of Examining Boards, State Department of Health, Attn: Board of Pharmacy, 301 Centennial Mall South, P.O. Box 95007, Lincoln, NE 68509; (402) 471-2115.

Nevada
State Board of Pharmacy, 1201 Terminal Way, Suite 212, Reno, NV 89502; (702) 322-0691.

New Hampshire
State Board of Pharmacy, 57 Regional Drive, Concord, NH 03301; (603) 271-2350.

New Jersey
Board of Pharmacy, 124 Halsey Street, Newark, NJ 07102; (201) 504-6450.

New York
Office of Professional Discipline, One Park Ave., New York, NY 10016; (212) 951-6400.

North Carolina
Board of Pharmacy, P.O. Box 459, Carrboro, NC 27510; (919) 942-4454.

North Dakota
State Board of Pharmacy, P.O. Box 1354, Bismarck, ND 58502; (701) 258-1535.

Ohio
State Board of Pharmacy, 77 South High St., 17th Floor, Columbus, OH 43266-0320; (614) 466-4143.

Oklahoma
State Board of Pharmacy, 4545 N. Lincoln, Suite 112, Oklahoma City, OK 73105; (405) 521-3815.

Oregon
Board of Pharmacy, 800 NW Oregon Street #9, Suite 425, Portland, OR 97232; (503) 731-4032.

Pennsylvania
Board of Pharmacy, P.O. Box 2649, Harrisburg, PA 17105; (717) 783-7157.

Rhode Island
State Department of Health and Drug Control, 304 Cannon Bldg., 3 Capitol Hill, Providence, RI 02908; (401) 277-2837.

South Carolina
State Board of Pharmacy, 1026 Sumter St., Room 209, P.O. Box 11927, Columbia, SC 29211; (803) 734-1010.

South Dakota
State Board of Pharmacy, P.O. Box 518, Pierre, SD 57501; (605) 224-2338.

Tennessee
Board of Pharmacy, 500 James Robertson Pkwy., Nashville, TN 37243-1143; (615) 741-2718.

Texas
State Board of Pharmacy, 8505 Cross Park Drive, Suite 110, Austin, TX 78754; (512) 832-0661.

Utah
Board of Pharmacy, Heber Wells Building, 160 East 300 South, P.O. Box 45805, Salt Lake City, UT 84145-0805; (801) 530-6628.

Vermont
State Board of Pharmacy, c/o Carla Preston, 109 State Street, Montpelier, VT 05609-1106; (802) 828-2875.

Virginia
State Board of Pharmacy, 6606 W. Broad, 6th Floor, Richmond, VA 23230-1717; (804) 662-9911.

Washington
Board of Pharmacy, 1300 Quince SE, Mail Stop 7863, Washington Education Association Building, Olympia, WA 98504-7863; (206) 753-6834.

West Virginia
State Board of Pharmacy, 236 Capital St., Charleston, WV 25301; (304) 348-0558.

Wisconsin
State Department of Regulation and Licensing, P.O. Box 8935, Madison, WI 53708; (608) 266-2112.

Wyoming
State Board of Pharmacy, 1720 South Poplar St., Suite 5, Casper, WY 82601; (307) 234-0294.

PRESCRIPTION FRAUD

Type of Complaint

- Your friend brags to you that his doctor sells her prescriptions for valium under the table.

- Your doctor offers to sell you a prescription for codeine.

- Even though you've recovered from your depression, your doctor offers to sell you anti-depressants directly whenever you want them at half the normal price.

☎ **Contact:**
Office of Diversion Control
Drug Enforcement Agency
Washington, DC 20537
(202) 307-8010

Help Available
Information: yes
Investigation: yes
Mediation/Arbitration: n/a

Legal advice: no
Legal representation: no

If you know of a doctor who's got his or her own drug dealership going on the side, selling drugs or prescriptions for drugs that are controlled substances, the Drug Enforcement Agency (DEA) wants to know about it. Not only does the DEA investigate drug dealers on the street, they also respond to complaints involving physicians who are abusing their privileged access to drugs that under any other circumstances would be illegal.

Upon receiving your complaint about a doctor, DEA investigators will look into it and try to determine if there's evidence to support your report. If they believe there is evidence that the doctor is dealing illegally in prescription drugs, they can bring criminal charges against the doctor, and if he's found guilty, have his license revoked or send him to prison.

PRODUCT SAFETY DEFECTS

Type of Complaint

- The paint on a toy doll is peeling off, and your kid eats it.

- You buy a new high chair that has sharp metal screws exposed that scratch your baby's legs.

- Your new electric blender falls apart when you puree.

- A halloween mask interferes with your child's breathing.

- The smoke detector you just bought won't go off even when you set fire to it.

- Your son is injured when his all terrain vehicle flips over at a low speed.

☎ **Contact:**
Consumer Product Safety Commission
5401 Westbard Ave.

Washington, DC 20207
(800) 638-2772

Help Available
Information: yes
Investigation: yes
Mediation/Arbitration: no
Legal advice: yes
Legal representation: no

There are a few steps you should take to complain about the safety of a product that you've bought. First report the defective product to the store from which you bought it, and then report it to the U.S. Consumer Product Safety Commission's (CPSC) toll-free hotline. The CPSC will review your complaint, and depending on the circumstances and the number of similar complaints they are getting, they might decide to begin an investigation of the product and the manufacturer.

The CPSC, however, will not sue a company for you or help you get compensation from it for any injuries you may have suffered from one of their defective products. What they can do is investigate a company on the behalf of the general public, and order a recall of the products, or if necessary, seek legal action against it to stop them from manufacturing and distributing their unsafe products.

☎ **Contact:**
State Consumer Protection Offices
See page 647 for the office nearest you

Help Available
Information: yes
Investigation: yes
Mediation/Arbitration: yes
Legal advice: yes
Legal representation: no

As far as your own particular complaint against the company, you should contact your state's Consumer Protection Office. They will help by investigating your complaint and trying to work out a solution with the manufacturer or seller of the defective product. Also keep in mind that when negotiating a settlement with a company concerning a defective product, you can get plenty of useful statistics on product-related injuries from the Consumer Product Safety Commission to support your case.

RADON

Type of Complaint

■ Your neighbor says he has radon gas in his basement and thinks you should get your house tested.

■ You can't find a contractor whom you trust to fix the radon problem in your home.

■ You don't know where to find a reliable radon detection kit.

☎ **Contact:**
Radon Division (6604-J)
Office of Radon Programs
U.S. Environmental Protection Agency
401 M St., SW
Washington, DC 20460
(202) 233-9370
(800) SOS RADON

Help Available
Information: yes
Investigation: no
Mediation/Arbitration: no
Legal advice: yes
Legal representation: no

Since 1985 when dangerous levels of radon gas were found in homes all across the U.S., homeowners have been asking a lot of questions about their safety. To better address this large demand for information and assistance, the U.S. Environmental Protection Agency and each state have set up special Radon Offices (see listing below for the Radon office in your state). Although these offices won't come out and test your home for radon for you, they can answer any questions you might have, including how to test your home, where to find a licensed contractor to do any needed repairs, and information on whether or not high levels of radon have been discovered in the homes in your area.

State Radon Offices

Alabama
Division of Radiation Control, Alabama Department of Public Health, 434 Monroe #510, Montgomery, AL 36130; (205) 242-5315, (800) 582-1866.

Alaska
Radiological Health Program, Alaska Department of Health and Social Services, Box 110613, Juneau, AK 99811-0613; (907) 465-3019.

Arizona
Arizona Radiation Regulatory Agency, 4814 S. 40th St., Phoenix, AZ 85040; (602) 255-4845.

Arkansas
Division of Radiation Control and Emergency Management, Arkansas Department of Health, 4815 W. Markham St., Little Rock, AR 72205-3867; (501) 661-2301.

California
California Department of Health Services, Room 334, 2151 Berkeley Way, Berkeley, CA 94704; (510) 540-3014.

Radiation Management, County of Los Angeles, Department of Health Services, 2615 S. Grand Ave., Los Angeles, CA 90007; (213) 744-3244.

Colorado
Radiation Control Division, Colorado Department of Health, 4300 Cherry Creek Dr. South, Denver, CO 80222-1530; (303) 692-3057.

Connecticut
Radon Program, Toxic Hazards Section, Connecticut Department of Health Services, 150 Washington St., Hartford, CT 06106; (203) 566-3122.

Delaware
Division of Public Health, Delaware Bureau of Environmental Health, P.O. Box 637, Dover, DE 19901; (302) 739-5410, or (800) 554-4636 (toll-free in DE).

District of Columbia
D.C. Department of Consumer and Regulatory Affairs, 613 G St., NW, Room 1014, Washington, DC 20001; (202) 727-7000.

Florida
Office of Radiation Control, Department of Health and Rehabilitative Services, 1317 Winewood Blvd., Tallahassee, FL 32399-0700; (904) 488-1525, or (800) 543-8279 (toll-free in FL).

Georgia
Environmental Protection Division, Georgia Department of Human Resources, 878 Peachtree St., Room 100, Atlanta, GA 30309; (404) 894-6644, (800) 745-0037.

Hawaii
Environmental Protection and Health Services Division, Hawaii Department of Health, 591 Ala Moana Blvd., Honolulu, HI 96813; (808) 586-4424.

Idaho
Office of Environmental Health, Division of Health, Idaho Department of Health and Welfare, 4th Floor, 450 W. State St., Boise, ID 83720; (208) 334-6584 or (800) 445-8647.

Illinois
Illinois Department of Nuclear Safety, Office of Environmental Safety, 1301 Knotts St., Springfield, IL 62703; (217) 786-6384 or (800) 325-1245.

Indiana
Division of Industrial Hygiene & Radiological Health, Indiana State Board of Health, 1330 W. Michigan St., P.O. Box 1964, Indianapolis, IN 46206-1964; (317) 633-0153, or (800) 272-9723 (toll-free in IN).

Iowa
Bureau of Radiological Health, Iowa Department of Public Health, Lucas State Office Bldg., Des Moines, IA 50319-0075; (515) 281-7781, or (800) 383-5992 (toll-free in IA).

Kansas
Bureau of Air Quality and Radiation Control, Kansas Department of Health and Environment, 109 SW 9th Street, Mills Building, #602, Topeka, KS 66612-1274; (913) 296-1560.

Kentucky
Radiation Control Branch, Division of Radiation and Product Safety, Department of Health

Services, Cabinet for Human Resources, 275 E. Main St., Frankfort, KY 40621; (502) 564-3700.

Louisiana
Louisiana Nuclear Energy Division, P.O. Box 14690, Baton Rouge, LA 70898-4690; (504) 765-0160.

Louisiana Radiation Pest Service, P.O. Box 82135, 7290 Blue Bonett, 2nd Floor, Baton Rouge, LA 70810.

Maine
Indoor Air Program, Division of Health Engineering, Maine Department of Human Services, 157 Capitol Street, State House Station 10, Augusta, ME 04333; (207) 289-3826 or (800) 232-0842.

Maryland
Center for Radiological Health, Maryland Department of Environment, 2500 Broening Highway, Baltimore, MD 21224; (410) 631-3300, or (800) 872-3666 (toll-free in MD).

Massachusetts
Radiation Control Program, Massachusetts Department of Public Health, 23 Service Center, North Hampton, MA 01060; (413) 586-7525, or (617) 727-6214 in Boston.

Michigan
Division of Radiological Health, Michigan Department of Public Health, 3423 N. Logan, P.O. Box 30195, Martin Luther King Jr. Blvd., Lansing, MI 48909; (517) 335-8190.

Minnesota
Section of Radiation Control, Environmental Health Division, Minnesota Department of Health, 925 Delaware St., SE, P.O. Box 59040, Minneapolis, MN 55459-0040; (612) 627-5033 or (800) 798-9050.

Mississippi
Division of Radiological Health, Mississippi Department of Health, 3150 Lawson St., P.O. Box 1700, Jackson, MS 39215-1700; (601) 354-6657 or (800) 626-7739.

Missouri
Bureau of Radiological Health, Missouri Department of Health, 1730 E. Elm, P.O. Box 570, Jefferson City, MO 65102; (314) 751-6083, or (800) 669-7236 (toll-free in MO).

Montana
Occupational Radiation Health Bureau, Montana Department of Health and Environmental Sciences, Cogswell Bldg., Helena, MT 59620; (406) 444-3671.

Nebraska
Division of Radiological Health, Nebraska Department of Health, 301 Centennial Mall South, P.O. Box 95007, Lincoln, NE 68509; (402) 471-2168 or (800) 471-0594.

Nevada
Radiological Health Section, Health Division, Nevada Department of Human Resources, 505 E. King St., #101, Carson City, NV 89710; (702) 687-5394.

New Hampshire
Bureau of Radiological Health, Division of Public Health Services, Health and Welfare Bldg., 6 Hazen Dr., Concord, NH 03301-6527; (603) 271-4674 or (800) 852-3345.

New Jersey
Radiation Protection Element, New Jersey Department of Environmental Protection, 729 Alexander Rd., Princeton, NJ 08540; (609) 987-6402, or (800) 648-0394 (toll-free in NJ).

New Mexico
Radiation Licensing and Registration Section, New Mexico Environmental Improvement Division, Box 26110, Market Place, Suite 4, Santa Fe, NM 87502; (505) 827-4301.

New York
Bureau of Environmental Radiation Protection, New York State Health Department, 2 University Plaza, Albany, NY 12237; (518) 458-6450, or (800) 458-1158.

North Carolina
Radiation Protection Section, Division of Facility Services, North Carolina Department of Human Resources, 3825 Barrett Dr., Raleigh, NC 27609; (919) 733-4141.

North Dakota
North Dakota Department of Health, Missouri Office Bldg., 1200 Missouri Ave., Room 304, P.O. Box 5120, Bismarck, ND 58502-5520; (701) 221-5188.

Ohio
Radiological Health Program, Ohio Department of Health, 35 E. Chestnut Street, P.O. Box 118, Columbus, OH 43266-0118; (614) 644-2727, or (800) 523-4439 (toll-free in OH).

Oklahoma
Radiation and Special Hazards Service, Consumer Protection Service #0202, 1000 NE 10th Street, Oklahoma City, OK 73117-1299; (405) 271-5221.

Oregon
Oregon State Health Department, Radiation Control Section, 800 NE Oregon, #705, Portland, OR 97232; (503) 731-5797 or (800) 422-6012.

Pennsylvania
Pennsylvania Department of Environmental Resources, Bureau of Radiation Protection, P.O Box 2063, Harrisburg, PA 17105-2063; (717) 787-2480, or (800) 23-RADON (in PA).

Puerto Rico
Puerto Rico Radiological Health Division, G.P.O. Call Box 70184, Rio Piedras, PR 00936; (809) 767-3563.

Rhode Island
Division of Occupational Health and Radiation, Rhode Island Department of Health, 206 Cannon Bldg., 3 Capitol Hill, Providence, RI 02908; (401) 277-2438.

South Carolina
Bureau of Radiological Health, South Carolina Department of Health and Environmental Control, 2600 Bull St., Columbia, SC 29201; (803) 734-4700/4631 or (800) 768-0362.

South Dakota
Division of Public Health, Licensing & Linesure, Radiation Protection, 445 E. Capitol, Pierre, SD 57501-3181; (605) 773-3364.

Tennessee
Division of Air Pollution Control, Bureau of Environmental Health, Department of Health and Environment, Custom House, 701 Broadway, Nashville, TN 37219-5403; (615) 522-0733 or (800) 232-1139.

Texas
Bureau of Radiation Control, Texas Department of Health, 1100 W. 49th St., Austin, TX 78756-3189; (512) 834-6688 or (800) 241-6688.

Utah
State of Utah, Division of Radiation Control, 168 North, 1950 West, P.O. Box 144850, Salt Lake City, UT 84114-4850; (801) 536-4250 or (800) 458-0145.

Vermont
Division of Occupational and Radiological Health, Vermont Department of Health, 10 Baldwin St., Montpelier, VT 05602; (802) 828-2886 or (800) 640-0601.

Virginia
Bureau of Radiological Health, Department of Health, 1500 E. Main Street, #104A, P.O. Box 2448, Richmond, VA 23218; (804) 786-5932, or (800) 468-0138 (toll-free in VA).

Virgin Islands
Division of Environmental Protection, Department of Planning and Natural Resources, 50 Nisky Center, #231,N, #458 Charlotte Amalie, St. Thomas, VI 00802; (809) 774-3320.

Washington
Environmental Protection Section, Washington Office of Radiation Protection, Thurston AirDustrial Center, Bldg. 5, P.O. Box 47827, Olympia, WA 98504; (206) 586-3303, or (800) 323-9727 (toll-free in WA).

West Virginia
Department of Environmental Health, West Virginia Department of Health, Radiological Division, 815 Quarrier Street, #418, Charleston, WV 25301; (304) 348-3526 or (800) 922-1255.

Wisconsin
Radiation Protection Section, Division of Health, Department of Health & Social Services, P.O. Box 309, Madison, WI 53701-0309; (608) 267-4795.

Wyoming
Environmental Health, Department of Health & Social Service, Hathaway Bldg., 4th Floor, Cheyenne, WY 82002-0710; (307) 777-6015.

TANNING DEVICES AND SALONS

Type of Complaint

■ An ad for a tanning lamp promises medical benefits such as reducing blood pressure, treating diabetes, improving your sex life, and promoting vitamin D production.

■ The timing device on a sun lamp in a tanning salon cannot be controlled by the customer.

■ A tanning salon does not provide you with protective eyewear because they claim it is perfectly safe without using any.

☎ **Contact:**
Food and Drug Administration
Center for Devices and Radiological Health
Office of Compliance and
Surveillance (HSV-312)
1390 Piccard Dr.
Rockville, MD 20850
(301) 427-1172

Help Available
Information: yes
Investigation: yes
Mediation/Arbitration: yes
Legal advice: yes
Legal representation: no

According to Food and Drug Administration (FDA) regulations, the only labeling claim that a tanning device can make is that it browns your skin. Any other claims, such as safety, reduced blood pressure, and so on, are illegal. If you find advertising or labeling that makes illegal claims, contact the FDA or the Federal Trade Commission, and if they find that the labels and ads are in fact misleading, they can order to have them stopped.

If you've noticed or experienced a health threat involving a tanning device, whether at a tanning salon or from a product advertised in a publication or on television, contact an FDA regional office nearest you (listed on page 639).

Depending on the case, the FDA may send out an agent to investigate the complaint, and if they find a violation has occurred, they will send the manufacturer of the tanning salon involved a cease and desist letter asking for them to correct the safety violation. Usually a letter from the FDA will do the trick, but if the company in question refuses to listen to the FDA's requests, the FDA may go to court and have the equipment seized.

Keep in mind, though, that the FDA will get involved with private tanning salons only if there is a serious health risk. They aren't going to get into complaints about billing or the quality of your tan or their service, nor will they represent you in court if you are injured at a tanning salon. You can, however, use whatever findings they come up with in an investigation if you plan to pursue the matter in court on your own.

GETTING INVOLVED IN CHANGING THE CURRENT HEALTH CARE SYSTEM

Are you interested in finding out more about current legislation on health care or ways that you can let your opinion be known? This is an election year, make your vote work for you. Look at where candidates stand on the issue of health care. Your representative and senators have information papers on their positions regarding health care and are just a phone call away (202-224-3121). There are also special interest groups that lobby on this issue, as well as citizen action groups. The following list is some suggestions of places to begin.

* Families USA
   1334 G St., NW
   Washington, DC 20005   (202) 737-6340

They have a special program called a.s.a.p. designed to get people involved.

* League of Women Voters

1730 M St., NW, 10th Floor
Washington, DC 20036   (202) 429-1965

They are currently in the middle of a study on the Universal Cost Containment for Health Care. They have many public education programs which they conduct at the local level. Contact a League near you for more information.

* National Commission on Children

1111 Eighteenth St., NW
Washington, DC 20036   (202) 254-3800

They have a free final report titled *Beyond Rhetoric: A New American Agenda for Children and Families*.

* Public Citizen

2000 P St., NW
Washington, DC 20036   (202) 833-3000

People can become members and receive a monthly magazine, notices regarding upcoming legislation, and information regarding becoming an activist. You can also receive a monthly newsletter, *Health Letter*, which discusses health care and health insurance issues.

* Children's Defense Fund

122 C St., NW
Washington, DC 20001   (202) 628-8787

They have publications and reports dealing with children's health and health insurance.

* Health Insurance Association of America

1025 Connecticut Ave., NW
Washington, DC 20036   (202) 223-7780

They publish an annual report of health insurance data.

* American Medical Association

515 N. State St.
Chicago, IL 60610   (312) 464-4416

They have information regarding their Health Access America proposal, which is the AMA's proposal to improve access to affordable, quality health care.

* American Academy of Pediatrics

Department of Child Health Care
Finance and Organization
141 Northwest Point Blvd.
P.O. Box 927
Elk Grove Village, IL 60009   (800) 433-9016

* Coalition for America's Children

American Academy of Pediatrics
1710 Rhode Island Ave., NW, 4th Floor
Washington, DC 20036   (202) 857-7829

160-member organization of local and state-based group has a broad agenda of children's issues. One of the focuses is on public education.

Appendix A:
1992 Clinical Studies

What follows is a listing of 1992 Clinical Studies being conducted at the National Institutes of Health. For more information on how to become a clinical trials patient, see the "Free Medical Care for Rich and Poor by the Best Doctors in the World" Section in the first chapter of this book.

1) National Institute on Aging

Mark B. Schapiro, M.D.
Deputy Clinical Director

Telephone referrals of patients
should be directed to:
Carol J. Fuchs-Kinslow, MSSW
Social Worker
(301) 496-4754

Laboratory of Neurosciences

Section on Brain Aging and Dementias
National Institute on Aging (NIA) has an eight-bed patient care unit to study brain function in relation to healthy aging and in patients with Alzheimer's disease, multi-infarct dementia, Pick's disease, geriatric depression and hypertension. Developmental neurological disorders, including Down, Fragile X and Turner syndromes, are examined. Studies are longitudinal and involve continued participation. The methods employed include positron emission tomography to examine brain metabolism and blood flow; magnetic resonance imaging and computer assisted tomography to examine brain anatomy; neuropsychology; and pharmacology and pharmacokinetics to study therapeutic approaches to brain disease. Post-mortem follow-up for verification of diagnosis is routine.

2) National Institute on Alcohol Abuse and Alcoholism

Gerald L. Brown, M.D.
Clinical Director

Telephone referrals of patients
should be directed to:
Section of Clinical Assessment
and Biological Correlates
(301) 496-1993

Laboratory of Clinical Studies

Chronic Organic Brain Syndromes of Alcoholism
Patients with brain dysfunction attributable to chronic alcohol consumption receive a complete neuropsychiatric evaluation. The evaluation includes various specialized measures of brain function: neuropsychological tests, electroencephalographic studies, measures of neuroendocrine function, and brain imaging techniques such as computerized tomography (CT), positron emission tomography (PET), and magnetic resonance imaging (MRI). Selected patients are eligible for drug treatment designed to ameliorate cognitive and other behavioral signs and symptoms of chronic organic brain syndromes, such as neurotransmitter replacement, neuropeptide or neurotropic agents.

Clinical and Family Studies
Families of alcoholic patients are evaluated by a multidisciplinary team for various aspects of biopsychosocial functioning. Selected patients and their family members are eligible for longitudinal studies to identify prospectively genetic, biological and social factors that contribute to the development of alcoholism: namely, cognitive development, neuropsychological functioning, electroencephalographic techniques, genetic and biochemical markers. Extensive family pedigrees will be constructed to evaluate genetic predisposing and protective factors in the development of alcoholism in individuals from

high-risk families. Studies on suicide risk in alcoholics as well as alcoholism in various racial and ethnic groups are ongoing. These groups include Caucasians, Blacks, Native Americans, and Irish. Studies of relationships between panic disorders, aggressive/impulsive disorders, nicotine and alcoholism are also ongoing.

Pharmacologic Reduction of Alcohol Consumption
Patients who are medically healthy but have serious alcohol-related problems and who wish to reduce their alcohol consumption are eligible for long-term drug studies designed to reduce their craving for alcohol.

Treatment of Alcohol Withdrawal
Selected patients with no serious medical problems who have been drinking prior to admission will be studied in the hospital during their withdrawal from alcohol. Patients will be studied to understand the alcohol withdrawal syndrome and develop new and more efficacious pharmacologic treatments. Biological characteristics of patients which may serve as prognostic indicators of recovery of the brain and other organ system function are studied, i.e., sleep electrophysiology, drug metabolism, neuropsychological functioning, intermediary carbohydrate metabolism, fatty acid and lipid metabolism, neuroendocrine function and immune response.

Neuropharmacology of Alcoholism
Selected patients who are medically fit are eligible for study of the neuropharmacological processes that may be changed by ethanol or may predispose to alcoholism. Patients are admitted and undergo three weeks of abstinence during which any withdrawal problems are assessed and treated. Tests will explore the neuropharmacological systems that evidence suggests are important targets for the action of alcohol. Patients must participate in a therapeutic program designed to minimize the chance of relapsing on discharge.

3) National Institute of Allergy and Infectious Diseases

H. Clifford Lane, M.D.
Clinical Director, AIDS Studies
(800) 243-7644

Acquired Immunodeficiency Syndrome (AIDS) and Other Syndromes Associated with Human Immunodeficiency Virus (HIV) Infection
An extensive clinical research program directed toward the treatment and prevention of HIV infection is underway. Areas currently being explored are the following:

Anti-retrovirals: Patients at all stages of HIV infection are recruited for clinical trials utilizing a variety of new agents either alone or in combination. Combinations of antiretroviral drugs with immunomodulators such as IL-2 are also studied.

Anti-infectives: Patients with CMV retinitis, PCP, toxoplasmosis, Mycobacterium avium intracellulare, cryptosporidiosis and microsporidiosis are recruited for clinical trials. Prophylaxis trials in several of these areas are also in progress.

Allergic Rhinitis
Nasal responses to provocative challenge with mediators and allergens are studied. Contact: Michael Kaliner, M.D., (301) 496-9314.

Anaphylaxis
Selected patients having recurring anaphylaxis or anaphylactoid reactions are studied to enumerate the responsible mediators. Contact: Michael Kaliner, M.D., (301) 496-9314.

Asthma and Allergic Diseases
Selected patients with bronchial asthma and other allergic diseases are studied. Seasonal allergic asthmatics, aspirin-sensitive patients and certain "intrinsic" asthmatics also are sought. Patients undergo studies designed to characterize their immunologic, biochemical and neurophysiologic responses. Contact: Michael Kaliner, M.D., (301) 496-9314.

Chediak-Higashi Syndrome
The role of lysosomal enzymes in the pathogenesis of Chediak-Higashi is under investigation. In addition, the function of the phagocytic system is measured. Contact: John Gallin, M.D., (301) 496-3006.

Cryptococcosis
Patients with untreated cryptococcosis are

requested for study of diagnostic methods, immunologic responses and therapy with various promising drugs. Patients with suspected cryptococcosis (meningitis or disseminated disease) not proven by culture but with convincing negative workup for other causes are considered. Contact: John Bennett, M.D., (301) 496-3461.

Eosinophilic Syndromes (Loeffler's Syndrome, Loeffler's Endocarditis, Polyarteritis with Eosinophilia, Tropical Eosinophilia, Eosinophilic Leukemia, Eosinophilic Collagen Vascular Disease, Allergic Disorders with Eosinophilia and Parasitic Infections with Eosinophilia

An intensive multidisciplinary study is under way to determine the pathophysiology of these diseases. Of special interest are patients with eosinophilic invasion of tissues, especially the heart, the most commonly involved organ. Cardiac involvement is the most frequent cause of morbidity and mortality. Several promising modes of therapy are employed and studied. Contact: Randi Leavitt, M.D. or Gary Hoffman, M.D., (301) 496-1124.

Epstein-Barr Virus

Patients with chronic Epstein-Barr Virus-related lymphoproliferative disorders are studied. Contact: Janet Dale, R.N., (301) 496-5221.

Food Additive Reactions

Selected patients with a clear history of adverse reaction to a food additive are studied to determine the reproducibility of the history and the pathogenesis of the reaction. Contact: Dean Metcalfe, M.D., (301) 496-2165.

Gluten-Sensitive Enteropathy (Coeliac Sprue)

Patients with gluten-sensitive enteropathy are studied for immunologic and genetic abnormalities. Contact: Warren Strober, M.D., (301) 496-9662.

Granulomatous Diseases

Immunological and biological functions in patients with sarcoidosis, granulomatous hepatitis and other granulomatous diseases are studied. The physiological capabilities of leukocytes are investigated. Improved therapeutic regimens are evaluated. Contact: John Gallin, M.D., (301) 496-3006.

Chronic Granulomatous Diseases of Childhood

Patients with chronic granulomatous disease are admitted for studies of host diseases and assessment of the genetic basis of the disease. Long-term management of acute and chronic problems is provided. Trials of therapeutic agents including interferon-gamma and oral antifungal agents are ongoing. Contact: John Callin, M.D., (301) 496-3006.

Herpes Simplex Virus Infections

patients with recurrent, chronic or severe herpes simplex virus infections are studied in outpatient or inpatient facilities. Viral pathogenesis, resistance to acyclovir, efficacy of new antiviral drugs and a recombinant vaccine are evaluated. Contact: Janet Dale, R.N., (301) 496-5221.

Hyperimmunoglobulin and Recurrent Infection (Job's) Syndrome

Patients with extreme elevation of IgE and recurrent cutaneous and deep-seated infections with Staphylococcus aureus are studied. These patients, who have "cold abscesses," are studied for their ability to mount an inflammatory response. Phagocytic cell, cytokine and immune parameters are monitored and therapeutic interventions are studied. Contact: John Gallin, M.D., (301) 496-3006.

Immunodeficiency Diseases

Patients with all forms of primary immunodeficiency, including patients with common variable hypogammaglobulinemia, IgA deficiency, hyper-IgM syndrome, are studied to determine the underlying immunologic mechanisms present and to select appropriate therapy. Contact: Warren Strober, M.D., (301) 496-9662.

Inflammatory Bowel Disease

Patients with inflammatory bowel disease (Crohn's disease or ulcerative colitis) are admitted for study of immunologic factors in the cause of diseases and the effect on patient in vitro function of various therapeutic agents. Contact: Warren Strober, M.D., (301) 496-9662.

Mastocytosis and Urticaria Pigmentosa

Patients are sought to assess the factors responsible for symptoms as well as the response to certain anti-histamine and anti-mast-cell drugs. Contact: Dean Metcalfe, M.D., (301) 496-2165.

Mycoses

Patients requiring therapy for aspergillosis, fungal sinusitis, histoplasmosis, blastomycosis, coccidioidomycosis and other deep mycosis refractory to conventional drugs are considered for treatment with new chemotherapeutic agents. Contact: John Bennett, M.D., (301) 496-3461.

Neutropenia

Patients with cyclic neutropenia and other forms of moderate to severe idiopathic neutropenia are admitted to assess the factors that may cause the defect in neutrophil production. Recombinant human G-CSF or GM-CSF are evaluated where applicable. Contact: John Gallin, M.D., (301) 496-3006.

Parasitic Diseases: Amebiasis, Chagas' Disease, Cryptosporidiosis, Cysticercosis, Echinococcosis, Filariasis, Giardiasis, Leishmaniasis, Malaria, Onchocerciasis, Schistosomiasis, Strongyloidiasis and Toxoplasmosis

Patients with parasitic infections are considered for evaluation and study. Specialized tests, procedures and medications are available to diagnose, characterize and treat parasitic infections. Contact: Eric Ottesen, M.D., (301) 496-5399.

Recurrent Pyogenic Infections

Patients with recurrent bacterial infections are admitted to study host defense mechanisms, with particular emphasis on leukocyte functions. Patients with eczema, elevated IgE and recurrent superficial and deep-seated staphylococcal infections are evaluated for defective leukocyte function. Contact: John Gallin, M.D., (301) 496-3006.

Varicella-Zoster Infections

Selected individuals with varicella-zoster infections are evaluated in outpatient or inpatient facilities. Viral pathogenesis, resistance to acyclovir and efficacy of new antiviral drugs are studied. Contact: Stephen Straus, M.D., (301) 496-5221.

Vasomotor Rhinitis

Patients with vasomotor rhinitis will be examined in order to determine the underlying cause. Contact: Michael Kaliner, M.D., (301) 496-9314.

Vasculitis

Selected patients with disseminated vasculitis, polyarteritis nodosa, Wegener's granulomatosis, Takayasu's arteritis, and other forms of inflammatory vascular diseases are accepted for study of various in vivo and in vitro immunologic parameters before, during and after treatment with corticosteroids and/or cytotoxic agents. Contact: Randi Leavitt, M.D. or Gary Hoffman, M.D., (301) 496-1124.

4) National Institute of Arthritis and Musculoskeletal and Skin Diseases

John H. Klippel, M.D.
Clinical Director

Telephone referrals should be directed to individuals listed under each subject area:

Polymyositis and Dermatomyositis and Related Myopathies

The genetic, immunologic and virologic factors of inflammatory muscle disease (polymyositis and dermatomyositis) are studied. Patients at the very onset of their illness and patients from families with other cases of autoimmune inflammatory muscle disease are of special interest. Patients at all stages of the illness may be considered for clinical therapeutic trials. Contact: Paul H. Plotz, M.D., Arthritis and Rheumatism Branch, (301) 496-1474.

Rheumatoid Arthritis

Neuroendocrine, paracrine and autocrine factors play critical roles in the pathogenesis of rheumatoid arthritis. Studies in progress are addressing these issues. Patients with recent onset disease, patients from families with a high incidence of autoimmune disease, and monozygotic and dizygotic twins discordant for rheumatoid arthritis are of special interest. Contact: Ronald L. Wilder, M.D., Ph.D., Arthritis and Rheumatism Branch, (301) 496-3373.

Systemic Lupus Erythematosus

The genetics, immune and environmental factors involved in the pathogenesis of systemic lupus erythematosus are studied. Investigations of cellular activation and function are performed on peripheral blood, bone marrow and lymph node cells. Classical genetic studies are complemented by molecular biological analyses. Patients with lupus glomerulonephritis or membranous nephropathy, lupus thrombocytopenia, or hypercholesterolemia will be considered for experimental therapeutic trials. Contact: John H. Klippel, M.D., (301) 496-3374; Alfred D. Steinberg, M.D., (301) 496-1961; Arthritis and Rheumatism Branch, James E. Balow, M.D., (301) 496-4181, Kidney Disease Section, National Institute of Diabetes and Digestive and Kidney Diseases (NIDDK).

Genodermatoses
Investigators are interested in determining the etiology of various genodermatoses, including but not limited to Darier's disease, the ichthyoses, basal cell nevus syndrome (Gorlin Syndrome), and albinism. Clinical, genetic, and molecular biologic approaches are used. Diagnosis and genetic counseling are available. Families with individuals affected with genodermatoses are eligible for study. Contact: Sherri J. Bale, Ph.D., Laboratory of Skin Biology, (301) 496-3375.

5) National Cancer Institute

Gregory A. Curt, M.D.
Clinical Director

Telephone referrals should be directed to physicians listed under each branch.

Biological Response Modifiers Program
Dan L. Longo, M.D.
Acting Chief, Clinical Research Branch
(301) 846-1520

Clinical testing of biological agents and their integration with combination chemotherapy in the treatment of cancer is under way. The agents examined include immunoaugmenting and immunomodulatory agents, lymphokines, interferons, maturation and differentiation factors, tumor vaccines, antitumor monoclonal antibodies and antitumor effector cells. The Clinical Research Branch is located in Frederick, MD, with the National Cancer Institute's Frederick Cancer Research and Development Center. There is a BRMP inpatient unit including a cytapheresis unit

and an intensive care monitoring unit in the Frederick Memorial Hospital. The outpatient center is located across the street from the hospital in the Frederick Memorial Hospital Cancer Treatment Center. Both units are staffed by NCI oncologists and research nurses.

Studies are focused on early clinical testing of interferons and antitumor monoclonal antibodies, lymphokines (alone, in combination, and in unique formulations) and cytotoxic T-cells and monocytes. The trials are open to patients with histologically proven cancer for which there is no known effective therapy or recurrent cancer of any type which is refractory to curative therapy. Patients must be ambulatory and not have received chemotherapy, radiation or corticosteriod therapy within three to four weeks of entering the trial. The trials are open to patients with colon cancer, ovarian cancer, malignant melanoma, renal cell carcinoma, malignant lymphoma, and hairy cell leukemia. Patients with other solid tumors are considered.

Another focus of research is previously untreated lymphoma patients: Hodgkin's disease, any stage or massive mediastinal non-Hodgkin's lymphoma, indolent as well as aggressive histologies. Refractory or relapsed non-Hodgkin's lymphoma are also eligible for studies.

Patients entering research trials of the Clinical Research Branch will be referred back to their primary physician after the trial completion for ongoing care and follow-up. Patients will receive funds to help defray hospitalization and travel expenses.

Dermatology Branch
Chief: Stephen I. Katz, M.D., Ph.D.
(301) 496-2481
Selected patients with the following diseases will be admitted for study:

Basal Cell carcinoma (especially nevoid basal cell carcinoma)
Benign Mucosal Pemphigoid (ocular pemphigoid)
Bullous Pemphigoid
Dermatitis Herpetiformis
Disorders of Keratinization (Ichthyoses, Darier's

Disease)
Epidermodysplasia Verruciformis (Genetic predisposition for flat warts and squamous cell carcinoma)
Epidermolysis Bullosa Acquisita
Erythema Elevatum Diutinum
Granuloma Faciale
Erythema Multiforme
Herpes Gestationis
Multiple Warts
Pemphigus Foliaceus
Pemphigus Vulgaris
Psoriasis
Sezary Syndrome
Vasculitis
Xeroderma Pigmentosum

Epidemiology Program
Chief: Joseph F. Fraumeni, Jr., M.D.
(301) 496-1611
Persons with cancer or at high-risk of cancer are sought for studies on the causes of cancer. Patients are considered for inclusion based on the following conditions:

1. Strong family history of malignant or benign neoplasia of an unusual type, pattern or frequency (e.g., three or more close relatives with cancer, particularly melanomas, sarcomas, lymphoproliferative neoplasms, ovarian, bladder and renal carcinomas);

2. Known or suspected factor(s) that predispose to neoplasia: environmental exposures (occupation, drugs, radiation, diet, viruses, etc.) or genetic and congenital factors (birth defects, chromosomal anomalies or Mendelian traits associated with neoplasia, especially Recklinghausen's neurofibromatosis and bilateral acoustic neurofibromatosis);

3. Tumors presenting with peculiar demographic or clinical features (unusual age of onset, bilaterality, unusual histopathology or response to therapy, or associated medical conditions);

4. Documented history of T-cell leukemia and/or lymphoma for study of human T-cell lymphotropic virus (HTLV) type I;

5. Elevated risk for acquired immune deficiency

syndrome (AIDS) to evaluate the predisposition to certain cancers (e.g., non-Hodgkin's lymphoma) and the role of human immunodeficiency virus (HIV).

Studies include verifying the patient's personal and family history through questionnaire, interview and review of records and histologic slides, and sometimes offering in-depth clinical and laboratory evaluation to clarify the mechanism of carcinogenesis. Studies may involve drawing blood, taking skin biopsy and radiographic examinations, and use of clinically available tissue for laboratory assays. No therapy beyond counseling is offered but referral to other National Cancer Institute (NCI) clinical branches will be expedited.

Experimental Immunology Branch
Chief: Alfred Singer, M.D.
(301) 496-5461

Malignant Disease
Treatment using autologous bone marrow transplantation is evaluated. The study is open to patients with T-cell malignancy who have failed to respond satisfactorily to conventional therapy. All patients must fail to meet criteria for entry into routine allogeneic bone marrow transplantation studies. Patient evaluations will include staging and determining the baseline immunologic function. The patient will be treated with total body irradiation and combination chemotherapy followed by the administration of autologous marrow depleted of tumor. After marrow infusion, follow-up studies include those tests useful in restaging or understanding the competence of the reconstituting immune system.

Medicine Branch
Chief: Robert E. Wittes, M.D.
(301) 496-4916

Patients with the following diseases are eligible for admission to the Medicine Branch for experimental treatment provided they have not received prior chemotherapy or, where indicated, prior radiotherapy. A serious underlying illness in addition to the patient's neoplasm will disqualify the patient from eligibility.

Hodgkin's Disease and Non-Hodgkin's Lymphoma
Patients with biopsy-proven diagnosis of these diseases not previously treated are eligible for treatment in collaboration with the Radiation Oncology Branch.

Ovarian Carcinoma
Patients who have epithelial tumors of the ovary are eligible. All stages of disease are acceptable, provided patients have had no prior chemotherapy or radiotherapy. Selected patients with minimal residual disease after initial treatment are considered.

Breast Carcinoma
Patients with primary breast masses or disseminated breast cancer with evaluable metastatic lesions, are eligible for chemotherapeutic trials. Primary breast cancer treatment studies to compare breast irradiation and lymph node dissection to modified radical mastectomy and chemotherapy.

AIDS/Kaposi's Sarcoma
Patients who develop Kaposi's sarcoma in the context of AIDS are admitted for experimental therapy.

Colon Cancer
Patients with measurable metastatic colon cancer are eligible for a range of primary and second line treatment protocols.

Clinical Pharmacology Branch
Chief: Charles E. Myers, M.D.
(301) 402-1357

Prostate Cancer
Patients with a good performance status and no serious medical problems are eligible for treatment with Suramin and other new agents.

Metabolism Branch
Chief: Thomas A. Waldmann, M.D.
(301) 496-6653

Agammaglobulinemia
Selected patients with X-linked Agammaglobulinemia and thymoma and agammaglobulinemia are studied.

Ataxia-Telangiectasia
Patients with Ataxis-telangiectasia are admitted for thorough evaluation and intensive study of immunologic function.

DiGeorge Syndrome (Thymic-Parathyroid Aplasia)
Selected patients with the DiGeorge syndrome are admitted for study and therapy.

Growth Hormone Deficiency
Selected patients between 4 and 20 years old with isolated growth hormone deficiency or growth hormone deficiency as part of panhypopituitarism are studied.

Hypogammaglobulinemia
Patients with common, variable hypogammaglobulinemia and different forms of dysgammaglobulinemia are studied.

Isolated IgA Deficiency
Selected patients with isolated IgA deficiency or IgA deficiency associated with autoimmune disorders are studied.

Severe Combined Immunodeficiency
Selected patients with severe combined immunodeficiency syndrome are admitted for study and therapy. Patients with adenosine deaminase deficiency (ADA) are admitted for gene therapy of their disease.

Cutaneous T-Cell Lymphomas (Sezary Syndrome)
Selected patients with cutaneous T-cell lymphomas are admitted for study and immunotherapy with monoclonal antibodies.

Adult T-Cell Leukemia
Selected patients with human T-cell lymphotropic virus-I-associated (HTLV-I) adult T-cell leukemia are admitted for study and immunotherapy with monoclonal antibodies.

Tropical Spastic Paraparesis
Selected patients with tropical spastic paraparesis (TSP) are admitted for study and immunotherapy with monoclonal antibodies.

Wiskott-Aldrich Syndrome
Patients are admitted for extensive evaluation of immunodeficiency and platelet defect. Splenectomy and/or high dose IV Ig therapy are evaluated.

NCI-NAVY Medical Oncology Branch
Acting Chief: Bruce Johnson, M.D.
(301) 496-0920
(301) 496-0901
Military and civilian patients with certain neoplastic diseases are referred to this branch for primary treatment studies. Combination chemotherapy, radiation therapy and immunotherapy, including antibodies directed against tumor growth factors, are investigated. In addition, basic research in tumor cell biology, genetics, cytogenetics and immunology is conducted on clinically available material.

Civilian and military patients with non-small cell and small cell lung cancer, and mycosis fungoides/Sezary syndrome are of particular interest.

Pediatric Branch
Chief: Philip A. Pizzo, M.D.
(301) 496-4256

The Pediatric Branch accepts patients with selected neoplasms who are between 1 and 25 years old. All patients accepted for admission may be enrolled in studies of optimal supportive care techniques. Clinically available materials are employed in basic studies of molecular biology, kinetics, cell biology, biochemistry, immunology and genetics.

Acute Leukemia
Untreated patients, usually under 25 years old, are considered for admission. In patients with acute lymphocytic leukemia, the therapeutic emphasis is on the evaluation of drug combinations, new agents and various methods for cranial prophylaxis. Previously treated patients are eligible for Phase I or II studies. Selected patients are eligible for allogeneic bone marrow transplantation using T-cell-depleted marrow.

Ewing's Sarcoma
Previously untreated patients with a biopsy-proven diagnosis are eligible for admission and treatment with radiation and chemotherapy. Current studies also evaluate GM-CSF in treatments of this neoplasm.

Brain Tumors
Patients with previously treated or untreated CNS

malignancies may be eligible for chemotherapy treatment protocols.

Neuroblastoma
Patients with metastatic disease are eligible for treatment with TIL (tumor infiltrating lymphocyte) therapy.

Non-Hodgkin's Malignant Lymphoma (especially Burkitt's Lymphoma)
Patients under 25 years old with a suspected or proven diagnosis of non-Hodgkin's lymphoma are sought. While untreated patients are preferred, certain treated patients are accepted. The treatment emphasis is on combined modality therapy including surgery, radiation and chemotherapy.

Osteogenic Sarcoma
Previously untreated patients with non-metastatic disease are offered surgery and adjuvant chemotherapy with the Surgery Branch.

Rhabdomyosarcoma and Undifferentiated Sarcomas
Previously untreated patients with extensive disease are considered for admission. Combined modality therapy is evaluated.

Acquired Immunodeficiency Syndrome (AIDS)
Children with AIDS or symptomatic HIV infection who are between 3 months and 18 years old are eligible for therapy with azidothymidine (AZT), ddC, ddI, or other antiviral agents alone or in combination.

Radiation Oncology Branch
Chief: Eli Glatstein, M.D.
(301) 496-5457

Breast Cancer
Patients with Stage I or II breast cancer receive either radical mastectomy or primary radiotherapy to the breast. This study is performed with the Surgery and Medicine Branch. Early breast cancer studies involve randomization between radiotherapy and operative therapy.

Unresectable Sarcomas
Patients with locally unresectable tumors of any histologic type receive radiation therapy and radiosensitizers.

Gliomas

Patients without prior radiation therapy are eligible for a variety of radiotherapy studies performed with the Neurological Surgery Branch of NINDS.

Hodgkin's Disease

Patients with previously untreated disease are eligible for full staging and therapy with radiation and/or combination chemotherapy. This study is performed with the Medicine Branch.

Non-Hodgkin's Malignant Lymphomas

Previously untreated patients with a biopsy-proven diagnosis of lymphoma are eligible for admission and treatment. This study is performed with the Medicine Branch.

Oat Cell Cancer

Patient with biopsy-proven oat cell carcinoma of the lung are eligible for treatment. This study is performed with the NCI-NAVY Medical Oncology Branch.

Gastric Cancer

Patients with these neoplasms and no distant metastases are eligible for studies involving intraoperative irradiation with radical surgery performed by the Surgery Branch.

Carcinoma of the Bladder

Patients without distant hematogenous metastases are eligible for studies dealing with phototherapy and/or interstitial irradiation with urologists in the Surgery Branch.

Abdominal Sarcomas

Patients with visceral or retroperitoneal sarcomas can be considered for protocol treatment with surgery and photodynamic therapy. This study is performed with the Surgery Branch.

Ovarian Cancer

Patients with ovarian cancer can be considered for treatment with chemotherapy and intraoperative photodynamic therapy. This study is performed with the Medicine and Surgery Branches.

Cervix Cancer

Patients with locally advanced cervix cancer without distant hematogenous metastases are eligible to receive radiation therapy and radiosensitizers.

Surgery Branch

Chief: Steven A. Rosenberg, M.D., Ph.D.
(301) 496-4164
Admitting Officer: David N. Danforth, Jr., M.D.
(301) 496-1534

Sarcomas of Bone and Soft Tissues

Patients with high grade sarcomas of the extremity or trunk, who may or may not have had definitive surgical therapy, are eligible for treatment under new radiotherapeutic and chemotherapeutic adjuvant combined modality studies. Patients with low grade sarcomas of either the extremity or the trunk who may or may not have had definitive surgical therapy are eligible for treatment under combined surgery and radiation therapy studies. Other studies evaluate new immunotherapeutic regimens for patients with sarcoma who have not responded to standard treatments.

Patients with high grade osteogenic sarcomas of the extremity are eligible for treatment under combined surgery and chemotherapy studies.

Breast Cancer

Patients with untreated stage I-II epithelial cancers of the breast and patients with breast masses which require biopsy to exclude malignancy are considered.

Patients with locally advanced stage III or stage IV epithelial cancers of the breast are considered for combined modality or immunotherapy trials.

Melanoma

Patients with disseminated melanoma without central nervous system involvement will be considered for adoptive immunotherapy trials.

Lung Cancer

Previously untreated patients with squamous cell carcinoma of the lung confined to one hemithorax with positive mediastinal nodes are considered for combined modality surgery-radiation therapy studies. Patients must not have had previous thoracotomy.

Renal Cancer

Patients with metastatic renal cell carcinoma are considered for adoptive immunotherapy trials.

Bladder Cancer
Patients with superficial or invasive bladder cancer are considered for phototherapy or interstitial implantation protocols.

Metastatic Colorectal Cancer
Patients with measurable metastatic colorectal cancer and good performance status will be considered for combinations of immunotherapy and chemotherapy.

Cancer of the Pancreas
Patients with documented localized or locally advanced (non-metastatic) adeno-carcinoma of the pancreas will be evaluated for combined modality multidrug chemotherapy and surgery. Eligibility requirements also include good performance status and no prior radiation or chemotherapy.

Cancer of the Stomach
Patients with newly diagnosed untreated carcinoma of the stomach are considered for a treatment strategy of pre- and post-operative chemotherapy in combination with surgery. Patients should have localized disease and be medically able to undergo surgery.

6) National Institute of Child Health and Human Development

Fernando Cassorla, M.D.
Clinical Director

NICHD is concerned with the biological and neurobiological, medical and behavioral aspects of normal and abnormal human development. Patients with genetic, metabolic or endocrine disorders are evaluated and admitted to the institute's inpatient wards and outpatient clinics.

Telephone referrals of patients should be directed to chiefs listed under each branch. General inquiries should be directed to:
Fernando Cassorla, M.D.
Clinical Director
(301) 496-1068

Human Genetics Branch
Chief: William A. Gahl, M.D., Ph.D.

(301) 496-6683
The Human Genetics Branch pursues the diagnosis and treatment of inborn metabolism errors including certain amino acidurias, lysosomal storage diseases, disorders of carbohydrate metabolism, disorders of secreted proteins, bone and connective tissue disorders, transport defects, and disorders of copper metabolism.

Selected patients are accepted into studies designed to investigate the following specific disorders:

Cystinosis
Individuals with nephropathic cystinosis are treated with cysteamine and related cystine-depleting agents. Growth, kidney function and effects of cysteamine therapy are monitored. The natural history of cystinosis is studied in cystinotic patients who have had a renal transplant. Individuals with late-onset and benign cystinosis, as well as infants with cystinosis diagnosed at birth are of special interest. The clinical concomitants of renal Fanconi syndrome are investigated.

Lysosomal Storage Disorders
Individuals with suspected but undiagnosed lysosomal storage disorders are sought for investigation. Deficiencies of two or more lysosomal enzymes, variant manifestations of a single lysosomal deficiency and the combination of a lysosomal enzyme deficiency with cystine storage are of special interest.

Lowe Syndrome (Oculocerebrorenal)
Patients and female carriers with Lowe syndrome are examined. The ophthalmic, renal, neurological and biochemical aspects of the syndrome are studied.

Amino Acid Disorders
Selected patients with amino-acidemias or aminoacidurias of unknown etiology are investigated.

α_1 Antritrypsin Deficiency
The natural history and pathogenesis of liver disease associated with α_1 antritrypsin deficiency is studied. Individuals with rare α_1-antritrypsin genes are identified and the molecular structures of these rare alleles are characterized.

Menkes' Disease
Individuals with Menkes' Disease are treated with copper histidinate, an experimental therapy of potential benefit in patients diagnosed and treated from an early age. The biochemical as well as clinical effects of copper histidinate therapy are monitored. Other disorders of copper metabolism are also studied.

Osteogenesis Imperfecta
Several types of osteogenesis imperfecta and Ehlers-Danlos syndrome are studied at the gene defect level. Collagen-specific nucleotide probes are used to study gene expression in skin and bone. Studies are conducted on the endocrine basis of short stature in osteogenesis imperfecta.

Ectodermal Dysplasia
Clinical and basic research aspects of ectodermal dysplasia are investigated.

Developmental Endocrinology Branch
Chief: Bruce C. Nisula, M.D.
(301) 496-4686
The Developmental Endocrinology Branch directs its efforts toward understanding the endocrine concomitants of growth, development and reproduction. Patients of any age are admitted.

Patients with the following disorders are of current interest:

Cushing's Syndrome
Patients with the tentative diagnosis of Cushing's syndrome are accepted for studies to assess the efficacy of several newly developed diagnostic and therapeutic approaches.

Nelson's Syndrome
Patients with Nelson's syndrome are studied to assess the effectiveness of several pharmacological agents in suppressing elevated ACTH secretion.

Congenital Adrenal Hyperplasia
Children and adults with congenital adrenal hyperplasia are studied to determine the optimum dose and dose schedule of glucocorticoid treatment, to develop improved biochemical criteria for monitoring the effectiveness of treatment, to assess the effect of supplemental dietary salt on the control of adrenal androgen

secretion, and to evaluate a new approach to treatment based upon antiandrogen combined with an inhibitor of androgen-to-estrogen conversion.

Adrenal Insufficiency
Prepubertal children with primary or secondary adrenal insufficiency (including panhypopituitarism) are accepted into studies to determine the optimal glucocorticoid dosage for growth.

Short Stature
Patients with growth hormone-deficient and non-growth hormone deficient short stature are accepted for studies to improve diagnostic methods and to evaluate new treatment approaches. Among these approaches are treatment with growth hormone-releasing hormone or growth hormone to accelerate growth rate, and luteinizing hormone-releasing hormone analog to delay epiphyseal closure.

Premature Ovarian Failure
Patients with premature ovarian failure are being studied to understand the cause of this disorder and to evaluate the effectiveness of new therapeutic approaches.

Congenital or Acquired Hypothyroidism
Prepubertal children with congenital or acquired hypothyroidism are studied to determine the optimum thyroid hormone dose for skeletal growth.

Turner Syndrome
Girls with Turner syndrome are studied to assess the effect of low dose estrogen and growth hormone on adult height.

Hypophosphatemic Rickets
Children with hypophosphatemic rickets are studied to evaluate the pathophysiology and treatment of growth failure.

Precocious Puberty
Patients with tentative diagnoses of premature thelarche, premature adrenarche, McCune-Albright syndrome and familial male-limited precocious puberty are studied. The pathophysiology of the disorders and new methods of treatment are investigated.

Delayed Puberty and Kallmann's Syndrome
Patients with delayed puberty or Kallmann's

syndrome are accepted into studied of the pathophysiology, diagnosis and treatment of these disorders. Studies include assessment of optimal androgen levels and estrogen levels for pubertal growth and accumulation of adult bone mass.

Hirsutism and Virilism
Patients with Hirsutism or virilism, including suspected adrenal or gonadal tumors, are accepted into studies of pathogenesis, diagnosis and treatment.

Multiple Miscarriages
Women with multiple miscarriages are studied to evaluate the pathophysiology of the disorder.

Infertility
Patients with polycystic ovarian syndrome who have not responded to clomiphene citrate treatment are evaluated and accepted into clinical trials evaluating other methods of treatment. Patients with other disorders of ovulation including premature ovarian failure may be candidates for ongoing clinical trials. Patients with idiopathic infertility are studied to determine the causes of this disorder.

Pituitary Tumors
Patients with pituitary tumors are studied to determine the optimum treatment modality. This study is carried out with the Neurosurgical Branch of NINDS.

Ambiguous Genitalia
Children and adults with ambiguous genitalia are evaluated to identify the causes of this disorder. Treatment is offered if appropriate.

Autoimmune Polyglandular Disorders
Children and adults with Type I or Type II auto-immune polyglandular disorder are studied to determine the etiologic mechanisms of this disease.

Cell Biology and Metabolism Branch
Chief: Richard D. Klausner, M.D.
(301) 496-6368
The Cell Biology and Metabolism Branch is concerned with abnormalities of metal metabolism. Of particular interest are patients with hereditary hemochromatosis. Patients can be referred for diagnosis and clinical evaluation, recommendations

concerning therapy and the management of multisystem involvement. Patients and family members are enrolled in studies to understand the molecular basis of the disease and to establish tools for early diagnosis.

Laboratory of Comparative Ethology
Chief: Stephen J. Suomi, Ph.D.
9301) 496-6833

Developmental Psychology
The Child and Family Research Section is conducting a series of normative and descriptive studies on children's behavioral development and their experiences in the natural home environment. Research participants are from the Washington, D.C. area. Mother-infant interactions are studied until the child is four years old. Background conditions, such as whether the mother is employed outside of the home, are evaluated for their influence on the child's psychological development. Longitudinal studies focus on events that motivate the child to develop competence.

The Section on Social and Emotional Development is conducting longitudinal research on the cultural, social, and physiological origins of individual differences in the behavioral styles and relationship patterns of infants between birth and 5 years of age.

7) National Institute on Deafness and Other Communication Disorders

Ralph Naunton, M.D.
Acting Clinical Director

Telephone referrals should be directed to:
Suzanne Lischynsky
(301) 496-7491
(301) 496-0771 (TDD)

Voice and Speech Section
Speech Disorders
Patients with speech production problems associated with neurological or laryngological

disorders or without apparent cause are studied. Special emphasis is on stuttering and oral-lingual dystonia. Studies investigate movements of the larynx, tongue, lips and jaw during speech and oral movement. Diagnosis and evaluation are available. Positron emission tomography is used to examine brain activity during normal and disordered speech. The effects of botulinum toxin injections and neuropharmacological treatments are evaluated in selected patients with the following disorders: stuttering, dysarthria, verbal apraxia, Tourette syndrome, dystonia, Parkinson's disease, Huntington's chorea, cerebellar disorders, and essential tremor. Contact: Christy Ludlow, Ph.D., (301) 496-9365; (301) 496-0771 (TDD).

Voice or Laryngeal Disorders
Patients with phonatory disorders associated with neurological or laryngological disorders or without apparent cause are studied. Comprehensive diagnostic evaluations are provided. Investigations include vocal fold movements, vibration, respiratory coordination, brain activation patterns while speaking and intrinsic laryngeal muscle function. The effects of intramuscular injections, nerve block and neuropharmacological treatment are determined for a few patients with the following disorders: Spastic or spasmodic dysphonia, voice tremor, vocal fold paralysis, and laryngeal nodules or polyps. Contact: Christy Ludlow, Ph.D., (301) 496-9365; (301) 496-0771 (TDD).

Hearing Section
Clinical Audiology Unit
Hearing Assessment
Patients and normal volunteers are studied for development and validation of clinical techniques to identify a significant change in the human hearing mechanism or provide an audiologic profile of patients with specific disorders. The purpose is to obtain normative data using certain test procedures and/or equipment from control subjects who are otologically and audiologically normal and to follow those patients who are being treated (medically and surgically) for hearing loss. This study uses equal numbers of age and sex matched subjects. Test procedures include various auditory evoked potential paradigms as well as manipulations of speech signal, especially studies of dichotic function over a wide age range. Also

included in this normative battery are studies of acoustic immittance, including tympanometry and acoustic reflexes. The data are used for comparison with various patient populations studied with the same audiologic techniques. Contact: Anita Pikus, M.A., (301) 496-7491; (301) 496-0771 (TDD).

Inherited Deafness
Patients with inherited deafness, specifically patients with Waardenburg syndrome type 1 and type 2 are sought for inclusion in a linkage analysis gene mapping study. Typical manifestations of the Waardenburg syndrome(s) include: dystopia canthorum, white forelock, prematurely gray hair, deafness or hearing impairment, heterochromia irides or iris bicolor, and hypopigmented areas of the skin. Evaluation will include audiologic, vestibular, ophthalmologic and genetic studies. Most helpful in the study will be individuals in families with sizable numbers of affected individuals, multigenerational structure, and ample sibships. Studies on inherited deafness disorders other than Waardenburg syndrome are planned and inquiries regarding potential referral of patients for study enrollment are welcomed. Contact: Kenneth M. Grundfast, M.D., (301) 496-7491; (301) 496-0771 (TDD).

8) National Institute of Dental Research

Bruce J. Baum, D.M.D., Ph.D.
Clinical Director

Telephone referrals should be directed to the investigators listed after each study description.

Salivary Gland Function and Dysfunction
Patients with suspected or actual alterations in salivary gland physiology are sought for evaluation of the etiology, sequelae and treatment of such disorders. Particular interest is focused on individuals with a complaint of dry mouth (xerostomia) related to Sjogren's syndrome or radiation-induced gland damage. Individuals with head and neck neoplasms whose regimen of therapy would consist of radiation of the oro-facial area (independent of chemotherapy) are needed

to be seen after the course of radiotherapy. Comprehensive oral evaluation and therapy is provided. Patients with hypofunctional salivary glands (especially those with primary Sjogren's syndrome) are sought for clinical trials of agents to increase salivary output. Contact: Philip C. Fox, D.D.S., (301) 496-4278.

Taste and Related Oral Sensory Disorders
Patients who are experiencing a persistent bad taste in their mouth (dysgeusia), other distortions (losses or reductions) or taste, or with olfactory disorders are needed for clinical studies. These disruptions of perception may occur as isolated symptoms or in conjunction with oral or systemic disease, salivary gland dysfunction or various therapeutic regimens. Patients with taste or olfactory disorders of unknown etiology are of special interest. Thorough oral and dental evaluations are made of each patient and gustatory and olfactory function clinically evaluated. Consultation or referral is offered as appropriate. Contact: James M. Weiffenbach, Ph.D., (301) 496-4278.

Oral Motor Dysfunction
Individuals with altered performance in orofacial muscular functions (swallowing, mastication, speech, irregular tongue movements), independent of generalized neurologic dysfunction are needed for studies of etiology, assessment and treatment. Oral motor dysfunctions that are drug induced and idiopathic are of special interest. Patients with general neuropathies who exhibit particularly disabling oral motor disorders are studied. Patients will receive a thorough oral evaluation as well as clinical dental examination. Noninvasive, quantitative assessments of tongue functions are made by ultrasound methodology. Patients will consult with medical specialists and speech pathologists as appropriate. Contact: Bruce J. Baum, D.M.D., Ph.D., (301) 496-1363.

Recurrent Herpes
Individuals with recurrent herpes simplex involving the face or other non-genital areas (buttocks and thighs) are needed for studies examining the pathogenesis and therapy of these lesions. Contact: James F. Rooney, M.D., (301) 496-0309.

Oral Surgery
Patients in need of removal of impacted third molars serve as subjects for a series of investigations to evaluate pharmacological methods of pain control. Novel analgesics, local anesthetics and sedative drugs are compared to standard drugs. Contact: Raymond Dionne, D.D.S., Ph.D., (301) 496-5483.

Chronic Facial Pain
Patients with chronic facial pain may be eligible for clinical studies evaluating novel diagnostic and therapeutic modalities. Patients with pain related to the muscles of mastication, temporomandibular joint or the trigeminal nerve, uncomplicated by prior treatments, may be eligible. Contact: Kevin Reid, D.D.S., M.S. and Raymond Dionne, D.D.S., Ph.D. (301) 496-5483.

Painful Diabetic Neuropathy
Patients with chronic pain from diabetic neuropathy may take part in controlled trials of conventional and experimental drugs that may relieve the pain. Contact: Mitchell Max, M.D., (301) 496-5484.

Reflex Sympathetic Dystrophy or Causalgia
Patients are sought for a 1-3 day program of detailed tests of sensory perception, with the intention of elucidating the underlying physiological abnormality. The findings may aid in suggesting treatment to the referring physician. Contact: Mitchell Max, M.D., (301) 496-5483 or 496-6695.

Oral Endosseous Implants
Partially and totally edentulous patients are sought to evaluate the clinical performance of a titanium implant system. The investigation also will evaluate diet, body image, personality profiles, denture satisfaction, gingival health and oral hygiene in patients with conventional dentures as well as those with implant supported dental prostheses. Contact: Jaime S. Brahim, D.D.S., M.S., (301) 496-4371.

9) National Institute of Diabetes and Digestive and Kidney Diseases

James E. Balow, M.D.
Clinical Director

Telephone referral should be directed to physicians listed under each subject area:

Blood Diseases
Studies of blood coagulation and platelet function are under way to develop therapy for various congenital and acquired hemorrhagic and thrombotic diseases. There is a special interest in immune thrombocytopenias and hemostatic disorders involving platelets. Patients with disorders such as drug-induced thrombocytopenia, post-transfusion purpura, neonatal thrombocytopenia, idiopathic thrombocytopenic purpura and lupus-associated thrombocytopenia are sought for serologic testing and treatment. Congenital and acquired platelet abnormalities and obscure, undiagnosed bleeding disorders are considered for evaluation. Patients with suspected thrombasthenia and Bernard-Soulier Syndrome are of particular interest. Contact: N. Raphael Shulman, M.D., Clinical Hematology Branch, (301) 496-4787.

Chronic Viral Hepatitis
Persons with chronic viral hepatitis—either type B, delta, or non-A, non-B hepatitis—are accepted into studies of anti-viral therapy. Patients should be between 18 and 70 years old and without other significant medical illnesses. Patients are evaluated in the outpatient clinics to assess chronic hepatitis disease activity and the status of hepatitis virus in the serum. Patients with high titers of virus and active disease may enter into a randomized controlled trial of an antiviral therapy. Contact: Jay H. Hoofnagle, M.D. and Adrian M. DiBisceglie, M.D., Liver Diseases Section, (301) 496-1721.

Pruritus of Cholestasis
Patients with severe itching due to cholestatic liver disease are admitted for evaluation and entry into controlled treatment trials, which include administering opiate antagonists. Contact: E. Anthony Jones, M.D., Liver Diseases Section, (301) 496-1721.

Diabetes Mellinus
Patients between 6 and 60 years old will be considered for study.

1. Both insulin-treated and non-insulin-treated patients with insulin resistance (patients with high endogenous insulin concentrations or patients who usually require more than 200 units per day of exogenous insulin). This includes patients with lipotrophic diabetes, syndrome of insulin resistance associated with acanthosis nigricans, acromegaly, Cushing's disease and excess antibody production.

2. Patients with hyperglycemic symptoms of an autoimmune disorder.

Severely ill patients may be referred by calling Richard Eastman, Derek LeRoith, and Simeon Taylor, M.E., Diabetes Branch, (301) 496-4658.

Gastrointestinal Diseases
The Gastroenterology Section is interested in conferring with outside physicians involved in gastroenterology problems that are unusual because of the rarity, complexity, associated features or family distribution. Of particular interest are patients with Zollinger-Ellison syndrome or other functional islet cell tumors. Zollinger-Ellison patients or patients with functional islet cell tumors who have disseminated tumor, localized disease or no apparent tumor are all of interest. Patients with atypical or refractory peptic ulcers are also sought. Contact: Robert T. Jensen, M.D., Gastroenterology Section, (301) 496-4201.

Hyperthyroidism with Carcinoma
Some patients with cancer develop increased concentrations of protein-bound- and thyroxine-iodine in their serum, typically unaccompanied by the usual physical findings of hyperthyroidism. This condition may be due to production by the neoplasm of an ectopic thyroid-stimulating hormone. Patients with this association are of interest for this study. Contact: Bruce Weintraub, M.D., Molecular, Cellular and Nutritional Endocrinology Branch, (301) 496-3405.

Hypoglycemia
Selected patients over 16 years old how have had fasting blood glucose of 45mg/100ml or less will be studied and treated. Of particular interest are hypoglycemic patients who have large intrathoracic and intra-abdominal tumors that do not secrete excess insulin. Patients with insulin-secreting tumors of the pancreas or autoantibodies to the insulin receptor are also sought. Fasting hypoglycemia of unknown etiology is studied. Contact: Richard C. Eastman (301) 496-4658, Derek LeRoith, M.D. (301) 496-4658, and Simeon Taylor, M.D., Diabetes Branch, (301) 496-4658.

Parathyroid Disorders and Metabolic Bone Diseases
Patients with hypercalcemia, hypophosphatemia, nephrocalcinosis, nephrolithiasis, multiple endocrine adenomatosis or other manifestations of hyperparathyroidism are sought. Familial hypercalcemia is of interest. Patients with mild asymptomatic hyperparathyroidism are studied prospectively. Patients with persistent or recurrent postoperative hyperparathyroidism will be evaluated with preoperative parathyroid gland localization methods.

Related methods are applied in selected cases of hypoparathyroidism, rickets, osteomalacia, vitamin D-resistant rickets, juvenile osteoporosis, and certain other abnormalities of bone metabolism. Patients with hereditary hypo-calcemic rickets with or without alopecia are sought. Patients with familial hypocalciuric hypercalcemia are sought for evaluation and investigation. Patients with pseudohypoparathyroidism also are studied.

Patients with acquired osteomalacia are sought. Selected patients with juvenile osteoporosis also are sought. Contact: S.J. Marx, M.D., Metabolic Diseases Branch, (301) 496-5051, and A.M. Spiegel, Molecular Pathophysiology Branch, (301) 496-0808.

Pituitary Tumors and Hypopituitarism
Pituitary tumors with growth hormone hypersecretion (acromegaly or gigantism) are studied and evaluated for therapy with transphenoidal surgery, supervoltage irradiation, bromergocryptine and somatostatin analog. In addition, patients with chromophobe adenomas (with or without galactorrhea) and various forms of anterior pituitary insufficiency are under study, including cases of isolated growth hormone deficiency or patients with apparently normal growth hormone who have growth retardation or growth excess. Contact: Richard C. Eastman, M.D., Derek LeRoith, M.D., and Simeon Taylor, M.D., Diabetes Branch, (301) 496-4658.

Primary Biliary Cirrhosis
Selected patients with primary biliary cirrhosis and other autoimmune chronic cholestatic liver diseases are admitted for diagnostic evaluation, studies of immunologic function and review of therapy. Patients participate in a randomized, controlled trial of an immunosuppressive therapy for this disease. Contact: E. Anthony Jones, M.D., Liver Diseases Section, (301) 496-1721.

Kidney Diseases
Selected patients with immunologically-mediated glomerulonephritis are admitted for study of humoral and cellular immune functions. Patients with membranous nephropathy idiopathic and secondary to lupus are sought for laboratory investigation and therapeutic studies. Contact: James E. Balow, M.D., Howard A. Austin III, M.D., and Karen MacKay, M.D., Kidney Disease Section, (301) 496-3092.

Thyroid Neoplasms
Patients with various types of goiter, thyroid nodules and thyroid carcinoma are studied. Patients with "high risk" forms of thyroid carcinoma and functional metastatic thyroid carcinoma are sought. Medical or surgical treatment is offered if appropriate. Contact: Jacob Robbins, M.D., Clinical Endocrinology Branch, (301) 496-5761.

Inappropriate Secretion of TSH, Hypothyroidism
Patients whose serum concentration of thyrotropin (TSH) does not appear to be appropriate for their clinical status and circulating levels of thyroid hormones are studied. Such patients include those with hyperthyroidism and detectable TSH or those with resistance to the action of thyroid hormone.

Patients with any form of hypothyroidism, particularly those with TSH deficiency and those who require high doses of thyroid hormone replacement are sought. Contact: Bruce D. Weintraub, M.D., Molecular, Cellular and Nutritional Endocrinology Branch, (301) 496-3405.

Zollinger-Ellison Syndrome
Patients with recurrent, ectopic, multiple or typical peptic ulcers associated with gastric hypersecretion, diarrhea or hypergastrinemia are admitted for diagnostic studies and therapy. Those already known to have Zollinger-Ellison syndrome will also be considered. Patients will be assigned to one of two therapies: acid secretory control and exploratory laparotomy for tumor resection or antitumor therapy (chemotherapy, interferon, somatostatin analogues) for those with extensive tumor or metastatic disease. Contact: Robert T. Jensen, M.D., Gastroenterology Section, (301) 496-4201.

Hemoglobinopathies

Studies are currently under way in collaboration with NHLBI to elevate fetal hemoglobin levels in sickle cell patients by pharmacological approaches. These include the use of agents, such as hydroxyurea, 5-azacytidine, or erythropoietin, alone or in combination. Responders will be offered the opportunity to continue on therapy, under close observation, on an extended basis. Patients with sickle cell anemia and related syndromes (S-β-thalassemia, hemoglobin SC or SD disease) are also being recruited to undergo several noninvasive studies aimed at characterizing blood flow abnormalities in the brain. Selected patients will undergo PET scanning and MRI imaging, in conjunction with neurologic and psychometric evaluations. Contact: Griffin P. Rodgers, M.D., Laboratory of Chemical Biology, (301) 496-5408.

10) National Eye Institute

Robert Nussenblatt, M.D.
Clinical Director

Telephone referral of patients
should be directed to:
Robert Nussenblatt, M.D.
Clinical Director
(301) 496-3123

Clinical Branch

Cataracts

Patients with cataracts are sought for clinical, biochemical, histochemical and histopathologic correlative studies. Pupillary membranes with laser pulses are assessed in selected children and adults.

Glaucoma: Studies of the Factors Controlling Intraocular Pressure

Patients with glaucoma, pigment dispersion syndrome, essential iris atrophy and ocular hypertension are studied.

Neuro-Ophthalmology

Patients with various ocular motor, visual or visuo-congenital disturbances of intracranial origin are studied by electro-oculography, pupillography, color testing and campimetric methods to test

neurophysiologic principles and diagnostic criteria. Selection is based on individual discussion with the referring physician.

Ophthalmic Congenital and Genetic Disease

Clinical, biochemical, psychophysical and electrodiagnostic studies of patients with retinal diagnostic problems, retinal degeneration such as retinitis pigmentosa, juvenile macular degeneration, fundus flavimaculatus, gyrate atrophy of the choroid and retina, etc., are conducted. Patients with inherited ocular disease or developmental abnormalities of the eye also are sought. Of special interest are patients and families with anterior chamber abnormalities such as Reiger's Peter's and Axenfeld's syndromes, aniridia, oculocutaneous albinism and ocular albinism.

Congenital and Acquired Color Vision Deficiencies

Patients with verified or suspected alterations of color vision, either congenital or secondary to retinal or intracranial disorder, are sought for study of the physiological concomitants of the alterations and to test neurophysiological principles and diagnostic criteria. Selection is based on individual discussion with the potential patient and on preliminary testing.

Vitreo-Retinal Disease

Patients with adult onset diabetes and minimal or no ocular changes are recruited. This study tests the efficacy of drugs to prevent the ocular manifestations of this disease. Additionally, diabetic patients with ocular changes such as macular edema are sought to participate in randomized laser studies.

Retinal Degeneration

Patients with senile macular and other acquired disorders of the macula, especially idiopathic central serous choroidopathy, are sought for studies of the pathogenesis of these conditions. Patients with retinitis pigmentosa, especially members of larger pedigrees, are also sought for clinical studies. Macular edema cases are of special interest.

Uveitis

Patients having anterior uveitis, ocular sarcoidosis, toxoplasmic chorioretinitis, pars planitis, ocular complications of Behcet's disease, Harada's disease, Intractable uveitis of unknown cause and severe recurrent anterior uveitis are sought for the study of immunologic concomitants of their disease and for therapeutic clinical trials. Patients with intermediate and posterior uveitis are sought for studies evaluating the efficacy of several therapeutic approaches.

11) National Heart, Lung, and Blood Institute

Harry R. Keiser, M.D.
Clinical Director

Telephone referrals should be directed
to the physicians listed under each branch.

Cardiology Branch
Chief: Stephen E. Epstein, M.D.
(301) 496-5817
Deputy Chief: Robert O. Bonow, M.D.
(301) 496-9895

Coronary Artery Disease
Patients under 80 years old with known or suspected coronary artery disease are studied by clinical techniques, exercise testing, radionuclide cineangiography, exercise thallium scintigraphy, and coronary arteriography to select appropriate candidates for surgical correction or balloon dilation. Appropriate patients will have the opportunity of undergoing studies to determine whether coronary collateral growth can be facilitated by pharmacologic interventions. Studies involving thallium imaging, positron emission tomography (PET), and magnetic resonance imaging (MRI) are in progress to identify viable myocardium in patients with previous infarction and left ventricular dysfunction.

Microvascular Angina
Patients with anginal-like chest pain and normal coronary arteries are evaluated by noninvasive and invasive techniques. The evaluation determines whether the pain is due to myocardial ischemia and, if so, to ascertain the precipitating mechanisms and optimal therapeutic approaches to microvascular angina.

Hypertrophic Cardiomyopathy (HCM, ASH, IHSS)
Selected patients having or suspected of having HCM are evaluated and followed medically. Electrophysiologic studies are in progress to identify patients at risk of sudden cardiac death. Family studies are underway to identify genetic markers for the disease. Operations will be performed on those patients requiring surgical intervention.

Valvular Heart Disease
An investigation to determine the optimal time for operative intervention is conducted in patients with aortic or mitral valvular regurgitation. Surgery will be performed in patients requiring surgical correction and studies will be conducted to determine those (echocardiographic, radionuclide, hemodynamic) measurements that most reliably reflect reversible or irreversible myocardial dysfunction.

Hypertension
Symptomatic patients with systemic hypertension are studied to assess the effects of blood pressure, left ventricular hypertrophy and coronary flow limitation on left ventricular systolic and diastolic function. The effects of hypertension treatments, regarding effects of blood pressure reduction and hypertrophy regression, on these variables also are assessed.

Hypertension-Endocrine Branch
Chief: Harry R. Keiser, M.D.
Hypertension
(301) 496-1518
As part of a broad program for the study of blood pressure control, this branch will admit for diagnosis, study and treatment, patients with hypertension. Under special study are:

Essential Hypertension
The pathologic physiology of idiopathic hypertension is under intensive study in a number of laboratories of the branch and a program is in progress to explore new pharmacological agents and regimens. Patients under 55 years old without advanced degenerative changes are preferred.

Familial Hypertension
Patients with the following types of familial hypertension are accepted: ACTH-dependent

(Laidlaw); low-renin, low-aldosterone (Liddle); DOCA-dependent with 11-hydroxylase deficiency (adrenogenital) or without (Biglieri).

Pheochromocytoma

A broad study of the biogenesis and pharmacology of epinephrine and norepinephrine that will contribute directly and indirectly to diagnosis and treatment is under way. In established cases, definitive therapy for either benign or malignant disease is available at the referring physician's request.

Renovascular Hypertension

Disorders of renin production and release are under investigation. In established cases of renovascular hypertension, definitive therapy is available at the request of the referring physician.

Steroid Hypertension

All forms of steroid hypertension are studied, including aldosteronism, Cushing's syndrome, DOCA hypertension and the hypertension resulting from enzymatic deficiency or block (17-hydroxylase, 11-hydroxylase) in adrenal steroidogenesis. The control of adrenal steroid biogenesis and the mechanism of steroid hypertension are currently investigated.

Other Areas of Interest

Hypokalemia

Patients with hypokalemia, whether or not associated with hypertension, are admitted for diagnosis and treatment. Patients with hypokalemia, normal blood pressure hyperreninemia and aldosteronism are extensively studied to determine if they have a tubulopathy such as Bartter's syndrome, magnesium-losing tubulopathy or calcium-losing tubulopathy or another cause of their abnormal renal function. Full diagnostic facilities are offered and assistance with management is available as desired.

Molecular Disease Branch

Chief: H. Bryan Brewer, Jr., M.D.
(301) 496-5095

Hyperlipidemia (Hyperlipoproteinemia)

A long-range clinical study is conducted, on an inpatient and an outpatient basis, of patients with hypercholesterolemia, hypertriglyceridemia or both. Familial cases and acquired hyperlipidemia (secondary to diet, dysglobulinemia, obstructive liver disease and certain other causes) may be accepted.

Both etiology and therapy are under investigation. Criteria for acceptance are: abnormally high cholesterol or triglyceride concentrations or xanthomatosis, especially when familial. Patients with early vascular disease are of special interest.

Hypolipidemia (Hypolipoproteinemia)

Familial disorders associated with deficiency of one or more lipids are being intensively studied. These include abetalipoproteinemia, hypobetalipoproteinemia, alpha lipoprotein deficiency (Tangier disease), lecithin cholesterol acyltranserase deficiency. Criteria for acceptance are: acanthocytes, very low concentrations of plasma cholesterol, cholesterol esters, triglycerides or foam cells in tonsils or other tissues.

Clinical Hematology Branch

Chief: Arthur W. Nienhuis, M.D.
(301) 496-5093

Aplastic Anemia and Myelodysplasia

Patients with aplastic anemia are accepted for therapeutic studies including administration of anti-thymocyte globulin, T-cell specific, toxin conjugated immunoglobulins, cyclosporine and hematopoietic growth factors. The pathogenesis of aplastic anemia is investigated. Patients with various myelodysplastic syndromes and significant pancytopenia are also candidates for therapeutic trials of hematopoietic growth factors.

Sickle Cell Anemia and Thalassemia

Investigation is focused on pharmacological manipulation of fetal hemoglobin synthesis. Clinical trials to determine the ability of various drugs and hematopoietic growth factors to increase HbF production are conducted. Hematological and clinical effects of increased fetal hemoglobin are also evaluated. Several non-invasive methods for defining the pathophysiological mechanisms of sickle cell anemia and evaluating clinical severity and therapeutic intervention are under active investigation. Patients with secondary hemochromatosis due to prolonged transfusion are candidates for chronic chelation therapy. Non-invasive measures of tissue iron deposition and toxicity are used.

Pulmonary Branch
Chief: Ronald Crystal, M.D.
(301) 496-3632

Interstitial Lung Disease
Clinical studies in the pathophysiology and biochemistry of pulmonary interstitial disease are under way. Patients with roentgenographic evidence of interstitial disease and/or evidence of restrictive disease by pulmonary function testing are accepted for diagnostic studies. Patients with known diagnoses are accepted on an inpatient and outpatient basis as part of a long-range study in the natural history and therapy of these disorders. Particular emphasis is placed on idiopathic pulmonary fibrosis, sarcoidosis, hypersensitivity, pneumonitis, inorganic dust diseases (pneumoconioses), drug-induced disease and chronic eosinophilic pneumonias.

Hereditary Emphysema (α-1 Antitrypsin Deficiency)
Patients with α-1 antitrypsin deficiency and associated emphysema are accepted for diagnostic and therapeutic studies.

Emphysema and Chronic Bronchitis
Patients with emphysema or chronic bronchitis associated with cigarette smoking are accepted as part of new studies concerning novel approaches to therapy of obstructive airway diseases.

Cystic Fibrosis
Patients with cystic fibrosis are accepted for evaluation of new forms of therapy of cystic fibrosis.

12) National Institute of Mental Health

David R. Rubinow, M.D.
Clinical Director

Telephone referrals of patients
should be directed to:

Jean H. Murphy, R.N., M.S.N.
or Nazli Haq, M.A.
(301) 496-1337

Depression and Mania
Studies in the psychobiology of affective disturbance are under way, including studies on alterations in biogenic amine metabolism, neuroendocrine function and disturbances in biological rhythms. In addition, a number of psychosocial and psychodynamic factors in depression and suicide are under investigation.

Programs are available for both inpatients and outpatients, and may involve an evaluation with biological studies and recommendations, an evaluation with treatment in collaboration with the referring therapist, or a full evaluation and treatment program. Patients with endogenous depression and/or bipolar affective disorder are usually eligible for participation. Specific studies address rapid-cycling, recurrent brief depressions, seasonal, or menstrually-related mood disorders. There is special interest in geriatric depressed patients up to the age of 85 who are otherwise in good health. The eligibility of individuals with more atypical presentations depends on their specific history and symptoms and on the status of specific research studies. Because of the variety of evaluation and treatment programs, referring physicians may call (301) 496-1337 or write the Office of the Clinical Director (Attn: Jean H. Murphy, R.N., M.S.N.) to determine the most suitable program.

Many treatments are under investigation in both inpatient and outpatient studies. Pharmacologic studies of standard and investigational antidepressants, lithium and carbamazepine are ongoing. Non-pharmacologic interventions such as sleep-deprivation and circadian shifts are used in other studies. Individual family, group and milieu therapies may be employed in the treatment program.

Genetic studies are conducted in selected families with a history of affective illness. Family members are evaluated using clinical and biochemical parameters to determine heritable as well as social factors that contribute to the development of affective illness. In addition, participating families are examined for possible "linkage" between known chromosomal markers and affective illness to further clarify the mode(s) of transmission within families. Contact: Jean H. Murphy, R.N., M.S.N., Office of the Clinical Director, (301) 496-1337.

Seasonal Affective Disorder (SAD)
Light treatment (phototherapy) and the relationship between mood changes and changes in seasons and climate are studied. Patients who experience recurrent depression in the winter and at other times of the year are studied. Ongoing studies explore new ways to treat "summer depression" and "winter depression" and to understand how the environment exerts its mood altering affects. Selected patients may participate in long or short term studies. Contact: Charlotte Brown, M.S., Clinical Psychobiology Branch, (301) 496-0500.

Obsessive-Compulsive Disorder
A comprehensive investigation is conducted into the psychobiology of adults with obsessive-compulsive disorder. Major areas of research include: (1) studies of the therapeutic efficacy and mechanism of action of clomipramine and other investigational treatments for this disorder; (2) studies of possible serotonergic and other neurotransmitter and neuromodulator involvement; (3) studies involving neuropsychiatric testing designed to elucidate potential structural and/or functional differences in OCD patients as compared to controls.

The investigations are almost exclusively conducted on an outpatient basis, with referred patients also followed by their own physicians during consultation and study. Contact: Teresa Pigott, M.D. or Suzanne Bernstein, M.D., Laboratory of Clinical Science, (301) 496-3421.

Borderline Personality Disorder
Researchers are examining a select group of men and women ages 18 to 45 who have been diagnosed as borderline and have episodes of behavioral dyscontrol or self-destructive acts. The evaluation includes neurological and physiological studies. Researchers are examining the possible relationship between limbic structure activation and the dysphorias that these patients experience in response to real or perceived rejection. All patients must receive ongoing treatment with the referring therapist. Psychopharmacological

treatment recommendations will be made to the referring therapist after the evaluation. Contact: Kathleen O'Leary, L.C.S. W., Neuroscience Center at St. Elizabeths, (202) 373-6068.

Schizophrenia
The psychobiology of both acute and chronic schizophrenia, is explored using clinical, pharmacological, biochemical, neurophysiological and genetic methods. Areas of study include: (1) the dopamine hypothesis of schizophrenia; (2) the biological predictors of response to antipsychotic drugs and the effects of these drugs on brain amine metabolism and neuroendocrine function; (3) the role of peptides in schizophrenia; (4) changes in brain structure and function, using PET, MRI, and SPECT; (5) innovative therapeutic modalities.

Of further interest are: (1) the study of persons adopted at an early age who have a biological or adoptive parent who is schizophrenic; (2) studies to identify possible genetic markers in schizophrenia that may help predict which offspring are vulnerable to the illness and thus provide a basis for early intervention.

There is one clinical research unit at the Clinical Center in Bethesda and three units at NIMH's research facility on the grounds of St. Elizabeths Campus. Both locations offer comprehensive hospital care for patients with acute and chronic schizophrenia. Contact: Judy Schrieber, M.S.W., Clinical Neuroscience Branch, Clinical Center, (301) 496-7128 or Denise Juliano, M.S.W., Neuroscience Center at St. Elizabeths, (202) 373-6100.

The Clinical Center in Bethesda has an outpatient program that utilizes novel agents to treat the negative and residual symptoms of schizophrenia. For more information, contact Kayleen Hadd, R.N., Experimental Therapeutics Branch, (301) 496-2082.

Schizoaffective Illness
Establishing the efficacy of alternative treatments for schizoaffective illness and development improved diagnostic tools are areas of interest. All patients receive an extensive diagnostic work-up which includes MRI and SPECT studies and at least one trial of an alternative medication.

Selected patients whose diagnoses have varied over time may be eligible. Contact: Denise Juliano, M.S.W., Neuroscience Center at St. Elizabeths, (202) 373-6100.

Tardive Dyskinesia and Other Movement Disorders
The neurobiology of tardive dyskinesia and other movement disorders is studied. Trials of a variety of potential new treatments are offered along with a comprehensive evaluation. Included in the evaluation are studies of structural and functional brain changes through brain-imaging and specialized neurologic and neuropsychological assessments. Patients of all psychiatric diagnoses will be considered for admission. Both inpatient and outpatient studies are available. Contact: Denise Juliano, M.S.W., Neuroscience Center at St. Elizabeths, (202) 373-6100.

Disorders of Attention and Cognition
Studies of attention disorders, learning and memory in a variety of patients with mood disorders, schizophrenias, learning disabilities, epilepsy and various forms of dementia are ongoing. The psychobiology of attention and other cognitive processes are examined using a variety of neuropsychological methods, including evoked response, psychophysiological techniques and learning-memory procedures. Contact: Laboratory of Psychology and Psychopathology, (301) 496-2551.

Rapid Cyclers
People who suffer from frequent episodes (cycles) of depression, hypomania, or mania are known as "rapid cyclers." Patients may develop rapid cycling because of disturbances in their daily (circadian) rhythms. This study will document patients' circadian rhythms and use the results to guide innovative treatments including light therapy. Patients with bipolar or unipolar depression (seasonal or non-seasonal), drug-free or medicated, are accepted. The study is conducted on an outpatient basis with brief, planned inpatient stays. The patient remains in treatment with their referring physician. Contact: Brigid Noonan, M.A., Clinical Psychobiology Branch, (301) 496-6981, or Ellen Leibenluft, M.D., (301) 496-2141.

Childhood Mental Illness
Several studies relate to the psychobiology of children who have attention-deficit hyperactivity disorder and Tourette syndrome. Children admitted partially on a day basis participate in a highly structured, comprehensive diagnostic program. The program includes medical, neurological and psychiatric evaluations, psychological testing and evaluation of psychomotor and psycholinguistic development. Pharmacokinetic and metabolic studies of psychoactive drugs, psychobiological studies involving sleep and neuroendocrine parameters and clinical studies involving FDA-approved experimental drugs are ongoing. Contact: Gail Ritchie, M.S.W., Child Psychiatry Branch, (301) 496-0851 or (301) 496-6080.

Other studies involve consultative follow-up of children in the inpatient program as well as children with obsessive-compulsive disorder. Children and adults with selected developmental disabilities are sought for brain imaging studies. There is an ongoing outpatient medication treatment study for children and adolescents with autism.

An inpatient program for childhood onset schizophrenia in 6 to 18-year-olds is underway. Studies of brain structure and function and a medication trial comparing haloperidol and clozapine are performed. Contact: Marge Lenane, M.S.W., Child Psychiatry Branch, (301) 496-7962.

Developmental Psychology
Studies on developmental psychology include research of children who present serious risks for development of psychopathology. Research on sexually-abused children investigates the psychological and biological mechanisms involved in the effects of abuse. Dissociative reactions in traumatized children and alterations in their physiology (i.e., immune and hormonal system dysregulation) are studied. Preschool-age children at risk for development of conduct disorders are studied using a spectrum of familial and biological measures in an attempt to develop a profile for targeting children for early intervention. Offspring of unipolar and bipolar depressed parents are studied longitudinally from early childhood to adolescence, to obtain prospective information on their development and on the familial factors to which they are exposed. The interaction of genetic vulnerabilities and environmental factors at various developmental stages is of special interest. The

development of diagnostic procedures for young children is a part of the research. Contact: Marian Radke Yarrow, Ph.D., Laboratory of Developmental Psychology, (301) 496-1091.

Anxiety Disorders
Patients with panic disorder, agoraphobia, social phobias, generalized anxiety disorder and related anxiety conditions are accepted for intensive medical and neuropsychiatric evaluation. Patients with night terrors or sleep-related panic attacks are also accepted for evaluation and treatment. Selected patients with physiological dependence to caffeine, other methylxanthines or benzodiazepines will also be considered for admission to the program. Facilities are available for both inpatients and outpatients. Treatment modalities may include drug therapy and individual or group therapy. Pharmacotherapy may include conventional and research drugs, usually administered under double-blind, placebo-controlled conditions. Treatment may involve specific research protocols but is individualized in the course of participation. Contact: Barbara Scupi, Biological Psychiatry Branch, (301) 496-6825.

Menstrual and Menopausal Mood and Behavioral Disorders
The Consultation-Liaison Service and Biological Psychiatry Branch are evaluating women who experience menstrual or menopausal mood behavior disorders. Evaluation of mood and endocrine function is performed. Patients who experience well defined menstrual or menopausal mood syndromes may participate in a study to evaluate the efficacy of several therapeutic agents—progesterone, estrogen, magnesium, GnRH agonist, and antidepressant agents. Evaluation of these agents will include periodic interviews, blood studies and daily symptom self-rating scales. All patients will have completed a baseline evaluation period prior to participating in the treatment study. The duration of the entire evaluation and treatment series is six to twelve months. Contact: Anne Bowles, Consultation-Liaison Service, (301) 496-9675.

Eating Disorders
Obese patients or normal weight patients with bulimia and underweight patients with anorexia nervosa are admitted for study. Obese, anorectic and bulimic patients are evaluated from clinical and biologic perspectives. Patients are admitted to a specialized inpatient clinical unit for research studies and then may participate in outpatient treatment programs that include nutritional evaluation, individual and group therapy and medication trials. Contact: Margaret Altemus, M.D., Unit on Eating Disorders, (301) 496-3421.

Alzheimer's Disease
Individual patients or twins with early or moderate dementia of the Alzheimer's type are evaluated in a wide variety of studies within the institute. The Alzheimer's program consists of both inpatient and outpatient evaluations. Patients are assessed in a comprehensive manner from a phenomenologic, biologic, and psychosocial perspective. In addition to complete diagnostic and neuropyschologic assessment, patients are offered treatment with new drugs affecting the cholinergic and other brain neurotransmitter systems. Researchers are also working to better understand the behavioral features of dementia, including depression. For relatives, the program emphasizes new mechanisms for coping with the stress Alzheimer's disease places on the family. All participants and their families are encouraged to remain involved in the longitudinal follow-up studies once they have completed the initial evaluation process. Contact: Sue Bell, M.S.W., Laboratory of Clinical Science, (301) 496-3421.

Genetic Studies
Large families with multiple members affected by manic-depressive illness, panic disorder or schizophrenia are studied for genetic factors that may make some family members susceptible to these illnesses. These studies require a two-hour diagnostic interview and a small blood sample. In general, there must be at least four ill individuals in an extended family. Contact: Liz Maxwell, Clinical Neurogenetics Branch, (301) 496-8977.

Medically Ill Depressed Patients
Patients with depression related to medical illness (AIDS, cancer, diabetes or other medical conditions) are studied. Studies evaluate the antidepressant effect of methylphenidate. Contact: Jean Murphy, R.N., M.S.N., (301) 496-1337 or D. Rosenstein, M.D., Biological Psychiatry Branch, (301) 496-9675.

13) National Institute of Neurological Disorders and Stroke

Mark Hallett, M.D.
Clinical Director

Telephone referrals should be directed to the individuals listed under each branch.

Developmental and Metabolic Neurology Branch
Chief: Roscoe O. Brady, M.D.
(301) 496-3285
Chief: Clinical Care Unit
Norman W. Barton, M.D., Ph.D.
(301) 496-1465

Sphingolipidoses, Mucopolysaccharidoses and other Storage Disorders
Patients with Gaucher's disease, Niemann-Pick disease, Fabry's disease, Tay-Sachs disease, metachromatic leukodystrophy, Krabbe's disease and those with the various types of mucopolysaccharidoses are studied. Of particular interest are patients with lysosomal cholesterol storage disorder (previously known as Types C and D Niemann-Pick disease). Diagnosis of the diseases and detection of the carrier states is available. Genetic counseling, antenatal diagnosis and basic biochemical and molecular genetic studies are carried out. Enzyme replacement studies are under way. Bone marrow transplantation and gene replacement are under investigation.

Neurologic Disease with Metabolic Abnormalities
Patients with a suspected metabolic basis of neurologic disease are admitted to the outpatient department or ward for diagnosis, study and therapy. Examples of conditions under investigation are heredofamilial acute or progressive ataxias, diurnal dystonia and ceroid lipofuscinosis, and mucolipidosis IV.

Progressive Dementia in Children
Infants and children suffering from delayed development, spasticity and signs of progressive dementia with or without seizure disorders will be considered for admission. Genetic counseling and detection of carrier states is offered where a metabolic defect is identified. A few patients will be accepted for basic and clinical research studies.

Neuroimmunology Branch
Chief: Dale E. McFarlin, M.D.
(301) 496-1801
Assistant Chief: Henry F. McFarland, M.D.
(301) 496-1801

Multiple Sclerosis
A few patients with early disease are selected for highly specific immunologic and virologic studies. Trials of experimental treatments are conducted in selected patients.

Familial Multiple Sclerosis
Genetic, immunologic and virologic studies are conducted in families with unequivocal occurrence of multiple sclerosis in more than one individual. Monozygotic and dizygotic twins who are discordant or concordant for MS are admitted.

Subacute Sclerosing Panencephalitis
A few patients are accepted for basic immunologic investigation.

Neurological Diseases Related to HTLV-1
Patients with neurological disorders associated with HTLV-1 infection are admitted for clinical and immunological evaluation.

Experimental Therapeutics Branch
Chief: Thomas N. Chase, M.D.
(301) 496-7993

Extrapyramidal Disorders
Individuals with Parkinson's disease and related disorders with parkinsonian symptoms including progressive supranuclear palsy and striationigral degeneration as well as those with Huntington's disease, tardive dyskinesia, Tourette syndrome, torsion dystonia, and cerebellar ataxia are admitted for diagnosis, biochemical study and experimental drug therapy. Investigations are conducted both on an inpatient and outpatient basis.

Dementing Disorders
Patients with Alzheimer's disease and related presenile or senile dementias, including multi-infarct dementia and Pick's disease, are accepted for diagnosis, pathogenetic study including cerebral imaging with positron emission tomography, and experimental therapeutic interventions.

Surgical Neurology Branch
Chief: Edward H. Oldfield, M.D.
(301) 496-5728

Brain Tumors
The cellular biology, endocrinology, immuno-biology and radiobiology of gliomas, pituitary tumors and other primary tumors of the central nervous system are investigated. Patients with primary tumors of the brain, spinal cord and pituitary are sought for operative removal of the tumor and subsequent investigation. A comprehensive program of investigational therapy is available for these patients.

Spinal and Intracranial Arteriovenous Malformations
Patients for diagnostic angiography and surgery are appropriate for referral.

Pituitary Tumors
Pituitary tumors are investigated. Patients with microadenomas as well as larger pituitary lesions are sought.

Medical Neurology Branch
Chief: Mark Hallett, M.D.
(301) 496-9526

Human Motor Control Section
Chief: Mark Hallett, M.D.
(301) 496-1561

Voluntary Movement Disorders
Patients with stroke, parkinsonism and cerebellar ataxia are accepted for physiological studies to understand the mechanisms for deranged movements. Patients undergo extensive clinical testing and physiological investigations including electromyographic studies, evoked potential studies and PET scanning. Patients will be offered therapy as appropriate and some patients with stroke followed serially will get rehabilitative therapy.

Involuntary Movement Disorders
Patients with action tremors that are refractory to conventional therapy are entered into therapeutic drug trials. Patients with myoclonus are studied physiologically, classified and offered appropriate therapy. Patients with focal dystonia such as writer's cramp are evaluated and given experimental therapy.

Neuromuscular Diseases Section
Chief: Marinos Dalakas, M.D.
(301) 496-9979

Post-Polio Syndrome and Other Related Motor Neuron Diseases
Studies are performed to investigate viral or immune factors in the pathogenesis of motor neuron dysfunction. Patients receive detailed clinical, electrophysiological, histological, immunological and virological evaluation. Experimental therapeutic drug trials are conducted in selected groups.

Chronic Demyelinating Polyneuropathies
Patients with chronic inflammatory demyelinating polyneuropathies (CIDP) and with paraproteinemic polyneuropatheis are studied to investigate viral and immune factors in the mechanisms of demyelination. Experimental therapeutic drug studies are conducted for selected patients.

Inflammatory Myopathies
Patients with polymyositis, dermatomyositis and inclusion-body myositis are studied to investigate viral or autoimmune causes in the mechanism of the disease. Several experimental therapeutic drug trials are conducted.

Neuromuscular Diseases
Patients with a variety of unusual, acquired or hereditary neuromuscular diseases that do not fall into one of the above categories are also studied with a series of clinical and electrophysiological investigations. A battery of enzymohistochemical, metabolic, morphological and immunocytochemical studies are performed on the muscle or nerve biopsies to define diagnosis, provide genetic counseling and advise on therapies.

HIV-related Neuromuscular Disorders
Patients with neuromuscular disorders related to HIV-infection or due to various antiretroviral therapies are accepted for virological and immunological studies. Select patients with primary HIV-related CNS diseases and patients with Tropical spastic paraparesis (TSP) due to HTLV-1 are also accepted for various studies.

Cognitive Neuroscience Section
Chief: Jordan Grafman, Ph.D.
(301) 496-0220

Brain Behavior Studies

Brain mechanisms that underlie human cognition and mood states are investigated. Patients with neurological problems such as memory disorders (amnesia); problems in reading (alexia), writing (agraphia), or naming (anomia); face and object recognition disorders (prosopagnosia and agnosia); specific difficulties in visual attention (neglect); and problems in social and interpersonal functioning (dysexecutive syndrome) are evaluated. Patients with anoxia, carbon monoxide poisoning, encephalitis, stroke, Alzheimer's Disease, Parkinson's Disease or head injury are especially sought for participation in brain-behavior studies. Patients will receive a through evaluation and diagnosis of their disorders, and in some cases, they will receive new insights into the nature of their particular difficulty. Investigators work closely with the patients, their families, and referring physicians, and offer recommendations for therapy when appropriate. In some cases (e.g., patients with amnesia), patients will be eligible to participate in experimental treatment protocols conducted with other NIH investigators.

Clinical Neuroscience Branch
Chief: Irwin Kopin, M.D.
(301) 496-4297

Autonomic Nervous System Disorders

Patients with neurogenic orthostatic hypotension, autonomic neuropathy and neurological diseases attended by autonomic dysfunction are accepted for biochemical and pharmacological studies. These studies investigate the pathophysiology and consequences of chronic autonomic failure. Conventional and experimental treatments of orthostatic hypotension are available.

Familial Alzheimer's Disease

Biochemical and genetic studies are conducted on patients with familial Alzheimer's disease and their at-risk relatives.

Epilepsy Research Branch
Acting Chief: William H. Theodore, M.D.
(301) 496-1505

Clinical Epilepsy Section
Chief: William H. Theodore, M.D.
(301) 496-1505

Epilepsy

Patients with intractable epilepsy, especially those with partial seizures, may be candidates for drug treatment or surgery. Fundamental studies of the brain that involve a series of projects employing neuro-imaging, psychological, neurological and neurophysiological procedures are conducted. Patients who are candidates for surgery are studied by an integrated group of neurologists, neurosurgeons, neuropsychologists and electroencephalographers. Patients with Lennox-Gastaut Syndrome are admitted to clinical, neurophysiologic, metabolic and therapeutic studies.

Neuroimaging Branch
Chief: Giovanni Di Chiro, M.D.
(301) 496-6801

Brain Tumors

Brain tumors are investigated for metabolic features and biological behavior. All patients will have Positron Emission Tomography (PET), Magnetic Resonance Imaging (MRI) and/or Magnetic Resonance Spectroscopy (MRS) to grade the tumor (benign vs. malignant) and assess treatment and possible complications. Studies are conducted on an outpatient basis.

Stroke Branch
Chief: John M. Hallenbeck, M.D.
(301) 496-6579

Stroke

Patients with acute thromboembolic or hemorrhagic stroke are admitted to the Neurointensive Care Unit at the National Naval Medical Center. Standardized stroke scale, CT, routine MRI, perfusion and diffusion-weighted MRI and blood flow measurements assess the efficacy of acute interventions.

At-Risk-For-Stroke

Patients with risk factors for stroke and transient ischemic attacks are studied. Biochemical assays, immunohistochemistry, tissue culture and molecular genetic techniques explore the risk factors for stroke.

14) Clinical Center

Saul W. Rosen, M.D., Ph.D.
Acting Director

Critical Care Medicine Department
Telephone referrals should be directed to:
Henry Masur, M.D.
Chief
(301) 496-9320 or
(800) 243-7644 (AIDS-NIH)

HIV and Acquired Immune Deficiency Syndrome
The etiology, pathogenesis and treatment of AIDS is investigated in a collaborative project with the Laboratory of Immunoregulation, National Institute of Allergy and Infectious Diseases. Clinically stable patients with documented HIV infection are considered for immunotherapy, antiretroviral therapy, and treatment of infectious complications.

Medical Genetics Program
Telephone referrals should be directed to
Sandra Schlesinger, M.S.
Clinical Coordinator
(301) 496-1380

William A. Gahl, M.D., Ph.D.
Dilys Parry, Ph.D.

Program Directors
(301) 496-6683 or
(301) 496-4947

The Interinstitute Medical Genetics Program
The program is a cooperative undertaking involving clinical branches and research laboratories of ten institutes. Senior investigators work on various genetic diseases, see patients of particular research interest and serve as consultants for other patients. The genetics clinic also accepts referrals of patients requiring diagnostic assessment and genetic counseling for genetic disorders. Studies include chromosomal abnormalities, congenital malformations and biochemical defects. Prenatal diagnosis is arranged if indicated.

Participating investigators include those with expertise in inborn errors of metabolism, cytogenetics, congenital anomalies and malformation syndromes, bone and connective tissue disorders, neurological disorders, eye disorders and cancer. Special interests currently include cystinosis, Lowe syndrome, neurofibromatosis 1 (von Recklinghausen's disease), neurofibromatosis 2 (bilateral acoustic neurofibromatosis), osteogenesis imperfecta, Ehlers Danlos syndrome, Fragile X syndrome, familial movement disorders and familial cancer.

Appendix B:
How To Get Drug Companies To Fill
Your Prescription For Free

In this Appendix, you'll find a comprehensive A to Z listing of all the drugs that are available to certain qualified groups free of charge directly from the manufacturers. First, find the drug you need and the corresponding manufacturer. Next, look up the address and telephone number of the appropriate drug manufacturer from the *Directory of Pharmaceutical Manufacturers*, which follows the A to Z drug listing. You'll need to contact the individual drug company to find out how to receive the drug free of charge. For more information about this free drug program, consult the Free Medical Care Section at the beginning of this book.

Alphabetical Listing of Drug

Drug . . . . *Manufacturer*

A
Aci-Jel	Ortho
Actovase	Genentech
Actimmune	Genentech
Adriamycin PFS	Adria
Adrucil	Adria
Aldactazide	Searle
Aldactone	Searle
Aldomet	Merck
Alupent	Boehringer
Anaprox	Syntex
Ansaid	Upjohn
Antivert	Pfizer #1
Anusol HC	Parke-Davis
Apresoline	Ciba-Geigy
Aralen	Sanofi-Winthrop
Artane	Lederle
Atrovent	Boehringer
Axid	Eli Lilly
Augmentin	SmithKline
AZT (Retrovir)	Burroughs-Wellcome

B
Bactrim	Hoffman-LaRoche
Bactrim DS	Hoffman-LaRoche
Bactroban	SmithKline
Beconase	Glaxo
Beconase AQ	Glaxo
Betagan	Allergan
BICNU	Bristol-Myers #3
Blenoxane	Bristol-Myers #3
Bleph-10	Allergan
Blephamide	Allergan
Bucladin-S	ICI-Stuart
BuSpar	Bristol-Myers #1

C
Calan	Searle
Calan SR	Searle
Capoten	Bristol-Myers #2
Capozide	Bristol-Myers #2
Carafate	Marion Merrell Dow
Cardene	Syntex
Cardizem	Marion Merrell Dow
Cardizem CD	Marion Merrell Dow
Cardizem SR	Marion Merrell Dow
Cardura	Pfizer
Catapres	Boehringer
Ceclor	Eli Lilly
CEENU	Bristol-Myers #3
Ceftin	Glaxo
Cefzil	Bristol-Myers #3
Ceredase	Genzyme
Cipro	Miles
Clinoril	Merck
Clozaril	Sandoz
Cogentin	Merck
Compazine	SmithKline
Cordarone	Wyeth-Ayerst
Corgard	Bristol-Myers #2
Corzide	Bristol-Myers #3
Coumadin	DuPont-Merck
Cyclospasmol	Wyeth-Ayerst
Cytotec	Searle
Cytovene	Syntex
Cytoxan	Bristol-Myers #3

D
Dalmane	Hoffman-LaRoche
Danocrine	Sanofi-Winthrop

Dantrium . . . . Norwich-Eaton
Desyrel . . . . Bristol-Myers #1
Diabinese . . . . Pfizer #1
Diamox . . . . Lederle
Dienestrol . . . . Ortho
Diflucan . . . . Pfizer #2
Dilantin . . . . Parke-Davis
Diprolene . . . . Schering-Plough
Diprosone . . . . Schering-Plough
Dolobid . . . . Merck
Duricef . . . . Bristol-Myers #1
Dyazied . . . . SmithKline #1
Dymelor . . . . Eli Lilly

E
E-Mycin . . . . Upjohn
Efudex (Fluorouracil
 Injection) . . . . Hoffman-LaRoche
Eldepryl . . . . Sandoz
Eminase . . . . SmithKline #2
Epogen . . . . Amgen
Ergamisol . . . . Janssen #2
Erycette . . . . Ortho
Estrace . . . . Bristol-Myers #1
Eulexin . . . . Schering-Plough

F
Flexeril . . . . Merck
Floxin . . . . Ortho
FML . . . . Allergan
Folex . . . . Adria
Fulvicin . . . . Schering-Plough

G
Gastrocrom . . . . Fisons
Glucotrol . . . . Pfizer #1

H
Halcion . . . . Upjohn
Haldol . . . . McNeil
Hismanal . . . . Janssen #1
HMS . . . . Allergan

I
Idamycin . . . . Adria
Ifex . . . . Bristol-Myers #3
Imuran . . . . Burroughs-Wellcome
Indocin . . . . Merck
Insulin Products . . . . Eli Lilly
Interferon-A

Recombinant . . . . . . Hoffman-LaRoche
Intron-A . . . . Schering-Plough
Isoptin . . . . Knoll
Isordil . . . . Wyeth-Ayerst

K
K-Lyte . . . . Bristol-Myers #1
Keflex . . . . Eli Lilly
Kerlone . . . . Searle
Kinesed . . . . ICI/Stuart
Klonopin . . . . Hoffman-LaRoche
Klotrix . . . . Bristol-Myers #1

L
Lanoxin . . . . Burroughs-Wellcome
Leucovorin Calcium . Lederle
Leukine . . . . Immunex
Librium . . . . Hoffman-LaRoche
Limbritol . . . . Hoffman-LaRoche
Lindane Lotion/
 Shampoo . . . . Reed and Carnick
Lioresal . . . . Ciba-Geigy
Lithobid . . . . Ciba-Geigy
Lo/Ovral . . . . Wyeth-Ayerst
Lopid . . . . Parke-Davis
Lopressor . . . . Ciba-Geigy
Lotrimin . . . . Schering-Plough
Lotrixone . . . . Schering-Plough
Loxapine . . . . Lederle
Lyophilized Cytoxan . Bristol-Myers #3
Lysodren . . . . Bristol-Myers #3

M
Macrodantin . . . . . . Norwich-Eaton
Maxzide . . . . Lederle
Meclan . . . . Ortho
Medrol . . . . Upjohn
Megace . . . . Bristol-Myers #3
Mesnex . . . . Bristol-Myers #3
Metrodin . . . . Ares-Serono
Micronase . . . . Upjohn
Minipress . . . . Pfizer #1
Minizide . . . . Pfizer #1
Minocin . . . . Lederle
Monistat . . . . Ortho
Monistat Derm . . . . Ortho
Monopril . . . . Bristol-Myers #3
Motrin . . . . Upjohn
Myambutol . . . . Lederle
Mycostatin . . . . Bristol-Myers #1

N

Naphcon-A	Allergan
Naprosyn	Syntex
Nasalide	Syntex
Natalins TX	Bristol-Myers #1
Nebupent	Fujisawa
Neosar	Adria
Neupogen	Amgen
Nicorette	Marion Merrell Dow
Nimotop	Miles
Nitrodisc	Searle
Nizoral	Janssen #1
Nolvadex	ICI/Stuart
Nordette	Wyeth-Ayerst
Normodyne	Schering-Plough
Norpace	Searle
Norpace CR	Searle
Noroxin	Merck
Norplant System	Wyeth-Ayerst

O

Oculinium	Allergan
Optimine	Schering-Plough
Orinase	Upjohn
Ortho-Dienestrol	Ortho
Orudis	Wyeth-Ayerst
Ovcon	Bristol-Myers #1

P

Pancrease	McNeil
Parafon Forte	McNeil
Paraplatin	Bristol-Myers #3
Parlodel	Sandoz
Pavabid	Marion Merrell Dow
Pepcid	Merck
Periactin	Merck
Persa-Gel	Ortho
Persantine	Boehringer
Pilogan	Allergan
Platinol	Bristol-Myers #3
Plendil	Merck
Ponstel	Parke-Davis
Pravochol	Bristol-Myers #2
Premarin	Wyeth-Ayerst
Prilosec	Merck
Prinivil	Merck
Procan	Parke-Davis
Procan SR	Parke Davis
Procardia	Pfizer #1
Procardia XL	Pfizer #1
Procrit	Ortho-Biotechnology

Prokine	Hoechst-Roussel
Pronestyl SR	Bristol-Myers #2
Propine	Allergan
Prostat	Ortho
Protropin	Genentech
Proventil	Schering-Plough
Provera	Upjohn
Prozac	Eli Lilly
Pyridium	Parke-Davis

Q

Questran	Bristol-Myers #2
Quinamm	Marion Merrell Dow

R

Relafen	SmithKline
Rheumatrex	Lederle
Rocaltrol	Hoffman-LaRoche
Rocephin	Hoffman-LaRoche
Rythmol	Knoll

S

Sandimmune	Sandoz
Sandoglobulin	Sandoz
Sandostatin	Sandoz
Santyl	Knoll
Sectral	Wyeth-Ayerst
Septra DS	Burroughs-Wellcome
Seldane	Marion Merrell Dow
Seldane D	Marion Merrell Dow
Sinemet	Du Pont-Merck
Sinemet Cr	Du Pont-Merck
Sorbitrate	ICI/Stuart
Spectazole	Ortho
Sporanox	Janssen #1
Sultrin	Ortho
Survanta	Abbott
Symmetrel	Du Pont-Merck
Synalar	Syntex
Synemol	Syntex
Synthroid	Boots

T

Tagamet	SmithKline
Tarabine	Adria
Tenormin	ICI/Stuart
Tenoretic	ICI/Stuart
Terazol	Ortho
TheraCys	Connaught Labs
Timolol	Merck

Timoptic . . . . Merck
Tofranil . . . . Ciba-Geigy
Tolectin . . . . McNeil
Trandate . . . . Glaxo
Tridesilon Cream . . . Miles
Triostat . . . . SmithKline
Triphasil . . . . Wyeth-Ayerst

V

Vagistat . . . . Bristol-Myers #1
Valium . . . . Hoffman-LaRoche
Vasocar . . . . McNeil
Vasodilan . . . . Bristol-Myers #2
Vasoretic . . . . Merck
Vasotec . . . . Merck
Vepesid . . . . Bristol-Myers #3
Verelan . . . . Lederle
Videx . . . . Bristol-Myers #4
Vincasar . . . . Adria
Voltaren . . . . Ciba-Geigy

W

Wellcovorin . . . . Burroughs-Wellcome
Winstrol . . . . Sanofi-Winthrop
Wytensin . . . . Wyeth-Ayerst

X

Xanax . . . . Upjohn

Z

Zantac . . . . Glaxo
Zarontin . . . . Parke-Davis
Zestril . . . . ICI/Stuart
Zestoretic . . . . ICI/Stuart
Zithromax . . . . Pfizer #1
Zoloft . . . . Pfizer #1
Zostrix . . . . Knoll
Zovirax . . . . Burroughs-Wellcome
Zyloprim . . . . Burroughs-Wellcome

Directory of Pharmaceutical Manufacturer Indigent Patient Programs

Abbott Laboratories/Ross Laboratories
Survanta Lifeline
Medical Technology Hotlines
555 13th Street NW
Suite 7E

Washington, DC 20004-1109   (800) 922-3255
(202) 637-6690 (fax)

Adria Laboratories, Inc.
Adria Laboratories
Patient Assistance Program
P.O. Box 16529   (614) 764-8100
Columbus, OH 43215-6529   (614) 764-8102 (fax)

Allergan Prescription Pharmaceuticals
Judy McGee
(800) 347-4500, ext. 6219
(714) 955-6976

Amgen, Inc.
Amgen Safety Net Programs
Medical Technology Hotlines   (800) 272-9376
637-6688 (Washington, DC)

Ares-Serono, Inc.
Gina Cella
Manager, Corporate Communications
Ares-Serono, Inc.
100 Longwater Circle   (617) 982-9000
Norwell, MA 02061   (617) 982-1269 (fax)

Astra Pharmaceuticals, Inc.
Linda Braun, Research Coordinator
FAIR Program (Foscavir Assistance and
 Information on Reimbursement)
State and Federal Associates   (800) 488-3247
(703) 683-2239 (fax)

Boehringer Ingleheim Pharmaceuticals, Inc.
Sam Quy   (203) 798-4131

Boots Pharmaceuticals
T.N. Thurman
Public Affairs
Boots Pharmaceuticals
300 TriState International Office Center
Suite 200   (800) 323-1817
Lincolnshire, IL 60069-4415   (708) 405-7400

Bristol-Myers Squibb #1
Bristol-Myers Squibb
Indigent Patient Program
P.O. Box 9445   (800) 736-0003
McLean, VA 22102-9998   (703) 760-0049 (fax)

Bristol-Myers Squibb #2
Cardiovascular Access Program

P.O. Box 9445   (800) 736-0003
McLean, VA 22102-9998   (703) 760--0049 (fax)

Bristol-Myers Squibb #3
Bristol-Myers Squibb
Cancer Patient Access Program
P.O. Box 9445   (800) 736-0003
McLean, VA 22102-9998   (703) 760-0049 (fax)

Bristol-Myers Squibb #4
Videx Temporary Assistance Program
                  (800) 788-0123
                  (703) 760-0049 (fax)

Burroughs-Wellcome
Jonas B. Daugherty
Manager, Professional Information Services
Burroughs-Wellcome Co.
3030 Cornwallis Road
Research Triangle Park, NC 27709
                  (919) 248-4418
                  (919) 248-0421 (fax)
       (800) 722-9294 (program enrollment)

or

Bernard Streed
Supervisor, Special Projects
Burroughs-Wellcome Co.
Patient Assistance Program
P.O. Box 52035   (602) 494-8725
Phoenix, AX 85072-9349   (602) 996-7731 (fax)
       (800) 722-9294 (program enrollment)

Ciby-Geigy Corporation, Pharmaceuticals Division
Jackie Laguardia
Senior Information Assistant
Ciba-Geigy Corporation
556 Morris Avenue
Summit, NJ 07901   (908) 277-5849

Connaught Laboratories, Inc.
David Hunt, Product Manager
Connaught Laboratories, Inc.
Route 611, P.O. Box 187
Swiftwater, PA 18370-0187
                  (717) 839-4617

Du Pont Merck
Du Pont Merck Pharmaceuticals
Barley Mill Plaza
P.O. Box 80027
Wilmington, DE 19880-0027

Fisons Pharmaceuticals
Gastrocrom Patient Assistance Program
Fisons Pharmaceuticals
P.O. Box 1766   (800) 234-5535
Rochester, NY 24603   (716) 475-9000

Fujisawa Pharmaceutical Company
Richard G. White
NebuPent Patient Assistance Program
Fujisawa Pharmaceutical Company
Parkway North Center
3 Parkway North   (708) 317-8638
Deerfield, IL 60015   (708) 317-5941 (fax)
       (800) 366-6323 (reimbursement hotline)

Genentech, Inc.
Genentech Reimbursement Information Program
Mailstop #99
c/o Genentech, Inc.
460 Point San Bruno Blvd.
S. San Francisco, CA 94080   (800) 879-4747

Genzyme Corporation
William Aliski
Director of Reimbursement
Genzyme Corporation
1 Kendall Square   (617) 252-7871
Cambridge, MA 02139   (617) 252-7600 (fax)

Glaxo, Inc.
Laura J. Newberry
Supervisor, Trade Communications
Glaxo, Inc.
P.O. Box 13438
Research Triangle Park, NC 27709
                  (800) GLAXO77
                  (919) 248-7932 (fax)

Hoechst-Roussel Pharmaceuticals, Inc.
Jannalee Smithey
Technology Assessment Group
                  (800) PROKINE

Hoffman-LaRoche, Inc.
Inge Shanahan
Medical Communications Associate
Roche Laboratories
340 Kingsland Street
Nutley, NJ 07110
       (800) 526-6367 (teleprompter #2)
                  (201) 235-5624 (fax)

ICI/Stuart Pharmaceuticals
Yvonne A. Graham
Manager, Professional Services
ICI Pharmaceuticals Group
P.O. Box 15197
Wilmington, DE 19850-5197   (302) 886-2231

Immunex Corporation
Michael L. Kleinberg
Director of Professional Services   (206) 587-0430
Immunex Corporation   (206) 343-8926 (fax)
                             (800) 321-4669

Janssen Pharmaceutica Inc. #1
Professional Services Department
Janssen Pharmaceutica Inc.
1125 Trenton-Harbourton Road
P.O. Box 200
Office A32000
Titusville, NJ 08560-0200   (800) 253-3682

Janssen Pharmaceutica Inc. #2
Ellen McDonald
Assistant Product Manager
Janssen Pharmaceutica Inc.
40 Kingsbridge Rd.   (908) 524-9409
Piscataway, NJ 08854   (908) 524-9118 (fax)

Knoll Pharmaceuticals
Knoll Pharmaceuticals
Indigent Patient Program
30 N. Jefferson Rd.
Whippany, NJ 07981   (800) 526-0710

Lederle Laboratories
Jerry Johnson, Pharm.D.
Director, Industry Affairs
American Cyanamid, Inc.
One Cyanamid Plaza   (800) 526-7870
Wayne, NJ 07470   (201) 831-4484 (fax)

Eli Lilly and Company
Indigent Patient Program Administrator
Eli Lilly and Company
Lilly Corporate Center
Drop Code 1844   (317) 276-2950
Indianapolis, IN 46285   (317) 276-9288 (fax)

McNeil Pharmaceutical
Laura Litzenberger
Senior Medical Information Specialist
Scientific Affairs

McNeil Pharmaceutical
Spring House, PA 19477   (215) 540-7803

Marion Merrell Dow, Inc.
Bill Lawrence
Supervisor of Product Contributions
P.O. Box 8480
Kansas City, MO 64114   (816) 966-4250

**Merck Sharp and Dohme
(Human Health Division, U.S.)**
Professional Information Department
Merck Human Health Division, U.S.
West Point, PA 19486   (215) 540-8627

Miles Pharmaceuticals
Professional Services
Attention: Miles Indigent Patient Program
400 Morgan Ave
West Haven, CT 06516   (203) 937-2000

**Norwich-Eaton Pharmaceuticals
(Proctor and Gamble)**
R.M. Brandt, Manager
Coverage and Reimbursement   (607) 335-2079
                             (607) 335-2020 (fax)
                             (800) 448-4878

Ortho Biotechnology
Carol Webb, Executive Director   (908) 704-5232
Hematopoietic Products   (908) 526-4997 (fax)

The Ortho Financial Assistance Program
1800 Robert Fulton Drive
Reston, VA 22091
          (800) 447-3437 (financial assistance)
          (800) 441-1366 (cost sharing program)

Ortho Pharmaceuticals
Jerald Holleman
Director, Government Affairs
ICOM Development Group
Johnson & Johnson
P.O. Box 300
Route 202 South
Raritan, NJ 08869-0602   (908) 218-6466

Parke-Davis
Parke-Davis
201 Tabor Road
Morris Plains, NJ 07950   (201) 540-2000

Pfizer Pharmaceuticals, Inc. Program #1:
Pfizer Labs, Roerig Division,
Pratt Pharmaceuticals
Richard Vastola
Manager, Professional and
 Consumer Programs
Pfizer, Inc.
235 East 42nd Street
New York, NY 10017   (212) 573-3954

Pfizer Inc. Program #2: Roerig Division
Diflucan Patient Assistance Program
                                   (800) 869-9979

Reed and Carnrick/Block Drug Company
Conrad Erdt
Customer Service Associate
Reed and Carnick Pharmaceutical Company
One New England Ave   (908) 981-0070
Piscataway, NJ 08854   (908) 981-1391 (fax)

Sandoz Pharmaceuticals
Gilbert Honigfeld, Ph.D.
Director of Scientific Affairs
59 Route 10
East Hanover, NJ 07936-1951   (201) 503-8341
                                (201) 503-7185 (fax)

Maria Hardin, Director
Sandoz Drug Cost Sharing Program (DCSP)
P.O. Box 8923   (203) 746-6518
New Fairfield, CT 06812   (800) 447-6673
                               (203) 746-6481 (fax)

Carol Lee-Kantor
Director, Clozaril Assistance Program
P.O. Box 8923
New Fairfield, CT 06812-1783   (800) 937-6673
                               (203) 746-6481 (fax)

Sanofi Winthrop Pharmaceuticals
Sanofi Winthrop
Product Information Department
90 Park Avenue
New York, NY 10016   (212) 907-2000

Schering-Plough
For Intron/Eulexin Products
Roger D. Graham, Jr.
Marketing Manager, Oncology/Biotech
Service Programs
Schering Laboratories

2000 Galloping Hill Road
Building K-5-2 B2
Kenilworth, NJ 07033

For Other Schering Products:
Drug Information Services
Indigent Program
Schering Laboratories/Key Pharmaceuticals
2000 Galloping Hill Road
Building K-5-1 C6   (908) 298-4000
Kenilworth, NJ 07033   (800) 822-7000

G.D. Searle and Co.
For health care professionals:
Michael Isaacson
Vice President, "Patients in Need" Foundation
Searle Co.   (800) 542-2526
5200 Old Orchard Rd.   (708) 470-3831
Skokie, IL 60077   (708) 470-6633 (fax)

Sigma-Tau Pharmaceuticals
Michael McCourt
Carnitor Drug Assistance Program
Administrator
National Organization for Rare Diseases
P.O. Box 8923   (800) 999-6673
New Fairfield, CT 06812-1783 (203) 746-6518
                              (203) 746-6481 (fax)

Barbara J. Bacon
Manager, Marketing Operations
Sigma-Tau Pharmaceuticals   (800) 447-0169
200 Orchard Ridge Drive   (301) 948-1041
Gaithersburg, MD 20878   (301) 948-1862 (fax)

SmithKline Beecham: Program #1
Jan Stilley
SmithKline Beecham
One Franklin Plaza FP1320
Philadelphia, PA 10101   (215) 751-5760

SmithKline Beecham: Program #2
Eminase and Triostat Programs
Helene Kennedy, Program Specialist
555 13th Street NW
Suite 700 East   (202) 508-6512
Washington, DC 20004   (202) 637-6690 (fax)

Syntex Laboratories, Inc.
Cytovene Medical Information Line:
                              (800) 444-4200
                    (Syntex Provisional Assistance

Program for Cytovene)
General Telephone Number to Inquire About
Indigent Patient Programs:

(800) 822-8255

Upjohn Company
Wendell Pierce
National Professional Services Manager
Upjohn Company
7000 Portage Rd.   (616) 323-6004
Kalamazoo, MI 49001   (616) 323-6332 (fax)

Wyeth-Ayerst Laboratories
Roger Eurbin
Associate Director, Professional Services
Wyeth-Ayerst
P.O. Box 8299
Philadelphia, PA 19101   (215) 971-5604

Appendix C:
State Health Statistics

Vital And Infectious Disease Statistics

The last few years have witnessed explosive growth in products and services aimed at the health-conscious baby-boomers and their aging parents. To better market products and services, many businesses use state health statistics and records. State health data are used to great success by insurance companies, individual medical providers and doctor groups, private health care clinics and rehabilitative service centers, diet and natural food producers, pharmaceutical and cosmetic companies, and even publishers.

A state's health care registration system is often the best place to start researching specific health data for an entire state's population. In addition, each state makes available its annual health report in a number of formats.

Some insurance companies use this information to steer away from areas where cancer rates are too high or to zero-in on areas where rates are lower than the national norm. Along this same line, a new doctor might search for an area where there is a greater demand for his or her specific medical expertise.

Exercise equipment manufacturers can use the data to target upscale markets for their sales campaigns -- or identify clusters of older hospitals with on-site physical therapy facilities that might need new equipment. Other examples include:

- *how many people have cancer, diabetes, or high blood pressure by zip code*
- *hospitals with CAT scans and other sophisticated medical equipment*
- *vaccination records to find which homes have babies, preschoolers, grade schoolers, etc.*
- *names, addresses and neighborhoods with the most senior citizens*
- *names and addresses of ambulatory care facilities and state-funded birth control/ venereal disease counseling clinics*
- *neighborhoods not immediately serviced by existing drug stores*

Data are collected and used to assess the current status of health and health care in a state and to help state officials better anticipate future health care needs and resources. In addition, the information provides baseline data for medical research, charts population shifts, and identifies specific groups, communities, neighborhoods, etc. for special state and federal health programs.

Annual reports, available from state vital statistics departments, contain information on births, deaths, marriages and divorces, with narrative and graphic highlights of emerging demographic and health issue trends.

Annual reports from a state's office of epidemiology contain specific data on the incidence of notifiable communicable diseases and related information reported by area physicians, hospitals and health clinics.

Computer printouts of selected data provide the most current health and health care information in detail, much of which does not make it into a state's annual reports. Data can be sorted and printed to assist individuals and businesses with statistical research projects. Most states are staffed with experts to help with individual research requests. Most offices prefer that information requests be placed in writing. State offices release aggregate data that includes no names or personal identifiers.

All states will provide computer printouts of selected data, at least on limited basis. In most instances, there is no charge for printouts. When requesting specific data not found in a state's annual report, place your information request in writing, be as specific as possible in what you are asking, and specify your computer system's requirements.

The following states provide information on magnetic tape or diskette. Fees vary from state to state depending upon the complexity of the request.

Magnetic tape: Arizona, California, Delaware, Florida, Georgia, Idaho, Illinois, Indiana, Kentucky, Maine, Maryland, Mississippi, Missouri, Montana, New Hampshire, New York, North Carolina, Oklahoma, South Carolina, South Dakota, Tennessee, Texas, Utah, Virginia, West Virginia, Washington, Wyoming

Diskette: Alaska, Arizona, California, Delaware, Florida, Georgia, Idaho, Illinois, Kentucky, Maine, Maryland, Minnesota, Mississippi, Missouri, Montana, Nebraska, New Hampshire, New Mexico, New York, North Carolina, Oklahoma, Oregon, South Carolina, South Dakota, Tennessee, Texas, Utah, Virginia, West Virginia, Wyoming

Offices For Vital And Infectious Disease Statistics

Alabama
Department of Public Health, Center for Health Statistics, P.O. Box 5625, Montgomery, AL 36130, (205) 242-5033. This office will provide computer printouts of selected data. There is a charge of $15 per printout. At present, data is not available on diskette or magnetic tape. Their publications include an *Annual Report*; *Teenage Birth Statistics*, and *Detailed Mortality Statistics*.

Bureau of Preventive Health Services, Epidemiology Division, Department of Health, 434 Monroe St., Rm. 900, Montgomery, AL 36130-1701, (205) 242-5131. Publications include their 1990 annual report, *Notifiable Diseases in Alabama*. The office can supply limited computer printouts of selected aggregate data on communicable diseases.

Alaska
State Department of Health, Division of Public Health, P.O. Box 110610, Juneau AK 99811-0610, (907) 465-3090. Publications include the *Vital Statistics Annual Report*. Information is available on computer printouts and on diskette on a limited basis. Fees vary according to the complexity of the request.

State Department of Health, Office of Epidemiology, P.O. Box 240249, Anchorage, AK 99524-0249, (907) 561-4406. Publications include the *Epidemiology Bulletin*. Information is available on computer printouts, usually free of charge.

Arizona
Department of Health Services, Office of Policy and Planning, 1740 West Adams St., Phoenix, AZ 85007, (602) 542-1216. Publications include *Abortion Surveillance Report*, *Accidental Deaths in Arizona*, and *Health Status and Vital Statistics*. The office provides aggregate data on computer printouts, free of charge. Special requests for selected data are handled on a limited basis. There is a minimum charge of $25 for computer programming time.

Department of Health Services, Office of Infectious Diseases, Epidemiology, 3008 N. 3rd St., Phoenix, AZ 85012, (602) 230-5927. Publications include *Communicable Diseases in Arizona*. This office provides computer printouts of selected data. If you send them a blank diskette they will transfer the information requested on to it, free of charge.

Arkansas
Department of Health, Office of Vital Records, State Health Building, 4815 W. Markham, Little Rock, AR 72205, (501) 661-2371. This office publishes an *Annual Report*. Computer printouts are available for certain items for a processing fee. If you provide the office with a diskette, they will process it for you.

Department of Health, Epidemiology Program, Division of Health Maintenance, 4815 W. Markham, Little Rock, AR 72205, (501) 661-2264. Publications include an *Annual Report, Annual Morbidity Report*, and *Physician's Bulletin* which contains 1991 data. The office provides computer printouts of selected data, free of charge.

California
California Department of Health Data and Services, 714 P. St., Sacramento, CA 95814, (916) 657-3057. Publications include: *Vital Statistics of California, General Fertility Rates and Age-Specific Live Births by Age of Mother, Suicides in California, Multiples Causes of Death*, and *California's Non-*

Licensed Marriages -- A First Look at Their Characteristics. Publication prices vary and a complete catalogue of titles can be obtained from this office. Specific computer searches are available. Information is provided on computer printout, diskette and magnetic tape. Fees vary according to the complexity of the request.

Colorado
Department of Health, Health Statistics Section, 4210 East 11th Ave., Denver, CO 80220, (303) 331-4895. Publications include the 400-page *Colorado Vital Statistics Report*. The office does provide specialized computer runs of extracted data at a minimum cost of $40. Computer printouts are provided, but no information is distributed on diskette or magnetic tape.

Department of Health, Division of Disease Control & Environmental Epidemiology, 4210 East 11th Ave., Denver, CO 80220, (303) 331-8330. Publications include the bi-monthly *Colorado Disease Bulletin* which contains yearly totals of infectious diseases.

Connecticut
Department of Health Services, Division of Health Surveillance and Planning, 150 Washington St., Hartford, CT 06106, (203) 566-7886. Publications include an *Annual Report*. Computer printouts and machine readable forms are offered through this office for a fee.

Department of Health Services, Epidemiology Program, 150 Washington St., Hartford, CT 06106, (203) 566-5058. Although this office provides information on infectious diseases such as hepatitis, separate statistics on AIDS, cancer and tuberculosis are handled through individual offices. There is no charge for computer printouts of statistical reports.

Delaware
Delaware Health Statistics Center, Bureau of Health Planning, Resource Management, P.O. Box 637, Dover, DE 19903, (302) 739-4776. Publications include an *Annual Report*. Computer printouts and information on diskette and magnetic tape are generally provided free of charge.

Bureau of Disease Prevention, Division of Public Health, P.O. 637, Dover, DE 19903, (302) 739-5617. This office's publications include a *Monthly Surveillance Report*. Computer printouts of data are generated, usually at no cost.

District of Columbia
Department of Human Services, Research and Statistics Division, 425 I St. N.W., Rm. 3007, Washington, DC 20001, (202) 727-0681. Publications include the *1990 Annual Report of Vital Statistics*. Statistical data tables are available on computer printout form.

Florida
Department of Health and Rehabilitative Services, Public Health Statistics, P.O. Box 210, Jacksonville, FL 32231-0042, (904) 359-6963. Publications include the: *Florida Vital Statistics, Vital News and Quarterly Vital Statistics Report*. This office can provide a computer printout of data records, at $.12 per record. Programming is $50.65 per hour. They will send two to three pages of data at no charge. Anything above that contains a handling charge of $18 per hour. Information is also provided on computer diskette. The fees are the same as those for computer printouts.

Department of Health and Rehabilitative Services, 1317 Winewood Blvd. Tallahassee, FL 32399-0700, (904) 487-2542. Publications include a *Monthly Report*, and *Florida Morbidity Statistics*. Computer printouts of selected data are provided on a limited basis.

Georgia
Department of Human Resources, Vital Records, 47 Trinity Ave., SW, Rm.. 217-H, Atlanta, GA 30334, (404) 894-6482. Publications include an *Annual Report*. Information requests must be made in writing. There is a $25 minimum charge for computer printouts of selected data. Information is available on diskette and on magnetic tape. Fees vary depending upon the scope of the project.

Department of Human Resources, Epidemiology Section, 878 Peachtree St. N.E., Room 210, Atlanta, GA 30309, (404) 894-6531. Publications include a *Communicable Disease Morbidity Annual Report* and *Annual Report*. Computer printouts on certain selected statistics are available.

Hawaii
Vital Records Section, State Dept of Health, P.O. Box 3378, Honolulu, HI, 96801-9984, (808) 586-4602. Publications include the *1990 Statistical Report*, which is free. Computer printouts of information are available on a limited basis. Detailed information requests should be in writing. The office can retrieve some information from databases on tape but it depends on the time frame involved and the resources available. At present, there is no charge for computer printouts.

Department of Health, Epidemiology Branch, Kinau Hale Building, 1250 Punchbowl St., Rm. 107, Honolulu, HI 96813, (808) 586-4586. Publications include *Communicable Disease Report* which is published bi-monthly.

Idaho
Department of Health and Welfare, Bureau of Vital Statistics, Statehouse, Boise, ID 83720, (208) 334-5980. Publications include an *Annual Report*. The office provides reports, free of charge, of existing data tables. Tables can also be placed on diskette for a fee of $25 to $50. There is a charge of $15 if computer programming runs over an hour. Records are legally confidential, so the use of magnetic tapes is possible only as long as data is not potentially identifying.

Department of Health and Welfare, Communicable Disease Prevention, Statehouse, Boise, ID 83720, (208) 334-5930. This office publishes a *Biweekly Disease Surveillance Report*. Computer printouts of information are available.

Illinois
Department of Public Health, Division of Vital Records, Division of Data Processing, 605 W. Jefferson, Springfield, IL 62702-5097, (217) 785-1064. Publications include the *Vital Statistics Annual Report*. Computer printouts of selected data are copied at $.25 per page. Magnetic tapes of birth/death data are available for a fee. If you supply the office with a blank diskette they will transfer the information on to it for a fee.

Department of Public Health, Division of Infectious Diseases, 525 W. Jefferson, Springfield, IL 62761, (217) 785-7165. Computer printouts are available through individual departments. You must fill out a data request form before information is released.

Indiana
State Board of Health, Division of Public Health Statistics, 1330 West Michigan St., P.O. Box 1964, Indianapolis, IN 46206-1964, (317) 232-0307 Publications include *Indiana Abortion Report*, and *1990 Indiana County Population Estimates*. Computer printouts and tapes are available on a limited basis. Programming fees vary depending upon the complexity of the request. The office also publishes an annotated list of publications.

State Board of Health, Disease Intervention, 1330 West Michigan St., P.O. Box 1964, Indianapolis, IN 46206, (317) 633-8414. Publications include an *Annual Report* Computer printouts are provided, if data exists.

Iowa
Department of Public Health, Statistic Services, 321 E. 12th St., Lucas State Office Building, Des Moines, IA 50319-0075, (515) 281-4945. Publications include a *Vital Statistics Annual Report*. This office provides yearly data tables. Information is available on computer printouts and fees vary according to the complexity of the request.

Department of Public Health, Epidemiology Section, Lucas State Office Building, Des Moines, IA 50319, (515) 281-5424. Weekly health updates are available through this office.

Kansas
Department of Health and Environment, Research and Analysis, Office of Communication Services, Forbes Field, Bldg. 740, Topeka, KS 66620, (913) 296-0632. Publications include an *Annual Report*. This office will provide printouts of selected data. There is a fee for reports over 25 pages. Information is available on computer diskette and there is a fee which is dependent upon the amount of programming time involved.

Department of Health and Environment, Bureau of Disease Control, Suite 605, Mills Building, 109 S.W. 9th St., Topeka, KS 66612, (913) 296-5586 Publications include their *Annual Report*. Computer printouts are available, free of charge.

Kentucky

Cabinet for Human Resources, Health Data Branch, 275 East Main St., Frankfort, KY 40621, (502) 564-2757. Publications include a monthly report and year-end summary table. Computer printouts of selected data are available for $10 per printout. Diskettes and magnetic tapes are available. The cost depends upon the scope of the request.

Cabinet for Human Resources, Division of Epidemiology, 275 East Main St., Frankfort, KY 40621, (502) 564-3418. Publications include monthly and year- end summary reports of specific diseases plus their *Monthly Epidemiologic Notes and Reports*. The office does provide computer printouts of selected data but information on diskette or magnetic tape is not available.

Louisiana

Department of Health and Human Resources, Public Health Statistics, P.O. Box 60630, New Orleans, LA 70160, (504) 568-5458. This office publishes an *Annual Report*. Computer printouts are available, if the data is complete. There is no charge.

Department of Health and Human Resources, Office of Epidemiology, P.O. Box 60630, New Orleans, LA 70160, (504) 568-5005. This office publishes an *Annual Report*. Computer printouts of 1991 data are provided free of charge.

Maine

Department of Human Services, Department of Vital Records, 221 State St., Augusta, ME 04333, (207) 624-5445. Publications include the *1991 Annual Report of Vital Statistics* which is available at $10.50. This office will provide raw data via printouts, diskettes and magnetic tapes. There is a base fee of $27.50 per diskette and $52 per magnetic tape. All request should be in writing, and be as specific as possible regarding the data that you request and the requirements of your computer system. The office encourages callers to provide their own disk or magnetic tape when possible.

Bureau of Health, Division of Disease Control, State House Station 11, Augusta, ME 04333, (207) 289-3591. Publications include the *Epigram* which is published every two months on topics of health concern to Maine residents. A limited amount of raw data can be provided to callers on computer printouts. All requests for detailed information should be in writing.

Maryland

Department of Health and Mental Hygiene, Division of Health Statistics, 201 West Preston St., Baltimore, MD 21201, (410) 225-5950. Publications include the *1989 Vital Statistics Preliminary Report*. Computer printouts of tables of selected data are provided. Requests for information should be in writing. Information is available on magnetic tape and diskette. Fees vary according to the amount of information requested.

Department of Health and Mental Hygiene, Communicable Diseases Surveillance, 201 West Preston St., 3rd Floor Baltimore, MD 21201, (410) 225-6712. This office publishes *Annual Report* that is free of charge.

Massachusetts

Department of Public Health, Division of Health Statistics and Research, 153 Tremont, 5th Floor, Jamaica Plains, MA 02111, (617) 239-4257. Publications include an *Annual Report*. Computer printouts of selected data are provided, free of charge.

Department of Public Health, Epidemiology Program, 305 South St., Jamaica Plains, MA 02130, (617) 522-3700. Publications include fact sheets on various communicable diseases.

Michigan

Department of Public Health, Office of State Registrar, Center for Health Statistics, Statistical Services Section, P.O. Box 300195, Lansing, MI 48909, (517) 335-8656. Publications include: *Health Statistics Pocket Guide, Abortions in Michigan, Cancer Incidence and Mortality, Michigan Perinatal Effectiveness Index, Infant and Maternal Health Statistics*, most of which are free. Requests for computer printouts should be placed in writing. There is a fee for services.

Department of Public Health, Division of Disease Surveillance, P.O. Box 30035, Lansing, MI 48909, (517) 335-8050. Publications include weekly surveillance reports of communicable diseases. These are available for researchers.

Minnesota
State Health Department, Center for Health Statistics, 717 Delaware St., S.E., P.O. Box 9441, Minneapolis, MN 55410-9441, (612) 623-5353. Publications include the *Annual Report of Health Statistics*. This office will provide you with selected tables from their annual report at no cost. The fees for information transferred to computer diskette would depend upon the complexity of the request.

State Health Department, Acute Epidemiology Department, 717 Delaware St., S.E., Minneapolis, MN 55414, (612) 623-5414. Publications include various statistical reports on all reportable diseases. Computer printouts of summary data can be obtained from the Center for Health Statistics, described above.

Mississippi
Department of Health, Vital Records Division, Statistical Services, P.O. Box 1700, 2423 N. State St., Jackson, MS 39205, (601) 960-7635. Publications include the *1990 Annual Report*. Computer printouts of specific information require a written request. The office will provide photocopies of tables at no charge. If you furnish your own magnetic tape or computer diskette they will transfer information on to it for you.

Department of Health, Office of Epidemiology, P.O. Box 1700, Jackson, MS 39215, (601) 960-7725. Publications include the *Mississippi Morbidity Report* which includes annual case tabulation. Aggregate data is available via computer printouts and diskettes.

Missouri
Department of Health, Vital Records Department, P.O. Box 570, Jefferson City, MO 65102, (314) 751-6400. Publications include the *Annual Report of Vital Statistics*. Requests for information should be in writing. Printouts of data, such as tables already printed in the annual report, are free of charge. A special computer run of a selected year of data is $43.50, including programming time and shipping and handling. Each additional year of data requested is $21. Information transferred to

floppy disk costs $100. Information transferred to magnetic tape costs $250.

Department of Health, Bureau of Communicable Disease Control, 1730 E. Elm St., P.O. Box 570, Jefferson City, MO 65102, (314) 751-6128. Publications include the *1991 Annual Report* and the bi-monthly *Missouri Epidemiologist*. The office will distribute data information included in their *Annual Report*, free of charge.

Montana
Department of Health, Bureau of Records and Vital Statistics, Helena, MT 59620, (406) 444-2614. Publications include the *Annual Report of Vital Statistics*. Specific data can be provided on computer printout, diskette and magnetic tape. Fees vary according to the complexity of the request and the amount of programming time involved.

Department of Health and Environmental Sciences, Communicable Disease Section of Preventive Health Services Bureau, Cogswell Building, Helena, MT 59620, (406) 444-2737. Computer printouts of aggregate data are available on a limited basis.

Nebraska
Department of Health, Bureau of Vital Statistics, P.O. Box 95007, Lincoln, NE 68509-5007, (402) 471-2871. Publications include the *1990 Annual Report of Vital Statistics*. The Health Data and Statistical Research Department will help with statistical information on the phone as well as provide information on computer printout and diskette. The cost of computer time is $20 per hour. Requests for selected data should be made in writing. Be as specific as possible, including your computer system's requirements as well as diskette size and density.

Department of Health, Division of Disease Control, 301 Centennial Mall South, P.O. Box 95007, Lincoln, NE 68509-5007, (402) 471-2937. Publications include the *Nebraska Morbidity Report*. Computer printouts of data are available on a limited basis.

Nevada
Department of Human Resources, Division of

Health, Section of Vital Statistics, 505 East King St., Carson City, NV 89710, (702) 687-4481. Publications include the *1990 Vital Statistics Report*. Computer printouts on selected data are available free of charge.

Department of Human Resources, Office of Disease Control, 505 East King St., Room 304 Carson City, NV 89710, (702) 687-4800. This office provides numerous publications on a variety of communicable diseases. They are not staffed to do selected computer runs.

New Hampshire
Department of Health and Welfare, Bureau of Vital Records and Health Statistics, Health and Human Services Building, 8 Hazen Drive, Concord, NH 03301, (603) 271-4651. Publications include an *Annual Report*. Requests are for specific information are handled on a case by case basis. Fees vary according to the amount of computer programming involved. Computer printouts, diskettes and magnetic tapes are available.

Department of Health and Welfare, Bureau of Communicable Disease Control, Health and Human Services Building, 6 Hazen Dr., Concord, NH 03301-6527, (603) 271-4477. Publications include several bimonthly bulletins. Computer printouts are available of selected data.

New Jersey
Department of Health, Bureau of Vital Statistics, CN 370, Trenton, NJ 08625, (609) 292-4087. Publications include an *Annual Report*. Computer printouts are available for a fee.

Department of Health, Division of Epidemiology and Disease Control, University Office Plaza, CN 369, Trenton, NJ 08625, (609) 588-7500. This office will answer specific questions over the phone, but does not provide computer printouts of information.

New Mexico
Department of Health and Environment, Office of Vital and Health Statistics, Public Health Division, P.O. Box 26110, Santa Fe, NM 87503-6110, (505) 827-2539. Publications include the *1990 Annual Report*. Detailed requests for information not

found in their annual report should be placed in writing. Information can be provided on diskette. Fees vary according to the complexity of the request.

Department of Health, Division of Epidemiology, P.O. Box 26110, Santa Fe, NM 87502, (505) 827-0006. Publications include their monthly *Epidemiology Report*. Requests for information not found in their monthly report should be placed in writing. If you provide them with a blank diskette they will download data on to it for you and omit any identifiers.

New York
Department of Health, Bureau of Biometrics, Empire State Plaza, Concourse Rm. C144, Albany, NY 12237-0044, (518) 474-3189. Publications include the *1989 Annual Report of Vital Statistics*. Requests for information should be placed in writing. Information that is readily available, such as tables printed in the 1989 Annual Report, are distributed at no cost. A specific data run of information is $191. Some information is available on diskette and magnetic tape. Fees vary, according to the complexity of the request.

Department of Health, Bureau of Communicable Disease Control, Tower Bldg., Rm 651, Empire State Plaza, Albany, NY 12237, (518) 474-3187. Publications include the *1998-1989 Annual Report*. The office will run computer searches of aggregate data, depending upon the purpose of the request.

North Carolina
North Carolina Center for Health and Environmental Statistics, P.O. Box 29538, Raleigh, NC 27626-0538, (919) 733-4728. Publications include an *Annual Report* and *1990 Vital Statistics Report*, among others. Information requests should be in writing. If requesting a magnetic tape, be sure to include your system requirements. Computer printouts, diskettes, and magnetic tapes are provided on a limited basis. The charge for magnetic tapes is the cost of the tape and the computer time involved.

North Dakota
Department of Health, Administrative Services Section, 600 E. Blvd., Second Floor, Judicial Wing, State Capitol, Bismarck, ND 58505-0200, (701)

224-2392. Publications include the *1990 Vital Statistics Annual Report*. Computer searches and printouts are provided free of charge.

Department of Health, Division of Disease Control, 600 E. Blvd., State Capitol, Bismarck, ND 58505-0200, (701) 224-2378. This office publishes a variety of publications on communicable diseases. Computer searches and printouts are not provided.

Ohio

Statistical Analysis Unit, Health Policy Data Center, Ohio Department of Health, P.O. Box 118, Columbus, OH 43266-0118, (614) 644-7800. Publications include the *1990 Annual Report of Vital Statistics* which is $9. The office also publishes a *Vital Statistics Summary Fact Sheet*, which is free. Special computer runs are $25 per data year. Extensive programming is extra, and the amount depends upon the complexity of the request. Information is provided via computer printouts.

Oklahoma

Department of Health, Division of Data Management, 1000 N.E. 10th St., P.O. Box 53551, Oklahoma City, OK 73117, (405) 271-4542. Publications include the *1990 Annual Report of Vital Statistics*. Computer searches and printouts are provided, usually free of charge. If you supply your own magnetic tape or diskette they will transfer information to if for you. Fees vary according to the complexity of the request. All information for specific data runs should be in writing. Be sure to include information describing your computer system's requirements.

Department of Health, Office of General Communicable Diseases-0305, 1000 N.E. 10th St., Oklahoma City, OK 73117-1299, (405) 271-4060. Publications include a monthly *Epidemiological Bulletin* and *Epidemiologic Annual Summary of Communicable Diseases*. Computer searches and printouts are provided free of charge. All requests for information should be submitted in writing at least two weeks before the data is needed. Fees vary according to the complexity of the request.

Oregon

State Health Department, Division of Vital Statistics, P.O. Box 14050, Portland, OR 97214,

(503) 731-4108. Publications include: *1990 Oregon Vital Statistics*, *Oregon Deaths Due to Drugs and Alcohol*, and their newsletter, *Oregon Health Trends*. Information is available on computer printout and diskette. Fees vary according to the complexity of the request.

State Health Department, Division of Epidemiology Control, P.O. Box 116, Portland, OR 97202, (503) 731-4025. Publications include the *Current Disease Summary* which is published every other week. The office is not equipped to provide printouts of selected data that do not already exist in published form.

Pennsylvania

Department of Health, Health Statistics and Research, State Health Data Center, P.O. Box 90, Harrisburg, PA 17108, (717) 783-2543. Publications include the *County Profile*. Computer searches and printout requests must be made in writing. Costs are $150 for one year of data, $75 for each additional year.

Department of Health, Division of Epidemiology, Health and Welfare Building, 7th and Forster Sts., P.O. Box 90, Harrisburg, PA 17120, (717) 787-3350. Publications include an *Annual Report*. Computer searches and printouts are available, free of charge.

Rhode Island

Department of Health, Vital Records, Room 101, 75 Davis St., Providence, RI 02908, (401) 277-2812. Publications include the *1988 Annual Report of Vital Statistics*. Printouts of information are available depending upon whether or not the data is available on computer. Requests for individualized reports must be made in writing. Fees vary and are based upon the amount of computer programming needed to fulfill a request.

Department of Health, Office of AIDS-Sexually Transmitted Diseases, 3 Cannon Building, Providence, RI 02908, (401) 277-2577. Publications include the bi-monthly *Disease Bulletin*. This office does not provide selected data printouts.

South Carolina

Department of Health and Environmental Control, Office of Vital Records and Public Health

Statistics, 2600 Bull St., Columbia, SC 29201, (803) 734-4810. Publications include the *South Carolina Vital and Morbidity Report*. Computer searches, printouts, and information on diskette and magnetic tape are provided. Information requests should be in writing, be sure to specify your computer system requirements. Each request is evaluated individually. Although in-house printouts are free, individual requests for selected data require a fee based on the complexity of the request and computer time involved.

Department of Health and Environmental Control, Communicable Disease Control Section, Robert Mills Complex, Box 101106, Columbia, SC 29211, (803) 737-4165. Publications include the *1991 South Carolina Reportable Diseases Report*. Computer searches and printouts of information are provided. Requests for information should be in writing. Information on diskette is provided on a limited basis. Since patient data is confidential, aggregate data is releases without any personal identifiers.

South Dakota
State Health Department, Center for Health Policy and Statistics, 445 E. Capitol St., Pierre, SD 57501-3185, (605) 773-3693. Publications include the *1990 Vital Statistics Annual Report* for $10.50. Once the office receives a written request for information they will respond with an estimate of computer charges. Information is available on diskette and magnetic tape on a limited basis.

State Health Department, Division of Public Health, 523 E. Capitol Bldg., Pierre, SD 57501, (605) 773-3361. Publications include a monthly newsletter and *1991 South Dakota Vital Statistics and Health Status* report. Computer reports of selected data are provided free of charge. Diskettes and magnetic tapes can be provided on a limited basis. All information requests should be in writing.

Tennessee
Department of Health and Environment, Center for Health Statistics, 419 Cordell Hull Building, Nashville, TN 37247-0360, (615) 741-1954. Publications include an *Annual Report of Vital Statistics*. There is also a series of four publications, *Tennessee's Health*, which gives a detailed health profile based on 1990 statistics. The series can be ordered in its entirety for $30. You can purchase the volumes separately, also. *Picture of the Present* is $5, *Picture of the Present, Part II*, $15, *Guidelines for Growth*, $5, and *Focus on the Future,* is also $5. Printouts are provided free of charge. The office will also download limited data to a magnetic tape or diskette at no charge, but you must supply them with the materials needed. All requests for information should be in writing, and be sure to include you computer system's specifications in your letter.

Texas
Department of Health, Bureau of Vital Statistics, Statistical Services Division, 1100 West 49th St., Austin, TX 78756, (512) 458-7111. Publications include *1990 Texas Vital Statistics*. The office will provide information on computer printouts, diskettes and magnetic tapes. Printouts are available at $150 per hour, diskettes at approximately $25 per tape. Programming charges are $30 per hour.

Department of Health, Bureau of Disease Control and Epidemiology, 1100 West 49th St., Austin, TX 78756, (512) 458-7455. Publications include their annual summary, *Reported Morbidity and Mortality in Texas*. Computer searches and printouts are provided at no cost.

Utah
Department of Health, Division of Vital Records, P.O. Box 16700, Salt Lake City, UT 84116, (801) 538-6186. Publications include the *1990 Vital Statistics Report*. Information is provided via computer printouts, diskettes and magnetic tapes. The office does charge for the use of the computer and the statistician's time. Fees vary according to the complexity of the request. If detailed information is required, requests should be made in writing. Be sue to include the specifications needed for diskettes or magnetic tapes.

Department of Health, Bureau of Epidemiology, P.O. Box 16660, Salt Lake City, UT 84116-0660, (801) 538-6191. Publications include the monthly *Epidemiology Newsletter*. The Department of Health is the process of creating a centralized statistics center. This should be in full operation as of Fall, 1992.

Vermont
Department of Health and Human Services, Vital Records Statistics, P.O. Box 70, Burlington, VT 05402, (802) 863-7275. Publications include the *1990 Vital Statistics Report*. Computer searches and printouts are available through this office.

Department of Health and Human Services, Division of Epidemiology and Disease Prevention, P.O. Box 70, Burlington, VT 05402, (802) 863-7240. Publications include the *Vermont Disease Control Bulletin* which is published bi-monthly. Reportable disease totals for the previous year are listed through this publication. The office releases county specific information.

Virginia
Department of Health, Center for Health Statistics, 109 Governors St., 307 Madison Bldg., P.O. Box 1000, Richmond, VA 23208-1000, (804) 786-6206. Publications include the *1990 Annual Report* for $10. Computer searches are available and information is provided via printouts, diskettes and magnetic tapes. The minimum charge for a selected data search is $25. All information requests should be in writing.

Department of Health, Office of Epidemiology, James Madison Building, P.O. Box 2448, 109 Governor St., Richmond, VA 23218, (804) 786-6261. Publications include the monthly *Virginia Epidemiology Bulletin*. The office provides county specific information. No diskettes or magnetic tapes are available.

Washington
Department of Health, Center for Health Statistics, Office Building #2, Olympia, WA 98504, (206) 753-5936. Publications include the *Annual Summary Report of Statistics for 1990, Selected Pregnancy Reports of Statistics for 1990, Age Adjusted Death Rates for 1986-1989,* and *Minority Health in Washington*. The office provides computer searches for selected data and computer printouts. Information is not provided on diskette. One year of aggregate data on magnetic tape costs $600.

West Virginia
State Health Department, Epidemiology and Health Promotion, Surveillance and Disease Control, State Capitol Complex, Charleston, WV 25305, (304) 558-9100. Publications include the *Annual Report of Vital Statistics* and the *1989 County Health Profile* which is being updated for publication in 1992. The office provides computer printouts of selected data, free of charge. Magnetic tapes and diskettes can be obtained on a limited basis for a fee.

Wisconsin
Department of Health and Social Services, Vital Statistics Department, 1 West Wilson St., Madison, WI 53701, (608) 266-1939. Publications include the *Annual Report of Vital Statistics*. Information requests should be in writing. Computer printouts of selected data are provided at no cost.

Department of Health and Social Services, Community Communicable Disease Section , P.O. Box 309, Madison, WI 53701, (608) 267-9003. Publications include the quarterly *Wisconsin Epidemiologic Bulletin*. Requests for information should be made in writing. Information is available on computer printout, free of cost.

Wyoming
Department of Health and Social Services, Division of Health and Medical Services, Vital Records Services, Hathaway Building, Cheyenne, WY 82002, (307) 777-7591. Publications include the *1990 Vital Statistics Report*. The office does provide computer searches and information is available on printouts, diskettes and magnetic tapes. There is a flat fee of $25 for computer searches. Diskettes and magnetic tapes require additional fees that vary with the complexity of the request.

Department of Health and Social Services, Division of Health and Medical Services, Preventive Medicine, Hathaway Building, Cheyenne, WY 82002, (307) 777-6004. Publications include the *Epidemiologic Bulletin*. Basic information is provided on computer printouts and diskette at no charge. Detailed requests should be in writing.

INDEX

7-Phone Call Rule, 5

Abdominal sarcoma, 685

Abetalipoproteinemia, 50, 695

Abnormal puberty, 360

Abortion, 50-51
　Freedom of Choice Act, 521
　statistics, 50

Abstinence, 51, 265

Acanthamoeba eye infections, 190

Accidents
　driving-while-intoxicated, 233
　prevention, 51
　traffic, 233

Acetaminophen, 51

Achondroplasia, 51-2

Aci-Jel, 705

Acidosis, 52

Acne, 52, 368
　see also Adolescent Health
　see also Cystic Acne
　see also Teenagers
　Acoustic neuroma, 52-3

Acquired hypothyroidism, 689

Acquired Immune Deficiency Syndrome
　see AIDS

Acquired osteomalacia, 692

Acromegaly, 53, 692

ACTH, 53

Actimmune, 705

Actovase, 705

Acupuncture, 53-4
　bibliography, 53
　chronic pain, 54, 172
　licensed professionals, 657-8, 660, 662
　research, 53

Acute leukemia, 54

Acute myocardial infarction, 54-5

Addison's disease, 55

Adenoma of the thyroid, 55

Adiposogenital dystrophy, 283

Adolescence
　see also Acne
　see also Puberty
　see also Teenagers
　abstinence, 51
　behavioral disorders, 418
　drug abuse, 55, 229

fatherhood, 57, 268
　health issues, 56-8
　mental health, 163
　pregnancy, 57, 190, 265

Adolescent Drug Abuse, 55
　see also Drug Abuse

Adoption
　Family Life Information Exchange, 58
　family planning, 191, 265
　mental health, 697

Adrenal gland disorders, 58-9

Adrenal hyperplasia, congenital, 184

Adrenal insufficiency, 687

Adrenarche, 687

Adrenoleukodystrophy, 59

Adriamycin PFS, 705

Adrucil, 705

Adult diabetes, 216

Advertising
　alcohol, 70
　tanning devices, 675

Advisory Mental Health Council, 539

Adynamia, 59

Affective disorders, 211

Agammaglobulinemia, 59, 683

Agency for Health Care Policy and Research, 311

Agency for Toxic Substances and
　Disease Registry, 308

Agenesis, 60

Agent Orange, 60, 221

Agents—progesterone, 699

Age-related macular degeneration, 59-60

Aging, 60-3
　see also Gerontology
　see also Living Wills
　see also Long-Term Care
　see also Nursing Homes
　aging process research, 60, 391
　Baltimore Longitudinal Study of
　　Aging, 60, 392
　brain function, 677
　constipation, 187
　family violence and abuse, 266
　gerontology research, 293
　hearing impairment, 317
　home care, 311
　parents, 61, 265

Aging (*con't*)
 residential facilities, 312
 skin, 552
 sleep disorders, 552
Agitans, paralysis, 473
Agnosia, 702
Agoraphobia, 699
Agranulocytosis, 63
Agraphia, 702
AIDS, 63-7
 AZT, free, 705
 barrier contraceptives, 190
 children with, 406
 clinical trials, 684
 contraception research, 190
 depression, 700
 dialysis, 218
 drug abuse and, 228
 drugs, 66
 etiology, 703
 food safety, 452
 health care costs, 312
 health care workers, 314
 HIV infection, 330
 hotline, 64
 immunomodulators, 678
 intravenous drug users, 65
 invasive dental procedures, 209
 military policy, 425
 nutrition, 66
 pediatric, 66, 161, 332
 research, 67
 Surgeon General's report, 66
 tuberculosis, 331
 women, 626
 workplace, 455
Air
 cleaners, 355, 549
 indoor pollution, 355
 pollution, 67-8
Alabama
 aging, 636
 consumer complaints, 647
 Health and Human Services, 645
 health statistics, 714
 insurance, 653
 licensed professionals, 656
 Medical board, 641
 nursing homes, 665
 pharmacies, 668
 radon, 672
Alaska

aging, 636
consumer complaints, 647
Health and Human Services, 645
health statistics, 714
insurance, 653
licensed professionals, 656
Medical board, 641
nursing homes, 665
pharmacies, 668
radon, 672
Albinism, 68, 681
Albright's syndrome, 68
Alcohol and alcoholism, 68-70
 see also Drug Abuse
 see also Pregnancy and Alcohol
 see also Workplace Drug Abuse
 abuse, 61, 69, 70
 accidents related to, 233
 advertising, 70
 aging, 70
 block grants, 230
 brain dysfunction, 677
 cancer connections, 69, 227
 children of alcoholics, 165
 chronic organic brain syndromes, 677
 cirrhosis of the liver, 173-4
 consumption, 677
 drug abuse and, 228
 family studies, 677
 genetic predisposition, 677
 hepatitis, 324
 high-risk families, 678
 hotline, 228
 juvenile abuse, 56
 minorities, 427
 mutual-help groups, 543
 National Clearinghouse for Alcohol
  and Drug Information, 69
 National Institute on Alcohol Abuse
  and Alcoholism, 69, 313
 Native Americans, 438
 neuropharmacology, 678
 pregnancy and, 503
 prevention and treatment, 69
 student use, 540
 teenagers, 583
 treatment, 228, 613
 withdrawal, 678
 women, 625
Aldactazide, 705
Aldactone, 705
Aldomet, 705

Aldosteronism, 71, 695
Alexander's syndrome, 71
Alexia, 702
Alglucerase therapy, 288
Alkaptonuria, 71
Alkylating agents, 71
Allergenics, 71-2, 596, 607
Allergic rhinitis, 72
Allergies, 72-3
    asthma and, 102
    dust, 72
    eye, 72
    food, 73
    disease, 72-3
    insect bites, 361
    mold, 72
Alopecia, 73
Alpers syndrome, 73-4
Alpha lipoprotein deficiency, 696
Alpha-1-antitrypsin Deficiency, 74
Alternative medical practices, 74, 333
Alupent, 705
Alveolar bone, 75
Alveolar microlithiasis, 75
Alveolar proteinosis, 75
Alzheimer's disease, 75-7
    see also Aging
    see also Dementia
    see also Presenile Dementia
    clinical studies, 699-700, 702
    Disease and Education Referral Center, 75
    long-term care services, 77
    publications, 61, 76, 702
Amalgam, dental, 209
Amaurotic idiocy, 77
Ambiguous genitalia, 77, 688
Amblyopia, 78
Amblyopia, strabismus, 569-70
Ambulatory health care, 507
Amebiasis, 78, 680
Amenorrhea, 460
Amino acid disorders, 78, 686
Amino acidurias, 686
Amnesia, 702
Amniocentesis, 78
    see also Pregnancy
Amosmia, 79
Amyloid polyneuropathy, 79
Amyloidosis, 79-80
Amyotonia congenita, 80, 457
Amyotrophic lateral sclerosis, 80-1
Analgesic-associated nephropathy, 81

Anaphoresis, 81
Anaphylactoid reactions, 678
Anaphylaxis, 678
Anaplasis, 81
Anaprox, 705
Anemia, 82, 365-66
    aplastic, 695
    hemolytic, 321
    pernicious, 481
    refractory, 524
    sickle cell, 549-50
    sideroblastic, 550
Anencephaly, 82
Aneurysms, 83, 363
Angelman's disease, 83
Angina
    pectoris, 83
    microvascular, 694
Angioedema, 84
Angiography, 84
    diagnostic, 701
    fluorescein, 275
Angioplasty, 84
    coronary, 192
    laser, 379
Aniline dyes, 84
Animal feed, 88, 279
Animals
    patents, 85
    research alternatives, 85
    transgenic, 85
Aniridia, 85, 693
Ankloglassia
    see Tongue-Tied
Ankylosing spondylitis, 85
Anomia, 702
Anonymous
    drug abuse hotline, 228
Anorexia nervosa, 85-6, 450, 454
    see also Eating Disorders
Anosmia, 86
Anoxia, 87, 702
Ansaid, 705
Antenatal diagnosis, 87
Anthrax, 87
Anti-addiction drugs, 423
Anti-cancer drugs, 88
    see also Cancer
Antialphatrypsin, 87
Antibiotics, 88
Anticoagulants, 88-9
Antidepressants, 696

Antidiuretic hormone syndrome, 353
Antidiuretic hormone, 89
Antifungal agents, oral, 679
Antihistamines, 89
Anti-inflammatories, 90
Antimetabolites, 89-90
Antineoplastic, 90
Antiretroviral therapies, 701
Antisocial behavior, 90
Antivert, 705
Antiviral substances, 90
Antritrypsin deficiency, 686
Anusol HC, 705
Anxiety disorders, 91, 419, 699
Aortic insufficiency, 91
Aortitis, 91
Aphakia, 91
Aphasia, 92
Aphthous stomatitis, 92
Aplasia, red cell, 517
Aplastic anemia, 92-3, 695
Apnea monitor, 574
Apnea, 93, 460, 553
    see also Sudden Infant Death Syndrome
Apple pesticides, 483
Appraisals, health risk, 387, 507
Apraxia, 93
Apresoline, 705
Aqua dynamics, 259
Arachnoiditis, 93
Arachnoiditis, spinal, 563
Aralen, 705
Aran Duchenne Spinal Muscular Dystrophy, 93-4
Arizona
    aging, 636
    consumer complaints, 647
    Health and Human Services, 645
    health statistics, 714
    insurance, 653
    licensed professionals, 656
    Medical board, 641
    nursing homes, 665
    pharmacies, 668
    radon, 672
Arkansas
    aging, 636
    consumer complaints, 647
    Health and Human Services, 645
    health statistics, 714
    insurance, 653
    licensed professionals, 657
    Medical board, 641

    nursing homes, 665
    pharmacies, 668
    radon, 672
Arnold-Chiari malformations, 94
Arrythmias, 94
Arsenic, 250
Artane, 705
Arteries, laser surgery, 379
Arteriosclerosis, 94-5
Arteriosus, truncus, 601
Arteriovenous malformations, 95
Arteritis, 95
    Takayasu's, 580
    temporal, 584
Arthritis, 95-6
    aging process, 61
    arthroscopy, 97
    bogus cures, 647
    childhood, 163
    diet, 452
    infectious, 72, 359
    lyme disease related, 398
    National Institute of Arthritis
        and Musculoskeletal and Skin
        Diseases, 367
    psoriatic, 514
    publications, 96
    rheumatoid, 532, 680
    videotape, 96, 299
Arthrogryposis multiplex cogenita, 96
Arthropathy, neurogenic, 444
Arthroplasty, 97
Arthroscopy, 97
Artificial
    blood vessels, 97
    hearts, 97
    joints, 98
    lungs, 98
Artificial insemination, 98
    see also In Vitro Fertilization
Artificial sweeteners
    aspartame, 100
    cyclamate, 100
    saccharin, 100
Asbestos, 99
    construction standards, 628
    Environmental Protection Agengy, 250
    hotline, 99
    occupational health, 99
    home exposure, 188
    worksite complaints, 646
Asbestosis, 99-100

Asians, 426
Asiatic Flu
    see Flu
Asparaginase, 100
Aspartame, 100, 279
Asperger's syndrome, 100
Aspergillosis, 101, 680
Asphyxia, 101
    neonatal, 440
Aspirin allergy, 101
Aspirin-sensitivity, 678
Asthma, 72, 101-02
Astigmatisms, 102-03
Asymmetric septal hypertrophy, 103
Ataxia, 103
    Friedreich's, 283
    heredofamilial acute, 700
    progressive, 700
    telangiectasia, 103
    telangiectasia, familial, 263, 683
Atelectasis, 104
Atherectomy, 104
Atherosclerosis, 104-05
Athlete's foot
    see Fungal Infections
Athetosis, 105
Atomic radiation exposure, 455
Atopic dermatisis, 105
Atrial fibrillation, 106
Atrovent, 705
Attention deficit disorder, 106
Attention disorders, 698
Attention-deficit hyperactivity, 698
Audiologists, 656
Augmentin, 705
Autism, 106-07, 305, 571, 698
Autoimmune disease, 107
Autoimmune polyglandular disorders, 688
Autonomic nervous system disorders, 702
Autosomal dominant disease
    see Huntington's Chorea
Axenfeld's syndrome, 693
Axid, 705

- **B** -

B-19 infection, 107
Baby bottle tooth decay, 108, 208
Baby monitors, 663
Bacillus Calmette-Guerin, 108
Back problems, 108

pain, 108-09
Bacteremia, 460
Bacterial meningitis, 109
Bacteriology, 110
Bactrim, 705
Bactroban, 705
Bad breath
    see Halitosis
Bag lunches, 452
Balance systems, 378
Balance, 182
Baltimore Longitudinal Study on
    Aging, 60, 61, 392
Barlow's syndrome, 110
Bartter's syndrome, 110, 695
Basal cell carcinoma, 111, 552, 681
Basal ganglia disease, degenerative, 206
Batten's disease, 111
Battered child
    see Child Abuse
Battered elderly
    see Aging
    see Elder Abuse
Battered spouses, 111-12
BCG, 108
Beach closings, 360
Beconase, 705
Bed wetting, 112
Bedsonia, 112
Behavior and health, 112-13
Behavior development, 113
Behavior modification, 113
Behavior patterns, 387
Behavioral disorders, 418
Behcet's disease, 113-14, 693
Bejel, 114
Bell's palsy, 114
Benign congenital hypotonia, 114-15
Benign mucosal pemphigoid, 115
Benign prostatic hyperplasia, 115
Benzene, 250
Benzo(a)pyrene, 115
Bereavement, perinatal, 574
Berger's disease, 116
Beriberi, 116
Bernard-Soulier syndrome, 116
Beta blocker drugs, 117
Beta-thalassemia, 117
Betagan, 705
BICNU, 705
Biliary cirrhosis, 117
Bilirubinemia, 117

Binocular vision, 117-18
Binswanger's disease, 118
Biochemical defects, 703
Biofeedback, 118
Biological pollutants, 355
Biomedical engineering, 118
Biomedical research
    at National Institutes of Health, 119
    cancer drug treatment, 141-2
    immune system, 72
    infectious diseases, 72
    kidney transplants, 373
    leprosy, 384
    orthopedics, 462
    stroke and trauma, 572
    stroke, 572
    tropical diseases, 601
Biophysics, 119
Biopsies, 119
Biopsy, breast, 133
Biostimulation, laser, 379
Biotechnology, 119-20, 451
Bipolar depression, 696
Bipolar disorders, 211
Birth, 120
    cesarean, 154
    defects, 120-21
    statistics, 50, 120
    weight, 121, 160, 393
Birth control
    see Contraception
    see Family Planning
    see Oral Contraceptives
Birth defects, 120-121
    see also Congenital Abnormalities
    see also Neural Tube Defects
Birth weight, 121
    see also Child Health
Black lung
    disease research, 122
    disability benefits, 122
    federal programs, 455
Blackheads, 181
Black tongue, 122
Blacks
    see Minority Health
Bladder cancer, 122-23, 686
    carcinoma, 685
Blastomycosis, 123, 680
Bleeding disorders, 691
Bleeding ulcers, 605
Blenoxane, 705

Bleomycin, 123
Bleph-10, 705
Blephamide, 705
Blepharitis, 123
Blepharospasm, 123
Blindness
    prevention, 261
    research, 124
Blistering, 124
Blisters, fever, 270
Bloch-Sulzberger syndrome, 124
Blood, 124-26
    abnormalities, 124
    blood brain barrier, 125
    Center for Biologics Evaluation and
        Research, 71
    cholesterol, 452
    coagulation, 125-26
    diseases, 126
    products, 71, 126, 596, 608
    substitutes, 126
    sugar, 216
    testing, 126
    transfusions, 596
    vessel prostheses, 511
    vessels, artificial, 97
Blood testing
    see Blood Products
Bloodborne pathogens, 67
Blue baby, 126-27
Body weight, 127
Bolivian hemorrhagic fever, 127
Bone
    cancer, 127
    disorders, 127-28
    Paget's disease, 469
    marrow transplantation, 128, 682, 700
    sarcoma, 530, 538
    thinning, 466
Bone, alveolar, 75
Borderline personality disorder, 697
Botulism, 128-29
Bovine growth hormone, 129
Bowel disease, 129
    see also Irritable Bowel Syndrome
Bowen's disease, 129-30
Brachial plexus injuries, 130
Bradycardia, 130
Brain, 130-31
    alcohol consumption, 678
    aging issues, 61
    behavior, 702

cancer, 131
dementia, 207
death, 131-32
disorders, 130
imaging techniques, 131, 419
injury, traumatic, 598
tumors, 132-33, 684, 701, 702
Breast cancer, 133-34,
see also Cancer
clinical trials, 684-85
Breast implants, 133, 135
FDA regulations, 626
Breast lumps
noncancerous, 133
Breast reconstruction, 133
Breastfeeding
health issues, 134-35
lactation, 160
nutrition, 502
PKU, 406
Surgeon General's report, 377
Bronchial asthma, 102, 678
Bronchiectasis, 135-36
Bronchitis, 136
Brown lung disease, 139
Brucellosis, 136
Bruxism, 136
Bubonic plague, 136
Bucladin-S, 705
Buerger's disease, 136-37
Building air quality, 549
Bulbar palsy, 137
Bulimia, 86, 137-38, 454, 699
see also Anorexia
see also Eating Disorders
Bullous pemphigoid, 138, 681
Bureau of Health Professions, 427
Burkitt's lymphoma, 138
Burn research, 138
Burning mouth syndrome, 138-39
Bursitis, 139
BuSpar, 705
Busulfan, 139
Byssinosis, 139

- C -

Cachexia, 460
Cadmium, 250
Caffeine, 139, 699
Calan, 705
Calcium, 140

Calcium-losing tubulopathy, 695
California
aging, 636
consumer complaints, 647
Food and Drug Administration, 639
Health and Human Services, 645
health statistics, 714
insurance, 653
licensed professionals, 657
Medical board, 641
nursing homes, 665
pharmacies, 668
radon, 672
Calories, 220
Canadian health care, 311
Canavan's disease, 140
Cancer, 140-42
see also Anti-Cancer Drugs
see also Radiation
see also specific type of Cancer
Annual Report on Carinogens, 145
Black Americans, 427
bladder, 686
breast, 685
Cancer Information Service, 140
colon polyps, 496
colorectal, 686
cures, bogus, 647
current research, 140
depression, 699
detection, 140
diet and cancer, 451
DNA, 226
environmental risks, 140, 143
financial assistance, 140
gastric, 685
genetics of, 291
interleukin-2 therapy, 363
kaposi's sarcoma, 370
kidney, 372
larynx, 378
laser surgery, 378
lung, 394, 685
occupational, 455
oral, 458
ovarian, 467
pain, 469
pancreatic, 470
pediatric, 142
physician referrals, 140
Pi-Mesons, 486
plasma cell, 489

Cancer (*con't*)
  prevention, 507
  prevention and diet, 451
  prostate, 510
  publications, 141
  renal, 460, 685
  respiratory, 527
  skin, 552
  smoking-related, 555
  squamous cell, 565
  stomach, 569
  teenagers, 583
  testicular, 585
  treatment video, 142
  trophoblastic, 600
  urinary tract, 606
  uterine, 606
Candida, 143
Canker sores, 143, 208, 234, 459
  and fever blisters, 270
Canned seafood, 643
Capoten, 705
Capozide, 705
Carafate, 705
Carbamazepine, 696
Carbohydrates, 143, 452
Carbon monoxide poisoning, 702
Carcalon, 143-44, 374
Carcinoembryonic antigen, 149
Carcinogens, 144
Carcinoma, 144
  ovarian, 683
Cardene, 705
Cardiac pacemakers, 468
Cardiogenic shock, 548
Cardiomegaly, 144-45
Cardiomyopathy, 145
Cardiopulmonary resuscitation, 145
Cardiovascular disease, 145, 450, 618
  see also Heart Disease
Carditis, 146
Cardizem, 705
Cardizem CD, 705
Cardizem SR, 705
Cardura, 705
Caries, 146
Carmustine, 146
Carnitine deficiency, 460
Carotid endarterectomy, 146
Carpal tunnel syndrome, 146-47, 455
Carpet fumes, 147
Carrier screening, CF, 201

Cat cry syndrome, 148
Cat scratch fever, 148
Cataphasia, 147
Cataplexy, 147-48
Catapres, 705
Cataracts, 148, 693
Catastrophic care, 312
Catastrophic health insurance, 311, 312
Catheterization, 148-49
Causalgia, 460, 690
CEA, 149
Ceclor, 705
CEENU, 705
Ceftin, 705
Cefzil, 705
Celiac disease, 149
Cellulite, 149-50
Centenarians, 150
Center for Biologics Evaluation
  and Research, 596, 608
Center for Developmental Disabilities, 214
Center for Devices and Radiological
  Health, 409, 421, 430, 631
Center for Drug Evaluation and Research, 231
Center for Population Research, 567
Central core disease, 150
Central processing dysfunctions, 151
Ceramic cookware, 381
Cerebellar arteriosclerosis, 150
Cerebellar ataxia, 150-51, 700-01
Cerebellar disorders, 689
Cerebellar lesions, 151
Cerebral arteriovenous malformations, 151
Cerebral atrophy, 151-52
Cerebral palsy, 152, 305
Cerebrotendious xanthomatosis, 152
Cerebrovascular disease, 152-53
Ceredase, 705
Ceroid lipofuscinosis, 153, 700
Cervical cancer, 153, 685
  see also Cancer
Cervical cap, 153, 191
  see also Contraception
Cervical disorders, 153-54
  see also Cervical Cancer
Cesarean birth, 154
Cestode
  see Tapeworm
Chagas' disease, 154, 680
Chalazion, 154-55
Chancroid, 155
Change of life

see Menopause
Chaparral tea, 155
Charcoal broiling meat, 155
Charcot-Marie-Tooth disease, 155-56
Charge syndrome, 156
Chediak-Higashi syndrome, 156, 678
Cheiloaschsis
    see Harelip
Chelation therapy, 156
Chemicals
    hazards, 455
    pesticide hotline, 482, 592
    spills, 156-57
Chemotherapy, 157, 614-15, 681
Chest
    pain, 694
    x-rays, 632
Chewing tobacco and snuff, 157, 555
    see also Smoking
    see also Smokeless Tobacco
Chicken pox, 157
Chilblain, 158
Child abuse and neglect, 158-59
    prevention, and treatment, 158
    research, 159
    sexual abuse, 159, 545
Child day care, 204
Child development, 159
Child health, 158-165
    see also Lead Poisoning
    AIDS, 406
    baby-bottle tooth decay, 208
    birth, 162
    chronic lung disease, 406
    colic, 178
    development issues, 159
    developmental psychology, 699
    federal programs, 162
    hyperactivity, 418
    injury prevention, 508
    Medicaid, 411
    medications, 411-12
    mental disorders, 164
    mental health services, 418
    mental illness, 698
    mentally retarded, 418
    metabolism disorders, 422
    nutrition, 134
    obesity, 145, 454
    PKU, 406
    progressive dementia, 700
    protective services, 223

    rearing, 162, 418
    special needs, 357, 406
    technology-dependent, 407
Child support, 162, 225
Childbearing families, 58, 264
Childbirth, 162, 163
    see also Postnatal Care
Childhood
    arthritis, 96, 163
    asthma
        see Asthma
    leukemia, 385
    mental disorders, 163, 164
    nutrition, 164, 165
Children of alcoholics, 69, 165
Chinese Restaurant Syndrome, 165
Chiropractors, 656
Chlamydia, 165
Chloasma, 165-66
Chlorambucil, 166
Chloride, 250
Cholecystectomy
    see Gallbladder
Cholelithotomy
    see Gallstone
Cholera, 166
Cholestatic liver disease, 691
Cholesterol, 166-67
    blood, 452
    database, 166
    education programs, 318
    nutritional guidelines, 452
    videos, 615
Chondrocalcinosis, 167
Chondromalacia, 167
Chondrosarcoma, 168
Chordoma, 168
Choriocarcinoma, 168
Chorionic villus sampling, 168
Choroid, gyrate atrophy, 694
Choroidal disease, 529
Choroiditis, 169
Chromium, 250
Chromophobe adenemas, 692
Chromosomal abnormalities, 703
Chronic
    bronchitis, 136, 169, 696
    cough, 169, 194
    diseases, 169-70, 264
    EBV, 170
    granulomatous disease, 171
    infections, 171

Chronic (*con't*)
    lung disease, 171-72
    pain management techniques, 54, 172
    renal failure, 526
Chronic fatigue syndrome, 170-71
Chrysotherapy, 172
Churg-Strauss syndrome, 172-73
Cicatricial pemphigoid, 173
Cigarette smoking, 556-57, 583, 696
Cipro, 705
Circulation disorders, 173
Circumcision, 173, 615
Cirrhosis, 173-74, 390
Cirrhosis, primary biliary, 692
Cisplatin, 174
Civil rights, 652
Claudication, 174
Claustrophobia, 174
Clearinghouse on Disability Information
    Program, 222
Clearinghouse on Disability Information, 38
Clearinghouse on Family Violence
    Information, 266
Clearinghouse on Postsecondary
    Education for Individual with Handicaps, 38
Clearinghouse on the Handicapped, 305
Cleft palate, 174
Climacteric
    see Menopause
Clinical laboratory improvements, 314
Clinical research, 175
Clinical trials
    acquired hypothyroidism, 687
    AIDS, 66, 176, 678, 682
    alcoholism, 677
    allergic diseases, 678
    allergic rhinitis, 678
    Alzheimer's, 677, 699
    amino acid disorders, 686
    anaphylaxis, 678
    asthma, 678
    brain aging, 677
    brain tumors, 684
    breast cancer, 683, 685
    cancer, 141
    cataracts, 693
    Chediak-Higashi syndrome, 678
    colitis, ulcerative, 679
    colon cancer, 683
    colorectal cancer, 686
    cryptococcosis, 678
    Cushing's syndrome, 687

    cystic fibrosis, 696
    cystinosis, 686
    demyelination, 701
    depression, 696
    dermatomyositis, 680
    eating disorders, 699
    emphysema, 696
    eosinophilia, 679
    Epstein-Barr virus, 679
    Ewing's sarcoma, 684
    facial pain, 690
    food additive reactions, 679
    genodermatoses, 681
    geriatric depression, 677
    gluten-sensitive enteropathy, 679
    granulomatous hepatitis, 679
    growth hormone deficiency, 683
    heart disease, 694
    hepatitis, viral, 691
    herpes simplex, 679, 690
    hirsutism, 688
    HIV, 678
    hypertension, 677, 695
    immunodeficiency, 679
    infertility, 360, 688
    inflammatory bowel disease, 679
    isolated IgA deficiency, 683
    leukemia, 684
    Lowe syndrome, 686
    lung cancer, 685
    lung disease, 696
    lupus erythematosus, 680
    lysosomal storage disorders, 686
    mania, 696
    mastocytosis, 679
    melanoma, 685
    Menkes' disease, 687
    menopause, 699
    mental illness, 696
    miscarriages, 688
    mycoses, 680
    neurologic diseases, 700
    neutropenia, 680
    osteogenesis imperfecta, 687
    ovarian cancer, 683
    parasitic diseases, 680
    Parkinson's disease, 700
    phobias, 699
    Pick's disease, 677
    pituitary tumors, 688
    polymyositis, 680
    precocious puberty, 687

premenstrual syndrome, 699
prostate cancer, 683
pruritus of cholestasis, 691
pyogenic infections, 680
recurrent infection syndrome, 679
rheumatoid arthritis, 680
salivary gland dysfunction, 689
sarcoidosis, 679
short stature, 687
sickle cell anemia, 693
staphylococcal infections, 680
stuttering, 689
taste disorders, 690
Varicella-zoster, 680
vasculitis, 680
vasomotor rhinitis, 680
Clinoril, 705
Clomiphene citrate treatment, 688
Cloning, 175
Clotting disorders, 175-76
Clozaril, 705
Cluster headache
see Histamine Headache
CMV
see Cytomegalovirus
CMV retinitis, 678
Coal workers' pneumoconiosis, 122
Coat's disease, 176
Cobalt, 176
Cocaine Anonymous, 228
Cocaine, 176-77
see also Drug Abuse
Coccidioidomycosis, 680
Cochlear implants, 316
Cockayne's syndrome, 177
Codeine, 51, 177
Coeliac sprue, 679
Coffee
see Caffeine
Cogan's syndrome, 177
Cogentin, 705
Cognition, 178
Cognitive development, 159, 418
Cold, common, 181-82
Cold sores
see Fever Blisters
Coley's mixed toxins, 178
Colic, 178
Colitis, 179
Colitis, ulcerative, 605
Collagen disease, 179
Collapsed lungs, 179

Colon
cancer, 180, 681, 683
disorders, 180
polyps, 496
Color blindness, 180
Color therapy 74
Color vision deficiency, 693
Colorado
aging, 637
consumer complaints, 648
Food and Drug Administration, 639
Health and Human Services, 645
health statistics, 715
insurance, 653
licensed professionals, 657
Medical board, 641
nursing homes, 665
pharmacies, 668
radon, 672
Colorectal
cancer, 686
neoplasms, 180
Colostomies, 180-81
Colpocystitis, 181
Comas, 181
Comedo
see Acne
Common cold, 181-82
Communicable diseases, 182, 713
Communication disorders, 160, 182-83, 406
Community
child abuse prevention grants, 158
health centers, 312, 507
mental health centers, 419
services, 312
Compazine, 705
Complaints
aging-related services, 636
cosmetics, 193, 639
defective products, 670-71
doctors, 640-43
fish and seafood, 643-44
health clubs, 650-51
health fraud, 647-50
health insurance, 652-55
health maintenance organizations
(HMOs), 650
hospitals, 335, 645, 651-52
licensed professionals, 655-62
medical bills, 662-63
medical devices, 663
Medicare, 664

Complaints (*con't*)
    nursing homes, 664-67
    pharmacists, 667-70
    prescription fraud, 670
    radon, 671-75
    tanning devices & salons, 675
    workplace safety, 645-47
Complex carbohydrates, 143, 452
Compulsion, 183
Computer access, 183
Computerized databases, 3
Condoms, 66, 184, 547
    advertising, 184
Congenital
    abnormalities, 184
        see also Birth Defects
    adrenal hyperplasia, 184-85, 687
    malformations, 184, 703
    heart disease, 185
    infections, 185
Congestive heart failure, 185
Conjunctivitis, 54, 186
Connecticut
    aging, 637
    consumer complaints, 648
    Health and Human Services, 645
    health statistics, 715
    insurance, 653
    licensed professionals, 657
    Medical board, 641
    nursing homes, 665
    pharmacy, 668
    radon, 672
Connective tissue disease, 186, 428, 686, 703
Constipation, 186-87
Constitutional rights, mental patients, 419
Construction hazards, 455
Consumer
    injury and illness data, 187
    organic and natural foods, 312
    product injuries, 187-89
Consumer Product Safety Commission, 187, 670
Consumer products
    blenders, 187
    clothes dryers, 187
    flammable fabrics, 187
    smoke detectors, 188
Contact dermatitis, 189, 522
Contact lenses, 189-90
Continuous Ambulatory Peritoneal Dialysis, 218
Contraception, 190-91
    family planning, 265-66

foams, 190
jellies, 190
oral, 458
safety and effectiveness, 190
sexually transmitted diseases, 190
steroid, 567
Convenience food markets, 276
Convulsions, febrile, 268
Cookbook, Healthy Heart, 452
Cooking, 61
    see also Food
Cookware safety, 191, 451
Cooley's anemia, 117, 161, 191-92, 406
Copper metabolism, 687
Cor pulmonale, 192
Cordarone, 705
Corgard, 705
Corneas
    disorders, 192
    transplants, 192, 597
Cornelia deLange syndrome, 192
Coronary angioplasty, 192-93
Coronary artery disease, 694
Coronary disease
    see Cardiovascular Disease
    see Heart Disease
Corpus callosum, 60
Corzide, 705
Cosmetic surgery
    see Face Lifts
Cosmetics, 193, 639
Cost containment, health, 311
Costochondritis, 193
Cot death
    see Sudden Infant Death Syndrome
Coughing, 169, 193
Coumadin, 705
Council for Exceptional Children, 305
Cowpox, 194
Coxsackie virus, 194
CPR, 145
Crack cocaine, 194-95
Cranial abnormalities, 195
Craniofacial malformations, 195
Cretinism, 195
Creutzfeldt-Jakob disease, 195-96
Crib death apnea, 574
Crigler-Najar syndrome, 196
Crime, family violence, 243
Critical care medicine, 196
Crohn's disease, 179, 196-97
Cross-eye, 197

Cryosurgery, eyes, 197-98
Cryptococcosis, 198, 678
Cryptosporidiosis, 198, 679, 680
Curvature of the spine, 109
    see also Scoliosis
Cushing's syndrome, 198-99, 687
Cutaneous infections, 679
Cutis laxa, 199
Cyanide, 250
Cyclamates, 100, 279
Cyclic idiopathic edema, 199
Cyclitis, 199-200
Cyclophosphamide, 200
Cyclospasmol, 705
Cyclosporine-associated hypertension, 200
Cystic acne, 200
Cystic fibrosis, 200-01, 289, 291, 696
Cystic mastitis
    see Fibrocystic Breast Disease
Cysticercosis, 680
Cystinosis, 201, 686, 703
Cystinuria, 201
Cystitis, 201-02
Cytarabine, 202
Cytomegalic inclusion, 202
Cytomegalovirus, 202-03
Cytotec, 705
Cytotoxic T-cells, 681
Cytovene, 705
Cytoxan, 705

- D -

D/ART, 210
Dacarbazine, 205
Dactinomycin, 203
Dalmane, 705
Daltonism
    see Color Blindness
Dandruff, 203
Dandy-Walker syndrome, 204
Danocrine, 705
Dantrium, 706
Darier's disease, 204
Databases
    cancer, 140
    cholesterol, 166
    family violence, 243, 266
    mental health, 91, 418
    National Electronic Injury Surveillance
        System, 187

smoking and health, 476, 555
Daunorubicin, 204
Day care, 158, 204-05
Deafness, 205, 689
Death, 205
    see also Living Wills
    accident prevention, 51
    alcohol and drug use, 233
    consumer products, 187
    highway fatalities, 233
    statistics, 205
    videos, 615
Decarbazine, 205-06
Decubitus ulcers, 206
Deductibles, insurance, 653
Deep-seated infections, 680
Degenerative basal ganglia disease, 206
Degenerative joint disease, 206
Deglutition, 206-07
Dejerine-Sottas disease, 207
Delaware
    aging, 637
    consumer complaints, 648
    Health and Human Services, 645
    health statistics, 715
    insurance, 653
    licensed professionals, 657
    Medical board, 641
    nursing homes, 665
    pharmacies, 668
    radon, 672
Dementia, 207
    see also Mental Illness
    see also Alzheimer's Disease
    see also Presenile Dementia
    aging-related, 61
    Alzheimer's, 75-7
    causes and treatment, 130, 207
    multi-infarct, 431
    presenile, 506
    research, 207-08
    senile, 543
Demyelinating diseases, 208
Demyelinating polyneuropathies, 701
Dengue, 208
Dental health
    amalgams, 209
    baby-bottle tooth decay, 208
    care, 208-10, 540
    dental disease prevention activity, 208
    dentists, complaints, 656
    dentures, 210, 690

Dental Health (*con't*)
   disease, 208-09, 234, 459
   fluoridation, 209
   hygienists, 656
   periodontal disease, 209
   plaque, 210, 489
   porcelain, 209
   procedures & AIDS, 67, 209
   restorative materials, 209
   sealants, 209-10
   x-rays, 210
Dentobacterial plaque infections, 210
Depression, 62, 210-11, 419, 696
   teenage, 211
Depth perception, 211
Dermagraphism, 211
Dermatitis herpetiformis, 212, 681
Dermatitis, contact, 189, 522
Dermatology, 212
Dermatomyositis, 212-13, 701
Dermographism, 212
DES, 213
Desserts, 452
Desyrel, 706
Developmental disabilities, 214, 482
Devic's syndrome, 214-15
Dextranase, 215
Dhobie itch, 215
Diabetes, 215-17
   adult, 216
   afro-americans, 216
   aging issues, 216
   Black Americans, 427
   blood sugar, 216
   complications of, 216
   cookbooks, 216
   depression, 699
   diet guidelines, 450
   education, 216
   foot care, 216
   gestational, 216, 294
   hispanics, 216, 427
   insulin-dependent, 216
   juvenile, 369
   kidney disease, 216
   mellinus, 691
   mellitus, 216
   National Diabetes Advisory Board, 216
   National Diabetes Information
      Clearinghouse, 216
   noninsulin-dependent, 216
   periodontal disease, 216, 584

   pregnancy, and, 217
   research, 215, 362
   retinopathy, 216
   tooth disease, 216
   video, 217
Diabetic neuropathy, 217
Diabinese, 706
Diagnostic angiography, 701
Diagnostic imaging, 218
   Diagnostic Imaging Research Program, 218
Dialysis, 218
Diamox, 706
Diaper rash, 218
Diarrhea, 218-19
   peptic ulcers, 692
   traveler's, 219
Dienestrol, 706
Diet and dieting, 219-20
   see also Food
   see also Nutrition
   arthritis, 96, 452
   books, 219, 220
   fads, 219
   low sodium, 451, 537
   nutrient data analysis, 453
   nutrition survey, 277
   nutritional strategies, 167
   programs, 220
   supplements, 219
   weight loss gimmicks, 220
   weight reduction products, 219
Dietary Analysis Program, 453
Diethylstilbestrol, 213
Dieticians, 656
Diffuse sclerosis, 220
Diflucan, 706
DiGeorge syndrome, 683
Digestive Diseases Advisory Board, National, 221
Digestive diseases, 180, 220-21, 238, 317
Dilantin, 706
Dioxin, 60, 221, 250
Diphtheria, 222
Diprolene, 706
Diprosone, 706
Disabilities, 35-48, 222-23
   benefits, 36
   handicap programs, 305-06
   infants with, 223
   job training, 36
   rehabilitation resource center, 222
Disaster victims, 223
Discoid lupus erythematosus, 224

Discrimination
    employment, 290
    hospitals, 652
    nursing homes, 664
Disease outbreaks, 182, 224, 609
Disease hotline
    Centers for Disease Control, 224
District of Columbia
    aging, 637
    consumer complaints, 648
    Health and Human Services, 645
    health statistics, 715
    insurance, 653
    licensed professionals, 657
    Medical board, 641
    nursing homes, 665
    pharmacies, 668
    radon, 672
Disturbed children, 418
Diuretics, 224
Diurnaldystonia, 224, 700
Diverticulitis, 225
Divorce, 50, 163, 225, 418
Dizygotic twins, 225
Dizziness, 225-26
DNA testing, 161, 226, 291, 407
Doctors
    complaints, 640-43, 656
    HMOs, 651
    medical bills, 662-63
    prescription fraud, 670
Dolobid, 706
Donor tissue damage, 460
Down's syndrome, 226, 677
Doxorrubicin, 226-27
DPT vaccine
    see Immunizations
Drinking water, 227
    radon in, 521
Dropsy
    see Edema
Drug abuse, 227-30
    see also Alcoholism
    see also specific drug
    see also Workplace Drug Abuse
    AIDS, 228
    anti-addiction, 423
    block grants, 230
    Cocaine Anonymous, 228
    hotlines, 228
    Narcotics Anonymous, 228
    National Clearinghouse for Alcohol

    and Drug Information, 228
    prevention, 229
    teen use, 583
    testing, 228, 232
    treatment programs, 228, 233
    veterans, 613
    video, 228
    workplace, 228, 233
Drug allergy, 230
Drugs (pharmaceuticals)
    allergies, 72, 230
    antiretroviral, 678
    antiviral, 679
    approval process, 230
    Center for Drug Evaluation and
        Research, 231
    development, 231
    evaluation, 231
    generic, 288
    interactions, 231, 412
    labeling, 231-32
    mental illness, 419
    nonprescription, 230, 412
    over-the-counter, 467-68
    prescription, 412
    purpura, 232
    resistence, 232
    transdermal delivery, 596
Drunk driving, 70, 160, 233-34, 407
Dry eyes, 234
Dry mouth, 234, 689
Duchenne muscular dystrophy, 235
Dupuytren's contracture, 235
Duricef, 706
Dust allergy, 72, 232-36
Dust inhalation diseases, 235
Dwarfism, 236
Dyazied, 706
Dying, 205
Dymelor, 706
Dysarthria, 689
Dysautonomia, 236
Dysentery, 236-37
Dysexecutive syndrome, 702
Dysgeusia, 690
Dyskinesia, 237
    tardive, 581
Dyslexia, 237-38, 569
Dysmenorrhea, 238, 490
Dyspepsia, 238
Dysphonia, spasmodic, 560
Dysphorias, 697

Dysplasia
   fibrous, 273
   polyostotic fibrous, 496
Dystonia, 238-39
   canthorum, 689
   musculorum deformans, 238
   torsion, 591

- E -

E-Mycin, 706
Ear infection, 239, 424
Eating disorders
   anorexia nervosa, 85-87, 240
   bulimia, 86, 239-40
   obesity, 454
Eating and aging, 62
Eaton-Lambert myasthenic syndrome, 240
Echinococcosis, 680
Echocardiography, 240
Eclampsia, 240
   see also Pregnancy
Economics Research Service, 276
Ectodermal dysplasia, 240-41, 687
Ectopic hormones, 241
Ectopic pregnancy, 241
Eczema, 241-42, 680
Edema, 242
Efudex, 706
Eggs, 242
   see also Food
Ehlers Danlos syndrome, 242, 703
Eisenmenger's syndrome, 242-43
EKGs, 243
Eldepryl, 706
Elder abuse, 243
   see also Aging
   nursing homes, 62, 243
Elderly
   see Aging
Electrical muscle stimulaters, 54, 243, 313
Electric blankets, 244
Electrocardiogram, 244
Electromagnetic fields, 244
Electro-Shock treatment, 244-45
Electrologists, 656
Electromagnetic fields, 244, 501
Elephantiasis, 245
Embolisms, 245
Embryo transplants, 120
Emergency medical personnel, 223

Emergency medical technicians, 656
Emergency rooms, 31, 187, 651
Eminase, 706
Emotional disorders, 62, 161, 418-19
Emphysema, 245
Empty nest families, 264
Enamel, tooth, 246
Encephalitis, 246, 416, 613
   clinical trials, 702
   lethargica, 247
   measles, 408
Encephalomyelitis, 247
Encephalopathy
   lead, 380
   Wernicke's, 623
Encopresis, 247
End-stage renal disease, 372
Endocarditis, 247
Endocrine
   glands, 247-48
   muscle disease, 248
Endodontics, 248
Endogenous depression
   see Depression
Endometriosis, 248-49, 360
Endoscopy, 587, 605
Energy metabolism, 422
Enigmatic blistering disorders, 124, 249
Enlargement of the prostate, 510
Enteric disease, 249-50
Environmental health issues, 250
Environmental Protection Agency, 250
Eosinophilic granuloma, 250-51
Eosinophilic pneumonias, 696
Epicondylitis
   see Tennis Elbow
Epidemiology, 251, 713
Epidermodysplasia verruciformis, 251
Epidermolysis bullosa, 251-52
Epiglottitis, 252
Epikeratophakia, 252
Epilepsy, 252-53
   dental implications, 160, 209, 406
   therapies, 252
Epinephrine, 695
Epistaxis
   see Nosebleeds
Epogen, 706
Epstein-Barr Virus, 170, 253, 679
Equine encephalitis, 253
Ergamisol, 706
Erycette, 706

Erythema
elevatum diutinum, 254, 682
multiforme, 254
nodosum, 254
Erythroblastosis fetalis, 254
Erythrocytes
see Blood
Esophageal disorders, 255
reflux, 255, 318
Esotropia
see Cross Eye
Essential hypertension, 694
Essential iris atrophy, 693
Essential tremor, 689
Estrace, 706
Estramustine, 255
Estreptozocina, 255
Estrogen, 256
aging-related, 61
clinical studies, 699
osteoporosis, 466
women's health, 626
Ethics, 257
Eulexin, 706
Euthanasia
see Living Wills
Ewing's sarcoma, 257, 684
Exercise, 257-59
arthritis, 96
obesity, 454
President's Council on Physical Fitness, 258
Exotropia, 259
Experimental allergic encephalomyelitis, 259
Experimental drugs, 230
Experts
getting information, 5
locating an, 3
7-Phone Call Rule, 5
Ten Basic Telephone Tips, 6
Extended care facility
see Long-Term Care
see Nursing Homes
Extended wear contact lenses, 190
Extracoporeal shock-wave lithotripsy, 260
Extrapyramidal disorders, 260, 700
Eyes, 260-61
allergies, 72
banks, 260
cancer, 198
care, 260-61
exercises, 261
fungus, 284

infections, 359
National Eye Institute, 260
research, 260-61
surgery, 379, 519
tumors, 261, 603
Eyeliners, 639

- F -

Fabry's disease, 261-62, 700
Face lifts, 262
Facial dystonia, 414
Facial pain, 690
Facial tics, 262
Fad diets, 219
Fainting, 263, 577
Falls, age-related, 61, 263
Familial ataxia telangiectasia, 263
Familial hypertension, 694
Familial multiple endocrine neoplasia, 264
Familial spastic paraparesis, 264
Families
childbearing, 265, 387
economics, 387
family planning, 265-66
genetics, 160-61, 165, 178
health, 264
marital relationships, 266, 387
support counselors, 656
violence, 158, 243, 266
Family leave, 264-65
Family Life Information Exchange, 190-91, 265
Family planning, 265
Fanconi's anemia, 266
Farmers lung, 266
Farsightedness, 266-67
Fascioliasis, 267
Fast food, 267, 276, 452
Fasting, 267
Fasting hypoglycemia, 691
Fat, dietary, 167
Fat substitutes, 268, 451
Fatherhood, 267-68
Febrile
convulsions, 268
seizures, 268
Federal Emergency Management Agency (FEMA), 223
Federal Trade Commission, 315
Feeding impairments, 268
Feet, 269

FEMA
   see Federal Emergency Management Agency
Feminine hygiene, 418
Fertility
   control, 190
   drugs, 269
   planning technologies, 497
   regulating products, 190
   research, 269
Fertilization, in vitro, 365
Fetal alcohol syndrome, 121, 269
Fetal monitoring, 269-70
Fetal research, 50, 270
Fever blisters, 143, 270
Fevers, 270
Fiber
   dietary, 270-71
   intake, 452
Fibrillation, 271
Fibrilnolysis, 271
Fibrocystic disease of the breast, 271
Fibroid tumors, 271-72
Fibroids, 360
Fibromuscular hyperplasia, 272
Fibromyalgia, 272
Fibrositis, 272
Fibrotic lung diseases, 272-73
Fibrous dysplasia, 273
Fifth disease, 273
Filariasis, 273, 680
Finance in health care, 310
Finger foods, 161, 406
Firework safety, 188
First aid, 274
Fish oil, 450
Fish, 451, 643-44
   see also Seafood
Fitness centers, 650
Flab removal, 313
Flexeril, 706
Floaters, eye, 274
Floppy baby, 274, 439
Florida
   aging, 637
   consumer complaints, 648
   Food and Drug Administration, 639
   Health and Human Services, 645
   health statistics, 715
   insurance, 653
   licensed professionals, 657
   Medical board, 641
   pharmacies, 668

   radon, 672
Flossing, 208
Floxin, 706
Floxiridine, 274
Flu, 61, 274-75, 610
Fluorescein angiography, 275
Fluorescent lamps, 275
Fluoridation, 275
Fluoride treatment, 227, 234, 275-76, 459
Fluoroscopy, 276
Fluorosis, 276
Fluorouracil, 276
FML, 706
Focal dystonia, 701
Folex, 706
Food, 276-82
   see also Nutrition
   additives, 280, 408, 500, 679
   adverse reactions, 277
   allergies, 73, 279
   antibiotics in, 279
   calories, 278
   children's literature, 450
   consumption survey, 277
   dietary analysis software, 453
   drug interactions, 278
   expenditures, 276
   fast, 267, 279
   finger, 161, 406
   handling, 278
   imported, 282
   inexpensive recipes, 451
   irradiation, 279-80, 281
   labels, 277, 278-80, 408, 500
   low-cost, 450
   microwave ovens, 281
   microwave safety, 424
   nutrient composition, 278
   organic foods, 312
   pesticide residues, 278, 483
   pesticides, 482
   poisoning, 277, 280-81, 408, 500
   potassium content, 499
   preparation, 277, 408, 451, 500
   preservatives, 279, 281, 452
   ready-prepared, 278
   safety, 65-66, 278, 281-82
   service, 278
   sodium content, 537
   sulfites, 279, 281, 575
   tropical oils, 280
   weight loss, 450-51

Food and Drug Administration, 230, 639
Food and Nutrition Information Center, 450
Food-borne illness, 278
Foot care, 61, 269
Formaldehyde, 282
Foster care, 282
Fracture healing, 282
Fragile X syndrome, 283, 677, 703
Frailty, 61
Frailty, age-related, 263
Fraud, health, 312-13
Freedom of Choice Act, 51
Friedreich's ataxia, 103, 283
Froehlich's syndrome, 283-84
Fruit, 282, 284, 368, 452
Fuch's dystrophy, 284
Fulvicin, 706
Fundus flavimaculatus, 693
Fungal disease, eye, 284
Fungal infections, 284-85
Fungal sinusitis, 680
Funnel chest, 285, 477
Furry tongue, 285

- G -

G6PD deficiency, 285
Galactorrhea, 285
Galactosemia, 285-86
Gallbladder disease, 286
Gallstones, 286-87
Garren gastric bubble, 220
Gas, 287
Gastric bubble, 287
Gastric cancer, 685
Gastric hypersecretion, 287, 692
Gastrinoma, 287-88
Gastritis, 288
Gastrocrom, 706
Gastrointestinal diseases, 692
Gaucher's disease, 288, 700
Gene splicing, 161, 291, 406
Gene therapy, 289
Generic drugs, 288-89, 311
Genetic pancrea, 289
Genetic risk, x-rays, 632
Genetic-metabolic diseases, 160, 407, 422
Genetics, 289-92
    cancer, 142, 291
    child development, 160
    counseling, 201, 406, 700-01
    diseases, 703
    disorder testing, 291
    engineering, 119, 291
    heritable mutations, 291
    mapping, 290
    research, 290
    services, 406
    spina bifida, 562-63
    testing, 161, 291, 406
    therapy, 290-91
Genital herpes, 292
Genital warts, 292
Genitalia, ambiguous, 77
Genodermatoses, 681
Georgia
    aging, 637
    consumer complaints, 648
    Food and Drug Administration, 640
    Health and Human Services, 645
    health statistics, 715
    insurance, 653
    licensed professionals, 657
    Medical board, 641
    nursing homes, 665
    pharmacies, 668
    radon, 672
Geriatric depression, 62, 677
Geriatrics
    see Aging
    see Gerontology
Germ cell tumors, 460
German measles, 293
Gerontology, 293
    see also Aging
    see also Long-Term Care
    Gerontology Research Center, 293
Gerson method, 293
Gerstmann's syndrome, 293-94
Gestation, 294
Gestational diabetes, 216, 294
Giardiasis, 294, 680
Gigantism, 294-95, 692
Gilbert's syndrome, 295
Gilles de la Tourette's disease, 295
Gillis W. Long Hansen's Disease Center, 384
Gingivitis, 295
Glaucoma, 148, 295-96, 405, 693
Gliomas, 296, 685, 701
Globoid cell leukodystrophy, 296
Glomerulonephritis, 296, 692
Glucose intolerance, 297
Glucotrol, 706

Gluten intolerance, 297
Gluten-sensitive enteropathy, 679
Glycogen storage disease, 297
GnRH agonist, 699
Goiter, 297-98, 692
Gonads, 298
Gonorrhea, 298
Goodpasture's syndrome, 298-99
Gorlin syndrome, 681
Gout, 299
Grains, 299
Grand Forks Human Nutrition Research
    Center, 595
Granulocytopenia, 300
Granuloma faciale, 682
Granulomatous disease, 171, 300, 680
Granulomatous hepatitis, 679
Grape cure, 300
Grave's disease, 300-01
Grief, 299
Grippe
    see Flu
Growth hormone deficiency, 301, 683
Guillain-Barre syndrome, 301-02, 495
Gum disease, 302, 480
Gynecology, 626
Gynecomastia, 302
Gyrate atrophy, 302-03, 693

- H -

Hailey's disease, 303
Hair loss, 303
Hair removal, 303-04
Hair spray, 304
Hairy tongue
    see Black Tongue
Halcion, 706
Haldol, 706
Halitosis, 304
Hallervorden-Spatz disease, 304
Hand-foot and mouth disease, 194, 304-05
Handicaps, 35-48, 305-06
    children, 305-06
    ERIC Clearinghouse, 305
    Handicapped Educational Exchange, 38
Hansen's disease, 306-07, 384
Happy puppet syndrome, 307
Harada's disease, 307, 693-94
Hardening of the arteries, 307
Harelip, 307-08

Hashimoto's disease, 308
Haverhill fever, 308
Hawaii
    aging, 637
    consumer complaints, 648
    Health and Human Services
    health statistics, 716
    insurance, 653
    Medical board, 641
    nursing homes, 665
    pharmacies, 668
    professionals, 658
    radon, 672
Hay fever, 308
Hazardous substances, 308-09
HDL, 329
Headaches, 18-20, 309, 615
Head,
    injuries, 309-10, 702
    lice, 310, 386
Healing, fracture, 282
Health administrators, 507-08
Health benefits, 63
Health care costs, 63, 310-11
Health Care Financing
    Administration, 310, 410, 651
Health care policy, 311-12
Health care workers, AIDS, 314
Health clubs, 315, 650
Health facilities, 312
Health foods, 312
Health fraud, 312-13, 647
Health insurance, 313-14
    AIDS, 66
    catastrophic, 312-14
    children with special needs, 406
    cost control, 310-11
    genetic testing, 290
    Medicare, 410
Health Maintenance Organizations, 314
    complaints, 651
    insurance, 313
    Medicare, 411
Health professions, 314-15
Health scams, 647
Health spas, 315
Health statistics, 315, 387, 391, 428
    see also Appendix C
Health, National Institutes of
    Aging, 60, 391, 677
    Alcohol Abuse and Alcoholism, 69, 313, 677
    Allergy and Infectious Diseases, 72, 678, 703

Arthritis and Musculoskeletal and Skin
    Disease, 52, 368, 514, 680
Cancer, 141, 681
Child Health and Human
    Development, 501, 686
Deafness and Other Communication
    Disorders, 688
Dental Research, 208, 689
Diabetes and Digestive and Kidney
    Diseases, 690
Eye, 617, 693
Heart, Lung, and Blood, 694
Mental Health, 91, 210, 418, 696
Neurological Disorders and Stroke, 53, 700
Hearing aid specialists, 656
Hearing aids, 315-16
Hearing
    communication disorders, 182
    conservation, 628
    loss, 316-17
Heartburn, 317
Heart defects, 353
Heart disease, 318
    see also Cardiovascular Disease
    attacks, 317
    congenital, 185
    congrestive failure, 185
    diagnosis and treatment, 318
    mitral valve prolapse, 428
    weight-related, 452
Heart prostheses, 511
Heart transplants, 319, 597
Heart-lung machines, 318-19
Heart murmurs, 319
Heart transplants, 319
Heat exhaustion, 342
Heat stroke, 319, 342
Heating bills, 636
Hebephrenia, 319
Hemiplegia, 320
    spastic, 560
Hemochromatosis, hereditary, 688
Hemodialysis, 320
Hemoglobin genetics, 320
Hemoglobinopathies, 320, 693
Hemoglobinuria, paroxysmal nocturnal, 475
Hemolytic anemia, 231, 321
Hemolytic disease, 321, 502
Hemophilia, 64, 67, 321-22
Hemophilus influenza, 322
Hemorrhagic diathesis, 322
Hemorrhagic shock, 548

Hemorrhoids, 322-23
Hemosiderosis, 323
    transfusional, 596
Hemostatic disorders, 691
Henoch-Schonlein purpura, 323
Hepatitis, 323-24, 691
    hepatitis B, 209
Herbal therapy, 74
Herbs, 277, 408, 500
Hereditary cerebellar lesions, 151
Hernias, 324-25
Herniated discs, 325
Heroin, 325
Herpes, 325-26
    genital, 292
    gestationis, 682
    recurrent, 690
    simplex infections, 679
    zoster, 326-27, 548
Heterochromia irides, 689
Hiatal hernia, 327
Hiccups, 327
High blood pressure, 327-28
    cholesterol, 166
    High Blood Pressure Information Center, 327
    minorities, 427
    salt, 536-37
    smoking, 328
    Spanish publications, 328
High cholesterol, 695
    see also Cholesterol
High density lipoproteins, 328-29
High risk youth, 56
High school drug use, 56, 229
Highway traffic accidents, 233
Hill-Burton law, 20, 645
Hirschsprung's disease, 329
Hirsutism, 329, 688
Hismanal, 706
Hispanics, 426
    see also Minority health care
Histiocytosis, 329
Histoplasmosis, 330, 680
HIV, 330-32
    see also AIDS
    clinical trials, 678
    hotline, 330
    neuromuscular disorders, 701
    pediatric, 332
    publications, 161
Hives, 330
HMS, 706

Hodeolum
  see Stye
Hodgkin's disease, 332, 682, 684-85
Holistic medicine, 615
  see Alternative Medicine Practices
Home
  care, elderly, 311
  drug infusion therapy, 334
  safety, 188
  test kits, 334
  water treatment units, 227
Homeless mentally ill, 420
Homelessness, 332-33
  medical conditions, 333
  mental illness, 333
Homemade saline solution, 190
Homeopathy, 333
Homeowners
  asbestos, 188
  indoor air quality, 188
  insulation safety, 188
Homocystinuria, 333
Homosexuality, 333-34
Hookworm disease, 334
Hormone therapy, 335, 417, 626
Hormones, 334-35
  see also Menopause
  growth, 683, 692
  sex, 334, 545
Hospice care, 335, 615
Hospitals
  complaints, 335, 652
  discrimination, 652
  food, 651
  free care, 20, 644
  infections, 335-36
  medicare payments, 314
  rural, 312
  waste disposal, 359
Hotlines
  AIDS clinical trials, 64
  alcoholism, 69
  asbestos, 99
  brain injury, 598
  cancer, 140
  child sexual abuse, 545
  children with disabilities, 223
  chronic fatigue syndrome, 182, 224, 609
  cytomegalovirus, 182, 224, 609
  disease, 182, 224, 609
  drug abuse, 228
  drug abuse and AIDS, 65, 330

  encephalitis, 182, 224, 609
  enteric diseases, 182, 224, 609
  Epstein-Barr, 182, 224, 609
  family health issues, 264
  handicapped, 39
  hepatitis, 182, 224, 609
  hospital complaints, 335
  infant health, 356
  laser surgery, 378
  lyme disease, 182, 224, 609
  malaria, 182, 224, 609
  meat and poultry, 277, 408, 500
  Medicare, 410
  minority health care, 426
  National Drug Abuse Information and
    Treatment, 228
  occupational safety and health, 455
  orphan drugs, 461
  pesticides, 592
  rabies, 182, 224, 609
  radon, 521
  rare diseases, 461, 522
  rehabilitation, 39, 598
  second surgical opinions, 576
  sexually transmitted diseases, 546
  spinal cord injuries, 563
  toxics, 592
  vaccine-preventable diseases, 182, 224, 609
  yellow fever, 182, 224, 609
House Select Committee on Narcotics Abuse
  and Control, 228
Household hazards, 336
HPV, 336
HTLV-1 infection, 700
Human fetal research, 270
Human growth hormone, 196, 336
Human guinea pigs, 175
Human Life Amendment, 51
Human papilloma virus, 336
Human parvovirus, 107
Hunger, 337, 453
Hunt's disease, 337
Hunter's syndrome, 337
Huntington's chorea, 337-38, 689, 700
Hurler's syndrome, 338
Hyaline membrane disease, 338-39
Hydrocephalus, 339
Hydroxyurea, 339
Hyperactivity, 164, 339-40, 418
Hyperbaric oxygenation, 340
Hyperbilirubinemia, 340-41
Hypercalcemia, 341, 692

see also Paget's Disease
Hypercalciuria, 341
   see also Osteoporosis
Hypercholesterolemia, 695
   see Cholesterol
Hyperglycemia, 341
Hyperkinesis, 341-42
Hyperlipidemia, 342, 695
Hyperlipoproteinemia, 342
Hyperparathyroidism, 342, 692
Hyperplasia
   fibromuscular, 272
   islet cell, 367
   juxtaglomerular, 369
   prostate, 510
Hyperpyrexia, 342-43
Hypersensitivity pneumonitis, 343
Hypersensitivity, 696
Hypertension
   see also High Blood Pressure
   cyclosporine-associated, 200
   essential, 694
   familial, 694
   geriatric, 677
   ocular, 456
   renovascular, 526, 695
   steroid, 567, 695
   systemic, 694
   systolic, 579
Hyperthermia, 343
Hyperthyroidism, 343-44
   with carcinoma, 691
Hypertriglyceridemia, 344
Hypertrophic cardiomyopathy, 694
Hyperuricemia, 344
Hyperventilation, 344
Hypo-calcemic rickets, 692
Hypobetalipoproteinemia, 344-45, 695
Hypocalciuric hypercalcemia, 692
Hypocomplementemic glomerulonephritis, 345
Hypogammaglobulinemia, 683
Hypoglycemia, 345, 691
Hypogonadism, 345-46
Hypokalemia, 346, 695
Hypokalemic periodic paralysis, 346
Hypolipidemia, 695
Hypolipoproteinemia, 346
Hypoparathyroidism, 347
Hypophosphatemia, 692
Hypophosphatemic rickets, 687
Hypopituitarism, 347
Hypospadias, 347

Hypotension
   see Low Blood Pressure
Hypothalamus, 347-48
Hypothermia, 348
Hypothyroidism, 348, 692
Hypotonia, 348-49
Hypoventilation, 349
Hypoxia, 349
Hypsarrhythmia, 349

- I -

IBD
   see Irritable Bowel Syndrome
IBS
   see Irritable Bowel Syndrome
Iceland disease, 349-50
Ichthyosis, 350
Identical twins
   see Twins
Idaho
   aging, 637
   Health and Human Services, 645
   health statistics, 716
   insurance, 653
   licensed professionals, 658
   Medical board, 641
   nursing homes, 665
   pharmacies, 668
   radon, 672
Idamycin, 706
Idiocy, 77
Idiopathic central serous choroidopathy, 693
Idiopathic edema, cyclic, 199
Idiopathic hypertrophic subaortic stenosis, 350
Idiopathic inflammatory myopathy, 350-51
Idiopathic pulmonary fibrosis, 696
Idiopathic thrombocytopenic purpura, 351
Ifex, 706
IGA deficiency, 367, 683
Ileitis, 351
Illinois
   aging, 637
   consumer complaints, 648
   Food and Drug Administration, 640
   Health and Human Services, 645
   health statistics, 716
   insurance, 653
   licensed professionals, 658
   Medical board, 642
   nursing homes, 665

Illinois (*con't*)
    pharmacies, 668
    radon, 672
Imaging devices, 430-31
Immobilized enzymes, 120
Immune deficiency disease, 351-52, 682
Immune thrombocytopenia purpura, 352, 691
Immunizations, 352-53
    requirements, 182, 224, 609
    Immunization Practices Advisory
        Committee, 352, 608
Impact resistant lenses, 190
Implants, orthopedic, 462
Impotence, 191, 353, 615-16
Imuran, 706
In vitro fertilization, 365
    see also Artificial Insemination
Inappropriate antidiuretic hormone
        syndrome, 353
Inborn heart defects, 353-54
Inborn metabolism errors, 686
Incest, 159
Inclusion-body myositis, 701
Incontinence, 354
Incontinentia pigmenti, 354-55
Independent living, 222
Indian health care, 438
    see also Native Americans
Indiana
    aging, 637
    consumer complaints, 648
    Food and Drug Administration, 640
    Health and Human Services, 645
    health statistics, 716
    insurance, 654
    licensed professionals, 658
    Medical board, 642
    nursing homes, 665
    pharmacies, 668
    radon, 672
Indocin, 706
Indoor air pollution, 355, 455
Induced movement disorders, 355
Infants, 356-58
    see also Sudden Infant Death Syndrome
    apnea, 574
    disabilities, 223, 358
    formula, 356
    health, 356
    mortality, 356
    muscular atrophy, 433
    nutrition, 357

Infections
    chronic, 171
    congenital, 185
Infectious arthritis, 359
Infectious diarrhea, 219
Infectious diseases, 182, 359
Infectious eye diseases, 359
Infectious waste, 359-60
Infertility
    clinical studies, 688
    treatments, 360
    services, 360
    videos, 615
Inflammatory bowel disease, 129, 361, 679
Inflammatory muscle disease, 680
Inflammatory myopathies, 701
Influenza
    see Flu
Inherited diseases, 291
Inherited metabolic diseases, 421-22
Injury clearinghouse, 187
Inorganic dust diseases, 696
Insect stings, 361
Insomnia, 361-62
Insulin products, 706
Insulin-dependent diabetes, 216, 362
Insulinomas, 362
Insurance
    see also Health insurance
    complaints, 652
    long-term care, 313
    agents, 656
Interactions, drug, 231
Interferon, 362-63, 681
Interferon-A Recombinant, 706
Interferon-gamma, 679
Interleukin-2 therapy, 363
Interstitial cystitis, 363
Interstitial lung disease, 696
Intestinal malabsorption syndrome, 363
Intra-abdominal tumors, 691
Intracervical insemination, 360
Intracranial aneurysm, 363-64
Intracranial arteriovenous malformations, 701
Intraocular lenses, 364
Intrauterine
    devices, 190
    growth retardation, 364
    insemination, 360
Intravenous drug therapy, 364
Intron-A, 706
Invasive dental procedures, 364-65

Involuntary movement disorders, 701
Iowa
    aging, 637
    consumer complaints, 648
    Health and Human Services, 645
    health statistics, 716
    insurance, 654
    licensed professionals, 658
    Medical board, 642
    nursing homes, 665
    pharmacies, 668
    radon, 672
Iridocyclitis, 365
Iris atrophy, 693
Iris bicolor, 689
Iritis, 365
Iron deficiency, 365-66
Irradiation
    see Food Irradiation
Irritable bowel syndrome, 129, 366
    see also Bowel Disease
Iscador, 366
Ischemia, 366-67
Ischemic attacks, 596-97
Islet cell hyperplasia, 367
Isolated growth hormone deficiency, 692
Isolated IGA deficiency, 367
Isoptin, 706
Isordil, 706
Itching, 691
IUDs, 190

- J -

Jakob-Creutzfeldt disease, 367
Japanese health care, 312
Job safety, 646
    see also Workplace safety
Job Accommodation Network, 39
Job training, handicapped, 36
Job's syndrome, 679
Joint disease, degenerative, 206
Joint replacement, 367-68
Joseph's disease, 368
Juicing, 368
Just Say No program, 229
Juvenile delinquency, 55-56, 368-69
Juvenile diabetes, 369
Juvenile rheumatoid arthritis, 369
Juxtaglomerular hyperplasis, 111, 369

- K -

K-Lyte, 706
Kallmann's syndrome, 687
Kanner's syndrome, 369-70
Kansas
    aging, 637
    consumer complaints, 648
    Health and Human Services, 645
    health statistics, 716
    insurance, 654
    licensed professionals, 658
    Medical board, 642
    nursing homes, 665
    pharmacies, 668
    radon, 672
Kaposi's sarcoma, 370, 683
    see also AIDS
Kawasaki disease, 370
Kearns-Sayre syndrome, 370
Keflex, 706
Kentucky
    aging, 637
    consumer complaints, 648
    Health and Human Services, 645
    health statistics, 717
    insurance, 654
    licensed professionals, 658
    Medical board, 642
    nursing homes, 665
    pharmacies, 668
    radon, 672
Keratinization disorders, 681
Keratitis, 370-71
Keratoconus, 371
Keratomileusis, 371
Keratoplasty, 371
Keratosis palmaris et plantaris, 371-72
Kerlone, 706
Kidneys, 372-73
    cancer, 372
    diabetes, 216, 218
    disease, 372
    extracorporeal shock wave, 373
    stones, 373
    transplants, 373
Kinesed, 706
Kleine-Levin syndrome, 373
Kleptomania, 374
Klinefelter's syndrome, 374
Klonopin, 706
Klotrix, 706

Koch antitoxins, 374
Krabbe's disease, 374, 700
Krebiozen, 143, 374-75
Kugelberg-Welander disease, 375
Kuru, 375

- L -

L-Tryptophan, 395
Labeling, drug, 231
Laboratory testing, 375
Labyrinthitis, 375-76
Lacrimal glands, 376
Lactation, 376-77
    breastfeeding, 160
    infant nutrition, 357, 406
    nutritional guidelines, 160
Lactose deficiency
    see Lactose Intolerance
Lactose intolerance, 377
Laetrile, 377
Lamaze method of childbirth
    see Childbirth
Language disorders, 182, 377-78, 560
Lanoxin, 706
Laparoscopic infertility surgery, 615
Laryngeal nodules, 689
Laryngological disorders, 689
Larynx cancer, 378
    see also Cancer
Lasers
    angioplasty, 379
    biostimulation, 379
    eye surgery, 379
    removal of tattoos, 378
    surgery hotline, 379
Laser surgery, 378-79
Lassa fever, 379
Lateral sclerosis, primary, 508
Laurence-Moon-Bardet-Biedl syndrome, 380
Lead encephalopathy, 380
Lead poisoning, 250, 380-81
Learning disabilities, 381-82, 698
Leber's disease, 382
Legal Services Corporation, 36
Legg-Perthes disease, 382
Legionella pneumophila, 382
Legionnaire's disease, 382
Leigh's disease, 383
Leishmaniasis, 383, 460, 680
Lennox-Gastaut syndrome, 383, 702

Lens implants, 383
Leprosy, 384
Lesch-Nyhan disease, 384
Leucovorin calcium, 706
Leukemia, 54, 384-85
    eosinophilic, 679
    hairy cell, 681
    myelogenous, 171
    T-cell, 682
Leukine, 706
Leukoaraiosis, 385
Leukodystrophy, 385
    globoid cell, 296
Leukoencephalopathy, 385-86, 509
Leukoplakia, 386
Librium, 706
Lice, 386
Licensed health professionals, 655
Lichen planus, 386-87
Life cycle, 264, 387
Life expectancy, 387
Life extension, 387
Life-sustaining technologies, 314, 390
    see also Living Wills
Lifestyle, 387-88
    cancer prevention, 142
    Health Risk Appraisals, 387, 507
    risk factors, 387
Limbritol, 706
Lindane lotion, 706
Lioresal, 707
Lipid research, 388
Lipid storage disease, 388
Lipid transport disorders, 388-89
Lipidemia, 389
Lipidosis, 389
Lipstick, 639
Listeriosis, 389
Lithium, 697
Lithobid, 706
Lithotripsy, 389-90
Liver, 73, 390
    cirrhosis, 174
    disorders, 390
    obstructive disease, 695
Living wills, 265, 390
    see also Aging
Lo/Ovral, 706
Lobster substitute, 643
Locked-in syndrome, 390
Lockjaw (Tetanus), 391
Loeffler's syndrome, 391, 679

Lomustine, 391
Long-term care, 391-92
   see also Aging
   see also Gerontology
   see also Nursing Homes
   aging issues, 62
   financing, 392
   insurance, 313
   nursing homes, 448
Longevity statistics, 391
Lopid, 706
Lopressor, 706
Lotrimin, 706
Lotrixone, 706
Lou Gehrig's disease, 81, 392
Louisiana
   aging, 637
   consumer complaints, 648
   Food and Drug Administration, 640
   Health and Human Services, 645
   health statistics, 717
   insurance, 654
   licensed professionals, 658
   Medical board, 642
   nursing homes, 665
   pharmacies, 668
   radon, 672
Low birthweight, 357, 393, 406
Low blood pressure, 393-94
Low density lipoproteins (LDL), 394
Low-calorie sweeteners, 279, 394
Low-cost food, 450
Low-fat diet, 394
Low-income women, 394-95
Low-sodium diet, 450
Lowe's syndrome, 395
Lower back pain, 392-93
Loxapine, 706
L-Tryptophan, 395
Lungs
   cancer, 395-96
   collapsed, 180
   disease, 170, 396, 456
Lupus, 397
   Black women, 426
   erythematosus, systemic, 397, 681
   hotline, 224
   neurological sequelae of, 397
Lyme disease, 397-98
Lymphadenopathy syndrome, 398
Lymphedema, 399
Lymphoblastic lymphosarcoma, 399

Lymphokines, 681
Lymphoma, non-Hodgkins, 399, 681
Lymphosarcoma, 399-400
Lymphosarcoma, lymphoblastic, 399
Lyophilized cytoan, 706
Lysodren, 706
Lysosomal cholesterol storage disorder, 700
Lysosomal storage disorders, 688

- M -

Macrodantin, 706
Macroglobulinemia, 400
Macular degeneration, 59, 400, 544
Macular edema, 693
Magnesium, 699
Magnesium-losing tubulopathy, 695
Maine
   aging, 637
   consumer complaints, 648
   Health and Human Services, 645
   health statistics, 717
   insurance, 654
   licensed professionals, 658
   Medical board, 642
   pharmacies, 668
   radon, 673
Makari test, 400
Malabsorptive disease, 400-01
Malaria, 401, 680
Malignancies, 401
   see also Cancer
Malnutrition, 401-02
Malocclusion, 402
Malpractice, 615
Mammograms, 402, 626
   see also Breast Cancer
Mandible disorders, 402-03
Mania, 403, 696
Manic-depressive illness, 211, 403
Maple syrup urine disease, 403
Marble bone disease
   see Osteopetrosis
Marburg virus disease, 403-04
Marfan syndrome, 404, 477
Marijuana, 404-05
   see also Drug Abuse
Marital relationships, 264, 387
Marriage counselors, 656
Marriages, 50
Maryland
   aging, 637

Maryland (*con't*)
    consumer complaints, 648
    Food and Drug Administration, 640
    Health and Human Services, 645
    health statistics, 717
    insurance, 654
    licensed professionals, 658
    Medical board, 642
    nursing homes, 665
    pharmacies, 668
    radon, 673
Massachusetts
    aging, 637
    consumer complaints, 648
    Food and Drug Administration, 640
    Health and Human Services, 645
    health statistics, 717
    insurance, 654
    licensed professionals, 659
    Medical board, 642
    nursing homes, 665
    pharmacies, 669
    radon, 673
Mastectomies, 405
    see also Breast Cancer
Mastication, 690
Mastocytosis, 405, 679
Masturbation, 615
Maternal and child health, 406-07
Maxzide, 706
Mayo Clinic, 142
McArdle's disease, 407
McCune-Albright syndrome, 687
Measles, 407-08
    see also Immunizations
Measles encephalitis, 407
Meat
    hotline, 277
    inspection, 408
    poultry, 500
Mechlorethamine, 408
Meclan, 706
Meconium aspiration syndrome, 408-09
Medicaid, 409-11
    child health, 411
    community services, 312
    hotline, 410
    HMO payments, 651
Medical
    bills, 640, 662-63
    devices, 243, 409, 663
    devices, quack, 409

economics, 310
imaging, 409, 419, 430
leave, 264-65
licensing boards, 641
radiation, 448
rehabilitation, 511
testing, 409
waste, 359-60
Medicare, 409-411
    catastrophic coverage, 312
    disability payments, 36
    HMOs, 651
    lab referals, 314
    medical bills, 662
    payments to hospitals and doctors, 314
    peer review organizations, 315
    physician payment reform, 314
    publications, 410-11
Medications, 411-13
    see also Drug Approval Process
    see also Drug Evaluation
    food interactions, 278
    generic drugs, 311
    patent law, 413
    prescription, 30
    publications, 412
Medicinal plants, 413
Mediterranean fever, 413
Medrol, 706
Megace, 706
Megaloblastic anemia
    see Anemia
Megavitamin therapy, 413-14
Meige's syndrome, 414
Melanoma, 414-15, 682, 685
    see also Cancer
    malignant, 142, 552
Melkerson's syndrome, 415
Melphalan, 415
Memory loss, 76, 415-16
Menier's disease, 416
Meningitis, 109, 416
Meningocele, 416-17
Menke's disease, 417, 687
Menopause, 335, 417, 626
    see also Estrogen
    clinical studies, 699
    videos, 615
Menstrual mood disorders (PMS), 616, 699
Menstrually-related mood disorders, 696, 699
Menstruation, 418
Mental handicaps, 525

Mental illness and health, 418-20
  block grants, 230
  childhood, 418, 698
  clinics, 419
  homeless, 333
  medications, 418
  President's Committee on Mental
    Retardation, 420
  Project D/ART, 210
  rehabilitation, 210
  research, 210
Mental retardation, 420-21
  assessment tools, 418
  birth defects, 120-21
  community services, 312
  developmental disabilities, 406
  handicap programs, 305
  Mental Retardation Research Centers, 420
  research, 420
Menu planning, 451
Mercaptopurine, 421
Mercury poisoning, 421
  see also Seafood Inspection
Mercury vapor lamps, 421
Mercy killing
  see Living Wills
Mesnex, 706
Metabolic bone disease, 692
Metabolic diseases, 160-61, 421-22
Metabolism, inborn errors, 422
Metachromatic leukodystrophy, 700
Metal halide lamps, 421
Metal metabolism, 688
Metastatic tumors, 422
  see also Cancer
Methadone, 423
Methotrexate, 423
Methylene, 250
Methylphenidate, 699
Metrodin, 706
Michigan
  aging, 637
  consumer complaints, 648
  Food and Drug Administration, 640
  Health and Human Services, 645
  health statistics, 717
  insurance, 654
  licensed professionals, 659
  Medical board, 642
  nursing homes, 665
  pharmacies, 669
  radon, 673

Microcephaly, 423
Micronase, 767
Microsporidiosis, 678
Microtropia, 423
Microvascular
  agina, 694
  surgery, 424
Microwaves, 244, 281, 424, 451
Middle ear infection, 424
Midwives, 656
Migraine headaches, 18-20, 424-25
Migrant health centers, 507
Military health care, 425
Milk, 425-26
  see also Lactose Intolerance
  intolerance, 425
  nonfat solids, 279
  standards, 425
Minamata disease, 421
Mind-body, 74
Mineral therapy, 74
Minipress, 706
Minizide, 706
Minnesota
  aging, 637
  consumer complaints, 648
  Food and Drug Administration, 640
  Health and Human Services, 645
  health statistics, 718
  insurance, 654
  licensed professionals, 659
  Medical board, 642
  nursing homes, 665
  pharmacies, 669
  radon, 673
Minocin, 706
Minority health, 426-27
  professionals, 427
Minority Health Resource Center, 426
Miracle cures, 647
Miscarriages, 688
Mississippi
  aging, 637
  consumer complaints, 648
  Health and Human Services, 645
  health statistics, 718
  insurance, 654
  licensed professionals, 659
  Medical board, 642
  nursing homes, 665
  pharmacies, 669
  radon, 673

Missouri
 aging, 638
 consumer complaints, 648
 Food and Drug Administration, 640
 Health and Human Services, 645
 health statistics, 718
 insurance, 654
 licensed professionals, 659
 Medical board, 642
 nursing homes, 665
 pharmacies, 669
 radon, 673
Mitochondrial myopathies, 427-28
Mitomycin, 428
Mitotane, 428
Mitral valve prolapse, 110, 428, 625
Mixed connective tissue disease, 428
Mobile home safety, 188
Modified fasts, 220
Molds, 72, 428-29
Mongolism
 see Down Syndrome
Monistat, 706
Monistat Derm, 706
Mononucleosis, 429
Monopril, 706
Monozygotic twins
 see Twins
Montana
 aging, 638
 consumer complaints, 648
 Health and Human Services, 645
 health statistics, 718
 insurance, 654
 licensed professionals, 659
 Medical board, 642
 nursing homes, 665
 pharmacies, 669
 radon, 673
Mood disorders, 696
Mortality rates, 429
Motor neuron disease, 429-30
Motrin, 706
Movement disorders, 355, 430
Moya-Moya disease, 430
MRIs, 430-31
MSG
 see Chinese Restaurant Syndrome
Mucolipidosis IV, 700
Mucopolysaccharidosis, 431, 700
Multi-infarct dementia, 431
Multiple endocrine neoplasia, 264

Multiple myeloma, 435
Multiple sclerosis, 431-32, 700
Mumps, 432
 see also Immunizations
Muscle stimulaters, 315
Muscular dystrophy, 432-33
Muscular fatigue, 433
Musculoskeletal injuries, 455
Mutations, heritable, 291
Mutual help groups, 69, 229, 419
Myambutol, 706
Myasthenia gravis, 433
Mycobacterial infections, 433-34
Mycobacterium avium intracellulare, 678
Mycoses, 434, 680
Mycosis fungoides, 434
Mycostatin, 706
Mycotoxins, 434
Myelitis, transverse, 597
Myelodysplasia, 695
Myelodysplastic syndrome, 434-35
Myelofibrosis, 435
Myelogenous leukemia, chronic, 171
Myeloma, 400, 435
Myocardial infarction, 55, 436
 see also Heart Disease
Myoclonus, 436, 460, 701
Myofascial pain syndrome, 436
Myopathies, mitochondrial, 427
Myopathy, idiopathic inflammatory, 350
Myopathy, thyrotoxic, 589
Myopia, 436
Myositis, 437
Myotonia
 atophica, 437
 congenita, 437

- N -

Naphcon-A, 707
Naprosyn, 707
Narcolepsy, 438
Narcotics Anonymous, 228
Nasalide, 707
Natalins TX, 707
National Center for Clinical Infant Programs, 356
National Center for Education in Maternal
 and Child Health, 376, 406
National Center for Environmental Health
 and Injury Control, 380
National Center for Medical Rehabilitation

Research, 511
National Cholesterol Education Program, 318
National Clearinghouse for Primary Care
    Information, 394, 508
National Clearinghouse on Alcohol and Drug
    Information, 228, 324
National Diabetes Advisory Board, 216
National Diabetes Information
    Clearinghouse, 215, 216, 362
National Electronic Injury Surveillance
    System, 187
National Genetic Voluntary Organizations, 406
National Head Injury Foundation, 598
National health insurance
see Health Insurance
National Health Service Corps, 315
National Information Center for Handicapped
    Children and Youth, 306
National Information Center for Orphan Drugs
    and Rare Diseases, 460
National Institutes of Health
    Aging, 60, 391, 677
    Alcohol Abuse and Alcoholism, 69, 313, 677
    Allergy and Infectious Diseases, 72, 678, 703
    Arthritis and Musculoskeletal and Skin
        Disease, 52, 368, 514, 680
    Cancer, 141, 681
    Child Health and Human
        Development, 501, 686
    Deafness and Other Communication
        Disorders, 688
    Dental Research, 208, 689
    Diabetes and Digestive and Kidney
        Diseases, 690
    Eye, 617, 693
    Heart, Lung and Blood, 694
    Mental Health, 91, 210, 418, 696
    Neurological Disorders and Stroke, 53, 700
National Institute for Occupational Safety
    and Health, 455
National Institute of Environmental Health
    Sciences, 592
National Institute on Disability and Rehabilitation
    Research, 305, 525
National Library of Medicine, 614
National Marine Fisheries Service, 643-44
National Pesticide Telecommunications
    Network, 592
National Rehabilitation Information
    Center, 39, 222, 525, 598
National Reproductive Medicine Network, 360
National Resource Center On Homelessness

    and Mental Illness, 332
National Resource Center on Worksite
    Health Promotion, 628
National Safety Council, 520
National Second Surgical Opinion Program, 576
National Sudden Infant Death Syndrome
    Clearinghouse, 574
Nationwide Food Consumption Survey, 277
Native Americans, 438-39
see also Minority Health Care
    diet and disease, 439
    hotline, 426
    nutrition, 453
Natural childbirth
see Childbirth
Nearsightedness, 439
Nebraska
    aging, 638
    consumer complaints, 649
    Health and Human Services, 645
    health statistics, 718
    insurance, 654
    licensed professionals, 659
    Medical board, 642
    nursing homes, 666
    pharmacies, 669
    radon, 673
Nebupent, 707
Needles, 66
Nelson's syndrome, 687
Nemaline myopathy, 274, 439
Neonatal
    asphyxia, 440
    intensive care, 393
    respiratory distress syndrome, 440
    thrombocytopenia, 691
Neoplasia, 439, 682
    familial multiple endocrine, 449
Neoplasms
    clinical studies, 682
    diseases, 684
    head, 689
    pediatric, 684
    thyroid, 692
Neosar, 707
Nephritis, 440
Nephrocalcinosis, 440-41, 692
Nephrolithiasis, 441, 692
Nephropathy, reflux, 524
Nephrotic syndrome, 441
Nerve damage, 441
Neupogen, 707

Neural tube defects, 441-42
see also Birth Defects
Neuralgia, 442
trigeminal, 589, 600
Neuro-Ophthalmology, 442, 693
Neuroaxonal dystrophy, 443
Neuroblastoma, 443, 684
Neurodermatitis, 442
Neurofibromatosis, 443-44
Neurogenic arthropathy, 444
Neurologic disease, 444, 700
Neuromuscular disorders, 701
Neuron disease, 429
Neuropathy, 444
diabetes, 691
peripheral, 481
Neuroscience, 445
Neurosclerosis, 445
Neurotoxic disorders, 445, 455
Neutropenia, 680
Nevada
aging, 638
consumer complaints, 648
Health and Human Services, 645
health statistics, 719
insurance, 654
licensed professionals, 659
Medical board, 642
nursing homes, 666
pharmacies, 669
radon, 673
New Hampshire
aging, 638
consumer complaints, 649
Health and Human Services, 645
health statistics, 719
insurance, 654
licensed professionals, 659
Medical board, 642
nursing homes, 666
pharmacies, 669
radon, 673
New Jersey
aging, 638
consumer complaints, 649
Food and Drug Administration, 640
Health and Human Services, 645
health statistics, 719
insurance, 654
licensed professionals, 660
Medical board, 642
pharmacies, 669

radon, 673
New Mexico
aging, 638
consumer complaints, 649
Health and Human Services, 645
health statistics, 719
insurance, 654
licensed professionals, 660
Medical board, 642
nursing homes, 666
radon, 673
New York
aging, 638
consumer complaints, 649
Food and Drug Administration, 640
Health and Human Services, 645
health statistics, 719
insurance, 654
licensed professionals, 660
Medical board, 642
nursing homes, 666
pharmacies, 669
radon, 673
Newborn screening, 357, 445
Nicorette, 707
Niemann-Pick disease, 445-46, 700
Night blindness, 446
Nimotop, 707
Nitrodisc, 707
Nizoral, 707
Noise, effects of, 446
Nolvadex, 707
Non-Hodgkins lymphoma, 399, 681
Non-traditional information sources, 3
Nonfat milk solids, 279
Nongonococcal urethritis, 447
Noninsulin-Dependent diabetes, 216
Non-ionizing radiation, 520
Nonprescription drugs, 230, 412, 447
see also Medications
Nordette, 707
Norepinephrine, 695
Normodyne, 707
Noroxin, 707
Norpace, 707
Norpace CR, 707
Norplant, 190, 265, 447-48, 707
see also Contraception
North Carolina
aging, 638
consumer complaints, 649
Health and Human Services, 645

health statistics, 719
insurance, 654
licensed professionals, 660
Medical board, 642
nursing homes, 666
pharmacies, 669
radon, 673
North Dakota
aging, 638
consumer complaints, 649
Health and Human Services, 645
health statistics, 720
insurance, 654
licensed professionals, 660
Medical board, 642
nursing homes, 666
pharmacies, 669
radon, 673
Nose jobs, 640
Nosebleeds, 448
Nosology, 572
Nuclear medicine, 448
Nurse training programs, 314
Nurses, complaints against, 651, 656
Nursing homes, 448-49
    see also Long-Term Care
    selecting, 61, 62, 449
    resident abuse, 62, 448
    complaints, 636, 664
Nutrients, 452
Nutrition, 449-53
    AIDS, 67
    aging-related, 62, 449
    behavior, 450
    cardiovascular disease, 450
    children, 134, 164, 451
    chronic diseases, 169
    consumer attitudes, 276
    dental health, 453
    education, 451, 629
    energy metabolism, 169
    hunger, 453
    infant, 357, 450-51
    lactation, 376, 406
    national monitoring, 453
    Native Americans, 438, 453
    Nutrition Labeling and Education Act, 280
    pregnant and lactating women, 134
    Recommended Daily Allowances, 452
    renal, 372
    research, 169
    sports, 258, 451, 565

vegetarian, 450, 611
women, 452
worksite, 628
Nutritional labeling
    see Food Labeling
Nystagmus, 453

- O -

Oat cell cancer, 685
Obesity, 145, 422, 454
    see also Dieting
Object recognition disorders, 702
Obscenity laws, 162
Obsessive-compulsive disorder, 455, 698
Obstructive lung disease, chronic, 171
Occupational disease, 455
Occupational Safety and Health
    Administration, 627, 646
Occupational safety, 455
Occupational therapists, 656
Ocular
    albinism, 693
    disease, 693
    hypertension, 456, 693
    motor disturbances, 693
    sarcoidosis, 693
Oculinium, 707
Oculocutaneous albinism, 693
Odor disorders, 456
Office of Cosmetics and Colors, 193
Office of Special Education Programs, 38
Office on Smoking and Health, 476, 501, 555
Office of Vocational Rehabilitation, 37
Office ventilation, 549
Ohio
    aging, 638
    consumer complaints, 649
    Food and Drug Administration, 640
    Health and Human Services, 645
    health statistics, 720
    insurance, 655
    licensed professionals, 660
    Medical board, 643
    nursing homes, 666
    pharmacies, 669
    radon, 673
Oklahoma
    aging, 638
    consumer complaints, 649
    Health and Human Services, 645

Oklahoma (con't)
   health statistics, 720
   insurance, 655
   licensed professionals, 660
   Medical board, 643
   nursing homes, 666
   pharmacies, 669
   radon, 674
Olivopontocerebellar atrophy, 456
Omega-3s, 450
Onchocerciasis, 456-57, 680
Oncology, 457
   see also Cancer
Ophthalmia neonatorum, 457
Opiate addiction, 423
Oppenheim's disease, 457
Optic atrophy, 457-58
Optic neuritis, 458
Optimine, 707
Optometric care, 617
Optometrists, 656
Oral cancer, 458
   see also Cancer
Oral contraceptives, 190, 458-59
   see also Contraception
Oral endosseous implants, 690
Oral health, 450, 459
Oral surgery, 690
Oral-facial pain, 469
Oral-lingual dystonia, 689
Oregon
   aging, 638
   consumer complaints, 649
   Health and Human Services, 645
   health statistics, 720
   insurance, 655
   licensed professionals, 661
   Medical board, 643
   nursing homes, 666
   pharmacies, 669
   radon, 674
Organs
   donation, 264, 459
   rejection, 597
   transplants, 459
Organic foods, 280, 312
Orinase, 707
Orotic aciduria, 460
Orphan diseases, 460
Orphan drugs, 460-61
Ortho-Dienestrol, 707
Orthodontics, 461, 462

Orthognathic surgery, 461
Orthokeratology, 461-62
Orthopedic implants, 462
Orthopedics, 462
Orthostatic hypotension, 462, 702
Orthotics, 463
Orudis, 707
Osteitis deformans, 463, 469
Osteoarthritis, 97, 299, 463
Osteogenesis, 464
Osteogenesis imperfecta, 464, 687, 703
Osteogenic sarcoma, 464, 685
Osteomalacia, 464, 692
Osteomyelitis, 464-65
Osteopaths, 656
Osteopetrosis, 465
Osteoporosis, 97, 465-66
Osteoporosis, juvenile, 692
Osteosarcoma, 466
   see also Papilloma Virus
Osteosclerosis, 466-67
Otitis Media
   see Ear Infections
Otosclerosis, 467
Ovarian cancer, 467, 681, 685
   see also Cancer
Ovarian failure, primary, 508
Ovcon, 707
Over-the-counter drugs, 230, 467-68
   see also Medications
Ovulation, 468

- P -

Pacemakers, 468, 663
Pacific Islanders, 426
Paget's disease, 468-69
Pain, 469-70
   acupuncture, 54
   elderly, 470
   cancer-related, 470
   facial, 690
   myofascial, 436
   oral-facial, 469
Palpitations, 470
Palsy
   supranuclear, 470
Pancreas, 707
Pancreatic cancer, 470-71, 686
   see also Cancer
Pancreatitis, 471

Panencephalitis, 471-72
Panic
    attacks, 471
    disorders, 471, 699
Panniculitis, 472
Pap tests, 472
Papilloma virus, 472-73
    see also Cancer
Parafon Forte, 707
Paralysis
    agitans, 473
    hypokalemic periodic, 346
    thyrotoxic, 589
Paramyotonia congenita, 473
Paranoia, 473
Paraparesis, tropical spastic, 601
Paraplatin, 707
Paraplegia, 473-74
Paraproteinemic polyneuropatheis, 701
Parasitic disease, 474
Parathyroid disorders, 474, 692
Parental leave, 264-65
Parents, aging, 63
Parkinson's disease, 474-75, 689, 700
Parkinson's, drug-induced, 475
Parlodel, 707
Paroxysmal atrial tachycardia, 475
Paroxysmal nocturnal hemoglobinuria, 475
Pars planitis, 476, 694
Parvovirus infections, 476
Passive smoking, 476
    see also Smoking
Patents, animal, 85
Pathophysiology, 565
Pavabid, 707
PCP, 476-77
    see also Drug Abuse
Pectus excavatum, 284, 477
Pediatric AIDS, 66, 332
    see also AIDS
Pediatric cancer, 142
Pediatric pulmonology, 396
Pediculosis
    see Lice
Pedodontics, 477-78
Pelizaeous-Merzbacher disease, 478
Pelvic inflammatory disease, 478
Pemphigoid, 478
Pemphigus foliaceus, 682
Penicillin, 479
Penile implants, 615-16
Pennsylvania

aging, 638
    consumer complaints, 649
    Food and Drug Administration, 640
    Health and Human Services, 645
    health statistics, 720
    insurance, 655
    licensed professionals, 661
    Medical board, 643
    nursing homes, 666
    pharmacies, 669
    radon, 674
Pepcid, 707
Peptic ulcers, 479, 604
    refractory, 691
Periactin, 707
Periarteritis nodosa, 479
Pericardial tamponade, 480
Pericarditis, 479-80
Perinatal bereavement, 574
Perinatal services, 161, 406, 480, 505
    see also Prenatal
Periodontal disease, 480
Peripheral Neuropathy, 209, 233, 459, 481
Peripheral vascular disease, 481
Pernicious anemia, 481
Persa-Gel, 707
Persantine, 707
Personality disorders, 481-82, 697
Pertussis, 482
    see also Immunizations
Pervasive Developmental Disorders, 482
    see also Developmental Disabilities
Pesticides, 482-83
    drinking water, 227
    food, 483
    fruits and vegetables, 284
    hotline, 482, 592
    National Pesticides Telecommunications
        Network, 482
    residues, 278
    toxicology, 592
Peter's syndrome, 693
Peyronie's disease, 483
Pharmaceutical Manufacturer's Association, 30
Pharmaceuticals
    see Medications
    see Drug Approval Process
    see Drug Evaluation
Pharmacists, 412, 656
Pharmacology
    research, 483
Pharyngeal disabilities, 484

Pheochromocytoma, 484, 695
Phenylketonuria
    see PKU
Phlebitis, 484-85
Phlebothrombosis, 485
Phobias, 471, 485
Phonatory disorders, 689
Physical fitness, 258, 419
    see also Exercise
Physical frailty, 61
Physical therapists, 656
Physicians, 651, 652
    see also Doctors
Pi-Mesons, 486
Pick's disease, 485-86, 700
Pigment dispersion syndrome, 693
Pigmentosum, xeroderma, 631
Pill, the, 191
    see also Oral Contraceptives
Pilogan, 707
Pimples
    see Acne
Pink eye, 486
Pinta, 486
Pinworms, 486-87
Pituitary tumors, 487-88, 688, 692, 701
Pityriasis
    rosea, 487
    rubra pilaris, 487
PKD
    see Polycystic Kidney Disease
PKU, 488
    breastfeeding, 134
    dental health, 406
    dietary guidelines, 488
    treatment programs, 161
    metabolism diseases, 422
Placenta disorders, 488
Plaque
    dental, 210, 489
Plasma, 125
Plasma cell cancer, 489
Plastic Surgery
    see Face Lifts
Platelet abnormalities, 125, 691
Platinol, 707
Play, 159, 418
Playground safety, 407, 489
Plendil, 707
Pleurisy, 489
Plicamycin, 489-90
PMS, 490, 616

Pneumococcal infections, 490
Pneumonitis, 696
Pneumothorax, 490-91
Podiatrists, 656
Poison Control Centers, 491-92
Poison ivy, 493
Poison prevention, 187, 491
Poisoning, 491-93
Polioencephalitis, 493
Poliomyelitis, 493
    cerebral, 493
Pollen allergy, 73, 493-94
Pollution, indoor air, 355
Polyaromatic hydrocarbons, 250
Polyarteritis, 494, 680
Polychlorinated biphenyls, 250
Polycystic kidney disease (PKD), 494
Polycystic ovary syndrome, 494
Polycythemia, 494
Polymyalgia rheumatica, 495
Polymyositis, 495, 680, 701
Polyneuritis, 301, 495-96
Polyostotic fibrous dysplasis, 496
Polyps
    colon, 496
Polyserositis, 496-97
Pompe's disease, 497
Ponstel, 707
Pools, 188
Population control, 497
Porcelain, dental, 209
Pornography, child, 162
Porphyria, 497-98
Positron emission tomography, 498
Post-polio syndrome, 499, 701
Post-transfusion purpura, 691
Postnatal care, 498-99
    see also Childbirth
    see also Child Health
Postural hypotension, 499
Potassium, 499
Pott's disease, 500
Poultry inspection, 277, 408, 500
    see also Meat
Power lines, 244, 500-01
Practitioners, 508
Prader-Willi syndrome, 501
Pravochol, 707
Pre-term babies, 504
    Healthy Start Program, 356
    low birthweight, 393
    nutrition, 407

Prednisone, 501
Pregnancy, 501-03
　　see also Amniocentesis
　　adolescent, 265
　　counselors, 265
　　diabetes, 215
　　discrimination, 503
　　drinking, 502
　　drugs, 502
　　environmental exposures, 406
　　exercise, 502
　　gestational diabetes, 502
　　high blood pressure, 503
　　nutrition, 502
　　smoking, 502
　　sonograms, 604
　　teenage, 503, 583, 584
　　tubal, 360
　　ultrasound, 502, 604
　　vitamins, 502
　　weight gain, 502
　　x-rays, 502, 503
Pregnancy and alcohol, 503-04
　　see also Alcoholism
　　see also Drug Abuse
Premarin, 707
Premature babies, 504
　　see also Pre-term babies
Premenstrual syndrome
　　see PMS
Premiums, insurance, 652
Prenatal care, 160, 407, 505
Prenatal drug exposure, 503
Presbycusis, 505-06
Presbyopia, 506
Prescription drugs
　　see Medications
　　see Appendix B
Prescription fraud, 670
Prescriptions, free, 30
Presenile dementia, 506-07
　　see also Dementia
　　see also Alzheimer's Disease
Preservatives
　　see Food
President's Committee on Mental
　　Retardation, 420
President's Council on Physical Fitness and
　　Sports, 258
Prevention, 507
　　adolescent drug use, 229
　　aging-related disease, 63

alcoholism, 69
cancer, 142, 507
cancer and diet, 451
disease, 507
hepatitis B, 324
kidney stones, 373
occupational disease, 455
sports injuries, 565
Prilosec, 707
Primary biliary cirrhosis, 692
Primary care, 507-08
　　block grants, 312
Primary lateral sclerosis, 508
Primary ovarian failure, 508
Prinivil, 707
Procan SR, 707
Procan, 707
Procarbazine, 509
Procardia, 707
Procrit, 707
Produce, 284
Product safety, 670
Professional education, health, 314
Progeria, 509
Progesterone, 509
Progestins, 509
Progressive multifocal leukoencephalopathy, 509
Progressive supranuclear palsy, 509
Project Zero to Three, 356
Prokine, 707
Pronestyl SR, 707
Propine, 707
Prosopagnosia, 702
Prostat, 707
Prostate cancer, 510, 683
　　see also Cancer
Prostate problems, 510, 616
Prostheses, 511
　　blood vessel, 511
　　heart, 511
Prosthodontics, 511
Proteinosis, pulmonary alveolar, 516
Protropin, 707
Proventil, 707
Provera, 707
Prozac, 707
Prurigo nodularis, 511
Pruritus 512
Pseudogout, 512
Pseudohypertrophic dystrophy
　　see Muscular Dystrophy
Pseudohypoparathyroidism, 512, 692

Pseudomonas infections, 512-13
Pseudosenility, 513
Pseudotumor cerebri, 513
Pseudoxanthoma elasticum, 513
Psittacosis, 514
Psoriasis, 514, 682
Psoriatic arthritis, 514
Psychiatric hospitals, 420
Psychologists, 656
Psychology, developmental, 688
Psychotic episodes, 514-15
Pterygium, 515
Ptosis, 515
Puberty
    see also Adolescent Health
    see also Teenagers
    delayed, 515
    precocious, 515, 687
Public Health Service Act, 266
Puerto Rico
    aging, 638
    consumer complaints, 649
    Food and Drug Administration, 640
    Health and Human Services, 645
    insurance, 655
    Medical board, 643
    nursing homes, 666
    radon, 674
Pulmonary alveolar proteinosis, 516
Pulmonary disease, 516
Pulmonary toxicants, 396, 516-17
Pure red cell aplasia, 517
Purpura, 517
    drug, 232
    Henoch-Schonlein, 323
    idiopathic thrombocytopenic, 351
Pyelonephritis, 517
Pyogenic infections, 517-18, 680
Pyorrhea, 518
Pyridium, 707

- Q -

Quack medical devices, 409
Quackery, 61, 313
Quadriplegia, 518
Questran, 707
Quinamm, 707

- R -

Rabies
    information line, 182, 518-19
    research, 519
    video, 519
    vaccines, 609
Radial keratotomy, 519
Radiation, 519-20
    breast cancer, 521
    eyes, effects on, 520
    food irradiation, 520
    medical, 448
    microwave, 424
    non-ionizing, 520
    teeth, effects on, 519
    television, 632
    therapy, 520
Radiation-induced gland damage, 689
Radiography, scoliosis, 542
Radon, 520-21
    legislation, 355, 521
    hotline, 520-21
Ramsey Hunt syndrome, 521
Rape, 522
Rapid cyclers, 698
Rare diseases, 522
Rashes, 189, 522
Raynaud's disease, 522-23
Reactivity, 571
Reading disorders, 523
Read method of childbirth
    see Childbirth
Recombinant DNA, 119
Rectum cancer, 180
Recurrent fever, 270, 523
Reflex sympathetic dystrophy syndrome, 524
Reflux nephropathy, 524
Refractory anemia, 524-25
Refsum's disease, 525
Regional enteritis
    see Crohn's Disease
Rehab Centers, drug, 65, 330
Rehabilitation, 525
    see also Disabilities
    aging-relating, 525
    clearinghouse, 222
    Rehabilitation Services Administration, 37
Reiger's syndrome, 693
Reiter's syndrome, 525-26
Relafen, 707
Relaxation, 526, 569
Renal
    cancer, 461, 685

cell carcinoma, 681
  disorders, 526
  nutrition, 372
Renovascular hypertension, 526-27, 695
Repetitive stress syndrome, 527
Reproductive disorders, 455, 527
Resident abuse, 448
Resource Persons Network, 426
Respirators, 663
Respiratory diseases, 527-28
Respiratory distress syndrome, 440, 528
Respiratory protection, 628
Respiratory syncytial virus, 528
Restless leg syndrome, 529
Restorative materials, dental, 209
Retardation
  see Mental Retardation
Retinal disease, 529
Retinitis pigmentosa, 693
Retinopathy, diabetic, 216
Retirement, 264, 387
Retrovir, 707
Rett's syndrome, 529-30
Reye's syndrome, 530
Rh factor, 530
Rh isoimmunication, 502
Rhabdomyosarcoma, 530-31, 684
Rheumatic disease, 96, 531
Rheumatic fever, 531
Rheumatic heart, 531
Rheumatism, 531-32
Rheumatoid arthritis, 299, 369, 532
Rheumatrex, 707
Rhinitis, 532
  allergic, 72, 680
Rhode Island
  aging, 638
  consumer complaints, 649
  Health and Human Services, 645
  health statistics, 720
  insurance, 655
  licensed professionals, 661
  Medical board, 643
  nursing homes, 666
  pharmacies, 669
  radon, 674
Rhus dermatitis, 532
Rhytidoplasty
  see Face Lift
Rickets, 533, 692
  hypophosphatemic, 687
  vitamin-D resistant, 533

Riley-Day syndrome, 533
Ringworm, 533
River blindness, 534
Rocaltrol, 707
Rocephin, 707
Rocky mountain spotted fever, 534
Root caries, 534
Rosaceae, 534-35
Rotavirus, 535
Rothmund-Thompson syndrome, 535
Rubella, 293, 535
  see also Immunizations
Runaways, 535
  hotline, 535
Running, 259
Rural hospitals, 312
Rythmol, 707

- S -

Saccharin, 100, 279
Safe sex, 536
  see also AIDS
  see also Sexually Transmitted Diseases
Safety
  antennas, 188
  bicycles, 187
  chain saws, 188
  children's furniture, 187
  fireplaces, 188
  fireworks, 188
  home insulation, 188
  kerosene heaters, 188
  kitchen knives, 189
  lawn mowers, 188
  methylene chloride, 188
  mini bikes, 187
  on the job, 645-46
  playground equipment, 188
  pools, 188
  skateboards, 187
  space heaters, 188
  television fire and shock, 187
  toys, 189
  wood burning stoves, 188
Saline solution, homemade, 190
Salivary system disease, 536
Salmonella
  enteritidis, 500
  infections, 536
Salt, 61, 536-37

Sandimmune, 707
Sandoglobulin, 707
Sandostatin, 707
Santavuori disease, 537
Santyl, 707
Sarcoidosis, 537-38, 679, 693, 696
Sarcomas, 538, 682
Saturated fat, 166, 452, 538
Scabies, 538
Scarlet fever, 538
Schilder's disease, 539
Schistosomiasis, 539, 680
Schizoaffective illness, 697
Schizophrenia, 539
    genetic studies, 698
    medications, 419
    research, 539
    clinical studies, 697-99
School fluoride programs, 480
School health, 539-40
Schwanoma, 540-41
Sciatica, 393, 541
    see also Back Problems
Scleroderma, 541
Sclerosis, 541-42
Sclerosis, diffuse, 220
Sclerosis, progressive systemic, 579
Scoliosis, 542
Seafood inspection, 408, 542
Seafood processing, 451, 643-44
Sealants, dental restorative, 209
Seasonal affective disorders (SAD), 697
Second surgical opinion, 576
Second-hand smoke, 476
Secreted proteins, 686
Sectral, 707
Segawa's dystonia, 543
Seizures, 543
    see also Epilepsy
    febrile, 268
Seldane D, 707
Seldane, 707
Select Committee on Aging, 459
Self-help, 542-43
    alcoholism, 69
    children with special needs, 161
    Surgeon General's workshop, 407
Seminoma, 543
    see also Testicular Cancer
Senile macular degeneration, 544
Senility, 513, 543-44
    see also Aging

    see also Alzheimer's Disease
Septal defects, 544
Septra DS, 707
Sex changes, 545
Sex determination, 545
Sex hormones, 334, 545
Sexual abuse, 157, 545
    see also Child Abuse
    see also Family Violence
Sexual activity, teen, 583
Sexual development, 545
Sexual harrassment, 641
Sexuality, age-related, 545-46
Sexually transmitted diseases, 66, 190, 546-47
Sezary syndrome, 547, 682
    see also Safe Sex
Shaken baby syndrome, 158, 547
Shingles, 547-48
Shock
    cardiogenic, 547
    hemorrhagic 547
Short stature, 548, 687
Shy-Drager syndrome, 548-49
Siamese twins
    see Twins
Sibling incest, 159
Sick building syndrome, 549
Sickle cell, 549-50
    child health, 161
    clinical studies, 695
    family resources, 407
    therapy, 550
Sideroblastic anemia, 550
SIDS, 574
    see also Sudden Infant Death Syndrome
Silicone implants
    see Breast Implants
Sinemet, 707
Sinemet CR, 707
Sinusitis, 550
Sjogren's syndrome, 550-52
Skim milk, 357, 407
Skin
    aging, 552
    cancer, 552-53
    conditions, 553
    cream, 639
    ulcers, 460
Skull abnormalities, 195
Sleep apnea, 553
Sleep disorders, 553-54
Sleep-deprivation, 696

Slow viruses, 554
Smallpox, 554
Smell disorders, 182, 554-55, 581
Smoke detectors, 670
Smokeless tobacco, 555
   see also Smoking
Smoking, 556-57
   aging, 62
   cessation methods, 556-57
   heart disease, 556
   hypertension, 328
   parent guide, 583
   passive, 476-77
   research, 476, 556
   school programs, 540
   state and local programs, 556
Snacking, 452, 557
Snuff, 555
Social phobias, 699
Social Security Administration, 35, 557-59, 636
Sodium, 536-37
   see also Salt
   food content, 278
   high blood pressure, 537
   restrictive diets, 451
   meat preparation, 408, 500
   poultry preparation, 408, 500
Soft contact lenses, 190
Soft tissue sarcoma, 530, 538
Solar burns
   eye, 559-60
Somatization disorder, 508
Sonograms, 606
Sorbitrate, 707
South Carolina
   aging, 638
   consumer complaints, 649
   Health and Human Services, 645
   health statistics, 720
   insurance, 655
   licensed professionals, 661
   Medical board, 643
   nursing homes, 666
   pharmacies, 669
   radon, 674
South Dakota
   aging, 638
   consumer complaints, 649
   Health and Human Services, 645
   health statistics, 721
   insurance, 655
   licensed professionals, 661

   Medical board, 643
   nursing homes, 667
   pharmacies, 669
   radon, 674
Spasmotic dysphonia, 560
Spastic conditions, 560
Spastic paraparesis, familial, 264
Spectazole, 707
Speech
   disorders, 560-61
   assistive devices, 183
   developmental disorders, 378
   clinical studies, 689-90
   pathologists, 656
Sphingolipidoses, 561-62
Spielmeyer-Sjogren's disease, 562-63
Spina bifida, 121, 305, 562-63
Spinal arachnoiditis, 563
Spinal aneurysms, 83
Spinal arteriovenous malformations, 701
Spinal cord injuries, 563
Spinal cord tumors, 563-64, 701
Spinal curvature, 109, 542
   see also Scoliosis
Spinal muscular atrophy, 564
Spine joints
   see Ankylosing Spondylitis
Spinocerebellar degeneration, 564-65
Sporanox, 707
Sports
   mental health, 258-59
   injuries, 565
   medicine, 128, 259, 565
   nutrition, 258, 565
Spousal abuse, 111-12, 266
   see also Battered Spouses
   see also Family Violence
Squamous cell carcinomas, 552, 565-66
Stained teeth, 566
Staphylococcal (Staph) infections, 566, 680
State Indoor Air Contacts, 549
Statistics
   abortions, 50, 120, 205
   births, 50, 120, 205, 713
   deaths, 50, 120, 205, 713
   divorces, 50, 120, 205, 713
   Huntington's Disease, 337-38
   infectious diseases, 713
   marriages, 50, 120, 205, 713
   Medicaid and Medicare, 410
   smoking, 476, 556
   tobacco use, 476, 555

Stature disorders, 548

Steele-Richardson disease, 566

Steinerts disease
    see Muscular dystrophy

Stenosis, 350
    aortic, 91

Sterilization
    see also Vasectomies
    operations, 265
    safety and effectiveness, 567
    vasectomies, 611

Steroid contraceptives, 567

Steroid hypertension, 567, 695

Steroids, 56, 540, 568

Stevens-Johnson syndrome, 568

Stiff man syndrome, 568

Still's disease, 569

Stomach
    bubble, 287
    cancer, 569
    ulcers, 604

Stomatitis, 92, 569

Strabismus, 460, 569-70

Streptococcal (Strep) infection, 570

Streptokinase, 570

Stress, 223, 570-71, 629, 616

Striatonigral degeneration, 571

Stroke, 571-72, 701-03

Strongyloidiasis (Roundworm), 572, 680

Student health, 540

Sturge-Weber syndrome, 573

Stuttering, 573, 673, 689

Stye, 573

Subacute necrotizing encephal, 383

Subcommittee on Health on Long-Term
    Care, 311

Subcommittee on Housing and Consumer
    Interests, 135, 311

Subcommittee on Human Services, 453

Subcommittee on Retirement Income
    and Employment, 313

Substance abuse, 228

Sudden cardiac death, 573-74, 694

Sudden infant death syndrome, 574-75

Suicide, 575
    alcoholics, 678
    clinical studies, 696
    teenagers, 575

Sulfites, 279, 281, 575

Sultrin, 707

Summer depression, 697

Sun burns, 576

Sunlamps, 576, 675

Sunscreens, 553, 576

Supplemental Social Security Income, 36

Support groups, 264

Supranuclear palsy, 470, 509

Surgeon General, 556

Surgeons, 641

Surgery, 576
    aging patients, 61
    breast, 405
    complaints, 640
    cryosurgery, 197
    eye, 197
    microvascular, 424
    oral, 690
    orthognathic, 461
    second opinion, 576
    sterilization, 567

Surrogate motherhood, 576, 626

Survanta, 707

Swallowing, 690

Sweat gland disorders, 576-77
    see also Anaphoresis

Sweeteners, 279

Swine flu, 577
    see also Flu

Sydenham's chorea, 577

Symmetrel, 707

Synalar, 707

Syncope, 577
    see also Fainting

Synemol, 708

Synovitis, 577-78

Synthroid, 708

Syphilis, 578

Syringomyelia, 578

Systemic lupus erythematosus, 397
    see also Lupus

Systemic sclerosis, 579

Systolic hypertension, 579

- T -

T-cell leukemia, 682

Tachycardia, 579

Tachycardia, paroxysmal atrial, 475

Tagamet, 707

Takayasu's arteritis, 580, 680

Tamoxifen, 580

Tampons, 593

Tangier disease, 580, 695

Tanning, 580-81
   devices, 675
   lamps, 675
   risks, 581
Tapeworms, 581
Tarabine, 707
Tardive dyskinesia, 581, 698, 700
Taste disorders, 182, 581-82, 690
Tattoo removal, 379, 582
Tay-Sachs disease, 582-83, 700
TB, 65
Technology and aging, 63
Teenagers, 583
   see also Adolescent Health
   cigarette smoking test, 583
   depression, 211
   pregnancy, 265, 583-84
   sexual activity, 584
   smoking, 583
   suicide, 58, 573
Teeth
   problems, 584
   radiation effects on, 519
   stained, 566
Telemarketing fraud, 313
Television radiation, 632
Temporal arteritis, 584-85
Tendonitis, 585
Tennessee
   aging, 638
   consumer complaints, 649
   Food & Drug Administration, 640
   Health and Human Services, 645
   health statistics, 721
   insurance, 655
   licensed professionals, 661
   Medical board, 643
   nursing homes, 667
   pharmacies, 669
   radon, 674
Tennis elbow, 585
Tenoretic, 707
Tenormin, 707
Terazol, 707
Terminal illnesses, 264
Test tube babies, 585
Testicular cancer, 585-86
   see also Cancer
Tetanus, 586
Tetra-chloroethylene, 250
Tetralogy of fallot, 586
Texas

aging, 638
   consumer complaints, 650
   Food and Drug Administration, 640
   Health and Human Services, 645
   health statistics, 721
   insurance, 655
   licensed professionals, 661
   Medical board, 643
   nursing homes, 667
   pharmacies, 669
   radon, 674
Thalassemia, 586-87, 695
Thelarche, 687
TheraCys, 707
Therapeutic endoscopy, 587, 605
Thoracic-outlet syndrome, 587
Thrombasthenia, 587
Thromboangiitis obliterans, 137
Thrombocytopenia, 587-88
Thrombolysis, 588
Thrombophlebitis, 588
Thrombosis, 588
Thyroid, 55
   carcinoma, 692
   disorders, 588-89
   neoplasms, 692
Thyroma, 589
Thyrotoxic myopathy, 589
Thyrotoxic periodic paralysis, 589
Thyrotropin, 692
Tic douloureux, 262, 589-90
Ticks, 590
Timolol, 707
Timoptic, 708
Tinnitus, 590
Tissue transplantation, 270
Tobacco
   chewing, 555
   smoke, 549
   smoking clearinghouse, 556
   smokeless, 555
Tofranil, 708
Tolectin, 708
Tomography, positron emission, 498
Tongue movements, irregular, 690
Tongue tied, 590
Tooth decay, 208, 233, 459, 480
Torsion dystonia, 238, 591, 701
Torticollis, 591, 630
Tourette syndrome, 591-92, 689, 698, 700
Toxic shock syndrome, 593-94
Toxicants, pulmonary, 516-17

Toxicology, 592-93
   carcinogens, 144
   health effects, 592
   pesticides, 482
Toxics, 592
Toxocariasis, 594
Toxoplasmic chorioretinitis, 693
Toxoplasmosis, 594-95, 678, 680
Toys, 189, 670
Trace elements, 595
Trachoma, 595
Trandate, 708
Tranquilizers, 61, 595-96
Transdermal drug delivery, 596
Transfusional hemosiderosis, 596
Transfusions, 596
Transient ischemic attacks, 596-97
Transplants
   cornea, 597
   heart, 318, 597
   kidney, 373, 597
   liver, 597
   lung, 597
   pancreas, 597
Transport defects, 686
Transverse myelitis, 597-98
Traumatic brain injuries, 132, 598
   see also Head Injuries
Traveling
   diarrhea, 219
   immunizations, 598-99
Tremors, 599
Trench mouth, 599
Trichinosis, 599-600
Trichloroethylene, 250
Trichomoniasis, 600
Trichuriasis
   see Strongyloidiasis
Tridesilon, 708
Trigeminal neuralgia, 600
Triostat, 708
Triphasil, 708
Trophoblastic cancer, 600
Tropical diseases, 600-01
Tropical eosinophilia, 679
Tropical oils
   nutrition and health, 601
   labeling requirements, 280
Tropical spastic paraparesis, 683, 701
Truncus arteriosus, 601
Trypanosomiasis, 602
Trypsinogen deficiency, 602

TSH, 692
Tubal ligation
   see Contraception
   see Sterilization
Tubal pregnancy, 360
Tuberculosis, 67, 602
Tuberous sclerosis, 602-03
Tularemia, 603
Tumor vaccines, 681
Tumors, 603-04
   see also Cancer
   eye, 603
   fibroid, 271
   metastatic, 422
   pituitary, 487
   spinal cord, 563-64
Tuna, 643
Turner syndrome, 604, 677, 687
Twins, 604
Typhoid fever, 604

- U -

Ulcerative colitis, 179, 605, 679
Ulcers, 604-05
   corneal, 190
   decubitus, 206
   peptic, 479
   skin, 461
Ultrasound imaging, 221, 605-06
Unconventional cancer treatments, 142
Unconventional medical practices 74
Underground Injection Program, 227
Unipolar depression, 698
Unresectable sarcomas, 684
Uranium, dental, 209
Uremia, 606
Urinalysis, 232, 334
Urinary incontinence, 61, 354
Urinary stones, 373
Urinary tract disease, 606-07
Urine testing, 232
Urolithiasis, 607
Urticaria, 607
Urticaria pigmentosa, 679
Utah
   aging, 638
   consumer complaints, 649
   Health and Human Services, 645
   health statistics, 721
   insurance, 655
   licensed professionals, 661

Medical board, 643
nursing homes, 667
pharmacies, 669
radon, 674
Uterine cancer, 607-08
Uveitis, 606, 693

- V -

Vaccine-preventable diseases, 352
Vaccines, 72, 596, 608-09
Vaccines for travelers, 598
Vaginitis, 609
Vagistat, 708
Valium, 708
Valvular heart disease, 609, 694
Varicella-zoster infections, 610, 680
Varicose veins, 610
Vascular disease, peripheral, 481
Vasculitis, 610-11, 680
Vasectomies, 611, 616
    see also Contraception
    see also Sterilization
Vasocar, 708
Vasodilan, 708
Vasomotor rhinitis, 680
Vasoretic, 708
Vasotec, 708
VD
    see Venereal Disease
Vegetables, 282
Vegetables, juicing, 368
Vegetarianism
    see also Food
    see also Nutrition
    nutrition, 450, 611
Venereal disease, 611-12
Venezuelan equine encephalitis, 612
Vepesid, 708
Verbal apraxia, 689
Verelan, 708
Vermont
    aging, 639
    consumer complaints, 650
    health and human services, 645
    health statistics, 722
    insurance, 655
    licensed professionals, 662
    Medical board, 643
    nursing homes, 667
    pharmacies, 669

    radon, 674
Vertigo, 612
Vestibular systems, 378
Veterans
    atomic radiation exposure, 455
    drug addiction treatment 232, 613
    U.S. Department of Veterans Affairs, 420
Video display terminals, 455, 613-14
Videos, 614-16
    aging parents, 62
    aging process, 63-4
    AIDS & drugs, 228
    AIDS, 63-7, 331
    allergic diseases, 73
    brain imaging techniques, 131, 419
    bronchial asthma, 102
    cancer, 141-42
    cancer prevention, 142
    cancer treatment, 142
    chemical accidents, 592
    chemotherapy, 614
    cholesterol, 615
    chronic pain, 172, 470-71
    circumcision, 615
    community support, mental health, 419
    crohn's disease, 179
    death, 615
    dental health, 453
    dental health, aging, 208
    diabetes, 215
    drug abuse, workplace, 228
    drug-free workplace, 627
    feminine hygiene, 418
    flossing, teeth, 208
    foot care, 269
    genetic diseases, 291
    genetic engineering, 291
    headaches, 615
    hearing impairment, 317
    hearing loss, 317
    heart attacks, 317
    holistic health, 615
    home safety, 189
    infertility, 615
    lyme disease, 396
    male transsexual, 614
    malpractice, 615
    masturbation, 615
    Mayo Clinic, 142
    Medicare, 410
    menopause, 615
    mental illness, 419

Videos (*con't*)
 optometric care, 617
 orthodontics, 461
 panic disorders, 471
 Parkinson's disease, 475
 pediatric cancer, 142
 penile implants, 615-16
 periodontal disease, 209, 480
 phobias, 471
 premenstrual syndrome, 616
 prostate, 616
 rabies, 519
 seizures, 543
 skin cancer, 142
 sleep disorders, 554
 smokeless tobacco, 555
 sports injuries, feet, 269
 stress management, 616
 teeth care, 208
 turkey preparation, 453
 ulcerative colitis, 179
 vasectomies, 616
 venereal disease, 614
 vision changes, aging, 617
Videx, 708
Vinblastine, 616
Vincasar, 708
Vincent's infection, 616
Vincristine, 616-16
Vinyl chloride, 250
Virgin Islands
 aging, 639
 consumer complaints, 650
 Food and Drug Administration, 640
 Health and Human Services, 645
 insurance, 655
 Medical board, 643
 radon, 674
Virginia
 aging, 639
 consumer complaints, 650
 Food and Drug Administration, 640
 Health and Human Services, 645
 health statistics, 722
 insurance, 655
 licensed professionals, 662
 Medical board, 643
 nursing homes, 667
 pharmacies, 670
 radon, 674
Virilism, 688
Viruses, 617

Vision
 see also Eye Care
 aging-related, 617
 attention, 702
 impairment, 305, 617
 research, 192, 529
 video, 617
Vital statistics
 see Health Statistics
 See Appendix C
Vitamins, 618
Vitiligo, 618
Vitrectomy, 618-19
Vitreo-Retinal disease, 693
Vocal cord paralysis, 619
Vocational rehabilitation, 37
Vogt-Koyanagi disease, 619
Voice, 182
Voltaren, 708
Voluntary movement disorders, 701
Von Recklinghausen's disease, 619-20
Von Willebrand's disease, 620

- W -

Waardenburg syndrome, 620
Waldenstroms macroglobulinemia, 620
Walleye, 620-21
Warts, 621
Water
 see Drinking Water
Weber-Christian disease, 621-22
Wegener's granulomatosis, 622, 680
Weight control, 219, 450-52, 537
Weight loss
 see Dieting
Wellcovorin, 708
Werdnig-Hoffmann disease, 622
Werner's syndrome, 622-23
Wernicke's encephalopathy, 623
West Virginia
 aging, 639
 consumer complaints, 650
 Health and Human Services, 645
 health statistics, 722
 insurance, 655
 licensed professionals, 662
 Medical board, 643
 nursing homes, 667
 pharmacies, 670
 radon, 674

Whiplash, 623
Whooping cough, 623
Wife abuse
    see Battered Spouses
Wilms' tumor, 372, 624
Wilson's disease, 460, 624
Winstrol, 708
Winter depression, 697
Wisconsin
    aging, 639
    consumer complaints, 650
    Health and Human Services, 645
    health statistics, 722
    insurance, 655
    licensed professionals, 662
    medical board, 643
    nursing homes, 667
    pharmacies, 670
    radon, 674
Wiskott-Aldrich syndrome, 624-25
Wolf-Parkinson-White syndrome, 625
Women
    see also Battered Spouses
    aging, 625
    AIDS, 626
    alcohol use, 69, 504, 625
    cardiac health, 626
    dietary needs, 140
    heart disease, 318
    low-income, 394-95
    lupus, 397, 427
    medical research, 311
    menopause, 335
    nutrition, 452, 626
    sterilization operations, 265-66
    support groups, 161, 407, 626
    yeast infections, 632-33
Women, Infants, and Children (WIC), 164-65
Workplace drug abuse, 626
    see also Drug Abuse
    see also Alcoholism
Workplace health, 625-30
    AIDS, 455
    drugs and alcohol, 228, 233
    high risk disease, 455
    passive smoking, 557
    reproductive health hazards, 503
    video display terminals, 455
Writer's cramp, 701
Writing disorders, 702

Wryneck, 630
Wyoming
    aging, 639
    consumer complaints, 650
    Health and Human Services, 645
    health statistics, 722
    insurance, 655
    licensed professionals, 662
    medical board, 643
    nursing homes, 667
    pharmacies, 670
    radon, 675
Wytensin, 708

- X -

Xanax, 708
Xanthinuria, 630
Xanthomatosis, 630-31
Xeroderma pigmentosum, 631, 682
Xerophtalmia, 631
Xerostomia
    see Dry Mouth
X-rays
    see also Radiation
    dental exams, 209-10
    exposure, 631-32
    pregnancy, 503

- Y -

Yeast infections, 632
Yellow fever, 632-33

- Z -

Zantac, 708
Zarontin, 708
Zestorectic, 708
Zestril, 708
Zithromax, 708
Zollinger-Ellison syndrome, 633, 691
Zoloft, 708
Zoonoses, 633
Zostrix, 708
Zovirax, 708
Zyloprim, 708